SOLARO

STUDY GUIDE

Accelerated Algebra I

SOLARO Study Guide is designed to help students achieve success in school. The content in each study guide is 100% curriculum aligned and serves as an excellent source of material for review and practice. To create this book, teachers, curriculum specialists, and assessment experts have worked closely to develop the instructional pieces that explain each of the key concepts for the course. The practice questions and sample tests have detailed solutions that show problem-solving methods, highlight concepts that are likely to be tested, and point out potential sources of errors. ***SOLARO Study Guide*** is a complete guide to be used by students throughout the school year for reviewing and understanding course content, and to prepare for assessments.

Rao,Gautam,1961 –
SOLARO STUDY GUIDE – Accelerated Algebra I (2013 Edition) Common Core

1. Mathematics – Juvenile Literature. I. Title

Castle Rock Research Corporation
2410 Manulife Place
10180 – 101 Street
Edmonton, AB T5J 3S4

1 2 3 MP 15 14 13

Printed in the United States of America

Publisher
Gautam Rao

Dedicated to the memory of Dr. V. S. Rao

THE *SOLARO STUDY GUIDE*

The ***SOLARO Study Guide*** is designed to help students achieve success in school and to provide teachers with a road map to understanding the concepts of the Common Core State Standards. The content in each study guide is 100% curriculum aligned and serves as an excellent source of material for review and practice. The ***SOLARO Study Guide*** introduces students to a process that incorporates the building blocks upon which strong academic performance is based. To create this resource, teachers, curriculum specialists, and assessment experts have worked closely to develop instructional pieces that explain key concepts. Every exercise question comes with a detailed solution that offers problem-solving methods, highlights concepts that are likely to be tested, and points out potential sources of errors.

The ***SOLARO Study Guide*** is intended to be used for reviewing and understanding course content, to prepare for assessments, and to assist each student in achieving their best performance in school.

The ***SOLARO Study Guide*** consists of the following sections:

TABLE OF CORRELATIONS

The Table of Correlations is a critical component of the ***SOLARO Study Guide***.

Castle Rock Research has designed the ***SOLARO Study Guide*** by correlating each question and its solution to Common Core State Standards. Each unit begins with a Table of Correlations, which lists the standards and questions that correspond to those standards.

For students, the Table of Correlations provides information about how each question fits into a particular course and the standards to which each question is tied. Students can quickly access all relevant content associated with a particular standard.

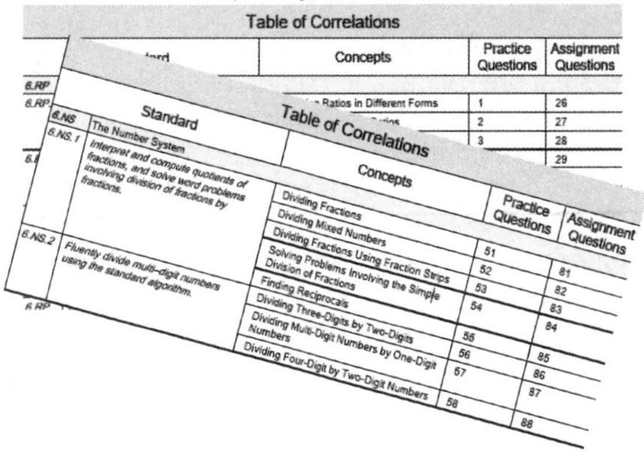

For teachers, the Table of Correlations provides a road map for each standard, outlining the most granular and measurable concepts that are included in each standard. It assists teachers in understanding all the components involved in each standard and where students are excelling or require improvement. The Table of Correlations indicates the instructional focus for each content strand, serves as a standards checklist, and focuses on the standards and concepts that are most important in the unit and the particular course of study.

Some concepts may have a complete lesson aligned to them but cannot be assessed using a paper-and-pencil format. These concepts typically require ongoing classroom assessment through various other methods.

LESSONS

Following the Table of Correlations for each unit are lessons aligned to each concept within a standard. The lessons explain key concepts that students are expected to learn according to Common Core State Standards.
As each lesson is tied to state standards, students and teachers are assured that the information will be relevant to what is being covered in class.

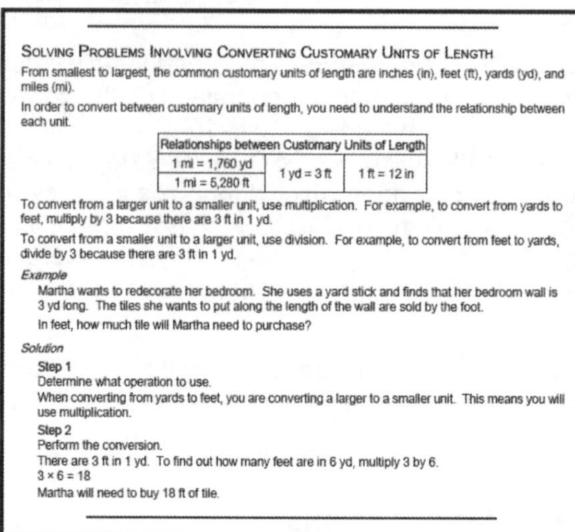

SOLVING PROBLEMS INVOLVING CONVERTING CUSTOMARY UNITS OF LENGTH

From smallest to largest, the common customary units of length are inches (in), feet (ft), yards (yd), and miles (mi).

In order to convert between customary units of length, you need to understand the relationship between each unit.

Relationships between Customary Units of Length		
1 mi = 1,760 yd	1 yd = 3 ft	1 ft = 12 in
1 mi = 5,280 ft		

To convert from a larger unit to a smaller unit, use multiplication. For example, to convert from yards to feet, multiply by 3 because there are 3 ft in 1 yd.

To convert from a smaller unit to a larger unit, use division. For example, to convert from feet to yards, divide by 3 because there are 3 ft in 1 yd.

Example

Martha wants to redecorate her bedroom. She uses a yard stick and finds that her bedroom wall is 3 yd long. The tiles she wants to put along the length of the wall are sold by the foot.

In feet, how much tile will Martha need to purchase?

Solution

Step 1
Determine what operation to use.
When converting from yards to feet, you are converting a larger to a smaller unit. This means you will use multiplication.

Step 2
Perform the conversion.
There are 3 ft in 1 yd. To find out how many feet are in 6 yd, multiply 3 by 6.
$3 \times 6 = 18$
Martha will need to buy 18 ft of tile.

EXERCISE QUESTIONS

Each set of lessons is followed by two sets of exercise questions that assess students on their understanding of the content. These exercise questions can be used by students to give them an idea of the type of questions they are likely to face in the future in terms of format, difficulty, and content coverage.

DETAILED SOLUTIONS

Some study guides only provide an answer key, which will identify the correct response but may not be helpful in determining what led to the incorrect answer. Every exercise question in the ***SOLARO Study Guide*** is accompanied by a detailed solution. Access to complete solutions greatly enhances a student's ability to work independently, and these solutions also serve as useful instructional tools for teachers. The level of information in each detailed solution is intended to help students better prepare for the future by learning from their mistakes and to help teachers discern individual areas of strengths and weaknesses.

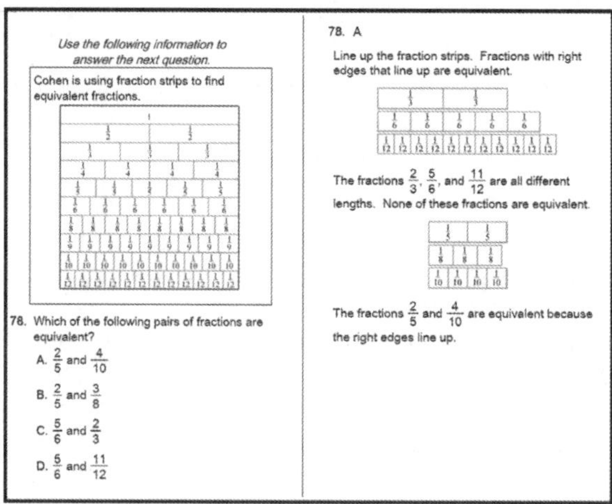

Use the following information to answer the next question.

Cohen is using fraction strips to find equivalent fractions.

78. Which of the following pairs of fractions are equivalent?
A. $\frac{2}{5}$ and $\frac{4}{10}$
B. $\frac{2}{5}$ and $\frac{3}{8}$
C. $\frac{5}{6}$ and $\frac{2}{3}$
D. $\frac{5}{6}$ and $\frac{11}{12}$

78. A

Line up the fraction strips. Fractions with right edges that line up are equivalent.

The fractions $\frac{2}{3}$, $\frac{5}{6}$, and $\frac{11}{12}$ are all different lengths. None of these fractions are equivalent.

The fractions $\frac{2}{5}$ and $\frac{4}{10}$ are equivalent because the right edges line up.

For the complete curriculum document, visit www.corestandards.org/the-standards.

SOLARO Study Guides are available for many courses. Check www.solaro.com/orders for a complete listing of books available for your area.

For more enhanced online resources, please visit www.SOLARO.com.

Student-Oriented Learning, Assessment, and Reporting Online

SOLARO is an online resource that provides students with regionally and age-appropriate lessons and practice questions. Students can be confident that SOLARO has the right materials to help them when they are having difficulties in class. SOLARO is 100% compliant with each region's core standards. Teachers can use SOLARO in the classroom as a supplemental resource to provide remediation and enrichment. Student performance is reported to the teacher through various reports, which provide insight into strengths and weaknesses.

TABLE OF CONTENTS

CREDITS

Every effort has been made to provide proper acknowledgement of the original source and to comply with copyright law. However, some attempts to establish original copyright ownership may have been unsuccessful. If copyright ownership can be identified, please notify Castle Rock Research Corp so that appropriate corrective action can be taken.

Some images in this document may be from www.clipart.com, copyright (c) 2013 Getty images

Some images in this document may be from www.nasa.com.

Some images may be from National Atmospheric and Oceanic Administration http://www.noaa.gov/.

Some images may be from www.usgs.gov/.

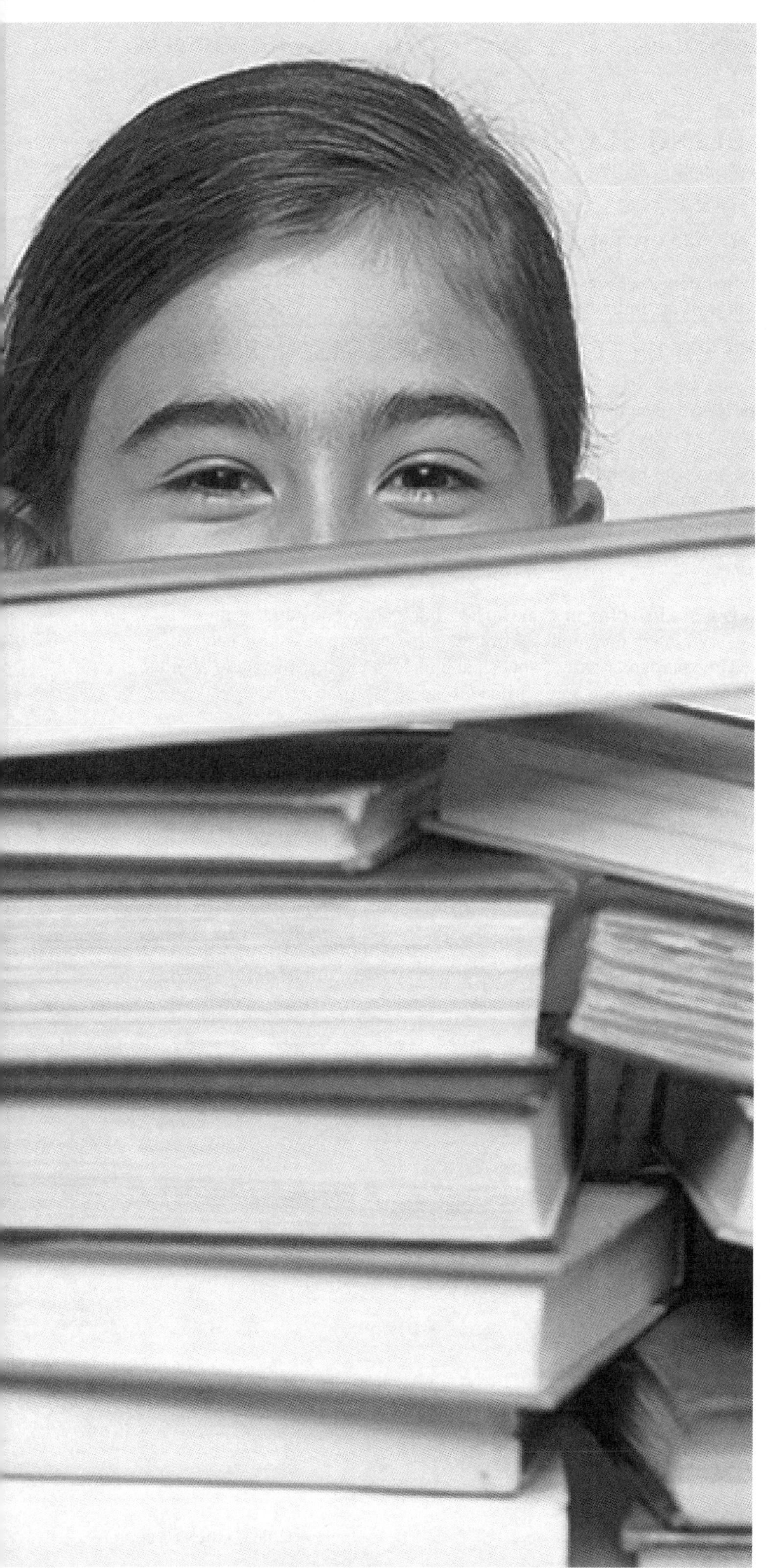

Key Tips for Being Successful at School

KEY TIPS FOR BEING SUCCESSFUL AT SCHOOL

KEY FACTORS CONTRIBUTING TO SCHOOL SUCCESS

In addition to learning the content of your courses, there are some other things that you can do to help you do your best at school. You can try some of the following strategies:

- **Keep a positive attitude:** Always reflect on what you can already do and what you already know.
- **Be prepared to learn:** Have the necessary pencils, pens, notebooks, and other required materials for participating in class ready.
- **Complete all of your assignments:** Do your best to finish all of your assignments. Even if you know the material well, practice will reinforce your knowledge. If an assignment or question is difficult for you, work through it as far as you can so that your teacher can see exactly where you are having difficulty.
- **Set small goals for yourself when you are learning new material:** For example, when learning the parts of speech, do not try to learn everything in one night. Work on only one part or section each study session. When you have memorized one particular part of speech and understand it, move on to another one. Continue this process until you have memorized and learned all the parts of speech.
- **Review your classroom work regularly at home:** Review to make sure you understand the material you learned in class.

- **Ask your teacher for help:** Your teacher will help you if you do not understand something or if you are having a difficult time completing your assignments.
- **Get plenty of rest and exercise:** Concentrating in class is hard work. It is important to be well-rested and have time to relax and socialize with your friends. This helps you keep a positive attitude about your schoolwork.
- **Eat healthy meals:** A balanced diet keeps you healthy and gives you the energy you need for studying at school and at home.

How to Find Your Learning Style

Every student learns differently. The manner in which you learn best is called your learning style. By knowing your learning style, you can increase your success at school. Most students use a combination of learning styles. Do you know what type of learner you are? Read the following descriptions. Which of these common learning styles do you use most often?

- **Linguistic Learner:** You may learn best by saying, hearing, and seeing words. You are probably really good at memorizing things such as dates, places, names, and facts. You may need to write down the steps in a process, a formula, or the actions that lead up to a significant event, and then say them out loud.
- **Spatial Learner:** You may learn best by looking at and working with pictures. You are probably really good at puzzles, imagining things, and reading maps and charts. You may need to use strategies like mind mapping and webbing to organize your information and study notes.
- **Kinesthetic Learner:** You may learn best by touching, moving, and figuring things out using manipulatives. You are probably really good at physical activities and learning through movement. You may need to draw your finger over a diagram to remember it, tap out the steps needed to solve a problem, or feel yourself writing or typing a formula.

SCHEDULING STUDY TIME

You should review your class notes regularly to ensure that you have a clear understanding of all the new material you learned. Reviewing your lessons on a regular basis helps you to learn and remember ideas and concepts. It also reduces the quantity of material that you need to study prior to a test. Establishing a study schedule will help you to make the best use of your time.

Regardless of the type of study schedule you use, you may want to consider the following suggestions to maximize your study time and effort:

- Organize your work so that you begin with the most challenging material first.
- Divide the subject's content into small, manageable chunks.
- Alternate regularly between your different subjects and types of study activities in order to maintain your interest and motivation.
- Make a daily list with headings like "Must Do," "Should Do," and "Could Do."
- Begin each study session by quickly reviewing what you studied the day before.
- Maintain your usual routine of eating, sleeping, and exercising to help you concentrate better for extended periods of time.

Creating Study Notes

Mind-Mapping or Webbing

Use the key words, ideas, or concepts from your reading or class notes to create a mind map or web (a diagram or visual representation of the given information). A mind map or web is sometimes referred to as a knowledge map. Use the following steps to create a mind map or web:

1. Write the key word, concept, theory, or formula in the centre of your page.

2. Write down related facts, ideas, events, and information, and link them to the central concept with lines.

3. Use coloured markers, underlining, or symbols to emphasize things such as relationships, timelines, and important information.

The following examples of a Frayer Model illustrate how this technique can be used to study vocabulary.

Definition	**Notes**
• Perimeter is the distance around the outside of a polygon.	• Perimeter is measured in linear units (e.g., metres, centimetres, and so on).
Perimeter	
Examples	**Non-Examples**
• The length of a fence around a yard • The distance around a circle (circumference)	• The area of grass covering a lawn • The size of a rug lying on a floor

Definition	**Notes**
• A cube is a solid 3-D object with six faces.	• A cube is different from other shapes because it has six equally-sized square faces, eight vertices, and twelve equal edges.
Cube	
Examples	**Non-Examples**
B	

INDEX CARDS

To use index cards while studying, follow these steps:

1. Write a key word or question on one side of an index card.
2. On the reverse side, write the definition of the word, answer to the question, or any other important information that you want to remember.

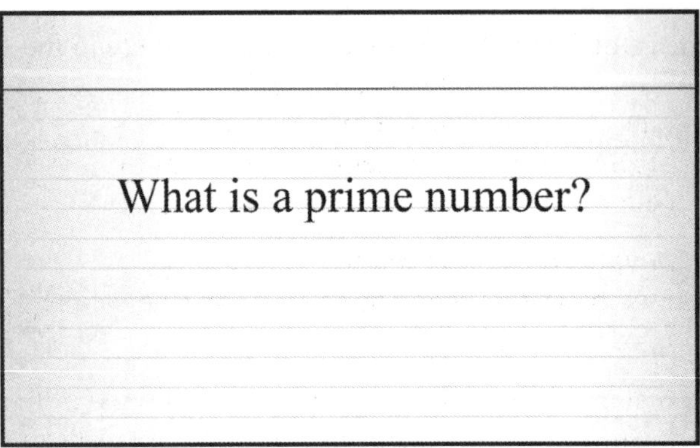

What is a prime number?

A prime number is any number that has exactly 2 factors.
A prime number can be divided evenly only by itself and one.
For example, 2, 3, 5, 7, 19.
The number 1 is not a prime number.

SYMBOLS AND STICKY NOTES—IDENTIFYING IMPORTANT INFORMATION

Use symbols to mark your class notes. The following are some examples:

- An exclamation mark (!) might be used to point out something that must be learned well because it is a very important idea.
- A question mark (?) may highlight something you are not certain about
- A diamond (◊) or asterisk (*) could highlight interesting information that you want to remember.

Sticky notes are useful in the following situations:

- Use sticky notes when you are not allowed to put marks in books.
- Use sticky notes to mark a page in a book that contains an important diagram, formula, explanation, or other information.
- Use sticky notes to mark important facts in research books.

MEMORIZATION TECHNIQUES

- **Association** relates new learning to something you already know. For example, to remember the spelling difference between dessert and desert, recall that the word *sand* has only one *s*. So, because there is sand in a desert, the word *desert* has only one *s*.
- **Mnemonic** devices are sentences that you create to remember a list or group of items. For example, the first letter of each word in the phrase "Every Good Boy Deserves Fudge" helps you to remember the names of the lines on the treble-clef staff (E, G, B, D, and F) in music.

- **Acronyms** are words that are formed from the first letters or parts of the words in a group. For example, RADAR is actually an acronym for Radio Detecting and Ranging, and MASH is an acronym for Mobile Army Surgical Hospital. HOMES helps you to remember the names of the five Great Lakes (Huron, Ontario, Michigan, Erie, and Superior).
- **Visualizing** requires you to use your mind's eye to "see" a chart, list, map, diagram, or sentence as it is in your textbook or notes, on the chalkboard or computer screen, or in a display.
- **Initialisms** are abbreviations that are formed from the first letters or parts of the words in a group. Unlike acronyms, an initialism cannot be pronounced as a word itself. For example, GCF is an initialism for **G**reatest **C**ommon **F**actor.

KEY STRATEGIES FOR REVIEWING

Reviewing textbook material, class notes, and handouts should be an ongoing activity. Spending time reviewing becomes more critical when you are preparing for a test. You may find some of the following review strategies useful when studying during your scheduled study time:

- Before reading a selection, preview it by noting the headings, charts, graphs, and chapter questions.
- Before reviewing a unit, note the headings, charts, graphs, and chapter questions.
- Highlight key concepts, vocabulary, definitions, and formulas.
- Skim the paragraph, and note the key words, phrases, and information.
- Carefully read over each step in a procedure.
- Draw a picture or diagram to help make the concept clearer.

KEY STRATEGIES FOR SUCCESS: A CHECKLIST

Reviewing is a huge part of doing well at school and preparing for tests. Here is a checklist for you to keep track of how many suggested strategies for success you are using. Read each question, and put a check mark (✓) in the correct column. Look at the questions where you have checked the "No" column. Think about how you might try using some of these strategies to help you do your best at school.

Key Strategies for Success	Yes	No
Do you attend school regularly?		
Do you know your personal learning style—how you learn best?		
Do you spend 15 to 30 minutes a day reviewing your notes?		
Do you study in a quiet place at home?		
Do you clearly mark the most important ideas in your study notes?		
Do you use sticky notes to mark texts and research books?		
Do you practise answering multiple-choice and written-response questions?		
Do you ask your teacher for help when you need it?		
Are you maintaining a healthy diet and sleep routine?		
Are you participating in regular physical activity?		

Quantitative Reasoning

QUANTITATIVE REASONING

Table of Correlations

Standard		Concepts	Exercise #1	Exercise #2
Unit1.1	Reason quantitatively and use units to solve problems.			
N-Q.1	*Use units as a way to understand problems and to guide the solution of multi-step problems; choose and interpret units consistently in formulas; choose and interpret the scale and the origin in graphs and data displays.*	Graphing Data Using Technology	1	10
		Solving Linear Measurement Problems	2	11
		Displaying Data in a Scatter Plot	3	12
		Creating and Comparing Bar Graphs, Histograms, and Line Graphs	4	13
		Creating Circle Graphs	5	14
N-Q.2	*Define appropriate quantities for the purpose of descriptive modeling.*	Identifying Referents for Linear Measurements for the Imperial System	6	15
		Comparing SI and Imperial Units Using Referents	7	
		Estimating Linear Measurement Using a Referent	8	16
N-Q.3	*Choose a level of accuracy appropriate to limitations on measurement when reporting quantities.*	Calculating the Relative Error in Measuring Square and Cubic Units	9	17

N-Q.1 Use units as a way to understand problems and to guide the solution of multi-step problems; choose and interpret units consistently in formulas; choose and interpret the scale and the origin in graphs and data displays.

Graphing Data Using Technology

Continuous data includes all values between the measured points as well as the measure points. For example, if a child's height is measured at 105 cm one year and 109 cm the next year, it is understood that during that year, the child passed through each of the heights between 105 cm and 109 cm.

Discrete data does not include all the in-between data. For example, if a can of pop costs $1.00, it is assumed that 1.32 cans of pop cannot be purchased for $1.32. It does not make sense to think of partial cans of pop being sold.

When graphing continuous information, the data must be connected by a line to indicate the inclusion of all the information between the points.

Graphs of discrete points should not have the points connected. The exception is when the range of numbers is large relative to the space between them. For example, with respect to the $1.00 can of pop, it would not be reasonable to graph 1,000 separate points to represent the sale of 1,000 cans of pop.

Linear and non-linear data can be graphed using a graphing calculator, such as the T1-83 Plus.

Using technology, such as a T1-83 Plus calculator, to graph linear and non-linear data requires the use of proper window settings and the appropriate selection of calculator buttons.

For example, to graph the data in the given table, follow these general steps:

Time (min)	Length (m)
0	0
2	10
4	20
6	30
8	40

Step 1: Delete the previous data in the calculator.

Press 2nd + to access the MEMORY menu.

Select 4:ClrAllLists.

Press ENTER two times. Any data that was contained in the lists will be cleared.

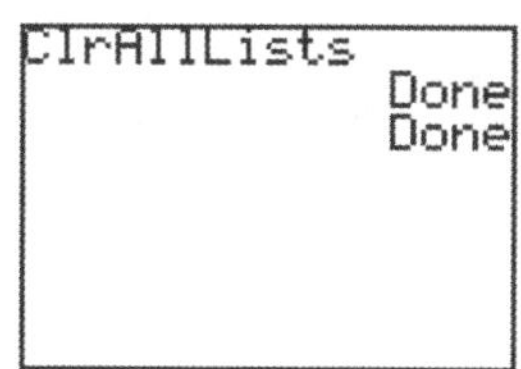

Step 2: Enter the appropriate data into the list editor.

Press STAT to view the EDIT menu.

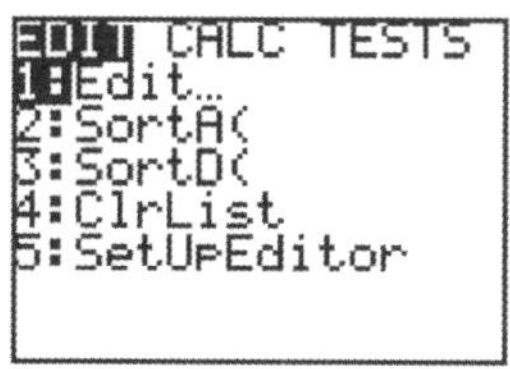

Select 1:Edit…

If there is data in the columns, press  to move the cursor onto L1.

Press CLEAR ENTER. Move to L2 using ▶, and repeat the process.

Using the cursor keys, move the cursor to the first column, as highlighted in the given screen shot.

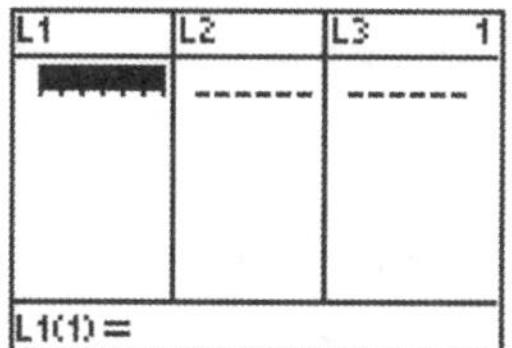

Enter the numbers representing the *x*-values (independent variables) in L1.

Press ENTER after each data entry to move the cursor to the next row. Continue this process until all the *x*-values are entered.

Press ▶ to move to column L2.

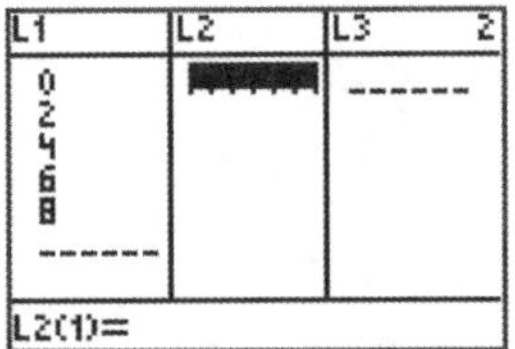

Enter the numbers representing the *y*-values (dependent variables) in L2.

Step 3: Choose a graph.

Press 2nd Y = to view the STAT PLOTS menu.

Select 1:Plot 1…On

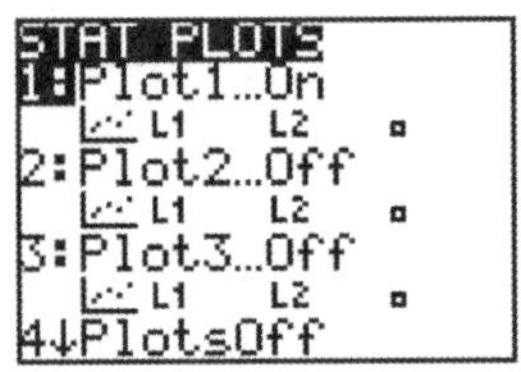

Turn on the STAT PLOT by pressing ENTER if the cursor is highlighting ON.

Use the cursor keys to navigate through each of the rows.

Select from the following options you want by highlighting that option, and then press ENTER.

- "On" means STAT PLOT is on and the data will be plotted by pressing GRAPH.
- "Type" shows icons of how the graph will be displayed. Select the first graph if the data is discrete. Select the second graph if the data is continuous. In the given example, the data is continuous, so select the second graph.
- "Xlist" should read "L1" to tell the calculator that the data from list 1 goes on the *x*-axis.
- "Ylist" should read "L2" to tell the calculator that the data from list 2 goes on the *y*-axis.
- "Mark" shows icons of how each point will be plotted.

Step 4: Set an appropriate window setting for the graph so that all the data will be displayed appropriately. Setting the window is the graphing calculator's equivalent to choosing and labeling the scale. The minimum, maximum, and scale for each axis must be entered.

Press WINDOW.

Type in appropriate minimum, maximum, and scale values. For instance, in the given example, press ENTER after each entry and navigate through the rows.

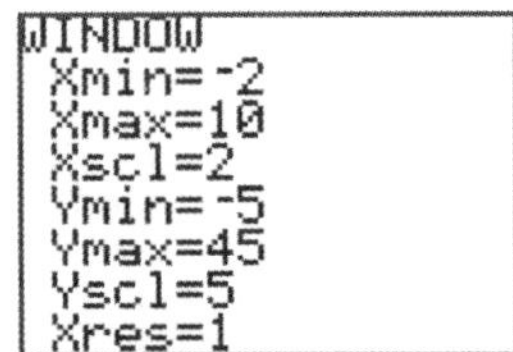

- "Xmin" is the smallest value represented on the *x*-axis. Choose a value one increment smaller than the smallest *x*-value in the table of values.
- "Xmax" is the largest value represented on the *x*-axis. Choose a value one increment larger than the largest *x*-value in the table of values.
- "Xscl" is the scale or spacing between tick marks on the *x*-axis. Choose an increment that is a factor of most of the values in the table of values.

- "Ymin" is the smallest value represented on the *y*-axis. Choose a value one increment smaller than the smallest *y*-value in the table of values.
- "Ymax" is the largest number represented on the *y*-axis. Choose a value one increment larger than the largest *y*-value in the table of values.
- "Yscl" is the scale or spacing between the tick marks on the *y*-axis.
- "Xres" defines the distance, in pixels, between consecutive evaluated *x*-values. The default is set at 1.

A shorthand method of communicating the window setting is in the form of
$X[x_{min}, x_{max}, x_{scl}]Y[y_{min}, y_{max}, y_{scl}]$.

For most data, a good starting window setting can be created by pressing the ZOOM button and selecting 9:ZoomStat or 0:Fit feature.

Step 5: Press the GRAPH button to view the graph of the data represented by the table of values. A possible graph is as shown.

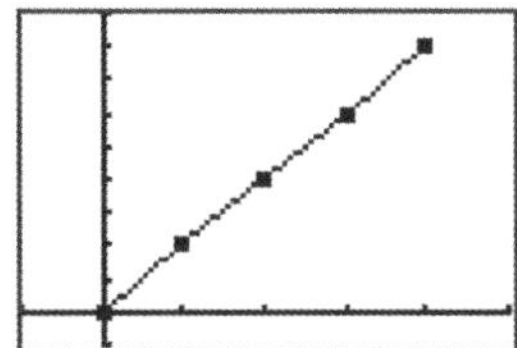

Solving Linear Measurement Problems

To estimate a linear measure, it is important to select the most appropriate **imperial** or SI unit of measure. A personal **referent** can then be used to approximate the length of an object or the distance between two points.

Example

To estimate the length of her car, Fiona could use the length of her thumb to the first joint or her stride length.

Which referent and corresponding imperial unit would be the **most appropriate** choice?

Solution

Using the thumb as a referent would be far too tedious, impractical, and prone to measurement error. Therefore, the stride, corresponding approximately to the imperial unit of 1 yd, would be the most appropriate referent to use in order to estimate the length of a car.

When solving problems involving linear measurement, use an appropriate instrument (ruler, tape measure, etc.), use necessary formulas, and use an effective problem-solving strategy.

Example

Conrad wanted to buy enough border material for his circular garden plot. Since he had no measuring instrument, he used his shoe to estimate the diameter of the garden plot to be 9.5 shoe lengths. When he got to the store, he measured his shoe with a tape measure, and determined its length to be $10\frac{3}{8}$ in.

To the nearest inch, what is the approximate length of the border material required?

Solution

Step 1

Calculate the diameter, d, of the garden plot.

d = shoe length × # of shoe lengths

$$\begin{aligned} d &= 10\frac{3}{8} \times 9.5 \\ &= 10.375 \times 9.5 \\ &= 98.5625 \text{ in} \end{aligned}$$

Step 2

Determine the length of the border material by calculating the circumference, C, of the garden plot.

$$\begin{aligned} C &= \pi d \\ &= \pi \times 98.5625 \\ &\approx 309.6432 \text{ in} \end{aligned}$$

The approximate length of the border material required is 310 in.

Displaying Data in a Scatter Plot

A **scatter plot** is a graphical method of displaying the relationship or correlation between two variables from given data. The two axes are labeled with the variables that are being compared: the x-axis represents the independent variable, and the y-axis represents the dependent variable. In a scatter plot, each point represents one ordered pair.

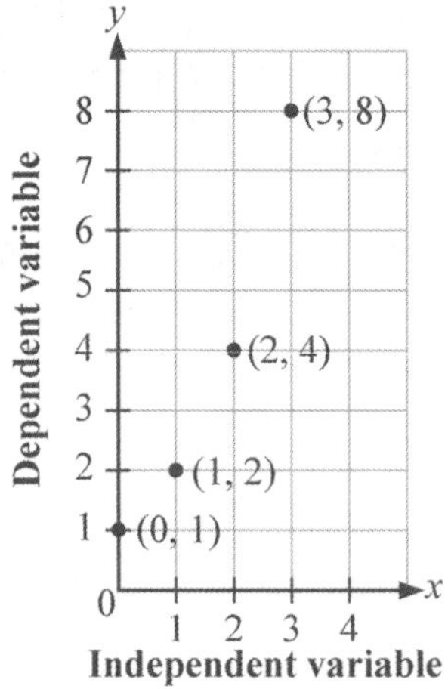

It is useful to display data in a scatter plot when you need to determine the type and strength of the relationship between the variables.

To represent data in a scatter plot, follow these general steps:

1. Write the ordered pairs to be plotted.
2. Choose suitable increments to mark both axes for the data.
3. Draw the axes, and plot the points.
4. Label the axes, and give the scatter plot a title.

(Note that steps 3 and 4 can be combined into one step.)

Example

A certain isotope of phosphorus has a half-life of 14 days. This means that half the isotope decays every 14 days. The given table shows the percentage of phosphorus left after a certain number of days.

Number of Days	Percentage of Phosphorus (%)
0	100
14	50
28	25
42	12.5
56	6.25
70	3.125
84	1.5625

Create a scatter plot for the data.

Solution

Step 1

Write the ordered pairs to be plotted.

The independent variable is the x-value, and the dependent variable is the y-value.

Number of Days	Percentage of Phosphorus	Ordered Pair
0	100	(0, 100)
14	50	(14, 50)
28	25	(28, 25)
42	12.5	(42, 12.5)
56	6.25	(56, 6.25)
70	3.125	(70, 3.125)
84	1.5625	(84, 1.5625)

Step 2

Choose a suitable scale (intervals) for numbering the axes.

The scale on the x-axis will be 14, but the scale for the y-axis is not obvious. If you can, choose a scale that is a factor of the majority of the values given. In this case, there is no obvious factor to use, so a scale that is easy to work with is 10.

Step 3
Draw the axes lines, and plot the points. Label the axes according to the set of data they represent, and give the scatter plot a title.

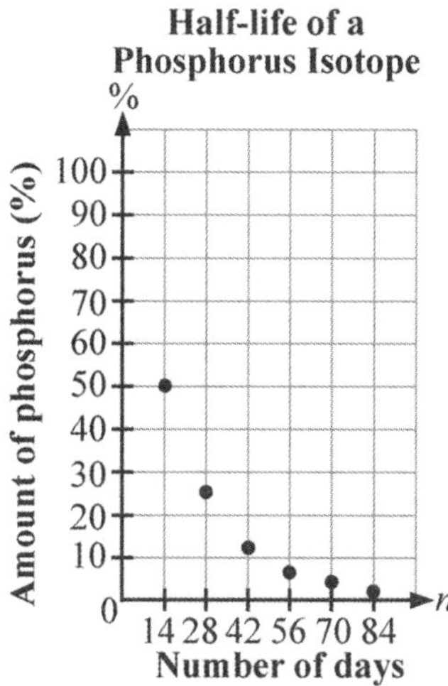

Observe that the scatter plot represents data that is non-linear.

Example

The table represents the relationship between each person's mass and his or her IQ for seven individuals.

Mass (kg)	65	70	75	80	85	90	100
IQ	125	85	140	95	100	130	95

Create a scatter plot for the data.

Solution

Step 1
Write the ordered pairs to be plotted.

The independent variable is the x-value, and the dependent variable is the y-value.

Mass (kg)	IQ	Ordered Pair
65	125	(65, 125)
70	85	(70, 85)
75	140	(75, 140)
80	95	(80, 95)
85	100	(85, 100)
90	130	(90, 130)
100	95	(100, 95)

Step 2
Choose a suitable and equal scale (intervals) for numbering the axes.

The independent variable (mass) will be on the horizontal x-axis. It increases by 5 kg at each point. All the data will be clearly displayed if the minimum x-value is 65 to a maximum x-value of 100.

The dependent variable (IQ) will be on the vertical y-axis. It increases by 10 at each point. All the data will be displayed if the minimum y-value is 85 to a maximum y-value of 140.

Step 3
Draw the axes lines, and plot the points.

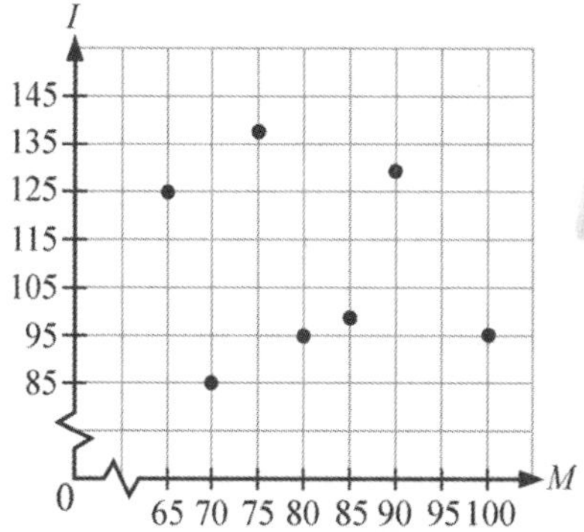

Step 4
Label the axes according to the set of data they represent, and give the scatter plot a title.

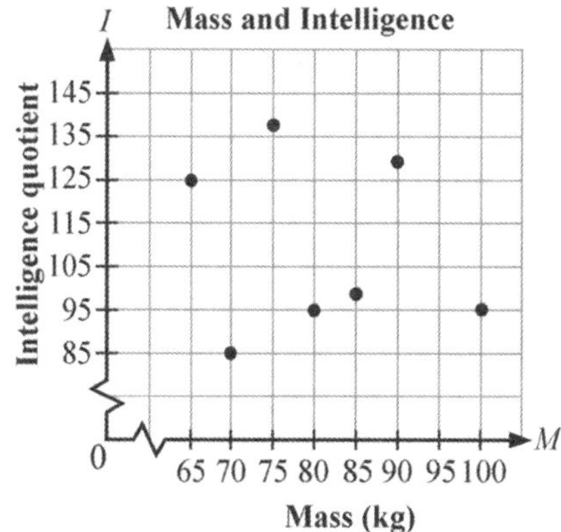

Observe that the scatterplot represents data that is non-linear.

Creating and Comparing Bar Graphs, Histograms, and Line Graphs

Data can be displayed in bar graphs, histograms, and line graphs. The type of graph used depends on the type of data.

Bar Graphs

Bar graphs are used to display categorical data, which is data that fits into separate and distinct categories. Each bar represents a category. Bar graphs are drawn with spaces between the bars.

Follow these steps to construct a bar graph:

1. Choose suitable increments to mark both axes for the data.
2. Label and draw the axes. Give the bar graph a title.
3. Draw bars to represent data from each category. Leave an appropriate amount of space between the bars.

Example

A gym teacher surveyed 105 students in a junior high school to determine which sport students most prefer playing. The following table shows the results of this survey.

Sport	Number of Students
Volleyball	15
Badminton	20
Soccer	30
Dodgeball	40

Construct a bar graph to illustrate the given data.

Solution

Step 1
Choose suitable increments to mark both axes for the data.

In this case, the four different sports should be spread out along the horizontal axis.
The number of students who chose each sport should be represented on the vertical axis.
Since the data ranges from 15 to 40, a suitable scale would be from 0 to 45, going up by five units.

Step 2
Label and draw the axes. Give the bar graph a title.

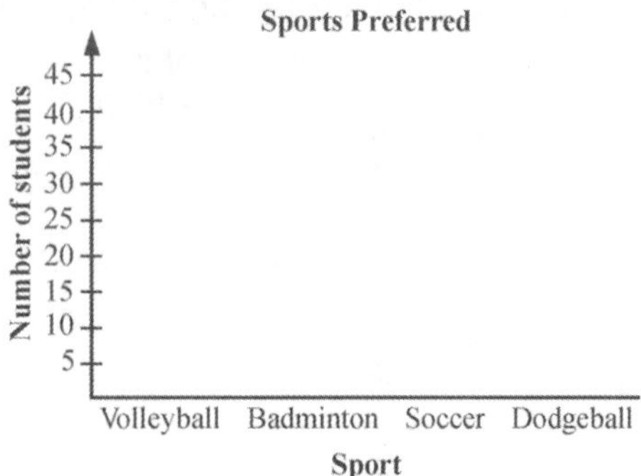

Step 3
Draw bars to represent data from each category. Leave an appropriate amount of space between each bar.

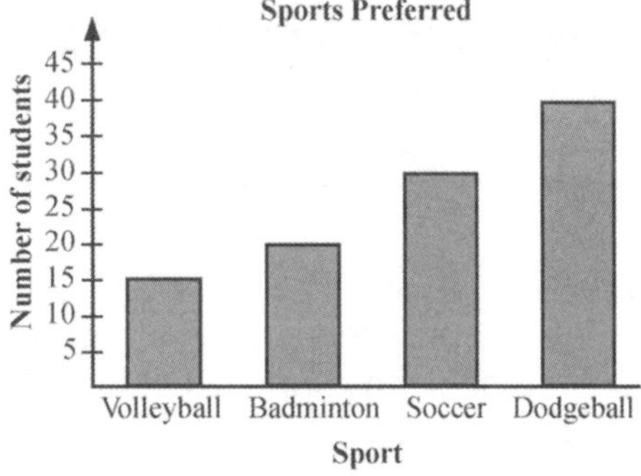

Histograms

Histograms are used to represent continuous data found in a frequency table. Continuous data usually represents something that can be measured. A histogram looks similar to a bar graph, but since the data is continuous, there are no gaps between the bars.

The horizontal axis of a histogram represents the intervals, and the vertical axis represents the frequency of the data. To construct a histogram, follow these steps:

1. Construct a frequency table for the given data set.
2. Draw and label the axes. Give the histogram a title.
3. Draw bars to represent each interval.

Example

A track and field coach recorded the time it took for 25 high school students to complete a 400 m race. The following table gives the times to the nearest tenth of a minute.

Time Taken to Complete a 400 m Race (min)

1.6	1.3	1.8	0.9	1.4
1.7	1.7	1.4	1.2	2.1
2.6	1.9	1.4	1.8	2.2
2.4	2.7	1.9	1.8	2.3
2.6	1.9	2.4	2.1	2.7

Construct a histogram from the given data.

Solution

Step 1

Construct a frequency table. Set an appropriate interval width. In this case, an interval width of 0.5 min can be used, starting at 0.5.

Time (min)	Frequency
0.5–0.9	1
1.0–1.4	5
1.5–1.9	9
2.0–2.4	6
2.5–2.9	4

Step 2

Draw and label the axes. Give the histogram a title.

The horizontal axis of a histogram represents the intervals, and the vertical axis represents the frequency of the data. Label the horizontal axis "Time" and the vertical axis "Frequency." Use the same interval width as the frequency table.

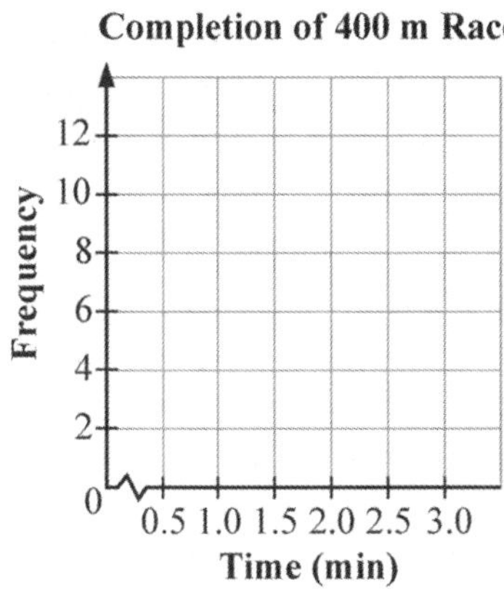

Step 3

Draw bars to represent each interval.

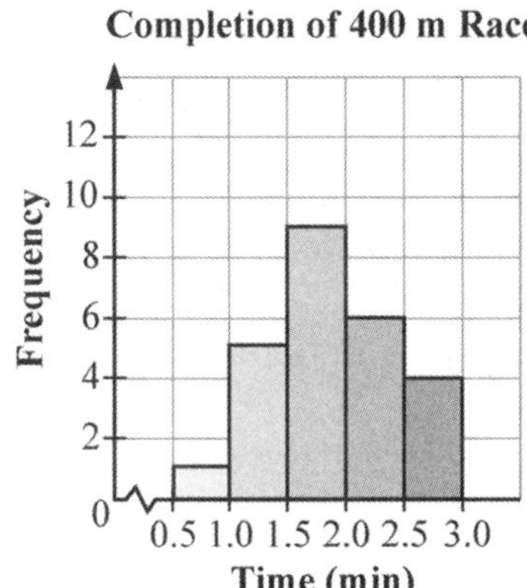

The following graph shows another way to represent the intervals on the horizontal axis.

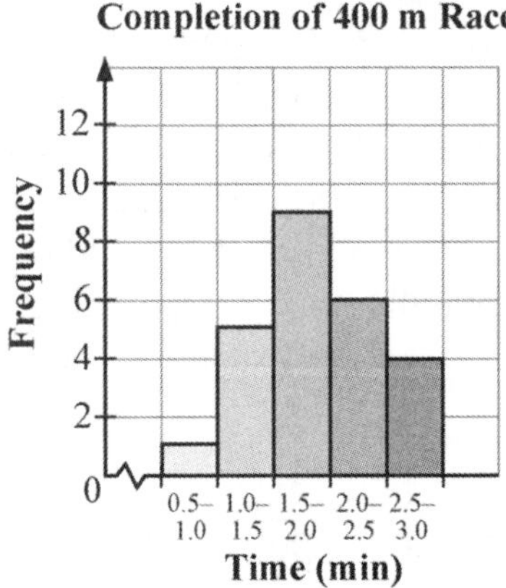

Histograms are useful for graphing large sets of data and for displaying the distribution of the data set.

Line Graphs

Line graphs are used to show trends in data over time. They often show continuous data.

To represent data in a line graph, follow these steps:

1. Write the ordered pairs to be plotted.
2. Choose suitable increments to mark both axes for the data.
3. Draw and label the axes. Give the line graph a title.
4. Plot the points, and draw a line to connect them.

Example

The following table lists the highest temperatures reached over a 10-day period in the month of May.

Day	Temperature (°C)
1	15
2	13
3	18
4	20
5	12
6	11
7	19
8	25
9	16
10	26

Graph the given data using an appropriate graph type.

Solution

Since the given data covers a 10-day period, it is best displayed using a line graph.

Step 1

Write the ordered pairs to be plotted.

The independent variable, the *x*-value, is the day. The dependent variable, the *y*-value, is the temperature.

Day	Temperature (°C)	Ordered Pair
1	15	(1, 15)
2	13	(2, 13)
3	18	(3, 18)
4	20	(4, 20)
5	12	(5, 12)
6	11	(6, 11)
7	19	(7, 19)
8	25	(8, 25)
9	16	(9, 16)
10	26	(10, 26)

Step 2
Choose suitable increments to mark both axes for the data.

Choose a scale that is a factor of the majority of the values given. Since the days go up by 1, the scale on the x-axis will be 1. There is no set pattern for the temperature, so the scale on the y-axis can start at 10 and go up by 2.

Step 3
Draw and label the axes. Give the line graph a title.

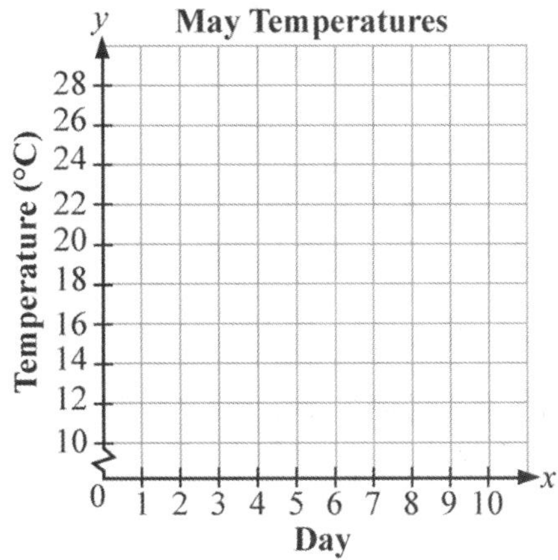

Step 4
Plot the points, and draw a line to connect them.

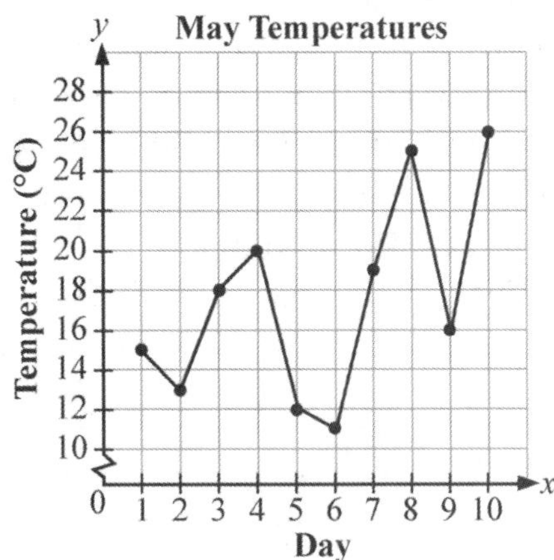

Creating Circle Graphs

Circle graphs represent data that constitutes parts of a whole. This data is divided into parts called wedges or sectors. The circle represents 100%, and each sector represents a part of 100%. This allows you to easily compare one sector to another. Each percentage corresponds to an equivalent number of degrees in the circle.

Circle graphs are generally used to represent data with different values for given variables. This type of data is referred to as categorical data. Examples of categorical data are size (small, medium, large), music style (pop, jazz, rock, hip hop), or age group (infant, toddler, adolescent, adult, senior).

To construct a circle graph, follow these steps:

1. Convert the data into percentages.
2. Calculate each percentage as an angle in degrees.
3. Draw a circle, and add each of the angles using a protractor and straight edge.
4. Label the circle graph.

Example

The number of goals in a season made by each player on the Fury, a local co-ed hockey team, is shown in the given table.

Player	Number of Goals
Tyler	11
Vickie	29
Minh	3
Matt	23
Ed	8
Chandra	17
Natalie	35
Lucas	6
Darren	2

Build a circle graph from the given data.

Solution

Step 1

Convert the data into percentages.

The total number of goals scored in the season is 134. 11 + 29 + 3 + 23 + 8 +17 + 35 + 6 + 2 = 134

Player	Number of Goals	Percentage of Goals (%)
Tyler	11	$\frac{11}{134}(100) \approx 8.21$
Vickie	29	$\frac{29}{134}(100) \approx 21.64$
Minh	3	$\frac{3}{134}(100) \approx 2.24$
Matt	23	$\frac{23}{134}(100) \approx 17.16$
Ed	8	$\frac{8}{134}(100) \approx 5.97$
Chandra	17	$\frac{17}{134}(100) \approx 12.69$
Natalie	35	$\frac{35}{134}(100) \approx 26.12$
Lucas	6	$\frac{6}{134}(100) \approx 4.48$
Darren	2	$\frac{2}{134}(100) \approx 1.49$

Step 2

Calculate each percentage as an angle in degrees, and order them from largest to smallest.

Multiply each percentage by $\frac{360°}{100\%}$.

Natalie—$26.12\% \times \frac{360°}{100\%} \approx 94.03°$

Vickie—$21.64\% \times \frac{360°}{100\%} \approx 77.90°$

Matt—$17.16\% \times \frac{360°}{100\%} \approx 61.78°$

Chandra—$12.69\% \times \frac{360°}{100\%} \approx 45.68°$

Tyler—$8.21\% \times \frac{360°}{100\%} \approx 29.56°$

Ed—$5.97\% \times \frac{360°}{100\%} \approx 21.49°$

Lucas—$4.48\% \times \frac{360°}{100\%} \approx 16.13°$

Minh—$2.24\% \times \frac{360°}{100\%} \approx 8.06°$

Darren—$1.49\% \times \frac{360°}{100\%} \approx 5.36°$

Step 3

Draw a circle, and add each of the angles using a protractor and straight edge.

Be sure to make a circle large enough to label all the sectors. Use a protractor to draw each of the angles or sectors. Start at the top of the circle graph, using the largest angle. Move in a clockwise direction until the smallest angle is drawn.

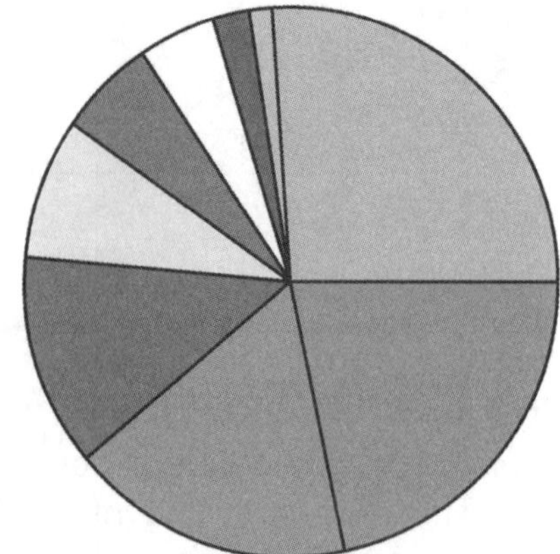

Step 4

Label the circle graph.

Include the category and percentage for each sector. Give the graph a title.

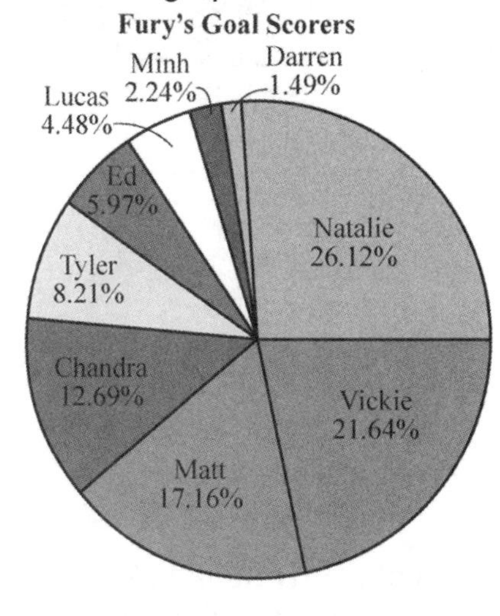

N-Q.2 Define appropriate quantities for the purpose of descriptive modeling.

Identifying Referents for Linear Measurements for the Imperial System

The imperial system of measure is sometimes referred to as the **human system** because the basic units are often lengths and quantities most people are familiar with. There are many common referents for imperial measurement based on measurements of the body.

For example, a yard is about the distance from a man's breastbone to the end of his outstretched arm. Another example is that one foot is about the length from a wrist to an elbow. Using such referents can simplify measuring a distance.

Example

What is a good referent for measuring the length of one inch?

Solution

A good referent for one inch is the distance from the tip of the thumb to the first joint.

What is a good referent for measuring the length of one foot?

Solution

A good referent for one foot is the length of a grown man's foot.

Example

Chelsea wants to build a fence around her yard. She needs to estimate the total length of fencing required in feet before she can buy her supplies.

Describe how Chelsea could estimate the total length of the fencing she needs using a referent.

Solution

Chelsea could use her stride length as a referent if she knows her stride length is about three feet. Chelsea could count the number of strides as she walks around the perimeter of her yard until she returns to her starting point. Then she could multiply the number of strides that she counted as she walked by 3. This will give her an estimate of the distance around her yard in feet.

Example

Using a referent, estimate the height of a doorway in feet. Explain your answer.

Solution

A good referent for one foot is the length from your elbow to your wrist. Place your elbow at the bottom end of the doorway, and point your arm upward. Mark the position of your wrist. Then, place your elbow at this mark, point your arm upward again, and mark the position of your wrist. Repeat this process until you reach the top of the doorway (you may have to stand on a chair). This will give you an estimate of the height of the doorway.

Using a referent, estimate the width of a doorway in feet. Explain your answer.

Solution

A good referent for the length of one foot is your foot. Place one foot at the edge of the doorway and place the other foot in front of it. Count how many foot steps it takes to cross the width of the doorway. This will give you an estimate for the width of the doorway in feet.

Comparing SI and Imperial Units Using Referents

It is important to use only one measurement system in technical occupations. However, most people use both SI and imperial units in their everyday lives. For example, people may describe their height in feet and inches, even if they describe the distance between two towns in kilometers. Therefore, you must be able to compare SI and imperial units. You can use referents to compare these distances easily. It is much easier to compare units of similar sizes, such as centimeters and inches, meters and yards, and kilometers and miles. Use referents of an appropriate scale for these comparisons.

A centimeter is about the width of your fingernail. The length from the tip of the thumb to the first joint is about an inch.

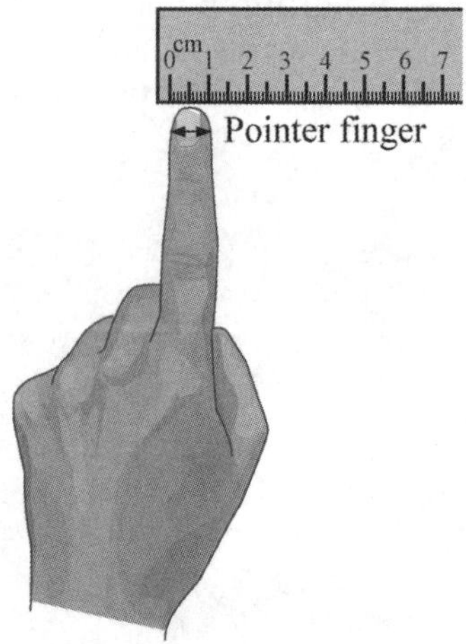

Some other common referents for 1 cm include the length or width of a die and the length or width of a sugar cube. Another referent for 1 inch in length or width is an ice cube.

Example

Compare the lengths of one inch and one centimeter using their referents.

Solution

An inch is about the length from the tip of the thumb to the first joint. A centimeter is about the length of the thumbnail. Therefore, an inch is a little more than twice as long as a centimeter.

Compare the sizes of one kilometer and one mile using their referents.

Solution

A kilometer is about 7 city blocks long, while a mile is about 12 city blocks long. A mile is almost twice as long as a kilometer.

Estimating Linear Measurement Using a Referent

A **referent** used to estimate a measurement must be easily accessible. After selecting an appropriate referent, use it as a standard measurement instrument to measure the unknown length.

For example, if a tape measure is unavailable when purchasing a piece of furniture to fit in a living room, simply measuring its length in numbers of hand spans will be a good approximation. If the measure of a hand span is approximately eight inches, the approximate length of the furniture in inches can be easily calculated.

Example

Explain how to estimate the length of a dining room table in centimeters using a referent.

Solution

Use your hand width with fingers together as a referent for 10 cm. Measure the length of the table using your hand widths. You can then approximate the length of the table based on the number of hand widths and the length of one hand width. For example, if the length of the table is 16 hand widths, then the table measures approximately $10 \times 16 = 160$ cm.

Explain how to estimate the width of a putting green at a golf course using a referent.

Solution

An appropriate unit for measuring the width of a putting green is a meter. Use the length of a large stride as a referent for one meter. Count the number of large steps from one edge of the putting green to the other to measure its width.

Explain how to estimate the length of a paper-clip using a referent.

Solution

An appropriate unit for measuring the length of a paper-clip is a millimeter. The thickness of a credit card is about one millimeter, so it can be used as a referent. Place a credit card, on edge, successively side by side to measure the length of a paper clip.

Example

Jani wants to know the height of the ceiling, but she cannot reach high enough to use her meter stick. She knows that the distance from the floor to the doorknob is about 1 m.

By looking at the given picture, estimate the height of the ceiling using the distance from the floor to the doorknob as a referent for 1 m.

Solution

Jani would see that the ceiling is about 3 times the distance from the floor to the doorknob. The ceiling is about 3 m high.

N-Q.3 Choose a level of accuracy appropriate to limitations on measurement when reporting quantities.

Calculating the Relative Error in Measuring Square and Cubic Units

When errors are made in linear measurements, these errors are compounded in square and cubic measurements.

Example

A cube with 9 cm sides will have a surface area of $9 \times 9 \times 6 = 486$ cm^2 and a volume of $9 \times 9 \times 9 = 729$ cm^3. If the cube is incorrectly measured as having 11 cm sides, the surface area will be calculated as $11 \times 11 \times 6 = 726$ cm^2 and the volume will be $11 \times 11 \times 11 = 1{,}331$ cm^3.

In this case, a 2 cm error in linear measurement results in a 240 cm^2 error in calculated surface area and a 602 cm^3 error in calculated volume.

The relative error of these measurements can be determined by comparing the measured value to the actual value.

The relative error is calculated using the following formula:

$$\text{relative error} = \frac{|\text{measured value} - \text{actual value}|}{\text{actual value}}$$

The error is commonly represented as a percentage, and the formula used to calculate the percent error is as follows:
percent error = relative error × 100

When calculating relative or percent error, try to use exact values until the final calculation is performed, since rounding prior to it will add to the errors.

Example

For the cube with 9 cm sides, the percent errors in linear measurement, calculated surface area, and calculated volume can all be calculated.

Percent error in linear measurement:

$$\frac{|11 - 9|}{9} \times 100 \approx 22.2\%$$

Percent error in calculated surface area:

$$\frac{|726 - 486|}{486} \times 100 \approx 49.4\%$$

Percent error in calculated volume:

$$\frac{|1{,}331 - 729|}{729} \times 100 \approx 82.6\%$$

Example

A cylinder and its dimensions are given.

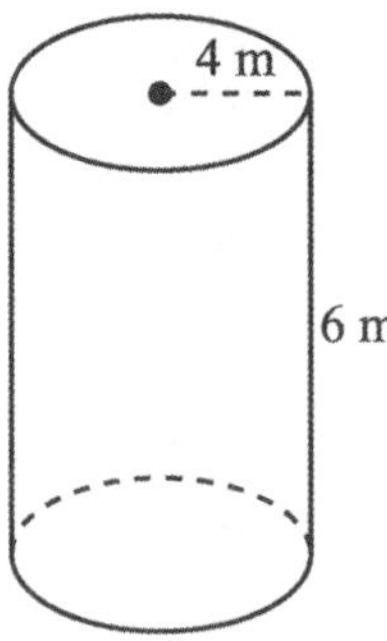

If someone accidentally measured the radius as 3.5 m, what would be the percent error of the calculated volume?

Solution

Step 1

Calculate the actual volume of the cylinder.

Apply the formula $V = \pi r^2 h$.

$V = \pi(4^2)6$
$V = 96\pi$

The actual volume is 96π m^2.

Step 2

Calculate the measured volume.

Apply the formula $V = \pi r^2 h$.

$V = \pi r^2 h$
$V = \pi(3.5^2)6$
$V = 73.5\pi$

The measured volume is 73.5π m^3.

Step 3

Calculate the percent error.

$$\% \text{ error} = \frac{|\text{measured value-actual value}|}{\text{actual value}} \times 100\%$$

$$\% \text{ error} = \frac{|73.5\pi - 96\pi|}{96\pi} \times 100\%$$

$\%$ error = 23.4375%

The percent error of the calculated volume would be about 23.4%.

EXERCISE #1—QUANTITATIVE REASONING

Use the following information to answer the next question.

A model rocket was launched from a platform and its height, *h*, in meters above the ground with respect to time, *t*, in seconds, was recorded. Some of the data obtained is shown in the following table.

Time (s)	Height (m)
0	0
1	148
3	410
8	880
14	1,140
20	1,030
25	660
29	148
30	0

1. Which of the following graphs **best** represents the data shown in the table?

A.

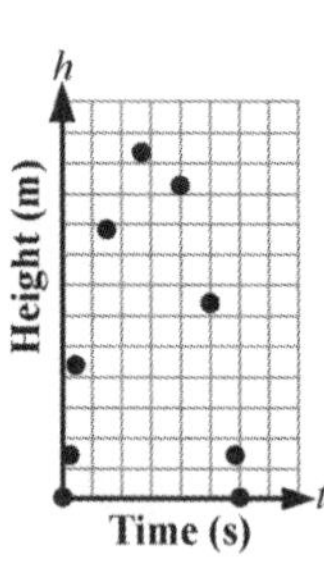

B.

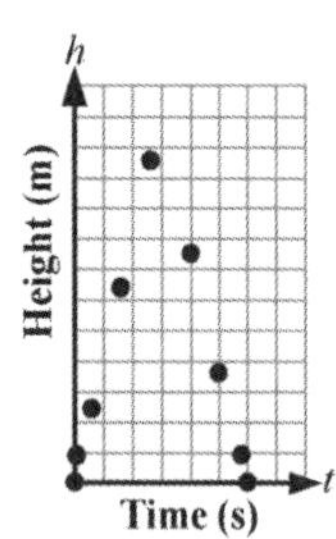

C.

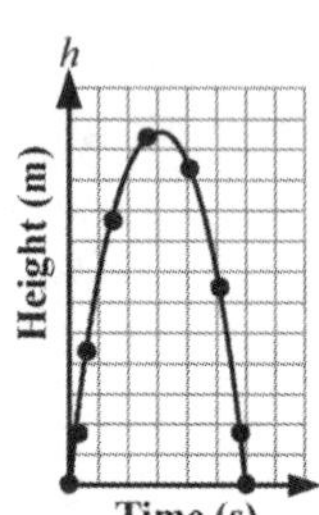

D.

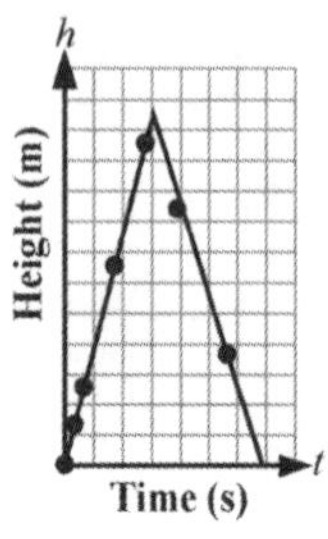

Use the following information to answer the next question.

Amanda built her own trundle wheel using the lid of an ice-cream pail. The diameter of the lid was a good referent for 1 ft. She used it to measure the distance from point *A* to point *B*.

2. If her trundle wheel made exactly $12\frac{3}{4}$ revolutions from point *A* to point *B*, then the length of the curve, to the nearest foot, is

A. 20 ft
B. 26 ft
C. 40 ft
D. 52 ft

Use the following information to answer the next question.

Shoe Sizes of Students of Different Ages

Age	Shoe Size
10	5, 6, 7
11	7, 8
12	7, 8, 9
13	8, 9
14	9, 10
15	9, 10, 11

3. Which of the following scatter plots illustrates the data in the given table?

A. B.

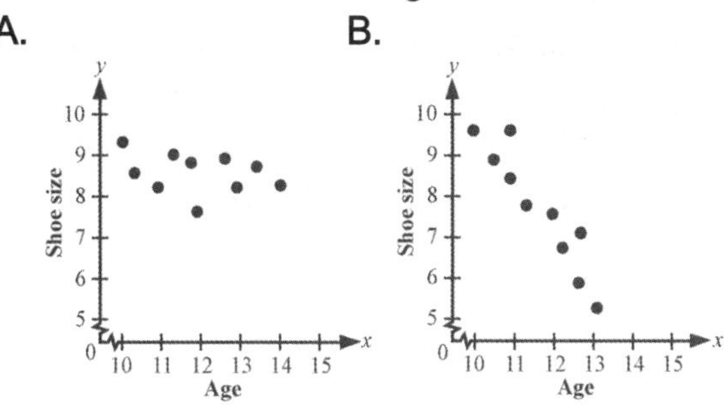

C. D.

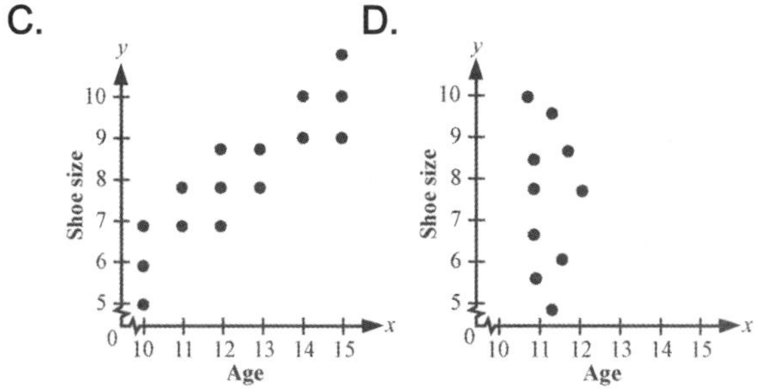

Use the following information to answer the next question.

Colin's teacher asked his students about their means of getting to school. Then, he asked Colin to make a graph to display the information he collected.

Means of Getting to School	Number of Students
Walk	8
Bus	12
Bicycle	3
Ride from parents	9

4. Which of the following types of graphs is **most appropriate** for Colin to use to display this information?

A. Bar graph
B. Histogram
C. Line graph
D. Line plot

Use the following information to answer the next question.

Gena surveys 200 high school students about how they get to school. She collects her results in this table.

Method of Getting to School	Number of Students	Degrees in Circle Graph (°)
Public transit	60	*p*
Walk	50	90
Bicycle	20	36
Car	30	*q*
School bus	*m*	64.8
Other	*n*	7.2

She also makes this circle graph based on her collected data.

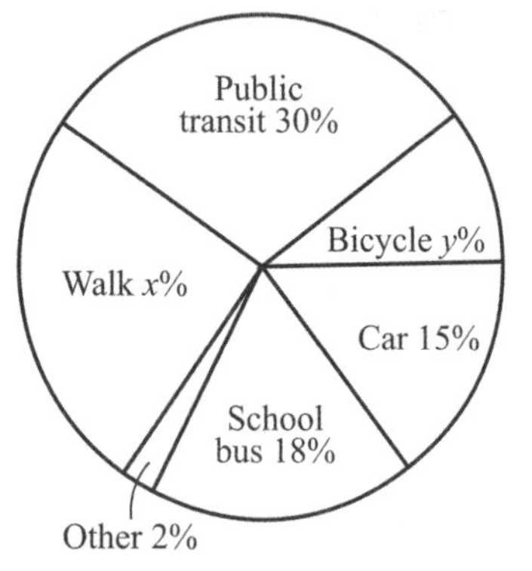

5. What are the numerical values represented by the letters *n*, *p*, and *y*?

   A. $n = 4$, $p = 108$, $y = 10$

   B. $n = 4$, $p = 108$, $y = 12$

   C. $n = 6$, $p = 110$, $y = 10$

   D. $n = 6$, $p = 110$, $y = 12$

Use the following information to answer the next question.

Gladys wants to replace her rectangular doormat that sits at her back door. In order to do so, she needs to estimate the length of the rug that needs replacing.

6. Which of the following referents would **best** assist Gladys to estimate the length of her doormat?
   A. Length of a broom handle
   B. Her walking stride length
   C. Width of a credit card
   D. Her foot length

7. Which of the following imperial units is the **most appropriate** for measuring the height of a flag pole?
   A. Inch
   B. Foot
   C. Mile
   D. Yard

8. Which of the following referents would be the **best** to use to estimate the height of a drinking glass?
   A. Length of your foot
   B. Thickness of your finger nail
   C. Distance from your elbow to your wrist
   D. Distance from the end of your thumb to the knuckle

Use the following information to answer the next question.

The given diagram represents a trapezoidal desktop with the manufacturer's stated approximate dimensions. Dwayne purchased one of the desktops and decided to check the manufacturer's measurements. His measurements agreed with the manufacturer's, except for the side indicated as 50 cm in length, which was actually 48 cm in length.

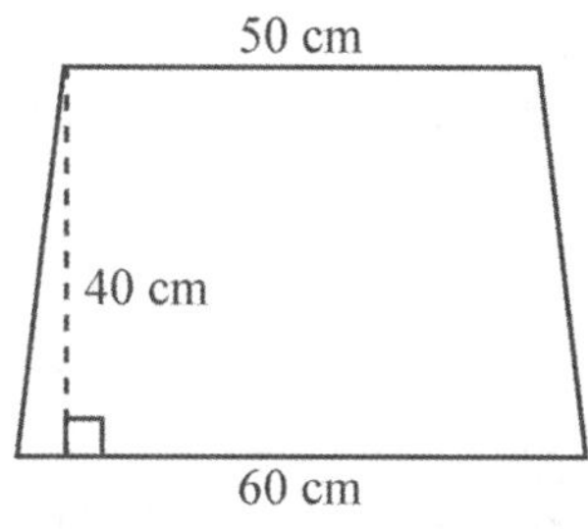

9. Given that the area of a trapezoid can be found using the formula $A = \frac{1}{2}(a + b)h$, and assuming that Dwayne's measurements are correct, what is the percent error of the manufacturer's approximate area of the desktop to the nearest tenth?

   A. 1.8% B. 1.9%

   C. 2.1% D. 2.2%

EXERCISE #1—QUANTITATIVE REASONING ANSWERS AND SOLUTIONS

1. C	4. A	7. B
2. C	5. A	8. D
3. C	6. D	9. B

1. C

Step 1
The shape of the graph can be determined by sketching by hand or by using technology.

Using a TI-83 Plus graphing calculator, enter the data as lists L_1 and L_2 in the STAT EDIT mode.

Then, use ZOOM STAT to get the following graph:

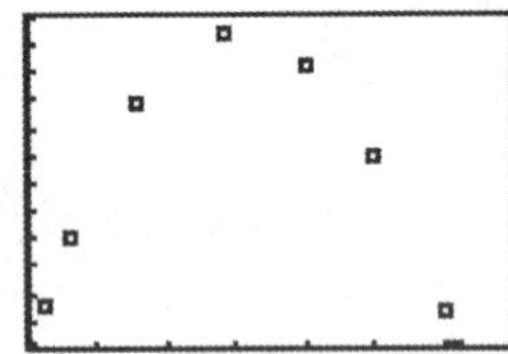

Step 2
Determine the shape of the curve.

The shape of the graph models a curve. Since the model rocket has heights at real number values of t between the restricted domain values of 0 s to 30 s while the rocket is in the air, the data is continuous and should have the points connected as a solid curved line.

This graph best represents the data in this context.

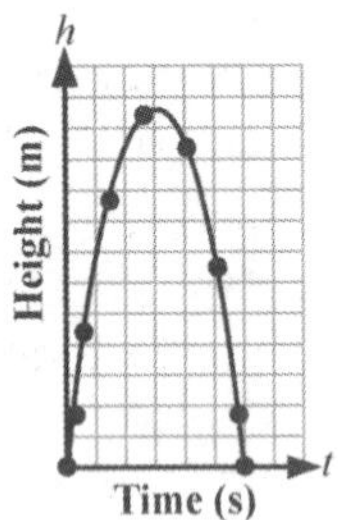

2. C

Determine the distance from point A to point B along the curve.

Step 1
Using the formula for the circumference of a circle, $c = \pi d$, where c is the circumference and d is the diameter, determine the distance covered by one revolution of the trundle wheel.

Remember that the diameter of the trundle wheel is a referent for 1 ft.

$$C = \pi d$$
$$= \pi(1)$$
$$\approx 3.1416 \text{ ft}$$

Step 2
Determine the distance, d, from point A to point B.

$$d = 12\frac{3}{4} \times 1 \text{ revolution}$$
$$\approx 12.75 \times 3.1416$$
$$\approx 40.0554 \text{ ft}$$

The distance from point A to point B, to the nearest foot, is 40 ft.

3. C

Step 1
Write the ordered pairs to be plotted.

Age	Shoe Size	Ordered Pairs
10	5, 6, 7	(10, 5), (10, 6), (10, 7)
11	7, 8	(11, 7), (11, 8)
12	7, 8, 9	(12, 7), (12, 8), (12, 9)
13	8, 9	(13, 8), (13, 9)
14	9, 10	(14, 9), (14, 10)
15	9, 10, 11	(15, 9), (15, 10), (15, 11)

Step 2
Choose suitable increments to mark both axes for the data.

The independent variable, age, will be on the horizontal x-axis. It increases by 1 year at each point. All the data will be clearly displayed if the x-minimum value is 10 and the x-maximum value is 16.

The dependent variable, shoe size, will be on the vertical y-axis. It shows an increase of 1 size at each point. All the data will be displayed if the y-minimum value is 0 and the y-maximum value is 12.

Step 3

Draw and label the axes, plot the points, and give the scatter plot a title.

Plot the ordered pairs with the first number representing age and the second number representing shoe size.

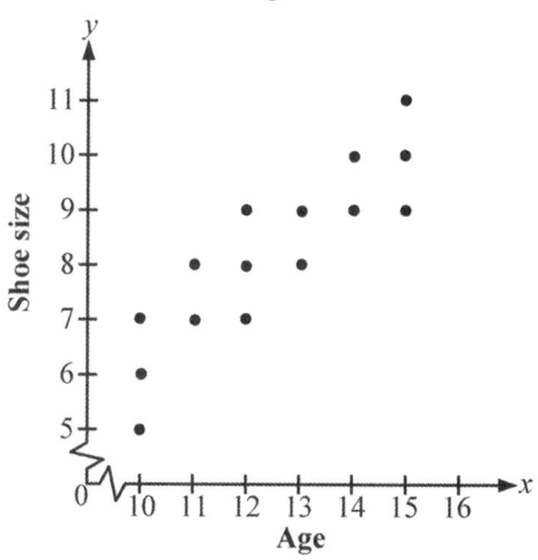

4. A

Examine each type of graph in turn.

A bar graph is used for categorical data. The categories are spread out on the horizontal axis and the numerical data is displayed on the vertical axis. From the given table, the data fits into four distinct categories: walk, bus, bicycle, and ride from parents. This makes the bar graph appropriate for the given data.

A histogram requires continuous data on the horizontal axis. Since the given data is categorical, Colin could not use a histogram to display the information his teacher collected.

A line graph is appropriate when the information on the horizontal axis is numerical. Because the horizontal axis should display the information about the means of getting to school, this is not an appropriate type of graph for Colin to use.

A line plot is used for discrete data, which means the information on the horizontal axis should be numerical. This is not an appropriate type of graph for Colin to use.

Therefore, the only appropriate type of graph for Colin to use to display the information is a bar graph.

5. A

Step 1

Determine the numerical value of n.

The circle graph shows that 2% of students stated they used other means of transportation to get to school. Since 200 students were surveyed, it follows that the value of n is 2% of 200.

$0.02 \times 200 = 4$

The value of n is 4.

Step 2

Determine the numerical value of p.

The circle graph shows that 30% of the students surveyed used public transit to get to school. Therefore, the degree allocation for public transit in the circle graph must be 30% of 360°.

$0.30 \times 360° = 108°$

The value of p is 108.

Step 3

Determine the numerical value of y.

The table shows that 36° represents the number of students riding bicycles to school.

$\frac{36°}{360°} \times 100\% = 10\%$

The value of y is 10.

Therefore, $n = 4$, $p = 108$, and $y = 10$.

6. D

From the given alternatives, the best referent to use to determine the length of the doormat is the length of Gladys' foot. She could start at one end of the mat and then, successively placing one foot in front of the other, count the number of foot steps required to reach the opposite end of the mat.

Using the width of her credit card as a referent would be far too tedious and subject to measurement error. Since a doormat is smaller than a yard she would not be able to use the length of her walking stride or the length of her broom handle as referents.

7. B

The inch is too small to measure the height of the flag pole. The yard and mile are too large. Therefore, the most appropriate unit is the foot.

8. D

The distance from the end of your thumb to the knuckle is approximately 1 inch. As most drinking glasses are between 3 and 7 inches in height, this would be the best referent to use.

9. B

Step 1
Determine the area of the desktop, as approximated by the manufacturer, using the formula
$A = \frac{1}{2}(a + b)h$.

Substitute 50 for *a*, 60 for *b*, and 40 for *h*. Solve for *A*.

$A = \frac{1}{2}(50 + 60)(40)$

$A = \frac{1}{2}(110)(40)$

$A = (55)(40)$

$A = 2{,}200 \text{ cm}^2$

Step 2
Determine the actual area of the desktop, as calculated by Dwayne, using the formula
$A = \frac{1}{2}(a + b)h$.

Substitute 48 for *a*, 60 for *b*, and 40 for *h*. Solve for *A*.

$A = \frac{1}{2}(48 + 60)(40)$

$A = \frac{1}{2}(108)(40)$

$A = (54)(40)$

$A = 2{,}160 \text{ cm}^2$

Step 3
Determine the percent error of the area of the desktop, using the manufacturer's approximate measurements.
Apply the formula for percent error.

$\% \text{ error} = \frac{|\text{measured value} - \text{actual value}|}{\text{actual value}} \times 100\%$

$\% \text{ error} = \frac{|2{,}200 - 2{,}160|}{2{,}160} \times 100\%$

$\% \text{ error} = \frac{40}{2{,}160} \times 100\%$

$\% \text{ error} \approx 0.0185 \times 100\%$

$\% \text{ error} \approx 1.85\%$

To the nearest tenth, the percent error of the area of the desktop measured by the manufacturer is 1.9%.

EXERCISE #2—QUANTITATIVE REASONING

Use the following information to answer the next question.

A model rocket was launched from a platform and its height, *h* meters, above the ground with respect to time, *t* seconds, was recorded. Some of the data obtained is shown in the table.

Time (s)	Height (m)
0	3
1	148
3	410
8	890
14	1,140
20	1,025
25	700

10. Which of the following graphs **best** represents the data shown in the table?

A. B.

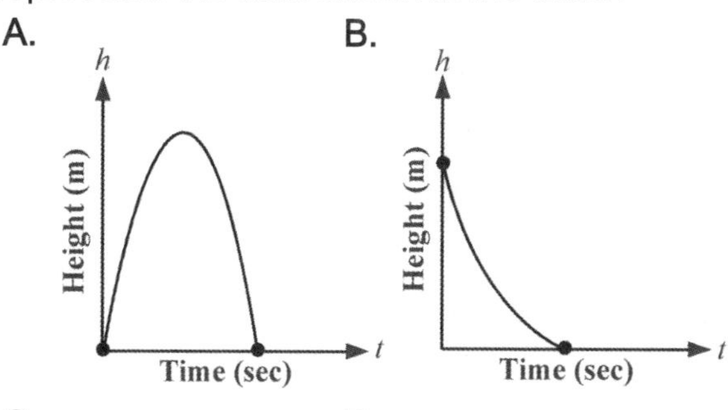

C. D.

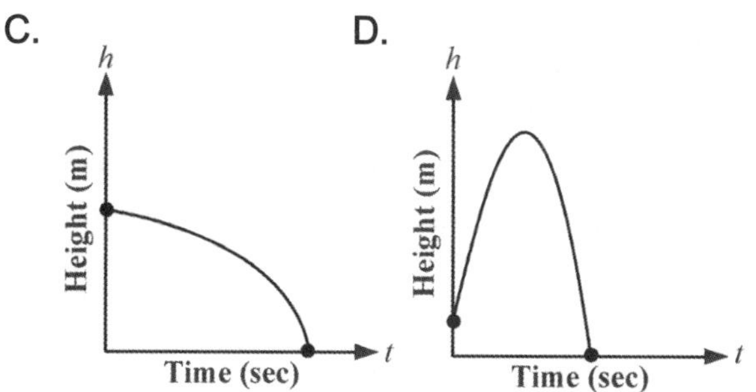

Use the following information to answer the next question.

Anjuli wanted to determine the perimeter of the given shape. Anjuli estimated the perimeter to be 72 yd. She used her stride as a referent, and each stride was about 1 yd.

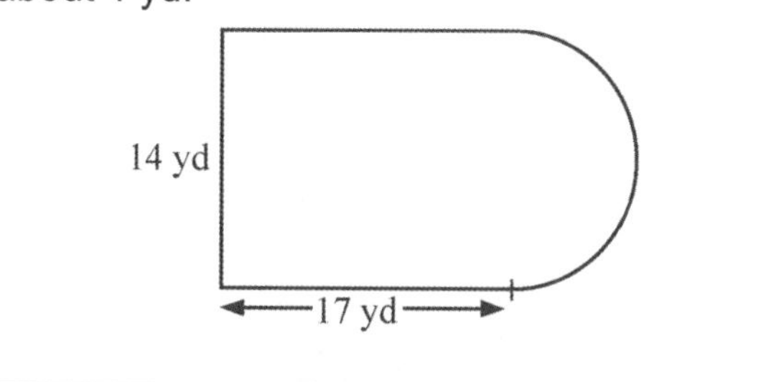

11. Based on the actual perimeter of the shape, what was the error of Anjuli's estimation, in terms of stride lengths?

A. 1 stride B. 2 strides
C. 3 strides D. 4 strides

Use the following information to answer the next question.

Snowflakes Cereal Company Annual Profits

Year	Profit (million $)
1	4.82
2	5.00
3	2.15
4	1.04
5	6.08
6	2.09
7	1.17
8	6.25
9	6.93

12. Which of the following scatter plots correctly illustrates the data in the given table?

A. B.

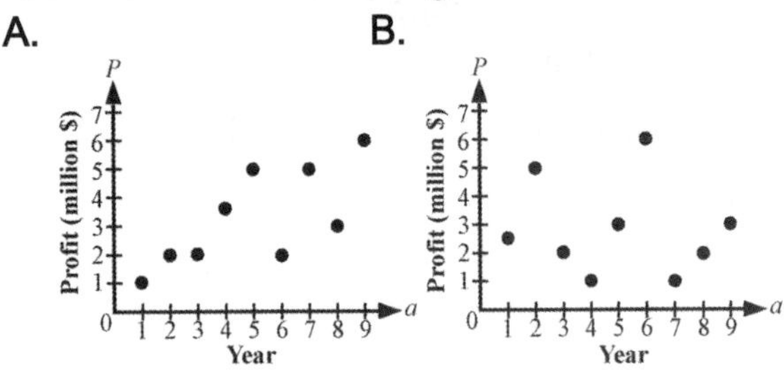

C. D.

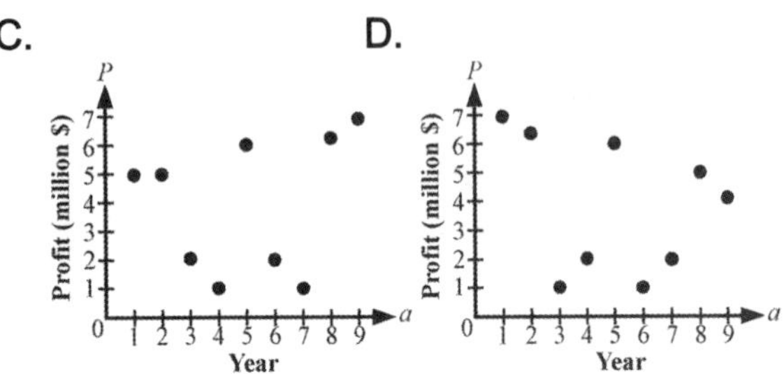

Use the following information to answer the next question.

At a summer fair, a circus tent was set up. Performances occurred continuously from 7:00 P.M. to 11:00 P.M. Each hour, the type of performance changed. The given table shows the times of the different performances and the number of people who attended each performance.

Time	Performance	Attendance
7:00 P.M.	Clowns	125
8:00 P.M.	Lions	300
9:00 P.M.	Jugglers	250
10:00 P.M.	Trapeze	325

The given display shows data from the table.

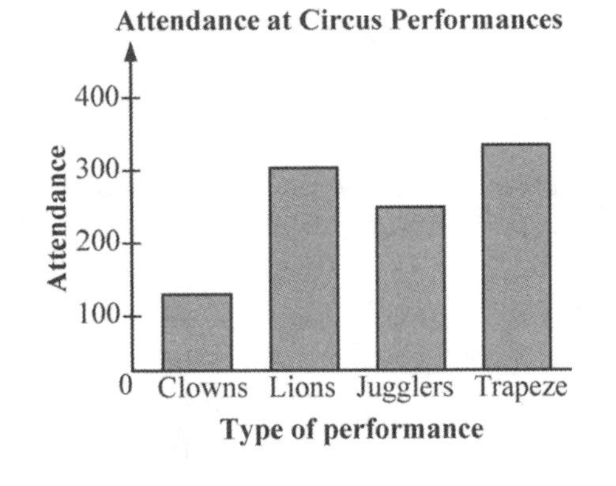

13. The given display is an example of a
    A. histogram, since the data fit into distinct categories
    B. bar graph, since the data fit into distinct categories
    C. histogram, since the data fit into intervals
    D. bar graph, since the data fit into intervals

Use the following information to answer the next question.

The given table represents the results of a survey of 120 Grade 9 students with regard to their favorite type of movie.

Favorite Type of Movie	Number of Students
Comedy	36
Action	30
Drama	24
Romance	12
Horror	8
Science fiction	6
Foreign	4

14. If the data in the given table is to be illustrated in a circle graph, then the number of degrees allocated for comedy will exceed the number of degrees allocated for drama by

A. 12° **B.** 16°
C. 32° **D.** 36°

Use the following information to answer the next question.

Suzanne is in an appliance store and is about to purchase a refrigerator. However, before she makes the purchase, she needs to ensure that the refrigerator will fit into a designated location in her kitchen.

15. Which of the following referents would be **most appropriate** for Suzanne to use when determining the height of the refrigerator?

A. The width of her little finger
B. The length of her foot
C. Her hand span
D. Her wrist size

Use the following information to answer the next question.

Kareem went to a building supply store to purchase some bricks for his new sidewalk. He used quarters as a referent to estimate the length of one brick and found that the brick was 8 quarters long.

16. Which of the following lengths is the **best** estimate for the length of one brick?

A. 8 mm **B.** 8 cm
C. 8 in **D.** 8 ft

Use the following information to answer the next question.

In order to determine the radius of a playground ball, Joel deflated the ball and measured its radius with a ruler. He found the radius to be 15.9 cm. He used this value to calculate the volume of the ball when it is inflated using the formula for the volume of a sphere, $V = \frac{4}{3}\pi r^3$.

17. If the radius of the playground ball is actually 15 cm, what is the percent error of Joel's calculated volume to the nearest tenth?

A. 16.0% **B.** 17.4%
C. 18.0% **D.** 19.1%

EXERCISE #2—QUANTITATIVE REASONING ANSWERS AND SOLUTIONS

10. D	12. C	14. D	16. C
11. B	13. B	15. C	17. D

10. D

The shape of the graph can be determined either by using technology or by sketching the graph by hand. If a TI-83 graphing calculator is used the resulting graph will display as shown.:

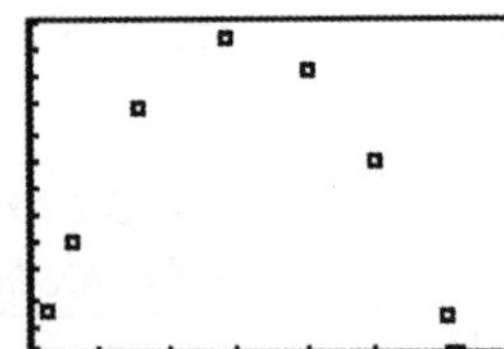

The shape of the graph models a parabola. Examine the first set of ordered pairs from the table to see that when time is 0, the height is 3. Therefore, the graph that best represents the data is graph D.

11. B

Determine the perimeter, *P*, of the shape. This consists of three sides of a rectangle and the circumference of a semicircle. Compare it to Anjuli's estimated perimeter.

Step 1
Calculate the perimeter of the shape using the formula $C = \pi d$ for the circumference of a circle.

$$\begin{aligned} P_{\text{shape}} &= P_{\text{rectangle (sides)}} + P_{\text{semicircle}} \\ &= l + l + w + \frac{\pi d}{2} \\ &= 17 + 17 + 14 + \frac{\pi(14)}{2} \\ &= 48 + 7\pi \\ &\approx 48 + 21.99115 \\ &\approx 70.0 \text{ yd} \end{aligned}$$

Step 2
Compare the actual perimeter to the estimated perimeter of the shape.

$$\begin{aligned} P_{\text{difference}} &= P_{\text{estimate}} - P_{\text{actual}} \\ &= 72 \text{ yd} - 70 \text{ yd} \\ &= 2 \text{ yd} \end{aligned}$$

Since 1 yd = 1 stride, the error in Anjuli's estimation is about 2 strides.

12. C

Step 1
Write the ordered pairs to be plotted.

Take the years as *x*-values and the profit in millions as the *y*-values in the ordered pairs.

Year	Profit (million $)	Ordered Pair
1	4.82	(1, 4.82)
2	5.00	(2, 5.00)
3	2.15	(3, 2.15)
4	1.04	(4, 1.04)
5	6.08	(5, 6.08)
6	2.09	(6, 2.09)
7	1.17	(7, 1.17)
8	6.25	(8, 6.25)
9	6.93	(9, 6.93)

Step 2
Choose suitable increments to mark both axes for the data.

Plot the independent variable along the horizontal *x*-axis.

The independent variable (year) will be on the horizontal *x*-axis. It increases by 1 at each point. All the data will be clearly displayed if the *x*-minimum value is 1 to a maximum *x*-value of 9.

The dependent variable, the profit, will be on the vertical *y*-axis. It ranges from $1.04 million to $6.93 million. All the data will be displayed if the minimum *y*-value is $1.04 million to a maximum *y*-value of $6.93 million.

Step 3
Draw and label the axes, and plot the points.

Snowflakes Cereal Company Annual Profits

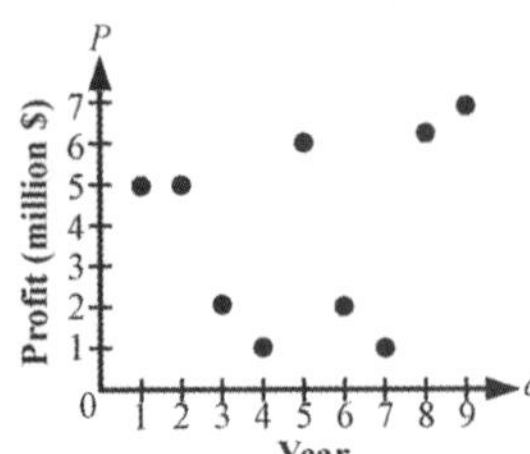

13. B

Bar graphs are used to display categorical data, which are data that fit into separate and distinct categories. Each bar represents a category. Bar graphs are drawn with spaces between the bars.

This display of data shows categorical data with spaces separating the bars, which indicates that it is a bar graph.

A histogram would show bars representing intervals, not categories. These bars would not have spaces between them. Although there are similarities between histograms and bar graphs, this display cannot be classified as a histogram.

14. D

Step 1
Determine the number of degrees in the circle graph allocated for comedy.
Since 36 students stated that their favorite type of movie was comedy, it follows that
$\frac{36}{120} \times 100\% = 30\%$ of the students surveyed preferred comedy movies. Thus, 30% of 360° must be allocated for comedy in the circle graph.
$0.30 \times 360° = 108°$

Step 2
Determine the number of degrees in the circle graph allocated for drama.
Since 24 students stated that their favorite type of movie was drama, it follows that
$\frac{24}{120} \times 100\% = 20\%$ of the students surveyed preferred drama movies. Thus, 20% of 360° must be allocated for drama in the circle graph.
$0.20 \times 360° = 72°$

Step 3
Determine how many more degrees must be allocated for comedy compared to drama in the circle graph.
$108° - 72° = 36°$
The number of degrees allocated for comedy in the circle graph exceeds the number of degrees allocated for drama in the circle graph by 36°.

15. C

The best referent for Suzanne to use to determine the height of the refrigerator is her hand span. She could start at the bottom of the refrigerator and count the number of successive hand spans required to reach the top. Suzanne could then multiply the number of hand spans taken to reach the top of the refrigerator by the length of one hand span in order to determine the height of the refrigerator. To use the width of her little finger as a referent would be too tedious and prone to measurement error. To use either the length of her foot or her wrist size as referents would be impractical.

16. C

The diameter of a quarter is approximately 1 in. Since 8 quarters were used to measure the length of the brick, the brick is about 8 in long.

17. D

Step 1
Determine the actual volume of the playground ball, using $V = \frac{4}{3}\pi r^3$.

Substitute 15 for r.

$V = \frac{4}{3}\pi(15)^3$

$V = \frac{4}{3}\pi(3{,}375)$

$V = 4{,}500\pi \text{ cm}^3$

Step 2
Determine the volume of the ball using Joel's value for the radius, 15.9 cm.

$V = \frac{4}{3}\pi r^3$

$V = \frac{4}{3}\pi(15.9)^3$

$V = \frac{4}{3}\pi(4{,}019.679)$

$V = 5{,}359.572\pi \text{ cm}^3$

Step 3
Determine the percent error of Joel's calculated volume.

Apply the formula to find percent error.

$\% \text{ error} = \frac{|\text{measured value} - \text{actual value}|}{\text{actual value}} \times 100\%$

$\% \text{ error} = \frac{|5{,}359.572\pi - 4{,}500\pi|}{4{,}500\pi} \times 100\%$

$\% \text{ error} = \frac{859.572\pi}{4{,}500\pi} \times 100\%$

$\% \text{ error} = 0.191016 \times 100\%$

$\% \text{ error} = 19.1016\%$

The percent error of the calculated volume is about 19.1%.

NOTES

Interpreting Expressions

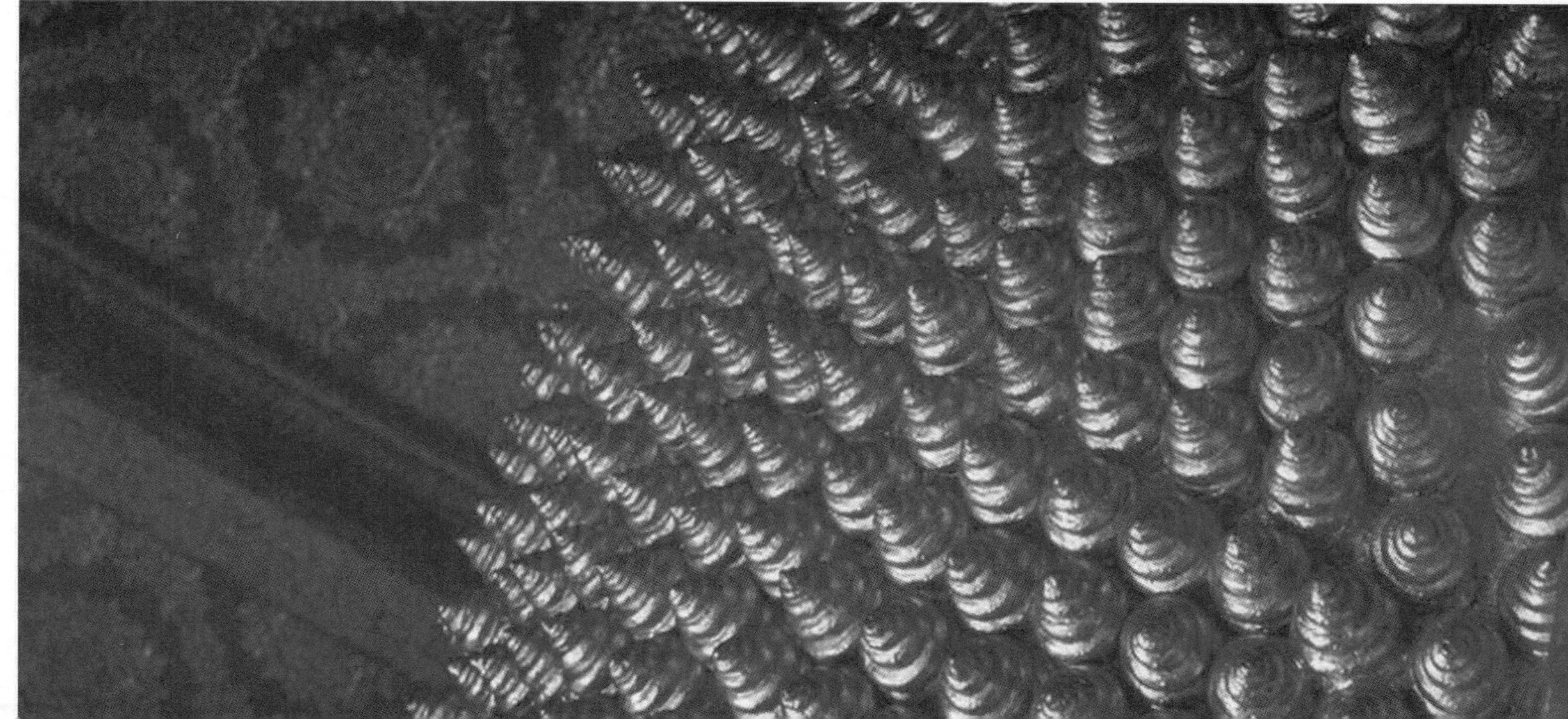

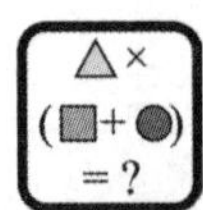

INTERPRETING EXPRESSIONS

Table of Correlations

Standard		Concepts	Exercise #1	Exercise #2
Unit1.2	Interpret the structure of expressions.			
A-SSE.1ai	*Interpret expressions that represent a quantity in terms of its context. Interpret parts of an expression, such as terms, factors, and coefficients.*	Meaning of y-intercept and Slope in Graphs of Real Situations	18	24
		Identifying the Significance of m and b	19	25
		Understanding Terms in Algebra	20	26
A-SSE.1bii	*Interpret expressions that represent a quantity in terms of its context. Interpret complicated expressions by viewing one or more of their parts as a single entity.*	Calculating Simple Interest	21	27
		Solving Compound Interest Problems Using a Formula	22	28
		Factoring Trinomials of the Form $x^2 + bx + c$	23	29

A-SSE.1ai Interpret expressions that represent a quantity in terms of its context. Interpret parts of an expression, such as terms, factors, and coefficients.

Meaning of *y*-Intercept and Slope in Graphs of Real Situations

The slope and variables in the equation $y = mx + b$ can be used to represent a rate and quantities, respectively, in realistic situations. Doing so does not affect the linear relationship. For example, a local plumber charges $100.00 to come to your home plus $65.00 / h for the time that he spends fixing the problem. The equation to calculate his total cost is $C = 100 + 65h$.
The equation rewritten in slope *y*-intercept form is $C = 65h + 100$. In this equation, the following substitutions are made:

- *C* replaces *y* (dependent variable)
- 100 replaces *b* (*y*-intercept)
- 65 replaces *m* (slope or constant rate of change)
- *h* replaces *x* (independent variable)

Because no variable has an exponent greater than 1, the equation is linear. This equation represents partial variation, where the *y*-intercept (100) represents the initial cost.

You can also be faced with problems where you have to come up with a realistic situation for a given linear relation.

For example, consider $C = 500 + 28n$.
One possible interpretation of the equation could be that it costs $500.00 plus $28.00 / person to rent a hall for a wedding reception.

Identifying the Significance of *m* and *b*

If given a graph, the slope (*m*) and *y*-intercept (*b*) are determined through inspection of the points.

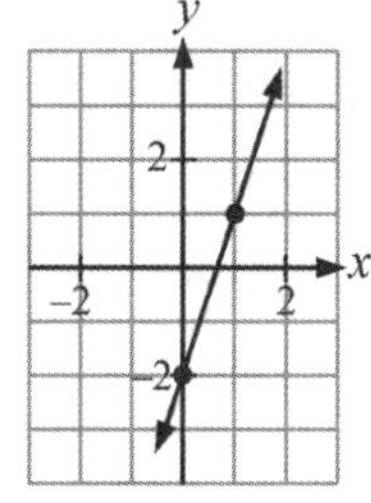

The *y*-intercept (*b*) is the *y*-value that sits on the *y*-axis when *x* is 0: (0, −2). That is, $b = -2$

To find the slope, use two points from the graph and apply the slope formula.

$$m = \frac{y_2 - y_1}{x_2 - x_1}$$

$$m = \frac{1 - (-2)}{1 - 0}$$

$$m = 3$$

Given *m* and *b*, it is possible to plot the points and write the equation of the line.

Example

What is the equation of the line where $m = -\frac{3}{4}$ and $b = 2$?

Start by plotting the *y*-intercept. Then, use the slope to rise and run to the next point. Because the slope is negative, you can either fall 3 units and run four units right, or rise 3 units and run 4 units left.

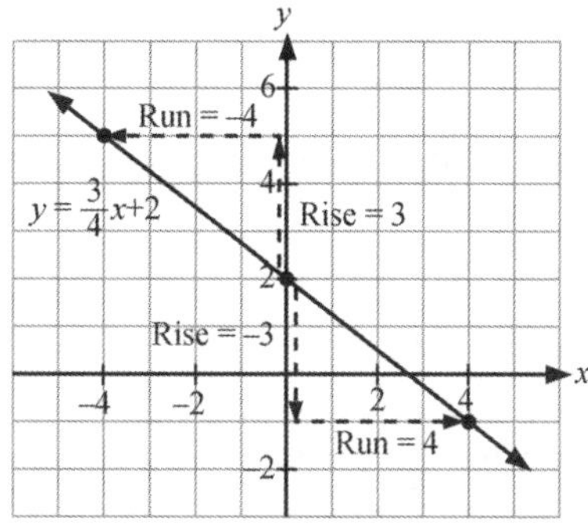

Both movements follow the same line.

Substitute the values into the slope *y*-intercept form to express the equation of the line.

$$y = -\frac{3}{4}x + 2$$

Understanding Terms in Algebra

Algebra allows you to represent known and unknown values in an expression or an equation. **Terms** in algebraic expressions are separated by addition or subtraction signs.

A **variable** in a term is any letter of the alphabet that stands in place of an unknown value. Examples of variables are *x*, *y*, or *n*. The number in front of a variable is a **coefficient** and indicates multiplication of an unknown value by the known value.
For example, in $4x$, the coefficient is 4. It is multiplying the variable *x*.

This chart shows different examples of terms with rational numbers.

Form of Term	Examples
Rational numbers	$2, -3, -\frac{1}{4}, 2\frac{3}{5}$
Rational numbers with a variable	$2x, -\frac{1}{3}xy, -12xy, \frac{6xy}{3}$
Rational numbers with a variable and an integral exponent	$2x^2, -4x^2y^3, -9p^6q^{-3}$

In algebraic expressions, a **constant** is a number that is known.

Example

Identify the variable, numerical coefficient, and constant term in the expression $4x - 6$.

Solution

- *x* is the variable because it is a letter that is taking the place of a number.
- 4 is the numerical coefficient because it multiplies the variable *x*.
- 6 is the constant term because it is being subtracted from the variable term, and it cannot be manipulated or changed.

A-SSE.1bii Interpret expressions that represent a quantity in terms of its context. Interpret complicated expressions by viewing one or more of their parts as a single entity.

Calculating Simple Interest

When dealing with financial institutions, interest is usually calculated on loans and deposits. If you borrow money from a bank, you are charged interest for using their money. If you deposit money into a bank, they pay you interest for using your money. The **interest rate** is stated as a percentage of the amount borrowed or deposited for a **period** of time (week, month, or year).
The amount of money borrowed or deposited is called the **principal**. **Simple interest** is calculated on the principal only. It is paid out at the end of the time the money is being invested.

To calculate the interest, use the formula:

interest = principal (original amount) × interest rate (percentage converted to a decimal) × time (period)
OR
$i = p \times r \times t$ usually written $i = prt$.

Example

Sally puts $200 in a bank account. Each year, the account earns 8% simple interest.

How much interest will Sally earn in three years?

Solution

Step 1
Match the number with the corresponding part of the formula.
i = the amount of interest is the unknown.
p = she deposited $200.
r = the rate was 8%, which is equal to 0.08.
t = the period is one year, and she will be saving for 3 periods.

Step 2
Substitute the numbers into the formula, and solve for the unknown.

$$\begin{aligned} i &= prt \\ &= \$200.00 \times 0.08 \times 3 \\ &= \$48.00 \end{aligned}$$

Sally will earn $48.00 at the end of 3 years.

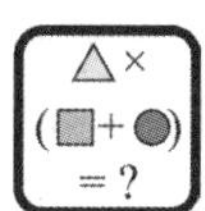

Solving Compound Interest Problems Using a Formula

When solving compound interest problems, the resulting amount, A, or final value, FV, can be found using the following compound interest formula:

$A = P(1 + i)^n$ or $FV = PV(1 + i)^n$, in which A or FV is the accumulated amount, P or PV is the principal or original investment, i is the interest rate (as a decimal) per compounding period, and n is the number of compounding periods over the total time of the investment.

Compound interest is often added to the principal more than once a year. The time when interest is calculated and added to the principal is called the **compounding period**.

The interest rate, r, is usually quoted as an annual rate, but can be compounded more than once a year. To calculate the interest, i, that is added per compounding period, divide the annual interest rate by the frequency, f, of the compounding periods in a year.

To calculate the number of compounding periods, n, over the total time of the investment, multiply the number of years by the frequency, f, of the compounding periods in a year.

The following chart illustrates the concept of compounding.

r	f	i	n
5 %/a annually for 3 years	1	$= \frac{0.05}{f}$ $= \frac{0.05}{1}$ $= 0.05$	$= 3 \times f$ $= 3 \times 1$ $= 3$
6 %/a semi-annually for 4 years	2	$= \frac{0.06}{f}$ $= \frac{0.06}{2}$ $= 0.03$	$= 4 \times f$ $= 4 \times 2$ $= 8$
12 %/a quarterly for 2 years	4	$= \frac{0.12}{f}$ $= \frac{0.12}{4}$ $= 0.03$	$= 2 \times f$ $= 2 \times 4$ $= 8$
9 %/a monthly for 6 years	12	$= \frac{0.09}{f}$ $= \frac{0.09}{12}$ $= 0.0075$	$= 6 \times f$ $= 6 \times 12$ $= 72$
10 %/a daily for 1 year	365	$= \frac{0.10}{f}$ $= \frac{0.10}{365}$ (leave as fraction)	$= 1 \times f$ $= 1 \times 365$ $= 365$

The designation "a" in the quoted interest rate stands for *annum*, which means "year."

Example

Natasha wants to invest \$60,000. She has the following two account options:

1. 10%/a, compounded semi-annually for four years
2. 10%/a, compounded daily for four years

Determine which option is the best choice.

Solution

Use the formula $A = P(1 + i)^n$ to calculate the total amount for each option after four years.

Option 1: Compounded semi-annually $\Rightarrow f = 2$

$$i = 0.10 \div f = 0.10 \div 2 = 0.05$$
$$n = 4 \times f = 4 \times 2 = 8$$
$$\begin{aligned} A &= P(1 + i)^n \\ &= 60{,}000(1 + 0.05)^8 \\ &= 60{,}000(1.05)^8 \\ &= \$88{,}647.33 \end{aligned}$$

Option 2: Compounded daily $\Rightarrow f = 365$

$$\begin{aligned} i &= 0.10 \div f \\ &= 0.10 \div 365 = \frac{0.10}{365} \end{aligned}$$
$$n = 4 \times f = 4 \times 365 = 1{,}460$$

Use brackets around i when it is a fraction.

$$\begin{aligned} A &= P(1 + i)^n \\ &= 60{,}000\left(1 + \left(\frac{0.10}{365}\right)\right)^{1{,}460} \\ &= \$89{,}504.58 \end{aligned}$$

The best choice is for Natasha to invest the \$60,000 into the account with the daily compounded interest, since more interest accumulates over the four years than in the option that is compounded semi-annually. You can expect a larger final amount with an option that gives you interest more often during the year.

Example

Determine the present value (PV) when the future value (FV) after 15 years in an investment is \$40,000, and the interest earned is 8%/a, compounded annually.

Solution

Compounded annually $\Rightarrow f = 1$

$$i = 0.08 \div f = 0.08 \div 1 = 0.08$$
$$n = 15 \times f = 15 \times 1 = 15$$
$$\begin{aligned} FV &= PV(1 + i)^n \\ 40{,}000 &= PV(1 + 0.08)^{15} \\ 40{,}000 &= PV(3.172169114) \\ \frac{40{,}000}{3.172169114} &= PV \\ 12{,}609.67 &= PV \end{aligned}$$

The present value is \$12,609.67.

Factoring Trinomials of the Form $x^2 + bx + c$

Trinomials are algebraic expressions with three terms.

When factoring trinomials of the form $x^2 + bx + c$, write the trinomial as a product of two binomials, if possible.

Consider the following product of binomials: $(x + 3)(x - 5)$.

$$\begin{aligned} &= (x)(x) + (x)(-5) + (3)(x) + (3)(-5) \\ &= x^2 - 5x + 3x - 15 \\ &= x^2 - 2x - 15 \end{aligned}$$

Notice that the first two terms of the binomials are multiplied to get the first term of the trinomial: $(x)(x) = x^2$.

The last two terms of the binomials are multiplied to give the last term in the trinomial: $(3)(-5) = -15$. The product of the coefficient of the first term and the last term in the trinomial is called the **product**.

Since the middle term in the trinomial is found by adding the like terms together, the coefficient of the middle term in the trinomial is called the **sum**.

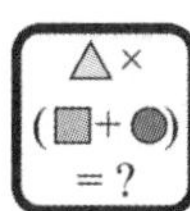

Example

Factor $x^2 + 6x + 8$.

Solution

Step 1
The product value is the product of the coefficient of the first term and the last term in the polynomial.
Product = 1 × 8

The sum value is the coefficient of the middle term in the polynomial.
Sum = 6

Step 2
List all the factors of the product until you find two numbers that multiply to a product of 8 and add to a sum of 6.

Product	Sum
1 × 8 = 8	1 + 8 = 9
2 × 4 = 8	2 + 4 = 6
−1 × −8 = 8	−1 + (−8) = −9
−2 × −4 = 8	−2 + (−4) = −6

The numbers that add to 6 and have a product of 8 are 4 and 2.

Step 3
Write the factored solution of two binomials.

Since $(x)(x) = x^2$, x is the first term in the binomials.
$(x + \_\_\_\_\_\_\_\_)(x + \_\_\_\_\_\_\_\_)$
Insert one of the numbers in the first binomial and the other number in the second binomial. The order does not matter.
$(x + 2)(x + 4)$

Step 4
Check the solution by using FOIL.
$(x + 2)(x + 4) = x^2 + 4x + 2x + 8$
$(x + 2)(x + 4) = x^2 + 6x + 8$
Verification can also be done using vertical multiplication.

$$\begin{array}{r} x+2 \\ \times \quad x+4 \\ \hline 4x+8 \\ \underline{x^2+2x+0} \\ x^2+6x+8 \end{array}$$

Factor $x^2 - 11x + 18$.

Solution

Step 1
Identify the product and sum values in the trinomial.

The product value is the product of the first term and the last term of the trinomial.
Product = 1 × 18

The sum value is the coefficient of the middle term of the trinomial.
Sum = −11

Step 2
List all the factors of the product until two numbers are identified that multiply to a product of 18 and add to a sum of −11.

Product	Sum
1 × 18 = 18	1 + 18 = 19
2 × 9 = 18	2 + 9 = 11
3 × 6 = 18	3 + 6 = 9
−1 × −18 = 18	−1 + (−18) = −19
−2 × −9 = 18	−2 + −9 = −11
−3 × −6 = 18	−3 + (−6) = −9

The two numbers that work are −2 and −9.

Step 3
Write the factored solution of two binomials.

Since $(x)(x) = x^2$, x is the first term in the binomials.
$(x\_)(x\_)$
Place one of the numbers in the first set of brackets and the other number in the second set.

The order does not matter, but the proper sign of the number must be inserted. Since both numbers are negative, a subtraction sign must be used in each binomial.

The factored answer is $(x - 2)(x - 9)$.

Step 4
Check the solution by using FOIL.
$$\begin{aligned}(x - 2)(x - 9) &= x^2 - 9x - 2x + 18 \\ &= x^2 - 11x + 18\end{aligned}$$

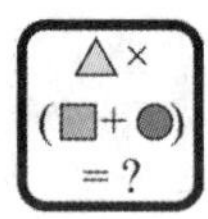

EXERCISE #1—INTERPRETING EXPRESSIONS

Use the following information to answer the next question.

The cost of renting a car, C, in dollars is given by the linear relation $C = 0.12n + 33$, where n is the number of kilometers driven.

18. When the graph of the equation $C = 0.12n + 33$ is drawn, the slope of the line representing the relation is

A. \$33/km B. 33 km/\$

C. \$0.12/km D. 0.12 km/\$

19. Which of the following equations represents the line with the **greatest** slope value?

A. $y = 3$ B. $y = 2x$

C. $y = -x + 3$ D. $y = \frac{1}{2}x - 3$

20. What are the terms in the expression $5z + 6yz + 3$?

A. 3 B. $5z$

C. $5z$ and $6yz$ D. $5z$, $6yz$, and 3

Use the following information to answer the next question.

Anson borrows some money from a bank at a rate of 10% simple interest for 1 year. Jenny borrows \$1,000 more than Anson from another bank at 8% simple interest for 6 months.

21. If the total interest paid by both Anson and Jenny is \$740, what is the amount of money Anson borrowed?

A. \$1,250 B. \$3,750

C. \$4,070 D. \$5,000

22. If interest is compounded quarterly for 3 years at 5% per annum, how much interest is earned by an investment of \$1,100?

A. \$173.39 B. \$176.83

C. \$241.33 D. \$875.44

23. One factor of $x^2 - 9x + 20$ is

A. $(x - 10)$ B. $(x + 5)$

C. $(x - 4)$ D. $(x + 2)$

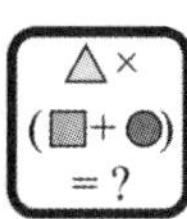

EXERCISE #1—INTERPRETING EXPRESSIONS ANSWERS AND SOLUTIONS

18. C	20. D	22. B
19. B	21. D	23. C

18. C

Identify the slope of the graph of the function $C = 0.12n + 33$.

The slope-intercept form of a linear relation is $y = mx + b$, where m is the slope and b is the y-intercept.

By comparison, the slope must be 0.12. Since the cost C is in dollars and n is the number of kilometers driven, the units for slope must be dollars per kilometer ($/km).

19. B

Step 1
Determine the slope of each of the given lines.
Each of the given lines is written in the slope-intercept form $y = mx + b$ where m represents the slope and b represents the y-intercept.
Therefore, the slopes of the lines defined by the equations are determined as follows:

- $y = 3r \rightarrow y = 0x + 3$. The slope of this line is 0 and the y-intercept is 3.
- $y = 2x \rightarrow y = 2x + 0$. The slope of this line is 2 and the y-intercept is 0.
- $y = -x + 3$. The slope of this line is -1 and the y-intercept is 3.
- $y = \frac{1}{2}x - 3$. The slope of this line is $\frac{1}{2}$ and the y-intercept is -3.

Step 2
Determine the greatest value of the slope.
The greatest slope value is 2. Therefore, the graph of the line in alternative B will have the greatest value for the slope.

20. D

Terms in an algebraic expression are separated by addition or subtraction signs.

An addition sign separates $5z$, $6yz$, and 3, so they are all terms in the expression $5z + 6yz + 3$.

21. D

Step 1
Determine the amount that Anson borrowed.
Anson borrowed money at a rate of 10% interest for 1 year.
Use the interest formula $i = prt$. Let p stand for the amount that Anson borrowed.

$$\begin{aligned} i &= p \times 0.1 \times 1 \\ &= 0.1p \end{aligned}$$

Step 2
Determine the amount that Jenny borrowed.
Jenny borrowed some money at a rate of 8% for half a year.
Recall that Jenny borrowed $1,000 more than Anson.
Use the formula $i = prt$. Let p stand for the amount that Anson borrowed.

$$\begin{aligned} i &= (p + 1{,}000) \times 0.08 \times 0.5 \\ &= 0.04(p + 1{,}000) \\ &= 0.04p + 40 \end{aligned}$$

Step 3
Add the two amounts together to determine the missing value.
The sum of the two interest amounts is $740.
Add both expressions together to determine the amount that Anson originally borrowed.

$$\begin{aligned} 0.1p + (0.04p + 40) &= 740 \\ 0.14p + 40 &= 740 \\ 0.14p + 40 - 40 &= 740 - 40 \\ 0.14p &= 700 \\ \frac{0.14p}{0.14} &= \frac{700}{0.14} \\ p &= 5{,}000 \end{aligned}$$

Anson originally borrowed $5,000.

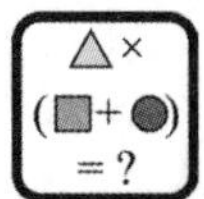

22. B

Step 1
Calculate the accumulated amount of the investment using the compound interest formula.
The principal is \$1,100. Since the interest rate is 5 % compounded quarterly, $i = \frac{0.05}{4}$. Since the investment is compounded quarterly for 3 years, the number of compounding periods is $n = 3 \times 4 = 12$.

$A = P(1 + i)^n$
$A = 1{,}100\left(1 + \frac{0.05}{4}\right)^{12}$
$A = 1{,}100(1.1607545)$
$A = 1{,}276.83$

Therefore, the accumulated value of the investment is \$1,276.83.

Step 2
Calculate the interest earned.
Subtract the principal from the accumulated value of the investment.

$1{,}276.83 - 1{,}100 = 176.83$

Therefore, the interest earned is \$176.83.

23. C

Step 1
Determine which two numbers have a sum of −9 and a product of +20.
$(-5) + (-4) = -5 - 4 = -9$ and $(-5) \times (-4) = +20$.
The two numbers are −5 and −4.

Step 2
Open two sets of brackets. Inside each set of brackets, write the same variable that was used in the given trinomial.
(x__________)(x__________)

Step 3
Place one of the numbers in the first set of brackets and the other number in the second set.
$(x - 5)(x - 4)$
One of the factors of $x^2 - 9x + 20$ is $(x - 4)$.

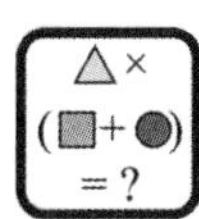

EXERCISE #2—INTERPRETING EXPRESSIONS

Use the following information to answer the next question.

The Linear Dinner is a popular restaurant for breakfast and lunch. The relationship between the number of people in the restaurant, y, and the number of people eating in the restaurant, x, at any point in time between 12 P.M. and 1 P.M. is given by the equation $y = 2x + 10$.

24. The number 10 in the equation represents the number of people

A. that work in the restaurant

B. that had breakfast in the restaurant

C. waiting in line outside the restaurant

D. who had lunch in the restaurant before 12 P.M.

25. Which of the following graphs illustrates the line defined by the equation $y = -\frac{5}{2}x + 4$?

A.

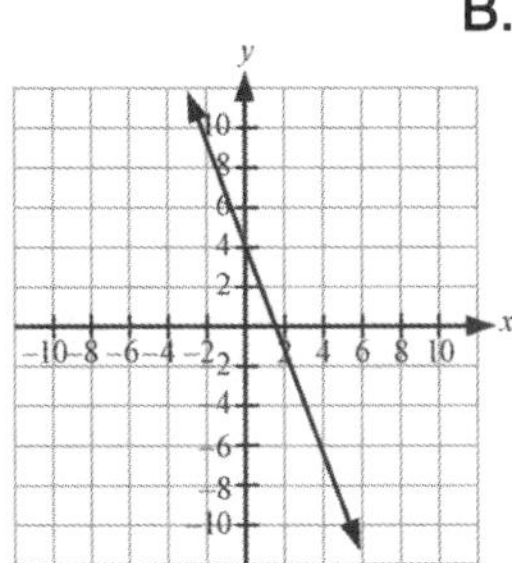

B.

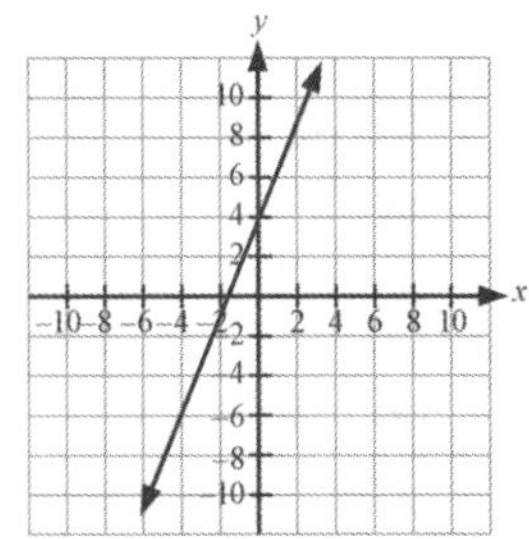

C. D.

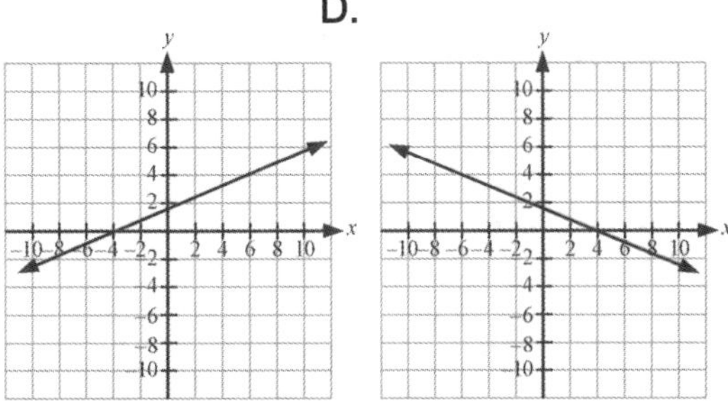

26. The coefficient of y in the expression $7x - 2y + 3$ is

A. –2

B. 2

C. 3

D. 7

Use the following information to answer the next question.

An investment of $7,600 earns an interest rate of 4.5% per year.

27. How long will it take for the investment to earn $1,368 in interest? __________ years

28. Rounded to the nearest hundredth, the amount of interest earned by an investment of $725 when interest is compounded semiannually for 2 years at 6% per year is $__________.

29. When the expression $x^2 + 3x - 40$ is factored, the result is

A. $(x + 8)(x - 5)$

B. $(x - 8)(x + 5)$

C. $(x + 8)(x + 5)$

D. $(x - 8)(x - 5)$

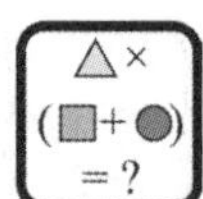

EXERCISE #2—INTERPRETING EXPRESSIONS ANSWERS AND SOLUTIONS

24. A	26. A	28. 90.99
25. A	27. 4	29. A

24. A

In this situation, y represents the number of people in the restaurant, while x represents the number of people that are eating in the restaurant.

If the value of x is 0, it means there are no people eating in the restaurant, but y is still equal to 10. Regardless of how many people are eating in the restaurant, there will always be 10 more people in the restaurant than the number of people eating.

The number 10 represents the number of people that work in the restaurant.

25. A

The slope-intercept form of the equation that defines the graph of a line is $y = mx + b$ where m represents the slope and b represents the y-intercept of the line.

The equation $y = -\frac{5}{2}x + 4$ is written in the slope-intercept form. Since $m = -\frac{5}{2}$ in the equation, the line should have a slope of $-\frac{5}{2}$, which means it should fall from the left to the right. As well, since $b = 4$ in the equation, the line should intercept the y-axis at 4. Graph A is the only graph that represents a line with a negative slope (falling from left to right) and a y-intercept of 4.

Note: Upon further analysis it can be verified that the slope of the line shown in graph A is $-\frac{5}{2}$.

26. A

In the expression $7x - 2y + 3$, there are three terms: $7x$, $-2y$, and 3. Examine the expression to find the coefficient of y.

When the term has only a number, it is the constant. In the given expression, the constant is 3.

When the term has a variable and a number, the number is called the coefficient. Positive and negative signs are part of the coefficient. Therefore, the coefficient of x is 7, and the coefficient of y is –2.

27. 4

Use the simple interest formula $i = prt$ to find the solution.

Step 1
Match the number with the corresponding part of the formula.

- The amount of interest, i, is $1,368.
- The original investment, p, is $7,600.
- The rate, r, is 4.5%, which is equal to 0.045.
- The period, t, is the unknown value.

Step 2
Substitute the numbers into the formula, and solve for the unknown.

$$i = prt$$
$$1,368 = 7,600 \times 0.045 \times t$$
$$1,368 = 342t$$
$$\frac{1,368}{342} = t$$
$$t = 4$$

It will take 4 years for the investment to earn the given amount of interest.

28. 90.99

Step 1
Calculate the accumulated amount of the investment using the compound interest formula.

The principal, P, is $725. Since the interest rate is 6% compounded semiannually, $i = \frac{0.06}{2}$. Since the investment is compounded semiannually for 2 years, the number of compounding periods is $n = 2 \times 2 = 4$.

$$A = P(1 + i)^n$$
$$A = 725\left(1 + \frac{0.06}{2}\right)^4$$
$$A \approx 725(1.126)$$
$$A \approx 815.99$$

Therefore, the accumulated amount of the investment is $815.99.

Step 2
Calculate the compound interest.

Subtract the amount of money in the account after 2 years from the principal amount.

$815.99 - 725 \approx 90.99$

Therefore, the compound interest is $90.99.

29. A

Step 1
Determine which two numbers have a sum of +3 and a product of −40.
+8 − 5 = +3 and +8 × −5 = −40
The two numbers are +8 and −5.

Step 2
Open two sets of brackets. Inside each set of brackets, write the same variable that was used in the given trinomial.
$(x\_)(x\_)$

Step 3
Place the two numbers inside each set of brackets.
$(x+8)(x-5)$

NOTES

Describing Relationships with Equations

DESCRIBING RELATIONSHIPS WITH EQUATIONS

Table of Correlations

Standard		Concepts	Exercise #1	Exercise #2
Unit1.3	Create equations that describe numbers or relationships.			
A-CED.1ii	*Create equations and inequalities in one variable and use them to solve problems. Include equations arising from linear and quadratic functions, and simple rational and exponential functions.*	Solving Problems Using Linear Inequalities	30	48
		Representing Situations Using Quadratic Expressions in One Variable	31	49
		Using Inequalities to Represent Situations Described in Words	32	50
		Writing Equations to Represent Real-Life Relationships with One Variable	33	51
		Modeling and Solving Real-World Problems with Linear Equations	34	51, 52
		Writing and Solving Simple Non-Contextual Word Problems	35	53
		Solving Real-World Quadratic Problems	36	54
A-CED.2	*Create equations in two or more variables to represent relationships between quantities; graph equations on coordinate axes with labels and scales.*	Determining other Representations of a Linear Relation	37	55
		Determining the Equation that Models Quadratic Data Algebraically	38	56
		Writing Algebraic Expressions for Given Situations	39	57
		Modeling Linear Relations of Contextual Problems	40	58
		Modeling Exponential Functions of Growth	41	59
		Modeling Exponential Functions of Decay	42	60
A-CED.3i	*Represent constraints by equations or inequalities, and by systems of equations and/or inequalities, and interpret solutions as viable or non-viable options in a modeling context.*	Using Inequalities to Represent Situations Described in Words	32	50
		Writing Algebraic Expressions for Given Situations	39	57
		Expressing Problems as a System of Equations	43	61
		Determining the Reasonableness of Solutions to Linear Equations	44	62
		Determining the Reasonableness of Solutions to Systems of Linear Equations	45	63
		Representing Situations as a System of Linear Inequalities in Two Variables	46	64
A-CED.4	*Rearrange formulas to highlight a quantity of interest, using the same reasoning as in solving equations.*	Rearranging Formulas	47	65

A-CED.1ii Create equations and inequalities in one variable and use them to solve problems. Include equations arising from linear and quadratic functions, and simple rational and exponential functions.

Solving Problems Using Linear Inequalities

A mathematical sentence that does not have an exact value is called an **inequality**. Inequalities are written using the symbols $>$, $<$, $\geq$, $\leq$, and $\neq$.

Inequalities can be used to model and solve problems about real-life situations. To solve problems involving inequalities, follow these steps:

1. Create an inequality to model the problem. Assign meaningful variables to the quantities involved, and use keywords from the problem to determine the type of inequality and the mathematical operations involved.

Symbol	Meaning
$>$	greater than, more than
$\geq$	greater than or equal to, minimum, at least, cannot fall below
$<$	less than, fewer than
$\leq$	less than or equal to, maximum, at most, cannot exceed
$\neq$	not equal, does not equal

Operation	Keywords
Add	add, increased by, sum, total, altogether, more than
Subtract	minus, decreased by, difference, less than, take away, taken from
Multiply	of, times, times greater than, product, by
Divide	quotient, times less than, divided into, groups

2. Apply inverse operations to isolate the variable.
3. Verify the solution set using a test point.

Example

Lindsay has to go to a workshop for a project she is working on in school. While at the workshop, she has to park her car underground. The cost of parking underground is $3.00 for the first hour and $4.25 for each additional hour or portion of an hour. She has $20.00 to spend on parking.

What is the maximum number of additional hours Lindsay can park?

Solution

Step 1

Create an inequality to model the problem.

Let h represent the additional hours Lindsay can park. It costs $4.25 for each additional hour of parking, so this can be represented as $4.25h$ in the inequality.

The total cost of parking includes $3.00 for the first hour, which can be represented as $+3$ in the inequality.

The total amount of money that Lindsay can spend on parking is $20; therefore, the maximum number of additional hours that she can park can be represented by

$4.25h + 3 \leq 20$.

Step 2

Apply inverse operations to isolate the variable.

$$4.25h + 3 \le 20$$
$$4.25h + 3 - 3 \le 20 - 3$$
$$\frac{4.25h}{4.25} \le \frac{17}{4.25}$$
$$h \le 4$$

Step 3

Verify the solution set using a test point.

Since $3 \le 4$, one test point that can be used is 3.

$$4.25h + 3 \le 20$$
$$4.25(3) + 3 \le 20$$
$$12.75 + 3 \le 20$$
$$15.75 \le 20$$

Since the resulting statement is true, the solution set is correct.

Lindsay can park for a maximum of 4 additional hours.

Representing Situations Using Quadratic Expressions in One Variable

Some problems can be represented by quadratic expressions in one variable that can be expanded and simplified.

Example

A 2×3 picture is to be framed with a matte that has a width of x and a frame with a length of l and a width of w. All the measures are in inches.

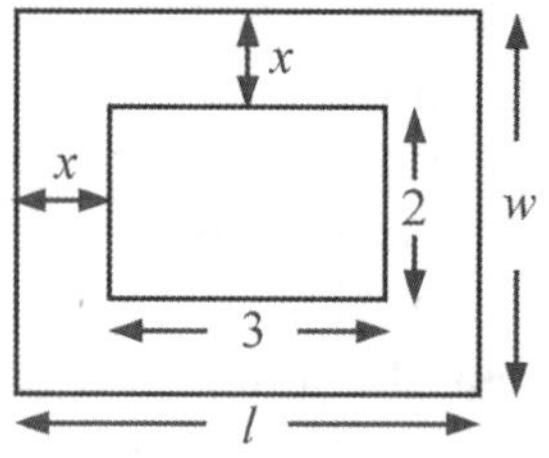

Determine the algebraic expression in terms of x that represents the total area of the picture frame, including the matte.

Solution

The length, l, can be expressed as $x + 3 + x = 2x + 3$, and the width, w, can be expressed as $x + 2 + x = 2x + 2$.

The area of the frame is $A = lw$.

$$A = lw$$
$$A = (2x + 3)(2x + 2)$$

Simplify the expression for the area of the picture frame.

Solution

The expression for the area of the picture frame is $(2x + 3)(2x + 2)$.

Expand the expression using the FOIL method, and then collect like terms.

$$(2x + 3)(2x + 2) = (2x)(2x) + (2)(2x) + (3)(2x) + (3)(2)$$

$$= 4x^2 + 4x + 6x + 6$$
$$= 4x^2 + 10x + 6$$

The simplified expression representing the area of the picture frame is $4x^2 + 10x + 6$.

Using Inequalities to Represent Situations Described in Words

A mathematical sentence that does not have an exact value is called an **inequality**. Inequalities are written using the symbols $>$, $<$, $\ge$, $\le$, and $\ne$.

Inequalities represent relationships between different quantities. When a relationship between different quantities is initially described in words, it is useful to write an inequality that represents the relationship. The inequality can then be used for further problem solving.

When inequalities are initially described in words, they can be translated into mathematical expressions by following these steps:

1. Assign meaningful variables to the quantities involved.
2. Find keywords that describe the type of inequality involved.

Symbol	Keywords
>	greater than, more than
≥	greater than or equal to, minimum, at least, cannot fall below
<	less than, fewer than
≤	less than or equal to, maximum, at most, cannot exceed
≠	not equal to

3. Find keywords that describe the operations involved.

Operation	Keywords
Add	add, increased by, sum, total, altogether, more than
Subtract	minus, decreased by, difference, less than, take away, taken from
Multiply	of, times, times greater than, product, by
Divide	quotient, times less than, divided into, groups

4. Write the inequality.

Example

For her birthday, Charlene received a $500.00 gift card to a local sporting goods store. She wants to buy a pair of basketball shoes that cost $250.00, and she would like to spend the rest of the money on track suits, which are on sale for $20.00 each.

Write an inequality to describe the maximum number of track suits that Charlene can buy.

Solution

Step 1
Assign meaningful variables to the quantities involved.
Let t represent the number of tracksuits Charlene can buy.

Step 2
Find keywords that describe the type of inequality involved.
The phrase “maximum number of track suits” indicates a value less than or equal to a number, so the symbol to use in the inequality will be ≤ .

Step 3
Find keywords that describe the operations involved.
Track suits are on sale for $20.00 each, which can be expressed as $20t$ in the inequality.
The basketball shoes cost $250.00, which can be expressed as +250 in the inequality.

Step 4
Write the inequality.
$20t + 250 \leq 500$

Example

Maria is going on a ski trip, and she wants to save at least $100.00 for spending money for the trip. She currently has $35.00 set aside for this purpose, and she plans to save $2.50 per day from her wages from her part-time job in order to reach her goal.

Write an inequality to represent the number of days that Maria needs to work in order to save at least $100.00.

Solution

Step 1
Assign meaningful variables to the quantities involved.

Let d represent the number of days Maria will have to work.

Step 2
Find keywords that describe the type of inequality involved.

The phrase "at least $100.00" implies a value greater than or equal to $100, so the symbol to use in the inequality will be ≥ .

Step 3
Find keywords that describe the operations involved.

Maria wants to save $2.50 per day, which can be expressed as $2.50d$ in the inequality.

She currently has $35.00 saved, which can be expressed as +35 in the inequality.

Step 4
Write the inequality.
$2.50d + 35 \geq 100$

Writing Equations to Represent Real-Life Relationships with One Variable

Mathematical expressions can consist of numbers, variables, and operational symbols (+, −, ×, and ÷). Expressions can be as short as a single term, or they can consist of two or more terms joined by an operation. For example, $3x + 5$ has two terms ($3x$ and 5) and the addition operation.

You write an **equation** by putting an equal sign between two expressions. The equal symbol means that the expressions on both the left side and right side of the equal sign have the same value.

To convert a word problem into an equation, follow these steps:

1. Define the variable that represents the unknown value for which you need to solve.
2. Identify mathematical keywords, and translate them into mathematical symbols.
3. Using the variable, create an equation to represent the problem.

Some examples of mathematical keywords are listed in this table.

Add (+)	Increase, more than, sum, all together, greater than
Subtract (−)	Minus, remaining, reduce, less than, decrease, difference
Multiply (×)	Times, per, rate, of, product
Divide (÷)	Into, quotient, how many times, divided by
Equal to (=)	Result, answer, sum, total

Example

The cost to rent a DVD player is $5 per day, plus a $15 deposit. Bill paid $30 for his DVD player rental. Write an equation to find the number of days that he rented the DVD player for.

Solution

Step 1
Define the variable.

Let x = the number of days that Bill rented the DVD player for.

Step 2
Identify the keywords.

"$5 per day" → $5x$

"Plus $15" → +15

"Paid $30" → = 30

Step 3
Write the equation.
$5x + 15 = 30$

Example

The area of Lake Superior is 5 times the area of Lake Ontario. The sum of the areas of the two lakes is 105,000 km^2. Write an equation that represents this word problem.

Solution

Step 1
Define the variable.
Let x = the area of Lake Ontario.

Step 2
Identify the keywords.
"5 times the area of Lake Ontario" → $5x$
"Sum of the areas of the two lakes is 105,000 km^2" → = 105,000

Step 3
Write the equation.
$x + 5x = 105{,}000$

Modeling and Solving Real-World Problems with Linear Equations

Linear equations can be written to represent real-world situations. You can use these equations to find unknown values in real-world problems.

Use the following steps to solve real-world problems with linear equations:

1. Define the variable (the unknown value for which you need to solve).
2. Create an equation by using the variable to represent the situation.
3. Solve the equation.
4. Check the solution.

Example

Jonah wants to complete a long-distance race of 25 km. He begins at 9:00 A.M. and jogs at a steady rate of 4 km/h.

How far will Jonah still have left to walk at 1:15 P.M. if he is to finish the race?

Solution

Step 1
Define the variable.
Let x represent the number of kilometers Jonah has left to walk at 1:15 P.M., or the distance remaining.

Step 2
Create the equation.
At 1:15 P.M., Jonah will have been walking for $4\frac{1}{4}$ or 4.25 h at a steady rate of 4 km/h.
Since distance = rate × time, the distance he will have traveled is (4 × 4.25) km.
$x = 25 -$ distance traveled
$x = 24 - (4 \times 4.25)$

Step 3
Solve the equation.
$x = 25 - (4 \times 4.25)$
$x = 25 - 17$
$x = 8$
Jonah has 8 km left to walk to complete the race.

Step 4
Check the solution.
If Jonah has walked for 4.25 h at 4 km/h, then he has walked 17 km. That leaves 8 km left to walk in order for Jonah to reach his goal.

Example

Jillian bought four candles for her neighbor's housewarming party. She paid $1.20 in sales tax, and her total bill came to $25.20.

What is the cost of each of the candles Jillian bought?

Solution

Step 1
Define the variable.
Let c be the cost of each candle that Jillian bought.

Step 2
Create an equation by using the variable to represent the situation.
Jillian bought four candles. Multiply c by the total number of candles she bought, and then add the amount of sales tax to find the amount of the total bill.
$4c + 1.20 = 25.20$

Step 3
Solve the equation.

$$\begin{aligned} 4c + 1.20 &= 25.20 \\ 4c &= 25.20 - 1.20 \\ 4c &= 24.00 \\ \frac{4c}{4} &= \frac{24.00}{4} \\ c &= 6.00 \end{aligned}$$

Each candle cost $6.00

Step 4
Check the solution.

Substitute the calculated value into the original equation.

$$\begin{aligned} 4c + 1.20 &= 25.20 \\ 4(6.00) + 1.20 &= 25.20 \\ 24.00 + 1.20 &= 25.20 \\ 25.20 &= 25.20 \end{aligned}$$

Writing and Solving Simple Non-Contextual Word Problems

Linear equations can be used to represent non-contextual word problems. You can use these equations to solve for unknown values in the given word problems.

Use the following steps to solve non-contextual word problems:

1. Define the variable (the unknown value for which you need to solve).
2. Create an equation using the variable to represent the problem.
3. Solve the equation.
4. Find the unknown values.
5. Check the answer.

Example

The sum of two numbers is 90. If one number is 5 less than 4 times the other, what are the numbers?

Solution

Step 1
Define the variable.
Let x represent the first number.

Step 2
Create the equation.
The other number is four times the first number minus 5, or $4x - 5$.

Therefore, the equation is $x + (4x - 5) = 90$, since the sum of the two numbers is 90.

Step 3
Solve the equation.

$$\begin{aligned} x + (4x - 5) &= 90 \\ x + 4x - 5 &= 90 \\ 5x - 5 &= 90 \\ 5x - 5 + 5 &= 90 + 5 \\ 5x &= 95 \\ \frac{5x}{5} &= \frac{95}{5} \\ x &= 19 \end{aligned}$$

Step 4
Find the two numbers.

Since $x = 19$, the first number is 19.
Since the second number is defined by $4x - 5$ its value, N_2, can be found as follows:

$$\begin{aligned} N_2 &= 4x - 5 \\ &= 4(19) - 5 \\ &= 76 - 5 \\ &= 71 \end{aligned}$$

Step 5
Check the answer.
$19 + 71 = 90$

Therefore, the two numbers are 19 and 71.

Example

The difference between two numbers is 12. The larger number is three more than two times the smaller number.

Determine the two numbers.

Solution

Step 1
Define the variable.

Let x represent the smaller number.

Step 2
Create an equation.

The larger number is three more than two times the smaller number, or $2x + 3$.

Since the difference between the two numbers is 12, the equation is $(2x + 3) - x = 12$.

Step 3
Solve the equation.

$$(2x + 3) - x = 12$$
$$x + 3 = 12$$
$$x = 9$$

Step 4
Find the two numbers.
Since $x = 9$, the smaller number is 9.
The larger number, N_1, is defined by $2x + 3$, and its value can be found by substituting in the value of x.

$$N_1 = 2(9) + 3$$
$$= 18 + 3$$
$$= 21$$

Step 5
Check the answer.
$21 - 9 = 12$
Therefore, the two numbers are 21 and 9.

Solving Real-World Quadratic Problems

Quadratic functions can be used to describe real-world situations. Problems can be modeled using a quadratic equation, which can then be solved.

To use a quadratic function to solve a real-world problem, follow these general steps:

1. Write an equation to represent the situation.
2. Simplify the equation, and write it in $ax^2 + bx + c = 0$
3. Factor the quadratic.
4. Set each factor equal to 0, and solve for the variable.
5. Determine the solution to the problem.

Example

A crate of soda cans holds 10 cans. The length of the crate has three more cans than the width.

$x + 3$

x

How many cans fit along the length and width of the crate?

Solution

Step 1
Write an equation to represent the area of the crate.
The bottom of the crate is in the shape of a rectangle. The area of a rectangle is $A = l \times w$.
The length of the crate has three more cans than the width. From the diagram, the number of cans along the length of the crate is $x + 3$. The number of cans along the width of the crate is x. The crate can hold 10 cans of soda, so the area of the crate is 10.
The area of the crate can be written as follows:

$$A = l \times w$$
$$10 = (x + 3)x$$

Step 2
Simplify the area equation.
Use the distributive property to simplify the right-hand side of the equation.

$$10 = (x + 3)x$$
$$10 = x^2 + 3x$$

Write the equation in $ax^2 + bx + c = 0$ form.

$$10 = x^2 + 3x$$
$$0 = x^2 + 3x - 10$$

Step 3
Factor the trinomial.
The method of decomposition can be used to factor the trinomial.

$$0 = x^2 + 3x - 10$$
$$0 = x^2 + 5x - 2x - 10$$
$$0 = x(x + 5) - 2(x + 5)$$
$$0 = (x - 2)(x + 5)$$

Step 4
Solve for x.
Set each factor equal to 0, and solve for x.

$$x - 2 = 0$$
$$x = 2$$

OR

$$x + 5 = 0$$
$$x = -5$$

Step 5

Determine the solution.

There are two possible answers for x. Since x represents the number of cans along the width, x must be a positive integer. Therefore, $x = 2$.

Since $x = 2$, the number of cans along the width of the crate is 2. The number of cans along the length of the crate is three more than along the width. Therefore, the number of cans along the length is 5.

A-CED.2 Create equations in two or more variables to represent relationships between quantities; graph equations on coordinate axes with labels and scales.

Determining Other Representations of a Linear Relation

When you are given a relation in a table of values, as a graph, or as an algebraic expression, you can present the relation in one of the other two forms.

For example, the table of values below represents the distance, d, from a lightning flash, to the time, t, between seeing the lightning and hearing the thunder.

Time (s)	3	6	9	12	15
Distance (km)	1	2	3	4	5

This linear relation can then be represented graphically.

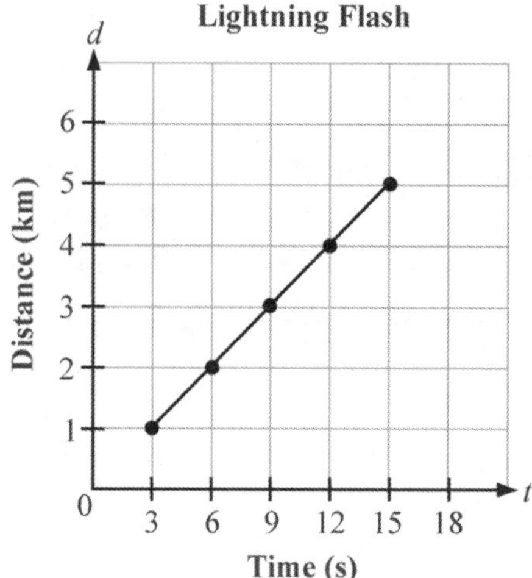

Recall that the rate of change is the ratio of the y-value to its x-value, also known as the slope of the line.

It is clear that the constant rate of change is $\frac{1}{3}$, since the distance increases 1 km (y-value) for every 3 s (x-value). If the line is extended back, it passes through the origin (0, 0). This means the initial value is (0, 0).

This linear relation can be represented algebraically in the form $y = mx + b$:

$d = \frac{1}{3}t + 0 \rightarrow d = \frac{1}{3}t$

DETERMINING THE EQUATION THAT MODELS QUADRATIC DATA ALGEBRAICALLY

The equation of the quadratic function representing the set of points or curve of best fit can be found using the following general steps:

1. If a graph of the data is not given, begin by plotting the data points on graph paper and sketching a curve that best represents the points.
2. Find the vertex (h, k) of the curve by locating the highest or lowest point of the parabola.
3. Choose another point from the graph (e.g., y-intercept, x-intercept, etc.).
4. Substitute the values of x, y, h, and k into the equation $y = a(x - h)^2 + k$.
5. Determine the stretch factor, a.
6. Write the equation in the form $y = a(x - h)^2 + k$.

Example

Number of Registered Apprentices in Building Construction Trades in Canada from 1991 to 2003

Year	Year (Number)	Number of Apprentices
1991	1	46,925
1992	2	43,703
1993	3	40,996
1994	4	36,679
1995	5	34,786
1996	6	33,394
1997	7	32,957
1998	8	33,395
1999	9	36,496
2000	10	39,090
2001	11	42,109
2002	12	47,545
2003	13	53,606
Source: Statistics Canada, Registered Apprenticeship Information System		

Determine the equation in the form $y = a(x - h)^2 + k$ of the quadratic function representing the curve of best fit that represents the data.

Solution

Step 1

Plot the points on graph paper, and sketch a curve by hand that best represents the points. This is illustrated on the given diagram.

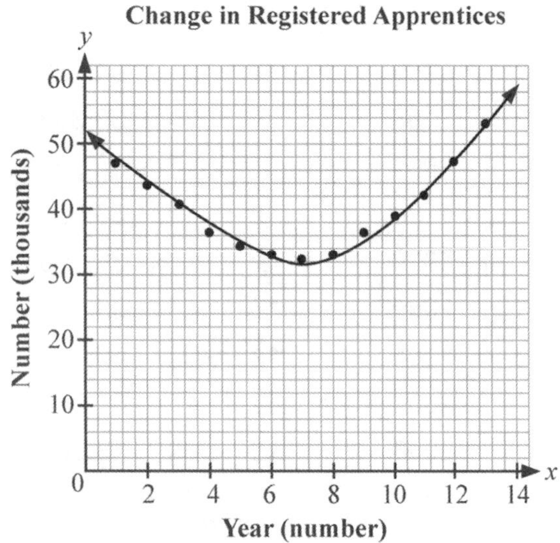

Step 2

Determine the equation in the form $y = a(x - h)^2 + k$.

Find the vertex (h, k) by identifying the lowest point on the curve, which is approximately (7, 31,500). Then, choose another point that the curve passes through. For example, the curve passes through the y-intercept (0, 52,000).

Substitute the value of the vertex into h and k, and the values of the y-intercept for x and y. Then, solve for a.

$$y = a(x - h)^2 + k$$
$$52{,}000 = a(0 - 7)^2 + 31{,}500$$
$$52{,}000 = a(-7)^2 + 31{,}500$$
$$52{,}000 - 31{,}500 = 49a$$
$$20{,}500 = 49a$$
$$a = \frac{20{,}500}{49}$$

Therefore, the equation modeling the curve is

$$y = \frac{20{,}500}{49}(x - 7)^2 + 31{,}500.$$

To find the equation describing the factored form $y = a(x - r)(x - s)$, substitute the x-intercepts for r and s, and substitute a particular point that lies on the curve, $P(x, y)$, in for x and y. Then, solve for a.

Example

At a water park, a particular water jet follows a parabolic path. The relationship between the height, y, in meters and the horizontal distance from the edge of the park, x, in meters of the water jet is shown.

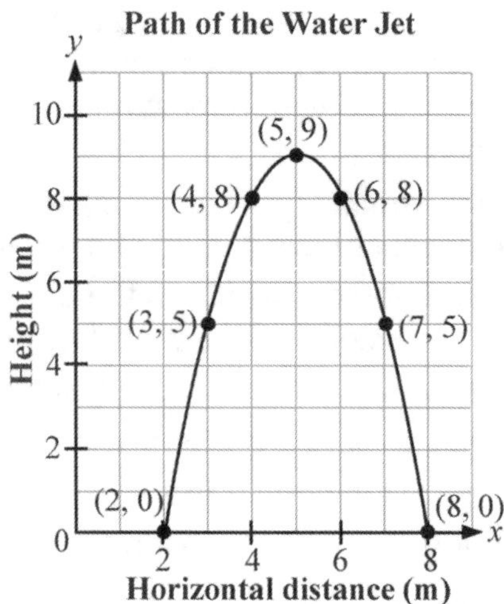

Determine the quadratic function in the form $y = a(x - r)(x - s)$ that models the relationship between the height and the horizontal distance.

Solution

From the graph, the x-intercepts are 2 and 8. To find the equation describing the factored form $y = a(x - r)(x - s)$, substitute the x-intercepts for r and s, and substitute another point, for example (3, 5), for x and y. Then, solve for a.

$$y = a(x - r)(x - s)$$
$$5 = a(3 - 2)(3 - 8)$$
$$5 = a(1)(-5)$$
$$5 = -5a$$
$$a = -1$$

Therefore, the equation in factored form representing the graph of the path of the water jet is

$y = -(x - 2)(x - 8)$.

Writing Algebraic Expressions for Given Situations

Mathematical **expressions** can consist of numbers, variables, and operational symbols (+, −, ×, and ÷). Expressions can be as short as a single term, or they can consist of two or more terms joined by an operation.

Variables are letters used to represent numbers when the values in an expression are not known.

An expression can be used to represent a real-life situation. This type of expression often involves the interaction of more than one variable that represents real things. To help keep track of what each variable represents, it is useful to assign meaningful variables to the unknowns. For example, cost may be represented by C, time may be represented by t, and height may be represented by h. (Note that it is not incorrect to assign non-meaningful variables to the unknowns as long as the variables used are defined for what they represent.)

To write an expression based on the description of a real-life situation, use the following steps:

1. Assign meaningful letters for the variables.
2. Determine the operations.
3. Write the expression.

Example

John has a landscaping business. He charges $20.00 per load of dirt and $30.00 per hour for any work he does.

Write the expression that represents the given situation.

Solution

Step 1

Assign meaningful letters for the variables.

Let l represent the loads of dirt.
Let h represent the hours worked.

Step 2

Determine the operations.

The $20 per load indicates multiplication—$20l$.
The $30 per hour indicates multiplication—$30h$.
The *and* in the problem indicates addition.

Step 3

Write the expression.

The expression that represents the given situation is $20l + 30h$.

Terri has a large number of coins in her pocket. She knows that she has only quarters, dimes, and nickels, but she does not know the exact number of each.

Write an expression to represent the value in cents of the change in Terri's pocket.

Solution

Step 1

Assign meaningful letters for the variables.

- Let q equal the number of quarters.
- Let d equal the number of dimes.
- Let n equal the number of nickels.

Step 2

Determine the operations.

- Since quarters are 25 cents per coin, the number of quarters, q, is multiplied by 25 to find the value of all the quarters—$25q$.
- Since dimes are 10 cents per coin, the number of dimes, d, is multiplied by 10 to find the value of all the dimes—$10d$.
- Since nickels are 5 cents per coin, the number of nickels, n, is multiplied by 5 to find the value of all the nickels—$5n$.

Since the total value of the change is the sum of all the coins, the values of the three groups of coins will be added together.

Step 3

Write the expression.

The expression that represents the value of the change in Terri's pocket is $25q + 10d + 5n$.

Modeling Linear Relations of Contextual Problems

A linear relation may be presented in context. The relationship between the two variables in any given situation can be used to determine a linear equation and generate a graph that describes the situation.

Example

Walter is researching the cost of renting a car for one week because he is getting his car repainted. Company I charges $75 per week plus $0.20 for each kilometer driven. Company II charges $100 per week plus $0.10 for each kilometer driven.

Write an equation of the line formed by each relation, and solve graphically. Explain the conditions under which each plan is better.

Solution

The equation for each company can be written in slope y-intercept form ($y = mx + b$). The y-intercept is the weekly charge, and the slope is the rate per kilometer.

Step 1
Determine the equation of the line for company I.
Since the y-intercept is 75 and the slope is 0.2, substitute 75 for b and 0.2 for m in the equation $y = mx + b$.

$$\begin{aligned} y &= mx + b \\ &= 0.2x + 75 \end{aligned}$$

Step 2
Determine the equation of the line for company II.
Since the y-intercept is 100 and the slope is 0.10, substitute 100 for b and 0.1 for m in the equation $y = mx + b$.

$$\begin{aligned} y &= mx + b \\ &= 0.1x + 100 \end{aligned}$$

Step 3
Graph each relation.
First, plot the y-intercept. Then, use the slope or substitute values into the equation to determine other points on the line.

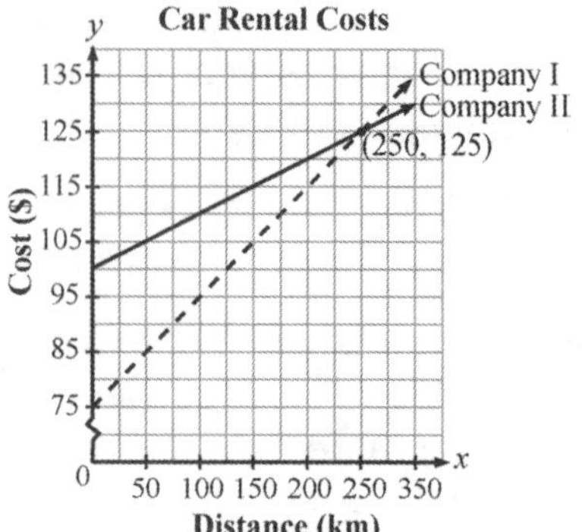

Step 4
Determine the conditions under which each plan is better.
Company I is the better value if Walter travels less than 250 km. Company II is the better value if Walter travels more than 250 km.

Modeling Exponential Functions of Growth

Applications of exponential functions often involve exponential growth. Equations, graphs, and tables of values of exponential functions are often used to model real-life examples in which quantities increase or grow at an exponential rate.

A common example in which an exponential function is used to model exponential growth is population growth.

Example

The population in an ant colony doubles every 3 hours. At time $t = 0$, the population is 50.

Create a table of values showing the population growth of the ant colony.

Solution

Create a table of values.

Time, t (h)	Population, P	Calculation
0	50	Given
3	100	$50(2) = 50(2^1)$
6	200	$50(2)(2) = 50(2^2)$
9	400	$50(2)(2)(2) = 50(2^3)$
12	800	$50(2)(2)(2)(2) = 50(2^4)$
15	1,600	$50(2)(2)(2)(2)(2) = 50(2^5)$
18	3,200	$50(2)(2)(2)(2)(2)(2) = 50(2^6)$

The population behaves as an exponential function of time, t. The amount of time it takes for the population to double is called the **doubling period**.

Example

The population in an ant colony doubles every 3 h. At time $t = 0$, the population is 50.

Determine the equation of the exponential function representing the population growth of the ant colony in terms of time elapsed, t.

Solution

The equation of an exponential function can be expressed in the form $y = ab^x$, where a is the value of the function when $x = 0$ and $b > 0$, $b \neq 1$.

For the equation of an exponential growth function, $b > 1$.

At any given time, the ant colony's population, P, is given by $P = 50(2^n)$, where n is the number of doubling periods. Since the population doubles every 3 h, the number of doubling periods is equal to $\frac{t}{3}$, where t is the elapsed time.

The general population equation for the ant colony can be rewritten as $P = 50\left(2^{\frac{t}{3}}\right)$.

If the growth of the ant colony's population can be modeled by the equation $P = 50\left(2^{\frac{t}{3}}\right)$, where P is the population and t is the elapsed time in hours, use a graphing calculator to sketch the graph of the population function.

Solution

Using the [Y =] feature of a TI-83 Plus graphing calculator, enter the function Y = 50(2)^(x/3). Use a window setting of X:[0, 50, 10], Y:[0, 1,000,000, 100,000]. The graph is shown.

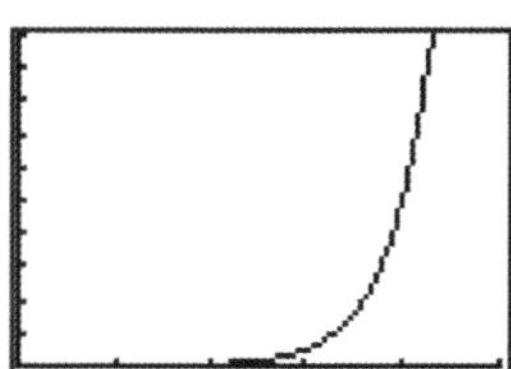

If the growth of the ant colony's population can be modeled by the equation $P = 50\left(2^{\frac{t}{3}}\right)$, where P is the population and t is the elapsed time in hours, what will the population of the colony be after 40 h?

Solution

Since the elapsed time is 40 h, substitute 40 for t in the formula, and solve for P.

$P = 50\left(2^{\frac{t}{3}}\right)$
$P = 50\left(2^{\frac{40}{3}}\right)$
$P \approx 50(10,321.27)$
$P \approx 516,063.7$

The population after 40 h will be approximately 516,064 ants.

If the growth of the ant colony's population can be modeled by the equation $P = 50\left(2^{\frac{t}{3}}\right)$, where P is the population and t is the elapsed time in hours, how long will it take, to the nearest hour, for the ant colony to reach a population of 10,000,000?

Solution

Step 1
Substitute 10,000,000 for P.

$10,000,000 = 50\left(2^{\frac{t}{3}}\right)$

Step 2
Divide both sides by 50.

$200,000 = 2^{\frac{t}{3}}$

Step 3
Take the common logarithm of both sides of the equation.

$\log 200,000 = \log\left(2^{\frac{t}{3}}\right)$

Step 4
Apply the power law of logarithms.

$\log 200,000 = \frac{t}{3}\log 2$

Step 5
Divide both sides of the equation by log 2.

$\frac{\log 200,000}{\log 2} = \frac{t}{3}$

Step 6
Multiply both sides by 3.

$\frac{3\log 200,000}{\log 2} = t$

Step 7
Evaluate using a calculator.

$52.83 \approx t$

It will take approximately 53 h for the colony to reach a population of 10,000,000.

A general formula that defines a quantity growing exponentially is given by $N_t = N_0 \times R^{\frac{t}{p}}$, where the following apply:

- N_t—The quantity at time t
- N_0—The initial size or value (when $t = 0$)
- R—The growth rate, $R > 1$. For example, when a quantity doubles in size, $R = 2$; when it triples, $R = 3$; when it increases by 25 %, $R = 1.25$, and so on.
- t—The elapsed time
- p—The period of time that it takes the quantity to grow by rate R. For example, if it takes 3 h for a population to double, $p = 3$.

The general formula $N_t = N_0 \times R^{\frac{t}{p}}$ can be used to determine the exponential equation that defines a particular problem.

To begin, the variables that have defined values need to be determined from the given problem.

Example

A certain island has 30 spiders.

If the population quadruples every 9 days, what is the island's spider population after 100 days?

Solution

Step 1
Determine the exponential equation that defines the problem.
Define the variables whose values are given in the problem with respect to the general formula

$N_t = N_0 \times R^{\frac{t}{p}}$.

- At time zero, the population is 30: $N_0 = 30$.
- If the population quadruples, then the growth rate is 4: $R = 4$.
- The population after 100 days needs to be determined: $t = 100$.
- It takes 9 days for the population to quadruple, so the period is 9: $p = 9$.

Step 2
Substitute the values $N_0 = 30$, $R = 4$, $t = 100$, and $p = 9$ into the general formula

$N_t = N_0 \times R^{\frac{t}{p}}$.

$N_{100} = 30 \times 4^{\frac{100}{9}}$

Step 3
Evaluate N_{100}.

$$\begin{aligned} N_{100} &= 30 \times 4^{\frac{100}{9}} \\ &\approx 146{,}783{,}323 \end{aligned}$$

After 100 days, the spider population is approximately 146,783,323.

Modeling Exponential Functions of Decay

Applications of exponential functions often involve exponential decay. Equations, graphs, and tables of values of exponential functions can also be used to model real-life examples in which quantities decrease or decay at an exponential rate. Common examples in which exponential functions are used to model exponential decay are depreciating assets or investments and radioactive half-lives.

The general formula for exponential growth $N_t = N_0 \times R^{\frac{t}{p}}$ also applies when a quantity or value is decreasing at an exponential rate. However, for exponential decay, the variable R refers to the rate of decay and will have a value of $0 < R < 1$. For example, when a quantity decreases to half its original value, $R = \frac{1}{2}$; when it depreciates by 25%, $R = 0.75$, and so on.

The general formula can be used to determine the exponential decay equation that defines a particular problem as a function of time. To begin, the variables that have defined values need to be determined from the given problem.

Example

A car that was originally worth $50,000 depreciates at a rate of 15% each year.

What is the exponential equation that defines the value of the car as a function of time?

Solution

The general formula for exponential decay is given by $N_t = N_0 \times R^{\frac{t}{p}}$.

Step 1

Define the variables that have values given in the problem.

- At time 0, the car's value is $50,000, so $N_0 = 50{,}000$.
- If the car depreciates at 15%, the growth rate is 0.85. In other words, each year the car is worth 85% of what its value was the previous year. Thus, $R = 0.85$.
- It takes 1 year for the car's value to reduce to 85% of the previous year's value, so $p = 1$.
- The number of years is defined by t.

Step 2

Substitute the values $N_0 = 50{,}000$, $R = 0.85$, and $P = 1$ into the general formula.

$$N_t = 50{,}000 \times (0.85)^{\frac{t}{1}}$$

Example

The value of a car after t years is given by the function $N_t = 50{,}000 \times (0.85)^{\frac{t}{1}}$.

What will the value of the car be after 14 years?

Solution

Substitute 14 for t in the equation $N_t = 50{,}000 \times (0.85)^{\frac{t}{1}}$, and evaluate.

$$\begin{aligned} N_{14} &= 50{,}000 \times (0.85)^{\frac{14}{1}} \\ &\approx 5{,}138.48 \end{aligned}$$

The car's value after 14 years is represented by N_{14}.

The car will be worth approximately $5,138.48 in 14 years.

The amount of time that it takes for a radioactive substance to decrease to half its original mass is called its half-life.

Radioactive decay questions are approached in a similar manner to a depreciating asset. When a radioactive substance decays, the substance's mass decreases.

Example

The mass of a certain radioactive substance is currently 300 g, and its half-life is 7 years.

To the nearest thousandth of a gram, what will its mass be in 100 years? __________

Solution

Step 1

Determine the exponential equation that defines the problem.

Define the variables whose values are given in the problem with respect to the general formula $N_t = N_0 \times R^{\frac{t}{p}}$.

- At time 0, the mass is 300 g.
  $N_0 = 300$
- The substance is reduced to $\frac{1}{2}$ its mass during each period.
  $R = \frac{1}{2}$
- The mass in 100 years needs to be determined, so $t = 100$.
- It takes 7 years for the substance to reduce to $\frac{1}{2}$ its mass, so the period is 7:
  $p = 7$

Step 2

Substitute the values $N_0 = 300$, $R = \frac{1}{2}$, $t = 100$, and $p = 7$ into the general formula $N_t = N_0 \times R^{\frac{t}{p}}$.

$$N_{100} = 300 \times \left(\frac{1}{2}\right)^{\frac{100}{7}}$$

Step 3
Evaluate N_{100}.

$$N_{100} = 300 \times \left(\frac{1}{2}\right)^{\frac{100}{7}}$$
$$\approx 0.0150208$$

The mass of the substance will be approximately 0.015 g in 100 years.

A-CED.3i Represent constraints by equations or inequalities, and by systems of equations and/or inequalities, and interpret solutions as viable or non-viable options in a modeling context.

Expressing Problems as a System of Equations

A system of equations consists of two or more equations. Problems can be expressed as a system of equations in order to find a solution. Even problems dealing with complicated situations can be simplified when they are expressed as a system of equations.

Example

The sum of two numbers is 11. Multiplying the same two numbers equals 24.

Write a system of equations that represents this situation.

Solution

Step 1
Identify the given information, and express the unknown numbers as variables.

- The sum of two numbers equals 11.
- Multiplying the same two numbers equals 24.
- Let the first number be x and the second number be y.

Step 2
Write an equation to represent the sum.

Use x and y for the two numbers.
The equation representing the sum is $x + y = 11$.

Step 3
Write an equation to express the multiplication.

Use x and y for the same two numbers.
The equation representing the product is $xy = 24$.

Step 4
Identify the system of equations.

The system of equations that represents the given situation is $x + y = 11$ and $xy = 24$.

Problem solving can be organized using systems of equations when there is more than one unknown. Use the information given in the problem to write equations in two variables that represent the problem. Pay attention to what is the same and what is different in the problem.

Example

A motorboat takes 1 h to travel 10 km downstream and 1.5 h to return to its point of departure upstream. The boat is set to travel at the same speed in both directions.

Write a system of linear equations that can be used to determine the actual speed of the motorboat and the speed of the current.

Solution

Step 1
Identify the given information.

Distance traveled is 10 km.
Time taken to travel downstream is 1 h.
Time taken to travel upstream is 1.5 h.

Step 2
Represent the unknowns with variables

Let m equal the speed of the motorboat in kilometers per hour (km/h).
Let c equal the speed of the current in kilometers per hour (km/h).

Step 3
Write an equation to represent the trip downstream.

When traveling downstream, the speed of the current helps the boat move faster than the speed of the motor. Add the speed of the current to the speed of the boat.
The linear equation representing the speed downstream is $(m + c)(1) = 10$.

Step 4

Write an equation to represent the trip upstream.

When traveling upstream, the speed of the current acts as resistance and slows the boat down, making the speed slower than the speed of the motor. Subtract the speed of the current from the speed of the boat.

The linear equation representing the speed upstream is $(m - c)(1.5) = 10$.

The system of linear equations that can be used to determine the actual speed of the boat and the speed of the current is $(m + c)(1) = 10$ and $(m - c)(1.5) = 10$.

Determining the Reasonableness of Solutions to Linear Equations

In order for solutions to linear equations to be reasonable, they must fit the given context of the equation. In addition, when the equation is verified with the solution, both sides of the equation must be equal.

Example

Consider the equation $2x - 4y = -12$, defined where $x > 0$. A solution of (2, 4) is given. In order for the solution to be reasonable, both sides of the equation must equal −12 when values of (x, y) are substituted into the equation.

To verify the given solution, substitute 2 for x and 4 for y into the equation.

$$2x - 4y = -12$$
$$2(2) - 4(4) = -12$$
$$4 - 16 = -12$$
$$-12 = -12$$

Since there is a restriction on the domain $(x > 0)$, any ordered pair that is a solution to the equation must have an x-value greater than 0. The solution (2, 4) is a reasonable solution since the x-value is greater than 0 and both sides equal −12 when verified.

Example

The standard rate to rent a hall is \$100 plus \$10 per guest that attends. If the hall is booked and no one attends, a fee is still charged. This situation can be represented by the equation $C(n) = 100 + 10n$.

John rents the hall for a party and thinks that if no one shows up, it will cost him nothing. Explain why John's estimate of the cost is **not** reasonable.

Solution

If the hall is rented and no one attends the event, $n = 0$.

$$C(n) = 100 + 10n$$
$$C(0) = 100 + 10(0)$$
$$C(0) = 100 + 0$$
$$C(0) = 100$$

If no one attends, it will still cost John \$100 to rent the hall. Therefore, it is not reasonable for him to think it will cost nothing if no one attends.

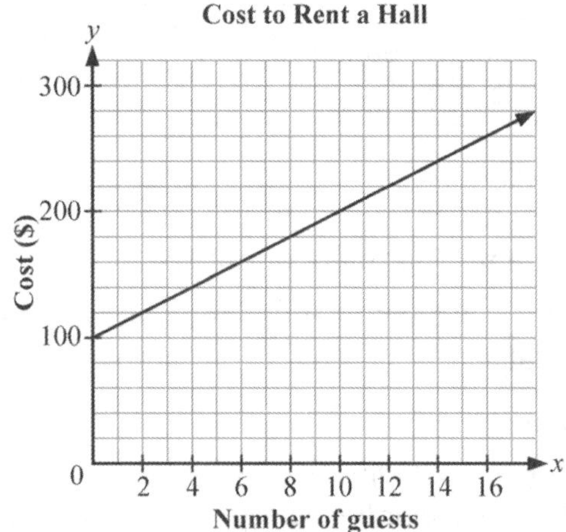

Determining the Reasonableness of Solutions to Systems of Linear Equations

A set of two or more linear equations is a linear system. The solution to a linear system is the set of ordered pairs, usually (x, y), that satisfies all equations in the system. On a graph, the solution is the point (or points) of intersection on the graphs of the equations.

A reasonable solution to a system of linear equations must satisfy all the equations in the system and be appropriate to the context of the question.

Example

Consider the given system of equations with a solution of (1, 1).

$$2x + 4y = 6$$
$$x + y = 2$$

In order to determine whether the solution is reasonable, the x- and y-coordinates must be substituted into each equation.

$$\begin{aligned} 2x + 4y &= 6 \\ 2(1) + 4(1) &= 6 \\ 2 + 4 &= 6 \\ 6 &= 6 \end{aligned}$$

The LHS equals the RHS, so the solution (1, 1) satisfies the equation $2x + 4y = 6$.

$$\begin{aligned} x + y &= 2 \\ 1 + 1 &= 2 \\ 2 &= 2 \end{aligned}$$

The LHS equals the RHS, so the solution (1, 1) satisfies the equation $x + y = 2$.

Since the solution satisfies both equations, it is a reasonable solution to the system of equations.

Example

Sara is asked to solve the following problem: How many dimes and quarters are there if the total value of the dimes and quarters is $12.50 and there are 15 more quarters than dimes?

Sara lets x represent the number of quarters and y represent the number of dimes. She then correctly sets up the system of linear equations shown, which she will use to solve the problem.

$$25x + 10y = 1{,}250$$
$$x = 15 + y$$

Which of the ordered pairs (75, −60), $\left(\frac{95}{2}, 30\right)$, or (40, 25) is a reasonable solution to Sara's system of equations?

Solution

Step 1

Determine whether the ordered pair (75, −60) is a reasonable solution to the given problem.

The value of y in the ordered pair (75, −60) is −60. Since y represents the number of dimes, this would imply that there are −60 dimes, which is impossible. Thus, there is no need to determine whether the ordered pair (75, −60) satisfies the provided system of equations. The ordered pair (75, −60) is not a reasonable solution to the given problem.

Step 2

Determine whether the ordered pair $\left(\frac{95}{2}, 30\right)$ is a reasonable solution to the given problem.

The value of x in the ordered pair $\left(\frac{95}{2}, 30\right)$ is $\frac{95}{2}$. Since x represents the number of quarters, this would imply that there are $\frac{95}{2}$, or $47\frac{1}{2}$, quarters, which is impossible. Once again, there is no need to determine whether the ordered pair $\left(\frac{95}{2}, 30\right)$ satisfies the provided system of equations. The ordered pair $\left(\frac{95}{2}, 30\right)$ is not a reasonable solution to the given problem.

Step 3

Determine whether the ordered pair (40, 25) is a reasonable solution to the given problem.

The numbers 40 and 25 are both whole numbers and thus potential solutions to the given problem. Next, it is necessary to determine whether the ordered pair (40, 25) satisfies the provided system of linear equations.

Substitute 40 for x and 25 for y in each of the provided linear equations, and simplify.

$$25x + 10y = 1{,}250$$
$$25(40) + 10(25) = 1{,}250$$
$$1{,}000 + 250 = 1{,}250$$
$$1{,}250 = 1{,}250$$

$$x = 15 + y$$
$$40 = 15 + 25$$
$$40 = 40$$

Since 1,250 = 1,250 and 40 = 40, the ordered pair (40, 25) satisfies the system of equations. It is, therefore, the only one of the three given ordered pairs that is a reasonable solution to Sara's problem.

Representing Situations as a System of Linear Inequalities in Two Variables

A system of linear inequalities in two variables consists of two or more linear inequalities.

A relationship between different quantities that is described in words can be represented mathematically using an inequality symbol. Based on the particular situation or scenario, a system of linear inequalities can be created and used for problem solving.

There are specific keywords to be aware of that will indicate the use of a particular inequality symbol. The given table relates keywords to inequality symbols.

Symbol	Keywords
$>$	Greater than, more than
$\geq$	Greater than or equal to, minimum, at least, cannot fall below
$<$	Less than, fewer than
$\leq$	Less than or equal to, maximum, at most, cannot exceed
$\neq$	Not equal to

An inequality described in words can be translated into mathematical expressions by following these steps:

1. Assign meaningful variables to the quantities involved.
2. Find keywords that describe the type of inequalities involved.
3. Write the inequalities.

For the most part, systems of linear inequalities representing real-life situations deal with quantities of an item or passing time. Both types of situations are measured in a unit that cannot have a negative quantity. The system of inequalities representing scenarios like these must include the restrictions $x \geq 0$ and $y \geq 0$.

Example

Sansa is setting up her first apartment. She has space for at most 6 chairs. Wooden chairs cost $40 each, and leather chairs cost $80 each. Sansa has budgeted up to $400 to spend on chairs.

Set up a system of linear inequalities to represent how many of each type of chair Sansa can afford in the available space.

Solution

Step 1

Assign meaningful variables to the quantities involved.

Let x be the number of wooden chairs, and let y be the number of leather chairs.

Step 2
Find keywords that describe the type of inequalities involved.

There are two phrases that deal with inequalities. The phrase "at most" indicates a value less than or equal to a number, so the symbol to use in the inequality will be $\leq$. The phrase "budgeted up to" indicates a value less than or equal to a number, so the symbol to use in the inequality will be $\leq$.

The question also deals with quantities of chairs, and there cannot be negative quantities of chairs. These inequalities will use the symbol $\geq$.

There will be a total of four inequalities.

Step 3
Write the inequalities.

There are four inequalities in the system that represents the given situation. The first inequality deals with the amount of money Sansa budgeted. The next one deals with the number of chairs Sansa has space for. The last two limit the number of chairs so that negative quantities are not counted.

$40x + 80y \leq 400$
$x + y \leq 6$
$x \geq 0$
$y \geq 0$

A-CED.4 Rearrange formulas to highlight a quantity of interest, using the same reasoning as in solving equations.

Rearranging Formulas

Sometimes you will be asked to solve for a variable in an equation that has multiple variables in it, like in a formula. A formula can be used to find the value of any of its variables if you know how to manipulate it.

Follow the same steps to solve these types equations as those used for solving single-variable equations.

1. Identify the variable that is to be isolated.
2. Isolate that variable by performing inverse operations to both sides of the equation.

Example

Solve the equation $P = 2l + 2w$ for w.

Solution

Step 1
Identify the variable that is to be isolated.

In this case, w needs to be isolated.

Step 2
Isolate the variable by performing inverse operations on both sides of the equation.

To isolate the term containing w, subtract both sides of the equation by $2l$.

$P - 2l = 2l + 2w - 2l$
$P - 2l = 2w$

Divide both sides of the equation by 2, the numerical coefficient of w.

$\frac{P-2l}{2} = \frac{2w}{2}$

$\frac{P-2l}{2} = w$

Since w is alone on one side of the equation, the equation is solved for w.

Example

The circumference of a circle is given by the formula $C = 2\pi r$. Solve for r.

Solution

Step 1
Identify the variable that is to be isolated.

In this case, r is to be isolated.

Step 2
Isolate r by performing the inverse operation on both sides of the equation.

Divide both sides by 2π so that r remains on the right side of the equation by itself.

$\frac{C}{2\pi} = \frac{2\pi r}{2\pi}$

$\frac{C}{2\pi} = r$

Since r is alone on one side of the equation, the equation has been solved for r.

Example

Solve the equation $h(a-k) = y$ for a.

Solution

Step 1

Identify the variable that is to be isolated.

In this case, a is to be isolated.

Step 2

Isolate the variable by performing inverse operations on both sides of the equation.

Divide both sides of the equation by h.

$$\frac{h(a-k)}{h} = \frac{y}{h}$$

$$a-k = \frac{y}{h}$$

Add k to both sides of the equation.

$$a-k+k = \frac{y}{h} + k$$

$$a = \frac{y}{h} + k$$

Since a is alone on one side of the equation, the equation has been solved for a.

EXERCISE #1—DESCRIBING RELATIONSHIPS WITH EQUATIONS

Use the following information to answer the next question.

Sean and Dave ate at a local pizza parlor on all-you-can-eat pizza night. Sean ate at least six more than triple the number of slices of pizza Dave ate.

30. If Sean ate 18 slices of pizza, which inequality represents the number of slices of pizza Dave ate?

A. $x \geq 8$ B. $x \leq 8$

C. $x \geq 4$ D. $x \leq 4$

Use the following information to answer the next question.

The design of the side view of a specialized cement staircase is shown, with expressions for all side lengths.

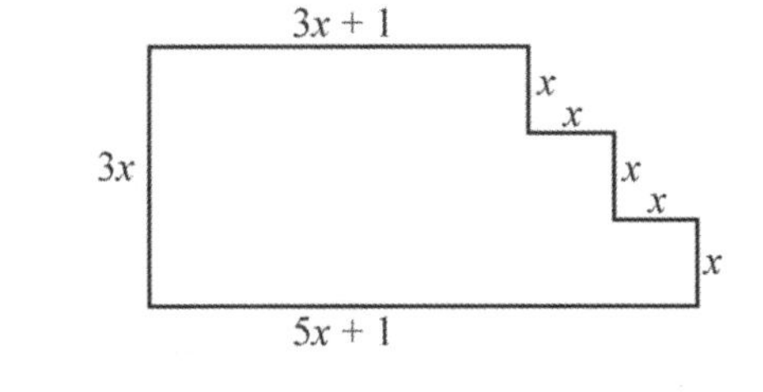

31. Which of the following simplified expressions describes the area of the side view of the staircase?

A. $6x^2$ B. $15x^2$

C. $12x^2 + 3x$ D. $13x^2 + 3x$

Use the following information to answer the next question.

For a class he is taking, Jayson has to complete at least 35 h of volunteer work. He has already completed 7 h at the food bank. He wants to finish his hours at a local animal shelter, where all the shifts are 4 h long.

32. Which of the following inequalities expresses the number of shifts that Jayson needs to volunteer for to complete his class?

A. $4s + 7 \leq 35$ B. $4s + 7 \geq 35$

C. $4s - 7 \leq 35$ D. $4s - 7 \geq 35$

33. Jill works in a shoe store where she makes \$96 / day plus \$3 in commission for each pair of shoes that she sells. If Jill makes \$500 in one week and sells n pairs of shoes, which of the following equations represents her earnings for the 5-day work week?

A. $5(3 + 96n) = 500$

B. $5(96 + 3n) = 500$

C. $96(3 + 5n) = 500$

D. $96(5 + 3n) = 500$

Use the following information to answer the next question.

Danielle has 7 fewer than 6 times as many marbles as Katherine.

34. If Danielle has 119 marbles, how many marbles does Katherine have? __________

Use the following information to answer the next question.

The difference between two numbers is 13. The larger number is 7 less than 6 times the smaller number.

35. What are the two numbers?

A. 17, 4 B. 18, 5

C. 19, 6 D. 20, 7

Use the following information to answer the next question.

Contractors are asked to install wall-to-wall carpet on the floor of each of two square rooms. One side of the larger square room is 4 m longer than a side of the smaller square room.

36. If the total area of the two square rooms is 208 m^2, then the side length of the smaller square room is

A. 8 m **B.** 9 m

C. 12 m **D.** 13 m

Use the following information to answer the next question.

x	−5	−3	−1	0	1	3	5
y	y_1	5	1	−1	y_2	y_3	−11

37. What are the values of y_1, y_2, and y_3, respectively?

Show your work.

Use the following information to answer the next question.

The captain of a small yacht fires a rescue flare into the air. The given table shows the height of the flare in relation to the time elapsed after the flare is fired.

Time (s)	Height of Flare (m)
0	0
1	150
2	240
3	270
4	240
5	150
6	0

38. Written in the form $y = a(x - r)(x - s)$, which of the following functions **best** models the height of the flare in relation to the time elapsed?

A. $y = -20x(x - 6)$

B. $y = -30x(x - 6)$

C. $y = -80x(x - 6)$

D. $y = -120x(x - 6)$

Use the following information to answer the next question.

An airplane takes 3 h to travel a particular distance with the wind. Measured in kilometers per hour, the speed of the airplane in still air is represented by a and the speed of the wind is represented by w.

39. Which of the following expressions represents the distance traveled in kilometers by the airplane in 3 h?

A. $3(aw)$ **B.** $\frac{a + w}{3}$

C. $3a + w$ **D.** $3(a + w)$

Use the following information to answer the next question.

The boiling temperature of pure water is 100°C at sea level and 97.2°C at an altitude of 0.335 km above sea level.
The relationship between the boiling temperature of pure water and the altitude above sea level is linear.

40. If T represents the boiling temperature of pure water in degrees Celsius and h represents the height in kilometers above sea level, which of the following equations and graphs show the relationship between T and h?

A. $T = -2.8h + 100$

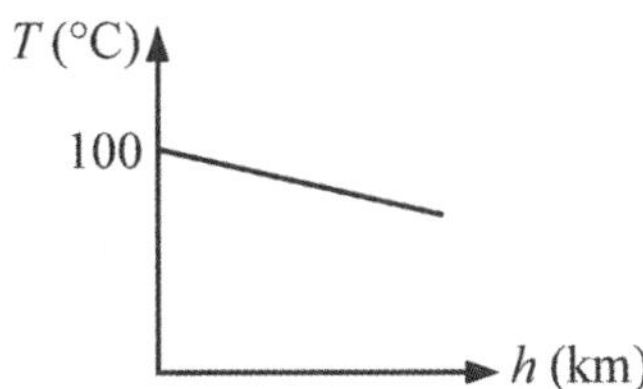

B. $T = -8.36h + 100$

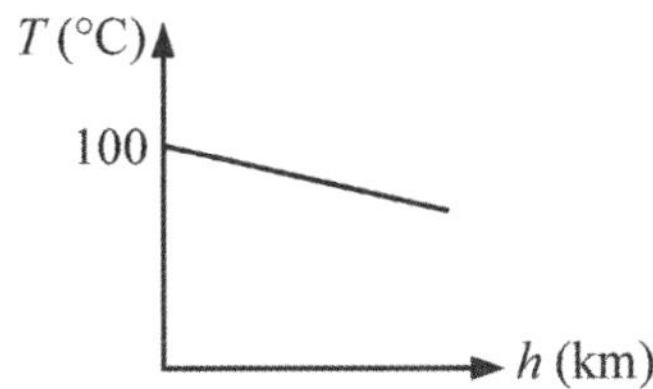

C. $T = -2.8h + 100$

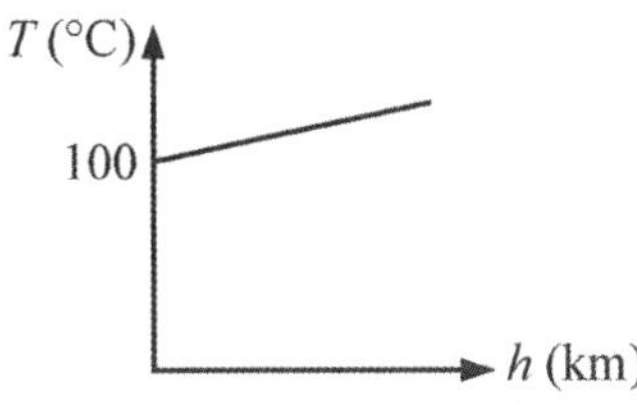

D. $T = -8.36h + 100$

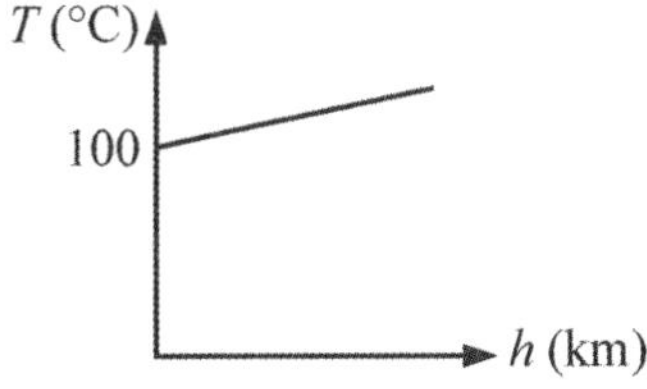

Use the following information to answer the next question.

The population of a small town is 1,400 people, and the population of the town doubles every 20 years.

41. The number of years it will take for the population of the town to reach 50,000 people is between

A. 80 and 90 years

B. 90 and 100 years

C. 100 and 110 years

D. 110 and 120 years

Use the following information to answer the next question.

When a large block of ice is put in a tub of water, it melts such that the volume of ice is halved every 12 minutes.

42. Using a graphical approach, determine the amount of time, to the nearest minute, that it takes for the block of ice to melt to one-tenth of its original volume?

A. 3 min
B. 24 min
C. 33 min
D. 40 min

Use the following information to answer the next question.

Miguel's math tests are always out of 100. The sum of the marks on his last three tests was 199. His mark on the first math test was 60. The product of his marks on the second and third tests was equal to 80 times his mark on the first test. Miguel wanted to create a system of equations that could help him determine his marks on his second and third tests.

43. If x represents Miguel's mark on the second math test and y represents his mark on the third math test, which of the following systems of equations can be used to solve the given problem?

A. $x + y = 139$
$xy = 140$

B. $x + y = 139$
$xy = 4{,}800$

C. $x + y = 199$
$xy = 80$

D. $x + y = 199$
$xy = 4{,}800$

Use the following information to answer the next question.

A landscaping company, DesignCO, charges a \$45 consultation fee and \$50/h for labor to do basic landscaping. These charges can be represented by the linear equation $C(t) = 50t + 45$, where $C(t)$ is the total cost of landscaping and t is the number of hours to complete the task. Tom would like DesignCO to landscape his backyard but wants the total cost of landscaping to be less than \$900.

44. In order to stay within Tom's budget of \$900, the length of time DesignCO could take to complete the task is

A. –17.5 h
B. 0 h
C. 16 h
D. 19.5 h

Use the following information to answer the next question.

Two oceanfront docks in the Atlantic Ocean are 152 mi apart. A sailboat leaves the northern dock at the same time as an empty fishing boat leaves the southern dock.
The two boats travel toward each other, and they meet 4 h after leaving their respective docks. The sailboat is traveling 8 mph faster than the fishing boat.
The given system of linear equations can be used to determine the speed of each boat, where x represents the speed of the sailboat and y represents the speed of the fishing boat.
$4x + 4y = 152$
$x - y = 8$

45. Which of the following ordered pairs is a reasonable solution to the given problem?

A. (24.5, 16.5)
B. (18, –10)
C. (14, 22)
D. (23, 15)

Use the following information to answer the next question.

Henry is trying to organize a one-day golf tournament at a particular golf course. From a survey he conducted, he knows that fewer than 50 golfers are interested in participating. He also determined that at least 34 golfers will use a golf cart, while at most 16 golfers will walk the course. The cost of using a cart is $42 per player, while the cost of walking the course is $30 per player. Henry must collect more than $1,920 in golf fees from the players in order for the tournament to take place.

46. If x represents the number of golfers who will walk the course and y represents the number who will use a golf cart, which of the following inequalities could be part of a system of inequalities that represents the given information?

A. $x + y \leq 50$

B. $0 \leq x \leq 16$

C. $34 < y < 50$

D. $30x + 42y \geq 1{,}920$

47. Rewrite the equation $A = \frac{bh}{2}$ to isolate h.

EXERCISE #1—DESCRIBING RELATIONSHIPS WITH EQUATIONS ANSWERS AND SOLUTIONS

30. D	35. A	40. B	45. D
31. C	36. A	41. C	46. B
32. B	37. See solution	42. D	47. See solution
33. B	38. B	43. B	
34. 21	39. D	44. C	

30. D

Let the variable x represent the number of slices of pizza Dave ate.

The phrase "six more than triple the slices of pizza Dave ate" can be represented by the expression $3x + 6$. Therefore, Sean ate at least $3x + 6$ slices of pizza. Since Sean ate 18 slices of pizza, the problem can be represented by the inequality $3x + 6 \le 18$.

Solve the inequality by applying inverse operations.

$$3x + 6 \le 18$$
$$3x + 6 - 6 \le 18 - 6$$
$$3x \le 12$$
$$\frac{3x}{3} \le \frac{12}{3}$$
$$x \le 4$$

The inequality $x \le 4$ represents the number of slices of pizza Dave ate. In other words, Dave ate a maximum of 4 slices of pizza.

31. C

Method 1

Multiply $3x(5x + 1)$ to find the total rectangular area and then subtract three squares represented by $(x)(x)$.

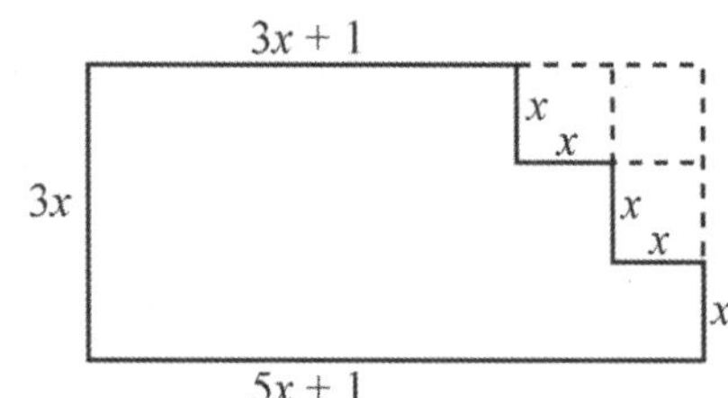

$$A_{rectangle} = 3x(5x + 1)$$
$$= 15x^2 + 3x$$
$$A_{square} = (x)(x) = x^2$$
$$A_{3\ squares} = 3(x^2) = 3x^2$$
$$A_{staircase} = A_{rectangle} - A_{3\ squares}$$
$$= 15x^2 + 3x - 3x^2$$
$$= 12x^2 + 3x$$

Method 2

Multiply three horizontal strips (A, B, and C), making up the stair as shown below.

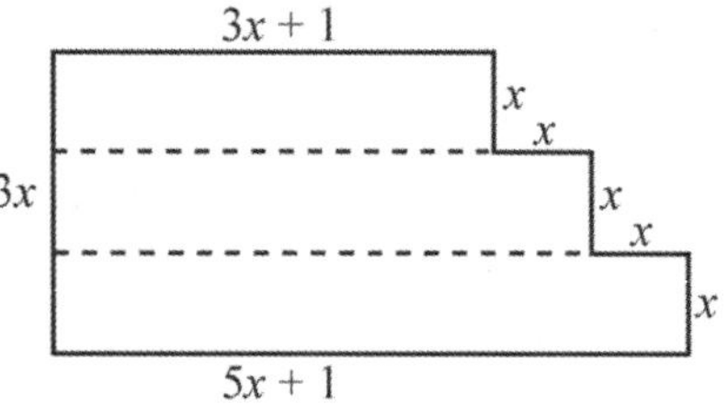

$$Area_A = (x)(3x + 1)$$
$$Area_B = (x)(3x + 1 + x)$$
$$Area_C = (x)(5x + 1)$$
$$Area_{staircase} = Area_A + Area_B + Area_C$$
$$= (x)(3x + 1) + (x)(4x + 1) + (x)(5x + 1)$$
$$= 3x^2 + x + 4x^2 + x + 5x^2 + x$$
$$= 12x^2 + 3x$$

The simplified expression describing the area of the staircase is $12x^2 + 3x$.

32. B

Step 1

Assign meaningful variables to the quantities involved.

Let s equal the number of shifts that Jayson will need to work at the animal shelter.

Step 2

Find the keywords that describe the type of inequality involved.

Since the question asks for at least 35 h, the type of inequality will be greater than or equal to, ≥ .

Step 3

Find the keywords that describe the operations involved.

The shifts at the animal shelter are 4 h long. You can write this as $4s$.

Jayson has already completed 7 h at the food bank. You can write this as +7.

Step 4
Write the inequality.
$4s + 7 \geq 35$

33. B

Identify keywords that will help to create a mathematical equation to represent the situation.

Jill makes $96 / day plus another $3 in commission for each pair of shoes she sells. This is represented by $96 + 3n$.

In one work week, Jill will work 5 days. The expression becomes $5(96 + 3n)$.

If she makes a total of $500 in one week, the equation now becomes $5(96 + 3n) = 500$.

34. 21

Step 1
Define the variable.
Let k be the number of marbles that Katherine has.

Step 2
Create the equation.
Danielle has 6 times as many ($6k$) minus 7 marbles (-7). Danielle has 119 marbles.
$6k - 7 = 119$

Step 3
Solve the equation.
To remove a term from an equation, perform the inverse operation to both sides. Remove the constant term by adding 7 to both sides of the equation.

$$\begin{aligned} 6k - 7 &= 119 \\ 6k - 7 + 7 &= 119 + 7 \\ 6k &= 126 \end{aligned}$$

Remove the coefficient by dividing both sides of the equation by 6.

$$\begin{aligned} 6k &= 126 \\ \frac{6k}{6} &= \frac{126}{6} \\ k &= 21 \end{aligned}$$

Step 4
Check the solution.
Substitute 21 for k in the equation. Solve each side of the equation to ensure the right side is equal to the left side.

$$\begin{aligned} 6k - 7 &= 119 \\ 6(21) - 7 &= 119 \\ 126 - 7 &= 119 \\ 119 &= 119 \end{aligned}$$

Since the left side equals the right side, Katherine has 21 marbles.

35. A

Step 1
Define the variable.
Let x represent the smaller number.

Step 2
Create the equation.
The larger number is 7 less than 6 times the smaller number, or $6x - 7$. Therefore, the equation is $(6x - 7) - x = 13$ since the difference between the two numbers is 13.

Step 3
Solve the equation.

$$\begin{aligned} (6x - 7) - x &= 13 \\ 5x - 7 &= 13 \\ 5x &= 20 \\ x &= 4 \end{aligned}$$

Step 4
Find the two numbers.
Since $x = 4$, the smaller number is 4.
Since the larger number is defined by $6x - 7$, its value, N_1, can be found as follows:

$$\begin{aligned} N_1 &= 6x - 7 \\ N_1 &= 6(4) - 7 \\ N_1 &= 24 - 7 \\ N_1 &= 17 \end{aligned}$$

Step 5
Check the solution.
$17 - 4 = 13$
The first number is 17, and the second number is 4.

36. A

Step 1
Write an equation that represents the information in the given problem.
If x represents the side length of the smaller square room, then the side length of the larger square room can be represented by $x + 4$. Recall that the area, A, of a square can be determined by applying the formula $A = s^2$, where s represents the side length of the square.
The area of the smaller square room can be expressed as x^2, and the area of the larger square room can be expressed as $(x + 4)^2$. Since the total area of the two square rooms is 208 m^2, an equation that can represent the information in the given problem is $x^2 + (x + 4)^2 = 208$.

Step 2

Simplify the equation $x^2 + (x+4)^2 = 208$, and then write the resulting equation equal to zero.

$$\begin{aligned} x^2 + (x+4)^2 &= 208 \\ x^2 + (x+4)(x+4) &= 208 \\ x^2 + x^2 + 4x + 4x + 16 &= 208 \\ 2x^2 + 8x + 16 &= 208 \\ 2x^2 + 8x - 192 &= 0 \end{aligned}$$

Each term in the equation $2x^2 + 8x - 192 = 0$ is divisible by 2, so the equation $2x^2 + 8x - 192 = 0$ is equivalent to the equation $x^2 + 4x - 96 = 0$.

Step 3

Factor the trinomial $x^2 + 4x - 96$.

Since the trinomial $x^2 + 4x - 96$ is in the general quadratic form $x^2 + bx + c$, it can be factored by first determining the two numbers that multiply to equal -96 and that add to equal 4. These two numbers are 12 and –8. Therefore, the trinomial $x^2 + 4x - 96$ can be expressed in factored form as $(x+12)(x-8)$.

Step 4

Solve for x.

Set each factor equal to 0, and solve for x.

$x + 12 = 0$
$x = -12$

OR

$x - 8 = 0$
$x = 8$

Step 5

Determine the solution to the given problem.

Since x represents the side length of the smaller square room, the value of x must be positive. Therefore, $x = 8$. It then follows that the side length of the larger square room, $x + 4$, is $8 + 4 = 12$ m.

The side length of the smaller square room is 8 m.

37.

Write the equation of the line first by calculating the rate of change and the y-intercept.

$$\begin{aligned} \text{Rate of change} &= \frac{\text{vertical separation}}{\text{horizontal separation}} \\ &= \frac{y_2 - y_1}{x_2 - x_1} \\ &= \frac{5-1}{(-3)-(-1)} \\ &= \frac{4}{-2} \\ &= -2 \end{aligned}$$

According to the table the y-intercept is –1, which means the equation is $y = -2x - 1$.

To complete the table, substitute the values of x into the equation $y = -2x - 1$ and solve for y.

- For $x = -5$: $y = -2(-5) - 1 = 9$
- For $x = 1$: $y = -3$
- For $x = 3$: $y = -2(3) - 1 = -7$

x	–5	–3	–1	0	1	3	5
y	9	5	1	–1	–3	–7	–11

Therefore, $y_1 = 9$, $y_2 = -3$, and $y_3 = -7$.

38. B

Begin by plotting the points and drawing a curve that best represents the points.

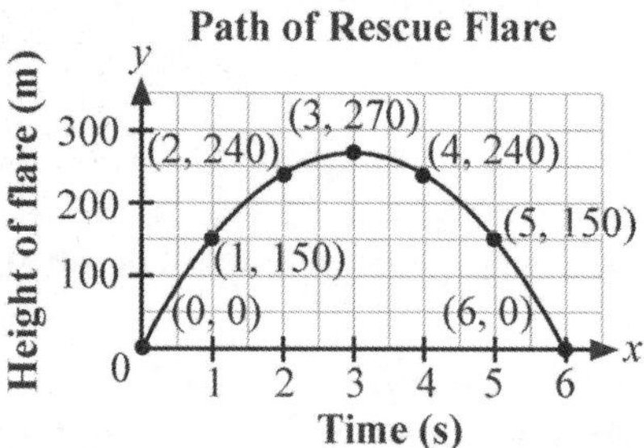

From the data table and the graph, the x-intercepts are 0 and 6. To find the equation describing the factored form $y = a(x - r)(x - s)$, substitute the x-intercepts for r and s, and substitute another point, for example (2, 240), for x and y. Then, solve for a.

$$\begin{aligned} y &= a(x-r)(x-s) \\ 240 &= a(2-0)(2-6) \\ 240 &= a(2)(-4) \\ 240 &= -8a \\ a &= -30 \end{aligned}$$

The equation in factored form representing the graph of the rescue flare's path is $y = -30(x - 0)(x - 6)$, which simplifies to $y = -30x(x - 6)$.

39. D

The distance traveled by an object is equal to the speed of the object multiplied by the time traveled.

Step 1

Determine an expression for the speed of the airplane with the wind.

The speed of the airplane with the wind is equal to the speed of the airplane in still air, a, plus the wind speed, w. Thus, the speed of the airplane with the wind can be represented by the expression $a + w$.

Step 2
Determine an expression for the distance traveled by the airplane in 3 h.
The distance traveled by the airplane is equal to the speed of the airplane with the wind (represented by $a + w$) multiplied by the travel time, 3 h. Thus, an expression for the distance traveled in kilometers by the airplane in 3 h is $3(a + w)$.

40. B

Step 1
Determine the equation in the form $y = mx + b$.
The boiling temperature decreases $100 - 97.2 = 2.8°\text{C}$ as the altitude increases by 0.335 km; therefore, the slope m is equal to

$$\frac{-2.8°\text{C}}{0.335 \text{ km}} \approx -8.36°\text{C/km}.$$

The boiling temperature at sea level $(h = 0)$ is 100°C, so $b = 100$.
The equation is approximately $T = -8.36h + 100$.

Step 2
Determine the correct graph.
As the altitude increases, the boiling temperature decreases from a vertical intercept of 100. Therefore, the graph must slope down to the right as shown in the given graph.

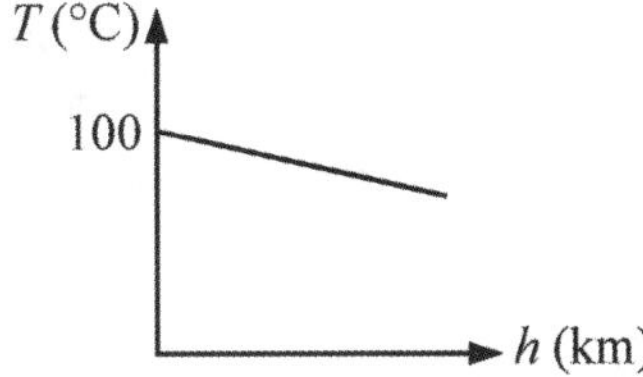

41. C

Step 1
Determine what the town's population is every 20 years, and enter the data in a table of values as shown:

Years	Population
0	1,400
20	2,800
40	5,600
60	11,200
80	22,400
100	44,800
120	89,600

Step 2
Graph the ordered pairs as points on a graph, and join the points with a smooth curve. The following is the graph of the relationship between the number of years and the population. From the graph, the population reaches 50,000 between 100 and 110 years.

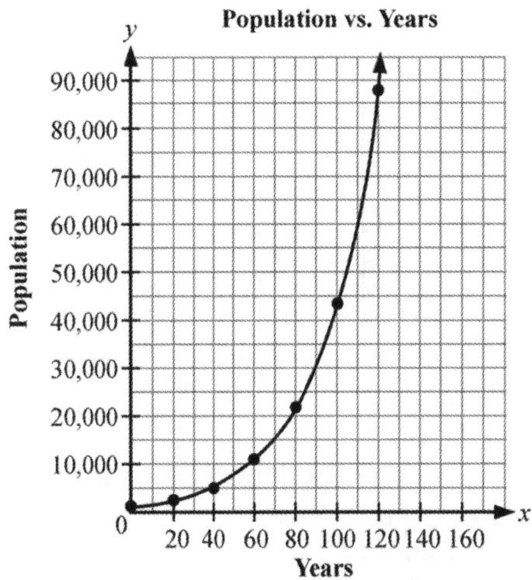

42. D

Step 1
Determine the percentage volume of the block of ice after every 12 minutes, and place the data in a table of values.

Time (min)	Volume (%)
0	100.0
12	50.0
24	25.0
36	12.5
48	6.3
60	3.1
72	1.6

Step 2
Plot the ordered pairs as points on a graph, and join the points with a smooth line. The graph generated is shown.

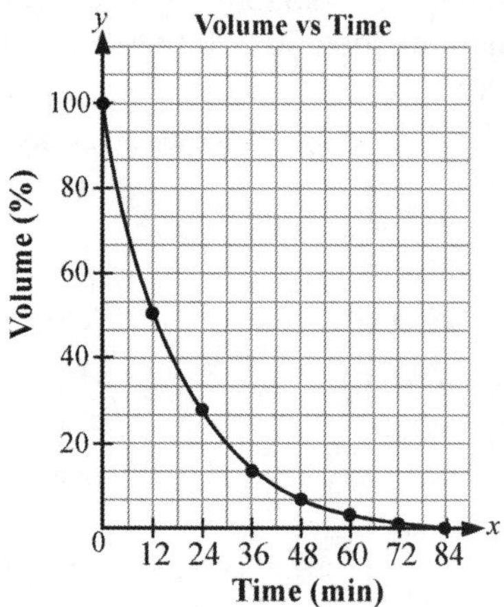

The graph shows that the time it takes for the block of ice to melt to one-tenth, or 10%, of its original volume is about 40 min.

43. B

Step 1
Identify the given information.

The sum of the marks on Miguel's last three math tests is 199.

Miguel's mark on his first test is 60.

The product of Miguel's marks on the second and third tests is 80 times the mark on his first test.

Step 2
Write an equation to represent the sum of Miguel's marks on the last three math tests.

The word *sum* implies addition. Given that Miguel's mark on the first test is 60 and his marks on the second and third tests are represented by x and y, respectively, then an equation in terms of x and y that represents the sum of Miguel's marks on the last three math tests is $60 + x + y = 199$.

The equation $60 + x + y = 199$ is equivalent to the equation $x + y = 139$, since $199 - 60 = 139$.

Step 3
Write an equation to represent the fact that the product of Miguel's marks on the second and third math tests is 80 times the mark on his first math test.

Both the word *product* and the word *times* imply multiplication. Thus, the product of Miguel's marks on the second and third tests can be represented by xy. Also, 80 times Miguel's mark on the first test is $80 \times 60 = 4{,}800$.

It follows that the required equation could be $xy = 4{,}800$.

Step 4
Write a system of equations that Miguel can use to solve the given problem.

The system of equations that can be used to solve the given problem is as follows:

$x + y = 139$
$xy = 4{,}800$

44. C

To solve this problem, you must determine the reasonableness of the possibilities and then calculate the solution.

Step 1
Determine whether –17.5 h is a reasonable solution.

A solution of –17.5 h implies that the landscapers worked negative hours, which is impossible. Therefore, –17.5 h is not a reasonable solution, and no calculations are required.

Step 2
Determine whether 0 h is a reasonable solution.

A solution of 0 h implies that no actual landscaping was done and only the consultation fee was charged. Since Tom decided to get basic landscaping done, 0 h of labor is not a reasonable solution, and no calculations are required.

Step 3
Determine whether 19.5 h is a reasonable solution.

Calculate the total cost of landscaping, $C(t)$, with 19.5 h of labor. Substitute 19.5 for t in the linear equation.

$C(t) = 50t + 45$
$C(t) = 50(19.5) + 45$
$C(t) = 975 + 45$
$C(t) = \$1{,}020$

Since \$1,020 > \$900, Tom would have spent more than \$900 on landscaping using 19.5 h of labor. Therefore, 19.5 h is not a reasonable solution.

Step 4
Determine whether 16 h is a reasonable solution.

Calculate the total cost of landscaping, $C(t)$, with 16 h of labor. Substitute 16 for t in the linear equation.

$C(t) = 50t + 45$
$C(t) = 50(16) + 45$
$C(t) = 800 + 45$
$C(t) = \$845$

Since \$845 < \$900, Tom would have spent less than \$900 on landscaping using 16 h of labor. Therefore, 16 h is a reasonable solution.

The length of time DesignCO could take to complete the landscaping is 16 h.

45. D

Step 1

Determine whether the ordered pair (24.5, 16.5) is a reasonable solution.

Since 24.5 is 8 more than 16.5, determine whether the ordered pair (24.5, 16.5) satisfies the given system of linear equations.

Substitute 24.5 for x and 16.5 for y in each of the linear equations, and then simplify.

$$\begin{aligned} 4x+4y &= 152 \\ 4(24.5)+4(16.5) &= 152 \\ 98+66 &= 152 \\ 164 &\neq 152 \end{aligned}$$

$$\begin{aligned} x-y &= 8 \\ 24.5-16.5 &= 8 \\ 8 &= 8 \end{aligned}$$

Since $164 \neq 152$, the ordered pair (24.5, 16.5) does not satisfy the given system of equations; therefore, it is not a reasonable solution.

Step 2

Determine whether the ordered pair (18, −10) is a reasonable solution.

The value of y in the ordered pair (18, −10) is −10. Since y represents the speed of the fishing boat, this implies that the speed of the fishing boat is −10 mph, which is impossible. Therefore, the ordered pair (18, −10) is not a reasonable solution, so there is no need to determine whether this ordered pair satisfies the given system of linear equations.

Step 3

Determine whether the ordered pair (14, 22) is a reasonable solution.

The values of x and y in the ordered pair (14, 22) are 14 and 22, respectively. Since x represents the speed of the sailboat and y represents the speed of the fishing boat, this implies that the speed of the sailboat is 14 mph and the speed of the fishing boat is 22 mph. This contradicts the statement in the problem that the sailboat travels 8 mph faster than the fishing boat. Therefore, the ordered pair (14, 22) is not a reasonable solution, so there is no need to determine whether this ordered pair satisfies the given system of linear equations.

Step 4

Determine whether the ordered pair (23, 15) is a reasonable solution.

Since 23 is 8 more than 15, determine whether the ordered pair (23, 15) satisfies the given system of linear equations.

Substitute 23 for x and 15 for y in each of the linear equations, and then simplify.

$$\begin{aligned} 4x+4y &= 152 \\ 4(23)+4(15) &= 152 \\ 92+60 &= 152 \\ 152 &= 152 \end{aligned}$$

$$\begin{aligned} x-y &= 8 \\ 23-15 &= 8 \\ 8 &= 8 \end{aligned}$$

Since 152 = 152 and 8 = 8, the ordered pair (23, 15) satisfies the given system of linear equations; therefore, it is a reasonable solution.

46. B

Step 1

Identify keywords or phrases in the problem that describe the types of inequalities involved.

Four phrases in the problem describe inequalities:

1. The phrase "fewer than 50 golfers" indicates a value smaller than 50.
2. The phrase "at most 16 golfers will walk the course" indicates a value less than or equal to 16 (but greater than or equal to 0, since it is not possible to have a negative number of golfers).
3. The phrase "at least 34 golfers will use a golf cart" indicates a value greater than or equal to 34 (but less than 50, because fewer than 50 golfers will play in the tournament).
4. The phrase "collect more than $1,920 in golf fees" indicates a value greater than, but not equal to, $1,920.

Step 2

Write the inequalities that represent the four phrases.

Since x represents the number of golfers who will walk and y represents the number who will use a golf cart, the inequality that represents phrase 1 is $x+y<50$.

The inequality that represents phrase 2 is $0 \leq x \leq 16$.

The inequality that represents phrase 3 is $34 \leq y < 50$.

Given that the cost per golfer to walk is $30 and the cost per golfer to use a golf cart is $42, the inequality that corresponds to phrase 4 is $30x+42y>1,920$.

Step 3

From the given alternatives, identify the inequality that could be part of the system of inequalities that represents the given information.

A system of inequalities that could represent the given information is as follows:

$$x + y < 50$$
$$0 \le x \le 16$$
$$34 \le y < 50$$
$$30x + 42y > 1{,}920$$

It follows that the inequality $0 \le x \le 16$ could be part of a system of inequalities that represents the given information.

47.

Step 1

Multiply both sides of the equation by 2 to eliminate the fraction.

$$A = \frac{bh}{2}$$
$$2(A) = \left(\frac{bh}{2}\right)2$$
$$2A = bh$$

Step 2

Divide both sides of the equation by b to isolate h.

$$\frac{2A}{b} = \frac{bh}{b}$$
$$\frac{2A}{b} = h$$

EXERCISE #2—DESCRIBING RELATIONSHIPS WITH EQUATIONS

Use the following information to answer the next question.

Rachelle and Lisa are flying to Vancouver. When they weigh their bags at the airline counter, they discover that Rachelle's bag weighs no more than double Lisa's bag decreased by 5 kg.

48. If Rachelle's bag weighs 45 kg, which of the following inequalities represents the possible weight of Lisa's bag?

A. $x \geq 25$ B. $x \leq 25$

C. $x \geq 20$ D. $x \leq 20$

Use the following information to answer the next question.

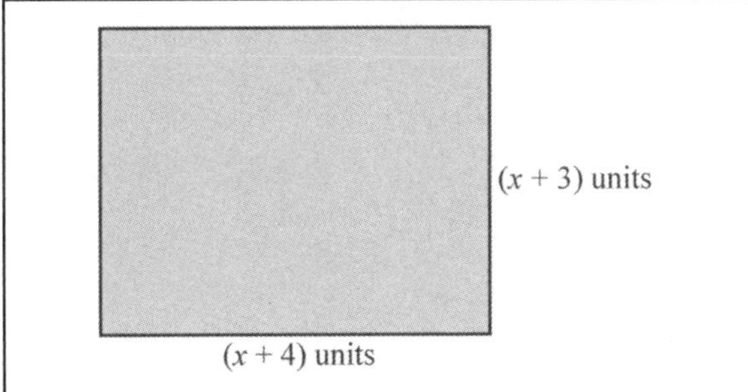

49. The area of the rectangle is

A. $x^2 + 7x + 12$

B. $x^2 + 7x + 7$

C. $x^2 + 12$

D. $x^2 + 7x$

Use the following information to answer the next question.

Maria wants to save $100. She has already saved $35. She saves $2.50 every day from her wages.

50. Which of the following inequalities shows the minimum number of days Maria needs to work to earn $100?

A. $35 + 2.50x \geq 100$

B. $35 + 2.50x \leq 100$

C. $35x + 2.50 \geq 100$

D. $35x + 2.50 \leq 100$

Use the following information to answer the next question.

Vivian has 14 fewer quarters than nickels.

51. If the total value of Vivian's coins is $8.80, which of the following equations could be used to solve for the number of quarters that Vivian has?

A. $0.25x + 0.05(x + 14) = 8.80$

B. $0.05x + 0.25(x - 14) = 8.80$

C. $0.05x + 0.25(x + 14) = 8.80$

D. $0.25x - 0.05(x - 14) = 8.80$

Use the following information to answer the next question.

Robyn bought a used car for $5,500. To pay for the car, she borrowed $3,500 and spent one-third of the money in her savings account.

52. How much money was in Robyn's savings account before she bought the car?

A. $19,500 B. $16,500

C. $6,000 D. $3,000

53. The sum of two numbers is 84. If the second number is 10 more than the first number, what is the value of the larger number? __________

Use the following information to answer the next question.

A particular theater has a total of 736 seats. The number of rows of seats is 9 less than the number of seats in each row.

54. The number of rows of seats in the theater is

A. 21 B. 23

C. 28 D. 32

Use the following information to answer the next question.

Kilograms (x)	10	15	20	25
Pounds (y)	22	33	44	55

55. Which equation may be used to convert kilograms to pounds?

A. $y = x + 2.2$ B. $x = y + 2.2$

C. $y = 2.2x$ D. $x = 2.2y$

Use the following information to answer the next question.

The curve of the arch spanning the High Bridge over the Harlem River in New York City can be modeled by the quadratic function $y = a(x - h)^2 + k$. The bottom of the arch at both ends is 28.5 ft above the water. The total span of the bridge is 450 ft with a maximum height of 114 ft in the middle.

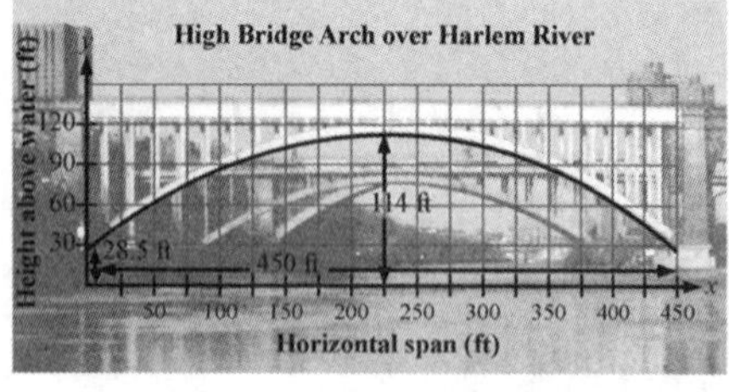

56. Which of the following quadratic functions in the form $y = a(x - h)^2 + k$ **best** models the arch?

A. $y = -0.00295(x - 225)^2 + 114$

B. $y = -0.00169(x - 225)^2 + 114$

C. $y = -0.0151(x - 114)^2 + 225$

D. $y = -0.0308(x - 114)^2 + 225$

Use the following information to answer the next question.

A box containing 48 golf balls has a total mass of 1,400 g. Twelve golf balls are removed from the box. Measured in grams, the mass of a golf ball is g and the mass of the box is b.

57. Which of the following expressions represents the total mass of the box and the golf balls that remain after 12 have been removed?

A. $12g + b$

B. $36g + b$

C. $12g + 1{,}400b$

D. $36g + 1{,}400b$

Use the following information to answer the next question.

For every 1 km increase in altitude above Earth's surface, the temperature of the atmosphere, T, in degrees Celsius, decreases by 5°C.

58. If h represents the height above Earth's surface in kilometers, then on a day when the temperature at Earth's surface is 15°C, the equation and graph relating T and h are

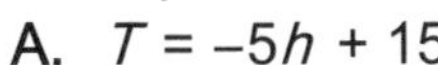

A. $T = -5h + 15$

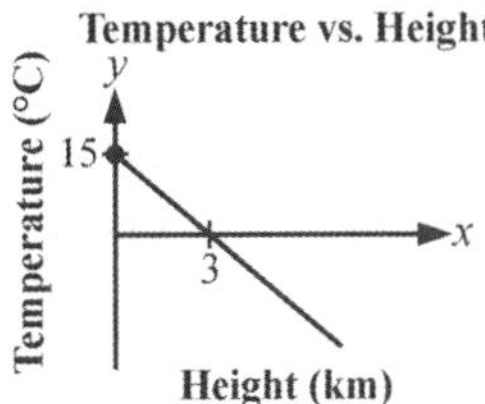

B. $T = -5h + 15$

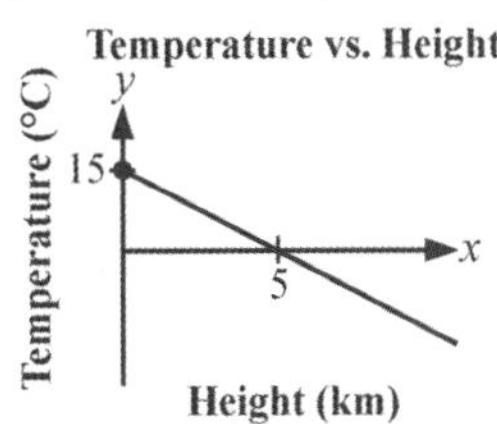

C. $T = -5 + 15h$

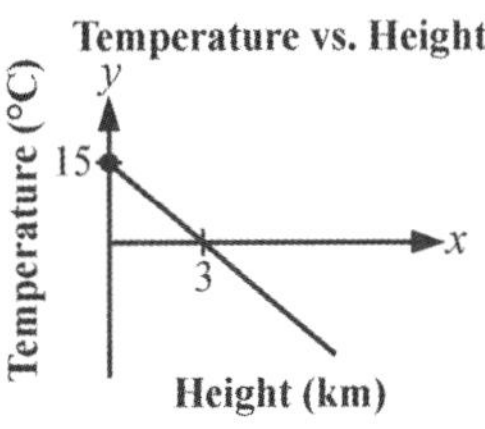

D. $T = -5 + 15h$

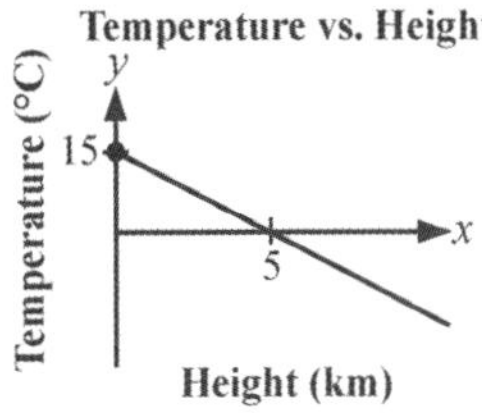

Use the following information to answer the next question.

The exponential equation $R = 3.7(1.171)^n$, can be used to represent the number of rats, R, in millions, in a certain region, after n number of years since 1997.

59. If the rat population continues to grow at the given rate, then what will be the approximate number of rats in that region in the year 2010?

A. 12.6 million
B. 14.4 million
C. 28.8 million
D. 32.3 million

Use the following information to answer the next question.

An equation for determining radioactive decay is $A = A_0\left(\frac{1}{2}\right)^{\frac{t}{h}}$, where

A = the mass present at time t
A_0 = the original mass
t = the time in days
h = the half-life of the material in days
The half-life of iodine-126 is 13 days.

60. To the nearest tenth of a gram, what is the mass of iodine-126 remaining from a 10 g sample after 86 days?

A. 0.1 g
B. 0.3 g
C. 5.0 g
D. 9.0 g

Use the following information to answer the next question.

Leonardo is asked to solve the following problem:
A teacher treated her class to hot dogs and hamburgers. If every student in the class would have eaten only hot dogs, which cost \$2.75 each, the teacher's cost would have been \$71.50. Also, if the boys in the class would have eaten hot dogs and the girls would have eaten hamburgers, which cost \$3.25 each, the teacher's cost would have been \$77.50. How many boys and how many girls are in the teacher's class?

61. If b represents the number of boys and g represents the number of girls in the teacher's class, which of the following systems of equations could Leonardo use to solve the given problem?

A. $\begin{aligned} 2.75b + 2.75g &= 71.50 \\ 2.75b + 3.25g &= 77.50 \end{aligned}$

B. $\begin{aligned} 2.75bg &= 71.50 \\ 2.75b + 3.25g &= 77.50 \end{aligned}$

C. $\begin{aligned} 2.75b + 2.75g &= 71.50 \\ b + 3.25g &= 77.50 \end{aligned}$

D. $\begin{aligned} 2.75bg &= 71.50 \\ b + 3.25g &= 77.50 \end{aligned}$

Use the following information to answer the next question.

Luka is on vacation and decides to rent a car for seven days. The car rental agency he uses has the following two rental plans to choose from:

- Plan A—the cost, C, in dollars, is represented by the linear equation $C = 35d + 0.08m$, where d equals the number of days the car is rented for and m equals the number of miles the car is driven.
- Plan B—the cost, C, in dollars, is represented by the linear equation $C = 0.85m$, where m equals the number of miles the car is driven.

Luka decided on plan B and returned the car after seven days.

62. Assuming that Luka saved money by choosing plan B, which of the following distances **most likely** equals the distance Luka drove during his vacation?

A. –330 mi B. –320 mi

C. 315 mi D. 325 mi

Use the following information to answer the next question.

At a particular movie theater, an adult ticket costs $12 and a student ticket costs $8. For a certain show, twice as many student tickets as adult tickets were sold. The total receipts for the show were $2,100.
The given system of linear equations can be used to determine how many adult tickets (represented by x) and student tickets (represented by y) were sold.

$$2x = y$$
$$12x + 8y = 2{,}100$$

63. Which of the following ordered pairs is a reasonable solution to the given problem?

A. $\left(\frac{135}{2}, 135\right)$

B. (80, −160)

C. (130, 65)

D. (75, 150)

Use the following information to answer the next question.

A sporting goods store sells two types of road bicycles, type R and type S. From past records, the manager of the store knows that during the month of May, the sales team can sell more than 15, but less than 32, type R bicycles. During the same time, they can sell at most 12 type S bicycles. Type R bicycles sell for $1,800, and type S bicycles sell for $1,200.
To meet the store's goal for the month of May in the coming year, the store must sell at least a total of 30 road bicycles and the sales from the two types of bicycles must exceed $43,800.

64. If x represents the number of type R road bicycles sold and y represents the the number of type S road bicycles sold, then which of the following inequalities could **not** be part of a system of inequalities that represents the given information?

A. $1{,}800x + 1{,}200y > 43{,}800$

B. $15 < x < 32$

C. $0 \leq y \leq 12$

D. $x + y > 30$

65. Rewrite the equation $y = mx + b$ to isolate m.

EXERCISE #2—DESCRIBING RELATIONSHIPS WITH EQUATIONS ANSWERS AND SOLUTIONS

48. A	53. 47	58. A	63. D
49. A	54. B	59. C	64. D
50. A	55. C	60. A	65. See solution
51. B	56. B	61. A	
52. C	57. B	62. C	

48. A

Let the weight of Lisa's bag be x. The relationship between the weights of the girls' bags can be represented by the inequality $2x - 5 \geq 45$.

Solve the inequality by applying inverse operations.

$$2x - 5 \geq 45$$
$$2x - 5 + 5 \geq 45 + 5$$
$$\frac{2x}{2} \geq \frac{50}{2}$$
$$x \geq 25$$

The weight of Lisa's bag is greater than or equal to 25 kg.

49. A

Step 1
Substitute the given values into the area formula for a rectangle.
$A = l \times w$
$A = (x + 3)(x + 4)$

Step 2
Multiply each term of the first binomial by each term in the second binomial.
$= (x + 3)(x + 4)$
$= x(x + 4) + 3(x + 4)$
$= x^2 + 4x + 3x + 12$

Step 3
Collect like terms and simplify.
$= x^2 + 4x + 3x + 12$
$= x^2 + 7x + 12$

50. A

Step 1
Look for keywords.
Since the question asks for a minimum, the inequality will be "greater than or equal to."

Step 2
Set up the inequality.
Let x stand for the number of days that Maria needs to work.
The total amount of money Maria will save from her wages will be her daily savings multiplied by the number of days she works: $2.50x$.
The inequality will be the sum of the amount she has already saved plus the amount she saves from her wages each day compared to the total amount of money she wishes to save.
$35 + 2.50x \geq 100$

51. B

Step 1
Define the variable.
Let x = the number of nickels Vivian has.

Step 2
Create an equation using the variable to represent the situation.
Since x is defined as the number of nickels that Vivian has, $x - 14$ = the number of quarters Vivian has.
value of nickels & quarters = \$8.80
(value of nickels) = $0.05x$
(value of quarters) = $0.25(x - 14)$
Given this information it is now possible to put together an equation that satisfies the situation described.
$0.05x + 0.25(x - 14) = 8.80$
When dealing with coins, decide whether you will treat everything as dollars or as cents. If you choose to represent the values as cents, then the expression would be as follows:
$5x + 25(x - 14) = 880$

52. C

Step 1

Determine the equation that represents the situation.

Let x represent the money Robyn had in her savings account before buying the car.

The sum of the loan and one-third of her savings will equal the amount she paid for the car.

The equation is $\frac{x}{3} + 3{,}500 = 5{,}500$.

Step 2

Solve the equation for x.

Remove the constant by completing the inverse operation.

The constant is 3,500. The inverse of adding is subtracting, so subtract 3,500 from both sides.

$$\frac{x}{3} + 3{,}500 = 5{,}500$$
$$\frac{x}{3} + 3{,}500 - 3{,}500 = 5{,}500 - 3{,}500$$
$$\frac{x}{3} = 2{,}000$$

Step 3

Isolate the variable.

Multiply both sides of the equation by 3.

$$\frac{x}{3} = 2{,}000$$
$$\frac{x}{3} \times 3 = 2{,}000 \times 3$$
$$x = 6{,}000$$

Robyn had $6,000 in her savings account before buying the car.

53. 47

Step 1

Define the variable.

Let x represent the first number.

Step 2

Create the equation.

The second number is 10 more than the first number, or $x + 10$. Therefore, the equation is $x + (x + 10) = 84$ since the sum of the two numbers is 84.

Step 3

Solve the equation.

$$x + (x + 10) = 84$$
$$2x + 10 = 84$$
$$2x = 74$$
$$x = 37$$

Step 4

Find the value of the larger number.

Since $x = 37$, the first number is 37.

The larger number, N_2, is equal to $x + 10$. Substitute 37 for x.

$$N_2 = x + 10$$
$$N_2 = 37 + 10$$
$$N_2 = 47$$

Step 5

Check the solution.

$37 + 47 = 84$

Therefore, the first number is 37 and the second (larger) number is 47.

54. B

Step 1

Write an equation that represents the information in the given problem.

If x represents the number of seats in each row, then the number of rows of seats can be represented by $x - 9$.

Since there are a total of 736 seats in the theater, an equation that represents the information in the given problem is $x(x - 9) = 736$.

Step 2

Simplify the equation $x(x - 9) = 736$, and then write the resulting equation equal to zero.

$$x(x - 9) = 736$$
$$x^2 - 9x = 736$$
$$x^2 - 9x - 736 = 0$$

Step 3

Factor the trinomial $x^2 - 9x - 736$.

Since the trinomial $x^2 - 9x - 736$ is in the general quadratic form $x^2 + bx + c$, it can be factored by first determining the two numbers that multiply to equal -736 and that add to equal -9. These two numbers are -32 and 23. Therefore, the trinomial $x^2 - 9x - 736$ can be expressed in factored form as $(x - 32)(x + 23)$.

Step 4

Solve for x.

Set each factor equal to 0, and solve for x.

$$x - 32 = 0$$
$$x = 32$$

OR

$$x + 23 = 0$$
$$x = -23$$

Step 5
Determine the solution to the given problem.

Since x represents the number of seats in each row, the value of x must be positive. Therefore, $x = 32$. It then follows that the number of rows of seats, $x - 9$, is $32 - 9 = 23$.

There are 23 rows of seats in the theater.

55. C

Rate of change is the ratio of a y-value to an x-value. Dividing the number of pounds (y) by the number of kilograms (x) results in:

$$\frac{22}{10} = \frac{33}{15} = \frac{44}{20} = \ldots = 2.2$$

1 kg = 2.2 lbs

In the form of an equation, the rate of change between pounds (y) and kilograms (x) is $y = 2.2x$.

56. B

To find the quadratic function that best models the arch of the bridge, find the vertex, (h, k), and another point, $P(x, y)$.

Since the whole length of the arch is 450 ft, the maximum is located at the midpoint, which has an x-coordinate of $\frac{450}{2} = 225$. The y-coordinate of the maximum is 114. Therefore, the vertex is (225, 114).

Another point is the y-intercept, which is $P(0, 28.5)$ according to the diagram. Substitute these values into h, k, x, and y to determine the value of a in $y = a(x - h)^2 + k$.

$$\begin{aligned} y &= a(x-h)^2 + k \\ 28.5 &= a(0-225)^2 + 114 \\ 28.5 &= a(50{,}625) + 114 \\ -85.5 &= 50{,}625a \\ -0.00169 &\approx a \end{aligned}$$

Therefore, the equation that best models the arch of the bridge is $y = -0.00169(x - 225)^2 + 114$.

57. B

Step 1
Determine an expression that represents the total mass of the golf balls that remain after 12 have been removed from the box.

If 12 golf balls are removed from the box, the number of golf balls that remain in the box is $48 - 12 = 36$. Since the mass of a golf ball is represented by the variable g, the mass of 36 golf balls will be represented by the expression $36 \times g = 36g$.

Step 2
Determine an expression that represents the total mass of the box and the 36 remaining golf balls.
The mass of the box is represented by the variable b, and the mass of the 36 remaining golf balls is represented by $36g$. Therefore, the total mass of the box and the remaining golf balls can be represented by the expression $36g + b$.

58. A

Step 1
Determine the equation in the form $y = mx + b$.
The temperature is decreasing by 5°C for every 1 km increase in altitude. This means the slope is $m = -5$.
The temperature at an altitude of zero is 15°C; therefore, $b = 15$.
The equation is $T = -5h + 15$.

Step 2
Determine the correct graph.
Both of the graphs in the alternatives with the correct equation have the correct vertical intercept of 15 °C. They differ in the altitude at which the temperature reaches zero. If the temperature is decreasing by 5 °C for every kilometer increase in altitude, then it should take an increase in altitude of 3 km to cause the temperature to decrease to 0. This is shown in the given graph.

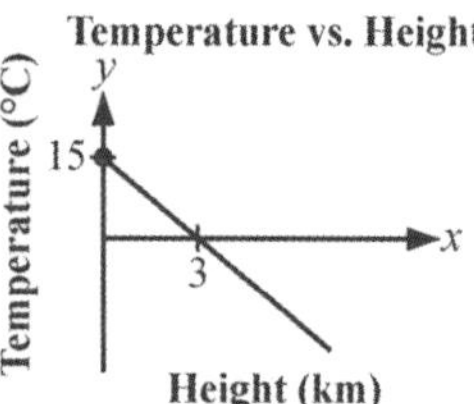

59. C

Step 1
Determine the number of years from 1997 to 2010.
$2{,}010 - 1{,}997 = 13$

Step 2
Substitute 13 for n into the given equation.

$$\begin{aligned} R &= 3.7(1.171)^n \\ &= 3.7(1.171)^{13} \\ &= 3.7(7.784659762) \\ &= 28.8 \end{aligned}$$

In the year 2010, the approximate number of rats in a certain region will be 28.8 million.

60. A

Step 1

Identify the variables whose values are given.

$A_0 = 10$
$t = 86$
$h = 13$

Step 2

Substitute the values into the given equation, and evaluate.

$$A = A_0\left(\frac{1}{2}\right)^{\frac{t}{h}}$$
$$= 10\left(\frac{1}{2}\right)^{\frac{86}{13}}$$
$$= 10(0.0102)$$
$$= 0.1 \text{ g}$$

61. A

Step 1

Identify the given information.

If each student had eaten a hot dog, the teacher's cost would have been \$71.50.

If the boys had eaten hot dogs and the girls had eaten hamburgers, the teacher's cost would have been \$77.50.

Step 2

Write an equation that represents the teacher's cost if each student had eaten a hot dog.

Since there are b boys in the class and hot dogs cost \$2.75 each, the cost of the hot dogs for the boys would have been represented by $2.75b$. Similarly, the cost of the hot dogs for the girls, represented by g, would have been represented by $2.75g$. Therefore, an equation that would represent the teacher's cost if each student in the class had eaten a hot dog, in terms of b and g, is $2.75b + 2.75g = 71.50$.

Step 3

Write an equation that represents the teacher's cost if the boys had eaten hot dogs and the girls had eaten hamburgers.

Since the cost of each hot dog is \$2.75, the cost of the hot dogs for the boys would be represented by $2.75b$. Given that the cost of each hamburger is \$3.25, the cost of the hamburgers for the girls would be represented by $3.25g$. Thus, an equation that would represent the teacher's cost if the boys had eaten hot dogs and the girls had eaten hamburgers, in terms of b and g, is $2.75b + 3.25g = 77.50$.

Step 4

Write a system of equations that Leonardo could use to solve the given problem.

A system of equations that Leonardo could use to solve the given problem is as follows:

$2.75b + 2.75g = 71.50$
$2.75b + 3.25g = 77.50$

62. C

Step 1

Determine whether –330 mi is a reasonable solution.

A solution of –330 mi implies that the car traveled a negative distance, which is impossible. Therefore, –330 mi is an unreasonable solution and no calculations are required.

Similarly, the other negative value given, –320 mi, is also an unreasonable solution.

Step 2

Determine whether 315 mi is a reasonable solution.

Determine the cost of driving a rental car 315 mi according to both plan A and B.

In plan A, $C = 35d + 0.08m$. Substitute 7 for d and 315 for m.

$C = 35(7) + 0.08(315)$
$C = 245 + 25.20$
$C = \$270.20$

In plan B, $C = 0.85m$. Substitute 315 for m.

$C = 0.85(315)$
$C = \$267.75$

Since \$267.75 < \$270.20, Luka would have saved money by choosing plan B if the car had been driven 315 mi. Therefore, 315 mi is a reasonable solution.

Step 3

Determine whether 325 mi is a reasonable solution.

Determine the cost of driving a rental car 325 mi according to both plan A and B.

In plan A, $C = 35d + 0.08m$. Substitute 7 for d and 325 for m.

$C = 35(7) + 0.08(325)$
$C = 245 + 26$
$C = \$271.00$

In plan B, $C = 0.85m$. Substitute 325 for m.

$C = 0.85(325)$
$C = \$276.25$

Since \$276.25 > \$271.00, Luka would not have saved money by choosing plan B if the car had been driven 325 mi. Therefore, 325 mi is not a reasonable solution.

Since 315 mi is the only reasonable solution of those given, it is most likely equal to the distance Luka drove during his vacation.

63. D

Step 1

Determine whether the ordered pair $\left(\frac{135}{2}, 135\right)$ is a reasonable solution.

The value of x in $\left(\frac{135}{2}, 135\right)$ is $\frac{135}{2}$. Since x represents the number of adult tickets sold, this would imply that $\frac{135}{2}$, or $67\frac{1}{2}$, adult tickets were sold, which is impossible. Therefore, $\left(\frac{135}{2}, 135\right)$ is not a reasonable solution, and there is no need to determine whether it satisfies the given system of linear equations.

Step 2

Determine whether the ordered pair (80, −160) is a reasonable solution.

The value of y in (80, −160) is −160. Since y represents the number of student tickets sold, this would imply that −160 student tickets were sold, which is impossible. Therefore, (80, −160) is not a reasonable solution, and there is no need to determine whether it satisfies the given system of linear equations.

Step 3

Determine whether the ordered pair (130, 65) is a reasonable solution.

The values of x and y in (130, 65) are 130 and 65, respectively. Since x represents the number of adult tickets sold and y represents the number of student tickets sold, this would imply that 130 adult tickets and 65 student tickets were sold. This contradicts the given information, which states that twice as many student tickets as adult tickets were sold. Therefore, (130, 65) is not a reasonable solution, and there is no need to determine whether it satisfies the given system of linear equations.

Step 4

Determine whether the ordered pair (75, 150) is a reasonable solution.

The numbers 75 and 150 are both whole numbers, and 150 is twice as large as 75. Thus, 75 and 150 are potential solutions to the given problem. In order to determine whether 75 and 150 are reasonable solutions, it is necessary to determine whether the ordered pair (75, 150) satisfies the given system of linear equations.

Substitute 75 for x and 150 for y in each of the given linear equations, and then simplify.

$$\begin{aligned} 2x &= y \\ 2(75) &= 150 \\ 150 &= 150 \end{aligned}$$

$$\begin{aligned} 12x + 8y &= 2{,}100 \\ 12(75) + 8(150) &= 2{,}100 \\ 900 + 1{,}200 &= 2{,}100 \\ 2{,}100 &= 2{,}100 \end{aligned}$$

Since 150 = 150 and 2,100 = 2,100, the ordered pair (75, 150) satisfies the given system of equations. Therefore, it is a reasonable solution to the given problem.

64. D

Step 1

Identify keywords or phrases in the problem that describe the types of inequalities involved.

In the problem, there are four phrases that deal with inequalities.

1. The phrase “The sales team can sell more than 15, but less than 32, type R bicycles” indicates a value greater than 15 and smaller than 32.
2. The phrase “at most sell 12 type S bicycles” indicates a value between 0 and 12, inclusive.
3. The phrase “sell at least a total of 30 road bicycles” indicates a value greater than or equal to 30.
4. The phrase “sales from the two types of bicycles must exceed $43,800” indicates a value greater than $43,800.

Step 2

Write the inequality that corresponds to each of the four indicated phrases.

Since x represents the number of type R bicycles sold, the inequality that corresponds to phrase 1 is $15 < x < 32$.

Given that y represents the number of type S bicycles sold, the inequality that corresponds to phrase 2 is $0 \le y \le 12$.

The word "total" implies an addition, so the inequality that corresponds to phrase 3 is $x + y \ge 30$.

Each type R bicycle sells for $1,800, and each type S bicycle sells for $1,200; therefore, the inequality that corresponds to phrase 4 is $1{,}800x + 1{,}200y > 43{,}800$.

Step 3

From the given alternatives, identify the inequality that could not be part of a system of inequalities representing the given information.

A system of inequalities that could represent the given information is as follows.

$$\begin{aligned} 15 < x &< 32 \\ 0 \le y &\le 12 \\ x + y &\ge 30 \\ 1{,}800x + 1{,}200y &> 43{,}800 \end{aligned}$$

It follows that the inequality $x + y > 30$ does not represent the information; therefore, it cannot be part of a system of inequalities that represents the given information.

65.

Step 1

Determine which variables or numbers will move.

To isolate m, first subtract b from both sides of the equation.

$$\begin{aligned} y &= mx + b \\ y - b &= mx + b - b \\ y - b &= mx \end{aligned}$$

Step 2

Divide both sides of the equation by x.

$$\frac{y-b}{x} = \frac{mx}{x}$$

$$\frac{y-b}{x} = m$$

NOTES

Solving Equations by Reasoning

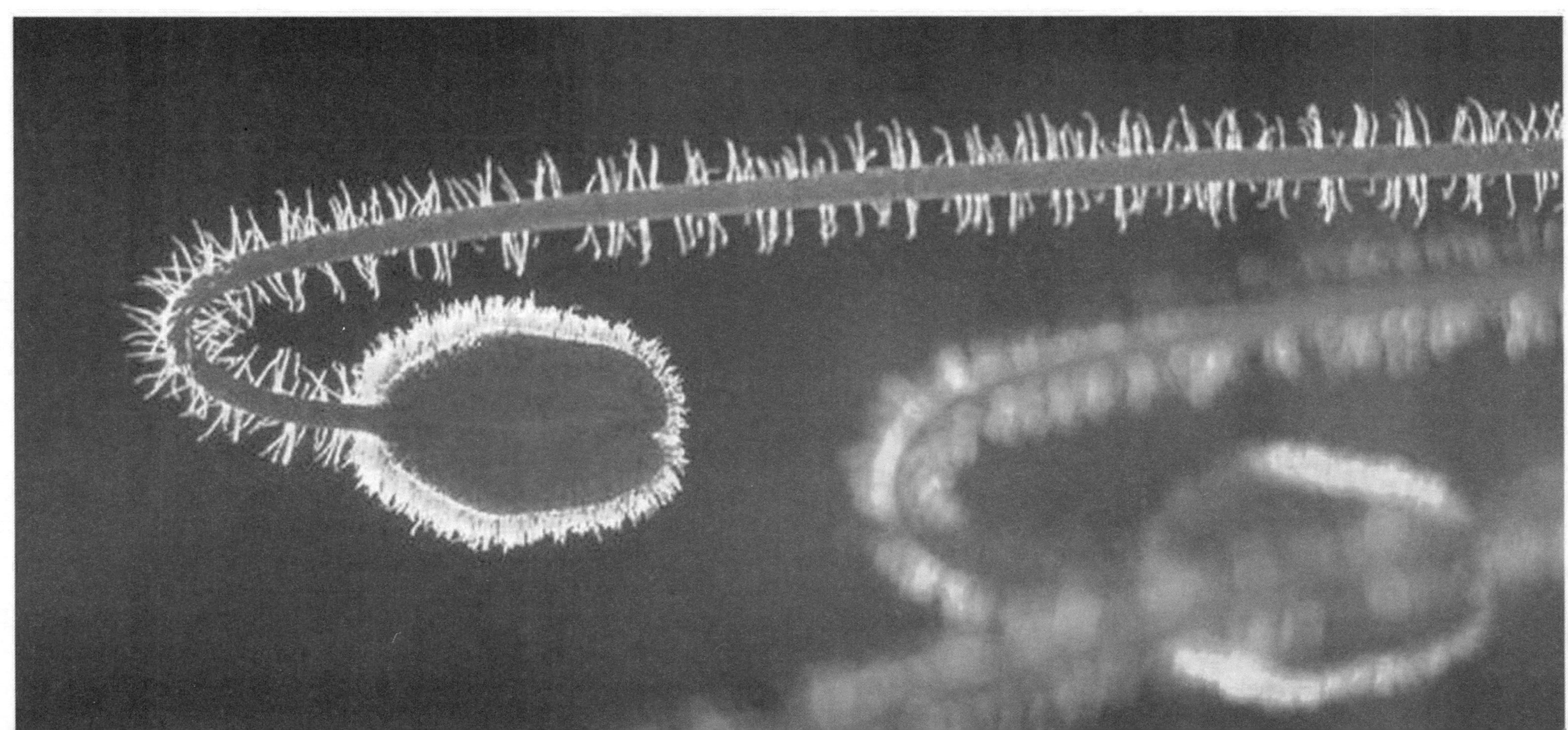

SOLVING EQUATIONS BY REASONING

Table of Correlations

Standard		Concepts	Exercise #1	Exercise #2
Unit1.4	Understand solving equations as a process of reasoning and explain the reasoning.			
A-REI.1	*Explain each step in solving a simple equation as following from the equality of numbers asserted at the previous step, starting from the assumption that the original equation has a solution. Construct a viable argument to justify a solution method.*	Determining if an Argument is Valid by Applying Properties of the Real Number System and Order of Operations	66	68
		Equality of Real Numbers	67	69

A-REI.1 Explain each step in solving a simple equation as following from the equality of numbers asserted at the previous step, starting from the assumption that the original equation has a solution. Construct a viable argument to justify a solution method.

Determining if an Argument is Valid by Applying Properties of the Real Number System and Order of Operations

When evaluating or simplifying mathematical expressions or equations containing more than one operation, it is important to apply the properties of real numbers correctly and to follow the correct order of operations.

Recall some key properties of real numbers:

Commutative Properties	for addition: $a + b = b + a$
	for multiplication: $a \times b = b \times a$
Associative Properties	for addition: $(a + b) + c = a + (b + c)$
	for multiplication: $(a \times b) \times c = a \times (b \times c)$
Distributive Property	for multiplication over addition: $a(b + c) = ab + ac$ and $(b + c)a = ba + ca$
Identity Properties	for addition: $a + 0 = a$
	for multiplication: $a \times 1 = a$
Inverse Properties	for addition: $a + (-a) = 0$
	for multiplication: $a \times \frac{1}{a} = 1,\ a \neq 0$

Also, recall the order of operations, commonly referred to as **BEDMAS**:

- **B**rackets
  Carry out all operations inside the brackets first. If there are brackets inside of brackets, start on the innermost set of brackets first.
- **E**xponents
  Evaluate all powers.
- **D**ivision and **M**ultiplication
  Carry out division and multiplication operations in the order in which they appear from left to right (reading order).
- **A**ddition and **S**ubtraction
  Carry out addition and subtraction operations in the order in which they appear from left to right (reading order).

In order to determine whether an argument in an expression or equation is valid, analyze each step in the calculation and identify mistakes made by applying the properties of real numbers incorrectly or by not following the correct order of operations.

Example

A student shows the following work in solving the equation $7x - 21 = 42$.

$$\frac{7}{7}x - 21 = \frac{42}{7}$$
$$x - 21 = 6$$
$$x - 21 + 21 = 6 + 21$$
$$x = 27$$

The student then checks her work by evaluating the initial equation with $x = 27$.

$$7(27) - 21 = 42$$
$$7 \times 27 - 21 = 42$$
$$7 \times 6 = 42$$
$$42 = 42$$

Identify the two mistakes that the student made.

Solution

The first mistake was made in the first step. To solve an equation, the opposite order of operations must be applied.

- In this case, 21 should have been added to both sides of the equation first before dividing by 7.
- Also, when dividing by 7, all terms in the equation must be divided by 7, not just the far left and right terms.

The second mistake occurs when the student was checking the third step.

- In this case, the student does not follow the correct order of operations when evaluating the equation.
- The number 7 should have been multiplied by 27 first instead of subtracting 21 from 27.

Equality of Real Numbers

The equality of real numbers is demonstrated with the equals sign (=). An equals sign means that the values on each side of the sign are the same. The following properties apply to the equality of real numbers:

- Reflexive property—$a = a$
- Symmetric property—if $a = b$, then $b = a$.
- Transitive property—if $a = b$ and $b = c$, then $a = c$.
- Addition property—if $a = b$, then $a + c = b + c$.
- Subtraction property—if $a = b$, then $a - c = b - c$.
- Multiplication property—if $a = b$, then $a \times c = b \times c$.
- Division property—if $a = b$, then $\frac{a}{c} = \frac{b}{c}$.

Example

Consider the equations $x = \frac{1+4+6-7}{2}$ and $\frac{1+4+6-7}{2} = 2$. From the transitive property it can be determined that $x = 2$.

Example

According to the addition and subtraction properties, if you add or subtract the same number on both sides of an equation, the two sides will still be equal.

Consider the equation $2 \times 4 = 3 + 5$. If 6 is added to both sides of the equation, both sides are still equal.

$$2 \times 4 = 3 + 5$$
$$2 \times 4 + \underline{6} = 3 + 5 + \underline{6}$$
$$14 = 14$$

Example

According to the multiplication and division properties, if you multiply or divide the same number on both sides of an equation, the two sides will still be equal.

Consider the equation $3 \times 4 = 7 + 5$. If both sides of the equation are divided by 2, then both sides will still be equal.

$$3 \times 4 = 7 + 5$$
$$\frac{3 \times 4}{2} = \frac{7+5}{2}$$
$$\frac{12}{2} = \frac{12}{2}$$
$$6 = 6$$

To solve an equation with a variable, you need to **isolate** the variable. This means that you need to get the variable by itself on one side of the equation. You always do the **inverse** of the operation on a number to get rid of it.

Example

On the left side of the equation $x + 8 = 15$, there is an 8 added to the x. The inverse of addition is subtraction. If you subtract 8 from the left side, then the x will be by itself. To keep the equation equal, you must also subtract 8 from the right side of the equation.

$$x + 8 = 15$$
$$x + 8 \underline{- 8} = 15 \underline{- 8}$$
$$x = 7$$

In this equation, the variable was isolated by subtracting 8 from both sides. You can test your answer by substituting 7 into the equation to see if it is correct.

$$x + 8 = 15$$
$$7 + 8 = 15$$
$$15 = 15$$

EXERCISE #1—SOLVING EQUATIONS BY REASONING

Use the following information to answer the next question.

Mildred has to evaluate the expression $(3 - 1) \times 4 - (4 + 8)^2 \div 4$. Her solution is shown.

1. $(2) \times 4 - (12)^2 \div 4$
2. $8 + 24 \div 4$
3. $8 + 6$
4. 14

66. Which of the following statements about Mildred's solution is **true**?

A. Mildred's solution is correct.
B. Mildred made a mistake in step 2.
C. Mildred made a mistake in step 3.
D. Mildred made a mistake in step 4.

67. If $12 + 24 + a = 100$ and $10 + 26 + b = 100$, which of the following equations is **true**?

A. $a - b = 0$
B. $a + b = 0$
C. $a - b = 36$
D. $a + b = 36$

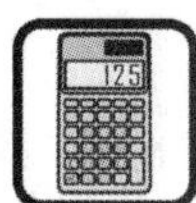

EXERCISE #1—SOLVING EQUATIONS BY REASONING ANSWERS AND SOLUTIONS

66. B	67. A

66. B

Step 1

Analyze step 1.

In the first step, Mildred correctly simplified the expression in the brackets as per the order of operations.

$(2) \times 4 - (12)^2 \div 4$

Step 2

Analyze step 2.

In the second step, Mildred carried out the multiplication operation in the order in which it appears from left to right. She made a mistake when she multiplied the squared term $-(12)^2$ and got an answer of +24. The 12 should have been squared and since the negative sign is not part of the power expression, the answer should have been −144.

$8 - 144 \div 4$

Step 3

Carry out the division operation in the order in which it appears from left to right.

$8 - 36$

Step 4

Evaluate the resulting expression.

Subtract the remaining terms to evaluate the expression.

-28

Therefore, Mildred made a mistake in step 2.

67. A

If $12 + 24 + a = 100$, it follows that $36 + a = 100$. If $10 + 26 + b = 100$, it follows that $36 + b = 100$, or $100 = 36 + b$.

Since $36 + a = 100$ and $100 = 36 + b$, the transitive property can be applied, resulting in the equation $36 + a = 36 + b$.

Now, apply the subtraction property.

$$36 + a = 36 + b$$
$$36 + a - 36 = 36 + b - 36$$
$$a = b$$

The equation $a = b$ is equivalent to $a - b = 0$.

EXERCISE #2—SOLVING EQUATIONS BY REASONING

Use the following information to answer the next question.

Martha has to evaluate the expression $(4 + 5) \times 2 + 4 + 7 \times 3$. Her solution is shown.

1. $9 \times 2 + 4 + 7 \times 3$
2. $18 + 4 + 7 \times 3$
3. 29×3
4. 87

68. Which of the following statements about Martha's solution is **true**?

A. Martha's solution is correct.

B. Martha made a mistake in step 1.

C. Martha made a mistake in step 2.

D. Martha made a mistake in step 3.

Use the following information to answer the next question.

Rafi would like to make up an equation that could be solved by using the properties of equality in the following order:

1. Addition property
2. Multiplication property
3. Subtraction property
4. Division property

69. Which of the following equations can be solved by using the properties of equality in the order Rafi requires?

A. $\frac{3x}{2} - 4 = 5$

B. $\frac{2x - 5}{3} = 9$

C. $3x - \frac{5}{2} = \frac{7}{2}$

D. $\frac{2x + 7}{3} - 4 = 1$

EXERCISE #2—SOLVING EQUATIONS BY REASONING ANSWERS AND SOLUTIONS

68. D	69. D

68. D

Step 1

Analyze step 1.

In the first step, Martha correctly simplified the expression in the brackets as per the order of operations.

$9 \times 2 + 4 + 7 \times 3$

Step 2

Analyze step 2.

In the second step, Martha correctly carried out the multiplication operation in the order in which it appears from left to right.

$18 + 4 + 7 \times 3$

Step 3

Analyze step 3.

In the third step, Martha incorrectly carried out the addition operation before carrying out the remaining multiplication operation. According to the order of operations, the multiplication of 7 × 3 should have been performed before the addition process.

$18 + 4 + 21$

Step 4

Evaluate the resulting expression.

Add the remaining terms to evaluate the expression.

43

69. D

Step 1

Solve $\frac{3x}{2} - 4 = 5$.

Apply the addition property.

$\frac{3}{2}x - 4 + 4 = 5 + 4$

$\frac{3}{2}x = 9$

Apply the multiplication property.

$2 \times \frac{3}{2}x = 2 \times 9$

$3x = 18$

Apply the division property.

$\frac{3x}{3} = \frac{18}{3}$

$x = 6$

This equation cannot be solved by using the properties of equality in the order Rafi requires.

Step 2

Solve $\frac{2x-5}{3} = 9$.

Apply the multiplication property.

$3 \times \left(\frac{2x-5}{3}\right) = 3 \times 9$

$2x - 5 = 27$

Apply the addition property.

$2x - 5 + 5 = 27 + 5$

$2x = 32$

Apply the division property.

$\frac{2x}{2} = \frac{32}{2}$

$x = 16$

This equation cannot be solved by using the properties of equality in the order Rafi requires.

Step 3

Solve $3x - \frac{5}{2} = \frac{7}{2}$.

Apply the addition property.

$3x - \frac{5}{2} + \frac{5}{2} = \frac{7}{2} + \frac{5}{2}$

$3x = \frac{12}{2}$

$3x = 6$

Apply the division property.

$\frac{3x}{x} = \frac{6}{3}$

$x = 2$

This equation cannot be solved by using the properties of equality in the order Rafi requires.

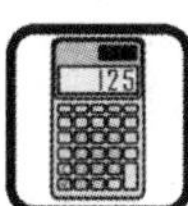

Step 4

Solve $\frac{2x+7}{3} - 4 = 1$.

Apply the addition property.

$$\frac{2x+7}{3} - 4 + 4 = 1 + 4$$
$$\frac{2x+7}{3} = 5$$

Apply the multiplication property.

$$3 \times \frac{2x+7}{3} = 3 \times 5$$
$$2x + 7 = 15$$

Apply the subtraction property.

$$2x + 7 - 7 = 15 - 7$$
$$2x = 8$$

Apply the division property.

$$\frac{2x}{2} = \frac{8}{2}$$
$$x = 4$$

Therefore, of the given equations, $\frac{2x+7}{3} - 4 = 1$ is the only one that can be solved by using the properties of equality in the order Rafi requires.

NOTES

One Variable Equations and Inequalities

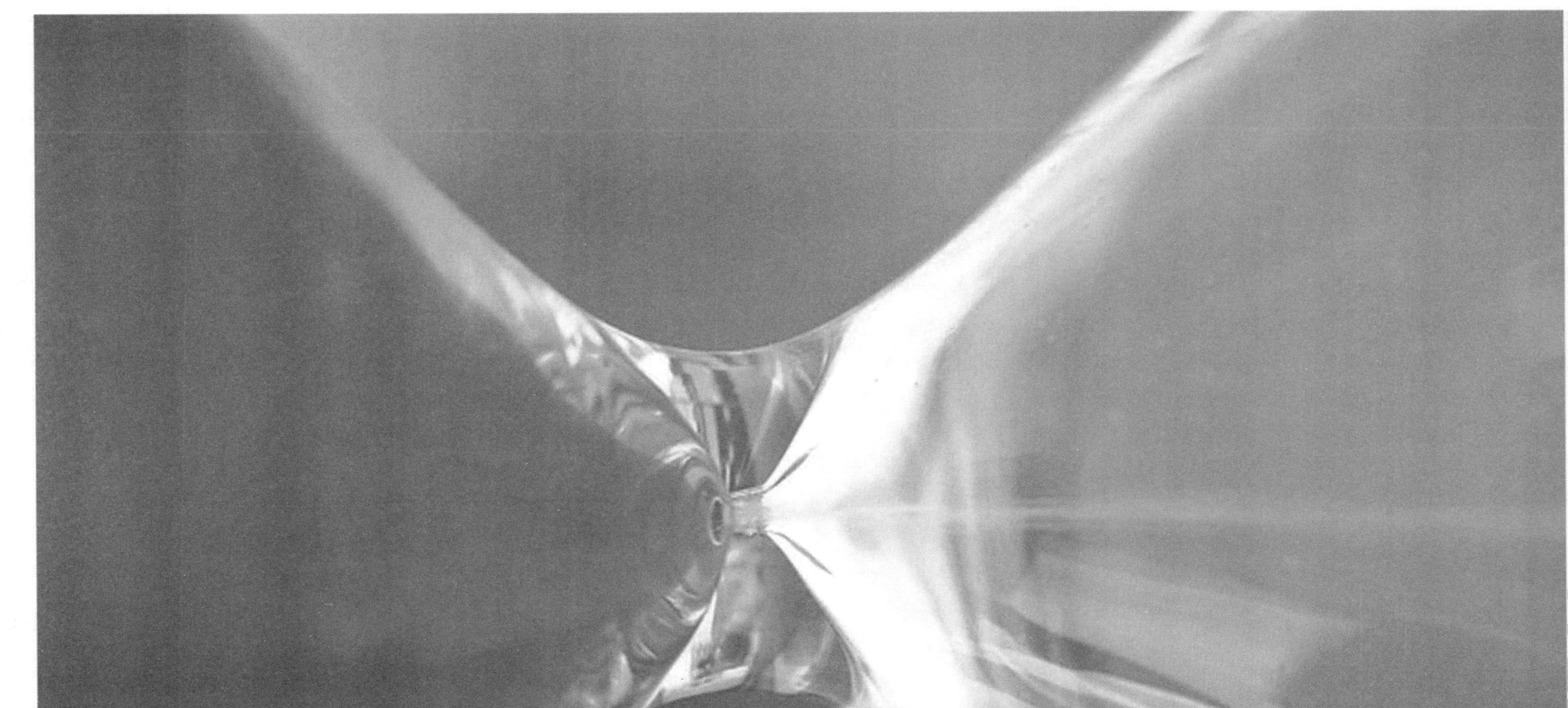

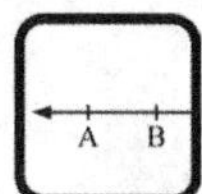

ONE VARIABLE EQUATIONS AND INEQUALITIES

Table of Correlations

Standard		Concepts	Exercise #1	Exercise #2
Unit1.5	Solve equations and inequalities in one variable.			
A-REI.3	*Solve linear equations and inequalities in one variable, including equations with coefficients represented by letters.*	Rearranging Formulas	47	65
		Solving Equations of the Form $a(bx + c) = d(ex + f)$ for x	70	77
		Solving Linear Inequalities Using a Number Line	71	78
		Solving Linear Inequalities by Adding and Subtracting	72	79
		Solving Linear Inequalities Using Positive Multipliers and Divisors	73	80
		Solving Linear Inequalities Using Negative Multipliers and Divisors	74	81
		Solving Multistep Linear Inequalities	75	82
		Solving Equations of the Form $\frac{a}{x} = b$	76	83

A-REI.3 Solve linear equations and inequalities in one variable, including equations with coefficients represented by letters.

Solving Equations of the Form $a(bx + c) = d(ex + f)$ for x

To solve for the variable in equations of the form $a(bx + c) = d(ex + f)$, follow these steps:

1. Use the distributive property to simplify the equation. When using this property, the each term inside the brackets is multiplied by the term outside the brackets. For example, the equation $2(x + 4) = 7$ is simplified to $2x + 8 = 7$ by applying the distributive property.

Use inverse operations for the next three steps. Remember that whatever operation is done to one side of an equation must be applied to the other side.

2. Move all the variables to the left side of the equation by completing the inverse (or opposite) operation, and simplify.
3. Move all the constants to the right side of the equation by completing the inverse operation, and simplify.
4. Isolate the variable by completing the inverse operation. In most cases, the inverse operation is division.

Example

$3(2x + 5) = -2(-4x + 7)$

Solve the given equation. Express the answer as a fraction in lowest terms and as a decimal.

Solution

Step 1

Distribute the term outside the brackets to each term inside the brackets, and simplify.

$$3(2x) + 3(5) = -2(-4x) - 2(7)$$
$$6x + 15 = 8x - 14$$

Step 2

Move all the variables to the left side of the equation by subtracting $8x$ from both sides.

$$6x - 8x + 15 = \cancel{8x} - \cancel{8x} - 14$$
$$-2x + 15 = -14$$

Step 3

Move the constant to the right side of the equation by subtracting 15 from both sides.

$$-2x + \cancel{15} - \cancel{15} = -14 - 15$$
$$-2x = -29$$

Step 4

Isolate the variable by dividing both sides of the equation by −2.

$$\frac{-2x}{-2} = \frac{-29}{-2}$$
$$x = 14\frac{1}{2}$$

Expressed as a decimal, $14\frac{1}{2} = 14.5$.

Step 5

Verify the answer by substituting the value of the variable back into the equation. If the answer is correct, the left side of the equation should equal the right side.

$$3(2x + 5) = -2(-4x + 7)$$
$$3(2 \times 14.5 + 5) = -2(-4 \times 14.5 + 7)$$
$$3(29 + 5) = -2(-58 + 7)$$
$$3(34) = -2(-51)$$
$$102 = 102$$

Since the left and right side of the equation are equal, the solution $x = 14\frac{1}{2} = 14.5$ is correct.

Solving Linear Inequalities Using a Number Line

Inequalities are equations that use $>$, $<$, $\geq$, $\leq$, or $\neq$ in place of the equal sign. An inequality means one side does not have to equal the other side. When solving, both sides must satisfy the inequality sign.

left $<$ right	left is less than right
left $\leq$ right	left is less than or equal to right
left $>$ right	left is greater than right
left $\geq$ right	left is greater than or equal to right
left $\neq$ right	left is not equal to right

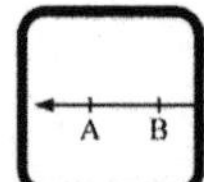

Inequalities are solved in the same way that equations are solved: all the variables are moved to the left side of the equation and all of the numbers to the right side. However, there is one important difference. When multiplying or dividing both sides of an inequality by a negative value, *reverse* the inequality sign.

To demonstrate this point, start with a true statement.

$5 > 3$

Multiply both sides by −1, and simplify.

$(-1)(5) > (-1)(3)$

$(-5) > (-3)$

This is a false statement because −5 is to the left of −3 on a number line.

−5 −4 −3 −2 −1 0

To make it true, reverse the sign.

$(-5) < (-3)$

Example

Solve and graph the solution to $2x - 2 \leq 3x + 1$.

Solution

Step 1

Move all the variables to the left side of the equation by subtracting $3x$ from both sides, and simplify.

$2x - 3x - 2 \leq 3x - 3x + 1$

$-1x - 2 \leq 1$

Step 2

Move the constant to the right side by adding 2 to both sides of the equation.

$-1x - 2 + 2 \leq 1 + 2$

$-1x \leq 3$

Step 3

Isolate the variable by dividing both sides of the equation by −1.

$$\frac{-1x}{-1} \geq \frac{3}{-1}$$

$x \geq -3$

Notice the $\leq$ sign reversed to $\geq$ because both sides of the equation were divided by a negative value.

$x \geq -3$

To graph the solution:

Step 4

Place the solution number (−3) in the middle of the line. Write the next three numbers in the sequence on either side of the middle number.

−6 −5 −4 −3 −2 −1 0

Step 5

Draw a shaded circle at −3 on the number line. The circle is shaded because the solution includes −3. (An unshaded circle means the solution begins at −3, but does not equal −3.)

−6 −5 −4 −3 −2 −1 0

Step 6

Draw the arrow in the direction that satisfies the solution.

To check that the direction is correct, substitute numbers from both sides of the solution number (−3) for *x*. Make sure the arrow goes in the direction that makes the statement true.

For example, $-4 \geq -3$ is not true. Do not point the arrow in the direction of −4.

Since $-2 \geq -3$, point the arrow in the direction of −2.

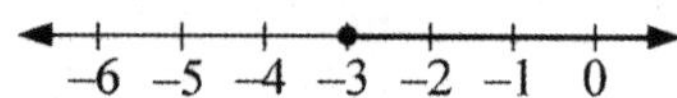

Example

Graph the solution to $x < 5$.

Solution

Step 1

Place the solution number (5) in the middle of the line. Write the next three numbers in the sequence on either side of the middle number.

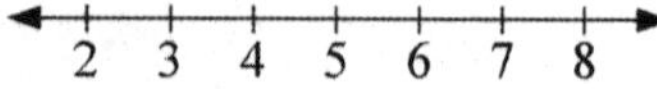

Step 2

Draw an unshaded circle at 5 on the number line. The circle is unshaded because the solution begins at 5 but does not equal 5.

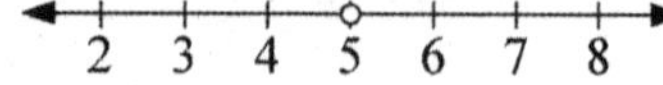

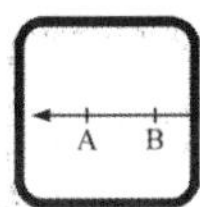

Step 3

Draw the arrow in the direction that satisfies the solution.

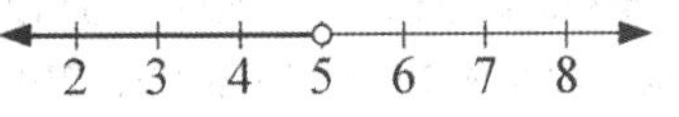

Example

Solve $2x - 3 > 5$, and then identify which of the numbers –3, –4, –7, or 7 belongs to the solution set. ________

Solution

Step 1

Move the constant to the right side of the equation by adding 3 to both sides of the equation.

$$2x - 3 > 5$$
$$2x - \cancel{3} + \cancel{3} > 5 + 3$$
$$2x > 8$$

Step 2

Isolate the variable by dividing both sides of the equation by 2.

$$2x > 8$$
$$\frac{\cancel{2}x}{\cancel{2}} > \frac{8}{2}$$
$$x > 4$$

Notice both sides of the equation were divided by a positive value. The inequality sign did not change.

Step 3

Determine the answer.

The solution set is all the values that satisfy the inequality. The only given number that is greater than 4 is 7.

Solving Linear Inequalities by Adding and Subtracting

Inequalities are solved in much the same way that equations are solved: all the variables are moved to one side of the equation, and all the numbers are moved to the other side by applying inverse operations.

To solve linear inequalities using addition and subtraction, follow these steps:

1. Isolate the variable by completing the inverse operation.
2. Verify the solution set using a test point.

Example

Solve for x in the linear inequality $x + 4 < 10$.

Solution

Step 1

Isolate the variable by completing the inverse operation.

$$x + 4 < 10$$
$$x + 4 - 4 < 10 - 4$$
$$x < 6$$

Step 2

Verify the solution set using a test point.

Since $4 < 6$, 4 can be used as the test point.

$$x + 4 < 10$$
$$(4) + 4 < 10$$
$$8 < 10$$

The resulting statement is true, so it can be assumed that all numbers less than 6 are part of the solution set.

Example

Solve for x in the linear inequality $x - 7 \geq 25$.

Solution

Step 1

Isolate the variable by completing the inverse operation.

$$x - 7 \geq 25$$
$$x - 7 + 7 \geq 25 + 7$$
$$x \geq 32$$

Step 2

Verify the solution set using a test point.

Since $35 \geq 32$, 35 can be used as the test point.

$$x - 7 \geq 25$$
$$(35) - 7 \geq 25$$
$$28 \geq 25$$

The resulting statement is true; therefore, it can be assumed that all numbers greater than or equal to 32 are part of the solution set.

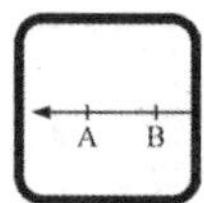

Solving Linear Inequalities Using Positive Multipliers and Divisors

Inequalities are solved in much the same way that equations are solved: all the variables are moved to one side of the equation, and all the numbers are moved to the other side by applying inverse operations. Once a solution is obtained, a test point within the solution set can be substituted into the inequality to verify that the solution is correct.

To solve linear inequalities using positive multipliers and divisors, follow these steps:

1. Isolate the variable by completing the inverse operation.
2. Verify the solution set using a test point.

Example

Solve for x in the linear inequality $15x \geq 120$.

Solution

Step 1

Isolate the variable by completing the inverse operation.

$$15x \geq 120$$
$$\frac{15x}{15} \geq \frac{120}{15}$$
$$x \geq 8$$

Step 2

Verify the solution set using a test point.

Since $10 \geq 8$, 10 will be the test point.

$$15x \geq 120$$
$$15(10) \geq 120$$
$$150 \geq 120$$

The resulting statement is true, so it can be assumed that all numbers greater than or equal to 8 are part of the solution set.

Example

Solve for x in the linear inequality $\frac{x}{9} < 36$.

Solution

Step 1

Isolate the variable by completing the inverse operation.

$$\frac{x}{9} < 36$$
$$9\left(\frac{x}{9}\right) < 9(36)$$
$$x < 324$$

Step 2

Verify the solution set using a test point.

Since $270 < 324$, 270 will be the test point.

$$\frac{x}{9} < 36$$
$$\frac{270}{9} < 36$$
$$30 < 36$$

The resulting statement is true, so it can be assumed that all numbers less than 324 are part of the solution set.

Solving Linear Inequalities Using Negative Multipliers and Divisors

Inequalities are solved in the same way that equations are solved: all the variables are moved to one side of the equation, and all the numbers are moved to the other side by applying inverse operations.

However, if an inequality is multiplied or divided by a negative number, the direction of the inequality symbol must be reversed.

To solve linear inequalities using negative multipliers and divisors, follow these steps:

1. Isolate the variable by completing the inverse operation.
2. Reverse the direction of the inequality symbol.
3. Verify the solution set using a test point.

Example

Solve for x in the linear inequality $\frac{x}{-3} \leq 27$.

Solution

Step 1
Isolate the variable by completing the inverse operation.

$$\frac{x}{-3} \leq 27$$
$$-3\left(\frac{x}{-3}\right) \leq -3(27)$$
$$x \leq -81$$

Step 2
Reverse the direction of the inequality symbol.
$x \leq -81 \Rightarrow x \geq -81$

Step 3
Verify the solution set using a test point.
Since $-30 \geq -81$, -30 can be used as a test point.

$$\frac{x}{-3} \leq 27$$
$$\frac{-30}{-3} \leq 27$$
$$-10 \leq 27$$

The resulting statement is true, so it can be assumed that all numbers greater than or equal to -81 are part of the solution set.

Example

Solve for x in the linear inequality $-9x \geq 12$.

Solution

Step 1
Isolate the variable by completing the inverse operation.

$$-9x \geq 12$$
$$\frac{-9x}{-9} \geq \frac{12}{-9}$$
$$x \geq -\frac{4}{3}$$

Step 2
Reverse the direction of the inequality symbol.

$x \geq -\frac{4}{3} \Rightarrow x \leq -\frac{4}{3}$

Step 3
Verify the solution set using a test point.

Since $-4 \leq -\frac{4}{3}$, -4 can be used as a test point.

$$-9x \geq 12$$
$$-9(-4) \geq 12$$
$$36 \geq 12$$

The resulting statement is true; therefore, it can be assumed that all numbers less than or equal to $-\frac{4}{3}$ are part of the solution set.

Solving Multistep Linear Inequalities

Inequalities are solved in the same way that equations are solved: use inverse operations to move the variables to one side of the equation and the numbers to the other side.

When solving multistep linear inequalities, follow these steps:

1. Isolate the variable by applying inverse operations. Operations must be completed in the following order:
   i. Addition and subtraction
   ii. Multiplication and division
   iii. Exponents
   iv. Brackets

Remember that if any step involves multiplying or dividing by a negative number, the direction of the inequality symbol must be reversed.

2. Verify the solution set using a test point.

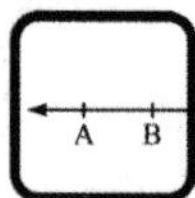

Example

Solve for x in the linear inequality $15 - 12x \geq 63$.

Solution

Step 1

Isolate the variable by applying inverse operations.

Subtract 15 from both sides.

$$15 - 12x \geq 63$$
$$15 - 15 - 12x \geq 63 - 15$$
$$-12x \geq 48$$

Divide both sides by -12.

Since the operation is division by a negative number, the inequality symbol must be reversed.

$$-12x \geq 48$$
$$\frac{-12x}{-12} \leq \frac{48}{-12}$$
$$x \leq -4$$

Step 2

Verify the solution set using a test point.

Since $-10 \leq -4$, one test point that can be used is -10.

$$15 - 12x \geq 63$$
$$15 - 12(-10) \geq 63$$
$$15 + 120 \geq 63$$
$$135 \geq 63$$

The resulting statement is true; therefore, it can be assumed that all numbers less than or equal to -4 are part of the solution set.

Example

Solve for x in the linear inequality $6x - 6 \geq 2x + 2$.

Solution

Step 1

Isolate the variable by applying inverse operations.

Add 6 to both sides.

$$6x - 6 \geq 2x + 2$$
$$6x - 6 + 6 \geq 2x + 2 + 6$$
$$6x \geq 2x + 8$$

Subtract $2x$ from both sides.

$$6x \geq 2x + 8$$
$$6x - 2x \geq 2x - 2x + 8$$
$$4x \geq 8$$

Divide both sides by 4.

$$4x \geq 8$$
$$\frac{4x}{4} \geq \frac{8}{4}$$
$$x \geq 2$$

Step 2

Verify the solution set using a test point.

Since $5 \geq 2$, one test point that can be used is 5.

$$6x - 6 \geq 2x + 2$$
$$6(5) - 6 \geq 2(5) + 2$$
$$30 - 6 \geq 10 + 2$$
$$24 \geq 12$$

The resulting statement is true; therefore, it can be assumed that all numbers greater than or equal to 2 are part of the solution set.

Solving Equations of the Form $\frac{a}{x} = b$

To solve for the variable in equations of the form $\frac{a}{x} = b$, follow these steps:

1. Multiply both sides of the equation by x.
2. Isolate the variable by dividing both sides of the equation by the numerical coefficient of x.
3. Verify the solution by substitution.

In all steps of the solution, apply the **inverse operation** to both sides of the equation. Always verify that the solution is correct by substituting the value of the variable back into the equation. If the solution is correct, the left side of the equation will equal the right side.

Example

Solve the equation $\frac{96}{x} = 12$, and verify the solution.

Solution

Step 1

Multiply both sides of the equation by x.

$$x\left(\frac{96}{x}\right) = (12)x$$

$$96 = 12x$$

Step 2

Isolate the variable by dividing both sides of the equation by the numerical coefficient of x.

The numerical coefficient of x is 12.

$$96 = 12x$$

$$\frac{96}{12} = \frac{12x}{12}$$

$$8 = x$$

Step 3

Verify the solution.

Substitute $x = 8$ into the original equation.

If both sides of the equation are equal, the solution is correct.

$$\frac{96}{x} = 12$$

$$\frac{96}{8} = 12$$

$$12 = 12$$

The solution has been verified, so $x = 8$.

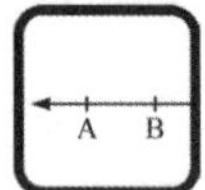

EXERCISE #1—ONE VARIABLE EQUATIONS AND INEQUALITIES

70. What is the value of x in the equation $2(3x + 5) = 5(x - 7)$?
   A. –2
   B. –17
   C. –25
   D. –45

Use the following information to answer the next question.

Adrian wants to purchase a new MP3 player that costs $45.00, including taxes. She has $5.00 saved and can save an additional $5.00 for every hour that she works.

71. If Adrian uses the inequality $5x + 5 \geq 45$, where x is the number of hours she works, then what is the minimum number of hours of work that it will take her to reach her goal?

72. The solution set for $7 + x < 67$ is
   A. $x < 60$
   B. $x > 60$
   C. $x < 74$
   D. $x > 74$

73. What is the solution set for the inequality $80 < \frac{5}{t}$?
   A. $t < \frac{1}{400}$
   B. $t < \frac{1}{16}$
   C. $t < 16$
   D. $t < 400$

74. What is the solution to the inequality $\frac{-x}{4} < -5$?
   A. $x > 20$
   B. $x < 20$
   C. $x > -20$
   D. $x < -20$

75. What is the value of x in the inequality $5(x - 2) > 4x + 3$?
   A. $x > -7$
   B. $x < -7$
   C. $x > 13$
   D. $x < 13$

76. What is the value of x in the equation $\frac{3(4 - 6) - 2}{x} = 4(4 - 2)$?
   A. 6
   B. 5
   C. 0
   D. –1

EXERCISE #1—ONE VARIABLE EQUATIONS AND INEQUALITIES ANSWERS AND SOLUTIONS

70. D	72. A	74. A	76. D
71. See solution	73. B	75. C	

70. D

Step 1
Distribute the term outside the brackets to each term inside the brackets, and simplify.

$$2(3x+5) = 5(x-7)$$
$$2(3x)+2(5) = 5(x)-5(7)$$
$$6x+10 = 5x-35$$

Step 2
Move all the variables to the left side of the equation by subtracting $5x$ from both sides, and simplify.

$$6x-5x+10 = 5x-5x-35$$
$$x+10 = -35$$

Step 3
Move the constant to the right side of the equation by subtracting 10 from both sides, and simplify.

$$x+10-10 = -35-10$$
$$x = -45$$

Step 4
Verify the answer by substituting the value of the variable back into the equation. If the answer is correct, the left side of the equation should equal the right side.

$$2(3x+5) = 5(x-7)$$
$$2[3(-45)+5] = 5[(-45)-7]$$
$$2(-135+5) = 5(-52)$$
$$2(-130) = -260$$
$$-260 = -260$$

Since the left and right side of the equation are equal, the solution $x = -45$ is correct.

71.

Step 1
Solve for x in the linear inequality.
Move the constant to the right side by subtracting 5 from both sides of the inequality, and simplify.

$$5x+5 \geq 45$$
$$5x+5-5 \geq 45-5$$
$$5x \geq 40$$

Isolate the variable by dividing both sides by 5, and solve for x.

$$\frac{5x}{5} \geq \frac{40}{5}$$
$$x \geq 8$$

Step 2
Graph the solution on a number line.
Place the solution number 8 in the middle of the line.
Write the next three numbers in the sequence on either side of the middle number.
Draw a shaded circle at 8 on the number line.
The circle is shaded because the solution set includes 8.
Draw the arrow in the direction that satisfies the solution.

Step 3
Answer the question.
After 8 hours or more of work, Adrian will have enough money to purchase the MP3 player.

72. A

For linear inequalities, the inequality sign can be treated like an equal sign if not multiplying or dividing by a negative value. Whatever operation is done to one side must be done to the other side.

$$7+x < 67$$
$$7-7+x < 67-7$$
$$x < 60$$

73. B

To solve this inequality, isolate the variable (t). When isolating a variable, be sure that the same operations are performed on both sides of the inequality.

$$80 < \frac{5}{t}$$
$$80(t) < \left(\frac{5}{t}\right)t$$
$$80t < 5$$
$$\frac{80t}{80} < \frac{5}{80}$$
$$t < \frac{1}{16}$$

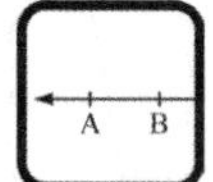

74. A

A linear inequality can be solved like a linear equation by applying inverse operations to isolate the variable. However, when multiplying or dividing a linear inequality by a negative number, the direction of the inequality sign must be changed.

$$\frac{-x}{4} < -5$$
$$\frac{-x}{4} \times 4 < -5 \times 4$$
$$-x < -20$$
$$\frac{-x}{-1} < \frac{-20}{-1}$$
$$x > 20$$

75. C

Step 1
Simplify the left side of the inequality by applying the distributive property.
$$5(x-2) > 4x+3$$
$$5(x) - 5(2) > 4x+3$$
$$5x - 10 > 4x+3$$

Step 2
Isolate the variable by applying inverse operations.
$$5x - 10 > 4x+3$$
Add 10 to both sides.
$$5x - 10 > 4x+3$$
$$5x - 10 + 10 > 4x+3+10$$
$$5x > 4x+13$$
Subtract $4x$ from both sides.
$$5x - 4x > 4x - 4x + 13$$
$$x > 13$$

Step 3
Verify the solution set using a test point.
Since 20 > 13, one test point that can be used is 20.
$$5(20-2) > 4(20)+3$$
$$5(18) > 80+3$$
$$90 > 83$$
The resulting statement is true; therefore, it can be assumed that all numbers greater than 13 are part of the solution set.

76. D

Step 1
Simplify any expressions inside the brackets.
$$\frac{3(4-6)-2}{x} = 4(4-2)$$
$$\frac{3(-2)-2}{x} = 4(2)$$
$$\frac{(-6)-2}{x} = 8$$
$$\frac{-8}{x} = 8$$

Step 2
Multiply both sides of the equation by the lowest common denominator (LCD).
The LCD is x.
$$(x)\frac{-8}{x} = 8(x)$$
$$-8 = 8x$$

Step 3
Move all the variables to the left side of the equation, and simplify.
Subtract $8x$ from both sides.
$$-8 - 8x = 8x - 8x$$
$$-8 - 8x = 0$$

Step 4
Move all the constants to the right side, and simplify.
Add 8 to both sides.
$$-8 + 8 - 8x = 0 + 8$$
$$-8x = 8$$

Step 5
Isolate the variable by dividing both sides by −8.
$$\frac{-8x}{-8} = \frac{8}{-8}$$
$$x = -1$$

EXERCISE #2—ONE VARIABLE EQUATIONS AND INEQUALITIES

77. Solve the equation $3(4x + 7) = 3(5x + 5)$.

78. Which of the following inequalities has a solution set of $g > 2$?

A. $10 - g < 12$ B. $28g > 54$
C. $43g > 86$ D. $g > 6$

79. What is the solution set for $x + 3 > 4$?

A. $x > 1$ B. $x > 7$
C. $x > 12$ D. $x < 12$

80. What is the solution set for $3x < 51$?

A. $x < 17$ B. $x > 17$
C. $x < 47$ D. $x > 54$

81. What is the solution set for the inequality $\frac{w}{-2} \geq 32$?

A. $w \leq -16$ B. $w \geq -16$
C. $w \geq -64$ D. $w \leq -64$

82. What is the value of y in the inequality $20 - 2y \geq 3y$?

A. $y \geq 6$ B. $y \leq 6$
C. $y \geq 4$ D. $y \leq 4$

83. What is the value of x in the equation $\frac{6}{3x} = 4(7 - 5)$?

A. $\frac{1}{4}$ B. $\frac{1}{2}$
C. $\frac{2}{3}$ D. 1

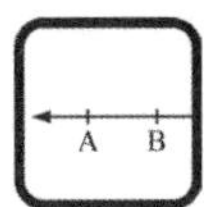

EXERCISE #2—ONE VARIABLE EQUATIONS AND INEQUALITIES ANSWERS AND SOLUTIONS

77. See solution	79. A	81. D	83. A
78. C	80. A	82. D	

77.

Step 1
Distribute the term outside the brackets to each term inside the brackets, and simplify.

$3(4x) + 3(7) = 3(5x) + 3(5)$
$12x + 21 = 15x + 15$

Step 2
Move all the variables to the left side of the equation by subtracting $15x$ from both sides, and simplify.

$12x - 15x + 21 = 15x - 15x + 15$
$-3x + 21 = 15$

Step 3
Move the constant to the right side of the equation by subtracting 21 from both sides, and simplify.

$-3x + 21 - 21 = 15 - 21$
$-3x = -6$

Step 4
Isolate the variable by dividing both sides of the equation by -3.

$\frac{-3x}{-3} = \frac{-6}{-3}$
$x = 2$

Step 5
Verify the answer by substituting the value of the variable back into the equation. If the answer is correct, the left side of the equation should equal the right side.

$3(4x + 7) = 3(5x + 5)$
$3[4(2) + 7] = 3[5(2) + 5]$
$3(8 + 7) = 3(10 + 5)$
$3(15) = 3(15)$
$45 = 45$

Since the left and right sides of the equation are equal, the solution $x = 2$ is correct.

78. C

For linear inequalities, the inequality sign can be treated like an equal sign if not multiplying or dividing by a negative value. Whatever operation is done to one side must also be done to the other side. When multiplying or dividing a linear inequality by a negative number, change the direction of the inequality sign.

Solve each inequality to find out which one has a solution set equal to $g > 2$.

Step 1
$g > 6$
This solution set is not equal to $g > 2$.

Step 2
$28g > 54$
$\frac{28g}{28} > \frac{54}{28}$
$g > 1.9$
This solution set is not equal to $g > 2$.

Step 3
$10 - g < 12$
$10 - 10 - g < 12 - 10$
$-g < 2$
$\frac{-g}{-1} < \frac{2}{-1}$
$g > -2$
This solution set is not equal to $g > 2$.

Step 4
$43g > 86$
$\frac{43g}{43} > \frac{86}{43}$
$g > 2$
This solution set is equal to $g > 2$.

79. A

When solving linear inequalities, the inequality sign can usually be treated like an equal sign. Whatever operation is done to one side must be done to the other side. The inequality needs to be reversed if multiplying or dividing by a negative value.

$x + 3 > 4$
$x + 3 - 3 > 4 - 3$
$x > 1$

80. A

For linear inequalities, the inequality sign can be treated like an equal sign if the inequality is not being multiplied or divided by a negative value. Whatever operation is done to one side must be done to the other side.

$3x < 51$
$\frac{3x}{3} < \frac{51}{3}$
$x < 17$

81. D

A linear inequality can be solved like a linear equation by applying inverse operations to isolate the variable. However, when multiplying or dividing a linear inequality by a negative number, remember to change the direction of the inequality sign.

$$\frac{w}{-2} \geq 32$$

$$\frac{w}{-2}(-2) \geq 32(-2)$$

$$w \leq -64$$

82. D

Step 1

Isolate the variable by applying inverse operations.

Add $2y$ to both sides of the equation

$$20 - 2y \geq 3y$$

$$20 - 2y + 2y \geq 3y + 2y$$

$$20 \geq 5y$$

Divide both sides by 5.

$$\frac{20}{5} \geq \frac{5y}{5}$$

$$4 \geq y$$

$$y \leq 4$$

Step 2

Verify the solution set using a test point.

Since $2 \leq 4$, one test point that can be used is 2.

$$20 - 2(2) \geq 3(2)$$

$$20 - 4 \geq 6$$

$$16 \geq 6$$

The resulting statement is true; therefore, it can be assumed that all numbers less than or equal to 4 are part of the solution set.

83. A

Step 1

Simplify any expressions inside the brackets.

$$\frac{6}{3x} = 4(7 - 5)$$

$$\frac{6}{3x} = 4(2)$$

$$\frac{6}{3x} = 8$$

Step 2

Multiply both sides of the equation by the lowest common denominator (LCD).

The LCD is $3x$.

$$(3x)\frac{6}{3x} = 8(3x)$$

$$6 = 24x$$

Step 3

Move all the variables to the left side of the equation, and simplify.

Subtract $24x$ from both sides.

$$6 - 24x = 24x - 24x$$

$$6 - 24x = 0$$

Step 4

Move all the constants to the right side, and simplify.

Subtract 6 from both sides.

$$6 - 6 - 24x = 0 - 6$$

$$-24x = -6$$

Step 5

Isolate the variable by dividing both sides by −24.

$$\frac{-24x}{-24} = \frac{-6}{-24}$$

$$x = \frac{1}{4}$$

NOTES

Rational Exponents

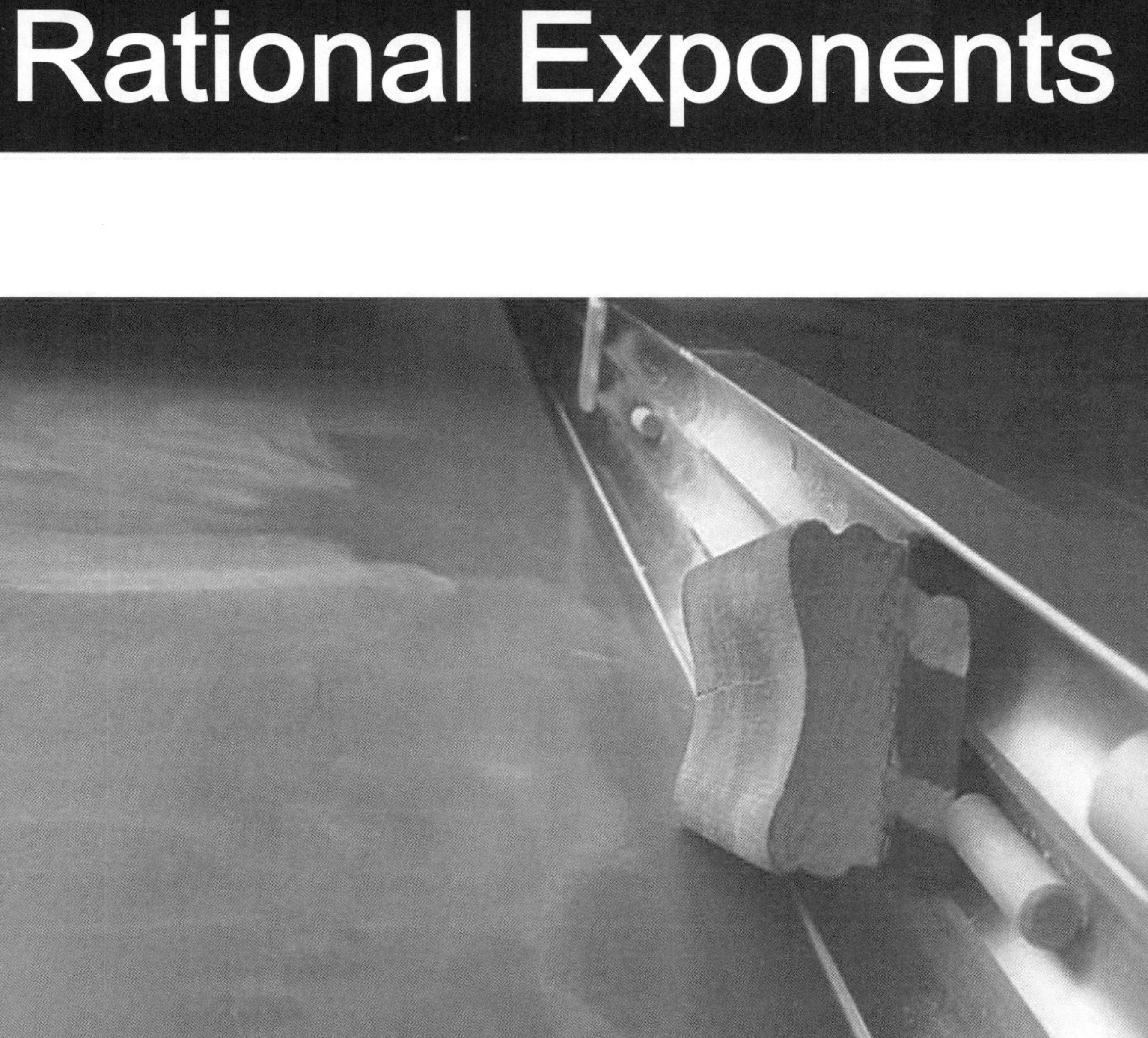

RATIONAL EXPONENTS

Table of Correlations

<table>
<tr><th colspan="2">Standard</th><th>Concepts</th><th>Exercise #1</th><th>Exercise #2</th></tr>
<tr><td>Unit2.1</td><td colspan="4">Extend the properties of exponents to rational exponents.</td></tr>
<tr><td rowspan="2">N-RN.1</td><td rowspan="2">Explain how the definition of the meaning of rational exponents follows from extending the properties of integer exponents to those values, allowing for a notation for radicals in terms of rational exponents.</td><td>Applying the Laws of Exponents, Including Radical Bases and Rational Exponents</td><td>84</td><td>86</td></tr>
<tr><td>Understanding the Laws of Rational Exponents</td><td>85</td><td>87</td></tr>
<tr><td>N-RN.2</td><td>Rewrite expressions involving radicals and rational exponents using the properties of exponents.</td><td>Applying the Laws of Exponents, Including Radical Bases and Rational Exponents</td><td>84</td><td>86</td></tr>
</table>

N-RN.1 Explain how the definition of the meaning of rational exponents follows from extending the properties of integer exponents to those values, allowing for a notation for radicals in terms of rational exponents.

Applying the Laws of Exponents, Including Radical Bases and Rational Exponents

Basic Laws and Properties of Exponents

The basic laws of exponents are as follows:

- Product law: $x^m \times x^n = x^{m+n}$
- Quotient law: $x^m \div x^n = x^{m-n}$
- Power law (often referred to as the "power of a power law"): $(x^m)^n = x^{m \times n} = x^{mn}$
- Power of a product law: $(xy)^n = x^n y^n$
- Power of a quotient law: $\left(\frac{x}{y}\right)^n = \frac{x^n}{y^n}$

There are two basic properties of exponents with which you must be familiar:

- Zero exponent property: $x^0 = 1$
- Negative exponent property: $x^{-1} = \frac{1}{x^n}$

Rational Exponents

Up to this point, $\sqrt{2}$ has simply been called "root two," or "the square root of two"—it is now defined as a radical. As well, $\sqrt[3]{8}$, the cube root of eight, is also a radical.

In the expression $\sqrt[3]{16}$, the number 16 is the radicand. The small number, 3, is called the index. The root sign is now called the radical sign. Any number or value that contains a radical sign is called a radical.

It follows that in the general expression $\sqrt[n]{x}$, the unknown variable x is the radicand, the unknown variable n is the index, and the familiar radical sign is present.

The index is not always shown. In square roots, which are the most common, the index of 2 is simply understood. It can be written, but it does not have to be. This is similar to writing x instead of $1x$.

Example

Can the radical expression $\sqrt{4}$ be written in exponential form?

To answer this question, begin by evaluating $\sqrt{4} \times \sqrt{4}$.

$$\begin{aligned}\sqrt{4} \times \sqrt{4} &= 2 \times 2 \\ &= 4\end{aligned}$$

Next, it is possible to solve for x in the equation $4^x \times 4^x = 4$ by applying the product law for exponents as follows:

$$\begin{aligned}4^x \times 4^x &= 4 \\ 4^{x+x} &= 4^1 \\ 4^{2x} &= 4^1\end{aligned}$$

For the equation $4^{2x} = 4^1$ to be valid, it follows that $2x$ must equal 1. Therefore, to determine the value of x, it is only necessary to solve the equation $2x = 1$. The solution to the equation $2x = 1$ is $x = \frac{1}{2}$.

Thus, $4^{\frac{1}{2}} \times 4^{\frac{1}{2}} = 4$.

Since $\sqrt{4} \times \sqrt{4} = 4$ and $4^{\frac{1}{2}} \times 4^{\frac{1}{2}} = 4$, it can be observed that $\sqrt{4}$ must be equivalent to $4^{\frac{1}{2}}$.

Similarly, $\sqrt[3]{8}$ can be written in exponential form.

The value of $\sqrt[3]{8} \times \sqrt[3]{8} \times \sqrt[3]{8}$ is 8(2 × 2 × 2). Now, solve for x in the equation $8^x \times 8^x \times 8^x = 8$ by applying the product law for exponents.

$$\begin{aligned}8^x \times 8^x \times 8^x &= 8 \\ 8^{x+x+x} &= 8^1 \\ 8^{3x} &= 8^1 \\ 3x &= 1 \\ x &= \frac{1}{3}\end{aligned}$$

Thus, $8^{\frac{1}{3}} \times 8^{\frac{1}{3}} \times 8^{\frac{1}{3}} = 8$. Since $\sqrt[3]{8} \times \sqrt[3]{8} \times \sqrt[3]{8} = 8$ and $8^{\frac{1}{3}} \times 8^{\frac{1}{3}} \times 8^{\frac{1}{3}} = 8$, it follows that $\sqrt[3]{8}$ is equivalent to $8^{\frac{1}{3}}$. In general, it can be shown that $\sqrt[n]{x} = x^{\frac{1}{n}}$. For example, $\sqrt[4]{25}$ is equivalent to $25^{\frac{1}{4}}$, and $\sqrt[5]{37}$ is equivalent to $37^{\frac{1}{5}}$. In order to write a more complex expression such as $(\sqrt[5]{26})^6$ in exponential form, apply the property that $\sqrt[n]{x} = x^{\frac{1}{n}}$, followed by the power of a power law for examples. Using this procedure an equivalent exponential form to the radical expression $(\sqrt[5]{32})^6$ can be determined as follows:

$$\begin{aligned}(\sqrt[5]{32})^6 &= \left(32^{\frac{1}{5}}\right)^6 \\ &= 32^{\frac{1}{5} \times \frac{1}{6}} \\ &= 32^{\frac{6}{5}}\end{aligned}$$

The expression $(\sqrt[n]{x})^m$ can also be written as $\sqrt[n]{x^m}$. Therefore, in general, the rational exponent property is $x^{\frac{m}{n}} = \sqrt[n]{x^m} = (\sqrt[n]{x})^m$.

The application of the rational exponent property can be observed in the following four examples.

Example

Evaluate $16^{\frac{3}{4}}$ without using a calculator.

Solution

Step 1

Write the term in radical form.

$$16^{\frac{3}{4}} = (\sqrt[4]{16})^3$$

Step 2

Evaluate.

Since $\sqrt[4]{16} = 2$, the value of $(\sqrt[4]{16})^3$ can be determined as follows:

$$\begin{aligned}(\sqrt[4]{16})^3 &= (2)^3 \\ &= 8\end{aligned}$$

Example

Evaluate $(0.001)^{-\frac{2}{3}}$ without using a calculator.

Solution

Step 1

Determine the fractional equivalent to 0.001.

$$0.001 = \frac{1}{1{,}000}$$

Step 2

Substitute $\frac{1}{1{,}000}$ for 0.001 in the given expression, then apply the negative exponent property.

$$\begin{aligned}(0.001)^{-\frac{2}{3}} &= \left(\frac{1}{1{,}000}\right)^{-\frac{2}{3}} \\ &= (1{,}000)^{\frac{2}{3}}\end{aligned}$$

Step 3

Evaluate $(1{,}000)^{\frac{2}{3}}$ by applying the rational exponent property.

$$\begin{aligned}(1{,}000)^{\frac{2}{3}} &= (\sqrt[3]{1{,}000})^2 \\ &= (10)^2 \\ &= 100\end{aligned}$$

Example

Express $x^{0.6}$ in radical form.

Solution

Step 1

Determine the fractional equivalent to 0.6.

$$\begin{aligned}0.6 &= \frac{6}{10} \\ &= \frac{3}{5}\end{aligned}$$

Step 2

Substitute $\frac{3}{5}$ for 0.6 in the given expression.

$$x^{0.6} = x^{\frac{3}{5}}$$

Step 3

Express $x^{\frac{3}{5}}$ in radical form by applying the rational exponent property.

$x^{\frac{3}{5}} = (\sqrt[5]{x})^3 = \sqrt[5]{x^3}$

Thus, $x^{0.6}$ is equivalent to $\sqrt[5]{x^3}$.

Example

Express $\left(\sqrt[4]{x^3}\right)\left(\sqrt[8]{x}\right)$ in a simplified exponential form.

Solution

Step 1
Rewrite the given expression in exponential form by applying the rational exponent property in reverse.

$\left(\sqrt[4]{x^3}\right)\left(\sqrt[8]{x}\right) = \left(x^{\frac{3}{4}}\right)\left(x^{\frac{1}{8}}\right)$

Step 2
Simplify the expression by applying the product law for exponents.

$$\begin{aligned}\left(x^{\frac{3}{4}}\right)\left(x^{\frac{1}{8}}\right) &= x^{\frac{3}{4}+\frac{1}{8}}\\ &= x^{\frac{6}{8}+\frac{1}{8}}\\ &= x^{\frac{7}{8}}\end{aligned}$$

In a simplified exponential form, $\left(\sqrt[4]{x^3}\right)\left(\sqrt[8]{x}\right)$ can be written as $x^{\frac{7}{8}}$.

Understanding the Laws of Rational Exponents

A rational exponent is an exponent that can be written in the form of a rational number, $\frac{a}{b}$, where a and b are integers and $b \neq 0$.

Example

Evaluate the expression $4^{\frac{1}{2}}$.

Solution

Step 1

Create an equation in which multiples of $4^{\frac{1}{2}}$ equal 4^m, where m is a whole number exponent.

$4^{\frac{1}{2}} \times 4^{\frac{1}{2}} = 4^{\frac{1}{2}+\frac{1}{2}} = 4^1$

Step 2

Substitute x for $4^{\frac{1}{2}}$.

$(x)(x) = 4^1$

$x^2 = 4$

Step 3
Solve for x.

$x = \pm\sqrt{(4)}$

Note: Dismiss $-\sqrt{4}$, since the base is greater than 0.

Since $x = 4^{\frac{1}{2}}$, $4^{\frac{1}{2}} = \sqrt{(4)^1} = 2$.

Example

Evaluate the expression $64^{-\frac{1}{3}}$.

Solution

Step 1

Create an equation in which multiples of $64^{-\frac{1}{3}}$ equal 64^m, where m is a whole number.

$64^{-\frac{1}{3}} \times 64^{-\frac{1}{3}} \times 64^{-\frac{1}{3}} = 64^{-\frac{3}{3}} = 64^{-1}$

Step 2

Substitute x for $64^{-\frac{1}{3}}$.

$$(x)(x)(x) = 64^{-1}$$

$$x^3 = \frac{1}{(64)^1}$$

Step 3

Solve for x by taking the cube root of both sides.

$$x = \frac{1}{\sqrt[3]{64}}$$

$$64^{-\frac{1}{3}} = \frac{1}{\sqrt[3]{(64)^1}} = \frac{1}{4}$$

Radicals can be written as powers with rational exponents, and powers with rational exponents can be written as radicals.

In general, the rational exponent property is $x^{\frac{m}{n}} = \sqrt[n]{x^m} = \left(\sqrt[n]{x}\right)^m$.

Once a radical is expressed as a power with a rational exponent, the regular laws of exponents can be applied. These laws are stated as follows:

- When multiplying powers with the same bases, add the exponents together.
  $b^x \times b^y = b^{x+y}$
- When dividing powers with the same bases, subtract the exponents.
  $\frac{b^x}{b^y} = b^{x-y}$, in which $b \neq 0$
- When a power is raised to a power, multiply the exponents.
  $\left(b^x\right)^y = b^{xy}$
- When the product of powers inside brackets is raised to a power, each power in the brackets is raised to the power outside the brackets.
  $(ab)^x = a^x b^x$
- When the quotient of powers inside brackets is raised to a power, each power in the numerator and denominator in the brackets is raised to the power outside the brackets.
  $\left(\frac{a}{b}\right)^x = \frac{a^x}{b^x}$, in which $b \neq 0$
- When a base is raised to a negative exponent, it can be represented as 1 over the base raised to a positive exponent.
  $b^{-x} = \frac{1}{b^x}$, in which $b \neq 0$
- Any base other than 0 raised to the exponent 0 is equal to 1.
  $b^0 = 1[b \neq 0]$
- Zero raised to any exponent (except 0) is equal to 0.
  $0^x = 0[x \neq 0]$
- The expression 0^0 is undefined.

EXERCISE #1—RATIONAL EXPONENTS

84. What is the value of the expression
$81^{\frac{5}{4}}+(0.01)^{-\frac{1}{2}}-(-64)^{\frac{1}{3}}$?

A. 237
B. 247.1
C. 249
D. 257

85. Written using a single radical, what is the expression $\sqrt[5]{w^2}\times\sqrt{w^4}$?

A. $\sqrt[5]{w^{12}}$
B. $\sqrt[5]{w^4}$
C. $\sqrt[12]{w^5}$
D. $\sqrt[4]{w^5}$

EXERCISE #1—RATIONAL EXPONENTS ANSWERS AND SOLUTIONS

84. D	85. A

84. D

Step 1
Evaluate each term in the given expression by applying the rational exponent property, where $x^{\frac{m}{n}} = \left(\sqrt[n]{x}\right)^m$.

$$81^{\frac{5}{4}} = \left(\sqrt[4]{81}\right)^5 = (3)^5 = 243$$

$$(0.01)^{-\frac{1}{2}} = \left(\frac{1}{100}\right)^{-\frac{1}{2}} = (100)^{\frac{1}{2}} = \sqrt{100} = 10$$

$$(-64)^{\frac{1}{3}} = \sqrt[3]{-64} = -4$$

Step 2
Substitute 243 for $81^{\frac{5}{4}}$, 10 for $(0.01)^{-\frac{1}{2}}$, and −4 for $(-64)^{\frac{1}{3}}$ in the given expression, and then evaluate the resulting expression.

$$81^{\frac{5}{4}} + (0.01)^{-\frac{1}{2}} - (-64)^{\frac{1}{3}}$$
$$= 243 + 10 - (-4)$$
$$= 243 + 10 + 4$$
$$= 257$$

85. A

Step 1
Write the radicals as rational exponents.

$$\sqrt[5]{w^2} \times \sqrt{w^4} = w^{\frac{2}{5}} \times w^{\frac{4}{2}}$$

Step 2
Use the product law of exponents.

$$w^{\frac{2}{5}} \times w^{\frac{4}{2}} = w^{\frac{2}{5}+\frac{4}{2}} = w^{\frac{2}{5}+\frac{2}{1}} = w^{\frac{2}{5}+\frac{10}{5}} = w^{\frac{12}{5}}$$

Step 3
Write the rational expression as a radical.

$$w^{\frac{12}{5}} = \sqrt[5]{w^{12}}$$

EXERCISE #2—RATIONAL EXPONENTS

86. The expression $\sqrt{2} \times \sqrt[3]{2}$ is equivalent to

    A. $\sqrt[3]{4}$ B. $\sqrt[3]{16}$

    C. $\sqrt[6]{32}$ D. $\sqrt[5]{64}$

87. The expression $x^{-\frac{4}{3}}$ is equivalent to

    A. $\sqrt[4]{x^3}$ B. $-\sqrt[3]{x^4}$

    C. $-\frac{1}{\sqrt[4]{x^3}}$ D. $\frac{1}{\sqrt[3]{x^4}}$

EXERCISE #2—RATIONAL EXPONENTS ANSWERS AND SOLUTIONS

86. C	87. D

86. C

Step 1
Write the given expression as an equivalent expression with rational exponents.
Apply the rational exponent property (in reverse) where $x^{\frac{m}{n}} = \sqrt[n]{x^m}$. Thus, $\sqrt{2} = 2^{\frac{1}{2}}$ and $\sqrt[3]{2} = 2^{\frac{1}{3}}$.
The expression $\sqrt{2} \times \sqrt[3]{2}$ is equivalent to $2^{\frac{1}{2}} \times 2^{\frac{1}{3}}$.

Step 2
Apply the product law for exponents where $x^m \times x^n = x^{m+n}$.

$$\begin{aligned} 2^{\frac{1}{2}} \times 2^{\frac{1}{3}} &= 2^{\frac{1}{2}+\frac{1}{3}} \\ &= 2^{\frac{3}{6}+\frac{2}{6}} \\ &= 2^{\frac{5}{6}} \end{aligned}$$

Step 3
Apply the rational exponent property.

$$\begin{aligned} 2^{\frac{5}{6}} &= \sqrt[6]{2^5} \\ &= \sqrt[6]{32} \end{aligned}$$

87. D

Step 1
Apply the negative exponent property.
$x^{-\frac{4}{3}}$ can be written as $\frac{1}{x^{\frac{4}{3}}}$.

Step 2
Apply the rational exponent property.
$\frac{1}{x^{\frac{4}{3}}}$ is equivalent to $\frac{1}{\sqrt[3]{x^4}}$.

Linear Equations

LINEAR EQUATIONS

Table of Correlations

Standard		Concepts	Exercise #1	Exercise #2
Unit2.2	Analyze and solve linear equations and pairs of simultaneous linear equations.			
8.EE.8a	*Analyze and solve pairs of simultaneous linear equations. Understand that solutions to a system of two linear equations in two variables correspond to points of intersection of their graphs, because points of intersection satisfy both equations simultaneously.*	Solving a Linear System of Equations Using the Graphing Method	88	94
		Graphically Solving Systems of Linear Equations in the Form $y = mx + b$	89	95
8.EE.8b	*Analyze and solve pairs of simultaneous linear equations. Solve systems of two linear equations in two variables algebraically, and estimate solutions by graphing the equations. Solve simple cases by inspection.*	Algebraically Solve Systems of Linear Equations in Two Variables by Substitution	90	96
		Solve Systems of Linear Equations Algebraically by Elimination	91	97
8.EE.8c	*Analyze and solve pairs of simultaneous linear equations. Solve real-world and mathematical problems leading to two linear equations in two variables.*	Solving Problems Involving Systems of Linear Equations Algebraically	92	98
		Solving Problems with Systems of Linear Equations by Graphing	93	99
Unit2.3	Solve systems of equations.			
A-REI.5	*Prove that, given a system of two equations in two variables, replacing one equation by the sum of that equation and a multiple of the other produces a system with the same solutions.*	Solve Systems of Linear Equations Algebraically by Elimination	91	97
A-REI.6	*Solve systems of linear equations exactly and approximately, focusing on pairs of linear equations in two variables.*	Solving a Linear System of Equations Using the Graphing Method	88	94
		Algebraically Solve Systems of Linear Equations in Two Variables by Substitution	90	96
		Solve Systems of Linear Equations Algebraically by Elimination	91	97

8.EE.8a Analyze and solve pairs of simultaneous linear equations. Understand that solutions to a system of two linear equations in two variables correspond to points of intersection of their graphs, because points of intersection satisfy both equations simultaneously.

Solving a Linear System of Equations Using the Graphing Method

A set of two or more linear equations is a **linear system**. The solution to a linear system is the set of ordered pairs, usually (x, y), that satisfies all equations in the system. Graphically, the solution is the point (or points) of intersection of the graph of the lines defined by the linear system. A linear system can be solved using several graphing methods.

One method for solving a linear system is sketching the graph of the lines by hand on grid paper. This is a valuable tool to aid in understanding various aspects of the solution such as location, number of ordered pairs, and approximate values. However, for some linear systems, determining the solution by approximating and testing values can be tedious.

The graphing method of using a graphing calculator is often a more efficient method of determining the solution to a linear system. However, in some cases, the calculator will give a rounded answer because the coordinates are given as decimals. For example, the solution to the system of equations $y = \frac{3}{2}x$ and $y = -\frac{3}{2}x + 2$ from a calculator is $x = 0.66666667$, $y = 1$. The x-value has been rounded and is actually $\frac{2}{3}$. The solution can be verified by testing the x- and y-values in the original equations.

Example

$y = x + 4$
$y = -x + 3$

Use a graphical procedure to determine the solution to the given system of equations.

Solution

Method 1: Using Grid Paper

1. Determine the x- and y-intercepts.For $y = x + 4$, find the x-intercept by setting $y = 0$ and solving for x.
   $0 = x + 4$
   $x = -4$
   By setting $x = 0$, the y-intercept is found to be 4. Recall that the y-intercept is the b-value when the equation is written in the form $y = mx + b$. Therefore, since b is 4, the y-intercept must also be 4 in $y = x + 4$.For $y = -x + 3$, the y-intercept is 3.

2. Draw a line through the points corresponding to these intercepts.The graphs of the two equations are plotted here.

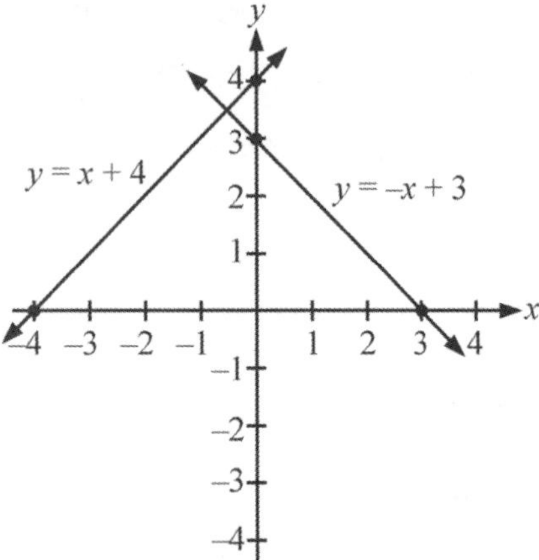

The solution to the system is the ordered pair $(x,\ y)$ that is represented by the point that is common to both lines. It appears that this point is approximately (–0.5, 3.5).

3. Verify the solution.Substitute $x = -0.5$ and $y = 3.5$ into both equations. Check that the left side of the equation equals the right side of the equation after performing the necessary calculations.

Left Side	Right Side
y	$x + 4$
3.5	$(-0.5) + 4$
3.5	3.5

The left side is equal to the right side in the equation $y = x + 4$.

Left Side	Right Side
y	$-x + 3$
3.5	$-(-0.5) + 3$
3.5	3.5

The left side is equal to the right side in the equation $y = -x + 3$.Since (–0.5, 3.5) satisfies both equations, the solution is the set of ordered pairs (–0.5, 3.5).The solution is often written in set notation using braces { }. In this case, the solution could also be written {(–0.5, 3.5)}.

Method 2: Using Technology

An alternative to sketching, approximating, and testing the potential solution points is to use a graphing calculator or computer.

The following steps illustrate how to use a T1-83 graphing calculator to obtain the solution to the given system of equations.

1. Press $y =$
2. Type $Y_1 = x + 4$
3. Type $Y_2 = -x + 3$
4. Press GRAPH

It may be necessary to adjust the window settings in order to display the graphs.
For example, if the ZOOM 6:*Z* standard window is chosen, the calculator screen should look like this.

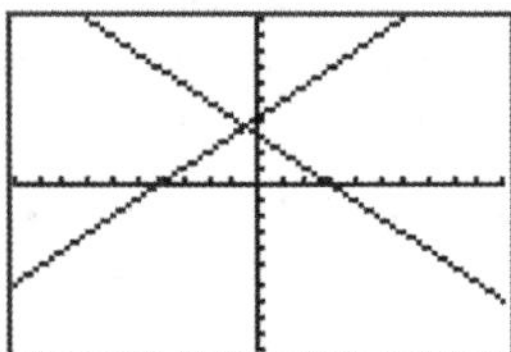

Press 2nd CALC. Choose: 5: intersect.
Press ENTER.

Using the left and right arrows, position the cursor just left or right of the intersection point.
Press ENTER ENTER ENTER.

The intersection point is shown at the bottom of the calculator screen as $x = -0.5,\ y = 3.5$.

Thus, the solution to the system of equations is {(–0.5, 3.5)}.

Example

Two linear equations are given as $4x + 3y = -4$ and $y = 8x - 13$.

Determine the solution to the given system of linear equations by sketching the graphs on grid paper and testing the apparent point of intersection.

Solution

For $4x + 3y = -4$, the x-intercept is determined by setting $y = 0$. The result is that the x-intercept is -1. Thus, $(-1, 0)$ is a point on the graph.

The y-intercept is determined by setting $x = 0$. The result is $4(0) + 3y = -4$. This gives $y = -\frac{4}{3}$, which is not a convenient intercept to graph.

Alternatively, a point that is easier to graph can be obtained by choosing another value for x or y that gives an ordered pair containing integers. For example, $y = 4$ works well.

$$\begin{aligned} 4x + 3y &= -4 \\ 4x + 3(4) &= -4 \\ 4x &= -16 \\ x &= -4 \end{aligned}$$

Thus, $(-4, 4)$ is another point on the graph.

For $y = 8x - 13$, the y-intercept is -13. Thus, the point $(0, -13)$ is on the graph. This time, the x-intercept is not a convenient value to graph. Choosing a value such as $x = 2$ works well. Substitute $x = 2$ into the equation to get $y = 8(2) - 13 = 3$. Thus, the point $(2, 3)$ is on the graph.

Graph the first equation by drawing a line through the points $(-1, 0)$ and $(-4, 4)$. Graph the second equation by drawing a line through the points $(0, -13)$ and $(2, 3)$.

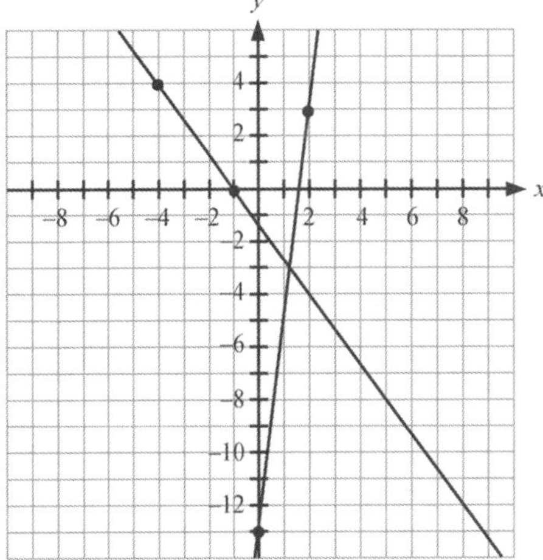

It appears that the point of intersection is an x-value of approximately 1.2 or 1.3 and a y-value of -3. Substituting $x = 1.2$ and $y = -3$ into the second equation gives this result.

Left Side	Right Side
y	$8x - 13$
-3	$8(1.2) - 13$
-3	$9.6 - 13$
-3	-3.4

Since $-3 \neq -3.4$, the ordered pair $(1.2, -3)$ is not the solution. By testing different values in the equations, determine whether or not an ordered pair is going to work.

Test $(1.25, -3)$ in both equations.

Left Side	Right Side
y	$8x - 13$
-3	$8(1.25) - 13$
-3	$10 - 13$
-3	-3

Left Side	Right Side
$4x + 3y$	-4
$4(1.25) + 3(-3)$	-4
$5 - 9$	-4
-4	-4

Since the test values for x and y satisfy both equations, the solution to the system is {(1.25, −3)}.

Example

Use a graphing calculator to determine the solution to the system of linear equations $4x + 3y = -4$ and $y = 8x - 13$.

Solution

Before you enter the equations into the graphing calculator, ensure that they are written in the form $y = mx + b$.

Step 1
Rewrite $4x + 3y = -4$.

$$4x + 3y = -4$$
$$3y = -4x - 4$$
$$y = -\frac{4}{3}x - \frac{4}{3}$$

Step 2
Enter the equations into a graphing calculator, and find the intersection point.

- Press [y =]
- Type $Y_1 = -\frac{4}{3}x - \frac{4}{3}$. Type $Y_2 = 8x - 13$
- Press [GRAPH]. Press [2nd][CALC]
- Choose: 5: intersect. Press [ENTER]
- Using the left and right arrows, position the cursor just left or right of the intersection point
- Press [ENTER][ENTER][ENTER].

If the [ZOOM] 6:Z standard window is chosen, the calculator screen should look like this.

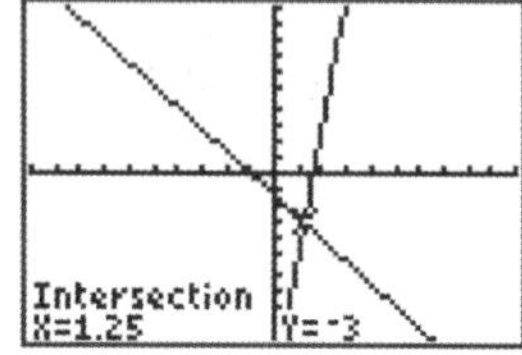

The calculator indicates that the point of intersection of the two lines is at $x = 1.25$, $y = -3$.
The solution to the system of linear equations is {(1.25, −3)}.

Example

When he applied for a job at the Super Snowboard Shop, Terry had his choice of two pay options:

1. $300/week plus 5% of sales
2. $200/week plus 13% of sales

Use technology to graph the two functions, and determine the amount of sales required to make option 2 most advantageous for Terry.

Solution

Step 1
Write equations to represent each plan in the form $y = mx + b$.
The equation $Y_1 = 300 + 0.05x$ represents option 1, and the equation $Y_2 = 200 + 0.13x$ represents option 2. In each equation, Y_1 and Y_2 represent the total weekly pay for each option with respect to the total amount of weekly sales x.

Step 2
Enter the equations into a graphing calculator, and find the intersection point.

- Press [y =].
- Type $Y_1 = 300 + 0.05x$. Type $Y_2 = 200 + 0.13x$.
- Press [GRAPH]. Press [2nd][CALC].
- Choose: 5: intersect. Press [ENTER].
- Using the left and right arrows, position the cursor just left or right of the intersection point.
- Press [ENTER][ENTER][ENTER].

A graphing calculator with window settings such as x:[0, 2,000, 10], y:[0, 500, 10] will yield the graphs shown with an intersection point of $x = 1{,}250$, $y = 362.5$.

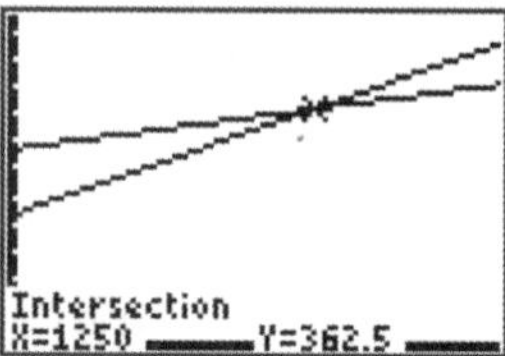

Step 3
Determine when option 2 becomes most advantageous for Terry by analyzing the graph.
To the right of the point of intersection on the graph, the line representing option 2 is above the line representing option 1.
Therefore, it is most advantageous for Terry to use option 2 when the total weekly sales are more than \$1,250.

Graphically Solving Systems of Linear Equations in the Form $y = mx + b$

A set of two or more linear equations is a **linear system**. The solution to a linear system is the set of ordered pairs, usually (x, y), that satisfies all equations in the system. On a graph, the solution is the point or points of intersection of the graphs of the equations.

To solve a system of linear equations graphically, follow these steps:

1. Graph the equations.
2. Determine the point of intersection.

A system of two different linear equations can have one or no solutions.

Example

A system of linear equations is given.
$y = 2x - 5$
$y = x - 1$
What is the solution to the given system of linear equations?

Solution

Step 1
Graph the equations.
Use the slope and y-intercept to graph each line. Use the y-intercept or another point and count off the slope as $\frac{\text{rise}}{\text{run}}$ to obtain additional points.

- For the equation $y = 2x - 5$, the slope is 2 and the y-intercept is –5. Some of the points on this line are (0, –5), (1, –3), (2, –1), (3, 1), and (4, 3).
- For the equation $y = x - 1$, the slope is 1 and the y-intercept is –1. Some of the points on this line are (0, –1), (1, 0), (3, 2), and (4, 3).

Draw a line through the points to obtain the following graph.

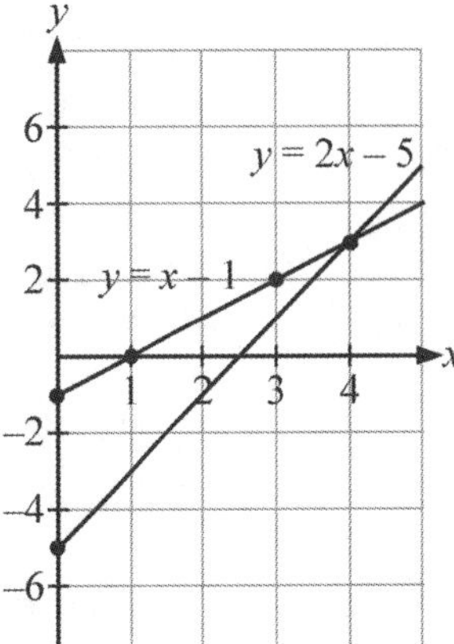

Step 2

Determine the point of intersection.

From the graph, it appears that the point of intersection is at (4, 3).

The point of intersection, (4, 3), is the solution to the system of equations.

8.EE.8b Analyze and solve pairs of simultaneous linear equations. Solve systems of two linear equations in two variables algebraically, and estimate solutions by graphing the equations. Solve simple cases by inspection.

Algebraically Solve Systems of Linear Equations in Two Variables by Substitution

Solving systems of linear equations involves only working with first-degree equations.

Algebraic methods of solving linear equations allow for exact value solutions.

The solution to the system is the ordered pair (x, y) that satisfies both equations.

From a graphical standpoint, the solution represents the intersection point of the graphs of the two related functions.

To solve a system of linear equations using the substitution method, follow these steps:

1. Write one of the equations (labeled as 1 or 2) so that one variable is isolated in terms of the other variable.
2. Substitute this replacement expression into the other equation (labeled as 2 or 1) so it can be solved as a first-degree equation in one variable.
3. Substitute the solved value in either one of the original equations, and then solve for the other variable.
4. Write the solution as an ordered pair in set notation. Verify where necessary.

Example

A linear system of equations is given as follows:

$$3x - 4y + 2 = 0$$
$$2x = 6y - 3$$

Solve the given system using the method of substitution.

Solution

Step 1

Label the equations.

(1) $3x - 4y + 2 = 0$

(2) $2x = 6y - 3$

Step 2

Isolate the chosen variable in one of the equations.

In this case, x has been chosen in equation (2).

Isolate x in terms of y.

$$(2) \rightarrow 2x = 6y - 3$$
$$\rightarrow x = 3y - \frac{3}{2}$$

Step 3

Substitute $3y - \frac{3}{2}$ for x in equation (1).

$$(1) \rightarrow 3x - 4y + 2 = 0$$
$$\rightarrow 3\left(3y - \frac{3}{2}\right) - 4y + 2 = 0$$

Step 4

Solve for y.

$$3\left(3y - \frac{3}{2}\right) - 4y + 2 = 0$$
$$9y - \frac{9}{2} - 4y + 2 = 0$$
$$5y - \frac{5}{2} = 0$$
$$5y = \frac{5}{2}$$
$$y = \frac{1}{2}$$

Step 5

Substitute $y = \frac{1}{2}$ into equation (1) (or (2)), and solve for x.

$$3x - 4y + 2 = 0$$
$$3x - 4\left(\frac{1}{2}\right) + 2 = 0$$
$$3x - 2 + 2 = 0$$
$$3x = 0$$
$$x = 0$$

Step 6
State the solution in set notation.

The solution in set notation is $\left\{\left(0,\ \frac{1}{2}\right)\right\}$.

Solve Systems of Linear Equations Algebraically by Elimination

Solving systems of linear equations involves only working with first-degree equations.
Algebraic methods of solving linear equations allow for exact value solutions.
The solution to the system is the ordered pair $(x,\ y)$ that satisfies both equations.
From a graphical standpoint, the solution represents the intersection point of the graphs of the two related functions.

To solve a linear system using the elimination method, follow these steps:

1. Label the equations, and choose a variable to be eliminated.
2. Eliminate the variable by adding or subtracting the equations in the system. In order to eliminate the variable, the multiplication of one equation or both equations may be required to produce two equations where the coefficients of the eliminated variable are the same (for subtraction) or additive inverses (for addition).
3. Solve for the remaining variable.
4. Substitute the value back into one of the original equations, and solve for the other variable.
5. State the solution as an ordered pair in set notation. Verify where necessary.

Example

A system of linear equations is given as follows:

$3x - 4y = 20$
$x + 3y = -2$

Solve the given system using elimination, and verify the solution.

Solution

Step 1
Label the equations, and choose which variable is to be eliminated.

(1) $3x - 4y = 20$
(2) $x + 3y = -2$

In this case, x is the easiest variable to eliminate.

Step 2
Eliminate x by subtraction, multiply equation (2) by 3.

$3 \times (2) \rightarrow\ 3(x + 3y = -2)$
$\rightarrow\ 3x + 9y = -6$

Let $3x + 9y = -6$ represent equation (3).

Step 3
Subtract equation (3) from equation (1) to eliminate x.

$(1) \rightarrow 3x - 4y = 20$
$(3) \rightarrow \underline{3x + 9y = -6}$
$0x - 13y = 26$

Step 4
Solve for y.

$0x - 13y = 26$
$-13y = 26$
$y = -2$

Step 5
Substitute $y = -2$ into one of the original equations, and solve for x.

$x + 3y = -2$
$x + 3(-2) = -2$
$x - 6 = -2$
$x = 4$

The solution to the system in set notation is $\{(4,\ -2)\}$.

Step 6
Verify the solution.
Substitute $(4,\ -2)$ into both original equations, and check that these values satisfy the equations.

$(1) \rightarrow 3(4) - 4(-2) = 20$
$12 + 8 = 20$
$20 = 20$

$(2) \rightarrow (4) + 3(-2) = -2$
$4 - 6 = -2$
$-2 = -2$

As verified, the solution to this system is $\{(4,\ -2)\}$.

Example

A system of linear equations is given as follows:

$2x + 3y = -10$
$5x - 2y = 13$

Solve the given system using elimination, and verify the solution.

Solution

Step 1

Label the equations, and choose which variable is to be eliminated.

$(1) 2x + 3y = -10$
$(2) 5x - 2y = 13$

In this case, y has been chosen.

Step 2

To eliminate y by addition, determine the least common multiple of the coefficients of $3y$ and $2y$.

The least common multiple of 2 and 3 is 6.

Step 3

Multiply equation (1) by 2 and equation (2) by 3 to produce the terms $6y$ and $-6y$, respectively.

$2 \times (1) \rightarrow 2(2x + 3y = -10)$
$\rightarrow 4x + 6y = -20$

$3 \times (2) \rightarrow 3(5x - 2y = 13)$
$\rightarrow 15x - 6y = 39$

Let $4x + 6y = -20$ represent equation (3), and let $15x - 6y = 39$ represent equation (4).

Step 4

Add equations (3) and (4) to eliminate y.

$(3) \rightarrow 4x + 6y = -20$
$(4) \rightarrow \underline{15x - 6y = 39}$
$19x + 0y = 19$

Step 5

Solve for x.

$19x + 0y = 19$
$19x = 19$
$x = 1$

Step 6

Substitute $x = 1$ into one of the original equations, and solve for y.

$2x + 3y = -10$
$2(1) + 3y = -10$
$3y = -12$
$y = -4$

Step 7

State the solution in set notation.

The solution in set notation is $\{(1, -4)\}$.

Step 8

Verify the solution.

Substitute $(1, -4)$ into both original equations, and check that these values satisfy the equations.

$(1) \rightarrow 2(1) + 3(-4) = -10$
$2 - 12 = -10$
$-10 = -10$

$(2) \rightarrow 5(1) - 2(-4) = 13$
$5 + 8 = 13$
$13 = 13$

As verified, the solution to this system is $\{(1, -4)\}$.

8.EE.8c Analyze and solve pairs of simultaneous linear equations. Solve real-world and mathematical problems leading to two linear equations in two variables.

Solving Problems Involving Systems of Linear Equations Algebraically

Systems of linear equations can be used to solve problems that arise in everyday life. Use the following steps to solve a system of linear equations algebraically:

1. Assign a different variable to each of the unknown quantities.
2. Set up a system of two linear equations.
3. Solve the system using an algebraic method.
4. Clearly state the solution to the given problem.

Example

At a grocery store, 4 cabbages and 5 heads of lettuce cost \$8.40, while 6 cabbages and 2 heads of lettuce cost \$8.20.

Determine the respective prices of a cabbage and a head of lettuce.

Solution

Step 1

Assign a different variable to each of the unknown quantities.

- Let x equal the price in dollars of one cabbage.
- Let y equal the price in dollars of one head of lettuce.

Step 2
Set up a system of two linear equations.
① $4x + 5y = 8.40$
② $6x + 2y = 8.20$

Step 3
Solve the system using an algebraic method, such as elimination.

Begin by finding a common coefficient for y.
Multiply equation 1 by 2.
$2(4x + 5y) = 2(8.40)$
$8x + 10y = 16.80$
Let $8x + 10y = 16.80$ represent equation 3.
Multiply equation 2 by 5.
$5(6x + 2y) = 5(8.20)$
$30x + 10y = 41.00$
Let $30x + 10y = 41.00$ represent equation 4.
Subtract equation 4 from equation 3.
③ $8x + 10y = 16.80$
④ $\underline{30x + 10y = 41.00}$
$-22x + 0y = -24.20$
Solve for x.
$x = \frac{-24.20}{-22}$
$x = 1.10$
Substitute 1.10 for x in equation 1.
$4(1.10) + 5y = 8.40$
$4.40 + 5y = 8.40$
$5y = 4.00$
$y = 0.80$

Step 4
State the solution to the given problem.

The price of a cabbage is \$1.10, and the price of a head of lettuce is \$0.80.

Example

A car rental company offers two plans to rent compact cars at a weekly rate. Plan A costs \$50 plus \$0.05 for each kilometer driven. Plan B costs \$80 plus \$0.03 for each kilometer driven.

Determine the distance that must be driven for plan B to be more economical than plan A.

Solution

Determine the distance a rental car must be driven in one week so that the cost of plan B equals the cost of plan A. For plan B to be more economical than plan A, the total distance driven in one week must be greater than this distance.

Step 1
Assign a different variable to each of the unknown quantities.

- Let x equal the number of kilometers driven.
- Let C equal the weekly cost.

Step 2
Set up a system of two linear equations.

- Plan A will be represented by $C = 50 + 0.05x$.
- Plan B will be represented by $C = 80 + 0.03x$.

Step 3
Solve the system using an algebraic method.
$80 + 0.03x = 50 + 0.05x$
$30 + 0.03x = 0.05x$
$30 = 0.02x$
$1{,}500 = x$

Step 4
State the solution to the given problem.

Plan B is more economical than plan A if the car is driven more than 1,500 km in one week.

Solving Problems with Systems of Linear Equations by Graphing

A set of two or more linear equations is a **linear system**. The solution to a linear system is the set of ordered pairs that solves each equation in the system.

A linear system can be solved by graphing. The solution to a graph of a linear system is the point, or points, of intersection of the graphs of the equations.

Sometimes, linear equations can be used to solve real-life problems. The following steps show how to graph a linear system to solve a problem:

1. Determine the equations that represent the problem.
2. Graph the equations.
3. Determine the point of intersection, and use this to solve the problem.

Example

Skyler wants to purchase a gym membership. The first gym he goes to, Gym Jam, requires a payment of $15 per month plus $5 for each visit. The second gym he visits, Fitness Folk, requires a payment of $1 per month plus $12 for each visit.

What is the minimum number of times that Skyler must go to the gym in one month for Gym Jam to be the least expensive choice?

Solution

Step 1
Determine the equations that represent the problem.
Let C represent the total monthly cost to attend a gym. Let n represent the number of visits to the gym in one month.
The equation for Gym Jam is $C = 15 + 5n$.
The equation for Fitness Folk is $C = 1 + 12n$.

Step 2
Graph the equations.

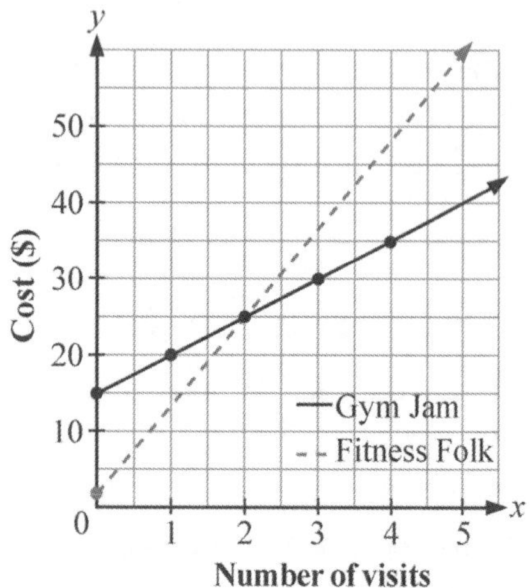

Step 3
Determine the point of intersection, and use this to solve the problem.
The intersection point is the ordered pair (2, 25).
This means that if Skyler goes to either gym exactly 2 times, it will cost $25. Skyler must go to the gym at least 3 times in a month for Gym Jam to be the least expensive choice.

Example

A car rental company offers two plans to rent compact cars at a weekly rate:

- Plan A: $50 plus $0.05/km
- Plan B: $80 plus $0.03/km

Use a graphing calculator to determine the distance that must be driven in a week for plan B to be more economical than plan A.

Solution

Step 1
Determine the equations that represent the problem.
Let x represent the number of kilometers driven. Let C represent the weekly cost.
The equation for plan A is $C = 50 + 0.05x$.
The equation for plan B is $C = 80 + 0.03x$.

Step 2
Graph the equations.

Press [Y =] and input each equation.

$y_1 = 50 + 0.05x$
$y_2 = 80 + 0.03x$

Press [WINDOW] and input the window settings x: $[0, 2{,}000, 250]$ and y: $[0, 200, 50]$. Then, press [GRAPH].

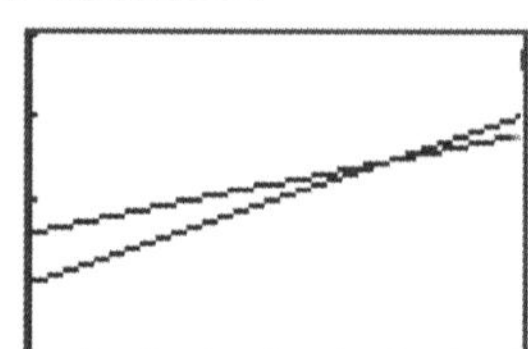

Step 3
Determine the point of intersection, and use this to solve the problem.

Press [2nd] [TRACE], and choose 5:intersect.

For "First curve?," position the cursor just left or right of the intersection point, and press [ENTER].

For "Second curve?," position the cursor just left or right of the intersection point, and press [ENTER].

For "Guess," press [ENTER].

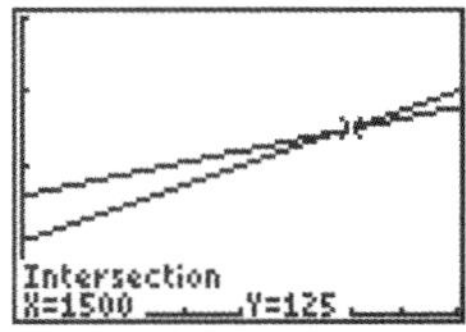

The point of intersection is (1,500, 125).
This means that after driving 1,500 km, plan A and plan B will both cost $125. Therefore, plan B is more economical if the car is driven more than 1,500 km in one week.

EXERCISE #1—LINEAR EQUATIONS

Use the following information to answer the next question.

Shefali is asked to solve the system of equations $5.6x + 2y = 12.9$ and $3x - 7.5y - 25.4 = 0$. Upon analysis of the system of equations, she decides to solve it with her graphing calculator.

88. In the solution to the system of the equations, what is the value of x to the nearest hundredth? __________

89. One line has a slope of $-\frac{3}{2}$ and a y-intercept of 6. A second line, drawn on the same coordinate grid, has a slope of $-\frac{1}{2}$ and a y-intercept of 0. Which of the following coordinates is the intersection point between the two lines?

A. (−3, −6) **B.** (−2, −5)
C. (5, −2) **D.** (6, −3)

Use the following information to answer the next question.

A system of linear equations is given.
$\frac{1}{2}x - 3y = -1$
$2x - 5y = 10$

90. Solve using the method of substitution.

Use the following information to answer the next question.

The ordered pair (x, y) is the solution to the system of linear equations $4x - 3y = 10$ and $-5x + 7y = -32$. The teacher instructs the class to solve the system using elimination.

91. For the given system of equations, the value of y is

A. −6 **B.** $-\frac{2}{3}$
C. $\frac{2}{3}$ **D.** 6

Use the following information to answer the next question.

One train leaves a station heading east. A second train, heading west, leaves the same station two hours later at an average of 10 km/h faster than the first train. The trains are 890 km apart 4 h after the second train departed.

92. What is the average speed of the train heading west?

A. 85 km/h **B.** 87 km/h
C. 92 km/h **D.** 95 km/h

Use the following information to answer the next question.

Kenya and Maria are going to run a race, but Maria would like a head start because Kenya is quite fast. Kenya runs 6 m in 1 s, while Maria runs 4 m in 1 s. Kenya offers to give Maria a 100-meter head start.

93. How long will it take Kenya to run the same distance as Maria?

A. 10 s **B.** 50 s
C. 140 s **D.** 300 s

EXERCISE #1—LINEAR EQUATIONS ANSWERS AND SOLUTIONS

88. 3.07	90. See solution	92. D
89. D	91. A	93. B

88. 3.07

Step 1
Re-write both equations in terms of y.

$$5.6x + 2y = 12.9$$
$$2y = -5.6x + 12.9$$
$$y = -\frac{5.6}{2}x + \frac{12.9}{2}$$

$$3x - 7.5y = 25.4$$
$$-7.5y = -3x + 25.4$$
$$y = \frac{3}{7.5}x - \frac{25.4}{7.5}$$

Step 2
Use a TI–83 graphing calculator to graph the system of equations.

- Press [y=].
- Type $y_1 = -\frac{5.6}{2}x + \frac{12.9}{2}$.
- Type $y_2 = \frac{3}{7.5}x - \frac{25.4}{7.5}$.

Step 3
Use [2nd] [CALC] [5:intersect] to determine the point of intersection.

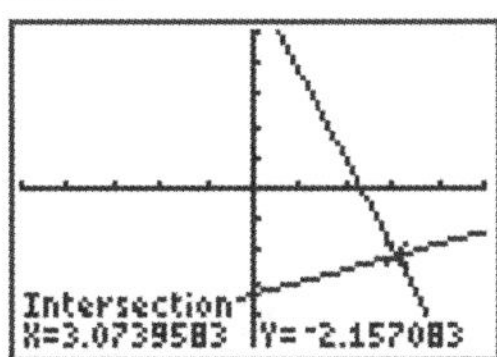

Window setting: x:[−5, 5, 1] y:[−5, 5, 1]
The graph shows that the point of intersection is exactly at $x = 3.0739583$, $y = -2.157083$.
Therefore, in the solution to the system of equations, the value of x, rounded to the nearest hundredth, is 3.07.

89. D

Step 1
Graph each of the given lines on the same coordinate system.
Each line can be drawn by using the slope (recall that slope is equal to $\frac{\text{rise}}{\text{run}}$) and the y-intercept.
The following graph shows the two lines on the same coordinate system.

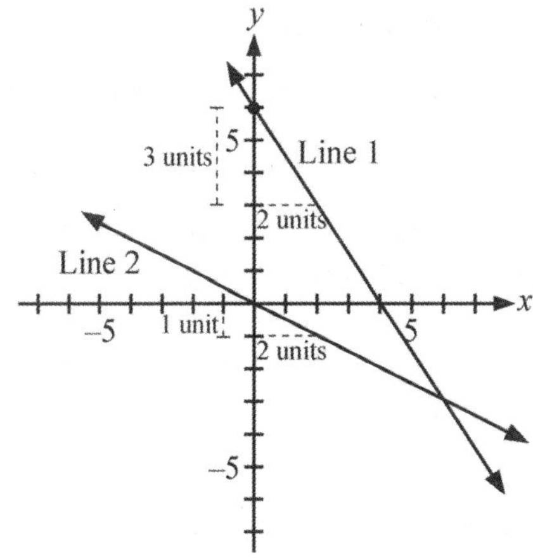

Step 2
Determine where the two lines intersect.
The two lines intersect at the ordered pair (6, −3).

90.

Step 1
Label the equations.

① $\frac{1}{2}x - 3y = -1$

② $2x - 5y = 10$

Step 2
Choose which variable to isolate.
In this solution, x has been chosen in equation 2.
Solve for x in terms of y.

$$2x - 5y = 10$$
$$2x = 10 + 5y$$
$$x = 5 + \frac{5}{2}y$$

Step 3

Substitute $5 + \frac{5}{2}y$ for x in equation 1.

$$\frac{1}{2}\left(5 + \frac{5}{2}y\right) - 3y = -1$$

Solve for y.

$$\begin{aligned}\frac{5}{2} + \frac{5}{4}y - 3y &= -1\\ 10 + 5y - 12y &= -4\\ -7y &= -10 - 4\\ -7y &= -14\\ y &= 2\end{aligned}$$

Step 4

Substitute $y = 2$ into one of the original equations. In this case, $y = 2$ has been substituted into equation 2.

$$\begin{aligned}2x - 5(2) &= 10\\ 2x - 10 &= 10\\ 2x &= 20\\ x &= 10\end{aligned}$$

State the solution in set notation.

$\{(10, 2)\}$

91. A

Step 1

Label the equations.

① $4x - 3y = 10$
② $-5x + 7y = -32$

Multiply both sides of equation 1 by 5 and both sides of equation 2 by 4.

③ $20x - 15y = 50$
④ $-20x + 28y = -128$

Step 2

Eliminate the x-terms from the two equations.

Add the two equations. Note that $20x + (-20x) = 0$.

$$\begin{aligned}&③\quad 20x - 15y = 50\\ &④\quad \underline{-20x + 28y = -128}\\ &\qquad\qquad 13y = -78\end{aligned}$$

Step 3

Solve for y.

$$\begin{aligned}13y &= -78\\ y &= -6\end{aligned}$$

92. D

The distance traveled by an object is equal to the rate (speed) of the object multiplied by the travel time.

Step 1

Assign a different variable to each of the unknown quantities.

- Let x represent the average speed of the train heading east.
- Let y represent the average speed of the train heading west.

Step 2

Set up a system of two linear equations that represents the information in the given problem.

The train heading west travels 10 km/h faster than the train heading east, which can be represented by the equation $y = x + 10$.

When the two trains are 890 km apart, the train heading east will have been traveling for 6 h, and the train heading west will have been traveling for 4 h.

Therefore, the distance traveled by the train heading east after 6 h can be represented by $x \times 6 = 6x$, and the distance traveled by the train heading east after 4 h can be represented by $y \times 4 = 4y$. Thus, $6x + 4y = 890$.

The resulting system of equations is as follows:

① $y = x + 10$
② $6x + 4y = 890$

Step 3

Solve the derived system of equations using the method of substitution.

Substitute $x + 10$ for y in equation 2, and solve for x.

$$\begin{aligned}6x + 4y &= 890\\ 6x + 4(x + 10) &= 890\\ 6x + 4x + 40 &= 890\\ 10x + 40 &= 890\\ 10x &= 850\\ x &= 85\end{aligned}$$

Solve for y by substituting 85 for x in the equation $y = x + 10$.

$$\begin{aligned}y &= x + 10\\ y &= (85) + 10\\ y &= 95\end{aligned}$$

Step 4

State the average speed of the train heading west (represented by y).

The average speed of the train heading west is 95 km/h.

93. B

Step 1

Determine the equations to represent the problem. Let D represent distance, and let x represent time.

- The total distance Kenya ran is given by the equation $D = 6x$.
- The total distance Maria ran is given by the equation $D = 4x + 100$.

Step 2
Graph the equations.

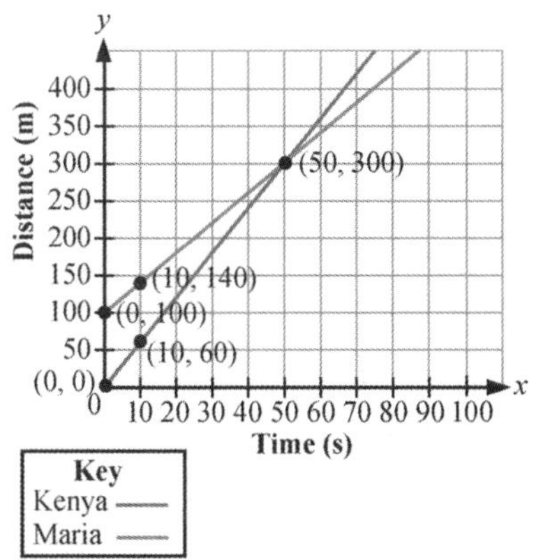

Step 3
Determine the point of intersection, and use this information to solve the problem.

The question asks for the amount of time it will take Kenya to run the same distance as Maria.

The intersection point is the ordered pair (50, 300).

At 50 s, both girls will be at the 300 m point on the track.

It will therefore take Kenya 50 s to run the same distance as Maria.

EXERCISE #2—LINEAR EQUATIONS

Use the following information to answer the next question.

Jasmine is asked to solve the system of equations $3.4x - 2.5y = 8.6$ and $2.7x + 4y = 20.9$. Upon analysis of the system of equations, Jasmine decides to solve it with her graphing calculator.

94. In the solution to the system of equations, what is the value of y to the nearest hundredth? __________

Use the following information to answer the next question.

Aelyn is asked to solve a linear system of equations. She uses a graphical approach to solve the given system. One of the equations that Aelyn graphs correctly is shown below.

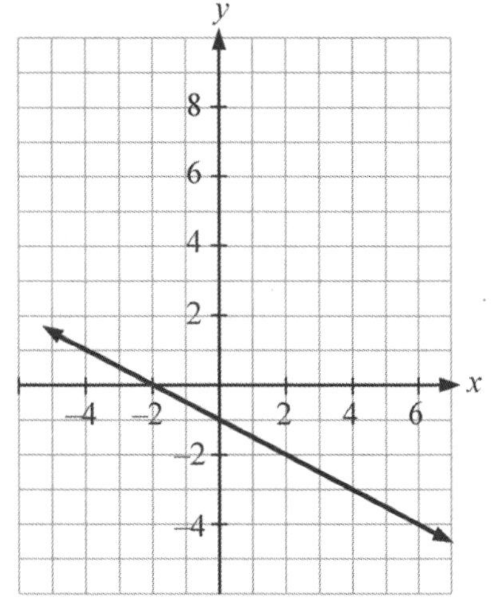

95. If the other equation in the system is $y = 2x + 9$, then the solution to the system is the point $(-a, b)$. The value of $a + b$ is __________.

Use the following information to answer the next question.

A system of linear equations is given.
$x + 2y = 7$
$2x - y = 9$

96. Using the method of substitution, solve this system algebraically.

97. Use the algebraic method of elimination to solve the following system:

$$\frac{x+6}{4} + \frac{y-3}{2} = 5$$
$$3x + y = 15$$

98. For a music concert, there was a total of 15,360 adult and student tickets sold. If there were fifteen times more student tickets than adult tickets sold, how many student tickets were sold?

A. 13,725 B. 13,800

C. 14,400 D. 14,475

Use the following information to answer the next question.

Holly and Heather want to rent a hall for a party. In their neighborhood, there are two halls they could rent. Hall A costs $100, plus an additional $5 per person. Hall B costs $45, plus an additional $10 per person.

99. What is the minimum number of guests that must attend the party in order for hall A to cost less than hall B?

A. 11 **B.** 12

C. 15 **D.** 16

EXERCISE #2—LINEAR EQUATIONS ANSWERS AND SOLUTIONS

94. 2.35	96. See solution	98. C
95. 5	97. See solution	99. B

94. 2.35

Step 1
Re-write both equations in terms of y.

$3.4x - 2.5y = 8.6$
$-2.5y = -3.4x + 8.6$
$y = \frac{3.4}{2.5}x - \frac{8.6}{2.5}$

$2.7x + 4y = 20.9$
$4y = -2.7x + 20.9$
$y = -\frac{2.7}{4}x + \frac{20.9}{4}$

Step 2
Use a TI–83 graphing calculator to graph the system of equations.

- Press $\boxed{y=}$.
- Type $y_1 = \frac{3.4}{2.5}x - \frac{8.6}{2.5}$.
- Type $y_2 = -\frac{2.7}{4}x + \frac{20.9}{4}$.

Step 3
Use $\boxed{\text{2nd}}\boxed{\text{CALC}}\boxed{\text{5:intersect}}$ to determine the point of intersection.

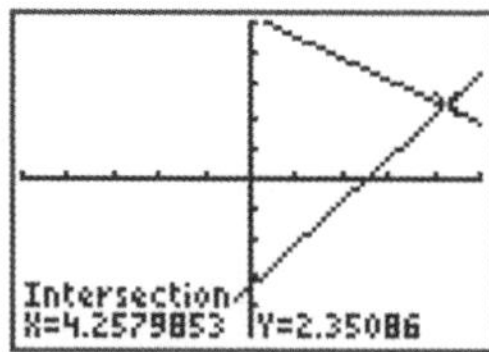

Window setting: x:[−5, 5, 1] y:[−5, 5, 1]
The graph shows that the point of intersection is at exactly $x = 4.2579853$, $y = 2.35086$.
Therefore, in the solution to the system of equations, the value of y, rounded to the nearest hundredth, is 2.35.

95. 5

The equation is given in slope y-intercept form $y = mx + b$.

Use the y-intercept to plot (0, 9). Use the slope (2) to determine the second and third points, such as (−1, 7) and (−2, 5). Join the points and extend the line through that of the first equation.

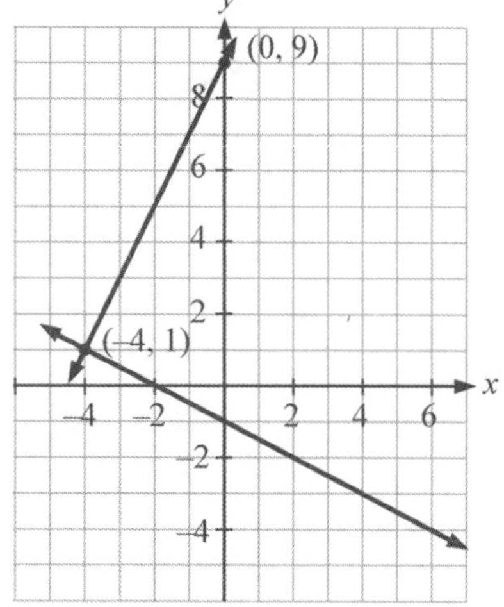

The intersection point or solution is (−4, 1).

Therefore, the value of $a + b$ is 4 + 1 = 5.

96.

Step 1
Label each equation.

① $x + 2y = 7$
② $2x - y = 9$

Choose which variable is to be isolated. In this solution, x can be chosen in equation 1.
Solve for x in terms of y by subtracting $2y$ from both sides of equation 1.

① → $x = 7 - 2y$

Step 2
Substitute $7 - 2y$ for x in equation 2, and solve for y.

$2(7 - 2y) - y = 9$
$14 - 4y - y = 9$
$14 - 5y = 9$
$-5y = -5$
$y = 1$

Step 3
Substitute $y = 1$ into one of the original equations. Use equation 1 in this case.

$$x + 2(1) = 7$$
$$x + 2 = 7$$
$$x = 5$$

Write the solution in set notation.
$\{(5, 1)\}$

97.

Step 1
Label the equations.

$$① \rightarrow \frac{x+6}{4} + \frac{y-3}{2} = 5$$
$$② \rightarrow 3x + y = 15$$

Step 2
Rewrite equation 1 in standard form by multiplying the equation by the lowest common denominator (LCD) of 4. Label the new equation as 3.

$$(x+6) + 2(y-3) = 20$$
$$x + 6 + 2y - 6 = 20$$
$$x + 2y = 20 \rightarrow ③$$

Step 3
Choose which variable to eliminate. In this solution, x will be eliminated.

Multiply equation 3 by 3, and then subtract to solve for y.

$$③ \times 3 \rightarrow 3x + 6y = 60$$
$$② \rightarrow \underline{3x + y \quad = 15}$$
$$5y = 45$$
$$y = 9$$

Step 4
Substitute $y = 9$ into one of the original equations.
Use equation 2 in this case.

$$3x + 9 = 15$$
$$3x = 15 - 9$$
$$3x = 6$$
$$x = 2$$

Write the solution in set notation.
$\{(2, 9)\}$

98. C

Step 1
Assign a different variable to each of the unknown quantities. The unknown quantities are the number of adult tickets sold and the number of student tickets sold.

Let x represent the number of adult tickets sold, and let y represent the number of student tickets sold.

Step 2
Set up a system of two linear equations that represents the information in the given problem.

The total number of adult and student tickets sold was 15,360, which can be represented by the equation $x + y = 15{,}360$.

The phrase "there were fifteen times more student tickets than adult tickets sold" implies that the number of student tickets sold is equal to the number of adult tickets sold, multiplied by 15. Thus, $y = 15x$.

The resulting system of equations is as follows:

$$① \quad x + y = 15{,}360$$
$$② \quad y = 15x$$

Step 3
Solve the derived system of equations using an algebraic procedure.

Solve using the method of substitution.

$$① \quad x + y = 15{,}360$$
$$② \quad y = 15x$$

Substitute $15x$ for y in equation 1, and solve for x.

$$x + y = 15{,}360$$
$$x + (15x) = 15{,}360$$
$$16x = 15{,}360$$
$$x = 960$$

Solve for y by substituting 960 for x in the equation $y = 15x$.

$$y = 15x$$
$$y = 15(960)$$
$$y = 14{,}400$$

Step 4
State the number of student tickets sold (represented by y).

There were 14,400 student tickets sold.

99. B

Step 1
Determine the equations to represent the problem.

Let C represent the total cost to rent the hall. Let n represent the number of people attending the party.

$$C_{\text{Hall A}} = 100 + 5n$$
$$C_{\text{Hall B}} = 45 + 10n$$

Step 2

Graph the equations.

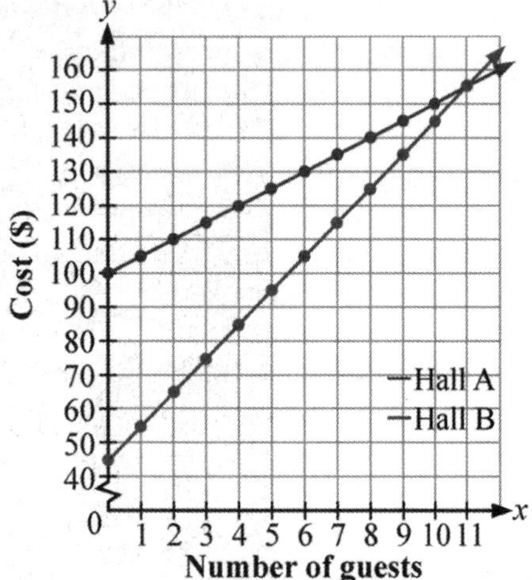

Step 3

Find the point of intersection, and use this to solve the problem.

The intersection point is the ordered pair (11, 155). This means that if 11 people attend the party, Holly and Heather can rent either hall for the same price. Therefore, at least 12 people must attend the party in order for hall A to cost less than hall B.

Graphic Equations and Inequalities

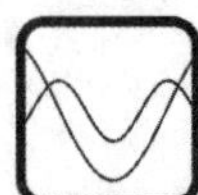

GRAPHIC EQUATIONS AND INEQUALITIES

Table of Correlations				
Standard		**Concepts**	**Exercise #1**	**Exercise #2**
Unit2.4	Represent and solve equations and inequalities graphically			
A-REI.10i	*Understand that the graph of an equation in two variables is the set of all its solutions plotted in the coordinate plane, often forming a curve (which could be a line).*	Determining the Reasonableness of Solutions to Linear Equations	44	62
		Graphing Exponential Relations and Defining Them as Functions	100	105
		Graphing a Linear Function Using a Graphing Calculator	101	106
A-REI.11ii	*Explain why the x-coordinates of the points where the graphs of the equations y = f(x) and y = g(x) intersect are the solutions of the equation f(x) = g(x); find the solutions approximately.*	Graphing a Linear Function Using a Graphing Calculator	101	106
		Solving Quadratic Equations Using Technology	102	107
A-REI.12	*Graph the solutions to a linear inequality in two variables as a half-plane (excluding the boundary in the case of a strict inequality), and graph the solution set to a system of linear inequalities in two variables as the intersection of the corresponding half-planes.*	Solving a System of Two Linear Inequalities in Two Variables	103	108
		Graphing Solutions to Linear Inequalities in Two Variables	104	109

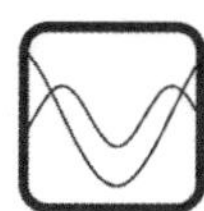

A-REI.10i Understand that the graph of an equation in two variables is the set of all its solutions plotted in the coordinate plane, often forming a curve (which could be a line).

Graphing Exponential Relations and Defining Them as Functions

An exponential relation is given as $y = a^x$, where $a > 0$ and $a \neq 1$. These relations can be graphed for different base values, a, by hand or with the use of a graphing calculator.

Example

Draw a sketch of the relation $y = 2^x$, and examine the graph on your graphing calculator.

x	-2	-1	0	1	2
y	$\frac{1}{4}$	$\frac{1}{2}$	1	2	4

Solution

To sketch $y = 2^x$, substitute values for x to define values of y in a table of values.

To graph $y = 2^x$ on your graphing calculator, follow these steps:

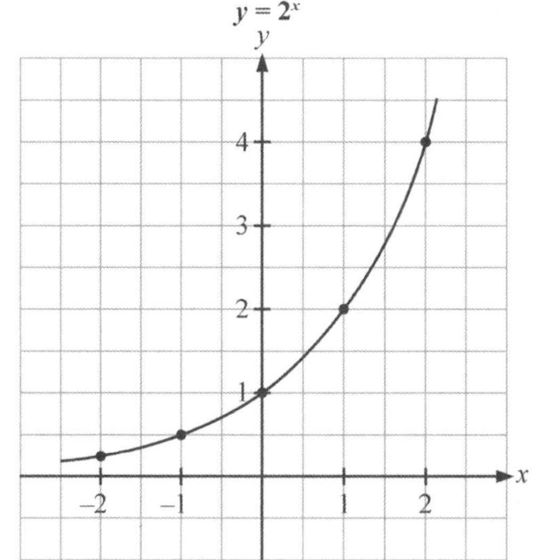

1. Set your WINDOW as x:[−3, 3, 1], y:[−2, 6, 1].
2. Enter the equation into [Y_1 =] as follows:
   $Y_1 = 2^\wedge x$
3. Press GRAPH to see the following screen.

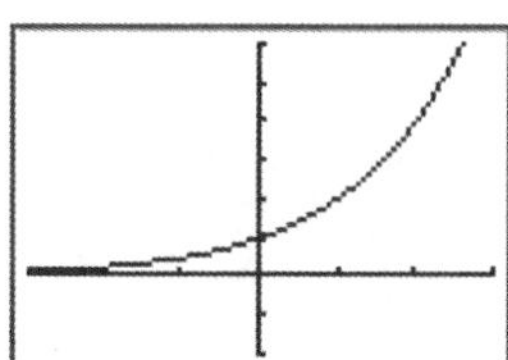

The relation $y = 2^x$ is a function and can be written as $f(x) = 2^x$ based on the following reasons:

- For every x-value in the table or on the graph, there is only one corresponding y-value.
  Note: This can be observed by tracing along your graph on your graphing calculator using the TRACE feature.
- If a vertical line ($x = a$, where $a \in \mathbb{R}$) were to be drawn through any place on the graph, it would only pass through a single point.

Therefore, it can be concluded that the relation $y = a^x$, where $a > 0$ and $a \neq 1$, is also a function and can be written as $f(x) = a^x$.

Graphing a Linear Function Using a Graphing Calculator

A graphing calculator will display the graph of a given equation and is a convenient device for graphing a linear function. There is a definite procedure to use to effectively graph a linear function from an equation.

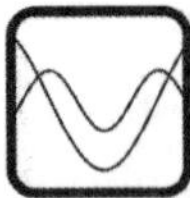

Use the following procedure to graph the equation $y = 5x - 3$.

First, clear the STAT PLOT to make sure there is no data in the lists, and turn the STAT PLOT function off.

[2nd] [Y =] Select Off using the cursor.

[ENTER]

Next, press [Y =], and clear any equations that might be present. Type the equation into Y_1. Use the key [x, t, θ, n] for x.

```
Plot1 Plot2 Plot3
\Y1=5X-3
\Y2=
\Y3=
\Y4=
\Y5=
\Y6=
\Y7=
```

Then, set the window size by pressing [WINDOW].

The following settings are for the standard window:

- **Xmin = –10** is the lowest value of x.
- **Xmax = 10** is the highest value of x.
- **Xscl = 1** is the value of each tick on the x-axis.
- **Ymin = –10** is the lowest value of y.
- **Ymax = 10** is the highest value of y.
- **Yscl = 1** is the value of each tick on the y-axis.

This is the view of the screen.

```
WINDOW
 Xmin=-10
 Xmax=10
 Xscl=1
 Ymin=-10
 Ymax=10
 Yscl=1
 Xres=1
```

Once each parameter is set, press [ENTER] for the calculator to acknowledge the new data.

Finally, press [GRAPH] to view the graph.

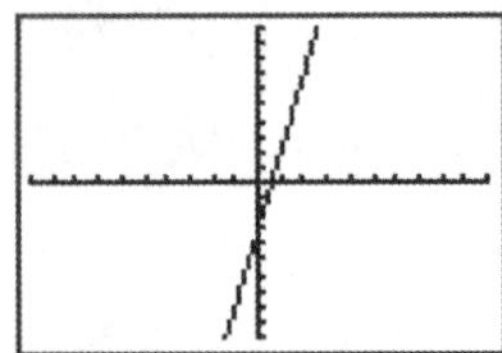

Note that any values can be entered for the window scale, depending on the type of function being graphed.

Other Function Options

The TABLE function gives the table of values that corresponds to the function entered in [Y =] and the displayed graph. To use the TABLE function, press [2nd] [GRAPH]. Once in the table of values screen, any ordered pair can be located.

To change the interval of the x-values in the table of values that the table starts with and the increments that the x-values increase by, press [2nd] [WINDOW] to change the table of values as required.

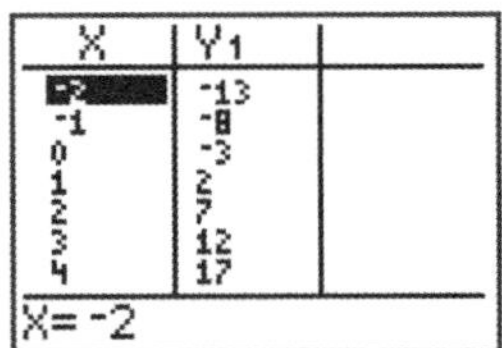

X	Y1
-2	-13
-1	-8
0	-3
1	2
2	7
3	12
4	17

X= -2

To use the TRACE function on a graphing calculator, press [TRACE]. A cursor that indicates the x- and y-coordinates for a particular point is displayed. Press the arrows left and right to move the cursor. At the bottom of the screen, x and y indicate the ordered pair for the point.

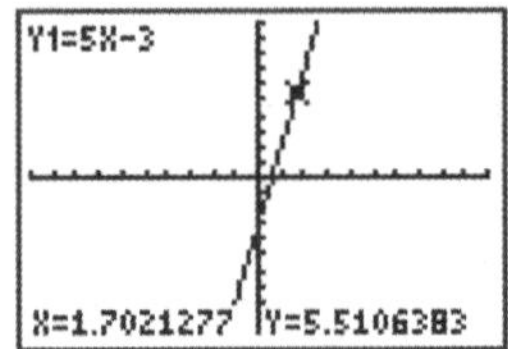

In some situations, it is necessary to change the [WINDOW] settings to get a better view of the graph.

Sometimes, the equations or graphs are not given in terms of y. To enter an equation into the Y = screen, the equation needs to be in terms of y. In other words, y must be isolated on one side of the equal sign. If the equation is not in that format, manipulate the equation so it is expressed in terms of y. Remember to do the same operation to both sides of the equation.

Use the following procedure to graph the equation $y + x = 3$ and fill in the table shown.

x	y
2	
1	
0	
−1	
−2	

Rearrange the equation to isolate the y-variable.

$$y + x = 3$$
$$y + x - x = 3 - x$$
$$y = 3 - x$$

The equation $y = 3 - x$ can now be entered into the calculator.

Enter the equation into Y = .

```
Plot1 Plot2 Plot3
\Y1■3-X
\Y2=
\Y3=
\Y4=
\Y5=
\Y6=
\Y7=
```

Set the window to the default setting.

```
WINDOW
 Xmin=-10
 Xmax=10
 Xscl=1
 Ymin=-10
 Ymax=10
 Yscl=1
 Xres=1
```

Press GRAPH. The graph of the equation should be similar to the one shown.

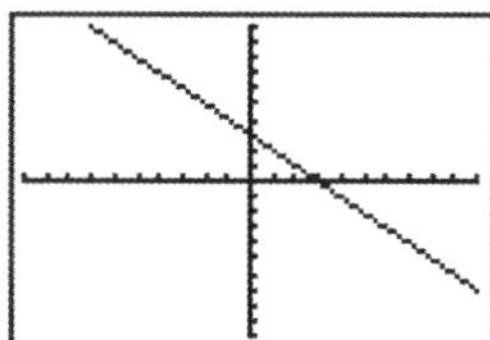

Use the table feature to compare the table of values.

```
X   | Y1
-3  | 6
-2  | 5
-1  | 4
0   | 3
1   | 2
2   | 1
3   | 0
X=-3
```

Fill in the table.

x	y
2	1
1	2
0	3
−1	4
−2	5

Example

A charitable organization organizes a dinner party to raise money for their cause. The net profit from the party is related to the number of people who attend. The equation that represents this relationship is $P = 20n - 500$, where n is the number of people attending and P is the net profit, in dollars.

Graph this equation using a graphing calculator, and use the graph to determine the profit earned when 1,000 people attend the party.

Solution

Remember that in real-life settings, values such as time, distance, and number of people cannot be negative. Therefore, the window setting should reflect this in the x-values. At the same time, profit may be negative representing a loss (y-values may be negative and positive).

Rewrite the equation in terms of x and y.
$y = 20x - 500$

Enter the equation into Y = .

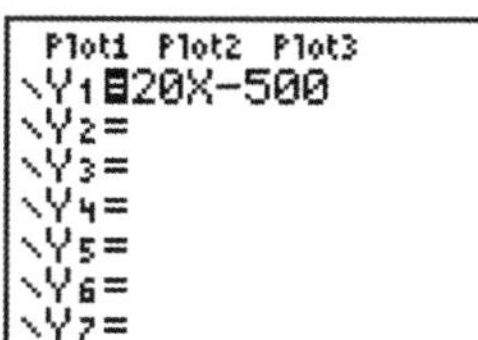

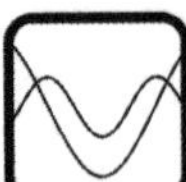

Adjust the window to view the graph. This may require a few adjustments. If necessary, use the TABLE feature for assistance in determining the window settings.

The Xscl and Yscl should be adjusted if the difference between the maximum and minimum settings is a large number. A possible window setting for the equation $y = 20x - 500$ is shown.

```
WINDOW
 Xmin=0
 Xmax=50
 Xscl=10
 Ymin=-500
 Ymax=600
 Yscl=100
 Xres=1
```

The graph of the equation $y = 20x - 500$ should be similar to this graph.

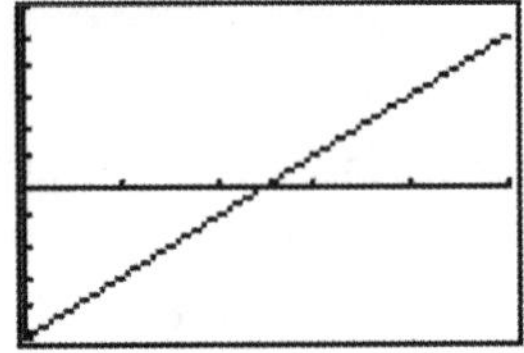

The graph shows that in order for the charitable organization to break even (when net profit is \$0), 25 people must attend the party (the value of x is 25 when $y = 0$).

To find out how many people must attend the party in order for the organization to have a profit of \$1,000, select the table feature and scroll up or down the table until you reach the y-value of 1,000 and then determine the corresponding value for x.

A profit of \$1,000 would be made if 75 people attended the party.

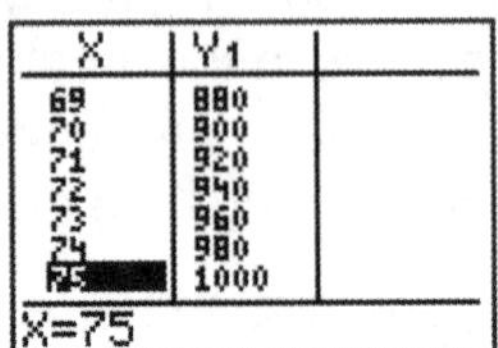

X	Y1
69	880
70	900
71	920
72	940
73	960
74	980
75	1000

X=75

A-REI.11ii Explain why the x-coordinates of the points where the graphs of the equations y = f(x) and y = g(x) intersect are the solutions of the equation f(x) = g(x); find the solutions approximately.

Solving Quadratic Equations Using Technology

Quadratic equations in the form of $0 = ax^2 + bx + c$, in which a, b, and c are real numbers and $a \neq 0$, can be solved using technology.

One technique is to graph the function $y = ax^2 + bx + c$ with a graphing calculator and then find the x-intercepts.

Example

Solve the quadratic equation $0 = x^2 - 4$ using a graphing calculator.

Solution

Step 1

Graph the corresponding quadratic function for the given equation using technology.

The corresponding quadratic function for the quadratic equation $0 = x^2 - 4$ is $y = x^2 - 4$ or $y = (x - 0)^2 - 4$.

The graph of this quadratic function is a parabola that opens upward, and its vertex is at (0, −4).

Enter the function $y = x^2 - 4$ into the graphing utility of the TI-83+ calculator. Choose an appropriate window such as ZOOM | 6:ZStandard.

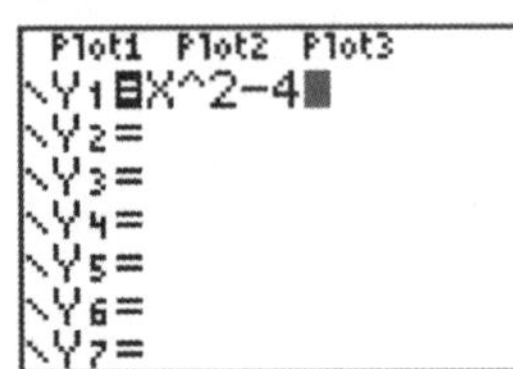

The graph created is similar to the one shown.

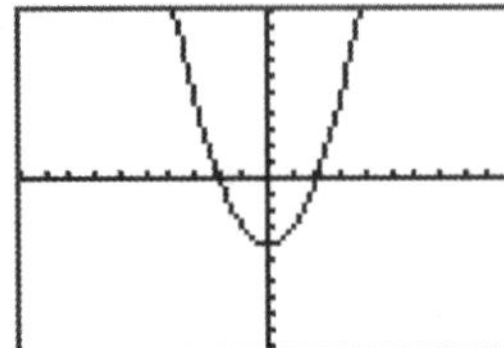

Step 2

Find the zeros of the quadratic function using technology.

The solutions, or roots, of the quadratic equation are the zeros of the corresponding quadratic function.

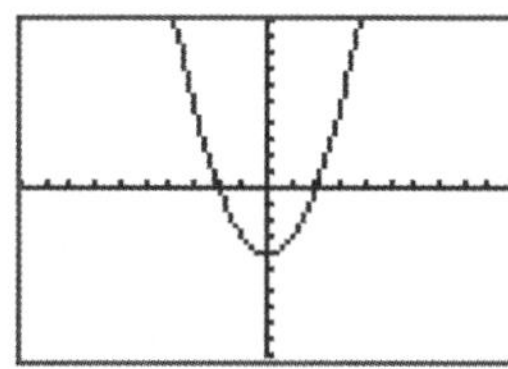

Press 2nd TRACE to enter the CALCULATE menu. Choose 2:zero, and press ENTER.

Move the cursor to the left of the zero when asked for a left bound, and press ENTER.

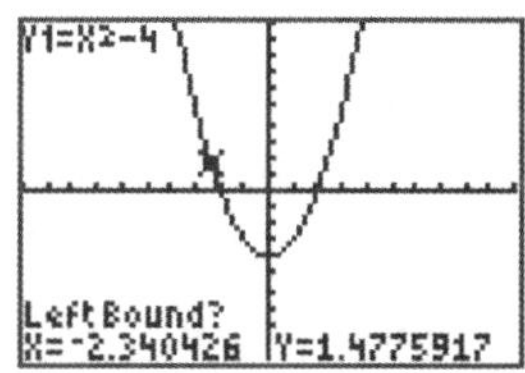

Move the cursor to the right of the zero when asked for a right bound, and press ENTER.

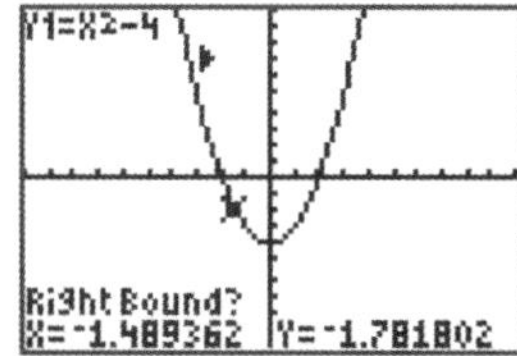

Press ENTER after the "Guess?" prompt.

Repeat the given procedure to determine the other zero.

The calculator will indicate that the x-intercepts of the graph, or zeros of the function, are $x = -2$ and $x = 2$.

The solutions to the given quadratic equation are $x = -2$ and $x = 2$.

Example

Using a graphing calculator, solve the equation $0 = x^2 + 4x - 21$.

Solution

Enter the equation in the TI-83+ graphing calculator's Y = window.

Access the CALC menu by pressing 2nd Trace. Choose 2:Zero to determine the x-intercepts of the graph (the zeros of the related function, $y = x^2 + 4x - 21$).

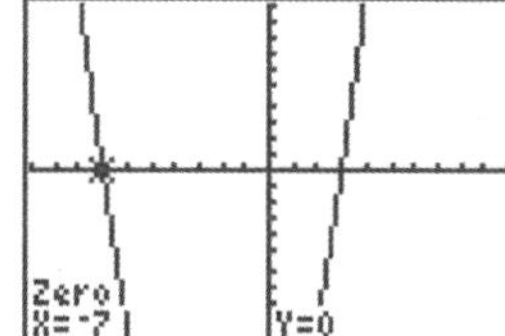

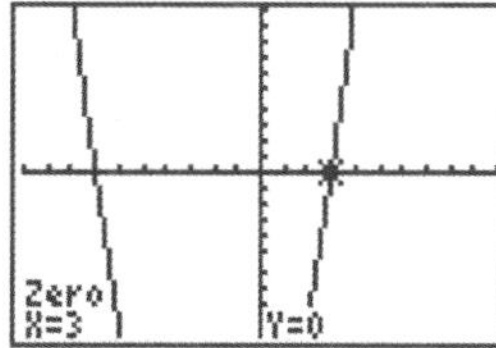

Using the ZERO feature, the x-intercepts, or zeros, are $x = 3$ and $x = -7$.

The solution to the equation $0 = x^2 + 4x - 21$ is $x = 3$ or $x = -7$.

When using a graphing calculator, solutions to quadratic equations can also be obtained by entering different parts of the equation as separate functions in the Y= feature of the graphing calculator.

Using this technique, it is not necessary to rewrite a quadratic equation in the form of $ax^2 + bx + c = 0$. Often, it is easier to enter two parts of an equation as two separate functions and determine the x-coordinates of their point or points of intersection.

Example

Enter $8x^2 + 4x - 3 = 0$ as two separate functions, and use a graphing calculator to solve the equations to the nearest hundredth.

Solution

Since $8x^2 + 4x - 3 = 0$ is equivalent to $8x^2 = -4x + 3$, one possibility is to enter the two functions, $Y_1 = 8x^2$ and $Y_2 = -4x + 3$, into the graphing utility. Then, find the *x*-coordinates of the points of intersection.

Adjust the window settings to x:$[-3, 3, 1]$ and y:$[-5, 10, 1]$ to obtain the graphs shown.

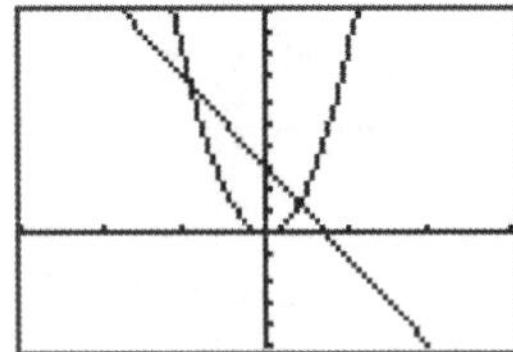

Using the graphing calculator feature 2nd | TRACE 5:Intersect, move the cursor to one point of intersection. Press ENTER three times. The result is the coordinates of that point of intersection of the two graphs.

The *x*-coordinate is one solution to the equation. Repeat this process for the second point of intersection to find the second solution value.

The solutions to the equation are $x \approx -0.91$ and $x \approx 0.41$.

Example

Use technology to solve $(3x - 5)(2x + 1) = 2x^2 - 7x$ to the nearest hundredth.

Solution

Instead of rewriting the equation to make one side equal to zero, enter the functions $Y_1 = (3x - 5)(2x + 1)$ and $Y_2 = 2x^2 - 7x$ into the graphing utility of a TI-83+ calculator. The *x*-values at the intersection points of the two graphs will be the solutions.

There are many appropriate window settings. The ones used here are x:$[-3, 3, 1]$, y:$[-10, 15, 1]$.

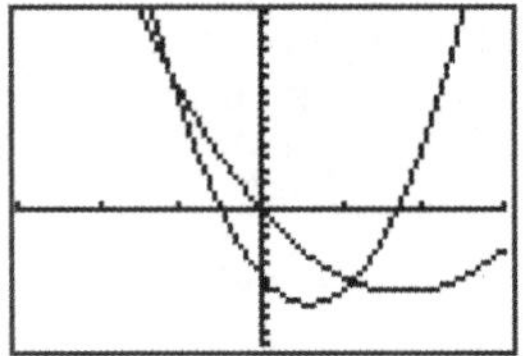

Using the graphing calculator feature 2nd | TRACE 5:Intersect, move the cursor to one point of intersection. Press ENTER three times. The result is the coordinates of that point of intersection of the two graphs.

The *x*-coordinate is one solution to the equation. Repeat this process for the second point of intersection to find the second solution value.

The solutions to the equation are $x \approx -1.12$ and $x \approx 1.12$.

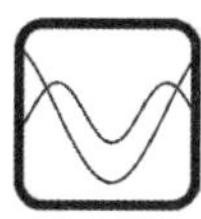

A-REI.12 Graph the solutions to a linear inequality in two variables as a half-plane (excluding the boundary in the case of a strict inequality), and graph the solution set to a system of linear inequalities in two variables as the intersection of the corresponding half-planes.

Solving a System of Two Linear Inequalities in Two Variables

Systems of linear inequalities are represented graphically by overlapping regions on a coordinate plane that have boundaries defined by linear equations. The overlapping region of a solution depends on the type of inequality.

For the inequality $y > mx + b$, the solution region is the half-plane above the boundary line $y = mx + b$.

For the inequality $y < mx + b$, the solution region is the half-plane below the boundary line $y = mx + b$. In these two cases, the boundary line is not part of the solution, and is denoted by a **dotted** line.
For the inequalities $y \geq mx + b$ and $y \leq mx + b$, the boundary line is included in the solution region, and is denoted by a **solid** line.

Example

Graph the solution region to the system of linear inequalities $y > 2x + 3$ and $y \leq -2x + 6$, where $y \geq 0$, and use a test point to verify the solution region.

Solution

Step 1
Graph the linear inequality $y > 2x + 3$, where $y \geq 0$.
The solution region is the half-plane above the boundary line $y = 2x + 3$. Since the boundary line is not part of the solution (y is greater than, but NOT equal to $2x + 3$), it is denoted by a dotted line.

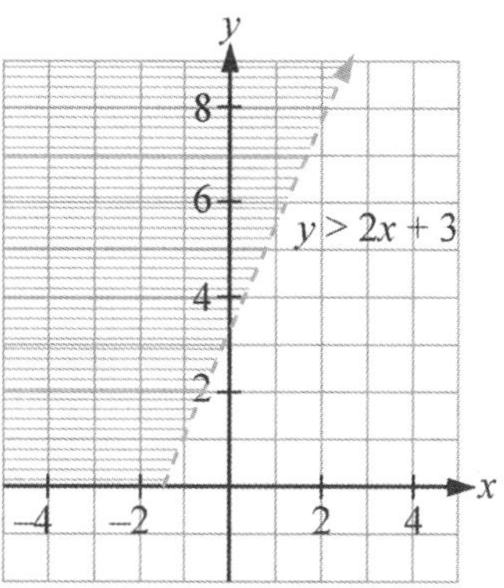

Step 2
On the same grid, graph the linear inequality $y \leq -2x + 6$, where $y \geq 0$.
Since the boundary line is part of the solution, it is denoted by a solid line.

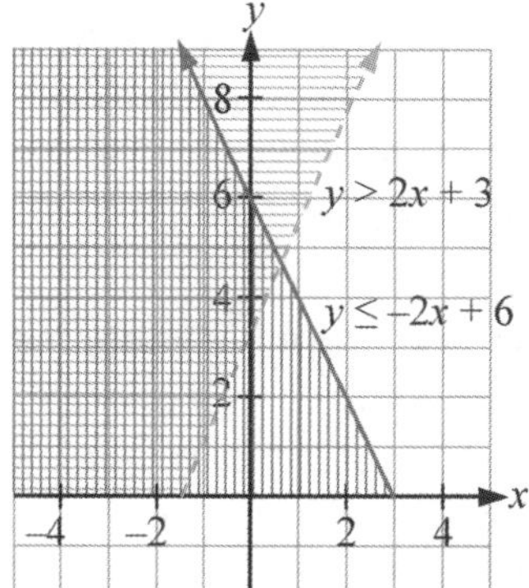

The solution is the shaded region where the two graphs overlap.

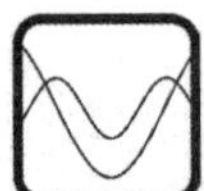

Step 3

Use a test point to verify the solution region. To choose a test point, select a point that appears to clearly lie within the overlapping shaded regions.

Test Point (0, 4)	Test Point (0, 4)
$y > 2x + 3$	$y \leq -2x + 6$
$4 > 2(0) + 3$	$4 \leq -2(0) + 6$
$4 > 3$, true	$4 < 6$, true

Graphing Solutions to Linear Inequalities in Two Variables

In a linear inequality, one side of the inequality is greater than or less than the other side of the inequality. In an equation, both sides of the equation are equal.

There are many solutions to a linear inequality, instead of one specific answer that is obtained from an equation. Since the solution to a linear inequality consists of a set of solutions, graphing the linear inequality shows where the solution set is located.

The graph always shows a **boundary line** corresponding to the inequality. The graph is shaded on one side of the boundary line to show the location of where the solution set lies.

If the inequality is $<$ or $>$, the boundary line is not part of the solution set, and is drawn as a dotted line. If the inequality is $\leq$ or $\geq$, then the boundary line is part of the solution set, and is drawn as a solid line.

When solving and graphing linear inequalities in two variables, use the same principles as solving and graphing equations, with one important difference—when both sides of an inequality are multiplied or divided by a **negative** number, the direction of the inequality sign is **reversed**.

Example

Fred and Andy decide to pool their money to buy a used motorcycle. The most they will pay for a motorcycle is $500.

If the amount of money that Fred contributes is represented by x and the amount of money Andy contributes is represented by y, then the amount of money they contribute together can be represented by the inequality $x + y \leq 500$. Graph this inequality.

Solution

The solution consists of all ordered pairs on the line $x + y = 500$, as well as ordered pairs that lie in the region bounded by $x + y = 500$, the x-axis, and the y-axis. Solutions are limited to positive values with two decimal places (dollars and cents).

The solution is all ordered pairs of numbers on the boundary line and in the shaded region.

The ordered pairs represent amounts of money that could be contributed by Fred (x-values) and Andy (y-values).

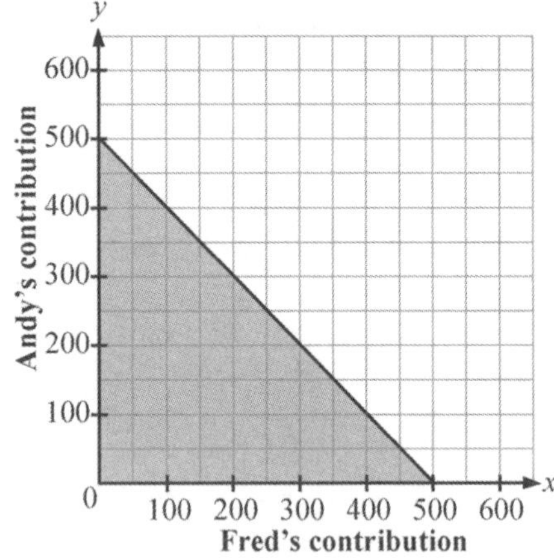

Techniques for Graphing Linear Inequalities in Two Variables

Using a Test Point

The boundary line splits the coordinate plane into two half planes. One method of knowing which half plane is the solution involves choosing a point that is not on the boundary line and testing to see if it satisfies the inequality. If the point does satisfy the inequality, then that region is the solution; if it does not satisfy the inequality, then the other region is the solution.

Often, the **origin**, or (0, 0), is a convenient point to test.

Example

Graph $3x - 2y > 24$.

Solution

The boundary line can be drawn by converting the inequality to an equality and determining the *x*- and *y*-intercepts. The *x*-intercept is 8, and the *y*-intercept is −12.

Use the origin (0, 0) as a test point.
$3(0) - 2(0) > 24$
$0 > 24$

This does not satisfy the inequality. This point is not in the solution, so the region on the other side of the boundary line is the solution and is shaded.

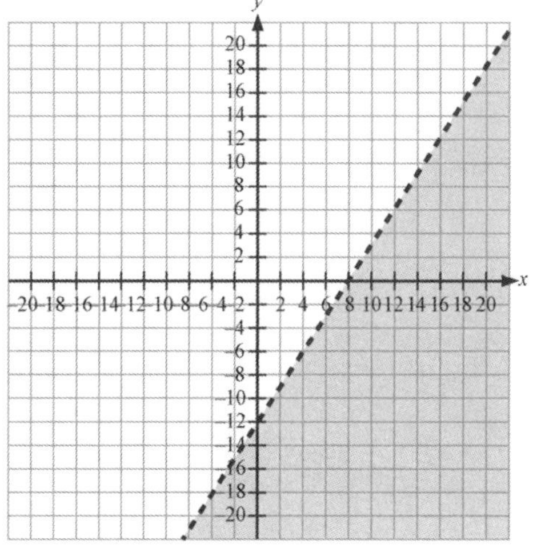

Isolating One Variable

If the equation is written with *y* isolated in the form $y >$ or $y \geq$, the region to be shaded is above the boundary line; if the form is $y <$ or $y \leq$, the region to be shaded is below the boundary line. Thus, the boundary line can be written as an equation in slope-intercept form to help determine the graph of the solution.

Example

Graph $\frac{1}{2}y \geq 3x - 5$.

Solution

$$\frac{1}{2}y \geq 3x - 5$$
$$y \geq 6x - 10$$

The boundary line is $y = 6x - 10$. This is in slope-intercept form, with a *y*-intercept of −10 and a slope of 6.

This boundary line is graphed as a solid line, and the region above is shaded.

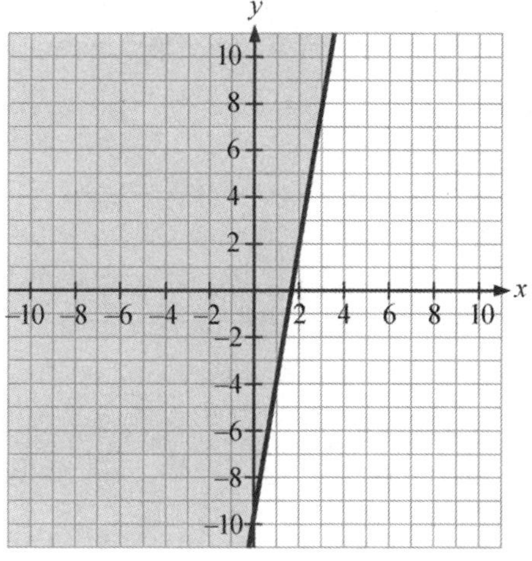

Using a Graphing Calculator

A graphing calculator, such as the TI-83, has a built-in feature that will shade the region above or below a boundary line.

Example

Use a graphing calculator to graph $6x + 3y < 9$.

Solution

Step 1

Rearrange the equation into $y < mx + b$ form.

$3y < -6x + 9$

$y < -2x + 3$

Step 2

Enter the equation of the boundary line into the graphing calculator as if it were a linear function (relation) in slope-intercept form.

$y = -2x + 3$

Step 3

Using the arrow keys, move the cursor to the left where the dotted line flashes.

Press ENTER three times or until the following image appears: .

Step 4

Press GRAPH.

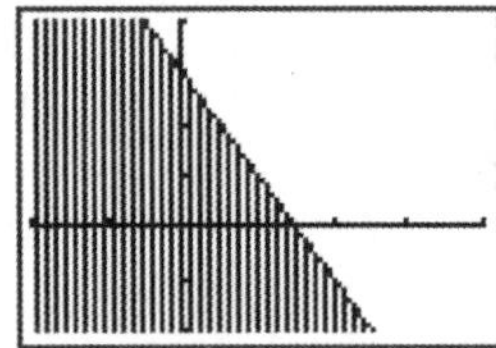

The graph of the solution is displayed; however, the calculator cannot distinguish between a solid or broken boundary line.

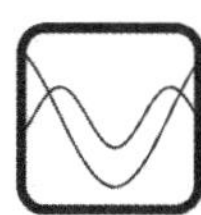

EXERCISE #1—GRAPHIC EQUATIONS AND INEQUALITIES

100. On the given grid, sketch and label the graphs of $f(x) = \left(\frac{1}{4}\right)^x$ and $g(x) = 4^x$.

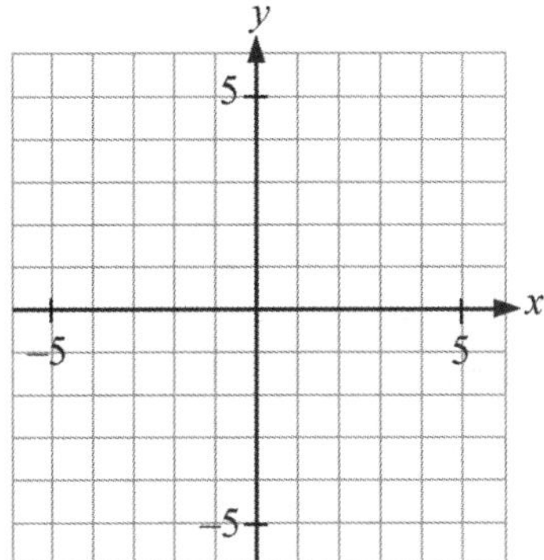

Use the following information to answer the next question.

A linear function has the equation $y = 2x + 4$.

101. Determine the x-intercept of the given function using the TABLE feature on a TI-83 calculator.

102. Using a graphing calculator, the solution to the quadratic equation $\frac{3}{2}(2 - x)\left(2x + \frac{1}{4}\right) = \frac{x}{6} + 2$, in which $x > 1$, expressed to the nearest hundredth, is

A. $x = 0.27$ **B.** $x = 1.55$

C. $x = 2.00$ **D.** $x = 2.26$

Use the following information to answer the next question.

A student is asked to graph the solution region to the system of linear inequalities $3x - 2y \leq 6$ and $5x + 4y + 20 \geq 0$.
The student's partial graph is given.

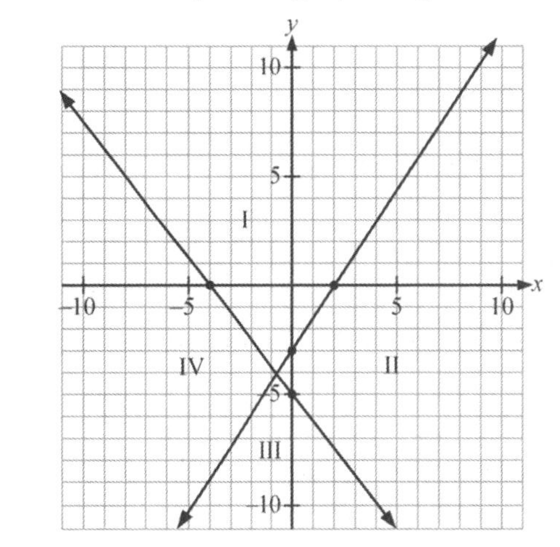

103. To correctly graph the solution region for the given system of linear inequalities, which region should the student shade?

A. I **B.** II

C. III **D.** IV

104. Use technology to graph the solution to the inequality $4x + 2y > 8$.

EXERCISE #1—GRAPHIC EQUATIONS AND INEQUALITIES ANSWERS AND SOLUTIONS

100. See solution	102. B	104. See solution
101. See solution	103. A	

100.

The graphs of $f(x) = \left(\frac{1}{4}\right)^x$ and $g(x) = 4^x$ are shown on the grid.

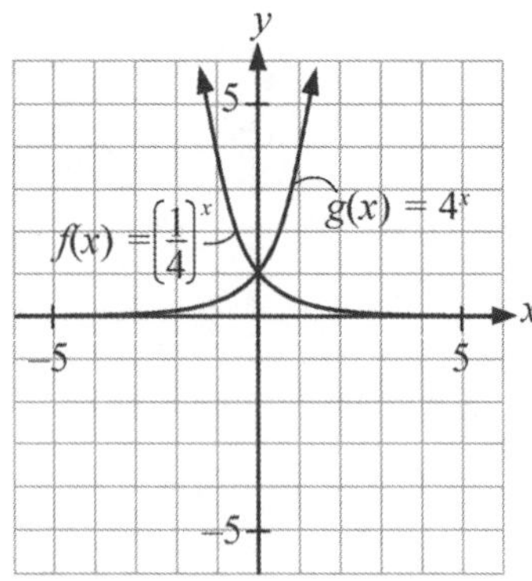

101.

Step 1
Enter the equation into the calculator.

Press Y =, and enter $2x + 4$ into Y_1.

Step 2
Determine the x-intercept using the TABLE feature.

Press 2nd GRAPH to access the TABLE menu.

Scroll down the X column to find the x-value when $y = 0$.

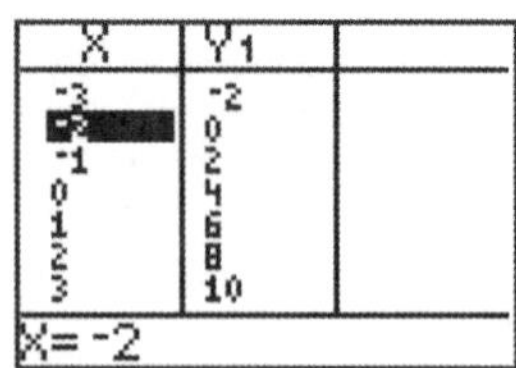

X	Y1
-3	-2
-2	0
-1	2
0	4
1	6
2	8
3	10

X= -2

According to the table, the x-intercept of the given function is −2.

Note that if you need to change the intervals of the x-coordinates shown in the table, press 2nd WINDOW to access the TABLE SETUP menu and type in the appropriate interval beside ΔTbl.

102. B

Step 1
Graph the corresponding quadratic functions for the given equation with a graphing calculator.

In this case, it is less work to graph two functions than to simplify the equation and graph one function.

The corresponding quadratic functions for the quadratic equation $\frac{3}{2}(2 - x)\left(2x + \frac{1}{4}\right) = \frac{x}{6} + 2$ are $Y_1 = \frac{3}{2}(2 - x)\left(2x + \frac{1}{4}\right)$ and $Y_2 = \frac{x}{6} + 2$.

Press Y= on the TI-83 Plus calculator, and enter the functions into the graphing utility.

Choose an appropriate window such as ZOOM 6:ZStandard.

Step 2
Find the x-value of the intersection point of the quadratic functions, when $x > 1$.

The solution to the quadratic equation is the intersection point of the corresponding quadratic functions.

Press 2nd TRACE to enter the CALCULATE menu, and choose 5:intersect, from the list.

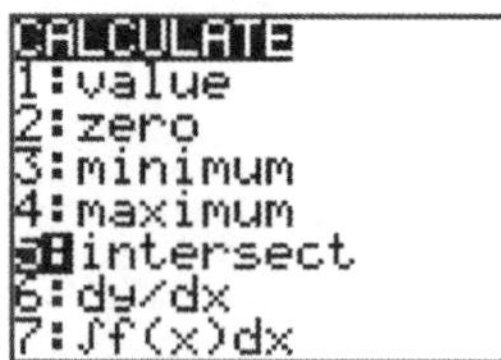

Since $x > 1$, find the intersection point on the right side of $x = 1$.

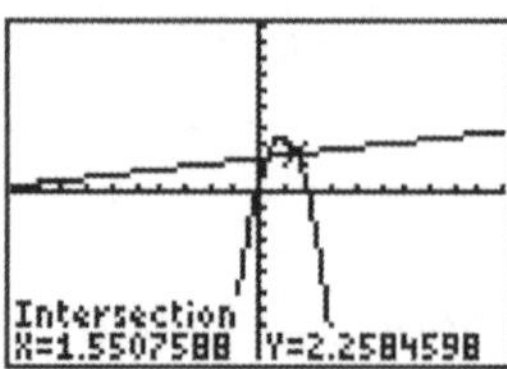

Move the cursor as close to the point of intersection as possible and press ENTER three times.

The calculator will indicate that the intersection point of the functions is approximately (1.55, 2.26).

Since it is the x-value that is needed, the solution is $x = 1.55$.

103. A

Step 1

An ordered pair located in the solution region of an inequality will satisfy the inequality.

Use point (0, 0) as a test point for each inequality.

Substitute the test point into the inequality $3x - 2y \leq 6$.

$3(0) - 2(0) \leq 6$
$0 \leq 6$

This inequality is true; the point satisfies the inequality.

The point (0, 0) is in the region that should be shaded. Therefore, the half-plane that includes regions I and IV should be shaded.

Substitute the test point into the inequality $5x + 4y + 20 \geq 0$.

$5(0) + 4(0) + 20 \geq 0$
$20 \geq 0$

The inequality is true; the point satisfies the inequality.

The point (0, 0) is in the region that should be shaded. Therefore, the half-plane that includes regions I and II has to be shaded.

Step 2

Identify the solution region.

The solution of a system of inequalities is the intersecting region of the solutions of the individual inequalities.

Because region I contains the point (0, 0) and is the region common to the solutions of the individual inequalities, region I is the solution region to the given system of linear inequalities.

104.

Step 1

Rewrite the given inequality in terms of *y*.

$$4x + 2y > 8$$
$$4x + 2y > 8 - 4x$$
$$2y > -4x + 8$$
$$\frac{2y}{2} > \frac{-4x + 8}{2}$$
$$y > -2x + 4$$

Step 2

Use a TI-83 or similar graphing calculator to graph the inequality.

- Press the ZOOM button, and select the 6:ZStandard to set the window setting.
- Press Y =, and enter in the equation $Y_1 = -2X + 4$.

Use the arrow keys to move the cursor to the left where the dotted line flashes. Press ENTER two times or until the following image appears: ◥.

Press GRAPH.

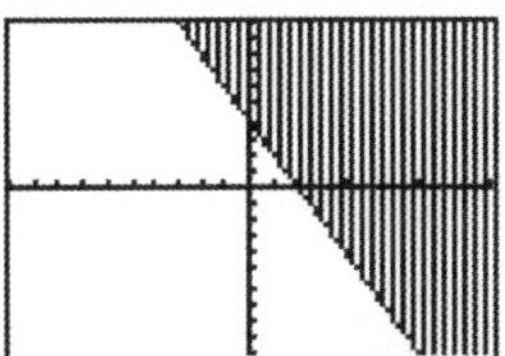

The graph of the solution is displayed; however, the calculator cannot distinguish between a solid or broken boundary line.

EXERCISE #2—GRAPHIC EQUATIONS AND INEQUALITIES

105. Which of the following statements correctly explains why $y = (15)^x$ can be written as the function $f(x) = (15)^x$?

A. When the line $y = x$ is drawn through any place on the graph, it passes through a single point.

B. When the line $y = -x$ is drawn through any place on the graph, it passes through a single point.

C. When the line $x = a,\ x \in \mathbb{R}$ is drawn through any place on the graph, it passes through a single point.

D. When the line $y = a,\ x \in \mathbb{R}$ is drawn through any place on the graph, it passes through a single point.

Use the following information to answer the next question.

A linear function has the equation $y - \frac{1}{5}x + 6x = 0$.

106. Determine the y-intercept of the given function using the TABLE feature of a TI-83 calculator.

107. Expressed to the nearest hundredth, the solution of the quadratic equation $2(x-2)(3x+1) = \frac{5x^2}{6} - 3x$, where $x > 0$, is

A. $x = .83$ B. $x = 1.79$

C. $x = 2.00$ D. $x = 3.60$

Use the following information to answer the next question.

A student is asked to graph the solution region to the system of linear inequalities $3x - 2y < 6$ and $4x + 5y + 20 \le 0$.
The student's partial graph is given.

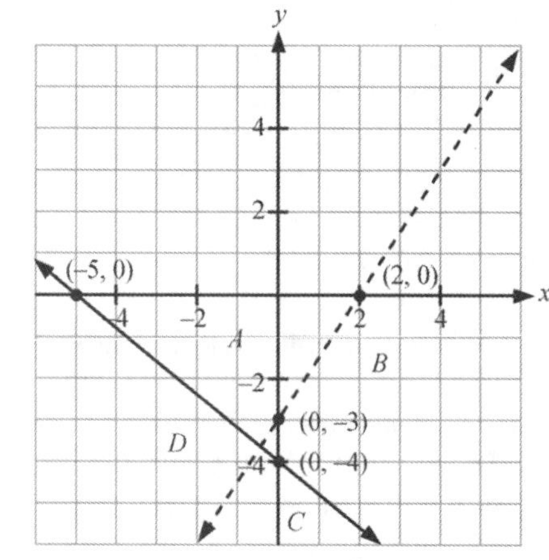

108. In order to correctly complete the graph of the solution region to the given system of linear inequalities, which region must the student shade in?

A. A B. B

C. C D. D

109. The solution set to the inequality $2y + 3x \le 10$ is **best** illustrated by which of the following graphs?

A.

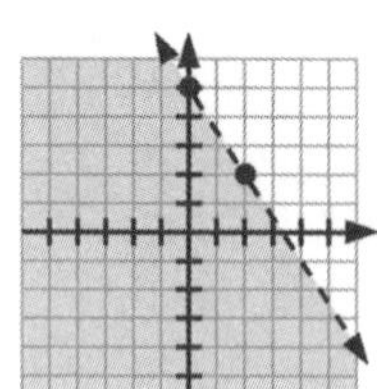

B.

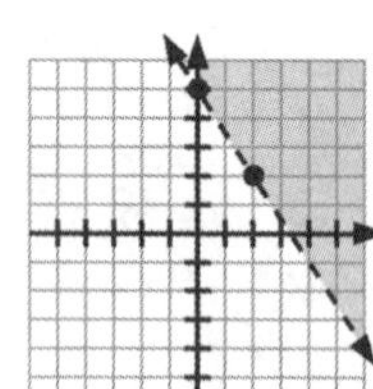

C.

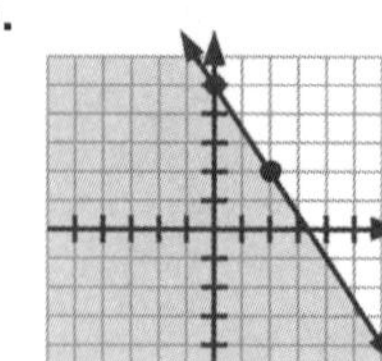

D.

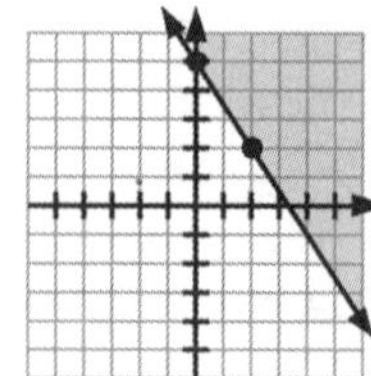

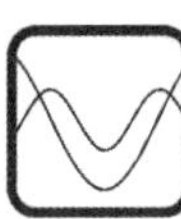

EXERCISE #2—GRAPHIC EQUATIONS AND INEQUALITIES ANSWERS AND SOLUTIONS

105. C	107. B	109. C
106. See solution	108. D	

105. C

To be a function, any vertical line, defined by $x = a$, that is drawn through any part of the graph, can only pass through a single point. Since the domain of the exponential relation $y = (15)^x$ is $x \in \mathbb{R}$, then $y = 15^x$ can be written as the function $f(x) = 15^x$, since every vertical line defined by $x = a$, $x \in \mathbb{R}$, will only pass through a single point.

106.

Step 1
Rewrite the given equation to isolate y.

$y = \frac{1}{5}x - 6x$

Step 2
On a TI-83 calculator, press [Y =], and then enter $\frac{1}{5}x - 6x$ into Y_1.

Step 3
Determine the y-intercept using the TABLE feature. Press [2nd] [GRAPH] to access the TABLE menu. Scroll down the X column to find when $x = 0$.

X	Y1	
-4	23.2	
-3	17.4	
-2	11.6	
-1	5.8	
0	0	
1	-5.8	
2	-11.6	

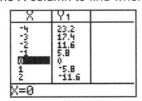

X=0

According to the table, the y-intercept of the given function is 0.

107. B

Step 1
Graph the corresponding quadratic functions for the given equation with a graphing calculator.

This is a situation where it is less work to graph two functions than to simplify the equation and graph one function.

The corresponding quadratic functions for the quadratic equation $2(x-2)(3x+1) = \frac{5x^2}{6} - 3x$ are

$y_1 = 2(x-2)(3x+1)$ and $y_2 = \frac{5x^2}{6} - 3x$.

Press [Y=], and enter the functions into the graphing utility.

Choose an appropriate window, such as [ZOOM] 6:ZStandard.

Step 2
Find the x-value of the intersection point of the quadratic functions when $x > 0$ using the calculator.

The solutions of the quadratic equation are the intersection points of the corresponding quadratic functions. Press [2nd] [TRACE] to enter the CALCULATE menu, choose 5:intersect, and press [ENTER].

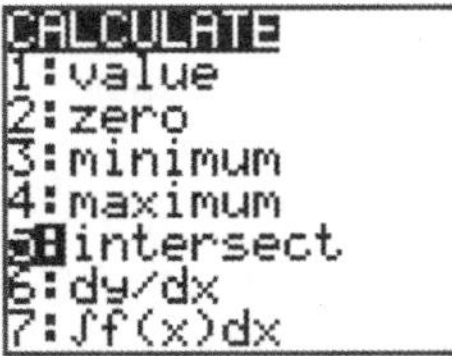

Since $x > 0$, find the intersection point on the right side of the y-axis. Move the cursor as close to the point of intersection as possible, and press [ENTER] three times.

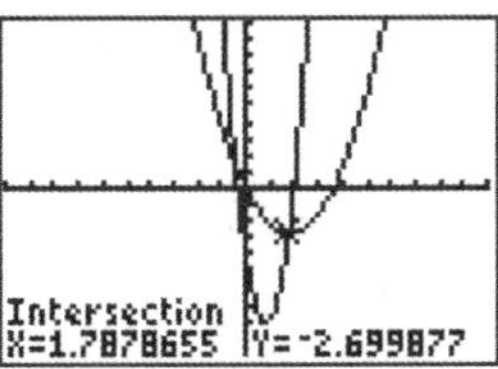

The calculator will indicate that the intersection point of the functions, to the nearest hundredth, is (1.79, −2.70). Since it is the x-value that is needed, the solution is $x = 1.79$.

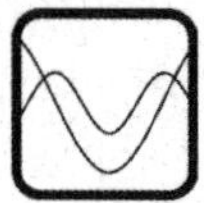

108. D

An ordered pair located in the solution region of an inequality will satisfy the inequality.

Step 1
Use (0, 0) as a test point in the inequality $3x - 2y < 6$.

$3(0) - 2(0) < 6$
$0 < 6$

The inequality is true, so the point satisfies the inequality.
Therefore, (0, 0) is in the region to be shaded. That is, the half-plane labeled A and D has to be shaded.

Step 2
Use (0, 0) as a test point in the inequality $4x + 5y + 20 \leq 0$.

$4(0) + 5(0) + 20 \leq 0$
$20 \leq 0$

The inequality is false, so the point does not satisfy the inequality.
Therefore, (0, 0) is not in the region to be shaded. That is, the other half-plane labeled D and C has to be shaded.
The solution of a system of inequalities is the intersection region of the solutions of individual inequalities.
Therefore, the solution region to the given system of linear inequalities is shown by shading in the region labeled D.

109. C

Step 1
Determine any two points on the boundary line $2y + 3x = 10$. These can be obtained by substituting two values for x in the equation and solving for the corresponding y-values.
Let $x = 0$ and $x = 2$. Substitute each into the equation to solve for the corresponding y-values.

$2y + 3(0) = 10$
$2y + 0 = 10$
$2y = 10$
$y = 5$

$2y + 3(2) = 10$
$2y + 6 = 10$
$2y = 4$
$y = 2$

The points (0, 5) and (2, 2) lie on the boundary line. Since the inequality has the symbol $\leq$, the boundary line is solid because the line itself is part of the solution region.

Step 2
Use (0, 0) as a test point. Substitute the point in the inequality to check whether the point lies in the solution region of the inequality.

$2(0) + 3(0) \leq 10$
$0 \leq 10$

The point satisfies the inequality. Therefore, the point (0, 0) lies in the solution region of the inequality, and thus the half plane that contains the point (0, 0) has to be shaded.
The solution to the inequality is represented by a solid boundary line, and the region below it shaded.

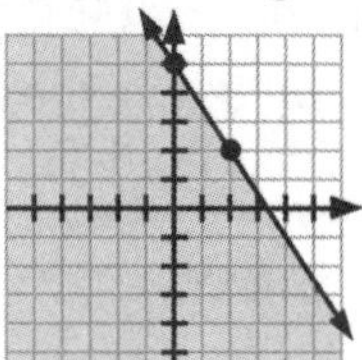

Functions

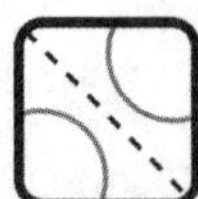

FUNCTIONS

Table of Correlations

Standard		Concepts	Exercise #1	Exercise #2
Unit2.5	Define, evaluate, and compare functions.			
8.F.1	*Understand that a function is a rule that assigns to each input exactly one output. The graph of a function is the set of ordered pairs consisting of an input and the corresponding output.*	Identifying a Function Using a Graph	110	120
		Identifying a Function Using a Table of Values	111	121
		Identifying a Function Using a Set of Ordered Pairs	112	122
		Identifying a Function from an Equation	113	123
		Identifying a Function from a Mapping Diagram	114	124
8.F.3	*Interpret the equation y = mx + b as defining a linear function, whose graph is a straight line; give examples of functions that are not linear.*	Graphing Linear and Non-Linear Data by Hand	115	126
		Determining the Characteristics of the Graph of a Linear Function	116	127
		Equations of Linear Relations versus Non-Linear Relations	118	125
		Defining Function Notation for a Linear Function in Two Variables	119	128
		Defining Equations in Slope-Intercept Form	117	129

8.F.1 Understand that a function is a rule that assigns to each input exactly one output. The graph of a function is the set of ordered pairs consisting of an input and the corresponding output.

Identifying a Function Using a Graph

Various graphs that you see can represent a relationship between two quantities.

The input is the independent variable (x), and the output is the dependent variable (y).

A **function** is a special type of relation in which each input has only one output.

Example

The relation in the given graph is a function because each input number has only one output number.

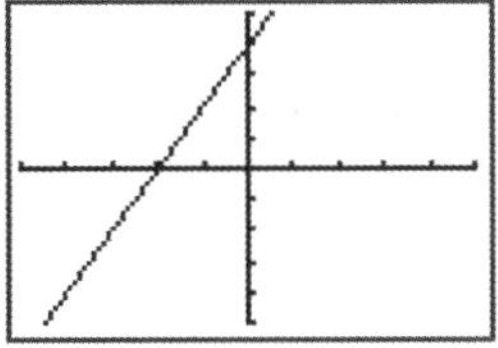

A **vertical line test** can be used to determine whether a relation defined by a graph is a function. If two points on the graph of a relation can be joined by a vertical line, the relation is not a function. If no two points on the graph can be can be joined by a vertical line, the relation is a function.

Example

This information can be used to determine whether or not each of the given graphs is a function.

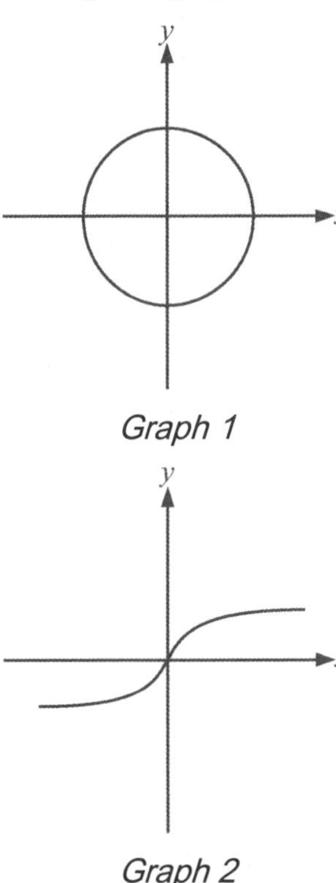

Graph 1

Graph 2

In the case of graph 1, the relation is not a function, since a vertical line will intersect the graph more than once, as shown in the given illustration.

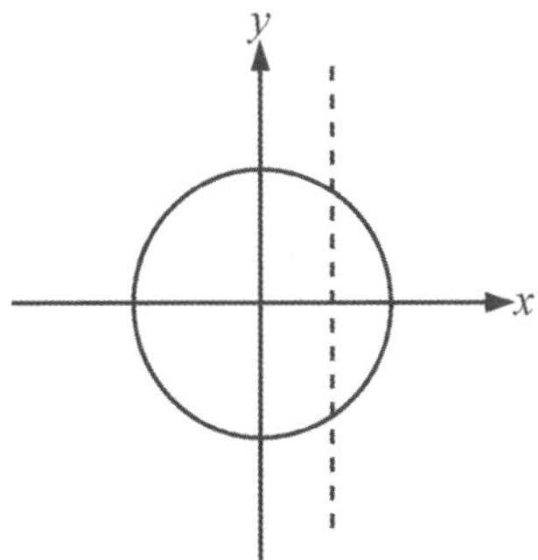

Graph 1 intersected by a vertical line

In the case of graph 2, the relation is a function because a vertical line will not intersect the graph more than once. This is illustrated in the given graph.

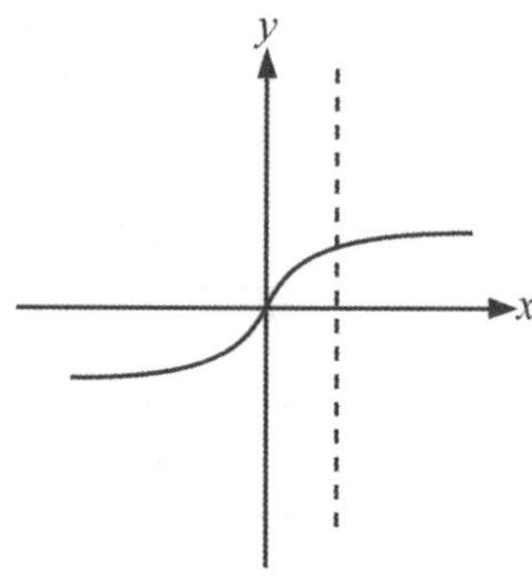

Graph 2 intersected by a vertical line

Example

Determine if the given linear graph is a function.

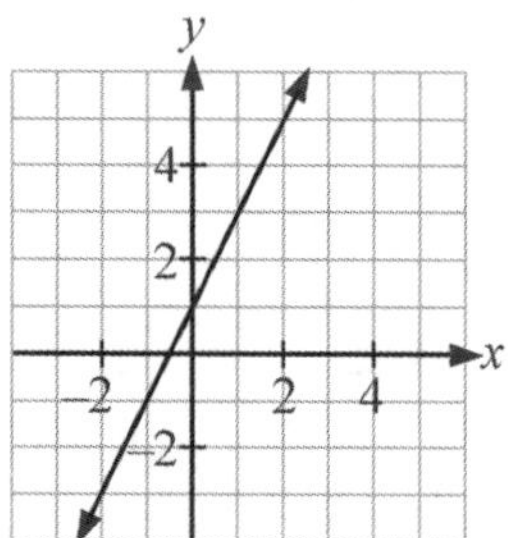

Solution

Use the vertical line test to determine if the given graph represents a function.

The vertical line test states that if a vertical line drawn anywhere on the graph crosses the graph more than once, that graph does not represent a function.

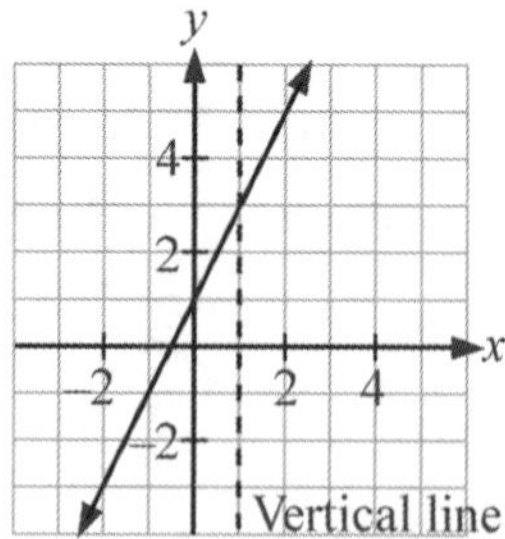

The graph passes the vertical line test; therefore, the linear graph represents a function.

Example

Determine if the given graph represents a function.

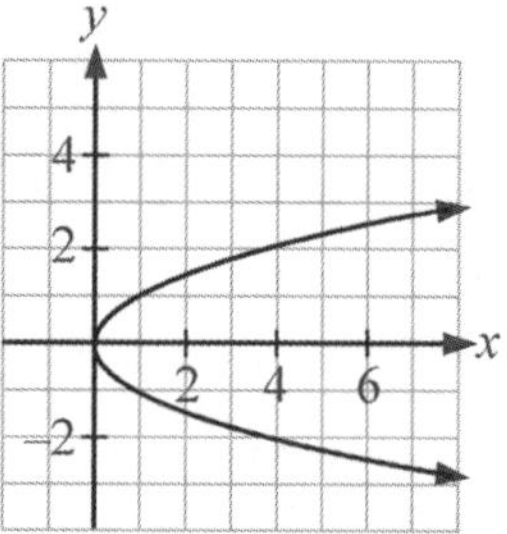

Solution

Use the vertical line test to determine if the given graph represents a function.

The vertical line test states that if a vertical line drawn anywhere on the graph crosses the graph more than once, that graph does not represent a function.

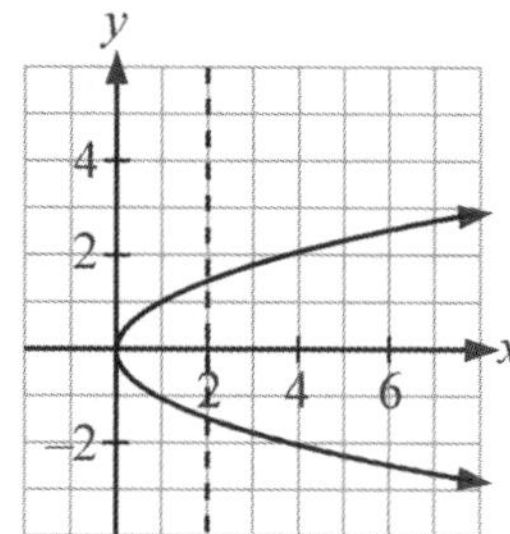

The given graph does not pass the vertical line test; therefore, the graph does not represent a function.

IDENTIFYING A FUNCTION USING A TABLE OF VALUES

A function is a special relation. It has one output number for each input number. Another way of stating this is that a function is a set of ordered pairs in which there is only one y-value for every x-value.

Determining if a given table of values represents a function is easy because the data is organized in such a way that it can be clearly seen whether or not there is only a single output for each input number.

Example
Consider the data in the following table of values:

x	y
−2	0
−1	1
0	2
1	3
2	4

Notice how each x-value has its own y-value. In other words, each input has only one output. Therefore, the given table of values represents a function.

Example
The data in this table of values represents a relation.

x	y
1	10
1	20
2	40
3	50

Does the given table of values represent a function?

Solution
This table of values does not represent a function. The input value of 1 has two separate outputs: 10 and 20. Thus, each input does not have its own output.

Identifying a Function Using a Set of Ordered Pairs

In order for a relation to be a function, each input must have its own unique output. Look carefully at each relation to see if there is a duplicate in the input values.

Example
The following two relations are stated as sets of ordered pairs:

- Relation A contains (2, 3), (4, 5), (6, 7), and (8, 9).
- Relation B contains (6, 2), (6, 4), (8, 6), and (10, 8).

Relation A is a function because for each x value, there is only one y value.

Relation B is not a function because when x is 6, there are two possible values of y, namely 2 and 4.

Example
Determine if the set of ordered pairs {(4, 8), (3, −4), (−7, 0), (5, 11), (3, 8), (9, 2)} represents a function, and explain your reasoning.

Solution
The relation described by the given list is not a function because two ordered pairs, (3, −4) and (3, 8), have the same x-value (input), but the y-values (output) are different.

Example
Determine whether or not the relations {(3, 2), (8, 2), (−9, 2), (2, 2)} are functions, and explain your reasoning.

Solution
The relation described by the given list is a function because no two ordered pairs have the same first component.

Identifying a Function from an Equation

Identifying whether a relation written as an equation is a function is done in the same way as identifying a function using words. Create either a table of values, ordered pairs, or a graph to better understand the pattern. Mental math and estimation will help you see if each input has only one output.

Example

State whether or not the relation defined by the equation $y = 2x + 5$ is a function.

Solution

Using mental math, it can be determined that each x-value chosen will only give one possible y-value.

Therefore, the given equation represents a function. Each value substituted in for x will have a single output: y.

Using technology can also help you understand whether or not a relation written as an equation is a function.

Example

Determine if the equation $y = 3x - \frac{1}{4}$ represents a function.

Solution

Using a graphing calculator, complete the following steps in the order given.

Press [Y=] and enter the equation as $Y_1 = 3x - \frac{1}{4}$.

Press [2nd] [GRAPH] to display a table of values similiar to the following:

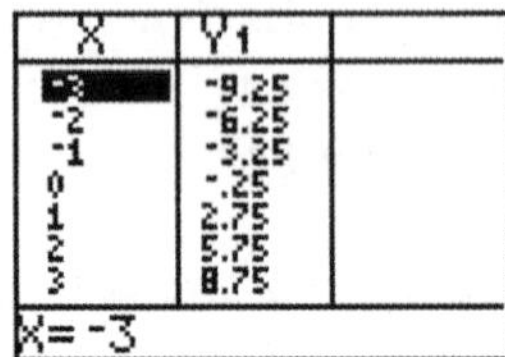

X	Y1	
-3	-9.25	
-2	-6.25	
-1	-3.25	
0	-.25	
1	2.75	
2	5.75	
3	8.75	

X=-3

Display the graph by pressing [GRAPH] and applying the vertical line test.

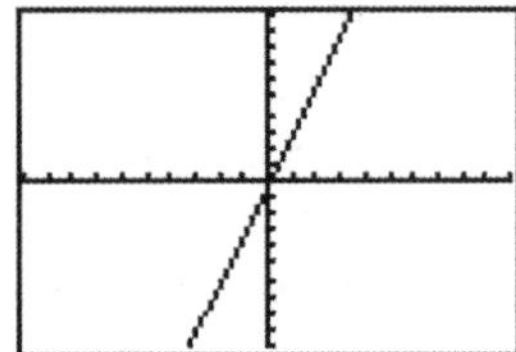

From the table of values and the graph of the function, it can be seen that each x-value (input) has only one y-value (output). Therefore, the equation represents a function.

Example

Determine if the relation $x = y^2$ represents a function.

Solution

Step 1

Isolate y.

Take the square root of both sides.

$$x = y^2$$
$$\pm\sqrt{x} = \pm\sqrt{y^2}$$
$$y = \pm\sqrt{x}$$

Step 2

Using a graphing calculator, graph $y = \pm\sqrt{x}$.

Press [Y=], and enter the equation as $Y_1 = \sqrt{x}$ and $Y_2 = -\sqrt{x}$.

Display the graph by pressing [GRAPH].

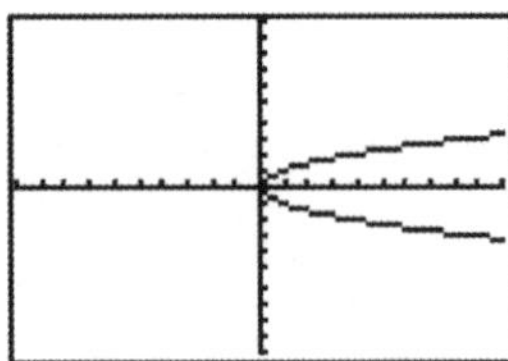

Step 3

Apply the vertical line test to the graph.

Notice that a vertical line would cross the curve at two distinct points. In other words, at least one x-value (input) has more than one y-value (output). Therefore, the equation $y = \pm\sqrt{x}$ does not represent a function.

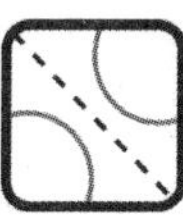

Identifying a Function from a Mapping Diagram

A mapping diagram can be used to identify a function by showing arrows pointing from values in one region to values in a second region.

Each x-value (located in the first region) can only be joined to a distinct y-value (located in the second region), and this relationship is symbolized by an arrow.

Example

The given mapping diagram defines a function.

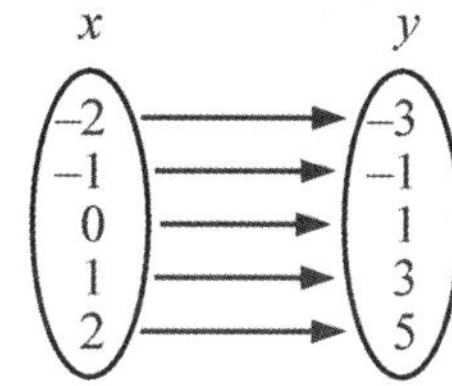

One arrow relates each x-value to a unique y-value.

Example

The given mapping diagram does not define a function.

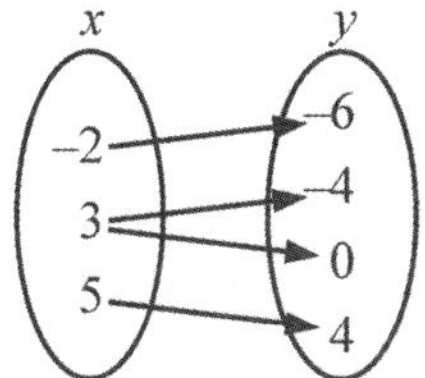

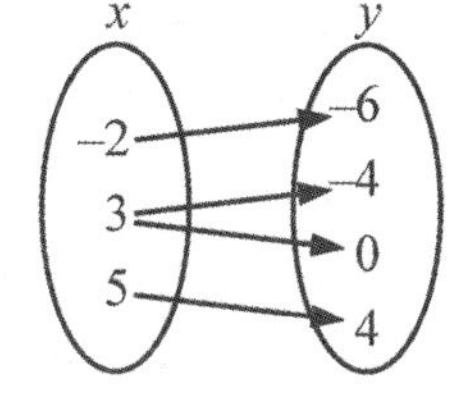

There are two arrows that relate the x-value of 3 to two different y-values, –4 and 0.

Example

Draw a mapping diagram of the ordered pairs {(7, 3), (4, 3), (4, 6), (–3, 6), (–3, –7), (–6, 6)}, and determine if it represents a function.

Solution

Step 1

Draw a mapping diagram that represents the set of ordered pairs.

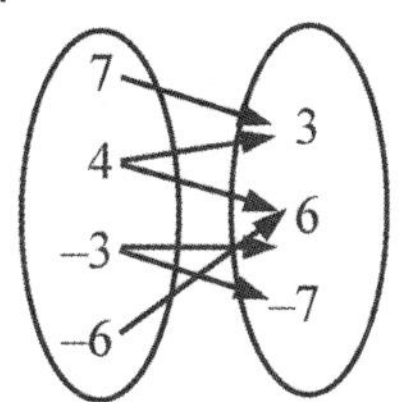

Step 2

Determine if the relation described by the mapping diagram represents a function.

The relation described by the mapping diagram is not a function because there are two arrows that relate the x-value of 4 to two different y-values, 3 and 6. Similarly, there are two arrows that relate the x-value of –3 to 6 and –7.

8.F.3 Interpret the equation $y = mx + b$ as defining a linear function, whose graph is a straight line; give examples of functions that are not linear.

Graphing Linear and Non-Linear Data by Hand

Continuous data includes all values between the measured points. For example, if a child's height is measured to be 105 cm one year and 109 cm the next year, it is understood that during that year, the child passed through each of the heights in between.

Discrete data does not include all the in-between data. For example, if a can of pop costs \$1.00, it is assumed that 1.32 cans of pop cannot be purchased for \$1.32. It does not make sense to think of partial cans of pop being sold.

When graphing continuous information, the data must be connected by a line to indicate the inclusion of all of the information between the points.

Graphs of discrete points should not have the points connected. The exception is when the range of numbers is large relative to the space between them. For example, with the \$1.00 can of pop, it would not be reasonable to graph 1,000 separate points to represent the sale of 1,000 cans of pop.

To represent data in a line graph, follow these steps:

1. Choose suitable increments to mark both axes for the data.
2. Draw the axes, and plot the points.
3. Label the axes, and give the graph a title.

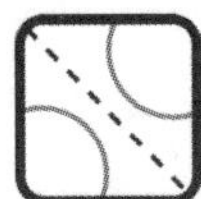

Once the ordered pairs have been plotted, the resulting pattern indicates the type and strength of the relationship between the variables.

The graph of the data can form a straight diagonal line that heads either up (positive direction) or down (negative direction). If this is the case, then the relationship is said to be linear.

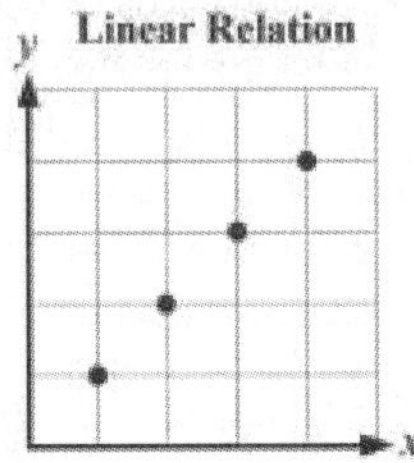

When the graph of the data forms a curved line, which can be either straight or smooth, the relationship is said to be non-linear.

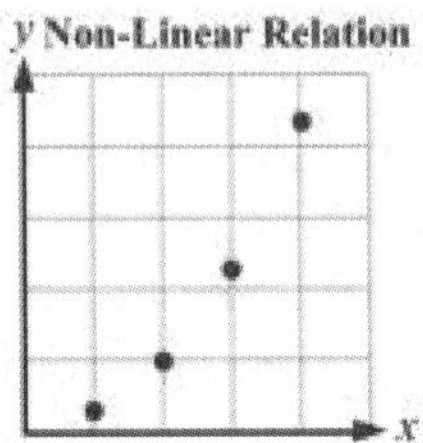

Example

A loom weaves bolts of fabric that are measured in meters. The following table shows the length in meters that is produced after given intervals of time in minutes.

Time (min)	Length (m)
2	10
4	20
6	30
8	40

Prove graphically whether this data is linear or non-linear.

Solution

Step 1

Choose suitable increments to mark the axes.

Plot the independent variable t on the horizontal axis. All data will be clearly displayed if the axis scale goes from 0 to 10 min in intervals of 2 min.

Plot the dependent variable l on the vertical axis. All data will be shown if the scale on the axis goes from 0 to 50 m in intervals of 10 m.

Step 2

Draw and label the axes.

Plot the points, and give the graph a title.

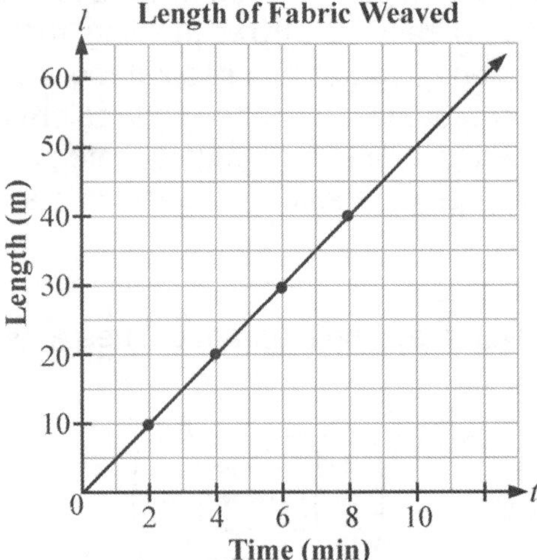

This is a linear relationship because the line created is a straight diagonal line that is headed in the positive direction.

The following example shows how to graph non-linear data. Identify whether or not the data is continuous or discrete. This will help determine whether or not the plotted points need to be connected with a line.

Example

The following table of values shows the height in meters of an object that has been thrown in the air and eventually falls back down to the ground relative to the time in seconds.

Time (s)	Height (m)
0	5.0
0.5	6.8
1.0	8.1
1.5	7.0
2.0	3.4
2.5	0

Prove graphically whether this relationship is linear or non-linear.

Solution

Step 1
Choose suitable increments to mark both axes for the data.

Plot the independent variable, time, on the horizontal axis. All data will be clearly displayed if the axis scale goes from 0 to 3 min in intervals of 0.5 s.

Plot the dependent variable, height, on the vertical axis. All data will be shown if the scale on the axis goes from 0 to 10 m in intervals of 1 m.

Step 2
Draw and label the axes.

Plot the points, and give the graph a title.

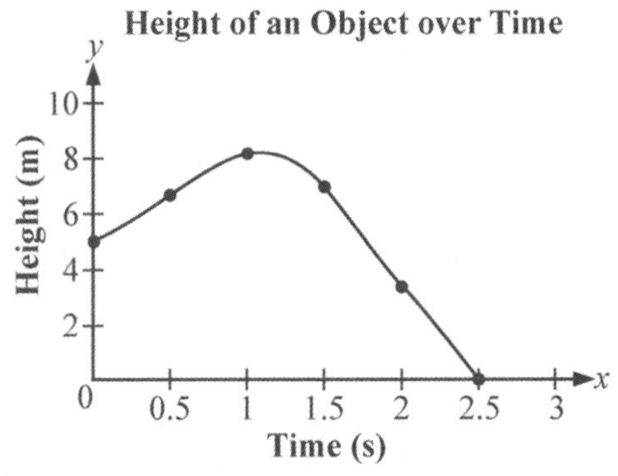

The data points should be connected since it is continuous data.

This relationship is non-linear because the data point forms a curve.

Determining the Characteristics of the Graph of a Linear Function

Having the ability to identify certain characteristics of the graph of a linear function allows you to make quick mental calculations, answer questions efficiently, and determine if a given answer is reasonable. These are only a few of the ways in which an understanding of the characteristics of a linear function can be used.

Some important characteristics of the graph of a linear function are with respect to the intercepts, slope, domain, and range of the graph.

Intercepts

Identifying the x- and y-intercepts of the graph of a linear function is extremely important because they are required for any further calculations.

A x-intercept is a point where the graph touches or crosses the x-axis. At this point, $y = 0$.
A y-intercept is a point where the graph touches or crosses the y-axis. At this point, $x = 0$.

In the graph shown here, point A is the x-intercept, and point B is the y-intercept.

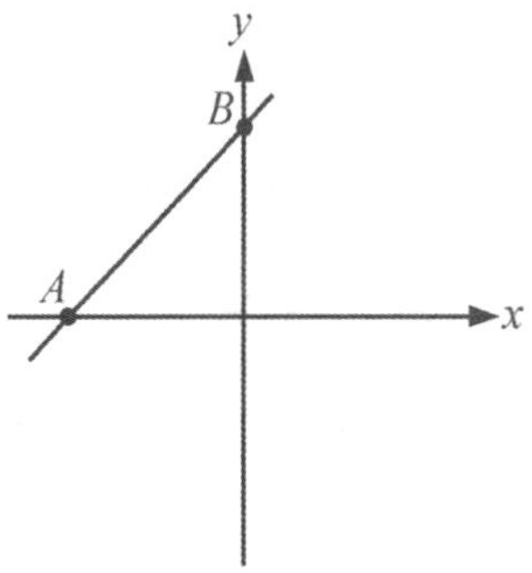

The x-intercept can be expressed as an ordered pair in the form $(x, 0)$, and the y-intercept can be expressed in the form $(0, y)$.

To determine the value of an x-intercept of the graph of a linear function, written in terms of x and y, make the y-value equal to zero and solve for x. Similarly, to determine the value of a y-intercept, make the x-value equal to zero and solve for y.

Example

Determine the x- and y-intercepts of the graph of the function $2x - 3y = 12$.

Solution

Step 1
Determine the x-intercept.
Since the x-intercept is at the point $(x, 0)$, substitute 0 for y into the equation, and solve to find the value of x.

$$\begin{aligned} 2x - 3y &= 12 \\ 2x - 3(0) &= 12 \\ 2x &= 12 \\ x &= 6 \end{aligned}$$

The x-intercept is 6 or $(6, 0)$.

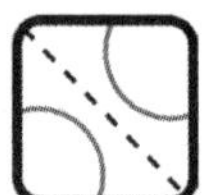

Step 2

Determine the y-intercept.

Since the y-intercept is at the point $(0, y)$, substitute 0 for x into the equation, and solve to find the value of y.

$$\begin{aligned} 2x - 3y &= 12 \\ 2(0) - 3y &= 12 \\ -3y &= 12 \\ y &= -4 \end{aligned}$$

The y-intercept is -4 or $(0, -4)$.

SLOPE

Slope is an important characteristic of the graph of a linear function. It describes the rate that the output (responding) variable is changing with respect to the input variable. Here are some examples of rates that the slope commonly represents:

- Speed/velocity (distance versus time)
- Rate of pay (earning versus time)
- Cost per item (cost versus number of items)

The slope of a linear function can always be determined from a graph or table of values by using two points and the slope formula $m = \frac{y_2 - y_1}{x_2 - x_1}$.

The slope can also be determined from the equation of a function by arranging the equation into the slope-intercept form $y = mx + b$, where m is the slope and b is the y-intercept.

To interpret the slope, it is helpful to look at the units. For example, $m = \frac{\text{rise}}{\text{run}} = \frac{\$}{\text{h}}$ (dollars per hour).

Example

The given table of values represents David's earnings as a function of the number of hours he worked.

Number of Hours	Earnings ($)
2	15.90
4	31.80
6	47.70
8	63.60

Determine the slope of the graph of the function.

Solution

Apply the slope formula using any two ordered pairs from the table of values.

If the points (2, 15.9) and (4, 31.8) are used, the calculation is:

$$\begin{aligned} m &= \frac{y_2 - y_1}{x_2 - x_1} \\ &= \frac{31.8 - 15.9}{4 - 2} \\ &= \frac{15.9}{2} \\ &= 7.95 \end{aligned}$$

The slope of the graph of the given function is 7.95.

DOMAIN AND RANGE

Domain and range are two terms that are commonly used in describing linear functions. **Domain** is the set of all first, or input, values and is often represented by the variable x. **Range** is the set of all second, or output, values and is often represented by the variable y.

The domain is found by examining all the values that x can assume, and the range is found by examining all the values that y can assume. For example, examine the partial graph of the linear function defined by the equation $y = x + 6$, as shown.

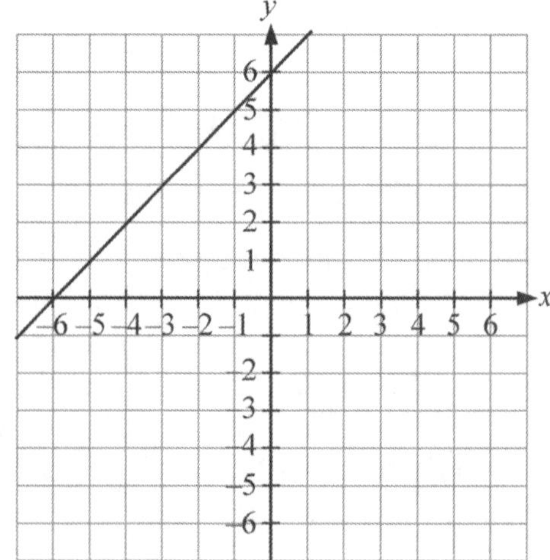

Since the line is infinite in both directions, both the domain and the range contain all real numbers.

The domain and range for the graph of this linear function can then be written as:

- Domain—
  $x \in \mathrm{R}$(x is an element of the real numbers)
- Range—
  $y \in \mathrm{R}$(y is an element of the real numbers)

Sometimes, the graphs of linear functions are not infinite in both directions, or they are discontinuous. In such cases, the following inequality symbols can be used where necessary:

- Greater than
  $>$
- Greater than or equal to
  $\geq$
- Less than
  $<$
- Less than or equal to
  $\leq$

Example

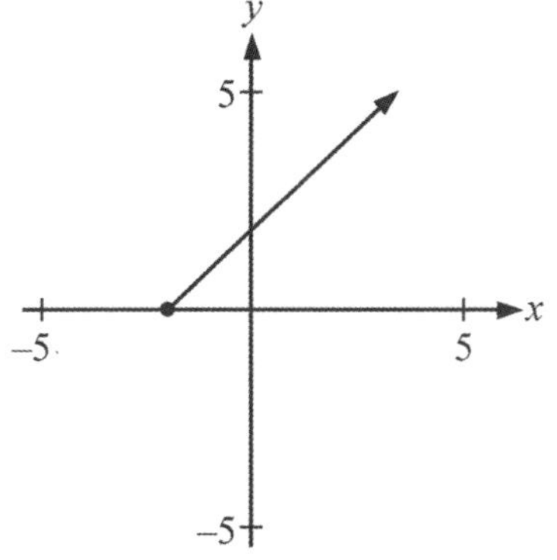

The given graph is the graph of a particular linear function.

State the domain and range of this function.

Solution

For the domain, the x-values start at −2 and increase infinitely. This statement can be written as $x \geq -2$. The given inequality means that x is greater than or equal to −2.

For the range, the y-values start at 0 and increase infinitely. This statement can be written as $y \geq 0$. The given inequality means that y is greater than or equal to 0.

Equations of Linear Relations versus Non-Linear Relations

Linear and non-linear relations can be distinguished by the equation of a line and by inspecting the graphs of the equations.

There are two general forms of equations for linear relations: standard form and slope y-intercept form.

- Standard form: $Ax + By + C = 0$, in which A, B, and C are integers
- Slope y-intercept form: $y = mx + b$

To differentiate between the equations of linear and non-linear relations, look at the exponents in the equation.

For **linear equations**, the largest exponent on the x-variable will be 1 or 0. For example, $y = x + 2$ is a linear equation because the highest exponent on the x-variable is 1.

For **non-linear equations**, the exponent on the x-variable can be any number except 0 or 1. For example, $y = x^2 - 2x + 1$ is a non-linear equation because the largest exponent on the x-variable is 2.

The equation $y = 3x$ has 1 as the largest exponent on the x-variable. The graph of $y = 3x$ is a straight line with a slope of 3 and a y-intercept of 0. Thus, it is a linear relation.

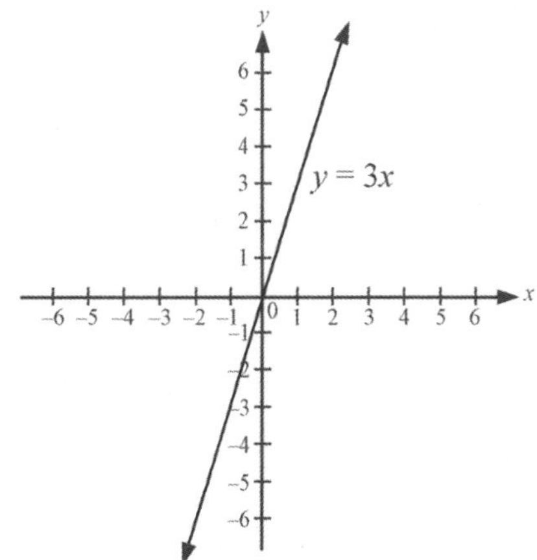

An example of a graph of a non-linear relation is a parabola, defined by the equation $y = 3x^2$. The largest exponent in this equation is 2, it has a *y*-intercept of 0, and its vertex or minimum point occurs at (0, 0).

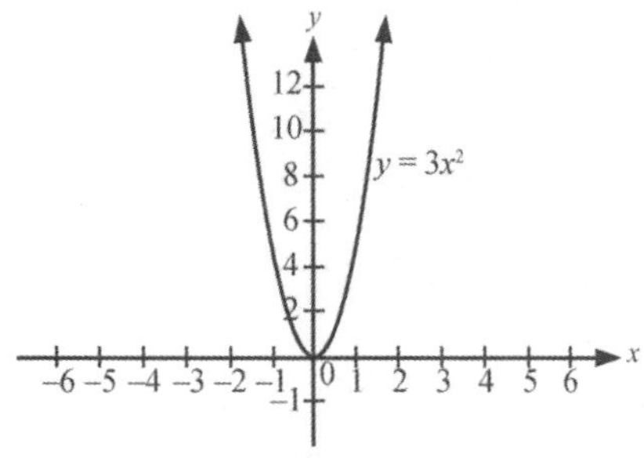

Defining Function Notation for a Linear Function in Two Variables

Function notation involves the use of symbols such as $f(x)$ and $g(x)$ to represent the dependent variable (often *y*) in a function. For example, $y = 3x - 4$ may be written as $f(x) = 3x - 4$.

While *f* is the most common function letter, any letter can be used. Often *g* and *h* are also used to represent generic functions. Sometimes the letter is selected for its connection to a real-world situation. If the question has cost represented as a function of the number of items sold, $C(n)$ might be used. To represent height as a function of time, $h(t)$ could be used.

The symbol $f(x)$ is read as "*f* of *x*" or "*f* at *x*." This notation emphasizes that the function values (output values) are produced from values of *x* (input values).

Example

The graph of $y = f(x)$ is shown.

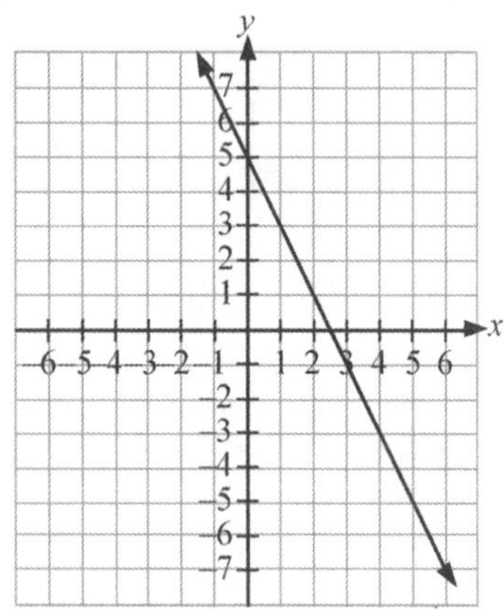

What is the value of $f(4)$?

Solution

Another way of thinking of $f(4)$ is "what is the value of *y* when *x* is equal to 4?"

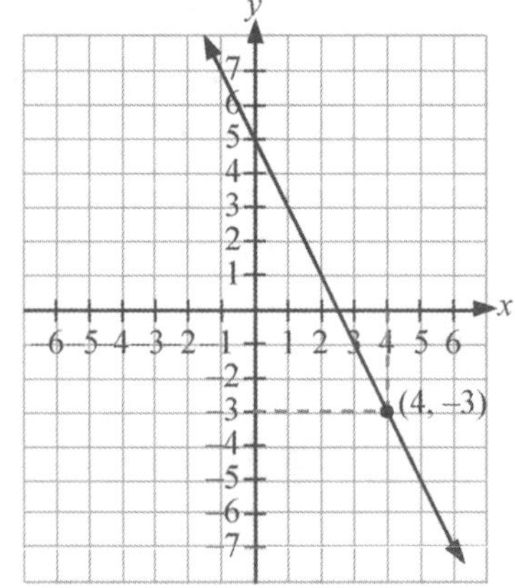

From the graph, when *x* is equal to 4, the value of *y* is –3. Therefore, $f(4) = -3$.

Example

A table of values is given.

x	$g(x)$
–3	–16
–2	–8
–1	–2
0	2
1	4
2	4
3	2

Determine the value of $g(-2)$.

Solution

In the given table, the values of $g(x)$ (output values) are produced from values of *x* (input values).

The value of $g(-2)$ is the output value when *x* is equal to –2. From the table, an input value of –2 yields an output value of –8. Therefore, $g(-2) = -8$.

You can convert between other forms of equations of linear functions and function notation.
For example, a function that is in general form, $Ax + By + C = 0$, can be converted to function notation by solving for y and then replacing y with $f(x)$.

Example

Write $5x - 2y + 6 = 0$ using function notation.

Solution

Step 1
Solve for y.

$$5x - 2y + 6 = 0$$
$$-2y = -5x - 6$$
$$y = \frac{-5}{-2}x - \frac{6}{-2}$$
$$y = \frac{5}{2}x + 3$$

Step 2
Replace y with $f(x)$.

$$f(x) = \frac{5}{2}x + 3$$

Defining Equations in Slope-Intercept Form

All linear relations that are functions can be written in the form $y = mx + b$, in which m represents the slope, and b represents the y-intercept of the line forming the graph of the relation.

Example

What is the equation of the line that has a slope of $-\frac{4}{3}$ and a y-intercept of $\frac{1}{2}$ in slope-intercept form?

Solution

Substitute $m = -\frac{4}{3}$ and $b = \frac{1}{2}$ into the slope-intercept form of the equation of a line.

$$y = mx + b$$
$$y = -\frac{4}{3}x + \frac{1}{2}$$

Example

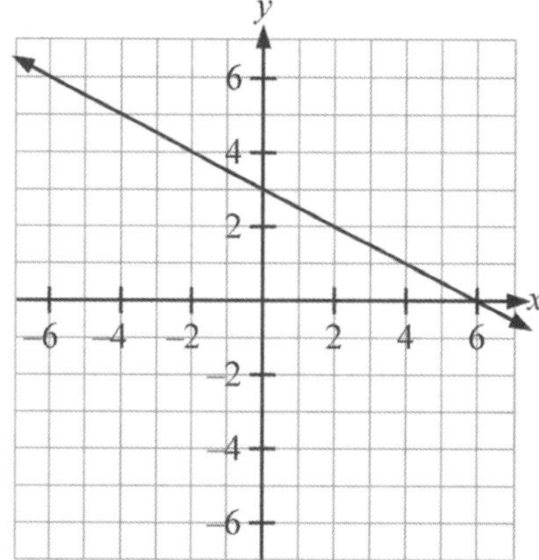

What is the equation of the line in the given graph in slope-intercept form?

Solution

From the given graph, the y-intercept is 3.

Count to another readable point on the line to obtain the slope of the line (the slope is equal to the rise divided by the run). The distance between the y-intercept and the x-intercept is 3 units down and 6 units to the right. Therefore, the slope is $\frac{-3}{6} = -\frac{1}{2}$.

Substitute $m = -\frac{1}{2}$ and $b = 3$ into the equation $y = mx + b$.

$$y = -\frac{1}{2}x + 3$$

EXERCISE #1—FUNCTIONS

110. Which of the following graphs is **not** the graph of a function?

A.

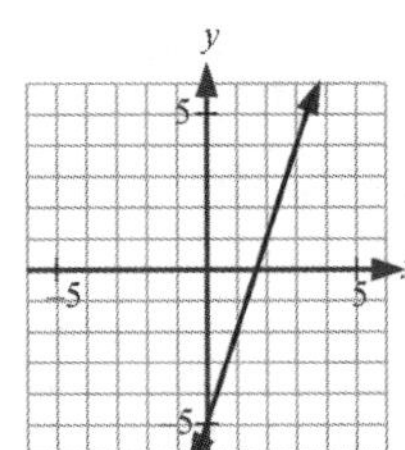

B.

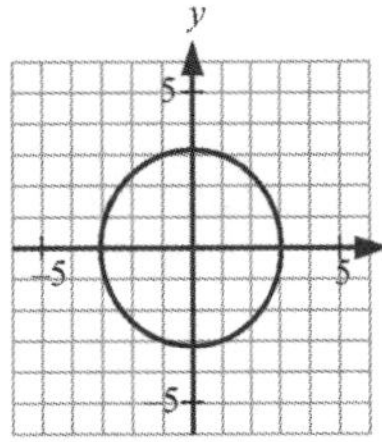

C.

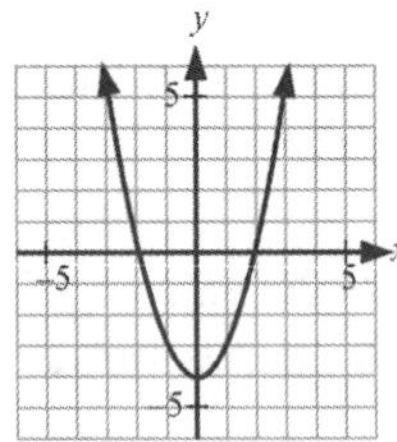

D.

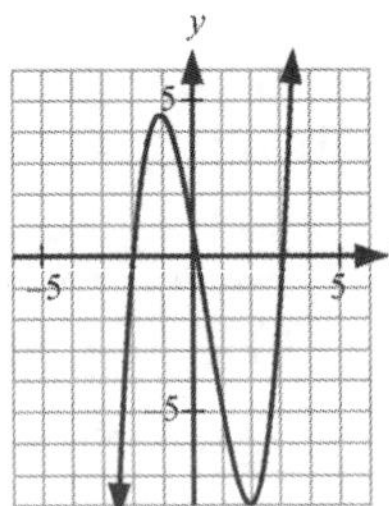

Use the following information to answer the next question.

A relation is given as a table of values.

Input	Output
2	3
4	8
5	9
6	9
7	12

111. Which of the following statements about the relation is **true**?

A. The relation is a function because each output has only one input.

B. The relation is a function because each input has only one output.

C. The relation is not a function because one input has two different outputs.

D. The relation is not a function because there are two identical outputs for different inputs.

112. Which of the following sets of ordered pairs is **not** a function?

A. {(2, 30), (1, 1), (1, −2), (8, 2)}

B. {(5, 8), (8, 9), (11, 10), (14, 11)}

C. {(−7, 16), (−6, 11), (−3, 10), (1, 8)}

D. {(−10, −1), (−8, 4), (−4, 7), (0, −8)}

113. Which of the following relations is **not** a function?

A. $y + 13 = -2x^2 + 12x$

B. $7x + 4y - 6 = 0$

C. $5x - 4y = 20$

D. $x = y^2$

114. Which of the following mapping diagrams represents a function with a range of {1, 2, 3}?

A.

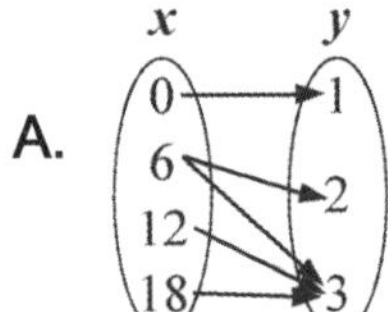

B.

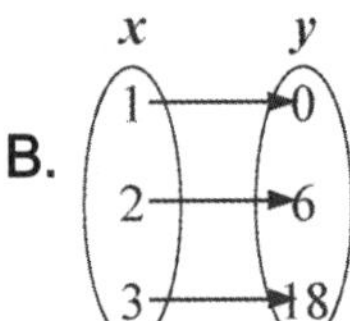

C.

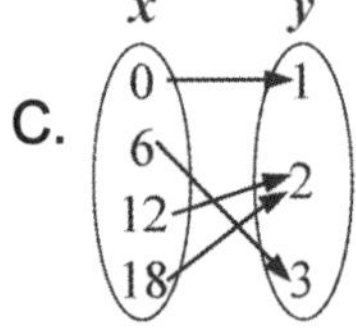

D.

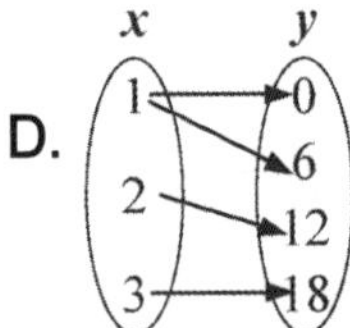

115. A ball is dropped from an initial height of 10 m. Which of the following partial graphs illustrates the rebound heights of the ball as a function of time?

A. 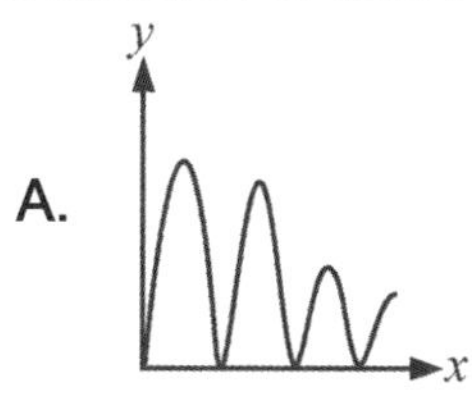

B. 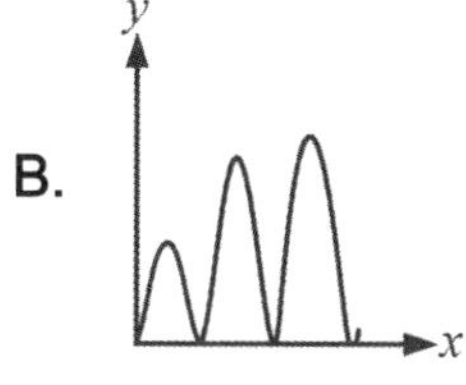

C. 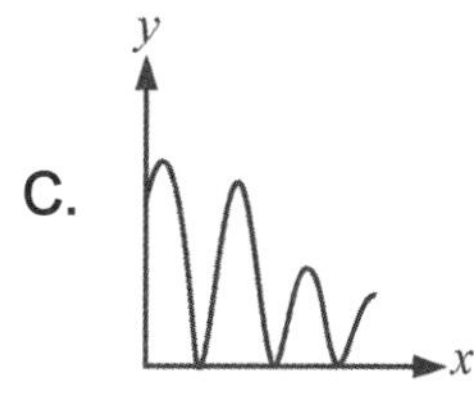

D. 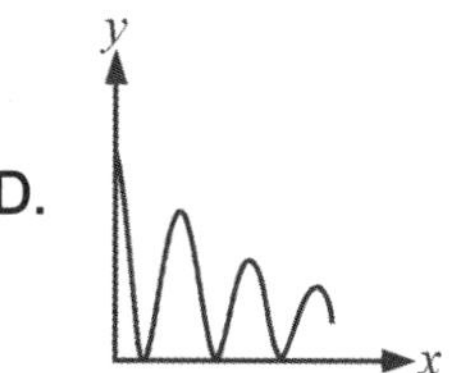

Use the following information to answer the next question.

> As a computer saleswoman, Diane receives a salary of $600 each month and earns a commission of 6% of her total monthly sales. Her monthly wage is represented by the equation $W = 0.06s + 600$, where W represents her wage and s represents her total monthly sales.

116. If Diane's commission is raised to 8%, the graph of the equation that represents Diane's monthly wage will have a

A. slope of 800

B. slope of 0.08

C. y-intercept of 800

D. y-intercept of 0.08

117. Which of the following equations represents a line with a slope of –4 and a y-intercept of 7?

A. $y = -4x + 7$ B. $y = -7 + 4x$

C. $y = -4 - 7x$ D. $y = 7x - 4$

Use the following information to answer the next question.

> A list of equations is given.
>
> $y = \frac{x}{y}$ $y = -5x + 2$
>
> $x = -2$ $3x - 2y + 7 = 0$
>
> $y = x(x + 3)$ $4x^2 - 3y + 6 = 0$
>
> $y = 3(x - 2)$

118. How many equations in this list represent linear relations?

A. 2 B. 3

C. 4 D. 5

Use the following information to answer the next question.

> The graph of a linear function is shown.
>
> 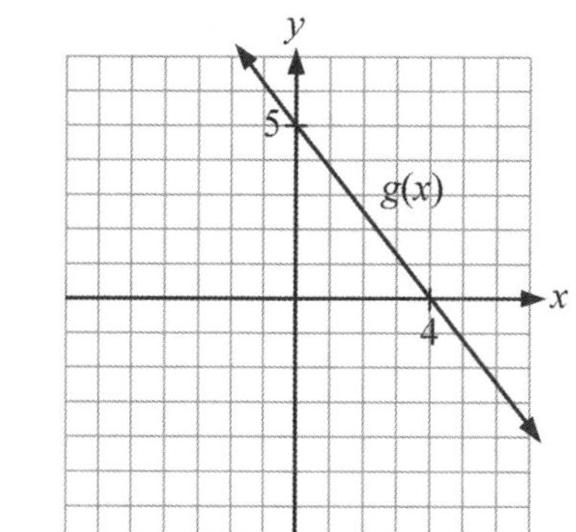
>

119. When expressed in function notation, the equation of the linear function is

A. $g(x) = -\frac{4}{5}x + 5$

B. $g(x) = -\frac{5}{4}x + 5$

C. $g(x) = 4x + 5y - 25$

D. $g(x) = 5x + 4y - 20$

EXERCISE #1—FUNCTIONS ANSWERS AND SOLUTIONS

110. B	113. D	116. B	119. B
111. B	114. C	117. A	
112. A	115. D	118. C	

110. B

A graph that is intersected by a vertical line at two or more points is not a function. Use this vertical line test to determine which of the given graphs are not functions.

In graph B, at almost any place a vertical line is drawn, it will either intersect the graph in two locations or not at all. Therefore, the graph does not represent a function.

Since a vertical line does not intersect the other graphs more than once, the relations in graphs A, C, and D are functions.

111. B

A relation is a function if each input value gives only one output value. The given relation fits this criterion, so it is a function.

112. A

A relation is a function if for every *x*-value, there is a single *y*-value.

The set of ordered pairs $\{(2, 30), (1, 1), (1, -2), (8, 2)\}$ is not a function because for the input value (*x*-value) of 1, there are two different output values (*y*-values): 1 and –2.

113. D

Rewrite the four equations in terms of *y*, and enter them into a graphing calculator. Use the vertical line test to determine which of the given equations are functions.

Step 1
Perform the vertical line test on $y + 13 = -2x^2 + 12x$.

$$y + 13 = -2x^2 + 12x$$
$$y = -2x^2 + 12x - 13$$

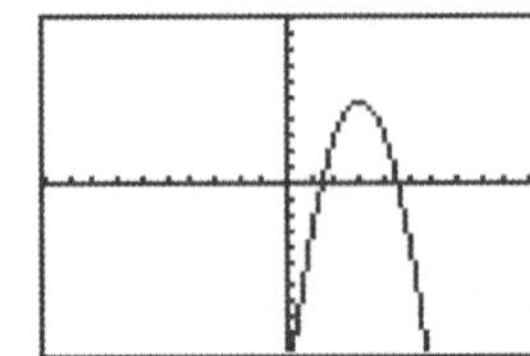

The graph of this relation passes the vertical line test; therefore, the relation is a function.

Step 2
Perform the vertical line test on $7x + 4y - 6 = 0$.

$$7x + 4y - 6 = 0$$
$$4y = -7x + 6$$
$$y = -\frac{7}{4}x + \frac{6}{4}$$
$$y = -\frac{7}{4}x + \frac{3}{2}$$

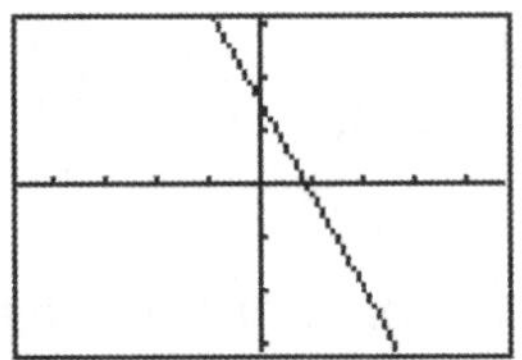

The graph of this relation passes the vertical line test; therefore, the relation is a function.

Step 3
Perform the vertical line test on $5x - 4y = 20$.

$$5x - 4y = 20$$
$$-4y = -5x + 20$$
$$y = \frac{5}{4}x - 5$$

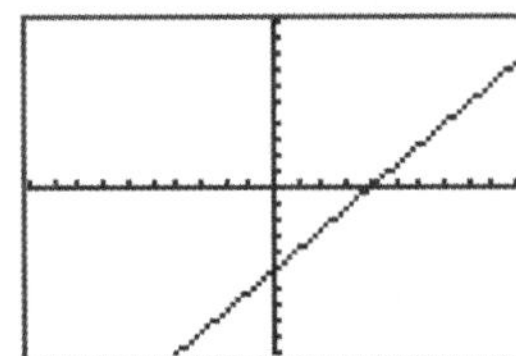

The graph of this relation passes the vertical line test; therefore, the relation is a function.

Step 4
Perform the vertical line test on $x = y^2$.

$$x = y^2$$
$$y = \pm\sqrt{x}$$

This function can be graphed by entering $Y_1 = \sqrt{X}$ and $Y_2 = -\sqrt{X}$ into the graphing calculator.

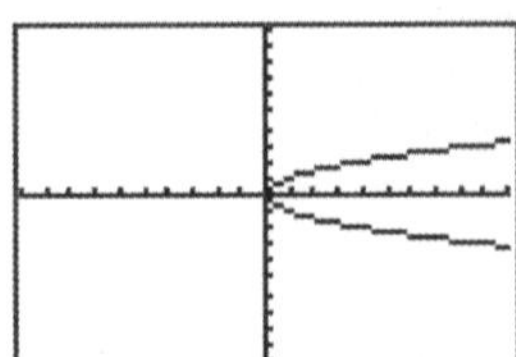

The graph of this relation does not pass the vertical line test; therefore, the relation is not a function.

114. C

In order for a mapping diagram to be a function, each input must have its own output. Given that the domain is {1, 2, 3}, these values are the output values.

Diagram A is not the correct solution because even though the given domain of {1, 2, 3} is in the output column, each input does not have only one output value. (Notice how 6 has the values 2 and 3 assigned to it.)

Diagram B is not the correct solution because the given range of {1, 2, 3} is in the input column.

Diagram C is the correct solution because the given range of {1, 2, 3} is in the output column and each input value has only one output value.

Diagram D is not the correct solution because the given range of {1, 2, 3} is in the input column.

115. D

If a ball is dropped from an initial height of 10 m, then the graph must have a y-intercept of 10 m. As time goes on, the rebound height of the ball will decrease. The only graph that meets these requirements is the following graph:

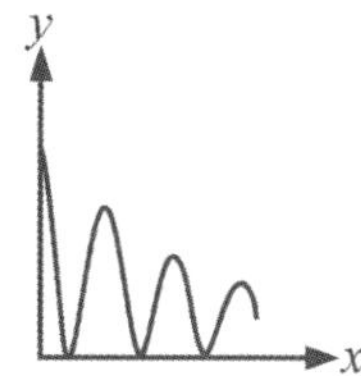

The following graph does not show a y-intercept of 10 m, even though the height decreases over time.

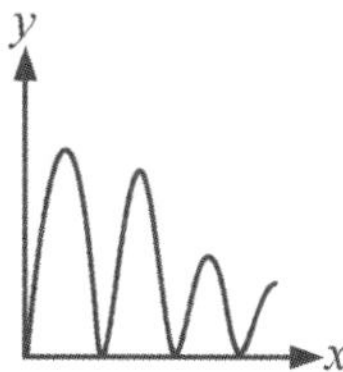

The following graph shows that the height increases over time; it is also incorrect because it has a y-intercept of 0 m.

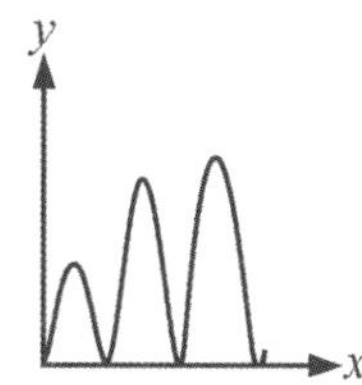

The following graph shows a decrease in height over time, but it indicates that when the ball was dropped, it first went up and then fell, which is incorrect.

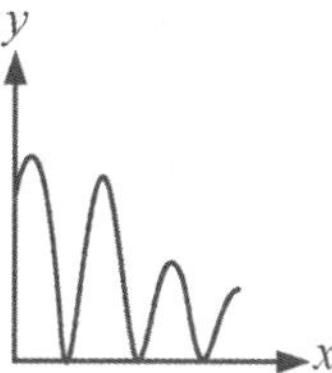

116. B

Step 1
Convert 8% to a decimal.
8% = 0.08

Step 2
Write the new equation.
$W = 0.08s + 600$

The slope of the corresponding graph is the coefficient of s in the equation.

Therefore, the slope is 0.08.

117. A

The slope-intercept form of the equation of a line is $y = mx + b$, where m represents the slope and b represents the y-intercept.

Since the given line has a slope of −4 and a y-intercept of 7, the value of m in the equation $y = mx + b$ is −4 and the value of b is 7.

Thus, the equation that represents the given line is $y = -4x + 7$.

118. C

A linear relation has the form $Ax + By + C = 0$, where A, B, and C are real numbers. The degree of each term must be either 0 or 1.

There are four equations that can be expressed in the form $Ax + By + C = 0$ and which have terms with degrees of either 1 or 0. These are $3x - 2y + 7 = 0$, $y = -5x + 2$, $x = -2$, and $y = 3(x - 2)$.

The other three equations do not represent linear relations:

- The equation $y = \frac{x}{y}$ is equivalent to $y^2 = x$. The term y^2 has a degree of 2.
- The equation $4x^2 - 3y + 6 = 0$ contains the term $4x^2$, which has a degree of 2.
- The equation $y = x(x + 3)$ is equivalent to $y = x^2 + 3x$. The term x^2 has a degree of 2.

119. B

Step 1
Determine the equation in the form $y = mx + b$.
From the graph, the y-intercept is 5; therefore, $b = 5$.
According to the triangle formed by the axes and intercepts, the rise is −5 and the run is 4; therefore, the slope, m, is $-\frac{5}{4}$.

The equation of the function is $y = -\frac{5}{4}x + 5$.

Step 2
Write the equation in function notation.
To express the equation in function notation, replace y with $g(x)$.
$g(x) = -\frac{5}{4}x + 5$

EXERCISE #2—FUNCTIONS

120. Which of the following graphs is **not** the graph of a function?

A.

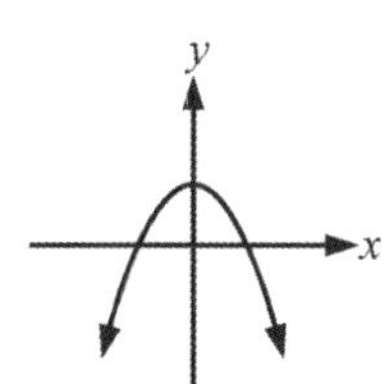

B.

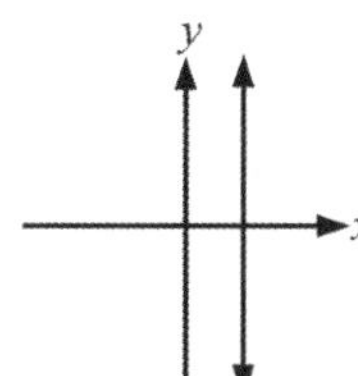

C.

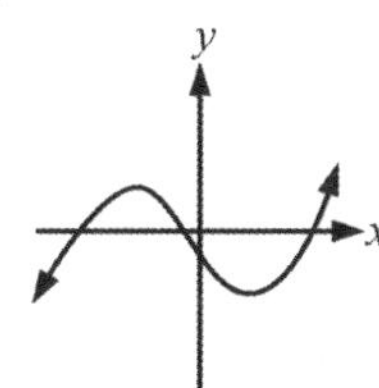

D.

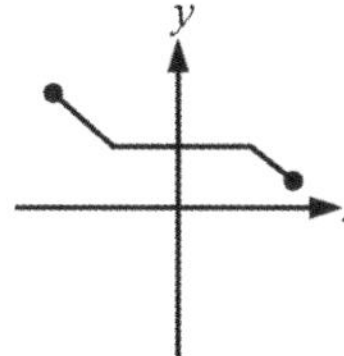

121. Which of the following sets of data does **not** represent a function?

A.

x	y
3	4
5	4
7	8
9	8
11	12

B.

x	y
−2	4
−1	1
0	0
1	1
2	4

C. {(1, 4), (3, 8), (1, 5), (6, 8)}

D. {(−4, 7), (−3, 8), (3, 9), (4, 10)}

Use the following information to answer the next question.

> A set of ordered pairs is given.
> {(6, 3), (8, 0), (k, 10), (2, 7)}

122. Which of the following values of k makes the given set of ordered pairs a function?

A. 2 B. 3
C. 6 D. 8

123. Which of the following quadratic relations is also a quadratic function?

A. $y^2 - 2x = 0$

B. $y - \sqrt{2}x^2 = 0$

C. $x - 2y^2 = 0$

D. $(y-2)^2 - x = 0$

124. Which of the following mapping notations represents a function with a domain of {−2, 3, 5}?

A.

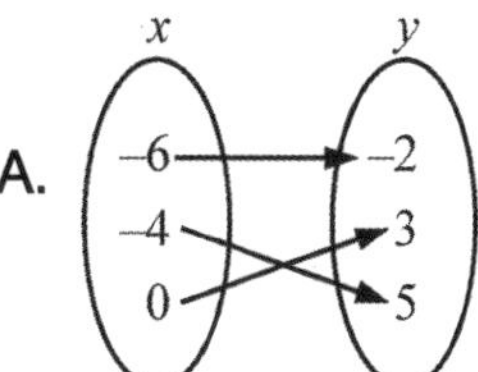

B.

x y
−2 −6
3 −4
5 0
4

C.

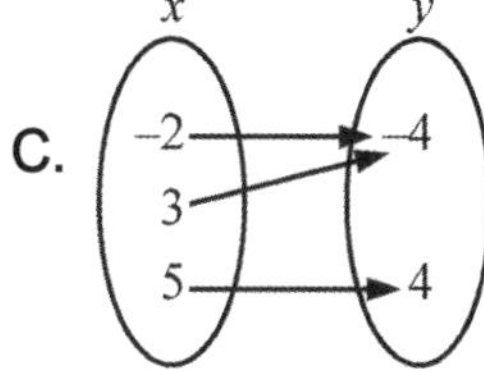

D.

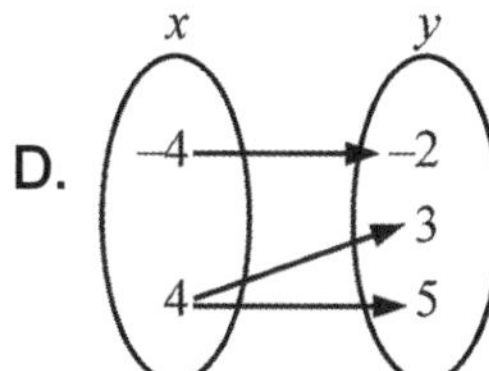

125. Which of the following equations is a linear relation?

A. $y = -\dfrac{5}{x}$

B. $y = -\dfrac{3}{2}x$

C. $y = x^3 + 5$

D. $y = (x-2)(x+2)$

Use the following information to answer the next question.

The captain of a small yacht fires a rescue flare into the air. The given table shows the height of the flare in relation to the time elapsed after the flare is fired.

Time (s)	Height of Flare (m)
0	0
1	150
2	240
3	270
4	240
5	150
6	0

126. Which of the following graphs **best** represents the information in the given table?

A. Path of Rescue Flare

y
300
200
100
0
1 2 3 4 5 6 x
Height of flare (m)
Time (s)

B.

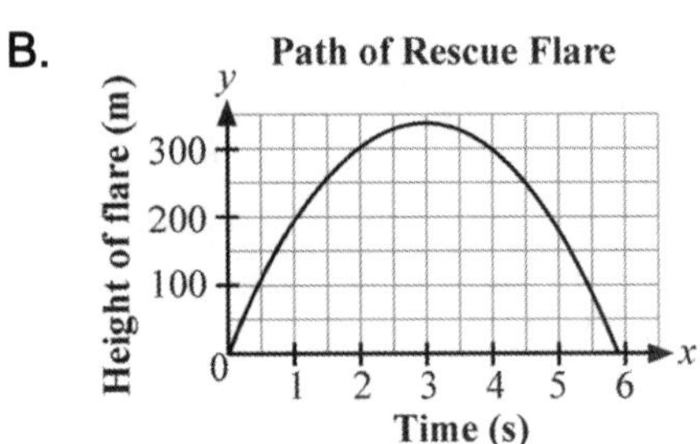

C. Path of Rescue Flare

y
300
200
100
0
1 2 3 4 5 6 x
Height of flare (m)
Time (s)

D.

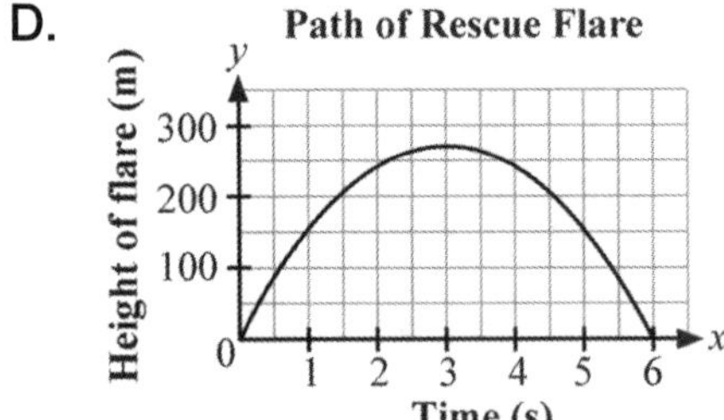

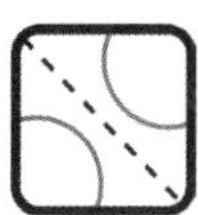

Use the following information to answer the next question.

A company that sells textbooks determines the total cost of an order based on the function
$C(t) = 46t + 552$, where C is the cost of the textbook order, and t is the number of textbooks purchased.

127. The slope of the graph of the function $C(t) = 46t + 552$ is the number

A. 46, which represents the cost of each textbook

B. 552, which represents the cost of each textbook

C. 46, which represents the company's setup fee for the order

D. 552, which represents the company's setup fee for the order

Use the following information to answer the next question.

The given table shows the speed of sound, v, in meters per second for a number of different air temperatures, t, measured in degrees Celsius.

t(°C)	v(m/s)
5	334.4
10	337.4
15	340.4
20	343.4
25	346.4

128. If the given relationship is linear, which of the following equations represents the relationship between v and t in function notation?

A. $v(t) = 0.6t + 331.4$

B. $v(t) = 3t + 334.4$

C. $v(t) = 5v - 3t - 1{,}657$

D. $v(t) = 5v - 6t - 1{,}672$

129. The slope and the y-intercept of the graph of the line $5x - 2y = 6$ are, respectively,

A. $\frac{5}{2}$ and -3

B. $\frac{3}{2}$ and 6

C. $-\frac{2}{5}$ and -3

D. $-\frac{3}{2}$ and 5

EXERCISE #2—FUNCTIONS ANSWERS AND SOLUTIONS

120. B	123. B	126. D	129. A
121. C	124. C	127. A	
122. B	125. B	128. A	

120. B

Apply the vertical line test to each of the graphs in the alternatives to determine which of them are functions.

The vertical line test states that if a vertical line drawn anywhere on the graph crosses the graph more than once, then that graph does not represent a function.

This graph passes the vertical line test; therefore, it is the graph of a function.

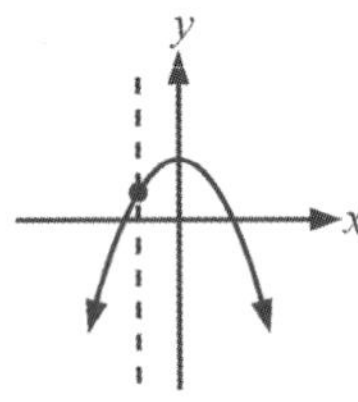

This graph is itself a vertical line, which means that it does not pass the vertical line test because a vertical line would touch the graph at infinitely many points. Therefore, this graph is not a function.

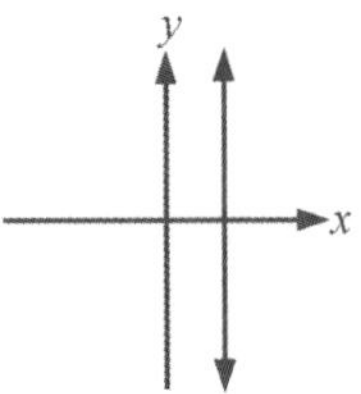

This graph passes the vertical line test; therefore, it is the graph of a function.

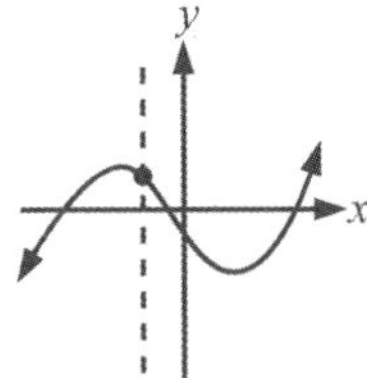

This graph passes the vertical line test; therefore, it is the graph of a function.

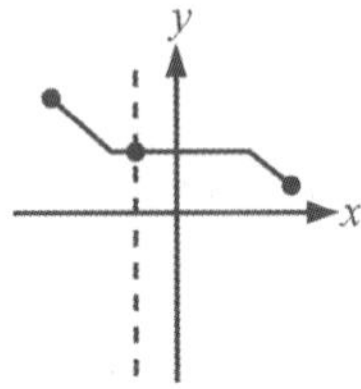

121. C

In order for a relation to be a function, each x-value (input) must have its own y-value (output).
The relation {(1, 4), (3, 8), (1, 5), (6, 8)} does not represent a function because the x-value of 1 has two y-values. The other alternatives all have one y-value for each x-value.

122. B

A relation is a function if for every x-value there is a single y-value. If $k = 2$, the input value would have two output values: 10 and 7. If $k = 3$, each input value of the relation will have a single output value. If $k = 6$, the input value would have two output values: 3 and 10. If $k = 8$, the input value would have two output values: 0 and 10. Therefore, $k = 3$.

123. B

If each relation is isolated for y you would get the following results.

Choice A: $y^2 - 2x = 0 \rightarrow y^2 = 2x \rightarrow y = \pm\sqrt{2x}$

Choice B: $y - \sqrt{2}x^2 = 0 \rightarrow y = \sqrt{2}x^2$

Choice C: $x - 2y^2 = 0 \rightarrow -2y^2 = -x \rightarrow y = \pm\sqrt{\frac{x}{2}}$

Choice D: $(y-2)^2 - x = 0 \rightarrow (y-2)^2 = x \rightarrow$
$y - 2 = \pm\sqrt{x} \rightarrow y = 2 \pm \sqrt{x}$

To determine which of these quadratic relations is also a function, use a mapping diagram or function machine for a given x-value.

Choice A

For $x = 2$, $y = +\sqrt{(2)(2)} = 2$
$y = -\sqrt{(2)(2)} = -2$

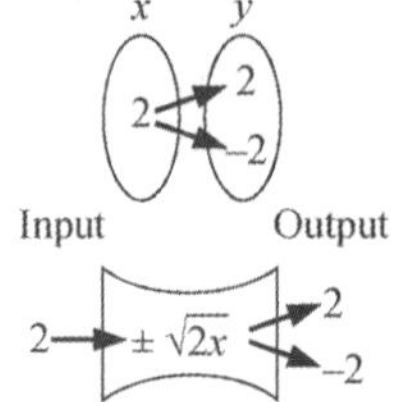

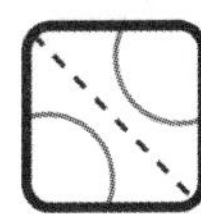

Choice B

For $x = 1$, $y = \sqrt{2}(1)^2 = \sqrt{2}$

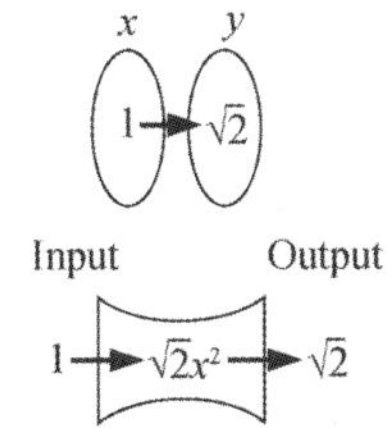

Choice C

For $x = 2$, $y = +\sqrt{\frac{2}{2}} = 1$

$y = -\sqrt{\frac{2}{2}} = -1$

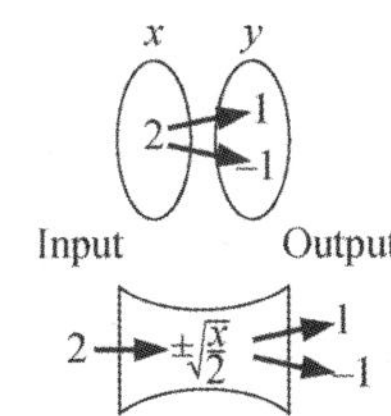

Choice D

For $x = 1$, $y = 2 + \sqrt{1} = 3$

$y = 2 - \sqrt{1} = 1$

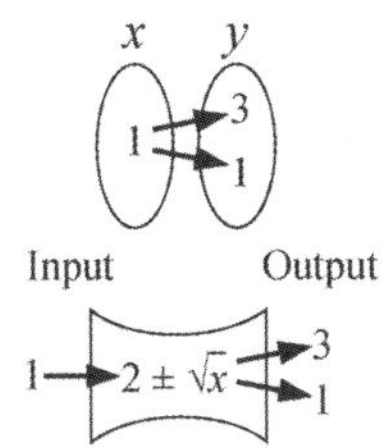

Look at all four mapping diagrams and function machines. Choices A, C, and D have two output y-values for a single x-value, whereas choice B has one output value for the single x-value. This shows that only choice B represents a quadratic function.

124. C

Step 1

Define a function in terms of mapping notation.

In order for a mapping to be a function, each input must have its own output. Given that the domain is {−2, 3, 5}, these values are the input values.

Step 2

Analyze alternative A.

This is not the correct solution, as the required domain of {−2, 3, 5} is in the output column.

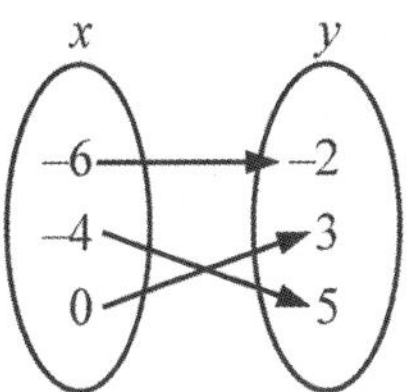

Step 3

Analyze alternative B.

This is not the correct solution because even though the given domain of {−2, 3, 5} is in the input column, each input does not have only one output value. Notice how 3 has the values −4 and 0 assigned to it.

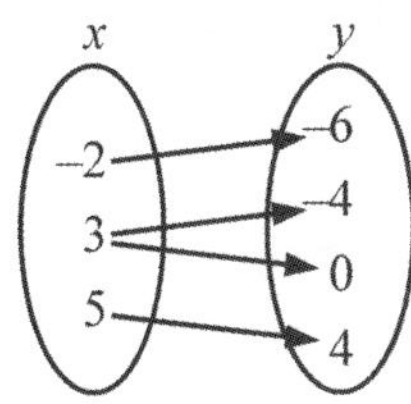

Step 4

Analyze alternative C.

This is the correct solution because the given domain of {−2, 3, 5} is in the correct input column, and each input value has only one output value.

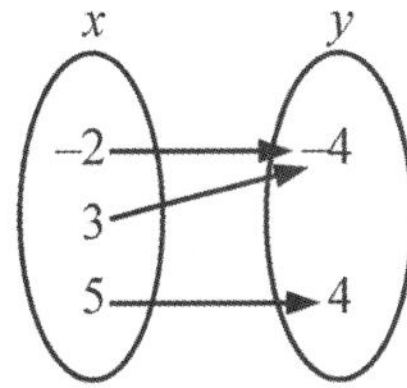

Step 5

Analyze alternative D.

This is not the correct solution, as the required domain of {−2, 3, 5} is in the output column.

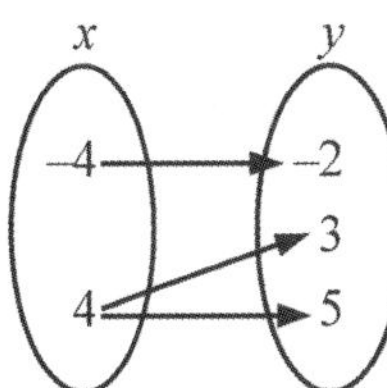

125. B

A linear relation has the form $Ax + By + C = 0$, where A, B, and C are real numbers. The degree of the terms must be either 0 or 1.

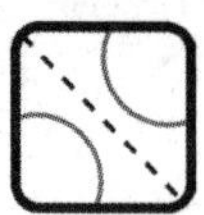

The only relation in which the terms have a degree of either 1 or 0 and can be expressed in the form $Ax + By + C = 0$ is the relation $y = -\frac{3}{2}x$.

The relation $y = (x - 2)(x + 2)$ is equivalent to $y = x^2 - 4$. The term x^2 has a degree of 2.

The relation $y = -\frac{5}{x}$ is equivalent to $xy = -5$.

The term xy has a degree of 2. Finally, the relation $y = x^3 + 5$ has the term x^3, which has a degree of 3.

126. D

Label the specified ordered pairs in the graph

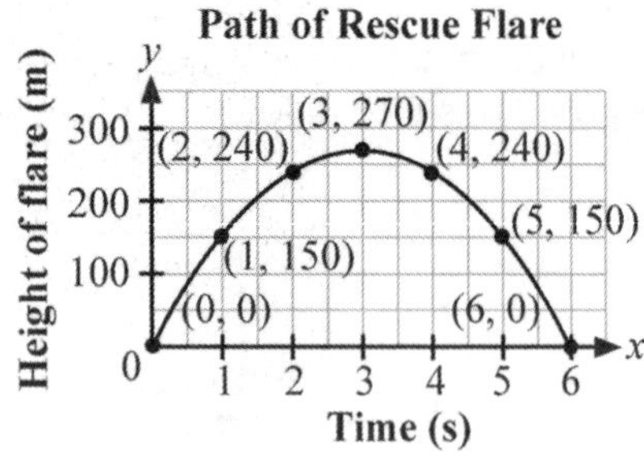

Therefore, graph D is the graph that best represents the information in the table.

127. A

Identify the slope of the graph of the function $c(t) = 46t + 552$.

The slope-intercept form of the line is $y = mx + b$, where m is the slope and b is the y-intercept.

Therefore, the slope of the function is 46. Here, 46 is the cost of each textbook.

128. A

Step 1
Determine the slope by using any two pairs of coordinates and the formula $m = \frac{y_2 - y_1}{x_2 - x_1}$.

Substitute (5, 334.4) for (x_1, y_1) and (10, 337.4) for (x_2, y_2).

$m = \frac{y_2 - y_1}{x_2 - x_1}$
$m = \frac{337.4 - 334.4}{10 - 5}$
$m = 0.6$

The slope of the relation is $0.6 \frac{\text{m/s}}{°\text{C}}$.

Step 2
Determine the value of b in the linear equation $y = mx + b$.
Substitute 0.6 for m and the coordinates of any point, such as (5, 334.4), for x and y.

$y = mx + b$
$334.4 = 0.6(5) + b$
$334.4 = 3.0 + b$
$331.4 = b$

The vertical intercept is 331.4 m/s.

Step 3
Write the equation in function notation.
If $m = 0.6$ and $b = 331.4$, the equation in $y = mx + b$ form is $y = 0.6x + 331.4$.
Substituting v for y and t for x, the equation becomes $v = 0.6t + 331.4$.
Since the speed of sound, v, is a function of the temperature, t, the equation is $v(t) = 0.6t + 331.4$.

129. A

The equation of the given line is $5x - 2y = 6$.
$2y = 5x - 6$
$y = \frac{1}{2}(5x - 6)$
$y = \frac{5}{2}x - 3$

In the equation $y = mx + b$, m is the slope and b is the y-intercept made by the line.

Comparing the equation with the equation $y = mx + b$, Slope of the line $= \frac{5}{2}$

y-intercept $= -3$

Function Notation

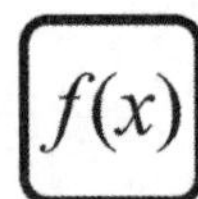

FUNCTION NOTATION

Table of Correlations

Standard		Concepts	Exercise #1	Exercise #2
Unit2.6	Understand the concept of a function and use function notation.			
F-IF.1	*Understand that a function from one set (called the domain) to another set (called the range) assigns to each element of the domain exactly one element of the range. If f is a function and x is an element of its domain, then f(x) denotes the output of f corresponding to the input x. The graph of f is the graph of the equation y = f(x).*	Identifying a Function Using a Graph	110	120
		Identifying a Function Using a Table of Values	111	121
		Identifying a Function Using a Set of Ordered Pairs	112	122
		Identifying a Function from an Equation	113	123
		Identifying a Function from a Mapping Diagram	114	124
		Identifying a Function Using Words	130	140
F-IF.2i	*Use function notation, evaluate functions for inputs in their domains, and interpret statements that use function notation in terms of a context.*	Evaluating a Linear Function Algebraically Given an Input Value	131	141
		Evaluating a Linear Function Algebraically Given an Output Value	132	142
		Evaluating a Linear Function Using a Graph	133	143
		Evaluating Linear Functions Arising from Real-World Applications	134	144
		Connecting Equation Notation With Function Notation	135	145
F-IF.3	*Recognize that sequences are functions, sometimes defined recursively, whose domain is a subset of the integers.*	Relating Arithmetic Sequences and Linear Functions	136	146
		Generating Arithmetic Sequences	137	147
		Generating Geometric Sequences	138	148
		Finding the Terms of a Sequence Given the Recursive Definition	139	149

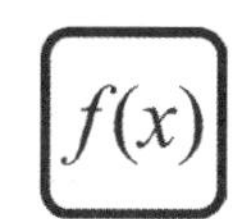

F-IF.1 Understand that a function from one set (called the domain) to another set (called the range) assigns to each element of the domain exactly one element of the range. If f is a function and x is an element of its domain, then f(x) denotes the output of f corresponding to the input x. The graph of f is the graph of the equation y = f(x).

Identifying a Function Using Words

It is important to recognize that there are many patterns in mathematics and that certain equations written in words will have a specific look to them. This method of identifying a function initially requires the use of a table of values, a set of ordered pairs, or a graph to identify the relationship between two given quantities. However, with practice, you will be able to identify these patterns and determine if a relation is a function without having to rely on tables, ordered pairs, or graphs.

Example

A relation is described as "the second number is two less than five times the first number." To determine whether or not the given relation is a function, you can either create a table of values, a set of ordered pairs, or a graph to illustrate the pattern of the words.

A possible list of ordered pairs could be (2, 8), (1, 3), (0, −2), and (−2, −12). Notice how each input value only gives one output value; therefore, this relation is a function.

Another possible way to answer these types of questions is to use mental math.

Example

A relation is stated with the words "a number is three times another number minus five."

State whether or not the given relation is a function.

Solution

The words represent a function because every value that is multiplied by three and has five subtracted from it (input) will have only one resulting value (output).

F-IF.2i Use function notation, evaluate functions for inputs in their domains, and interpret statements that use function notation in terms of a context.

Evaluating a Linear Function Algebraically Given an Input Value

When functions are represented as equations, special notation is often used. The ordered pairs (x, y) that satisfy the equation $y = 2x + 3$ form a function. Function notation is a short way of writing a rule or relationship between variables.

Functions can be represented by x-y notation, such as $y = 2x + 3$.

Function notation is shown in the equation $f(x) = 2x + 3$.

In function notation, f represents a function, and $f(x)$ can be considered as y (the dependent variable). The advantage of using function notation is that the value of the independent variable being used for any computation or analysis is readily visible. The symbol $f(x)$ is the value of the function, f, at x, and it can be read as "the value of f at x" or "f of x".

When an x-value in the domain of the function f is entered into the equation of the function, the output is $f(x)$. The output $f(x)$ is determined by the rule of the function.

Another benefit of this notation is the ease with which substitution can be communicated.

Function notation can also be used in cases in which the value of the input is known but the value of the output variable is not. For a linear function, an algebraic approach can be used to solve for an unknown output variable, $f(x)$, when given an input variable, x.

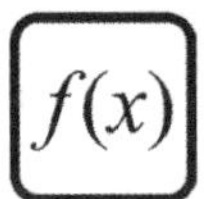

Example

Given the function $f(x) = 3x + 2$, determine the value of $f(-1)$, and state the corresponding coordinate point on the graph of $f(x) = 3x + 2$.

Solution

Substitute −1 for x in the equation.

$$\begin{aligned} f(x) &= 3x + 2 \\ f(-1) &= 3(-1) + 2 \\ &= -3 + 2 \\ &= -1 \end{aligned}$$

Since $f(x)$ represents the value of y, the corresponding coordinate point on the graph of $f(x) = 3x + 2$ is $(-1, -1)$.

Example

Given the function $f(x) = 2x - 3$, determine $f(5a)$.

Solution

Substitute $5a$ for x in the given function and simplify.

$$\begin{aligned} f(x) &= 2x - 3 \\ f(5a) &= 2(5a) - 3 \\ f(5a) &= 10a - 3 \end{aligned}$$

Example

Given the function $f(x) = 2x - 3$, determine $f(a - 6)$.

Solution

Substitute $a - 6$ in for x in the given function.

$$\begin{aligned} f(x) &= 2x - 3 \\ f(a-6) &= 2(a-6) - 3 \\ f(a-6) &= 2a - 12 - 3 \\ f(a-6) &= 2a - 15 \end{aligned}$$

Evaluating a Linear Function Algebraically Given an Output Value

In function notation, f represents a function, and $f(x)$ can be considered as y (the dependent variable). The advantage of using function notation is that the value of the independent variable being used for any computation or analysis is readily visible. The symbol $f(x)$ is the value of the function, f, at x, and it can be read as "the value of f at x" or "f of x."

When an x-value in the domain of the function f is entered into the equation of the function, the output is $f(x)$. The output, $f(x)$, is determined by the rule of the function.

Function notation can also be used in cases in which the value of the output is known but the value of the input variable is not. For a linear function, an algebraic approach can be used to solve for an unknown input variable, x, when given an output variable, $f(x)$.

Example

Given the function $g(x) = 6x - 4$, determine the value of x when $g(x) = 8$.

Solution

Determine the input, x, if the output is 8. Substitute 8 for $g(x)$, and solve for x.

$$\begin{aligned} g(x) &= 6x - 4 \\ 8 &= 6x - 4 \\ 12 &= 6x \\ x &= 2 \end{aligned}$$

Evaluating a Linear Function Using a Graph

Function notation can be used to understand values and points on linear graphs.

Example

The graph of a function, $y = f(x)$, is given.

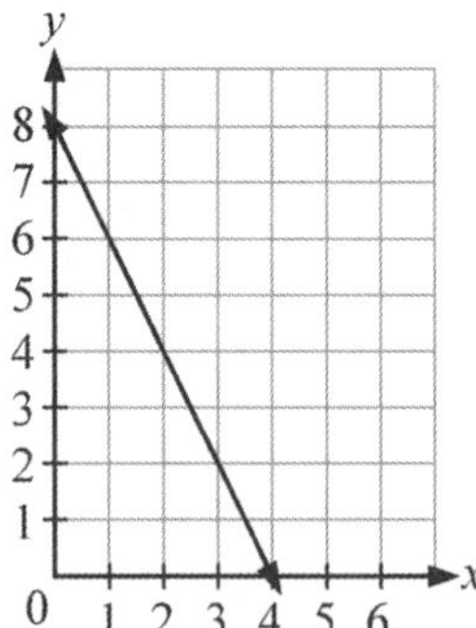

For the linear graph, determine $f(2)$.

Solution

The value of $f(2)$ is the value of y on the graph when $x = 2$.

On the graph of the function, $y = 4$ when $x = 2$.

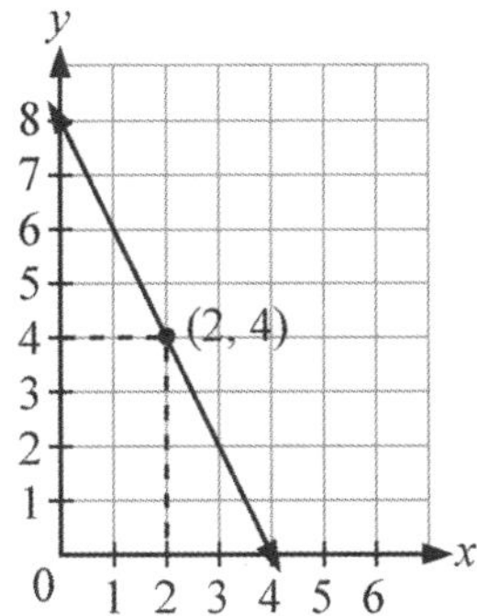

Therefore, $f(2) = 4$.

Evaluating Linear Functions Arising from Real-World Applications

While f is the most common letter used to represent a function, any letter can be used. Often, g and h are used to represent generic functions. Sometimes, the letter is selected for its connection to the question.

For example, if the question has cost represented as a function of the number of items sold, $C(n)$ might be used. To represent height as a function of time, $h(t)$ could be used.

Example

A blue whale can travel under water at a speed of about 9 m/s. The equation for the distance traveled, d meters, under water by a blue whale, in the time of t seconds is $d(t) = 9t$.

Determine the distance a blue whale can travel under water in 11 s.

Solution

To determine the distance traveled, find the value of $d(11)$. Substitute 11 for t in the equation $d(t) = 9t$.

$$\begin{aligned} d(t) &= 9t \\ d(11) &= 9(11) \\ &= 99 \text{ m} \end{aligned}$$

The blue whale can travel 99 m under water in 11 s.

Connecting Equation Notation With Function Notation

Function notation involves the use of symbols such as $f(x)$ and $g(x)$ to represent the dependent variable (often y) in a function. For example, the equation $y = 3x - 4$ may be written as $f(x) = 3x - 4$.

The advantage of using function notation is that the value of the independent variable being used for any computation or analysis is readily visible. The symbol $f(x)$ refers to the value of the function, f, at x, and it can be read as "the value of f at x" or "f of x". This notation emphasizes that the function values (output values) are produced from values of x (input values).

Example

Write the equation $y = 6x + 5$ in function notation.

Solution

An equation can be written in function notation by replacing y with $f(x)$.

Written in function notation, the equation $y = 6x + 5$ is $f(x) = 6x + 5$.

You can convert between other forms of equations and function notation. A function that is in general form, $Ax + By + C = 0$, can be converted to function notation by solving for y and replacing y with $f(x)$.

Example

Write the equation $7x - 3y + 18 = 0$ in function notation.

Solution

Step 1

Solve for y.

$$7x - 3y + 18 = 0$$
$$-3y = -7x - 18$$
$$y = \frac{-7x}{-3} - \frac{18}{-3}$$
$$y = \frac{7x}{3} + 6$$

Step 2

Replace y with $f(x)$.

$$f(x) = \frac{7x}{3} + 6$$

F-IF.3 Recognize that sequences are functions, sometimes defined recursively, whose domain is a subset of the integers.

Relating Arithmetic Sequences and Linear Functions

Consider the following arithmetic sequence:
4, 1, −2, −5, ...

The value of $a = 4$ and the value of $d = -3$.

By substituting these values into the general term formula, the general term of the sequence is produced.

$$t_n = a + (n - 1)d$$
$$t_n = 4 + (n - 1)(-3)$$
$$t_n = 4 + -3n + 3$$
$$t_n = -3n + 7$$

If t_n is replaced with y and n is replaced with x, then the equation for this general term, and for all arithmetic sequences, models a linear function. In other words, the equation of the general term will produce linear functions with graphs that are straight lines and have domains in the natural number set.

To graph the arithmetic sequence, $t_n = -3n + 7$, create a table of values where x is the term number and y is the term, and then graph the ordered pairs using the LIST editor on a graphing calculator.

x	y
1	4
2	1
3	−2
4	−5
5	−8
6	−11

The arithmetic sequence will produce the following graph:

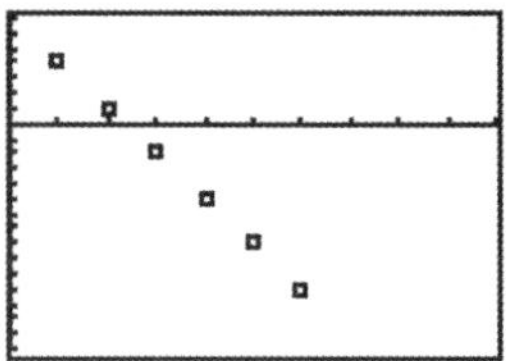

Enter the general term $t_n = -3n + 7$ into a graphing calculator in the form of $y = -3x + 7$.

This function will produce the following graph:

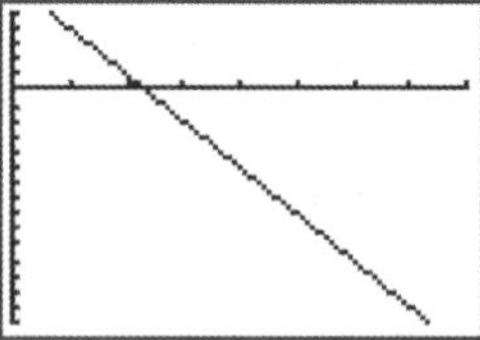

Note, that the table feature on a graphing calculator allows for a list of the entire sequence to be displayed.

$f(x)$

An arithmetic sequence produces a linear function in which each x-value has its own distinct y-value. An arithmetic sequence also passes the vertical line test, and it graphs a straight, diagonal line.

Since the general term of an arithmetic sequence is related to the equation of a linear function, it is possible to relate the common difference of an arithmetic sequence to the slope of a linear function.

Example

Several terms of the arithmetic sequence are shown below:

a	t_2	t_3	t_4	...
-4	1	6	11	...

Determine the slope of the graph for the terms of the arithmetic sequence.

Solution

Step 1

Determine the common difference.

$$\begin{aligned} d &= t_4 - t_3 \\ &= t_3 - t_2 \\ &= t_2 - a \\ &= 5 \end{aligned}$$

Step 2

Determine the general of the arithmetic sequence.

$$\begin{aligned} t_n &= a + (n-1)d \\ &= -4 + (n-1)5 \\ &= -4 + 5n - 5 \\ &= 5n - 9 \end{aligned}$$

Step 3

Write the corresponding linear function.

The arithmetic sequence consists of discrete points on the graph of the linear function $y = 5x - 9$ for the x-values of 1, 2, 3, 4, ... (all Natural numbers).

Step 4

Determine the slope.

The slope of the graph of the arithmetic sequence $t_n = 5n - 9$ is the same as the slope of the linear function $y = 5x - 9$ and is equal to 5.

The slope of a linear function is the same as the common difference. In general, the common difference d of an arithmetic sequence $t_n = a + (n-1)d$ is equal to the slope m of the corresponding linear function $y = mx + b$.

It is also possible to relate the y-intercept to the first term of an arithmetic sequence.

Example

Several terms of the arithmetic sequence are shown below:

a	t_2	t_3	t_4	...
14	8	2	-4	...

Determine the difference between the first term of the arithmetic sequence and the y-intercept of the corresponding linear function.

Solution

Step 1

Determine the common difference.

$$\begin{aligned} d &= t_4 - t_3 \\ &= t_3 - t_2 \\ &= t_2 - a \\ &= -6 \end{aligned}$$

Step 2

Determine the general term of the arithmetic sequence.

$$\begin{aligned} t_n &= a + (n-1)d \\ &= 14 + (n-1)(-6) \\ &= 14 - 6n + 6 \\ &= -6n + 20 \end{aligned}$$

Step 3

Write the corresponding linear function.

The arithmetic sequence consists of discrete points on the graph of the linear function $y = -6x + 20$ for the x-values of 1, 2, 3, 4, ... (all Natural numbers).

Step 4

Determine the difference between the first term of the arithmetic sequence and the y-intercept of the corresponding linear function.

$$\begin{aligned} a - b &= (14) - (20) \\ &= -6 \\ &= d \end{aligned}$$

The difference is -6, which is the same value as the common difference.

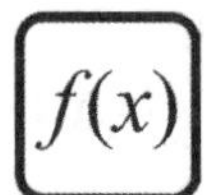

Since the difference between term number 1 and the y-intercept is the common difference of the arithmetic sequence, it is possible to describe the y-intercept b as the zero term of an arithmetic sequence. In practical terms, the zero term is the starting value, such as a flat fee for a service or the initial position of a moving object.

Generating Arithmetic Sequences

In order to generate an arithmetic sequence, a starting value and the common difference are required. All terms can then be generated by repeatedly adding the same amount to each term.

Example

Generate the first five terms of the arithmetic sequence that starts with 14 and has a common difference of 7.

Solution

$14 + 7 = 21$
$21 + 7 = 28$
$28 + 7 = 35$
$35 + 7 = 42$

The first five terms of this arithmetic sequence are 14, 21, 28, 35, and 42.

Example

Generate the first five terms of the arithmetic sequence that starts with 1.3 and has a common difference of −2.4.

Solution

$1.3 + (-2.4) = -1.1$
$-1.1 + (-2.4) = -3.5$
$-3.5 + (-2.4) = -5.9$
$-5.9 + (-2.4) = -8.3$

The first five terms in this arithmetic sequence are 1.3, −1.1, −3.5, −5.9, and −8.3.

Example

Generate the first five terms of the arithmetic sequence that starts with $\frac{1}{3}$ and has a common difference of $\frac{2}{3}$.

Solution

$\frac{1}{3} + \frac{2}{3} = 1$
$1 + \frac{2}{3} = 1\frac{2}{3}$
$1\frac{2}{3} + \frac{2}{3} = 2\frac{1}{3}$
$2\frac{1}{3} + \frac{2}{3} = 3$

The first five terms in this arithmetic sequence are $\frac{1}{3}$, 1, $1\frac{2}{3}$, $2\frac{1}{3}$, and 3.

Generating Geometric Sequences

In order to generate a geometric sequence, a starting value and the common ratio, r, are required. All terms can then be generated by repeatedly multiplying the common ratio to each term.

Example

Generate the first five terms of the geometric sequence that starts with 11 and has a common ratio of 3.

Solution

$11 \times 3 = 33$
$33 \times 3 = 99$
$99 \times 3 = 297$
$297 \times 3 = 891$

The first five terms of this geometric sequence are 11, 33, 99, 297, and 891.

Example

Generate the first five terms of the geometric sequence that starts with 1.5 and has a common ratio of –3.5.

Solution

$$1.5 \times (-3.5) = -5.25$$
$$-5.25 \times (-3.5) = 18.375$$
$$18.375 \times (-3.5) = -64.3125$$
$$-64.3125 \times (-3.5) = 225.09375$$

The first five terms in this geometric sequence are 1.5, –5.25, 18.375, –64.3125, 225.09375

Alternatively, when at least two consecutive terms of a geometric sequence are given, other terms in the geometric sequence can be determined.

Example

Find the next three terms of the geometric sequence 4, 20, 100, ...

Solution

Find r.

$$r = \frac{20}{4}$$
$$r = 5$$

Calculate the next three terms by multiplying the preceding term by the value of r.

$t_4 = 100 \times 5 = 500$

$t_5 = 500 \times 5 = 2,500$

$t_6 = 2,500 \times 5 = 12,500$

Example

Find the next three terms of the geometric sequence $\sqrt{5}, \sqrt{10}, 2\sqrt{5}, ...$

Solution

Find r.

$$r = \frac{\sqrt{10}}{\sqrt{5}}$$
$$r = \sqrt{2}$$

Calculate the next three terms by multiplying the preceding term by the value of r.

$t_4 = 2\sqrt{5} \times \sqrt{2} = 2\sqrt{10}$

$t_5 = 2\sqrt{10} \times \sqrt{2} = 2\sqrt{20}$

$t_6 = 2\sqrt{20} \times \sqrt{2} = 2\sqrt{40}$

Example

Find the next three terms of the geometric sequence $\frac{3}{2}, \frac{3}{4}, \frac{3}{8}, ...$

Solution

Find r.

$$r = \frac{\frac{3}{4}}{\frac{3}{2}}$$
$$r = \frac{3}{4} \times \frac{2}{3}$$
$$r = \frac{1}{2}$$

Calculate the next three terms by multiplying the preceding term by the value of r.

$t_4 = \frac{3}{8} \times \frac{1}{2} = \frac{3}{16}$

$t_5 = \frac{3}{16} \times \frac{1}{2} = \frac{3}{32}$

$t_6 = \frac{3}{32} \times \frac{1}{2} = \frac{3}{64}$

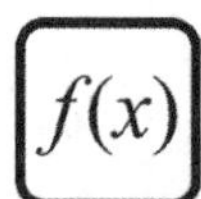

Finding the Terms of a Sequence Given the Recursive Definition

A **recursive pattern** is a sequence that uses one term to find the next term in the sequence. An operation is performed on the first term of the sequence to obtain the next term. For example, in order to determine the tenth term in a recursive sequence, you need to know the ninth term.

To determine unknown terms of a recursive sequence, a recursive definition is required.

Example

A recursive sequence is defined as $t_{n+1} = 8 + 3t_n$, with the first term equal to 6.

What is the fourth term of the sequence?

Solution

In this case, the first term is 6. Since the recursive sequence is defined as $t_{n+1} = 8 + 3t_n$, substitute the first term into the formula to find the next term.

Step 1
Calculate the second term.
Let $t_1 = 6$.

$$\begin{aligned} t_{n+1} &= 8 + 3t_n \\ t_{1+1} &= 8 + 3t_1 \\ t_2 &= 8 + 3(6) \\ t_2 &= 8 + 18 \\ t_2 &= 26 \end{aligned}$$

Step 2
Calculate the third term.
Let $t_2 = 26$.

$$\begin{aligned} t_{n+1} &= 8 + 3t_n \\ t_{2+1} &= 8 + 3t_2 \\ t_3 &= 8 + 3(26) \\ t_3 &= 8 + 78 \\ t_3 &= 86 \end{aligned}$$

Step 3
Calculate the fourth term.
Let $t_3 = 86$.

$$\begin{aligned} t_{n+1} &= 8 + 3t_n \\ t_{3+1} &= 8 + 3t_3 \\ t_4 &= 8 + 3(86) \\ t_4 &= 8 + 258 \\ t_4 &= 266 \end{aligned}$$

Therefore, the fourth term of this sequence is 266.

Example

A recursive sequence is defined as $t_n = 3(t_{n-1} + 7)$, where $n > 1$.

If the third term is equal to 138, determine the value of t_1.

Solution

It is given that the third term is 138. Substitute the third term into the formula $t_n = 3(t_{n-1} + 7)$ to find the previous term.

Step 1
Calculate the second term.
Let $t_3 = 138$.

$$\begin{aligned} t_3 &= 3(t_{3-1} + 7) \\ 138 &= 3(t_2 + 7) \\ 46 &= t_2 + 7 \\ 39 &= t_2 \end{aligned}$$

Step 2
Calculate the first term.
Let $t_2 = 39$.

$$\begin{aligned} t_2 &= 3(t_{2-1} + 7) \\ 39 &= 3(t_1 + 7) \\ 13 &= t_1 + 7 \\ 6 &= t_1 \end{aligned}$$

Therefore, the first term in the recursive sequence is 6.

$f(x)$

EXERCISE #1—FUNCTION NOTATION

130. For a certain relation, each input value has exactly two output values. Which of the following statements about the relation is **true**?

A. The relation is a function because each input has two outputs.

B. The relation is not a function because each input has two outputs.

C. The relation is a function because there are two inputs for each output.

D. The relation is not a function because there are two inputs for each output.

131. If two linear functions are defined as $f(x) = -2x - 11$ and $g(x) = 6x + 18$, the sum of $f(-4)$ and $g(10)$ is __________.

Use the following information to answer the next question.

A linear function is given.

$$f(x) = \frac{ax}{4} + \frac{11}{4}$$

132. If $f(1) = 2$, what is the value of a?

A. −9 **B.** −3

C. 1 **D.** 3

Use the following information to answer the next question.

The graph of the linear function $y = g(x)$ is shown.

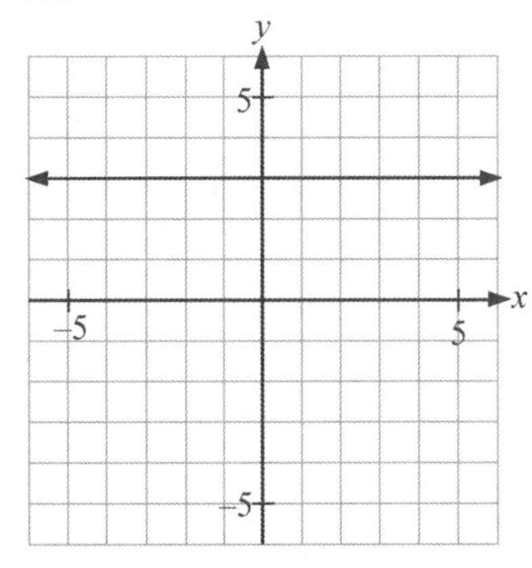

133. The value of $g(0)$ is

A. 0

B. −3

C. undefined

D. equal to the value of $g(-5)$

Use the following information to answer the next question.

The owner of a 40-unit apartment building has calculated that his monthly profit from the rental of the building is based on the total revenue from the monthly apartment rentals minus his monthly expenses of $19,500. Expressed as a function of the number of apartments rented, n, the monthly profit, $P(n)$, in dollars is given by the equation $P(n) = 900n - 19{,}500$.

134. Based on the given equation, what is the owner's monthly profit when all but 2 units are rented?

A. $13,800 **B.** $14,700

C. $15,600 **D.** $16,500

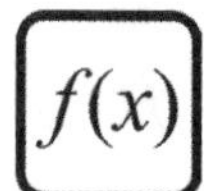

135. The function $f(x) = 5x - 3$ is equivalent to the equation

A. $-5x + y + 3 = 0$

B. $5x + y - 3 = 0$

C. $5x + y = 0$

D. $y + 3 = 0$

Use the following information to answer the next question.

Several terms of the arithmetic sequence are shown in the given chart:

a	t_2	t_3	t_4
–7	–4	–1	2

136. Determine the difference between the first term of the arithmetic sequence and the y-intercept of the corresponding linear function.

137. What are the first five terms of the arithmetic sequence that starts with $-\frac{2}{5}$ and has a common difference of $-\frac{4}{7}$?

A. $-\frac{2}{5}, \frac{34}{35}, -\frac{54}{35}, \frac{74}{35}, -\frac{94}{35}$

B. $-\frac{2}{5}, -\frac{34}{35}, -\frac{54}{35}, -\frac{74}{35}, -\frac{94}{35}$

C. $-\frac{2}{5}, \frac{8}{35}, -\frac{32}{245}, \frac{128}{1{,}715}, -\frac{512}{12{,}005}$

D. $-\frac{2}{5}, -\frac{8}{35}, -\frac{32}{245}, -\frac{128}{1{,}715}, -\frac{512}{12{,}005}$

138. If the first three terms of a geometric sequence are $\frac{\sqrt{2}}{x}$, a, and $2\sqrt{2}x^3$, what is the fourth term?

A. $\pm 4x^4$

B. $\pm 4x^5$

C. $\pm 4\sqrt{2}x^6$

D. $\pm 4\sqrt{2}x^7$

139. If a recursive sequence is defined as $t_{n+1} = 12 + 2t_n$ and the first term is equal to 5, the value of $t_2 + t_4$ is __________.

$f(x)$

EXERCISE #1—FUNCTION NOTATION ANSWERS AND SOLUTIONS

130. B	133. D	136. See solution	139. 146
131. 75	134. B	137. B	
132. B	135. A	138. B	

130. B

A relation is a function if each input value only gives one output value. In the given relation, each input has two outputs, which is not a characteristic of a function. Therefore, this relation is not a function.

131. 75

Step 1
Substitute −4 for x in the function $f(x) = -2x - 11$.

$$f(x) = -2x - 11$$
$$f(-4) = -2(-4) - 11$$

Step 2
Evaluate $f(-4)$.

$$\begin{aligned} f(-4) &= -2(-4) - 11 \\ &= 8 - 11 \\ &= -3 \end{aligned}$$

Step 3
Substitute 10 for x in the function $g(x) = 6x + 18$.

$$g(x) = 6x + 18$$
$$g(10) = 6(10) + 18$$

Step 4
Evaluate $g(10)$.

$$\begin{aligned} g(10) &= 6(10) + 18 \\ &= 60 + 18 \\ &= 78 \end{aligned}$$

Step 5
Calculate the sum of $f(-4)$ and $g(10)$.

$$\begin{aligned} f(-4) + g(10) &= -3 + 78 \\ &= 75 \end{aligned}$$

132. B

Step 1
Since $f(1) = 2$, substitute 1 for x and 2 for $f(x)$.

$$f(x) = \frac{ax}{4} + \frac{11}{4}$$
$$2 = \frac{a(1)}{4} + \frac{11}{4}$$
$$2 = \frac{a}{4} + \frac{11}{4}$$

Step 2
Solve for a.

$$\begin{aligned} 2 &= \frac{a}{4} + \frac{11}{4} \\ 4(2) &= 4\left(\frac{a}{4}\right) + 4\left(\frac{11}{4}\right) \\ 8 &= a + 11 \\ -3 &= a \end{aligned}$$

133. D

The value of $g(0)$ is the value of the y-coordinate on the graph when $x = 0$.

On the graph of the function $y = g(x)$, all the y-coordinates are 3. Therefore, $g(0) = 3$ and $g(-5) = 3$, so $g(0) = g(-5)$.

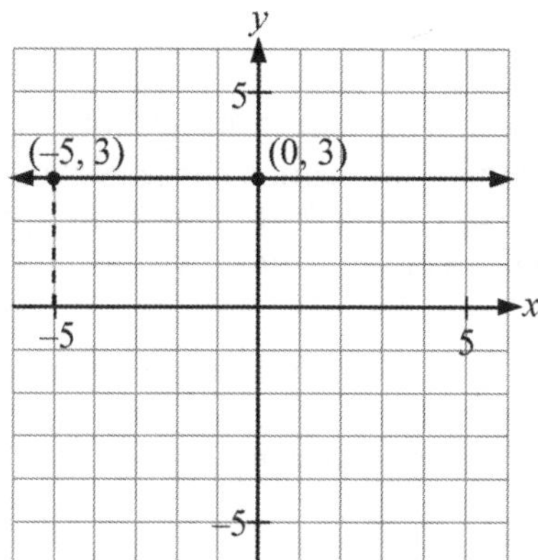

134. B

Step 1
Determine what the question is asking.

Since 2 units are not rented, 38 of the 40 units are rented.

To determine the monthly profit, find the value of $P(38)$.

Step 2
Substitute 38 for n in the equation $P(n) = 900n - 19{,}500$.

$$P(38) = 900(38) - 19{,}500$$
$$P(38) = 34{,}200 - 19{,}500$$
$$P(38) = 14{,}700$$

When all but 2 units are rented, the owner makes a monthly profit of $14,700.

135. A

Step 1
Replace $f(x)$ with y.
$y = 5x - 3$

Step 2
Convert to general form.

$$y = 5x - 3$$
$$-5x + y + 3 = 0$$

136.

Step 1
Determine the common difference.

$$\begin{aligned} d &= t_4 - t_3 \\ &= t_3 - t_2 \\ &= t_2 - a \\ &= -4 - -7 \\ &= +3 \end{aligned}$$

Step 2
Determine the general term of the arithmetic sequence.

$$\begin{aligned} t_n &= a + (n-1)d \\ &= -7 + (n-1)(3) \\ &= -7 + 3n - 3 \\ &= 3n - 10 \end{aligned}$$

Step 3
Write the corresponding linear function.

The arithmetic sequence consists of discrete points on the graph of the linear function $y = 3n - 10$ for the x-values of 1, 2, 3, 4, … (all natural numbers).

Step 4
Determine the difference between the first term of the arithmetic sequence and the y-intercept of the corresponding linear function.

$$\begin{aligned} a - b &= (-7) - (-10) \\ &= +3 \\ &= d \end{aligned}$$

The difference is +3, which is the same value as the common difference.

137. B

Step 1
Determine the value of the second term.

The first term is $-\frac{2}{5}$, and each subsequent term can be determined by adding $-\frac{4}{7}$ to the previous term.

$$t_1 = -\frac{2}{5}$$
$$\begin{aligned} t_2 &= -\frac{2}{5} + \left(-\frac{4}{7}\right) \\ &= -\frac{2}{5}\left(\frac{7}{7}\right) + \left(-\frac{4}{7}\right)\left(\frac{5}{5}\right) \\ &= -\frac{14}{35} - \frac{20}{35} \\ &= -\frac{34}{35} \end{aligned}$$

Step 2
Determine the third, fourth, and fifth terms.

$$t_2 = -\frac{34}{35}$$
$$\begin{aligned} t_3 &= -\frac{34}{35} + \left(-\frac{4}{7}\right) \\ &= -\frac{54}{35} \end{aligned}$$
$$\begin{aligned} t_4 &= -\frac{54}{35} + \left(-\frac{4}{7}\right) \\ &= -\frac{74}{35} \end{aligned}$$
$$\begin{aligned} t_5 &= -\frac{74}{35} + \left(-\frac{4}{7}\right) \\ &= -\frac{94}{35} \end{aligned}$$

The first five terms in this arithmetic sequence are $-\frac{2}{5}, -\frac{34}{35}, -\frac{54}{35}, -\frac{74}{35}$, and $-\frac{94}{35}$.

138. B

Step 1
Determine the value of a.

Since the given sequence is geometric, there is a common ratio between each pair of successive terms. As such, $\frac{t_2}{t_1} = \frac{t_3}{t_2}$.

$$\frac{a}{\frac{\sqrt{2}}{x}} = \frac{2\sqrt{2}x^3}{a}$$
$$\begin{aligned} a^2 &= \left(2\sqrt{2}x^3\right)\left(\frac{\sqrt{2}}{x}\right) \\ a^2 &= 2\sqrt{4}x^2 \\ a^2 &= 4x^2 \\ a &= \pm\sqrt{4x^2} \\ a &= \pm 2x \end{aligned}$$

Step 2

Since the second term is $a = \pm 2x$, there are two possible values for the common ratio r.

Find the common ratio when $a = 2x$.

$$\begin{aligned} r &= \frac{t_2}{t_1} \\ &= \frac{2x}{\frac{\sqrt{2}}{x}} \\ &= \frac{2x^2}{\sqrt{2}} \\ &= \sqrt{2}x^2 \end{aligned}$$

Find the common ratio when $a = -2x$.

$$\begin{aligned} r &= \frac{t_2}{t_1} \\ &= \frac{-2x}{\frac{\sqrt{2}}{x}} \\ &= \frac{-2x^2}{\sqrt{2}} \\ &= -\sqrt{2}x^2 \end{aligned}$$

The common ratio is $\pm\sqrt{2}x^2$.

Step 3

Determine the fourth term by multiplying the common ratio by the third term.

$$\begin{aligned} t_4 &= t_3 \times r \\ &= 2\sqrt{2}x^3 \times \sqrt{2}x^2 \\ &= 4x^5 \end{aligned}$$

$$\begin{aligned} t_4 &= t_3 \times r \\ &= 2\sqrt{2}x^3 \times (-\sqrt{2})x^2 \\ &= -4x^5 \end{aligned}$$

The fourth term is $\pm 4x^5$.

139. 146

Step 1

Calculate the second term of the sequence.

Using the formula $t_{n+1} = 12 + 2t_n$, let $t_1 = 5$ and find t_2.

$$\begin{aligned} t_{n+1} &= 12 + 2t_n \\ t_{1+1} &= 12 + 2t_1 \\ t_2 &= 12 + 2(5) \\ t_2 &= 12 + 10 \\ t_2 &= 22 \end{aligned}$$

Step 2

Calculate the third term of the sequence.

Let $t_2 = 22$, and determine t_3.

$$\begin{aligned} t_{n+1} &= 12 + 2t_n \\ t_{2+1} &= 12 + 2t_2 \\ t_3 &= 12 + 2(22) \\ t_3 &= 12 + 44 \\ t_3 &= 56 \end{aligned}$$

Step 3

Calculate the fourth term of the sequence.

Let $t_3 = 56$, and determine t_4.

$$\begin{aligned} t_{n+1} &= 12 + 2t_n \\ t_{3+1} &= 12 + 2t_3 \\ t_4 &= 12 + 2(56) \\ t_4 &= 12 + 112 \\ t_4 &= 124 \end{aligned}$$

Step 4

Determine the value of $t_2 + t_4$.

$$\begin{aligned} t_2 + t_4 &= 22 + 124 \\ t_2 + t_4 &= 146 \end{aligned}$$

The value of $t_2 + t_4$ is 146.

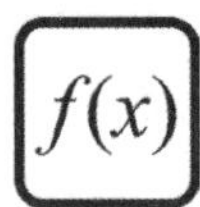

EXERCISE #2—FUNCTION NOTATION

140. For a certain relation, each output value is equal to an input value squared. Which of the following statements about this relation is **true**?

A. This relation is a function because each input has only one output.

B. This relation is a function because each output has only one input.

C. This relation is not a function because there are two outputs for each input.

D. This relation is not a function because two inputs can have the same output.

141. For the linear function $f(x) = -20x + 5$, the sum of $f(-2)$ and $f(-5)$ is __________.

Use the following information to answer the next question.

The function $g(x) = ax - 6$, and $g(4) = 124$.

142. To the nearest tenth, the value of a is __________.

Use the following information to answer the next question.

The graphs of the linear functions $y = f(x)$ and $y = g(x)$ are shown.

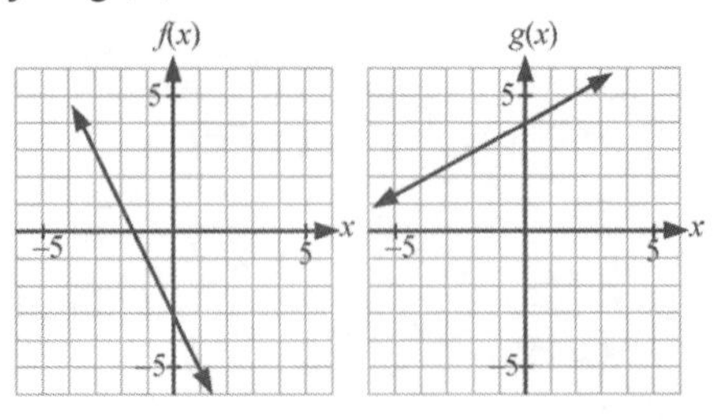

143. What is the value of $g(-4) + f(-2)$?

A. 2 **B.** 3

C. 7 **D.** 8

Use the following information to answer the next question.

A car initially traveling at a constant speed of 20 m/s begins to accelerate. While the car accelerates, the speed of the car as a function of time can be expressed by the equation $s(t) = 20 + 1.5t$, where $s(t)$ is the speed in meters per second and t is the time in seconds.

144. Expressed to the nearest tenth, the speed of the car 3.2 s after it starts accelerating is approximately __________m/s.

145. The equation $4x - 2y + 6 = 0$ in function notation is

A. $f(x) = -4x + 6$

B. $f(x) = -4x - 6$

C. $f(x) = 2x - 3$

D. $f(x) = 2x + 3$

146. Describe an investment that could be represented by the function $f(x) = 800(1 + 0.03x)$.

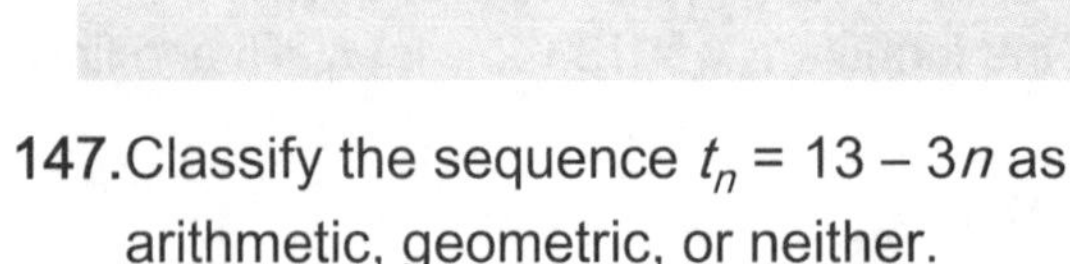

147. Classify the sequence $t_n = 13 - 3n$ as arithmetic, geometric, or neither.

148. If $\frac{3\sqrt{2}}{4}$ is the first term in a geometric sequence and the common ratio is $\sqrt{2}$, then the sixth term is

A. 6 **B.** 3

C. $6\sqrt{2}$ **D.** $3\sqrt{2}$

149. Which of the following sequences follows a recursive pattern defined by the formula $t_{n+1} = 4t_n - 7$, with the first term equal to 4?

A. 4, 2, 0, –2… **B.** 4, 1, –3, –6…

C. 4, 20, 36, 52… **D.** 4, 9, 29, 109…

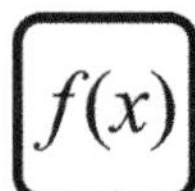

EXERCISE #2—FUNCTION NOTATION ANSWERS AND SOLUTIONS

140. A	143. B	146. See solution	149. D
141. 150	144. 24.8	147. See solution	
142. 32.5	145. D	148. A	

140. A

A relation is a function if each input value gives only one output value. The given relation generates a single output value by squaring the input value; therefore, it is a function.

141. 150

Step 1
Evaluate $f(-2)$ in $f(x) = -20x + 5$ by substituting -2 for x.

$$\begin{aligned} f(x) &= -20x + 5 \\ f(-2) &= -20(-2) + 5 \\ &= 40 + 5 \\ &= 45 \end{aligned}$$

Step 2
Evaluate $f(-5)$ in $f(x) = -20x + 5$ by substituting -5 for x.

$$\begin{aligned} f(x) &= -20x + 5 \\ f(-5) &= -20(-5) + 5 \\ &= 100 + 5 \\ &= 105 \end{aligned}$$

Step 3
Calculate the sum of $f(-2)$ and $f(-5)$.

$$\begin{aligned} f(-2) + f(-5) &= 45 + 105 \\ &= 150 \end{aligned}$$

142. 32.5

Step 1
Since $g(4) = 124$, substitute 4 for x and 124 for $g(x)$, in the equation $g(x) = ax - 6$.

$$\begin{aligned} g(x) &= ax - 6 \\ 124 &= a(4) - 6 \end{aligned}$$

Step 2
Solve for a.

$$\begin{aligned} 124 &= a(4) - 6 \\ 124 + 6 &= 4a - 6 + 6 \\ 130 &= 4a \\ \frac{130}{4} &= a \\ 32.5 &= a \end{aligned}$$

143. B

Step 1
Determine the value of $g(-4)$.

The value of $g(-4)$ is the value of the y-coordinate on the graph when $x = -4$.

On the graph of the function $y = g(x)$, $y = 2$ when $x = -4$. Therefore, $g(-4) = 2$.

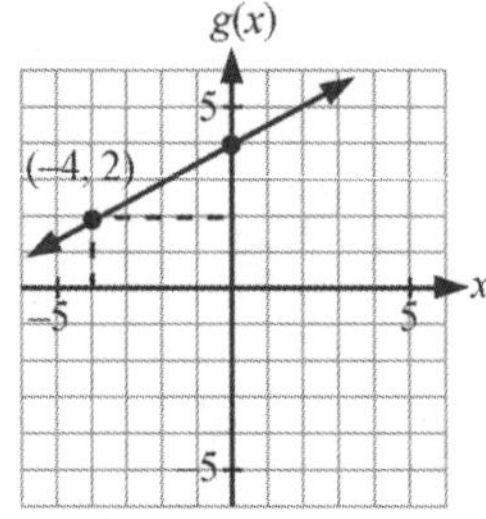

Step 2
Determine the value of $f(-2)$.

The value of $f(-2)$ is the value of the y-coordinate on the graph when $x = -2$.

On the graph of the function $y = f(x)$, $y = 1$ when $x = -2$. Therefore, $f(-2) = 1$.

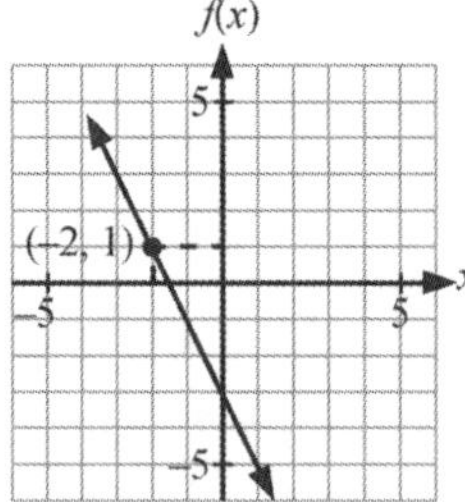

Step 3
Determine the value of $g(-4) + f(-2)$.

$$\begin{aligned} g(-4) + f(-2) &= 2 + 1 \\ &= 3 \end{aligned}$$

144. 24.8

To determine the speed, find the value of $s(3.2)$.

Substitute 3.2 for t in the equation $s(t) = 20 + 1.5t$.

$$\begin{aligned} s(3.2) &= 20 + 1.5(3.2) \\ s(3.2) &= 20 + 4.8 \\ s(3.2) &= 24.8 \end{aligned}$$

After accelerating for 3.2 s, the speed of the car is approximately 24.8 m/s.

145. D

Step 1
Solve for y.

$$4x-2y+6=0$$
$$-2y=-4x-6$$
$$\frac{-2y}{-2}=\frac{-4x-6}{-2}$$
$$y=2x+3$$

Step 2
Replace y with $f(x)$.

$$f(x)=2x+3$$

146.

The function $f(x) = 800(1 + 0.03x)$ has the following values:

$$f(1) = 800(1 + 0.03(1)) = 824$$
$$f(2) = 800(1 + 0.03(2)) = 848$$
$$f(3) = 800(1 + 0.03(3)) = 872$$

Since these values can continue according to the given function, these amounts represent the values of an investment with a principal amount of $800 invested at a simple interest rate of 3%/*a*, where $f(1)$ is the value of the investment at the end of the first year, $f(2)$ is the value of the investment at the end of the second year, and so on.

147.

Step 1
Determine the terms of the sequence.

$$t_n = 13 - 3n$$
$$t_1 = 13 - 3(1) = 10$$
$$t_2 = 13 - 3(2) = 7$$
$$t_3 = 13 - 3(3) = 4$$
$$t_4 = 13 - 3(4) = 1$$

Therefore, the sequence is 10, 7, 4, 1, …

Step 2
Determine the first differences of the sequence.

$$7 - 10 = -3$$
$$4 - 7 = -3$$
$$1 - 4 = -3$$

These are constant.

Step 3
Determine the ratio of consecutive terms.

$$\frac{7}{10} = 0.7$$
$$\frac{4}{7} \approx 0.57$$
$$\frac{1}{4} = 0.25$$

These are not constant.
Therefore, this sequence is arithmetic.

148. A

Generate the sequence to determine the sixth term.

To generate this sequence, multiply each successive term by $\sqrt{2}$, beginning with the first term, $\frac{3\sqrt{2}}{4}$.

$$t_2 = t_1 \times r = \frac{3\sqrt{2}}{4} \times \sqrt{2} = \frac{3}{2}$$
$$t_3 = t_2 \times r = \frac{3}{2} \times \sqrt{2} = \frac{3\sqrt{2}}{2}$$
$$t_4 = t_3 \times r = \frac{3\sqrt{2}}{2} \times \sqrt{2} = 3$$
$$t_5 = t_4 \times r = 3 \times \sqrt{2} = 3\sqrt{2}$$
$$t_6 = t_5 \times r = 3\sqrt{2} \times \sqrt{2} = 6$$

149. D

A pattern that uses the previous term to find the next term in a sequence is called a recursive pattern. In a recursive pattern, an operation is performed on the first term to obtain the next term. In this case, the first term is 4. Substitute the first term into the formula $t_{n+1} = 4t_n - 7$ to find the next term.

Step 1
Calculate the second term.

Let $t_1 = 4$.

$$t_{1+1} = 4t_1 - 7$$
$$t_2 = 4(4) - 7$$
$$t_2 = 16 - 7$$
$$t_2 = 9$$

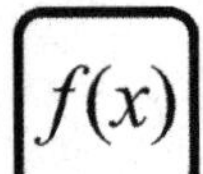

Step 2
Calculate the third term.
Let $t_2 = 9$.

$$t_{2+1} = 4t_2 - 7$$
$$t_3 = 4(9) - 7$$
$$t_3 = 36 - 7$$
$$t_3 = 29$$

Step 3
Calculate the fourth term.
Let $t_3 = 29$.

$$t_{3+1} = 4t_3 - 7$$
$$t_4 = 4(29) - 7$$
$$t_4 = 116 - 7$$
$$t_4 = 109$$

The sequence is 4, 9, 29, 109…

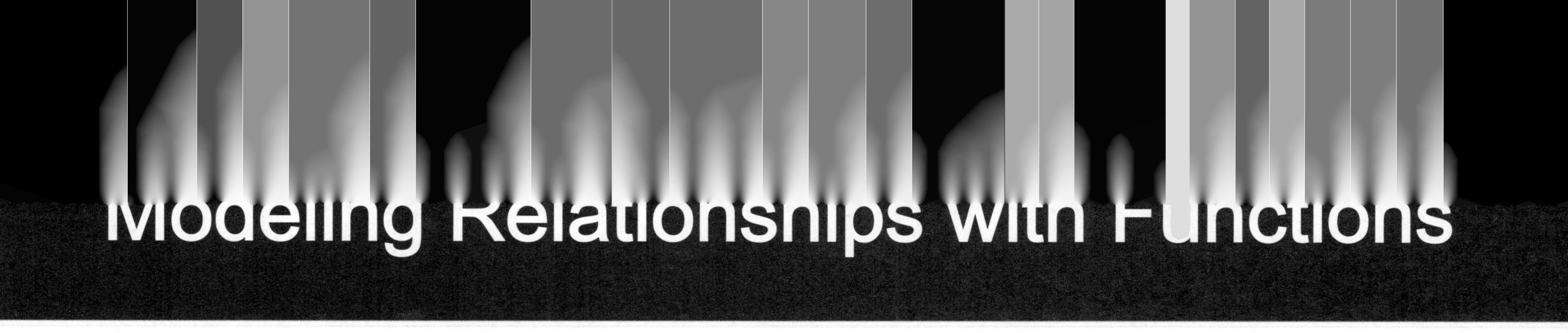
Modeling Relationships with Functions

MODELING RELATIONSHIPS WITH FUNCTIONS

<table>
<tr><th colspan="5">Table of Correlations</th></tr>
<tr><th colspan="2">Standard</th><th>Concepts</th><th>Exercise #1</th><th>Exercise #2</th></tr>
<tr><td>Unit2.7</td><td colspan="4">Use functions to model relationships between quantities.</td></tr>
<tr><td rowspan="9">8.F.4</td><td rowspan="9">Construct a function to model a linear relationship between two quantities. Determine the rate of change and initial value of the function from a description of a relationship or from two (x, y) values, including reading these from a table or from a graph. Interpret the rate of change and initial value of a linear function in terms of the situation it models, and in terms of its graph or a table of values.</td><td>Meaning of y-intercept and Slope in Graphs of Real Situations</td><td>18</td><td>24</td></tr>
<tr><td>Determining the Characteristics of the Graph of a Linear Function</td><td>116</td><td>127</td></tr>
<tr><td>Defining Function Notation for a Linear Function in Two Variables</td><td>119</td><td>128</td></tr>
<tr><td>Defining Equations in Slope-Intercept Form</td><td>117</td><td>129</td></tr>
<tr><td>Using Formulas to Determine the Slope of a Line</td><td>150</td><td>157</td></tr>
<tr><td>Writing a Linear Equation to Represent a Table of Values</td><td>151</td><td>158</td></tr>
<tr><td>Defining Equations in General Form</td><td>152</td><td>159</td></tr>
<tr><td>Writing an Equation in $y = mx + b$ Form from Its Given Graph</td><td>153</td><td>160</td></tr>
<tr><td>Writing Equations in Slope-Point Form</td><td>154</td><td>161</td></tr>
<tr><td rowspan="3">8.F.5</td><td rowspan="3">Describe qualitatively the functional relationship between two quantities by analyzing a graph. Sketch a graph that exhibits the qualitative features of a function that has been described verbally.</td><td>Determining the Characteristics of the Graph of a Linear Function</td><td>116</td><td>127</td></tr>
<tr><td>Graphing a Rate of Change</td><td>155</td><td>162</td></tr>
<tr><td>Interpreting Points on a Linear Graph</td><td>156</td><td></td></tr>
</table>

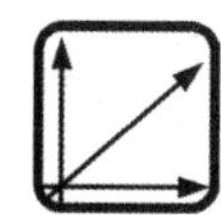

8.F.4 Construct a function to model a linear relationship between two quantities. Determine the rate of change and initial value of the function from a description of a relationship or from two (x, y) values, including reading these from a table or from a graph. Interpret the rate of change and initial value of a linear function in terms of the situation it models, and in terms of its graph or a table of values.

Using Formulas to Determine the Slope of a Line

The **slope** of a line is a measure of the line's steepness. Slope is usually represented by the lowercase letter *m*.

Finding Slope Graphically

The slope of a line can be determined graphically by comparing the vertical change to the horizontal change of the line. The vertical change is called the **rise**. Rise is the change in the *y*-values (indicated by the Greek letter delta, Δ).
The horizontal change is called the **run**. Run is the change in the *x*-values (indicated by the Greek letter delta, Δ).

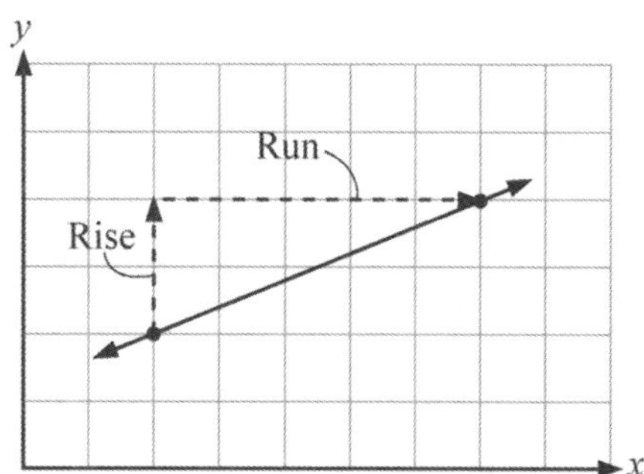

Slope (m) is the ratio of rise over run, and can be expressed as follows:

$$m = \frac{\text{rise}}{\text{run}} = \frac{\text{the change in } y}{\text{the change in } x} = \frac{\Delta y}{\Delta x}$$

Finding Slope Algebraically

When given the ordered pairs $(x_1,\ y_1)$ and $(x_2,\ y_2)$ of two points on a line, the slope can be calculated algebraically.

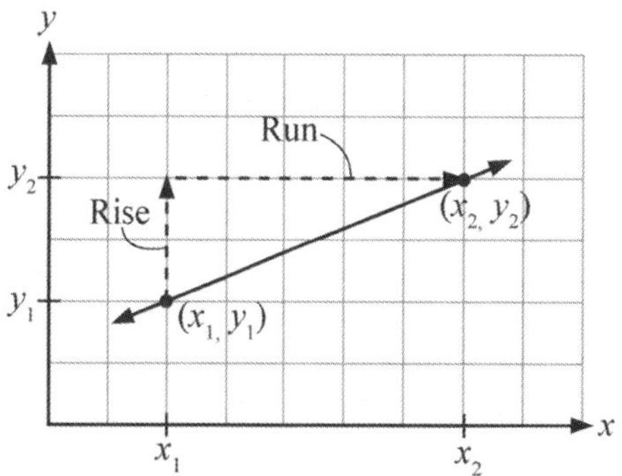

The change in the *x*- and *y*-values is found by calculating the differences between the *x*-coordinates $(x_2 - x_1)$ and the *y*-coordinates $(y_2 - y_1)$. The slope (m) is the ratio between these differences.

$$m = \frac{y_2 - y_1}{x_2 - x_1}$$

This process of determining slope is often referred to as the **slope formula**.

Example

A line passing through points *A* and *B* is shown.

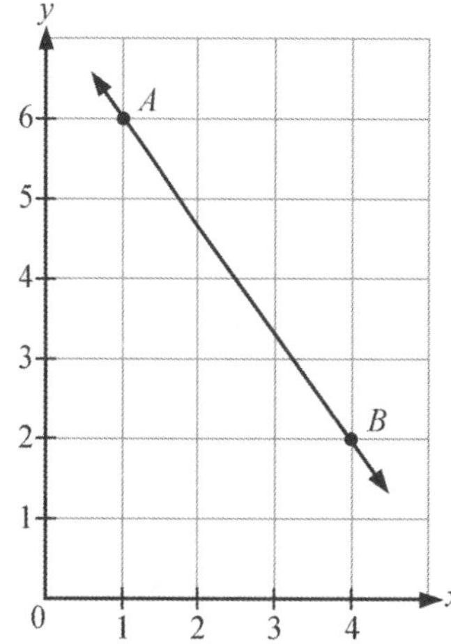

Find the slope of the line.

Solution

Graphically:

To get from point A to point B, go *down* (negative direction) 4 units, and then go *right* (positive direction) 3 units. The rise is −4 and the run is +3.

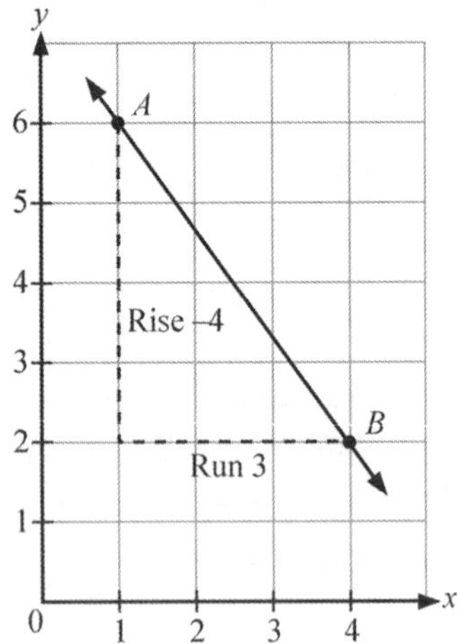

The slope is the ratio between the rise and the run.

$$m = \frac{\text{rise}}{\text{run}} = \frac{-4}{3} = -\frac{4}{3}$$

Algebraically:

Identify two points on the line.

Label the points.

$\underset{\text{Point 1}}{(1, 6)}$ and $\underset{\text{Point 2}}{(4, 2)}$

Label the coordinates.

$y_2 = 2,\ y_1 = 6$

$x_2 = 4,\ x_1 = 1$

Substitute the values into the slope formula and then solve.

$$m = \frac{y_2 - y_1}{x_2 - x_1} = \frac{2 - 6}{4 - 1} = \frac{-4}{3} = -\frac{4}{3}$$

Therefore, the slope of AB is $-\frac{4}{3}$.

Example

A line passing through the points M and N is shown.

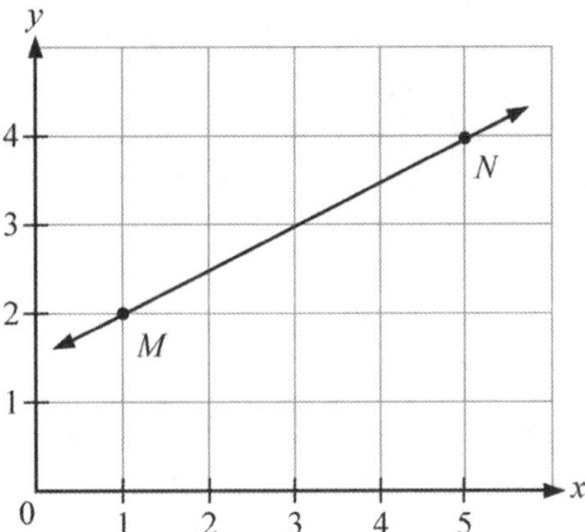

Find the slope of the line graphically and algebraically.

Solution

Graphically:

To get from point M to point N, go up (positive direction) 2 units, and then go right (positive direction) 4 units. Therefore, the rise is +2 and the run is +4.

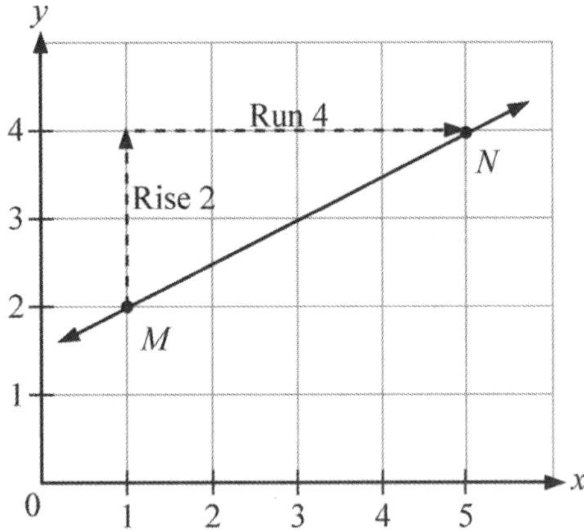

The slope is the ratio between the rise and the run.

$$\text{slope} = \frac{\text{rise}}{\text{run}} = \frac{2}{4} = \frac{1}{2}$$

Algebraically:
Identify two points on the line:
Point 1: (1, 2)
Point 2: (5, 4).

Label the coordinates.
$y_2 = 4,\ y_1 = 2$
$x_2 = 5,\ x_1 = 1$

Substitute the values into the slope formula and then solve.

$$m = \frac{y_2 - y_1}{x_2 - x_1} = \frac{4-2}{5-1} = \frac{2}{4} = \frac{1}{2}$$

Therefore, the slope of the line is $\frac{1}{2}$.

Writing a Linear Equation to Represent a Table of Values

An **expression** is an arrangement of numbers, variables, and mathematical symbols used to express a value or relationship. For example, $20t - 12$ is an expression.

An **equation** is an arrangement of two expressions separated by an equal sign (=). In an equation, the expressions on both sides of the equal sign are equal in value. For example, $a = 20t - 12$ is an equation expressing the fact that a is equal in value to $20t - 12$.

An equation can be used to represent a table of values. To write an equation based on a table of values, follow these steps:

1. Assign meaningful variables to the quantities involved.
2. Determine the relationship between the values of the first ordered pair.
3. Determine the relationship between the values of the second ordered pair.
4. Compare the relationship between the ordered pairs. If the relationship is the same, a linear equation can be written to express the relationship. If the relationship is different, a linear equation does not exist for the given table of values.
5. Write the equation.
6. Verify the equation using other values from the table.

Example

The given table of values represents a linear relation.

x	y
5	2
6	3
7	4
8	5
9	6

Write a linear equation that represents the pattern found in the given table of values, and verify the equation.

Solution

Solution

Step 1
Assign meaningful variables to the quantities involved.

In this problem, variables x and y have already been assigned.

Step 2
Determine the relationship between the values of the first ordered pair (5, 2).

The value of x is 5, and the value of y is 2.
The y-value is 3 less than the x-value.

Step 3
Determine the relationship between the values of the second ordered pair (6, 3).
The value of x is 6, and the value of y is 3.
The y-value is 3 less than the x-value.

Step 4
Compare the relationship between the ordered pairs.
The relationship between the values of the first ordered pair is the same as the relationship between the values of the second ordered pair. It is the same between all of the given ordered pairs; therefore, a linear equation can be written to represent the pattern in the table.

Step 5
Write the equation.
The y-values in the table are 3 less than the x-values.
Since the word *less* implies subtraction, the equation is written $y = x - 3$.

Step 6
Verify the equation using other values from the table.
The third ordered pair from the table is (7, 4).
Substitute the x- and y-values into the equation to verify that it is correct.
$y = x - 3$
$4 = 7 - 3$
$4 = 4$
The pattern in the table of values can be represented by the linear equation $y = x - 3$.

Defining Equations in General Form

All linear relations can be written in the general form $Ax + By + C = 0$, where A, B, and C are real numbers and where at least one of the numbers A or B is not equal to 0. A and B are called coefficients, and C is called the constant term.

The following equations are examples of linear relations written in general form.

- $3x + 5y - 8 = 0$
- $2.7x - 3.4y - 8 = 0$
- $\frac{3}{5}a - 6b + \pi = 0$
- $10x - 5 = 0$
- $3y + 29 = 0$

If a linear relation is not written in general form, it can be converted to general form. In many cases, the relation can be converted to general form with integral coefficients. Also, if the integral coefficients have a common factor, the coefficients can all be divided by that common factor to simplify the equation.

Example

Express the relation $14y = -6x - 22$ in simplest general form with integral coefficients.

Solution

Step 1
Add $6x$ and 22 to both sides.
$6x + 14y + 22 = 0$

Step 2
Divide both sides by 2.
$3x + 7y + 11 = 0$

Example

Express the relation $\frac{2}{3}x - 6 = 4y$ in simplest general form with integral coefficients.

Solution

Step 1
Multiply both sides by 3.
$2x - 18 = 12y$

Step 2
Subtract $12y$ from both sides.
$2x - 12y - 18 = 0$

Step 3
Divide both sides by 2.
$x - 6y - 9 = 0$

Example

Express the relation $y - 7 = \frac{5}{2}(x - 6)$ in simplest general form with integral coefficients.

Solution

Step 1
Multiply both sides by 2.
$2(y - 7) = 2\left(\frac{5}{2}(x - 6)\right)$
$2y - 14 = 5(x - 6)$

Step 2
Expand the right side of the equation.
$2y - 14 = 5x - 30$

Step 3
Subtract $5x$ and add 30 to both sides.
$-5x + 2y - 14 + 30 = 0$
$-5x + 2y + 16 = 0$

Step 4
Multiply both sides by -1.
$5x - 2y - 16 = 0$

It is often preferable to have a positive coefficient for the x-term (A).

Writing an Equation in $y = mx + b$ Form from Its Given Graph

To write an equation of a line in the form $y = mx + b$, it is necessary to find the slope of the line in order to form the equation. Finding the slope requires identifying two points on the line. Once the slope is determined, the equation of the line can be written.

The equation of a line from its given graph can be determined using the following steps:

1. Identify two points on the line, and determine the slope using the formula $m = \frac{y_2 - y_1}{x_2 - x_1}$.
2. Discard one of the two points. Use the calculated slope and the other point with the formula $m = \frac{y - y_1}{x - x_1}$ to determine the equation of the line.

The easiest points to use are the x- and y-intercepts, but any two points will work.

Example

A graph of a linear equation is given.

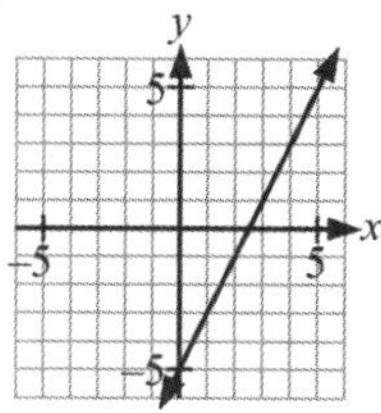

In the form $y = mx + b$, determine the equation of the line from its given graph.

Solution

Step 1
Identify two points on the line, and determine the slope using the formula $m = \frac{y_2 - y_1}{x_2 - x_1}$.

Two points on the line are (0, −5) and (3, 1). Substitute these points into the formula.

$$m = \frac{y_2 - y_1}{x_2 - x_1}$$
$$m = \frac{1 - (-5)}{3 - 0}$$
$$m = \frac{6}{3}$$
$$m = 2$$

Step 2
Use the calculated slope and one point with the formula $m = \frac{y - y_1}{x - x_1}$ to determine the equation of the line.
Use the point (0, −5).

$$m = \frac{y - y_1}{x - x_1}$$
$$2 = \frac{y - (-5)}{x - 0}$$
$$2(x) = y + 5$$
$$2x - 5 = y$$
$$y = 2x - 5$$

The equation of the line for the given graph in the form $y = mx + b$ is $y = 2x - 5$.
Notice that the value of b is equal to the y-coordinate of the y-intercept on the given graph.

Writing Equations in Slope-Point Form

Consider a line with a particular slope, m, a particular point on the line, $P(x_1, y_1)$, and any other point on the line, $Q(x, y)$.

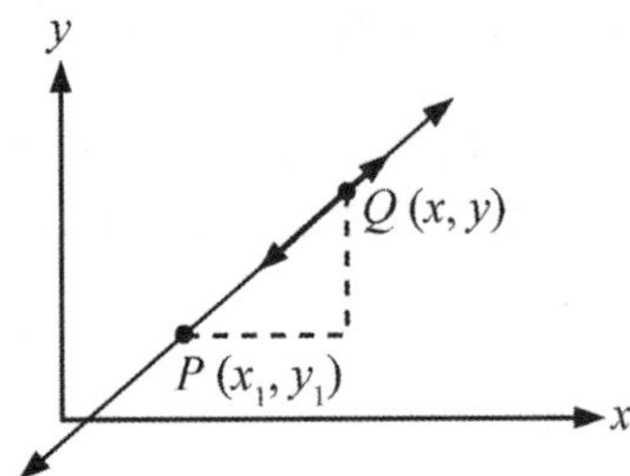

If the slope is represented by m, the slope between point P and point Q can be represented by the equation $\frac{y - y_1}{x - x_1} = m$. If point Q moves such that the slope between Q and P remains m, the equation $\frac{y - y_1}{x - x_1} = m$ describes the line with slope m that passes through point P. The form of the equation $\frac{y - y_1}{x - x_1} = m$ can be changed by multiplying both sides by $x - x_1$.

$$\frac{y - y_1}{x - x_1} = m$$

$$y - y_1 = m(x - x_1)$$

All linear relations that are functions can be written in the form $y - y_1 = m(x - x_1)$, in which m represents the slope, and (x_1, y_1) represents a point on the line.

When given a slope and a point on the line, the slope-point form can be used to determine the equation of the line in general form, $Ax + By + C = 0$.

Example

Determine the equation in simplest general form ($Ax + By + C = 0$) of the line that has a slope of -3 and passes through the point $P(1, -6)$.

Solution

Step 1

Substitute $m = -3$, $x_1 = 1$, and $y_1 = -6$ into the slope-point form equation.

$$y - y_1 = m(x - x_1)$$
$$y - (-6) = -3(x - 1)$$

Step 2

Simplify, and write in general form.

$$y + 6 = -3x + 3$$
$$3x + y + 3 = 0$$

Example

Determine the equation in simplest general form ($Ax + By + C = 0$) of the line that has a slope of $\frac{3}{2}$ and passes through the point $P(-4, 3)$.

Solution

Step 1

Substitute $m = \frac{3}{2}$, $x_1 = -4$, and $y_1 = 3$ into the slope-point form equation.

$$y - y_1 = m(x - x_1)$$
$$y - 3 = \frac{3}{2}(x - (-4))$$
$$y - 3 = \frac{3}{2}(x + 4)$$

Step 2

Multiply both sides by 2, and expand.

$$2(y - 3) = 2\left(\frac{3}{2}(x + 4)\right)$$
$$2y - 6 = 3(x + 4)$$
$$2y - 6 = 3x + 12$$

Step 3

Express in general form.

$$-3x + 2y - 18 = 0$$

Multiply both sides by -1.

$$3x - 2y + 18 = 0$$

8.F.5 Describe qualitatively the functional relationship between two quantities by analyzing a graph. Sketch a graph that exhibits the qualitative features of a function that has been described verbally.

Graphing a Rate of Change

A scenario that features a rate of change can be graphed to show the relationship between the two variables. Graphing the rate of change is useful for comparing how one quantity changes with respect to another.

The horizontal axis will have the independent variable, such as time, and the vertical axis will have the dependent variable, such as speed or distance.

Furthermore, the graph may be linear or non-linear, and it may or may not begin at the origin.

Example

Margaret was riding her bicycle at a constant speed on a level road. She came to a hill and decelerated while climbing it. Once she reached the top, the road became flat again, so she accelerated back to her original speed. She then slowed to a stop when she came to another, steeper hill.

Sketch a speed versus time graph of Margaret's bicycle trip.

Solution

Since Margaret is initially traveling at a constant speed, the graph will start from the vertical axis as a horizontal line.

To show her deceleration while climbing the first hill, the graph will curve downward. The graph will then begin to curve upward to show the point when she reached the top of the hill and began to accelerate again. Given that she accelerated back to her original speed, the graph will rise until it reaches the same height (speed) as it originally had. At this point, it will become a horizontal line again.

To show the point when she began to decelerate upon reaching the second hill, the graph will begin to curve downward. The graph will continue downward until it reaches the horizontal axis because her speed became zero when she came to a stop.

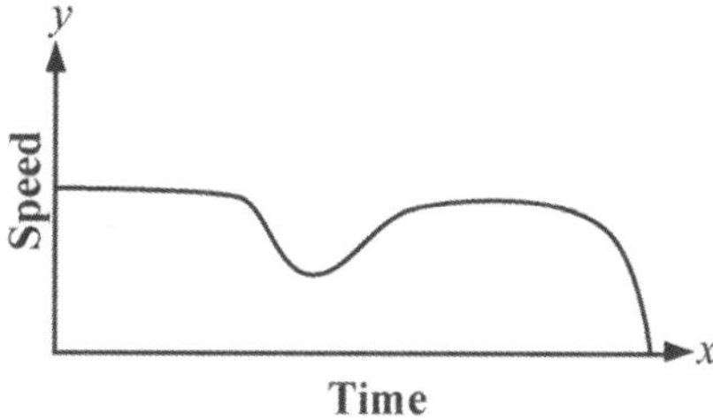

Sketch a distance versus time graph of Margaret's bicycle trip.

Solution

The graph can start from the origin if the distance traveled is measured from the instant the graph starts. Since Margaret is initially traveling at a constant speed, the graph will begin as an oblique line rising to the right from the origin.

The slope of the graph will begin to curve to the right to show her deceleration while climbing the first hill. However, even though the slope of the graph has decreased, the total distance traveled will still continue to increase.

The graph will then begin to curve upward to show her acceleration at the top of the first hill. To show her return to a constant speed, the graph will once again become an oblique line with the same slope as it originally had.

To show Margaret's final deceleration upon reaching the second hill, the graph will curve to the right again, and it will become horizontal at the point when she stopped. From here on, the slope of the graph is horizontal, indicating that she has stopped moving.

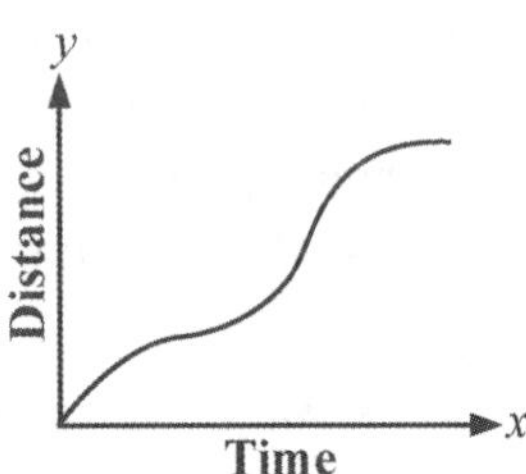

In the given examples, the graphs are approximate representations because the actual speed and distance traveled are not given. If these types of values are available, graph a more accurate representation of the rates of change by labeling the scales on the horizontal axis and the vertical axis.

When specific rates of change are given, it is possible to verify the accuracy of the resulting scaled graphs by using a combination of different technologies. For example, experiments can be conducted that involve the use of motion detectors and concrete materials, while other technologies, such as a graphing calculator or a calculator-based ranger (CBR), can also be used. Using these technologies, the data collected from experiments can be plotted, and the graphs compared, to verify accuracy.

Interpreting Points on a Linear Graph

You may be given a linear graph and asked to describe the relationship between the two variables.

There are three main patterns to look for in a linear graph:

1. As one variable increases, so does the other.

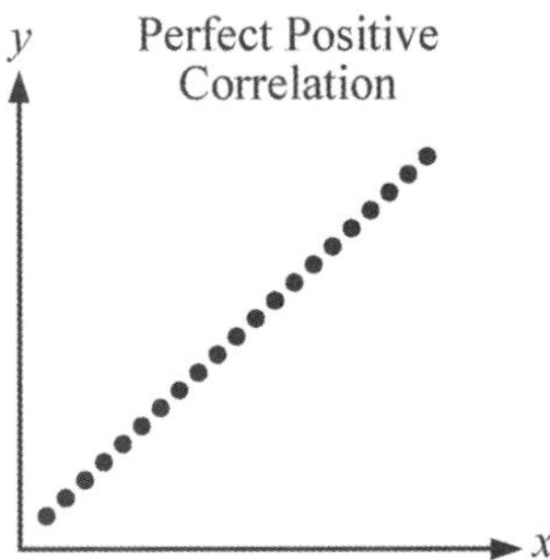

2. As one variable increases, the other decreases.

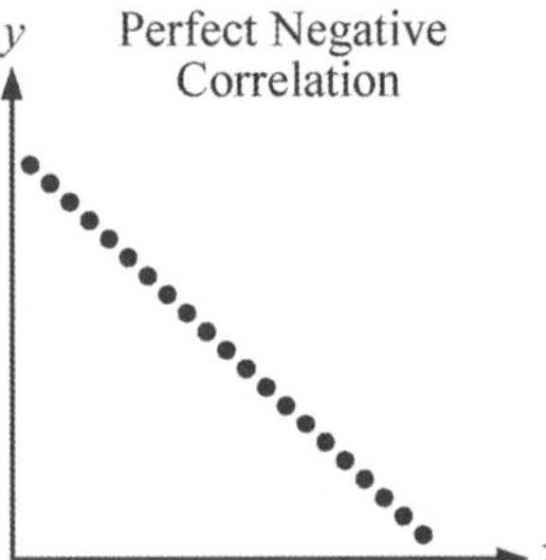

3. The points are scattered everywhere; there appears to be no relationship between the variables.

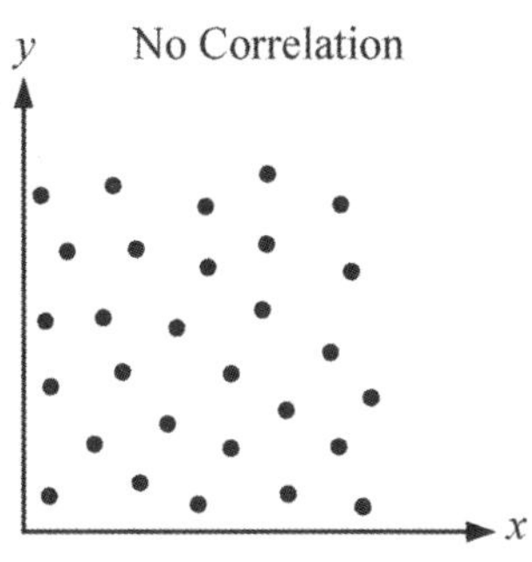

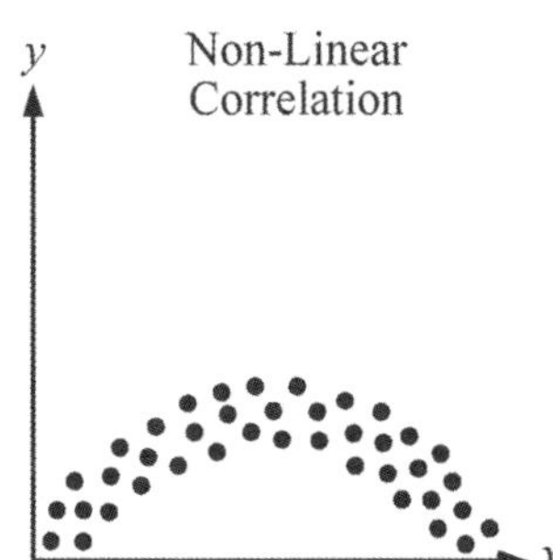

When interpreting a linear graph, observe the trend, identify the variables, and describe the relationship.

Example

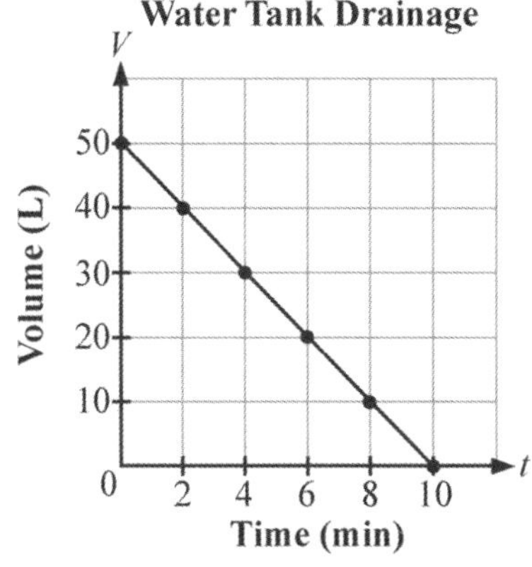

Describe the relationship between the variables of the linear graph.

Solution

Step 1

Observe whether the graphed points follow an upward, downward, or no trend.

The points follow a downward trend.

Step 2

Identify the independent and dependent variables.

Time is the independent variable.

The volume of water is the dependent variable.

Step 3

Describe the relationship between the variables.

The volume of water decreases as the number of minutes that pass increases.

EXERCISE #1—MODELING RELATIONSHIPS WITH FUNCTIONS

Use the following information to answer the next question.

Four line segments are shown on the given Cartesian plane.

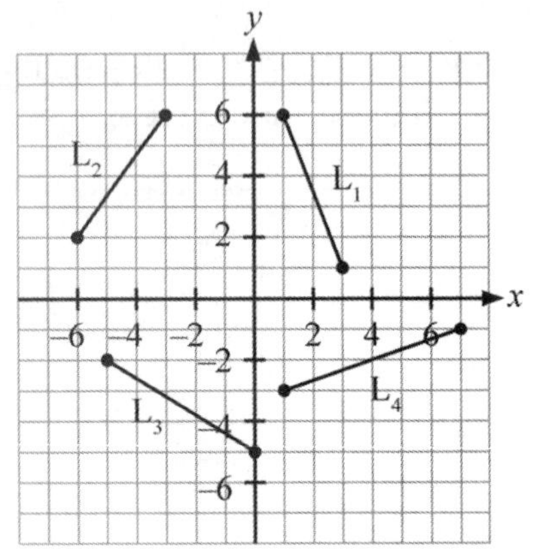

150. If the given line segments are placed in order of their ascending **steepness**, the order is __________, __________, __________, and __________. (Record your answer as a four-digit number.)

Use the following information to answer the next question.

The given table of values represents a linear relation.

x	y
5	2
6	3
7	4
8	5
9	6

151. Which of the following equations represents the linear relationship shown in the table?

A. $y = 2x + 1$ B. $y = 5x - 3$

C. $y = x + 1$ D. $y = x - 3$

152. Which of the following equations is written in general form?

A. $y = 3$

B. $y = 3x + 2$

C. $y = 3x$

D. $2x + \frac{y}{3} - 3 = 0$

Use the following information to answer the next question.

The graph of a line is given.

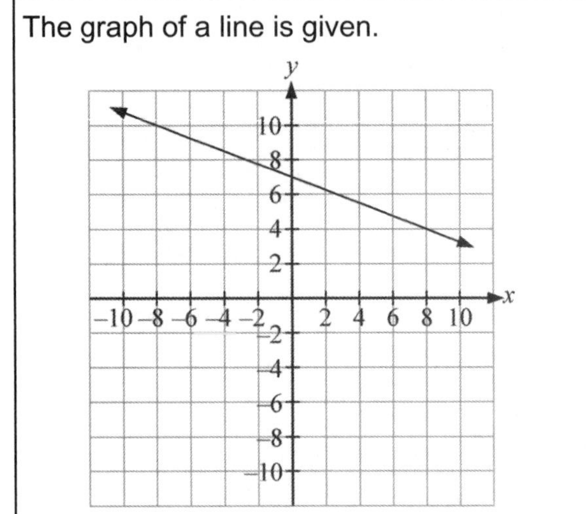

153. What is the equation of the given line in $y = mx + b$ form?

A. $y = -\frac{8}{3}x + 1$

B. $y = -\frac{8}{3}x + 7$

C. $y = -\frac{3}{8}x + 1$

D. $y = -\frac{3}{8}x + 7$

154. What is the standard form of the equation $y - \frac{2}{3} = \frac{3}{4}(x - 0)$?

A. $9x - y + 8 = 0$

B. $9x - 12y + 8 = 0$

C. $9x + 12y - 8 = 0$

D. $36x - 12y + 24 = 0$

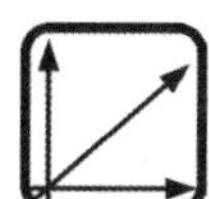

Use the following information to answer the next question.

While the cars of a train are being loaded, the train moves forward quickly, then backs up slowly just a little, and finally rolls forward to a stop.

155. Which of the following "total distance traveled vs. time" graphs best illustrates the situation described?

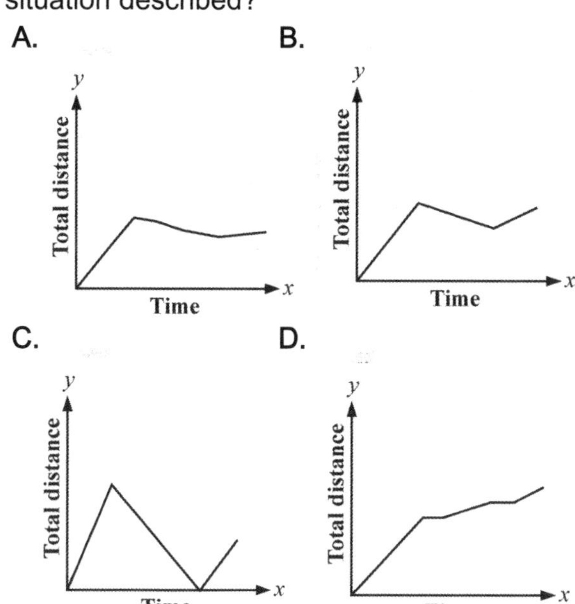

Use the following information to answer the next question.

The given graph shows the relationship between time and the height of a ride at a fair.

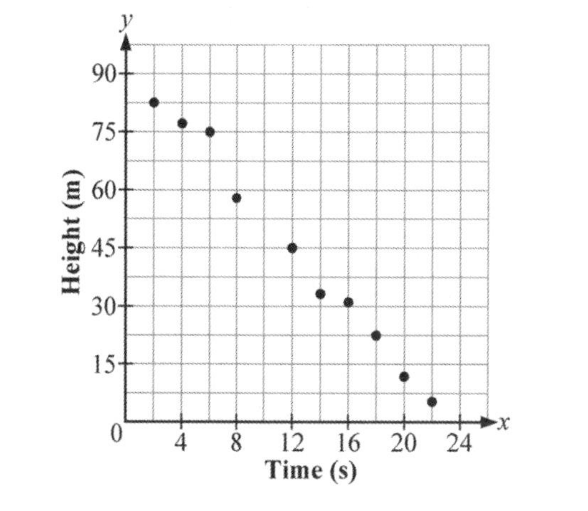

156. The given graph shows
A. non-linear correlation
B. negative correlation
C. positive correlation
D. no correlation

EXERCISE #1—MODELING RELATIONSHIPS WITH FUNCTIONS ANSWERS AND SOLUTIONS

150. 4321	152. D	154. B	156. B
151. D	153. D	155. D	

150. 4321

Step 1

Using the slope formula and the values of the endpoints, determine the slope, m, of each line segment.

$$L_1: m_1 = \frac{y_2 - y_1}{x_2 - x_1} = \frac{1-6}{3-1} = -\frac{5}{2}$$

$$L_2: m_2 = \frac{y_2 - y_1}{x_2 - x_1} = \frac{6-2}{-2-(-6)} = \frac{4}{4} = 1$$

$$L_3: m_3 = \frac{y_2 - y_1}{x_2 - x_1} = \frac{-5-(-2)}{0-(-5)} = -\frac{3}{5}$$

$$L_4: m_4 = \frac{y_2 - y_1}{x_2 - x_1} = \frac{-1-(-3)}{7-1} = \frac{1}{6}$$

Step 2

Order the steepness from least to greatest, according to the absolute values of the slopes.

$$m_4 = \frac{1}{6}$$

$$m_3 = \left|-\frac{3}{5}\right| = \frac{3}{5}$$

$$m_2 = 1$$

$$m_1 = \left|-\frac{5}{2}\right| = \frac{5}{2}$$

Therefore, the order of the steepness of the line segments from least to greatest is 4, 3, 2, and 1, or 4,321.

151. D

Step 1

Figure out what number is added to each term to get to the next term.

In the table, 1 is added to each term to get to the next term. This means the equation will have $1x$, which is equal to x.

Step 2

Multiply this number by any term number, and then add or subtract as necessary to equal the term.

Multiply 1 by the first term number.

$1 \times 5 = 5$

The first term is 2. To go from 5 to 2, you need to subtract 3.

This means that the equation is $y = x - 3$.

Step 3

Check your answer by using your rule with another term number and term.

Use your rule on the second term. If you substitute 6 for x, then $x - 3$ needs to equal 3.

$y = x - 3$
$y = 6 - 3$
$y = 3$

152. D

General form is $Ax + By + C = 0$. The equation $2x + \frac{y}{3} - 3 = 0$ is in general form.

153. D

Step 1
Identify two points on the line, and use them to determine the slope (m) using the formula
$m = \frac{y_2 - y_1}{x_2 - x_1}$.

Two points on the line are (−8, 10) and (8, 4). Substitute these points into the formula.

$$m = \frac{y_2 - y_1}{x_2 - x_1}$$
$$m = \frac{4 - 10}{8 - (-8)}$$
$$m = \frac{-6}{16}$$
$$m = -\frac{3}{8}$$

Step 2
Use the calculated slope, one point on the line, and the formula $m = \frac{y - y_1}{x - x_1}$ to determine the equation of the line.

Using the point (8, 4), calculate the equation of the line.

$$m = \frac{y - y_1}{x - x_1}$$
$$-\frac{3}{8} = \frac{y - 4}{x - 8}$$
$$-\frac{3}{8}(x - 8) = y - 4$$
$$-\frac{3}{8}x + 3 = y - 4$$
$$-\frac{3}{8}x + 7 = y$$
$$y = -\frac{3}{8}x + 7$$

Thus, the equation of the line in $y = mx + b$ form is $y = -\frac{3}{8}x + 7$.

154. B

The equation is currently in point-slope form.

Step 1
Simplify the right side.

$$y - \frac{2}{3} = \frac{3}{4}(x - 0)$$
$$y - \frac{2}{3} = \frac{3}{4}x$$

Step 2
Multiply each term by 12, the lowest common denominator, to eliminate the fractional coefficients.

$$12\left(y - \frac{2}{3}\right) = 12\left(\frac{3}{4}x\right)$$
$$12y - 8 = 9x$$

Step 3
Set the equation equal to 0 by moving all terms to the right side.

$$12y - 8 = 9x$$
$$12y - 12y - 8 + 8 = 9x - 12y + 8$$
$$0 = 9x - 12y + 8$$
$$9x - 12y + 8 = 0$$

Therefore, the equation in standard form is $9x - 12y + 8 = 0$.

155. D

The graph starts at the origin because the distance traveled is measured from the instant the graph begins. Since the train is initially traveling at a constant speed, the graph would begin as an oblique line rising to the right from the origin. Since the train was moving forward, it must stop in order to move backward. This is indicated by a short horizontal line.

Then, the train moves at a slower constant rate, which would be shown by an oblique line with a slight slope rising to the right from the horizontal line. The line is rising because the total distance covered increases despite the train's change in direction.

After moving backward, the train must stop again in order to roll forward. The stop is indicted by another short horizontal line.

As the train rolls forward, the graph will once again become an oblique line with a slight slope rising to the right from the previous horizontal line.

The explanation is illustrated in the following graph.

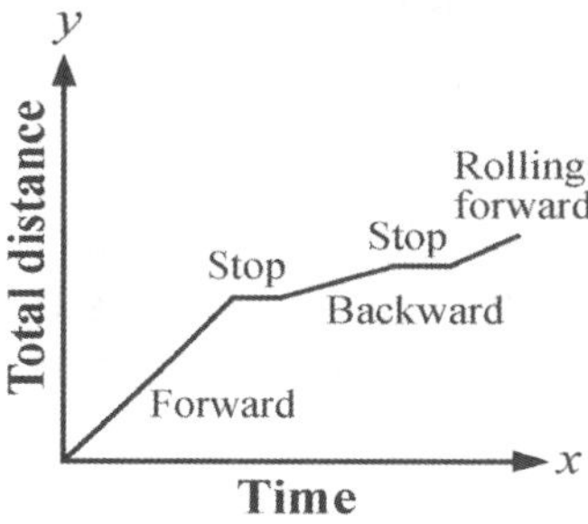

156. B

The points on this graph are all relatively close together and follow a downward trend. As one variable increases, the other variable decreases. The given graph shows negative correlation.

EXERCISE #2—MODELING RELATIONSHIPS WITH FUNCTIONS

Use the following information to answer the next question.

Points $A(3, -2)$ and $B(12, 1)$ are found on the same line.

157. Use the slope formula to determine the slope of AB.

Use the following information to answer the next question.

The given table of values displays the monthly cost of a long-distance cellphone plan compared to the number of long-distance minutes used each month.

Long-Distance Minutes	Cellphone Plan Cost
0	$50.00
50	$57.50
100	$65.00
150	$72.50
200	$80.00

158. Which of the following equations represents the relationship between the number of long-distance minutes used and the cost of the cellphone plan?

A. $C = 0.15m + 50$

B. $C = 0.15m - 50$

C. $C = 1.15m$

D. $C = 0.65m$

159. The linear relation $y - 5 = -\frac{5}{3}(x + 6)$ has a slope of $-\frac{5}{3}$ and passes through the point $(-6, 5)$. What is the equation of this linear relation expressed in general form?

A. $5x + 3y + 15 = 0$

B. $5x - 3y - 15 = 0$

C. $5x + 3y - 21 = 0$

D. $5x - 3y + 21 = 0$

Use the following information to answer the next question.

A graph of a linear equation is given.

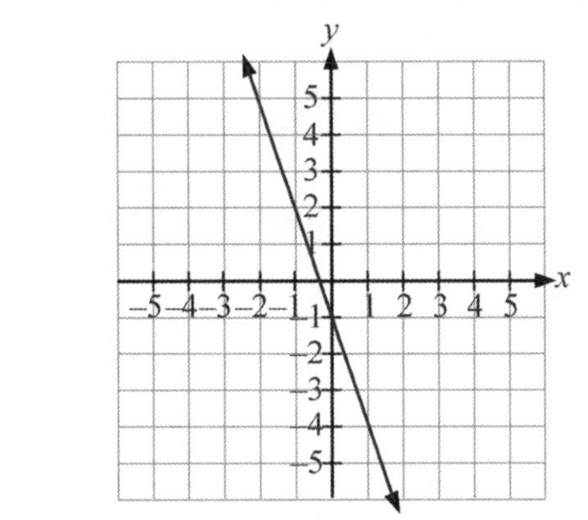

160. What is the equation of the line for the given graph in the form $y = mx + b$?

A. $y = -3x - 1$

B. $y = -2x - 1$

C. $y = -x - 3$

D. $y = -2x - 3$

Use the following information to answer the next question.

A line passes through the point $(-3, 4.5)$ and has a slope of 2.5.

161. When the equation of this line is written in the form $y = mx + b$, the value of b is __________. (Record your answer to the nearest tenth.)

Use the following information to answer the next question.

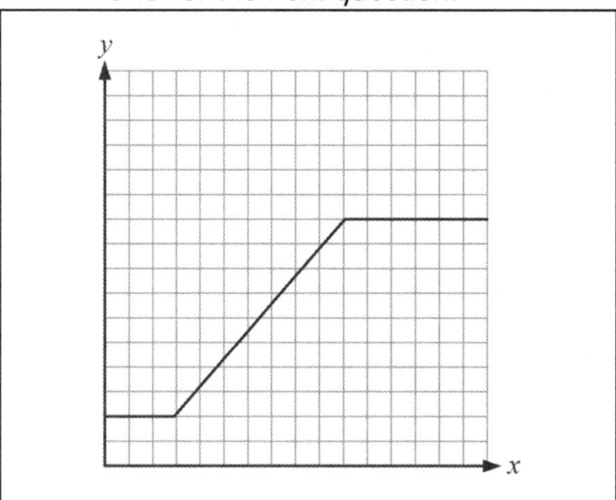

162. Which of the following situations is **best** represented by the given graph?

A. A car driving slowly on a side street, and accelerating onto a freeway where it can go faster.

B. A block of ice melting and then heating up to the boiling point of water.

C. A horse slowing down for the sharp corners on an oval race track.

D. A balloon increasing in size when it is exposed to constant heat.

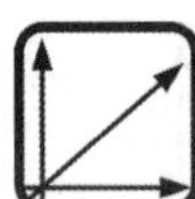

EXERCISE #2—MODELING RELATIONSHIPS WITH FUNCTIONS ANSWERS AND SOLUTIONS

157. See solution	159. A	161. 12.0
158. A	160. A	162. B

157.

Calculate the slope of the line using the slope formula $m = \frac{y_2 - y_1}{x_2 - x_1}$.

Substitute 1 for y_2, –2 for y_1, 12 for x_2, and 3 for x_1 into the formula. Then, simplify.

$$\begin{aligned} m_{AB} &= \frac{y_2 - y_1}{x_2 - x_1} \\ &= \frac{1-(-2)}{12-3} \\ &= \frac{1+2}{12-3} \\ &= \frac{3}{9} \\ &= \frac{1}{3} \end{aligned}$$

158. A

Step 1
Assign meaningful variables to the quantities involved.
Let m represent the number of long-distance minutes used, and let C represent the cost of using the long-distance cellphone plan.

Step 2
Determine if there is a fixed cost.
A fixed cost of $50 exists because the plan costs $50 if 0 min are used.

Step 3
Determine the cost per minute.
To determine the cost per minute, subtract the $50 fixed cost and divide by the number of minutes used.

$$57.50 - 50.00 = 7.50$$
$$\frac{7.50}{50} = 0.15$$

The cost per minute is $0.15.

Step 4
Write the equation.
$C = 0.15m + 50$

159. A

Convert $y - 5 = -\frac{5}{3}(x+6)$ into general form.

Step 1
Multiply both sides by 3.

$$3(y-5) = 3\left(-\frac{5}{3}(x+6)\right)$$
$$3y - 15 = -5(x+6)$$

Step 2
Expand.

$$3y - 15 = -5x - 30$$

Step 3
Add $5x$ and 30 to both sides, and simplify.

$$\begin{aligned} 5x + 30 + 3y - 15 &= -5x - 30 + 5x + 30 \\ 5x + 3y + 15 &= 0 \end{aligned}$$

160. A

Step 1
Identify two points on the line, and determine the slope by using the formula $m = \frac{y_2 - y_1}{x_2 - x_1}$.

Two points on the line are (–1, 2) and (1, –4). Substitute these points into the formula.

$$m = \frac{y_2 - y_1}{x_2 - x_1}$$
$$m = \frac{-4-(2)}{1-(-1)}$$
$$m = \frac{-6}{2}$$
$$m = -3$$

Step 2
Use the calculated slope and one point with the formula $m = \dfrac{y - y_1}{x - x_1}$ to determine the equation of the line.
Use the point (1, −4).

$$m = \frac{y - y_1}{x - x_1}$$
$$-3 = \frac{y - (-4)}{x - 1}$$
$$-3(x - 1) = y + 4$$
$$-3x + 3 = y + 4$$
$$-3x - 1 = y$$

The equation of the line for the given graph in the form $y = mx + b$ is $y = -3x - 1$.

161. 12.0

When given one point and the slope, use the form $y - y_1 = m(x - x_1)$.

Step 1
Substitute the values of the point (−3, 4.5) and the slope 2.5 into the formula.

$$y - y_1 = m(x - x_1)$$
$$y - 4.5 = 2.5(x - (-3))$$
$$y - 4.5 = 2.5(x + 3)$$

Step 2
Simplify to the equation of a line of the form $y = mx + b$.

$$y - 4.5 = 2.5(x + 3)$$
$$y - 4.5 = 2.5x + 7.5$$
$$y = 2.5x + 12.0$$

To the nearest tenth, the value of b is 12.0.

162. B

A car driving slowly at a constant speed on a side street could be represented by a straight line. However, when a car accelerates as it enters onto a freeway, its acceleration would cause the speed to increase in a curve similar to the following graph.

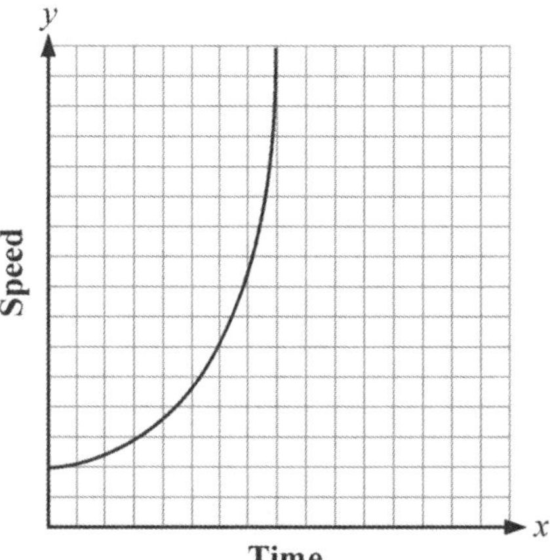

A horse slowing down for the corners on a horse race track will have a decrease in speed before the corner, but it will accelerate once the horse passes through the corner. These changes in speed as the horse slows down and then speeds up is often represented with a sinusoidal curve.

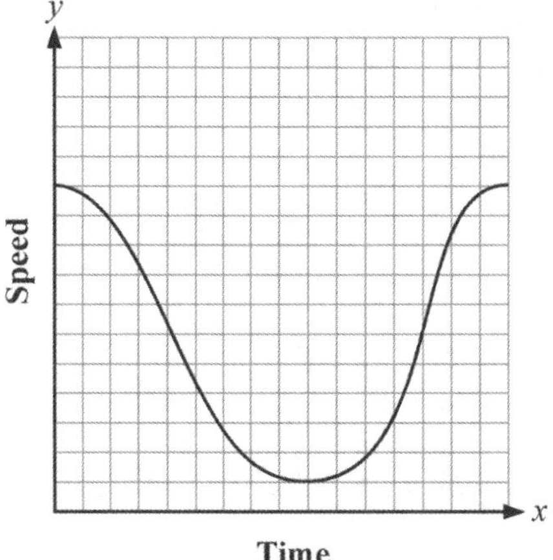

When a balloon is exposed to constant heat, it will increase in size at a constant rate. The description says nothing of a constant form before or after the increase, so this situation would be represented by a straight linear relationship.

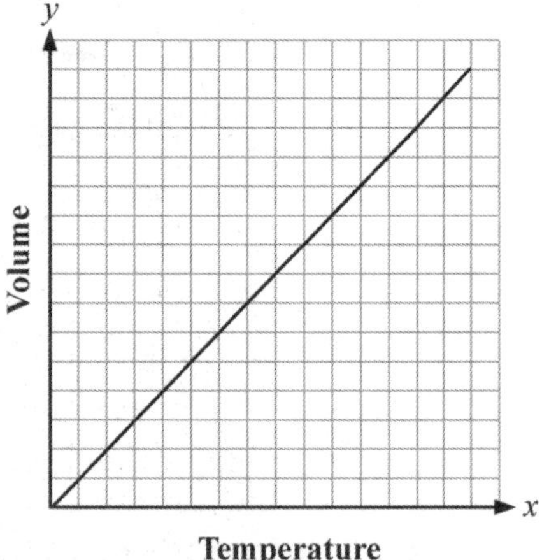

The temperature of a block of ice melting will remain at one temperature until the entire block has melted completely into water. The water will then increase in temperature as long as more energy is added to it by heating it up. Once the water reaches the boiling point of water, the heat will remain at the boiling point until the water has turned completely into steam. This relationship between temperature and energy added is a horizontal line during phase changes (energy is being added but the temperature remains constant) and an oblique line during a temperature increase.

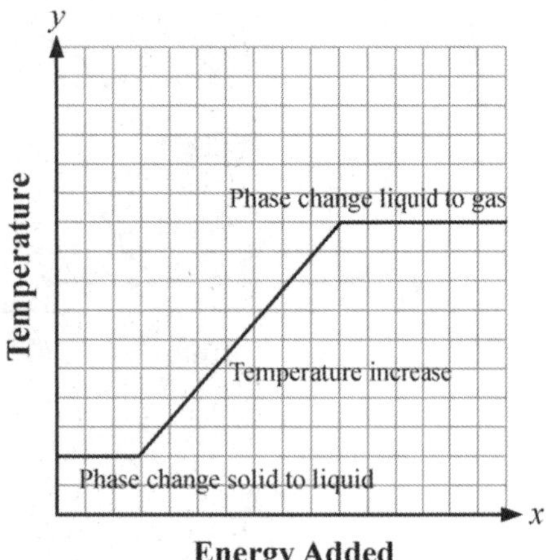

Interpreting Functions

INTERPRETING FUNCTIONS

Table of Correlations

Standard		Concepts	Exercise #1	Exercise #2
Unit2.8	Interpret functions that arise in applications in terms of a context.			
F-IF.4iii	*For a function that models a relationship between two quantities, interpret key features of graphs and tables in terms of the quantities, and sketch graphs showing key features given a verbal description of the relationship. Key features include: intercepts; intervals where the function is increasing, decreasing, positive, or negative; relative maximums and minimums; symmetries; end behavior; and periodicity.*	Determining the Characteristics of the Graph of a Linear Function	116	127
		Determining the Properties of Even and Odd Polynomial Functions	163	175
		Solve Problems Involving the Applications of Functions	164	176
		Properties of Exponential Functions	165	177
		Analyzing Polynomial Functions of Varying Degree and Their Graphs		
F-IF.5	*Relate the domain of a function to its graph and, where applicable, to the quantitative relationship it describes.*	Defining the Domain and Range of a Function	166	178
		Determining the Domain and Range for Discrete Data	167	179
		Determining the Domain and Range for Continuous Data	168	180
		Using a Graphing Calculator to Determine Domain and Range	169	181
		Determining the Domain and Range of Real-Life Situations	170	182
F-IF.6	*Calculate and interpret the average rate of change of a function (presented symbolically or as a table) over a specified interval. Estimate the rate of change from a graph.*	Understanding The Rate of Change for a Function	171	183
		Applications of Average Rates of Change	172	184
		Calculating Average Rates of Change Given a Graph	173	185
		Calculating Average Rates of Change Given a Table of Values	174	186

F-IF.4iii For a function that models a relationship between two quantities, interpret key features of graphs and tables in terms of the quantities, and sketch graphs showing key features given a verbal description of the relationship. Key features include: intercepts; intervals where the function is increasing, decreasing, positive, or negative; relative maximums and minimums; symmetries; end behavior; and periodicity.

Determining the Properties of Even and Odd Polynomial Functions

A function $f(x)$ is considered to be even if it satisfies the condition that $f(-x) = f(x)$ for all values of x in its domain. This means that the y-coordinate for any value of x must equal the y-coordinate at $-x$. For every point on the right side of the y-axis, a mirror image exists on the left side of the y-axis. Therefore, the graph of an even function is symmetrical about the y-axis.

Example

Since all the features of the graph $f(x) = x^4 - 18x^2 - 19$ on the left of the y-axis are duplicated in the reflection on the right, it is an even function.

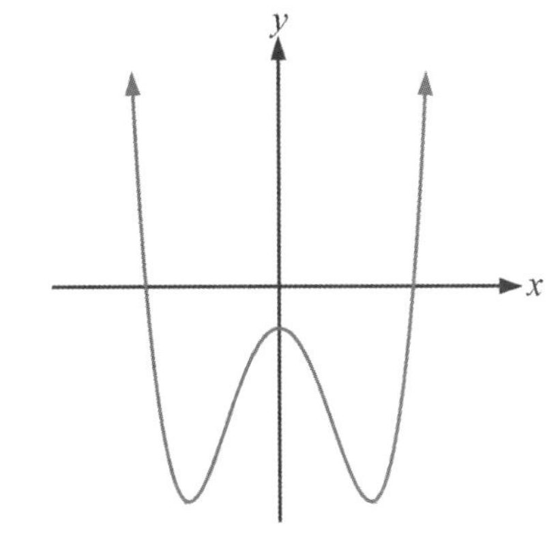

A function $f(x)$ is considered to be odd if it satisfies the condition that $f(-x) = -f(x)$ for all values of x in its domain. This means that the y-coordinate for any value of x must equal the negative of the y-coordinate at $-x$. For every point on the graph, there must be another point located directly through the origin, the same distance from the origin as the point itself. Therefore, the graph of an odd function is symmetrical about the origin.

Example

Since the graph $y = x^3 - 20x$ is symmetrical about the origin, it is an odd function.

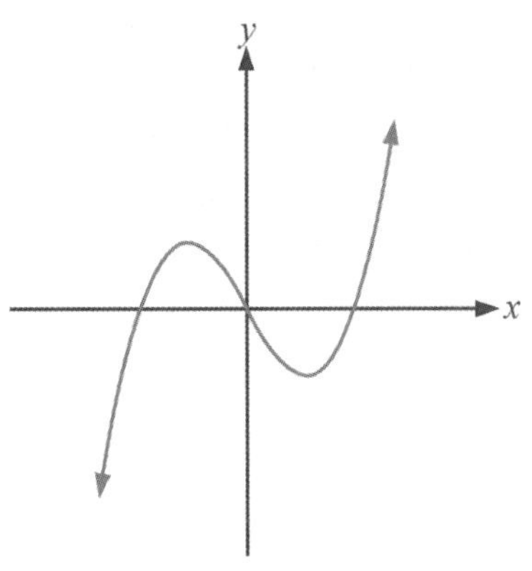

To determine whether or not a function $y = f(x)$ is even, find $y = f(-x)$. If $f(x) = f(-x)$, then the function is even. To determine if a function is odd, find both $f(-x)$ and $-f(x)$. If $f(-x) = -f(x)$, then the function is odd.

Example

Determine if the polynomial function $f(x) = 2x^3 - 5x$ is odd, even, or neither.

Solution

Substitute $-x$ for x into the equation $f(x) = 2x^3 - 5x$.

$$\begin{aligned} f(-x) &= 2(-x)^3 - 5(-x) \\ &= -2x^3 + 5x \\ &= -(2x^3 - 5x) \\ &= -f(x) \end{aligned}$$

Since $f(-x) = -f(x)$, $f(x)$ is an odd function and its corresponding graph is symmetrical about the origin.

It can be shown that any polynomial function whose terms consist of only odd degree monomials is an odd function and any polynomial function consisting of only even degree monomials is an even function. If the polynomial function has any combination of odd degree and even degree terms, then the function is neither odd nor even. For example, the function $f(x) = 2x^6 - 3x^4 + 5x^2 - 9$ is an even function since it consists of only even degree monomials. The function $g(x) = 2x^5 - 3x^4 + 5x^3 - 9$ consists of a combination of odd degree and even degree terms, so is neither even nor odd.

Solve Problems Involving the Applications of Functions

Different types of functions can be used to represent many types of real-world applications. Many strategies such as reasoning techniques, algebra, and technology can be used to solve problems involving functions.

Example

The distance that a particular car travels after the brakes are applied is measured for several different speeds. The data is given in the following table.

Speed (km/h)	Stopping Distance (m)
5	0.82
10	3.3
15	7.3
20	13.1
25	20.4
30	29.4
35	39.8

Technology can be used to investigate linear, quadratic, and exponential models for the relationship of speed and stopping distance.

Use technology to describe the possible models of the relationship between speed and stopping distance and predict the stopping distance for a speed of 50 km/h, for each.

Solution

Using a TI-83 calculator, graph the data by carrying out the following procedure.

Step 1
Input the data points.

Clear the lists by pressing [2nd] [+] and selecting 4:ClrAllLists. Press [ENTER].

Press [Y =] and clear any functions that were previously graphed. Then press [STAT] [ENTER]. Input the speeds in L1 and the stopping distances in L2.

Step 2
Graph the data.

Set the viewing window to x:[0, 60, 5] y:[0, 100, 10].

Press [2nd] [Y =] [ENTER] and turn Plot 1 on by pressing [ENTER] again.

The type of graph should be a scatter plot, the Xlist is L1, and the Ylist is L2.

Pressing [GRAPH] will show you the following graph.

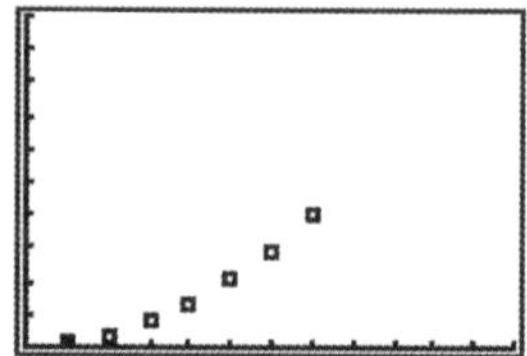

Step 3
Determine the best regression model for the data.

There is no need to do linear regression, since the graph is a curve. However, if you did need to, you would press [STAT], then scroll right to [CALC] and choose 4: LinReg ($ax + b$).

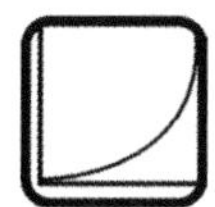

For quadratic regression press STAT, then scroll right to CALC and choose 5:QuadReg. Then press 2nd 1 , 2nd 2 , VARS, scroll right to Y-VARS, and press ENTER twice. The screen should now display QuadReg L1, L2, Y1.

Pressing ENTER will perform the regression and produce the following screen.

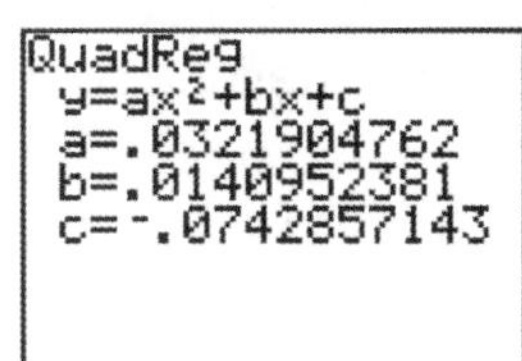

The quadratic function that best fits the data is approximately the equation
$y = 0.0321905x^2 + 0.0140952x - 0.0742857$.

If you press GRAPH, the calculator will draw the graph because you have stored the regression equation as Y_1.

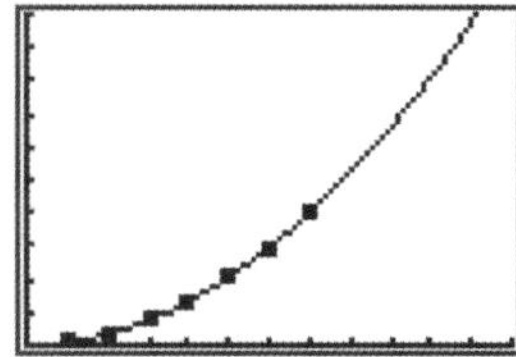

This function appears to be a fairly good fit to the given data.

To determine the predicted stopping distance for a speed of 50 km/h, press 2nd TRACE ENTER and input 50. Press ENTER.

The calculator gives a stopping distance of 81.1 m, to the nearest tenth, for the quadratic model.

To see how well an exponential function fits the data, press STAT, then scroll right to CALC and choose 0:ExpReg. Then press 2nd 1 , 2nd 2 , VARS, scroll right to Y-VARS, and press ENTER twice.
The screen will now display ExpReg L1, L2, Y1.

Press ENTER to perform the regression. The result should be an equation with approximate values of $y = 0.8178(1.1295)^x$
Press GRAPH to see how well this function fits the data.

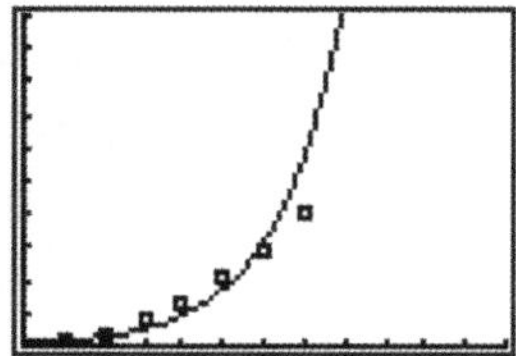

This function does not appear to fit the data as well as the quadratic function did since several points are above the curve and the graph rises rapidly to the right of the final point. To use this model to determine the predicted stopping distance for a speed of 50 km/h, again press 2nd TRACE ENTER and input 50. Press ENTER. The stopping distance for this model is approximately 360.3 m, which is unreasonably large.

The quadratic model is the more realistic relationship for this data.

Properties of Exponential Functions

The graphs of exponential functions of the form $y = b^x$, where the variable, x, is the exponent will be analyzed. The graph of $y = b^x$ changes depending on the value of the base, b. There are two sets of positive values for b:

- $b > 1$
- $0 < b < 1$

Negative values of b are not included because exponential expressions with negative bases do not always give real number values when the exponents are rational numbers. Consider the following examples.

1. Evaluate $(-125)^{\frac{1}{3}}$. Write $(-125)^{\frac{1}{3}}$ as $\sqrt[3]{-125}$, which is –5 because $(-5)^3 = -125$. There is no difficulty here.
2. Evaluate $(-4)^{\frac{3}{2}}$. Write $(-4)^{\frac{3}{2}}$ as $\sqrt{(-4)^3} = \sqrt{-64}$. $\sqrt{-64}$ cannot be evaluated because –64 is a negative number and there is no real number that when multiplied by itself gives a negative result. Thus, there is no real number value here.
3. Evaluate $(-8)^{\frac{2}{3}}$. Write $(-8)^{\frac{2}{3}}$ as $\sqrt[3]{(-8)^2}$. Now, $\sqrt[3]{(-8)^2} = \sqrt[3]{64} = 4$. Because this has a real number value, there is no difficulty here.

When the base is negative, some expressions can be evaluated and some cannot. In summary, the problem arises when the expression results in an even root of a negative number. To avoid problems associated with exponential functions of the form $y = b^x$, negative bases are avoided.

The graph of $y = 1^x$, where the base (b) is 1, is just a horizontal line.

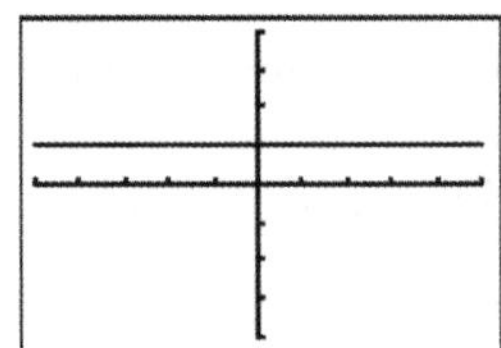

This graph is described by the constant function $y = 1$. Thus, exponential functions where the base is 1 are also not considered.

In general, the graphs of $y = b^x$ ($b > 0$, where $b \neq 1$) have the following characteristics:

- **Domain**: $x \in \mathrm{R}$, since all x-values are permissible.
- **Range**: $y > 0$, since each graph has y-values that get closer and closer to the y-axis, but never become 0.
- **Horizontal asymptote**: $y = 0$
  Note that an asymptote is the line a curve approaches but never touches, which in this case, is the x-axis defined by the equation $y = 0$.
- **y-intercept**: (0, 1) or 1, since for all exponential functions, $y = b^x$, $b^0 = 1$.
- **x-intercept**: None, since the graph never touches the x-axis.

The following are graphs of functions where the base, b, is greater than 1.

- $y = 2^x$:

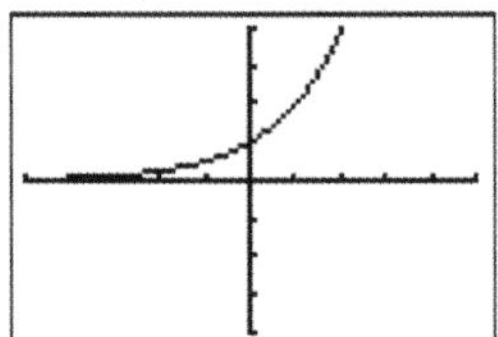

- $y = 3^x$:

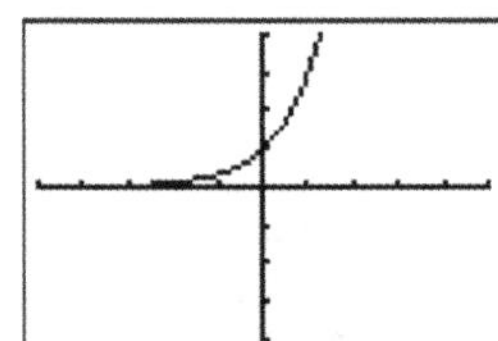

- $y = 9^x$:

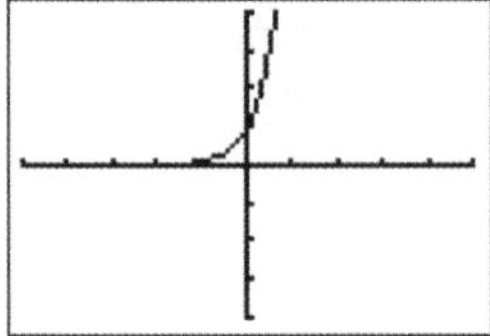

Notice that as the value of b increases, the graph of $y = b^x$ climbs more quickly from left to right.

When $b > 1$, the graph has these characteristics:

- It has this shape:

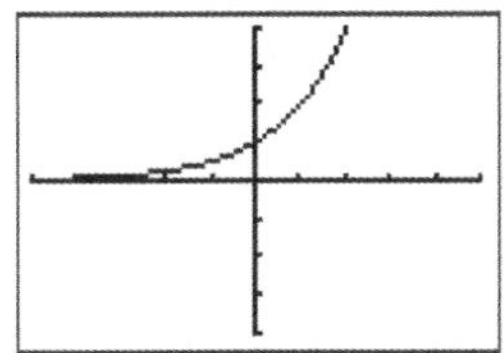

- It is an increasing function as you move from left to right through the domain.
- It is also flatter on the left side of the y-axis and steeper or increases more rapidly on the right side of the y-axis as the value of b increases.

Now, examine the following exponential graphs where the base, b, is between 0 and 1.

- $y = \left(\frac{1}{2}\right)^x$:

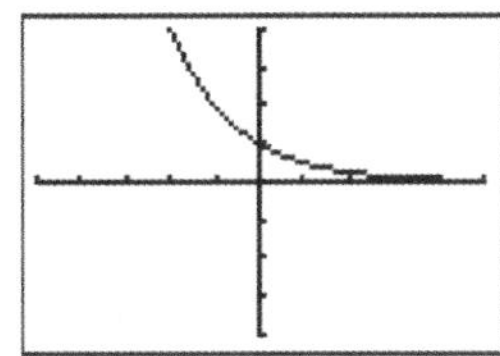

- $y = \left(\frac{1}{3}\right)^x$:

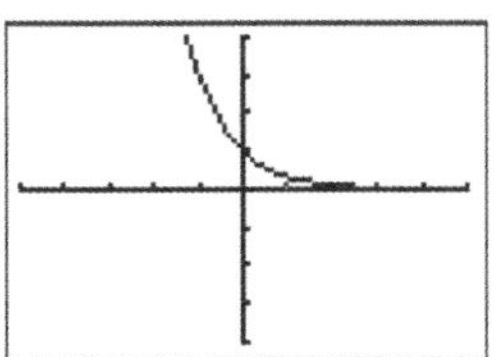

- $y = \left(\frac{1}{9}\right)^x$:

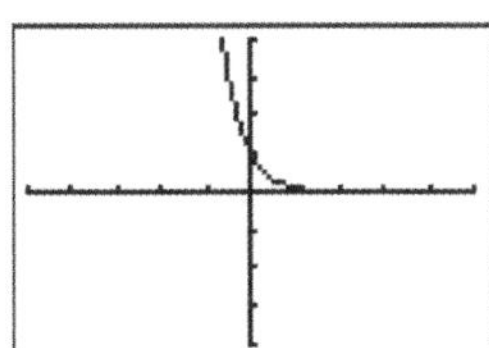

Notice that as the value of b decreases, the graph of $y = b^x$ falls more quickly from left to right.

When $0 < b < 1$, the graph has these characteristics:

- It has this shape:

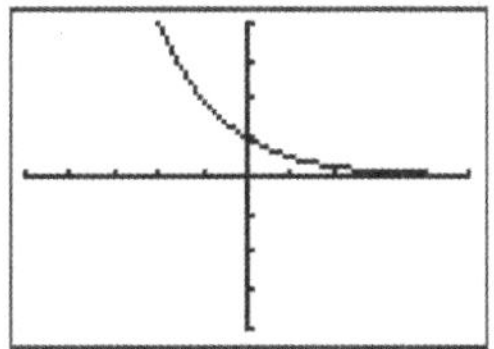

- It is a decreasing function as you move from left to right through the domain.
- It is also flatter on the right side of the y-axis and steeper or decreases more rapidly on the left side of the y-axis as the value of b decreases or gets closer to 0.

Notice that the graphs of the functions $y = b^x$ and $y = \left(\frac{1}{b}\right)^x$ are mirror reflections of each other in the y-axis. Observe that $y = \left(\frac{1}{b}\right)^x$ can be written as $y = \left(b^{-1}\right)^x = b^{-x}$.

Recall that when x is replaced with $-x$ in a function, the result is that the graph is a reflection of the original graph in the y-axis. Thus, the graph of $y = \left(\frac{1}{b}\right)^x = b^{-x}$ is a reflection of the graph of $y = b^x$ in the y-axis.

Analyzing Polynomial Functions of Varying Degree and Their Graphs

The graphs of polynomial functions change as the degree increases, beginning with degree 0 (the constant function). The sketches in this lesson will focus on the general shape of a graph along with the x- and y-intercepts, which are often all that is required to understand the main properties of the graph.

The sketches can usually be drawn by hand more quickly than by using a graphing calculator. Adjusting the window settings to appropriate values often slows down the calculator method. However, when a more exact graph is required, using a calculator or computer is the best approach.

The Constant Function

The constant function is defined by $f(x) = c$, where c is a constant.

The graph is a horizontal line, with the value of c equal to the y-intercept.

Example

Sketch the graph of $f(x) = -3$, and state the domain and range of the function.

Solution

The domain and range are $\{x|\ x\varepsilon\text{R}\}$, $\{y|\ y = -3\}$, respectively.

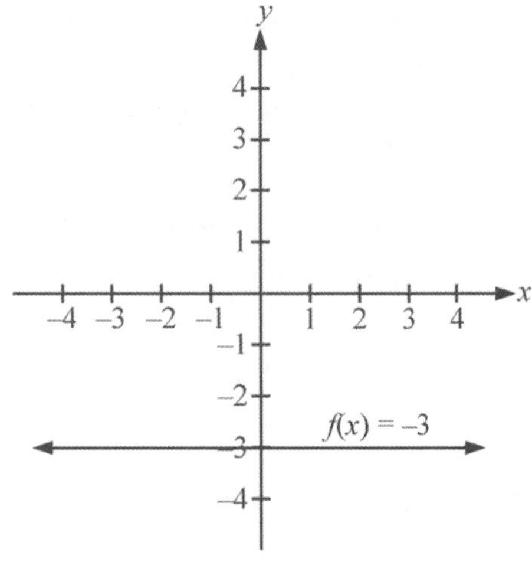

The Linear Function

The linear function is defined by $f(x) = ax + b$, where a and b are constants.

- If $a = 0$, the function is a constant function.
- If $a \neq 0$, the graph of the function is an oblique (slanted) line with a slope equal to a and a y-intercept equal to b.
- The domain and range for first-degree linear functions are $\{x|\ x\varepsilon\text{R}\}$, $\{y|\ y\varepsilon\text{R}\}$, respectively.

Example

Sketch the graph of $f(x) = -x + 1$.

Solution

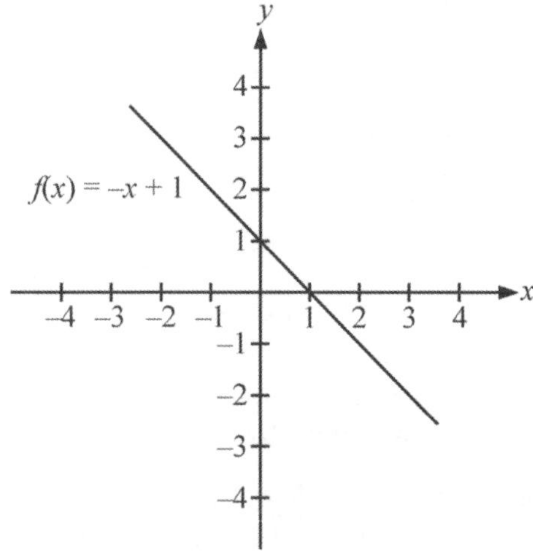

The Quadratic Function

The quadratic function is defined by $f(x) = ax^2 + bx + c$, where a, b, and c are constants.

- If $a = 0$, the function is a linear function.
- If $a \neq 0$, the graph of the function is a parabola opening either up ($a > 0$) or down ($a < 0$).

Example

Sketch the graph of $y = x^2 + 2x - 15$, and state the domain and range of the function.

Solution

The vertex of the parabola is located at $(-1, -16)$.

When written in factored form, the function $y = x^2 + 2x - 15$ is $y = (x - 3)(x + 5)$.

The following information can be obtained:

- The x-intercepts are 3 and –5 because these are the solutions to (or roots of) the equation $0 = (x - 3)(x + 5)$.
- The parabola opens up because $a > 0$.
- The y-intercept is –15 because the constant term in the function is –15.

Using the two x-intercepts and the y-intercept, the graph of the function can be sketched as shown. It follows from the location of the x- and y-intercepts that the parabola must open up (recall that $a > 0$).

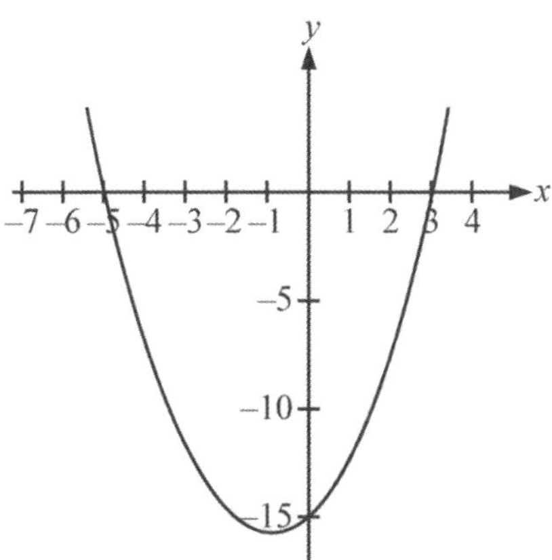

The domain and range are $\{x| \ x\varepsilon\mathrm{R}\}$, $\{y| \ y \geq -16, \ y\varepsilon\mathrm{R}\}$, respectively.

The Cubic Function

The cubic function is defined by $f(x) = ax^3 + bx^2 + cx + d$, where a, b, c, and d are constants.

- If $a = 0$, the function is a quadratic function.
- If $a > 0$, the graph of the function is an S curve that begins in quadrant III and continuously increases into quadrant I, as indicated by the X's in the graph.

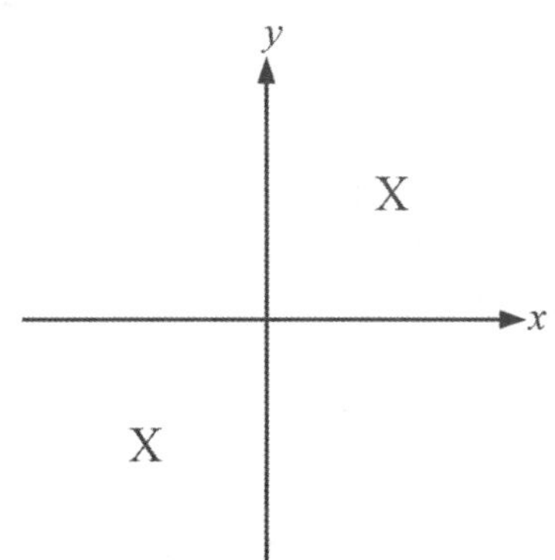

- If $a < 0$, the graph of the function is an S curve that begins in quadrant II and continuously decreases into quadrant IV, as indicated by the X's in the graph.

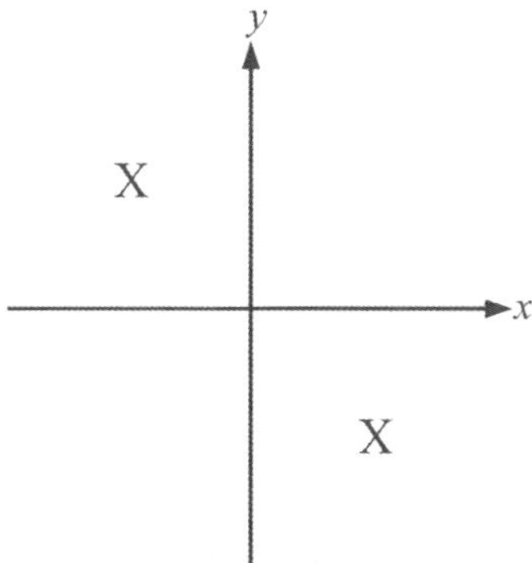

To understand why the graph of a cubic function begins and ends in particular quadrants, it is valuable to consider extreme values of x and the corresponding y-values of the function.

Consider the basic cubic function $y = x^3$. For very large negative values of x, the corresponding y-coordinate will be an even larger negative value. For example, if $x = -100$, $y = (-100)^3 = -1{,}000{,}000$, a quadrant III point of $(-100, -1{,}000{,}000)$ on the graph of $y = x^3$. Similarly, for very large positive values of x, the corresponding y-coordinate will be an even larger positive value. For example, if $x = 100$, $y = (100)^3 = 1{,}000{,}000$, a quadrant I point of $(100, 1{,}000{,}000)$ on the graph of $y = x^3$.

Now, consider the basic cubic function $y = -x^3$. For very large negative values of x, the corresponding y-coordinate will be an even larger positive value. For example, if $x = -100$, $y = -(-100)^3 = 1{,}000{,}000$, a quadrant II point of $(-100, 1{,}000{,}000)$ on the graph of $y = -x^3$. Similarly, for very large positive values of x, the corresponding y-coordinate will be an even larger negative value. For example, if $x = 100$, $y = -(100)^3 = -1{,}000{,}000$, a quadrant IV point of $(100, -1{,}000{,}000)$ on the graph of $y = -x^3$.

Even if there are other terms in the function (of lesser degree), the term with degree 3 is the dominant term and has the greatest effect on the value of the function for very extreme values of x.

In summary, a cubic function with a positive leading coefficient ($a > 0$) will begin in quadrant III and end in quadrant I. Also, a cubic function with a negative leading coefficient ($a < 0$) will begin in quadrant II and end in quadrant IV.

Sketching the graph of a cubic function, once factored, is very similar to graphing a quadratic function in factored form.

Example

Sketch the graph of the function $y = x^3 + x^2 - 9x - 9$, and state the domain and range of the function.

Solution

The function can be factored by grouping as follows:

$y = x^3 + x^2 - 9x - 9$
$y = x^2(x+1) - 9(x+1)$
$y = (x^2 - 9)(x+1)$
$y = (x+3)(x-3)(x+1)$

From the general and factored forms of the function, the following information about the intercepts of the graph can be obtained:

- The x-intercepts are -3, 3, and -1 (the solutions to the equation $0 = x^3 + x^2 - 9x - 9$).
- The y-intercept is -9 because the constant term in the function is -9.

Since the leading coefficient of this cubic function is positive (1), the graph will begin in quadrant III and continuously increase, ending in quadrant I.

Graphically, this means that for very negative x-values, the graph is in quadrant III, and for very positive x-values, the graph is in quadrant I.

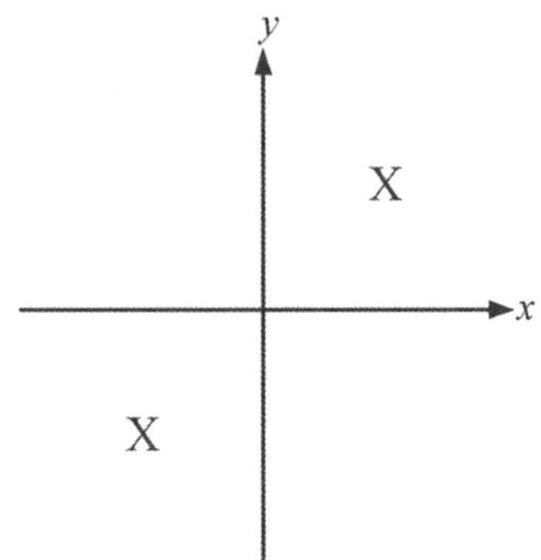

Plot the x-intercepts ($x = -3, -1, 3$) and y-intercept ($y = -9$), and trace a curve through the points, keeping in mind that the curve begins in quadrant III and ends in quadrant I.

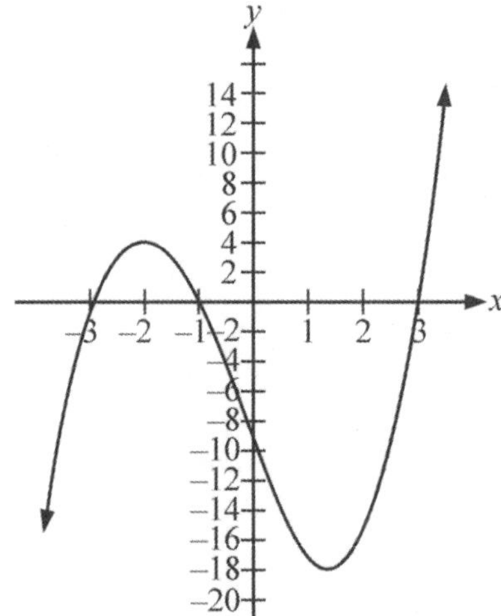

The domain and range are $\{x \mid x \varepsilon R\}$, $\{y \mid y \varepsilon R\}$, respectively.

The general shape of the graph is verified using a graphing calculator.

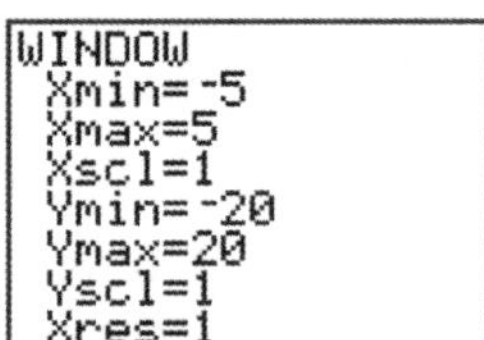

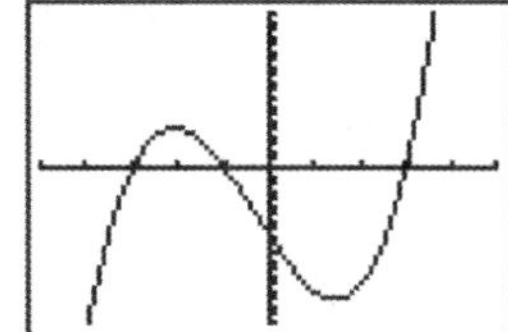

Note that for each of the examples given, the domain was always $\{x \mid x \varepsilon R\}$.

One additional property of polynomial functions is that the domain is always the set of real numbers. While the range may vary, as the examples showed, the domain is consistently the same. As such, polynomial functions are **continuous** functions.

There are no breaks or holes in the graph of a polynomial function. Simply put, the graphs of continuous functions can be sketched without having to take the pencil off the page midway through the sketch. Also, the graph of a polynomial function can be recognized as a smooth, continuous line or curve with a domain spanning the real numbers.

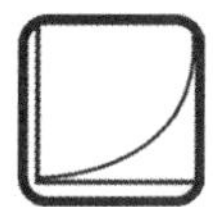

F-IF.5 Relate the domain of a function to its graph and, where applicable, to the quantitative relationship it describes.

Defining the Domain and Range of a Function

The **domain** of a function is the set of all possible x-values (valid input values) represented by the graph or the equation of the function. The **range** of a function is the set of all possible y-values (valid output values) represented by the graph or the equation of the function. On a graph, the domain is found by referring to the x-axis, and the range is found by referring to the y-axis.

Sometimes, the values contained in the domain and range can be stated in the form of a list. At other times, it is impossible to list all the values, and it is better to state the domain and range as intervals. The following inequality symbols are used when stating an interval:

- $>$ —greater than
- $\geq$ —greater than or equal to
- $<$ —less than
- $\leq$ —less than or equal to

Example

Find the domain and range of the function $y = x - 2$.

Solution

Graph or provide a table of values to visualize the domain and range of the given function.

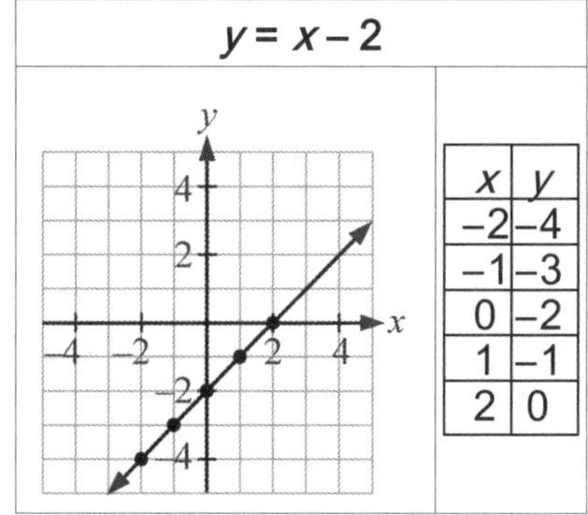

x	y
–2	–4
–1	–3
0	–2
1	–1
2	0

The graph continues infinitely to the right and left for all positive and negative real input elements, or x-values. Therefore, the domain is the set of real numbers. It is written as $x \in \mathbb{R}$, which reads as "x is defined by or belongs to the real numbers." The input values (x) of the table imply this reasoning as well.

The graph of the function $y = x - 2$ and sample output values (y) in the table show that the graph continues infinitely upward and downward for all positive and negative real numbers. Therefore, the range of this function is the set of all real numbers, $y \in \mathbb{R}$.

Example

Find the domain and range of the function $y = x^2 - 3$.

Solution

Graph or provide a table of values to visualize the domain and range of the given function.

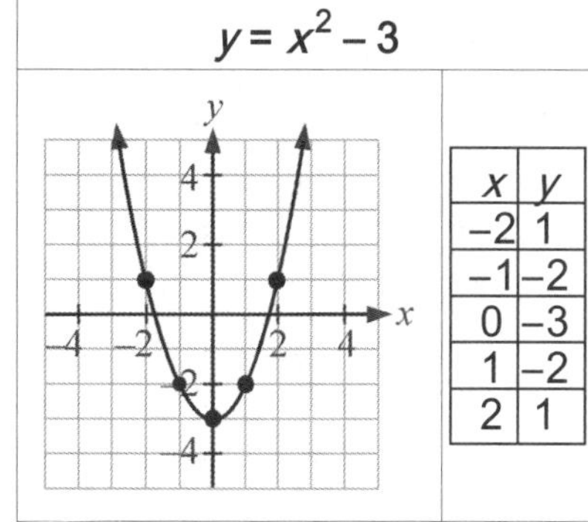

x	y
–2	1
–1	–2
0	–3
1	–2
2	1

The graph continues infinitely to the right and left for all positive and negative real input elements, or x-values. Therefore, the domain is the set of real numbers. It is written as $x \in \mathbb{R}$, which reads as "x is defined by or belongs to the real numbers." The input values (x) of the table imply this reasoning as well.

The graph of the function and sample output values $f(x)$ in the table show that the function's y-values do not go lower than –3, but increase infinitely for all real numbers above and including –3. This description of the range is written as $y \geq -3$.

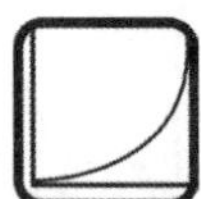

DETERMINING THE DOMAIN AND RANGE FOR DISCRETE DATA

Discrete data is data that can be categorized by distinct values. There are no values in between two consecutive values of the domain.

Example

The relation
$A = \{(-5, 1), (-3, 3), (0, 6), (3, 9), (5, 11)\}$
is given.

To determine the domain of relation A, write the x-coordinate of each ordered pair, and to identify the range, write the y-coordinate of each ordered pair as follows:

- Domain: $\{-5, -3, 0, 3, 5\}$
- Range: $\{1, 3, 6, 9, 11\}$

Graphing discrete data creates a set of distinct points. The points are not connected by a line or a curve because there are no data points between the graphed points.

Example

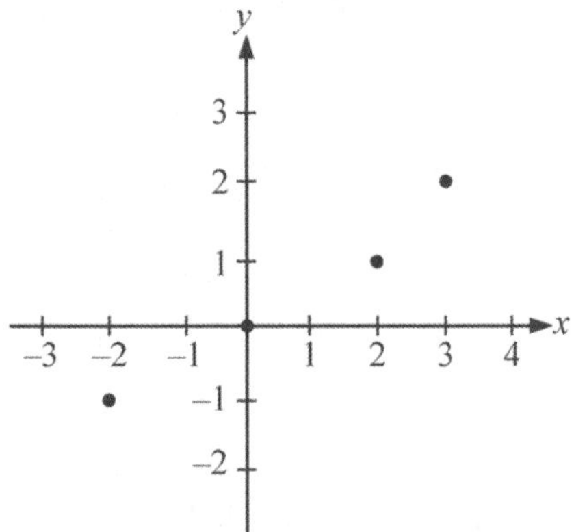

State the domain and range for the given graph.

Solution

To begin, determine the coordinate of each given ordered pair. The coordinates of the four ordered pairs are $(-2, -1)$, $(0, 0)$, $(2, 1)$ and $(3, 2)$. Therefore, the domain is $\{-2, 0, 2, 3\}$ and the range is $\{-1, 0, 1, 2\}$.

DETERMINING THE DOMAIN AND RANGE FOR CONTINUOUS DATA

A **continuous** relation includes all values between points.

Example

Since a linear graph continues indefinitely in both directions, both the domain and range contain the set of all real numbers.

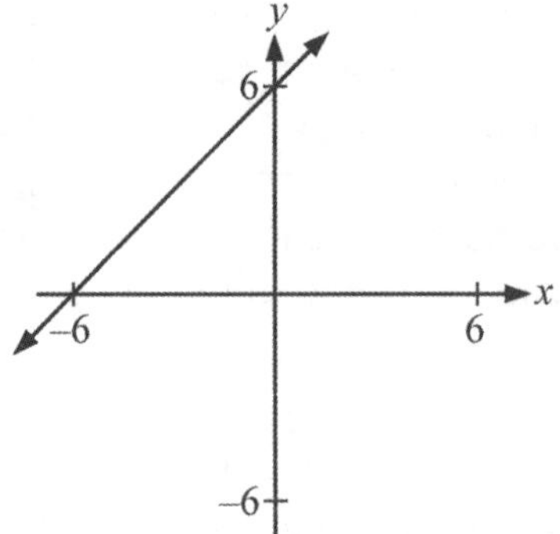

In this case, the domain can be written as $x \in \mathbb{R}$, and the range can be written as $y \in \mathbb{R}$.

The following inequality symbols are used when stating an interval:

- $>$ —greater than
- $\geq$ —greater than or equal to
- $<$ —less than
- $\leq$ —less than or equal to

Example

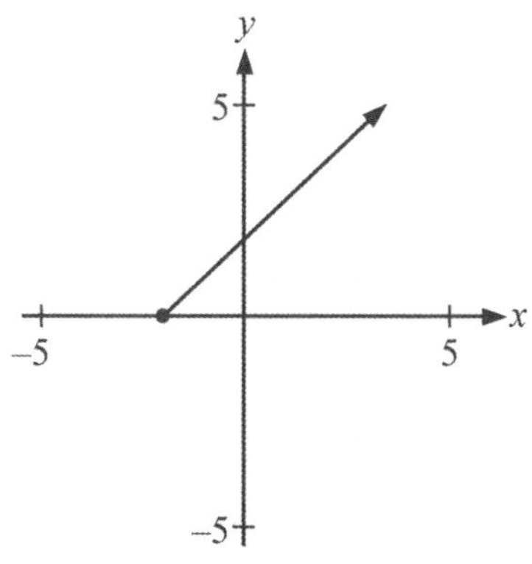

The given graph is the graph of a particular linear function.

State the domain and range of this function.

Solution

For the domain, the x-values start at -2 and increase infinitely. This statement can be written as $x \geq -2$. The given inequality means that x is greater than or equal to -2.

For the range, the y-values start at 0 and increase infinitely. This statement can be written as $y \geq 0$. The given inequality means that y is greater than or equal to 0.

Example

Consider the relation shown in the graph of $y = -x^2 + 4x + 2$.

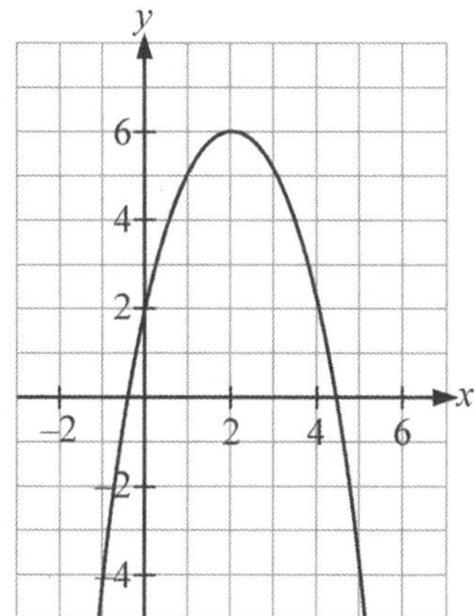

State the domain and range of the given relation.

Solution

The graph is continuous to the right and left for all positive and negative real input or x-values. The domain is the set of real numbers, which is written as $x \in \mathbb{R}$.

The graph also shows that the output or y-values decrease infinitely for all numbers less than or equal to 6. The range can be expressed as the inequality $y \leq 6$.

Using a Graphing Calculator to Determine Domain and Range

Using a graphing calculator is another way to determine the domain and range of a function. Graphing calculators are especially useful when the graph of a function is not given, and a visualization is required to find the domain and range.

To graph a function on a graphing calculator, follow these steps:

1. Make sure the function is written in terms of the y-variable or dependent variable.
2. Press the Y = button on your graphing calculator, and type in the function.
3. Set an appropriate WINDOW setting for the graph so that the resulting graph is adequately portrayed on the screen.
4. Press the GRAPH button to view the graph representing the function.

Example

Using a graphing calculator, determine the domain and range of the relation $15 - y = 0.5x^2 - 0.5x$.

Solution

Step 1

Determine the equation in terms of y.

$$15 - y = 0.5x^2 - 0.5x$$
$$-y = 0.5x^2 - 0.5x - 15$$
$$y = -0.5x^2 + 0.5x + 15$$

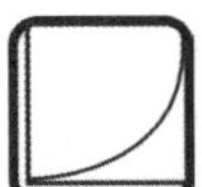

Step 2

Graph the relation $y = -0.5x^2 + 0.5x + 15$ using a graphing calculator.

Press [Y =]. If there are other functions entered in any of the Y = values, remove them by placing the cursor on them and pressing [CLEAR].

Type in the relation by pressing the following sequence of buttons:

[(–)] [0] [.] [5] [x, T, θ, n] [^] [2] [+] [0] [.] [5]
[x, T, θ, n] [+] [15]

Press the [ZOOM] button, and select 6:ZStandard. The graph should appear on the calculator screen as shown.

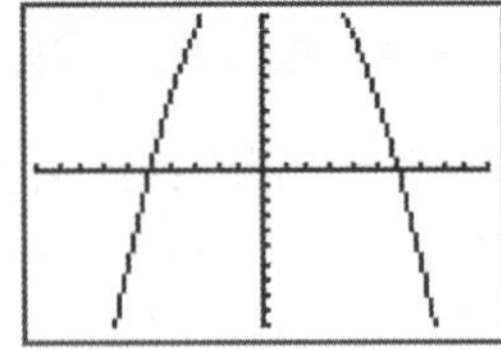

Step 3

Since the top part of the parabola is not visible, the window setting needs to be adjusted manually.

Press the [WINDOW] button. To see more of the upper part of the graph, the Ymax value needs to be increased. Press the down arrow key so that it highlights the Ymax value. Enter a greater value than 10, such as 20. Then press the [GRAPH] button. A more adequate graph of the parabola should appear on the screen.

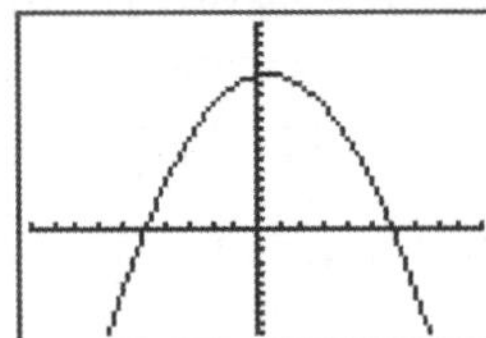

Step 4

State the domain of the graph.

The domain is $x \in \mathbb{R}$ since the graph is continuous and has no distinct largest or smallest value for x.

Step 5

State the range of the graph.

In order to state the range, it is necessary to know the y-value of the highest point on the graph. This can be found using the graphing calculator's maximum feature calculation.

Press [2nd] [TRACE] to enter the Calculate menu. Select 4:maximum from the list.

Using the left and right arrow keys, move to the left of the vertex when asked for a left-bound value, and press [ENTER].

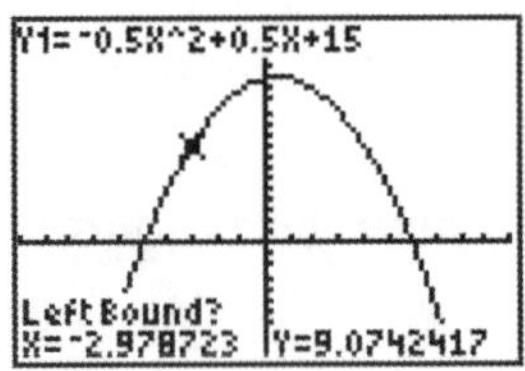

Move to the right of the vertex when asked for a right-bound value, and press [ENTER].

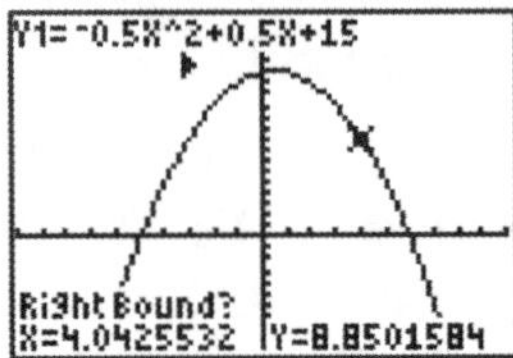

Press [ENTER] again when asked to guess.

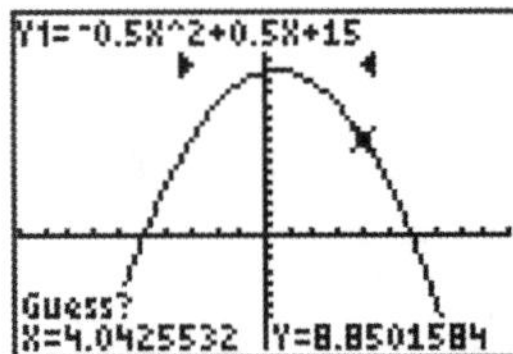

Rounding the nearest tenth, the maximum value is 15.1. Therefore, the range is $y \leq 15.1$.

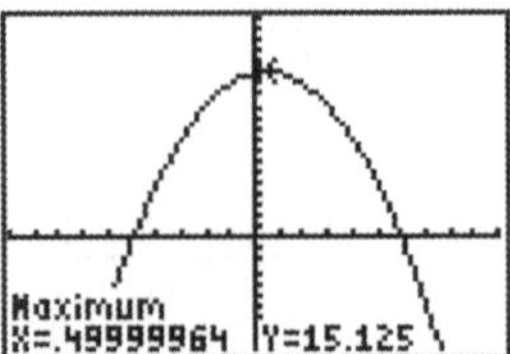

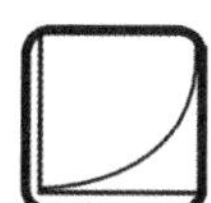

Example

State the domain and range of the function $f(x) = x^2 - 3$.

Solution

Since a graph was not provided and the graph of $f(x) = x^2 - 3$ can be graphed by using a graphing calculator.

Enter the given equation as $Y_1 = x^2 - 3$, press ZOOM and select 6:ZStandard.

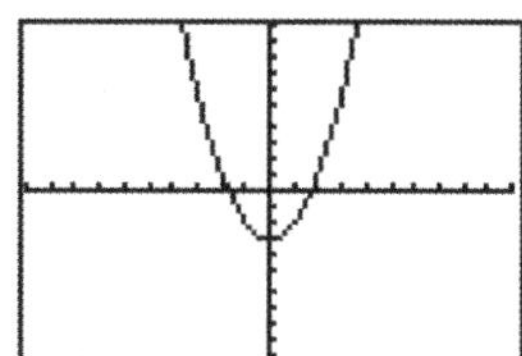

In order to state the range, it is necessary to know the value of the y-coordinate of the lowest point on the graph. This can be found using the graphing calculator's CALCULATE minimum feature.

In this case, the minimum value is −3. Therefore, the range is $y \geq -3$. The domain is $x \in \mathbb{R}$ since the graph is continuous and has no distinct largest or smallest value for x.

Determining the Domain and Range of Real-Life Situations

In real-life situations, there are often restrictions placed on both the domain and range of functions used to describe these situations. When the equation of a function describes a real-life situation, it is important to take the real-life elements of the question into account.

Example

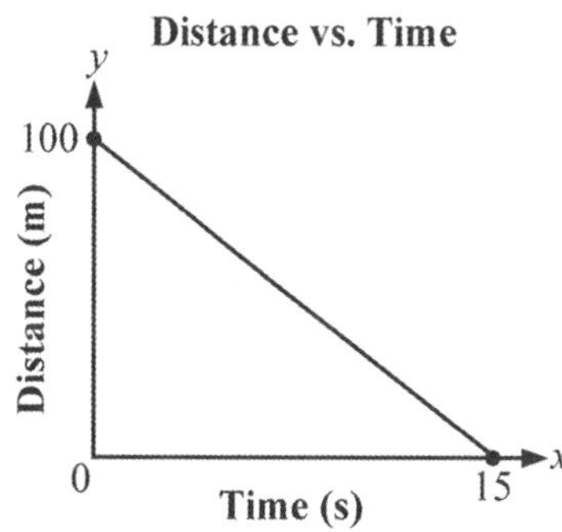

State the domain and range of the given function.

Solution

Since this example is modeling a real-life situation involving time and distance, it is important to leave out the negative values that occur if the graph is extended beyond the axes. Time and distance cannot be negative.

Domain: Time goes from 0 to 15 seconds, $0 \leq t \leq 15$ (t is greater than or equal to 0 and less than or equal to 15).

Range: Distance goes from 0 to 100 m, $0 \leq d \leq 100$ (d is greater than or equal to 0 and less than or equal to 100).

Sometimes, the values in the domain and range are discrete. Stating the number set that the values are a part of can indicate whether the values are discrete. A real-life situation dealing with discrete data is described in the example given here.

Example

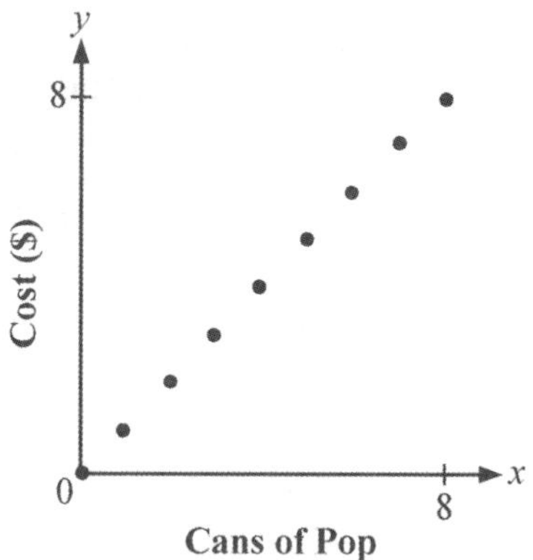

State the domain and range of the given function.

Solution

The domain can be written as
{0, 1, 2, 3, 4, 5, 6, 7, 8} or as $0 \leq x \leq 8$, $x \in I$.

The range can be written as
{0, 1, 2, 3, 4, 5, 6, 7, 8} or as $0 \leq y \leq 8$, $y \in I$.

F-IF.6 Calculate and interpret the average rate of change of a function (presented symbolically or as a table) over a specified interval. Estimate the rate of change from a graph.

Understanding The Rate of Change for a Function

Many real-world scenarios involve a rate of change.

The speed of an object is an example of a rate of change. **Speed** is defined as the rate of change of distance with respect to time.

Example

If an object travels at a constant speed of 5 m/s, this means that the distance changes by 5 m for every 1 s change in time. If v represents the speed, then the speed of the object can be written as $v = 5$ m/s.

The graph of speed versus time for this constant speed of 5 m/s is a horizontal line since the speed is not changing. In this case, the rate of change of speed, or the **acceleration**, is zero.

Whenever the rate of change of a quantity is zero, the corresponding graph is a horizontal line.

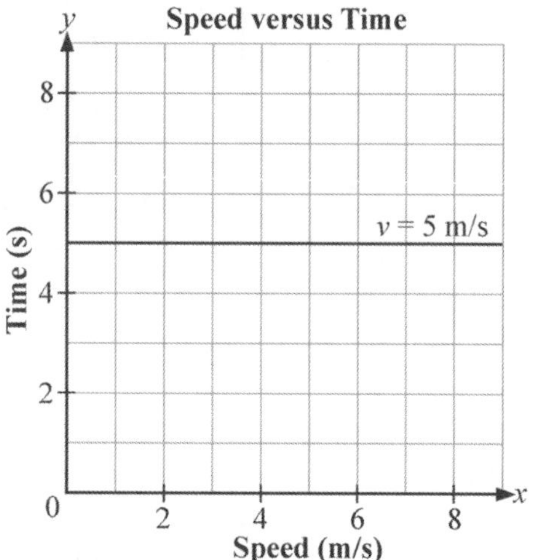

The graph of distance versus time for a constant speed of 5 m/s is an oblique line with a slope of 5 m/s, which is equal to the speed. Whenever the rate of change of a quantity is constant, or uniform, the graph will be an oblique line.

If d represents the distance, and t the amount of time passed, then the equation $d = 5t$ represents the situation algebraically.

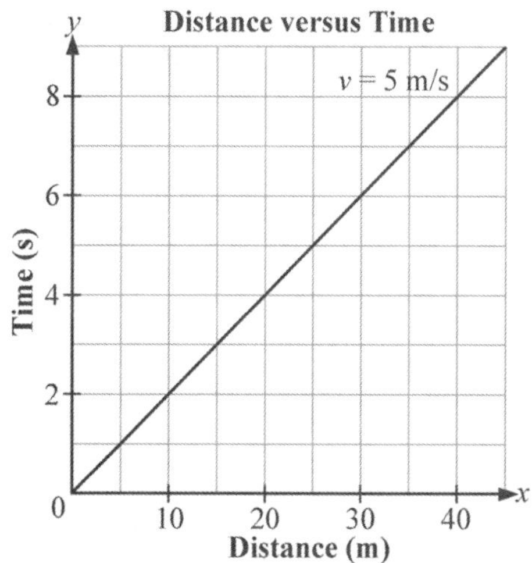

For functions of the form $y = f(x)$, the average rate of change of $f(x)$ with respect to x, between two values x_1 and x_2, is given by $\frac{f(x_2) - f(x_1)}{x_2 - x_1}$.

This ratio also represents the slope of the line joining these points on the graph of $y = f(x)$.

Example

A balloon is being inflated mechanically in such a way that the volume is increasing at a constant rate of 15 cm^3/s. If the volume of the balloon was originally 30 cm^3.

Compare the average rate of change of the volume of the balloon with respect to the radius of the balloon, to the nearest centimeter cubed per centimeter, between 0 s and 10 s, and between 10 s and 20 s.

Solution

It is given that the rate of change of volume with respect to time is a constant 15 cm^3/s.
For every 10 s, the volume will increase by 10 s × 15 cm^3/s = 150 cm^3.

After 10 s, the volume would be 30 cm^3 + 150 cm^3 = 180 cm^3, and after 20 s it would be 180 cm^3 + 150 cm^3 = 330 cm^3.

Next, determine the radius at 0 s, 10 s, and 20 s.

Using the formula for the volume of a sphere, $V = \frac{4}{3}\pi r^3$, solve for r, which gives $r = \sqrt[3]{\frac{3V}{4\pi}}$.
Substituting the three values for V, gives a radius of approximately 1.93 cm initially, 3.50 cm after 10 s, and 4.29 cm after 20 s.

The average rate of change of volume with respect to radius is calculated by $\frac{V_2 - V_1}{r_2 - r_1}$.

Therefore, between 0 s and 10 s, the average rate of change of volume with respect to radius is $\frac{180 - 30}{3.50 - 1.93} \approx 96$ cm^3/cm, and between 10 s and 20 s, it is $\frac{330 - 180}{4.29 - 3.50} \approx 190$ cm^3/cm.

These two values illustrate that the rate of change of volume with respect to radius is not constant.

APPLICATIONS OF AVERAGE RATES OF CHANGE

There are numerous applications and situations involving rate of change. The following list contains a few examples:

1. With the present day interest in global warming, there are many historical studies and a lot of research being done on the rate at which various regions of Earth are warming. On a related topic, there is research on how fast the ozone layer of the atmosphere is being depleted.
2. In medicine, there are studies on the rate of advancement of disease, and the rate of effectiveness of drugs and other treatments.
3. In finance and economics, there is interest in many rates of change, such as the rate of growth of economies and the rate of change of the values of stock markets.
4. The rate of change of displacement with respect to time is called velocity. When an object is dropped from a height of 200 m, its velocity, v m/s, toward the center of the earth after t s is given by the formula $v = -9.8t$. This formula disregards the effect of air friction on the object. Thus, after 3 s, the velocity of the object is $v = -9.8(3) = -29.4$ m/s. The negative sign indicates the direction is toward Earth rather than away from it.
5. Graphs are often used to show or emphasize rates of change. For example, consider what happens to the temperature in a barbecue when it is turned off.
   This graph shows the temperature, y (°C), in a particular barbecue x min after it has been turned off.

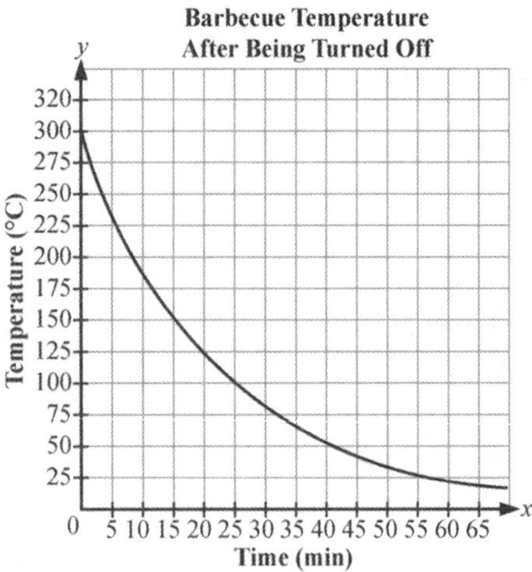

Notice how the temperature of the barbecue falls quickly initially (the graph is steep) and then much more slowly as time passes (the graph is getting flatter). This shows that the rate of change of the temperature with respect to time is greater initially (negatively) than it is after it gets closer to the temperature of the surrounding air.

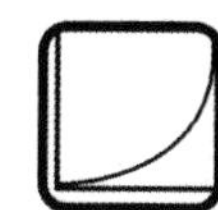

It is helpful to remember that the average rate of change between two given points is calculated using the formula $\frac{f(b)-f(a)}{b-a}$.

Example

The population of bacteria in a culture grows such that it can be modeled to the equation $N(t)=260(2)^{\frac{t}{6.5}}$, where t is the time in hours and $N(t)$ is the number of bacteria after t hours have passed.

Calculate and interpret the average rate of change of the bacteria population between 0 h and 20 h. Also calculate the average rate of change of the bacteria population between 0 h and 10 h and between 10 h and 20 h and then compare these rates to the rate of change over the 20 h interval.

Solution

Calculating gives

$N(0)=260(2)^{\frac{0}{6.5}}=260$

$N(10)=260(2)^{\frac{10}{6.5}}\approx 755$

$N(20)=260(2)^{\frac{20}{6.5}}\approx 2{,}194$

The average rate of change between 0 h and 20 h is

$\frac{N(20)-N(0)}{20-0}$
$=\frac{2{,}194-260}{20}$
$=96.7$ bacteria / h

This means that if the population increased uniformly by 96.7 bacteria every hour over the 20 h interval it would reach the same population of 2,194 bacteria, as previously calculated.

Between 0 h and 10 h, the average rate of change is

$\frac{N(10)-N(0)}{10-0}$
$=\frac{755-260}{10}$
$=49.5$ bacteria / h

Between 10 h and 20 h it is

$\frac{N(20)-N(10)}{20-10}$
$=\frac{2{,}194-755}{10}$
$=143.9$ bacteria / h

The average rate of change or the growth rate of the population is increasing as time passes since it changes from 96.7 bacteria/h over the first ten hours to 143.9 bacteria/h over the second ten hours. The average of these two rates equals the growth rate over the twenty hour interval.

Calculating Average Rates of Change Given a Graph

The average rate of change for a line or curve in a particular interval is the same as the slope between the two endpoints of the interval.

The formula for slope using two points, $P=(x_1,\ y_1)$ and $Q=(x_2,\ y_2)$, is $m_{PQ}=\frac{y_2-y_1}{x_2-x_1}$.

Substitute the values into the slope formula and solve. The result is the average rate of change between P and Q.

Example

Two points, A and B, are labeled on the given graph of a function.

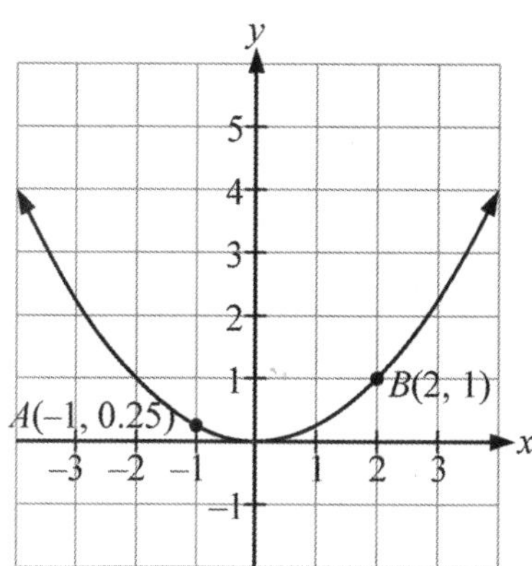

What is the average rate of change between A and B?

Solution

The average rate of change between A and B is the slope of $\overline{AB}$, as shown in the diagram.

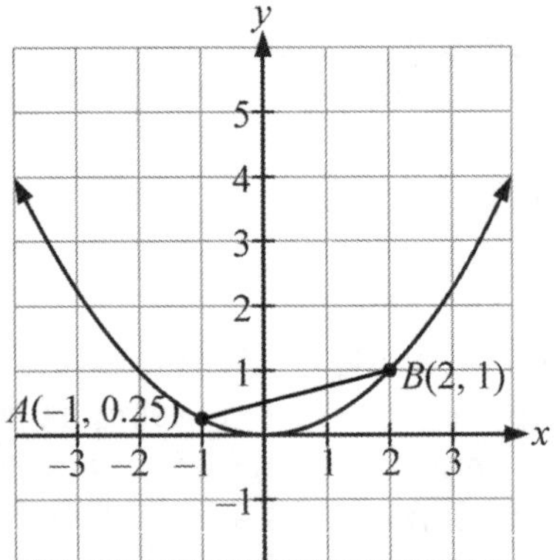

Substitute the values of points A and B into the slope formula and solve.

$$m_{AB} = \frac{y_B - y_A}{x_B - x_A}$$

$$m_{AB} = \frac{1 - 0.25}{2 - (-1)}$$

$$m_{AB} = \frac{0.75}{3}$$

$$m_{AB} = 0.25$$

Therefore, the average rate of change between A and B is 0.25.

If only the x-values are given, determine the corresponding y-values from the graph before calculating the slope.

Example

The diagram shows the graph of the function $f(x)$.

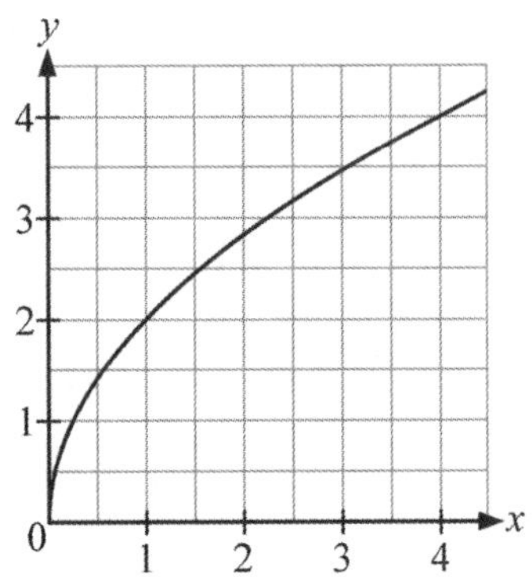

What is the average rate of change of the graph for the interval $1 \leq x \leq 4$?

Solution

Step 1

Determine the y-values for the endpoints of the interval.

The x-values for the endpoints of the interval are $x_1 = 1$ and $x_2 = 4$.

Find the corresponding y-values from the graph.

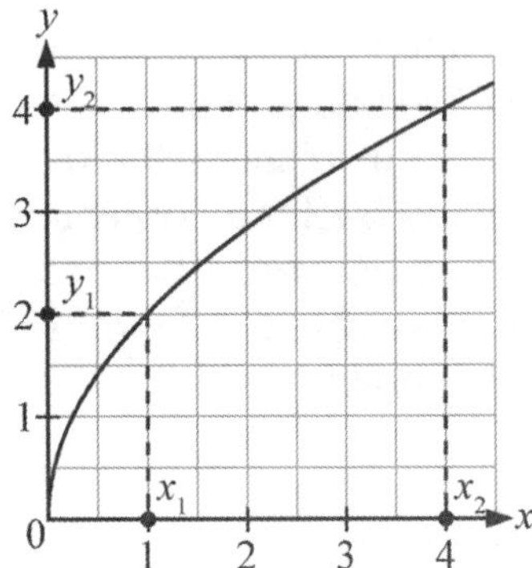

The y-values for the endpoints of the interval are $y_1 = 2$ and $y_2 = 4$.

Step 2

Calculate the slope of the line segment between the points shown in the diagram.

Substitute the values for (x_1, y_1) and (x_2, y_2) into the slope formula and solve.

$$m = \frac{y_2 - y_1}{x_2 - x_1}$$

$$m = \frac{4 - 2}{4 - 1}$$

$$m = \frac{2}{3}$$

The average slope of the graph for the interval $1 \leq x \leq 4$ is $\frac{2}{3}$.

CALCULATING AVERAGE RATES OF CHANGE GIVEN A TABLE OF VALUES

The average rate of change for a function over a certain interval can be determined by calculating the slope of the line between the end points of that interval.

The formula for slope between two points, (x_1, y_1) and (x_2, y_2), is $m = \frac{y_2 - y_1}{x_2 - x_1}$.

To calculate the average rate of change for the ordered pairs for a given interval, follow these steps:

1. Determine which values to use.
2. Calculate the average rate of change by using the slope formula.

Example

The table of values represents ordered pairs for the function $f(x) = 0.1x^3 - x$. Each row corresponds to one ordered pair, (x, y), which is a point on the curve $f(x)$.

x	y
–3	0.3
–2	1.2
–1	0.9
0	0
1	–0.9
2	–1.2
3	–0.3

What is the average rate of change for the interval $-2 \le x \le 3$?

Solution

Step 1
Determine which values to use.

Use the table of values to determine the y-values for the two ends of the interval. Since $x_1 = -2$ and $x_2 = 3$, then $y_1 = 1.2$ and $y_2 = -0.3$.

Therefore, the two ordered pairs are (–2, 1.2) and (3, –0.3).

Step 2
Calculate the average rate of change by using the slope formula.

Substitute the ordered pairs into the slope formula, and evaluate.

$$m = \frac{y_2 - y_1}{x_2 - x_1}$$
$$m = \frac{-0.3 - 1.2}{3 - (-2)}$$
$$m = \frac{-1.5}{5}$$
$$m = -0.3$$

Therefore, the average rate of change for the function f is –0.3.

EXERCISE #1—INTERPRETING FUNCTIONS

163. Which of the following equations is an even function?

A. $y = x^2 + 3 + \frac{3x}{4x^4}$

B. $y = \frac{1}{3} + \frac{1}{3x} + \frac{1}{3x^4}$

C. $y = x^2 + \frac{5x^5}{x} + \frac{1}{x^2}$

D. $y = 2x + 4x + 6x^2$

Use the following information to answer the next question.

The value of a truck decreases over time, as shown in the given table.

Time Since Purchase (years)	Value of Truck ($)
2	28,000
3	20,000
5	11,600
6	8,400
7	5,000

164. If this trend continues, what will the price of the truck be 7 years and 9 months after the time of purchase?

A. $3,965.80 **B.** $3,985.20

C. $4,025.60 **D.** $4,355.57

165. Sketch the graph of $y = 5^{x-4} + 1$, and state the domain, range, and equation of the asymptote.

Use the following information to answer the next question.

The equations for four different functions are shown:

1. $y = 3$
2. $y = 3x$
3. $y = x^2 - 3$
4. $y = 3 - x^2$

166. Which of the following statements about the given functions is **false**?

A. All the functions have domains of $x \in \mathrm{R}$.

B. The linear functions have a range of $y \in \mathrm{R}$.

C. The quadratic functions do not have a range of $y \in \mathrm{R}$.

D. Only one function has a domain of $x \in \mathrm{R}$ and a range of $y \in \mathrm{R}$.

167. The range of the function $G = \{(-5, 5), (-1, 1), (2, -3), (3, -4), (4, 3)\}$ is

A. $\{-4, -3, 1, 3, 5\}$

B. $\{-5, -1, 2, 3, 4\}$

C. $-4 \le y \le 5$

D. $-5 \le y \le 4$

Use the following information to answer the next question.

The air pressure in a car tire changes during a trip, as shown in the graph. The graph consists of five line segments.

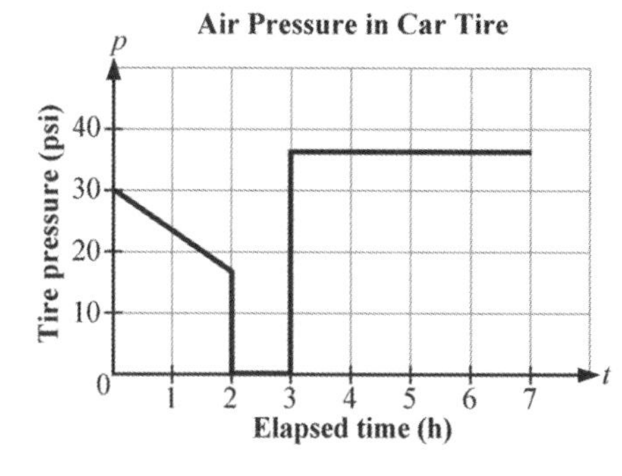

168. If the maximum tire pressure is 37 psi, what are the domain and range of the relation?

A. D:$\{0 \le t \le 2\}$ and R:$\{0 \le p \le 30\}$

B. D:$\{0 \le t \le 7\}$ and R:$\{0 \le p \le 37\}$

C. D:$\{0 \le p \le 30\}$ and R:$\{0 \le t \le 2\}$

D. D:$\{0 \le p \le 37\}$ and R:$\{0 \le t \le 7\}$

169. What is the range of the function $f(x) = x^2 + 6x - 11$?

A. $y \le -20$

B. $y \ge -20$

C. $y = -20$

D. $y \in \mathbb{R}$

Use the following information to answer the next question.

The cost of operating a small delivery service is given by the equation $C(x) = 80\sqrt{x+25}$, where x is the number of parcels delivered per day and $C(x)$ is the cost in dollars per day. The maximum number of parcels that the delivery service can deliver in one day is 200.

The domain of the given function is ____*i*____, and the range is ____*ii*____.

170. Which of the following tables contains the information that completes the given statement?

A.

i	*ii*
$25 \le x \le 200$ $x \in \mathrm{I}$	$\{400, 80\sqrt{26}, 80\sqrt{27}$ $80\sqrt{28}\ldots1{,}200\}$

B.

i	*ii*
$25 \le x \le 200$ $x \in \mathrm{I}$	$0 \le C(x) \le 1{,}200$ $C(x) \in \mathrm{I}$

C.

i	*ii*
$0 \le x \le 200$ $x \in \mathrm{I}$	$\{400, 80\sqrt{26}, 80\sqrt{27}$ $80\sqrt{28}\ldots1{,}200\}$

D.

i	*ii*
$0 \le x \le 200$ $x \in \mathrm{I}$	$0 \le C(x) \le 1{,}200$ $C(x) \in \mathrm{I}$

Use the following information to answer the next question.

The table shown gives the population of a city over a 29-year period.

Year	Population
1965	128,445
1970	166,408
1980	219,494
1990	266,406
1994	282,133

171. The average yearly rate of change of the population of the city was **greatest** between

A. 1965 and 1970

B. 1970 and 1980

C. 1980 and 1990

D. 1990 and 1994

Use the following information to answer the next question.

A population of bacteria is growing according to the function $P(t) = 20(1.33)^t$, where $P(t)$ is the population and t is the number of hours that have elapsed since there were exactly 20 bacteria.

172. What is the average rate of increase of the bacteria population during the sixth hour after the population was exactly 20?

A. 17 bacteria/h

B. 18 bacteria/h

C. 28 bacteria/h

D. 34 bacteria/h

Use the following information to answer the next question.

A ball is thrown straight upward with a speed of 8 m/s. The height of the ball (in meters) as a function of time (in seconds) is given by the function $h(t) = -4.9t^2 + 8t + 2$.

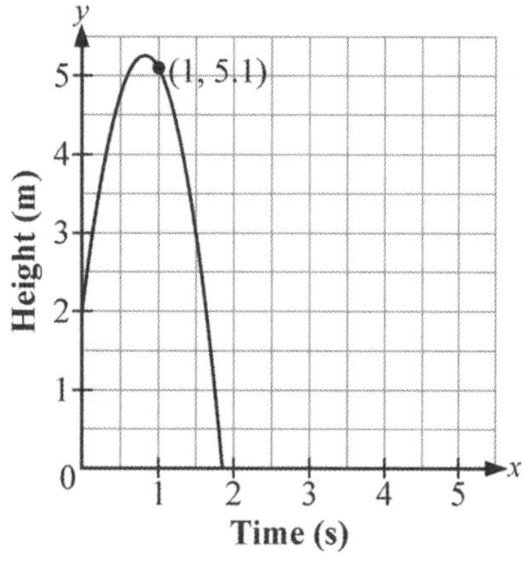

173. During the first second of the ball's flight, what is the average rate of change in height with respect to time?

A. 0.3 m/s　　**B.** 3.1 m/s

C. 5.3 m/s　　**D.** 7.1 m/s

Use the following information to answer the next question.

A partial table of values for a function $y = f(x)$ is shown.

x	y
1	2
2	6
3	?
4	10

174. If the average rate of change in the interval $1 \leq x \leq 3$ is 2.5, what is the value of $f(3)$?

A. 4　　**B.** 5

C. 6　　**D.** 7

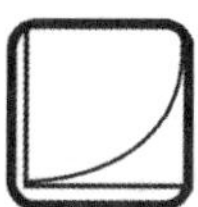

EXERCISE #1—INTERPRETING FUNCTIONS ANSWERS AND SOLUTIONS

163. C	166. B	169. B	172. C
164. D	167. A	170. C	173. B
165. See solution	168. B	171. A	174. D

163. C

Any polynomial function consisting of only even-degree monomials is an even function, and any polynomial function whose terms consist of only odd-degree monomials is an odd function. If the polynomial function has any combination of odd-degree and even-degree terms, it is neither odd nor even.

The equation $y = x^2 + \frac{5x^5}{x} + \frac{1}{x^2}$ is an even function. Since $\frac{5x^5}{x}$ simplifies to $5x^4$, the equation contains only even-degree monomials.

The other equations are neither odd nor even functions. The equation $y = \frac{1}{3} + \frac{1}{3x} + \frac{1}{3x^4}$ contains the odd-degree monomial $\frac{1}{3x}$.

The equation $y = x^2 + 3 + \frac{3x}{4x^4}$ contains $\frac{3x}{4x^4}$, which simplifies to the odd-degree monomial $\frac{3}{4x^3}$.

The equation $y = 2x + 4x + 6x^2$ contains the odd-degree monomials $2x$ and $4x$, which simplify to $6x$.

164. D

Step 1

Plot the points on a graph.

Press STAT, and select 1:Edit. Enter the values for the year in *L1* and the values for price in *L2*.

Press 2nd Y =, and select 1:Plot1. Press ENTER to turn on Plot1.

Clear any equations from Y =, and set an appropriate window. In this case, X:[0, 8, 1] and Y:[5,000, 29,000, 1] would be appropriate.

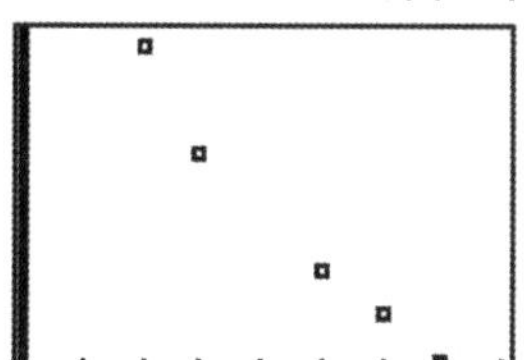

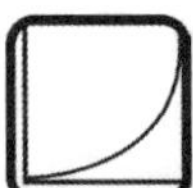

Step 2

Determine the best regression model for the data. The points in the graph follow a downward trend. The value of the truck decreasing over time is a situation in which the downward trend will continue. Therefore, the exponential regression model would be the best model to use.

Before doing the regression, however, make sure the Diagnostics are on so the value of the correlation coefficient is given. This will indicate the accuracy of the regression model (the closer the value is to 1 or −1, the better the equation fits the data). Press [2nd] [0] and then the [x^{-1}] key. Scroll down to DiagnosticON. Press [ENTER] twice.

Perform the exponential regression. Press [STAT], and scroll to the CALC menu. Select 0:ExpReg. The screen should show ExpReg. Press the [VARS] key, scroll right to the Y-VARS menu, and select 1:Function and then 1:Y_1. This will put the regression equation into the Y = feature. Press [ENTER], and the equation and correlation coefficient should appear.

The regression coefficient for an exponential regression, to the nearest thousandth, is $r \approx -0.993$. Press [GRAPH] to watch as the graph of the equation passes nearly through the center of all points in the data.

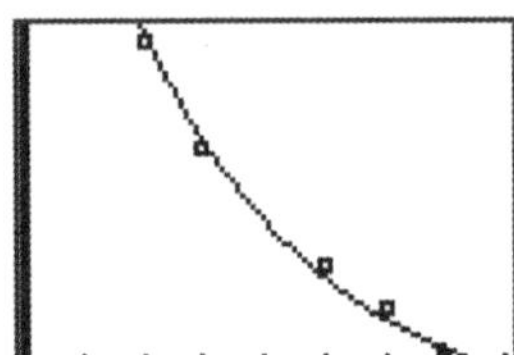

A quadratic model can be used, but because of the reality of the situation it is not the best model because the value of the truck will not increase after decreasing.

Step 3

Determine the price of the truck 7 years and 9 months after the time of purchase.

On the graph screen, press [2nd] [TRACE] to access the CALC menu, and select 1:Value. Enter 7.75 (for 7 and $\frac{9}{12}$ years), and press [ENTER].

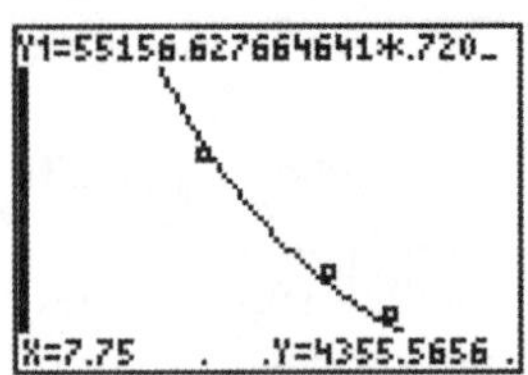

The coordinates of the point are (7.75, 4,355.57). The car will be worth $4,355.577 years and 9 months after the time of purchase.

165.

Step 1

Sketch the graph of $y = 5^x$.

Step 2

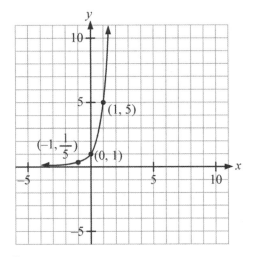

Determine the transformations required to produce the graph of $y = 5^{x-4} + 1$.

The equation $y = 5^{x-4} + 1$ can be written as $y - 1 = 5^{x-4}$. To arrive at the equation $y - 1 = 5^{x-4}$, it is necessary to substitute $y - 1$ for y and $x - 4$ for x in the equation $y = 5^x$. The graph of $y = 5^{x-4} + 1$ is produced by translating the graph of $y = 5^x$1 unit up and 4 units to the right.

Step 3

Sketch the graph of $y = 5^{x-4} + 1$.

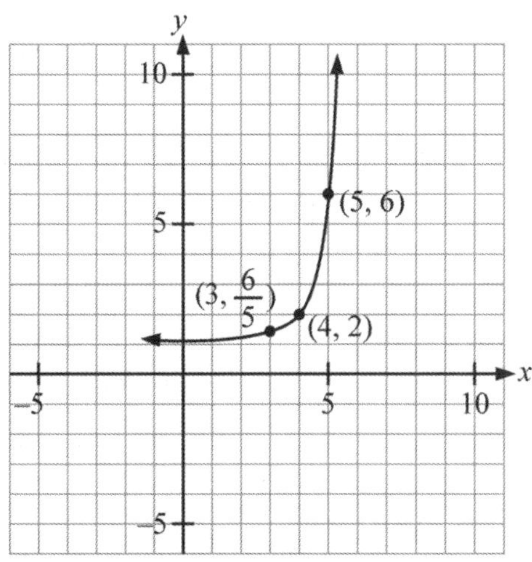

Step 4

From the graph of $y = 5^{x-4} + 1$, state the domain, range, and equation of the asymptote.

The domain is $x \in R$.

The range is $y > 1$. The range of the function $y = 5^x$ is $y > 0$. The graph of the function $y = 5^{x-4} + 1$ is $y > (0 + 1)$ or $y > 1$ since the graph of $y = 5^x$ is translated 1 unit up.

The equation of the horizontal asymptote is $y = 1$. The equation of the horizontal asymptote of the graph of the function $y = 5^x$ is $y = 0$. The equation of the horizontal asymptote of the graph of the function $y = 5^{x-4} + 1$ is $y = (0 + 1)$ or $y = 1$ since the graph of $y = 5^x$ is translated 1 unit up.

166. B

Step 1

Draw the graph of function 1, and determine the type of function, the domain, and the range of the graph.

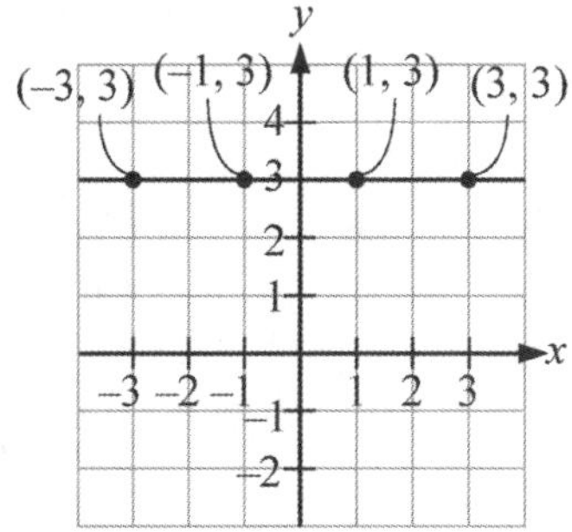

This is a linear function, where the domain is $x \in \mathrm{R}$ and the range is $y = 3$.

Step 2

Draw the graph of function 2, and determine the type of function, the domain, and the range of the graph.

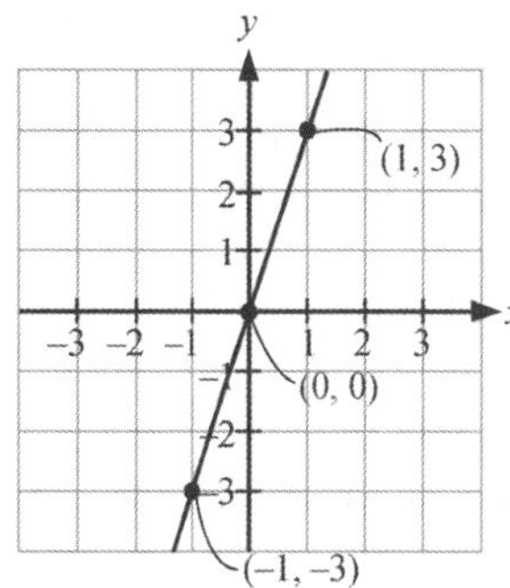

This is a linear function, where the domain is $x \in \mathrm{R}$ and the range is $y \in \mathrm{R}$.

Step 3

Draw the graph of function 3, and determine the type of function, the domain, and the range of the graph.

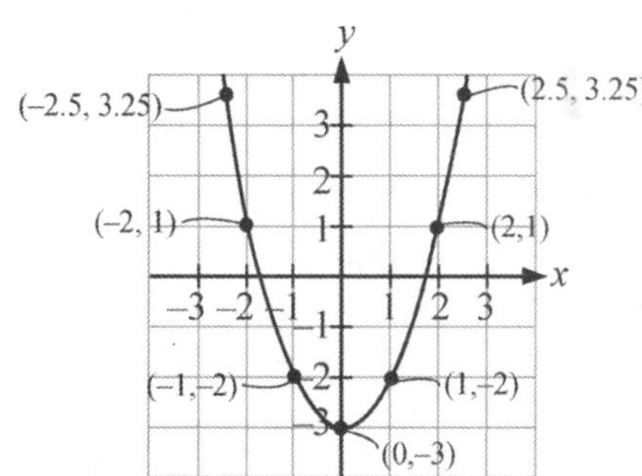

This is a quadratic function, where the domain is $x \in \mathrm{R}$ and the range is $y \geq -3$.

Step 4

Draw the graph of function 4, and determine the type of function, the domain, and the range of the graph.

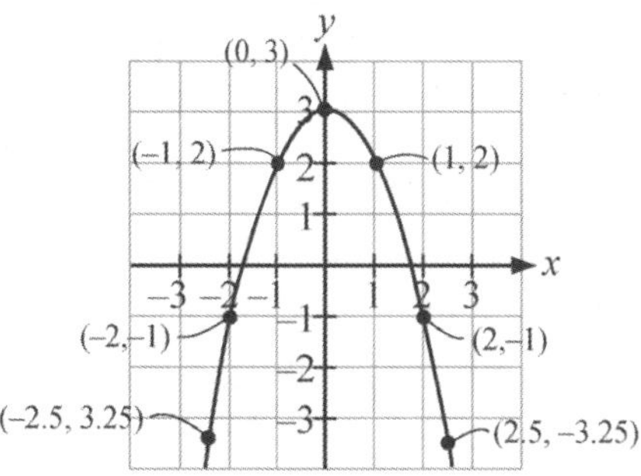

This is a quadratic function, where the domain is $x \in \mathrm{R}$ and the range is $y \leq 3$.

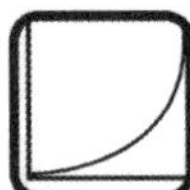

Step 5
Examine all graphs, and determine which statement is false.
All the functions have domains of $x \in \mathrm{R}$, so that statement is true.
Quadratic functions 3 and 4 do not have a range of $y \in \mathrm{R}$, so that statement is true.
Only function 2 has a domain of $x \in \mathrm{R}$ and a range of $y \in \mathrm{R}$, so that statement is true.
The linear functions (functions 1 and 2) do not have a range of $y \in \mathrm{R}$ since the range of function 1 is $y = 3$.
Therefore, the statement that the linear functions have a range of $y \in \mathrm{R}$ is false.

167. A

To identify the range of the given list of ordered pairs, list the y-values.

The y-values are 5, 1, −3, −4, and 3.

The range is therefore {−4, −3, 1, 3, 5}.

168. B

Step 1
Determine the domain of the relation.
Looking at the graph, the horizontal axis starts at 0 h and continues to 7 h before it stops. Therefore, the domain is 0 h to 7 h inclusive. If t represents the time, the domain is D:$\{0 \le t \le 7\}$.

Step 2
Determine the range of the relation.
Looking at the vertical axis, the lowest value is 0 psi, and the highest value is 37 psi. Therefore, the range is 0 psi to 37 psi inclusive. If p represents the tire pressure, the range is R:$\{0 \le p \le 37\}$.
Thus, the domain and range of the relation are D:$\{0 \le t \le 7\}$ and R:$\{0 \le p \le 37\}$.

169. B

Use a graphing calculator to determine the range of the given function.

Graph $f(x) = x^2 + 6x - 11$ on your graphing calculator by pressing [Y =] and entering the function into $[Y_1 =]$.

Press [WINDOW] and enter in the following min and max values:
Xmin = −10
Xmax = 4
Xscl = 1
Ymin = −25
Ymax = 5
Yscl = 2

Press [GRAPH] to view the graph.

Since the graph of this quadratic function opens upward infinitely, find the minimum y-value of the graph by pressing [2nd] [TRACE] and selecting 3:minimum.

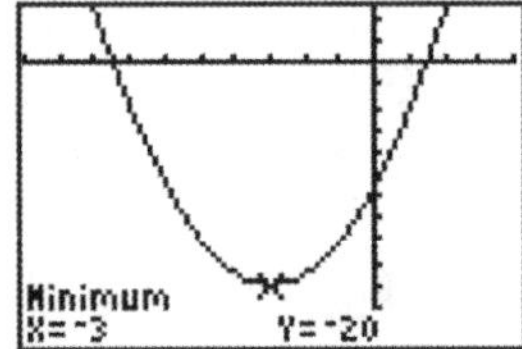

At an x-value of −3, the minimum y-value is −20. Therefore, the range of the graph is $y \ge -20$.

170. C

Step 1
Determine the domain of the given function.
The domain of the given function is the set of permissible values for the independent variable, the number of parcels delivered per day, x. Since it is impossible to deliver a negative number of parcels (or part of a parcel) and the maximum number of parcels that can be delivered in a day is 200, it follows that the domain of the given function is $0 \le x \le 200,\ x \in \mathrm{I}$.

Step 2
Determine the range of the given function.
The range of the given function is the set of permissible values for the dependent variable, the daily cost to operate the delivery service, $C(x)$. The permissible values for $C(x)$ can be obtained by sequentially substituting the numbers from 0 to 200, inclusive, for x in the equation $C(x) = 80\sqrt{x + 25}$.

- If $x = 0$, $C(x) = 80\sqrt{0 + 25} = \$400$.
- If $x = 1$, $C(x) = 80\sqrt{1 + 25} = \$80\sqrt{26}$.
- If $x = 2$, $C(x) = 80\sqrt{2 + 25} = \$80\sqrt{27}$.
- If $x = 3$, $C(x) = 80\sqrt{3 + 25} = \$80\sqrt{28}$.

This pattern would continue until 200 is substituted for x.
If $x = 200$, $C(x) = 80\sqrt{200 + 25} = \$1{,}200$.
Therefore, the range of the given function can be written as $\{400, 80\sqrt{26}, 80\sqrt{27}, 80\sqrt{28} \ldots 1{,}200\}$.

171. A

Determine the average yearly rate of change of the population for each time interval using the ratio $\frac{P_2 - P_1}{t_2 - t_1}$, where P_1 and P_2 are populations and t_1 and t_2 are the years in which those populations occurred.

Step 1
Calculate the average yearly rate of change between 1965 and 1970.

$$\begin{aligned}\frac{P_2 - P_1}{t_2 - t_1} &= \frac{166{,}408 - 128{,}445}{1{,}970 - 1{,}965}\\ &= \frac{37{,}963}{5}\\ &= 7{,}592.6\end{aligned}$$

Step 2
Calculate the average yearly rate of change between 1970 and 1980.

$$\begin{aligned}\frac{P_2 - P_1}{t_2 - t_1} &= \frac{219{,}494 - 166{,}408}{1{,}980 - 1{,}970}\\ &= \frac{53{,}086}{10}\\ &= 5{,}308.6\end{aligned}$$

Step 3
Calculate the average yearly rate of change between 1980 and 1990.

$$\begin{aligned}\frac{P_2 - P_1}{t_2 - t_1} &= \frac{266{,}406 - 219{,}494}{1{,}990 - 1{,}980}\\ &= \frac{46{,}912}{10}\\ &= 4{,}691.2\end{aligned}$$

Step 4
Calculate the average yearly rate of change between 1990 and 1994.

$$\begin{aligned}\frac{P_2 - P_1}{t_2 - t_1} &= \frac{282{,}133 - 266{,}406}{1{,}994 - 1{,}990}\\ &= \frac{15{,}727}{4}\\ &= 3{,}931.75\end{aligned}$$

The average yearly rate of change of the population was greatest between 1965 and 1970, when the population increased at an average of 7,592.6 people per year.

172. C

Step 1
Determine when the sixth hour occurs.

The first hour is between $t = 0$ and $t = 1$, the second hour is between $t = 1$ and $t = 2$, and the third hour is between $t = 2$ and $t = 3$. By extending the pattern, the sixth hour must be between $t = 5$ and $t = 6$.

Step 2
Determine the population of bacteria at $t = 5$ and $t = 6$.

- At $t = 5$, the population is as follows:
  $P(5) = 20(1.33)^5$
  $P(5) \approx 83.232$
- At $t = 6$, the population is as follows:
  $P(6) = 20(1.33)^6$
  $P(6) \approx 110.698$

Therefore, to the nearest whole number, the population is 83 after 5 h and 111 after 6 h.

Step 3
Determine the rate of change of population by using the ratio $\frac{P_2 - P_1}{t_2 - t_1}$.

$$\begin{aligned}\frac{P_2 - P_1}{t_2 - t_1} &= \frac{P(6) - P(5)}{6 - 5}\\ &= \frac{111 - 83}{1}\\ &= 28\end{aligned}$$

During the sixth hour, the population is increasing at an average rate of 28 bacteria/h.

173. B

Step 1
Determine which points on the graph to use.
Since the question is only concerned with the average rate of change during the first second of flight, the corresponding interval is $0 < x \leq 1$.
From the graph, $h(0) = 2$ and $h(1) = 5.1$, so the points are (0, 2) and (1, 5.1).

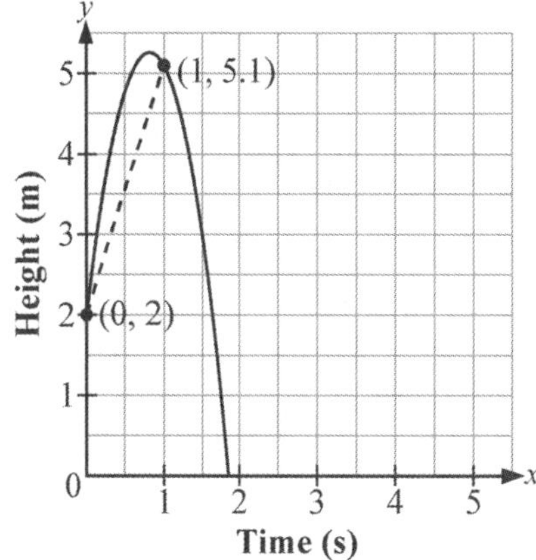

Step 2
Calculate the slope between the two points.
Substitute the coordinate values into the slope formula, and evaluate.

$$m = \frac{h(1) - h(0)}{1 - 0}$$

$$m = \frac{5.1 - 2}{1 - 0}$$

$$m = \frac{3.1}{1}$$

$$m = 3.1$$

Therefore, the average rate of change in height with respect to time is 3.1 m/s.

174. D

Step 1
Determine which values to use.
Use the table of values to determine the y-values for the two ends of the interval $1 \le x \le 3$.
When $x_1 = 1$, it follows that $y_1 = f(1) = 2$, and when $x_2 = 3$, $y_2 = f(3)$.

Step 2
To determine the value of $f(3)$, substitute the known values into the slope formula, and solve for $f(3)$.

$$\frac{y_2 - y_1}{x_2 - x_1} = m$$

$$\frac{f(3) - 2}{3 - 1} = 2.5$$

$$\frac{f(3) - 2}{2} = 2.5$$

$$f(3) - 2 = 5$$

$$f(3) = 7$$

EXERCISE #2—INTERPRETING FUNCTIONS

175. Which of the following functions is odd?

A. $f(x) = x^2 - 3x + 2$

B. $f(x) = -x^4 - x^3 - x^2$

C. $f(x) = 5x^5 + 2x^3 - 3x$

D. $f(x) = 3x^3 + 4x^2 - 5x - 1$

Use the following information to answer the next question.

The data in the given table shows the speed, v, in kilometers per hour, of an athlete running a 200 m sprint over a time period, t, in seconds.

Time (t)	Speed (v)
1	5.00
2	8.00
3	12.80
4	20.48
5	32.77

176. If this trend continues, after how many seconds will the athlete's speed reach 40 kilometers per hour?

A. 5.36 B. 5.42

C. 5.68 D. 5.77

177. Which of the following functions has a base of 3, a y-intercept of 4, and a range of $y > 1$?

A. $f(x) = 4(3)^{x+1}$

B. $f(x) = (3)^x + 3$

C. $f(x) = 4(3)^x + 1$

D. $f(x) = (3)^{x+1} + 1$

Use the following information to answer the next question.

The graph of the function $f(x) = 0x + 3$ is shown.

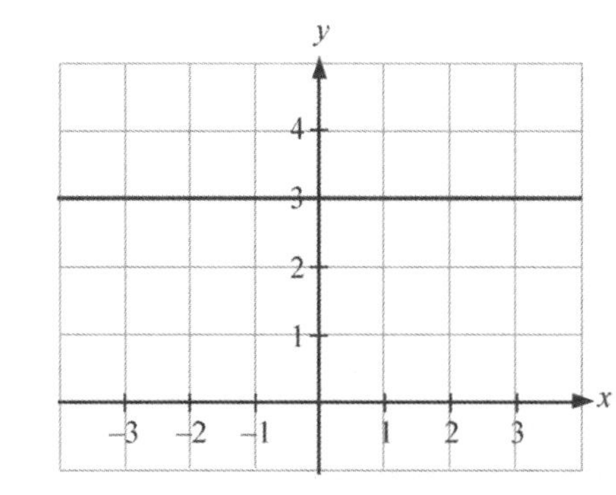

178. The domain (D) and range (R) of this linear function, respectively, are

A. D: $x \in \mathbb{R}$
R: $y \in \mathbb{R}$

B. D: $x = 3$
R: $y \in \mathbb{R}$

C. D: $x \in \mathbb{R}$
R: $y = 3$

D. D: $x \geq -4$
R: $y = 3$

Use the following information to answer the next question.

A set of points is plotted on a graph.

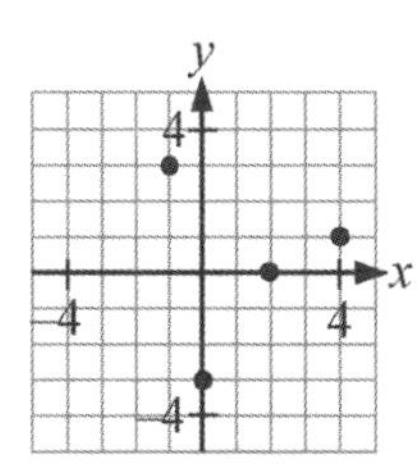

179. State the domain and range for the given graph.

Use the following information to answer the next question.

Sandy likes to take walks. One day, she decided to make a graph of the distance she walked in relation to the time it took. She plotted these three points for reference.

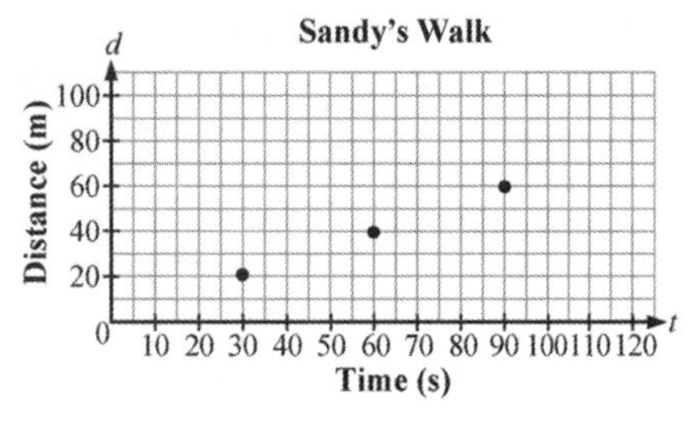

180. What are the domain and range of the relation if she walks for 2 min?

A. D:{$0 \le t \le 90$} and R:{$0 \le d \le 60$}

B. D:{30, 60, 90} and R:{20, 40, 60}

C. D:{$0 \le t \le 120$} and R:{$0 \le d \le 80$}

D. D:{30, 60, 90, 120} and R:{20, 40, 60, 80}

181. What are the domain and range of the relation $-y + 400x = 2x^2$?

A. The domain is $x \le 100$, and the range is $y \le 20{,}000$.

B. The domain is $x \in \mathbb{R}$, and the range is $y \le 20{,}000$.

C. The domain is $x \le 100$, and the range is $y \in \mathbb{R}$.

D. The domain is $x \in \mathbb{R}$, and the range is $y \in \mathbb{R}$.

Use the following information to answer the next question.

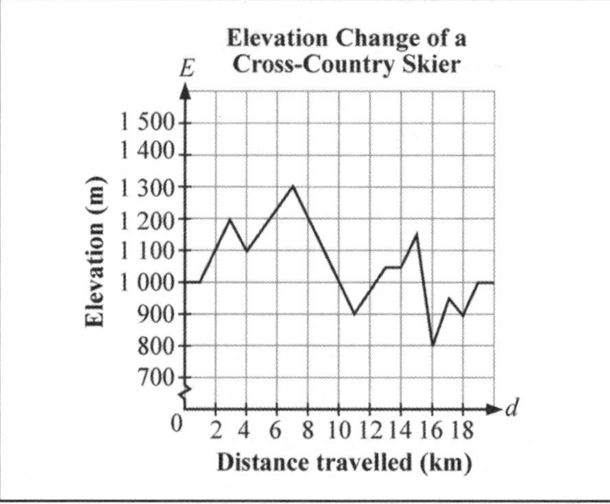

182. Assuming that the elevation is a function of the distance traveled, what is the range of the given function?

A. $E \le 800$ or $E \ge 1{,}000$, $E \in \mathbb{R}$

B. $1{,}000 \le E \le 1{,}300$, $E \in \mathbb{R}$

C. $800 \le E \le 1{,}300$, $E \in \mathbb{R}$

D. $E \ge 800$, $E \in \mathbb{R}$

Use the following information to answer the next question.

The given table shows the rate of change of some entity with respect to time for a particular situation.

Time	1	4	8	10
Rate of change with respect to time	2	16	256	1,024

183. Which of the following situations would **most likely** create the data in the given table?

A. A farmer recording population numbers when breeding rabbits

B. A passenger recording speeds as a vehicle accelerates to highway speeds

C. A pilot recording the air temperature as an airplane descends from 37,000 ft

D. A student recording the temperature on a thermometer when it is placed in a pot of boiling water

Use the following information to answer the next question.

The depth of water at an ocean dock is represented by the function $d(t) = -5.6\cos\left(\frac{\pi}{6}t\right) + 12.8$, where $d(t)$ is the depth in meters and t is the number of hours after midnight.

184. What is the average rate of change of the depth of the water between 2 A.M. and 4 A.M.?

A. 1.4 m/h **B.** 2.8 m/h

C. 4.3 m/h **D.** 5.6 m/h

Use the following information to answer the next question.

The graph of a function is shown.

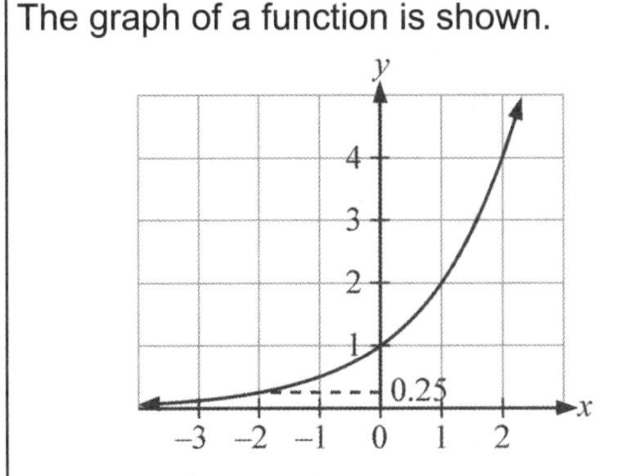

185. What is the average rate of change for the graph of the function for $-2 \le x \le 2$?

A. −1.0667 **B.** −0.9375

C. 0.9375 **D.** 1.0667

Use the following information to answer the next question.

Yolanda and her dad built a model rocket together. Their design included electronics to record the rocket's height during its launch and descent. The electronics inside the rocket recorded the time after launch in seconds and the height from the ground in meters. This data is organized in the following table:

Time (s)	Height (m)
0	0
1	10
2	30
3	75
4	80
5	70
6	55
7	48

186. To the nearest hundredth, what was the rate of change for Yolanda's model rocket from 4 s to 7 s?

A. −10.67 m/s **B.** −3.75 m/s

C. 6.86 m/s **D.** 16.00 m/s

EXERCISE #2—INTERPRETING FUNCTIONS ANSWERS AND SOLUTIONS

175. C	178. C	181. B	184. B
176. B	179. See solution	182. C	185. C
177. D	180. C	183. A	186. A

175. C

A function $f(x)$ is odd if and only if $f(-x) = -f(x)$. Evaluate each of the given functions to determine which is odd.

Step 1

Evaluate the function $f(x) = x^2 - 3x + 2$, when $f(-x)$.

$$f(x) = x^2 - 3x + 2$$
$$f(-x) = (-x)^2 - 3(-x) + 2$$
$$f(-x) = x^2 + 3x + 2$$

Since $f(-x) \neq -f(x)$, $f(x) = x^2 - 3x + 2$ is not an odd function.

Step 2

Evaluate the function $f(x) = -x^4 - x^3 - x^2$, when $f(-x)$.

$$f(x) = -x^4 - x^3 - x^2$$
$$f(-x) = -(-x)^4 - (-x)^3 - (-x)^2$$
$$f(-x) = -x^4 + x^3 - x^2$$

Since $f(-x) \neq -f(x)$, $f(x) = -x^4 - x^3 - x^2$ is not an odd function.

Step 3

Evaluate the function $f(x) = 5x^5 + 2x^3 - 3x$, when $f(-x)$.

$$f(x) = 5x^5 + 2x^3 - 3x$$
$$f(-x) = 5(-x)^5 + 2(-x)^3 - 3(-x)$$
$$f(-x) = -5x^5 - 2x^3 + 3$$

Since $f(-x) = -f(x)$, $f(x) = 5x^5 + 2x^3 - 3x$ is an odd function.

Step 4

Evaluate the function $f(x) = 3x^3 + 4x^2 - 5x - 1$, when $f(-x)$.

$$f(x) = 3x^3 + 4x^2 - 5x - 1$$
$$f(-x) = 3(-x)^3 + 4(-x)^2 - 5(-x) - 1$$
$$f(-x) = -3x^3 + 4x^2 + 5x - 1$$

Since $f(-x) \neq -f(x)$, $f(x) = 3x^3 + 4x^2 - 5x - 1$ is not an odd function.

176. B

Step 1

Plot the data points using a graphing calculator. This can be done by pressing STAT and selecting 1:Edit. Put the values for time in L1 and the values for speed in L2. Press 2nd Y = and select 1:Plot1. Press ENTER to turn on Plot 1. Clear out any equations from Y = and set an appropriate window (in this case X:[0, 8, 1], Y:[0, 50, 5] would be appropriate). Press GRAPH and the points should appear.

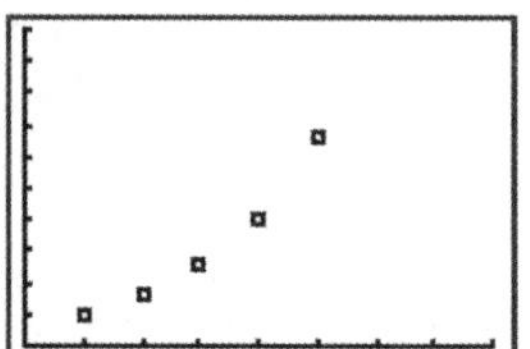

Step 2
Determine the best regression model for the data. Looking at the path of the points, it is clear that the best regression model to begin with is an exponential one. Make sure the Diagnostics are ON so that the value of the correlation coefficient is given before you do the regression. This will indicate the accuracy of the regression model (the closer the value is to 1 or −1, the better the equation fits the data). To do this, press 2nd 0 and then the x^{-1} key. Scroll down to DiagnosticON. Press ENTER twice.
When done correctly, your screen should say Done. Now, perform the exponential regression. Press STAT, scroll right to the CALC menu, and select 0:ExpReg. The screen should show ExpReg. Press the VARS key, scroll right to the Y-VARS menu, select 1:Function, and then 1:Y_1. This will put the exponential regression equation into the Y = feature. Press ENTER and the equation and correlation coefficient should appear.
Note that in this case, $r \approx 1$ which means that the data fits perfectly to an exponential model. Press GRAPH and notice the graph of the equation passes through the center of nearly all 5 points in the data.

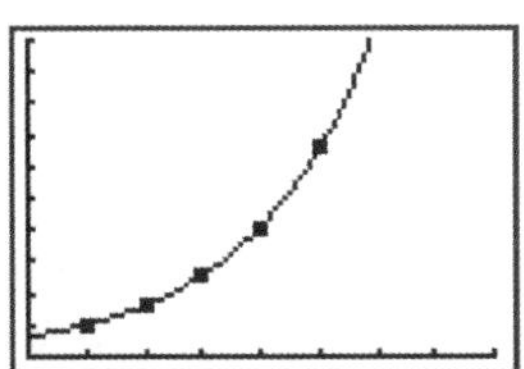

Note: if a quadratic regression is used, then $R^2 = .998$. This represents a very close fit for the data, but the exponential regression is still slightly better.

Step 3
Determine the time when the athlete's speed will reach 40 kilometers per hour.
To determine when the athlete's speed will reach 40 kilometers per hour, it is necessary to graph $Y_2 = 40$ and find the point of intersection between that line and the curve graphed from the exponential regression.
To find the point of intersection, press 2nd TRACE to access the CALC menu, select 5:intersect and move the cursor until it lies on the point of intersection, then press ENTER. Press ENTER two more times and the coordinates of the point are given.
The coordinates of the point are (5.42, 40).

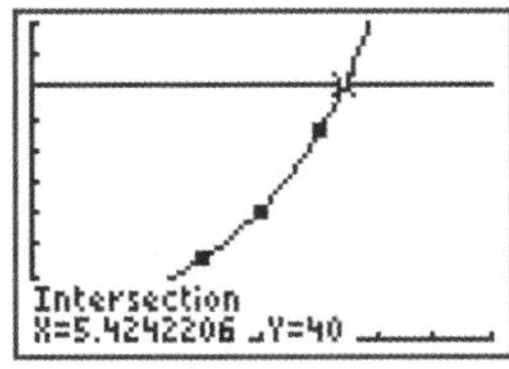

The athlete will reach 40 kilometers per hour, after 5.42 seconds.

177. D

Step 1
Interpret the required range in terms of transformations to the graph of an exponential function of the form $y = b^x$, $b > 1$.
Eliminate any functions that do not have a range of $y > 1$.
Since the desired exponential function has a range of $y > 1$, the function has been vertically translated up 1 unit ($y = b^x$ has a range of $y > 0$).
The function $f(x) = 4(3)^{x+1}$ has not been vertically translated, so its range is $y > 0$, not $y > 1$.
The function $f(x) = (3)^x + 3$ has been vertically translated up 3 units, so the range is $y > 3$, not $y > 1$.
The functions $f(x) = 4(3)^x + 1$ and $f(x) = (3)^{x+1} + 1$ have both been translated up 1 unit, and both functions will have a range of $y > 1$.

Step 2
Determine which of the remaining two functions have a y-intercept of 4.
If the desired function has a y-intercept of 4, $f(0) = 4$.

Using the function $f(x) = 4(3)^x + 1$, determine the value of $f(0)$.

$$\begin{aligned} f(x) &= 4(3)^x + 1 \\ f(0) &= 4(3)^0 + 1 \\ &= 4(1) + 1 \\ &= 4 + 1 \\ &= 5 \end{aligned}$$

Using the function $f(x) = (3)^{x+1} + 1$, determine the value of $f(0)$.

$$\begin{aligned} f(x) &= (3)^{x+1} + 1 \\ f(0) &= (3)^{0+1} + 1 \\ &= (3)^1 + 1 \\ &= 3 + 1 \\ &= 4 \end{aligned}$$

Therefore, $f(x) = (3)^{x+1} + 1$ is the correct function.

178. C

Any linear function, except for $x = a$, has a domain that is $x \in \mathbb{R}$. Thus, the function $f(x) = 0x + 3$ has a domain of $x \in \mathbb{R}$. This is shown in the graph that extends left and right infinitely due to the fact that all real numbers can be substituted for x to give a corresponding y-value. For all values of x, the corresponding y-values are always 3 (e.g., $f(1) = 0(1) + 3 = 3$, $f(-3) = 0(-3) + 3 = 3$). Therefore, the range of this function is $y = 3$.

179.

Step 1
Identify the ordered pairs on the graph.
$\{(-1, 3), (0, -3), (2, 0), (4, 1)\}$

Step 2
Determine the domain of the graph.
Write the x-coordinate of each ordered pair in ascending order.
$-1, 0, 2, 4$
The domain is $\{-1, 0, 2, 4\}$.

Step 3
Identify the range.
Write the y-coordinate of each ordered pair in ascending order.
$-3, 0, 1, 3$
The range is $\{-3, 0, 1, 3\}$.

180. C

Step 1
Connect the points by a line segment.

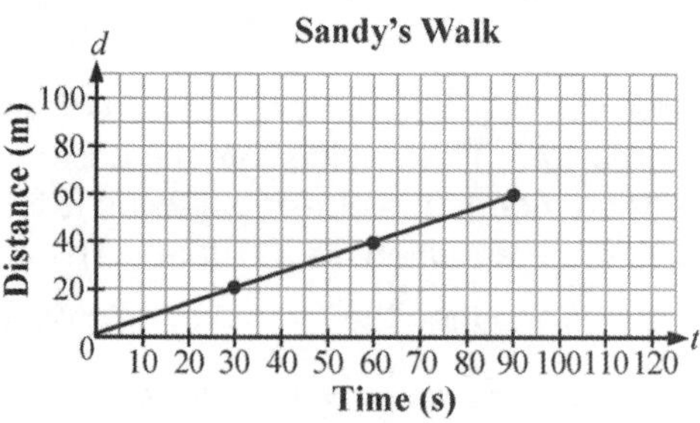

Step 2
Extend the line segment.

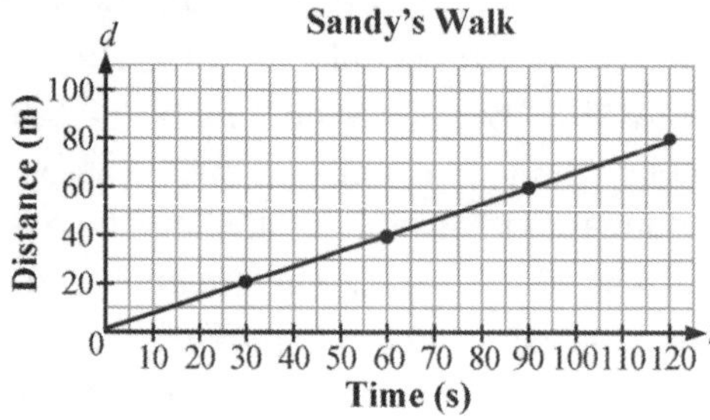

Identify the point on the line segment that corresponds to the x-coordinate of 120 (2 min). This point is (120, 80).

Step 3
Determine the domain and range of the relation.
The domain is 0 to 120 s inclusive. If t represents the time, the domain is $D:\{0 \le t \le 120\}$.
The range is 0 to 80 m inclusive. If d represents the distance, the range is $R:\{0 \le d \le 80\}$.

181. B

Step 1
Isolate y in the given relation.

$$\begin{aligned} -y + 400x &= 2x^2 \\ -y &= 2x^2 - 400x \\ y &= -2x^2 + 400x \end{aligned}$$

Step 2

Graph the function using a graphing calculator.

Press Y =, and enter the function into the editor as shown.

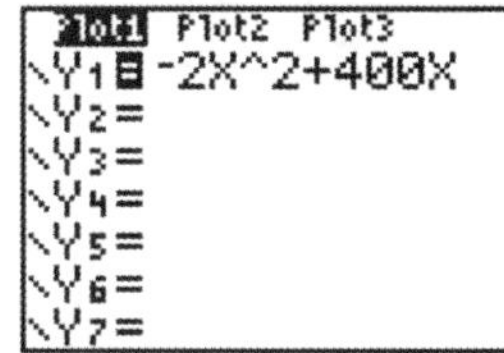

Adjust the window settings so that the vertex of the parabola is visible on the screen. You can use the ZoomFit function by pressing ZOOM and selecting 0:ZoomFit from the list. If needed, press WINDOW to adjust the settings so that the vertex is more clearly visible. Possible window settings are as shown.

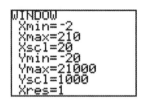

```
WINDOW
 Xmin=-2
 Xmax=210
 Xscl=20
 Ymin=-20
 Ymax=21000
 Yscl=1000
 Xres=1
```

Step 3

Find the domain and range of the function.

Since the graph of this function is a parabola, the domain is $x \in \mathbb{R}$.

Press 2nd Trace to access the CALC menu.

Choose 4:maximum, and move the cursor according to the calculator directives to determine the vertex of the parabola.

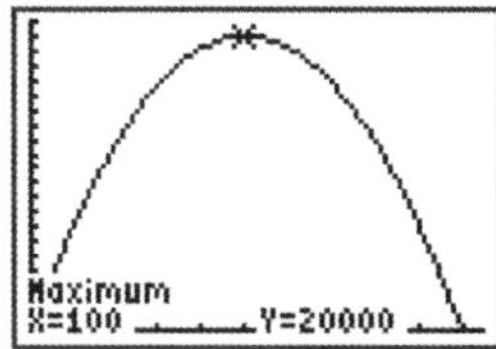

At an x-value of 100, the maximum y-value is 20,000. Therefore, the range of the relation is $y \le 20{,}000$.

182. C

The range of the given function is the set of permissible values for the dependent variable, the elevation, E. From the graph, it can be observed that the maximum value of E is approximately 1,300 m and the minimum value of E is approximately 800 m. Also, since there are no breaks or holes in the line graph, all values between 800 m and 1,300 m are possible values for E. Thus, the range of the given function could be written as $800 \le E \le 1{,}300,\ E \in \mathbb{R}$.

183. A

The population of rabbits breeding over time is the only given situation that increases exponentially. This would mean that the rate of change increases rapidly, as illustrated in the given table.

184. B

Step 1

Determine the depth of the water at 2 A.M. and at 4 A.M.

Determine $d(t)$ at 2 A.M.

$$\begin{aligned} d(2) &= -5.6\cos\left(\frac{\pi}{6}(2)\right) + 12.8 \\ &= -5.6\cos\left(\frac{\pi}{3}\right) + 12.8 \\ &= -5.6\left(\frac{1}{2}\right) + 12.8 \\ &= -2.8 + 12.8 \\ &= 10.0 \text{ m} \end{aligned}$$

Determine $d(t)$ at 4 A.M.

$$\begin{aligned} d(4) &= -5.6\cos\left(\frac{\pi}{6}(4)\right) + 12.8 \\ &= -5.6\cos\left(\frac{2\pi}{3}\right) + 12.8 \\ &= -5.6\left(-\frac{1}{2}\right) + 12.8 \\ &= 2.8 + 12.8 \\ &= 15.6 \text{ m} \end{aligned}$$

At 2 A.M., the depth of the water is 10.0 m, and at 4 A.M., the depth of the water is 15.6 m.

Step 2

Determine the average rate of change in depth between 2 A.M. and 4 A.M. by using the ratio $\frac{d_2 - d_1}{t_2 - t_1}$.

$$\begin{aligned} \frac{d_2 - d_1}{t_2 - t_1} &= \frac{d(4) - d(2)}{4 - 2} \\ &= \frac{15.6 - 10.0}{2} \\ &= 2.8 \text{ m/h} \end{aligned}$$

The average rate of change of the depth of the water between 2 A.M. and 4 A.M. is 2.8 m/h.

185. C

Step 1

Determine which points on the graph to use.

Determine the x-values from the interval given in the question. The x-values will be the ends of the interval.

$x_1 = -2$

$x_2 = 2$

Look at the graph to determine the corresponding y-values using $x_1 = -2$ and $x_2 = 2$.

The corresponding y-values are $y_1 = 0.25$ and $y_2 = 4$.

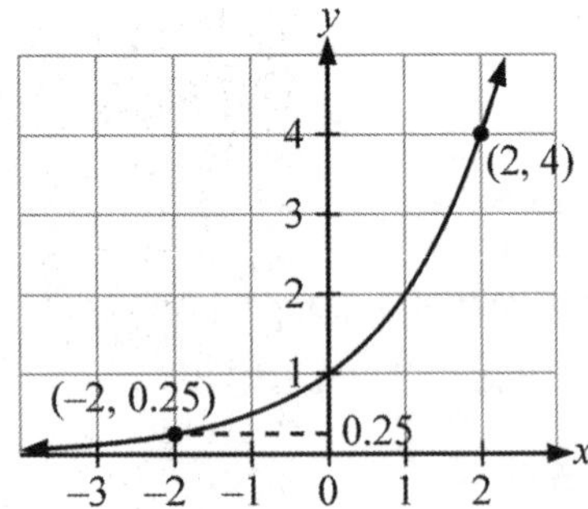

Therefore, the points are (−2, 0.25) and (2, 4).

Step 2

Calculate the slope between the two points.

Substitute the coordinate values into the slope formula, and evaluate.

$m = \dfrac{y_2 - y_1}{x_2 - x_1}$

$m = \dfrac{4 - 0.25}{2 - (-2)}$

$m = \dfrac{3.75}{4}$

$m = 0.9375$

The average rate of change of the function for $-2 \leq x \leq 2$ is 0.9375.

186. A

Step 1

Determine which values to use.

The question asks for the rate of change between 4 s and 7 s, so the time values will be $t_1 = 4$ and $t_2 = 7$.

The height values will be those that correspond to t_1 and t_2 in the table. Therefore, $h_1 = 80$ and $h_2 = 48$.

Step 2

Calculate the average rate of change.

Substitute the values for time and height into the slope formula, and evaluate. Since time is the independent variable, it will replace the x-values. Height will replace the y-values.

$m = \dfrac{y_2 - y_1}{x_2 - x_1}$

$m = \dfrac{h_2 - h_1}{t_2 - t_1}$

$m = \dfrac{48 - 80}{7 - 4}$

$m = \dfrac{-32}{3}$

$m \approx -10.666667$

The average rate of change for Yolanda's rocket between 4 s and 7 s was approximately −10.67 m/s.

Analyzing Functions

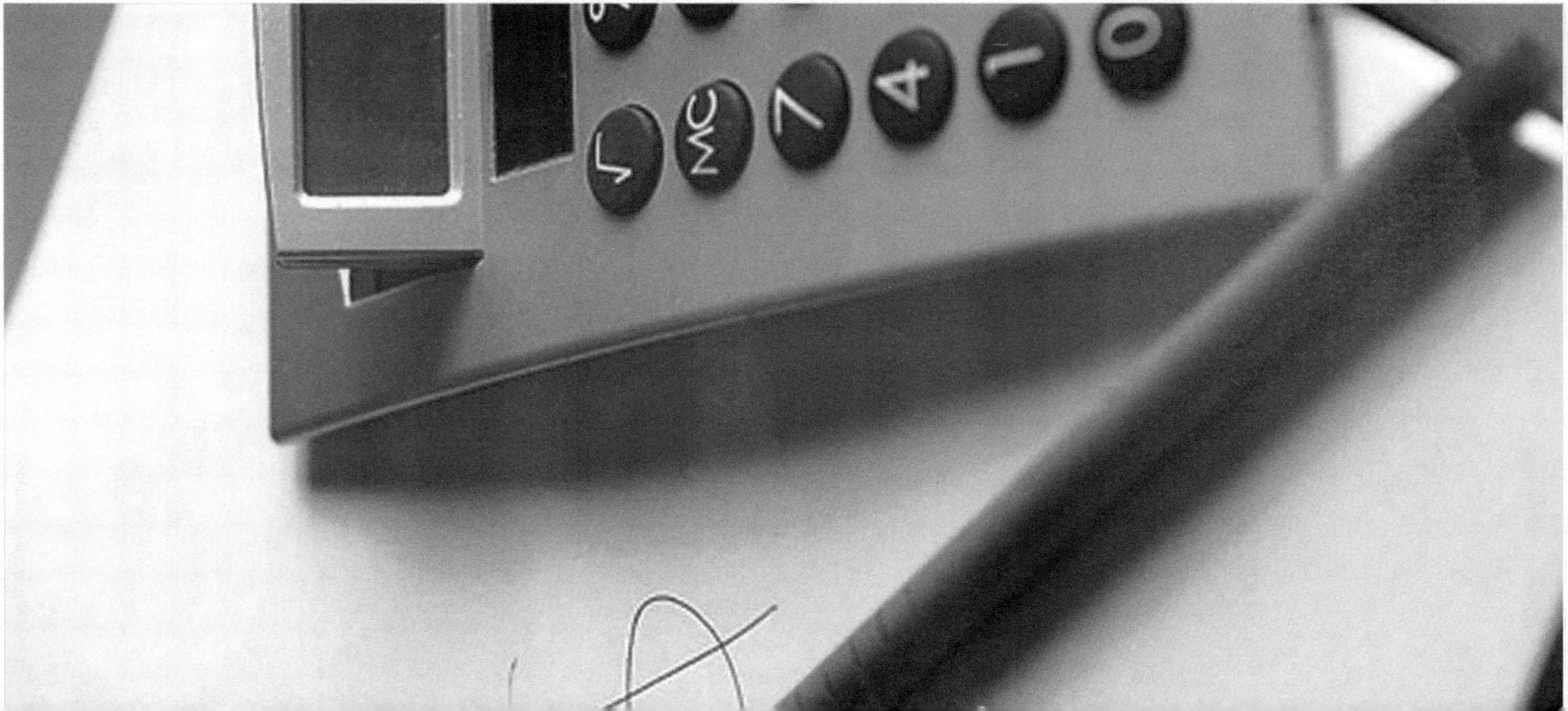

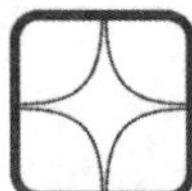

ANALYZING FUNCTIONS

Table of Correlations

Standard		Concepts	Exercise #1	Exercise #2
Unit2.9	Analyze functions using different representations.			
F-IF.7a	*Graph functions expressed symbolically and show key features of the graph, by hand in simple cases and using technology for more complicated cases. Graph linear and quadratic functions and show intercepts, maxima, and minima.*	Graphing a Linear Function Using a Graphing Calculator	101	106
		Graphing Various Forms of the Quadratic Function Using Technology	187	195
		Sketching the Graph of $y = a(x - r)(x - s)$ Using the Key Features	188	196
		Graphing a Linear Relation Given in Slope-Intercept Form	189	197
		Graphing a Linear Relation Given in General Form With and Without Technology	190	198
		Graphing a Linear Relation Given in Slope-Point Form	191	199
		Graphing Quadratic Functions by Hand by Completing the Square	192	200
		Determining Key Points on the Graph of a Quadratic Function	193	201
		Sketching the Quadratic Function of the Form $y = a(x - h)^2 + k$	194	202
F-IF.7e	*Graph functions expressed symbolically and show key features of the graph, by hand in simple cases and using technology for more complicated cases. Graph exponential and logarithmic functions, showing intercepts and end behavior, and trigonometric functions, showing period, midline, and amplitude.*	Graphing Exponential Relations and Defining Them as Functions	100	105
		Properties of Exponential Functions	165	177

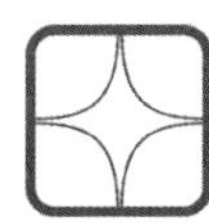

F-IF.7a Graph functions expressed symbolically and show key features of the graph, by hand in simple cases and using technology for more complicated cases. Graph linear and quadratic functions and show intercepts, maxima, and minima.

Graphing Various Forms of the Quadratic Function Using Technology

Using technology, such as a TI-83 Plus calculator, to graph a quadratic function requires the use of proper window settings and the appropriate selection of calculator buttons.

To graph a quadratic function on a graphing calculator, follow these steps:

1. Make sure the function is written in terms of the *y*-variable or unsquared variable.
2. Press the [Y =] button on your graphing calculator, and type in the function.
3. Set an appropriate WINDOW setting for the graph so that the resulting parabolic graph will be adequately portrayed on the screen. For most quadratic functions, a good starting WINDOW setting can be created by pressing the [ZOOM] button and selecting either the 6:ZStandard or 0:Zoom Fit feature.
4. Press the [GRAPH] button if necessary to view the parabolic graph representing the quadratic function.

Example

Graph $y = 2(x - 3)^2 - 5$ on a graphing calculator.

Solution

Step 1

Press the [Y =] button.

Type in the function by pressing the following sequence of buttons:

[2] [(] [x, T, θ, n] [–] [3] [)] [x^2] [–] [5]

Step 2

Set an appropriate WINDOW setting.

Press the [ZOOM] button, and select the 6:ZStandard feature. This graph should appear on the calculator screen.

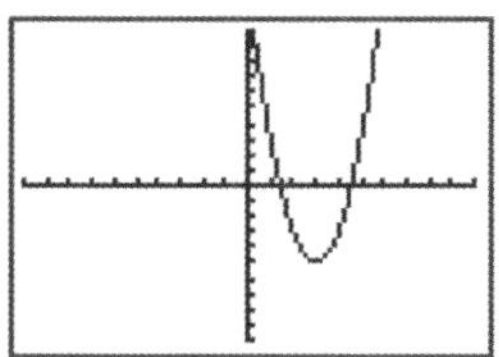

An adequate graph of the parabola representing the function is visible.

Example

Graph $P = -25s^2 + 1{,}010s - 3{,}253$ using technology.

Solution

Step 1

Press the [Y =] button.

When a function like $P = -25s^2 + 1{,}010s - 3{,}253$ is not defined in terms of *x*- and *y*-variables, it can still be entered into a graphing calculator as though it was, namely as $y = -25x^2 + 1{,}010x - 3{,}253$.

Type in the function by pressing the following sequence of buttons:

[(–)] [2] [5] [x, T, θ, n] [x^2] [+] [1] [0] [1] [0] [x, T, θ, n] [–] [3] [2] [5] [3]

Step 2

Set an appropriate WINDOW setting.

Press the [ZOOM] button, and select the 0:Zoom Fit feature. This graph should appear on the calculator screen.

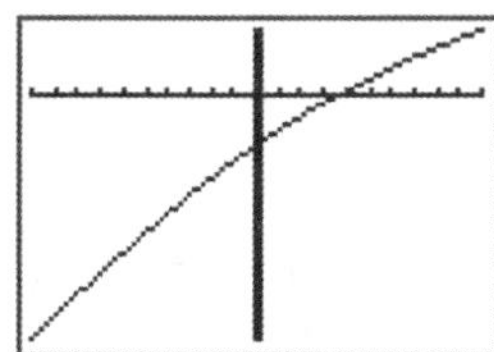

Since there is an inadequate amount of the parabola visible, the WINDOW setting needs to be adjusted manually.

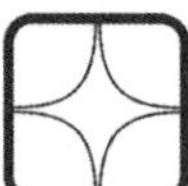

Step 3

Press the WINDOW button.

To see more of the graph, the top and right side of the graph needs to be made more visible. To do so, increase the Xmax value by pressing the down arrow key so that it highlights the Xmax value.

Enter a greater value than 10, such as 50. Then, press ZOOM again, and highlight the 0:Zoom Fit feature again. A more adequate parabola will appear on the screen.

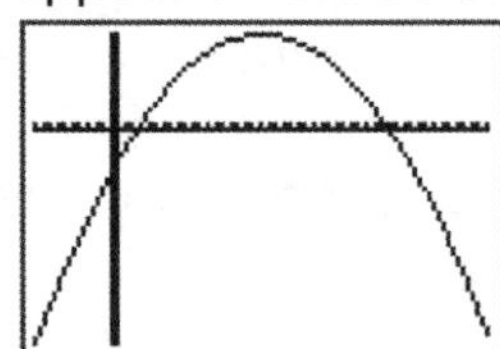

The WINDOW setting can be continually adjusted as necessary by pressing the WINDOW button and entering values for Xmin, Xmax, Xscl, Ymin, Ymac, or Yscl.

Example

Graph $y = -0.5(x-6)(x+5)$ using a graphing calculator.

Solution

Step 1

Press the Y = button.

Type in the function by pressing the following sequence of buttons:

(–) 0 . 5 (x, T, θ, n – 6) (

x, T, θ, n + 5)

Step 2

Set an appropriate WINDOW setting.

Press the ZOOM button, and select the 6:ZStandard feature. This graph should appear on the calculator screen.

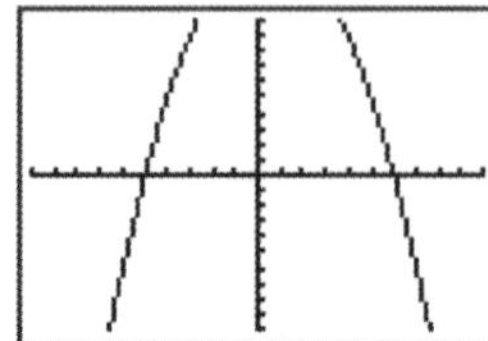

Since the top part of the parabola is not visible, the WINDOW setting needs to be adjusted manually.

Step 3

Press the WINDOW button.

To see more of the upper part of the graph, the Ymax value needs to be increased. Press the down arrow key so that it highlights the Ymax value. Enter a greater value than 10, such as 20. Then, press the GRAPH button. A more adequate graph of the parabola should appear on the screen.

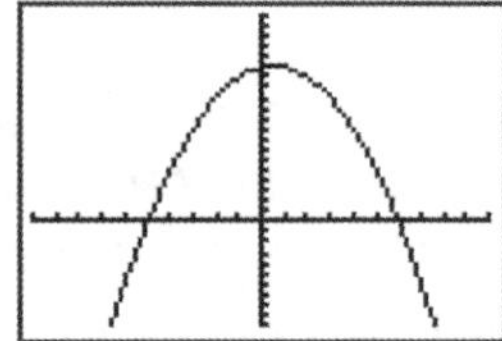

SKETCHING THE GRAPH OF $y = a(x-r)(x-s)$ USING THE KEY FEATURES

When the graph of a quadratic function has two distinct x-intercepts r and s, the axis of symmetry lies *halfway* between these x-intercepts. Therefore, the equation of the axis of symmetry, which is defined by the vertex (h, k), is $x = h = \frac{r+s}{2}$, and the vertex, with respect to the x-intercept, is $\left(\frac{r+s}{2}, k\right)$.

Using this understanding, you can sketch the graph of a quadratic function in factored form $f(x) = a(x-r)(x-s)$, where r and s are distinct x-intercepts.

Example

Sketch the graph of $f(x) = -2(x-3)(x+1)$ by using the x-intercepts and vertex defined by this function.

Solution

The x-intercepts are zeros of the factors of the function.

$x - 3 = 0$
$x = 3$
and
$x + 1 = 0$
$x = -1$

Therefore, the x-intercepts are 3 and –1.

Find the equation of the axis of symmetry, which is located halfway between the x-intercepts.

$x = h = \dfrac{3+(-1)}{2}$
$x = 1$

Find the vertex $(h,\ k)$ by substituting the value of h, corresponding to the equation of the axis of symmetry $x = 1$, into the function to determine the y-coordinate k.

$f(x) = -2(x-3)(x+1)$
$k = -2(1-3)(1+1)$
$k = -2(-2)(2)$
$k = 8$

The vertex is (1, 8).

Sketch the graph of the function using the x-intercepts (3, 0) and (–1, 0) and the vertex (1, 8).

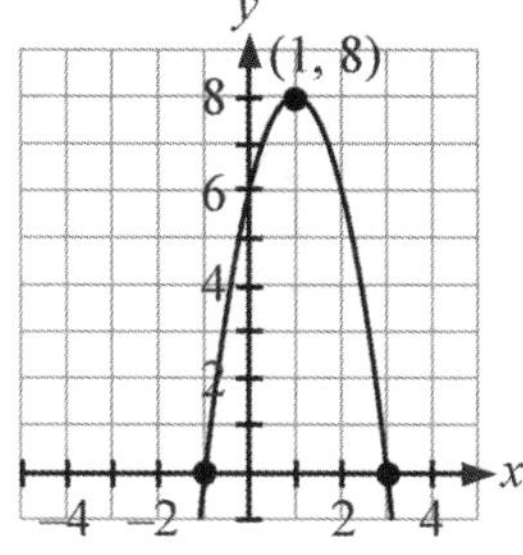

Graphing a Linear Relation Given in Slope-Intercept Form

The slope-intercept form of the equation of a line is $y = mx + b$.

Use the following steps to graph the linear relation of an equation given in slope-intercept form:

1. Determine the slope, m, and the y-intercept, b, from the slope-intercept form of the equation of a line, $y = mx + b$.
2. Plot the y-intercept.
3. Use the slope to locate a second point.
4. Draw arrows on each end of the line to show that it continues infinitely in both directions.

Example

Graph the line defined by the equation $y = \dfrac{2}{3}x - 4$.

Solution

Step 1

Determine the slope and the y-intercept of the line.

Using the information in the given equation, the slope of the line is $m = \dfrac{2}{3}$, and the y-intercept is $b = -4$.

Step 2

Plot the y-intercept, $b = -4$.

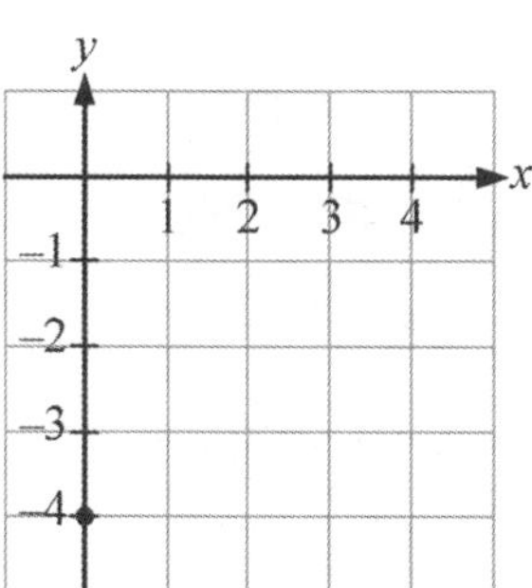

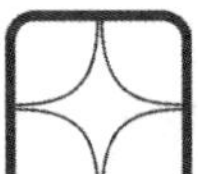

Step 3
Use the slope to locate a second point on the line.

The slope of the line is $m = \frac{2}{3}$. Therefore, from the y-intercept, a rise of 2 and a run of 3 in the positive direction will locate another point on the line at (3, −2).

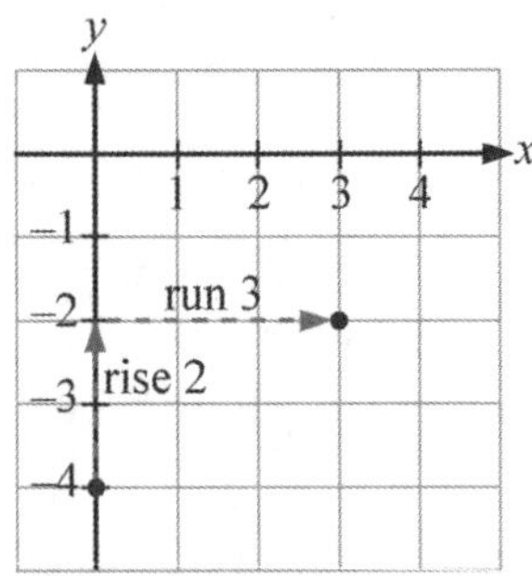

Step 4
Draw a line that passes through both points. Add arrows to each end of the line to show that it continues infinitely in both directions.

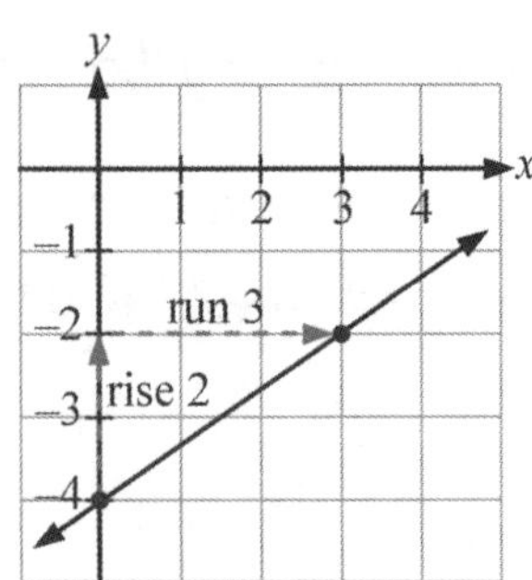

Graphing a Linear Relation Given in General Form With and Without Technology

To graph a linear relation from general form without the use of technology, follow these general steps:

- Determine the x-intercept.
- Determine the y-intercept.
- Plot the two intercepts on a graph.
- Connect the points with a straight edge, extending the lines and placing arrowheads on each end.

Example

Sketch the graph of the function defined by the equation $2x - 3y - 12 = 0$.

Solution

Step 1
Determine the x-intercept.
Since the x-intercept is of the form $(x, 0)$, substitute 0 for y into the equation.
The equation can then be solved to find the value of x.

$$\begin{aligned} 2x - 3y - 12 &= 0 \\ 2x - 3(0) - 12 &= 0 \\ 2x &= 12 \\ x &= 6 \end{aligned}$$

The x-intercept is at 6, or (6, 0).

Step 2
Determine the y-intercept.
Since the y-intercept is of the form $(0, y)$, substitute 0 for x into the equation.
The equation can then be solved to find the value of y.

$$\begin{aligned} 2x - 3y - 12 &= 0 \\ 2(0) - 3y - 12 &= 0 \\ -3y &= 12 \\ y &= -4 \end{aligned}$$

The y-intercept is at −4, or (0, −4).

Step 3
Sketch the graph.
Plot the x- and y-intercepts, and join the points with a line.

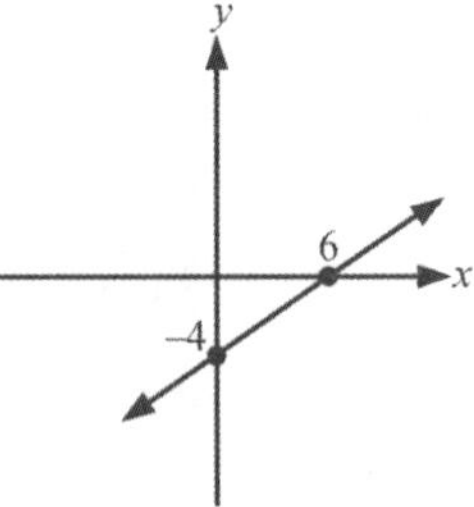

Another method is to first rearrange the equation into slope-intercept form. This method can be used when graphing by hand and when graphing using technology.

Example

Graph the line described by the equation $3x + 2y - 8 = 0$.

Solution

Step 1

Rearrange the equation into the form $y = mx + b$.

$$3x + 2y - 8 = 0$$
$$2y = -3x + 8$$
$$y = -\frac{3}{2}x + 4$$

The slope is $m = -\frac{3}{2}$ and can be treated as $\frac{-3}{2}$ or $\frac{3}{-2}$.

The y-intercept is $b = 4$.

Step 2

Graph the equation by plotting the y-intercept at $(0, 4)$ and then finding a second point on the line by rising -3 (or falling 3) and running 2. Join the points with a line.

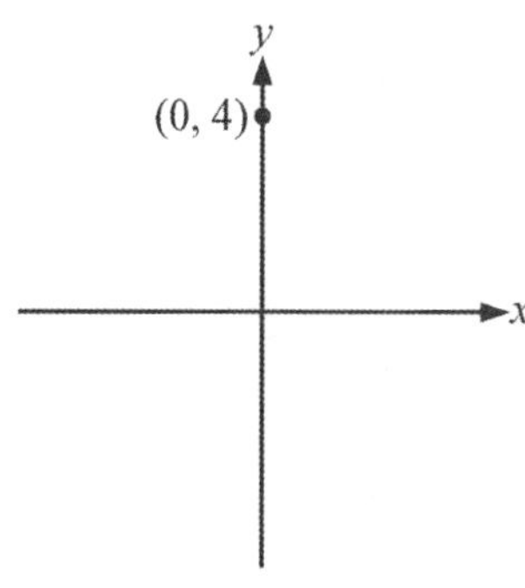

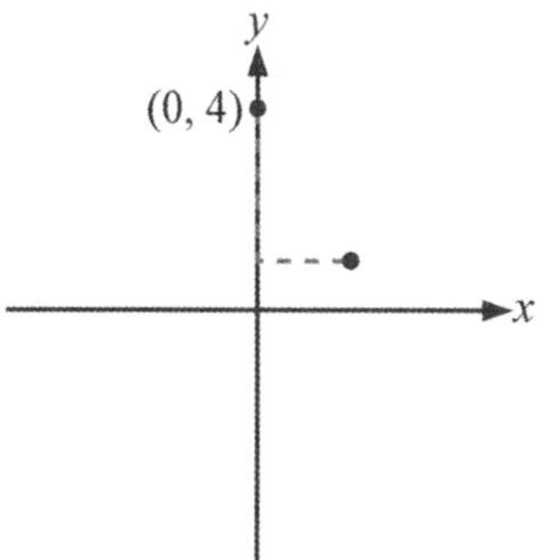

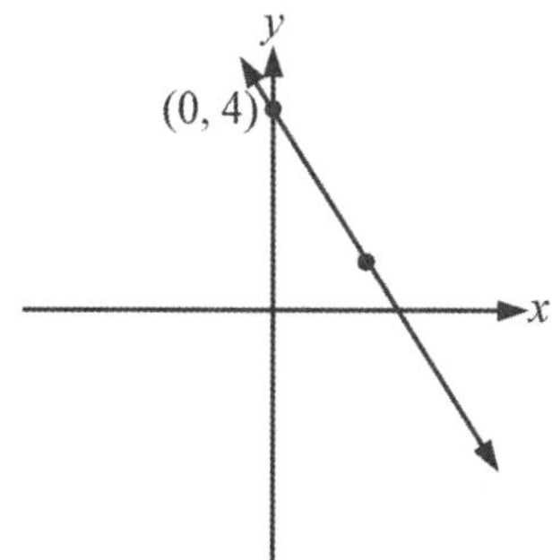

Example

Sketch the graph of the linear relation $x + y - 3 = 0$ using technology.

Solution

Step 1

Rearrange the equation to isolate the y-variable.

$$x + y - 3 = 0$$
$$x - x + y - 3 + 3 = 3 - x$$
$$y = 3 - x$$

The equation $y = 3 - x$ can now be entered into the calculator.

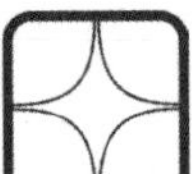

Step 2

Enter the equation into Y = .

```
Plot1 Plot2 Plot3
\Y1=3-X
\Y2=
\Y3=
\Y4=
\Y5=
\Y6=
\Y7=
```

Use standard window settings.

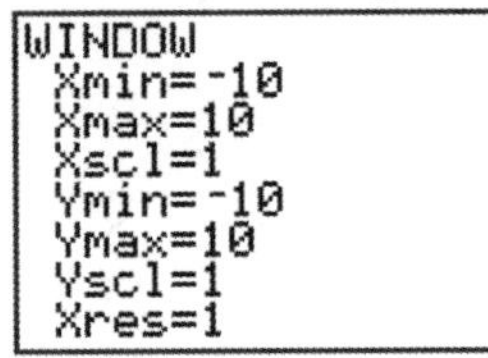

Step 3

Press GRAPH .

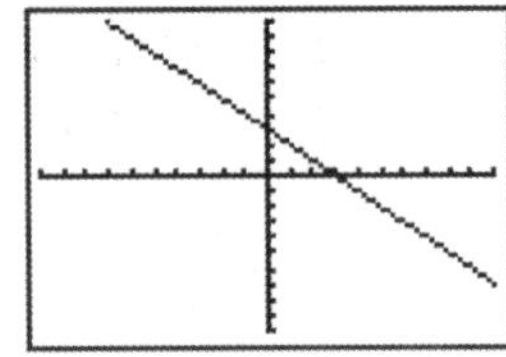

Graphing a Linear Relation Given in Slope-Point Form

A linear relation can be graphed using slope-point form. Equations written in the form $y - y_1 = m(x - x_1)$ have a slope of m and a point on the line at (x_1, y_1).

Use the following steps to graph a linear relation given in slope-point form:

1. Plot the given point.
2. Use the slope to locate the second point.
3. Draw a line passing through both points. Draw arrows on each end of the line to show that it continues infinitely in both directions.

Example

Sketch the graph of the equation $y + 2 = \frac{2}{3}(x - 3)$.

Solution

By comparing the equation $y + 2 = \frac{2}{3}(x - 3)$ to the form $y - y_1 = m(x - x_1)$, it can be determined that the coordinates of the point (x_1, y_1) are (3, −2).

Step 1

Plot the point (3, −2) on a Cartesian plane.

Step 2

Use the slope to find another point on the line. Since the slope is $m = \frac{2}{3}$, a rise of 2 and a run of 3 from the point will locate points at (6, 0) and (0, −4). Plot another point at either of these coordinates.

Step 3

Draw a line that passes through these two points. Draw arrows on each end of the line to show that it continues infinitely in both directions.

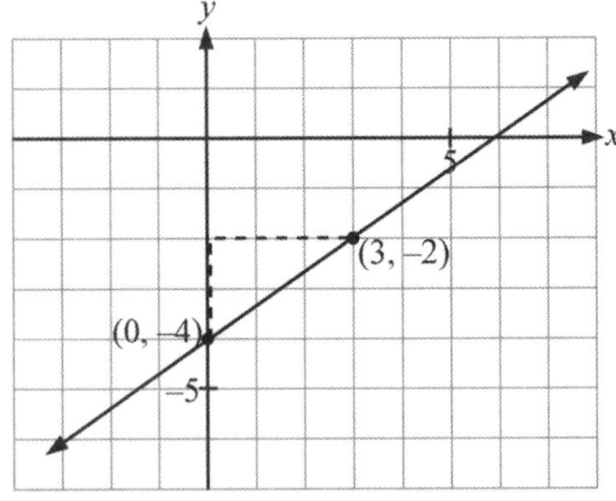

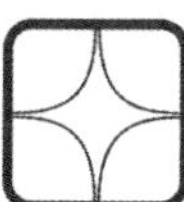

Graphing Quadratic Functions by Hand by Completing the Square

When you are graphing a quadratic function, you can gain useful information that will help you sketch the graph by completing the square and writing the function in the form $f(x) = a(x-h)^2 + k$, where $a \neq 0$.

From the completed square form, you can determine the coordinates of the vertex and the x- and y-intercepts.

Example

Graph the function $y = -x^2 - 6x - 8$ by completing the square.

Solution

Step 1

Complete the square.

$$y = -x^2 - 6x - 8$$
$$y = -(x^2 + 6x) - 8$$
$$y = -(x^2 + 6x + 9 - 9) - 8$$
$$y = -(x^2 + 6x + 9) + 9 - 8$$
$$y = -(x+3)^2 + 1$$

Step 2

Identify the vertex.

For a function of the form $f(x) = a(x-h)^2 + k$, the coordinates of the vertex are (h, k). For the function $y = -(x+3)^2 + 1$, the vertex has coordinates $(-3, 1)$.

Step 3

Find the y-intercept by setting x equal to zero.

$$y = -(0+3)^2 + 1$$
$$y = -9 + 1$$
$$y = -8$$

Step 4

Find the x-intercepts by setting y equal to zero.

$$0 = -(x+3)^2 + 1$$
$$(x+3)^2 = 1$$
$$x + 3 = \pm\sqrt{1}$$
$$x = \pm 1 - 3$$
$$x = -2 \text{ and } -4$$

Step 5

Use the vertex, y-intercept, and x-intercepts to sketch the graph of $y = -x^2 - 6x - 8$.

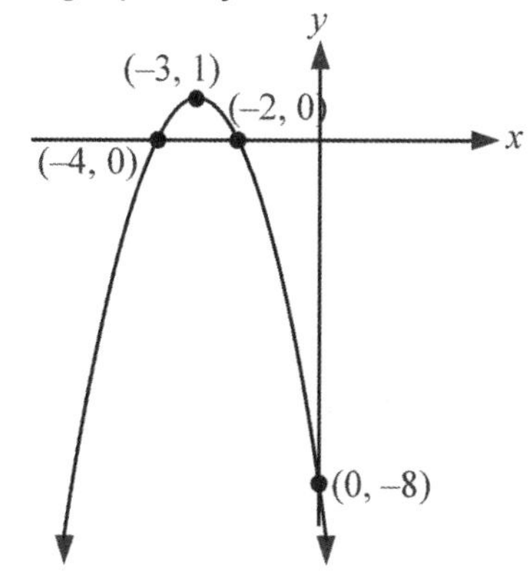

Determining Key Points on the Graph of a Quadratic Function

The key points of a quadratic function can be determined by examining its graph. These points include the x-intercepts, the y-intercept, and the vertex.

The x-intercepts are the points at which the graph crosses the x-axis, where the value of the y-coordinate is 0. These locations are also referred to as the zeros of the function. The zeros of a function of the form $y = ax^2 + bx + c$ are also the solutions, or roots, of the related equation $0 = ax^2 + bx + c$.

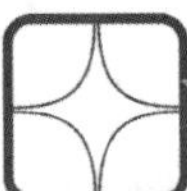

The y-intercept is the point at which the graph crosses the y-axis, where the value of the x-coordinate is 0.

The vertex is the maximum or minimum of the graph of a quadratic function.

Example

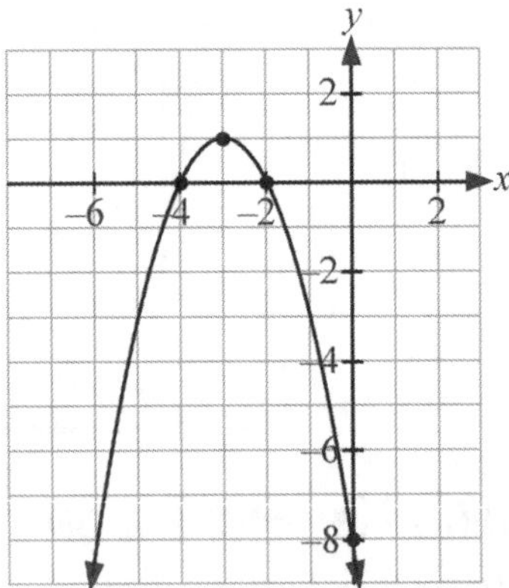

The graph of a function

Determine the coordinates of the x-intercepts, y-intercept, and the vertex of the graph.

Solution

Step 1

Determine the x-intercepts.

The x-intercepts are the points at which the graph crosses the x-axis, where the value of y is 0. This occurs at two locations, (–4, 0) and (–2, 0).

Step 2

Determine the y-intercept.

The y-intercept is the point at which the graph crosses the y-axis, where the value of x is 0. This only happens at one location, (0, –8).

Step 3

Determine the coordinates of the vertex.

The vertex is found at the maximum or minimum of the graph of a quadratic function. There is a maximum for the given graph, and its coordinates are (–3, 1).

You can also find these key points with a graphing calculator. Use the TRACE function to find the coordinates of the y-intercept by entering zero for the value of x. The CALC menu gives the option of finding the zeros and the minimum and maximum values of a graph. This menu can be reached by pressing 2nd TRACE.

Example

Determine the coordinates of the vertex of the function $y = x^2 + 3x - 5$ using a graphing calculator.

Solution

Step 1

Graph the equation $y = x^2 + 3x - 5$ using a graphing calculator.

Enter the equation in the TI-83+ graphing calculator's Y = window.

Select a ZOOM 6:ZStandard window setting, and then press GRAPH.

Step 2

Determine the coordinates of the vertex.

It can been seen from the graph that the vertex is a minimum. Access the CALC menu by pressing 2nd TRACE, and choose 3:Minimum to determine coordinates of the minimum of the graph.

Move the cursor to the left of the vertex when asked for a left bound, and press ENTER.

Move the cursor to the right of the vertex when asked for a right bound, and press ENTER.

Press ENTER a third time, and the result is as given.

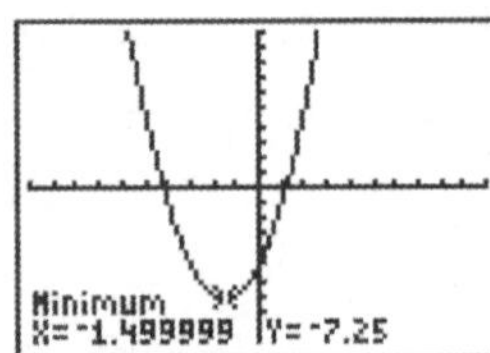

The coordinates of the vertex of the graph of the function $y = x^2 + 3x - 5$ are (–1.5, –7.25).

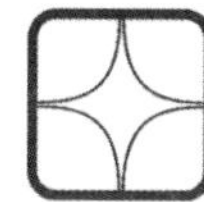

Sketching the Quadratic Function of the Form $y = a(x - h)^2 + k$

The graph of a quadratic function of the form $y = a(x - h)^2 + k$, $a \neq 0$ can be sketched from a given equation once the key features are identified.

The following key features can be used to sketch the graph of a quadratic function of the form $y = a(x - h)^2 + k$:

- The vertex is (h, k).
- The y-intercept occurs when $x = 0$.
- The x-intercepts occur when $y = 0$.
- The axis of symmetry occurs when $x = h$.
- When $a > 0$, the parabola opens upward.
- When $a < 0$, the parabola opens downward.

The x-intercepts will not be necessary if the graph does not cross the x-axis.

Example

Using key features of the equation, sketch the graph of the function $y = \frac{1}{4}(x - 4)^2 + 3$.

Solution

Step 1
Determine the vertex.
Since an equation of the form $y = a(x - h)^2 + k$ has a vertex of (h, k), the equation $y = \frac{1}{4}(x - 4)^2 + 3$ has a vertex of $(4, 3)$.

Step 2
Determine the direction the parabola opens.
In an equation of the form $y = a(x - h)^2 + k$, the parabola opens upward when $a > 0$. Since $\frac{1}{4} > 0$, the parabola will open upward.

Since the parabola opens upward and the vertex is above the x-axis, there are no x-intercepts.

Step 3
Determine the y-intercept.
The y-intercept occurs when $x = 0$.

$y = \frac{1}{4}(x - 4)^2 + 3$

$y = \frac{1}{4}(0 - 4)^2 + 3$

$y = \frac{1}{4}(16) + 3$

$y = 4 + 3$

$y = 7$

The coordinates of the y-intercept are $(0, 7)$.

Step 4
Sketch the graph.

The graph of the function $y = \frac{1}{4}(x - 4)^2 + 3$ is shown.

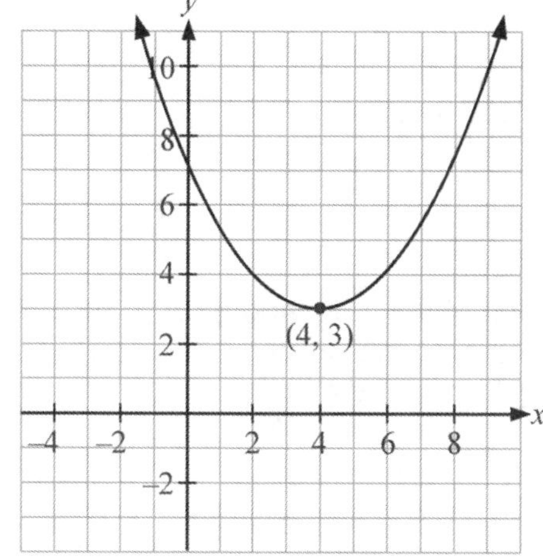

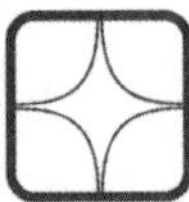

EXERCISE #1—ANALYZING FUNCTIONS

187. Which of the following graphs could be a sketch of the quadratic function $y = -24x^2 + 1{,}000x - 3{,}250$?

A.

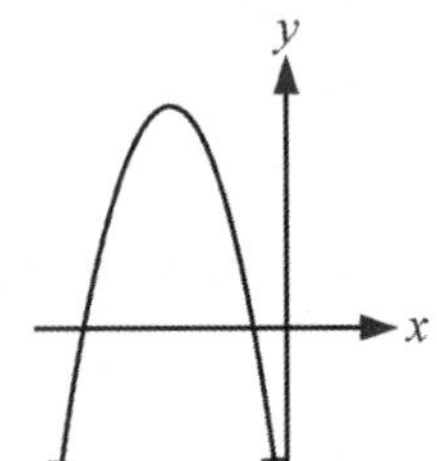

B.

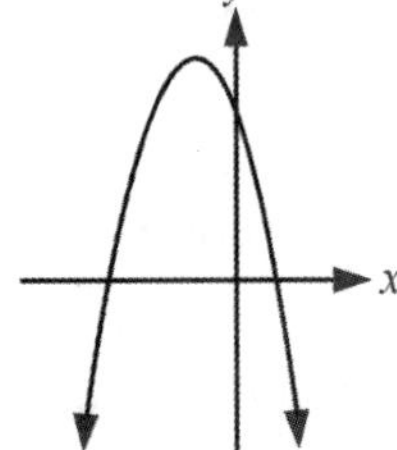

C.

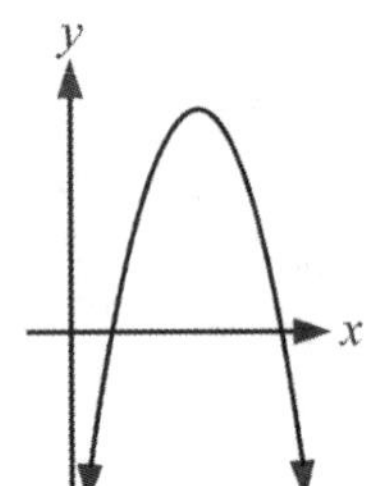

D.

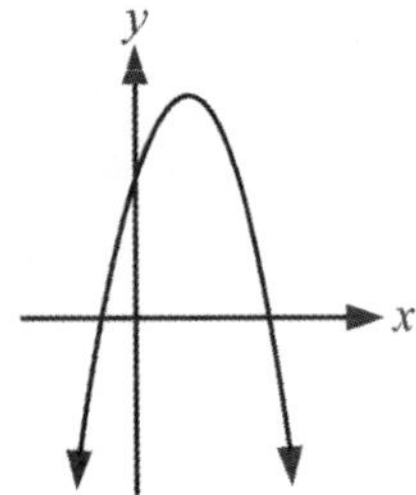

188. Which of the following graphs correctly represents the graph of the quadratic function $f(x) = (x+1)(x-5)$?

A.

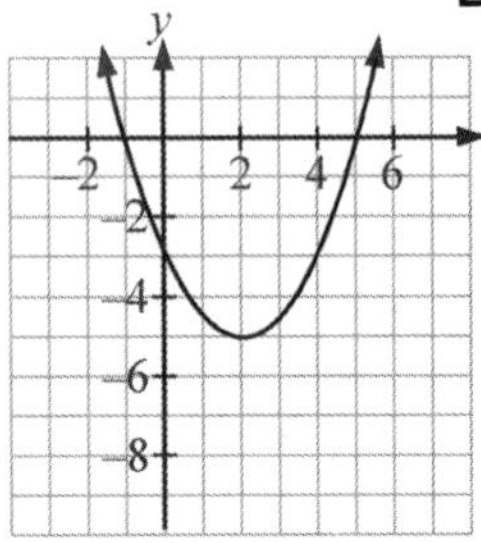

B.

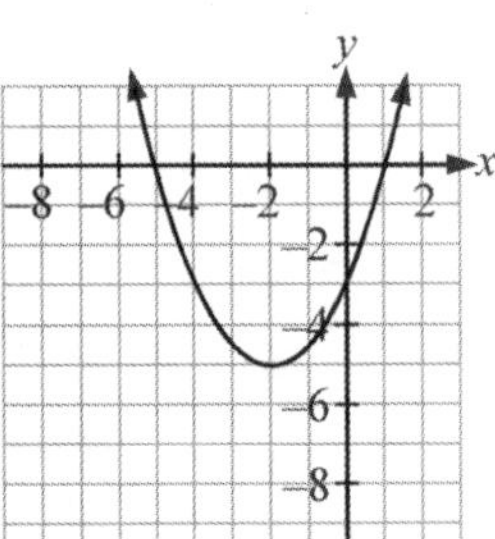

C.

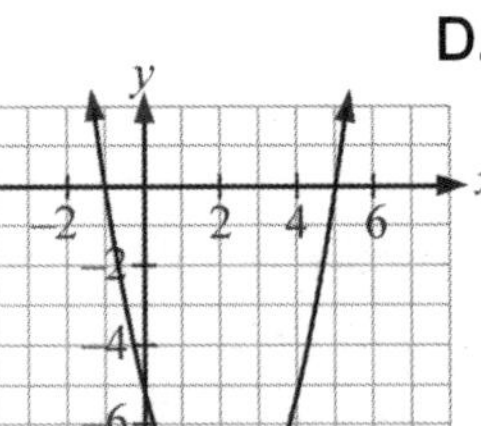

D.

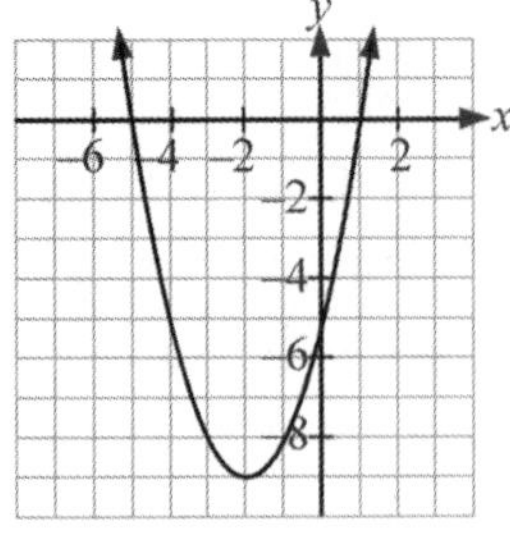

189. Which of the following graphs could represent the line defined by the equation $y = \frac{2}{3}x - 3$?

A.

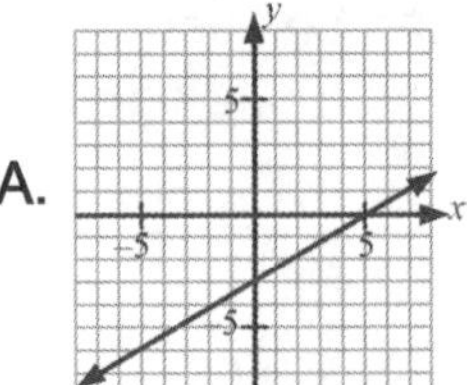

B.

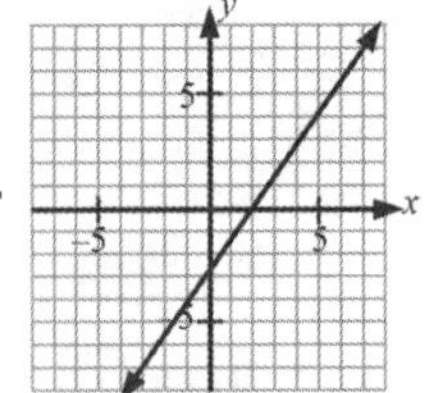

C.

D.

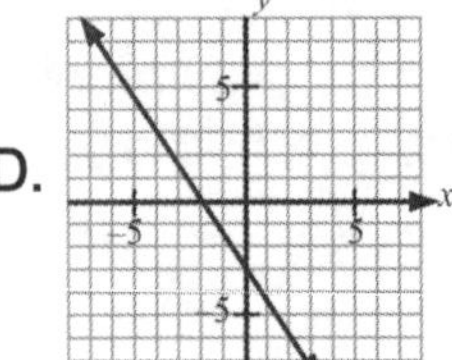

190. Which of the following graphs represents the line defined by the equation $-2x + 3y + 9 = 0$?

A.

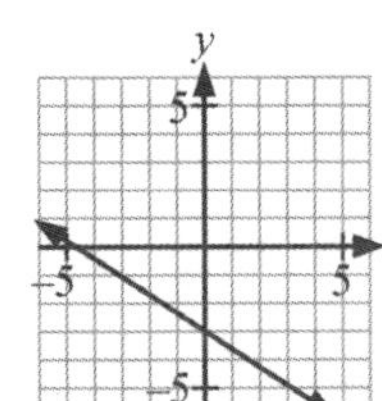

B.

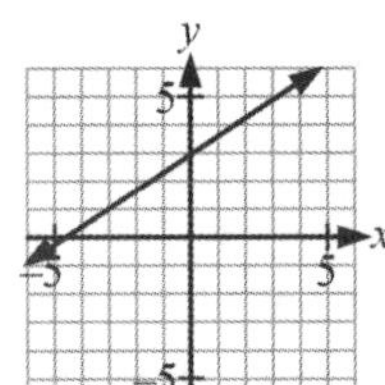

C.

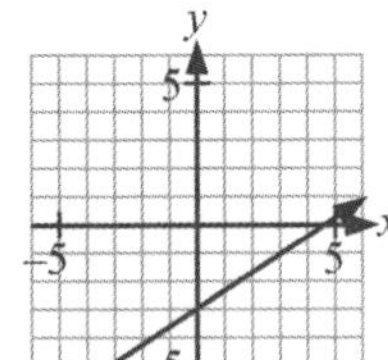

D.

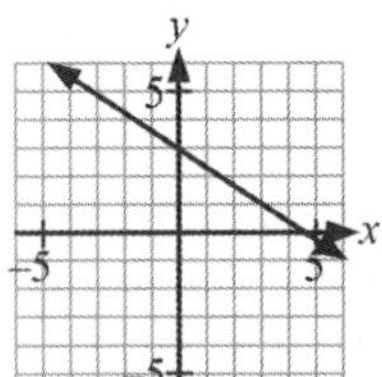

Use the following information to answer the next question.

Janelle is asked to use technology to graph the line defined by the equation $y + 3 = \frac{5}{6}(x - 2)$.

191. Which of the following equations could Janelle enter into her graphing calculator in order to obtain the desired graph?

A. $y = 5(x - 2) \div 6 - 18$

B. $y = (5x \div 6) - 13$

C. $y = (5x - 13) \div 6$

D. $y = (5x - 28) \div 6$

Use the following information to answer the next question.

Vera was asked to sketch the graph of the quadratic function $y = x^2 - 2x + 1$.
The steps in Vera's solution are as follows:

1. Determine the coordinates of the vertex by writing the equation in completed square form.
   $y = x^2 - 2x + 1$
   $y = (x^2 - 2x + 1 - 1) + 1$
   $y = (x^2 - 2x + 1) - 1 + 1$
   $y = (x - 1)^2 + 0$
   The vertex of $y = x^2 - 2x + 1$ is at (1, 0).
2. Determine the y-intercept.
   $y = (0)^2 - 2(0) + 1$
   $y = 1$
   The y-intercept of $y = x^2 - 2x + 1$ is 1.
3. Determine the x-intercepts.
   $y = (x - 1)^2 + 0$
   $0 = (x - 1)^2 + 0$
   $0 = (x - 1)^2$
   $\pm\sqrt{0} = x - 1$
   $0 = x - 1$
   $1 = x$
   The x-intercept of $y = x^2 - 2x + 1$ is 1.
4. Draw a graph of the function.

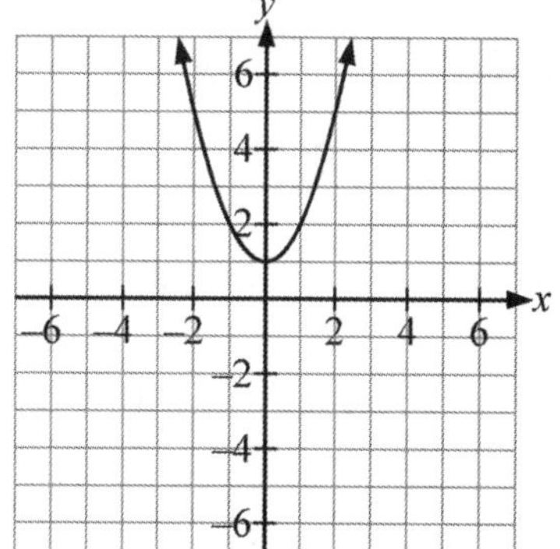

When Vera analyzed her solution, she realized that it was incorrect.

192. Vera's first error occurred in step

A. 1 B. 2

C. 3 D. 4

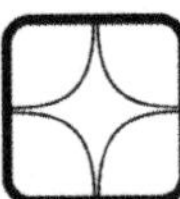

Use the following information to answer the next question.

The given graph of a quadratic function shows the coordinates of several points.

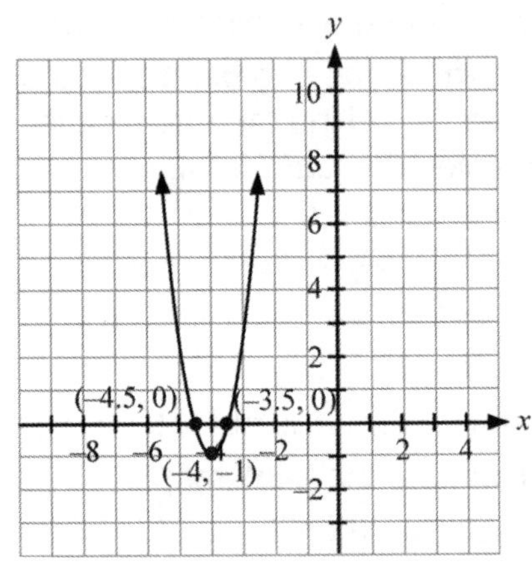

193. Which of the following points does **not** have its coordinates identified in the graph?

A. A zero
B. A vertex
C. A *y*-intercept
D. An *x*-intercept

194. Which of the following statements about the graph of the quadratic function $y = 3(x - 4)^2 - 41$ is **true**?

A. The equation of the axis of symmetry of the graph is $y = 4$.

B. The vertex of the graph is located at $(-4, -41)$.

C. The *y*-intercept of the graph is located at $(0, 7)$.

D. The graph opens downward.

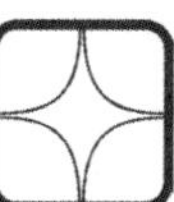

EXERCISE #1—ANALYZING FUNCTIONS ANSWERS AND SOLUTIONS

187. C	189. A	191. D	193. C
188. C	190. C	192. D	194. C

187. C

Use a graphing calculator to get the following graph of the function $y = -24x^2 + 1{,}000x - 3{,}250$.

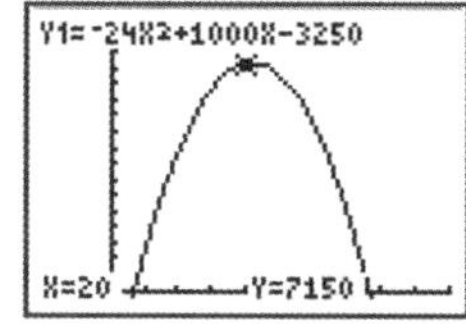

The graph is displayed using these window settings: x:[−10, 50, 5] y:[−200, 8,500, 500]

Therefore, this graph could be a sketch of the quadratic function $y = -24x^2 + 1{,}000x - 3{,}250$.

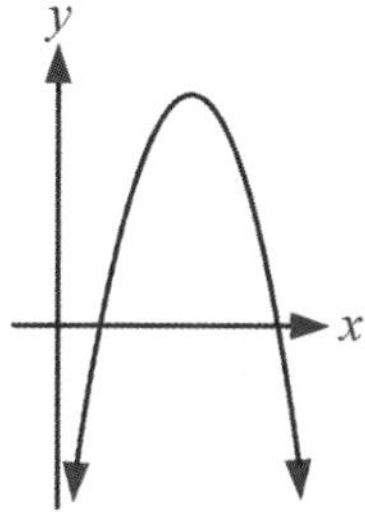

188. C

The x-intercepts of the quadratic function written in the factored form $f(x) = (x + 1)(x - 5)$ are found by setting each factor to zero.

$$x + 1 = 0 \quad\quad x = -1 \qquad \text{and} \qquad x - 5 = 0 \quad\quad x = 5$$

The equation of the axis of symmetry is located halfway between the x-intercepts, so it would be defined as

$$x = \frac{-1 + 5}{2} = \frac{4}{2} = 2$$

To find the vertex $(2, k)$, substitute the x-value into the function, and solve for k.

$$f(x) = (x + 1)(x - 5)$$
$$k = (2 + 1)(2 - 5)$$
$$k = (3)(-3)$$
$$k = -9$$

The vertex of the graph is (2, −9). The graph with x-intercepts of −1 and 5 and with the correct vertex is given in choice C.

189. A

Step 1

Determine the slope and y-intercept of the line defined by the equation $y = \frac{2}{3}x - 3$.

The equation $y = \frac{2}{3}x - 3$ is in the slope-intercept form $y = mx + b$. The slope, m, is $\frac{2}{3}$, and the y-intercept, b, is −3.

Step 2

Given that the slope of the line is $\frac{2}{3}$ and the line passes through the point (0, −3), determine another point on the line.

Another point on the line will be two units up and three units to the right of the point (0, −3). This point is (3, −1).

Step 3

Look at the given graphs, and determine which one shows a line that passes through the points (0, −3) and (3, −1).

The required line is as shown.

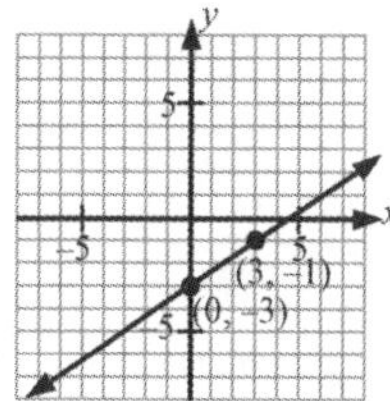

190. C

Step 1

Determine the x-intercept of the line defined by the equation $-2x + 3y + 9 = 0$.

Substitute 0 for y in the equation $-2x + 3y + 9 = 0$, and solve for x.

$$-2x + 3y + 9 = 0$$
$$-2x + 3(0) + 9 = 0$$
$$-2x + 9 = 0$$
$$-2x = -9$$
$$x = \frac{9}{2}$$
$$x = 4.5$$

The x-intercept is 4.5. In other words, the line passes through the ordered pair (4.5, 0).

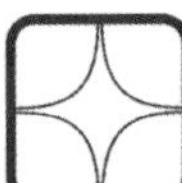

Step 2
Determine the y-intercept of the line defined by the equation $-2x + 3y + 9 = 0$.
Substitute 0 for x in the equation $-2x + 3y + 9 = 0$, and solve for y.

$$\begin{aligned} -2x + 3y + 9 &= 0 \\ -2(0) + 3y + 9 &= 0 \\ 3y + 9 &= 0 \\ 3y &= -9 \\ y &= -3 \end{aligned}$$

The y-intercept is –3. In other words, the line passes through the ordered pair (0, –3).

Step 3
Draw the line that passes through the points (4.5, 0) and (0, –3).
This graph shows the resulting line.

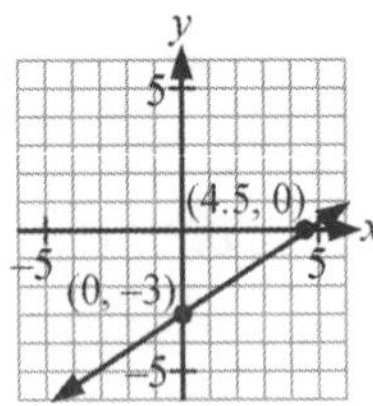

191. D

In order to enter the equation $y + 3 = \frac{5}{6}(x - 2)$ into a graphing calculator, isolate y.

$$\begin{aligned} y + 3 &= \frac{5}{6}(x - 2) \\ 6(y + 3) &= 6\left(\frac{5}{6}(x - 2)\right) \\ 6y + 18 &= 5(x - 2) \\ 6y + 18 &= 5x - 10 \\ 6y &= 5x - 28 \\ y &= \frac{5x - 28}{6} \end{aligned}$$

The equation $y = \frac{5x - 28}{6}$ can be entered into a graphing calculator as $y = (5x - 28) \div 6$.

192. D

Vera made her first error in step 4. On her graph of $y = x^2 - 2x + 1$, she plotted the vertex and x-intercept incorrectly. Given that the y-intercept is 1, the x-intercept is 1, and the vertex is at (1, 0), the graph should have been drawn as shown here.

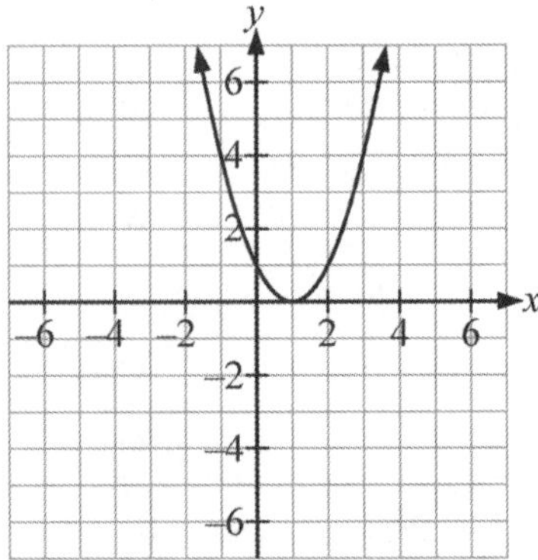

193. C

The x-intercepts are the locations where the graph intersects the x-axis. These are identified as (–4.5, 0) and (–3.5, 0).

The zeros are the same locations as the x-intercepts. These are also identified as (–4.5, 0) and (–3.5, 0).

The vertex is the location of the maximum or minimum point on the graph. This is identified as (–4, –1).

The y-intercept is the location where the graph intersects the y-axis. This is not identified.

194. C

The equation $y = 3(x - 4)^2 - 41$ is of the general quadratic form $y = a(x - h)^2 + k$. Thus, in the equation $y = 3(x - 4)^2 - 41$, the value of a is 3, the value of h is 4, and the value of k is –41.

Step 1
Determine the equation of the axis of symmetry for the graph of $y = 3(x - 4)^2 - 41$.
In general, the equation of the axis of symmetry for the graph of a quadratic function of the form $y = a(x - h)^2 + k$ is $x = h$. Thus, the equation for the axis of symmetry for the graph of $y = 3(x - 4)^2 - 41$ is $x = 4$, not $y = 4$.

Step 2
Determine the y-intercept for the graph of $y = 3(x - 4)^2 - 41$.

The y-intercept for the graph of $y = 3(x - 4)^2 - 41$ can be determined by substituting 0 for x and then solving for y.

$y = 3(x - 4)^2 - 41$
$y = 3((0) - 4)^2 - 41$
$y = 3(-4)^2 - 41$
$y = 3(16) - 41$
$y = 48 - 41$
$y = 7$

The y-intercept of the graph of $y = 3(x - 4)^2 - 41$ is located at the ordered pair (0, 7).

Step 3
Determine the vertex of the graph of $y = 3(x - 4)^2 - 41$.
In general, the vertex of the graph of a quadratic function of the form $y = a(x - h)^2 + k$ is at (h, k).
Thus, the vertex of the graph of $y = 3(x - 4)^2 - 41$ is located at the ordered pair (4, −41), not at (−4, −41).

Step 4
Determine the direction in which the graph of $y = 3(x - 4)^2 - 41$ opens.
In general, the graph of a quadratic function of the form $y = a(x - h)^2 + k$ opens upward if $a > 0$ and downward if $a < 0$. Thus, since $3 > 0$, the graph of $y = 3(x - 4)^2 - 41$ opens upward, not downward.

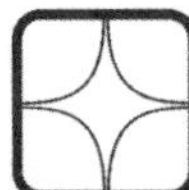

EXERCISE #2—ANALYZING FUNCTIONS

Use the following information to answer the next question.

Gladys would like to graph the quadratic function $y = -4.9x^2 + 30x + 1$ using her graphing calculator. Four possible window settings are given.

	Window Setting			
	I	II	III	IV
x_{min}	–10	–20	–15	–10
x_{max}	10	20	15	10
x_{scl}	1	2	2	1
y_{min}	–10	–30	–10	–20
y_{max}	10	30	40	60
y_{scl}	1	3	2	4
x_{res}	1	1	1	1

195. In order to display the graph with its vertex in view, Gladys must use window setting

A. I
B. II
C. III
D. IV

Use the following information to answer the next question.

Brad is attempting to sketch the graph of the quadratic function $f(x) = -2(x+4)(x+2)$. He makes the following four statements:

Statement I: The x-intercepts of the graph are –4 and –2.

Statement II: The equation of the axis of symmetry of the graph is $x = -3$.

Statement III: The vertex of the graph is (–3, 8).

Statement IV: The graph opens downward.

196. Which of the statements is **incorrect**?

A. I
B. II
C. III
D. IV

197. Which of the following graphs could represent the line defined by the equation $y = -x - 2$?

A.

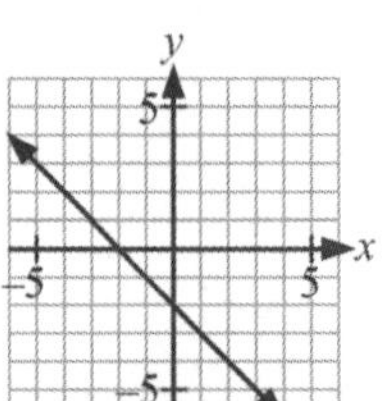

B.

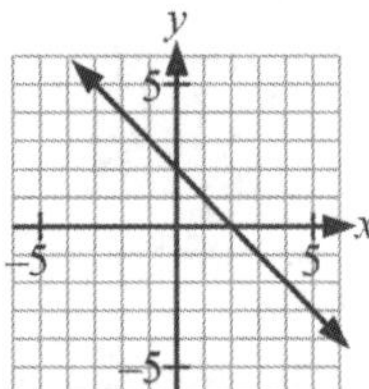

C.

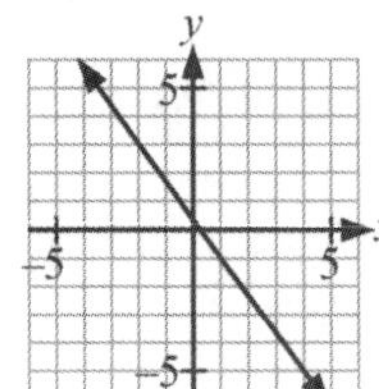

D.

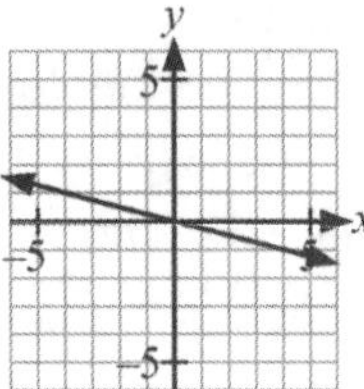

198. Which of the following graphs represents the equation $2x - y - 5 = 0$?

A.

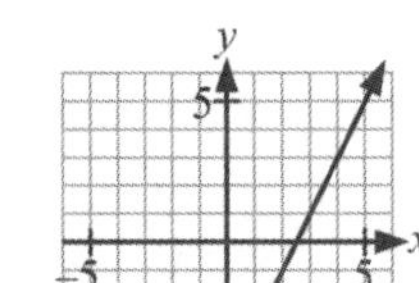

B.

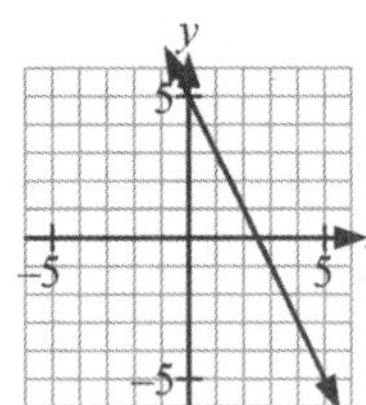

C.

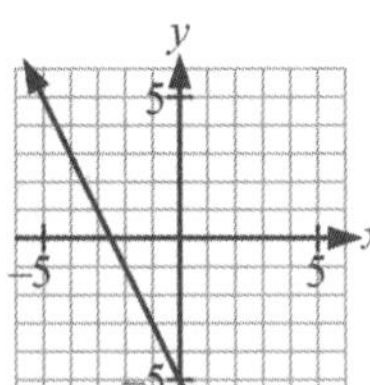

D.

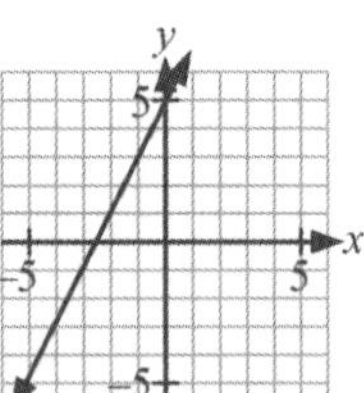

199. Which of the following lines represents the line defined by the equation $y - 3 = -\frac{2}{5}x$?

A.

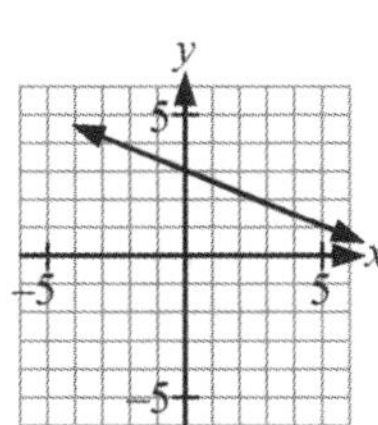

B.

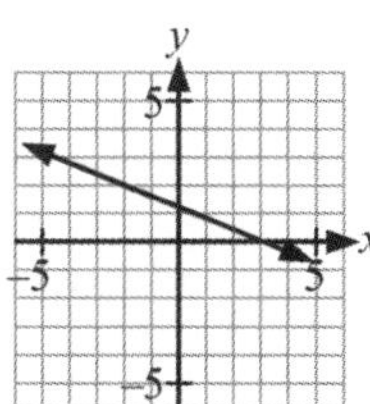

C.

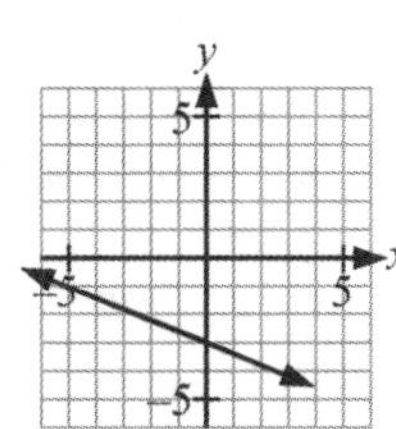

D.

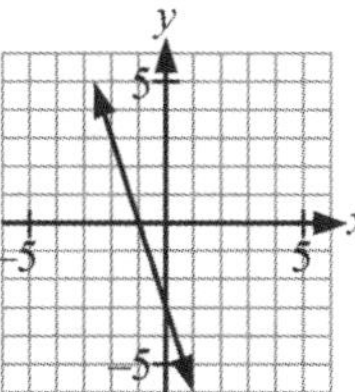

200. Which of the following graphs could represent the quadratic function $y = -2x^2 + 4x + 6$?

A.

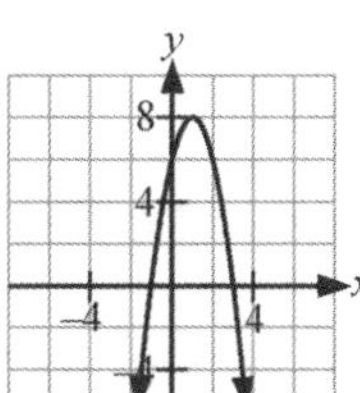

B.

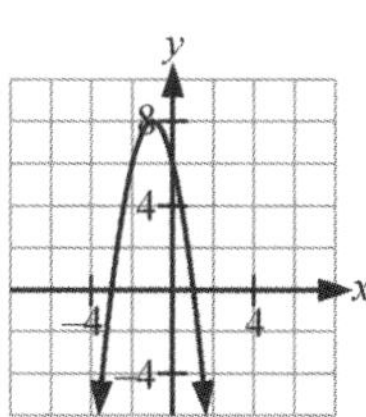

C.

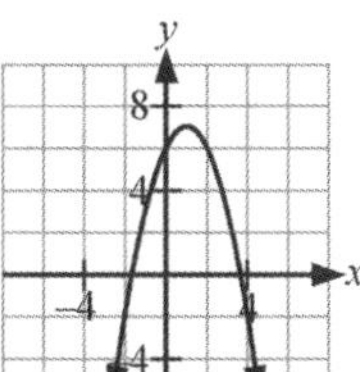

D.

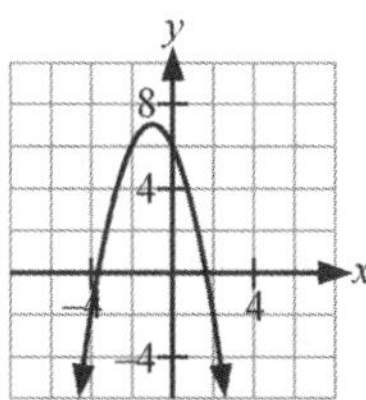

Use the following information to answer the next question.

A graph of a quadratic function is given.

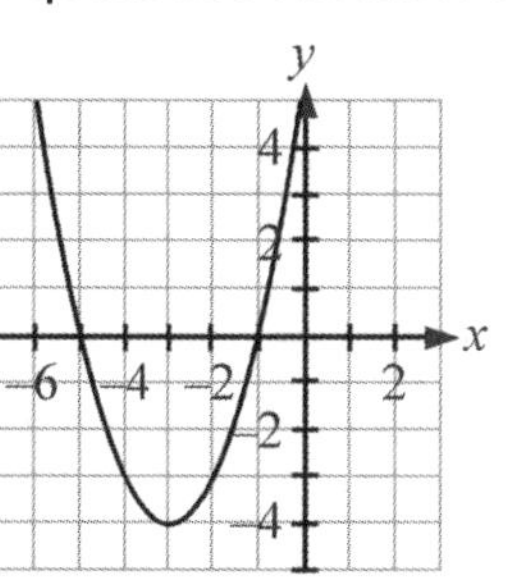

201. What are the coordinates of the *x*-intercepts?

A. (−5, 0) and (−1, 0)

B. (0, −5) and (0, −1)

C. (−3, −4) and (0, 5)

D. (5, 0) and (1, 0)

202. Which of the following graphs could represent the function $y = -3(x - h)^2 + k$, given that $h > 0$, $k < 0$, and both h and k are integers?

A.

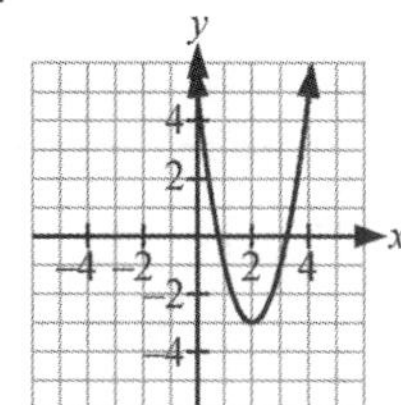

B.

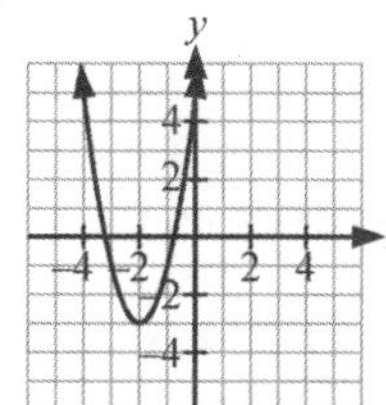

C.

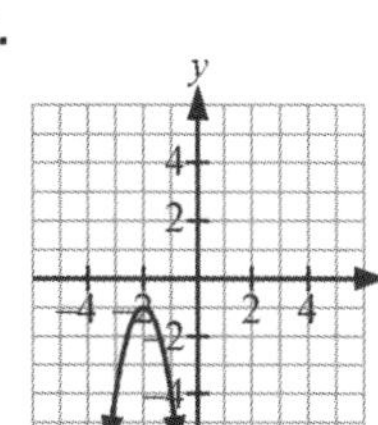

D.

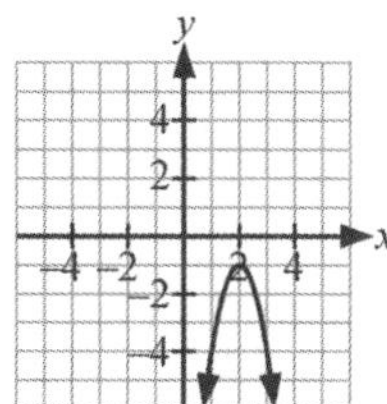

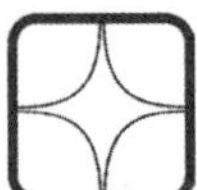

EXERCISE #2—ANALYZING FUNCTIONS ANSWERS AND SOLUTIONS

195. D	197. A	199. A	201. A
196. C	198. A	200. A	202. D

195. D

The graph of the quadratic function $y = -4.9x^2 + 30x + 1$ is displayed with each of the given window settings.

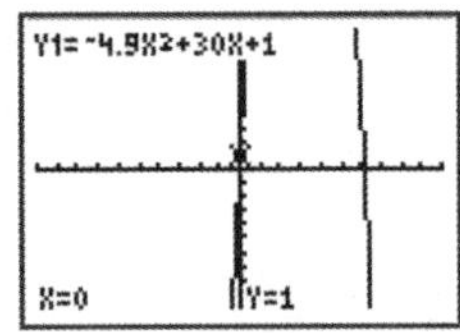

Window setting I

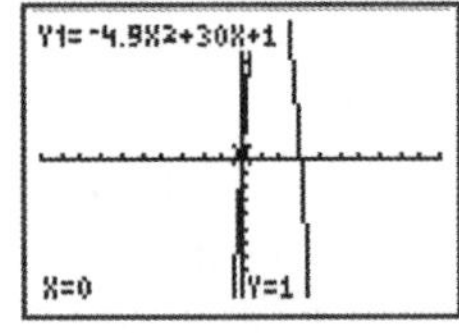

Window setting II

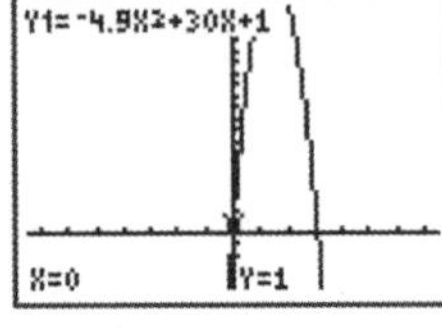

Window setting III

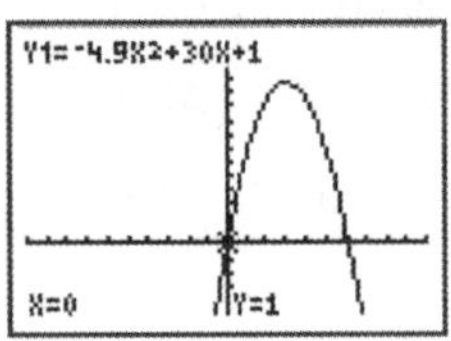

Window setting IV

Window setting IV will display the graph with its vertex in view.

196. C

For the quadratic function given in the factored form $f(x) = -2(x+4)(x+2)$, determine the following features of its graph:

- The x-intercepts are -4 and -2, since these values make each factor equal 0.

$$x + 4 = 0 \quad x = -4 \qquad \text{and} \qquad x + 2 = 0 \quad x = -2$$

- The equation of the axis of symmetry is located halfway between the x-intercepts:
$$x = h = \frac{r+s}{2} = \frac{-4+(-2)}{2} = -3$$
- The graph of the function opens downward since the numerical coefficient $a < 0$.
- The vertex of the graph (h, k) can be found, since it lies on the axis of symmetry $(x = -3)$. Substitute $x = -3$, and solve for k in the function.
$$f(x) = -2(x+4)(x+2)$$
$$k = -2(-3+4)(-3+2)$$
$$= -2(1)(-1)$$
$$= 2$$
The vertex is $(-3, 2)$.

In statement III, Brad incorrectly states that the vertex of the graph is $(-3, 8)$.

197. A

Step 1

Determine the slope and y-intercept of the line defined by the equation $y = -x - 2$.

The equation $y = -x - 2$ is in the slope-intercept form $y = mx + b$. Therefore, the slope (m) is -1, and the y-intercept (b) is -2.

Step 2

Given that the slope of the line is -1 and the line passes through the point $(0, -2)$, determine another point on the line.

Another point on the line will be 2 units down and 2 units to the right of the point $(0, -2)$. This point is $(2, -4)$.

Step 3

Draw a line passing through the points $(0, -2)$ and $(2, -4)$.

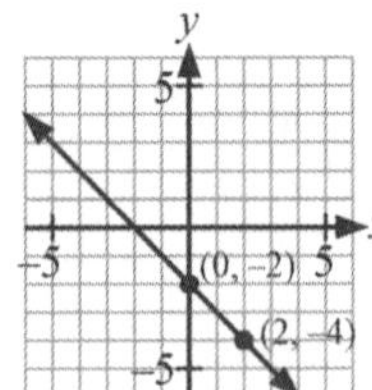

198. A

Step 1
Rewrite the equation in $y = mx + b$ form.

$$2x - y - 5 = 0$$
$$-y = -2x + 5$$
$$y = 2x - 5$$

Step 2
Determine the appropriate graph.

According to the equation, the slope is 2 and the y-intercept is -5.

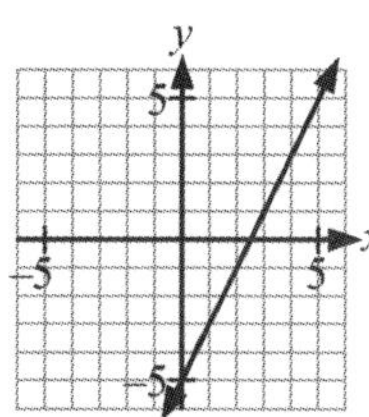

199. A

Step 1
Identify the slope, m, and the coordinates of the point (x_1, y_1) with respect to the line defined by the equation $y - 3 = -\frac{2}{5}x$.

Since the equation $y - 3 = -\frac{2}{5}x$, or $y - 3 = -\frac{2}{5}(x - 0)$, is in the slope-point form $y - y_1 = m(x - x_1)$, it can be observed that the slope is $-\frac{2}{5}$ and the coordinates of the point (x_1, y_1) are (0, 3).

Step 2
Determine a second point (x_2, y_2) on the line defined by the equation $y - 3 = -\frac{2}{5}x$.

Given that the slope of the line is $-\frac{2}{5}$ and the line passes through the point (0, 3), another point (x_2, y_2) on the line will be 2 units down and 5 units to the right of the point (0, 3). This point is (5, 1).

Step 3
Draw the line that passes through the points (0, 3) and (5, 1).

The correct line is shown here.

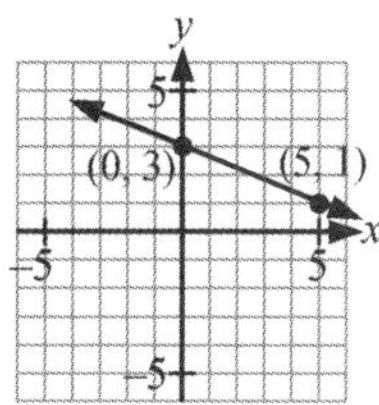

200. A

Step 1
Complete the square of the given quadratic function.

$$y = -2x^2 + 4x + 6$$
$$y = -2(x^2 - 2x) + 6$$
$$y = -2(x^2 - 2x + 1 - 1) + 6$$
$$y = -2(x^2 - 2x + 1) + 2 + 6$$
$$y = -2(x - 1)^2 + 8$$

The completed square form of the given quadratic function is $y = -2(x - 1)^2 + 8$.

Step 2
Identify the vertex of the graph.

The coordinates of the vertex of the graph of a quadratic function of the form $y = a(x - h)^2 + k$ are (h, k). Therefore, the coordinates of the vertex of the graph of $y = -2(x - 1)^2 + 8$ are (1, 8).

Step 3
Determine the y-intercept of the graph.

Substitute 0 for x in the equation $y = -2(x - 1)^2 + 8$, and then solve for y.

$$y = -2(x - 1)^2 + 8$$
$$y = -2(0 - 1)^2 + 8$$
$$y = -2(1) + 8$$
$$y = -2 + 8$$
$$y = 6$$

The y-intercept of the graph of $y = -2x^2 + 4x + 6$ is 6.

Step 4
Determine the x-intercepts of the graph.

Substitute 0 for y in the equation $y = -2(x - 1)^2 + 8$, and then solve for x.

$$y = -2(x - 1)^2 + 8$$
$$0 = -2(x - 1)^2 + 8$$
$$2(x - 1)^2 = 8$$
$$(x - 1)^2 = 4$$
$$x - 1 = \pm\sqrt{4}$$
$$x - 1 = \pm 2$$
$$x = 1 \pm 2$$
$$x = 3 \text{ or } x = -1$$

The x-intercepts of the graph of $y = -2x^2 + 4x + 6$ are 3 and -1.

Step 5
Identify the graph that could represent the function $y = -2x^2 + 4x + 6$.

Graph A has x-intercepts of 3 and -1, a y-intercept of 6, and a vertex at (1, 8).

Therefore, graph A could represent the quadratic function $y = -2x^2 + 4x + 6$.

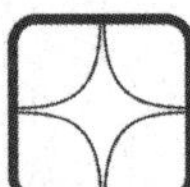

201. A

The x-intercepts are the points where the graph intersects the x-axis.

The coordinates of these points are (–5, 0) and (–1, 0).

202. D

The equation $y = -3(x - h)^2 + k$ is of the general quadratic form $y = a(x - h)^2 + k$. In general, the graph of a quadratic function of the form $y = a(x - h)^2 + k$ has a vertex of (h, k). The graph opens upward if $a > 0$ and downward if $a < 0$.

Since $a = -3$ in the equation $y = -3(x - h)^2 + k$, the graph of $y = -3(x - h)^2 + k$ opens downward. Also, given that $h > 0$ and $k < 0$, the vertex of the graph must be located in quadrant IV. For example, the vertex of the graph of $y = -3(x - h)^2 + k$ could be located at the ordered pair (2, –1).

The only graph that has a vertex in quadrant IV and opens downward is graph D.

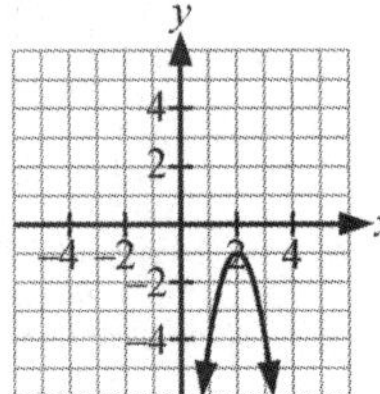

Building Functions

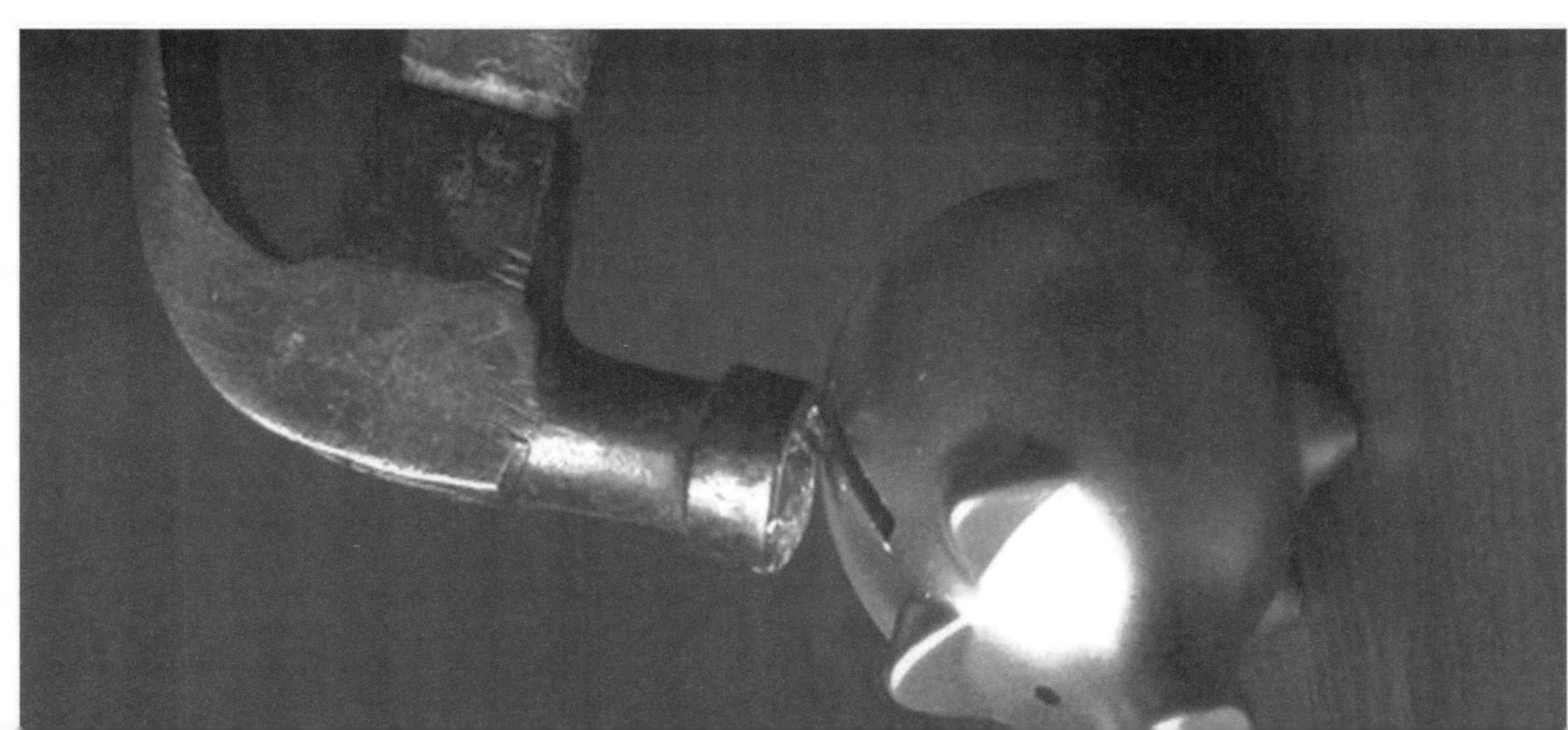

BUILDING FUNCTIONS

Table of Correlations

Standard		Concepts	Exercise #1	Exercise #2
Unit2.10	Build a function that models a relationship between two quantities.			
F-BF.1a	*Write a function that describes a relationship between two quantities. Determine an explicit expression, a recursive process, or steps for calculation from a context.*	Analyzing Non-Recursive and Recursive Data Tables	203	213
		Extract a Pattern From a Sequence and Find its Recursive Pattern	204	214
		Defining Functions as Recursive	205	215
F-BF.1b	*Write a function that describes a relationship between two quantities. Combine standard function types using arithmetic operations.*	Combining Functions Using Arithmetic Operations	206	216
F-BF.2	*Write arithmetic and geometric sequences both recursively and with an explicit formula, use them to model situations, and translate between the two forms.*	Finding the Terms of a Sequence Given the Recursive Definition	139	149
		Determine the General Term of an Arithmetic Sequence	207	217, 221
		Identify Arithmetic Sequences	208	218
		Identify Geometric Sequences	208, 209	219
		Determine the General Term of a Geometric Sequence	210	219
		Solving Problems Using Geometric Sequences	209	219
		Solving Problems Using Basic Arithmetic Sequences	211	220
		Solving Problems Using the General Term Formula for an Arithmetic Sequence	212	221

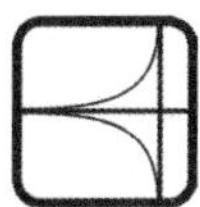

F-BF.1a Write a function that describes a relationship between two quantities. Determine an explicit expression, a recursive process, or steps for calculation from a context.

Analyzing Non-Recursive and Recursive Data Tables

One of the best ways to organize groups of data that are mathematically related is in a chart or table. The rows and columns of the table or chart should have headings that clarify the contents and help make the trends, patterns, and interrelationships more accessible.

Two types of data tables will be examined: non-recursive and recursive.

Non-Recursive Data Tables

A non-recursive data table is a table in which the values in each row or column are calculated independently of the other ones.

Example

The following table shows the price, number of sales and revenue for 4 particular products in a specialty coffee shop.

Product	Price ($)	Number of Sales	Revenue ($)
Coffee	1.85	75	138.75
Tea	1.35	50	67.50
Latte	3.25	68	221.00
Mocha	3.50	32	112.00

In words as well as by using a formula, describe how revenue is calculated.

Solution

Revenue is equal to the price charged for an item times the number of that item sold.

- Let R represent the revenue.
- Let p represent the price of an item.
- Let n represent the number of the items sold.

The formula for calculating revenue is $R = pn$.

What is the projected revenue from coffee sales if the managers of the coffee shop are planning to increase the price of coffee from $1.85 to $1.95 and the number of sales remains the same?

Solution

$R = pn$
$R = \$1.95(75)$
$= \$146.25$

If the number of coffee sales stays the same, the projected revenue is $146.25.

If the price of an item increases, will revenue also increase? Why or why not?

Solution

If the number of sales of an item stay the same following the price increase, then the revenue will increase. However, if the price increases too much, sales will likely decrease, and so revenue will also most likely decrease.

Example

A music store is having a sale. CDs that normally sell for $15.00 are being sold at 20% off, DVDs that normally sell for $25.00 are being sold at 15% off, and MP3 players that normally sell for $220.00 are being sold at 10% off.

The following data table illustrates the Item, Original Price, Discount (%), Sale Price, Sales (number of items sold), and Revenue generated from the sale.

Item	Original Price ($)	Discount (%)	Sale Price ($)	Sales	Revenue ($)
CD	15.00	20	12.00	85	1,020.00
DVD	25.00	15	21.25	50	1,062.50
MP3	220.00	10	198.00	22	4,356.00

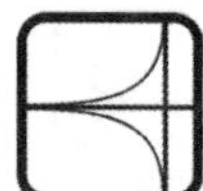

Write an equation to show how the sale price is calculated and then determine the revenue from the sale.

Solution

Sale Price:

- Let s represent the sale price.
- Let d represent the discount, as a decimal.
- Let p represent the original price.
- Sale price = (original price − (original price × discount))
- $s = p - pd$

Total Revenue:

Total = \$1,020.00 + \$1,062.50 + \$4,356.00
= \$6,438.50

The total revenue for the sale is \$6,438.50.

Recursive Data Tables

A recursive data table is a table in which subsequent rows or columns are dependent upon calculations in the previous one.

Example

Lexi's parents start an education savings account for her with an initial deposit of \$1,000. At the end of each year thereafter, Lexi's parents deposit \$2,000 into the account. Interest is paid and added to the balance at the end of each year at a rate of 2%.

The following table shows the details of the first four years of this savings account.

	Year 1	Year 2	Year 3	Year 4
Opening Balance	\$1,000.00	\$3,020.00	\$5,080.40	\$7,182.01
Interest Rate	2%	2%	2%	2%
Deposit	\$2,000.00	\$2,000.00	\$2,000.00	\$2,000.00
Closing Balance	\$3,020.00	\$5,080.40	\$7,182.01	\$9,325.65

How much money is in the account at the end of the fourth year?

Solution

At the end of the fourth year, the account contains \$9,325.65.

How much interest was earned over the four years?

Solution

Add up the interest earned for each of the four years.
Interest
= \$20 + \$60.40 + \$101.61 + \$143.64
= \$325.65

Notice that this amount could also be found by subtracting the original opening balance and all of the deposits from the final balance:
Interest
= \$9,325.65 – \$1,000 – 4(\$2,000)
= \$325.65

Describe how the closing balance is calculated for any given year.

Solution

The closing balance is found by first calculating the interest earned on the opening balance, and then adding this interest and the deposit amount to the opening balance.

Example

Stephen has $3,500.00 in the bank.
He decides to add to this amount by depositing $1,800 at the end of each year.
He has found a bank that will pay 2.5% interest per year at the end of each year.

Complete a recursive table that displays the following information for three years: year, opening balance, interest rate (%), interest earned, deposit, closing balance.

Solution

Step 1

Determine the closing balance for the first year.

Interest Earned = $3,500 × 2.5%
= $3,500 × 0.025
= $87.50

Opening Balance = $3,500.00
The closing balance is equal to:
the opening balance + interest earned + amount of deposit

Thus, the closing balance for the first year was $3,500.00 + $87.50 + $1,800 = $5,387.50

Step 2

Calculate the closing balance for year 2.

Openning balance = closing balance from year 1

The opening balance is $5,387.50.
Interest Earned = $5,387.50 × 2.5%
= $5,387.50 × 0.025
= $134.69

Deposit = $1,800.00

Closing Balance
= $5,387.50 + $134.69 + $1,800.00
= $7,322.19

Step 3

Calculate the closing balance for year 3.

Openning balance = closing balance from year 2

The opening balance is $7,322.19.
Interest Earned = $7,322.19 × 2.5%
= $5,387.50 × 0.025
= $183.05

Deposit = $1,800.00

Closing Balance
= $7,322.19 + $183.05 + $1,800.00
= $9,305.24

Step 4

By making use of the derived values, set up the required recursive table.

	Year 1	Year 2	Year 3
Opening Balance	$3,500.00	$5,387.50	$7,322.19
Interest Rate	2.5%	2.5%	2.5%
Interest Earned	$87.50	$134.69	$183.05
Deposit	$1,800.00	$1,800.00	$1,800.00
Closing Balance	$5,387.50	$7,322.19	$9,305.24

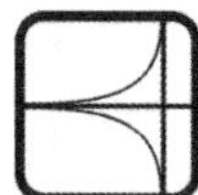

When borrowing money instead of investing, the goal is to have the balance decrease. Interest is still added to the opening balance, but the payments are then subtracted from the opening balance.

Example

The following table shows the repayment of a loan over a period of five years.

Year 1	
Opening Balance	$2,000.00
Interest Rate	5.0%
Interest Charged	$100.00
Payment	$550.00
Closing Balance	$1,550.00
Year 2	
Opening Balance	$1,550.00
Interest Rate	5.0%
Interest Charged	$77.50
Payment	$550.00
Closing Balance	$1,077.50
Year 3	
Opening Balance	$1,077.50
Interest Rate	5.0%
Interest Charged	$3.88
Payment	$550.00
Closing Balance	$531.38
Year 4	
Opening Balance	$531.38
Interest Rate	5.0%
Interest Charged	$29.07
Payment	$550.00
Closing Balance	$60.45
Year 5	
Opening Balance	$60.45
Interest Rate	5.0%
Interest Charged	$3.02
Payment	$63.47
Closing Balance	$0.00

Why was the payment at the end of the fifth year different from the payment in other years?

Solution

The opening balance plus the interest charged totaled $63.47.

Since this was all of the debt that remained, that was the amount of the payment at the end of the fifth year.

How much interest was paid on this loan?

Solution

Total interest = $100 + $77.50 + $53.88 +$29.07+$3.02
Total interest = $263.47

Notice that the interest paid may also be calculated using the following method:
Total Interest = total payments made – opening balance
= 4($550.00) + $63.47 – $2,000 = $263.47

Extract a Pattern From a Sequence and Find its Recursive Pattern

A **sequence** is an ordered list of numbers separated by commas. Each number in a sequence is called a **term**. A sequence contains a pattern, which can be used to predict the next number in the sequence.

Using mathematical notation, the first term in a sequence is equal to t_1 and the second term is equal to t_2. Each term in a sequence can be referred to as t_n, which is the nth term or the general term. The variable n is equal to all positive integers. An equation can be used to define the sequence.

Example

In the sequence 6, 11, 16, 21…, $t_1 = 6$ and $t_2 = 11$. The sequence can be defined by the equation $t_n = 5n + 1$.

$t_1 = 5(1) + 1$
$t_1 = 6$
$t_2 = 5(2) + 1$
$t_2 = 11$
$t_3 = 5(3) + 1$
$t_3 = 16$
$t_4 = 5(4) + 1$
$t_4 = 21$

A **recursive pattern** is a sequence that uses one term to find the very next term in the sequence. An operation is performed on the first term of the sequnce to obtain the next term.

Example

In the sequence 4, 8, 12, 16…, each term is found by adding 4 to the previous term.

$t_1 = 4$
$t_2 = t_1 + 4$
$t_2 = 4 + 4$
$t_2 = 8$
$t_3 = t_2 + 4$
$t_3 = 8 + 4$
$t_3 = 12$
$t_4 = t_3 + 4$
$t_4 = 12 + 4$
$t_4 = 16$

The formula for each term is found by using the term that came before it. If the general term is t_n, then the next term in the sequence is t_{n+1}. The given pattern can be written in mathematical notation as $t_{n+1} = t_n + 4$.

Example

Write the recursive pattern for the sequence 18, 15, 12, 9… in mathematical notation.

Solution

Step 1

Determine the recursive pattern in the given sequence.

$18 - 15 = 3$
$15 - 12 = 3$
$12 - 9 = 3$

The difference between each term is 3. Therefore, subtract 3 from the previous term to find the next term.

Step 2

Write the pattern in mathematical notation.

The pattern in the given sequence can be written as $t_{n+1} = t_n - 3$.

Once you have found the recursive pattern, you can use it to find unknown terms in the sequence.

Defining Functions as Recursive

When a recursive function is expanded to its first few terms, it may simplify to a pattern that takes the form of another type of function. You can then take the simplified pattern of the recursive function to the nth term, and rewrite it as a different type of function, such as a linear or exponential function.

Use the following steps when determining another form of a recursive function:

1. Expand the recursive function.
2. Substitute each calculated value into its preceding equation, and simplify the values into a predictable pattern.
3. Extend the pattern of the function to the nth term.

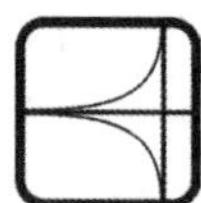

Example

A teacher writes the recursive function $a_n = 3a_{n-1}$, where $n > 0$, on the board.

Determine the equivalent exponential function.

Solution

Step 1
Expand the recursive function.
$a_1 = 3a_0$
$a_2 = 3a_1$
$a_3 = 3a_2$
$a_4 = 3a_3$

Step 2
Substitute the values of a_1, a_2, and a_3 into their respective equations, and simplify.
$a_4 = 3a_3$
$a_4 = 3(3a_2)$
$a_4 = 3(3(3a_1))$
$a_4 = 3(3(3(3a_0)))$
$a_4 = a_0(3)^4$

Step 3
Extend the pattern of the function to the nth term.

Observe the recursive function, $a_4 = a_0(3)^4$. The subscript value of a is equal to the exponent of 3. Therefore, the pattern from Step 2 can be continued until the nth term, giving the exponential equation $a_n = a_0(3)^n$.

F-BF.1b Write a function that describes a relationship between two quantities. Combine standard function types using arithmetic operations.

Combining Functions Using Arithmetic Operations

Functions are often created by applying the four basic operations to combine other simpler functions. Operations with functions are performed according to the rules and operations for polynomial, rational, and other representations of real numbers. Non-permissible values must be considered when working with rational functions and should be determined for the original function before any simplification occurs.
The non-permissible values are retained for the function after the common factors have been removed.

Example

It is given that $g(x) = x^2 - x - 12$ and $h(x) = x + 3$.

Determine $f(x)$ if $f(x) = g(x) + h(x)$.

Solution

Step 1
Substitute $x^2 - x - 12$ for $g(x)$ and $x + 3$ for $h(x)$ into the equation $f(x) = g(x) + h(x)$.
$f(x) = (x^2 - x - 12) + (x + 3)$

Step 2
Combine like terms and simplify.

$$\begin{aligned} f(x) &= (x^2 - x - 12) + (x + 3) \\ &= x^2 - x - 12 + x + 3 \\ &= x^2 - 9 \end{aligned}$$

Determine $f(x)$ if $f(x) = g(x) - h(x)$.

Solution

Step 1
Substitute $x^2 - x - 12$ for $g(x)$ and $x + 3$ for $h(x)$ into the equation $f(x) = g(x) - h(x)$.
$f(x) = (x^2 - x - 12) - (x + 3)$

Step 2
Combine like terms and simplify.

$$\begin{aligned} f(x) &= (x^2 - x - 12) - (x + 3) \\ &= x^2 - x - 12 - x - 3 \\ &= x^2 - 2x - 15 \end{aligned}$$

Determine $f(x)$ if $f(x) = g(x) \cdot h(x)$.

Solution

Step 1
Substitute $x^2 - x - 12$ for $g(x)$ and $x + 3$ for $h(x)$ into the equation $f(x) = g(x) \cdot h(x)$.

$$f(x) = (x^2 - x - 12)(x + 3)$$

Step 2
Expand using the distributive property and then simplify by combining like terms.

$$\begin{aligned} f(x) &= (x^2 - x - 12)(x + 3) \\ &= x^3 + 3x^2 - x^2 - 3x - 12x - 36 \\ &= x^3 + 2x^2 - 15x - 36 \end{aligned}$$

Determine $f(x)$ if $f(x) = \dfrac{g(x)}{h(x)}$.

Solution

Step 1
Substitute $x^2 - x - 12$ for $g(x)$ and $x + 3$ for $h(x)$ in the equation $f(x) = \dfrac{g(x)}{h(x)}$.

$$f(x) = \frac{x^2 - x - 12}{x + 3}$$

Step 2
Factor the numerator and denominator, and reduce.

$$\begin{aligned} f(x) &= \frac{x^2 - x - 12}{x + 3} \\ &= \frac{(x - 4)(x + 3)}{x + 3} \\ &= x - 4 \end{aligned}$$

State the non-permissible values.

$$\begin{aligned} x + 3 &\neq 0 \\ x &\neq -3 \end{aligned}$$

The non-permissible value of x is -3.

F-BF.2 Write arithmetic and geometric sequences both recursively and with an explicit formula, use them to model situations, and translate between the two forms.

Determine the General Term of an Arithmetic Sequence

The **general term formula** for an arithmetic sequence is as follows: $t_n = a + (n - 1)d$

This formula will generate any specified term for which a and d and n are known.

- a represents the first term in the series
- n represents the term number
- d represents the common difference between sequential terms in the sequence
- t_n represents the value of the term in the nth position

To determine the general term for any given sequence, identify the values of a and d, substitute them into the general term formula, and simplify.

Example

For the arithmetic sequence −5, 2, 9, 16, …, find the general term.

Solution

Step 1
In order to apply the general term formula, $t_n = a + (n - 1)d$, identify the values of a and d.

$$\begin{aligned} a &= -5 \\ d &= 2 - (-5) = 7 \end{aligned}$$

Step 2
Substitute the derived values for a and d into the general term formula and simplify.

$$\begin{aligned} t_n &= a + (n - 1)d \\ t_n &= -5 + (n - 1)(7) \\ t_n &= -5 + 7n - 7 \\ t_n &= 7n - 12 \end{aligned}$$

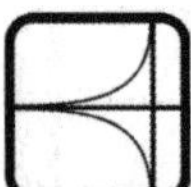

Example

For the arithmetic sequence 4, 1, −2, −5,..., determine the value of the 20th term (t_{20}).

Solution

Identify the values of a, d, and n.

$a = 4$
$d = 1 - 4 = -3$
$n = 20$

Substitute the derived values for a, d and n into the general term formula for an arithmetic sequence.

$$\begin{aligned} t_n &= a + (n-1)d \\ t_{20} &= 4 + (20-1)(-3) \\ &= 4 + (19)(-3) \\ &= -53 \end{aligned}$$

The value of the 20th term is −53.

In addition to being able to find the value of a desired term, the general term formula can be used to calculate the value of a, d or n, given the other three values.

Example

Which term in the arithmetic sequence −5, 2, 9, 16, ..., has a value of 79?

Solution

Identify the values of a, d and t_n.

$a = -5$
$d = 2 - (-5) = 7$
$t_n = 79$

Substitute the derived values for a, d and t_n into the general term formula for an arithmetic sequence and solve for n.

$$\begin{aligned} t_n &= a + (n-1)d \\ 79 &= -5 + (n-1)(7) \\ 79 &= -5 + 7n - 7 \\ 79 &= -12 + 7n \\ 91 &= 7n \\ 13 &= n \end{aligned}$$

The 13th term in the sequence is 79.

Example

A particular arithmetic sequence has a common difference of −2.5. In the same sequence, $t_{41} = -64$.

What is the first term in the given sequence?

Solution

Step 1

Identify the values of t_n, n, and d.

$t_n = -64$
$n = 41$
$d = -2.5$

Step 2

Substitute the derived values into the general term formula, and solve for a.

$$\begin{aligned} t_n &= a + (n-1)d \\ -64 &= a + (41-1)(-2.5) \\ -64 &= a - 100 \\ a &= 36 \end{aligned}$$

The first term is 36.

IDENTIFY ARITHMETIC SEQUENCES

A **number sequence** is a list of numbers that are separated by commas. Some sequences follow rules or patterns. In particular, an **arithmetic sequence** is one in which each term is increasing or decreasing by a constant amount, d, called the **common difference**.

Some examples of arithmetic sequences are given in the following list:

- In the sequence 2, 5, 8, 11 ... the number 3 is added to each term to get the subsequent term; thus $d = 3$.
- In the sequence 4, 3.5, 3, 2.5, 2 ... the number −0.5 is added to each term to get the subsequent term; thus $d = -0.5$.
- In the sequence $\frac{1}{3}, \frac{1}{2}, \frac{2}{3}, \frac{5}{6}, \ldots$, the number $\frac{1}{6}$ is added to each term to get the subsequent term; thus $d = \frac{1}{6}$.

The following sequences are not arithmetic:

- 1, 3, 6, 10, 15 ...
- 100, 50, 25, 12.5 ...

Although the above sequences follow a pattern, it is not the repeated addition of the same number, so these sequences are not arithmetic.

It is important to distinguish arithmetic sequences from other types of sequences.

Example

Determine whether or not the sequence 4, 9, 14, 19 … is an arithmetic sequence. If it is arithmetic, determine the common difference, d.

Solution

This sequence is arithmetic because 5 is being added to each term to get the subsequent term. Therefore, $d = 5$.

Example

Determine whether the sequence 3, 6, 12, 24 … is an arithmetic sequence. If it is arithmetic, determine the common difference, d.

Solution

This sequence is not an arithmetic sequence because the same number is not being added each time to get the subsequent term.

Example

Determine whether the sequence 10, 4, −2, −8 … is an arithmetic sequence. If it is arithmetic, determine the common difference, d.

Solution

The sequence is arithmetic because −6 is added to each term to get the subsequent term. Therefore, $d = -6$.

Example

Determine whether the sequence $\frac{1}{3}, \frac{2}{3}, \frac{4}{3}, \frac{8}{3}$ … is an arithmetic sequence. If it is arithmetic, determine the common difference, d.

Solution

This is not an arithmetic sequence because the same number is not being added each time to get the subsequent term.

Identify Geometric Sequences

A **sequence** is an ordered list of numbers that are separated by commas.

A common type of number sequence is a geometric sequence.

A sequence is **geometric** if each successive term is obtained by multiplying the previous term by a constant. This constant is called the **common ratio** and is denoted by r.

For example, in the sequence 3, 6, 12, 24, 48, each successive term is obtained by multiplying the previous term by 2. Therefore, the sequence is geometric with a common ratio, r, of 2.

$t_1 = a = 3$
$t_2 = t_1 \times 2 = 3 \times 2 = 6$
$t_3 = t_2 \times 2 = 6 \times 2 = 12$
$t_4 = t_3 \times 2 = 12 \times 2 = 24$
$t_5 = t_4 \times 2 = 24 \times 2 = 48$

The following sequences are examples of geometric sequences:

- 2, 4, 8, 16, 32 … $r = 2$
- −5, −15, −45, −135 … $r = 3$
- 100, 50, 25, 12.5 … $r = 0.5$

Any two successive terms in a sequence can be used to find the common ratio. Terms 1 and 2 are often used, so a possible formula is $r = \frac{t_2}{t_1}$.

When $r > 1$, the terms of a geometric sequence are increasing in value. This is referred to as **geometric growth**.

When $0 \le r < 1$, the terms of a geometric sequence are decreasing in value. This is called **geometric decay**.

When $r < 0$, the terms of a geometric sequence alternate between positive and negative values if the first term is positive or alternate between negative and positive values if the first term is negative.

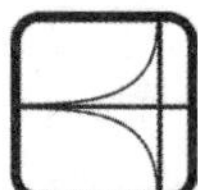

Example

For the geometric sequence 7, 21, 63, ..., determine the value of the common ratio and classify the sequence as growth or decay.

Solution

Find r.

$r = \frac{21}{7}$

$r = 3$

Since $r > 1$, this sequence is an example of geometric growth.

Example

For the geometric sequence 6, 3, $\frac{3}{2}$, ..., determine the value of the common ratio and classify the sequence as growth or decay.

Solution

Find r.

$r = \frac{3}{6}$

$r = \frac{1}{2}$

Since $0 < r < 1$, this sequence is an example of geometric decay.

To determine whether a sequence is geometric, look at the first two ratios. Check whether $\frac{t_2}{t_1} = \frac{t_3}{t_2}$. If the two ratios are equal, then quickly scan the other terms of the sequence to verify that the same common ratio applies to them as well. If it does, then the sequence is geometric.

A sequence, t_1, t_2, t_3, t_4, ... t_{n-1}, t_n, is geometric if it satisfies this condition:

$$\frac{t_2}{t_1} = \frac{t_3}{t_2} = \frac{t_4}{t_3} = \ldots = \frac{t_n}{t_{n-1}}$$

Example

Given the sequence $\frac{1}{2}, \frac{1}{4}, \frac{1}{8}, \ldots$, explain whether the sequence is geometric.

Solution

Step 1

Determine the common ratio using t_1 and t_2.

$$\frac{t_2}{t_1} = \frac{\left(\frac{1}{4}\right)}{\left(\frac{1}{2}\right)} = \frac{1}{4} \times \frac{2}{1} = \frac{2}{4} = \frac{1}{2}$$

Step 2

Determine the common ratio using t_2 and t_3.

$$\frac{t_3}{t_2} = \frac{\left(\frac{1}{8}\right)}{\left(\frac{1}{4}\right)} = \frac{1}{8} \times \frac{4}{1} = \frac{4}{8} = \frac{1}{2}$$

Step 3

Compare the common ratios.

$$\frac{t_2}{t_1} = \frac{1}{2} = \frac{t_3}{t_2}$$

Since the ratios are the same, the sequence $\frac{1}{2}$, $\frac{1}{4}, \frac{1}{8}, \ldots$ is a geometric sequence with a common ratio, r, of $\frac{1}{2}$.

Determine the General Term of a Geometric Sequence

The formula for the general term of a geometric sequence is as follows:

$t_n = ar^{n-1}$

This formula will generate any specified term for which a and r and n are known.

To determine the general term for any given geometric sequence, identify the values of a and r, substitute them into the general term formula, and simplify.

Example

What is the general term of the geometric sequence 54, 36, 24, 16, …?

Solution

Step 1

Determine the value of a, the first term.
In this sequence, the first term is 54.
Therefore, $a = 54$.

Step 2

Determine the common ratio, r.

$$\begin{aligned} r &= \frac{t_2}{t_1} \\ &= \frac{36}{54} \\ &= \frac{2}{3} \end{aligned}$$

Step 3

Substitute 54 for a and $\frac{2}{3}$ for r in the formula $t_n = ar^{n-1}$.

The general term is $t_n = 54\left(\frac{2}{3}\right)^{n-1}$.

Example

To the nearest hundredth, the 7th term of the geometric sequence 54, 36, 24, 16, … is _________.

Solution

Substitute 7 for n in the formula $t_n = 54\left(\frac{2}{3}\right)^{n-1}$, and then evaluate.

$$t_7 = 54\left(\frac{2}{3}\right)^{7-1}$$
$$t_7 = 54\left(\frac{2}{3}\right)^{6}$$
$$t_7 \approx 54(0.08779)$$
$$t_7 \approx 4.74$$

The 7th term is 4.74.

In addition to being able to find the value of a desired term, the general term formula can be used to calculate the value of a, r or n, given the other three values.

Example

The number of terms in the geometric sequence 4, 12, 36, 108, …, 78,732 is _______.

Solution

Since this is a finite sequence and the last term is 78,732, then for some value of n, $t_n = 78{,}732$. The number of terms in the sequence can be determined by solving for n.

Step 1

Determine the value of a, the first term.
In this sequence, the first term is 4. Therefore, $a = 4$.

Step 2

Determine the common ratio, r.

$$\begin{aligned} r &= \frac{t_2}{t_1} \\ &= \frac{12}{4} \\ &= 3 \end{aligned}$$

Step 3

Determine the general term.
Substitute 4 for a and 3 for r in the formula $t_n = ar^{n-1}$.

The general term is $t_n = 4(3)^{n-1}$.

Step 4

Substitute 78,732 for t_n in the formula $t_n = 4(3)^{n-1}$.

$$78{,}732 = 4(3)^{n-1}$$

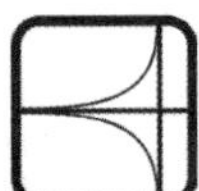

Step 5

Solve for n.

Divide both sides of the equation by 4.

$(3)^{n-1} = 19{,}683$

Take the common logarithm of both sides of the equation.

$\log (3)^{n-1} = \log 19{,}683$

Apply the power law of logarithms.

$(n - 1)\log 3 = \log 19{,}683$

Divide both sides by log 3.

$$n - 1 = \frac{\log 19{,}683}{\log 3}$$

Add 1 to both sides.

$$n = \frac{\log 19{,}683}{\log 3} + 1$$

Evaluate.

$n = 10$

The sequence has 10 terms, and 78,732 is the 10th term.

Since n must be a natural number, 19,683 must be a power of 3. The value of n could therefore be determined as follows:

$$3^{n-1} = 19{,}683$$
$$3^{n-1} = 3^9$$
$$n - 1 = 9$$
$$n = 10$$

Solving Problems Using Geometric Sequences

You can find many instances of geometric growth in real-life situations. Some of these situations include the following:

- Inflation
- Investments that grow
- Chain letters
- Bacterial growth
- Animal populations

Example

Stephen has a job that pays $25,000 per year in the first year and increases by 5% each year thereafter.

How much will Stephen earn in his fifth year of employment?

Solution

In this instance, the common ratio is 100% + 5% = 105% or 1.05, when 105% is written as a decimal.

First year	$25,000
Second year	$25,000 × 1.05 = $26,250
Third year	$26,250 × 1.05 = $27,562.50
Fourth year	$27,562.50 × 1.05 = $28,940.63
Fifth year	$28,940.63 × 1.05 = $30,387.66

Stephen will earn $30,387.66 in his fifth year of employment.

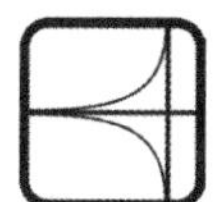

You can also find geometric decay in situations involving job raises, radioactive isotopes, or the depreciation of vehicles.

Example

A car is originally worth $25,000. Each year it depreciates by 18%.

At the end of which year will the car first be worth less than $10,000?

Solution

If the value of the car decreases 18% each year, then the common ratio is 100% – 18% = 82% or 0.82 when 82% is written as a decimal.

	Value ($)
Initial value	$25,000
End of year 1	$25,000(0.82) = $20,500
End of year 2	$20,500(0.82) = $16,810
End of year 3	$16,810(0.82) = $13,784.20
End of year 4	$13,784.20(0.82) = $11,303.04
End of year 5	$11,303.04(0.82) = $9,268.50

At the end of the fifth year, the car will be worth less than $10,000, for the first time.

Solving Problems Using Basic Arithmetic Sequences

There are many real-world situations that provide examples of arithmetic growth. When a problem arises in which the desired term number of the arithmetic sequence is small, it can be solved by generating the sequence required and then answering the given question.

Example

Each year on his birthday, David's grandparents give him money.

They started on his first birthday by giving him $10. Each birthday after that, they give him $5 more than they did the previous year.

How much money will David receive on his 10th birthday?

Solution

First, generate the pattern.

Add 5 to each term to get the subsequent term. 10, 15, 20, 25, 30, 35, 40, 45, 50, 55

On his 10th birthday, David will receive $55.00.

Solving Problems Using the General Term Formula for an Arithmetic Sequence

The general term of an arithmetic sequence is given by $t_n = a + (n - 1)d$, where t_n is the value of the nth term, a is the value of the first term in the sequence, and d is the common difference.

When solving problems using the general term formula, start by identifying all the given information, and decide what information is necessary to generate the general term.
The general term for each situation is different, so it is important to do this step first. Then, substitute the values of the known variables into the general term formula, and solve for the required (unknown) variable.

Example

Amorita starts working for a company at a yearly salary of $19,000. Each year, she gets a raise of $1,800.

How much will she be making during her fifth year with the company?

Solution

Step 1

Identify the values of a, d and n from the given information.

$a = 19{,}000$ (her starting salary)
$d = 1{,}800$ (her annual raise)
$n = 5$ (her 5th year)

Step 2

Substitute the derived values for a, d and n into the general term formula for an arithmetic sequence.

$t_n = a + (n - 1)d$
$t_5 = 19{,}000 + (5 - 1)(1{,}800)$

Step 3

Find the value of t_5.

$t_5 = 19{,}000 + (5 - 1)(1{,}800)$
$= 19{,}000 + 4(1{,}800)$
$= 19{,}000 + 7{,}200$
$= 26{,}200$

Amorita will make $26,200 in her fifth year.

During which year will she make $40,600?

Solution

Step 1

Identify the values of a, d and t_n from the given information.

$a = 19{,}000$ (her starting salary)
$d = 1{,}800$ (her annual raise)
$t_n = 40{,}600$ (the given salary)

Step 2

Substitute the derived values for a, d and t_n into the general term formula for an arithmetic sequence.

$t_n = a + (n - 1)d$
$40{,}600 = 19{,}000 + (n - 1)(1{,}800)$

Step 3

Solve for n.

$40{,}600 = 1{,}900 + (n - 1)(1{,}800)$
$40{,}600 = 19{,}000 + 1{,}800n - 1{,}800$
$40{,}600 = 1{,}800n + 17{,}200$
$23{,}400 = 1{,}800n$
$13 = n$

Amorita will make $40,600 in her 13th year of work.

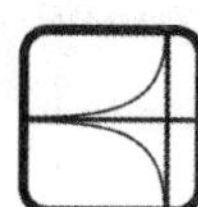

EXERCISE #1—BUILDING FUNCTIONS

Use the following information to answer the next question.

The following table shows some of the items in the inventory of a health-food store.

1	2	3	4
Item	Muesli cereal boxes	Trail mix bags	Dried fruit bags
Quantity	75	140	120
Wholesale Prices	\$2.95	\$1.80	\$3.40
Total Cost	\$221.25	\$252.00	\$408.00
Number Sold	68	125	94
Retail Price	\$4.50	\$3.40	\$5.60
Total Sales	\$306.00	\$425.00	\$526.40
Net Profit	\$84.75	\$173.00	

203. The total net profit from the three items given in the table is

A. \$118.40 B. \$376.15
C. \$665.75 D. \$784.15

204. What is the recursive formula for the sequence 47, 43, 39, 35...?

A. $t_n = 4 - t_{n-1}$

B. $t_{n+1} = t_n - 4$

C. $t_n = t_{n-1} - 2$

D. $t_{n+1} = t_n - 2$

205. A recursive function is defined by $a_n = a_{n-1} + a_{n-1}$, where $n > 0$. Which of the following functions is an equivalent function?

A. $a_n = (a_0)2n$

B. $a_n = (a_0)2^n$

C. $a_n = (a_0)n^2$

D. $a_n = (a_0)n$

206. If $f(x) = x^2 + 2x - 4$, $g(x) = x^2 + 25$, and $h(x) = f(x)g(x)$, what is $h(x)$ in simplified form?

A. $x^4 + 2x^3 - 21x^2 + 50x - 100$

B. $x^4 - 2x^3 - 29x^2 - 50x + 100$

C. $x^4 + 2x^3 + 29x^2 + 50x + 100$

D. $x^4 + 2x^3 + 21x^2 + 50x - 100$

207. Which of the following equations represents the value of a \$500 investment with a simple interest rate of 6%/*a* over several years?

A. $t_n = 30n$

B. $t_n = 3{,}000n$

C. $t_n = 500(1 + 6n)$

D. $t_n = 500(1 + 0.06n)$

208. Which of the following sequences is neither arithmetic nor geometric?

A. $\frac{1}{2}, 1, \frac{3}{2}, 2, \ldots$

B. $\frac{1}{2}, 1, \frac{3}{2}, \frac{5}{2}, \ldots$

C. $\frac{1}{2}, -1, 2, -4, \ldots$

D. $\frac{1}{2}, -1, -\frac{5}{2}, -4, \ldots$

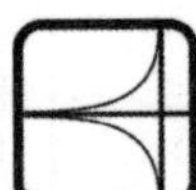

Use the following information to answer the next question.

The yearly value for the first four years of an initial investment of $800.00 is given by the sequence $824.00, $848.72, $874.18, and $900.41.

209. Which of the following investments describes the sequence?

A. $800 invested at simple interest of 3%/*a*

B. $800 invested at simple interest of 1.03%/*a*

C. $800 invested at 3%/*a* compounded annually

D. $800 invested at 6%/*a* compounded semi-annually

210. Determine the general term of the sequence $\frac{1}{64}, \frac{1}{32}, \frac{1}{16}, \frac{1}{8}, \ldots$, and then find the 12th term.

Use the following information to answer the next question.

Leroy is learning how to walk on his hands. After 1 week, he can walk for 3 seconds (s) before falling over.

211. If Leroy adds 4 s to the time he can walk on his hands for each additional week of practice, for how many seconds will he be able to walk on his hands after 6 weeks? __________ s

Use the following information to answer the next question.

In order to save money to buy a car, Renee decides to start an annuity. She deposits $500 the first month and increases the amount of each monthly deposit by $50 for a period of 15 months.

212. The value of the last deposit Renee makes is

A. $1,200 **B.** $1,900

C. $12,750 **D.** $13,125

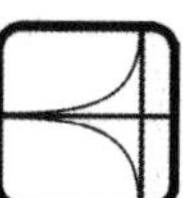

EXERCISE #1—BUILDING FUNCTIONS ANSWERS AND SOLUTIONS

203. B	206. D	209. C	212. A
204. B	207. D	210. See solution	
205. B	208. B	211. 23	

203. B

Step 1

Calculate the net profit for the dried fruit bags.

Net profit = Total sales − Total cost
= $526.40 − $408.00
= $118.40

Step 2

Calculate the net profit for all three items.

Add the net profit values for muesli, trail mix, and dried fruit.

$84.75 + $173.00+$118.40 = $376.15

204. B

Step 1

Determine the recursive pattern in the sequence.

The sequence is decreasing with each term.

Find the difference between each term.

$47 - 43 = 4$
$43 - 39 = 4$
$39 - 35 = 4$

To find the next term, subtract 4 from the previous term.

Step 2

Write the recursive formula.

The pattern in the given sequence can be written as $t_{n+1} = t_n - 4$.

205. B

Step 1

Expand the recursive function.

$a_1 = a_0 + a_0$

$a_2 = a_1 + a_1$

$a_3 = a_2 + a_2$

$a_4 = a_3 + a_3$

Step 2

Substitute the values of a_1, a_2, and a_3 into their respective equations, and simplify.

$a_1 = a_0 + a_0$

$a_1 = 2(a_0)$

$a_2 = a_1 + a_1$

$a_2 = 2(a_0) + 2(a_0)$

$a_2 = 4(a_0)$

$a_3 = a_2 + a_2$

$a_3 = 4(a_0) + 4(a_0)$

$a_3 = 8(a_0)$

$a_4 = a_3 + a_3$

$a_4 = 8(a_0) + 8(a_0)$

$a_4 = 16(a_0)$

Step 3

Extend the pattern of the function to the nth term. Notice that the coefficient of each term is equal to 2^n and a_0 is multiplied by this number. Therefore, the pattern from step 2 can be continued until the nth term, resulting in the exponential equation $a_n = (a_0)2^n$.

206. D

Step 1

Substitute $x^2 + 2x - 4$ for $f(x)$ and $x^2 + 25$ for $g(x)$ into the equation $h(x) = f(x)g(x)$.

$h(x) = (x^2 + 2x - 4)(x^2 + 25)$

Step 2

Expand by using the distributive property, and simplify by combining like terms.

$$\begin{aligned} h(x) &= (x^2 + 2x - 4)(x^2 + 25) \\ &= x^4 + 2x^3 - 4x^2 + 25x^2 + 50x - 100 \\ &= x^4 + 2x^3 + 21x^2 + 50x - 100 \end{aligned}$$

207. D

Step 1

Calculate the interest earned each year.

$$\begin{aligned} I &= Prt \\ &= (500)(0.06)(1) \\ &= \$30 \end{aligned}$$

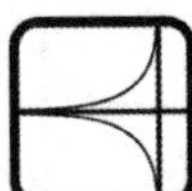

Step 2
Determine the sequence.
The value of the investment at the end of each year would form the arithmetic sequence \$530, \$560, \$590,… with a common difference of \$30.

Step 3
Determine the general term equation using the formula $t_n = a + (n-1)d$.

Substitute 530 for a and 30 for d.

$$\begin{aligned} t_n &= a + (n-1)d \\ &= 530 + (n-1)(30) \\ &= 500 + 30n \\ &= 500(1 + 0.06n) \end{aligned}$$

208. B

Step 1
Determine the first differences of the sequences.

- $\frac{1}{2}, 1, \frac{3}{2}, 2, \ldots 1 - \frac{1}{2} = \frac{1}{2}$
  $\frac{3}{2} - 1 = \frac{1}{2}$
  $2 - \frac{3}{2} = \frac{1}{2}$
  The sequence has a common difference of $\frac{1}{2}$; therefore, it is arithmetic.
- $\frac{1}{2}, -1, 2, -4, \ldots -1 - \frac{1}{2} = -1.5$
  $2 - (-1) = 3$
  $-4 - 2 = -6$
  The sequence has no common difference; therefore, it is not arithmetic.
- $\frac{1}{2}, 1, \frac{3}{2}, \frac{5}{2}, \ldots 1 - \frac{1}{2} = \frac{1}{2}$
  $\frac{3}{2} - 1 = \frac{1}{2}$
  $\frac{5}{2} - \frac{3}{2} = 1$
  The sequence has no common difference; therefore, it is not arithmetic.
- $\frac{1}{2}, -1, -\frac{5}{2}, -4, \ldots -1 - \frac{1}{2} = -1.5$
  $-\frac{5}{2} - (-1) = -1.5$
  $-4 - \left(-\frac{5}{2}\right) = -1.5$
  The sequence has a common difference of −1.5; therefore, it is arithmetic.

Step 2
Determine the ratio of consecutive terms of only the sequences $\frac{1}{2}, -1, 2, -4, \ldots$ and $\frac{1}{2}, 1, \frac{3}{2}, \frac{5}{2}, \ldots$ since the other two sequences have been determined to be arithmetic.

- $\frac{1}{2}, -1, 2, -4, \ldots$
  $\frac{-1}{\frac{1}{2}} = -2$
  $\frac{2}{-1} = -2$
  $\frac{-4}{2} = -2$
  There is a common ratio between consecutive terms of −2; therefore, it is geometric.
- $\frac{1}{2}, 1, \frac{3}{2}, \frac{5}{2}, \ldots$
  $\frac{1}{\frac{1}{2}} = 2$
  $\frac{\frac{3}{2}}{1} = \frac{3}{2}$
  $\frac{\frac{5}{2}}{\frac{3}{2}} = \frac{5}{3}$
  There is no common ratio between consecutive terms; therefore, it is not geometric.

The sequence $\frac{1}{2}, 1, \frac{3}{2}, \frac{5}{2}, \ldots$ is neither arithmetic nor geometric.

209. C

Step 1
Determine the common difference between consecutive terms in the sequence.

$$\begin{aligned} 848.72 - 824 &= 24.72 \\ 874.18 - 848.72 &= 25.46 \\ 900.41 - 874.18 &= 26.23 \end{aligned}$$

There is no common difference since the differences are not constant (24.72, 25.46, and 26.23).

Step 2
Determine the common ratio between consecutive terms.

$$\frac{848.72}{824} = 1.03$$
$$\frac{874.18}{848.72} = 1.03$$
$$\frac{900.41}{80{,}074.18} = 1.03$$

The common ratio is 1.03.

Step 3
Determine the interest rate.
Because the given sequence is geometric, the function that represents the sequence must represent compound interest.

The function $f(x) = 800(1.03)^x$ will generate the terms of the sequence.
Comparing the function to the compound interest formula $A = P(1 + i)^n$, this function describes a principal amount of $800 invested at 3%/*a* compounded annually.

210.

Step 1
Determine the general term of the sequence.
The sequence is geometric. The first term (a) is $\frac{1}{64}$, and the common ratio (r) is 2. Substitute the values into the formula for the general term $t_n = ar^{n-1}$, and solve.

$$\begin{aligned} t_n &= \frac{1}{64}(2)^{n-1} \\ &= \left(2^{-6}\right)(2)^{n-1} \\ &= 2^{-6+n-1} \\ &= 2^{n-7} \end{aligned}$$

Therefore, the general term of the sequence is $t_n = 2^{n-7}$.

Step 2
Find the 12th term.

$$\begin{aligned} t_{12} &= 2^{12-7} \\ &= 2^5 \\ &= 32 \end{aligned}$$

Therefore, the 12th term is 32.

211. 23

To calculate the time he can walk on his hands after 6 weeks, add 4 s to his total time for each week until he reaches 6 weeks.

Week of Practice	Time (s)
1	3
2	3 + 4 = 7
3	7 + 4 = 11
4	11 + 4 = 15
5	15 + 4 = 19
6	19 + 4 = 23

After practicing for 6 weeks, Leroy should be able to walk on his hands for 23 s.

212. A

The 15 deposits form an arithmetic sequence with a first term of a = $500 and a common difference of d = $50.

The last deposit is the 15th term, so substitute $n = 15$ into the formula $t_n = a + (n - 1)d$.

$$\begin{aligned} t_n &= a + (n - 1)d \\ t_{15} &= 500 + (15 - 1)50 \\ &= \$1,200 \end{aligned}$$

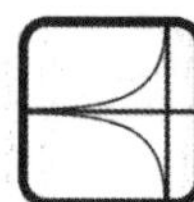

EXERCISE #2—BUILDING FUNCTIONS

Use the following information to answer the next question.

The following table shows the monthly sales activity for certain products in an electronic store.

Item	Number Sold	Price	Revenue
Printers	62	$89.99	$5,579.38
Printer cables	105	$12.39	$1,300.95
Ink cartridges	347	$21.95	$7,616.65
USB cables	93	$9.79	$910.47
Memory sticks	52	$59.99	$3,119.48

213. If the number of USB cables sold for the month had increased to 105 and the selling price remained the same, the difference in revenue for the month would have been

A. $117.48　　B. $132.95

C. $1,027.95　　D. $1,938.42

214. What is the recursive formula for the sequence 4, 10, 22, 46,...?

A. $t_{n+1} = t_n + 2$

B. $t_{n+1} = t_n + 6$

C. $t_{n+1} = 3(t_n - 1)$

D. $t_{n+1} = 2(t_n + 1)$

215. A recursive function is defined by $a_n = \frac{a_{n-1}}{2} + 1$, where $n > 0$. Which of the following functions is an equivalent function?

A. $a_n = \frac{a_0 + 2}{2^n} + 1$

B. $a_n = \frac{a_0 + 2^n - 2}{2^n} + 1$

C. $a_n = \frac{a_0 + 2^n - n}{2^n} + n$

D. $a_n = \frac{a_0 + 2^{n-1} + 1}{2^n} + n$

Use the following information to answer the next question.

A function is given by $f(x) = \frac{g(x)}{h(x)}$, where $g(x) = x^2 - 25$, $h(x) = x + 5$, and $h(x) \neq 0$.

216. The simplified form of $f(x)$ is

A. $x + 5,\ x \neq 5$

B. $x - 5,\ x \neq 5$

C. $x - 5,\ x \neq -5$

D. $x + 5,\ x \neq -5$

217. The 30th term of the sequence 4, 8, 12, 16, … is __________.

218. Which of the following sequences is arithmetic?

A. 5, 25, 125, 625, …

B. 5, 10, 15, 20, …

C. 5, 10, 20, 40, …

D. 5, 7, 11, 17, …

219. The eighth term of the sequence $\frac{1}{2}$, 2, 8, 32, … is __________.

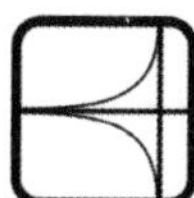

Use the following information to answer the next question.

The cost of renting a full-sized car is $38 per day plus 14 ¢ per kilometer for any distance traveled beyond 100 km per day. This chart illustrates the cost of driving a full-sized car up to 350 km per day.

Distance per Day (km)	Cost ($)
100	38.00
150	t_2
200	t_3
250	t_4
300	t_5
350	t_6

220. What is the cost of renting a full-sized car for one day and driving 350 km?

A. $66.00 **B.** $73.00

C. $80.00 **D.** $87.00

Use the following information to answer the next question.

A display of baseball cards is arranged in rows in such a way that the number of cards in each row forms an arithmetic sequence. There are 85 cards in row 1, 78 cards in row 2, 71 cards in row 3, and so on.

221. Which row will contain 15 cards?

A. Row 11 **B.** Row 10

C. Row 9 **D.** Row 8

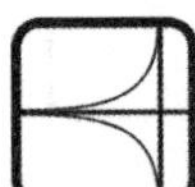

EXERCISE #2—BUILDING FUNCTIONS ANSWERS AND SOLUTIONS

213. A	216. C	219. 8192
214. D	217. 120	220. B
215. B	218. B	221. A

213. A

Step 1
Calculate the new revenue.
The total number of USB cables sold increases to 105, and the selling price remains the same ($9.79).
105 × $9.79 = $1,027.95

Step 2
Calculate the difference in revenue for the month.
$1,027.95 – $910.47 = $117.48
The difference in revenue for the month is $117.48.

214. D

Step 1
Determine the recursive pattern in the given sequence, 4, 10, 22, 46.

$$\frac{10}{2} - 1 = 5 - 1 = 4$$

$$\frac{22}{2} - 1 = 11 - 1 = 10$$

$$\frac{46}{2} - 1 = 23 - 1 = 22$$

To obtain the next term, you add 1 to the previous term and then multiply it by 2.

Step 2
Write the pattern in mathematical notation.
The pattern in the given sequence can be written as $t_{n+1} = 2(t_n + 1)$.

215. B

Step 1
Expand the recursive function.

$$a_1 = \frac{a_0}{2} + 1$$

$$a_2 = \frac{a_1}{2} + 1$$

$$a_3 = \frac{a_2}{2} + 1$$

$$a_4 = \frac{a_3}{2} + 1$$

Step 2
Substitute the values of a_1, a_2, and a_3 into their respective equations, and simplify.

$$a_1 = \frac{a_0}{2} + 1$$

$$a_2 = \frac{a_1}{2} + 1$$

$$a_2 = \frac{\frac{a_0}{2} + 1}{2} + 1$$

$$a_2 = \frac{a_0 + 2}{4} + 1$$

$$a_3 = \frac{a_2}{2} + 1$$

$$a_3 = \frac{\frac{a_0 + 2}{4} + 1}{2} + 1$$

$$a_3 = \frac{a_0 + 6}{8} + 1$$

$$a_4 = \frac{a_3}{2} + 1$$

$$a_4 = \frac{\frac{a_0 + 6}{8} + 1}{2} + 1$$

$$a_4 = \frac{a_0 + 14}{16} + 1$$

Step 3
Extend the pattern of the function to the nth term.
Notice that each term has a similar appearance.
The denominator always has a value of 2^n, and the number in the numerator is always 2 less than the denominator $2^n - 2$. The other values in the term, a_0 and +1, remain constant for every term.
Therefore, the pattern from step 2 can be continued until the nth term, resulting in the function

$$a_n = \frac{a_0 + 2^n - 2}{2^n} + 1.$$

216. C

Step 1

Substitute $x^2 - 25$ for $g(x)$ and $x + 5$ for $h(x)$ in the equation $f(x) = \frac{g(x)}{h(x)}$.

$$f(x) = \frac{x^2 - 25}{x + 5}$$

Step 2

State the non-permissible values.

$$x + 5 \neq 0$$
$$x \neq -5$$

The non-permissible value of x is -5.

Step 3

Factor the numerator, and reduce.

$$\begin{aligned} f(x) &= \frac{x^2 - 25}{x + 5} \\ &= \frac{(x - 5)(x + 5)}{x + 5} \\ &= x - 5 \end{aligned}$$

217. 120

The sequence is arithmetic with a first term of $a = 4$ and a common difference of $d = 4$. Substitute these values into the formula $t_n = a + (n - 1)d$.

$$\begin{aligned} t_n &= a + (n - 1)d \\ t_{30} &= 4 + (30 - 1)(4) \\ t_{30} &= 4 + 116 \\ t_{30} &= 120 \end{aligned}$$

218. B

Step 1

Determine the first differences of the sequence 5, 25, 125, 625, ...

$$\begin{aligned} 25 - 5 &= 20 \\ 125 - 25 &= 100 \\ 625 - 125 &= 500 \end{aligned}$$

The differences are not constant; therefore, the sequence is not arithmetic.

Step 2

Determine the first differences of the sequence 5, 10, 20, 40, ...

$$\begin{aligned} 10 - 5 &= 5 \\ 20 - 10 &= 10 \\ 40 - 20 &= 20 \end{aligned}$$

The differences are not constant; therefore, the sequence is not arithmetic.

Step 3

Determine the first differences of the sequence 5, 7, 11, 17, ...

$$\begin{aligned} 7 - 5 &= 2 \\ 11 - 7 &= 4 \\ 17 - 11 &= 6 \end{aligned}$$

The differences are not constant; therefore, the sequence is not arithmetic.

Step 4

Determine the first differences of the sequence 5, 10, 15, 20, ...

$$\begin{aligned} 10 - 5 &= 5 \\ 15 - 10 &= 5 \\ 20 - 15 &= 5 \end{aligned}$$

The differences are constant; therefore, the sequence is arithmetic.

219. 8192

Step 1

Determine the first differences of the sequence.

$$\begin{aligned} 2 - \frac{1}{2} &= 1.5 \\ 8 - 2 &= 6 \\ 32 - 8 &= 24 \end{aligned}$$

The differences are not constant, so this sequence is not arithmetic.

Step 2

Determine the ratio of consecutive terms of the sequence.

$$\frac{2}{\frac{1}{2}} = 4$$
$$\frac{8}{2} = 4$$
$$\frac{32}{8} = 4$$

The ratios are constant, a common ratio, so this sequence is geometric.

Step 3

Determine the general term formula for the given sequence using $t_n = ar^{n-1}$.

The sequence is geometric with a first term of $a = \frac{1}{2}$ and a common ratio of $r = 4$. Substitute into the formula $t_n = ar^{n-1}$.

$$\begin{aligned} t_n &= ar^{n-1} \\ &= \frac{1}{2}(4)^{n-1} \end{aligned}$$

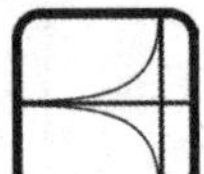

Step 4

Substitute 8 for n, and solve.

$$t_n = \frac{1}{2}(4)^{n-1}$$
$$t_8 = \frac{1}{2}(4)^{8-1}$$
$$t_8 = \frac{1}{2}(4)^{7}$$
$$t_8 = \frac{1}{2}(16{,}384)$$
$$t_8 = 8{,}192$$

220. B

Step 1

Determine the common difference.

The amount of money charged for each 50 km over the daily amount of kilometers is the common difference.

$0.14 / km × 50 km = $7.00

Therefore, the common difference is $7.00.

Step 2

Finish the table, and determine the value of t_6.

This process is illustrated in the given table.

Distance per Day (km)	Cost ($)
100	38.00
150	$t_2 = 38.00 + 7.00$ $= 45.00$
200	$t_3 = 45.00 + 7.00$ $= 52.00$
250	$t_4 = 52.00 + 7.00$ $= 59.00$
300	$t_5 = 59.00 + 7.00$ $= 66.00$
350	$t_6 = 66.00 + 7.00$ $= 73.00$

Therefore, it costs $73.00 to rent a full-sized car for one day and drive 350 km.

221. A

An arithmetic sequence is one that increases or decreases at a constant rate. The difference between two successive terms is called the common difference.

The nth term of an arithmetic sequence is defined by the formula $t_n = a + (n - 1)d$, where n is a positive integer, t_n is the nth term, and d is the common difference.

Step 1

Identify the first term and the common difference of the sequence.

The number of cards in the first row is 85. So, $a = 85$.

Find the common difference, d, by subtracting successive terms.

$78 - 85 = -7$
$71 - 78 = -7$

The value of d is -7.

Step 2

Apply the general term formula.

Since the number of cards in the nth row is 15, the value of t_n is 15.

Substitute the known values into the general term formula, and solve for n.

$$t_n = a + (n - 1)d$$
$$15 = 85 + (n - 1)(-7)$$
$$15 = 85 - 7n + 7$$
$$15 = -7n + 92$$
$$-77 = -7n$$
$$11 = n$$

The 11th row will contain 15 cards.

Modifying Functions

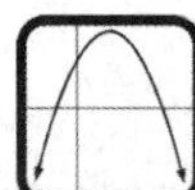

MODIFYING FUNCTIONS

Table of Correlations				
Standard		Concepts	Exercise #1	Exercise #2
Unit2.11	Build new functions from existing functions.			
F-BF.3	*Identify the effect on the graph of replacing f(x) by f(x) + k, k f(x), f(kx), and f(x + k) for specific values of k (both positive and negative); find the value of k given the graphs. Experiment with cases and illustrate an explanation of the effects on the graph using technology. Include recognizing even and odd functions from their graphs and algebraic expressions for them.*	Determining the Properties of Even and Odd Polynomial Functions	163	175
		Horizontal Stretches	222	229
		Vertical Stretches	223	230
		Horizontal Translations	224	231
		Vertical Translations	225	232
		Reflections in the *y*-axis	226	233
		Reflections about the *x*-Axis	227	234
		Describing the Role of *d* in the Exponential Function of the Form $y = B^{x} + d$, $B > 0$	228	235

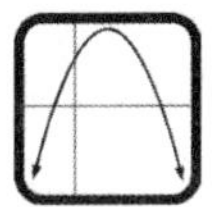

F-BF.3 Identify the effect on the graph of replacing f(x) by f(x) + k, k f(x), f(kx), and f(x + k) for specific values of k (both positive and negative); find the value of k given the graphs. Experiment with cases and illustrate an explanation of the effects on the graph using technology. Include recognizing even and odd functions from their graphs and algebraic expressions for them.

Horizontal Stretches

A horizontal stretch occurs when a graph is stretched horizontally about a vertical line by a specific factor. The graph is usually stretched about the *y*-axis. When the graph of $y = f(x)$ is transformed to the graph of $y = f(bx)$, the value of b causes a horizontal stretch about the *y*-axis by a factor of $\frac{1}{|b|}$, where $b \neq 0$. If $b < 0$, there is a reflection in the *y*-axis.

The *x*-coordinate of a transformed point is equal to $\frac{1}{b}$ times the value of the *x*-coordinate of the original corresponding point. The *y*-coordinates of the original and the corresponding transformed point are equal.

Example

When the graph of $y = \sqrt{x} + 3$ is stretched horizontally about the *y*-axis by a factor of $\frac{1}{2}$, the resulting graph is $y = \sqrt{2x} + 3$.

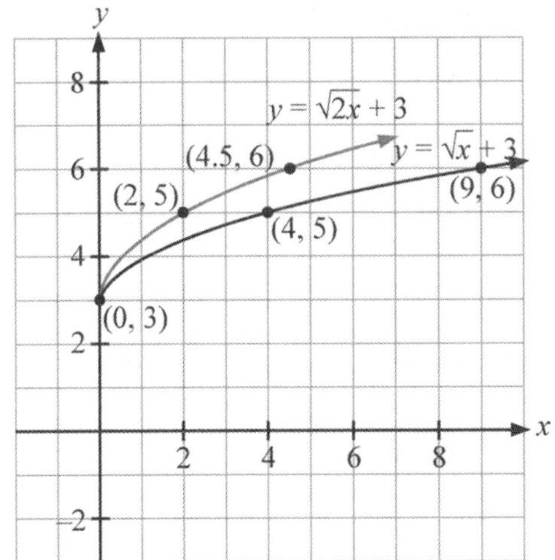

To produce the equation $y = \sqrt{2x} + 3$ from $y = \sqrt{x} + 3$, it is necessary to replace x with $2x$. Observe that the *y*-coordinate of any ordered pair on the original graph is equal to the *y*-coordinate of the corresponding ordered pair on the transformed graph. However, the *x*-coordinates of the ordered pairs on the transformed graph of $y = \sqrt{2x} + 3$ are $\frac{1}{2}$ the value of the *x*-coordinates of the corresponding ordered pairs on the graph of $y = \sqrt{x} + 3$. The *y*-intercept of each graph, (0, 3), does not change, so it is an invariant point.

When a graph is stretched horizontally about the *y*-axis by a factor of b, the horizontal distance from the *y*-axis to each transformed point is b times the original horizontal distance.

Example

If the graph of $y = f(x)$ contains the point (2, 5), then the corresponding point on the graph of $y = f\left(\frac{1}{2}x\right)$ is (4, 5). The horizontal distance from (4, 5) to the *y*-axis is 4 units, which is twice the horizontal distance from (2, 5) to the *y*-axis.

Example

How does the graph of $y = f(3x)$ compare with the graph of $y = f(x)$?

Solution

In order to transform the equation $y = f(x)$ to the equation $y = f(3x)$, x is replaced with $3x$ in the equation $y = f(x)$. When x is replaced with $3x$ in the equation $y = f(x)$, the graph of $y = f(x)$ will be horizontally stretched about the *y*-axis by a factor of $\frac{1}{3}$. Thus, $y = f(3x)$ is the graph of $y = f(x)$ stretched horizontally about the *y*-axis by a factor of $\frac{1}{3}$.

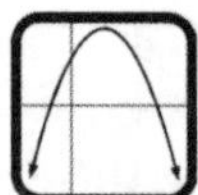

When a graph is stretched horizontally, the y-coordinates remain constant. It follows that the y-intercepts are not affected by a horizontal stretch about the y-axis. Since the y-coordinates are constant, the range of the graph is also constant.

When a graph is stretched horizontally by a factor of b, the x-coordinates are replaced by bx. It follows that the x-intercepts change from $(x, 0)$ to $(bx, 0)$. Since the x-coordinates change, the domain of the graph will be changed from $m \le x \le n$ to $bm \le x \le bn$.

Example

The graph of $y = f(x)$ is given.

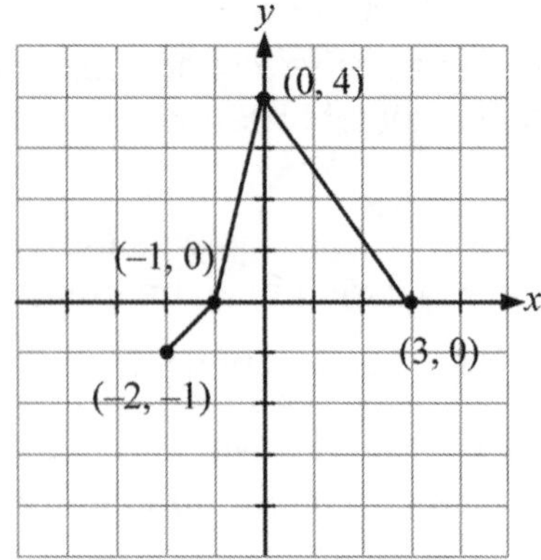

Determine the domain and range of the function after a horizontal stretch about the y-axis by a factor of 3.

Solution

Step 1

Determine the domain and range of $y = f(x)$.

- The domain of $y = f(x)$ is $-2 \le x \le 3$.
- The range of $y = f(x)$ is $-1 \le y \le 4$.

Step 2

Determine the domain and range of $y = f(x)$ after a horizontal stretch about the y-axis by a factor of 3.

When a graph is stretched about the y-axis by a factor of b, the domain of the graph will be changed from $m \le x \le n$ to $bm \le x \le bn$.

It follows that the domain of the transformed function is $3(-2) \le x \le 3(3)$, or $-6 \le x \le 9$.

The range of a function does not change after a horizontal stretch about the y-axis; therefore, the range of the stretched function is $-1 \le y \le 4$.

Determine the x- and y-intercepts of the given function after a horizontal stretch about the y-axis by a factor of 3.

Solution

Step 1

Determine the x and y-intercepts of $y = f(x)$.

- The x-intercepts of $y = f(x)$ are $(-1, 0)$ and $(3, 0)$.
- The y-intercept of $y = f(x)$ is $(0, 4)$.

Step 2

Determine the x- and y-intercepts of the stretched function.

When a graph is stretched horizontally by a factor of b, the x-intercepts change from $(x, 0)$ to $(bx, 0)$. The x-intercepts of the stretched function are $(3(-1), 0)$ and $(3(3), 0)$, or $(-3, 0)$ and $(9, 0)$.

Since y-intercepts are not affected by a stretch about the y-axis, the y-intercept of the stretched function is $(0, 4)$.

To sketch the graph of $y = f(bx)$ by transforming the graph of $y = f(x)$, take the following steps:

1. Select appropriate ordered pairs located on the graph of $y = f(x)$.
2. Apply the stretch factor to the x-coordinate of each selected ordered pair on the graph of $y = f(x)$. Since the graph is stretched horizontally about the y-axis by a factor of $\frac{1}{|b|}$, a point, (x, y), on the graph of $y = f(x)$ will be transformed to the corresponding point $\left(\frac{1}{b}x, y\right)$ on the graph of $y = f(bx)$. The reciprocal of b is $\frac{1}{b}$.
3. Plot the corresponding ordered pairs on a grid, and join the points to form the transformed graph.

Example

The graph of $y = x + 4$ is shown.

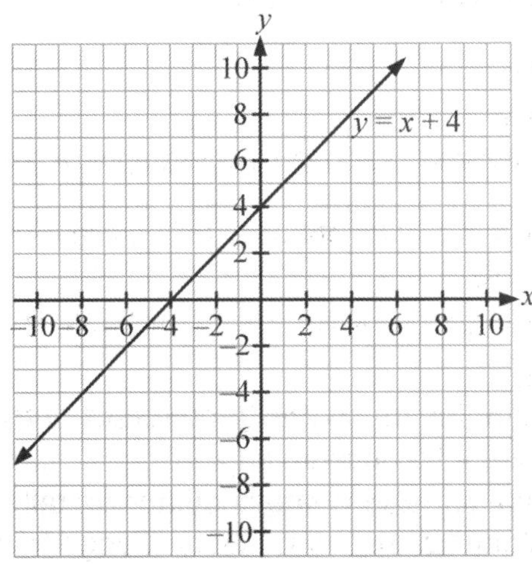

On the same axis, sketch the graph of the transformed function $y = \frac{1}{2}x + 4$.

Solution

Step 1

Determine the transformations applied to the graph of $y = x + 4$ in order to transform it to the graph of $y = \frac{1}{2}x + 4$.

Since the graph of $y = x + 4$ is transformed to the graph of $y = \frac{1}{2}x + 4$, x has been replaced by $\frac{1}{2}x$ in the equation $y = x + 4$. Thus, the graph of $y = x + 4$ will be horizontally stretched about the y-axis by a factor of 2. (The reciprocal of $\frac{1}{2}$ is 2.)

Step 2

Select appropriate ordered pairs located on the graph of $y = x + 4$.

One option is to choose the ordered pairs (2, 6), (0, 4), (–4, 0), and (–5, –1).

Step 3

Apply the stretch factor to the x-coordinate of each ordered pair on the graph of $y = x + 4$.

Since the graph is stretched horizontally about the y-axis by a factor of 2, a point (x, y) on the graph of $y = x + 4$ will be transformed to the corresponding point $(2x, y)$ on the graph of $y = \frac{1}{2}x + 4$. (The reciprocal of 2 is $\frac{1}{2}$.)

- Point (2, 6) becomes $(2 \times 2, 6) = (4, 6)$.
- Point (0, 4) becomes $(2 \times 0, 4) = (0, 4)$.
- Point (–4, 0) becomes $(2 \times -4, 0) = (-8, 0)$.
- Point (–5, –1) becomes $(2 \times -5, -1) = (-10, -1)$.

Step 4

Plot the corresponding ordered pairs on a grid, and join the points to form the basis for creating the graph of the transformed graph.

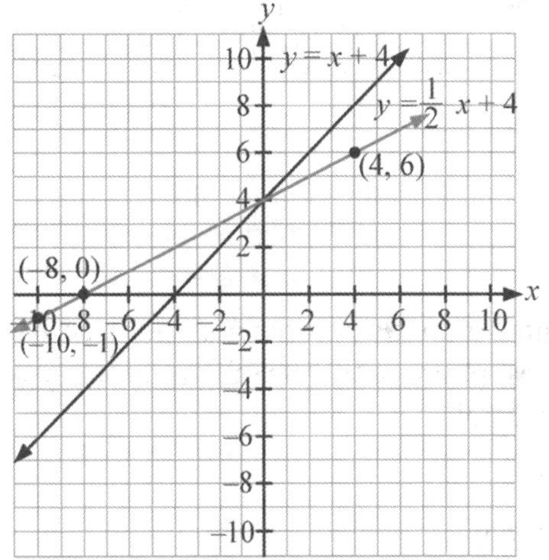

Vertical Stretches

A vertical stretch occurs when a given graph is stretched vertically about a horizontal line (usually the x-axis) by a certain factor. When the graph of $y = f(x)$ is transformed to the graph of $\frac{1}{a}y = f(x)$, or $y = af(x)$, the value of a causes a vertical stretch about the x-axis by a factor of $|a|$, $a \neq 0$. If $a < 0$, there is a reflection in the x-axis.

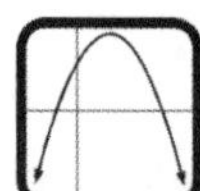

Example

When the graph of $y = \sqrt{x}$ is stretched vertically about the x-axis by a factor of 2, the resulting graph is $\frac{1}{2}y = \sqrt{x}$.

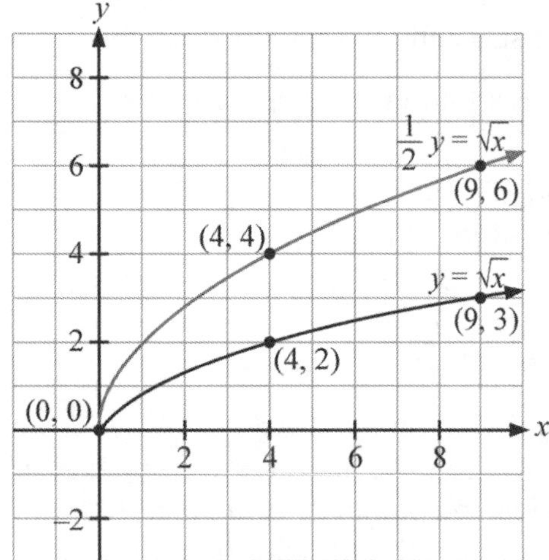

To produce the equation $\frac{1}{2}y = \sqrt{x}$ from $y = \sqrt{x}$, y is replaced with $\frac{1}{2}y$. The x-coordinate of an ordered pair on the original graph and the x-coordinate of the corresponding ordered pair on the transformed graph are equal. However, the y-coordinate of an ordered pair on the transformed graph, $\frac{1}{2}y = \sqrt{x}$, is twice the value of the y-coordinate of the corresponding ordered pair on the graph of $y = \sqrt{x}$.

When y is replaced with $\frac{1}{a}y$ in the equation $y = f(x)$, the graph of $y = f(x)$ is stretched vertically about the x-axis by a factor of $|a|$, resulting in the graph of $\frac{1}{a}y = f(x)$, or $y = af(x)$. As a result, a point (x, y) on the graph of $y = f(x)$ will be transformed to the point (x, ay) on the graph of $\frac{1}{a}y = f(x)$ because the reciprocal of $\frac{1}{a}$ is a. Thus, the y-coordinate of a transformed point is equal to a times the value of the y-coordinate of the original point, and the x-coordinates of the original and transformed points are equal.

When a graph is stretched vertically about the x-axis, the x-intercept is an invariant point.

Example

How can the graph of $\frac{1}{3}y = f(x)$ be obtained from the graph of $y = f(x)$?

Solution

In order to transform the equation $y = f(x)$ to the equation $\frac{1}{3}y = f(x)$, y is replaced with $\frac{1}{3}y$ in the equation $y = f(x)$.

Since $\frac{1}{a} = \frac{1}{3}$, the vertical stretch factor is 3.

Thus, the graph of $y = f(x)$ is stretched vertically about the x-axis by a factor of 3 to give the graph of $\frac{1}{3}y = f(x)$.

Since $\frac{1}{3}y = f(x)$ is usually changed to $y = 3f(x)$, the coefficient 3 is the vertical stretch factor.

In order to transform the graph of $y = f(x)$ into the graph of $\frac{1}{a}y = f(x)$, follow these steps:

1. Determine the vertical stretch factor.
2. Select appropriate ordered pairs located on the graph of $y = f(x)$.
3. Apply the stretch factor to the y-coordinate of each selected ordered pair on the graph of $y = f(x)$. Since the graph is stretched vertically about the x-axis by a factor of a, a point (x, y) on the graph of $y = f(x)$ will be transformed to the corresponding point (x, ay) on the graph of $\frac{1}{a}y = f(x)$, or $y = af(x)$, because the reciprocal of a is $\frac{1}{a}$.
4. Plot the corresponding ordered pairs on a grid, and use these ordered pairs to create the necessary graph.

Example

The graph of $y = x^2 - 4$ is shown.

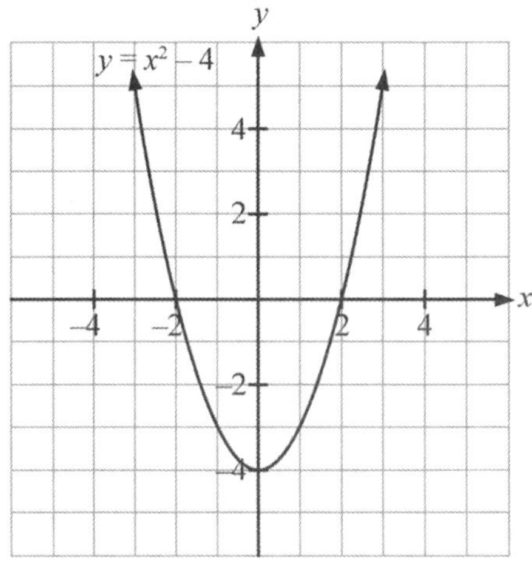

On the same axis, sketch the graph of the transformed function $y = \frac{1}{2}x^2 - 2$.

Solution

Step 1

Determine the stretch factor by rewriting the transformed equation of the function in the form $\frac{1}{a}y = f(x)$.

The equation $y = \frac{1}{2}x^2 - 2$ can be written as $y = \frac{1}{2}(x^2 - 4)$ by factoring out $\frac{1}{2}$ from the expression $\frac{1}{2}x^2 - 2$. The equation $y = \frac{1}{2}(x^2 - 4)$ is equivalent to $2y = x^2 - 4$.

Since the graph of $y = x^2 - 4$ is transformed to the graph of $2y = x^2 - 4$, y has been replaced by $2y$ in the equation $y = x^2 - 4$.

Thus, the graph of $y = x^2 - 4$ will be vertically stretched about the x-axis by a factor of $\frac{1}{2}$.

(The reciprocal of 2 is $\frac{1}{2}$.)

Step 2

Select appropriate ordered pairs located on the graph of $y = x^2 - 4$.

One option is to choose the ordered pairs $(-3, 5)$, $(-2, 0)$, $(0, -4)$, $(2, 0)$, and $(3, 5)$.

Step 3
Apply the stretch factor to the y-coordinate of each selected ordered pair on the graph of $y = x^2 - 4$.
Since the graph is stretched vertically about the x-axis by a factor of $\frac{1}{2}$, a point (x, y) on the graph of $y = x^2 - 4$ will be transformed to the corresponding point $\left(x, \frac{1}{2}y\right)$ on the graph of $2y = x^2 - 4$. (The reciprocal of 2 is $\frac{1}{2}$).

- Point $(-3, 5)$ becomes $\left(-3, \frac{1}{2} \times 5\right) = (-3, 2.5)$.
- Point $(-2, 0)$ becomes $\left(-2, \frac{1}{2} \times 0\right) = (-2, 0)$.
- Point $(0, -4)$ becomes $\left(0, \frac{1}{2} \times -4\right) = (0, -2)$.
- Point $(2, 0)$ becomes $\left(2, \frac{1}{2} \times 0\right) = (2, 0)$.
- Point $(3, 5)$ becomes $\left(3, \frac{1}{2} \times 5\right) = (3, 2.5)$.

Step 4
Plot the corresponding ordered pairs on the grid, and use these points to create the necessary graph.

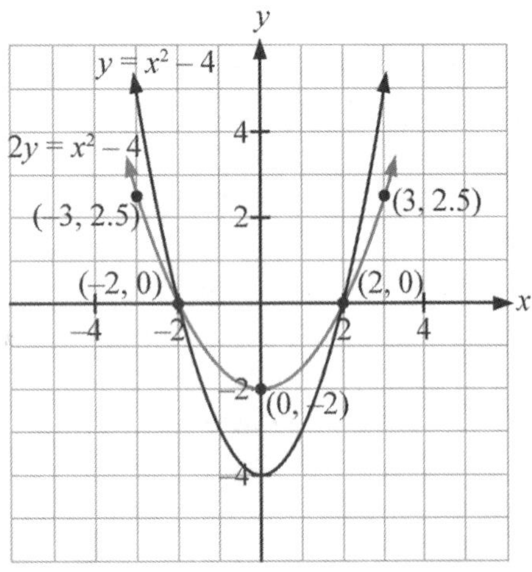

When a graph is stretched vertically about the x-axis by a factor of 2, the vertical distance from the x-axis to each transformed point is twice the original vertical distance.

Example
If the graph of $y = f(x)$ contains the point $(2, 5)$, the corresponding point on the graph of $y = 2f(x)$ is $(2, 10)$. The vertical distance from $(2, 10)$ to the x-axis is 10 units, which is twice the vertical distance from $(2, 5)$ to the x-axis.

When a graph is stretched vertically, the x-coordinate remains constant.

Horizontal Translations

A horizontal translation occurs when a graph is shifted left or right a certain number of units. When the graph of $y = f(x)$ is transformed into the graph of $y = f(x - h)$, the value of h causes a horizontal translation. When $h < 0$, the graph of $y = f(x)$ is translated to the left $|h|$ units, and when $h > 0$, the graph is translated to the right h units.

In general, to produce the equation $y = f(x - h)$ from $y = f(x)$, x is replaced with $x - h$.

Example

The graphs of $f(x) = x^2$ and $f(x) = (x - 2)^2$ are given.

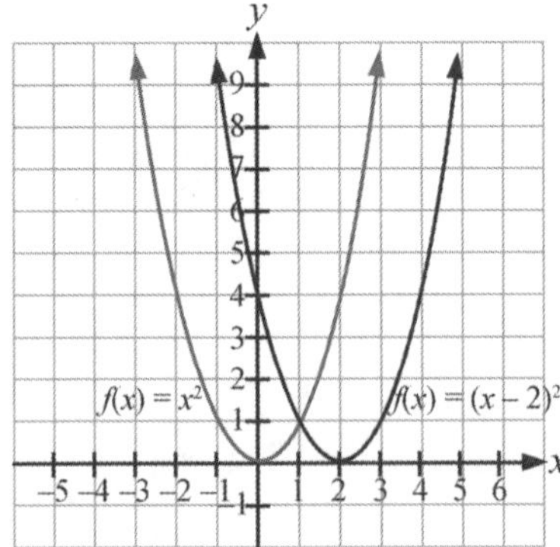

How can the graph of $f(x) = (x - 2)^2$ be obtained by translating the graph of $f(x) = x^2$?

Solution

The graph of $f(x) = (x - 2)^2$ is translated 2 units to the right of $f(x) = x^2$. This is because the equation $f(x) = (x - 2)^2$ is produced from $f(x) = x^2$ by replacing x with $(x - 2)$.

Example

The graphs of $f(x) = x^2$ and $f(x) = (x + 2)^2$ are given.

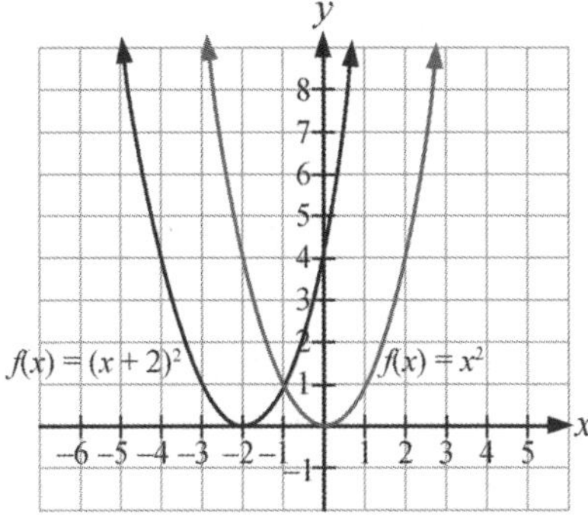

Describe how the graph of $f(x) = (x + 2)^2$ can be obtained by translating the graph of $f(x) = x^2$.

Solution

The graph of $f(x) = (x + 2)^2$ is translated 2 units to the left of $f(x) = x^2$. This is because the equation $f(x) = (x + 2)^2$ is produced from $f(x) = x^2$ by replacing x with $(x - (-2))$, or simply $(x + 2)$.

Example

Use a graphing calculator to graph $y = \sqrt{x}$ and $y = \sqrt{x + 6}$. Describe how the second graph can be obtained by translating the first graph.

Solution

The graphs of $y = \sqrt{x}$ and $y = \sqrt{x + 6}$ are shown using a window setting of x:$[-10, 10, 1]$ and y:$[-5, 5, 1]$.

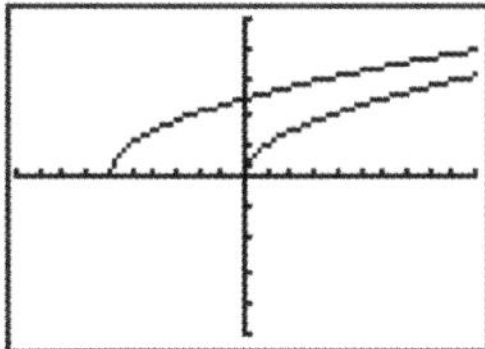

$y = \sqrt{x + 6}$ can be rewritten in the general form $y = f(x - h)$ as $y = \sqrt{x - (-6)}$. Since $h = -6$, the horizontal translation is 6 units to the left.

Thus, the graph of $y = \sqrt{x + 6}$ can be obtained from the graph of $y = \sqrt{x}$ by translating the graph of $y = \sqrt{x}$ 6 horizontal units to the left.

When a graph is translated horizontally, the y-coordinate of a given point will remain constant. Only the x-coordinate of that point changes. A coordinate point (x, y) on the graph of $y = f(x)$ will be transformed to the point $(x + h, y)$ on the graph of $y = f(x - h)$. For example, if the coordinate point $(-4, 1)$ is on the graph of $y = f(x)$, the corresponding point on the graph of $y = f(x + 2)$ is $(-4 - 2, 1) = (-6, 2)$. Remember that $y = f(x + 2)$ is equivalent to $y = f(x - (-2))$.

It follows that the x-intercepts are transformed from $(x, 0)$ to $(x + h, 0)$. There are no special rules for determining y-intercepts after a horizontal translation.

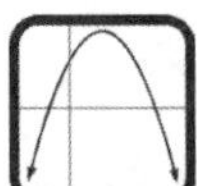

Example

Point (3, 9) is on the graph of $y = x^2$.
If $y = x^2$ is changed to $y = (x - 2)^2$, how will the point (3, 9) change?

Solution

When the graph of $y = x^2$ is transformed to the graph of $y = (x - 2)^2$, the graph of $y = x^2$ will be horizontally translated 2 units to the right. Thus, every point (x, y) on the graph of $y = x^2$ will be transformed to the point $(x + 2, y)$ on the graph of $y = (x - 2)^2$. Since the point (3, 9) is on the graph of $y = x^2$, the graph of $y = (x - 2)^2$ will contain the point $(3 + 2, 9) = (5, 9)$.

The point (3, 9) will be translated 2 units to the right.

Since the y-coordinates of $y = f(x - h)$ are the same as $y = f(x)$, the range of the translated graph does not change. The domain of the graph will be transformed h units to the right, from $m \le x \le n$ to $m + h \le x \le n + h$.

Example

The graph of $y = f(x)$ has a domain of $6 \le x \le 11$ and a range of $4 \le y \le 8$.

Determine the domain and range of $y = f(x + 6)$.

Solution

The domain of the graph of $y = f(x - h)$ will be $m + h \le x \le n + h$, where $m \le x \le n$ is the domain of $y = f(x)$. The value of h is –6 because $y = f(x + 6)$ is equivalent to $y = f(x - (-6))$. The domain of $y = f(x + 6)$ is $(6 - 6) \le x \le (11 - 6)$, or $0 \le x \le 5$.

Since the y-coordinates have not changed, the range of the translated graph will not change. The range is $4 \le y \le 8$.

Vertical Translations

A vertical translation occurs when a given graph is shifted down or up a certain number of units. When the graph of $y = f(x)$ is transformed to the graph of $y - k = f(x)$, the value of k causes a vertical translation. The equation $y - k = f(x)$ can also be written as $y = f(x) + k$. When $k < 0$, the graph of $y = f(x)$ is translated down $|k|$ units, and when $k > 0$, the graph is translated up k units.

For example, compare the graph of $f(x) = x^2$ with the graph of $f(x) = x^2 - 2$.

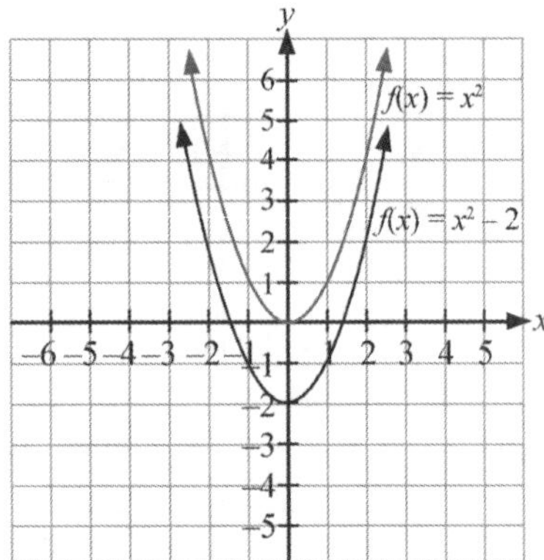

The graph of $f(x) = x^2 - 2$ is the graph of $f(x) = x^2$ translated 2 units down.

Next, compare the graph of $f(x) = x^2$ with the graph of $f(x) = x^2 + 2$.

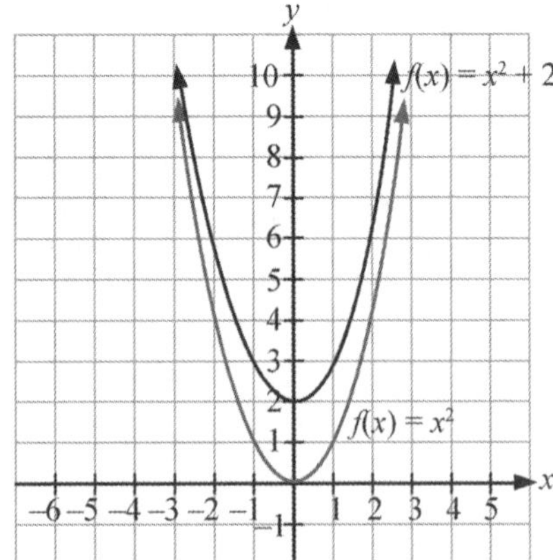

The graph of $f(x) = x^2 + 2$ is the graph of $f(x) = x^2$ translated 2 units up.

To produce the equation $f(x) = x^2 - 2$ from $f(x) = x^2$, follow these steps:

1. Write $f(x) = x^2$ as $y = x^2$.
2. Since the graph of $y = x^2$ is translated 2 units down, replace y with $y + 2$. Remember that $y + 2$ is equivalent to $y - (-2)$. $y + 2 = x^2$
3. Solve for y. $y = x^2 - 2$
4. Write $y = x^2 - 2$ in function notation. $f(x) = x^2 - 2$

Similarly, to produce the equation $f(x) = x^2 + 2$ from $f(x) = x^2$, follow these steps:

1. Write $f(x) = x^2$ as $y = x^2$.
2. Since the graph of $y = x^2$ is translated 2 units up, replace y with $y - 2$. Remember that $y - 2$ is equivalent to $y - (+2)$. $y - 2 = x^2$
3. Solve for y. $y = x^2 + 2$
4. Write $y = x^2 + 2$ in function notation. $f(x) = x^2 + 2$

In general, to produce the equation $y - k = f(x)$ from $y = f(x)$, replace y with $y - k$.

Example

Use a graphing calculator to graph $y = \sqrt{x}$ and $y = \sqrt{x} + 5$. Describe how the second graph can be obtained by translating the first graph.

Solution

The graphs of $y = \sqrt{x}$ and $y = \sqrt{x} + 5$ are shown using a window setting of x:[−5, 5, 1] and y:[−2, 10, 1].

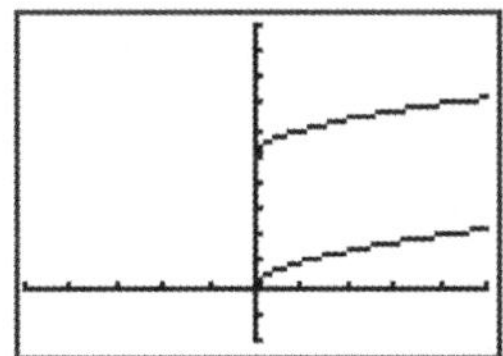

Recall that the function $y = \sqrt{x} + 5$ can be written in the general form, $y - k = f(x)$, as $y - 5 = \sqrt{x}$. Notice that $k = 5$ so the vertical translation is 5 units up. In the form $y = \sqrt{x} + 5$, the constant 5 is used to describe the vertical translation. Thus, the graph of $y = \sqrt{x} + 5$ can be obtained from the graph of $y = \sqrt{x}$ by translating the graph of $y = \sqrt{x}$ 5 vertical units up.

When a graph is translated vertically, the x-coordinate of a given point remains constant, but the y-coordinate of that point will change. A coordinate point (x, y) on the graph of $y = f(x)$ will be transformed to the point $(x, y + k)$ on the graph of $y - k = f(x)$. For example, if the coordinate point (3, −1) is on the graph of $y = f(x)$, then the corresponding point on the graph of $y + 4 = f(x)$ is $(3, -1 - 4) = (3, -5)$. Since $y + 4 = f(x)$ is equivalent to $y - (-4) = f(x)$, $k = -4$.

It follows that the y-intercepts are transformed from $(0, y)$ to $(0, y + k)$. There are no special rules for determining x-intercepts after a vertical translation.

Example

The point (3, 9) is on the graph of $y = x^2$. If $y = x^2$ is changed to $y - 2 = x^2$, how will the point (3, 9) change?

Solution

When the graph of $y = x^2$ is transformed to the graph of $y - 2 = x^2$ (or $y = x^2 + 2$), the graph of $y = x^2$ will be translated 2 units up. Thus, every point (x, y) on the graph of $y = x^2$ will be transformed to the point $(x, y + 2)$ on the graph of $y - 2 = x^2$. Since (3, 9) is on the graph of $y = x^2$, the graph of $y - 2 = x^2$ will contain the point $(3, 9 + 2) = (3, 11)$.

The point (3, 9) will be translated vertically 2 units up.

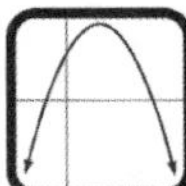

Since the x-coordinates of $y - k = f(x)$ are the same as $y = f(x)$, the domain of the translated graph will not change. The range of the graph will be transformed from $s \le y \le t$ to $s + k \le y \le t + k$.

Example

The graph of $y = f(x)$ has a domain of $6 \le x \le 11$ and a range of $4 \le y \le 8$.

Determine the domain and range of $y - 3 = f(x)$.

Solution

Since the x-coordinates have not changed, the domain of the translated graph will not have changed. The domain is $6 \le x \le 11$.

The range of the graph $y - k = f(x)$ will be $s + k \le y \le t + k$, where $s \le y \le t$ is the range of $y = f(x)$. The range of $y - 3 = f(x)$ is $(4 + 3) \le y \le (8 + 3)$, or $7 \le y \le 11$.

Reflections in the y-axis

A **horizontal reflection** occurs when a graph is reflected in the y-axis in such a way that the y-axis acts like a mirror. When x is replaced with $-x$ in the equation $y = f(x)$, the graph of $y = f(x)$ will be reflected in the y-axis, resulting in the graph of $y = f(-x)$.

Compare the graph of $y = 2x + 4$ with the graph of $y = 2(-x) + 4$, which is equivalent to $y = -2x + 4$.

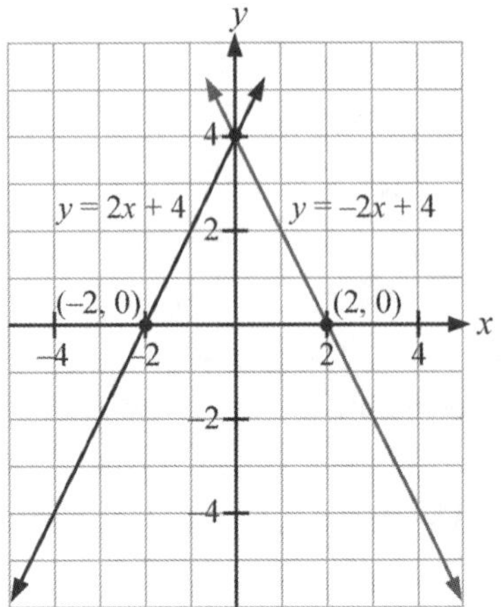

Observe that the graph of $y = -2x + 4$ is the graph of $y = 2x + 4$ reflected in the y-axis. This will always be true when x is replaced with $-x$. Notice that the y-intercept (0, 4) does not change, but the x-intercept changes from (–2, 0) to (2, 0). For a horizontal reflection, the y-coordinate of any point on the original graph will remain constant, but the x-coordinate will change signs. Therefore, the y-intercept is an invariant point, since it remains constant after a horizontal reflection.

In a horizontal reflection, a coordinate point (x, y) on the graph of $y = f(x)$ will be transformed to the point $(-x, y)$ on the graph of $y = f(-x)$.
For example, the graph of $y = 2x + 4$ contains the point (–1, 2). The graph of $y = 2(-x) + 4$, or $y = -2x + 4$, contains the corresponding point (1, 2).
$(-1 \times -1, 2) = (1, 2)$

Example

Using a graphing calculator to graph $y = (x - 2)^3$ and $y = (-x - 2)^3$, how are the points on the original graph transformed to the points on the second graph?

Solution

The equation of the transformed graph $y = (-x - 2)^3$ is derived from the equation of the original graph by substituting $-x$ for x in $y = (x - 2)^3$. Thus, the second graph is the first graph reflected in the y-axis. The graphs of $y = (x - 2)^3$ and $y = (-x - 2)^3$ are shown using a window setting of x:[–5, 5, 1] y:[–20, 20, 4].

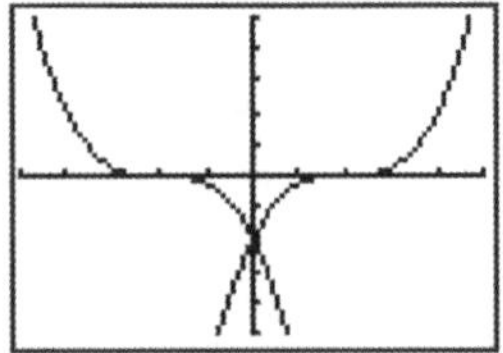

For every point on the original graph, the y-coordinate remains the same, but the x-coordinate has a sign change.
For example, the x-intercept changed from (2, 0) to (–2, 0). The y-intercept remained as (0, –8).

When a graph is reflected horizontally, the y-coordinates remain constant. Since the y-coordinates are constant, the range of the graph does not change.

When a graph is reflected about the y-axis, the x-coordinates are replaced with $-x$. Since the x-coordinates change sign, the largest x-value will become the smallest, and the smallest will become the largest. Therefore, the domain of the graph will be changed from $m \le x \le n$ to $-n \le x \le -m$.

Example

The graph of $y = f(x)$ is given.

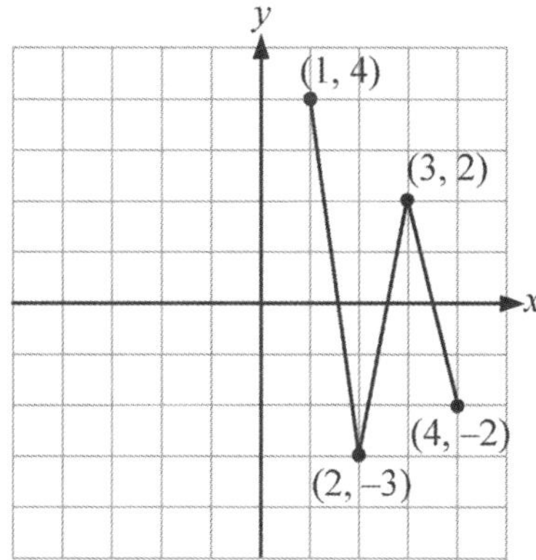

Determine the domain and range of the function after a reflection in the y-axis.

Solution

Step 1

Determine the domain and range of $y = f(x)$.

The domain of $y = f(x)$ is $1 \le x \le 4$.

The range of $y = f(x)$ is $-3 \le y \le 4$.

Step 2

Determine the domain and range of the reflected function.

When a graph is reflected in the y-axis, the domain of the graph will be changed from $m \le x \le n$ to $-n \le x \le -m$.

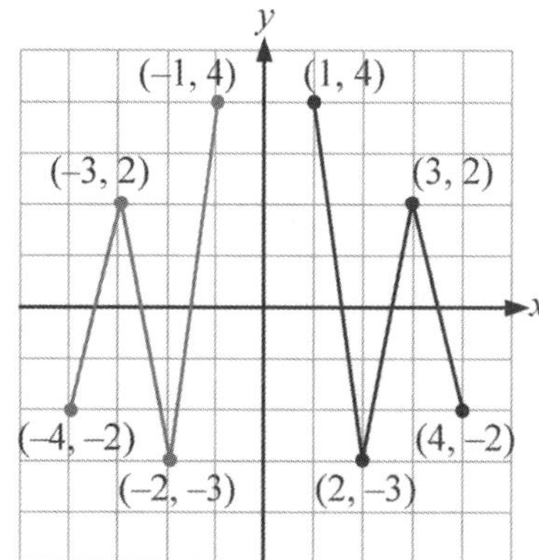

The domain of the reflected function is $-4 \le x \le -1$.

The range of the reflected graph does not change. The range is $-3 \le y \le 4$.

Reflections about the x-Axis

A **vertical reflection** occurs when a graph is reflected about the x-axis in such a way that the x-axis acts like a mirror.

When y is replaced with $-y$ in the equation $y = f(x)$, the graph of $y = f(x)$ will be reflected about the x-axis. This will result in the graph of $-y = f(x)$ or $y = -f(x)$.

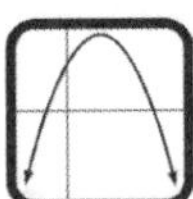

Example

Compare the graph of $y = x^2 - 4$ with the graph of $-y = x^2 - 4$, which is the same as $y = -(x^2 - 4)$, or $y = -x^2 + 4$. The graph of $y = x^2 - 4$ is reflected about the *x*-axis to produce the graph of $y = -x^2 + 4$.

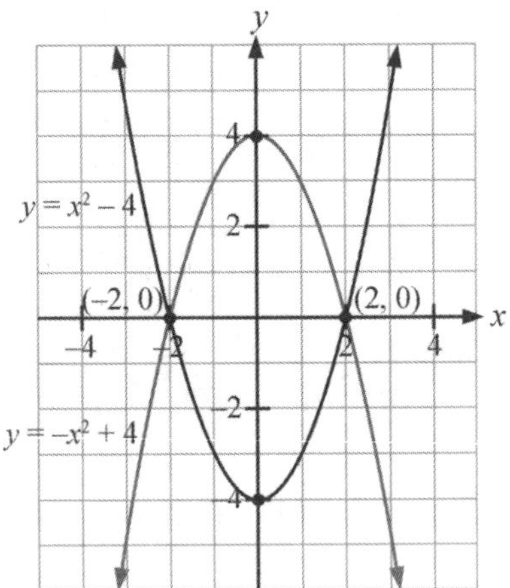

In a vertical reflection, the *x*-value of any point on the original graph will remain constant but the *y*-value will change signs. For example, the *x*-intercepts (2, 0) and (−2, 0) do not change, but the *y*-intercept changes from (0, −4) to (0, 4). Since the *x*-intercepts remain the same for both graphs, the *x*-intercepts are **invariant points**, which are points that remains constant after a transformation.

In a vertical reflection, a point (x, y) on the graph of $y = f(x)$ will be transformed to the point $(x, -y)$ on the graph of $-y = f(x)$. For example, the graph of $y = x^2 - 4$ contains the point (3, 5). The reflected graph $-y = x^2 - 4$ (or $y = -x^2 + 4$) contains the corresponding point $(3, -1 \times 5) = (3, -5)$.

Example

The graph of $y = \sqrt{x} + 2$ is reflected about the *x*-axis. What is the equation of the transformed graph?

Solution

Step 1

Since the graph is reflected about the *x*-axis, the equation of the transformed graph can be obtained by replacing *y* with $-y$ in the equation $y = \sqrt{x} + 2$.

Substitute $-y$ for *y* in the equation $y = \sqrt{x} + 2$.

$-y = \sqrt{x} + 2$

Step 2

Simplify $-y = \sqrt{x} + 2$ by dividing both sides of the equation by −1.

$$\frac{-y}{-1} = \frac{\sqrt{x} + 2}{-1}$$

$$y = \frac{\sqrt{x}}{-1} + \frac{2}{-1}$$

$$y = -\sqrt{x} - 2$$

The equation of the transformed graph is $y = -\sqrt{x} - 2$.

When a graph is reflected vertically, the *x*-coordinates remain constant.
Since the *x*-coordinates are constant, the domain of the graph does not change.

When a graph is reflected about the *x*-axis, the *y*-coordinates are replaced with $-y$.
Since the *y*-coordinates change sign, the largest *y*-value will become the smallest and the smallest will become the largest. Therefore, the range of the graph will be changed from $s \le x \le t$ to $-t \le x \le -s$.

Example

The graph of $y = f(x)$ is given.

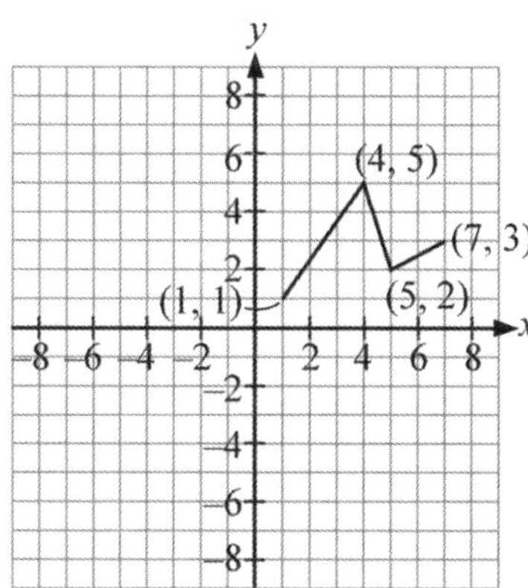

Determine the domain and range of the function after a reflection in the x-axis.

Solution

Step 1

Determine the domain and range of $y = f(x)$.

- The domain of $y = f(x)$ is $1 \le x \le 7$.
- The range of $y = f(x)$ is $1 \le y \le 5$.

Step 2

Determine the domain and range of the reflected function.

When a graph is reflected in the x-axis, the domain of the graph does not change. The domain is $1 \le x \le 7$.

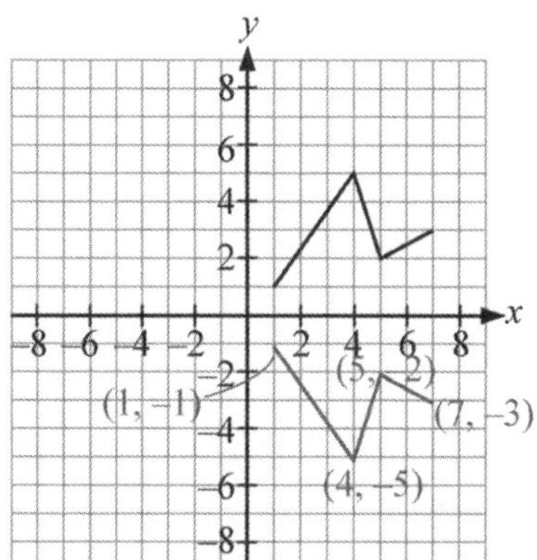

The range of the reflected graph will be changed from $s \le y \le t$ to $-t \le y \le -s$. The range of the reflected function is $-5 \le y \le -1$.

Describing the Role of d in the Exponential Function of the Form $y = B^x + d$, $B > 0$

When the graph of $y = B^x$, $B > 0$, is transformed to the graph of $y = B^x + d$, $B > 0$. The change in d-value causes a vertical translation.

The parameter d, in the exponential function $y = B^x + d$, $B > 0$, represents the vertical shift. It has the following effects on the curve:

- If $d > 0$, the curve is shifted upwards d units.
- If $d < 0$, the curve is shifted downwards $|d|$ units.
- If $d = 0$, the curve remains unaffected.

Example

The given graph shows three related curves.

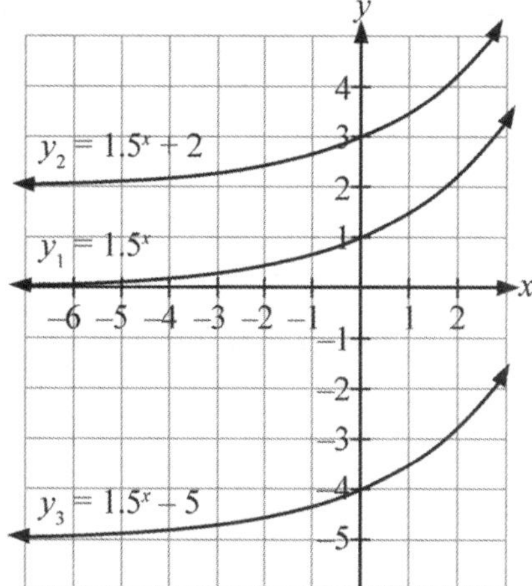

The curves have the following relations:

- Curve y_1 is the original curve.
- Curve y_2 has been shifted upwards by 2 units from y_1. This is because $d > 0$.
- Curve y_3 has been shifted downwards by 5 units from y_1. This is because $d < 0$.

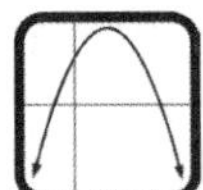

The parameter d also controls the y-intercept. The y-intercept occurs when the curve crosses the y-axis, or when $x = 0$.

$y = B^x + d$
$y = B^0 + d$
$y = 1 + d$

Therefore, the y-intercept is equal to $d + 1$.

Exponential functions of the form $y = B^x + d$, $B > 0$,have a horizontal asymptote at $y = d$. As x gets more and more negative, the graph of the function approaches this line but does not cross it.

Example

In the case of $y_3 = 1.5^x - 5$ from the previous example, $d = -5$; therefore, the horizontal asymptote (H.A.) is the line $y = -5$.

The domain of $y = B^x + d$, $B > 0$, is $x \in \mathbb{R}$.

To find the range of $y = B^x + d$, $B > 0$, start by looking at the range of $y = B^x$, $B > 0$, which is $y > 0$.

$B^x > 0$
$B^x + d > 0 + d$
$B^x + d > d$

Since $B^x + d > d$, the range of $y = B^x + d$, $B > 0$, must be $y > d$.

Example

The equation $y = 2.1^x - 3.5$ is an exponential function.

What is the vertical shift of the given function?

Solution

Since the function is in the format $y = B^x + d$, $B > 0$, the value of d is -3.5.

Therefore, the vertical shift is downwards by 3.5 units.

What is the y-intercept of the given function?

Solution

The y-intercept of an exponential function in the form $y = B^x + d$, $B > 0$, is $d + 1$.

The value of d from the equation is -3.5.

$d + 1 = -3.5 + 1$
$= -2.5$

Therefore, the y-intercept of the curve is -2.5.

What is the horizontal asymptote of the given function?

Solution

The horizontal asymptote of an exponential function in the form $y = B^x + d$, $B > 0$, is the line $y = d$.

Since $d = -3.5$, the horizontal asymptote is $y = -3.5$.

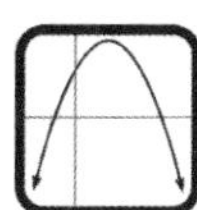

EXERCISE #1—MODIFYING FUNCTIONS

Use the following information to answer the next question.

The graph of $y = 9x^2 - 1$ is stretched horizontally about the y-axis by a factor of 6.

222. The equation of the transformed graph is

A. $y = \frac{1}{4}x^2 - 1$

B. $y = 54x^2 - 1$

C. $y = 54x^2 - 6$

D. $y = 324x^2 - 1$

Use the following information to answer the next question.

The partial graph of $y = f(x)$ is as shown.

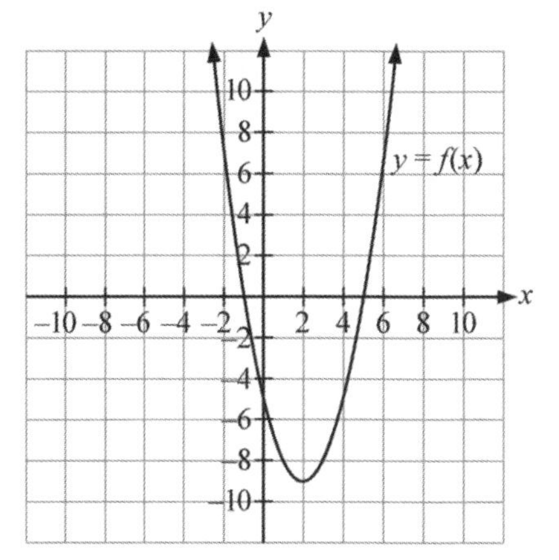

223. If the graph of $y = f(x)$ is vertically stretched about the x-axis by a factor of $\frac{1}{5}$, the x-intercepts of the transformed graph will be located at the ordered pairs

A. $\left(-\frac{1}{5}, 0\right)$ and $(25, 0)$

B. $\left(-\frac{1}{5}, 0\right)$ and $(1, 0)$

C. $(-5, 0)$ and $(25, 0)$

D. $(-1, 0)$ and $(5, 0)$

Use the following information to answer the next question.

The graph of $y = f(x)$ is given.

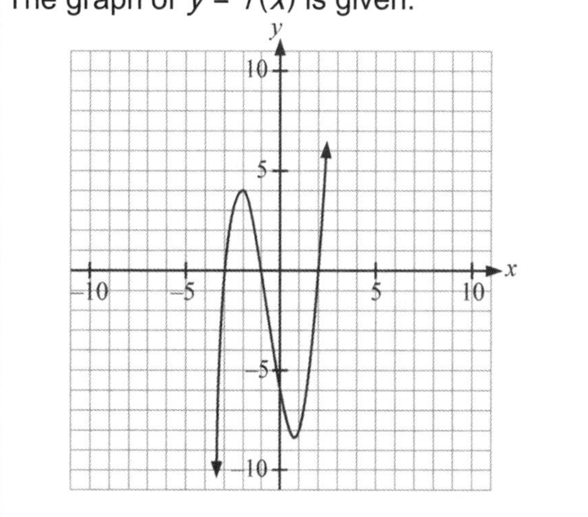

224. One x-intercept of the graph of $y = f(x - 7)$ is located at the ordered pair

A. $(-8, 0)$

B. $(-7, 0)$

C. $(6, 0)$

D. $(7, 0)$

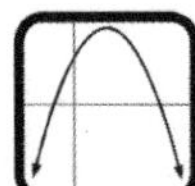

Use the following information to answer the next question.

The graph of $y = f(x)$ is given.

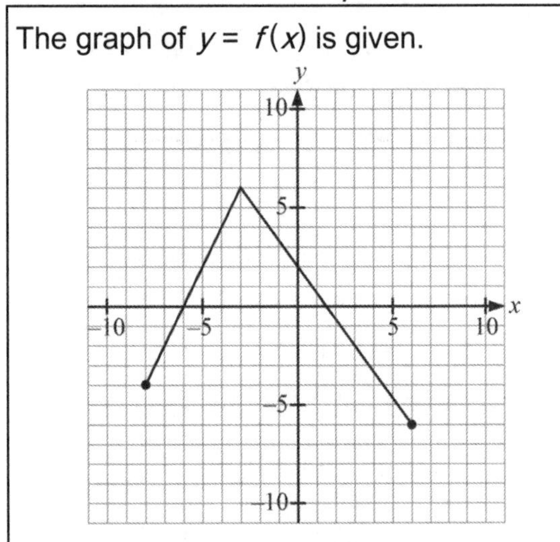

225. On the grid provided, sketch the graph of $y = f(x) + 2$.

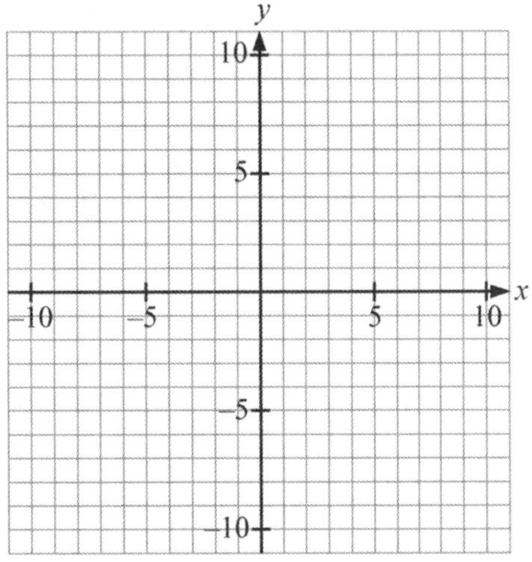

226. When the graph $y = f(x)$ is reflected about the y-axis, the resulting equation is

A. $-y = f(x)$ B. $y = f(-x)$

C. $y = -f(x)$ D. $y = \frac{1}{f(x)}$

227. If $y = f(x)$, where $f(x) = \sqrt{x+4} - 3$, then what is the x-intercept of $y = -f(x)$?

Use the following information to answer the next question.

The graph of the exponential function $y = \left(\frac{3}{4}\right)^x$ is translated so that the equation of the graph of the transformed function is written as $y - 4 = \left(\frac{3}{4}\right)^x$.

228. What is the y-intercept of the graph of the transformed function?

A. –4 B. –3

C. 4 D. 5

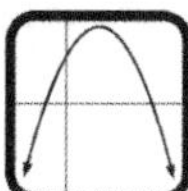

EXERCISE #1—MODIFYING FUNCTIONS ANSWERS AND SOLUTIONS

222. A	224. C	226. B	228. D
223. D	225. See solution	227. See solution	

222. A

Since the graph of $y = 9x^2 - 1$ is stretched horizontally about the y-axis by a factor of 6, the equation of the transformed graph can be obtained by substituting $\frac{1}{6}x$ (the reciprocal of 6 is $\frac{1}{6}$) for x in the equation $y = 9x^2 - 1$.

$$\begin{aligned} y &= 9x^2 - 1 \\ &= 9\left(\frac{1}{6}x\right)^2 - 1 \\ &= 9\left(\frac{1}{36}x^2\right) - 1 \\ &= \frac{1}{4}x^2 - 1 \end{aligned}$$

The equation of the transformed graph is $y = \frac{1}{4}x^2 - 1$.

223. D

Step 1

Identify the ordered pairs that define the x-intercepts of the graph $y = f(x)$.

Since the graph of $y = f(x)$ crosses the x-axis where $x = -1$ and $x = 5$, the x-intercepts of the graph of $y = f(x)$ are located at the ordered pairs $(-1, 0)$ and $(5, 0)$.

Step 2

Determine the x-intercepts of the transformed graph.

Since the graph of $y = f(x)$ is vertically stretched about the x-axis by a factor of $\frac{1}{5}$, a point (x, y) on the graph of $y = f(x)$ will be transformed to the corresponding point $\left(x, \frac{1}{5} \times y\right) = \left(x, \frac{1}{5}y\right)$ on the graph of the transformed function. Thus, the ordered pair $(-1, 0)$ corresponds to the point $\left(-1, 0 \times \frac{1}{5}\right) = (-1, 0)$, and the point $(5, 0)$ corresponds to the point $\left(5, 0 \times \frac{1}{5}\right) = (5, 0)$ on the graph of the transformed function. It then follows that the x-intercepts of the graph of the transformed function are also located at the ordered pairs $(-1, 0)$ and $(5, 0)$.

224. C

Step 1

Determine the x-intercepts of the graph of $y = f(x)$.

The x-intercepts of the graph are $(-3, 0)$, $(-1, 0)$, and $(2, 0)$.

Step 2

Determine how the graph of $y = f(x - 7)$ can be obtained from the graph of $y = f(x)$.

In order to generate the equation $y = f(x - 7)$ from the equation $y = f(x)$, it is necessary to substitute $x - 7$ for x in the equation $y = f(x)$. Therefore, the graph of $y = f(x)$ must be translated 7 units to the right in order to arrive at the graph of $y = f(x - 7)$.

Step 3

Determine the x-intercepts of the graph of $y = f(x - 7)$.

Since the graph of $y = f(x - 7)$ is 7 units to the right of the graph of $y = f(x)$, the x-intercepts of $y = f(x - 7)$are located at the ordered pairs $(-3 + 7, 0) = (4, 0)$, $(-1 + 7, 0) = (6, 0)$, and $(2 + 7, 0) = (9, 0)$. Only alternative C gives one of these x-intercepts.

225.

Step 1

Rewrite the equation $y = f(x) + 2$ as $y - 2 = f(x)$.

Step 2

Determine what transformation has been applied to the graph of $y = f(x)$.

To obtain the equation $y - 2 = f(x)$ from $y = f(x)$, $y - 2$ is substituted for y in $y = f(x)$. As a result, the graph of $y = f(x)$ will be translated 2 units up, and every ordered pair (x, y) on the graph of $y = f(x)$ will be translated to the ordered pair $(x, y + 2)$ on the graph of $y - 2 = f(x)$.

Step 3

Determine at least 3 points that best represent the graph of $y = f(x)$.

Select the endpoints $(-8, -4)$, $(-3, 6)$, and $(6, -6)$ on the graph of $y = f(x)$. These points will become $(-8, -4 + 2) = (-8, -2)$, $(-3, 6 + 2) = (-3, 8)$ and $(6, -6 + 2) = (6, -4)$ on the graph of $y = f(x) + 2$.

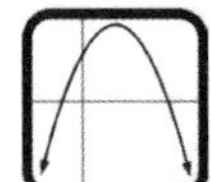

Step 4
Sketch the translated graph.
Plot the new endpoints, and sketch the graph of $y = f(x) + 2$.

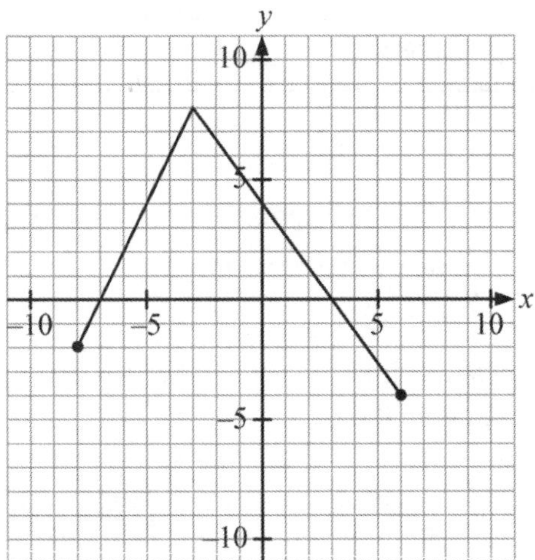

226. B

When x is replaced by $-x$ in the equation $y = f(x)$, the graph of $y = f(x)$ will be reflected in the y-axis, resulting in the graph of $y = f(-x)$.

227.

Step 1
Determine the x-intercept of the graph of $y = f(x)$.
Substitute 0 for y in the equation $y = \sqrt{x+4} - 3$, and solve for x.

$$y = \sqrt{x+4} - 3$$
$$0 = \sqrt{x+4} - 3$$
$$3 = \sqrt{x+4}$$
$$9 = x + 4$$
$$5 = x$$

The x-intercept occurs at the ordered pair (5, 0).

Step 2
Determine the x-intercepts of the transformed equation.
The graph of $y = -f(x)$ is the reflection of the graph of $y = f(x)$ about the x-axis. As a result, a point (x, y) on the graph of $y = f(x)$ becomes point $(x, -y)$ on the graph of $y = -f(x)$.
Thus, the x-intercept (5, 0) on the graph of $y = f(x)$ becomes point $(5, -0) = (5, 0)$ on the graph of $y = -f(x)$.
Note that the x-intercepts of the graph of $y = f(x)$ are invariant points when the graph of $y = f(x)$ is reflected in the x-axis.
The x-intercept of $y = -f(x)$ is also (5, 0) or $x = 5$.

228. D

The equation $y - 4 = \left(\frac{3}{4}\right)^x$ is equivalent to the equation $y = \left(\frac{3}{4}\right)^x + 4$. The equation $y = \left(\frac{3}{4}\right)^x + 4$ is of the general exponential form $y = b^x + d$, where $b = \frac{3}{4}$ and $d = 4$.

In general, the y-intercept of an exponential function $y = b^x + d$, $b > 0$ is $d + 1$. Therefore, the y-intercept of the function $y = \left(\frac{3}{4}\right)^x + 4$ (the equation of the graph of the transformed function) is $4 + 1 = 5$.

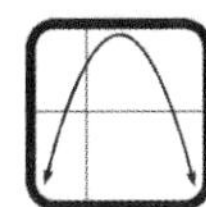

EXERCISE #2—MODIFYING FUNCTIONS

Use the following information to answer the next question.

Two graphs are as shown. Graph 2 is a transformation of graph 1.

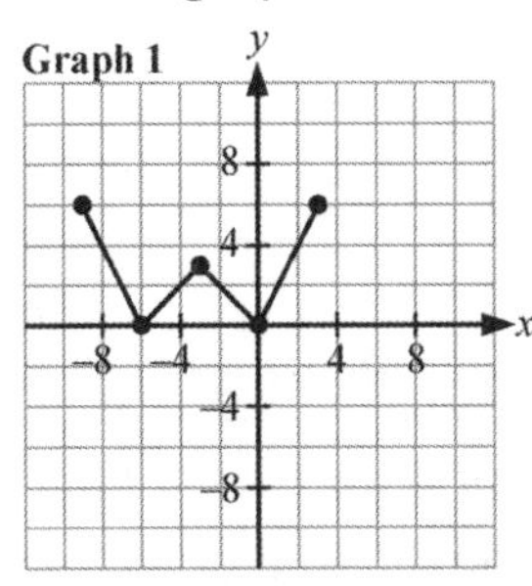

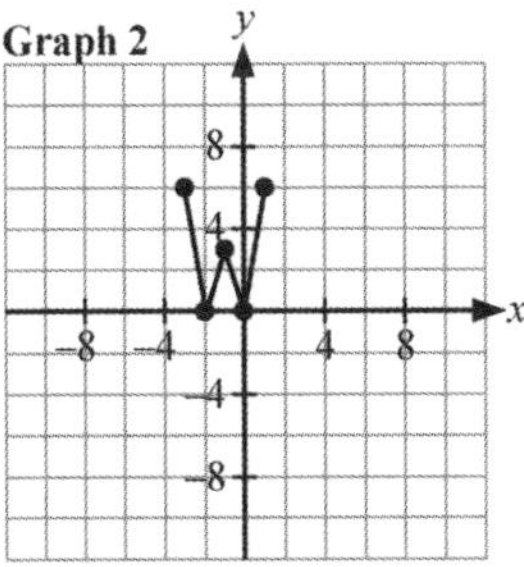

229. If the equation of graph 1 is $y = f(x)$, then the equation of graph 2 could be

A. $y = f(3x)$

B. $y = f\left(\frac{1}{3}x\right)$

C. $y = 3f(x)$

D. $y = \frac{1}{3}f(x)$

Use the following information to answer the next question.

The graph of $y = f(x)$ is shown.

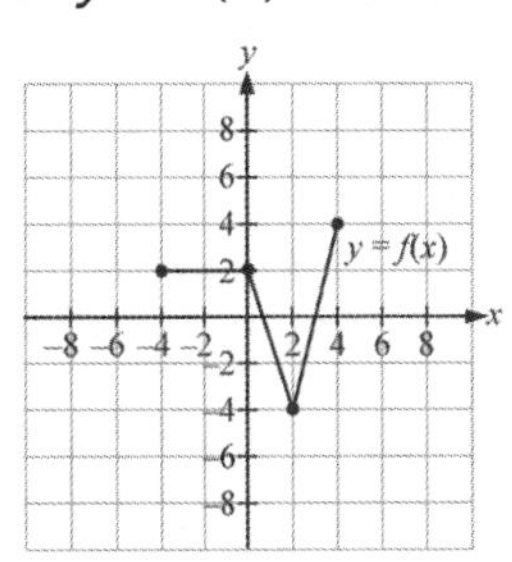

230. Which of the following graphs could be the graph of $y = 2f(x)$?

A.
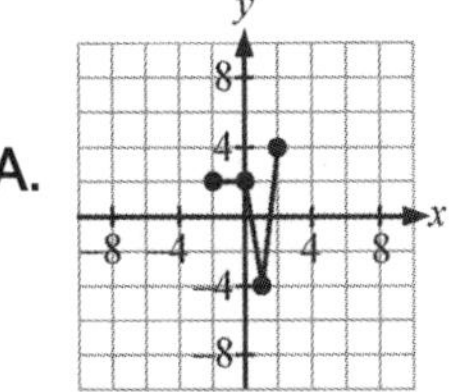

B.
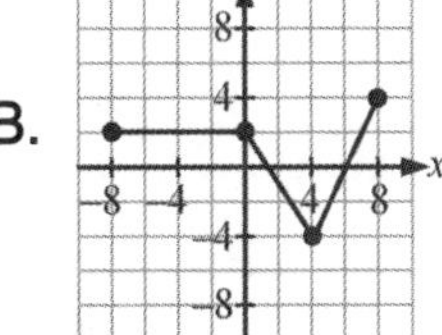

C.
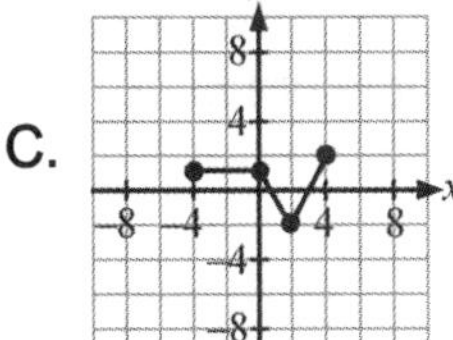

D.
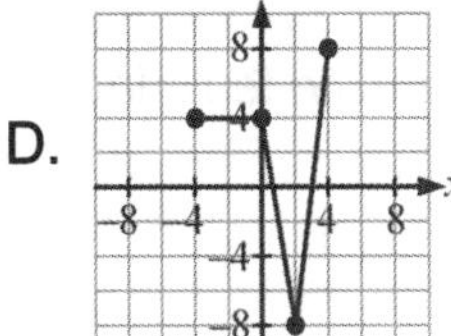

Use the following information to answer the next question.

The graph of $y = f(x)$ is translated to the graph of $y = f(x - 8)$. If the ordered pair (12, 7) is on the graph of $y = f(x - 8)$, then the corresponding ordered pair (k, 7) is on the graph of $y = f(x)$.

231. The value of k is _________.

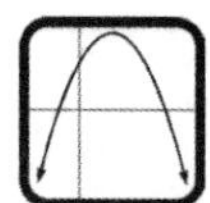

232. Given the graph of $y = f(x)$, the graph of $y + 1 = f(x) - 4$ can be drawn by translating the graph of $y = f(x)$ vertically

A. down by 4 units

B. down by 5 units

C. up by 4 units

D. up by 5 units

Use the following information to answer the next question.

The partial graph of the exponential function $y = f(x)$ is shown.

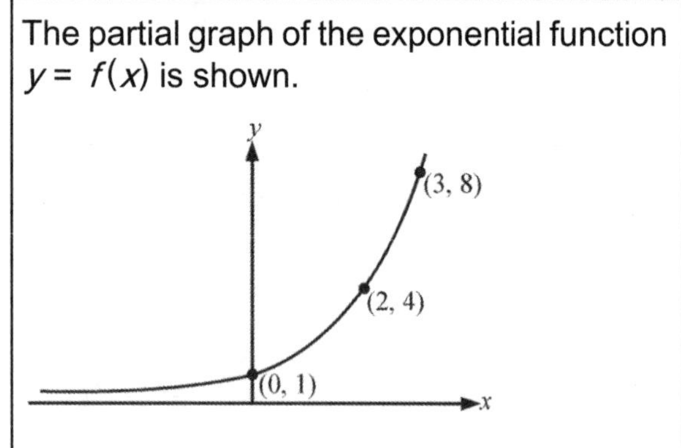

233. Show the transformation for each given point, and sketch the graph if the graph of $y = f(x)$ is reflected in the y-axis.

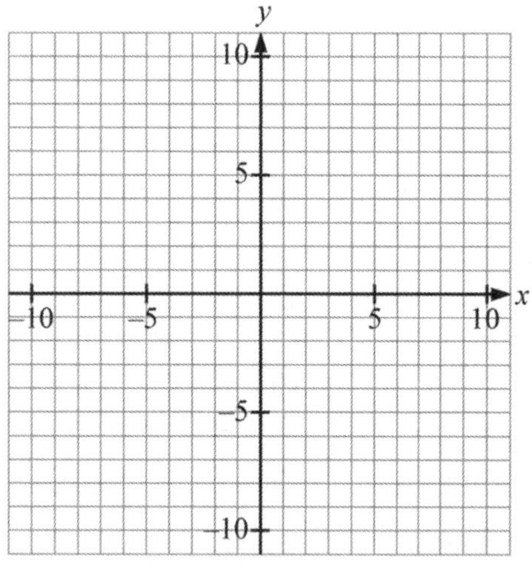

234. If the graph of the function $y = 2(x + 3)^2 - 4$ is reflected in the x-axis, then the equation of the graph of the resulting transformed function will be

A. $y = -2(x + 3)^2 - 4$

B. $y = -2(x + 3)^2 + 4$

C. $y = -2(x - 3)^2 - 4$

D. $y = -2(x - 3)^2 + 4$

Use the following information to answer the next question.

The graph of the exponential function $y = 7^x$ is translated 3 units upward.

235. The domain of the transformed graph is

A. $x > 3$ B. $x < 3$

C. $x > 4$ D. $x \in \mathbb{R}$

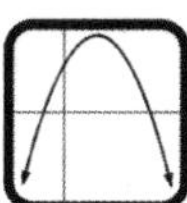

EXERCISE #2—MODIFYING FUNCTIONS ANSWERS AND SOLUTIONS

229. A	231. See solution	233. See solution	235. D
230. D	232. B	234. B	

229. A

Step 1

Identify appropriate points on graph 1.

Possible points on graph 1 include (−9, 6), (−6, 0), (−3, 3), (0, 0), and (3, 6).

Step 2

For each of the points (−9, 6), (−6, 0), (−3, 3), (0, 0), and (3, 6), identify the corresponding point on graph 2.

Point (−9, 6) corresponds to point (−3, 6), point (−6, 0) corresponds to point (−2, 0), point (−3, 3) corresponds to point (−1, 3), point (0, 0) corresponds to point (0, 0), and point (3, 6) corresponds to point (1, 6).

Step 3

Determine how each transformed point can be obtained from the corresponding point on graph 1.

Notice that the y-coordinate of any point on graph 2 is the same as the y-coordinate of the corresponding point on graph 1. Also, notice that the x-coordinate of any point on graph 2 is $\frac{1}{3}$ the x-coordinate of the corresponding point. Point (x, y) on graph 1 is transformed to point $\left(\frac{1}{3}x, y\right)$ on graph 2.

Step 4

Determine a possible equation for graph 2.

Since point (x, y) on graph 1 is transformed to point $\left(\frac{1}{3}x, y\right)$ on graph 2, graph 2 is obtained by horizontally stretching graph 1 about the y-axis by a factor of $\frac{1}{3}$. The equation of graph 2 can be arrived at by substituting $3x$ for x (the reciprocal of $\frac{1}{3}$ is 3) in the equation $y = f(x)$. Thus, a possible equation of graph 2 is $y = f(3x)$.

230. D

Step 1

Determine the transformation required to transform the graph of $y = f(x)$ to the graph of $y = 2f(x)$.

To arrive at the equation $y = 2f(x)$ (which is equivalent to $\frac{y}{2} = f(x)$) from the equation $y = f(x)$, substitute $\frac{y}{2}$ for y in the equation $y = f(x)$. When $\frac{y}{2}$ (or $\frac{1}{2}y$) is substituted for y in the equation $y = f(x)$, the graph of $y = f(x)$ will be vertically stretched about the x-axis by a factor of 2 (the reciprocal of $\frac{1}{2}$ is 2).

Step 2

Identify appropriate ordered pairs on the graph of $y = f(x)$.

Some ordered pairs on the graph of $y = f(x)$ are (−4, 2), (0, 2), (2, −4), and (4, 4).

Step 3

For each of the ordered pairs (−4, 2), (0, 2), (2, −4), and (4, 4), determine the corresponding point on the graph of $y = 2f(x)$.

Since the graph of $y = f(x)$ must be stretched vertically about the x-axis by a factor of 2 to obtain the graph of $y = 2f(x)$, a point (x, y) on the graph of $y = f(x)$ will be transformed to the corresponding point $(x, 2 \times y) = (x, 2y)$ on the graph of $y = 2f(x)$.

Thus, for the ordered pairs (−4, 2), (0, 2), (2, −4), and (4, 4), the corresponding points are as follows:

- Point (−4, 2) corresponds to $(-4, 2 \times 2) = (-4, 4)$.
- Point (0, 2) corresponds to $(0, 2 \times 2) = (0, 4)$.
- Point (2, −4) corresponds to $(2, -4 \times 2) = (2, -8)$.
- Point (4, 4) corresponds to $(4, 4 \times 2) = (4, 8)$.

Step 4

Determine which graph passes through points (−4, 4), (0, 4), (2, −8), and (4, 8).

Graph D passes through these four points; therefore, it is the graph of $y = 2f(x)$.

231.

The equation $y = f(x - 8)$ can be obtained from the equation $y = f(x)$ by substituting $x - 8$ for x in the equation $y = f(x)$.

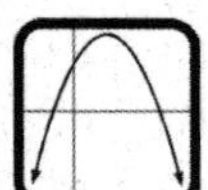

When $x - 8$ is substituted for x in the equation $y = f(x)$, the graph of $y = f(x)$ will be translated 8 units to the right. Therefore, the ordered pair $(k,7)$, which is on the graph of $y = f(x)$, will be transformed to the ordered pair$(k + 8,\ 7)$ on the graph of $y = f(x - 8)$.

Since it is given that $(k,7)$ is transformed to the ordered pair $(12,\ 7)$, the value of k can be determined as follows:

$$k + 8 = 12$$
$$k = 4$$

232. B

The equation $y + 1 = f(x) - 4$ can be written as $y + 5 = f(x)$.

To obtain the equation $y + 5 = f(x)$ from the equation $y = f(x)$, it is necessary to substitute $y + 5$ for y in the equation $y = f(x)$.

When $y + 5$ is substituted for y, the graph of $y = f(x)$ will be translated vertically 5 units down.

233.

The graph of $y = f(-x)$ is the graph of $y = f(x)$ reflected in the y-axis. Thus, the ordered pair $(x,\ y)$ on the graph of $y = f(x)$ becomes the ordered pair $(-x,\ y)$ on the graph of $y = f(-x)$. As a result, the ordered pairs (0, 1), (2, 4), and (3, 8), which are on the graph of $y = f(x)$, become the ordered pairs (0, 1), (−2, 4), and (−3, 8) when the graph of $y = f(x)$ is reflected in the y-axis. The resulting graph is as follows.

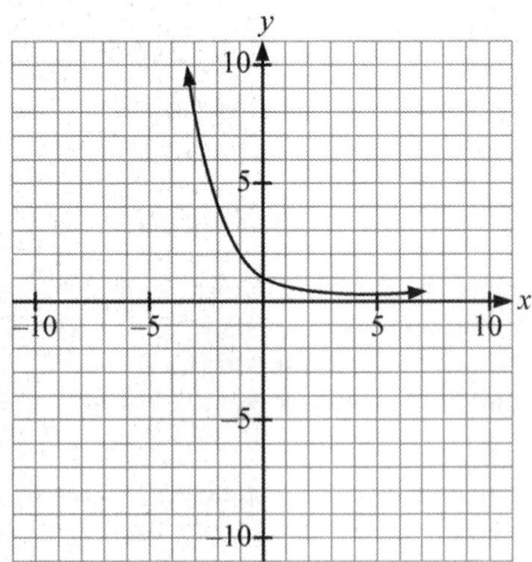

234. B

If the graph of the function $y = 2(x + 3)^2 - 4$ is reflected in the x-axis, then the equation of the transformed function can be obtained by substituting $-y$ for y in the equation $y = 2(x + 3)^2 - 4$.

Step 1
Substitute $-y$ for y in $y = 2(x + 3)^2 - 4$.

$$-y = 2(x + 3)^2 - 4$$

Step 2
Divide both sides of the equation by −1.

$$\frac{-y}{-1} = \frac{2(x + 3)^2}{-1} - \frac{4}{-1}$$

Step 3
Simplify.

$$y = -2(x + 3)^2 + 4$$

235. D

The domain of the graph of an exponential function of the form $y = b^x + d$, $b > 0$, $b \neq 1$ is $x \in \mathbb{R}$.

The function $y = 7^x$ is of the form $y = b^x + d$, where $b = 7$ and $d = 0$. When the graph of the function $y = 7^x$ is translated 3 units upward, the value of b in the equation $y = b^x + d$ remains as 7, but the value of d becomes 3. Therefore, the equation of the graph of the transformed function is $y = 7^x + 3$.

The range of the graph of $y = 7^x + 3$ is $y > (0 + 3)$, or $y > 3$.

However, the domain of the graph of the function $y = 7^x + 3$ is the same as the domain of the graph of the function $y = 7^x$, which is $x \in \mathbb{R}$.

Linear, Quadratic, and Exponential Functions

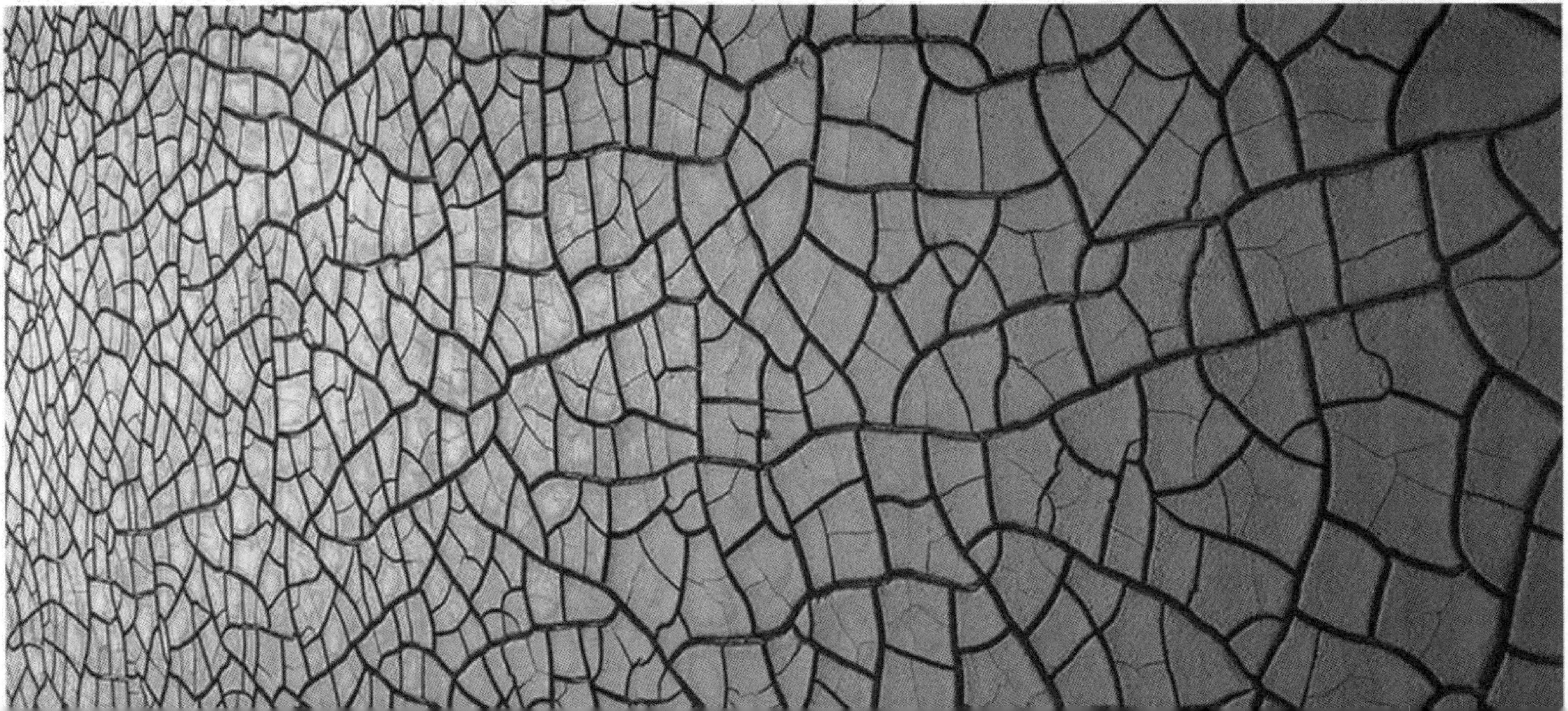

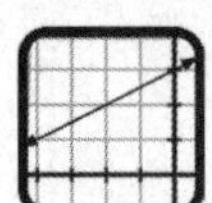

LINEAR, QUADRATIC, AND EXPONENTIAL FUNCTIONS

Table of Correlations

Standard		Concepts	Exercise #1	Exercise #2
Unit2.12	Construct and compare linear, quadratic, and exponential models and solve problems.			
F-LE.1ai	*Distinguish between situations that can be modeled with linear functions and with exponential functions. Prove that linear functions grow by equal differences over equal intervals; and that exponential functions grow by equal factors over equal intervals.*	Identifying a Rate of Change	236	239
F-LE.1b	*Distinguish between situations that can be modeled with linear functions and with exponential functions. Recognize situations in which one quantity changes at a constant rate per unit interval relative to another.*	Identifying a Rate of Change	236	239
		Comparing Rates	237	240
F-LE.1c	*Distinguish between situations that can be modeled with linear functions and with exponential functions. Recognize situations in which a quantity grows or decays by a constant percent rate per unit interval relative to another.*	Modeling Exponential Functions of Growth	41	59
		Modeling Exponential Functions of Decay	42	60
F-LE.2	*Construct linear and exponential functions, including arithmetic and geometric sequences, given a graph, a description of a relationship, or two input-output pairs (include reading these from a table).*	Relating Arithmetic Sequences and Linear Functions	136	146
		Generating Arithmetic Sequences	137	147
		Generating Geometric Sequences	138	148
		Defining Functions as Recursive	205	215
		Determine the General Term of an Arithmetic Sequence	207	217, 221
		Identify Arithmetic Sequences	208	218
		Identify Geometric Sequences	208, 209	219
		Determine the General Term of a Geometric Sequence	210	219
F-LE.3iii	*Observe using graphs and tables that a quantity increasing exponentially eventually exceeds a quantity increasing linearly, quadratically, or (more generally) as a polynomial function.*	Properties of Exponential Functions	165	177
		Comparing the Features of the Functions $y = x^2$ and $y = 2^x$	238	241

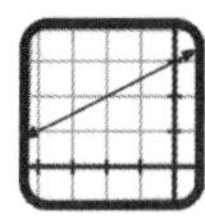

F-LE.1ai Distinguish between situations that can be modeled with linear functions and with exponential functions. Prove that linear functions grow by equal differences over equal intervals; and that exponential functions grow by equal factors over equal intervals.

IDENTIFYING A RATE OF CHANGE

Rate of change is a ratio between the change of two related variables.

$$\text{rate of change} = \frac{\Delta\text{in dependent variable}}{\Delta\text{in independent variable}}$$

Some common examples of a rate of change are:

- Speed/Velocity (distance versus time)
- Rate of pay (earning versus time)
- Cost per item (cost versus number of items)

Two variables are related by a **constant** rate of change if the relation is linear. That is, when corresponding pairs of independent and dependent variables are graphed, the points form a straight line.

When the data of a linear relation is graphed as ordered pairs (x, y) on the Cartesian plane, the change in the dependent variable (rise) is the same for a consistent change in the independent variable (run).

constant rate of change

$$= \frac{\Delta\text{in dependent variable}}{\Delta\text{in independent variable}}$$

$$= \frac{\text{rise}}{\text{run}}$$

$$= \text{slope}$$

Example

Susan worked at a golf course and made \$49.00 after working 7 hours.

Assuming Susan's wage is a constant hourly rate, determine Susan's rate of pay.

Solution

The rate is comparing money and hours worked. The dependent variable is the amount of money made (y-value), and the independent variable is the number of hours worked (x-value):

constant rate of change

$$= \frac{\Delta \text{ in dependent variable}}{\Delta \text{ in independent variable}}$$

$$= \frac{\Delta \$}{\Delta t}$$

$$= \frac{49}{7}$$

$$= \$7/\text{h}$$

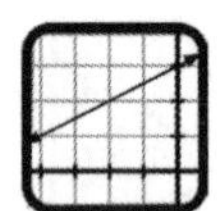

Example

Graph the relation.

Solution

You are given one ordered pair (7, 49).
If Susan did not work any hours, her pay would be $0.00. Thus, the second ordered pair is (0, 0).

The constant rate of change is the slope of the graph. Use the slope to place other points located on the line. To find a point that would occur after point (0, 0) on the line, increase the *y*-coordinate by 7 (rise) and increase the *x*-coordinate by 1 (run). This will give you the new point (0 + 1, 0 + 7) = (1, 7). Continue this along the graph. When the rate of change between each pair of successive points is the same, the slope is called the constant rate of change.

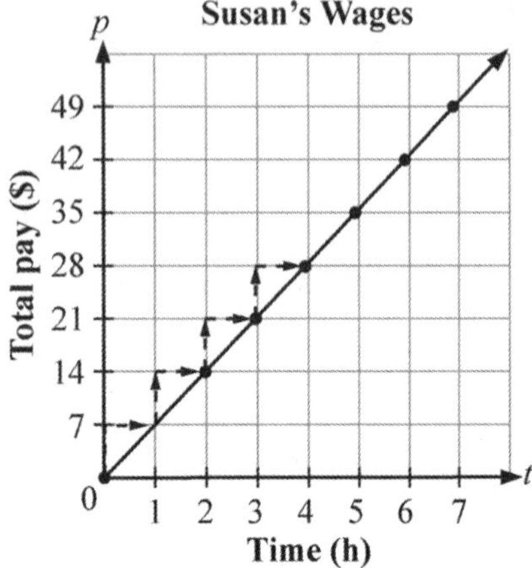

Notice that the data is continuous, so the points are joined in a straight line. Typically, when the independent variable is time, the data is continuous. In practice, however, employers often round hours worked to the nearest hour, half-hour or quarter of an hour. Continuous data includes all the values between the measured points. Discrete data excludes all the data between the measured points.

Another way to determine if two variables have a constant rate of change is to find the first differences of *y*-coordinates in a table of values.

First differences are differences between *successive* *y*-values in a table with evenly spaced *x*-values. To find the first differences, subtract each *y*-value by the previous *y*-value in the table.

To find the constant rate of change, divide the first differences of the *y*-values by the change in the *x*-values.

constant rate of change

$$= \frac{\text{first differences of the } y\text{-values}}{\Delta \text{in the } x\text{-values}}$$

Example

To maintain a hot water tank, it is a good idea to drain it once a year.

The table shows the volume of water remaining after an elapsed time when a hot water tank is drained.

Time (min)	Volume (L)
0	50
2	40
4	30
6	20
8	10
10	0

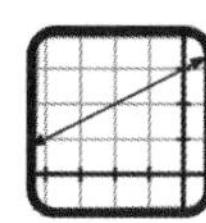

What is the constant rate of change using first differences? Show your work.

Solution

Time (min)	Volume (L)	First Differences
0	50	
2	40	40 – 50 = –10
4	30	30 – 40 = –10
6	20	20 – 30 = –10
8	10	10 – 20 = –10
10	0	0 – 10 = –10

constant rate of change

$$= \frac{\text{first differences of the } y\text{-values}}{\Delta \text{in the } x\text{-values}}$$

$$= \frac{-10}{5}$$

$$= -5 \text{ L/min}$$

Graph the data of this relation.

Solution

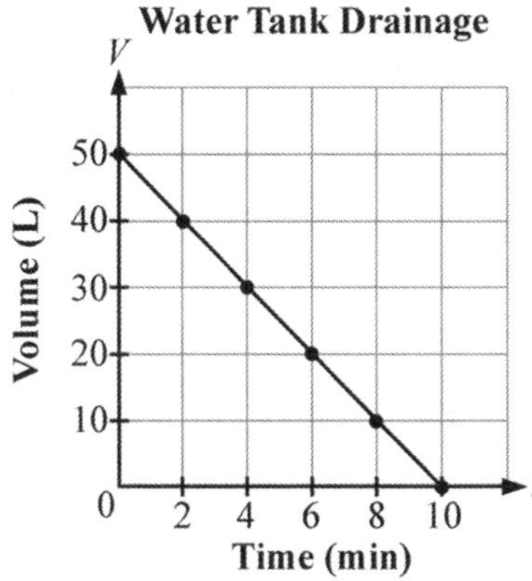

The rate of change can be positive or negative. It is logical here that the rate of change is negative because the tank is losing its water.

Even though the data is continuous, there are no arrows on either end of the line. The tank is full at 50 L and cannot increase in volume. Once the tank is empty at 0 L, it cannot empty any more.

F-LE.1b Distinguish between situations that can be modeled with linear functions and with exponential functions. Recognize situations in which one quantity changes at a constant rate per unit interval relative to another.

Comparing Rates

A **rate** is a comparison of two items that are measured in different units. A **unit rate** compares two items, but the second item must have a unit of 1. The rate someone charges per hour is a common unit rate. The cost of fruit per kilogram is another common unit rate.

When comparing the cost of merchandise, a unit rate must be calculated before determining the better value. To calculate the better value, follow these steps:

1. From the given rate, calculate the unit rate of each item.
2. Compare the unit rates.

Example

In a local grocery store, tuna is sold in packs of 6 or in cases of 24. The pack of 6 costs $7.68 before tax. The case of 24 costs $26.88 before tax.

Which is the better value?

Solution

Step 1
From the given rate, calculate the unit rate of each item.

Divide the numerator by the denominator.

Rate	Unit Rate
$7.68 / 6 cans	7.68 ÷ 6 = $1.28 / can
$26.88 / 24 cans	26.88 ÷ 24 = $1.12 / can

Step 2
Compare the unit rates.

Since $1.28 per can is more than $1.12 per can, buying the tuna by the case is the better value.

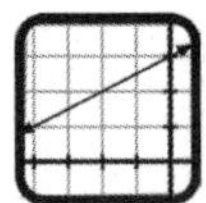

F-LE.3iii Observe using graphs and tables that a quantity increasing exponentially eventually exceeds a quantity increasing linearly, quadratically, or (more generally) as a polynomial function.

Comparing the Features of the Functions $y = x^2$ and $y = 2^x$

A **quadratic function** of the form $y = ax^2 + bx + c$ $(a \neq 0)$ differs in several ways when compared to an **exponential function** of the form $y = ab^x$.

To see how the two functions differ, compare the equations of each graph and the features of the graph of each function including the vertex, maximum value, minimum value, the x- and y-intercepts, and the axis of symmetry. Also, compare the second differences of each function.

When examining the equations of the two functions, notice that in an exponential function such as $y = ab^x$, the variable x is an exponent rather than part of the base as in the equation $y = ax^2 + bx + c(a \neq 0)$.

Using a TI-83 Plus graphing calculator, these graphs of $y = x^2$ and $y = 2^x$ are shown.

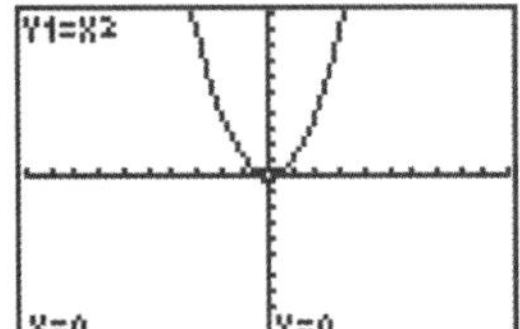

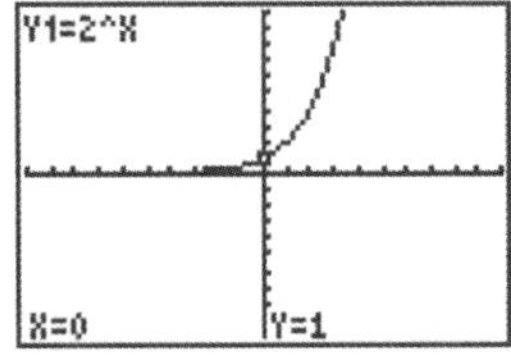

The graph of the function $y = x^2$ is a parabola opening upward. The vertex is located at (0, 0). The minimum value is 0, and the equation of the axis of symmetry is $x = 0$.

The graph of the exponential function $y = 2^x$ is a continuous curve that rises from the left to the right but never intersects the x-axis. The graph is asymmetrical and does not have a maximum or a minimum value; therefore, it does not have a vertex.

The x-intercept for the graph of the function $y = x^2$ is $x = 0$.

The function $y = 2^x$ does not cross or touch the x-axis. Thus, the graph of $y = 2^x$ has no x-intercept.

The y-intercept for the graph of the function $y = x^2$ is $y = 0$.

For the function $y = 2^x$, the graph crosses the y-axis at (0, 1). Therefore, the intercept is $y = 1$.

The first and second differences for the equation $y = x^2$ are shown in this table of values.

$y = x^2$

x	y	1st diff	2nd diff
−3	9		
		−5	
−2	4		2
		−3	
−1	1		2
		−1	
0	0		2
		1	
1	1		2
		3	
2	4		2
		5	
3	9		

Since the table of values is for a quadratic function of the form $y = ax^2 + bx + c$, the second difference is a constant. In this case, the second difference is 2.

The first and second differences for the equation $y = 2^x$ are shown in this table of values.

$y = 2^x$

x	y	1st diff	2nd diff
−3	0.125		
		0.125	
−2	0.25		0.125
		0.25	
−1	0.5		0.25
		0.5	
0	1		0.5
		1	
1	2		1
		2	
2	4		2
		4	
3	8		

For this function, neither the first nor second difference has a constant value. Therefore, the function is not linear or quadratic.

Note: Each y-value in the table can be obtained by multiplying the previous y-value by 2.

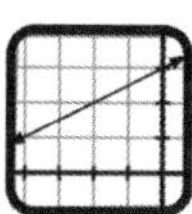

EXERCISE #1—LINEAR, QUADRATIC, AND EXPONENTIAL FUNCTIONS

236. In the linear relation $14x - 4y + 3 = 0$, what will the rate of change of y with respect to x be, to the nearest tenth?

Use the following information to answer the next question.

> Tom, Diana, Enrique, and Ahmad tested the fuel efficiency of their vehicles. Tom drove 320 km on 40 L of fuel, Diana drove 390 km on 50 L of fuel, Enrique drove 222 km on 30 L of fuel, and Ahmad drove 152 km on 20 L of fuel.

237. Who has the **most fuel-efficient** vehicle?

A. Tom
B. Diana
C. Ahmad
D. Enrique

Use the following information to answer the next question.

> Katrina's teacher wrote the functions $y = x^2$ and $y = 2^x$ on the whiteboard.

238. Which of the following statements about the given functions is **true**?

A. The function $y = x^2$ has a constant second difference of 2, and the function $y = 2^x$ does not have a constant second difference.

B. The function $y = x^2$ does not have a constant second difference, and the function $y = 2^x$ has a constant second difference of 2.

C. The function $y = x^2$ has a constant second difference of 2, and the function $y = 2^x$ has a constant second difference of 0.

D. Both functions $y = x^2$ and $y = 2^x$ have a constant second difference of 2.

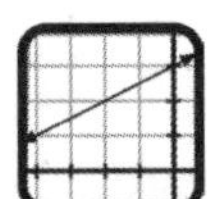

EXERCISE #1—LINEAR, QUADRATIC, AND EXPONENTIAL FUNCTIONS ANSWERS AND SOLUTIONS

236. 3.5	237. A	238. A

236. 3.5

The rate of change of a linear equation is the slope of the line.

Write the given linear relation in the slope-intercept form $y = mx + b$, where m is the slope and b is the y-intercept.

$$14x - 4y + 3 = 0$$
$$4y = 14x + 3$$
$$y = \frac{14x+3}{4}$$
$$y = \frac{7}{2}x + \frac{3}{4}$$
$$y = 3.5x + 0.75$$

The slope of the line $y = 3.5x + 0.75$ is 3.5.

Therefore, the rate of change of y with respect to x is 3.5.

237. A

Step 1
Calculate the unit rate for each vehicle.

- Tom's fuel efficiency is $\frac{320 \text{ km}}{40 \text{ L}} = 8$ km/L.
- Diana's fuel efficiency is $\frac{390 \text{ km}}{50 \text{ L}} = 7.8$ km/L.
- Enrique's fuel efficiency is $\frac{222 \text{ km}}{30 \text{ L}} = 7.4$ km/L.
- Ahmad's fuel efficiency is $\frac{152 \text{ km}}{20 \text{ L}} = 7.6$ km/L.

Step 2
Compare the unit rates.
Since Tom can travel 8 km on 1 L of fuel, his vehicle is the most fuel efficient.

238. A

A quadratic function of the form $y = ax^2 + bx + c$ has a constant second difference. Since $y = x^2$ is a quadratic relation, it has a constant second difference of 2.

An exponential relation such as $y = 2^x$ does not have a constant first or second difference.

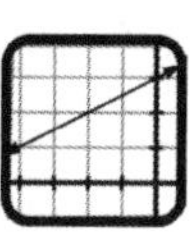

EXERCISE #2—LINEAR, QUADRATIC, AND EXPONENTIAL FUNCTIONS

Use the following information to answer the next question.

A cylindrical tank with a 200 L capacity is filled with water. The tank has an outlet pipe that drains the water out of the tank at a constant rate.

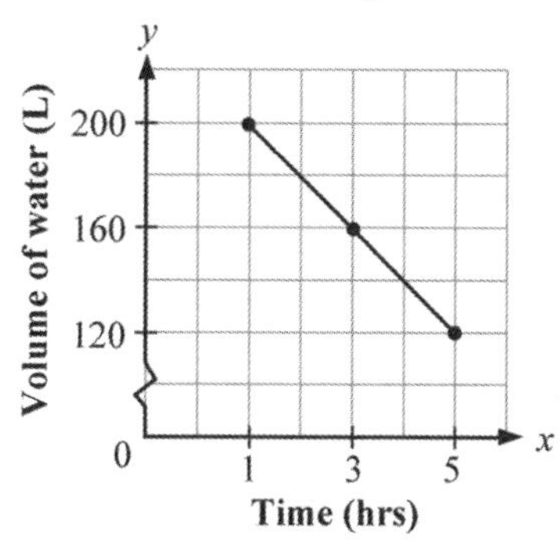

239. At what rate does the water drain out of the tank?

A. 8 L/h B. 9 L/h
C. 20 L/h D. 21 L/h

Use the following information to answer the next question.

Amanda is baking bread and needs to buy flour. She checks four grocery stores to see which offers the best price.

Grocery A	10 kg for $10.00
Grocery B	15 kg for $15.15
Grocery C	20 kg for $19.00
Grocery D	25 kg for $24.50

240. Which grocery store offers the **best** price for flour?

A. Grocery A B. Grocery B
C. Grocery C D. Grocery D

Use the following information to answer the next question.

The equation of the axis of symmetry for the graph of $y = x^2$ is ____*i*____, and the equation for the axis of symmetry for the graph of $y = 2^x$ is ____*ii*____.

241. This statement is completed by the information in which of the following tables?

A.

i	*ii*
undefined	$x = 0$

B.

i	*ii*
$x = 0$	undefined

C.

i	*ii*
undefined	$y = 0$

D.

i	*ii*
$x = 0$	$y = 0$

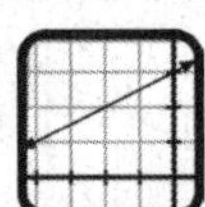

EXERCISE #2—LINEAR, QUADRATIC, AND EXPONENTIAL FUNCTIONS ANSWERS AND SOLUTIONS

239. C	240. C	241. B

239. C

The water drains out at a constant rate. Use the constant rate of change formula to determine the rate of drainage.

Constant rate of change

$$= \frac{\Delta \text{ in dependent variable}}{\Delta \text{ in independent variable}}$$

$$\text{Rate of drainage} = \frac{\text{Change in volume of water}}{\text{Change in time}}$$

$$= \frac{200 - 160}{3 - 1}$$

$$= \frac{40}{2}$$

$$= 20 \text{ L/h}$$

The water drains out of the tank at a rate of 20 L/h.

240. C

Step 1

Calculate the unit rate for each rate.

- Grocery A: 10 kg for $10.00

  $\frac{\$10.00}{10\text{kg}} = \$1.00/\text{kg}$
- Grocery B: 15 kg for $15.15

  $\frac{\$15.15}{15\text{kg}} = \$1.01/\text{kg}$
- Grocery C: 20 kg for $19.00

  $\frac{\$19.00}{20\text{kg}} = \$0.95/\text{kg}$
- Grocery D: 25 kg for $24.50

  $\frac{\$24.50}{25\text{kg}} = \$0.98/\text{kg}$

Step 2

Compare the unit rates.

Grocery C has the lowest unit rate where flour costs $0.95/kg.

241. B

The equation of the axis of symmetry for the graph of $y = x^2$ is $x = 0$. The graph of $y = 2^x$ is asymmetrical, and thus the equation of the axis of symmetry for this graph is undefined.

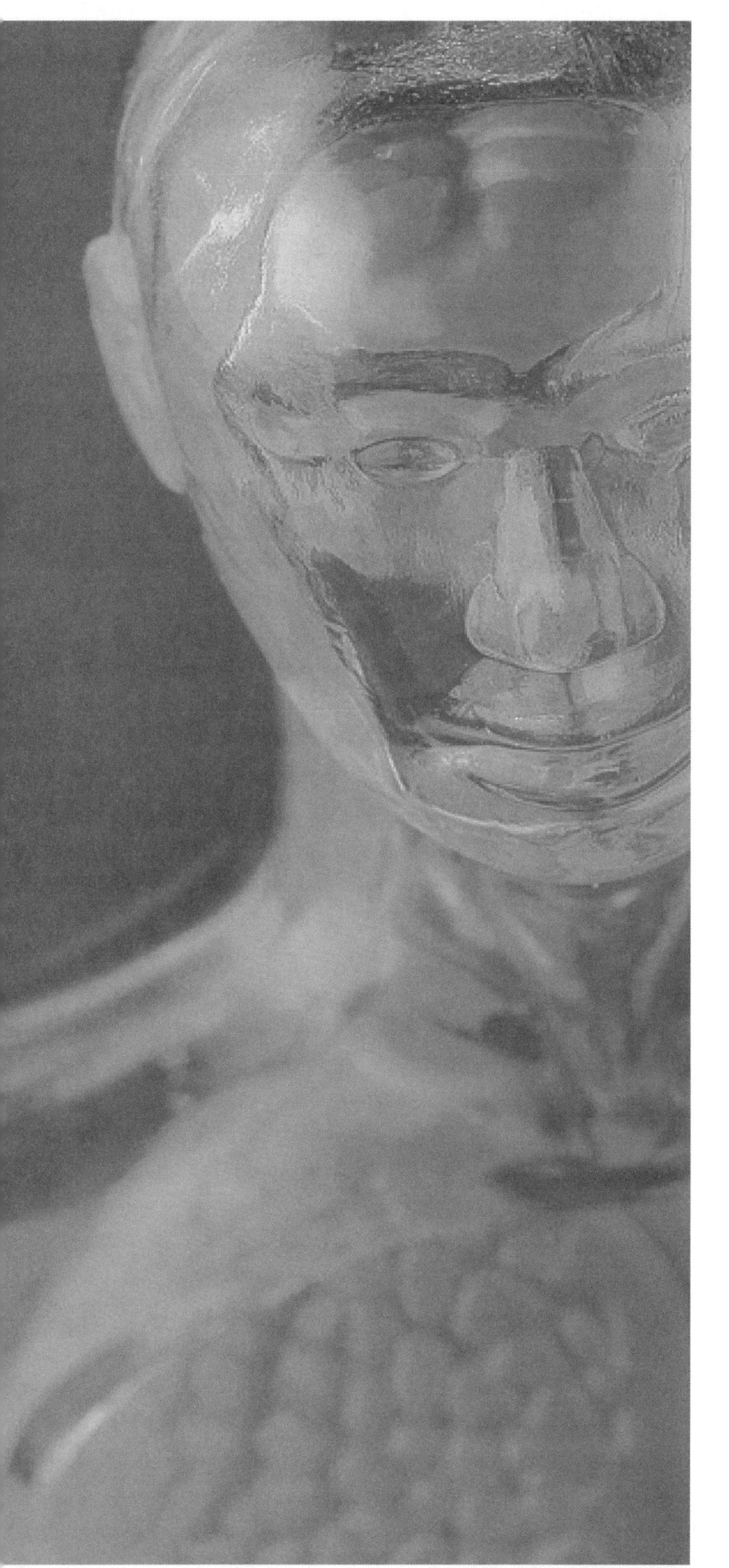

Interpreting Expressions for Functions

INTERPRETING EXPRESSIONS FOR FUNCTIONS

Table of Correlations				
Standard		**Concepts**	**Exercise #1**	**Exercise #2**
Unit2.13	Interpret expressions for functions in terms of the situation they model.			
F-LE.5	*Interpret the parameters in a linear or exponential function in terms of a context.*	Meaning of y-intercept and Slope in Graphs of Real Situations	18	24
		Modeling Exponential Functions of Growth	41	59
		Modeling Exponential Functions of Decay	42	60
		Solving Contextual Slope Problems	242	248
		Solving Linear Relations in Contextual Problems	243	249
		Solving Problems Involving Exponential Decay when Given a Graph	244	250
		Solving Problems Involving Exponential Decay	245	251
		Solving Problems Involving Exponential Growth Given an Equation	246	252
		Solving Problems Involving Exponential Growth Given a Graph	247	253

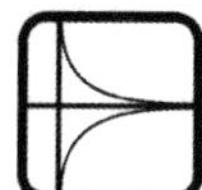

F-LE.5 Interpret the parameters in a linear or exponential function in terms of a context.

Solving Contextual Slope Problems

The slope of a linear relation can be referred to as the **rate of change**.

The rate of change is a ratio that represents the change in one variable relative to a corresponding change in another variable.

For any continuous relation whose graph contains a line segment, the slope of the line segment is the rate of change of the dependent variable with respect to the independent variable for the ordered pairs included in the line segment.

Traveling a certain distance over a period of time, being paid a certain wage per hour, and the cost of something per hour are examples of situations that can be described using the rate of change.

Example

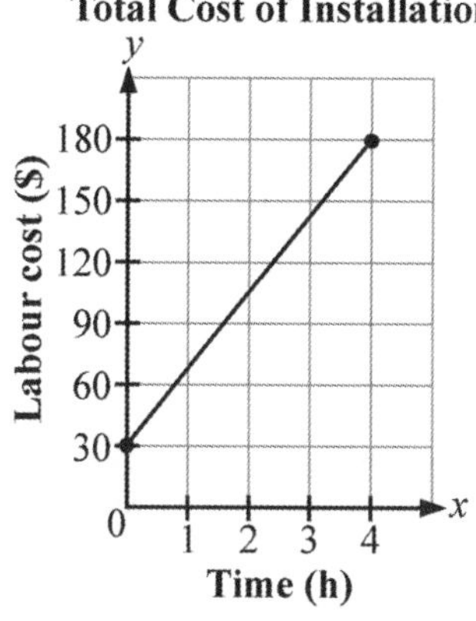

The graph shows the total labor cost of a plumber for the installation of a new water tank.

Determine the plumber's hourly rate of pay.

Solution

Step 1
Determine the slope of the linear relation.

Choose two points on the graph to use in the slope formula. Two points that can be chosen are (0, 30) and (4, 180).

Step 2
Substitute the points into the slope formula, and solve for the slope.

$$m = \frac{y_2 - y_1}{x_2 - x_1}$$
$$= \frac{180 - 30}{4 - 0}$$
$$= \frac{150}{4}$$
$$= 37.5$$

Since the slope is 37.5, the plumber's hourly rate of pay is \$37.50 /h.

Example

Amorita is traveling away from home for 5 h. The function $d = 80t + 40$ defines her distance (d) from home in kilometers as a function of time (t) in hours.

Determine the slope of the given function.

Solution

The equation $d = 80t + 40$ is of the form $y = mx + b$, in which m represents the slope of the line.

Therefore, the slope of the line is 80.

What does the slope of the given function represent?

Solution

The slope of the given function represents the speed Amorita is traveling, which is 80 km/h.

Example

The given table of values represents David's earnings as a function of the number of hours he worked.

Number of Hours	Earnings ($)
2	15.90
4	31.80
6	47.70
8	63.60

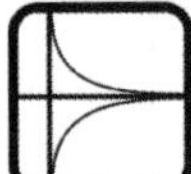

Determine the slope of the graph of the function.

Solution

Apply the slope formula using any two ordered pairs from the table of values.

If the points (2, 15.9) and (4, 31.8) are used, the calculation is:

$$\begin{aligned} m &= \frac{y_2 - y_1}{x_2 - x_1} \\ &= \frac{31.8 - 15.9}{4 - 2} \\ &= \frac{15.9}{2} \\ &= 7.95 \end{aligned}$$

The slope of the graph of the given function is 7.95.

What does the slope of the given situation represent?

Solution

The slope of the given situation represents David's rate of pay, which is \$7.95/h.

Solving Linear Relations in Contextual Problems

A linear relation may be presented in context. The intercepts, slope, domain, and range of the linear relation can be determined from the context in which it is presented.

Example

The cost for staging a dinner is \$200, plus \$12 for each guest. This situation can be represented by a relation in which the number of guests is the independent variable.

If n represents the number of guests, and C represents the total cost, what is the equation that describes the given relation?

Solution

The given relation can be described by the equation $C = 200 + 12n$.

Example

If the minimum number of guests is 10, and the maximum number of guests is 80, what are the domain and range of the given relation?

Solution

Since there can be between 10 and 80 guests, inclusively, the domain is $n = 10, 11, 12, 13, \ldots, 80$, which can also be expressed as $10 \le n \le 80,\ n \in I$.

Remember that the term $n \in I$ represents n being an element of the integers.

- When there are 10 guests, the cost can be calculated as follows:
  $C = 200 + 12(10)$
  $= \$320$
- When there are 11 guests, the cost can be calculated as follows:
  $C = 200 + 12(11)$
  $= \$332$
- When there are 12 guests, the cost can be calculated as follows:
  $C = 200 + 12(12)$
  $= \$344$
- When there are 80 guests, the cost can be calculated as follows:
  $C = 200 + 12(80)$
  $= \$1,160$

Therefore, the range of the given relation is $\{320, 332, 344, \ldots, 1160\}$.

Example

A banquet hall can hold up to 200 people for an event. The cost to rent the hall can be determined by the linear equation $C = 50 + 15P$, in which C represents the total cost in dollars, and P represents the amount of people attending the event.

What does the slope of the given equation represent?

Solution

The slope of the given equation represents the cost for each additional person in attendance. This cost is $15/person.

What does the y-intercept of the given relation represent?

Solution

The y-intercept corresponds to the value of the dependent variable, C, when the value of the independent variable, P, is 0.

In this situation, the y-intercept represents the cost to rent the hall when no people attend. It would cost $50 to rent the hall when no guests attend.

What do the domain and range of the given relation represent?

Solution

The domain of the relation represents all the possible values for the independent variable, P. In this relation, the domain is any whole number of people who attend the banquet to a maximum of 200.
$\{0, 1, 2, \ldots, 200\}$

The range of the relation represents all the possible values for the dependent variable, C. In this relation, the range represents the cost of the banquet hall in dollars, $50 + 15P$, based on how many people, P, attend.
$\{50, 65, 80, \ldots, 3{,}050\}$

Solving Problems Involving Exponential Decay when Given a Graph

Exponential graphs can be used to model real-life examples in which quantities decrease or decay at an exponential rate. Common examples in which exponential functions are used to model exponential decay include depreciating assets or investments and radioactive half-life.

Example

A group of doctors is testing the effectiveness of a new drug. The effectiveness of a drug decreases as the body metabolizes it.
The given graph represents the amount of the drug present in a test subject over a span of 50 h, with an initial dose of 275 mg.

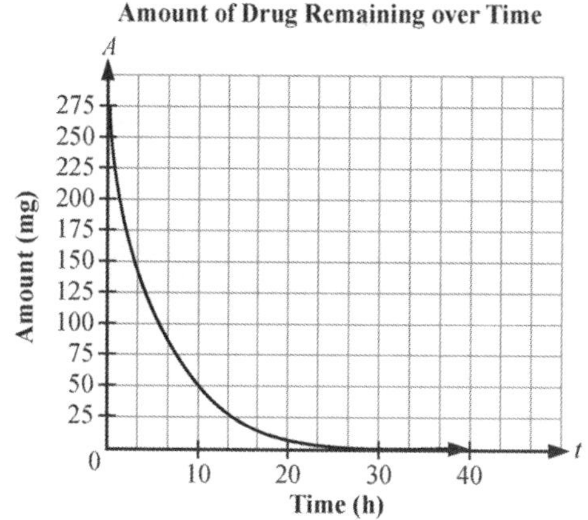

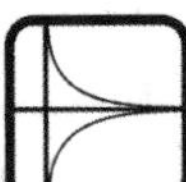

How long does it take until only 50 mg of the drug remain in the test subject?

Solution

Let variable A refer to the amount of drug present and t refer to the elapsed time.

Using the given graph of the relation, determine the value of t when $A = 50$.

The graph of the relation shows that $t = 10$ when $A = 50$.

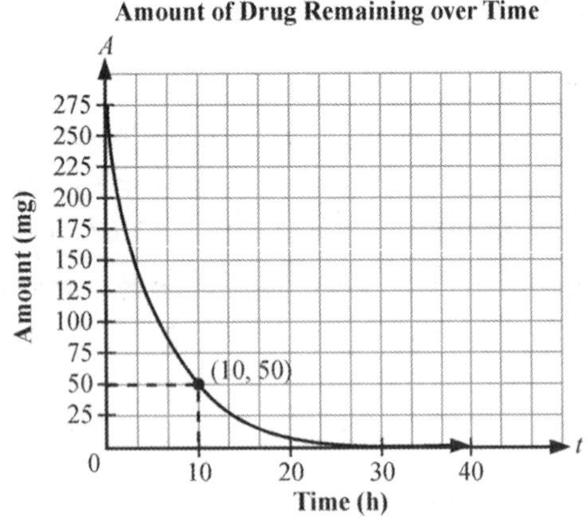

Therefore, it takes 10 h until only 50 mg of the drug remain in the test subject.

How much of the drug is metabolized after 3 h?

Solution

Let variable A refer to the amount of drug present and t refer to the elapsed time.

Step 1

Determine the amount of drug remaining, $A_{remaining}$, after 3 h.

Using the graph, determine the value of A when $t = 3$.

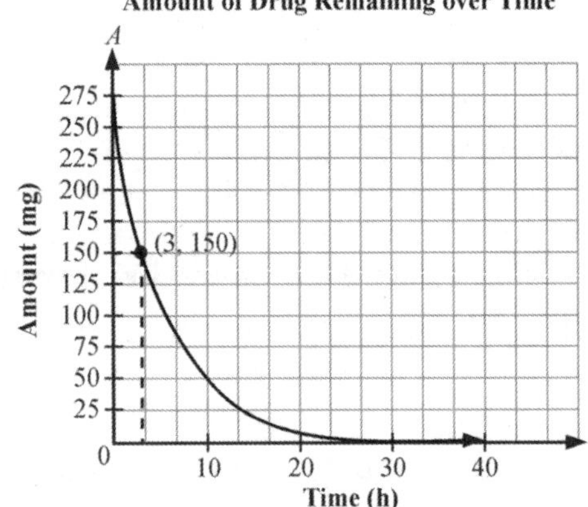

From the graph, $A = 150$ when $t = 3$.

Therefore, after 3 h, 150 mg of the drug remain in the test subject.

Step 2

Determine the amount of drug metabolized after 3 h.

To find the amount of drug metabolized after 3 h, subtract the amount of the drug remaining in the test subject from the initial amount given.

$A_{metabolized} = A_{initial} - A_{remaining}$

$A_{metabolized} = 275 - 150$

$A_{metabolized} = 125$

Therefore, the test subject metabolized 125 mg of the drug after 3 h.

Solving Problems Involving Exponential Decay

The form of an equation that models exponential decay is $N_t = N_0 \times R^{\frac{t}{p}}$, where N_t is the quantity at time t, N_0 is the initial size or value, R is the growth rate, t is the elapsed time, and p is the period of time that it takes the quantity to decay by rate R. This equation can be used to model exponential decay, solve problems, and predict the future behavior of certain quantities.

Example

A car was valued at \$43,750 at the time of its purchase. The value of the car depreciates at a rate of 12% per year. The formula that defines the value of the car as a function of time is $N(t) = 43{,}750(1 - 0.12)^t$, where t is the time in years and $N(t)$ is the value of the car after t years.

To the nearest dollar, determine the value of the car after 5 years.

Solution

Substitute 5 for t in the equation $N(t) = 43{,}750(1 - 0.12)^t$, and solve for $N(5)$.

$$N(5) = 43{,}750(1 - 0.12)^5$$
$$N(5) = 43{,}750(0.88)^5$$
$$N(5) = 43{,}750(0.52773\ldots)$$
$$N(5) = 230{,}888.271\ldots$$
$$N(5) \approx 23{,}088$$

To the nearest dollar, the car will be worth \$23,088 in 5 years.

Example

The half-life of iodine-126 is 13 days. (In other words, half of a sample of iodine-126 decays in 13 days.) Measured in grams, the amount, N_t, of iodine-126 with an initial mass of 10 g that remains after t days is given by the formula

$$N_t = 10\left(\frac{1}{2}\right)^{\frac{t}{13}}.$$

To the nearest tenth of a day, determine the time that it will take 10 g of iodine-126 to decay to 0.1 g.

Solution

The equation that represents the amount of iodine-126 after t days is $N_t = 10\left(\frac{1}{2}\right)^{\frac{t}{13}}$.

Use this formula to find the time it takes 10 g of iodine-126 to decay to 0.1 g.

Step 1

Substitute 0.1 for N_t in the equation $N_t = 10\left(\frac{1}{2}\right)^{\frac{t}{13}}$, and isolate the power.

$$0.1 = 10\left(\frac{1}{2}\right)^{\frac{t}{13}}$$

Divide both sides of the equation by 10.

$$\frac{0.1}{10} = \left(\frac{1}{2}\right)^{\frac{t}{13}}$$

$$0.01 = \left(\frac{1}{2}\right)^{\frac{t}{13}}$$

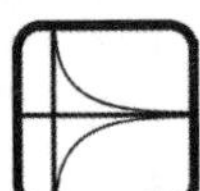

Step 2

Solve for t.

Take the common logarithm of each side of the equation.

$$\log(0.01) = \log\left(\left(\frac{1}{2}\right)^{\frac{t}{13}}\right)$$

Apply the power law of logarithms to the right side of the equation.

$$\log(0.01) = \frac{t}{13}\log\left(\frac{1}{2}\right)$$

Divide both sides of the equation by $\log\left(\frac{1}{2}\right)$.

$$\frac{\log(0.01)}{\log\left(\frac{1}{2}\right)} = \frac{t}{13}$$

Evaluate $\frac{\log(0.01)}{\log\left(\frac{1}{2}\right)}$, and solve for t.

$$\begin{aligned} 6.6438\ldots &= \frac{t}{13} \\ 6.6438\ldots(13) &= t \\ 86.3701\ldots &= t \\ 86.4 &\approx t \end{aligned}$$

To the nearest tenth of a day, it takes 86.4 days for 10 g of iodine-126 to decay to 0.1 g.

Solving Problems Involving Exponential Growth Given an Equation

You can use an equation in the form $N_t = N_0 \times R^{\frac{t}{p}}$ to model exponential growth, solve problems, and predict future behavior of certain quantities.

Example

A newly married couple invests \$20,000 into a variety of stocks in 1989. The exponential function describing the value, $V(t)$, in dollars over time, t, in years since Jan. 1, 1989 is $V(t) = 20{,}000(1.065)^t$.

According to the equation, what is the couple's annual average rate of return as a percentage?

Solution

The value of 1.065 in the equation describes the growth factor of 1.065 of their stock value. When the growth factor is converted to a percentage, it is $1.065 \times 100\% = 106.5\%$.

Since 100% means no growth (stays the same at 100% of its original amount), the annual average rate of return is $106.5 - 100 = 6.5\%$.

According to the function, what should the value of the stock be in 2000?

Solution

The value of t is the number of years since 1989. Therefore, in 2000, $t = 2{,}000 - 1{,}989 = 11$.

Substitute $t = 11$ into the equation, and solve for $V(t)$, the value of the stock.

$$\begin{aligned} V(11) &= 20{,}000(1.065)^{11} \\ &= 39{,}983.02801 \end{aligned}$$

To the nearest cent, the value of the stock in the year 2000 is \$39,983.03.

Solving Problems Involving Exponential Growth Given a Graph

A given graph relating to real world investigations can be used to solve problems. The graph representing a real life problem can be interpreted and analyzed to make accurate predictions and conclusions.

Example

The number of cellphone customers with a particular phone company increased by 20% every 6 months from 1996 to 2000. The given graph shows this exponential growth between the number of customers, *N*, and the time, *t*, in months from January 1, 1996.

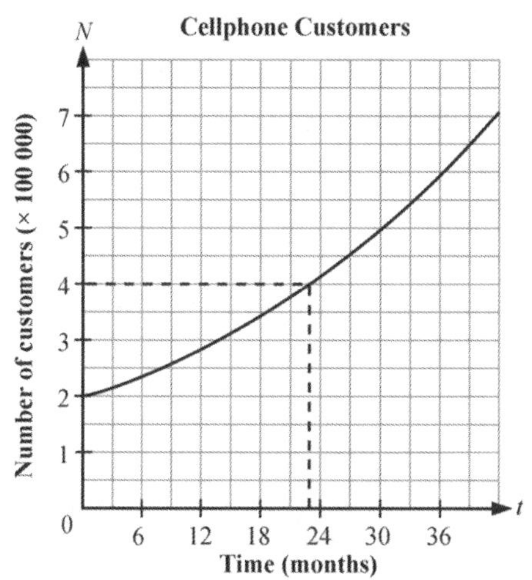

How many cellphone customers were with the company on January 1, 1996?

Solution

The *y*-intercept (value at $t = 0$) describes the number of cellphone customers on January 1, 1996.

This value is 200,000 customers.

Example

How long does it take for the number of cellphone customers to double?

Solution

If the number of cellphone customers at $t = 0$ was 200,000, find the approximate time, *t*, when there will be 400,000 customers. According to the dotted line on the graph, this occurs at about $t = 23$.

Therefore, it takes about 23 months for the number of cellphone customers to double.

Example

Write the exponential equation that represents the scenario portrayed by the given graph.

Solution

Since the given graph portrays a growth curve, the growth factor has to be larger than 1. Since 100% is a growth ratio of 1 (which means no change), then 120% (100% + 20% increase) is a growth ratio of 1.20, which is the ratio represented by the graph. Whenever a population increases by *i*%, the growth ratio is $\frac{(100\% + i\%)}{100}$.

This growth ratio occurs every 6 months. Since the original number of customers was 200,000, use the general formula of an exponential function, $N_t = N_0 \times R^{\frac{t}{p}}$. Substitute 200,000 for N_0, 1.20 for *R*, and 6 for *p*.

$$N_t = N_0 \times R^{\frac{t}{p}}$$

$$N_t = 200{,}000 \times (1.20)^{\frac{t}{6}}$$

$$N_t = 200{,}000(1.20)^{\frac{t}{6}}$$

Example

Determine the number of cellphone customers there would be on January 1, 2000.

Solution

The number of years between the starting time of January 1, 1996 to January 1, 2000 is 4 years or $4 \times 12 = 48$ months.

Therefore, you need to find the number of customers, N, at a time, $t = 48$. This can be found by substituting 48 for t and solving for N_t in the equation $N_t = 200{,}000(1.20)^{\frac{t}{6}}$.

$$\begin{aligned} N_t &= 200{,}000(1.20)^{\frac{t}{6}} \\ N_{48} &= 200{,}000(1.20)^{\frac{48}{6}} \\ &= 200{,}000(1.20)^8 \\ &= 859{,}963.392\ldots \\ &\approx 859{,}963 \text{ customers} \end{aligned}$$

Example

Use a graphing calculator to determine the month and year when there would be 650,000 customers.

Solution

To graph the function $N = 200{,}000(1.20)^{\frac{t}{6}}$, press the [$Y_1$ =] key and enter

$Y_1 = 200{,}000(1.20)$ ^ $(X/6)$.

Set your window to the following settings:

```
WINDOW
 Xmin=-5
 Xmax=50
 Xscl=5
 Ymin=0
 Ymax=1000000
 Yscl=100000
 Xres=1
```

Then, press GRAPH to get the following screen:

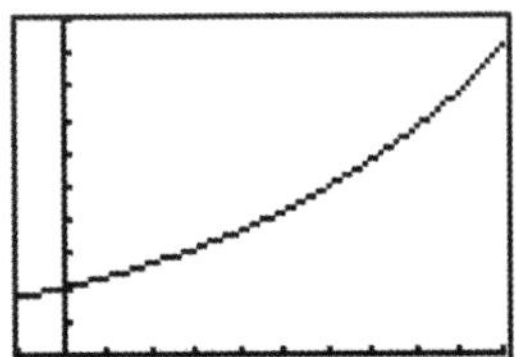

Using the TRACE feature, scroll to the right until the y-value is as close as possible to $y = 650{,}000$. The cursor should be at about $x = 38.882979$ when $y = 651{,}874.18$, as shown in the given diagram.

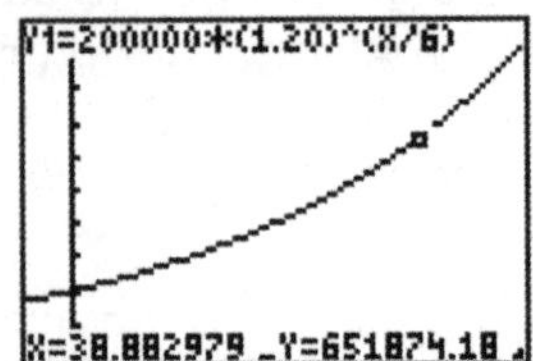

According to the graph, there would be 650,000 cellphone customers at about 38.88 months after January 1, 1996. Since there are 36 months in 3 years, this value occurs 3 years and 2.88 months after January 1, 1996, which would be at the end of March 1999.

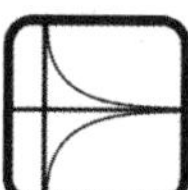

EXERCISE #1—INTERPRETING EXPRESSIONS FOR FUNCTIONS

Use the following information to answer the next question.

A contractor has building materials delivered from a lumberyard to various construction sites. The delivery cost, *C*, is based on a fixed amount plus a per-kilometer cost. The delivery cost and the distance, *d*, of the construction sites from the lumberyard are illustrated in the diagram shown.

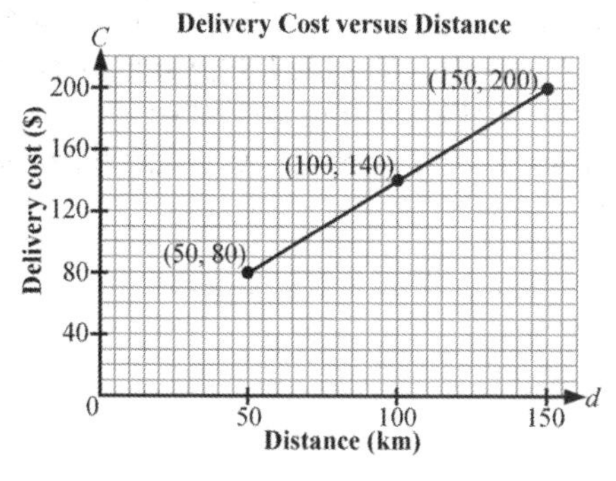

242. To the nearest dollar, the fixed delivery cost (y-intercept) is $__________.

Use the following information to answer the next question.

A rectangular water tank is being emptied at a uniform rate of 220 L/min. After 5 min, the volume of water remaining in the tank is 388 L. The variable V represents the number of liters of water in the tank, and t represents the number of minutes that have elapsed since the emptying of the tank began.

243. The linear relation that relates these two quantities is given by the equation

A. $V = 220t - 388$

B. $V = -220t + 388$

C. $V = 220t - 1{,}488$

D. $V = -220t + 1{,}488$

Use the following information to answer the next question.

An exponential graph is given.

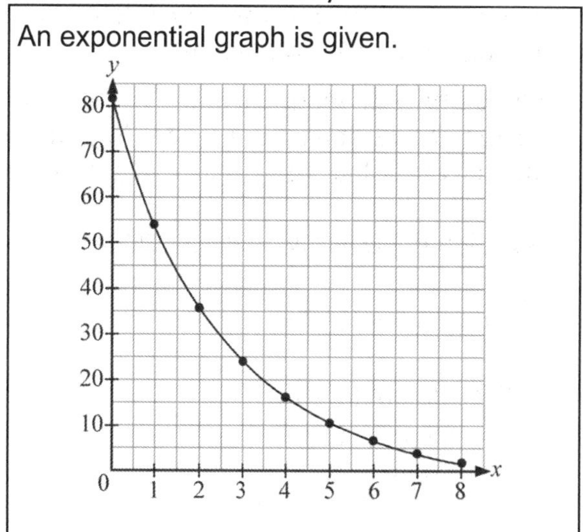

244. When $y = 16$, which of the following functions has the same x-value as the given graph?

A. $y = \frac{1}{2}x + 8$

B. $y = (x - 4)^2$

C. $y = -5x - 4$

D. $y = 2(x^2 - 8)$

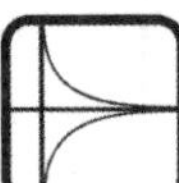

Use the following information to answer the next question.

A possible way to estimate the value of a car can be calculated using the formula $V_t = V_0(1 - r)^t$, where V_t is the value after t years, V_0 is the original value, and r is the depreciation rate expressed as a decimal. In 1996, a particular car was valued at \$27,500. Its value decreased exponentially each year afterward. For the first 7 years, the value of the car decreased by 24% of the previous year's value.

245. What will be the value of the car after 7 years?

A. \$942.85 **B.** \$3,060.75

C. \$4,027.43 **D.** \$5,299.25

Use the following information to answer the next question.

A bacteria culture grows at a rate proportional to its population. The growth rate, in bacteria/h, of the culture of bacteria is given by the function $g(t) = 1{,}000(2.5)^{\frac{t}{2}}$, in which t is the time measured in hours.

246. To the nearest whole number, what is the rate of growth of the bacteria culture after 5 h? __________ bacteria/h

Use the following information to answer the next question.

In the given graph, the mass of a certain bacteria, M, in grams, is graphed as a function of time, t, in days.

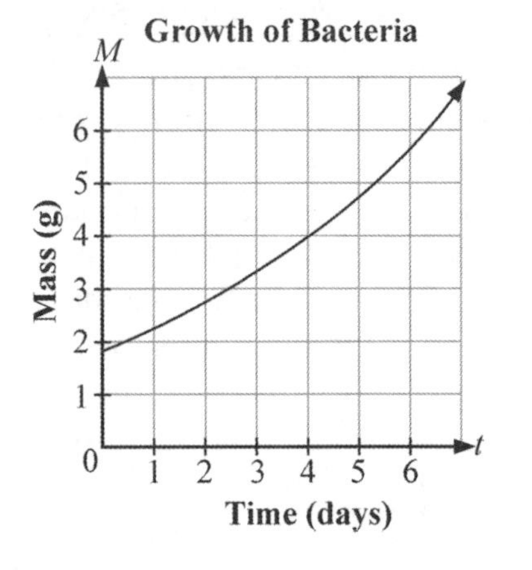

247. The initial amount of bacteria, to nearest tenth, is __________

A. 0.5 g **B.** 1.1 g

C. 1.9 g **D.** 2.2 g

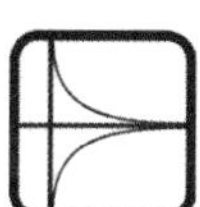

EXERCISE #1—INTERPRETING EXPRESSIONS FOR FUNCTIONS ANSWERS AND SOLUTIONS

242. 20	244. D	246. 9882
243. D	245. C	247. C

242. 20

Step 1

Choose any two points on the graph in order to determine the constant rate of change.

One possible choice is $P(50, 80)$ and $Q(100, 140)$.

Step 2

Substitute the values of these points into the slope formula, $m = \frac{y_2 - y_1}{x_2 - x_1}$, where m is the slope.

$$\begin{aligned} m &= \frac{y_2 - y_1}{x_2 - x_1} \\ &= \frac{140 - 80}{100 - 50} \\ &= \frac{60}{50} \\ &= \frac{6}{5} \end{aligned}$$

Step 3

Substitute the values of one point and the value of the slope into the slope formula, $m = \frac{y_2 - y_1}{x_2 - x_1}$, to find the fixed delivery cost (y-intercept), C, of the point $(0, C)$.

One option is to use the point (50, 80).

$$\begin{aligned} m &= \frac{y_2 - y_1}{x_2 - x_1} \\ \frac{6}{5} &= \frac{C - 80}{0 - 50} \\ \frac{6}{5} &= \frac{C - 80}{-50} \\ 6(-50) &= 5(C - 80) \\ -300 &= 5C - 400 \\ 100 &= 5C \\ \frac{100}{5} &= C \\ C &= 20 \end{aligned}$$

To the nearest dollar, the fixed delivery cost (y-intercept) is $20.

243. D

Step 1

Determine the form of the equation.

Since the volume of water in the tank depends on the amount of time that has elapsed since the emptying of the tank began, the equation has the form $V = mt + b$.

Step 2

Determine the value of m.

The tank is losing 220 L of water every minute, so the slope (or rate of change) is $m = -220$ L/min.

Step 3

Determine the value of b.

The value of b, the vertical-axis intercept, is the volume of water before the tank started emptying. This occurs when $t = 0$.

Since the tank is losing 220 L of water every minute, calculate how many liters of water were emptied from the tank in 5 min.

$5 \times 220 = 1{,}100$ L

Add 1,100 L to the volume of water remaining in the tank (388 L) to find the volume of water originally in the tank.

$388 + 1{,}100 = 1{,}488$ L

This means that $b = 1{,}488$.

Therefore, the linear equation that relates the two quantities is $V = -220t + 1{,}488$.

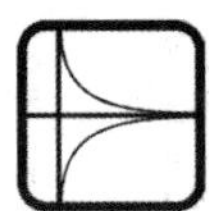

244. D

Step 1

Using the given exponential graph, determine the value of x when $y = 16$.

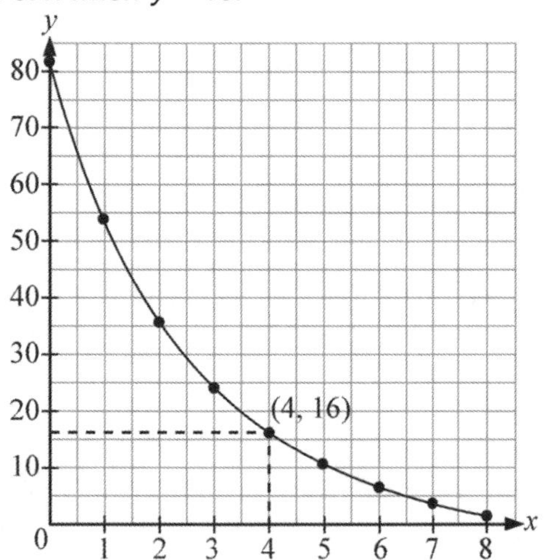

When $y = 16$, the value of x is 4.

Step 2

Substitute 16 for y into the given functions, and solve for x.

Solve for $y = \frac{1}{2}x + 8$.

$$y = \frac{1}{2}x + 8$$
$$16 = \frac{1}{2}x + 8$$
$$8 = \frac{1}{2}x$$
$$16 = x$$

Since $x = 16$, this function is not correct.

Solve for $y = (x - 4)^2$.

$$y = (x - 4)^2$$
$$16 = x^2 - 8x + 16$$
$$0 = x^2 - 8x$$
$$0 = x(x - 8)$$

Since $x = 0$ or $x = 8$, this function is not correct.

Solve for $y = -5x - 4$.

$$y = -5x - 4$$
$$16 = -5x - 4$$
$$20 = -5x$$
$$-4 = x$$

Since $x = -4$, this function is not correct.

Solve for $y = 2\left(x^2 - 8\right)$.

$$y = 2\left(x^2 - 8\right)$$
$$16 = 2x^2 - 16$$
$$32 = 2x^2$$
$$16 = x^2$$
$$\pm\sqrt{16} = x$$
$$\pm 4 = x$$

Since $x = 4$ or $x = -4$, this function is correct.

Therefore, the function $y = 2\left(x^2 - 8\right)$ has the same x-value as the given graph when $y = 16$.

245. C

Substitute 27,500 into the equation for V_0, 0.24 for r, and 7 for t, and then evaluate.

$$V_t = V_0(1 - r)^t$$
$$= 27{,}500(1 - 0.24)^7$$
$$= 27{,}500(0.76)^7$$
$$\approx 27{,}500(0.1464519457)$$
$$\approx 4{,}027.4285$$

Therefore, the value of the car after 7 years is \$4,027.43, to the nearest cent.

246. 9882

To determine the rate of growth of the bacteria after 5 h, evaluate $g(5)$.

$$g(t) = 1{,}000(2.5)^{\frac{t}{2}}$$

$$\begin{aligned} g(5) &= 1{,}000(2.5)^{\frac{5}{2}} \\ &= 1{,}000(2.5)^{2.5} \\ &= 9{,}882 \end{aligned}$$

The growth rate is 9,882 bacteria/h.

247. C

Using the given graph, determine the value of M when $t = 0$.

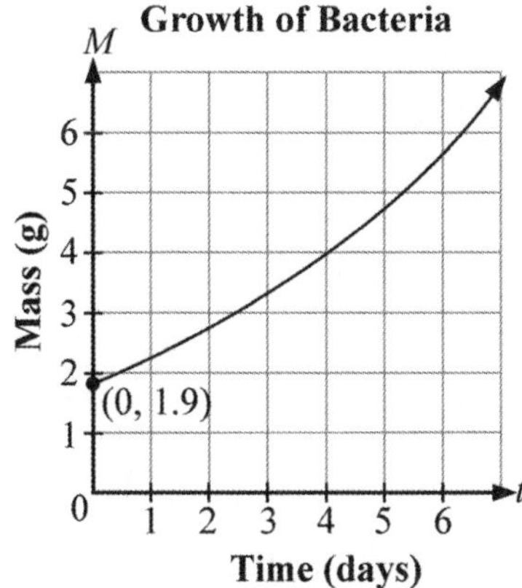

From the graph, $M = 1.9$ when $t = 0$.

Therefore, the initial amount of bacteria is 1.9 g.

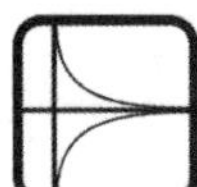

EXERCISE #2—INTERPRETING EXPRESSIONS FOR FUNCTIONS

Use the following information to answer the next question.

To hire a cab, Carla has to pay a fixed charge plus an additional constant rate for every kilometer driven.

248. If the cab driver charges \$23 for 10 km and \$33 for 15 km, what is the fixed charge to hire this cab?

A. \$1 **B.** \$2

C. \$3 **D.** \$4

Use the following information to answer the next question.

The temperature of Earth's atmosphere up to an altitude of 15 km above Earth's surface can be expressed as the linear relation $T = -5h + 15$, where T is the temperature measured in degrees Celsius and h is the altitude measured in kilometers.

249. What is the domain of this linear relation?

A. $-60°C \le T \le 15°C,\ T \in W$

B. $-60°C \le T \le 15°C,\ T \in R$

C. $0 \le h \le 15$ km, $h \in W$

D. $0 \le h \le 15$ km, $h \in R$

Use the following information to answer the next question.

A radioactive isotope technetium-99 is commonly used in various medical diagnoses. Given that a patient is injected with 10 mg of this isotope, the graph shows the amount of the isotope, m, in milligrams, remaining in her body over the next 24 hours, t.

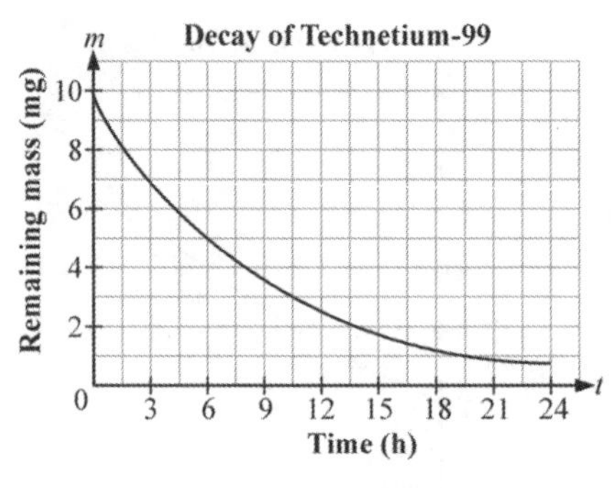

250. To the nearest 0.1 h, the half-life of the radioactive isotope is __________.

Use the following information to answer the next question.

The half-life of iodine-131 is every 8.04 days; that is, after 8.04 days, half of the iodine-131 decays. The amount, N_t, of iodine-131, in kilograms, with an initial mass of 12,600 kg, remaining after t days is given by the formula:

$$N_t = 12{,}600\left(\frac{1}{2}\right)^{\frac{t}{8.04}}$$

251. The approximate mass of iodine-131 remaining after 30 days, to the nearest whole kilogram, is

A. 131 kg **B.** 475 kg

C. 949 kg **D.** 3,378 kg

Use the following information to answer the next question.

A diamond ring was worth $12,000 and increased in value by 15% per year. Jasmine wrote the corresponding exponential equation as: $V = 12{,}000(a)^t$, where V is the value of the ring after t years.

252. The value of a in Jasmine's equation and the value, V, of the ring after 40 months, are

A. $a = 1.15$, $V = \$20{,}988$

B. $a = 1.50$, $V = \$46{,}361$

C. $a = 1.15$, $V = \$19{,}121$

D. $a = 1.50$, $V = \$60{,}750$

Use the following information to answer the next question.

The given graph shows the relationship between the wolf and rabbit populations, $P(t)$, in a Canadian forest over time, t, in months.

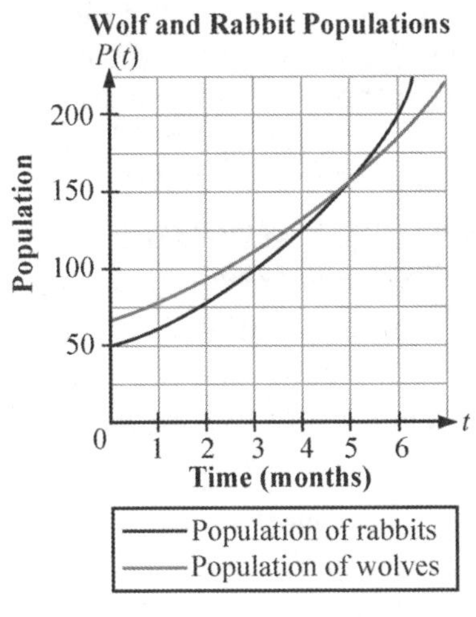

253. How many months did it take for the wolf population and the rabbit population to become equal?

A. 2

B. 3

C. 4

D. 5

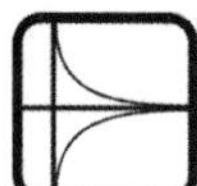

EXERCISE #2—INTERPRETING EXPRESSIONS FOR FUNCTIONS ANSWERS AND SOLUTIONS

248. C	250. 6.0	252. C
249. D	251. C	253. D

248. C

Step 1
Determine the constant rate of change, *m*.

Constant rate of change $(m) = \frac{\text{rise}}{\text{run}}$

The rise is the change in charge.
$33 - 23 = 10$
The run is the change in distance.
$15 - 10 = 5$

Constant rate of change $(m) = \frac{\$10}{5\text{ km}}$ or \$2/km

Step 2
Determine the fixed charge.
The initial value is the charge, *C*, at the start of the ride when the distance driven is 0 km. Use one of the other charge values and the value of *m* to find *c*.

$$m = \frac{\text{rise}}{\text{run}}$$
$$2 = \frac{23 - c}{10 - 0}$$
$$2 = \frac{23 - c}{10}$$
$$10(2) = 10\left(\frac{23 - c}{10}\right)$$
$$20 = 23 - c$$
$$c + 20 - 20 = 23 - c + c - 20$$
$$c = 3$$

The fixed charge, or initial value, is \$3.

249. D

The domain of a relation is the set of values for the independent variable, which in this case would be the altitude, *h*. The altitude at Earth's surface would be 0, and the information states that the relation holds up to an altitude of 15 km. The altitudes are not just the whole number altitudes (1 km, 2 km, 3 km … 15 km) but can be any real number between 0 and 15, such as 1.5 or 6.89. Thus, the domain of the given linear relation is $0 \le h \le 15$, $h \in \mathbb{R}$.

250. 6.0

If the original mass of the isotope is 10 mg at $t = 0$ h, then the half-life is the time taken for this mass to decay to half its original amount, namely $\frac{10}{2} = 5$ mg. According to the graph, the mass of 5 mg occurs at $t = 6.0$ h.

251. C

The formula for the decay of iodine-131 is given as:

$$N_t = 12{,}600\left(\frac{1}{2}\right)^{\frac{t}{8.04}}$$

where *t* is the time in days and N_t is the amount of iodine remaining after *t* days.

To find the amount of iodine remaining after 30 days, substitute $t = 30$ in the formula, and then evaluate.

$$N_{30} = 12{,}600\left(\frac{1}{2}\right)^{\frac{30}{8.04}}$$
$$\approx 12{,}600(0.0752928519)$$
$$\approx 948.6899342 \text{ kg}$$

Therefore, the approximate mass remaining after 30 days, to the nearest whole kilogram, is 949 kg.

252. C

The value *a* reflects the growth factor of the value of the ring each year. Since it increases 15% per year, $a = 115\%$ (to show how much above 100% the growth is), or as a decimal, $\frac{115\%}{100\%} = 1.15$

To find the value, *V*, of the ring after 40 months, you need to convert it to *t* years.

$\frac{40 \text{ months}}{12 \text{ months}} = 3.33333$ or $\frac{10}{3}$

Now, substitute $t = \frac{10}{3}$ into the equation to solve for value, *V*.

$$V = 12{,}000(1.15)^{\frac{10}{3}}$$
$$= 19{,}120.85819$$

The value of the ring, *V*, after 40 months, to the nearest dollar, is \$19,121.

253. D

The point at which the two populations are equal is given by the intersection point between the two curves.

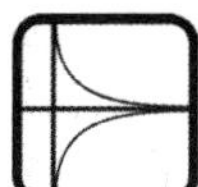

Determine the intersection point on the graph between the two curves.

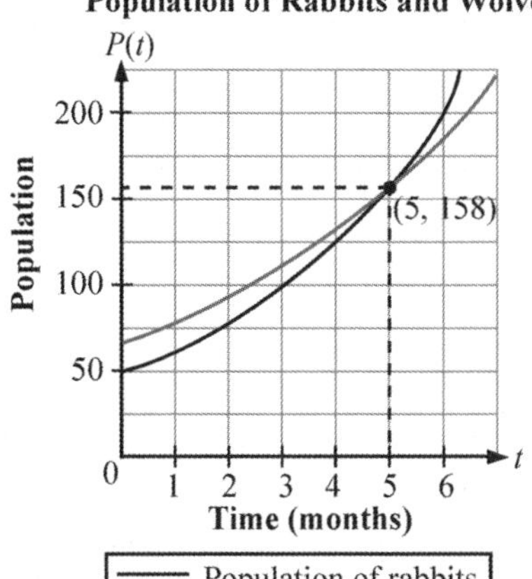

From the given graph, the intersection point between the two curves is (5, 158). Therefore, it took about 5 months for the wolf and rabbit populations to become equal.

NOTES

Single Variable Data

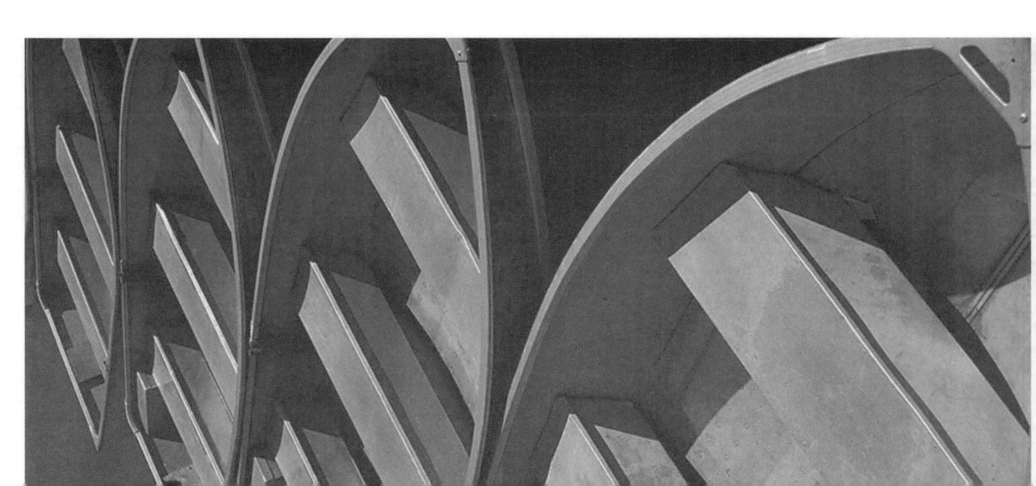

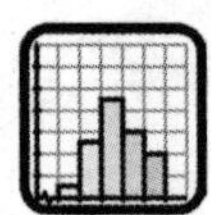

SINGLE VARIABLE DATA

Table of Correlations

Standard		Concepts	Exercise #1	Exercise #2
Unit3.1	Summarize, represent, and interpret data on a single count or measurement variable.			
S-ID.1	*Represent data with plots on the real number line (dot plots, histograms, and box plots).*	Displaying Data in a Scatter Plot	3	12
		Calculating Median, Range, and Quartiles of a Data Set	254	273
		Representing a Set of Data in a Box-and-Whisker Plot	255	274
		Representing Data in a Histogram	256	275
		Constructing a Double Line Graph	257	276
		Representing Data in a Line Plot	258	277
S-ID.2	*Use statistics appropriate to the shape of the data distribution to compare center (median, mean) and spread (interquartile range, standard deviation) of two or more different data sets.*	Calculating Mean	259	278
		Calculating Median	260	279
		Calculating Mode	261	280
		Applying Mean, Median, and Mode	262	281
		Calculating Variance and Standard Deviation of a Data Set	263	282
		Determine Quartiles and Interquartile Range for a Set of Data	264	283
		Calculating Standard Deviation and Variance in a Sample Data Set	265	284
		Interpreting the Range and Interquartile Range of a Set of Data	266	285
		Determining the Mean and Variance for Discrete Uniform Distribution	267	286
		Determining Mean and Variance for an Exponential Distribution	268	287
		Determining Mean and Variance for a Binomial Distribution	269	288
		Comparing Two Related Sets of Data Using Measures of Central Tendency	270	289
S-ID.3	*Interpret differences in shape, center, and spread in the context of the data sets, accounting for possible effects of extreme data points (outliers).*	Identifying Outliers for a Set of Data Given Graphically	271	290
		Identifying and Understanding the Effect of Outliers	272	291

S-ID.1 Represent data with plots on the real number line (dot plots, histograms, and box plots).

Calculating Median, Range, and Quartiles of a Data Set

A set of data can be analyzed to determine certain values. These values can be used to describe the data, organize the data to gain information, and make predictions about future data.

Median

The **median** is a number that represents the middle in a set of numbers. It is the middle number in a set of numbers arranged in order from least to greatest.

To calculate the median of a set of numbers, follow these steps:

1. List the numbers in order from least to greatest.
2. If there is an odd number of values, the median is the number in the middle. If there is an even number of values, the median will be the **mean** (or average) of the two middle numbers.

Example

14 18 16 12 13 17 15

Find the median of the given list of numbers. ________

Solution

List the numbers in order from least to greatest.
12 13 14 15 16 17 18

Since there is an odd number of values, the number in the middle is the median.
12 13 14 [15] 16 17 18

The median is 15.

Example

{20, 12, 16, 26, 15, 24}

Determine the median of the given data set.

Solution

Step 1
Place the values in order from least to greatest.
12, 15, 16, 20, 24, 26

Step 2
Determine the middle numbers.

There is an even number of values.

12 15 [16 20] 24 26

Calculate the average of the two middle numbers.
16 + 20 = 36
36 ÷ 2 = 18

The median is 18.

Range

In a set of numeric data, the upper extreme is the highest value and the lower extreme is the lowest value. The **range** is the difference between the upper and lower extremes.

Measures of central tendency are not the only thing to look at when examining data. The distribution of data organized in increasing order is also analyzed by looking at the upper and lower extremes, range, and upper and lower quartiles, and by looking at the data for gaps or clusters of data.

Example

{18, 32, 12, 45, 23, 54, 33, 31, 35, 45, 30, 21}.

Calculate the range of the data set using the highest and lowest values.

Solution

Step 1
Place the numbers in order from least to greatest.
12, 18, 21, 23, 30, 31, 32, 33, 35, 45, 45, 54

Step 2
Subtract the lowest value from the highest value in the set.

The lowest value is 12, and the highest value is 54.

Range = highest value – lowest value
= 54 – 12
= 42

The range is 42.

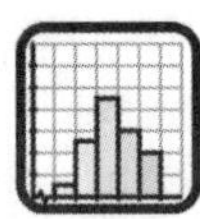

QUARTILES

The median divides the data so that 50% of the data is below the median and 50% of the data is above the median.

The upper and lower quartiles divide a set of data organized from smallest to largest into quarters. The lower quartile is the middle (or median) of the data values that lie below the median. The upper quartile is the middle (or median) of the data values that lie above the median.

To find the upper and lower quartiles, follow these steps:

1. Organize the data in increasing order.
2. Identify the median and the lower and upper extremes.
3. Find the lower quartile by finding the median of the numbers that lie below the data set's median.
4. Find the upper quartile by finding the median of the numbers that lie above the data set's median.

Example

A set of data is given.
18, 32, 12, 45, 23, 54, 33, 31, 35, 45, 30, 21

Find the upper and lower quartiles of this data.

Solution

Step 1
Organize the data in increasing order.
12, 18, 21, 23, 30, 31, 32, 33, 35, 45, 45, 54

Step 2
Identify the median and the lower and upper extremes.

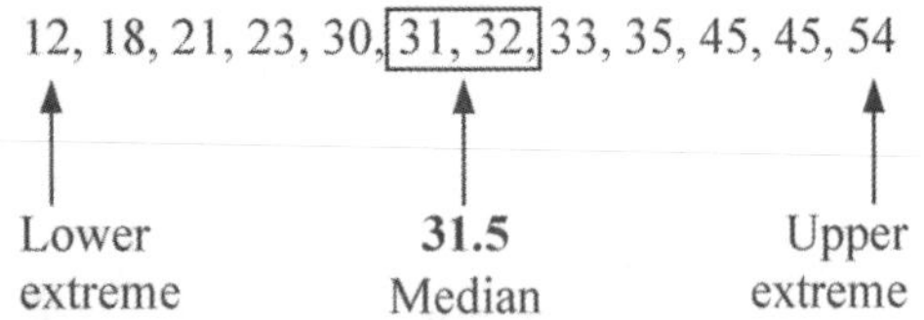

Step 3
Find the lower quartile by finding the median of the data between the lower extreme and the median.

12, 18, [21, 23,] 30, 31, 32, 33, 35, 45, 45, 54

↑
22

Step 4
Find the upper quartile by finding the median of the data between the median and the upper extreme.

12, 18, 21, 23, 30, 31, 32, 33, [35, 45,] 45, 54

↑
40

The lower quartile is 22, and the upper quartile is 40.

This diagram illustrates the relationship between the data distribution in the previous example and the lower and upper extremes, lower and upper quartiles, and the median.

Data Distribution

25%	25%	25%	25%

12, 18, 21, 23, 30, [31, 32,] 33, 35, 45, 45, **54**

Lower extreme: 12
22 Lower quartile
31.5 Median
40 Upper quartile
Upper extreme: 54

Example

A set of data is given.
18, 32, 12, 45, 23, 54, 32

Find the upper and lower quartiles of the given data.

Solution

Step 1
Organize the data in increasing order.
12, 18, 23, 32, 32, 45, 54

Step 2
Identify the median and lower and upper extremes.

The median is the value in the middle of the list of data. The lower extreme is the smallest value, and the upper extreme is the largest value.

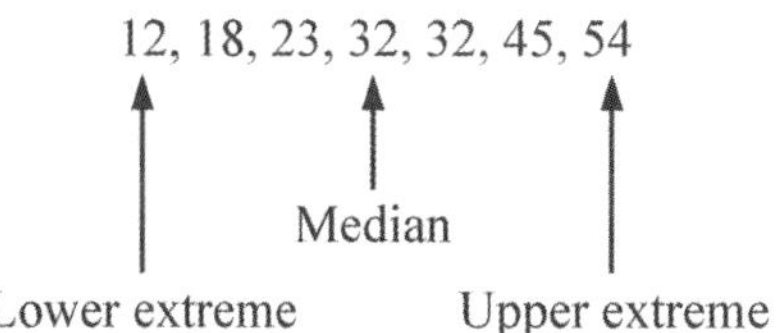

Step 3
Identify the lower quartile.

The lower quartile can be found by examining the list of values below the median and identifying the median of this group of data.

12, [18], 23, 32, 32, 45, 54

↑
18

The lower quartile is 18.

Step 4
Identify the upper quartile.

The upper quartile can be found by examining the list of values above the median and identifying the median of this group of data.

12, 18, 23, 32, 32, [45], 54

↑
45

The upper quartile is 45.

Representing a Set of Data in a Box-and-Whisker Plot

A box-and-whisker plot is often used in explanatory data analysis. It is a graphical representation of a data set created from the data's five-number summary. A box-and-whisker plot displays the data in a summary format. This type of format is useful for indicating whether a distribution is skewed, for determining the degree of data dispersion, and for identifying outliers.

The following diagram shows the locations of the five-number summary points plotted on a number line.

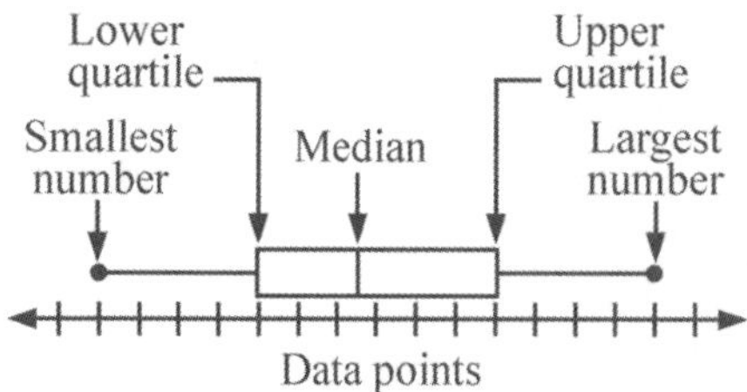

Make a box-and-whisker plot using the following five steps:

1. Determine the five-number summary. The five numbers are the five specific points used for making box-and-whisker plots. The five points are the smallest number, the largest number, the median, the lower quartile, and the upper quartile.
2. Make a number line based on the numbers presented in the data set.
3. Plot the five-number summary points above the line.
4. Join the smallest value and the lower quartile value to make one whisker, and join the upper quartile value and the largest value to make the other whisker.
5. Make a box around the median (middle value) using the lower and upper quartiles as end points of the box.

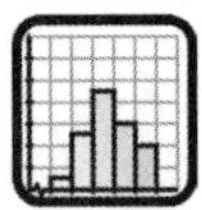

Example

A shoe store compiled a list of the shoe sizes in stock for a particular group of styles.

The following set of data represents the different shoe sizes:

3, 4, 4, 6, 7, 7, 8, 9, 10, 11, 11, 11, 12

Make a box-and-whisker plot using the given set of data.

Solution

Step 1

Look at the data set, and determine the five-number summary points.

I. Smallest value—3
II. Largest value—12
III. Median—8
IV. Lower quartile—5 (This is the median of the values less than the median of the entire set. Use 3, 4, 4, 6, 7, 7, and find the median. The middle numbers are 4 and 6, so add them and divide by 2 to find their mean.) 4 + 6 = 10 ÷ 2 = 5
V. Upper quartile—11 (This is the median of the numbers greater than the median of the entire set. Use 9, 10, 11, 11, 11, 12. The middle numbers are 11 and 11, so add them and divide by 2 to find their mean.)

Step 2

Draw a number line.

It is always a good idea to extend the number line past the smallest data value as well as past the largest data value to provide more room to work. Make sure that the numbers on the number line are evenly spaced.

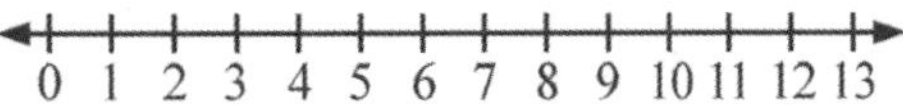

Step 3

Plot the five-number summary points on the line (3, 12, 8, 5, 11).

The points need to be above the line because the box still has to be drawn around the median.

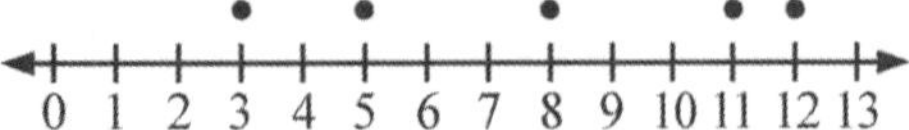

Step 4

Join the whiskers.

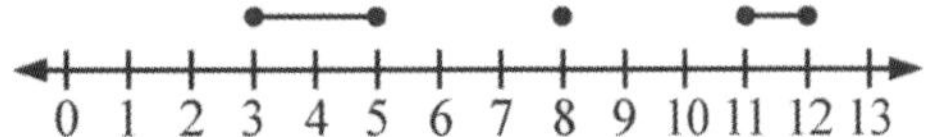

Step 5

Make the box around the median. Do not connect the median with anything; it should be inside the box. Then, give the box and whisker plot a title.

The complete box-and-whisker plot representing the given data is as shown.

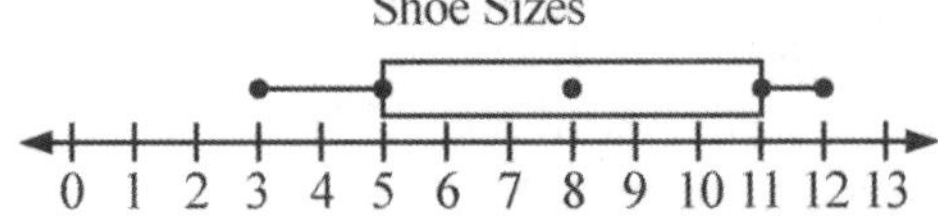

A box-and-whisker plot is divided into quartiles. This means that it is divided into four equal parts. Each whisker contains 25% of the data, and the box represents 50% of the data, 25% from the median to the lower quartile and 25% from the median to the upper quartile.

Even though each part represents 25% of the data, the lengths of the box and whiskers can vary from one set of data to another. Evenly distributed data has whiskers that are close to the same length and a box that is in the middle of the plot. In an evenly distributed set of data, the sum of the length of both whiskers should equal the length of the box. Unevenly distributed data usually has one whisker that is longer than the other and a box that is more on the left or the right side of the plot. Additionally, for unevenly distributed data, the dot for the median is closer to one edge of the box.

Example

The following set of data represents the ages of the players on a senior hockey team.
31, 33, 33, 34, 35, 37, 38, 38, 39, 40, 41, 57

Using the given data, make a box-and-whisker plot.

Solution

Step 1
Determine the five-number summary points.

I. Smallest value—31
II. Largest value—57 (Because this number is much larger than the number before it, the upper whisker of the plot will be much longer than the lower one.)
III. Median—37.5 ((37 + 38) ÷ 2 = 37.5)
IV. Lower quartile—33.5 ((33 + 34) ÷ 2 = 33.5)
V. Upper quartile—39.5 ((39 + 40) ÷ 2 = 39.5)

Step 2
Make a number line, and plot the five-number summary points on the line.

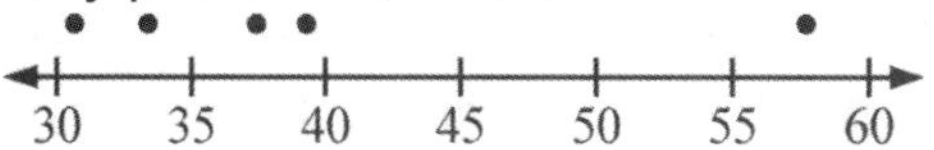

Step 3
Join the upper and lower whiskers, and draw a box around the median.
The following box-and-whisker plot represents the given data.

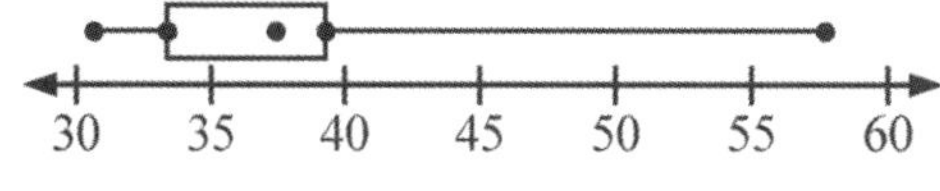

Sometimes, when certain data is represented in a plot, the whiskers are different in length.
Even though the upper whisker can be much longer than the lower whisker, it still represents 25% of the data.

By looking carefully at a box-and-whisker plot, it is possible to answer various questions about the data that is represented.

Example

A box-and-whisker plot is shown.

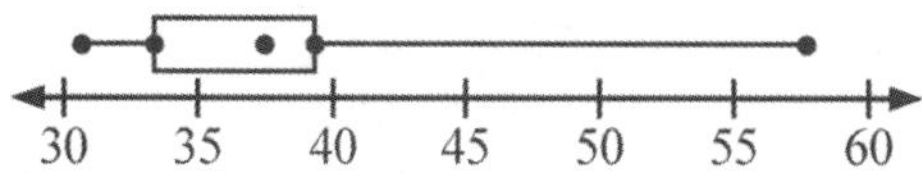

Approximately what percentage of the data is below 35?

Solution

Recall that a whisker represents 25% of the given data.

Since 35 is past the whisker, it represents more than 25%.
The next 25% of the data is cut off at the median. Because 35 is about a third of the way between the lower quartile and the median, estimate that it is about 8% more than the lower quartile.

$25 \times \frac{1}{3} \approx 8.33$

To determine the approximate percentage of data below 35, add 25% from the whisker and the 8% that is more than the lower quartile.
$25 + 8 = 33$

The percentage of data below 35 is approximately 33%.

A box-and-whisker plot is shown.

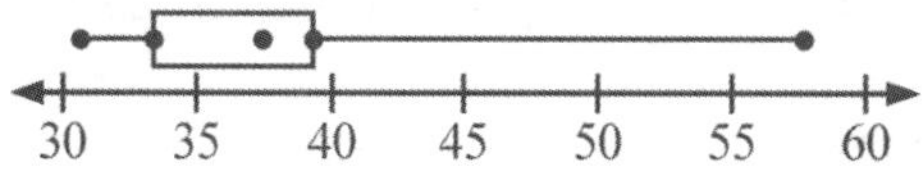

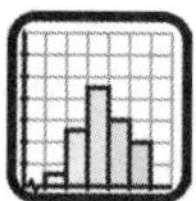

Approximately what percentage of the data lies between 45 and 55?

Solution

Recall that a whisker represents 25% of the data. The part between 45 and 55 is about half of the whisker, so it represents approximately 12.5% of the data.

Representing Data in a Histogram

A histogram looks similar to a bar graph, but since the data is continuous, there are no gaps between the bars. The bars in a histogram are used to represent continuous data found in a frequency table. The given graph is an example of a histogram.

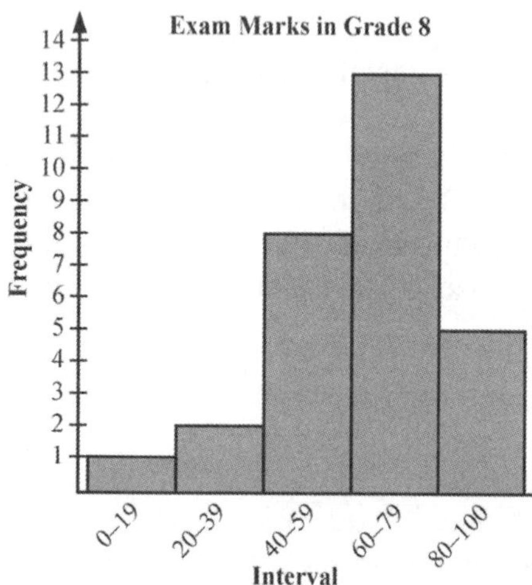

The horizontal axis of a histogram represents the intervals, and the vertical axis represents the frequency of the data.

In order to make a histogram, first collect the necessary data. Suppose that the objective is to try to measure the heights (in centimeters) of all 30 students in a class. The following measurements represent the data that might have been collected:
177 cm, 176 cm, 183 cm, 177 cm, 180 cm, 171 cm, 160 cm, 180 cm, 162 cm, 157 cm, 183 cm, 155 cm, 177 cm, 167 cm, 176 cm, 171 cm, 145 cm, 180 cm, 174 cm, 177 cm, 156 cm, 166 cm, 178 cm, 184 cm, 180 cm, 165 cm, 167 cm, 178 cm, 177 cm, 164 cm

Second, the data must be grouped into smaller, more manageable intervals.

The following intervals would be appropriate when organizing the heights of students in a class:
145–149 cm, 150–154 cm, 155–159 cm, 160–164 cm, 165–169 cm, 170–174 cm, 175–179 cm, 180–184 cm

When creating a histogram, the only relevant information is found in the numbers and their frequencies. The number of people in each height category is revealed by creating a frequency table with intervals.

Height (cm)	Tally	Frequency
145–149	|	1
150–154		0
155–159	|||	3
160–164	|||	3
165–169	||||	4
170–174	|||	3
175–179	~~||||~~ ||||	9
180–184	~~||||~~ ||	7

The number next to each height is the frequency with which that height occurs. The higher the frequency of each interval, the more people there are in that category.

By grouping data into intervals, there will be fewer bars on the graph, and each bar will contain a significant amount of data. More importantly, there is now a continuous range of heights, from 145 cm to 184 cm.

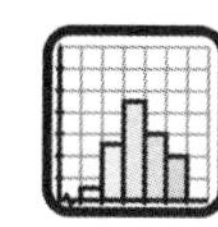

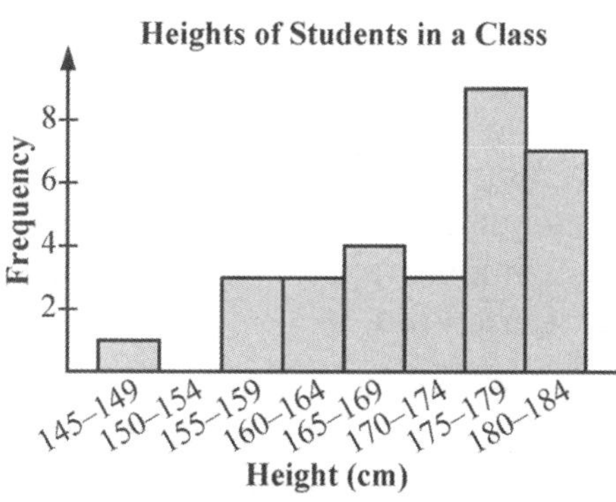

In a histogram, the bars must touch because the set of data is represented by numbers that are grouped to form a continuous range from left to right. There are no gaps in the numbers along the bottom axis because every possible height of the classmates can be located in one of the intervals.

Constructing a Double Line Graph

Line graphs are one of the most common ways of displaying data. They are best used for measuring data that is continuously changing. Double line graphs are used to compare two different categories of continuously changing data.

Keep the following points in mind when you create a double line graph:

- Give the graph a title.
- Label the x-axis and the y-axis.
- Use equal and appropriate intervals.
- Make and label a key to show the meaning of each line.

Example

Jordan was asked to compare a classmate's heart rate in two different classes: a mathematics class and a physical education (P.E.) class. He found a heart-rate monitor that recorded heart rate at five-minute intervals. Each class was 60 min in length. Jordan recorded all the data he collected from his classmate in the table shown.

Time (minutes)	Heart Rate during Math Class (beats per minute)	Heart Rate during P.E. Class (beats per minute)
0	72	75
5	70	80
10	77	143
15	74	134
20	75	151
25	73	145
30	75	143
35	73	138
40	72	137
45	71	143
50	73	135
55	72	117
60	73	90

Plot the given data on a double line graph.

Solution

Your double line graph for the given data should look like the graph shown. The red line represents the data collected during mathematics class, and the blue line represents the data collected during physical education class.

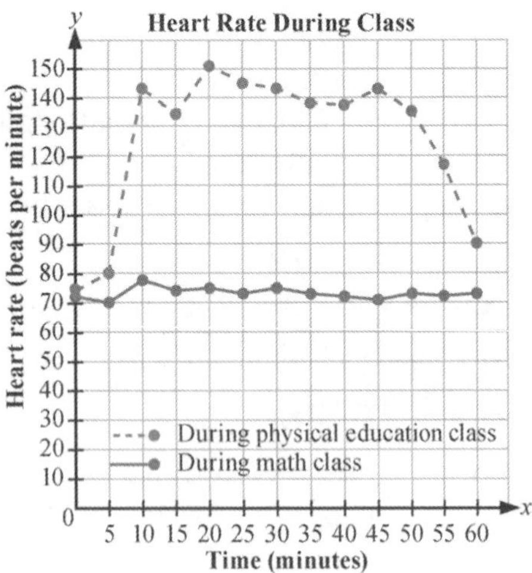

By looking at the graph, you can see that the heart rate of Jordan's classmate was much higher during the physical education class than it was during the mathematics class.

Representing Data in a Line Plot

A **line plot** is a sketch of data in which a check mark, X, or other symbol is drawn above a number line.

Example

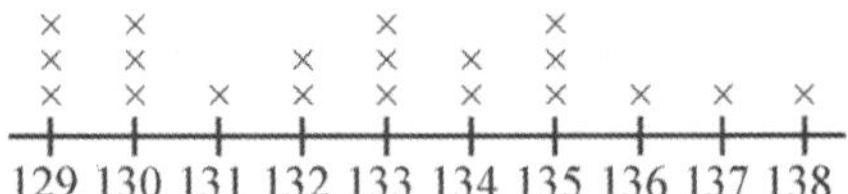

The bottom of a line plot is a number line. The number of Xs shows how many times that number appeared in the data set.

Line plots look similar to bar graphs, but they are used to show data that are given as a set of numbers. Examples of this type of data are the number of letters that your friends have in their names or your results when you roll a standard six-sided die.

To organize collected data on a line plot, follow these steps:

1. Draw a horizontal line segment. Label all the possible outcomes under the line segment.
2. Use a symbol to represent each time an outcome occurred.

Example

The given data shows the distance, to the nearest centimeter, that each student in a Grade 7 class can jump for the long jump.

434	440	429	427	439
430	434	434	435	428
427	431	432	435	431
430	440	437	431	438

Display the given data set on a line plot.

Solution

Step 1

Draw a horizontal line segment. Label all the possible outcomes under the line segment.

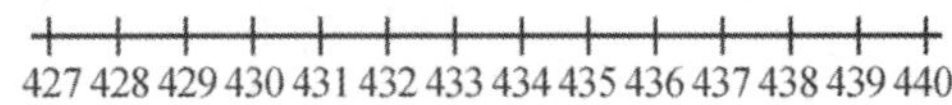

Step 2

Use a symbol to represent each time an outcome occurred.

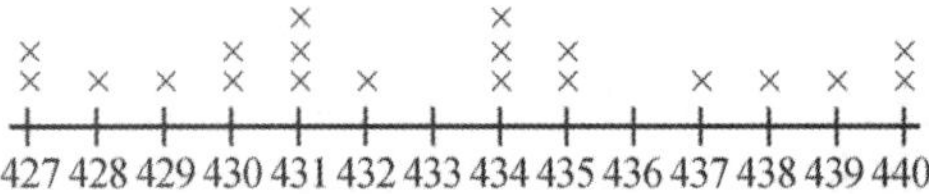

S-ID.2 Use statistics appropriate to the shape of the data distribution to compare center (median, mean) and spread (interquartile range, standard deviation) of two or more different data sets.

Calculating Mean

When given a set of data, statistical analysis can be performed to determine important information from the data. The mean, median, and mode are three measures of central tendency for a set of data. A set of data is an unordered collection of values. The set is usually within curly brackets { }.

The mean is often referred to as the average of a set of data.

To calculate the mean of a set of numbers, follow these steps:

1. Find the sum of the values.
2. Divide the sum of the values by the number of values.

Example

{12, 10, 14, 8, 16}

Calculate the mean of the given data set.

Solution

Step 1
Find the sum of the values.
12 + 10 + 14 + 8 + 16 = 60

Step 2
Divide the sum of the values by the number of values.

There are five values, so divide the sum by 5.
60 ÷ 5 = 12

The mean of the data set is 12.

Calculating Median

When given a set of data, statistical analysis can be performed to determine important information from the data. Central tendency is the tendency of data to merge around certain points near the middle of a set of data. The mean, median, and mode are three measures of central tendency for a set of data. A set of data is an unordered collection of values. The set is usually within curly brackets { }.

The median is the middle value in a set of data when the data is arranged in ascending order. It divides the data so that 50% of the data is above the median and 50% is below the median.

There are two possible results for median:

- Odd number of values—the number located exactly in the middle.
- Even number of values—the average of the two middle numbers.

To determine the median of a set of numbers, follow these steps:

1. Place the values in order from least to greatest.
2. Determine the middle number(s).

Example

{14, 18, 16, 12, 13, 17, 15}

Determine the median of the given data set.

Solution

Step 1
Place the values in order from least to greatest.
12, 13, 14, 15, 16, 17, 18

Step 2
Determine the middle number.

There is an odd number of values, so only one number is in the middle.
12, 13, 14, **15**, 16, 17, 18

The median is 15.

Example

{20, 12, 16, 26, 15, 24}

Determine the median of the given data set.

Solution

Step 1
Place the values in order from least to greatest.
12, 15, 16, 20, 24, 26

Step 2
Determine the middle numbers.

There is an even number of values.

12 15 [16 20] 24 26

Calculate the average of the two middle numbers.
16 + 20 = 36
36 ÷ 2 = 18

The median is 18.

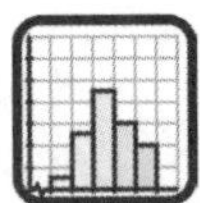

Calculating Mode

When given a set of data, statistical analysis can be performed to determine important information from the data. **Central tendency** is the tendency of data to merge around certain points near the middle of a set of data. The mean, median, and mode are three measures of central tendency for a set of data. A set of data is an unordered collection of values. The set is usually within curly brackets { }.

The mode of a set of data is the value in the set that occurs most often.

There are three possible results for mode:

- One mode—one number occurs more often than the other numbers.
- More than one mode—more than one number occurs the same number of times.
- No mode—all the numbers occur the same number of times.

To determine the mode of a set of numbers, follow these steps:

1. Place the values in order from least to greatest.
2. Determine which numbers occur most often, if any.

Example

{4, 9, 12, 7, 9, 2, 12, 8, 9, 4, 11, 3}

Determine the mode of the data set.

Solution

Step 1
Place the values in order from least to greatest.
2, 3, 4, 4, 7, 8, 9, 9, 9, 11, 12, 12

Step 2
Determine which numbers occur most frequently.

The numbers 4 and 12 occur twice and 9 occurs three times. The rest of the numbers occur once.

The mode is 9 because it occurs more often than any other number.

Example

{7, 3, 4, 8, 5, 4, 6, 3}

Determine the mode of the data set.

Solution

Step 1
Place the values in order from least to greatest.
3, 3, 4, 4, 5, 6, 7, and 8

Step 2
Determine which numbers occur most often.

The 3 and 4 occur twice, and the other numbers occur once.

The modes are 3 and 4.

Example

{5, 4, 2, 8, 6, 9, 7, 0}

Determine the mode of the data set.

Solution

Step 1
Place the values in order from least to greatest.

0, 2, 4, 5, 6, 7, 8, and 9

Step 2
Determine which numbers occur most often, if any.

Each number occurs once in the data set.

Since no number occurs more than any of the others, there is no mode.

Applying Mean, Median, and Mode

Statistical analysis is performed on data to extract information from it. Central tendency is the tendency of data to merge around certain points near the middle of a set of data. Most random sets of data when graphed will result in a bell curve with a few points at either end with the majority of the points in the middle.

The measures of central tendency include the mean, median, and mode. Which one you use to describe the data depends on the kind of data that is presented.

The **mean** is a good representation of central tendency for sets of data that have no major outliers. Because the mean is greatly affected by outliers, it is not a good representation for skewed data.

The **median** is a good representation of central tendency for data that contains outliers. Because the median is not greatly affected by outliers, it is a good representation for skewed data.

The **mode** is a good representation for central tendency for sets of categorical data. Categorical data is data that can be divided into groups. Examples of categorical data are size (small, medium, large), music style (pop, jazz, rock, hip hop), or age group (infant, toddler, adolescent, adult, senior).

To determine which measure of central tendency to use, follow these steps:

1. Assess the data.
2. Choose the best measure of tendency.

Example

A golfer wants to know the best representation of his golf score. The scores for ten rounds of 18 holes of golf were collected and arranged in ascending order.
63, 63, 71, 73, 75, 79, 79, 83, 86, 88

Which measure of central tendency is **best** used in this situation?

Solution

Step 1
Assess the data.
Look for outliers and type of data.
There are no major outliers, and the data is not categorical.

Step 2
Choose the best measure of tendency.
The mean is a good option to use to describe the golf score since there are no outliers.

$$\frac{63+63+71+73+75+79+79+83+86+88}{10} = \frac{760}{10} = 76$$

The golfer's average score is 76.
Mean is the best representation of his golf score using all of the scores because there is no outlier.

Example

Mr. Mellot wanted to know the average test score of his class, so he recorded these marks.
75%, 83%, 75%, 82%, 84%, 5%, 77%, 76%, 81%, 79%.

Which measure of central tendency is **best** used in this situation?

Solution

Step 1
Assess the data.
Look for outliers and type of data.
The data has an outlier of 5%, and the data is not categorical.

Step 2
Choose the best measure of tendency.
Median is the best measure of tendency when an average is required with an outlier in the data.
5%, 75%, 75%, 76%, 77%, 79%, 81%, 82%, 83%, 84%

$$\frac{77+79}{2} = 78$$

The average was approximately 78%.
Median is the best representation of the class's performance, leaving out the one test score that was unusually low.

Example

Evelyn works in a shoe store. She recorded the size of girls' shoes that were sold during the day.
6, 7, 6, 7, 7, 8, 7, 7, 9, 7, 7, 6, 6, 7

Which measure of central tendency is **best** used in this situation?

Solution

Step 1
Assess the data.
Look for outliers and type of data.
The data has no outliers. Since the shoes can be grouped into sizes, the data is categorical.

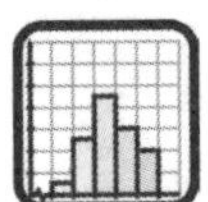

Step 2

Choose the best measure of tendency.

Mode is the best measure of central tendency for categorical data.

Place the values in order from least to greatest.
6, 6, 6, 6, 7, 7, 7, 7, 7, 7, 7, 7, 8, 9

Size 7 shoes were the most popular size of shoe sold.

Mode is the best representation of the size of shoe sold because the data can be categorized.

Calculating Variance and Standard Deviation of a Data Set

The variance and standard deviation of a data set are both measures of dispersion that represent how the data is spread about the mean. If the data values are spread out, the variance and standard-deviation value will be greater than if the data values are clustered together about the mean.

The variance is the average squared deviation of each number from the mean in a given data set. Variance is denoted by the small Greek letter sigma squared (σ^2). For the set of values $\{x_1, x_2, x_3, \ldots x_{n-1}, x_n\}$, the variance can be calculated as

$$\sigma^2 = \frac{(x_1 - \mu)^2 + (x_2 - \mu)^2 + \ldots + (x_n - \mu)^2}{n},$$ in which μ represents the mean.

The standard deviation is the square root of the variance. For the set of values $\{x_1, x_2, x_3, \ldots x_{n-1}, x_n\}$, the standard deviation can be calculated using the following formula:

$$\sigma = \sqrt{\frac{(x_1 - \mu)^2 + (x_2 - \mu)^2 + \ldots + (x_n - \mu)^2}{n}},$$ in which μ = the mean.

Example

A set of data is collected from 8 students who want to determine whether a new movie is worth seeing. Using a rating scale of 1 to 10, the set of data collected is $\{5, 7, 8, 5, 7, 6, 3, 9\}$.

To the nearest hundredth, determine the mean, the variance, and the standard deviation of the given movie ratings.

Solution

The mean is given by the formula

$$\mu = \frac{x_1 + x_2 + \ldots + x_n}{n}.$$

There are 8 data values, so $n = 8$.

Substitute the movie-rating values into the mean formula, and solve.

$$\begin{aligned}\mu &= \frac{5+7+8+5+7+6+3+9}{8}\\ &= \frac{50}{8}\\ &= 6.25\end{aligned}$$

The mean of the data set is 6.25.

Substitute these values (and the data values) into the variance formula

$$\sigma^2 = \frac{(x_1 - \mu)^2 + (x_2 - \mu)^2 + \ldots + (x_n - \mu)^2}{n},$$

and solve.

$$\sigma^2 = \frac{(5-6.25)^2 + (7-6.25)^2 + (8-6.25)^2 + (5-6.25)^2 + (7-6.25)^2 + (6-6.25)^2 + (3-6.25)^2 + (9-6.25)^2}{8}$$

$$\sigma^2 = \frac{(-1.25)^2 + (0.75)^2 + (1.75)^2 + (-1.25)^2 + (0.75)^2 + (-0.25)^2 + (-3.25)^2 + (2.75)^2}{8}$$

$$\sigma^2 \approx \frac{25.5}{8}$$

$$\sigma^2 \approx 3.1875$$

The variance of the data is approximately 3.19.

The standard deviation of the set of data is the square root of the variance. Take the square root of the variance.

$\sigma = \sqrt{\sigma^2}$
$\sigma \approx \sqrt{3.1875}$
$\sigma \approx 1.79$

The standard deviation of the data is approximately 1.79.

Recall that the standard deviation is a measure of how spread out the data values are from the mean. The larger the standard deviation, the more spread out the data values are from the mean.

In the original set of data {5, 7, 8, 5, 7, 6, 3, 9}, the mean is 6.25. Since the numbers are reasonably close together, a relatively small standard deviation of 1.79 results.

Compare the original set to the data set {2, 9, 8, 3, 10, 8, 1, 9}. This new set also has a mean of 6.25. However, it has a standard deviation of 3.38. The standard deviation is larger because the data values are more dispersed.

Consider a third set, {6, 6, 7, 5, 6, 6, 7, 7}. It also has a mean of 6.25, but has a standard deviation of 0.66. The data values are much closer together here, so the standard deviation is smaller.

Determine Quartiles and Interquartile Range for a Set of Data

A set of data can be split into four quarters. The first quartile, Q_1 or lower quartile, divides the first half of the data in half, so it is the first 25%, or 25th percentile. The second quartile, Q_2 or median, divides the data in half, so that exactly 50% of the data is above the second quartile and 50% of the data is below the second quartile, or the 50th percentile. The third quartile, Q_3 or upper quartile, divides the second half of the data in half, so it is the first 75%, or 75th percentile.

When you split up a data set like this, a quarter of the data is in each section and half of the data is between the first and third quartile. The difference between the third and first quartile is called the *interquartile range*, or IQR.

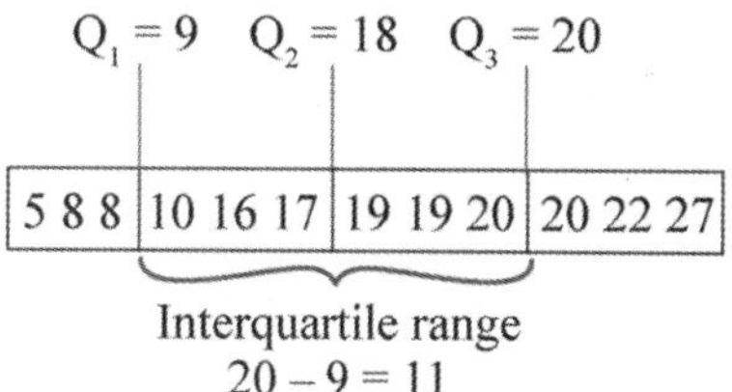

The first quartile, Q_1, is the middle (or median) of the data values that lie below the second quartile. The third quartile, Q_3, is the middle (or median) of the data values that lie above the second quartile.

Calculating Interquartile Range without a Calculator

To find the interquartile range, follow these steps:

1. Order the set from least to greatest.
2. Find the Q_2, or median.
3. Calculate the Q_1 by finding the middle of the data below the median.
4. Calculate the Q_3 by finding the middle of the data above the median.
5. Determine the interquartile range by finding the difference between the two quartiles, $IQR = Q_3 - Q_1$.

Example

A set of data is given.
153.4, 215.2, 248.7, 120.9, 198.6, 159.5, 187.4, 202.1, 227.3

Find the interquartile range of the data.

Solution

Step 1
Order the set of data from least to greatest.

120.9, 153.4, 159.5, 187.4, 198.6, 202.1, 215.2, 227.3, 248.7

Step 2
Find the Q_2, or median.

There are nine values in the data set, and the middle value is 198.6. Therefore, $Q_2 = 198.6$.

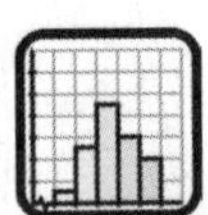

Step 3
Calculate the Q_1 by finding the middle of the data below the median.
Find the median of the numbers lower than 198.6.
120.9, **153.4**, **159.5**, 187.4
Calculate the average of the two middle numbers.

$$\frac{153.4 + 159.5}{2} = 156.45$$

Therefore, $Q_1 = 156.45$.

Step 4
Calculate the Q_3 by finding the middle of the data above the median.
Find the median of the numbers above 198.6.
202.1, **215.2**, **227.3**, 248.7
Calculate the average of the two middle numbers.

$$\frac{215.2 + 227.3}{2} = 221.25$$

Therefore, $Q_3 = 221.25$.

Step 5
Determine the interquartile range by finding the difference between the two quartiles.
$IQR = Q_3 - Q_1$
$IQR = 221.25 - 156.45$
$IQR = 64.8$

Calculating Interquartile Range with a Calculator

To find the interquartile range with a TI-83 or similar graphing calculator, follow these steps:

1. Enter the data into list L_1. Press STAT, then select 1:Edit.... Enter each data value in the set, pressing ENTER after each value.
2. Determine the value of the first and third quartiles. Press STAT, scroll to the right once to access the CALC menu, and select 1:1-Var Stats. Press ENTER. Scroll down until you can see Q_1 and Q_3. These are the first and third quartiles.
3. Calculate the interquartile range by finding the difference between the Q_3 and Q_1, $IQR = Q_3 - Q_1$.

Example

A set of data is given.
87.5, 45.2, 63.5, 62.1, 75.1, 53.9, 91.7, 69.5, 82.4, 73.4, 77.6, 71.2

Using a calculator, find the interquartile range of the data.

Solution

Step 1
Enter the data into list L_1.

Press STAT, then select 1:Edit.... Enter each data value in the set, pressing ENTER after each value.

L1	L2	L3 1
91.7		
69.5		
82.4		
73.4		
77.6		
71.2		

L1(13) =

Step 2
Determine the value of the first and third quartiles.

Press STAT, scroll to the right once to access the CALC menu, and select 1:1-Var Stats.

Press ENTER. Scroll down until you can see Q_1 and Q_3.

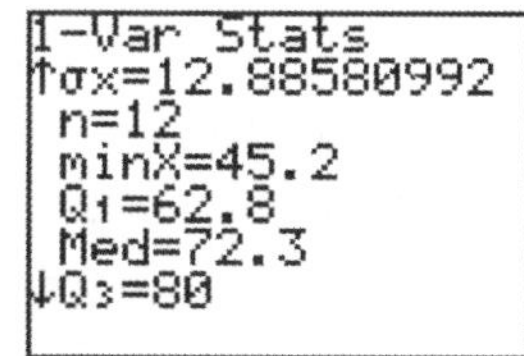

Therefore, $Q_1 = 62.8$ and $Q_3 = 80.0$.

Step 3
Calculate the interquartile range by finding the difference between Q_3 and Q_1.

$IQR = Q_3 - Q_1$
$IQR = 80.0 - 62.8$
$IQR = 17.2$

Calculating Standard Deviation and Variance in a Sample Data Set

The *variance* and *standard deviation* of a set of data are both measures of dispersion that represent how the data is spread about the mean. If the data values are spread out, the variance and standard deviation values will be greater than if the data values are clustered together about the mean.

A *sample data set* can be used to estimate the standard deviation and variance of data from an entire population. The calculation for variance using a sample data set of a population is different then the one made using the entire population.

The mean of a set of data is calculated by adding all the data values, then dividing by the number of data values in the set. The mean is often referred to as the average. When referring to a sample data set, mean is denoted by $\bar{x}$. The variance is the average squared deviation of each number from the mean in a given sample data set. Variance for a sample data set is denoted by s^2 (as opposed to σ^2 for an entire population). For the set of values in a sample, $\{x_1, x_2, x_3, \ldots x_{n-1}, x_n\}$, the variance can be calculated as

$$s^2 = \frac{(x_1 - \bar{x})^2 + (x_2 - \bar{x})^2 + \ldots + (x_n - \bar{x})^2}{n - 1}$$, in which

$\bar{x}$ represents the mean.

The standard deviation of a sample data set is denoted by s (as opposed to σ for an entire population) and can be calculated using the formula $s = \sqrt{\frac{(x_1 - \bar{x})^2 + (x_2 - \bar{x})^2 + \ldots + (x_n - \bar{x})^2}{n - 1}}$.

Example

Rick decides to collect data related to the amount of goals the top 50 hockey players in a league score in a season. Instead of determining the amount of goals from every player, he decides to collect data from a random sample of 10 hockey players. The sample set of data Rick collected is $\{12, 17, 13, 9, 15, 20, 12, 23, 19, 14\}$.

To the nearest hundredth, determine the standard deviation of the sample data set.

Solution

Step 1
Determine the mean of the set of data.

The mean formula is $\bar{x} = \frac{x_1 + x_2 + \ldots + x_n}{n}$.

There are 10 data values, so $n = 10$.

Substitute the data values into the mean formula, and solve.

$$\bar{x} = \frac{x_1 + x_2 + \ldots x_n}{n}$$
$$\bar{x} = \frac{12 + 17 + 13 + 9 + 15 + 20 + 12 + 23 + 19 + 14}{10}$$
$$\bar{x} = \frac{154}{10}$$
$$\bar{x} = 15.40$$

The mean of the set of data is 15.40.

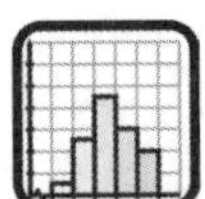

Step 2
Calculate the variance.

Substitute the data values and the mean into the variance formula

$$s^2 = \frac{(x_1 - \bar{x})^2 + (x_2 - \bar{x})^2 + \ldots + (x_n - \bar{x})^2}{n - 1},$$

and solve.

$$s^2 = \frac{(x_1 - \bar{x})^2 + (x_2 - \bar{x})^2 + \ldots + (x_n - \bar{x})^2}{n - 1}$$

$$s^2 = \frac{\begin{array}{l}(12 - 15.4)^2 + (17 - 15.4)^2 + (13 - 15.4)^2 \\ +(9 - 15.4)^2 + (15 - 15.4)^2 + (20 - 15.4)^2 \\ +(12 - 15.4)^2 + (23 - 15.4)^2 + (19 - 15.4)^2 \\ +(14 - 15.4)^2\end{array}}{10 - 1}$$

$$s^2 = \frac{\begin{array}{l}(-3.4)^2 + (1.6)^2 + (-2.4)^2 + (-6.4)^2 + (-0.4)^2 \\ +(4.6)^2 + (-3.4)^2 + (7.6)^2 + (3.6)^2 + (-1.4)^2\end{array}}{9}$$

$$s^2 = \frac{\begin{array}{l}11.56 + 2.56 + 5.76 + 40.96 + 0.16 \\ +21.16 + 11.56 + 57.76 + 12.96 + 1.96\end{array}}{9}$$

$$s^2 = \frac{166.4}{9}$$

$$s^2 \approx 18.489$$

The mean variance is 18.489.

Step 3
Calculate the standard deviation of the sample data set.

The standard deviation of the set of data is the square root of the variance. Take the square root of the variance.

$$s = \sqrt{s^2}$$
$$s \approx \sqrt{18.489}$$
$$s \approx 4.29988$$
$$s \approx 4.30$$

The standard deviation of the sample data set is approximately 4.30.

Interpreting the Range and Interquartile Range of a Set of Data

The range of a set of data is the difference between the largest and the smallest values. Range shows you how spread out the values in the data set are. Since the range looks at the two extreme values of the data, it can be greatly affected by outliers. Sometimes, this makes range a bad representation of the dispersion of data.

The interquartile range (IQR) is the difference between the third quartile (Q_3) and the first quartile (Q_1) of the data set, $IQR = Q_3 - Q_1$. Interquartile range shows you how spread out the values in the middle half of the data set are. Since the only data that affects the interquartile range is the middle 50%, it is not affected by extreme values or outliers, producing a more accurate representation of the dispersion of the data as compared to the range.

The following data interpretations are some conclusions you can make when looking at both the range and interquartile range of a set of data:

- If the interquartile range and the range are both large and close in value, it shows that the data has a high dispersion.
- If the interquartile range and the range are both small and close in value, it shows that the data has a low dispersion.
- If the range is large and the interquartile range is very small, it shows that a lot of the data points are around the median of the data, or there are outliers that are affecting the range.
- If the interquartile range is equal to half of the range, it shows that the data is fairly evenly distributed throughout the data set.

Example
The given data set represents the number of points a basketball player scores per game for 15 games: 4, 5, 5, 6, 11, 14, 20, 22, 30, 36, 38, 40, 42, 43, 44.

The range of this data set is 40(44 – 4 = 40), and the median is 22. The first quartile is 6, and the third quartile is 40. Therefore, the interquartile range of this data is 34(40 – 6 = 34).

The range shows that the spread of points scored is 40. The interquartile range of 34 is very close to the same spread as the range. Therefore, you can conclude that the number of points that this basketball player scores per game is very inconsistent. He either has a high-scoring game or a low-scoring game.

The interquartile range can be a more appropriate range to consider when you are given an extreme data point.

Example

Richard is looking at enrolling in a class, but it is taught by two different teachers. He wonders which class he would be more likely to get a better grade in. He has a list of grades from a previous semester in each teacher's class.

Teacher 1 (%)	Teacher 2 (%)
32.7	22.1
34.8	40.9
41.7	76.3
43.9	77.4
51.6	79.8
53.8	80.1
59.1	83.6
64.4	86.7
70.8	87.6
89.4	88.3
99.7	89.1

Explain which course Richard should enroll in for the best chance to get a higher grade based on range and interquartile range.

Solution

Step 1

Determine the range and interquartile range of the grades in teacher 1's class.

Find the range.

99.7 – 32.7 = 67%

The first quartile is 41.7%, and the third quartile is 70.8%.

Calculate the interquartile range.

$Q_3 - Q_1$

$= 70.8 - 41.7$

$= 29.1\%$

Step 2

Determine the range and interquartile range of the grades in teacher 2's class.

Find the range.

89.1 – 22.1 = 67%

The first quartile is 76.3%, and the third quartile is 87.6%.

Calculate the interquartile range.

$Q_3 - Q_1$

$= 87.6 - 76.3$

$= 11.3\%$

Step 3

Determine which course Richard should enroll in for the best chance for a higher grade.

The range of grades in each teacher's class is equal. However, the range of higher grades in each class differ. The highest and lowest mark in teacher 1's class are higher than the highest and lowest marks from teacher 2's class. Teacher 1's class has a larger interquartile range, 29.1%, with marks between 70.8 and 41.7 percent. In teacher 2's class, the interquartile range is 11.3%, with marks between 87.6 and 76.3. Student grades in teacher 1's class are lower and obtain a higher variation, and student grades in teacher 2's class are higher with smaller variation.

Therefore, Richard should enroll in teacher 2's class because the variation of the grades is smaller, and they are dispersed around a higher grade.

Determining the Mean and Variance for Discrete Uniform Distribution

A discrete uniform distribution can be represented by a sample space of equally spaced numbers with a minimum value, *a*, and a maximum value, *b*, and a total number of possible outcomes, *n*.

The mean, μ, and the variance, $Var(X)$, can be calculated by using the following formulas:

- $\mu = \dfrac{a+b}{2}$
- $Var(X) = \dfrac{n^2 - 1}{12}$

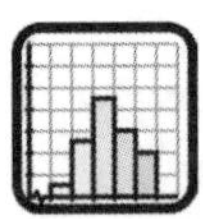

Example

The outcome of a fair die is an example of a uniform discrete distribution. The sample space, {1, 2, 3, 4, 5, 6}, contains six possible outcomes that are evenly spaced. All of the outcomes have the same probability,

$P(X) = \frac{1}{6}$, where X is one of the values from the sample space.

What is the mean of $P(X)$?

Solution

Substitute the minimum value, a, and the maximum value, b, from the sample space into the formula for mean (of a uniform discrete distribution), and evaluate.

$$\mu = \frac{a+b}{2}$$
$$\mu = \frac{1+6}{2}$$
$$\mu = \frac{7}{2}$$
$$\mu = 3.5$$

What is the variance of $P(x)$?

Solution

Substitute the number of outcomes, n, from the sample space into the formula for variance (of a uniform discrete distribution), and evaluate.

$$Var(X) = \frac{n^2 - 1}{12}$$
$$Var(X) = \frac{(6)^2 - 1}{12}$$
$$Var(X) = \frac{35}{12}$$
$$Var(X) \approx 2.9166667$$

In some cases, the total number of outcomes is not given, making it necessary to determine the value of n from the minimum and maximum values. This can be done by using the formula $n = (b - a) + 1$. Note that this formula only works when the difference between successive outcomes is 1.

Example

A random variable, X, can have any of the values in the set {–200, –199…349, 350}. $P(X)$ is a uniform distribution.

What is the variance of $P(X)$?

Solution

Step 1

Determine the value of n.

Substitute a and b into the formula for n (where the spacing is 1), and evaluate.

$$n = (b - a) + 1$$
$$n = (350 - (-200)) + 1$$
$$n = 551$$

Step 2

Calculate the variance.

Substitute 551 for n into the formula for variance (of a discrete uniform distribution).

$$Var(X) = \frac{n^2 - 1}{12}$$
$$Var(X) = \frac{(551)^2 - 1}{12}$$
$$Var(X) = \frac{303{,}601 - 1}{12}$$
$$Var(X) = 25{,}300$$

If the outcomes are spaced closer or further apart than 1, the formula for n becomes $n = \frac{(b-a)+1}{d}$, where d is the difference between successive outcomes in the sample space.

Example

A random variable, X, can have any of the values in the set {0, 0.25, 0.5...9.75, 10}. $P(X)$ is a uniform distribution.

What is the variance of $P(X)$?

Solution

Step 1

Determine the value of n.

Calculate d, the difference between two successive outcomes. Since $P(X)$ is a uniform distribution, it does not matter which two outcomes are selected as long as they come one right after the other.

$d = 0.5 - 0.25$
$d = 0.25$

Calculate n, using the formula for n, where the spacing is not 1.

$$n = \frac{(b-a)+1}{d}$$
$$n = \frac{(10-0)+1}{0.25}$$
$$n = \frac{11}{0.25}$$
$$n = 44$$

Step 2

Calculate the variance.

Substitute 44 for n in the formula for variance (of a discrete uniform distribution), and evaluate.

$$Var(X) = \frac{n^2-1}{12}$$
$$Var(X) = \frac{(44)^2-1}{12}$$
$$Var(X) = \frac{1,935}{12}$$
$$Var(X) = 161.25$$

Determining Mean and Variance for an Exponential Distribution

The probability density function for an exponential distribution is of the form $P(x) = \lambda e^{-\lambda x}$, $x \geq 0$.

The mean, μ, and the variance, $Var(X)$, can be calculated by using the following formulas:

- $\mu = \frac{1}{\lambda}$
- $Var(X) = \frac{1}{\lambda^2}$

Example

The function $P(x) = 1.5e^{-1.5x}$, $x \geq 0$ is the probability density function of an exponential distribution.

What is the mean of $P(x)$?

Solution

Substitute the value of λ into the formula for the mean.

Since $P(x)$ is already in the form $\lambda e^{-\lambda x}$, it follows that $\lambda = 1.5$.

$$\mu = \frac{1}{\lambda}$$
$$\mu = \frac{1}{1.5}$$
$$\mu = \frac{2}{3}$$

What is the variance of $P(x)$?

Solution

Substitute the value of λ into the formula for the variance.

Since $P(x)$ is already in the form $\lambda e^{-\lambda x}$, it follows that $\lambda = 1.5$.

$$Var(X) = \frac{1}{\lambda^2}$$
$$Var(X) = \frac{1}{1.5^2}$$
$$Var(X) = \frac{4}{9}$$

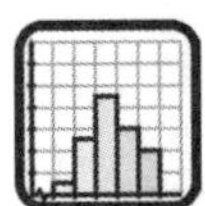

Determining Mean and Variance for a Binomial Distribution

A binomial distribution is a way of describing the number of successful outcomes of a series of trials with only two possible outcomes, where the probability of a successful outcome occurring is constant.

If the number of trials is n and the probability of success is p, the mean, μ, and the variance, $Var(X)$, can be calculated by using the following formulas:

- $\mu = np$
- $Var(X) = np(1 - p)$

Example

The number of times a tossed coin comes up heads is an example of binomial distribution.

What is the mean for the expected number of times a coin lands on heads if the coin is flipped 200 times?

Solution

Substitute the values for the number of trials, n, and the probability of success, p, into the formula for mean (of a binomial distribution).

Since $n = 200$ and $p = 0.5$, and both outcomes are equally likely, the mean can be calculated as follows.

$\mu = np$
$\mu = (200)(0.5)$
$\mu = 100$

What is the variance for the number of times a coin lands on heads if the coin is flipped 200 times?

Solution

Substitute the values for the number of trials, n, and the probability of success, p, into the formula for variance (of a binomial distribution).

Since $n = 200$ and $p = 0.5$, and both outcomes are equally likely, the variance can be calculated as follows.

$Var(X) = np(1 - p)$
$Var(X) = (200)(0.5)(1 - 0.5)$
$Var(X) = 50$

Comparing Two Related Sets of Data Using Measures of Central Tendency

Measures of central tendency can be quite useful when comparing related sets of data, such as age groups, genders, groups of people, etc. Measures of central tendency can also be used to determine if there is a benefit to doing one activity compared with another or if a specific group prefers things compared with a different group.

The measures of central tendency include the mean, median, and mode. The one that is selected to describe the data depends on the kind of data that is presented.

The mean is a good representation of central tendency for sets of data with no major outliers. Because the mean is greatly affected by outliers, it is not a good representation for skewed data.

The median is a good representation of central tendency for sets of data that contain outliers. Because the median is not greatly affected by outliers, it is a good representation for skewed data.

The mode is a good representation of central tendency for sets of categorical data. Categorical data is data that can be divided into groups. Examples of categorical data are size (small, medium, large), music style (pop, jazz, rock, hip hop), or age group (infant, toddler, adolescent, adult, senior).

Example

The results of a mathematics exam out of 25 are given. They have been divided into two groups: students who did and did not study. The students who studied received the following grades: 17, 23, 20, 13, 24, 25, 18, 25, 23, 19, 19, 21, 16, 22, 22, 21, and 10. The students who did not study received the following grades: 10, 20, 13, 4, 12, 9, 8, 9, 4, 7, and 10.

Make a conclusion about the grades of students who studied compared with students who did not study by measuring their central tendencies.

Solution

Step 1

Determine the measures of central tendency for the data on students who studied.

Calculate the mean.

$$\frac{\begin{pmatrix}17+23+20+13+24\\+25+18+25+23\\+19+19+21+16\\+22+22+21+10\end{pmatrix}}{17} \approx 19.88$$

The median is 21, and the mode is 19, 21, 22, and 23.

Step 2

Determine the measure of central tendency for the data on students who did not study.

Calculate the mean.

$$\frac{\begin{pmatrix}4+4+7\\+8+9+9+10\\+10+12+13+20\end{pmatrix}}{11} \approx 9.64$$

The median is 9, and the mode is 4, 9, and 10.

Step 3

Compare the central tendencies of the two sets of data.

On average, the students who studied got a mark of approximately 19.88 out of 25, which is quite high compared with the students who did not study. The students who did not study got an average mark of approximately 9.64 out of 25. Both the medians and modes of the data are close to their respective means. Therefore, the students who studied have central tendencies with greater values than the ones for students who did not study. A possible conclusion that can be made is that studying for an exam will get students a higher mark than they could expect if they did not study.

Example

Alphonso wants to start reading a music magazine. He is trying to choose between *The Guitar* and *The Drum*. He flips through both magazines and writes down a 1, 2, 3, 4, or 5 for each article. If the article is about rock and roll, he writes a 1. He writes a 2 for country, a 3 for alternative, a 4 for pop, and a 5 for rap. There are 20 articles in each magazine. His results are given.

The Guitar—2, 1, 5, 1, 3, 1, 2, 4, 1, 2, 2, 1, 1, 3, 1, 5, 1, 5, 1, 4

The Drum—5, 3, 5, 2, 5, 1, 5, 5, 3, 4, 5, 3, 4, 5, 1, 2, 3, 4, 5, 2

If Alphonso wants to read more articles on rock and roll than any other music style, which magazine should he read?

Solution

Alphonso wants to read one type of article more than the other types. This relates to the modes of the data.

Step 1

Determine the mode of the data for *The Guitar*.

The number 1 appears 9 times, the number 2 appears 4 times, the number 3 appears 2 times, the number 4 appears 2 times, and the number 5 appears 3 times.

Therefore, the mode is 1.

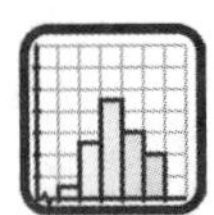

Step 2

Determine the mode of the data for *The Drum*.

The number 1 appears 2 times, the number 2 appears 3 times, the number 3 appears 4 times, the number 4 appears 3 times, and the number 5 appears 8 times.

Therefore, the mode is 5.

Step 3

Determine which magazine Alphonso should pick.

Since the mode for *The Guitar* is 1 and the number 1 identifies rock and roll articles, he should start reading *The Guitar*.

S-ID.3 Interpret differences in shape, center, and spread in the context of the data sets, accounting for possible effects of extreme data points (outliers).

Identifying Outliers for a Set of Data Given Graphically

An **outlier** for a set of data is any value that is distant from the rest of the values.

Example

A set of data is graphed on the Cartesian plane.

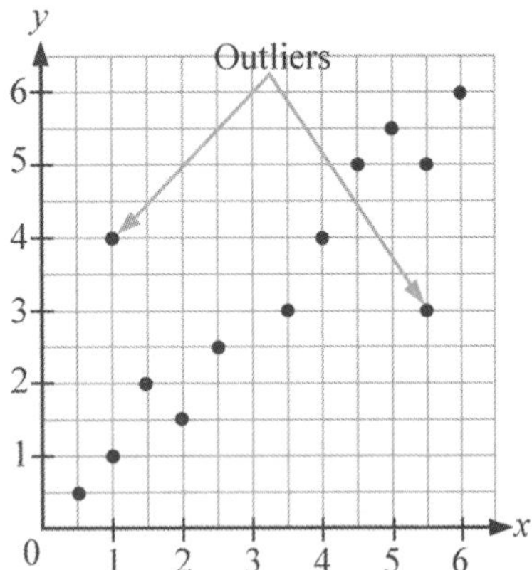

The outliers for the given set of data are located at points (1, 4) and (5.5, 3), because these points are distant from the rest of the values.

The measure of central tendency that is affected most by an outlier is the mean. The median can also be affected by outliers, but not as much as the mean. The values of the mean and median take into consideration the magnitude and number of values present in a set, so these measures can be affected by the presence or absence of an outlier. It is very rare that the mode of a set of data is affected by the presence of outliers. The mode would only be affected if the most common value in the set was an outlier.

Example

A set of data and a line of best fit are graphed on the Cartesian plane.

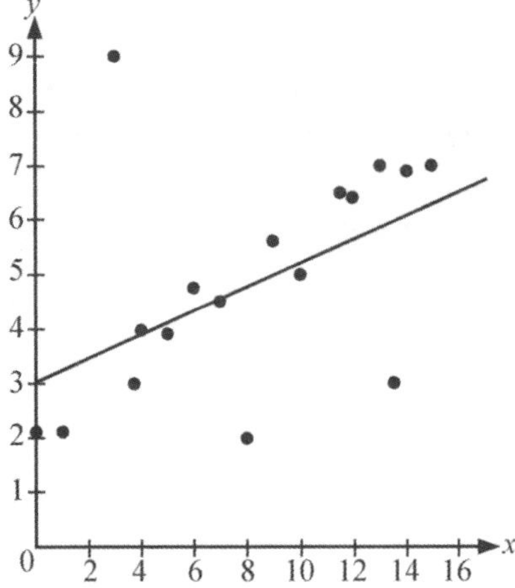

From the graph, the outliers are located at points (3, 9), (8, 2), and (13.5, 3).

If the outliers are not graphed, the line of best fit shifts to model the data more accurately.

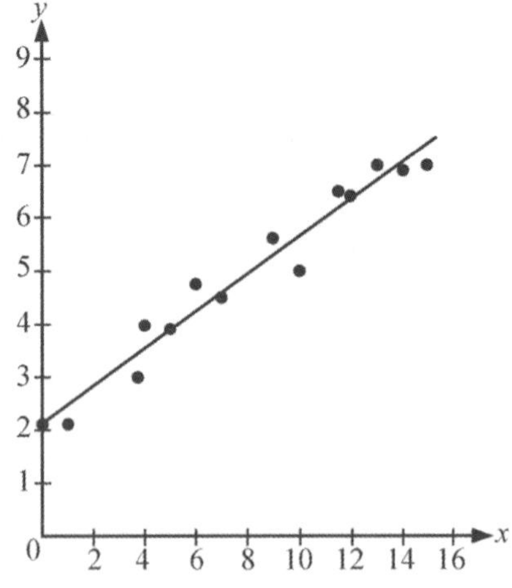

Example

Vanessa recorded her mountain-biking times for a particular trail in order to see her progress. She plotted her biking times for 12 consecutive days and created the given graph.

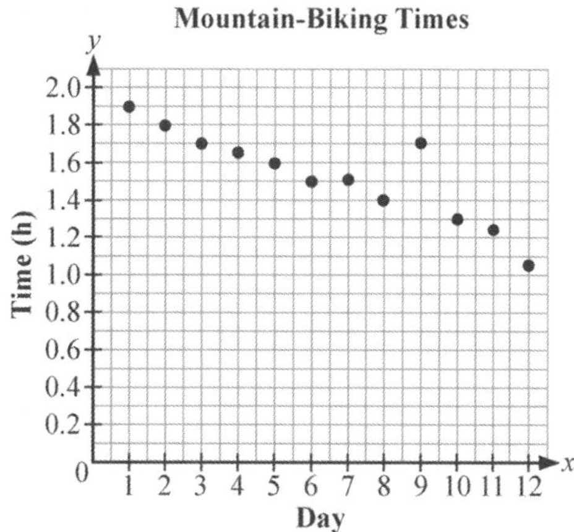

From the given graph, determine which day of mountain biking is an outlier.

Solution

An outlier for a set of data is a value that is distant from the rest of the values. From the graph, the outlier is located at point (9, 1.7).

Therefore, day 9 of mountain biking is an outlier.

Identifying and Understanding the Effect of Outliers

Outliers are values that are distant from the rest of the values in a set of data. To identify the outliers in a set of data by inspection, arrange the data in either ascending order or descending order.

Example

The following temperatures are given:
22°C, 8°C, 18°C, 2°C, 24°C, 26°C, 26°C, 24°C, 30°C

Determine the outliers.

Solution

Arrange data set in ascending order. 2, 8, 18, 22, 24, 24, 26, 26, 30. The outliers are 2°C and 8°C because both these values are distant from the others.

Outliers can affect measures of central tendency, such as the mean and median. Outliers do not usually influence mode values.

Example

A set of data is given.
41.27, 48.21, 12.32, 49.25, 8.76, 52.64, 130.25, 75.48, 63.21, 54.49, 75.48, 125.48, 78.12

Determine the effect of the outliers on the measures of central tendency for the given data set.

Solution

Step 1
Arrange the data in ascending order.
8.76, 12.32, 41.27, 48.21, 49.25, 52.64, 54.49, 63.21, 75.48, 75.48, 78.12, 125.48, 130.25

Step 2
Determine the outliers.

The outliers are 8.76, 12.32, 125.48, and 130.25. These are the numbers that are the most numerically distant from the remaining values.

Step 3
Determine the mean, median, and mode of the data set.
Calculate the mean.
The mean is equal to the sum of the values divided by the total number of values. Add the values together, and divide by 13.

$$\frac{814.96}{13} \approx 62.689$$

The median is the middle value of the data set.
The median is 54.49.
The mode is the value that occurs most frequently in a data set. In this set, the mode is 75.48 because this value occurs twice.

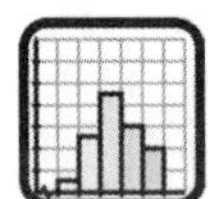

Step 4

Determine the mean, median, and mode of the data set without the outliers.

Without the outliers, the data set is 41.27, 48.21, 49.25, 52.64, 54.49, 63.21, 75.48, 75.48, 78.12.

Calculate the mean.

Add the values together, and divide by 9.

$$\frac{538.15}{9} \approx 59.794$$

Without the outliers, the mean of the data set is approximately 59.794.

The median is the middle value of the data set. Without the outliers, the median of the data set is 54.49.

The mode is the value that occurs most frequently in a data set. Without the outliers, the mode of this data set is 75.48 because this value occurs twice.

Step 5

Compare the results from both sets of calculations.

After the outliers were removed, the mean of the data set changed from approximately 62.69 to 59.79. The median and the mode remained the same after the outliers were removed. The only measure of central tendency that was affected by the outliers was the mean.

The measures of central tendency most likely to be affected by an outlier are the mean and median. The values of the mean and median take into consideration the magnitude and number of values present in a set, so these measures can be affected by the presence or absence of an outlier. It is very rare that the mode of a set of data is affected by the presence or absence of outliers. The mode is only affected if the most common value in a set is an outlier.

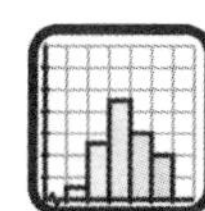

EXERCISE #1—SINGLE VARIABLE DATA

Use the following information to answer the next question.

A gym teacher created a sample set in which he recorded the weight, in kilograms, of 25 boys.
The sample set is as follows: 42, 50, 43, 42, 45, 42, 43, 50, 45, 45, 50, 43, 41, 42, 41, 50, 48, 42, 48, 48, 41, 42, 45, 42, 41

254. The range in weight of the 25 boys in this sample set is

A. 9 kg **B.** 15 kg
C. 41 kg **D.** 50 kg

Use the following information to answer the next question.

Clarissa surveys some of her classmates to find out how many hours of TV they watch each week.
3, 4, 7, 8, 8, 10, 11

255. Which of the following box-and-whisker plots represents this data?

A.
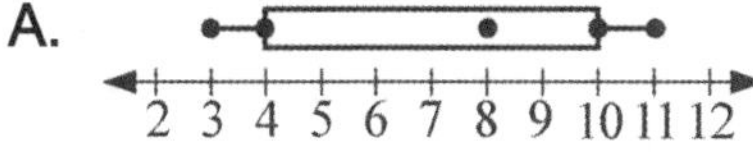

B.
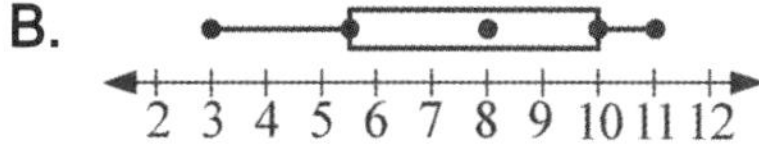

C.
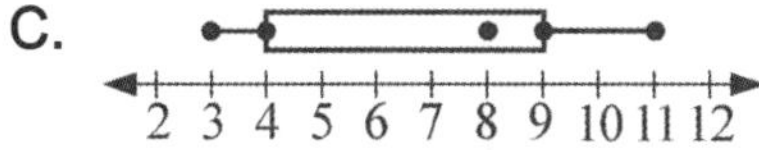

D.
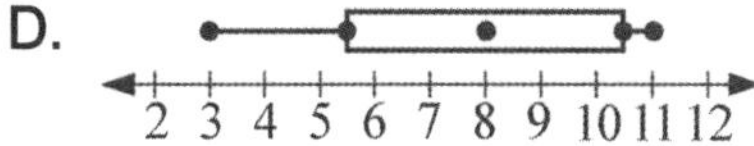

Use the following information to answer the next question.

In a particular school, the heights of 50 football players in fifth grade were measured. The given table shows the frequency distribution of their heights in centimeters (cm).

Height (cm)	Frequency
$140 < x \le 145$	6
$145 < x \le 150$	12
$150 < x \le 155$	18
$155 < x \le 160$	9
$160 < x \le 165$	5

256. Which of the following histograms represents the information in the given table?

A. **B.**
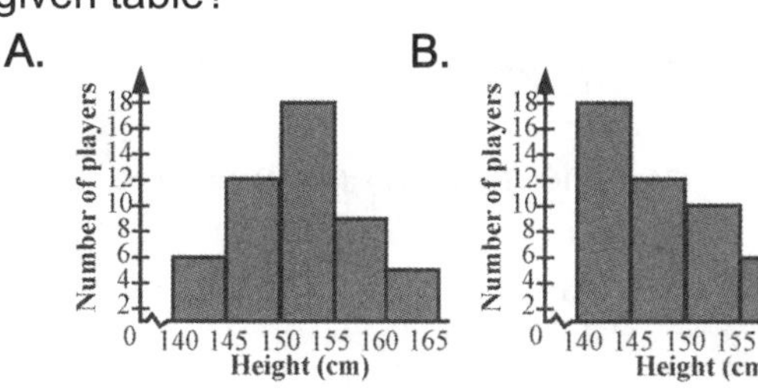

C.
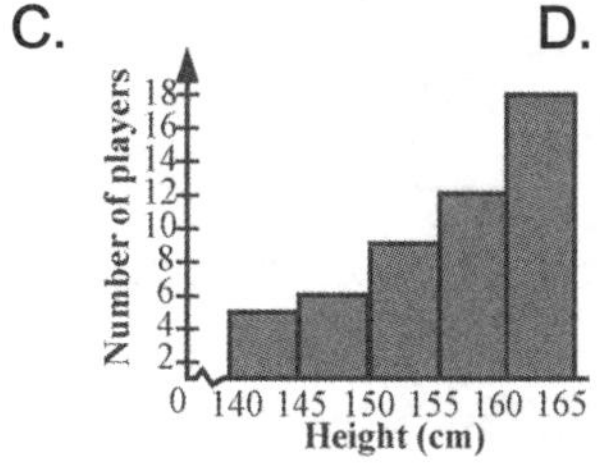

D.
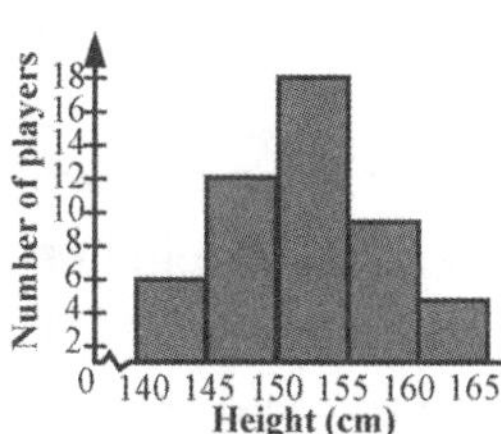

Use the following information to answer the next question.

The given table of values shows the number of new vehicles sold at a particular dealership during the first six months of the years 2010 and 2011.

Month	2010	2011
Jan	45	40
Feb	70	60
Mar	85	95
Apr	110	115
May	90	70
Jun	80	60

The data in the table of values is illustrated in the given double line graph.

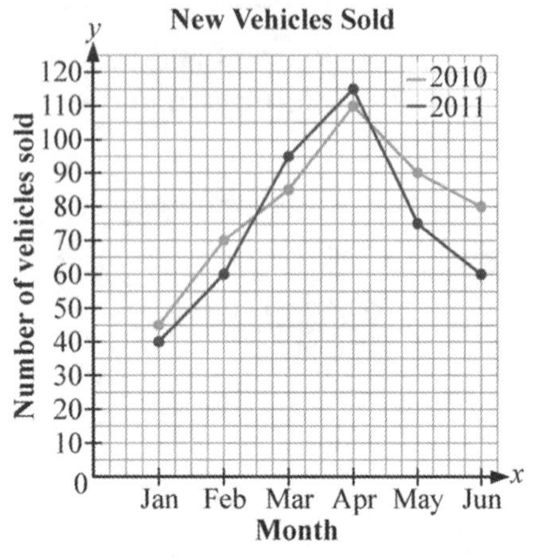

257. The double line graph is drawn incorrectly because one of the

A. data points for 2010 is not in the correct location

B. data points for 2011 is not in the correct location

C. axes has an incorrect scale

D. titles is wrong

Use the following information to answer the next question.

The given table shows some data that Keith collected.

15	11	14
17	15	15
12	11	12
17	12	15

Keith organized his data into the line plot shown. However, he realized that his line plot contained an error.

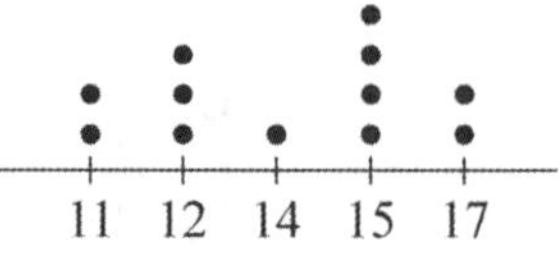

258. Which of the following statements **best** describes the error in Keith's line plot?

A. The line plot should be drawn vertically.

B. The data should be represented with Xs.

C. The data should be represented in a bar graph.

D. The numbers on the line plot should be consecutive.

259. Calculate the mean of the data set {125, 300, 150, 175, 50, 450, 150}.

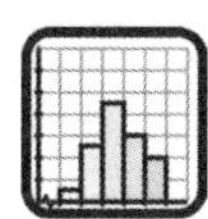

Use the following information to answer the next question.

The sets of data show the final scores for the last five games played by two basketball teams.

- Team *A*: 64, 79, 61, 86, 77
- Team *B*: 72, 89, 86, 75, 82

260. What is the difference between the median scores of the two teams?

A. 4 **B.** 5
C. 6 **D.** 7

Use the following information to answer the next question.

Stem	Leaf
5	0, 0, 3, 4, 5, 5, 8
6	1, 2, 2, 4, 6, 9, 9, 9
7	0, 0, 1, 1, 3, 5, 5, 8, 9, 9

261. Which of the following statements about the mode and frequency of the data displayed in the stem and leaf plot is **true**?

A. The mode is 9, and the frequency is 3.
B. The mode is 69, and the frequency is 5.
C. The mode is 69, and the frequency is 3.
D. The mode is 79, and the frequency is 2.

Use the following information to answer the next question.

20, 21, 25, 25, 30, 35

262. The values that **best** represent the measure of central tendency for this data are

A. mode and range
B. mean and range
C. mode and median
D. mean and median

Use the following information to answer the next question.

The table illustrates the percentage of time that a mathematics teacher spends talking to his students in six class periods.

Period	Percentage of Time (%)
1	85
2	78
3	90
4	65
5	82
6	88

263. To the nearest hundredth, the value of the standard deviation for the percentages is __________.

Use the following information to answer the next question.

A set of data is shown.

3, 13, 8, 16, 6

264. What is the interquartile range of this set of data?

A. 8 **B.** 9
C. 10 **D.** 11

Use the following information to answer the next question.

Dora takes the bus to school every day. She selected eight days at random from the school year and measured the amount of time, in seconds, that she waited for the bus. The times were 310, 250, 350, 300, 380, 290, 450, and 250.

265. Based on Dora's data, the estimate of the variance of the waiting times for the entire school year is

A. 4,650 **B.** 4,690
C. 4,710 **D.** 4,750

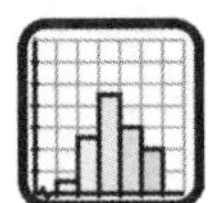

Use the following information to answer the next question.

The grades of 19 students on a test out of 20 marks are as follows: 17, 19, 18, 18, 17, 19, 18, 19, 20, 17, 19, 18, 18, 18, 17, 17, 20, 19, and 18. The teacher found that the range of the data set is 3 and the interquartile range (IQR) is 2.

266. Which of the following statements is the **best** conclusion that can be made about the test?

A. An even distribution of grades was produced, so the test was well designed.

B. An uneven distribution of grades was produced, so the test was poorly designed.

C. The test was too easy since it produced a low dispersion of grades around a set of grades with a small range.

D. The test was too difficult since it produced a low dispersion of grades around a set of grades with a large range.

Use the following information to answer the next question.

One student is randomly selected from a math class that contains 15 boys and 14 girls.

267. If x represents a discrete random variable in the sample space for this event, what is the variance of x?

A. 16.25 B. $18.\bar{6}$

C. 70 D. 75

Use the following information to answer the next question.

The time in minutes between individuals joining the teller lineup at a particular bank can be modeled as an exponential distribution. The associated probability density function was determined to be $P(t) = 0.65e^{-0.65t}$, $t \geq 0$, where t is the length of time in minutes.

268. To the nearest tenth, the variance of individuals joining the teller lineup at this bank is

A. 1.5 min B. 1.8 min

C. 2.4 min D. 2.7 min

Use the following information to answer the next question.

From past records, 85% of the students who took a driver education course in a particular rural high school obtained their driver's license on their first attempt.

269. If 200 students took the driver education course at this high school, what is the variance of the number of students who obtained their driver's license on their first attempt?

A. 25.5 B. 30.0

C. 144.5 D. 170.0

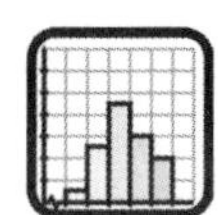

Use the following information to answer the next question.

Two hockey players are comparing the number of goals they scored in the last 10 seasons they played.
Player 1—10, 15, 20, 17, 22, 23, 28, 22, 27, 18
Player 2—14, 20, 18, 23, 21, 22, 25, 24, 20, 23

270. Which hockey player had the highest average goals per season?

A. Player 1 because the mean of his goals over the 10 seasons is higher than player 2.

B. Player 2 because the mean of his goals over the 10 seasons is higher than player 1.

C. Player 1 because the mode of his goals over the 10 seasons is higher than player 2.

D. Player 2 because the mode of his goals over the 10 seasons is higher than player 1.

Use the following information to answer the next question.

The forecast high temperature and the actual high temperature were recorded for a particular city over a two-week period. The given graph illustrates the data obtained and the partial corresponding line of best fit.

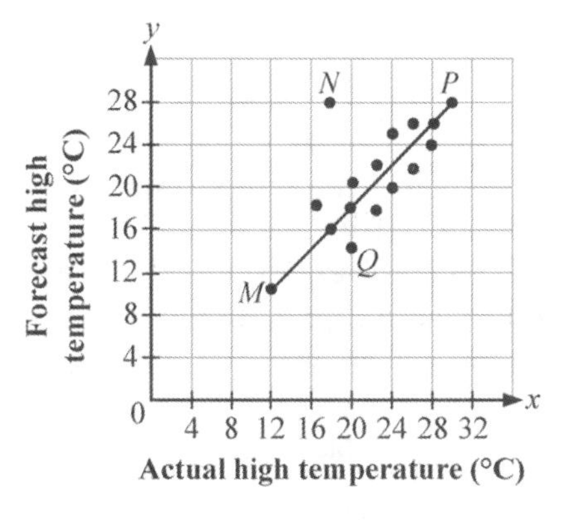

271. Which of the labeled points is an outlier for the given graph?

A. *M** **B.** *N*

C. *P* **D.** *Q*

Use the following information to answer the next question.

On her first five math tests, Andrea gets the following marks: 77%, 78%, 82%, 73%, and 80%. She calculates her average, treating all tests as having equal weight.

272. If the mark on her sixth test is 30%, by how many percentage points does her average change?

A. 6 **B.** 8

C. 10 **D.** 12

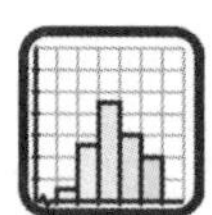

EXERCISE #1—SINGLE VARIABLE DATA ANSWERS AND SOLUTIONS

254. A	259. See solution	264. C	269. A
255. A	260. B	265. A	270. B
256. D	261. C	266. C	271. B
257. B	262. C	267. C	272. B
258. D	263. 8.28	268. C	

254. A

Step 1
Place the values in order from least to greatest.
41, 41, 41, 41, 42, 42, 42, 42, 42, 42, 42, 43, 43, 43, 45, 45, 45, 45, 48, 48, 48, 50, 50, 50, 50

Step 2
Subtract the lowest value from the highest value in the set.

Range = Highest value – Lowest value
= 50 – 41
= 9

The range in weight among the 25 boys is 9 kg.

255. A

Step 1
Determine the five-number summary.

- Lowest number—3
- Lower quartile—4
- Median—8
- Upper quartile—10
- Highest number—11

Step 2
Identify the box-and-whisker plot that correctly plots the five-number summary.

This box-and-whisker plot shows the five-number summary.

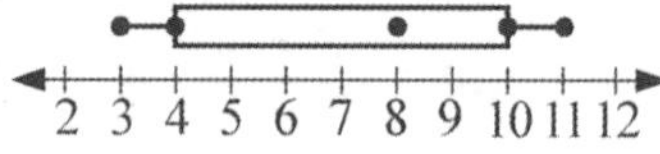

256. D

The histogram must display the following information from the table:

- A height of $140 < x \leq 145$ has a frequency of 6.
- A height of $145 < x \leq 150$ has a frequency of 12.
- A height of $150 < x \leq 155$ has a frequency of 18.
- A height of $155 < x \leq 160$ has a frequency of 9.
- A height of $160 < x \leq 165$ has a frequency of 5.

The following histogram correctly represents the information in the given table.

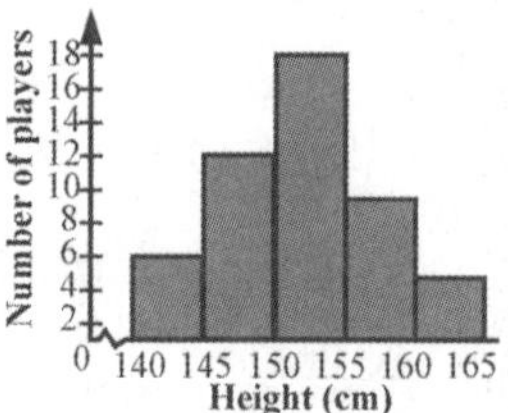

257. B

The double line graph is drawn incorrectly. The data point for May 2011 is not in the correct location. On the line graph, the point is located at 75 rather than 70.

258. D

The numbers on the line plot should be consecutive. Keith's line plot is incorrect because the numbers along the bottom of the line plot should be written consecutively. The number line should label all possible outcomes that could occur, not just the outcomes that did occur.

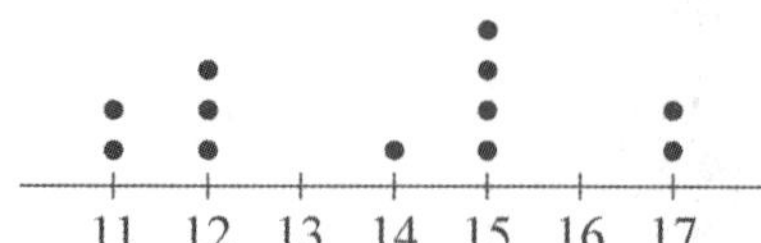

259.

Step 1
The mean of a set of data is defined as the ratio of the sum of the values to the number of values in the data set (in other words, taking the average of the data set).

Determine the sum of the given values.

$$\begin{pmatrix}125 + 300 + 150 + 175 \\ +50 + 450 + 150\end{pmatrix} = 1{,}400$$

Step 2
Divide the total sum by the number of values.

Since there are 7 values, divide by 7.
$1{,}400 \div 7 = 200$

Therefore, the mean of the data set is 200.

260. B

Step 1
Reorder the scores for the two teams from lowest score to highest score.

- Team *A*: 61, 64, 77, 79, 86
- Team *B*: 72, 75, 82, 86, 89

Step 2
Find the median.

The median of a data set is the value in the middle.

Since there is an odd number of scores (5), the value in the middle will be the third number in the list, with two lower scores to the left and two higher scores to the right.

- Team *A*: 61, 64, **77**, 79, 86
- Team *B*: 72, 75, **82**, 86, 89

The median score for team *A* is 77, and the median score for team *B* is 82.

Step 3
Find the difference.

Find the difference between the two medians by subtracting 77 from 82.
82 – 77 = 5

The difference between the median scores of the two teams is 5.

261. C

Step 1
Identify the mode.

The mode is the number that appears the most often.

Look at the numbers in the leaves. The number 9 in stem 6 appears three times, which is more than any other leaf.

The three 9s in stem 6 represent the number 69 three times.

The mode of the given set of data is 69.

Step 2
Identify the frequency.

The frequency is the number of times that the mode appears.

The number 69 appears three times. Therefore, the frequency of the mode (69) is 3.

The data displayed in the given stem and leaf plot has a mode of 69 and a frequency of 3.

262. C

Mode is the value that appears most often. For this data, the mode is 25, since it appears twice.

Median is the center value when data is arranged from least to greatest. For this data, the median is 25.

Mean is the average value of the data set.

For this data, the mean is

$$\frac{20+21+25+25+30+35}{6} = \frac{156}{6}$$
$$= 26$$

This value is not given in the data, so it is not representative.

Range is the spread of the data values. For this data, the range is 35 – 20 = 15. This does not represent central tendency.

Therefore, mode and median are the values that best represent the central tendency of this data.

263. 8.28

The standard deviation can be determined algebraically.

Step 1
Determine the mean of the data using the formula $\mu = \frac{x_1 + x_2 + \ldots + x_n}{n}$.

$$\mu = \frac{85+78+90+65+82+88}{6}$$

Simplify.

$$\mu = \frac{488}{6}$$
$$\mu \approx 81.33$$

Step 2
Substitute the required values into the standard deviation formula $\sigma = \sqrt{\frac{(x_1-\mu)^2 + (x_2-\mu)^2 + \ldots + (x_n-\mu)^2}{n}}$, where μ = the mean, and solve.

$$\sigma = \sqrt{\frac{(85-81.3\ldots)^2 + \ldots + (88-81.3\ldots)^2}{6}}$$
$$\sigma = \sqrt{\frac{411.33\ldots}{6}}$$
$$\sigma = 8.279828232$$

Step 3
Round the answer to the nearest hundredth.

The value of the standard deviation is 8.28.

264. C

Step 1
Order the set of data from least to greatest.
3, 6, 8, 13, 16

Step 2
Find Q_2, or the median.

There are five data values, so the median will be the middle number, which is 8.

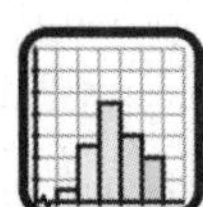

Step 3
Calculate Q_1 by finding the middle of the data below the median.
Find the median of the numbers less than 8.
The value of Q_1 will be the average of 3 and 6, which is 4.5.

$$\frac{3+6}{2} = 4.5$$

Step 4
Calculate Q_3 by finding the middle of the data above the median.
Find the median of the numbers greater than 8.
The value of Q_3 will be the average of 13 and 16, which is 14.5.

$$\frac{13+16}{2} = 14.5$$

Step 5
Determine the interquartile range by finding the difference between the two quartiles.

$IQR = Q_3 - Q_1$
$IQR = 14.5 - 4.5$
$IQR = 10$

The interquartile range of the given set of data is 10.

265. A

Step 1
Determine the mean of the set of data.
Substitute the data values into the mean formula, and solve.

$$\bar{x} = \frac{x_1 + x_2 + \ldots x_n}{n}$$

$$\bar{x} = \frac{310 + 250 + 350 + 300 + 380 + 290 + 450 + 250}{8}$$

$$\bar{x} = \frac{2{,}580}{8}$$

$\bar{x} = 322.5$

The mean of the set of data is 322.5.

Step 2
Calculate the variance.
Use the formula for variance of a sample data set.
Substitute the data values and the mean into the variance formula,

$$s^2 = \frac{(x_1 - \bar{x})^2 + (x_2 - \bar{x})^2 + \ldots + (x_n - \bar{x})^2}{n-1},$$

and solve.

$$s^2 = \frac{(x_1 - \bar{x})^2 + (x_2 - \bar{x})^2 + \ldots + (x_n - \bar{x})^2}{n-1}$$

$$s^2 = \frac{\begin{array}{c}(310-322.5)^2 + (250-322.5)^2 \\ +(350-322.5)^2 + (300-322.5)^2 \\ +(380-322.5)^2 + (290-322.5)^2 \\ +(450-322.5)^2 + (250-322.5)^2\end{array}}{8-1}$$

$$s^2 = \frac{\begin{array}{c}(-12.5)^2 + (-72.5)^2 + (27.5)^2 + (-22.5)^2 \\ +(57.5)^2 + (-32.5)^2 + (127.5)^2 + (-72.5)^2\end{array}}{7}$$

$$s^2 = \frac{\begin{array}{c}156.25 + 5{,}256.25 + 756.25 + 506.25 \\ +3{,}306.25 + 1{,}056.25 + 16{,}256.25 + 5{,}256.25\end{array}}{7}$$

$$s^2 = \frac{32{,}550}{7}$$

$s^2 = 4{,}650$

Therefore, the estimate of the variance of the waiting times for the entire school year is 4,650.

266. C

If the IQR and the range are both small and close in value, then the data has a low dispersion. The IQR is equal to 2, and the range is equal to 3. In the context of the given data, these values are both small and close in value, giving a low dispersion.
This shows that everyone in the class received roughly the same mark. The marks ranged from 17 to 20 out of 20, which would give all the students a fairly high grade. This could be a result of the test being too easy. Therefore, of the given statements, the best conclusion is that the test was too easy since it produced a low dispersion of grades around a set of grades with a small range.

267. C

Since there are 15 + 14 = 29 students in the class, the sample space for the given event contains 29 equally spaced possible outcomes, each with a probability of $\frac{1}{29}$. This is an example of a discrete uniform distribution.

Since x represents a discrete random variable in the sample space for this event, the variance of x, $Var(X)$, can be determined by applying the variance formula, $Var(X) = \frac{n^2 - 1}{12}$.

Substitute 29 for n (the number of possible outcomes), and solve for $Var(X)$.

$$Var(X) = \frac{29^2 - 1}{12}$$
$$Var(X) = \frac{841 - 1}{12}$$
$$Var(X) = \frac{840}{12}$$
$$Var(X) = 70$$

268. C

Since the probability density function $P(t) = 0.65e^{-0.65t}$ is of the general form $P(x) = \lambda e^{-\lambda x}$, the variance, $Var(X)$, in minutes of joining the teller lineup at the bank can be determined by applying the variance formula, $Var(X) = \frac{1}{\lambda^2}$.

Substitute 0.65 for λ, and then solve for $Var(X)$.

$$Var(X) = \frac{1}{\lambda^2}$$
$$Var(X) = \frac{1}{(0.65)^2}$$
$$Var(X) \approx 2.4$$

The variance of individuals joining the teller lineup at this bank is 2.4 min.

269. A

The variance, $Var(X)$, of the 200 students who took the driver education course and obtained their driver's license on their first attempt can be determined by applying the variance formula $Var(x) = np(1 - p)$, where n is the number of trials and p is the probability of success.

Substitute 200 for n and 0.85 for p, and solve for $Var(X)$.

$$Var(X) = (200)(0.85)(1 - 0.85)$$
$$Var(X) = (200)(0.85)(0.15)$$
$$Var(X) = 25.5$$

270. B

The average goals per season for each hockey player can be found by calculating the mean of each player's goals per season over the 10 seasons.

Step 1

Determine the mean of player 1's 10 seasons.

$$\frac{\begin{pmatrix} 10 + 15 + 20 + 17 + 22 \\ +23 + 28 + 22 + 27 + 18 \end{pmatrix}}{10} = \frac{202}{10}$$
$$= 20.2$$

Step 2

Determine the mean of player 2's 10 seasons.

$$\frac{\begin{pmatrix} 14 + 20 + 18 + 23 + 21 \\ +22 + 25 + 24 + 20 + 23 \end{pmatrix}}{10} = \frac{210}{10}$$
$$= 21$$

Step 3

Determine which player had the highest average goals per season.

Since player 2 has a mean of 21 goals per season over 10 seasons, he has the highest average goals per season.

271. B

An outlier for a set of data is the distant value from the rest of the data values. From the given graph, it can be observed that the outlier is located at point N.

272. B

Step 1

Determine the average without the outlier.

$$\frac{77 + 78 + 82 + 73 + 80}{5} = 78$$

Step 2

Determine the average with the outlier.

$$\frac{77 + 78 + 82 + 73 + 80 + 30}{6} = 70$$

Step 3

Determine the difference.

$78 - 70 = 8$

Therefore, the average changed by 8 percentage points.

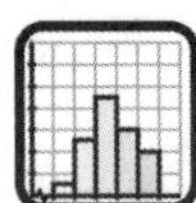

EXERCISE #2—SINGLE VARIABLE DATA

Use the following information to answer the next question.

A data set is given.
23, 45, 23, 67, 34, 35, 63, 25, 54, 31, 43, 56

273. What are the values of the lower and upper quartiles of this data set, respectively?

A. 31 and 54 **B.** 25 and 56
C. 23 and 39 **D.** 28 and 55

Use the following information to answer the next question.

Eight students count the number of pencils that they have in their pencil cases.
1, 2, 4, 8, 8, 10, 12, 13

274. Which of the following box-and-whisker plots represents this data?

A.
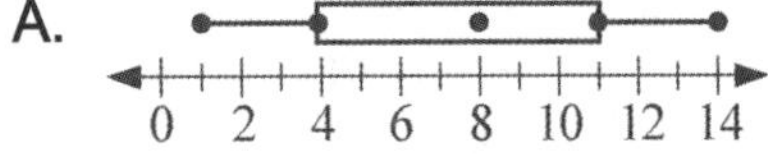

B.
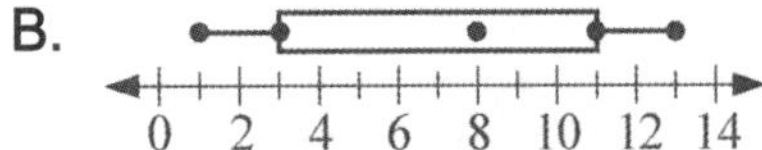

C.
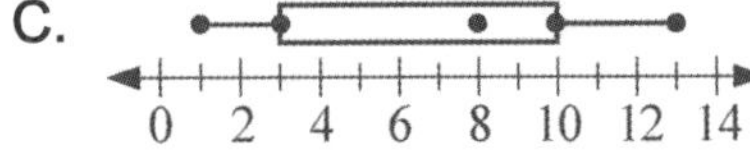

D.
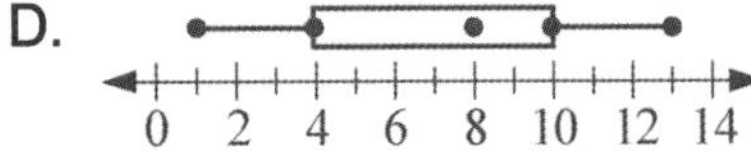

Use the following information to answer the next question.

Sherry makes a frequency chart to show how the number of sixth grade students attending her school has changed over five years. She uses the enrollment at the end of the second week of January for each of the five years.

Year	Frequency
2007	48
2006	43
2005	32
2004	37
2003	25

275. Which of the following histograms shows the changes in the sixth grade population?

A.
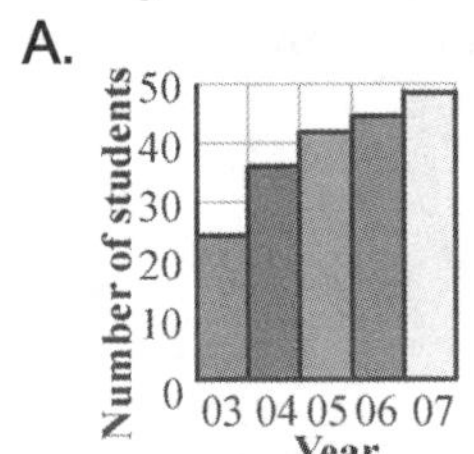

B.
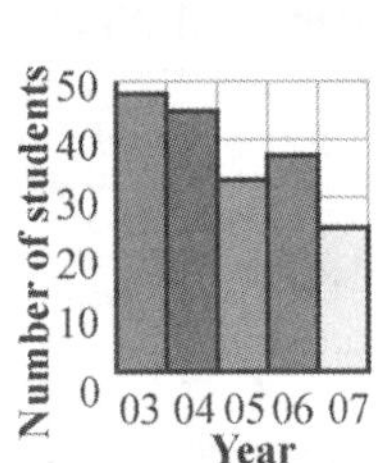

C.
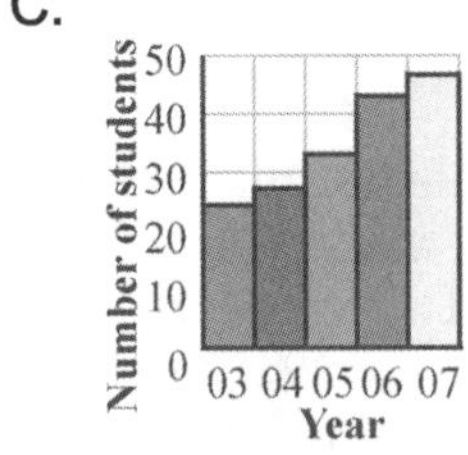

D.
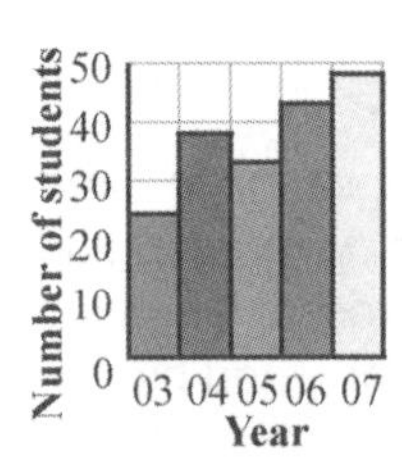

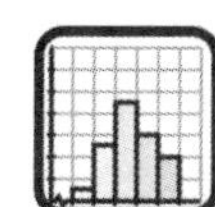

Use the following information to answer the next question.

Krystal began a new exercise routine using the treadmill. She made a table of values to show the time she spent walking and the time she spent running each morning over a 7-day period.

Day	Time Walking (min)	Time Running (min)
1	24	20
2	16	32
3	12	42
4	28	28
5	20	36
6	18	42
7	6	52

Krystal presented her data in the double line graph shown. While reviewing her graph, Krystal noticed that she had made an error.

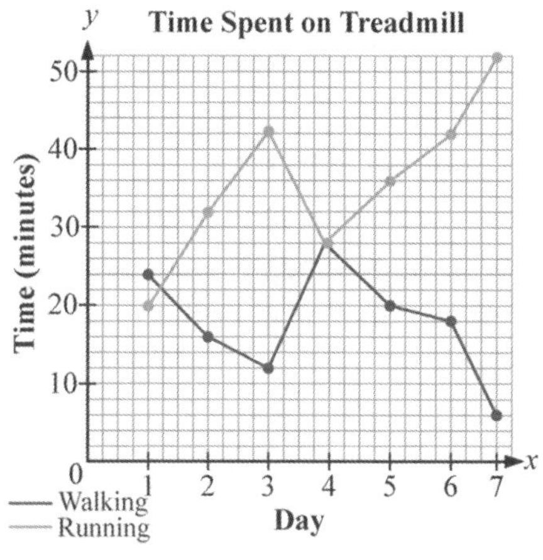

276. The given double line graph shows that Krystal made an error when she

A. plotted the data points for the time spent walking

B. plotted the data points for the time spent running

C. drew the scale on the x-axis

D. drew the scale on the y-axis

Use the following information to answer the next question.

Mr. Casey asked his students how many times they ordered the lunch special in the cafeteria that week, and he recorded the students' responses. The results from his survey are shown in the given data set.

1	2	4
2	2	1
4	2	5
5	5	5
4	2	3
2	1	4
3	5	2

277. Which of the following line plots represents Mr. Casey's data set?

A.

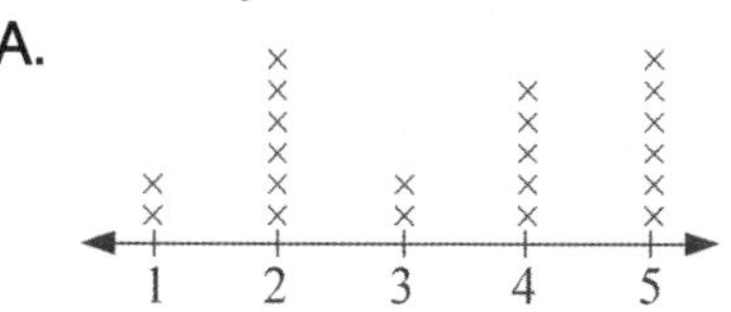

B.

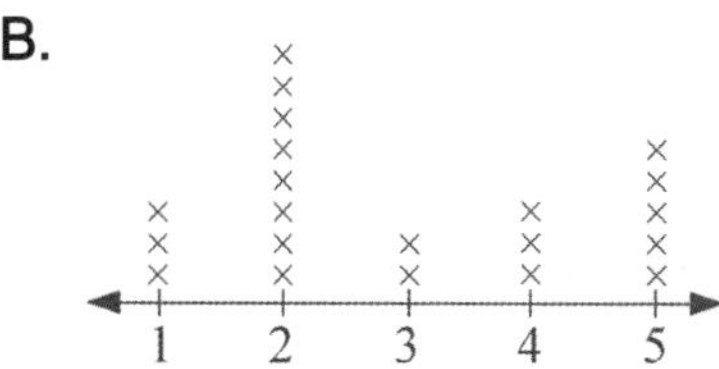

C.

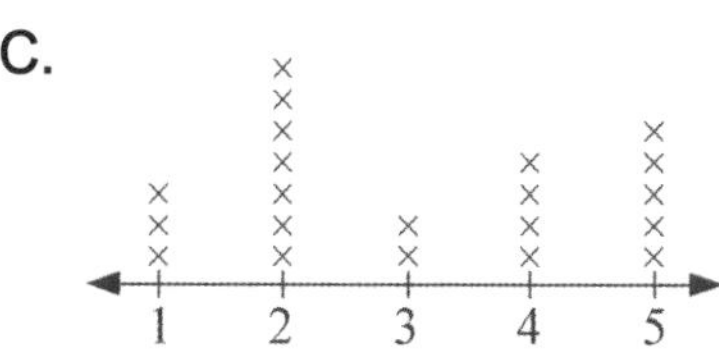

D.

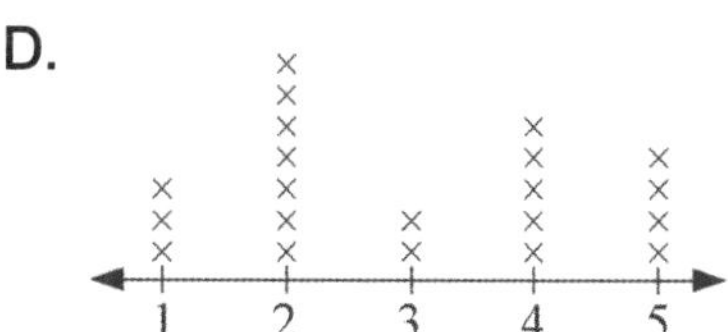

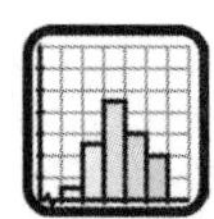

278. Calculate the mean of the data set {6, 13, 40, 23, 35, 27, 31}.

Use the following information to answer the next question.

The weights of 5 apples are recorded in the table.

	230 g
	170 g
	190 g
	220 g
	190 g

279. What is the median for the weights of the apples?

A. 170 g　　**B.** 190 g
C. 220 g　　**D.** 230 g

Use the following information to answer the next question.

This table shows the frequency of values used in a set of data.

Value	Frequency
2	4
8	3
5	1
3	1
6	1

280. The mode of the data in the given table is

A. 1　　**B.** 2
C. 4　　**D.** 8

Use the following information to answer the next question.

Manju decided to keep track of how many birds came to her birdfeeder everyday, and recorded the following numbers.
33, 27, 18, 33, 9, 8, 28, 13, 18, 6, 7, 33, 14

281. Which of the following statements about the given data set is **true**?

A. The mean is less than the mode.
B. The mode is less than the median.
C. The mean is greater than the mode.
D. The median is greater than the mean.

282. A set of 20 numbers has a standard deviation of 7. If 3 is added to each number in the set, the new standard deviation is __________.

Use the following information to answer the next question.

The ages in years of 12 people at a bus stop were 10, 10, 12, 16, 17, 20, 21, 24, 38, 50, and 56.

283. The value of the lower quartile for the data is

A. 12　　**B.** 14
C. 15　　**D.** 16

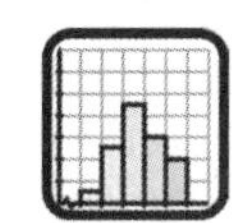

Use the following information to answer the next question.

In order to understand the study habits of his class of 200 mathematics students, a professor takes a random sample of 10 students and asks how many hours per week they usually spend on homework for his class. The results were 3, 2, 5, 2, 6, 3, 2, 8, 4, and 6.

284. If the professor uses this data to estimate the standard deviation of the homework time per week for the entire class, what will the calculated value be?

A. 1.90 **B.** 1.97

C. 2.01 **D.** 2.08

Use the following information to answer the next question.

The data set shown is the test scores out of 25 for 17 ninth grade students on a unit exam. The teacher found the interquartile range to be 10.
5, 8, 8, 11, 12, 12, 13, 15, 17, 18, 19, 20, 21, 22, 23, 24, 25

285. Which of the following statements about the interquartile range of the given data set is **true**?

A. It shows that a lot of the data points are around the median of the data.

B. It indicates that the test scores are fairly evenly distributed.

C. It indicates that the test scores have a low dispersion.

D. It is affected by the presence of outliers.

Use the following information to answer the next question.

Video game developers use random number generators to determine the position of power-ups and other items on the screen so that a game has increased challenge and replay value. Since a random number generator can only generate one number at a time, the *x*- and *y*-values of a 2-D coordinate must be generated separately.

286. If $0 \le x \le 719$, $x \in \mathbb{N}$, and every value is equally likely, what is the variance for the *x*-value?

A. 42,960 **B.** 43,080

C. 43,200 **D.** 43,320

Use the following information to answer the next question.

Every year, several new businesses are started, but many often fail. If the number of businesses in a particular country are continuously failing at a rate of 4 % per year, then the associated probability density function is $P(x) = 0.04e^{-0.04x}$, where x is measured in years.

287. The mean of $P(x)$ is __________.

Use the following information to answer the next question.

The computer help center for public service employees in a particular large city receives computer help requests on a daily basis. From past records, the help center knows that 70 % of the requests will be resolved on the day that they were received.

288. If 80 help requests are received on a particular day, then the mean number of help requests that will be resolved on that day is __________.

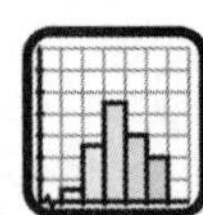

Use the following information to answer the next question.

The given table shows the average enrollment of students in School A and School B from 2004 to 2009.

Year	School A	School B
2004	110	105
2005	120	115
2006	117	123
2007	125	117
2008	130	125
2009	136	129

289. From 2004 to 2009, the difference between the mean enrollment of School A and the mean enrollment of School B is

A. 1 student **B.** 2 students

C. 3 students **D.** 4 students

Use the following information to answer the next question.

The following scatter plot displays the final mathematics exam marks for 21 students with respect to the corresponding number of hours studied for the exam.

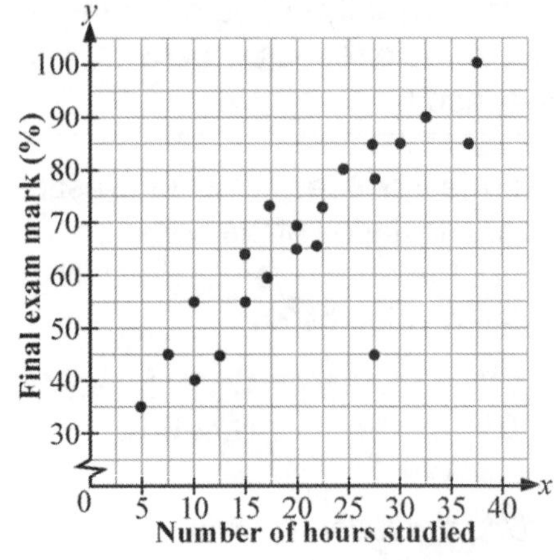

290. Which of the following pairs of coordinates represents an outlier point for the given graph?

A. (5, 35)

B. (27.5, 45)

C. (37, 85)

D. (37.5, 100)

Use the following information to answer the next question.

In order to estimate the average annual income in his neighborhood, Adam randomly selected seven nearby houses and asked what the income of the primary income earner was in the previous year. He received the following responses: \$45,000, \$40,000, \$48,000, \$40,000, \$55,000, \$52,000, and \$750,000. When he realized that the last homeowner won a lottery last year, Adam decided to eliminate the \$750,000 figure as an outlier.

291. Which of the following characteristics of the data will be **most** affected by eliminating the \$750,000 figure?

A. Mean **B.** Mode

C. Median **D.** Minimum

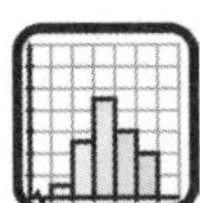

EXERCISE #2—SINGLE VARIABLE DATA ANSWERS AND SOLUTIONS

273. D	278. See solution	283. B	288. 56
274. B	279. B	284. D	289. D
275. D	280. B	285. B	290. B
276. C	281. A	286. C	291. A
277. C	282. 7	287. 25	

273. D

Step 1
Organize the data in increasing order.
23, 23, 25, 31, 34, 35, 43, 45, 54, 56, 63, 67

Step 2
Identify the median and lower and upper extremes.
23, 23, 25, 31, 34, [35, 43,] 45, 54, 56, 63, 67

The median is $\frac{35+43}{2}=39$. The lower extreme is 23, and the upper extreme is 67.

Step 3
Determine the lower quartile by finding the median of the numbers between the median and lower extreme.
23, 23, [25, 31,] 34, 35

The lower quartile is $\frac{25+31}{2}=28$.

Step 4
Find the upper quartile by finding the median of the numbers between the median and upper extreme.
43, 45, [54, 56,] 63, 67

The upper quartile is $\frac{54+56}{2}=55$.

Therefore, the lower quartile is 28, and the upper quartile is 55.

274. B

Step 1
Determine the five-number summary.

- Lowest number—1
- Lower quartile—3
- Median—8
- Upper quartile—11
- Highest number—13

Step 2
Identify the box-and-whisker plot that correctly plots the five-number summary.
This box-and-whisker plot correctly plots the five-number summary.

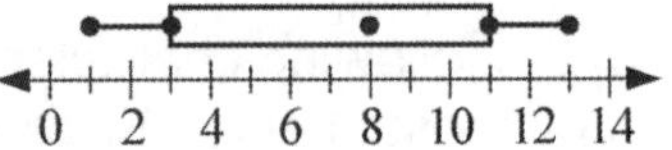

275. D

The correct histogram must show the given information.

- 2003 must reach a height of 25.
- 2004 must reach a height of 37.
- 2005 must reach a height of 32.
- 2006 must reach a height of 43.
- 2007 must reach a height of 48.

This histogram shows the changes in the sixth grade population.

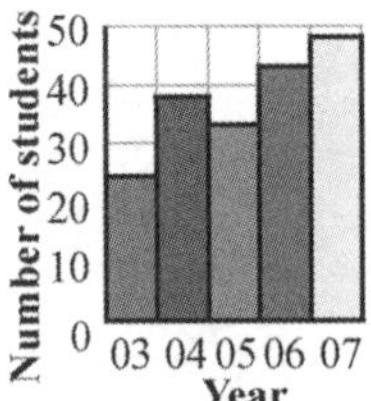

276. C

Krystal correctly drew the scale on the *y*-axis and plotted all the data points; however, on the *x*-axis, the distance between days 6 and 7 is narrower than the distance between the rest of the days. The distances between the days should all be equal.

Therefore, Krystal made an error when she drew the scale on the *x*-axis.

277. C

Step 1
Draw a horizontal line segment. From the data given, label all the possible outcomes under the line segment.

In this case, the numbers in the data go from 1 to 5, inclusive.

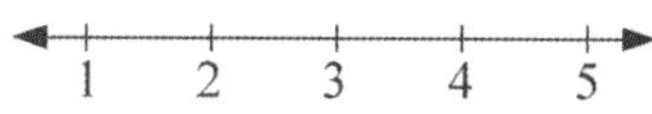

Step 2
Use a symbol to indicate each time an outcome occurred.

Based on the data given, a 1 occurred three times, a 2 occurred seven times, a 3 occurred two times, a 4 occurred four times, and a 5 occurred five times.

This is the line plot that correctly represents Mr. Casey's data set.

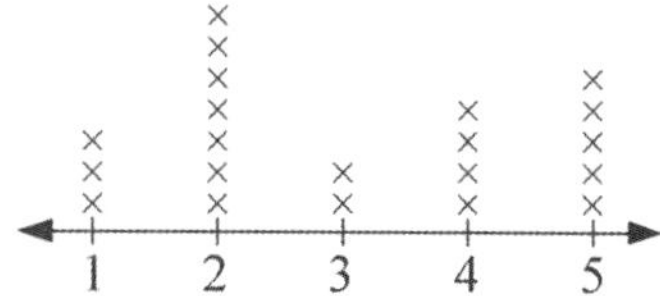

278.

Step 1
The mean of a set of data is defined as the ratio of the sum of the values to the number of values in the data set.

Determine the sum of the given values.
6 + 13 + 40 + 23 + 35+27 + 31 = 175

Step 2
Divide the total sum by the number of values.

Since there are 7 values, divide by 7.
175 ÷ 7 = 25

Therefore, the mean of the data set is 25.

279. B

Step 1
Place the values in order from least to greatest.
170, 190, 190, 220, 230

Step 2
Determine the middle number.

There is an odd number of values, so only one number is in the middle.
170, 190, 190, 220, 230

The median weight of the apples is 190 g.

280. B

The mode is the value that occurs most often.

The number in the frequency column of the table tells how many times the particular value appears in the set of data.

Since 4 is the number with the greatest value in the frequency column (4 > 3 > 1), that means the number value of 2 is used four times, which is more than any other number in this set of data.

Therefore, the mode of the data in the given table is 2.

281. A

To solve this problem, calculate the measures of central tendency and then compare them to each other.

Remember to arrange the data in ascending order to make the following calculations easier:
6, 7, 8, 9, 13, 14, 18, 18, 27, 28, 33, 33, 33

Median: There are 13 numbers in the data set which means the middle number will lay in the 7th position in the arrangement. The value in the 7th position, starting from the left or right side, is 18.

Mode: The number 33 appears three times, therefore, the mode is 33.

$$\text{Mean} = \frac{6+7+8+9+13+14+18+18+27+28+33+33+33}{13}$$
$$= \frac{247}{13}$$
$$= 19$$

The descending order of values for the measures of central tendency is as follows: mode, mean, median.

282. 7

Since 3 is added to each number in the set, the spread of the numbers about the mean stays the same. The standard deviation remains 7 because the dispersion of numbers has not changed.

283. B

Since the data is already ordered and there are an even number of numbers, the value of the lower quartile, Q_1, will be the median of the lowest six numbers: 10, 10, 12, 16, 17, and 20.

The median of this set is the average of the two middle numbers: 12 and 16.

$$Q_1 = \frac{12+16}{2}$$
$$Q_1 = \frac{28}{2}$$
$$Q_1 = 14$$

The value of the lower quartile for the data is 14.

284. D

Step 1

Determine the mean of the set of data.

The mean formula is $\bar{x} = \dfrac{x_1 + x_2 + \ldots + x_n}{n}$.

There are 10 data values, so $n = 10$.

Substitute the data values into the mean formula, and solve.

$$\bar{x} = \frac{3+2+5+2+6+3+2+8+4+6}{10}$$
$$\bar{x} = \frac{41}{10}$$
$$\bar{x} = 4.1$$

Step 2

Calculate the standard deviation of the sample data set.

Substitute the data values and the mean into the formula $s = \sqrt{\dfrac{(x_1 - \bar{x})^2 + (x_2 - \bar{x})^2 + \ldots + (x_n - \bar{x})^2}{n-1}}$, and solve.

$$s = \sqrt{\frac{(x_1 - \bar{x})^2 + (x_2 - \bar{x})^2 + \ldots + (x_n - \bar{x})^2}{n-1}}$$
$$s = \sqrt{\frac{\begin{array}{l}(3-4.1)^2 + (2-4.1)^2 + (5-4.1)^2 \\ +(2-4.1)^2 + (6-4.1)^2 + (3-4.1)^2 \\ +(2-4.1)^2 + (8-4.1)^2 + (4-4.1)^2 \\ +(6-4.1)^2\end{array}}{10-1}}$$
$$s = \sqrt{\frac{\begin{array}{l}(-1.1)^2 + (-2.1)^2 + (0.9)^2 + (-2.1)^2 + (1.9)^2 \\ +(-1.1)^2 + (-2.1)^2 + (3.9)^2 + (-0.1)^2 + (1.9)^2\end{array}}{9}}$$
$$s = \sqrt{\frac{\begin{array}{l}1.21 + 4.41 + 0.81 + 4.41 + 3.61 \\ +1.21 + 4.41 + 15.21 + 0.01 + 3.61\end{array}}{9}}$$
$$s = \sqrt{\frac{38.9}{9}}$$
$$s \approx \sqrt{4.32}$$
$$s \approx 2.08$$

For 10 sample values, $x_1, x_2, \ldots, x_{10}$ with the mean of the samples $\bar{x}$, the population standard deviation is approximately 2.08.

285. B

The range of the given data is equal to 25 – 5 = 20. The interquartile range is equal to 10, which is half of the range. This shows that the data is fairly evenly distributed throughout the data set.

286. C

Step 1

Determine the number of values, n.

$$n = (b - a) + 1$$
$$n = (719 - 0) + 1$$
$$n = 720$$

Step 2

Substitute 720 for n into the formula for variance (of a uniform discrete distribution), and evaluate.

$$Var(X) = \frac{n^2 - 1}{12}$$
$$Var(X) = \frac{720^2 - 1}{12}$$
$$Var(X) = \frac{518{,}399}{12}$$
$$Var(X) \approx 43{,}200$$

The variance for the x-value is 43,200.

287. 25

The function $P(x) = 0.04e^{-0.04x}$ is the probability density function of an exponential distribution.

To find the mean, simply substitute the value of λ into the formula for the mean, $\mu = \dfrac{1}{\lambda}$.

Since $P(x)$ is already in the form $\lambda e^{-\lambda x}$, it follows that $\lambda = 0.04$.

$$\mu = \frac{1}{\lambda}$$
$$\mu = \frac{1}{0.04}$$
$$\mu = 25$$

288. 56

The mean, μ, of the 80 help requests that will be resolved on the given day can be determined by applying the mean formula $\mu = np$, where the number of trials is n and the probability of success is p.

Substitute 80 for n and 0.70 for p, and then solve for μ.

$$\mu = np$$
$$\mu = (80)(0.70)$$
$$\mu = 56$$

The mean number of help requests that will be resolved on that day is 56.

289. D

Step 1
Determine the mean of the data set for School A.
Find the sum of all the values in the set, and divide the sum by the total number of values in the set.
110 + 120 + 117 + 125 + 130 + 136 = 738
738 ÷ 6 = 123
The mean enrollment for School A is 123 students.

Step 2
Determine the mean of the data set for School B.
Find the sum of all the values in the set, and divide the sum by the total number of values in the set.
105 + 115 + 123 + 117 + 125 + 129 = 714
714 ÷ 6 = 119
The mean enrollment for School B is 119 students.

Step 3
Determine the difference between the two means.
123 – 119 = 4
The mean enrollment for School A is 4 students greater than the mean enrollment for School B.

290. B

An outlier for a set of data is a value that is distant from the rest of the data values. This means an outlier point lies far from the data's line of best fit. On the given graph, it can be observed that the most distant data point from the rest of the data is located at (27.5, 45), making this point an outlier.

291. A

Examine each characteristic to see how much it changes with the elimination of the outlier.

Step 1
Examine the minimum value.
The minimum is $40,000. This is unchanged when the outlier is removed.

Step 2
Examine the mode.
The mode is $40,000. This is unchanged when the outlier is removed.

Step 3
Examine the mean.
The original mean (rounded to the nearest thousand) can be calculated as follows:
(45,000 + 40,000 + 48,000
+40,000 + 55,000 + 52,000
+750,000) ÷ 7 ≈ $147,000
When the outlier is removed, the mean (rounded to the nearest thousand) will be much smaller.
(45,000 + 40,000 + 48,000+40,000 + 55,000
+52,000) ÷ 6 ≈ $47,000
Thus, the mean is changed by
147,000 – 47,000 = $100,000.

Step 4
Examine the median.
Order the original data from least to greatest.
$40,000, $40,000, $45,000, $48,000, $52,000, $55,000, $750,000
The median of this data set is the middle term, which is $48,000.
When the outlier is removed, the data will then be ordered as follows:
$40,000, $40,000, $45,000, $48,000, $52,000, $55,000
The median then becomes the average of $45,000 and $48,000, which is $47,000 (rounded to the nearest thousand), so the median is changed by $1,000.
Therefore, the mean will be most affected by eliminating the outlier.

NOTES

Patterns in Bivariate Data

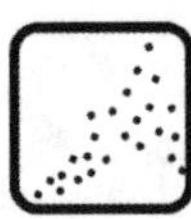

PATTERNS IN BIVARIATE DATA

Table of Correlations

Standard		Concepts	Exercise #1	Exercise #2
Unit3.2	Investigate patterns of association in bivariate data.			
8.SP.1	*Construct and interpret scatter plots for bivariate measurement data to investigate patterns of association between two quantities. Describe patterns such as clustering, outliers, positive or negative association, linear association, and nonlinear association.*	Representing Data in a Scatter Plot	292	299
		Investigating the Correlation between Two Variables	293	300
8.SP.2	*Know that straight lines are widely used to model relationships between two quantitative variables. For scatter plots that suggest a linear association, informally fit a straight line, and informally assess the model fit by judging the closeness of the data points to the line.*	Drawing a Line of Best Fit	294	301
		Approximating the Equation of a Line of Best Fit	295	302
		Interpreting a Line of Best Fit	296	303
8.SP.3	*Use the equation of a linear model to solve problems in the context of bivariate measurement data, interpreting the slope and intercept.*	Meaning of y-intercept and Slope in Graphs of Real Situations	18	24
		Approximating the Equation of a Line of Best Fit	295	302
		Interpreting a Line of Best Fit	296	303
		Extrapolating From a Line of Best Fit	297	304
		Interpolating from a Line of Best Fit	298	305

8.SP.1 Construct and interpret scatter plots for bivariate measurement data to investigate patterns of association between two quantities. Describe patterns such as clustering, outliers, positive or negative association, linear association, and nonlinear association.

Representing Data in a Scatter Plot

A **scatter plot** is a graphical method of displaying the relationship or correlation between two variables. In a scatter plot, two sets of data are plotted as ordered pairs on a coordinate plane, which are identified as (x, y). The x-axis (horizontal axis) represents the independent variable.
The y-axis (vertical axis) represents the dependent variable. The x- and y-axes are labeled with the variables that are being compared.

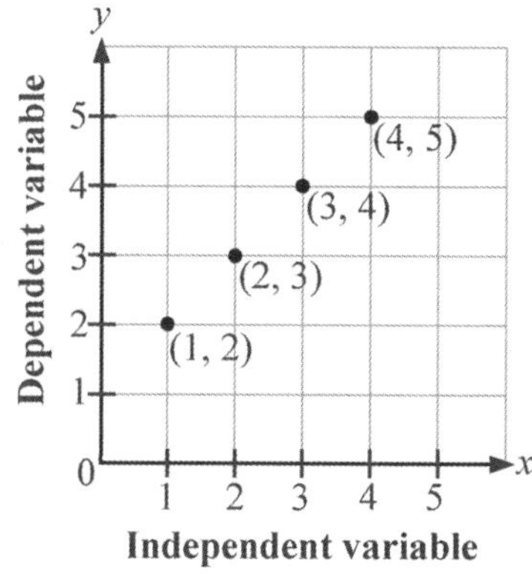

To represent data in a scatter plot, follow these steps:

1. Write the ordered pairs to be plotted.
2. Choose suitable increments to mark both axes for the data.
3. Draw the axes and plot the points.
4. Label the axes and give the scatter plot a title.

Example

Jashandeep wants to understand the relationship between the Celsius scale and the Fahrenheit scale. He goes onto the Internet, collects the following data, and organizes it into the given table.

Temperature (°C)	Temperature (°F)
−10	14
−5	23
0	32
5	41
10	50
15	59
20	68
25	77

Plot the data in a scatter plot.

Solution

Step 1

Write the ordered pairs to be plotted.
The independent variable is the x-value.
The dependent variable is the y-value.

Temperature (°C)	Temperature (°F)	Ordered Pair
−10	14	(−10, 14)
−5	23	(−5, 23)
0	32	(0, 32)
5	41	(5, 41)
10	50	(10, 50)
15	59	(15, 59)
20	68	(20, 68)
25	77	(25, 77)

Step 2

Choose a suitable and equal scale (intervals) for numbering the axes.

The independent variable, °C, will be on the horizontal *x*-axis. It increases by 5° at each point. All the data will be clearly displayed if the minimum *x*-value is −10°C to a maximum *x*-value of 25°C.

The dependent variable, °F, will be on the vertical *y*-axis. It increases by 9° at each point. All the data will be displayed if the minimum *y*-value is 14°F to a maximum *y*-value of 77°F.

Step 3

Draw the axes lines and plot the points.

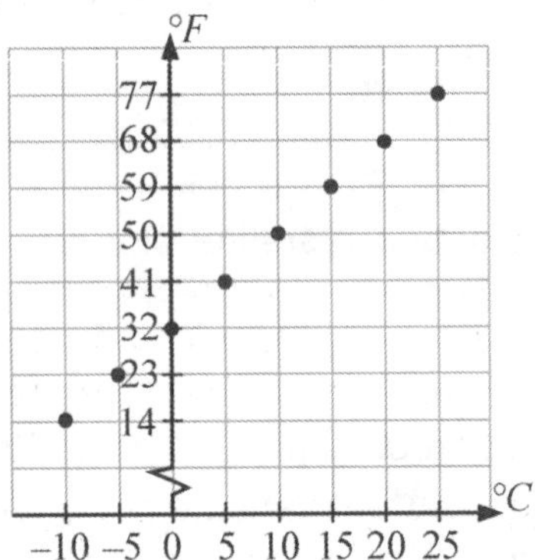

Step 4

Label the axes according to the set of data they represent, and give the scatter plot a title.

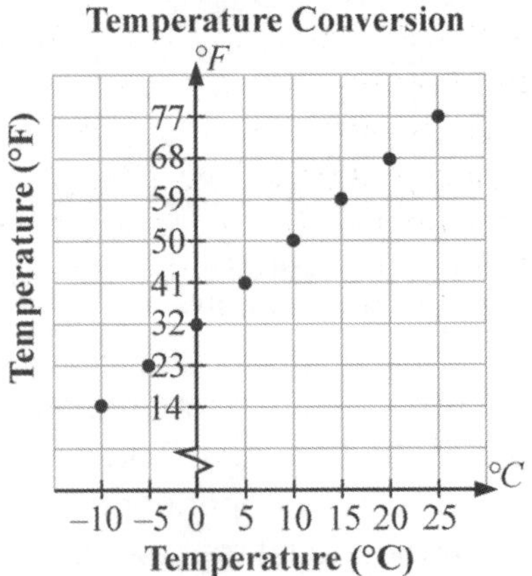

Notice the following:

- The axes are labeled according to the variables they represent, °C and °F, instead of *x* and *y*.
- The Fahrenheit axis has a break. This allows numbers that are not needed to be left out. Here, the temperatures from 0°F to 13°F are left out.

Investigating the Correlation between Two Variables

When a scatter plot is constructed from the data collected in an experiment, trends and relationships between two variables can be described. If the values of one variable consistently increase or decrease while the corresponding values of the other variable increase or decrease, then the scatter plot of the ordered pairs (points) will follow a linear pattern. The closer the points on the scatter plot come to forming a straight line, the stronger the correlation between the two variables. Also, the correlation is positive or negative, depending on the direction or trend of the points on the scatter plot.

When the points of a scatter plot follow a linear pattern, then inferences or conclusions can be made about the relationship between the two variables representing the data. These inferences can then be compared to the original hypotheses made about the relationship.

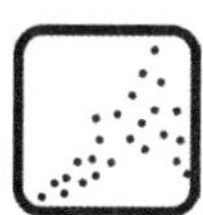

UPWARD TRENDS

If the points of a scatter plot move linearly from the lower left to the upper right of the graph, the graph shows an upward trend. There is a positive correlation between the two variables.
As the x-values increase, so do the corresponding y-values. The strength of the correlation is defined by the consistency of the linear pattern of the points or how close the points are to forming a straight line.

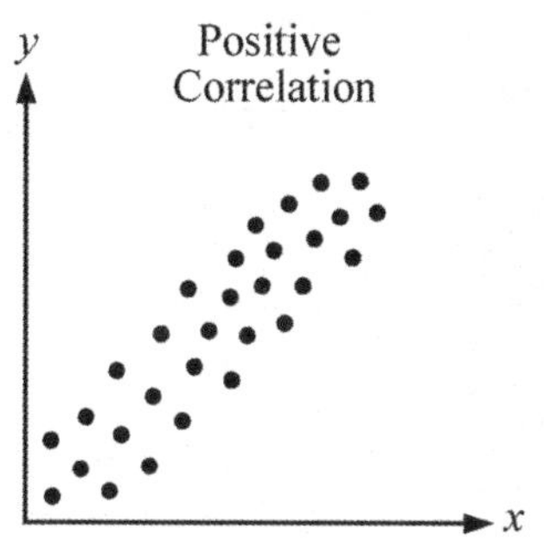

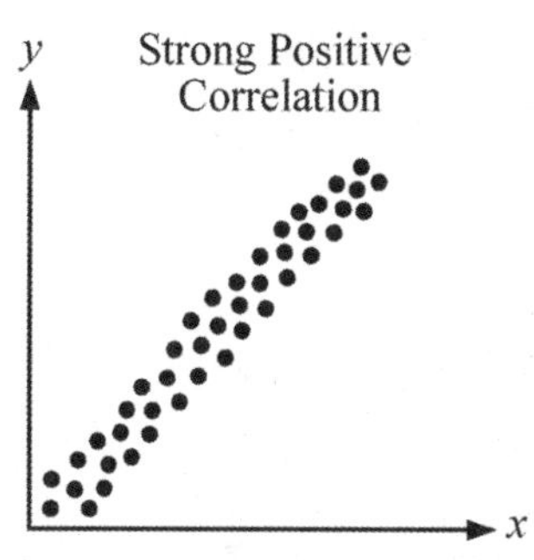

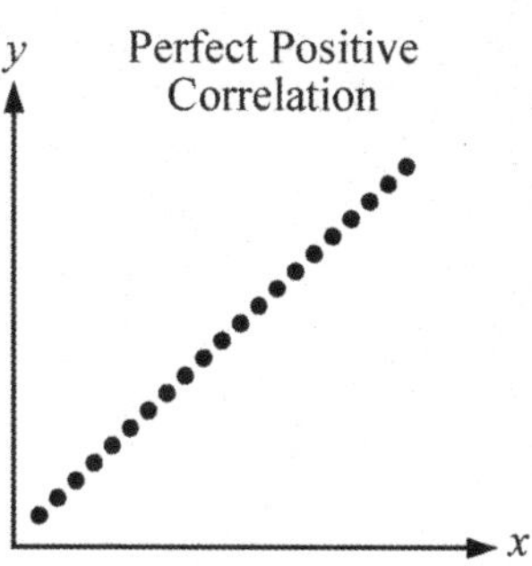

Example

A random group of individuals was surveyed to investigate the relationship between age, a, and yearly income, i.

Formulate three hypotheses about the relationship between the age of a person and his or her yearly income.

Solution

These hypotheses can be made:

- As a person's age increases, his or her income increases.
- As a person's age increases, his or her income decreases.
- There is no relationship between a person's age and yearly income

---

Example

A random group of individuals was surveyed to investigate the relationship between age, a, and yearly income, i. The given table displays the data collected.

Age (year)	Income ($ × 1,000)
18	10
21	20
24	10
27	25
30	35
33	40
36	25
39	30
42	46
45	40
48	58
51	50
54	10

Graph the data.

Solution

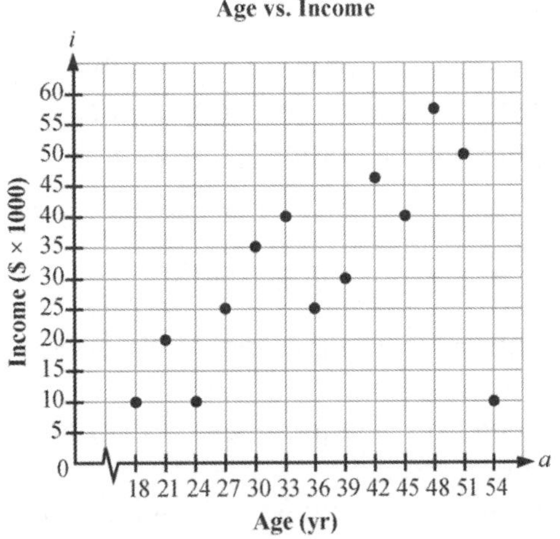

Notice a break was placed in the *x*-axis to show that the ages 0 to 17 were not needed in the graph.

Describe the relationship between the two variables, and state the correlation and trend of the data.

Solution

The points on the scatter plot show that as the person's age (independent variable) increases, the wage (dependent variable) also increases at various increments. The trend is upward, which indicates a positive correlation because the points move linearly upward from left to right.

However, the point at age 54 does not appear to follow the pattern. When a point like this is encountered, it is called an outlier. The outlier is not accurate because of a measurement error that occurred when collecting data or is non-representative because of other factors. In this case, the person may have lost his job and not made as much money as he normally would. Thus, this data would not be included when making inferences.

What inference can be made based on the trend of the data?

Solution

As a person's age increases, his or her income also increases. In other words, a person can expect to make more money as he or she gets older.

Downward Trend

If the points of a scatter plot move linearly from the upper left to the lower right of the graph, the graph shows a downward trend. There is a negative correlation between the two variables.
As the *x*-values increase, the corresponding *y*-values decrease. The strength of the correlation is defined by the consistency of the linear pattern of the points or how close the points are to forming a straight line.

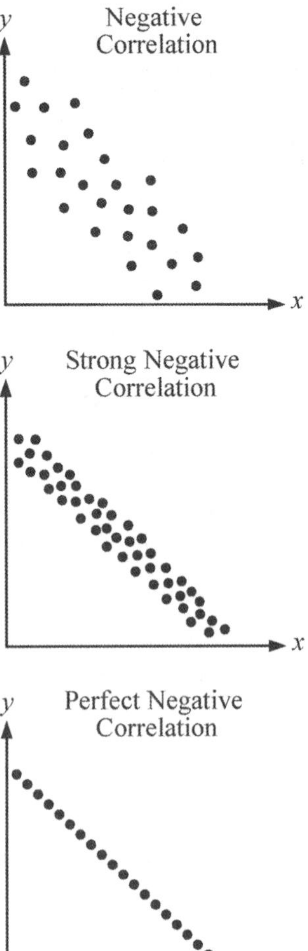

Example

Katrina is curious about how the temperature of hot chocolate changes as it sits on the counter.

Formulate two hypotheses about the relationship between the time a cup of hot chocolate sits on the counter and its temperature.

Solution

The following hypotheses can be made:

- The longer the hot chocolate sits on the counter, the colder it gets.
  As the independent variable (time) increases, the dependent variable (temperature) decreases.
- The longer the hot chocolate sits on the counter, the hotter it gets.
  As the independent variable (time) increases, the dependent variable (temperature) increases.

Katrina is curious about how the temperature of hot chocolate changes as it sits on the counter.

Time (min)	0	2	4	6	8
Temperature (°C)	50	40	27	22	20

Graph the data.

Solution

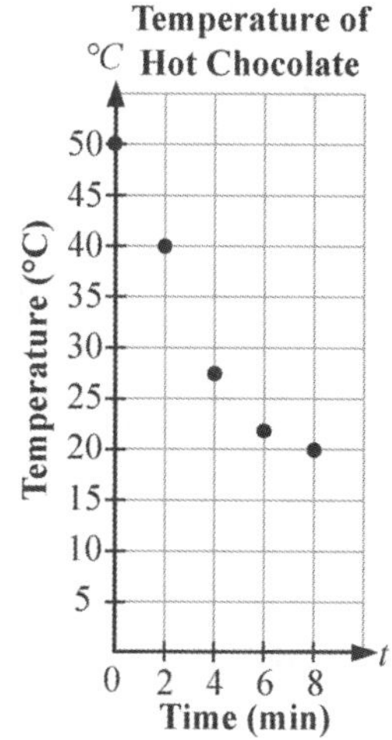

Describe the trend and correlation between the two variables as shown by the points on the scatter plot.

Solution

The points on the scatter plot show that the longer the hot chocolate sits on the counter, the cooler the temperature becomes.
The independent variable, time, is increasing while the dependent variable, temperature, is decreasing. This describes a negative correlation and a downward trend.

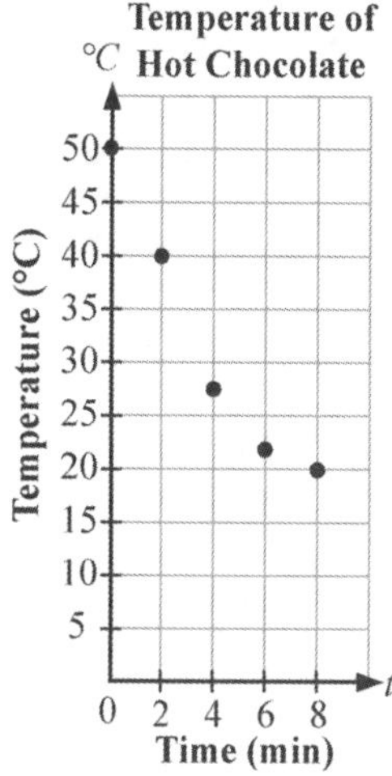

What inference can be made about the relationship between the two variables?

Solution

As time increases, the temperature of hot beverages decreases. It can also be noted that the temperature of the hot chocolate drops faster at the beginning and then begins to level off. The hot beverage initially cools off rapidly. As its temperature gets closer to the ambient room temperature, it stabilizes.

No Apparent Trend

If the points of a scatter plot appear scattered with no obvious upward or downward trend, then there is no relationship or no correlation between the variables. The data can also follow a non-linear pattern where one variable increases or decreases more than the other, resulting in a curved pattern. This would reflect a non-linear correlation between the two variables.

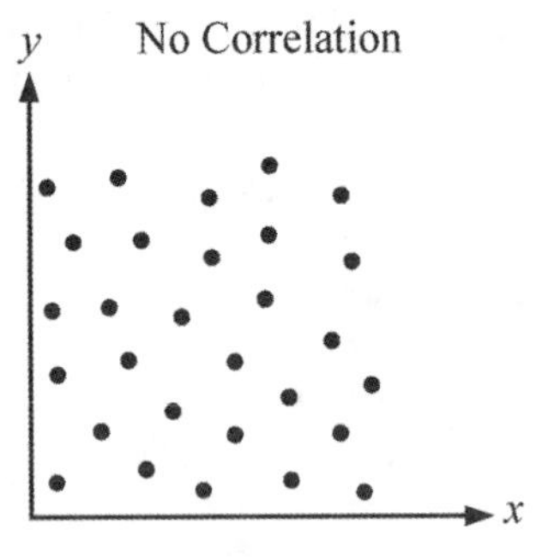

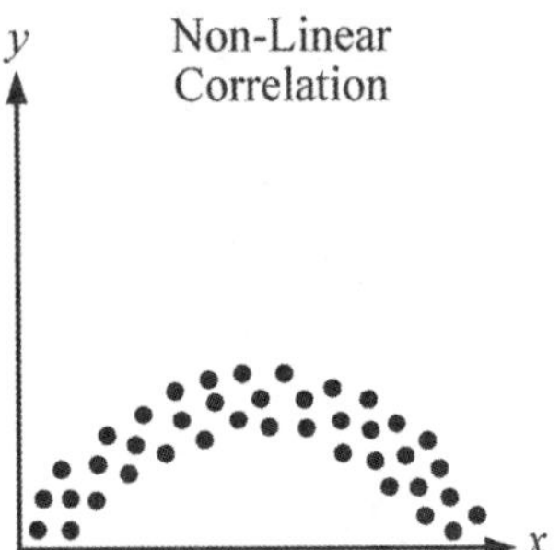

Example

John wanted to know if there was a lucky number that he should choose for his basketball jersey.

Formulate two hypotheses, and identify the relationship being described.

Solution

The following hypotheses can be made:

- The higher the jersey number, the greater the number of points scored.
  As the independent variable (jersey number) increases, the dependent variable (points scored) also increases.
- The higher the jersey number, the fewer the number of points scored.
  As the independent variable (jersey number) increases, the dependent variable (points scored) decreases.

There is no relationship between the jersey numbers and points scored.

John wanted to know if there was a lucky number that he should choose for his basketball jersey. The given data displays the jersey numbers, n, and points scored, p, of various members on the basketball team from the previous year.

Jersey Number	Points Scored
1	8
2	14
3	10
4	4
5	6
6	16
7	4
8	10
9	14
10	1
11	7

Graph the data.

Solution

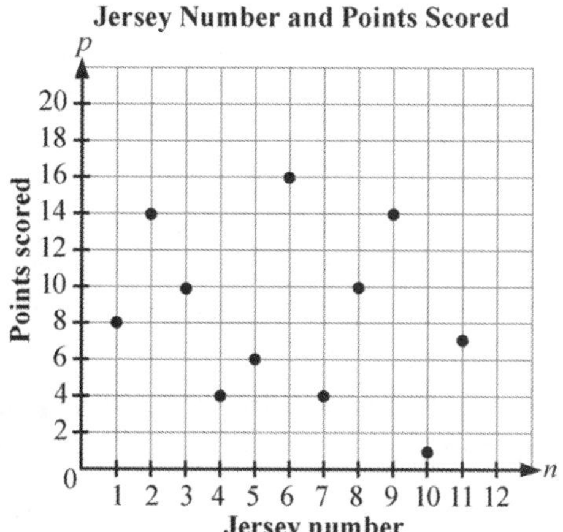

Describe the correlation and trend of the points shown on the scatter plot.

Solution

The points on the scatter plot do not form a pattern, so there is no correlation or trend between the points scored and the jersey number.

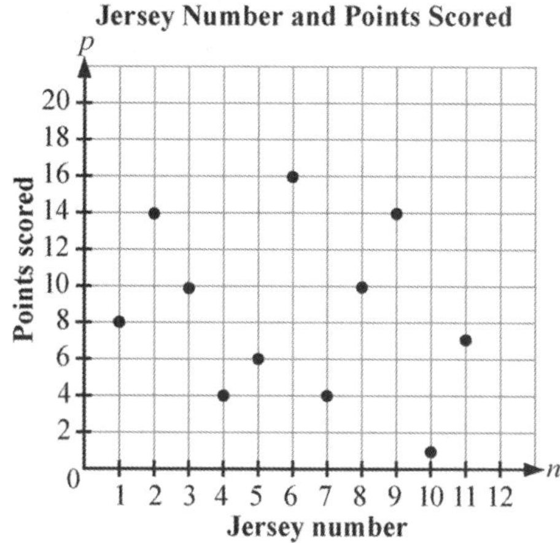

What inference can be made about the data?

Solution

The jersey number that John chooses or is given will not affect his ability to score more or fewer points during a basketball game.

A quick way to check whether the points on a scatter plot describe a positive (upward trend), negative (decreasing trend), or no correlation is to draw a line around the majority of the points and examine the shape formed. If the shape forms an oval that moves up to the right, it describes a positive correlation, and if the oval moves down to the right, it describes a negative correlation. If the shape forms a circle, there is no correlation.

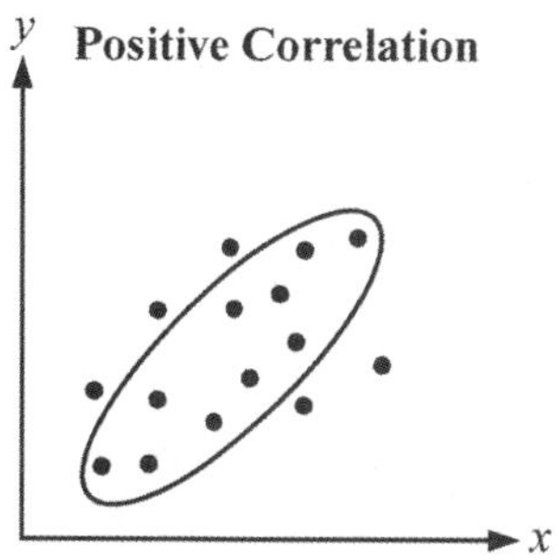

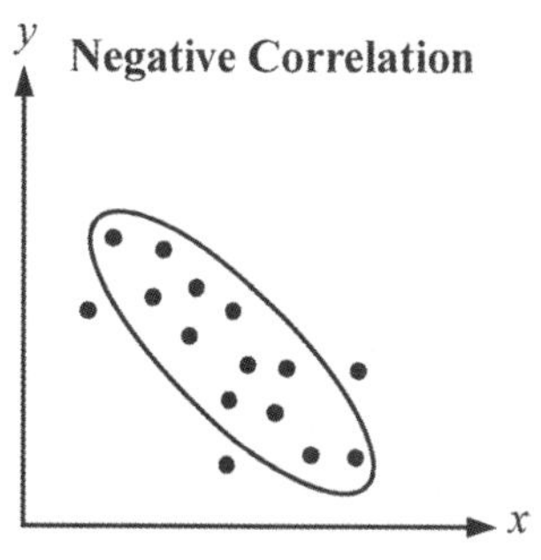

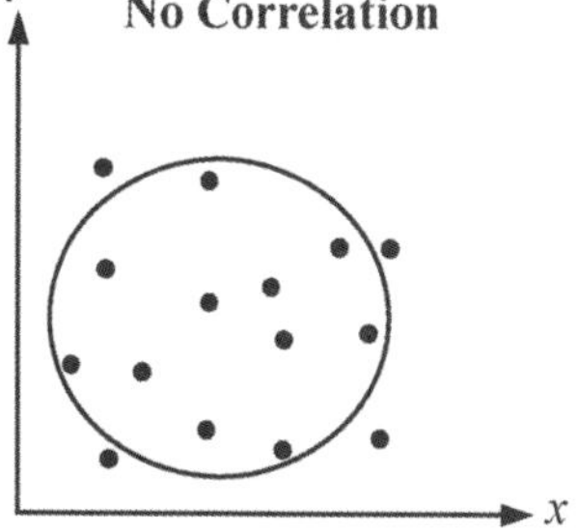

8.SP.2 Know that straight lines are widely used to model relationships between two quantitative variables. For scatter plots that suggest a linear association, informally fit a straight line, and informally assess the model fit by judging the closeness of the data points to the line.

Drawing a Line of Best Fit

A **line of best fit** is an average of the values represented by the points on a scatter plot. A line of best fit is of little use when the given variables have no relationship, because that means no trend is represented by the data.

If the relationship indicates that one variable increases as the other increases, the line on the graph will rise from left to right.

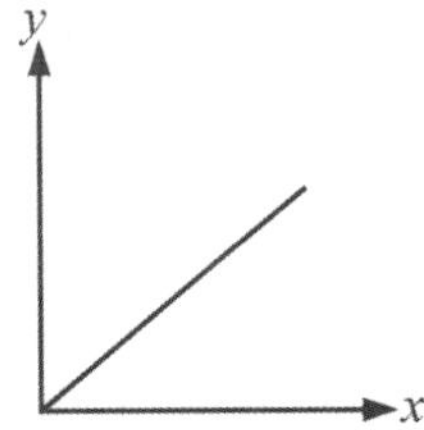

In a relationship in which a variable decreases as the other variable increases, the line on the graph will slope downward from left to right.

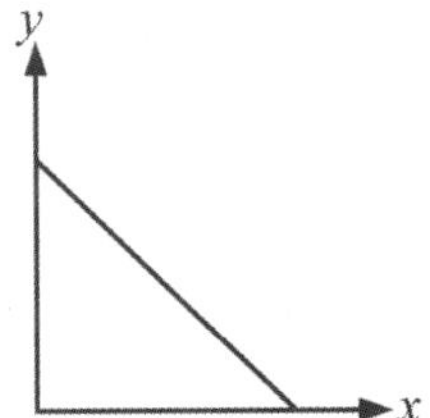

To add a line of best fit, line up your ruler so that it goes through the middle of the pattern formed by the points on the scatter plot. Follow the angle of the pattern as best as you can, then draw the line using your ruler. There may be some points that do not lie exactly on the line. In that case, draw your line of best fit so that an approximately equal number of points lie above and below the line. It is a good idea to extend the axes and the line of best fit beyond the data given so that predictions about future data can be made.

Example

Average Price per Liter of Gasoline at a Gas Station in Edmonton, Alberta, Over a Number of Years

Year	1970	1980	1990	2000	2005
Price per Liter	$0.10	$0.27	$0.35	$0.56	$0.73

Plot the given data on a scatter plot and add a line of best fit.

Solution

Step 1

Plot the data on a scatter plot.

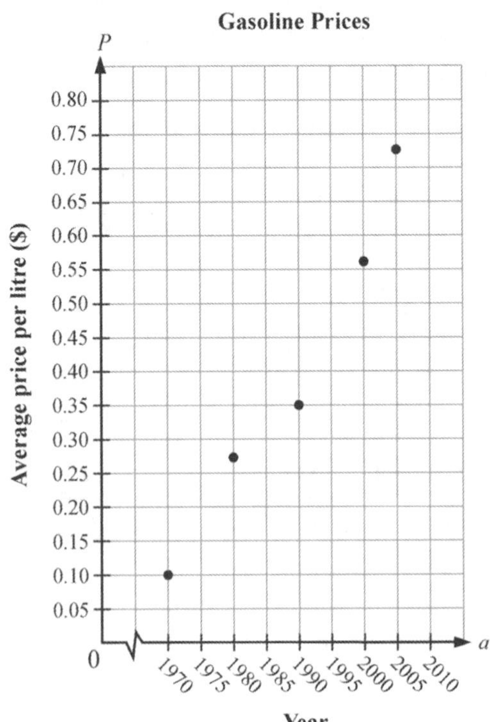

Step 2
Draw a line of best fit.

Place your ruler through the middle of the pattern formed by the points and draw a line.

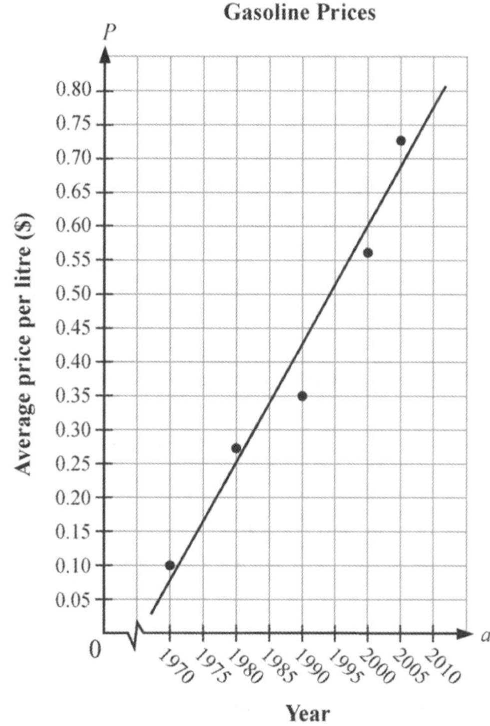

Approximating the Equation of a Line of Best Fit

When finding an equation for the line of best fit, it is important to remember that unless the data are perfectly linear, the equation will be a close approximation at best. Finding the slope of the line is necessary for forming an equation. This requires identifying or approximating two points on the line.

To approximate the equation of a line of best fit, follow these steps:

1. Identify two points on the line, and determine the slope by using the formula $m = \frac{y_2 - y_1}{x_2 - x_1}$.
2. Use the calculated slope and one of the two identified points with the formula $m = \frac{y - y_1}{x - x_1}$ to determine the equation of the line in either the standard or slope y-intercept form as required.

The best way to find the approximate equation of the line of best fit is to use points from the scatter plot that overlap the line of best fit. If possible, try to use points that are relatively far apart to minimize error.

Example

A line of best fit is shown.

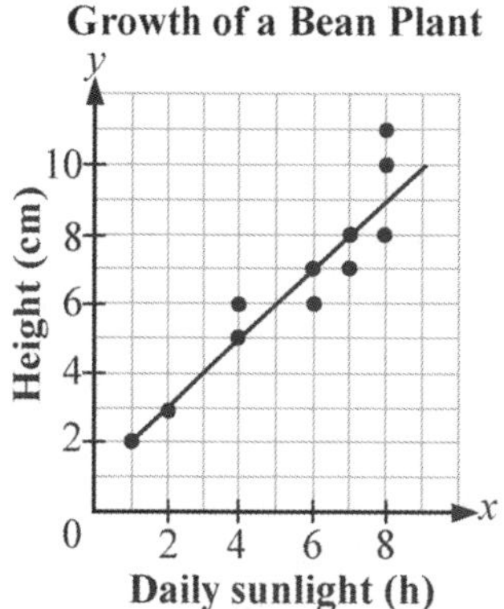

Determine an equation for the line of best fit.

Solution

Step 1
Identify two points on the line, and determine the slope by using the formula $m = \frac{y_2 - y_1}{x_2 - x_1}$.

Two points on the line are (1, 2) and (7, 8).

$$m = \frac{y_2 - y_1}{x_2 - x_1}$$
$$m = \frac{8 - 2}{7 - 1}$$
$$m = 1$$

Step 2
Use the calculated slope and one of the two identified points with the formula $m = \frac{y - y_1}{x - x_1}$ to determine the equation of the line.

Use the point (1, 2).

$$m = \frac{y - y_1}{x - x_1}$$
$$1 = \frac{y - 2}{x - 1}$$
$$x - 1 = y - 2$$
$$x + 1 = y$$

An equation for the line of best fit is $y = x + 1$.

When working with a line of best fit, the graph of the line will not always nicely overlap points from the scatter plot. In this situation, identify approximate points on the line that are easily recognizable.

Example

A line of best fit is shown.

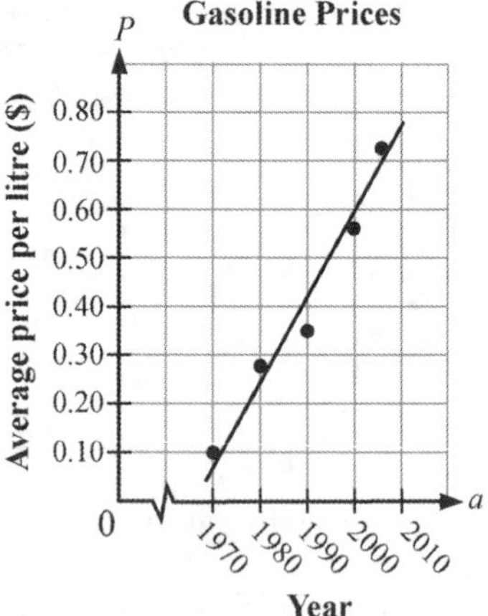

Determine an equation for the line of best fit.

Solution

Step 1

Identify two points on the line, and determine the slope by using the formula $m = \frac{y_2 - y_1}{x_2 - x_1}$.

Since none of the data points appear to overlap with the line, use two approximate points from the graph.

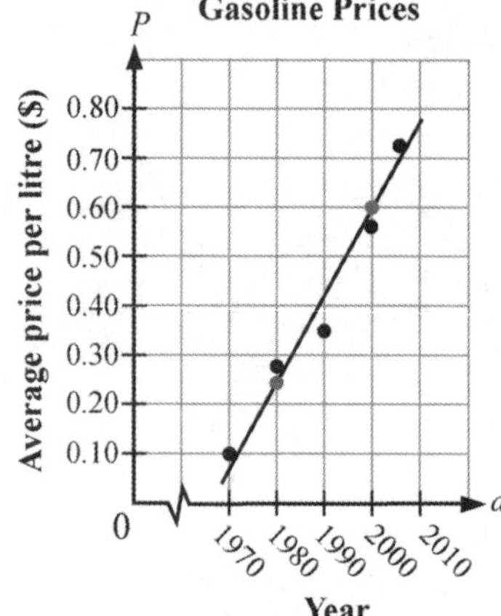

The coordinates (1,980, 0.25) and (2,000, 0.60) appear to be on the line.

$$m = \frac{y_2 - y_1}{x_2 - x_1}$$

$$m = \frac{0.60 - 0.25}{2,000 - 1,980}$$

$$m = 0.0175$$

Step 2

Use the calculated slope and one of the two points identified with the formula $m = \frac{y - y_1}{x - x_1}$ to determine the equation of the line.

Use the point (2,000, 0.60).

$$\begin{aligned} m &= \frac{y - y_1}{x - x_1} \\ 0.0175 &= \frac{y - 0.60}{x - 2,000} \\ 0.0175(x - 2,000) &= y - 0.60 \\ 0.0175x - 35 &= y - 0.60 \\ 0.0175x - 34.4 &= y \end{aligned}$$

A possible equation for the line of best fit is $y = 0.0175x - 34.4$.

Interpreting a Line of Best Fit

A **line of best fit** is an average of the values represented by the points on a scatter plot. It is useful for demonstrating trends in data.
The strength of the relationship between the variables is based on how closely the data points match the line. A line does not necessarily need to overlap any points to indicate a strong relationship. A line of best fit is of little use when the given variables have no relationship, because that means no trend is represented by the data. If data points are relatively far from the line, the relationship between the variables is weak or non-existent. A horizontal or vertical line indicates that there is no relationship, since one variable is constant regardless of the other.

The correlation of the data can be determined by looking at the value of the slope of a line of best fit. If the slope is negative, the data has a negative correlation. Similarly, if the slope is positive, the data has a positive correlation.

The slope of a linear regression is the same as the rate of change of a linear relation. The equations $m = \frac{\Delta \text{ dependent variable}}{\Delta \text{ independent variable}}$ and $m = \frac{y_2 - y_1}{x_2 - x_1}$ can be used to calculate the slope from the line.

The slope and a point on the graph can be used to determine the equation of the line if needed. The equation can be used to interpret the relationship between the two variables.

Example

In a recent hot dog eating competition, each competitor was asked how much time they spent training for the event. The given graph shows the number of weeks each competitor spent training and the amount of hot dogs they consumed in the contest. A line of best fit for the data is included.

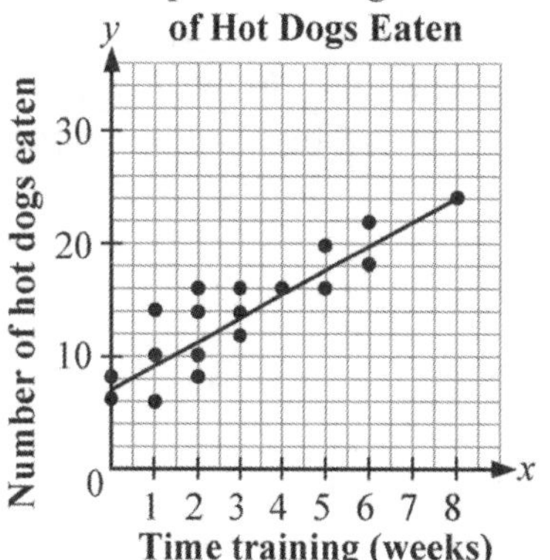

Interpret the line of best fit.

Solution

Step 1

Determine the equation of the line.

Identify two points on the line, and determine the slope by using the formula $m = \frac{y_2 - y_1}{x_2 - x_1}$.

Only the point (8, 24) appears to overlap with the line of best fit, so a second coordinate will need to be estimated from the line. A second coordinate that can be used to estimate the line is (0, 7).

$$m = \frac{y_2 - y_1}{x_2 - x_1}$$
$$m = \frac{24 - 7}{8 - 0}$$
$$m = \frac{17}{8}$$
$$m = 2.125$$

Use the calculated slope and one of the two points identified with the formula $m = \frac{y - y_1}{x - x_1}$ to determine the equation of the line.

$$m = \frac{y - y_1}{x - x_1}$$
$$2.125 = \frac{y - 24}{x - 8}$$
$$2.125(x - 8) = y - 24$$
$$2.125x - 17 = y - 24$$
$$2.125x + 7 = y$$

An approximate equation of the line of best fit is $y = 2.125x + 7$.

Step 2

Interpret the line of best fit.

Although the data does not perfectly match the line, it does appear to be correlated. Given the calculated slope of $m = 2.125$, there is a positive correlation between the variables. Each week of training undergone by a competitor appears to correlate with an additional 2.125 hot dogs consumed during the competition. Given that the y-intercept is approximately 7, a person who does not train at all for a competition should be able to eat an average of 7 hot dogs.

Example

In a recent hot dog eating competition, the body weight of each competitor was measured prior to the event. The given graph shows the body weight of the competitors and the amount of hot dogs they consumed during the contest. A line of best fit of the data is included.

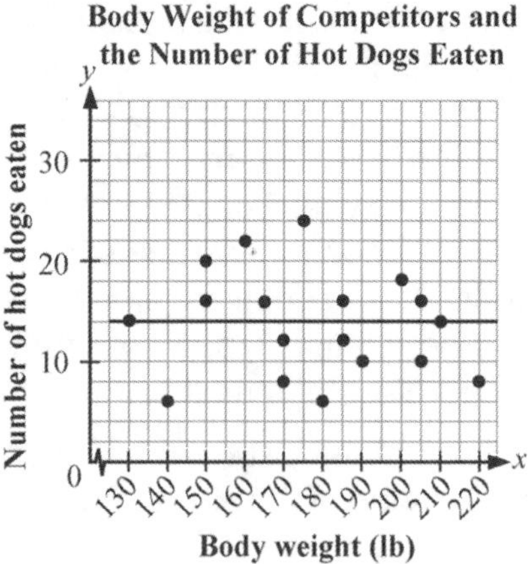

Interpret the line of best fit.

Solution

The given line of best fit is horizontal and does not align closely with the data points. Both of these factors indicate that there is no relationship between the weight of a competitor and how many hot dogs he or she can eat.

8.SP.3 Use the equation of a linear model to solve problems in the context of bivariate measurement data, interpreting the slope and intercept.

Extrapolating From a Line of Best Fit

A line of best fit is an average of the values represented by the points on a scatter plot. From the line of best fit, predictions can be made about values not directly given in the graph. To make predictions about a point beyond the given data is called **extrapolation**. To make predictions about a point within the given data is called **interpolation**.

When you extrapolate data, extend the given line of best fit far enough so that it goes beyond the piece of data required. Then, draw a vertical line up from the required data on the *x*-axis, and stop when it reaches the line of best fit. Then, draw a horizontal line from this point until it reaches the *y*-axis. Use this point to estimate your answer.

If the required point is found along the *y*-axis, draw a horizontal line toward the right, and stop when it reaches the line of best fit. Then, draw a vertical line down from this point until it reaches the *x*-axis. Use this point to estimate your answer.

Example

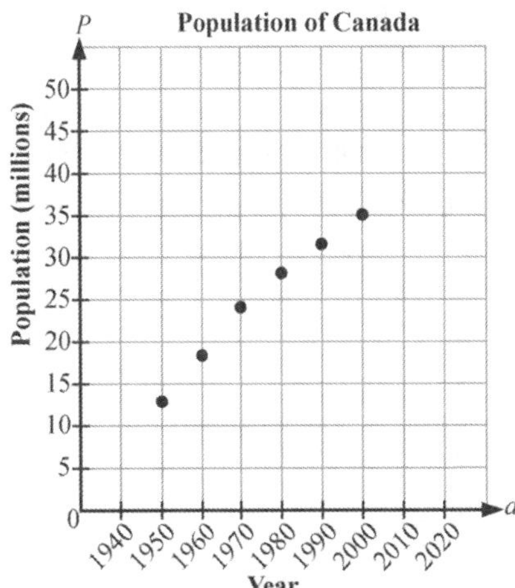

This scatter plot represents the population of Canada in six specific years.

Extrapolate the population of Canada in 2020.

Solution

Step 1

Draw a line of best fit that extends far enough beyond the data.

The question is asking for the population in 2020. The line of best fit must go beyond the year 2020.

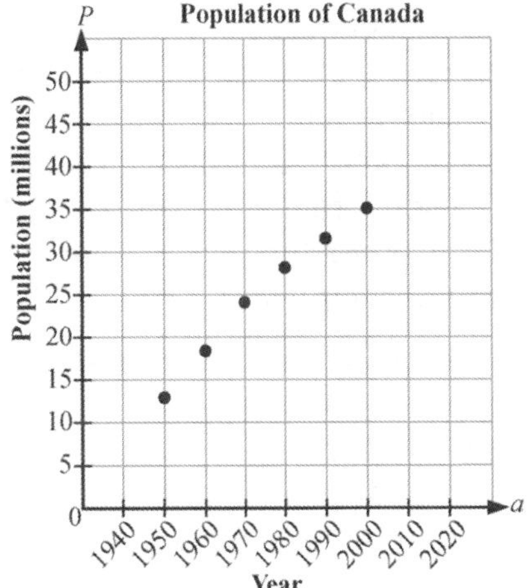

Step 2

Extrapolate the value.

Locate 2020 on the year axis. Draw a vertical line straight up until the line of best fit is reached. At this point, draw a straight horizontal line to intersect the population axis.

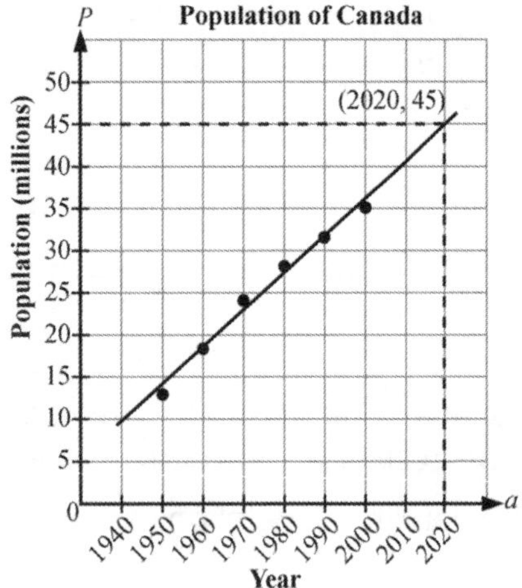

According to the line of best fit, the population of Canada in 2020 will be approximately 45 million.

Interpolating from a Line of Best Fit

When you interpolate data, you are locating information inside the existing graph. To do this, locate the point required along the *x*-axis, draw a vertical line up, and stop when it reaches the line of best fit. Then, draw a horizontal line from this point until it reaches the *y*-axis. Use this point to estimate the answer.

If the required point is found along the *y*-axis, draw a horizontal line toward the right and stop when it reaches the line of best fit. Then, draw a vertical line down from this point until it reaches the *x*-axis. Use this point to estimate the answer.

Example

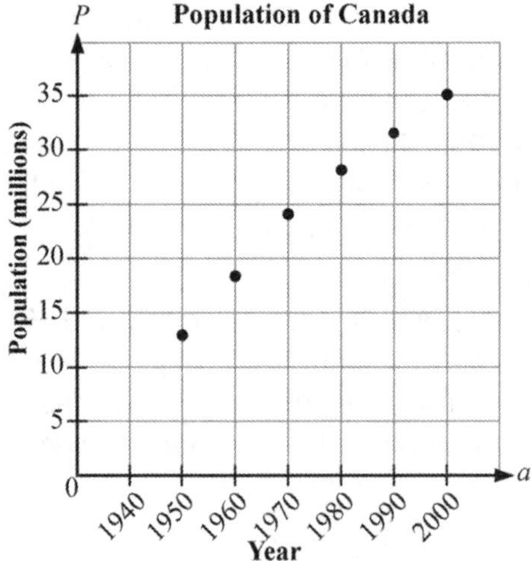

Interpolate the year the population of Canada was approximately 30 million.

Solution

Step 1

Draw a line of best fit that goes through the data.

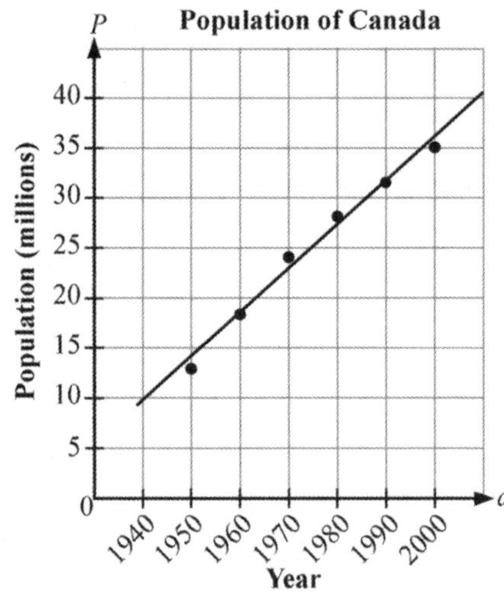

Step 2
Interpolate the value.
Locate 30 million on the population axis. Draw a horizontal line until the line of best fit is reached. At this point, draw a vertical line down to the year axis.

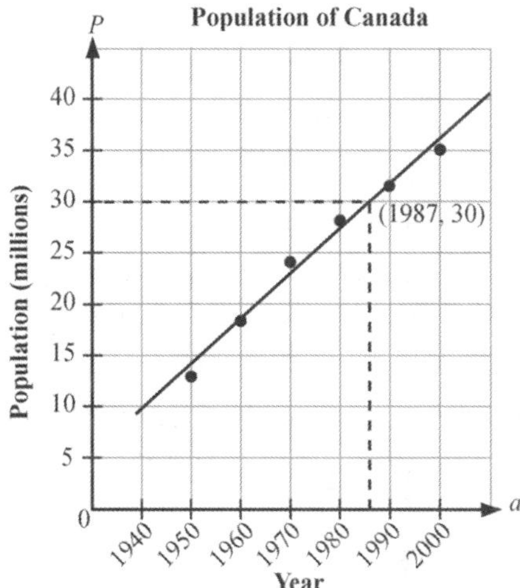

According to the line of best fit, the year that the population of Canada reached 30 million is approximately 1987.

EXERCISE #1—PATTERNS IN BIVARIATE DATA

Use the following information to answer the next question.

Elizabeth wanted to know if there was a correlation between the time, *t*, spent in the mall and the amount of money, *m*, she spends. She kept track of her spending in the following table.

Time (h)	Money Spent ($)
3	60
4	20
8	50
7	10
6	70
5	50
2	30
9	40

Elizabeth constructed the following scatter plot for the given data.

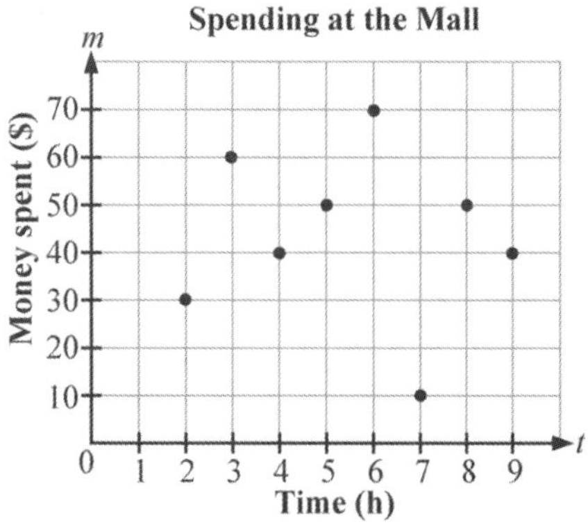

Upon analyzing her completed scatter plot, Elizabeth discovered that she had slotted one point incorrectly.

292. What is the *m*-coordinate of the point Elizabeth plotted incorrectly? __________

Use the following information to answer the next question.

Spring View Middle School conducted a study to determine whether the amount of time students spent studying affected their marks. The given scatter plot shows the results over one school year.

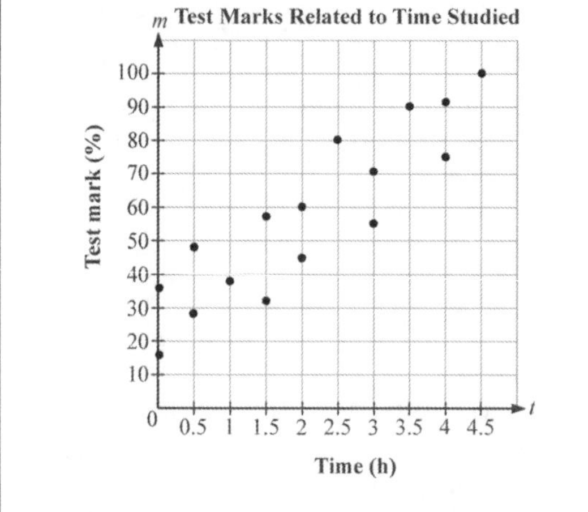

293. Which of the following statements is the **best** conclusion that can be drawn from the given graph?

A. No conclusion can be drawn from the data.

B. Test marks increased as the amount of studying increased.

C. Test marks decreased as the amount of studying increased.

D. Test marks are not affected by the amount of time spent studying.

Use the following information to answer the next question.

The given table shows how the value of a car changes over time.

Years after Purchase	Value of Car ($)
1	23,000
2	15,000
3	13,000
4	9,800
5	7,000
6	4,500

294. Plot the data on a scatter plot, and add a line of best fit.

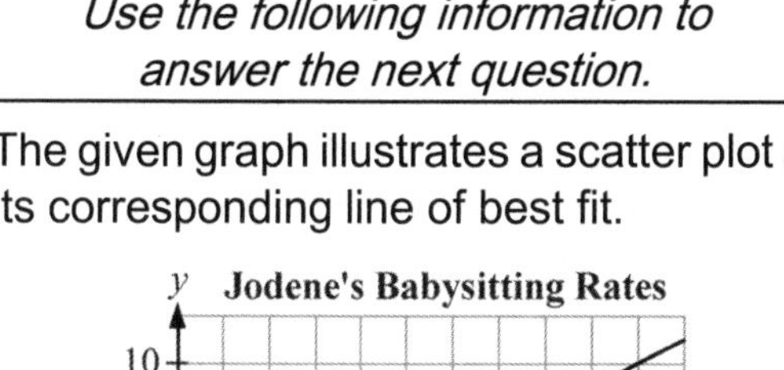

Use the following information to answer the next question.

The given graph illustrates a scatter plot and its corresponding line of best fit.

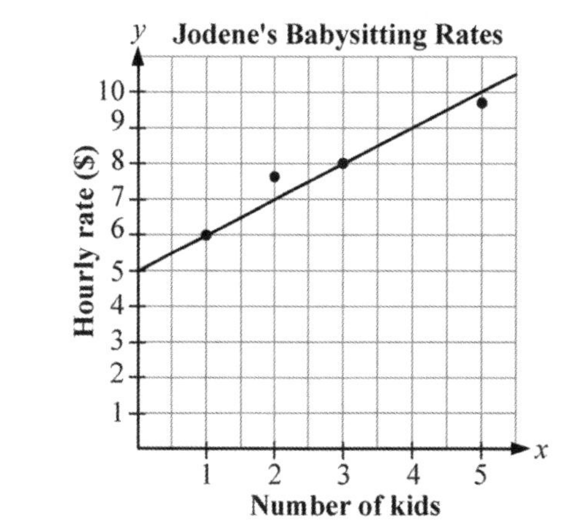

295. A possible equation for the line of best fit is

A. $y = x + 5$

B. $y = x + 6$

C. $y = \frac{3}{2}x + 5$

D. $y = \frac{3}{2}x + 6$

Use the following information to answer the next question.

The given graph shows the mathematics and chemistry marks of 10 randomly selected students and the line of best fit for the data.

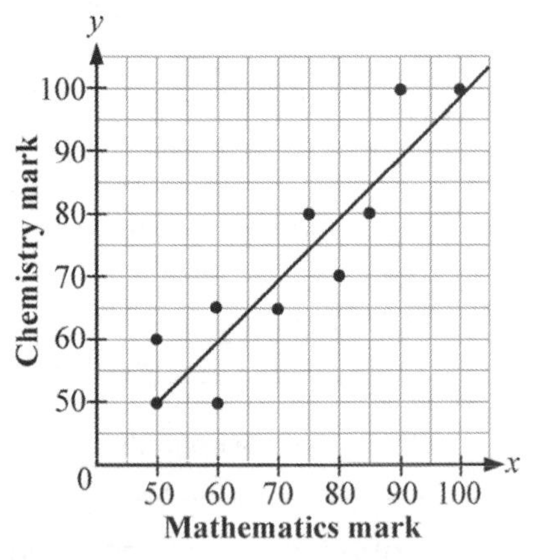

296. According to the graph, the correlation between the mathematics marks and the chemistry marks can **best** be described as

A. strong and negative

B. strong and positive

C. weak and negative

D. weak and positive

Use the following information to answer the next question.

The given table shows the attendance at a theme park over seven consecutive days.

Day	1	2	3	4	5	6	7
Attendance (thousands)	137	145	142	147	154	158	156

297. Use a scatter plot and line of best fit to determine which day should have an attendance of approximately 161,000 people.

Use the following information to answer the next question.

Jodene constructs a scatter plot showing her babysitting rates with respect to the number of kids. She then draws a possible line of best fit for the scatter plot.

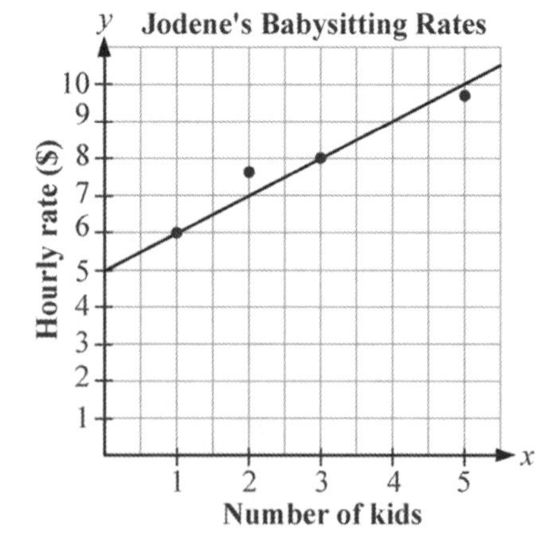

298. What is Jodene's approximate hourly rate when she babysits 4 kids?

A. \$8.50/h **B.** \$9.00/h

C. \$9.50/h **D.** \$10.00/h

EXERCISE #1—PATTERNS IN BIVARIATE DATA ANSWERS AND SOLUTIONS

292. 40	294. See solution	296. B	298. B
293. B	295. A	297. See solution	

292. 40

Look at all the ordered pairs of each point, and compare them to the given table.

The point with the coordinates (4, 40) is incorrect. The ordered pair should be (4, 20). Thus, the m-coordinate of the point plotted incorrectly is 40.

293. B

The scatter plot values are rising toward the right. This indicates that as the time spent studying increases, the resulting test marks also increase.

294.

Step 1
Plot the data on a scatter plot.

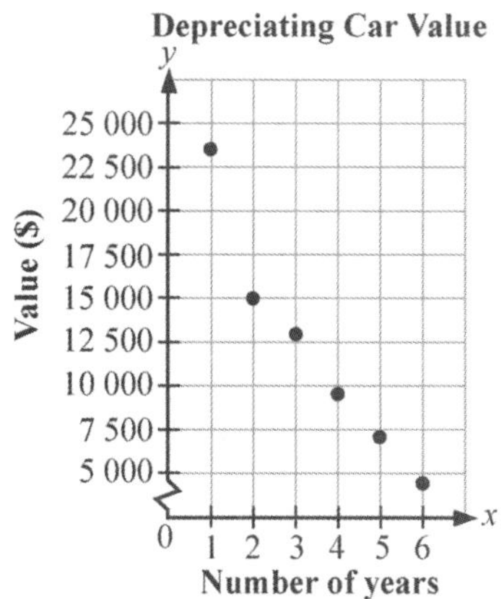

Step 2
Place the ruler through the middle of the pattern formed by the points, and add a line of best fit.

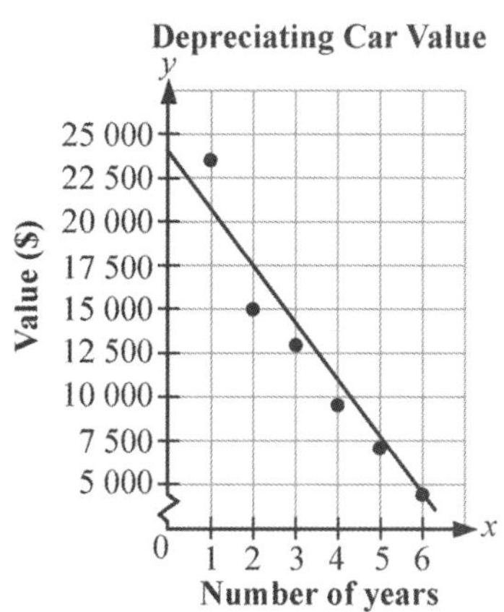

295. A

Step 1
Identify the initial value (the y-intercept) of the given line.
The line intersects the y-axis at the ordered pair (0, 5). Therefore, the initial value is 5.

Step 2
Identify two points on the line of best fit.
By observation, the line of best fit passes through the points (1, 6) and (3, 8).

Step 3
Determine the vertical separation $(y_2 - y_1)$ of the points (1, 6) and (3, 8).
The points (1, 6) and (3, 8) are vertically separated by 8 – 6 = 2 units.

Step 4
Determine the horizontal separation $(x_2 - x_1)$ of the points (1, 6) and (3, 8).
The points (1, 6) and (3, 8) are horizontally separated by 3 – 1 = 2 units.

Step 5
Write the equation of the line of best fit.
Apply the formula

$$y = \left(\frac{\text{vertical separation}}{\text{horizontal separation}}\right)x + \text{initial value}$$

Substitute 2 for the vertical separation, 2 for the horizontal separation, and 5 for the initial value.

$$y = \left(\frac{2}{2}\right)x + 5$$

$$y = x + 5$$

Therefore, the equation for the given line is $y = x + 5$.

296. B

Since the slope of the regression line is positive, the correlation is also positive. The points are grouped quite close to the line; therefore, the correlation is strong.

297.

Step 1

Draw the graph and plots the points.

The day of the measured period is the independent *x*-variable and the attendance is the dependent *y*-variable.

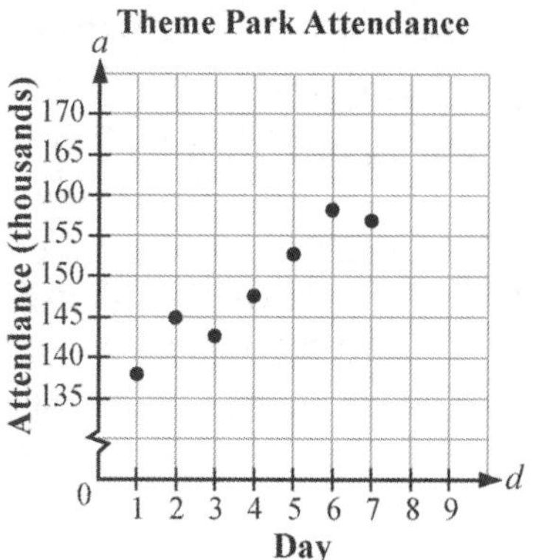

Step 2

Draw a line of best fit that extends beyond the scatter point data.

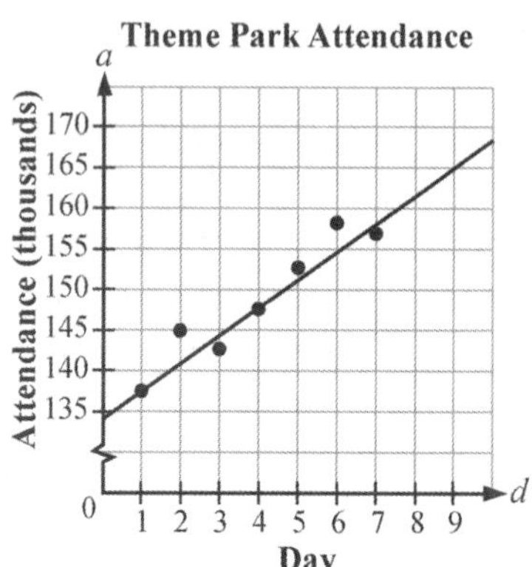

Step 3

Extrapolate the expected value.

Locate 161,000 on the attendance axis. Draw a straight horizontal line from that point on the attendance axis to the line of best fit. From this point on the line of best fit, draw a straight vertical line to the day axis.

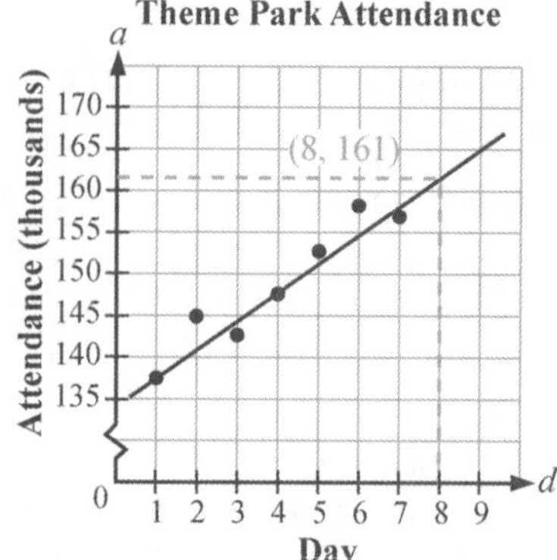

According to the line of best fit, the attendance on day 8 will be approximately 161,000.

298. B

Find the amount that Jodene charges by locating the number of kids on the *x*-axis and then finding the corresponding value of the *y*-axis by tracing a line straight upward until it intercepts the line.

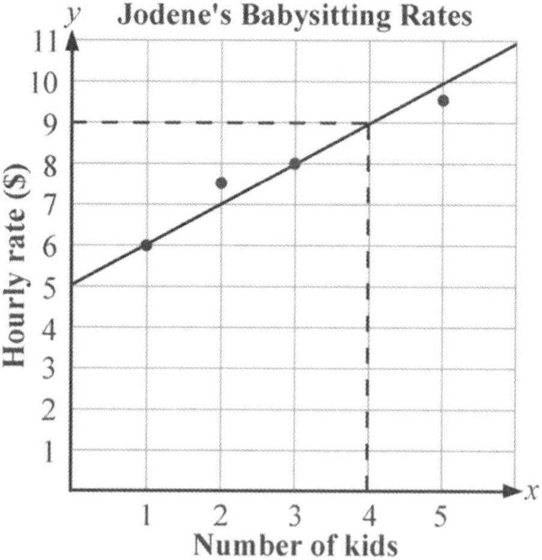

An hourly charge of $9.00 corresponds to 4 kids.

EXERCISE #2—PATTERNS IN BIVARIATE DATA

Use the following information to answer the next question.

Visitors to Niagra Falls

Year	Number of Visitors (× 10^6)
1960	45
1963	48
1970	80
1975	24
1980	50
1984	31
1986	27
2000	70
2002	71

299. Which of the following scatter plots illustrates the data in the given table?

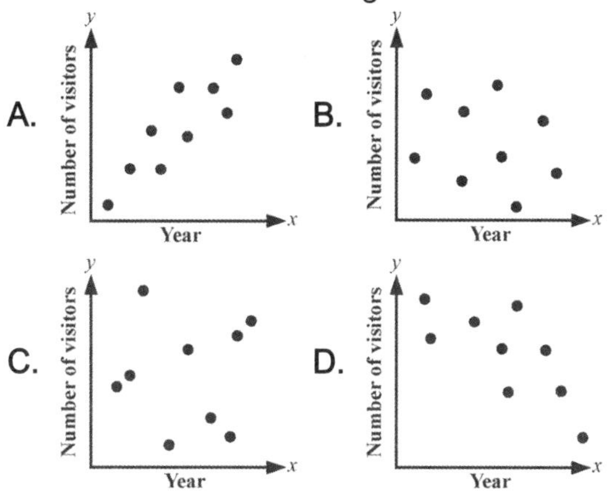

Use the following information to answer the next question.

The city of Guelph wants to determine how frequently a certain road is used. The given scatter plot shows the number of vehicles spotted at various times of the day. Each dot represents the number of vehicles recorded at a certain time.

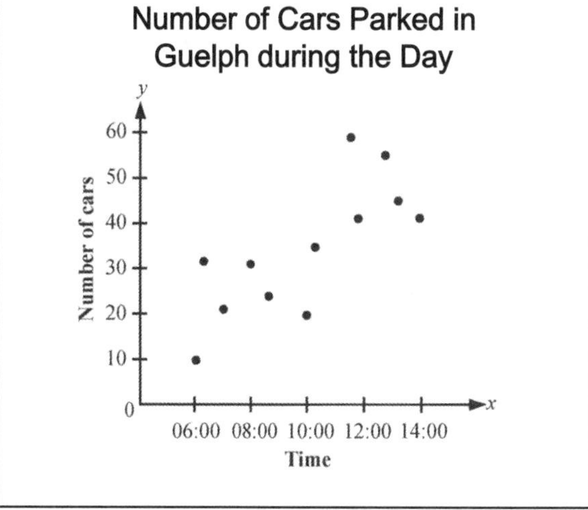

300. One conclusion that can be made from the given scatter plot is that the

A. number of vehicles using the road decreases as the day goes on

B. number of vehicles using the road increases as the day goes on

C. highest number of vehicles use the road at 13:00

D. highest number of vehicles use the road at 08:00

Use the following information to answer the next question.

A ball is dropped from a height of 2.7 m, and after each bounce (*n*), it rises to 80% of its previous height (*h*).

Number of bounces	Height (m)
0	2.7
1	2.7(0.80) = 2.16
2	2.16(0.80) = 1.728
3	1.728(0.80) = 1.3824
4	1.3824(0.80) = 1.10592
5	1.10592(0.80) = 0.884736

301. Plot the data from the given table on a scatter plot, and add a line of best fit.

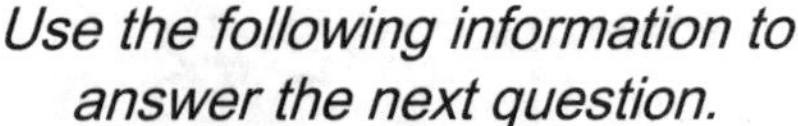

Use the following information to answer the next question.

The given scatter plot shows a line of best fit.

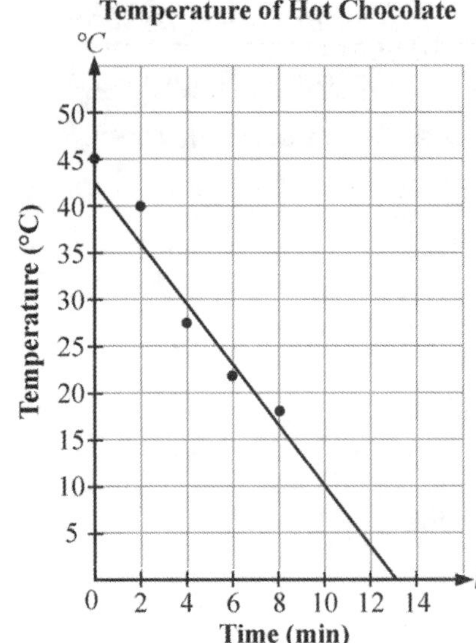

A close approximation of the equation of the line of best fit is $y = mx + 43$, where m is a real number.

302. A possible value of m is

A. $-\frac{9}{10}$

B. $-\frac{1}{2}$

C. $-\frac{9}{5}$

D. $-\frac{10}{3}$

Use the following information to answer the next question.

An auction house has kept track of the selling price of antique rotary phones over the last 10 years. The price and selling date of every antique phone was graphed, and a line of best fit has been drawn.

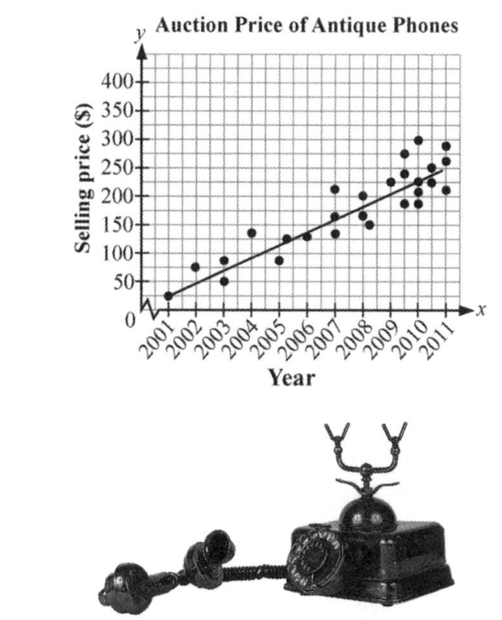

303. From the given graph, it can be concluded that over the past 10 years, the selling price of antique rotary telephones has increased by approximately

A. $50
B. $222
C. $50 per year
D. $222 per year

Use the following information to answer the next question.

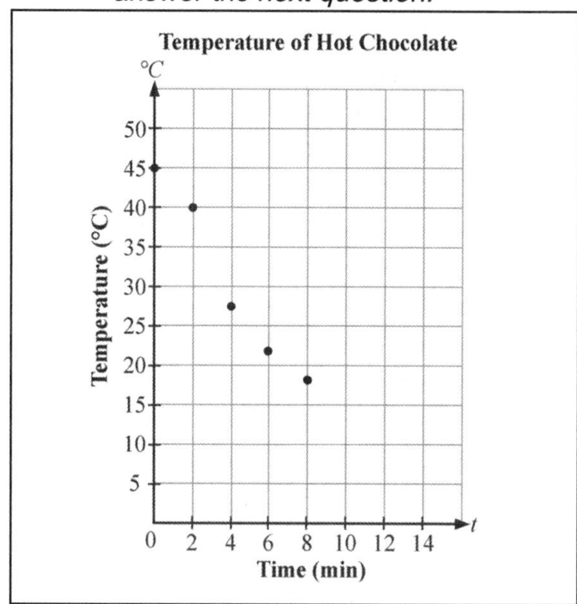

304. According to the graph, how long will it take for the temperature of the hot chocolate to reach 10°C?

A. 10 minutes
B. 12 minutes
C. 15 minutes
D. 20 minutes

Use the following information to answer the next question.

While outside on a winter day, a student measured the temperature of a cup of hot chocolate at two-minute intervals for 8 min. The student recorded the data in a scatter plot and drew a line of best fit as shown.

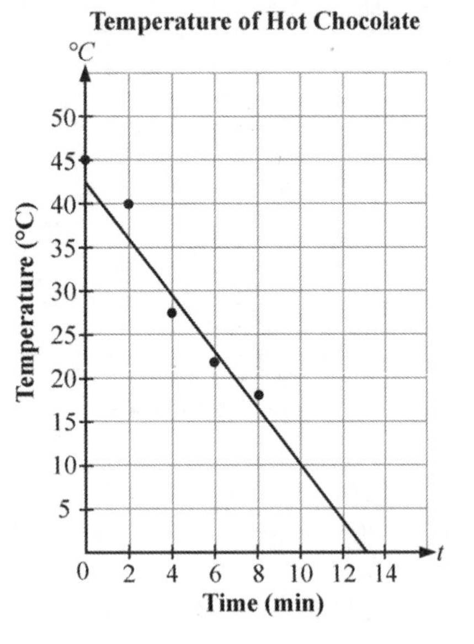

305. According to the line of best fit, how long will it take for the temperature of the hot chocolate to reach 10°C?

A. 10 min B. 12 min

C. 15 min D. 17 min

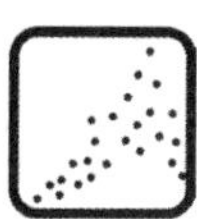

EXERCISE #2—PATTERNS IN BIVARIATE DATA ANSWERS AND SOLUTIONS

299. C	301. See solution	303. B	305. A
300. B	302. D	304. A	

299. C

Step 1
Write the ordered pairs to be plotted.

Visitors to Niagra Falls

Year	Number of Visitors $(\times 10^6)$	Frequency
1960	45	(1,960, 45)
1963	48	(1,963, 48)
1970	80	(1,970, 80)
1975	24	(1,975, 24)
1980	50	(1,980, 50)
1984	31	(1,984, 31)
1986	27	(1,986, 27)
2000	70	(2,000, 70)
2002	71	(2,002, 71)

Step 2
Choose suitable increments to mark both axes for the data.

The independent variable, year, will be on the horizontal x-axis.

The dependent variable, number of visitors, will be on the vertical y-axis.

Step 3
Draw and label the axes, plot the points, and give the scatter plot a title. This is the scatter plot that correctly illustrates the given data.

Visitors to Niagra Falls

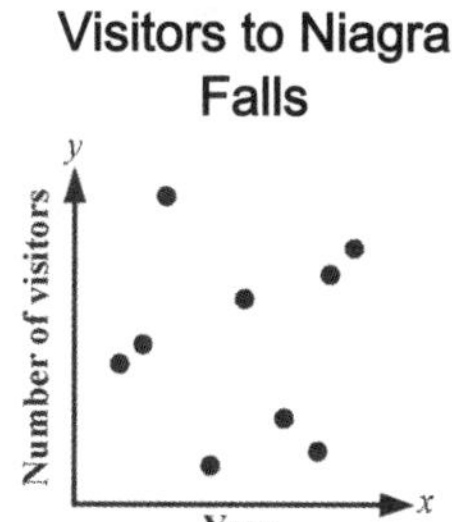

300. B

Step 1
Identify the correlation in the graph.

The data points show a positive correlation.

Step 2
Interpret the shape made by the points.

If the points are rising to the right, it means that as the x-values increase, the y-values increase as well. This indicates that as the day goes on, the number of vehicles using the road increases.

301.

Step 1
Plot the data on a scatter plot.

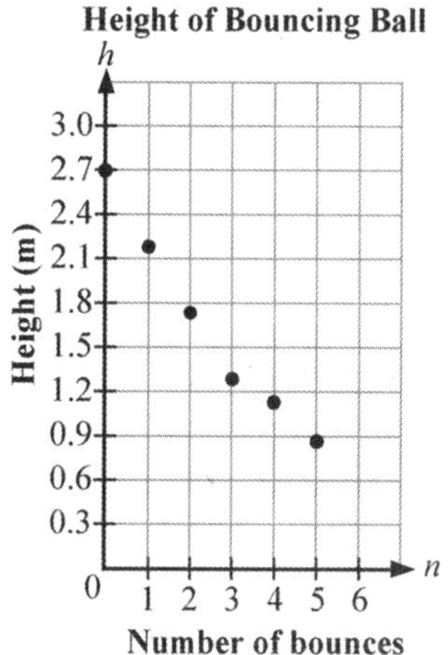

Step 2
Draw a line of best fit.

Place the ruler through the middle of the pattern formed by the points and draw a line.

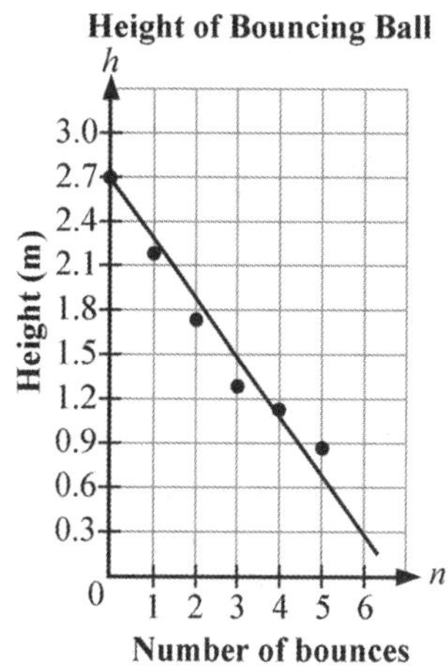

302. D

Step 1
Identify the initial value (the y-intercept) of the given line.
The line intersects the y-axis at approximately the ordered pair (0, 43). Therefore, the initial value is 43.

Step 2
Identify two points on the line of best fit.
The line of best fit passes approximately through the points (4, 30) and (10, 10).

Step 3
Determine the vertical separation $(y_2 - y_1)$ of the points (4, 30) and (10, 10).
The points (4, 30) and (10, 10) are vertically separated by 10 – 30 = –20 units.

Step 4
Determine the horizontal separation $(x_2 - x_1)$ of the points (4, 30) and (10, 10).
The points (4, 30) and (10, 10) are horizontally separated by 10 – 4 = 6 units.

Step 5
Write the equation of the line of best fit.
Apply the formula.

$$y = \left(\frac{\text{vertical separation}}{\text{horizontal separation}}\right)x + \text{initial value}$$

Substitute –20 for the vertical separation, 6 for the horizontal separation, and 43 for the initial value.

$$y = \left(\frac{-20}{6}\right)x + 43$$

$$y = -\frac{10}{3}x + 43$$

Step 6
Identify the value of m.

When the equation $y = -\frac{10}{3}x + 43$ is compared to the equation $y = mx + 43$, it can be seen that the value of m is $-\frac{10}{3}$.

303. B

Step 1
Determine the slope of the line. Two points on the line are needed to determine the slope.
The points (2,001, 25) and (2,010, 225) appear to overlap the line.

$$m = \frac{y_2 - y_1}{x_2 - x_1}$$

$$m = \frac{225 - 25}{2{,}010 - 2{,}001}$$

$$m = \frac{200}{9}$$

$$m \approx 22.222$$

Step 2
Use the slope to interpret the line.
The slope, $m \approx 22.222$, represents an average increase of \$22.22 per year. Over a 10-year period, this would result in a \$222.22, or approximately \$222, increase.

304. A

Step 1
Draw a line of best fit that extends far enough beyond the data.
The question is asking how long it will take for the temperature to reach 10°C. The line of best fit must go beyond 8 minutes.

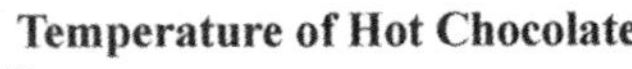

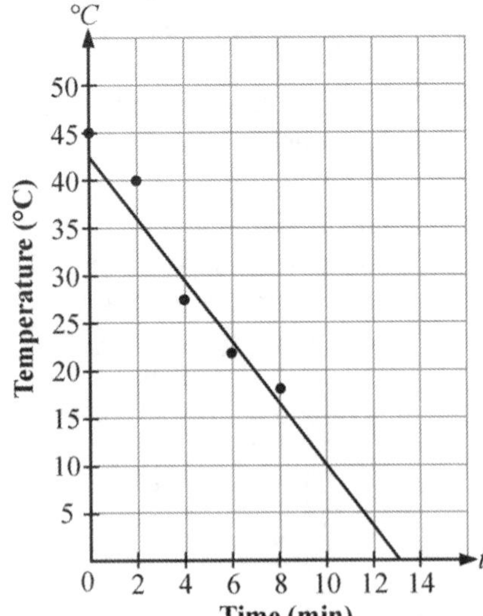

Step 2
Extrapolate the value.
Locate 10°C on the temperature axis. Draw a straight horizontal line until the line of best fit is reached. At this point, draw a straight vertical line to intersect the time axis.

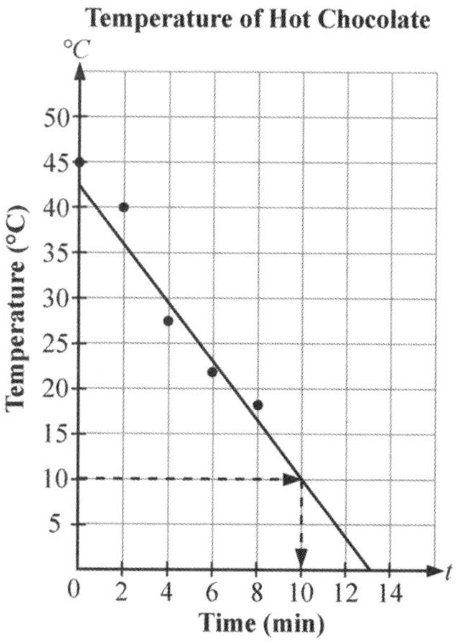

According to the line of best fit, it will take approximately 10 minutes for the temperature of the hot chocolate to become 10°C.

305. A

Locate 10°C on the temperature axis. Draw a straight horizontal line until the line of best fit is reached. At this point, draw a straight vertical line to intersect the time axis.

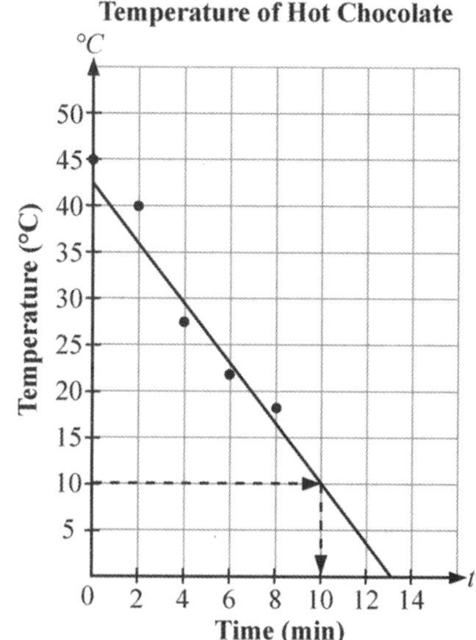

According to the line of best fit, it will take approximately 10 min for the temperature of the hot chocolate to reach 10°C.

NOTES

Two Variable Data

TWO VARIABLE DATA

Table of Correlations

Standard		Concepts	Exercise #1	Exercise #2
Unit3.3	Summarize, represent, and interpret data on two categorical and quantitative variables.			
S-ID.5	*Summarize categorical data for two categories in two-way frequency tables. Interpret relative frequencies in the context of the data (including joint, marginal, and conditional relative frequencies). Recognize possible associations and trends in the data.*	Determining the Frequency of Data	306	316
		Organizing Primary Data Using a Frequency Table	307	317
		Constructing a Cumulative Frequency Histogram	308	318
		Interpreting a Cumulative Frequency Distribution Table	309	319
		Selecting Appropriate Graphs to Display Data: Line Graphs, Bar Graphs, and Circle Graphs	310	320
S-ID.6ai	*Represent data on two quantitative variables on a scatter plot, and describe how the variables are related. Fit a function to the data; use functions fitted to data to solve problems in the context of the data. Use given functions or choose a function suggested by the context. Emphasize linear and exponential models.*	Deciding on an Appropriate Regression Based on a Scatter Plot	311	321
		Calculating the Correlation Coefficient for Linear Regression	312	322
		Interpreting the Correlation Coefficient for Linear Regression	313	323
		Solving Problems Using Exponential Regression	314	324
S-ID.6b	*Represent data on two quantitative variables on a scatter plot, and describe how the variables are related. Informally assess the fit of a function by plotting and analyzing residuals.*	Displaying Data in a Scatter Plot	3	12
		Drawing a Line of Best Fit	294	301
		Interpreting a Line of Best Fit	296	303
S-ID.6c	*Represent data on two quantitative variables on a scatter plot, and describe how the variables are related. Fit a linear function for a scatter plot that suggests a linear association.*	Calculating the Correlation Coefficient for Linear Regression	312	322
		Determining the Equation of the Least Squares Regression Line	315	325

S-ID.5 Summarize categorical data for two categories in two-way frequency tables. Interpret relative frequencies in the context of the data (including joint, marginal, and conditional relative frequencies). Recognize possible associations and trends in the data.

Determining the Frequency of Data

Graphs and charts can give a lot of information. In order to understand that information, you need to know how to interpret it. One way you can do that is by looking at the distribution of the data, specifically at the frequency.

The frequency of the data is the number of times a particular value appears in the data. For example, if four students receive a mark of 80% on a math quiz, then the mark of 80% is said to have a frequency of 4.

Example

11, 6, 3, 11, 7, 13, 6, 6, 9

Which of the given numbers occurs the most often and what is the frequency of this number?

Solution

Order the numbers from least to greatest value.
3, 6, 6, 6, 7, 9, 11, 11, 13

By looking at the data in numerical order, you can see that 6 is the number that occurs most often. It occurs three times, while the other numbers occur only once or twice.

The number that occurs the most often is 6 and its frequency is 3.

If the set of data contains a lot of values, then it is best to organize data into a frequency table.
A frequency table is constructed by arranging the data in ascending order with their corresponding frequencies totaled beside them.

To construct a frequency table, use the following steps:

1. Construct a table with three columns. In the first column, write all the data values in ascending order of magnitude.
2. Complete the second column by going through the list of data values and placing one tally mark beside that value of data. When the fifth tally is reached, draw a horizontal line through the first four tally marks. When the tallies are in groups of 5, it makes it easier to count them.
   Continue this process until all data values in the list are tallied.
3. Count the number of tally marks for each data value, and write it in the third column.

Example

The marks awarded for a math assignment for a Grade 9 class of 20 students were as follows:
6, 7, 5, 7, 7, 8, 7, 6, 9, 7, 4, 10, 6, 8, 8, 9, 5, 6, 4, 8

Present this information in a frequency table.

Solution

Step 1

Construct a table with three columns. In the first column, arrange the marks in ascending order.

Mark	Tally	Frequency
4		
5		
6		
7		
8		
9		
10		

Step 2
Go through the list of marks, and place a tally beside each mark as it comes up in the list. Continue this process until all marks in the list are tallied.

Mark	Tally	Frequency
4	𝍷𝍷	
5	𝍷𝍷	
6	𝍷𝍷𝍷𝍷	
7	𝍸	
8	𝍷𝍷𝍷𝍷	
9	𝍷𝍷	
10	𝍷	

Step 3
Count the number of tally marks for each mark, and write it in the third column.
The finished frequency table will look like this:

Mark	Tally	Frequency
4	𝍷𝍷	2
5	𝍷𝍷	2
6	𝍷𝍷𝍷𝍷	4
7	𝍸	5
8	𝍷𝍷𝍷𝍷	4
9	𝍷𝍷	2
10	𝍷	1

The information in the table shows that more students had a mark of 7 than any other mark.

Organizing Primary Data Using a Frequency Table

Information collected from a survey is often recorded on a survey sheet. Data is recorded as it is collected from people answering the survey by the use of tally marks, which are then added to give a frequency or total for each possible response. A sample survey sheet for the favorite type of music of students in a class is illustrated below.

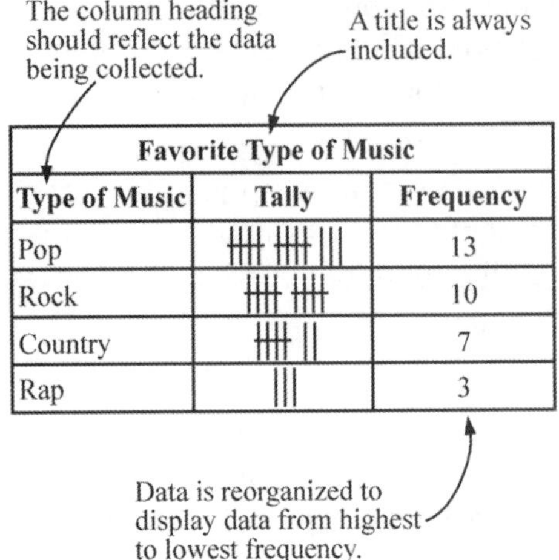

Favorite Type of Music		
Type of Music	**Tally**	**Frequency**
Pop	𝍸 𝍸 𝍷𝍷𝍷	13
Rock	𝍸 𝍸	10
Country	𝍸 𝍷𝍷	7
Rap	𝍷𝍷𝍷	3

The column heading should reflect the data being collected.
A title is always included.
Data is reorganized to display data from highest to lowest frequency.

The total number of people surveyed can be calculated by finding the sum of the frequency column. In this survey, there were 33 people surveyed.

Example

Vincent asked some students what their favorite subject is at school. Vincent used SC for science, M for mathematics, LA for language arts, and SS for social studies. He recorded the following results:
LA, M, SC, M, M, LA, M, SC, SC, SS, SS, SS, M, SC

Use the information provided to construct and complete a survey sheet to determine the subject that was most frequently chosen by the surveyed students.

Solution

Favorite Subject

Subject	Tally	Frequency
Mathematics	𝍸	5
Science	||||	4
Social studies	|||	3
Language arts	||	2

Mathematics was most frequently selected as the favorite subject of the students surveyed.

Example

Vincent asked some students what their favorite subject is at school. Vincent used SC for science, M for mathematics, LA for language arts, and SS for social studies. He recorded the following results:
LA, M, SC, M, M, LA, M, SC, SC, SS, SS, SS, M, SC

Use the information provided to construct and complete a survey sheet to determine the number of students that were surveyed.

Solution

Favorite Subject

Subject	Tally	Frequency
Mathematics	𝍸	5
Science	||||	4
Social studies	|||	3
Language arts	||	2

To find the number of students surveyed, find the sum of the frequency column.
$5 + 4 + 3 + 2 = 14$

Vincent surveyed 14 students.

Constructing a Cumulative Frequency Histogram

Histograms are used to represent continuous data. The horizontal axis of a histogram represents the intervals, and the vertical axis represents the frequency of the data. In a cumulative frequency histogram, each bar represents the sum of the given interval and all the intervals before it. The purpose of this is to show how much of a population is accounted for by the end of each interval. Cumulative frequency histograms also provide information about how much of the population is not accounted for.

Constructing a cumulative frequency histogram is similar to constructing a regular histogram. First, create a frequency table, and then add an additional column for cumulative frequency. The cumulative frequency will be the sum of each given frequency and the sum of all frequencies before it.

The histogram will be made with the cumulative frequency instead of the frequency for that interval. Usually, cumulative frequency histograms increase from left to right.

Example

The finishing times of 20 cross-country runners are given to the nearest minute.
30, 32, 33, 36, 37, 37, 38, 39, 40, 40, 40, 42, 43, 44, 44, 45, 48, 50, 54, 58

Construct a cumulative frequency histogram that represents the given data.

Solution

Step 1
Construct a frequency table with a column that shows the cumulative frequency.

Interval (Time in Minutes)	Frequency	Cumulative Frequency
30 – 34	3	3
35 – 39	5	8
40 – 44	7	15
45 – 49	2	17
50 – 54	2	19
55 – 59	1	20

Step 2
Create a histogram using the cumulative frequency values and the intervals they represent.

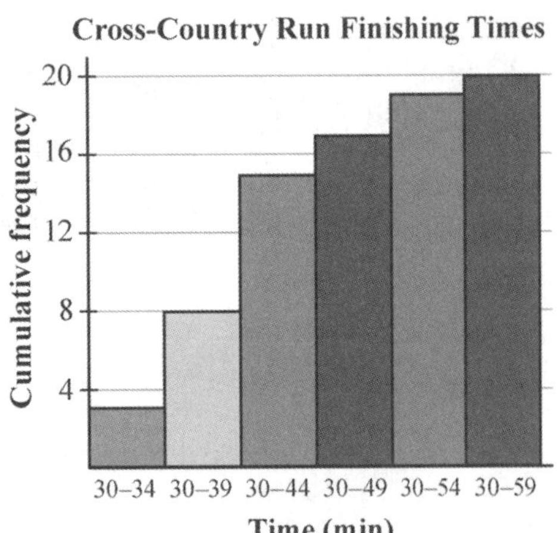

The following graph shows another way to represent the intervals on the horizontal axis.

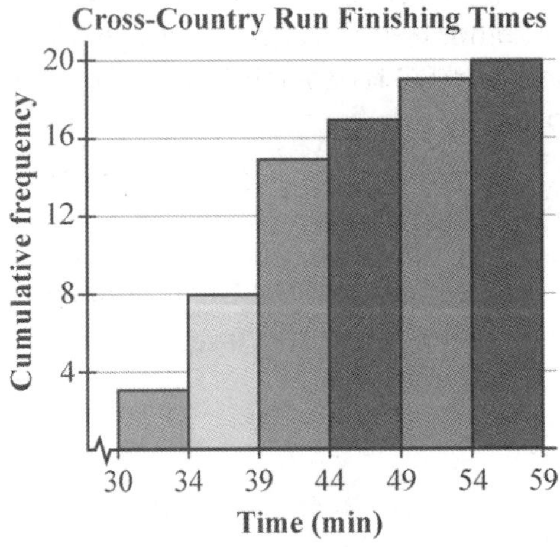

Interpreting a Cumulative Frequency Distribution Table

Cumulative frequency distribution tables are similar to normal frequency tables, except that each value represents the sum of the current interval as well as all the intervals before it.
The purpose for this type of table is to show how much of a population lies above or below a certain value.

Example

An intercity bus leaves the central station with 37 passengers. It will make six stops at various towns.

This cumulative frequency distribution table shows the number of passengers that get off at each station. It also keeps a running tally of the total number of passengers that have been dropped off.

Bus Station	Passengers Dropped Off	Cumulative Passengers Dropped Off
Springfield	4	4
Bloomington	5	4 + 5 = 9
Riverton	13	13 + 9 = 22
Rochester	7	22 + 7 = 29
Dawson	6	29 + 6 = 35
Grandview	2	35 + 2 = 37

Cumulative frequency distribution tables can also be created by increasing the size of the intervals to include the intervals before it. This can be done to illustrate the frequency of a population being less than or more than a value.

Example

A cumulative frequency table of class marks from a test is given.

Test Mark	Frequency
0–10	0
0–20	0
0–30	2
0–40	4
0–50	9
0–60	15
0–70	21
0–80	27
0–90	31
0–100	33

How many students received a mark of 50 or less?

Solution

The frequency table states that marks from 0 to 50 had a frequency of 9. Therefore, 9 students received a mark of 50 or less.

How many students received a mark between 71 and 80?

Solution

The frequency table states that 21 students received a mark of 70 or less and 27 students received a mark of 80 or less. The difference between these numbers will give the number of students who received a mark between 71 and 80.

$27 - 21 = 6$

Six students received a mark between 71 and 80.

Selecting Appropriate Graphs to Display Data: Line Graphs, Bar Graphs, and Circle Graphs

Data can be visually displayed by using a variety of graphs. Knowing what each kind of graph is used for can help you decide which graph to use to display data.

Bar Graphs

Bar graphs are best for displaying **categorical data**. Categorical data are organized according to categories, such as favorite sports or kinds of animals at the zoo.

The names of the categories are usually at the bottom of the graph, and the heights of the bars show how many items fall into each category.
In double bar graphs, each category has two bars and there is a legend that explains what each bar represents.

Example

In the given double bar graph, the different kinds of sports are the categories. The bars show how many boys and girls prefer each sport.

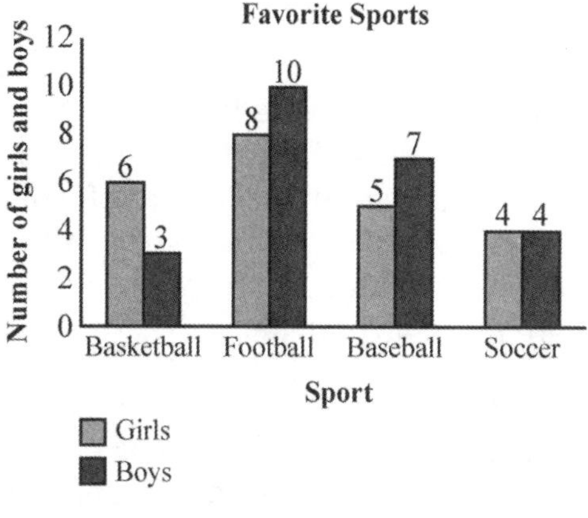

Circle Graphs

Circle graphs are also used to display categorical data. The most important difference between circle graphs and bar graphs is that bar graphs make it easy to compare the numbers in each category to one another but circle graphs make it easy to compare the number in each category to the whole.

In a circle graph, the numbers are usually given as percentages of the whole.

Example

In the given circle graph, the categories are still sports. Instead of telling you the exact number of students who like each sport, a circle graph tells you what percentage of students like each sport.

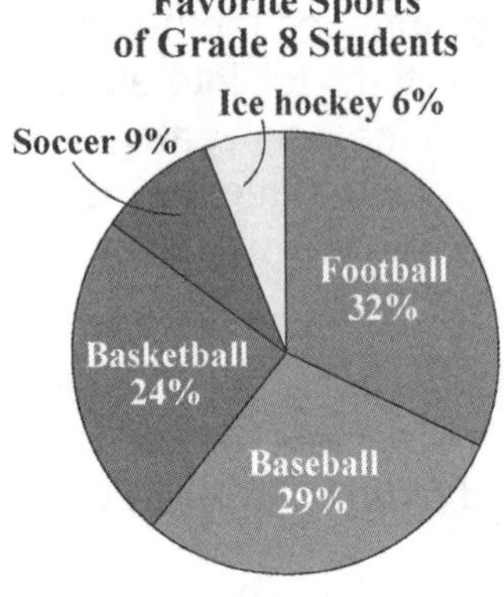

Another important difference is that bar graphs let you compare two sets of data. In the previous bar graph, you can compare the number of girls and the number of boys who like each sport. You would need to put two different circle graphs side by side to compare two sets of data.

Line Graphs

Line graphs are used to show changes over time. They often show **continuous data**. Continuous data can include whole numbers and decimals or fractions. For example, if a graph shows that the temperature rose from 15°C to 16°C, the temperature actually passed through all the temperatures between those points. A line graph shows this transition.

Continuous data is different from **discrete data**, which is always given as whole numbers. The number of pets that you own is an example of discrete data because you can own only a whole number of pets. Line graphs are usually not used to show discrete data.

Time is usually shown along the bottom of a line graph, and the number being measured is on the side. A double line graph shows two sets of data; a legend shows what each line represents.

Example

The given double line graph shows the average temperatures measured throughout the year in Washington, D.C., and Auckland, New Zealand.

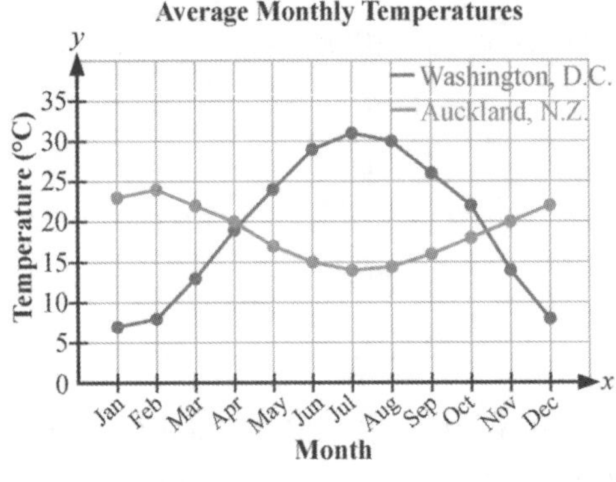

S-ID.6ai Represent data on two quantitative variables on a scatter plot, and describe how the variables are related. Fit a function to the data; use functions fitted to data to solve problems in the context of the data. Use given functions or choose a function suggested by the context. Emphasize linear and exponential models.

Deciding on an Appropriate Regression Based on a Scatter Plot

The following regressions can be done on a set of data consisting of ordered pairs:

- Linear
- Power
- Exponential
- Logarithmic

A regression may be a good fit for some sets of data and a bad fit for other sets of data. A good fit is preferred because it means the curve (or line) more accurately models the data.

Being able to predict which regression to use based on a scatter plot can save time. To predict which regression to use, match the characteristics of the data to characteristics of the curves (or line) produced by each type of regression.

Linear Regression

Linear regressions produce straight lines which are described by the equation $y = ax + b$. The slope of a line is usually denoted by m, but when dealing with regressions, a is used instead.

The graph shows an example of a linear regression.

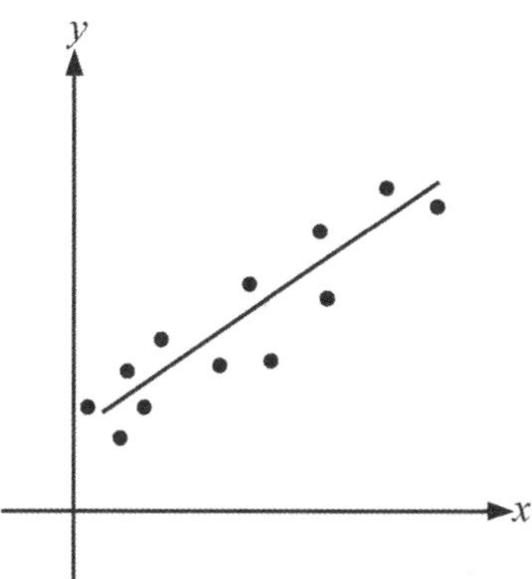

Use the following characteristics of a graph to identify data best modeled by a linear regression:

- The points tend to follow a straight line.
- If the line is extended there will be a y-intercept (unless the line is vertical).
- There will also be an x-intercept (unless the line is horizontal).

Power Regression

Power regressions produce curves which are described by the function $y = ax^b$. The graphs show two examples of power regressions.

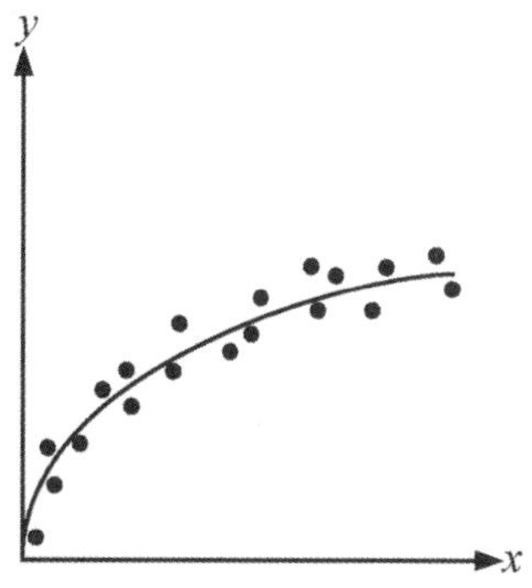

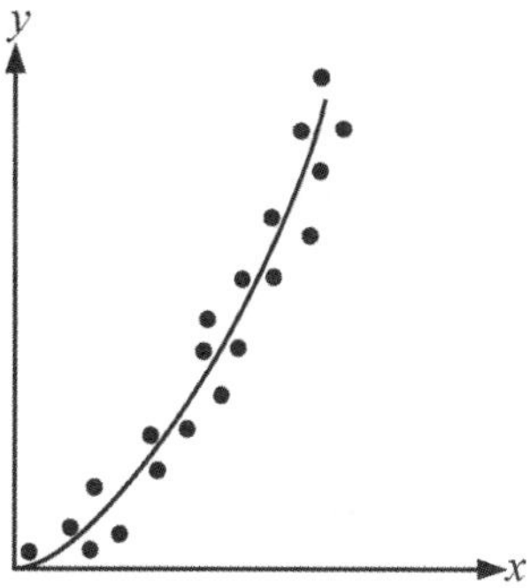

Data which follows a power regression can be distributed in a variety of ways. Use the following characteristics of a graph to identify data best modeled by a power regression:

- The points start close to the origin.
- The points appear to curve in one of the following ways:
  - They start out vertical and curve to the right.
  - They start out horizontal and curve up.

Since the data is often in the first quadrant, the given identifying characteristics assume that $x > 0$ and $y > 0$.

Exponential Regression

Exponential regressions produce curves which are described by the function $y = ab^x$. The graphs show two examples of exponential regressions.

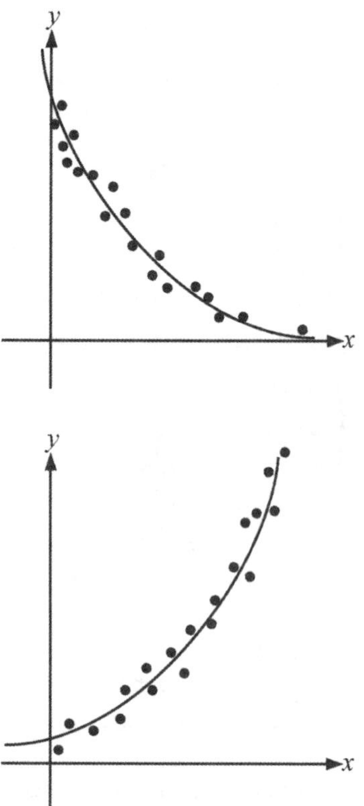

Use the following characteristics of a graph to identify data best modeled by an exponential regression:

- The points cross the y-axis.
- The points **never** cross the x-axis; therefore, there is a horizontal asymptote at $y = 0$.
- As x increases, the points can curve in one of the following ways:
  - They can flatten out and approach the x-axis but not cross it.
  - They can curve up (or down) toward positive (or negative) infinity.

Logarithmic Regression

Logarithmic regressions produce curves which are described by the function $a + b\ln x$, $x > 0$.
The graphs show some examples of logarithmic regressions.

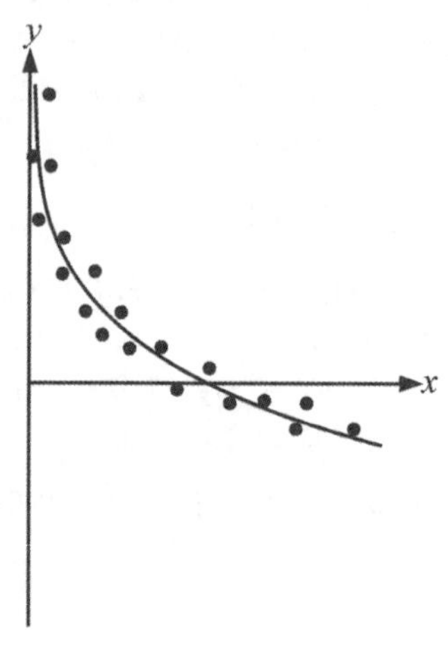

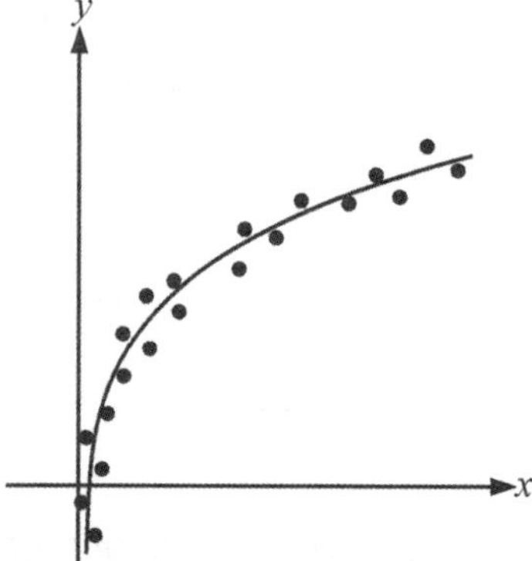

Use the following characteristics of a graph to identify data best modeled by a logarithmic regression:

- The x-values are always positive.
- The points cross the x-axis.
- The points curve to the right but never completely flatten out; therefore, there is no horizontal asymptote.

Choosing the Proper Regression

Use the following steps to choose the proper regression for a given scatter plot:

1. Sketch the curve (or line) of best fit on top of the scatter plot with roughly the same number of points on either side. The curve (or line) should be as close as possible to the points. If it is a curve, it should be smooth and curve in a single direction.
2. Match the sketched curve to one of the four types of regressions based on the identifying characteristics.

Example

Paul would like to do a regression on some data. He has graphed the points as a scatter plot.

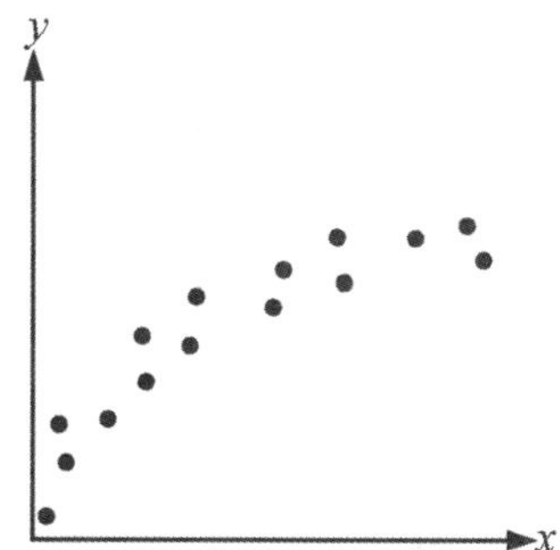

What regression should Paul use with his data?

Solution

Step 1

Sketch the line of best fit on top of the scatter plot.

The line of best fit in this case is a curve that starts close to the origin and curves up and then to the right.

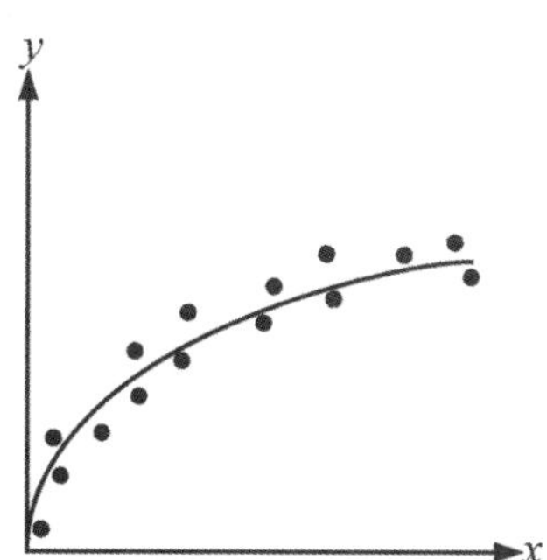

Step 2

Match the sketched curve to the correct regression.

The curve has the following properties:

- It starts at or close to the origin.
- It curves up and over to the right.

The curve is an example of a power function. Therefore, Paul should do a power regression.

Calculating the Correlation Coefficient for Linear Regression

The correlation coefficient is a measure of how close a set of data is to the line of best fit. Many graphing calculators can calculate the correlation coefficient, *r*. This value indicates how closely the data resembles a linear relation.

The formula for the correlation coefficient, *r*, is

$$r = \frac{1}{n-1}\sum_{i=1}^{n}\left(\frac{X_i - \overline{X}}{s_X}\right)\left(\frac{Y_i - \overline{Y}}{s_Y}\right).$$

The closer the *r*-value is to +1 or −1, the more accurate the line of best fit and the closer the data points are to the line.

Use the following steps to find the correlation coefficient with a TI-83 or similar calculator:

1. Press STAT and select 1:Edit… to access the list editor. Enter the values for the independent variable into list L_1 and the values for the dependent variable into list L_2.
2. Turn on diagnostics so that the correlation coefficient, *r*, will show up in the results of the regression. Press 2nd 0 to access the CATALOG menu, and scroll down to features beginning with the letter D by pressing x^{-1}. Select DiagnosticOn and press ENTER two times.
3. Calculate the linear regression, which also shows the correlation coefficient. Press STAT and the right arrow once to access the CALC menu. Select 4:LinReg($ax + b$) and press 2nd 1 , 2nd 2 to specify lists L_1 and L_2. Run the regression by pressing ENTER.

Example

A sporting goods store examined the amount spent on advertising compared with the amount earned in profit from sales over a nine-month period.

Month	Advertising ($)	Profit ($)
March	3,000	4,640
April	1,500	1,740
May	1,700	3,250
June	700	880
July	3,200	5,570
August	900	2,090
September	2,300	3,360
October	2,600	4,990
November	3,600	5,680

What is the correlation coefficient, *r*?

Solution

Step 1
Enter the values for the amount spent on advertising and the profit from sales into lists L_1 and L_2.
Start by clearing any lists already present.
Press 2nd +, select 4:ClrAllLists, and press ENTER.

Press STAT and select 1:Edit…. Enter the values for the amount spent on advertising and the profit from sales into lists L_1 and L_2, respectively.

Step 2
Turn on diagnostics so that the correlation coefficient, *r*, will show up in the results of the regression.

Press 2nd 0 to access the CATALOG menu. Scroll down to features beginning with the letter D by pressing x^{-1}, select DiagnosticOn, and press ENTER twice.

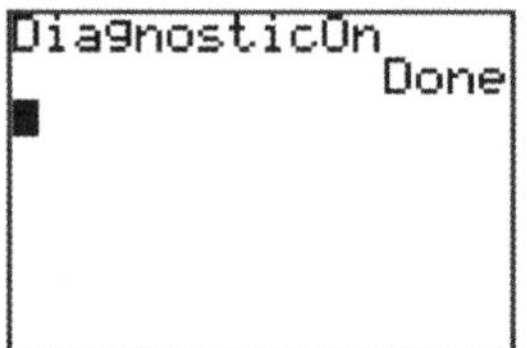

Step 3
Calculate the linear regression, which also shows the correlation coefficient, *r*.

Press STAT and the right arrow once to access the CALC menu. Select 4:LinReg ($ax + b$) and press 2nd 1 , 2nd 2 to specify lists L_1 and L_2.
Run the linear regression by pressing ENTER.

```
LinReg
 y=ax+b
 a=1.630252765
 b=45.56345445
 r²=.9142618582
 r=.9561704128
```

Since $r = 0.95617$ is reasonably close to 1, this equation represents a good line of best fit.

Interpreting the Correlation Coefficient for Linear Regression

The **correlation coefficient** for linear regression is a measure of how close a set of data is to a line. Many graphing calculators can calculate the correlation coefficient automatically.
The correlation coefficient is one way to show how closely the points are correlated, or mutually related. Sometimes, the data is very close to a line; other times, it is not.

The variable *r* represents the correlation coefficient. The closer the *r*-value is to +1 or –1, the more accurate the line of best fit and the closer the data points are to the line.

If the correlation coefficient is close to 1, the points are close to the line and the slope is positive. The data is said to have a strong positive correlation.

If the correlation coefficient is close to –1, the points are close to the line and the slope is negative. The data is said to have a strong negative correlation.

If the correlation coefficient is close to 0 and the points are distant from the line, the data is said to have a weak correlation.

Example
The given graph shows a set of data with a positive slope.

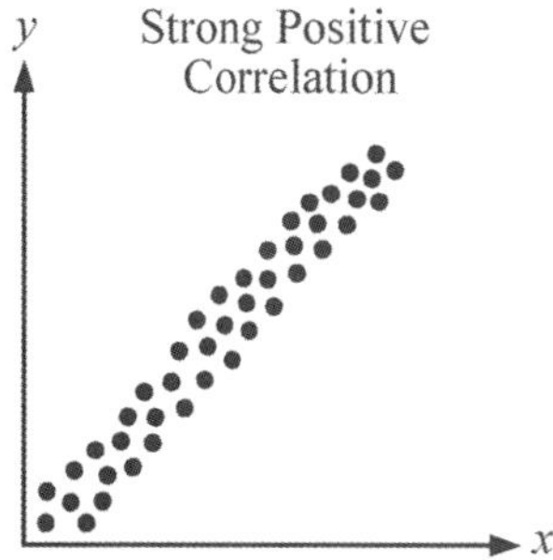

The line of best fit, or slope, is drawn in.

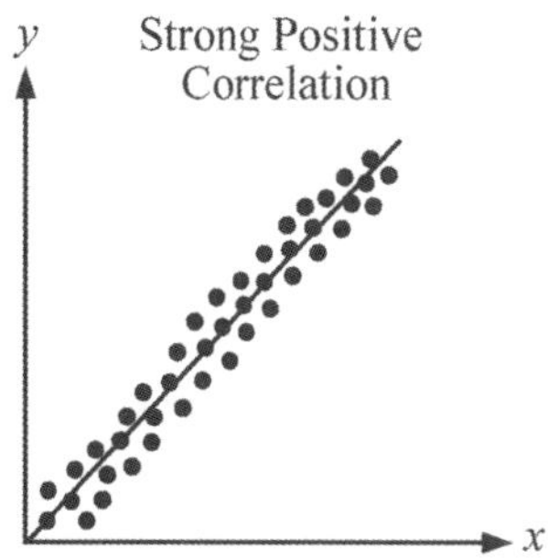

The points are quite close to the line and the slope is positive, which indicates a strong positive correlation. As such, the value of *r* would be close to 1.

Example
The given graph shows a set of data with a negative slope.

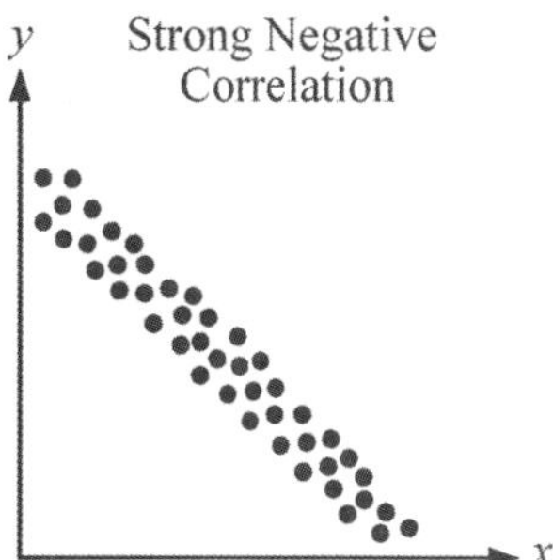

The line of best fit, or slope, is drawn in.

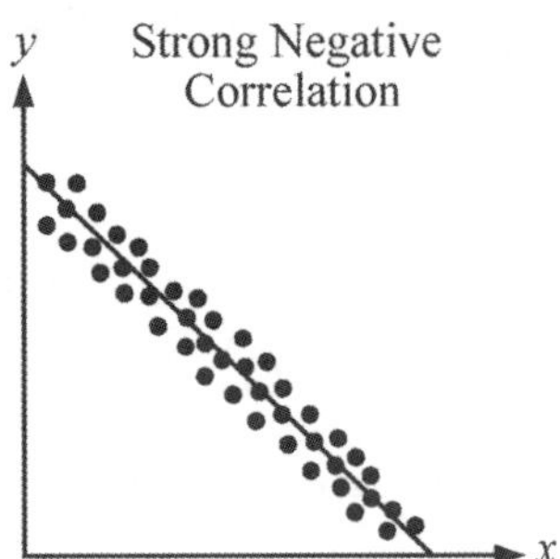

The points are quite close to the line and the slope is negative, which indicates a strong negative correlation. As such, the value of *r* would be close to –1.

Example

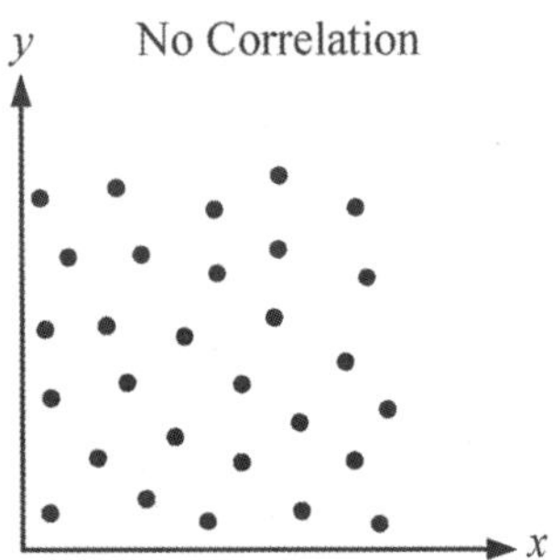

This particular set of data seems to have no relationship, which is why a line cannot be drawn. The data is neither increasing nor decreasing; therefore, there is no correlation. As such, the value of *r* would be near 0.

Solving Problems Using Exponential Regression

When ordered pairs or tables of values are used to model real-life examples of exponential data, exponential regression is often performed. Exponential regression is a technique for finding the best-fitting exponential graph that passes through a set of ordered pairs.

An exponential regression takes data and produces an equation of the form $y = ab^x$. The *a* variable represents either the *y*-intercept or the initial value. The *b* variable is always positive, that is $b > 0$. The *b* variable determines the rate of growth or decay in the following way:

- If $b > 1$, the function is growing. The larger *b* is, the faster it is growing.
- If $0 < b < 1$, the function is decaying. The closer *b* is to 0, the faster it is decaying.

The following steps can be used to perform an exponential regression with a TI-83 or similar calculator:

1. Determine which variable is the independent variable and which is the dependent variable.
2. Press STAT, and select 1:Edit… to access the list editor. Enter the values for the independent variable into list L_1 and the values for the dependent variable into list L_2.
3. Calculate the exponential regression. Press STAT and the right arrow once to access the CALC menu. Select 0:ExpReg, and specify lists L_1 and L_2 by pressing 2nd 1 , 2nd 2.
4. Run the regression by pressing ENTER.

Example

Terrence did an experiment in which he studied the growth rate of bacteria. He examined a bacterial culture through a microscope every ten minutes. He counted the number of bacteria in a small area and used that number to estimate the total number of bacteria. He recorded his observations in a table.

Time (min)	Bacteria Count
10	538
20	590
30	626
40	691
50	732
60	808

What is the rate of growth of the bacteria each hour?

Solution

First, determine which variable is the independent variable and which is the dependent variable.

- Since Terrence decided when to observe the bacteria, time is the independent variable.
- Therefore, the bacteria count is the dependent variable.

Next, enter the values for the independent variable into list L_1 and the values for the dependent variable into list L_2.

1. Start by clearing any lists already present. Press 2nd + , select 4:ClrAllLists, and press ENTER.
2. Press STAT , and select 1:Edit....
   Enter the values for time into L_1. Since the question is asking for the rate in hours, convert the given time from minutes by dividing each value by 60. This can be done directly in the list editor by typing the value in minutes divided by 60. The calculator will compute the value.

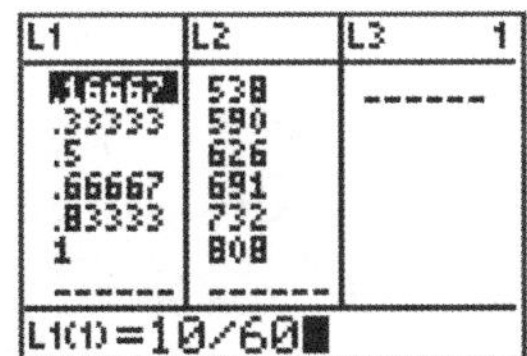

3. Enter the values for the bacteria count in L_2.

Next, calculate the exponential regression.

1. Press the STAT button, and then press the right arrow to access the CALC menu. Select 0:ExpReg.
2. Specify the lists L_1 and L_2 by pressing 2nd 1 , 2nd 2.

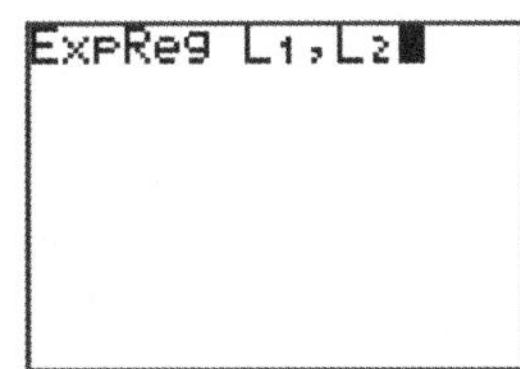

3. Press ENTER to run the exponential regression.

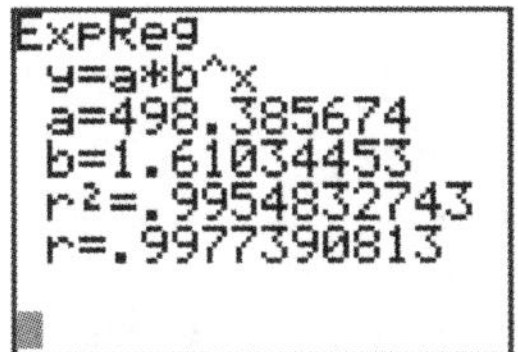

Finally, determine the growth rate.

- Since the value of *b* is about 1.61, the number of bacteria is increasing by 61% each hour.
- Therefore, the growth rate of the bacteria each hour is 61%.

After you find the values of *a* and *b*, you can use the regression function to make predictions.

Example

How many bacteria should Terrence expect to observe after 120 min?

Solution

First, substitute the values from the exponential regression into the exponential equation $y = ab^x$.

The results of the exponential regression are provided in this screen shot of a TI-83 graphing calculator.

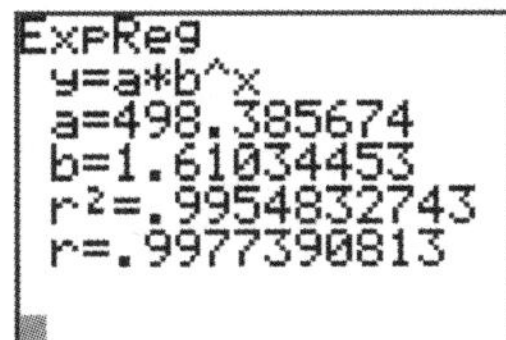

Substitute the values of a and b into $y = ab^x$.

$y = ab^x$
$y \approx (498)(1.61)^x$

Next, convert the given time from minutes to hours.

Divide the number of minutes by 60 to get the number of hours.

$x = \frac{120}{60}$
$x = 2$

Finally, substitute the time in hours for x in the exponential equation, and evaluate to find the value for y (the bacteria count).

Substitute $x = 2$ into $y \approx (498)(1.61)^x$, and evaluate.

$y \approx (498)(1.61)^x$
$y \approx (498)(1.61)^2$
$y \approx (498)(2.5921)$
$y \approx 1{,}290.8658$

Therefore, the number of bacteria Terrence should expect to observe after 120 min is approximately 1,291.

You can also use your graphing calculator to help make predictions from the exponential regression.

Example

What should the bacteria count be after 200 min?

Solution

First, enter the exponential equation that models the bacteria count into Y_1 on the calculator.

The calculator can do this automatically when calculating the exponential regression if a y-variable is specified to store the equation in.

1. Press the STAT button, and then press the right arrow to access the CALC menu. Select 0:ExpReg.Specify the lists L_1 and L_2 by pressing 2nd 1 , 2nd 2, but wait before actually running the command.

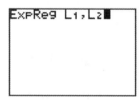

Run the exponential regression by pressing ENTER.

```
ExpReg
 y=a*b^x
 a=498.385674
 b=1.61034453
 r²=.9954832743
 r=.9977390813
```

If the ExpReg command is given a third variable, it will store the expression ab^x with a and b automatically substituted in that third variable. In this example, Y_1 will be used as the third variable.

2. Press , , and then specify the third variable.
3. Press VARS, and then the right arrow to move to the Y-VARS menu. Select 1:Function…, and then select 1:Y_1.

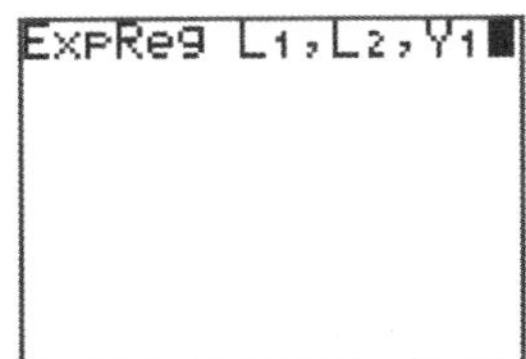

The exponential equation should now be stored in Y_1.

Next, set an appropriate window.

Before setting the window, turn on the stat plot.

1. Press 2nd Y= to access the STAT PLOTS menu. Select 1:Plot1, and press ENTER.
2. Highlight On, and press ENTER. Make sure that Xlist is set to L_1 and that Ylist is set to L_2.

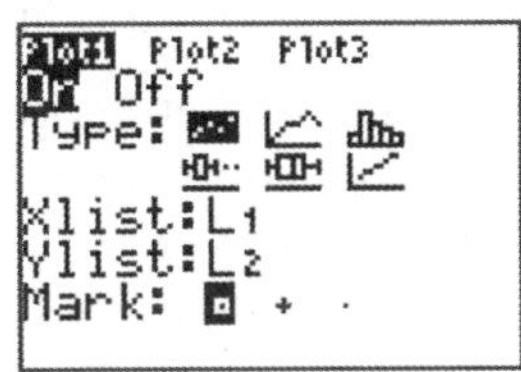

Ensure that both the equation for Y_1 and Plot1 are turned on in the Y= screen.

3. Press Y =, and verify that both Plot1 and the equals sign for Y_1 are highlighted in black. If either of them is not, move your cursor to the appropriate place and press ENTER to toggle that setting.

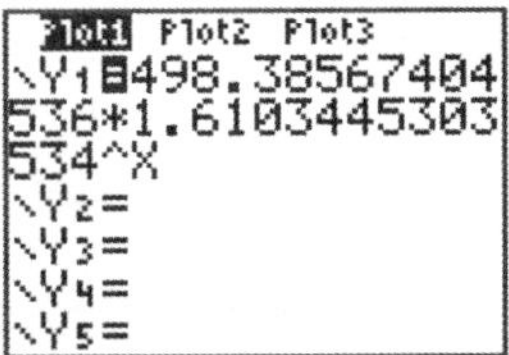

4. Set the window using ZoomStat. Press ZOOM, and select 9:ZoomStat.

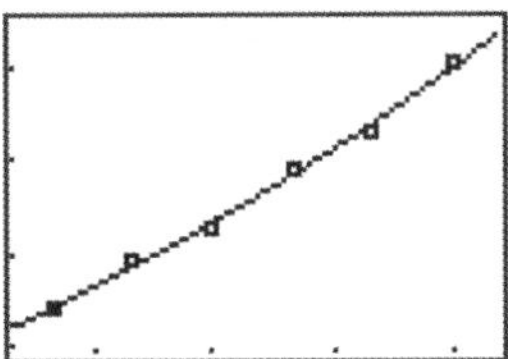

Adjust the window to include the desired value.

1. Calculate the time in hours by dividing the given time in minutes by 60. This will help determine what the window should be on the graphing calculator. Since time is the independent variable, the result will be an *x*-value.

   $x = \frac{200}{60}$

   $x \approx 3.33$

2. Change the Xmax of the window to be a value greater than 3.33.Press WINDOW, and set Xmin to 0 and Xmax to 4. Graph the function again.

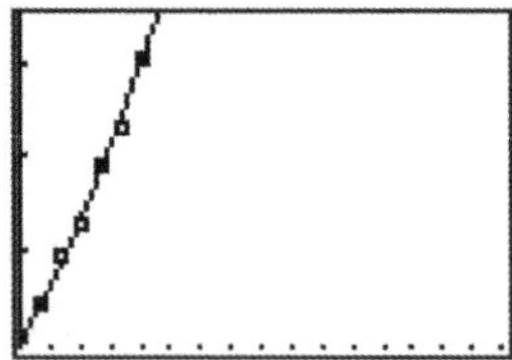

3. The Ymax has to be much larger so that more of the function is visible in the domain.Press WINDOW, and set Ymin to 400, Ymax to 4,000, and Yscl to 100. Graph the function again.

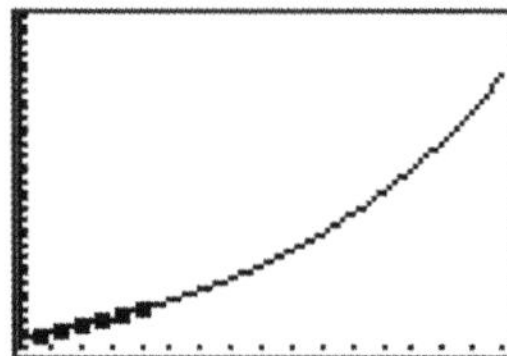

Finally use the trace function to determine the desired *y*-value.

1. Press TRACE, and use the up or down arrow to select the curve (instead of the points).
2. Type in 3.33, and press ENTER.

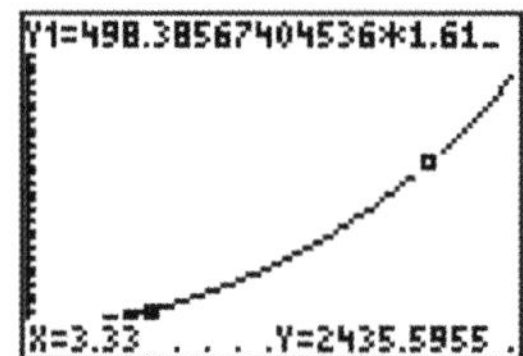

When $x = 3.33$, $y \approx 2{,}435.6$.

Therefore, after 200 min, Terrence should observe a bacterial count of approximately 2,436 bacteria.

S-ID.6c Represent data on two quantitative variables on a scatter plot, and describe how the variables are related. Fit a linear function for a scatter plot that suggests a linear association.

Determining the Equation of the Least Squares Regression Line

The **least squares regression line** for a set of data is the line that identifies where the sum of all of the squares of the distances between the points of data and the line is the smallest. It is also referred to as a line of best fit for a set of data.

The equation of a least squares regression line can be determined by performing a **linear regression** on a set of data. A TI-83 or similar calculator can perform a linear regression on a set of data and provide information about the fit of a line.

The **coefficient of determination**, r^2, indicates how well a least squares regression line models a set of data. The value of r^2 varies between 0 and 1. A value that is close to 1 indicates that the regression line is a good model for a set of data. A value that is close to 0 means that the regression line is not a good model for a set of data.

To determine the equation of the least squares regression line for a set of data, follow these steps:

1. Clear any list values already present in the calculator. Press 2nd + , select 4:ClrAllLists, and press ENTER.
2. Press 2nd 0 to access the CATALOG menu, then scroll down to DiagnosticOn. Press ENTER twice.
3. Press STAT and select 1:Edit… to access the list editor. Enter the values for the independent variable into list L_1 and the values for the dependent variable into list L_2.
4. Press STAT and press the right arrow once to access the CALC menu. Select 4:LinReg(ax +b) and press 2nd 1 , 2nd 2 to specify lists L_1 and L_2. Press ENTER.
5. Substitute the values of a and b into the equation of a line, $y = ax + b$.
6. Interpret the value of r^2 to determine how well the least squares regression line models the set of data.

In most cases, slope is denoted by m, but a TI-83 uses a to represent slope.

Example

Chen plots the daily closing values of a company he owns stock in. He is not sure whether he should keep the stock or sell it. Chen wants to determine the least squares regression line to help him decide if he should keep his stock. If the least squares regression line has a positive slope, Chen should hold on to his stock because the price is increasing. If the slope is negative, then the price is decreasing and Chen should sell his stock.

Day	Closing Value ($)
1	6.76
2	6.71
3	6.74
4	6.80
5	6.91

Determine if Chen should keep his stock using the equation of the least squares regression line that models the closing values of the stock.

Solution

Step 1

Clear any list values already present in the calculator. Press 2nd + , select 4:ClrAllLists, and press ENTER.

Step 2

Turn diagnostics on so that residual values will be displayed.

Press 2nd 0 to access the CATALOG menu, then scroll down to DiagnosticOn. Press ENTER twice.

Step 3

Enter the values for the independent variable into L_1 and the values for the dependent variable into L_2.

Press STAT and select 1:Edit…. Enter the values for day into L_1 and the closing values into L_2.

L1	L2	L3 2
1	6.76	------
2	6.71	
3	6.74	
4	6.8	
5	6.91	

L2(6) =

Step 4
Perform the linear regression.

Press STAT, press the right arrow to access the CALC menu, and select 4:LinReg($ax + b$).

Specify the two lists by pressing 2nd 1 , 2nd 2.

```
LinReg(ax+b) L1,
L2
```

Press ENTER to perform the linear regression.

```
LinReg
 y=ax+b
 a=.039
 b=6.667
 r²=.6305970149
 r=.7941013883
```

Step 5
Substitute the values of a and b into the equation of a line, $y = ax + b$.

Since $a = 0.039$ and $b = 6.667$, the equation for the least square regression line is $y = 0.039x + 6.667$.

Therefore, the least squares regression line for the data is $y = 0.039x + 6.667$.

Step 6
Interpret the value of r^2.

Since the value of r^2, 0.630…, is closer to 1.0 than 0, the line does a fair job of approximating the data. Since the line fairly approximates the data, an analysis of the slope would produce reliable information.

In this case, the slope of the line, 0.039, is slightly greater than 0. This means the price of the stock is increasing, but slowly. Therefore, Chen should keep his stock.

EXERCISE #1—TWO VARIABLE DATA

Use the following information to answer the next question.

The marks, in percentages, of a group of Grade 6 students on a mathematics test are 84, 75, 80, 96, 74, 96, 74, 80, 96, and 95.

306. Explain which mark has the **greatest** frequency.

Use the following information to answer the next question.

Ming spins this spinner 32 times.

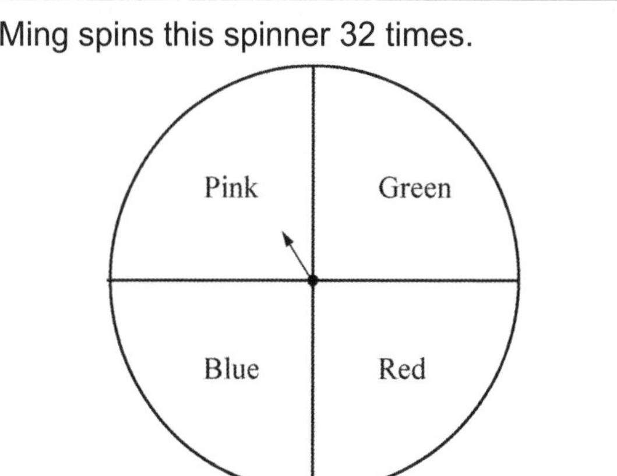

The outcome of all her spins are as follows: pink, pink, green, red, pink, pink, blue, blue, red, pink, green, pink, green, red, pink, red, blue, pink, green, pink, blue, pink, green, pink, pink, blue, red, pink, green, pink, red, pink.

307. Which of the following frequency charts shows the outcome of all of Ming's spins?

A.

Color	Pink	Green	Blue	Red
Frequency	15	6	5	6

B.

Color	Pink	Green	Blue	Red
Frequency	15	10	10	6

C.

Color	Pink	Green	Blue	Red
Frequency	15	6	8	8

D.

Color	Pink	Green	Blue	Red
Frequency	15	4	6	6

Use the following information to answer the next question.

A psychologist performed an experiment using 28 children as subjects. Each child was given a puzzle to solve, and the time taken to reach a solution to the puzzle was recorded to the nearest tenth of a minute. The psychologist constructed the given cumulative frequency histogram to represent the data that he obtained.

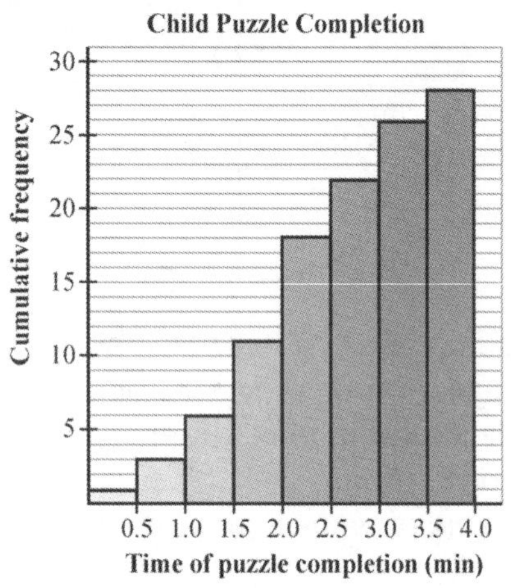

The times taken by the first 20 children to complete the puzzle are 0.8, 1.4, 1.8, 2.4, 2.1, 3.1, 2.6, 1.9, 1.2, 0.4, 0.9, 2.3, 2.9, 3.6, 3.2, 1.3, 1.8, 2.2, 1.7, and 3.8.

308. Which of the following lists could show the times taken by the other eight children to complete the puzzle?

A. 3.2, 2.4, 1.6, 2.7, 3.4, 2.8, 2.3, 2.1

B. 2.6, 1.8, 2.9, 2.3, 3.2, 1.6, 2.1, 3.3

C. 2.6, 2.9, 3.2, 2.8, 1.7, 3.6, 2.4, 2.1

D. 1.7, 2.8, 3.3, 2.4, 2.3, 0.7, 3.9, 1.9

Use the following information to answer the next question.

A hockey team recorded the number of goals they scored in each of the 60 games they played. The given cumulative frequency distribution table shows the data the hockey team collected.

Number of Goals Scored	Cumulative Frequency of Games with the Number of Goals Scored
0	2
1	10
2	27
3	43
4	52
5	56
6	59
7	60

309. In how many games did the hockey team score 3, 4, or 5 goals?

A. 13 **B.** 17

C. 25 **D.** 29

310. What type of graph would **best** represent a part of the whole?

Use the following information to answer the next question.

Two different scatter plots are shown.

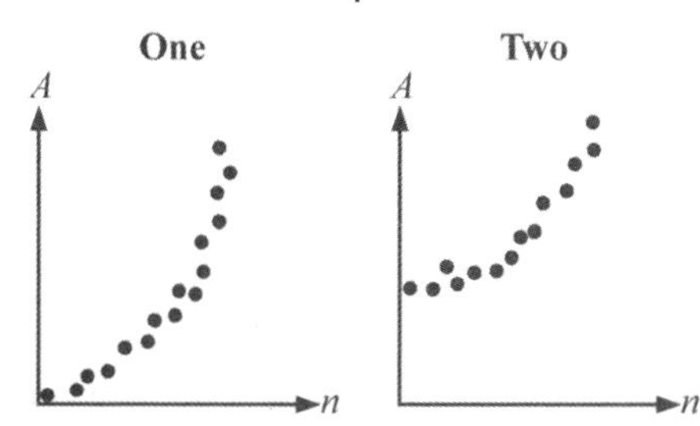

Gladys invested $10,000 at a variable interest rate, which is compounded at fixed intervals of time.

The value, A, in dollars, of Gladys's investment after n compound periods could be illustrated in scatter plot ____*i*____, and the best regression to choose to analyze the given data would be ____*ii*____ regression.

311. Which of the following tables contains the information that completes the given statement?

A.

i	ii
One	a linear

B.

i	ii
One	an exponential

C.

i	i
Two	a linear

D.

i	ii
Two	an exponential

Use the following information to answer the next question.

A golf handicap is a measure of how well a person plays golf. The lower the handicap, the better the player is. Handicaps are used to adjust golf scores so that players of different skill and ability can play against one another on more equal terms. The given chart shows the handicaps for a group of players with varying amounts of experience.

Years of Experience	Handicap
0	20
1	17
2	16
3	12
5	9

312. Rounded to the nearest thousandth, what is the correlation coefficient, r, between years of experience and a player's handicap?

A. –0.986 B. –0.972
C. 0.972 D. 0.986

Use the following information to answer the next question.

A set of data is graphed and found to have a linear relationship and a correlation coefficient, r, of –0.8.

313. Which of the following statements about the set of data is **true**?

A. The graphed data set points lie below the x-axis.

B. The data set is weakly correlated because the r-value is negative.

C. The graph for the data set has a line of best fit with a negative slope.

D. The graph for the data set has data points that lie far from the line of best fit.

Use the following information to answer the next question.

The sales staff at a magazine looked at the growth rate in the number of subscribers during the previous 10 years. They found the number of subscriptions had grown exponentially, as shown in the given chart.

Year Recorded	Subscriptions (millions)
1	0.430
2	0.456
3	0.474
4	0.512
5	0.601
6	0.685
7	0.765
8	0.812
9	0.906
10	1.012

An exponential regression was performed on the data to get a function that gives the number of subscriptions, y, in millions, as a function of x, the number of years before the magazine had one million subscribers.

314. Using the exponential regression function, what is the average growth rate percentage for the number of subscribers to the magazine during the past 10 years, to the nearest hundredth?

A. 0.37% B. 1.11%

C. 1.63% D. 2.27%

Use the following information to answer the next question.

Karen works at a recreation center that offers a month-long karate class for beginners. Since the class was first offered, the class size has steadily increased each month. Karen recorded the number of people who enrolled in the class each month, and her results are shown in the given chart.

Month Number	Number of People Enrolled
1	8
2	13
3	20
4	23
5	26
6	34
7	38
8	40

Karen performed a linear regression on her data, expressing the number of people enrolled, y, as a function of the month number, x.

315. Rounding all numbers to the nearest hundredth, what will Karen's equation be?

A. $y = 4.69x + 4.14$

B. $y = 4.14x + 0.99$

C. $y = 0.21x - 0.81$

D. $y = 6.90x + 0.99$

EXERCISE #1—TWO VARIABLE DATA ANSWERS AND SOLUTIONS

306. See solution	309. D	312. A	315. A
307. A	310. See solution	313. C	
308. A	311. D	314. B	

306.

Step 1
Reorder the marks from lowest percentage to highest percentage.
74, 74, 75, 80, 80, 84, 95, 96, 96, 96

Step 2
Count the number of times each mark appears.

- 74% appears twice.
- 75% appears once.
- 80% appears twice.
- 84% appears once.
- 95% appears once.
- 96% appears three times.

The mark with the greatest frequency is 96%.

307. A

Step 1
Create a tally chart to determine how many times the spinner landed on each color.

Color	Tally
Pink	𝍸 𝍸 𝍸
Green	𝍸 |
Blue	𝍸
Red	𝍸 |

According to the data, the spinner landed on pink 15 times, on green 6 times, on blue 5 times, and on red 6 times.

Step 2
Create a frequency chart using the data on the tally chart.

Color	Tally	Frequency
Pink	𝍸 𝍸 𝍸	15
Green	𝍸 |	6
Blue	𝍸	5
Red	𝍸 |	6

Therefore, table A is the frequency table showing the outcomes of Ming's spins.

308. A

Observe that the histogram shown has a starting point of 0 and an interval width of 0.5.

Step 1
Construct a cumulative frequency distribution table from the data given for the first 20 children, with intervals of width 0.5, starting at 0.

Interval	Frequency	Cumulative Frequency
0–0.5	1	1
0.5–1.0	2	3
1.0–1.5	3	6
1.5–2.0	4	10
2.0–2.5	4	14
2.5–3.0	2	16
3.0–3.5	2	18
3.5–4.0	2	20

Step 2
Using the given cumulative frequency histogram, determine the required frequency in each of the eight intervals.

Interval	Required Frequency
0–0.5	1
0.5–1.0	3 – 1 = 2
1.0–1.5	6 – 3 = 3
1.5–2.0	11 – 6 = 5
2.0–2.5	18 – 11 = 7
2.5–3.0	22 – 18 = 4
3.0–3.5	26 – 22 = 4
3.5–4.0	28 – 26 = 2

Step 3
Using the data from the derived frequency distribution table for the first 20 children and the derived required frequency for each interval, determine in which intervals the other 8 children must be located in order to construct the given cumulative frequency histogram.

In the cumulative frequency distribution table, the frequency in the first interval is 1, which corresponds to the required frequency for the first interval. Similarly, in the second and third intervals, the frequencies given in the cumulative frequency distribution table correspond to the required frequencies.

However, in the fourth interval, the given frequency is 4 and the required frequency is 5. Thus, one of the other eight children must have had a time between 1.5 and 2.0 min.

In the fifth interval, the frequency shown in the cumulative frequency distribution table is 4, but the required frequency is 7. Therefore, 3 of the other children must have had a time between 2.0 and 2.5 min.

In the sixth interval, the frequency shown in the cumulative frequency distribution table is 2, and the required frequency is 4. It follows that 2 of the other children must have had a time between 2.5 and 3.0 min.

In the seventh interval, the frequency shown in the cumulative frequency distribution table is 2, but the required frequency is 4. Therefore, 2 of the other children must have had a time between 3.0 and 3.5 min.

In the eighth interval, the frequency shown in the cumulative frequency distribution table is 2, which corresponds to the required frequency.

Step 4
From the provided lists, determine which set of data has one value between 1.5 and 2.0, three values between 2.0 and 2.5, two values between 2.5 and 3.0, and two values between 3.0 and 3.5.

The only alternative that has the necessary set of data is list A.

309. D

Step 1
Determine the number of games in which the hockey team scored less than 3 goals.

If the hockey team scored less than 3 goals, it follows that they scored 0, 1, or 2 goals. According to the given table, the cumulative frequency that corresponds to the number 2 is 27. Therefore, the hockey team scored less than 3 goals in 27 games.

Step 2
Determine the number of games in which the hockey team scored more than 5 goals.

If the hockey team scored more than 5 goals, it follows that they scored 6 or 7 goals. According to the given table, the cumulative frequency that corresponds to the number 5 is 56 and the cumulative frequency that corresponds to the number 7 is 60. Therefore, the hockey team scored more than 5 goals in 60−56 = 4 games.

Step 3
Determine the number of games in which the hockey team scored 3, 4, or 5 goals.

The team played a total of 60 games. Since they scored less than 3 goals in 27 games and more than 5 goals in 4 games, it follows that they scored 3, 4, or 5 goals in 60−(27 + 4) = 29 games.

310.

A circle graph shows a whole divided into separate parts. This allows for the comparison of each of the parts. Therefore, a circle graph is the best type of graph to use to represent a part of a whole.

311. D

Since Gladys initially invested $10,000, the related scatter plot cannot start at the origin. Therefore, scatter plot Two could illustrate the value, *A*, in dollars, of her investment after *n* compound periods.

Given that the points in scatter plot Two curve upward (toward positive infinity), an exponential regression (rather than a linear regression) would be the best regression to use in order to analyze the given data. If the given points tended to follow a straight line, then a linear regression would have been appropriate.

312. A

Use a TI-83 or similar calculator to calculate the correlation coefficient, *r*, for the given data.

Step 1
Enter the values for years of experience and handicap into the lists L_1 and L_2.
Start by clearing any lists already present. Press 2nd + , select 4:ClrAllLists, and press ENTER .

Push STAT , and select 1:Edit... from the EDIT menu. Enter the values for years of experience and handicap into the lists L_1 and L_2, respectively.

Step 2
Turn on the correlation coefficient, *r*.

Press 2nd 0 to access the CATALOG menu.
Scroll down to DiagnosticOn, and press ENTER twice.

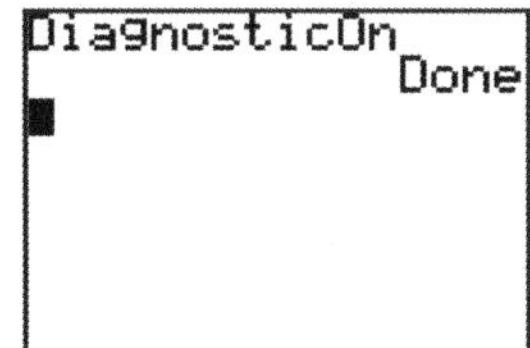

Step 3
Find the correlation coefficient, *r*.

Calculate the linear regression by pressing STAT and the right arrow once to bring up the CALC menu. Select 4:LinReg(ax+b).

Specify lists L_1 and L_2 by pressing 2nd 1 , 2nd 2 and then ENTER .

```
LinReg
 y=ax+b
 a=-2.216216216
 b=19.67567568
 r²=.9718167365
 r=-.985807657
```

Rounded to the nearest thousandth, the correlation coefficient, *r*, is –0.986.

313. C

If the correlation coefficient, *r*, is close to –1, the points are close to the line of best fit and the slope is negative. The data is said to have a strong negative correlation.

Therefore, a set of data with a correlation coefficient, *r*, of –0.8 indicates that the data has a strong negative correlation. The data set points are close to the line of best fit, and the line of best fit has a negative slope. The value of *r* is not affected by the location of the graph on the Cartesian plane.

314. B

Use a TI-83 or similar calculator to perform the exponential regression.

Step 1
Enter the *x*-values and *y*-values in lists L_1 and L_2, respectively.
Start by clearing any lists already present. Press 2nd + , select 4:ClrAllLists, and press ENTER .

Press STAT , and select 1:Edit... to edit the lists.
Enter the years recorded into list L_1 and the number of corresponding subscriptions in millions into list L_2. Press ENTER after entering each value.

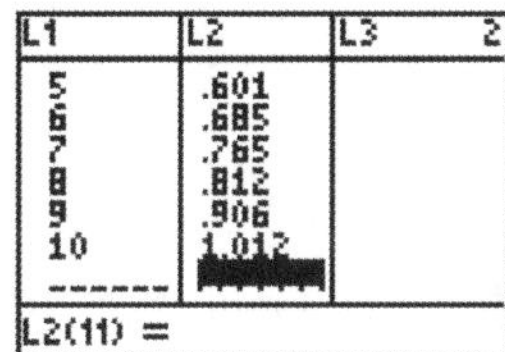

Step 2
Perform the exponential regression.

Press STAT , and then press the right arrow to access the CALC menu. Select 0:ExpReg.
Specify lists L_1 and L_2 to use with the exponential regression by pressing 2nd 1 , 2nd 2 .

Press ENTER to run the exponential regression.

quadratic regression, solution screen

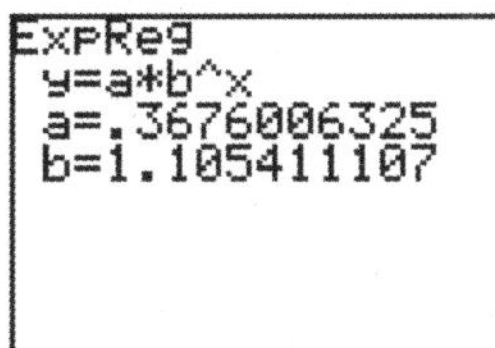

Step 3
Determine the average growth rate for the number of subscriptions.
The regression equation rounded to four decimal places is $y \approx 0.3676(1.1054)^x$. In an exponential function of the form $y = ab^x$, *b* represents the growth rate. Since $b \approx 1.1054$, this indicates a growth rate of 1.1054%, which rounds to 1.11%.

315. A

Use a TI-83 or similar calculator to perform a linear regression on the given data.

Step 1

Enter the values for the independent variable into L_1 and the values for the dependent variable into L_2. Start by clearing any lists already present. Press [2nd] [+], select 4:ClrAllLists, and press [ENTER].

Press [STAT], and select 1:Edit… from the Edit menu.

Enter the month numbers in L_1 and the values for the number of people in L_2. Press [ENTER] after entering each value.

Step 2

Turn on diagnostics so that residual values will be displayed.

Press [2nd] [0] to access the CATALOG menu. Scroll down to DiagnosticOn, and press [ENTER] twice.

Step 3

Perform the linear regression.

Press the [STAT] button and then the right arrow to access the CALC menu. Select 4:LinReg(ax+b). Specify lists L_1 and L_2 by pressing

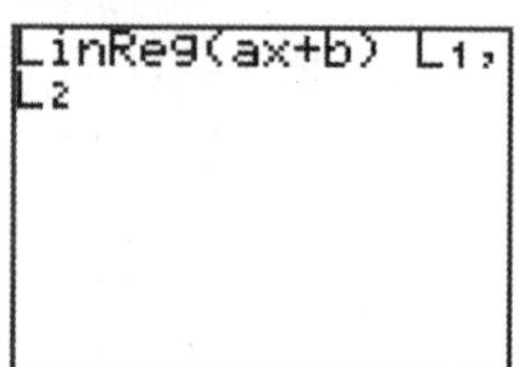

Press [ENTER] to run the linear regression.

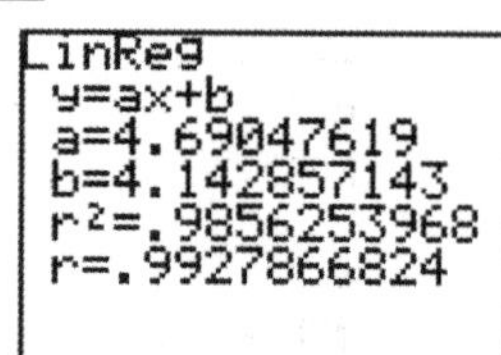

Step 4

Substitute a and b into the equation of a line, $y = ax + b$.

Since $a \approx 4.6905$ and $b \approx 4.1429$, write the formula for the least squares regression line.

$y = ax + b$

$y = 4.6905x + 4.1429$

Rounding to the nearest hundredth, the least squares regression line for the data is $y = 4.69x + 4.14$.

Step 5

Interpret the value of r^2.

Since $r^2 \approx 0.9856$ is very close to 1.0, the line approximates the data well.

EXERCISE #2—TWO VARIABLE DATA

Use the following information to answer the next question.

Marrissa recorded the number of seconds it took all the members of her swim team to swim 50 m.
31, 36, 34, 33, 36, 34, 31, 33, 34, 34, 31, 34, 36, 31

316. The time from the given data set that has a frequency of 3 is

A. 31 s
B. 33 s
C. 34 s
D. 36 s

Use the following information to answer the next question.

Nigel wants to know how many coins he has in his piggy bank. When Nigel flips the piggy bank upside down, coins with the following values fall out.
1, 1, 5, 5, 10, 1, 1, 25, 5, 25, 5, 10, 5, 25, 5, 25, 1, 1, 25, 1, 5, 5, 5, 5, 1, 1, 25, 1, 1, 25, 25, 10, 25, 1, 5, 10, 5, 10, 1, 25, 5, 5, 25, 5, 1, 10, 10, 5, 10, 1, 1, 1, 25, 25, 10, 10, 25, 1, 5, 1, 25, 1, 5, 1, 1, 5, 25, 5, 5, 10, 25, 10, 25, 25, 25, 1, 10, 25, 25, 5

317. Which of the following frequency charts organizes the given information?

A.

Coin (¢)	Frequency
1	23
5	20
10	17
25	24

B.

Coin (¢)	Frequency
1	23
5	22
10	15
25	23

C.

Coin (¢)	Frequency
1	23
5	22
10	13
25	22

D.

Coin (¢)	Frequency
1	23
5	21
10	15
25	22

Use the following information to answer the next question.

Beatrice studies every school night. To the nearest tenth of an hour, the number of hours that Beatrice studied each day for 20 school nights is shown in the given table.

Number of Hours Spent Studying over 20 School Days

Mon	Tue	Wed	Thu	Fri
1.3	0.6	2.3	2.9	1.7
2.4	0.8	0.4	2.7	1.8
0.7	1.2	1.6	2.3	1.9
2.8	1.1	1.7	1.4	2.1

318. Which of the following cumulative frequency histograms represents the given data?

A.
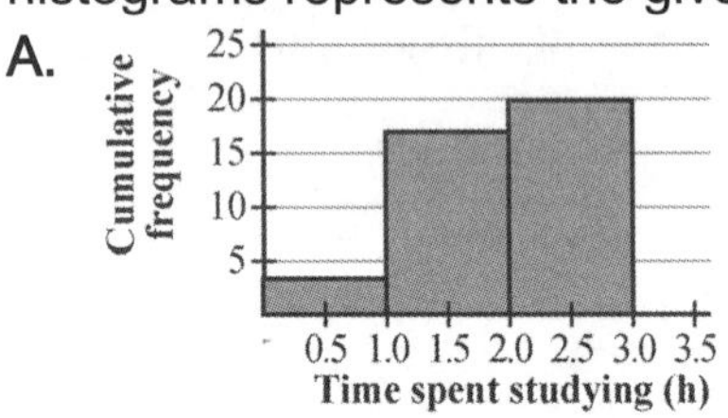

B.
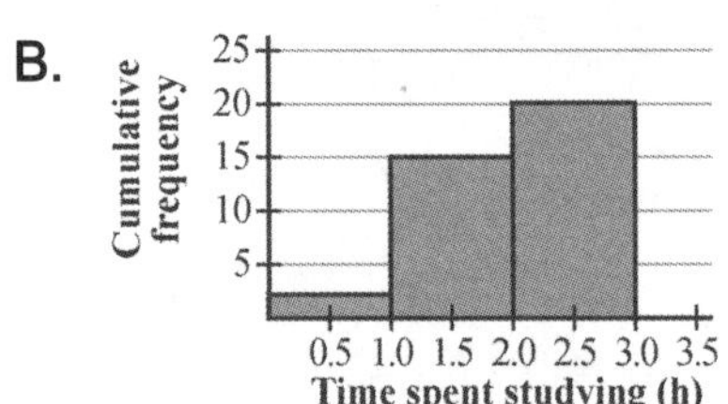

C.
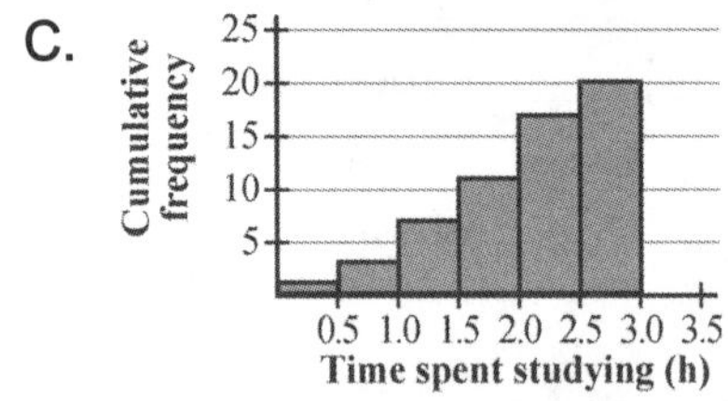

D.
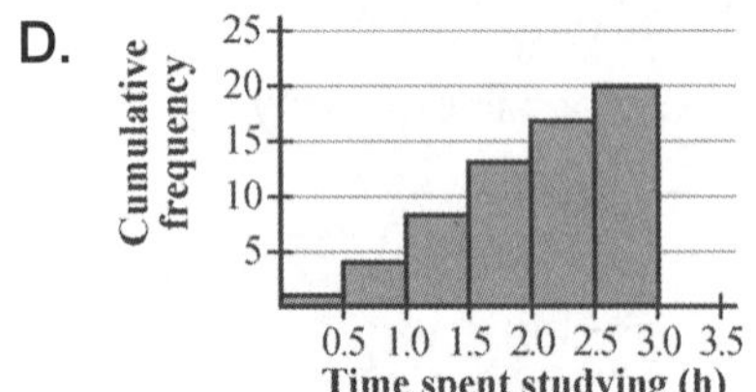

Use the following information to answer the next question.

For a particular city in June 2010, the daily high temperatures, to the nearest whole number in degrees Celsius, are recorded. The data is displayed using a cumulative frequency distribution table.

Daily High Temperatures (°C)	Frequency	Cumulative Frequency
23	4	4
24	3	7
25	5	12
26	6	18
27	4	22
28	2	24
29	0	25
30	3	27
31	2	29
32	1	30

319. What percentage of days in June 2010 was the city's high temperature more than 28°C?

A. $6.\bar{6}\%$ **B.** 18.75%

C. 20% **D.** $26.\bar{6}\%$

Use the following information to answer the next question.

Ivan created a table to show the points scored by his community league basketball team (Team A) and the team from a neighboring community (Team B) in their last five games.

Game	Team A	Team B
1	70	82
2	78	82
3	80	78
4	84	80
5	78	72

320. The **most appropriate** graph for Ivan to use in order to display his data is a

A. line plot

B. histogram

C. bar graph

D. double bar graph

Use the following information to answer the next question.

A team of scientists collected data about the relationship between the length and the midshaft diameter of the humerus bones of African antelopes. They constructed a scatter plot from the data, with the length along the x-axis and the midshaft diameter along the y-axis. The scientists determined that a power regression would be the best regression to use in analyzing the data.

321. Which of the following scatter plots shows the data collected by the scientists?

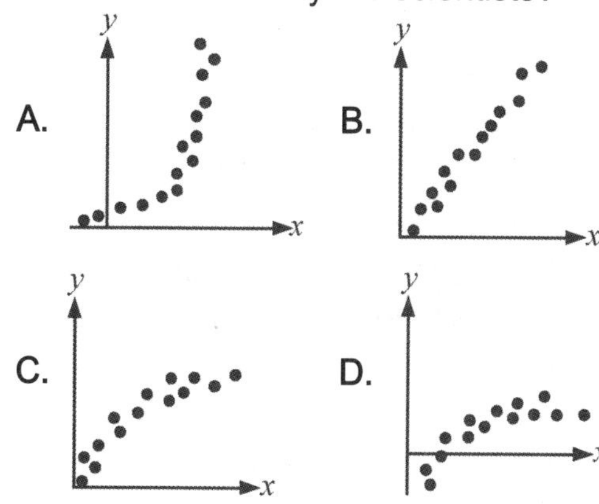

Use the following information to answer the next question.

The given graph shows the data that a student collected during an experiment.

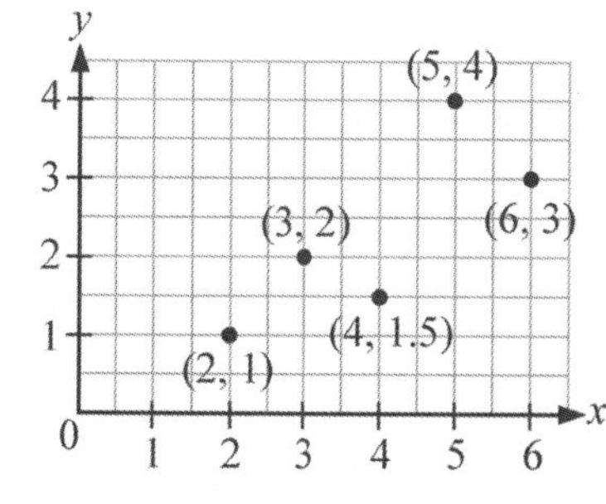

322. If a linear regression is performed on the given data, what is the value of the correlation coefficient, rounded to the nearest hundredth?

A. 0.62

B. 0.69

C. 0.72

D. 0.79

Use the following information to answer the next question.

Ryan decided to record the jersey number of each player on his hockey team along with the number of points each player scored during the first month of the season.

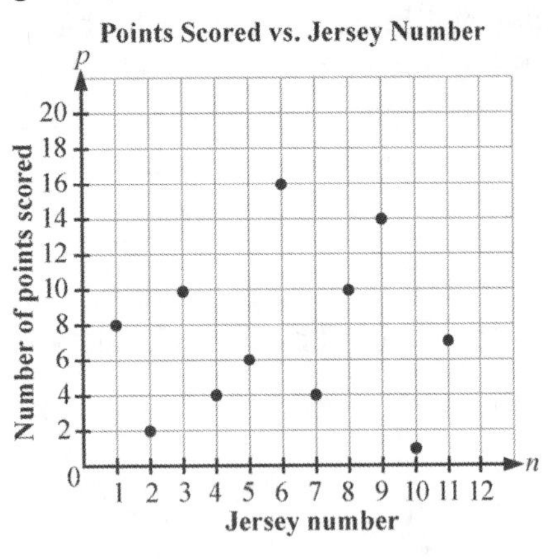

323. Which of the following correlation coefficients (r) **best** describes the data Ryan collected?

A. –0.5 B. 0

C. 0.5 D. 1

Use the following information to answer the next question.

A small publishing company initially recorded the number of titles it published every year since it opened in 1999, but it stopped collecting data after six years. The data collected by the company is shown in the given table.

Year	Year Number	Number of Titles Published
1999	0	310
2000	1	327
2001	2	345
2002	3	379
2003	4	402
2004	5	445

Exponential regression can be performed on this data to get a function that gives the number of titles published as a function of the number of years after 1999.

324. According to the regression equation, the number of titles published in 2005 could have been approximately

A. 455 B. 463

C. 471 D. 495

Use the following information to answer the next question.

In a survey, 13 car owners were asked about how many oil changes they had done in the previous calendar year and how much they had spent on car repairs during the same calendar year. The given table shows the data that were collected.

Oil Changes	Repair Costs ($)
3	300
5	200
2	500
3	400
1	700
4	400
6	100
4	200
3	450
2	650
0	650
10	0
8	100

A linear regression was performed on the data to express the cost, C, of repairs (in dollars) as a function of the number of oil changes, x.

325. Rounded to the nearest integer, the regression equation is

A. $C = -75x + 653$

B. $C = -75x - 653$

C. $C = 75x - 653$

D. $C = 75x + 653$

EXERCISE #2—TWO VARIABLE DATA ANSWERS AND SOLUTIONS

316. D	319. C	322. D	325. A
317. C	320. D	323. B	
318. D	321. C	324. C	

316. D

Step 1
Reorder the numbers from least to greatest.
31, 31, 31, 31, 33, 33, 34, 34, 34, 34, 34, 36, 36, 36

Step 2
Count the number of times each number appears.

- 31 appears four times.
- 33 appears two times.
- 34 appears five times.
- 36 appears three times.

The number that appears three times is the number 36.
The time from the given data set that has a frequency of 3 is 36 s.

317. C

Step 1
Carefully count the number of coins of each denomination and construct a tally chart using this information.

- There are 23 1-cent coins, this is represented with 23 tally marks.
- There are 22 5-cent coins, this is represented with 22 tally marks.
- There are 13 10-cent coins, this is represented with 13 tally marks.
- There are 22 25-cent coins, this is represented with 22 tally marks.

Coin (¢)	Tally
1	卌 卌 卌 卌 ǀ ǀ ǀ
5	卌 卌 卌 卌 ǀ ǀ
10	卌 卌 ǀ ǀ ǀ
25	卌 卌 卌 卌 ǀ ǀ

Step 2
Create a frequency chart using the information in the tally chart.

Coin (¢)	Frequency
1	23
5	22
10	13
25	22

Therefore, table C is the frequency table that organizes the given information.

318. D

All of the given histograms have the same starting point on the horizontal axis, 0. Two graphs have an interval width of 1.0 h and two graphs have an interval width of 0.5 h.

Step 1
Construct a cumulative frequency distribution table from the given data with intervals of 1.0, starting at 0.

Intervals	Frequency	Cumulative Frequency
0–1.0	4	4
1.0–2.0	9	13
2.0–3.0	7	20

Step 2
Construct a cumulative frequency distribution table from the given data with intervals of 0.5, starting at 0.

Intervals	Frequency	Cumulative Frequency
0–0.5	1	1
0.5–1.0	3	4
1.0–1.5	4	8
1.5–2.0	5	13
2.0–2.5	4	17
2.5–3.0	3	20

Step 3
Determine, from the given alternatives, which histogram represents the data in either of the derived cumulative frequency tables.

Neither of the graphs with an interval width of 1.0 h have a cumulative frequency of 4 in the first interval, 13 in the second interval, and 20 in the last interval.

The starting point of the two remaining histograms is 0, and the interval width is 0.5. However, only the histogram shown has a cumulative frequency of 1 in the first interval, 4 in the second interval, 8 in the third interval, 13 in the fourth interval, 17 in the fifth interval, and 20 in the last interval.

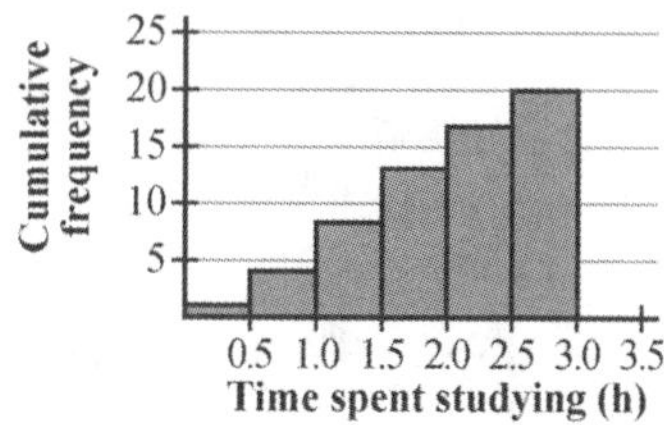

319. C

Step 1
Determine the number of days that the city's high temperature was more than 28 °C in June 2010.

The phrase "more than 28°C" means that the temperatures were 29°C or higher. The number in the cumulative frequency column for 28°C is 24.
It then follows that the number of days with a high temperature of more than 28°C is 30 – 24 = 6 days.
The sum of the frequencies for 29, 30, 31, and 32 (0 + 3 + 2 + 1) would also give the number of days the city's high temperature was more than 28°C.

Step 2
Determine the percentage of days.
The last entry in the cumulative frequency column corresponds to the number of days in the month of June.

$\frac{6}{30} \times 100\% = 20\%$

Therefore, 20 % of the days in June 2010 had a high temperature of more than 28 °C in the given city.

320. D

Some types of graphs are better suited to certain kinds of information.

The most appropriate choice would be a double bar graph because the main purpose of a double bar graph is to easily compare two separate pieces of information within the same category.

On this double bar graph, each team's wins and losses can be compared quickly and easily.

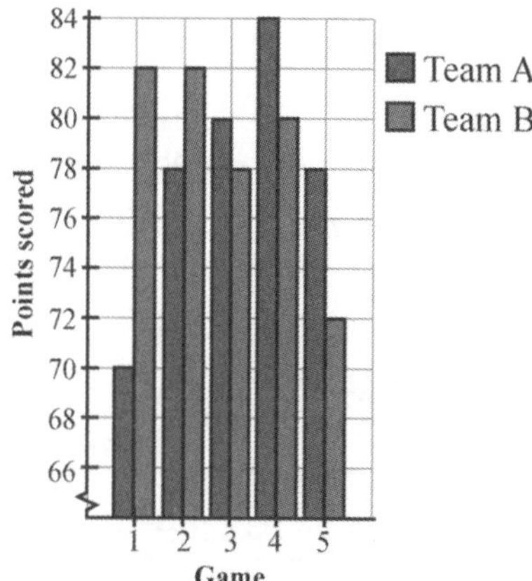

Although the data collected could be represented on two single bar graphs, this would not be the best choice.

321. C

Step 1
Sketch the line of best fit for the data in each scatter plot.

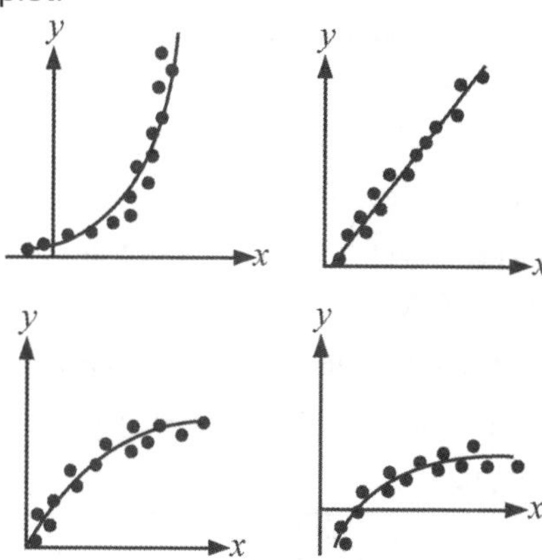

Step 2
Determine which scatter plot could have been constructed by the scientists.

Given that the scientists chose a power regression to analyze their data, the line of best fit for the data should start close to the origin. Initially, it should be almost vertical, and then it should curve to the right. The values of x and y must be positive.

Scatter plot C is the only one that satisfies these conditions.

322. D

Use a TI-83 or similar calculator to find the value of the correlation coefficient, *r*.

Step 1
Enter the values for the independent variable and the values for the dependent variable into different lists. Start by clearing any lists already present. Press [2nd] [+], select 4:ClrAllLists, and press [ENTER].

Press [STAT], and select 1:Edit… from the EDIT menu. Enter the *x*-values into L1 and the *y*-values into L2.

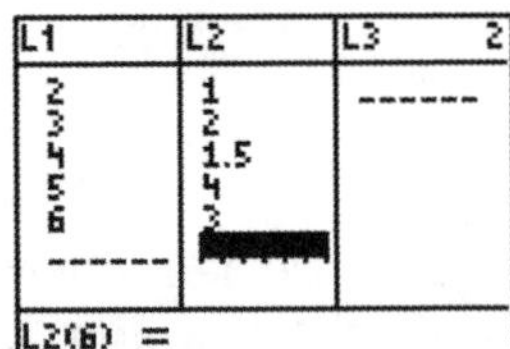

Step 2
Turn on diagnostics so that the correlation coefficient, *r*, will be displayed in the results of the regression.

Press [2nd] [0] to access the CATALOG menu. Scroll down to DiagnosticOn, and press [ENTER] twice.

Step 3
Perform the linear regression.

Press the [STAT] button, press the right arrow to access the CALC menu, and select 4:LinReg(ax+b). Specify the two lists to use by pressing [2nd] [1] [,] [2nd] [2]. Then, press [ENTER] to run the linear regression.

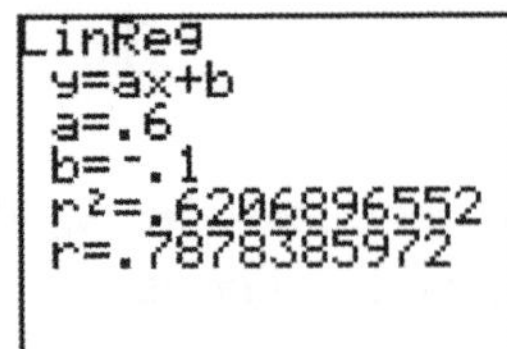

Rounded to the nearest hundredth, the value of the correlation coefficient, *r*, is 0.79.

323. B

The correlation coefficient (*r*) represents how correlated a set of data is, based on how close the data lies to its line of best fit. However, no line of best fit can be drawn for Ryan's data because there is no relationship between the jersey number of the player and the number of points scored. The data is neither increasing nor decreasing. Since there is no correlation between the two variables, the correlation coefficient (*r*) that best describes the data is 0.

324. C

Use a TI-83 or similar graphing calculator to perform the exponential regression and solve the regression equation.

Step 1
Enter the *x*-values and *y*-values in lists L_1 and L_2, respectively.
Start by clearing any lists already present. Press [2nd] [+], select 4:ClrAllLists, and press [ENTER].

Press [STAT], and select 1:Edit… to enter the lists. Enter the year numbers into list L_1 and the number of titles published into list L_2.

quadratic regression, data entry, list L1 L2, screen shot

L1	L2	L3 2
0	310	------
1	327	
2	345	
3	379	
4	402	
5	445	

L2(7) =

Step 2
Perform the exponential regression.

Press [STAT], and then press the right arrow to access the CALC menu. Select 0:ExpReg. Specify lists L_1 and L_2 to use with the exponential regression by pressing [2nd] [1] [,] [2nd] [2].

Press [ENTER] to run the exponential regression.

quadratic regression, solution screen

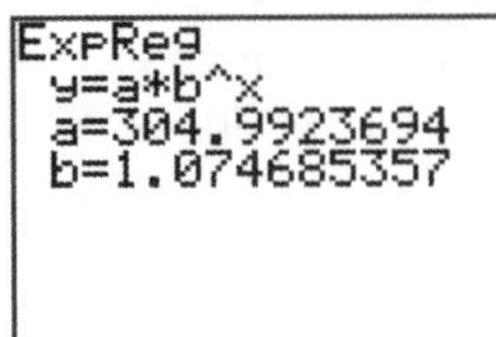

Step 3
Determine the number of books that could have been published in 2005.
Rounded to the nearest thousandth, the regression equation is $y \approx 304.992(1.075)^x$.
Since 2005 is 6 years after 1999, substitute 6 for *x* in the regression equation.

$y \approx 304.992(1.075)^x$
$y \approx 304.992(1.075)^6$
$y \approx 470.695$
$y \approx 471$

In 2005, the publishing company could have published approximately 471 books.

325. A

Use a TI-83 or similar calculator to solve the problem.

Step 1
Enter the values for the independent variable and the dependent variable into different lists.

Start by clearing any lists already present. Press [2nd][+], select 4:ClrAllLists, and press [ENTER].

Press [STAT], and select 1:Edit… from the EDIT menu. Enter the values from the Oil Changes column into L1 and the values from the Repair Costs column into L2.

Step 2
Turn on diagnostics so that residual values are displayed.

Press [2nd][0] to access the CATALOG menu. Scroll down to DiagnosticOn, and press [ENTER] twice.

Step 3
Perform the linear regression.

Press the [STAT] button and then the right arrow to access the CALC menu. Select 4:LinReg(ax+b).

Specify the two lists to use by pressing [2nd][1][,] [2nd][2].

Press [ENTER] to run the linear regression.

```
LinReg
 y=ax+b
 a=-75.24834437
 b=652.897351
 r²=.8296027293
 r=-.9108253012
```

Step 4
Substitute a and b into the equation of a line, $y = ax + b$.

Since the question asks for the values to be rounded to the nearest integer, $a \approx -75$ and $b \approx 653$.
The equation for the least squares regression line is thus as follows:
$y = ax + b$
$y = -75x + 653$

Therefore, the least squares regression line for the data, rounded to the nearest integer, is $C = -75x + 653$.

Step 5
Interpret the value of r^2.

Since $r^2 \approx 0.8296$ is relatively close to 1.0, the line approximates the data fairly well.

NOTES

Linear Models

LINEAR MODELS

Table of Correlations

Standard		Concepts	Exercise #1	Exercise #2
Unit3.4	Interpret linear models.			
S-ID.7	*Interpret the slope (rate of change) and the intercept (constant term) of a linear model in the context of the data.*	Meaning of y-intercept and Slope in Graphs of Real Situations	18	24
		Solving Contextual Slope Problems	242	248
		Interpreting a Line of Best Fit	296	303
		Interpreting Rate of Change	326, 327	330, 331
		Interpreting the Effects of Changing the Slope and y-intercept	328	332
S-ID.8	*Compute (using technology) and interpret the correlation coefficient of a linear fit.*	Calculating the Correlation Coefficient for Linear Regression	312	322
		Interpreting the Correlation Coefficient for Linear Regression	313	323
S-ID.9	*Distinguish between correlation and causation.*	Comparing Correlation and Causation	329	333

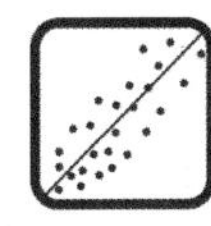

S-ID.7 Interpret the slope (rate of change) and the intercept (constant term) of a linear model in the context of the data.

Interpreting Rate of Change

Rate of change is a comparison between two quantities that have different units. Therefore, when stating a rate of change, units are required. Some common rates of change are speed/velocity (distance versus time), rate of pay (earning versus time), and cost per item (cost versus number of items). Two variables can be related by a constant rate of change (e.g., time and wages).

Tables are useful tools to help analyze data because they present the independent and dependent variables together, side by side. This allows you to see the relationship between the variables. This data is then used to describe trends and make predictions and conclusions based on that data.

To determine if two variables are related by a constant rate of change, follow these steps:

1. Determine the difference in the independent variable.
2. Determine the difference in the dependent variable.
3. Interpret the data and draw conclusions.

Example

Time (h)	Pay ($)
3	24
4	32
5	40
6	48
7	56
8	64

What conclusions can be made from the data in the given table?

Solution

Step 1

Determine the difference in the independent variable.

The independent variable is time.

$4 - 3 = 1$
$5 - 4 = 1$
$6 - 5 = 1$
$7 - 6 = 1$
$8 - 7 = 1$

The difference in the independent variable is 1, which means the time is increasing by 1 hour.

Step 2

Determine the difference in the dependent variable.

The dependent variable is pay.

$32 - 24 = 8$
$40 - 32 = 8$
$48 - 40 = 8$
$56 - 48 = 8$
$64 - 56 = 8$

The difference in the dependent variable is 8, which means the pay increases by $8.00.

Step 3

Interpret the data and draw conclusions.

The trend observed in the table is that the pay is going up by $8.00 per hour, which means that the rate of pay is $8.00 per hour.

If the difference between successive values of the dependent variable increases, then the rate of change increases as well.

Example

Time (h)	Pay ($)
3	36
4	48
5	60
6	72
7	84
8	96

Describe the trend displayed in the given table.

Solution

Step 1
Determine the difference in the independent variable.

The independent variable is time.
4 – 3 = 1
5 – 4 = 1
6 – 5 = 1
7 – 6 = 1
8 – 7 = 1

The difference in the independent variable is 1, which means the time is increasing by 1 hour.

Step 2
Determine the difference in the dependent variable.

The dependent variable is pay.
48 – 36 = 12
60 – 48 = 12
72 – 60 = 12
84 – 72 = 12
96 – 84 = 12

The difference in the dependent variable is 12, which means the pay is increasing by $12.00.

Step 3
Determine the trend.

The trend observed in the given table is that the pay is going up by $12.00, which means the rate of pay is $12.00 per hour.

As you can see, getting paid $12.00per hour is more than getting paid $8.00per hour. So, if the difference between the successive values of the variables increases, that means the rate of change increases as well. If the difference decreases, the rate of change decreases too.

The following relationships about rate of change can be determined using a line graph:

- If the line is rising to the right, this indicates growth. As one variable increases, so does the other.
- If the line is falling to the right, this indicates a decline. As one variable increases, the other decreases.

For example, study the given line graph.

Distance Walked in a Given Time Period

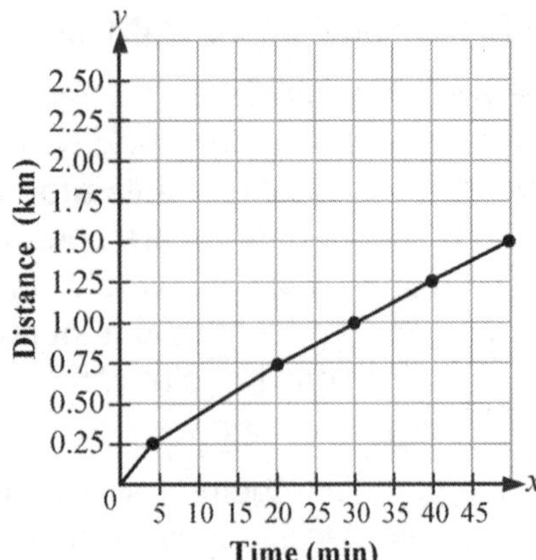

The line on the graph rises to the right.
This indicates that the variables are related—the longer you walk, the farther you will travel.

The steepness of the line also gives some information about the rate of change of the data. The steeper the line is, the more rapidly one variable changes in terms of the other variable. For example, study the given graph.

Height of Four Plants After Several Days of Growth

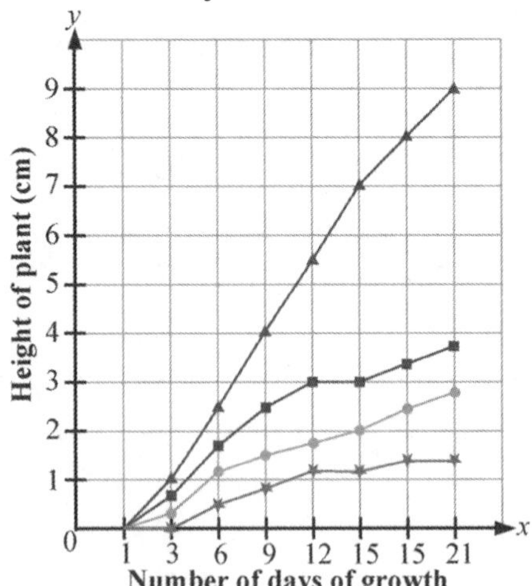

The first plant, represented by the purple line, grows much faster than the fourth plant, represented by the red line. This is because the purple line is a steeper line in that it rises to the right much quicker than any of the other lines.

This can be verified by inspecting the graph. The first plant grew 9 cm in 21 days, whereas the others grew between 1.5 cm to 3.8 cm in that same time.

Example

Don and Brett both go rock climbing and decide to race one another to the top. The given graph displays the results of their race.

Height versus Time in Rock Climbing

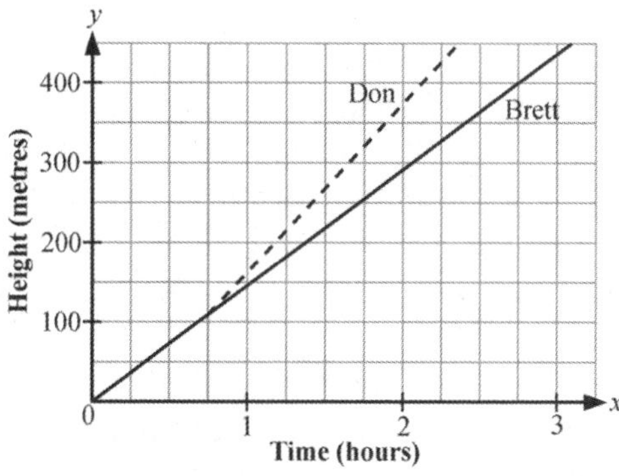

Which of the boys won the race?

Solution

The line that represents Don's progress is steeper than the line that represents Brett's progress. This means that Don climbed to the top in less time than Brett. Don climbed 450 m in a little over 2 h and 15 min, while it took Brett a little over 3 h to climb the same height.

Therefore, Don won the race.

Interpreting the Effects of Changing the Slope and *y*-Intercept

When an equation is in slope y-intercept form, $y = mx + b$, m equals the slope and b equals the y-intercept. If the slope and y-intercept of a line are changed, the line will become steeper or flatter and it will be translated up or down, depending on whether the values of m and b increased or decreased.

Example

Pablo sketched the graph of the line defined by the equation $y = 4x - 12$ on a grid. On the same grid, he would like to sketch the graph of a line that falls from left to right and is steeper than the line defined by the equation $y = 4x - 12$. He also wants the y-intercept of this line to be 15 units more than the y-intercept of the first line. In order for Pablo to sketch the graph of this second line, he must ensure that the value of m is less than P and that the value of b is equal to Q, where P and Q represent real numbers.

What are the numerical values of P and Q?

Solution

The equation $y = 4x - 12$ is written in slope y-intercept form, or $y = mx + b$. Therefore, the slope, m, of the line defined by the equation $y = 4x - 12$ is 4 and the y-intercept, b, is -12.

Step 1

Determine the numerical value of P.

Since the second line needs to fall from left to right, the value of m in the equation $y = mx + b$ must be negative. In order for the second line to be steeper than the first, the absolute value of the slope of the second line must be greater than 4, which is the slope of the first line. The value of m must be less than -4 because the absolute value of any number less than -4 is greater than 4. Therefore, the numerical value of P is -4.

Step 2
Determine the numerical value of Q.

In order for the y-intercept of the second line to be 15 units more than the y-intercept of the first line, the b-value in the defining equation of the second line must be 15 units more than the b-value in the defining equation of the first line, $y = 4x - 12$. The b-value in the equation $y = mx + b$ must equal $-12 + 15 = 3$. Therefore, the numerical value of Q is 3.

Example

The given graph shows a plumber's total labor cost for the installation of a new water tank.

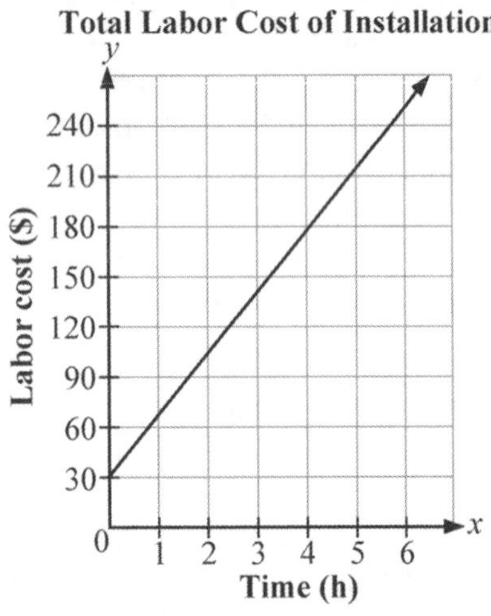

The line of the graph is defined by the equation $C(h) = 30 + 37.50h$.

If the plumber increases his initial labor cost to $45 and his pay rate to $50/h, how will the graph of the plumber's labor cost differ from the given graph?

Solution

Step 1
Determine the equation of the new line.

The plumber increased his initial labor cost to $45 and his pay rate to $50/h, which represents the rate of change.
The equation of the line becomes $C(h) = 45 + 50h$.

Step 2
Sketch the graph of the plumber's total labor cost by using the equation $C(h) = 45 + 50h$.

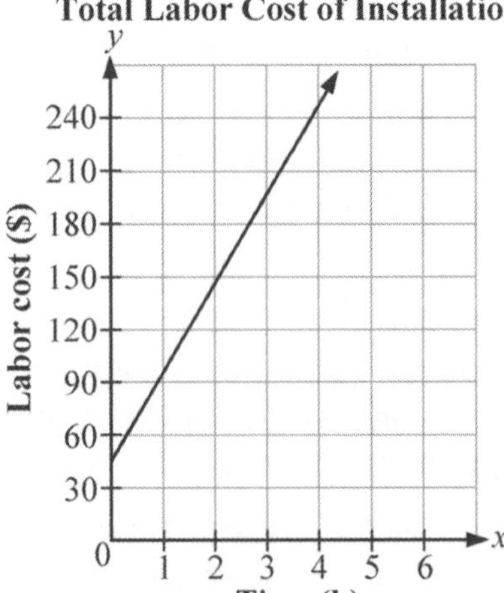

Step 3
Compare the graphs.

The change in the pay rate from $37.50/h to $50/h caused the graph of the second line to be steeper than the line of the first graph.

The first graph has a y-intercept at (0, 30), while the second graph has a y-intercept at (0, 45). The change in the initial labor cost from $30 to $45 caused the graph of the line to be vertically translated upward.

The increases in the initial cost and the pay rate increased the total cost of the installation.

S-ID.9 Distinguish between correlation and causation.

Comparing Correlation and Causation

Correlation between variables does not indicate the direction of causation. If two variables occur together, it does not necessarily mean that either one is causing the other. Two variables can be correlated because they are both caused by a third, unknown variable. For example, there is a high correlation between buckling a seatbelt and a car starting. However, starting a car does not buckle a seatbelt, and buckling a seatbelt does not start a car. If a person is planning on driving somewhere in the near future, this is a cause to both buckle up a seatbelt and start a car.

It can be tempting to assume a causal relationship exists when two events seem to occur together. This is a common fallacy. Causation requires proof that an independent variable has a direct impact on a dependent variable. When two events are correlated, consider what other variables might be at work.

Example

During the last year, there was a large increase in the number of forest fires during the same months as there was a large increase in the number of people water skiing.

Determine if this situation describes a correlation but **not** a causal relationship.

Solution

Neither of these events is a direct cause of the other. Both of these events do occur during summer months. It is most likely that warm weather is a variable that causes an increase in both the number of forest fires and the number of people water skiing. For this reason, the relationship between these two variables is correlative but not causal.

EXERCISE #1—LINEAR MODELS

Use the following information to answer the next question.

The birthrate and death rate of a country are shown in the given graph.

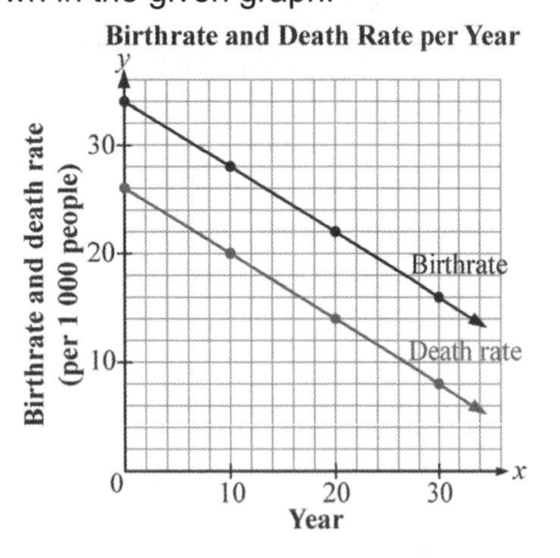

326. Which of the following statements is the **best** conclusion that can be drawn from the graph?

A. The death rate and birthrate have increased at the same rate.

B. The birthrate and death rate have fallen at the same rate.

C. The death rate has fallen more than the birthrate.

D. The birthrate has fallen more than the death rate.

Use the following information to answer the next question.

The given chart tracks how many laps Chelsea ran within a one-hour period.

Time (min)	Laps Run
10	12
20	22
30	30
40	38
50	46
60	54

327. Which of the following conclusions about the rate Chelsea is running can be made from the data?

A. Chelsea ran 1 lap/min.

B. Chelsea ran 1.2 lap/min for the first 10 min and then 1 lap/min afterward.

C. Chelsea ran 1 lap/min for the first 10 min and then 0.8 laps/min afterward.

D. Chelsea ran 1.2 laps/min for the first 10 min, 1 lap/min for the next 10 min, and then 0.8 laps/min afterward.

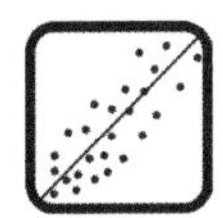

Use the following information to answer the next question.

Dakota works in a clothing store.
She earns $600 per week, plus a commission of 4% of her sales.
Stefan works in a car dealership.
He earns $200 per week, plus a commission of 5% of his sales.
An equation that represents Dakota's earnings, E, in dollars, per week would be $E = 600 + 0.04s$, in which s represents her sales in dollars. A similar equation that represents Stefan's weekly earnings would be $E = 200 + 0.05s$.

328. If the lines that represent the equations $E = 600 + 0.04s$ and $E = 200 + 0.05s$ are both drawn on the same grid, then the line that represents Dakota's earnings would be

A. not as steep and would have an E-intercept that is 400 more than the line that represents Stefan's earnings

B. not as steep and would have an E-intercept that is 400 less than the line that represents Stefan's earnings

C. steeper and would have an E-intercept that is 400 more than the line that represents Stefan's earnings

D. steeper and would have an E-intercept that is 400 less than the line that represents Stefan's earnings

Use the following information to answer the next question.

Data was collected with respect to the IQs of a group of students and the number of days of school these students missed in a particular school term. A scatter plot of the collected data is shown.

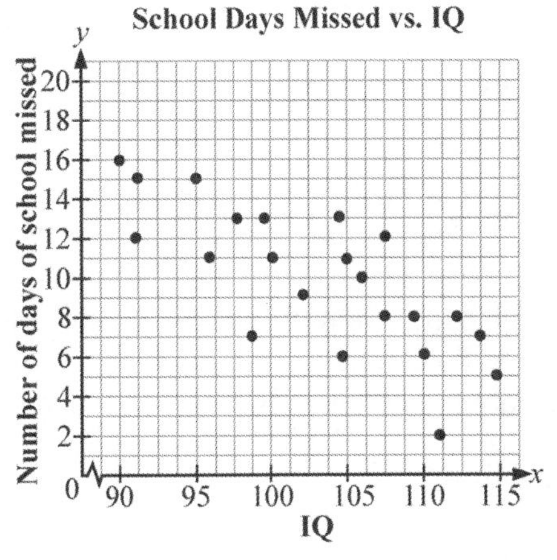

329. With regard to the relationship between IQ and the number of days of school a student missed in a particular school term, there is a

A. positive correlation and a causal relationship

B. negative correlation and a causal relationship

C. positive correlation and a non-causal relationship

D. negative correlation and a non-causal relationship

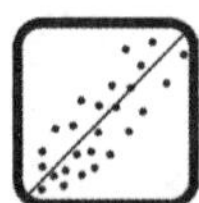

EXERCISE #1—LINEAR MODELS ANSWERS AND SOLUTIONS

326. B	327. D	328. A	329. D

326. B

The independent variable is time. The dependent variables are the birthrate and death rate.

Step 1
Determine the differences between the values of the independent variable.

$10 - 0 = 10$
$20 - 10 = 10$
$30 - 20 = 10$
$40 - 30 = 10$

Step 2
Determine the differences between the values of the dependent variables.

Calculate the differences between the values of the birthrate.

$34 - 28 = 6$
$28 - 22 = 6$
$22 - 16 = 6$

Calculate the differences between the values of the death rate.

$26 - 20 = 6$
$20 - 14 = 6$
$14 - 8 = 6$

Step 3
Interpret the data, and draw conclusions.

The birthrate remained higher than the death rate for the entire period. Calculating each rate shows that the birthrate and death rate both fell by 6 per 1,000 people per decade.

The trend is that even though the birthrate is always higher than the death rate, they are both falling at the same rate.

327. D

The independent variable is time. The dependent variable is the number of laps run.

Step 1
Determine the difference between the values of the independent variable.

$10 - 0 = 10$
$20 - 10 = 10$
$30 - 20 = 10$
$40 - 30 = 10$
$50 - 40 = 10$
$60 - 50 = 10$

Time is being measured in intervals of 10 minutes.

Step 2
Determine the difference between the values of the dependent variable.

$12 - 0 = 12$
$22 - 12 = 10$
$30 - 22 = 8$
$38 - 30 = 8$
$46 - 38 = 8$
$54 - 46 = 8$

Step 3
Interpret the data and draw conclusions.

For the first 10 minutes, Chelsea ran 12 laps.

This is a rate of $\frac{12 \text{ laps}}{10 \text{ min}} = \frac{1.2 \text{ laps}}{\text{min}}$.

For the second 10 minutes, Chelsea ran 10 laps.

This is a rate of $\frac{10 \text{ laps}}{10 \text{ min}} = \frac{1 \text{ lap}}{\text{min}}$.

For each of the next four sets of 10-minute intervals, Chelsea ran 8 laps each time.

This is a rate of $\frac{8 \text{ laps}}{10 \text{ min}} = \frac{0.8 \text{ laps}}{\text{min}}$.

328. A

The equations $E = 600 + 0.04s$ and $E = 200 + 0.05s$ are both in slope-intercept form, $y = mx + b$. Therefore, the slope and E-intercept of the line defined by the equation $E = 600 + 0.04s$ are 0.04 and 600, respectively. Also, the slope and E-intercept of the line defined by the equation $E = 200 + 0.05s$ are 0.05 and 200, respectively.

It then follows that the line that represents Dakota's earnings would not be as steep ($0.04 < 0.05$) and would have an E-intercept that is $600 - 200 = 400$ more than the E-intercept of the line that represents Stefan's earnings.

329. D

Since the data points in the given scatter plot primarily fall from left to right, and most of the data points would be reasonably close to a line of best fit if one were drawn, it appears that there is a negative correlation between IQ and the number of days of school a student missed during this particular school term.

However, a student's IQ does not necessarily directly affect the number of days of school the student missed. A student's health is not based on the student's IQ. A variety of other reasons for missing school, such as socioeconomic background, injuries, or sports tournaments, could affect a student's attendance at school. Therefore, the relationship between a student's IQ and the number of days of school missed during a particular school term is a non-causal relationship.

EXERCISE #2—LINEAR MODELS

Use the following information to answer the next question.

The given graph shows the distance that Dave rowed over a certain period of time.

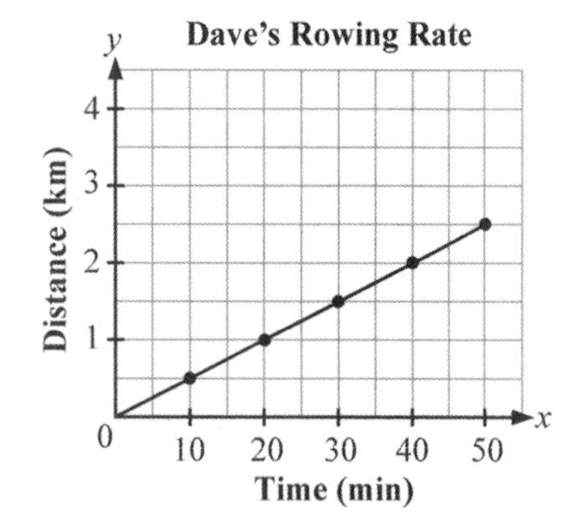

330. Over the period of time shown in the graph, Dave's rowing speed
   A. increased
   B. decreased
   C. remained constant
   D. increased and decreased

Use the following information to answer the next question.

The given table shows the distance that a car traveled over several hours.

Time (h)	Distance (km)
1	80
2	160
3	240
4	320
5	400

331. According to the data in the table, the speed of the car
   A. steadily increased
   B. remained constant
   C. decreased after the third hour
   D. decreased after the fourth hour

Use the following information to answer the next question.

The total cost of printing advertising brochures consists of a fixed cost and a variable cost, the number of brochures printed. For a particular advertising brochure, the total cost in dollars, T, is given by the equation $T = 40 + 0.10n$, where n is the number of brochures printed.

The partial graph that represents the equation $T = 40 + 0.10n$ is shown.

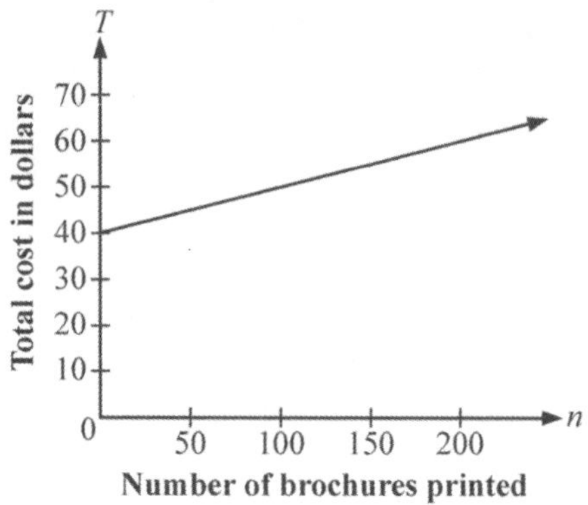

Upon further consultation, the total cost of printing the advertising brochure was revised. The fixed cost was raised to $60, and the variable cost was lowered to $0.08 per brochure.

332. Compared with the line shown, the line defined by the equation that represents the revised total cost would be
   A. steeper and have the same T-intercept
   B. steeper and have a different T-intercept
   C. less steep and have the same T-intercept
   D. less steep and have a different T-intercept

Use the following information to answer the next question.

At the end of the season, a basketball coach plotted the jersey numbers of his players and the average numbers of points the players scored per game. The graph is as shown.

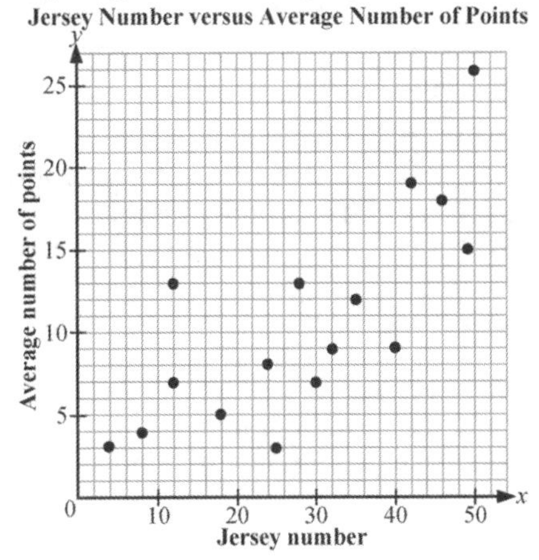

333. With regard to the relationship between a player's jersey number and the average number of points scored per game by that player, there is a

A. positive correlation and a causal relationship

B. negative correlation and a causal relationship

C. positive correlation and a non-causal relationship

D. negative correlation and a non-causal relationship

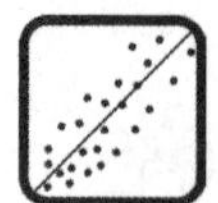

EXERCISE #2—LINEAR MODELS ANSWERS AND SOLUTIONS

330. C	331. B	332. D	333. C

330. C

The independent variable is time. The dependent variable is the distance rowed.

Step 1
Determine the difference between the values of the independent variable.
10 – 0 = 10
20 – 10 = 10
30 – 20 = 10
40 – 30 = 10
50 – 40 = 10

Step 2
Determine the difference between the values of dependent variable.
0.5 – 0 = 0.5
1 – 0.5 = 0.5
1.5 – 1 = 0.5
2 – 1.5 = 0.5
2.5 – 2 = 0.5

Step 3
Interpret the data, and draw conclusions.

Every 10 min that Dave rowed, he traveled 0.5 km. This rate remained constant for the entire 50 min that he rowed.

331. B

The independent variable is time. The dependent variable is distance.

Step 1
Determine the difference between the values of the independent variable.
2 – 1 = 1
3 – 2 = 1
4 – 3 = 1
5 – 4 = 1

The time interval measured in the table is every 1 h.

Step 2
Determine the difference between the values of the dependent variable.
160 – 80 = 80
240 – 160 = 80
320 – 240 = 80
400 – 320 = 80

During every time interval, the car traveled 80 km.

Step 3
Interpret the data, and draw conclusions.

The speed was 80 km/h for each of the five hours tracked. Therefore, the speed remained constant.

332. D

The equation $T = 40 + 0.10n$ is in slope-intercept form, $y = mx + b$. Thus, the slope of the line defined by the equation $T = 40 + 0.10n$ is 0.10 and the T-intercept is 40.

If the fixed cost is raised to \$60 and the variable cost is lowered to \$0.08, then the defining equation of the total cost to print the brochures becomes $T = 60 + 0.08n$. The slope of the line defined by the equation $T = 60 + 0.08n$ is 0.08, and the T-intercept is 60.

It follows that if the line defined by the equation that represents the revised total cost, $T = 60 + 0.08n$, is drawn on the same grid as the line shown, then this line would have a different T-intercept $(40 \neq 60)$ and would not be as steep $(0.08 < 0.10)$ as the line shown.

333. C

Since the data points in the given scatter plot rise from left to right, there is a positive correlation between a player's jersey number and the average number of points scored per game by that player. However, neither of these statistics is a direct cause of the other. The jersey number of a player has no direct impact on how many points the player scores per game. Therefore, the relationship between the jersey number and the average number of points scored per game is correlative but not causal.

The Structure of Expressions

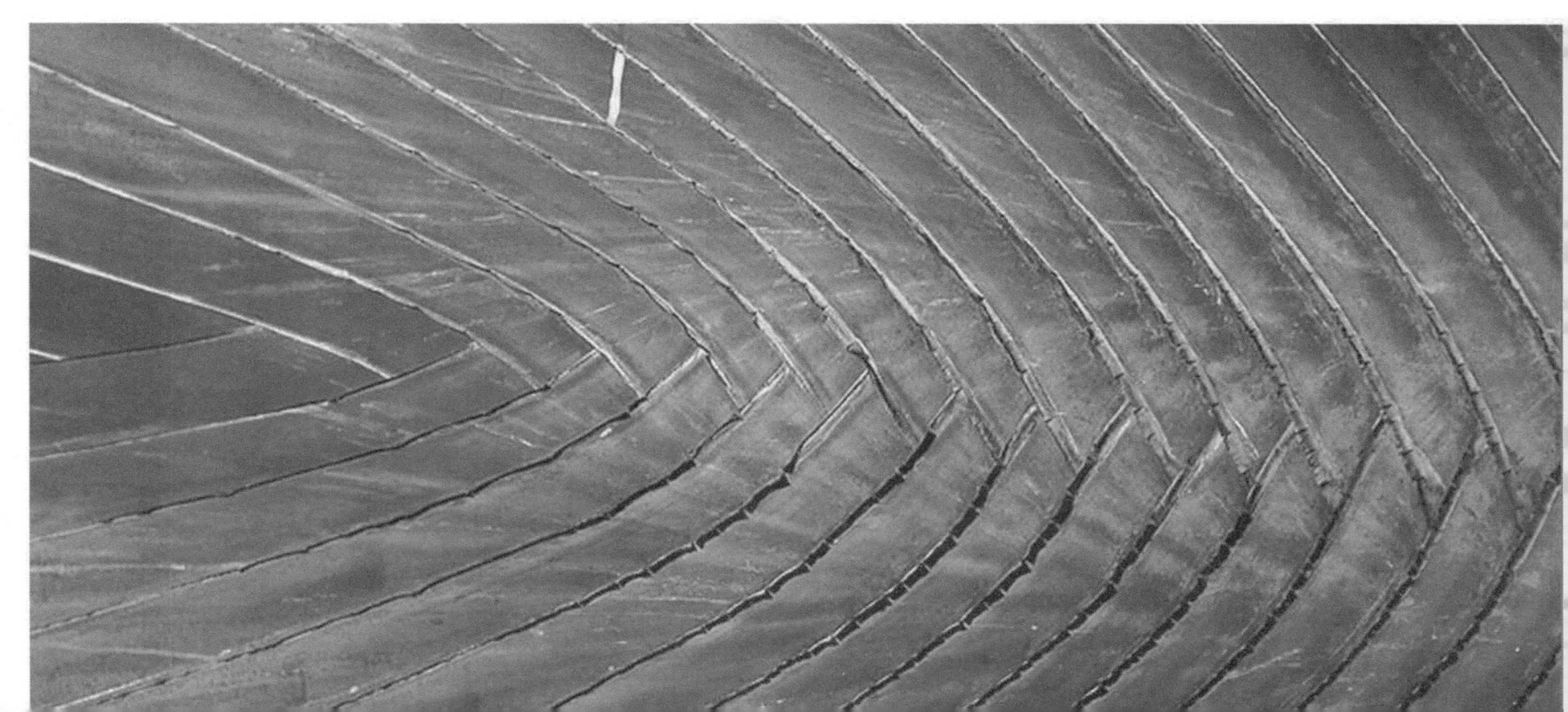

THE STRUCTURE OF EXPRESSIONS

Table of Correlations

Standard		Concepts	Exercise #1	Exercise #2
Unit4.1	Interpret the structure of expressions.			
A-SSE.2	*Use the structure of an expression to identify ways to rewrite it.*	Factoring Trinomials of the Form $x^2 + bx + c$	23	29
		Factoring Polynomials Using Common Factors	337, 341	343, 350
		Factoring Perfect Square Trinomials	334	344
		Factor a Sum of Cubes of the Form $a^3 + b^3$	335	345
		Factor a Difference of Cubes of the Form $a^3 - b^3$	336	346
		Factor Polynomials Using a Variety of Factoring Techniques	336, 337	349
		Factor a Difference of Squares of the Form $a^2 - b^2$, Where a and b Are Monomials of Degree 0 or 1	338	347
		Factor a Difference of Squares of the form $A^2 - B^2$, where A and B are Polynomials	339	348
		Factoring Trinomials of the Form $ax^2 + bx + c$ Using the Decomposition Method	337, 340	349
		Factoring by Grouping	341	350
		Factoring an Expression in the Form $a(f(x))^2 + b(f(x)) + c$, Where $a \neq 0$	342	351

x^2

A-SSE.2 Use the structure of an expression to identify ways to rewrite it.

Factoring Polynomials Using Common Factors

Polynomials are expressions containing three or more terms.

Factoring is the inverse operation of multiplying, in that the factors of the polynomial are identified through the process of division. Factors are two numbers (or in this case, expressions) that when multiplied result in the original polynomial. When factoring polynomials, first look for a greatest common factor (GCF).

When factoring out the GCF, look at the numbers and variables that are common in each term of the polynomial expression. Once the greatest common factor has been identified, divide it out of each term in the polynomial.

Example

Take, for example, the binomial, $6x^2 + 8x$. In order to determine its factors, first determine the greatest common factor (GCF) of each term.

- For the term $6x^2$, the factors are 1, 2, 3, 6, x, and x
- For the term $8x$, the factors are 1, 2, 4, 8, and x

Take the greatest number common to both coefficients and the greatest number of x's common to both terms.

The GCF of $6x^2$ and $8x$ is $2x$.

Factor $2x$ out of each term. Divide each term by the GCF, which in this case is $2x$.

$= 6x^2 + 8x$
$= (2x)(3x + 4)$

The factors of $6x^2 + 8x$ are $2x$ and $3x + 4$. When these terms are multiplied, the result will be the original binomial. They are written as a product.

Removing a common factor also applies to polynomial expressions that contain two variables. The same procedure is used as for polynomial expressions that contain one variable.

Follow these steps when removing a common factor from a polynomial expression:

1. Identify the GCF.
2. Divide each term by the GCF.
3. Multiply the GCF (the factor of the original polynomial) by the quotient (the answer to the division question).

Example

Factor $21x^2y - 14xy^2$.

Solution

Step 1

Determine the greatest common factor (GCF) of each term.

- $21x^2y$: 1, 3, 7, 21, x, x, and y.
- $14xy^2$: 1, 2, 7, 14, x, y, and y.

Take the greatest number common to both coefficients and the greatest number of variables common to both terms.

The GCF is $7xy$.

Step 2

Divide each term by the GCF.

$= \frac{21x^2y}{7xy} - \frac{14xy^2}{7xy}$
$= 3x - 2y$

Step 3

Multiply the GCF (the factor of the original polynomial) by the quotient (the answer to a division question).

$7xy(3x - 2y)$

Apply the same method when factoring a trinomial.

Example

Factor $21x^2y - 14xy^2 + 28x^3y^3$.

Solution

Step 1

Determine the GCF of each term.

$21x^2y$: 1, 3, 7, 21, x, x, and y.

$14xy^2$: 1, 2, 7, 14, x, y, and y.

$28x^3y^3$: 1, 2, 4, 7, 14, 28, x, x, x, y, y, and y.

The GCF is $7xy$

Step 2

Divide each term by the GCF.

$$\frac{21x^2y}{7xy} - \frac{14xy^2}{7xy} + \frac{28x^3y^3}{7xy}$$
$$= 3x - 2y + 4x^2y^2$$

Step 3

Multiply the GCF (the factor of the original polynomial) by the quotient (the answer to the division question).

$$= 21x^2y - 14xy^2 + 28x^3y^3$$
$$= 7xy(3x - 2y + 4x^2y^2)$$

Factoring a polynomial can also be done by regrouping, or rewriting, the polynomial so that it has an even number of terms. This way, a factor common to two terms in a group can be determined, and a binomial is formed. The factored form of the polynomial is then expressed as a product of two binomials.

To factor a polynomial by grouping, follow these steps:

1. Regroup the polynomial into smaller groups that contain a common factor.
2. Remove the GCF from each group.
3. Factor out the common binomial. The remainders form the second binomial.

Example

Factor the expression $x^2 + 2x + x + 2$ using grouping.

Solution

Step 1

Regroup the terms.

$(x^2 + x) + (2x + 2)$

Step 2

Remove the GCF from each group.

The GCF of $x^2 + x$ is x.

The GCF of $2x + 2$ is 2.

$x(x + 1) + 2(x + 1)$

Step 3

Factor out the common binomial.

The remaining terms form the second binomial.

$(x + 1)(x + 2)$

The factored form of $x^2 + 2x + x + 2$ is $(x + 1)(x + 2)$.

FACTORING PERFECT SQUARE TRINOMIALS

A perfect square trinomial can be expressed in the forms $a^2 + 2ab + b^2$ or $a^2 - 2ab + b^2$, where a and b are monomials.

The factored form of $a^2 + 2ab + b^2$ is the binomial $(a + b)$ squared:

$a^2 + 2ab + b^2 = (a + b)^2$

The factored form of $a^2 - 2ab + b^2$ is the binomial $(a - b)$ squared:

$a^2 - 2ab + b^2 = (a - b)^2$

Example

Factor the trinomial $9x^2 + 24x + 16$.

Solution

Step 1

The trinomial $9x^2 + 24x + 16$ is in the form $a^2 + 2ab + b^2$, so it is a perfect square trinomial. Therefore, determine a and b.

$a^2 = 9x^2$

$a = 3x$

$b^2 = 16$

$b = 4$

x^2

Step 2
Factor the trinomial.

The factored form of a perfect square trinomial is the binomial $(a+b)$ squared.

$a^2+2ab+b^2$
$=(a+b)^2$

$9x^2+24x+16$
$=(3x+4)^2$

The trinomial $9x^2+24x+16$ factors to $(3x+4)(3x+4)$, or $(3x+4)^2$.

If there is a greatest common factor in a trinomial, it should be factored out before applying other factoring strategies.

Example

Factor $8x^2-40x+50$.

Solution

Step 1
Since 2 is common to all terms in the trinomial, factor it from the trinomial.

$8x^2-40x+50=2(4x^2-20x+25)$.

Step 2
The factor $4x^2-20x+25$ is a trinomial in the form $a^2-2ab+b^2$, so it is a perfect square trinomial. Therefore, determine a and b.

$a^2=4x^2$
$a=2x$
$b^2=25$
$b=5$

Step 3
Factor the trinomial.

The factored form of a perfect square trinomial is the binomial $(a-b)$ squared.

$a^2-2ab+b^2$
$=(a-b)^2$

$2(4x^2-20x+25)$
$=2(2x-5)^2$

The trinomial $8x^2-40x+50$ factors to $2(2x-5)(2x-5)$, or $2(2x-5)^2$.

Factor a Sum of Cubes of the Form a^3+b^3

Recognition of perfect cube terms is the first step in factoring a sum of cubes.

A perfect cube is a term with exactly three identical factors.

Factoring a sum of cubes requires that the values $a=\sqrt[3]{a^3}$ and $b=\sqrt[3]{b^3}$ be determined and then substituted into the following formula:

$a^3+b^3=(a+b)(a^2-ab+b^2)$

Example

Factor the expression x^3+27.

Solution

Identify the given expression as a sum of cubes.

Both x^3 and 27 are perfect cubes with exactly three identical factors each.

$a^3=x^3$
$a=\sqrt[3]{x^3}$
$a=x$
$b^3=27$
$b=\sqrt[3]{27}$
$b=3$

Substitute the values of a and b into $a^3+b^3=(a+b)(a^2-ab+b^2)$.

$x^3+3^3=(x+3)(x^2-x(3)+(3)^2)$
$x^3+27=(x+3)(x^2-3x+9)$

Example

Factor the expression $64x^6 + 125y^3$.

Solution

Identify the given expression as a sum of cubes.

Both $64x^6$ and $125y^3$ are perfect cubes with exactly three identical factors each.

$a^3 = 64x^6$
$a = \sqrt[3]{64x^6}$
$a = 4x^2$
$b^3 = 125y^3$
$b = \sqrt[3]{125y^3}$
$b = 5y$

Substitute the values of a and b into $a^3 + b^3 = (a+b)(a^2 - ab + b^2)$.

$(4x^2)^3 + (5y)^3$
$= (4x^2 + 5y)((4x^2)^2 - 4x^2(5y) + (5y)^2)$
$64x^6 + 125y^3$
$= (4x^2 + 5y)(16x^4 - 20x^2y + 25y^2)$

Factor a Difference of Cubes of the Form $a^3 - b^3$

Identifying perfect cube terms is the first step in factoring a difference of cubes.

A perfect cube is a term with exactly three identical factors.

Factoring a difference of cubes requires that the values $a = \sqrt[3]{a^3}$ and $b = \sqrt[3]{b^3}$ be determined and then substituted into the following formula:
$a^3 - b^3 = (a-b)(a^2 + ab + b^2)$

Example

Factor the expression $8x^3 - y^3$.

Solution

Identify the given expression as a difference of cubes.

Both $8x^3$ and y^3 are perfect cubes with exactly three identical factors each.

$a^3 = 8x^3$
$a = \sqrt[3]{8x^3}$
$a = 2x$
$b^3 = y^3$
$b = \sqrt[3]{y^3}$
$b = y$

Substitute the values of a and b into $a^3 - b^3 = (a-b)(a^2 + ab + b^2)$.

$((2x)^3 - (y)^3) = (2x - y)((2x)^2 + (2x)(y) + (y)^2)$
$8x^3 - y^3 = (2x - y)(4x^2 + 2xy + y^2)$

Factor Polynomials Using a Variety of Factoring Techniques

Once a variety of factoring techniques have been learned, they can be used together to fully factor polynomial expressions requiring the use of more than one technique.

Most commonly, the identification of a greatest common factor (GCF) is the first step to fully factoring a polynomial.

Following the removal of the GCF, a number of factoring techniques may be required such as:

- Difference of Squares
- Grouping
- Decomposition
- Sum of Cubes
- Difference of Cubes

x^2

Example

Factor $6ax^2 - 24a$ completely.

Solution

Factor out the greatest common factor, $6a$.

$6ax^2 - 24a = 6a(x^2 - 4)$

Factor $x^2 - 4$ as a difference of squares.

$$\begin{aligned}6ax^2 - 24a &= 6a(x^2 - 4)\\ &= 6a(x^2 - 2^2)\\ &= 6a(x + 2)(x - 2)\end{aligned}$$

Example

Factor $9a^2 + 39a - 30$ completely.

Solution

Factor out the greatest common factor, 3.

$9a^2 + 39a - 30 = 3(3a^2 + 13a - 10)$

Factor the trinomial.

To factor the trinomial $3a^2 + 13a - 10$ using the decomposition method, find two numbers with a product of $3 \times (-10) = -30$ and a sum of $+13$.

The numbers are $+15$ and -2.

$$\begin{aligned}&9a^2 + 39a - 30\\ &= 3(3a^2 + 13a - 10)\\ &= 3(3a^2 + 15a - 2a - 10)\\ &= 3(3a(a + 5) - 2(a + 5))\\ &= 3(3a - 2)(a + 5)\end{aligned}$$

As with all factoring, the factored form can be verified by multiplying the factors to get the original polynomial.

$$\begin{aligned}&3(3a - 2)(a + 5)\\ &= 3(3a^2 + 15a - 2a - 10)\\ &= 3(3a^2 + 13a - 10)\\ &= 9a^2 + 39a - 30\end{aligned}$$

Factor a Difference of Squares of the Form $a^2 - b^2$, Where a and b Are Monomials of Degree 0 or 1

A polynomial expression in the form of $a^2 - b^2$ is called a **difference of squares**.

A difference of squares consists of a binomial in which a squared term is subtracted from another squared term. Factoring a difference-of-squares expression results in the product of two conjugates: $a^2 - b^2 = (a - b)(a + b)$

For example, to factor $x^2 - 1$, apply the formula $a^2 - b^2 = (a + b)(a - b)$.

$x^2 - 1 = (x + 1)(x - 1)$

Example

Factor the expression $x^2 - 64$.

Solution

The expression is a difference of squares, since it can be written as $x^2 - 8^2$. Apply the formula $a^2 - b^2 = (a + b)(a - b)$.

$x^2 - 8^2 = (x + 8)(x - 8)$

Therefore, the factored form of $x^2 - 64$ is $(x + 8)(x - 8)$.

Example

Factor the expression $4x^2 - 1$.

Solution

Step 1

Set up a product of two binomials as shown, one with an addition operation and one with a subtraction operation. The order of the binomials does not matter.

(_______ + _______)(_______ − _______)

Step 2

Determine the square root of the first term in the difference-of-squares expression, and use the root as the first term in each of the bracketed binomials.

$\sqrt{4x^2} = 2x \rightarrow (2x +$ _______$)(2x -$ _______$)$

Step 3
Calculate the square root of the second term in the difference-of-squares expression, and use the root as the second term in each of the bracketed binomials.
$\sqrt{1} = 1 \rightarrow \ (2x + 1)(2x - 1)$

The expression $4x^2 - 1$ can be factored as $(2x + 1)(2x - 1)$.

Example

Factor the difference of squares $16x^2 - 25y^2$.

Solution

Step 1
Set up a product of two binomials as shown, one with an addition operation and one with a subtraction operation. The order of the binomials does not matter.
(________+ ________)(________– ________)

Step 2
Determine the square root of the first term in the difference-of-squares expression, and use the root as the first term in each of the bracketed binomials.
$\sqrt{16x^2} = 4x \rightarrow = (4x +$ _______$)(4x -$ _______$)$

Step 3
Determine the square root of the second term in the difference-of-squares expression, and use the root as the second term in each of the bracketed binomials.
$\sqrt{25y^2} = 5y \rightarrow = (4x + 5y)(4x - 5y)$
Therefore, the factored form of the difference of squares $16x^2 - 25y^2$ is $(4x + 5y)(4x - 5y)$.

Factor a Difference of Squares of the Form $A^2 - B^2$, Where A and B Are Polynomials

A polynomial expression in the form of $a^2 - b^2$ is called a **difference of squares**.

A difference of squares consists of a binomial in which a squared term (or polynomial) is subtracted from another squared term (or polynomial).

Factoring a difference-of-squares expression results in the product of two conjugates:
$a^2 - b^2 = (a - b)(a + b)$

In general, the steps to factoring a difference-of-squares expression, $a^2 - b^2$, are as follows:

1. Set up a product of two binomials as shown, one with an addition operation and one with a subtraction operation. The order of the binomials does not matter.
   $(\square + \square)(\square - \square)$
2. Determine the square root of the first term (or polynomial) in the difference-of-squares expression, and use the result as the first term (or polynomial) in each of the bracketed binomials.
   $\sqrt{a^2} = a \rightarrow (a + \square)(a - \square)$
3. Determine the square root of the second term (or polynomial) in the difference-of-squares expression, and use the result as the second term (or polynomial) in each of the bracketed binomials.
   $\sqrt{b^2} = b \rightarrow (a + b)(a - b)$

The formula $a^2 - b^2 = (a + b)(a - b)$, in which a and b may represent variables, constants, or polynomials, can be applied to factor a difference-of-squares expression of any form.

Example

Fully factor $81x^2 - (yz - t)^2$.

Solution

To correctly factor the given expression, it must first be recognized as a difference of squares.

Step 1
Set up a product, one with an addition operation and one with a subtraction operation.
$(\square + \square)(\square - \square)$

Step 2
Determine the square root of the first polynomial in the difference-of-squares expression, and use the result as the first polynomial in each of the bracketed expressions.
$\sqrt{81^2} = 9x \rightarrow (9x + \square)(9x - \square)$

x^2

Step 3
Determine the square root of the second polynomial in the difference-of-squares expression, and use the result as the second polynomial in each of the bracketed expressions.

$\sqrt{(yz - t)^2}$
$= yz - t \rightarrow (9x + (yz - t))(9x - (yz - t))$

Distribute the addition and subtraction operations.

$(9x + yz - t)(9x - yz + t)$

FACTORING TRINOMIALS OF THE FORM $ax^2 + bx + c$ USING THE DECOMPOSITION METHOD

It is possible to factor many trinomials of the form $ax^2 + bx + c$ by using the inverse procedure of multiplication, i.e., the decomposition method.

This method will work for factoring all factorable trinomials in the form $ax^2 + bx + c$ into the product of two binomials.

Consider the product of two binomials, $(2x + 3)(x - 2)$.
Using the FOIL procedure, the result is:

$$\begin{aligned}(2x + 3)(x - 2) &= 2x^2 - 4x + 3x - 6 \\ &= 2x^2 - x - 6\end{aligned}$$

The inverse procedure would be as follows:

$$\begin{aligned}2x^2 - x - 6 &= 2x^2 - 4x + 3x - 6 \\ &= 2x(x - 2) + 3(x - 2) \\ &= (2x + 3)(x - 2)\end{aligned}$$

For the expression $2x^2 - x - 6$, observe that the product of the coefficient of the x^2-term and the constant term is $2 \times (-6) = -12$. Also, observe that the middle term, $-x$, is decomposed into $-4x + 3x$, and the product of these coefficients is also $-12(-4 \times 3 = -12)$.

Thus, the middle term is decomposed into two terms with coefficients whose product is equal to the product of the coefficient of the x^2-term and the constant term, and with a sum equal to the coefficient of the middle term.

Example

Factor $3x^2 + 10x - 8$ using the decomposition method. Verify the answer using multiplication.

Solution

In $3x^2 + 10x - 8$, the product of the coefficient of x^2 and the constant term is $3 \times (-8) = -24$. The middle term has a coefficient of $+10$. Find two integers that have a product of -24 and a sum of $+10$.

The pairs of integers with a product of -24, along with their respective sums, are as shown:

Product	Sum
$1 \times (-24) = -24$	$1 + (-24) = -23$
$2 \times (-12) = -24$	$2 + (-12) = -10$
$3 \times (-8) = -24$	$3 + (-8) = -5$
$4 \times (-6) = -24$	$4 + (-6) = -2$
$-1 \times 24 = -24$	$-1 + 24 = +23$
$-2 \times 12 = -24$	$-2 + 12 = +10$
$-3 \times 8 = -24$	$-3 + 8 = +5$
$-4 \times 6 = -24$	$-4 + 6 = +2$

The integers required are -2 and $+12$.

Express $10x$ as $-2x + 12x$, and then factor by grouping for a common factor as follows:

$$\begin{aligned}3x^2 + 10x - 8 &= 3x^2 - 2x + 12x - 8 \\ &= x(3x - 2) + 4(3x - 2) \\ &= (x + 4)(3x - 2)\end{aligned}$$

Verify by multiplying the factors (using the FOIL procedure).

$$\begin{aligned}(x + 4)(3x - 2) &= 3x^2 - 2x + 12x - 8 \\ &= 3x^2 + 10x - 8\end{aligned}$$

With practice, efficiency at finding the pair of numbers to use for splitting the middle term, without writing all the products and sums, will improve.

Example

Factor $6x^2 - 11x + 3$ using the decomposition method. Verify the answer using multiplication.

Solution

In $6x^2 - 11x + 3$, the product of the coefficient of x^2 and the constant term is $6 \times 3 = 18$. The middle term has a coefficient of -11. Find two integers that have a product of 18 and sum of -11.

The pairs of integers with a product of 18, along with their respective sums, are as shown.

Product	Sum
$1 \times 18 = 18$	$1 + 18 = 19$
$2 \times 9 = 18$	$2 + 9 = 11$
$3 \times 6 = 18$	$3 + 6 = 9$
$(-1) \times (-18) = 18$	$(-1) + (-18) = -19$
$(-2) + (-9) = -11$	$(-2) \times (-9) = 18$
$(-3) \times (-6) = 18$	$(-3) + (-6) = -9$

Thus, the two integers that are required are -2 and -9.

Express $-11x$ as $-2x - 9x$, and then factor by grouping for a common factor as follows:

$$\begin{aligned}6x^2 - 11x + 3 &= 6x^2 - 2x - 9x + 3\\ &= 2x(3x - 1) - 3(3x - 1)\\ &= (3x - 1)(2x - 3)\end{aligned}$$

Verify by multiplying the factors (using the FOIL procedure).

$$\begin{aligned}(3x - 1)(2x - 3) &= 6x^2 - 9x - 2x + 3\\ &= 6x^2 - 11x + 3\end{aligned}$$

Try This!

Factor $10x^2 + 19x + 6$ using the decomposition method. Verify the answer using multiplication.

Solution

In $10x^2 + 19x + 6$, the product of the coefficient of x^2 and the constant term is $10 \times 6 = 60$. The middle term has a coefficient of 19. Find two integers that have a product of 60 and sum of 19.

The pairs of integers with a product of 60, along with their respective sums, are as shown.

Product	Sum
$1 \times 60 = 60$	$1 + 60 = 61$
$2 \times 30 = 60$	$2 + 30 = 32$
$3 \times 20 = 60$	$3 + 20 = 23$
$4 \times 15 = 60$	$4 + 15 = 19$
$5 \times 12 = 60$	$5 + 12 = 17$
$6 \times 10 = 60$	$6 + 10 = 16$
$(-1) \times (-60) = 60$	$(-1) + (-60) = -61$
$(-2) \times (-30) = 60$	$(-2) + (-30) = -32$
$(-3) \times (-20) = 60$	$(-3) + (-20) = -23$
$(-4) \times (-15) = 60$	$(-4) + (-15) = -19$
$(-5) \times (-12) = 60$	$(-5) + (-12) = -17$
$(-6) \times (-10) = 60$	$(-6) + (-10) = -16$

Thus, the required integers are 4 and 15.

Express $19x$ as $4x + 15x$, and then factor by grouping for a common factor as follows:

$$\begin{aligned}10x^2 + 19x + 6 &= 10x^2 + 4x + 15x + 6\\ &= 2x(5x + 2) + 3(5x + 2)\\ &= (5x + 2)(2x + 3)\end{aligned}$$

Verify by multiplying the factors (using the FOIL procedure).

$$\begin{aligned}(5x + 2)(2x + 3) &= 10x^2 + 15x + 4x + 6\\ &= 10x^2 + 19x + 6\end{aligned}$$

---

x^2

Not all trinomials are factorable. Those that are not factorable are **prime polynomials**. The product and sum values from the method of decomposition can be used to determine whether a trinomial is prime.

For example, $2x^2 + x + 5$ is prime because there are no two integers that have a product of 10 and a sum of 1. For some trinomials it is necessary to calculate the product and possible sums in order to verify that the trinomial is prime.

Example

Factor $2x^2 - 3x - 6$ if possible.

If $2x^2 - 3x - 6$ is not factorable, show why the decomposition method does not work.

Solution

In $2x^2 - 3x - 6$ the product of the coefficient of x^2 and the constant term is $2 \times (-6) = -12$.
The middle term has a coefficient of -3.
If possible, find two integers that have a product of -12 and sum of -3.

The pairs of integers with a product of -12, along with their respective sums, are as shown.

Product	Sum
$1 \times (-12) = -12$	$1 + (-12) = -11$
$2 \times (-6) = -12$	$2 + (-6) = -4$
$3 \times (-4) = -12$	$3 + (-4) = -1$
$-1 \times 12 = -12$	$-1 + 12 = +11$
$-2 \times 6 = -12$	$-2 + 6 = +4$
$-3 \times 4 = -12$	$-3 + 4 = +1$

Since there are no two integers that have a product of -12 and sum of -3, $2x^2 - 3x - 6$ cannot be factored, and it is prime.

Try This!

Factor $3x^2 + 5x - 9$ if possible. If $3x^2 + 5x - 9$ is not factorable, show why the decomposition method does not work.

Solution

In $3x^2 + 5x - 9$, the product of the coefficient of x^2 and the constant term is $3 \times (-9) = -27$.

The middle term has a coefficient of 5. Find two integers, if possible, that have a product of -27 and a sum of 5.

The pairs of integers with a product of -27, along with their respective sums, are as shown.

Product	Sum
$1 \times (-27) = -27$	$1 + (-27) = -26$
$3 \times (-9) = -27$	$3 + (-9) = -6$
$-1 \times 27 = -27$	$-1 + 27 = 26$
$-3 \times 9 = -27$	$-3 + 9 = 6$

Since there are no two integers that have a product of -27 and a sum of 5, $3x^2 + 5x - 9$ cannot be factored, and it is prime.

Factoring by Grouping

Factoring by grouping involves rewriting a polynomial with an even number of terms into smaller groups. Most often, the polynomial is rewritten with groups of two terms. The pairing of the terms in the groups is chosen so that when the common factor in each group is removed, the resulting binomials are the same for all groups.

To use this method, remove the greatest common factor (GCF) from each group, and then factor out the common binomial.

Example

Factor the expression $x^2 + 2x + x + 2$.

Solution

Step 1
Group the terms.

$$x^2 + 2x + x + 2$$
$$= (x^2 + 2x) + (x + 2)$$

Step 2
Remove the GCF from each group.

$$(x^2 + 2x) + (x + 2)$$
$$= x(x + 2) + 1(x + 2)$$

Step 3
Factor out the common binomial.

$$x(x + 2) + 1(x + 2)$$
$$= (x + 2)(x + 1)$$

Example

Factor the expression $9mn - 5 + 3m - 15n$.

Solution

The first and third terms have a common factor, as do the second and fourth terms. Rearrange the terms so that these pairs of terms are together, and then factor by grouping.

$$9mn - 5 + 3m - 15n$$
$$= 9mn + 3m - 15n - 5$$
$$= 3m(3n + 1) - 5(3n + 1)$$
$$= (3n + 1)(3m - 5)$$

Notice that -5 was factored out of the last two terms in order to create a common factor of $(3n + 1)$.

Factoring an Expression in the Form $a(f(x))^2 + b(f(x)) + c$, Where $a \neq 0$

A trinomial can be written in the form $a(f(x))^2 + b(f(x)) + c$, where $a \neq 0$, and $f(x)$ represents a polynomial. The decomposition method can be used to factor trinomials of the form $a(f(x))^2 + b(f(x)) + c$. Once the expression is written as a product of two binomials, each can be simplified by collecting like terms.

Example

Factor $(x - 2)^2 - 3(x - 2) + 2$ using the decomposition method.

Solution

In $(x - 2)^2 - 3(x - 2) + 2$, the constant term is 2, and the middle term has a coefficient of -3.

Step 1
Find two integers with a product of 2 and a sum of -3. The pairs of integers with a product of 2 and their respective sums are given.

Product	Sum
$(-1) \times (-2) = 2$ $1 \times 2 = 2$	$(-1) + (-2) = -3$ $1 + 2 = 3$

The integers required are -1 and -2.

Step 2
Express $-3(x - 2)$ as $-(x - 2) - 2(x - 2)$.

$$(x - 2)^2 - 3(x - 2) + 2$$
$$= (x - 2)^2 - (x - 2) - 2(x - 2) + 2$$

Step 3
Group the terms, and remove the greatest common factor from each group.

$$(x - 2)^2 - (x - 2) - 2(x - 2) + 2$$
$$= [(x - 2)^2 - (x - 2)] + [-2(x - 2) + 2]$$
$$= (x - 2)[(x - 2) - 1] - 2[(x - 2) - 1]$$

Step 4
Factor out the common binomial.

$$(x - 2)[(x - 2) - 1] - 2[(x - 2) - 1]$$
$$= [(x - 2) - 1][(x - 2) - 2]$$

Step 5
Collect like terms in each binomial.

$$[(x - 2) - 1][(x - 2) - 2]$$
$$= (x - 3)(x - 4)$$

The trinomial $(x - 2)^2 - 3(x - 2) + 2$ factors to $(x - 3)(x - 4)$.

---

x^2

Example

Factor $-(x^2+4)^2+4(x^2+4)+21$ using the decomposition method.

Solution

In $-(x^2+4)^2+4(x^2+4)+21$, the product of the coefficient of $(x^2+4)^2$ and the constant term is $-21((-1)\times 21=-21)$. The middle term has a coefficient of 4.

Step 1

Find two integers that have a product of –21 and a sum of 4. The pairs of integers with a product of –21 and their respective sums are given.

Product	Sum
$(-1)\times 21=-21$	$(-1)+21=20$
$(-3)\times 7=-21$	**$(-3)+7=4$**
$1\times(-21)=-21$	$1+(-21)=-20$
$3\times(-7)=-21$	$3+(-7)=-4$

The integers required are –3 and 7.

Step 2

Express $4(x^2+4)$ as $-3(x^2+4)+7(x^2+4)$.

$$-(x^2+4)^2+4(x^2+4)+21$$
$$=-(x^2+4)^2-3(x^2+4)+7(x^2+4)+21$$

Step 3

Group the terms, and remove the greatest common factor from each group.

$$\left[-(x^2+4)^2-3(x^2+4)\right]+\left[7(x^2+4)+21\right]$$
$$=-(x^2+4)\left[(x^2+4)+3\right]+7\left[(x^2+4)+3\right]$$

Step 4

Factor out the common binomial.

$$-(x^2+4)\left[(x^2+4)+3\right]+7\left[(x^2+4)+3\right]$$
$$=\left[(x^2+4)+3\right]\left[-(x^2+4)+7\right]$$
$$=-\left[(x^2+4)+3\right]\left[(x^2+4)-7\right]$$

Step 5

Collect like terms in each binomial.

$$-\left[(x^2+4)+3\right]\left[(x^2+4)-7\right]$$
$$=-(x^2+7)(x^2-3)$$

The trinomial $-(x^2+4)^2+4(x^2+4)+21$ factors to $-(x^2+7)(x^2-3)$.

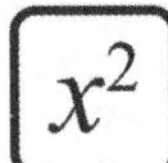

EXERCISE #1—THE STRUCTURE OF EXPRESSIONS

334. The area of a square is represented by $(9x^2 + 24x + 16)$ in^2. The perimeter of the square can be represented by

A. $(3x + 4)$ in

B. $(3x + 8)$in

C. $(12x + 16)$in

D. $(12x + 32)$in

335. One factor of the binomial $343 + 8n^3$ is

A. $7 - 2n$

B. $7 + 14n$

C. $49 - 28n + 4n^2$

D. $49 - 14n + 4n^2$

336. If the binomial $40z^4 - 135z$ can be factored as $az(bz - c)(dz^2 + ez + f)$, what is the value of $d + e + f$?

A. 7 B. 8

C. 19 D. 27

337. One factor of the trinomial $8x^3 - 20x^2 - 12x$ is

A. $2x - 3$ B. $2x + 3$

C. $x - 3$ D. $x + 3$

338. The factored form of $121d^2 - 144c^2$ is

A. $(11d - 12c)(11d - 12c)$

B. $(11d + 12c)(11d - 12c)$

C. $(11d + 12c)(12c - 11d)$

D. $(11d - 12c)(12c - 11d)$

339. Which of the following expressions is equivalent to the binomial $(m - n)^2 - (n - p)^2$?

A. $(m - p)^2$

B. $(m + p)^2$

C. $(m - 2n + p)(m - p)$

D. $(m - 2n - p)(m - p)$

340. When using the decomposition method, the factored form of the trinomial $2x^2 + 5x - 3$ is

A. $(x - 1)(x + 3)$

B. $(2x + 1)(x - 3)$

C. $(2x - 1)(x + 3)$

D. $2(x - 1)(x + 3)$

341. The polynomial $2xy - 3ay + 2xz - 3az$ can be written in factored form as

A. $(2x + 3a)(y - z)$

B. $(2x + 3a)(y + z)$

C. $(2x - 3a)(y - z)$

D. $(2x - 3a)(y + z)$

342. Which of the following factors is a factor of the trinomial $(x + 6)^2 - 8(x + 6) + 15$?

A. $(x - 3)$ B. $(x + 3)$

C. $(x - 5)$ D. $(x + 5)$

EXERCISE #1—THE STRUCTURE OF EXPRESSIONS ANSWERS AND SOLUTIONS

334. C	337. C	340. C
335. D	338. B	341. D
336. C	339. C	342. B

334. C

Step 1

Determine the length of one side of the square.
The area of a square is given by the formula $A = s^2$, in which A is the area and s is the length of each side of the square.

Since $A = 9x^2 + 24x + 16$, it follows that $s^2 = 9x^2 + 24x + 16$.

The expression $9x^2 + 24x + 16$ is a perfect square trinomial and can be factored as $(3x + 4)^2$.

Thus, $s^2 = (3x + 4)^2$ and $s = (3x + 4)$.

Step 2

Determine the perimeter of the square.
The perimeter of a square is given by the formula $P = 4s$, in which P is the perimeter and s is the length of each side of the square.

$P = 4s$

Substitute $3x + 4$ for s.

$P = 4(3x + 4)$

Apply the distributive property.

$P = 12x + 16$

The perimeter of the square is $(12x + 16)$in.

335. D

The binomial $343 + 8n^3$ is a sum of cubes and can be factored by using the formula $a^3 + b^3 = (a + b)(a^2 - ab + b^2)$.

Step 1

Determine the values of a and b.

$$a = \sqrt[3]{343} = 7$$

$$b = \sqrt[3]{8n^3} = 2n$$

Step 2

Apply the sum of cubes formula to determine the factors.

$$a^3 + b^3 = (a + b)(a^2 - ab + b^2)$$
$$343 + 8n^3 = (7 + 2n)((7)^2 - (7)(2n) + (2n)^2)$$
$$343 + 8n^3 = (7 + 2n)(49 - 14n + 4n^2)$$

The factors of $343 + 8n^3$ are $7 + 2n$ and $49 - 14n + 4n^2$.

336. C

Step 1

Remove the GCF$5z$ from $40z^4 - 135z$.

$$40z^4 - 135z = 5z(8z^3 - 27)$$

Step 2

Factor the binomial $8z^3 - 27$ as a difference of cubes by using the pattern $a^3 - b^3 = (a - b)(a^2 + ab + b^2)$.
Determine the cube root of each term.

$$\sqrt[3]{8z^3} = 2z$$
$$\sqrt[3]{27} = 3$$
$$8z^3 - 27 = \left(\begin{matrix} (2z - 3) \\ \times\ ((2z)^2 + (2z)(3) + (3)^2) \end{matrix}\right)$$
$$8z^3 - 27 = \left(\begin{matrix} (2z - 3) \\ \times\ (4z^2 + 6z + 9) \end{matrix}\right)$$
$$5z(8z^3 - 27) = 5z(2z - 3)(4z^2 + 6z + 9)$$

Step 3

Determine the value of $d + e + f$ for $az(bz - c)(dz^2 + ez + f)$.

Compare $dz^2 + ez + f$to $4z^2 + 6z + 9$. It follows that $d = 4$, $e = 6$, and $f = 9$.

$$d + e + f = 4 + 6 + 9 = 19$$

337. C

Step 1

Remove the greatest common factor, $4x$, from the trinomial $8x^3 - 20x^2 - 12x$.

$$8x^3 - 20x^2 - 12x = 4x(2x^2 - 5x - 3)$$

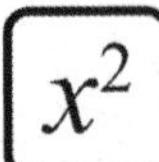

Step 2
Use decomposition to factor the trinomial $2x^2 - 5x - 3$ further.

Since $2 \times -3 = -6$, determine two numbers that have a product of −6 and a sum of −5.

The required numbers are −6 and 1.

Rewrite $-5x$ as $-6x + x$, and then factor by grouping.

$$\begin{aligned} 2x^2 - 5x - 3 &= 2x^2 - 6x + x - 3 \\ &= \left(2x^2 - 6x\right) + (x - 3) \\ &= 2x(x - 3) + 1(x - 3) \\ &= (x - 3)(2x + 1) \end{aligned}$$

The trinomial $8x^3 - 20x^2 - 12x$ factors to $4x(x - 3)(2x + 1)$.

338. B

Since both terms in the binomial are perfect squares, the binomial $121d^2 - 144c^2$ can be factored by applying the difference of squares factoring procedure, $a^2 - b^2 = (a + b)(a - b)$.

Step 1
Determine the square root of each term.

$\sqrt{121d^2} = 11d$

$\sqrt{144c^2} = 12c$

Step 2
Substitute this information into the formula $a^2 - b^2 = (a + b)(a - b)$.

$$\begin{aligned} &121d^2 - 144c^2 \\ &= (11d + 12c)(11d - 12c) \end{aligned}$$

The factored form of $121d^2 - 144c^2$ is $(11d + 12c)(11d - 12c)$.

339. C

Step 1
Factor the binomial $(m - n)^2 - (n - p)^2$.

The binomial is a difference of squares and can be factored by applying the difference of squares factoring procedure, where $a^2 - b^2 = (a + b)(a - b)$.

$$\begin{aligned} &(m - n)^2 - (n - p)^2 \\ &= [(m - n) - (n - p)][(m - n) + (n - p)] \end{aligned}$$

Step 2
Simplify.

$$\begin{aligned} &[(m - n) - (n - p)][(m - n) + (n - p)] \\ &= (m - n - n + p)(m - n + n - p) \\ &= (m - 2n + p)(m - p) \end{aligned}$$

340. C

For the trinomial $2x^2 + 5x - 3$, the product of the coefficient of the x^2 term and the constant term is $2 \times (-3) = -6$. The middle term has a coefficient of 5.

Step 1
Find two integers that have a product of −6 and sum of 5.

The pairs of integers with a product of −6, along with their respective sums, are as shown.

Product	Sum
$1 \times (-6) = -6$	$1 + (-6) = -5$
$2 \times (-3) = -6$	$2 + (-3) = -1$
$3 \times (-2) = -6$	$3 + (-2) = 1$
$6 \times (-1) = -6$	$6 + (-1) = 5$

The two integers required are −1 and 6.

Step 2
Express $5x$ as $-x + 6x$, and then factor by grouping to obtain a common factor.

$$\begin{aligned} 2x^2 + 5x - 3 &= 2x^2 - x + 6x - 3 \\ &= x(2x - 1) + 3(2x - 1) \\ &= (2x - 1)(x + 3) \end{aligned}$$

The complete factorization of $2x^2 + 5x - 3$ is $(2x - 1)(x + 3)$.

341. D

The polynomial $2xy - 3ay + 2xz - 3az$ can be factored by rearranging and grouping the terms in pairs.

Step 1
Group terms and factor out a greatest common factor.

Group the terms with the coefficients 2 together (the first and third terms) and the terms with the coefficients 3 together (the second and fourth terms).

$$\begin{aligned} &2xy - 3ay + 2xz - 3az \\ &= 2xy + 2xz - 3ay - 3az \end{aligned}$$

Once rearranged, a greatest common factor can be removed from each group, which is the greatest term that the coefficients can be divided by.

$$\begin{aligned} &2xy + 2xz - 3ay - 3az \\ &= 2x(y + z) - 3a(y + z) \end{aligned}$$

Step 2
Remove the common binomial factor $y + z$.

$$\begin{aligned} &2x(y + z) - 3a(y + z) \\ &\quad = (y + z)(2x - 3a) \end{aligned}$$

The factored form of the polynomial $2xy - 3ay + 2xz - 3az$ is $(y + z)(2x - 3a)$, which is equivalent to $(2x - 3a)(y + z)$.

x^2

342. B

In $(x+6)^2 - 8(x+6) + 15$, the constant term is 15 and the middle term has a coefficient of -8.

Step 1

Find two integers with a product of 15 and a sum of -8.

The pairs of integers with a product of 15 and their respective sums are as follows:

Product	Sum
$(-1) \times (-15) = 15$	$(-1) + (-15) = -16$
$(-3) \times (-5) = 15$	**$(-3) + (-5) = -8$**
$1 \times 15 = 15$	$1 + 15 = 16$
$3 \times 5 = 15$	$3 + 5 = 8$

The integers required are -3 and -5.

Step 2

Express $-8(x+6)$ as $-3(x+6) - 5(x+6)$.

$$(x+6)^2 - 8(x+6) + 15$$
$$= (x+6)^2 - 3(x+6) - 5(x+6) + 15$$

Step 3

Group the terms, and remove the greatest common factor from each group.

$$(x+6)^2 - 3(x+6) - 5(x+6) + 15$$
$$= \left[(x+6)^2 - 3(x+6)\right] + \left[-5(x+6) + 15\right]$$
$$= (x+6)\left[(x+6) - 3\right] - 5\left[(x+6) - 3\right]$$

Step 4

Factor out the common binomial.

$$(x+6)\left[(x+6) - 3\right] - 5\left[(x+6) - 3\right]$$
$$= \left[(x+6) - 3\right]\left[(x+6) - 5\right]$$

Step 5

Collect the like terms in each binomial.

$$\left[(x+6) - 3\right]\left[(x+6) - 5\right]$$
$$= (x+3)(x+1)$$

The trinomial $(x+6)^2 - 8(x+6) + 15$ factors to $(x+3)(x+1)$.

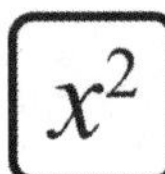

EXERCISE #2—THE STRUCTURE OF EXPRESSIONS

343. The expression $36x^2 + 18x$ written in factored form is $Ax(Bx + C)$, where A, B, and C are whole numbers. The value of $A + B + C$ is __________.

344. Which of the given expressions **cannot** be factored as a perfect square trinomial?

A. $4x^2 + 20x + 25$

B. $9x^2 + 12x + 16$

C. $64x^2 - 16x + 1$

D. $16x^2 - 56x + 49$

345. The factored form of the binomial $27m^3 + 64$ is

A. $(3m + 4)(9m^2 - 12m + 16)$

B. $(3m - 4)(9m^2 + 12m + 16)$

C. $(3m + 4)(9m^2 - 24m + 16)$

D. $(3m - 4)(9m^2 + 24m + 16)$

346. Which of the following expressions is a factor of the binomial $27m^3 - 64$?

A. $(9m^2 + 24m + 16)$

B. $(9m^2 - 24m + 16)$

C. $(9m^2 + 12m + 16)$

D. $(9m^2 - 12m + 16)$

347. One factor of the expression $16x^{64} - 49y^{36}$ is

A. $8x^{32} + 7y^{18}$

B. $4x^{32} + 7y^{18}$

C. $8x^8 - 7y^6$

D. $4x^8 - 7^6$

348. The expression $9x^2 - (4x - y)^2$ is equivalent to

A. $(7x - y)(-x + y)$

B. $(7x - y)(-x - y)$

C. $(5x - y)(x + y)$

D. $(5x - y)(x - y)$

349. What is the complete factored form of the trinomial $4mx^2 - 8mx - 12m$?

A. $4mx(x - 1)(2x - 3)$

B. $4mx(x + 1)(2x + 3)$

C. $4m(x - 1)(x + 3)$

D. $4m(x + 1)(x - 3)$

Use the following information to answer the next question.

One factor of the polynomial $12x^3 + kx^2 - 10x - 15$ is $2x + 3$.

350. If k is a whole number, then the value of k is __________.

351. Which of the following expressions is a factor of the trinomial $2(x - 9)^2 - 5(x - 9) - 3$?

A. $(2x - 17)$ B. $(2x - 15)$

C. $(2x - 13)$ D. $(2x - 11)$

x^2

EXERCISE #2—THE STRUCTURE OF EXPRESSIONS ANSWERS AND SOLUTIONS

343. 21	346. C	349. D
344. B	347. B	350. 18
345. A	348. A	351. A

343. 21

The greatest common factor of 36 and 18 is 18, and the greatest common factor of x^2 and x is x.

Thus $36x^2 + 18x$ can be factored as follows:

$$36x^2 + 18x$$
$$= 18x(2x + 1)$$

The value of $A + B + C = 18 + 2 + 1 = 21$.

344. B

A perfect square trinomial is a trinomial of the form $a^2 + 2ab + b^2$ or $a^2 - 2ab + b^2$. The factorization of $a^2 + 2ab + b^2$ is $(a + b)^2$. The factorization of $a^2 - 2ab + b^2$ is $(a - b)^2$.

Step 1

Determine if $4x^2 + 20x + 25$ will factor as a perfect square trinomial.

$$4x^2 + 20x + 25$$
$$= (2x)^2 + (2)(2x)(5) + (5)^2$$
$$= (2x + 5)^2$$

$4x^2 + 20x + 25$ is a perfect square trinomial.

Step 2

Determine if $9x^2 + 12x + 16$ will factor as a perfect square trinomial.

$$9x^2 + 12x + 16$$
$$\neq (3x)^2 + (2)(3x)(4) + (4)^2$$
$$\neq (3x + 4)^2$$

$9x^2 + 12x + 16$ is not a perfect square trinomial.

Step 3

Determine if $64x^2 - 16x + 1$ will factor as a perfect square trinomial.

$$64x^2 - 16x + 1$$
$$= (8x)^2 - 2(8x)(1) + (1)^2$$
$$= (8x - 1)^2$$

$64x^2 - 16x + 1$ is a perfect square trinomial.

Step 4

Determine if $16x^2 - 56x + 49$ will factor as a perfect square trinomial.

$$16x^2 - 56x + 49$$
$$= (4x)^2 - 2(4x)(7) + (7)^2$$
$$= (4x - 7)^2$$

$16x^2 - 56x + 49$ is a perfect square trinomial.

Therefore, the expression $9x^2 + 12x + 16$ will not factor as a perfect square trinomial.

345. A

As both terms are perfect cubes, the binomial $27m^3 + 64$ can be factored as a sum of cubes using the formula $a^3 + b^3 = (a + b)(a^2 - ab + b^2)$.

Step 1

Determine the values of a and b.

$$a = \sqrt[3]{27m^3}$$
$$= 3m$$
$$b = \sqrt[3]{64}$$
$$= 4$$

Step 2

Apply the sum of cubes formula to determine the factors.

$$a^3 + b^3 = (a + b)(a^2 - ab + b^2)$$
$$27m^3 + 64 = (3m + 4)((3m)^2 - (3m)(4) + 4^2)$$
$$27m^3 + 64 = (3m + 4)(9m^2 - 12m + 16)$$

346. C

The binomial $27m^3 - 64$ is a difference of cubes and can be factored using the formula $a^3 - b^3 = (a - b)(a^2 + ab + b^2)$.

Step 1

Determine the values of a and b.

$$a = \sqrt[3]{27m^3}$$
$$= 3m$$
$$b = \sqrt[3]{64}$$
$$= 4$$

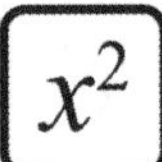

Step 2
Substitute the values for a and b into the difference of cubes formula.

$$a^3 - b^3 = (a-b)(a^2 + ab + b^2)$$
$$27m^3 - 64 = (3m-4)((3m)^2 + (3m)(4) + (4)^2)$$
$$27m^3 - 64 = (3m-4)(9m^2 + 12m + 16)$$

The two factors of the binomial $27m^3 - 64$ are $(3m-4)$ and $(9m^2 + 12m + 16)$.

347. B

Step 1
The binomial $16x^{64} - 49y^{36}$ is a difference of squares and can be factored by applying the difference of squares factoring procedure where $a^2 - b^2 = (a+b)(a-b)$. Write each term as a complete square.

$$16x^{64} - 49y^{36} = 4^2x^{64} - 7^2y^{36}$$
$$= (4x^{32})^2 - (7y^{18})^2$$

Step 2
Express $16x^{64} - 49y^{36}$ as a difference of squares.
$(4x^{32} - 7y^{18})(4x^{32} + 7y^{18})$
One of the factors is $4x^{32} + 7y^{18}$.

348. A

Step1
The binomial $9x^2 - (4x-y)^2$ is a difference of squares and can be factored by applying the difference of squares factoring procedure where $a^2 - b^2 = (a+b)(a-b)$.

Thus, $9x^2 - (4x-y)^2$ can be factored as shown:
$9x^2 - (4x-y)^2$
$= (3x)^2 - (4x-y)^2$
$= [3x + (4x-y)][3x - (4x-y)]$

Step 2
Simplify
$= (3x + 4x - y)(3x - 4x + y)$
$= (7x - y)(-x + y)$

349. D

Step 1
Remove the greatest common factor, $4m$, from $4mx^2 - 8mx - 12m$.
$4mx^2 - 8mx - 12m = 4m(x^2 - 2x - 3)$

Step 2
The trinomial $x^2 - 2x - 3$ can be factored by determining two integers whose product is -3 and whose sum is -2.
The required integers are -3 and 1.
$x^2 - 2x - 3 = (x+1)(x-3)$
When fully factored, the polynomial $4mx^2 - 8mx - 12m$ is $4m(x+1)(x-3)$.

350. 18

The polynomial $12x^3 + kx^2 - 10x - 15$ can be factored by grouping the terms.

Step 1
Factor out $2x + 3$ from the polynomial $12x^3 + kx^2 - 10x - 15$.
Remove the common factor -5 from the last two terms so $2x + 3$ is remaining.
$12x^3 + kx^2 - 10x - 15$
$= 12x^3 + kx^2 - 5(2x + 3)$
Because $2x + 3$ is a common binomial factor, $12x^3 + kx^2$ must be factored by this polynomial as well.

Determine the common factor of $12x^3 + kx^2$ so that $2x + 3$ is remaining. In other words, what is the factor that will be multiplied to $2x$ to get $12x^3$.
The term $(6x^2)(2x) = 12x^3$, so the next step is $6x^2(2x+3) - 5(2x+3)$.
Thus, $6x^2(2x+3)$ must equal $12x^3 + kx^2$.

Step 2
Equate the two polynomials and compare the coefficients in expanded form.
$6x^2(2x+3) = 12x^3 + kx^2$
$12x^3 + 18x^2 = 12x^3 + kx^2$
By comparison $18x^2 = kx^2$, so $k = 18$.

351. A

In $2(x-9)^2 - 5(x-9) - 3$, the product of the coefficient of $(x-9)^2$ and the constant term is $2 \times (-3) = -6$. The middle term has a coefficient of -5.

x^2

Step 1
Find two integers that have a product of –6 and a sum of –5.
The pairs of integers with a product of –6 and their respective sums are as follows:

Product	Sum
$(-1) \times 6 = -6$	$(-1) + 6 = 5$
$(-2) \times 3 = -6$	$(-2) + 3 = 1$
$(-3) \times 2 = -6$	$(-3) + 2 = -1$
$1 \times (-6) = -6$	**$1 + (-6) = -5$**
$2 \times (-3) = -6$	$2 + (-3) = -1$
$3 \times (-2) = -6$	$3 + (-2) = 1$

The integers required are 1 and –6.

Step 2
Express $-5(x-9)$ as $(x-9)-6(x-9)$.

$$2(x-9)^2 - 5(x-9) - 3$$
$$= 2(x-9)^2 + (x-9) - 6(x-9) - 3$$

Step 3
Group the terms, and remove the greatest common factor from each group.

$$\left[2(x-9)^2 + (x-9)\right] + \left[-6(x-9) - 3\right]$$
$$= (x-9)\left[2(x-9)+1\right] - 3\left[2(x-9)+1\right]$$

Step 4
Factor out the common binomial.

$$(x-9)\left[2(x-9)+1\right] - 3\left[2(x-9)+1\right]$$
$$= \left[2(x-9)+1\right]\left[(x-9)-3\right]$$

Step 5
Expand, and collect like terms in each binomial.

$$\left[2(x-9)+1\right]\left[(x-9)-3\right]$$
$$= (2x-18+1)(x-9-3)$$
$$= (2x-17)(x-12)$$

The trinomial $2(x-9)^2 - 5(x-9) - 3$ factors to $(2x-17)(x-12)$.

NOTES

Expressions in Equivalent Forms

EXPRESSIONS IN EQUIVALENT FORMS

Table of Correlations

Standard		Concepts	Exercise #1	Exercise #2
Unit4.2	Write expressions in equivalent forms to solve problems.			
A-SSE. 3a	*Choose and produce an equivalent form of an expression to reveal and explain properties of the quantity represented by the expression. Factor a quadratic expression to reveal the zeros of the function it defines.*	Factoring Trinomials of the Form $x^2 + bx + c$	23	29
		Factoring Trinomials of the Form $ax^2 + bx + c$ Using the Decomposition Method	337, 340	349
		Solving Quadratic Equations by Factoring	352	367
		Determining the x-intercepts of a Graph Given its Quadratic Equation in the Form $y = ax^2 + bx + c$	353	368
		Determining the x-Intercepts of the Graph of a Quadratic Function Given in Factored Form	354	369
A-SSE. 3b	*Choose and produce an equivalent form of an expression to reveal and explain properties of the quantity represented by the expression. Complete the square in a quadratic expression to reveal the maximum or minimum value of the function it defines.*	Expressing $y = ax^2 + bx + c$ in the Form $y = a(x - h)^2 + k$ by Completing the Square	355	370
		Determining the Maximum or Minimum Value of a Quadratic Function	356	371
		Determining the Maximum or Minimum of a Quadratic Function in Standard Form	357	372
A-SSE. 3c	*Choose and produce an equivalent form of an expression to reveal and explain properties of the quantity represented by the expression. Use the properties of exponents to transform expressions for exponential functions.*	Solving Problems Involving Exponential Decay	245	251
		Solving Problems Involving Exponential Growth Given an Equation	246	252
		Simplifying Numerical Expressions Using the Zero Exponent Law	358	373
		Identifying Compound Interest as an Exponential Function	359	374
		Simplifying Numerical Expressions Using the Product Law of Exponents	360	375
		Simplifying Numerical Expressions by Applying the Exponent Laws	361	376
		Simplifying Algebraic Expressions with Exponents	362	377
		Simplifying Numerical Expressions Using the Power of a Product Law	363	378
		Simplifying Numerical Expressions Using the Power of a Quotient Law	364	379
		Simplifying Numerical Expressions Using the Quotient Law of Exponents	365	380
		Simplifying Numerical Expressions Using the Power of a Power Law	366	381

A-SSE.3a Choose and produce an equivalent form of an expression to reveal and explain properties of the quantity represented by the expression. Factor a quadratic expression to reveal the zeros of the function it defines.

Solving Quadratic Equations by Factoring

A **quadratic equation** is any equation in the form of $0 = ax^2 + bx + c$, in which a, b, and c are real numbers and $a \neq 0$.

One method of solving a quadratic equation is to factor the equation, then set each factor equal to 0 and solve for the variable.

The solutions of a quadratic equation are also known as the roots of the equation.

Example

Solve the equation $0 = 2x^2 - 11x - 21$.

Solution

This equation can be solved by factoring the trinomial $2x^2 - 11x - 21$.

Step 1
Factor the trinomial in the form of $ax^2 + bx + c$. Decompose the middle term into two terms by finding two numbers whose product equals ac and whose sum equals b.
$a \times c = 2 \times (-21) = -42$
$b = -11$
Two numbers that have a product of −42 and a sum of −11 are −14 and +3.
Decompose $-11x$ into $-14x$ and $+3x$.
$0 = 2x^2 - 14x + 3x - 21$
Group the terms, and factor.
$0 = (2x^2 - 14x) + (3x - 21)$
$0 = 2x(x - 7) + 3(x - 7)$
$0 = (2x + 3)(x - 7)$

Step 2
Set each factor equal to 0 and solve for x.
$2x + 3 = 0$ or $x - 7 = 0$
$2x + 3 = 0$
$2x = -3$
$x = -\frac{3}{2}$
$x - 7 = 0$
$x = 7$
The values of x that satisfy the given equation are $-\frac{3}{2}$ and 7.

Example

Solve the quadratic equation $0 = x^2 - 4x - 45$ by factoring.

Solution

Step 1
Factor the trinomial.
$0 = x^2 - 4x - 45$
$0 = (x - 9)(x + 5)$

Step 2
Set each factor equal to 0 and solve for x.
$0 = x - 9$ or $0 = x + 5$
$x = 9$ or $x = -5$

Example

Solve the quadratic equation $0 = x^2 + 4x - 21$ by factoring.

Solution

Step 1
Factor the trinomial.
$0 = x^2 + 4x - 21$
$0 = (x - 3)(x + 7)$

Step 2
Set each factor equal to 0 and solve for x.
$0 = x - 3$ or $0 = x + 7$
$x = 3$ or $x = -7$

DETERMINING THE x-INTERCEPTS OF A GRAPH GIVEN ITS QUADRATIC EQUATION IN THE FORM $y = ax^2 + bx + c$

The **x-intercepts** are where the parabola crosses the x-axis. Sometimes, x-intercepts are also referred to as **zeros**.

The x-intercepts of a quadratic relation of the form $y = ax^2 + bx + c$, $(a \neq 0)$ are the value (or values) of x that make the quadratic relation equal to zero. In other words, to find the x-intercepts, set y equal to 0 and solve for x.

$y = ax^2 + bx + c \Rightarrow 0 = ax^2 + bx + c$

The x-coordinates of each ordered pair where the parabola touches or intersects the x-axis are the x-intercepts, or zeros. For a quadratic function, there can be 0, 1, or 2 distinct real zeros.

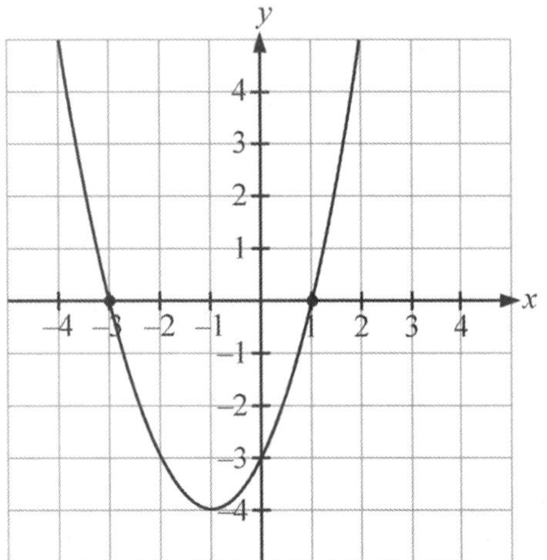

In the given graph, the x-intercepts are −3 and 1. The ordered pairs for the x-intercepts are (−3, 0) and (1, 0). Both y-values in the ordered pairs are 0.

Quadratic equations can be solved using factoring, the quadratic formula, or graphing.

Example

Solve the equation $0 = x^2 + 4x - 21$.

Solution

Method 1: Factoring

$0 = x^2 + 4x - 21$
$0 = (x - 3)(x + 7)$
$0 = (x - 3)$ or $0 = (x + 7)$
$x = 3$ or $x = -7$

Method 2: Using the quadratic formula
Substitute the values $a = 1$, $b = 4$, and $c = -21$, and then solve for x.

$$x = \frac{-b \pm \sqrt{b^2 - 4ac}}{2a}$$

$$x = \frac{-(4) \pm \sqrt{(4)^2 - 4(1)(-21)}}{2(1)}$$

$$x = \frac{-4 \pm \sqrt{16 + 84}}{2}$$

$$x = \frac{-4 \pm \sqrt{100}}{2}$$

$$x = \frac{-4 \pm 10}{2}$$

$$x = \frac{-4 + 10}{2} \text{ or } x = \frac{-4 - 10}{2}$$

$$x = \frac{6}{2} \text{ or } x = \frac{-14}{2}$$

$x = 3$ or $x = -7$

Method 3: Graphing
Enter the equation into the calculator by pressing the [Y =] button. Then, access the CALCULATE menu by pressing [2nd] [Trace], and choose 2:Zero to determine the x-intercepts of the graph.

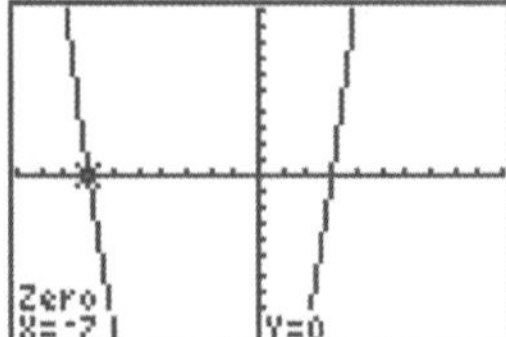

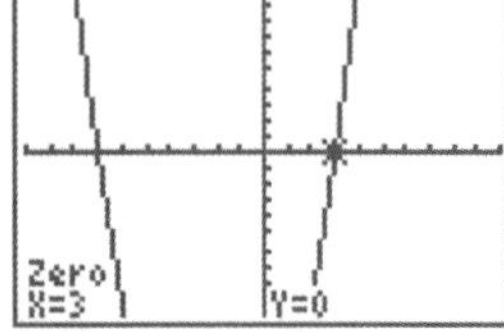

From the ZERO feature, the x-intercepts or zeros are $x = 3$ and $x = -7$.

Thus, the solution to the equation $0 = x^2 + 4x - 21$ is $x = 3$ or $x = -7$.

Determining the x-Intercepts of the Graph of a Quadratic Function Given in Factored Form

The factored form of a quadratic function is $f(x) = a(x - r)(x - s)$, where r and s are the x-intercepts.

To determine the x-intercepts from factored form, set the equation equal to zero, and apply the zero product of multiplication. If the product of two factors is zero, at least one of the factors is equal to zero. Set each factor to zero, and solve for x.

Example

Determine the exact values of the x-intercepts on the graph of the function $y = (4x - 3)(x + 1)$.

Solution

Determine the x-intercepts.

Let $y = 0$.
$0 = (4x - 3)(x + 1)$

Use the original factored form. If the product of two factors is zero, at least one of the factors is equal to zero.

Then, $4x - 3 = 0$ or $x + 1 = 0$.

$4x - 3 = 0$
$4x = 3$
$x = \frac{3}{4}$

$x + 1 = 0$
$x = -1$

Therefore, the x-intercepts are $\frac{3}{4}$ and -1.

A-SSE.3b Choose and produce an equivalent form of an expression to reveal and explain properties of the quantity represented by the expression. Complete the square in a quadratic expression to reveal the maximum or minimum value of the function it defines.

Expressing $y = ax^2 + bx + c$ in the Form $y = a(x - h)^2 + k$ by Completing the Square

Completing the square is the mathematical process used to change the form of a quadratic function from the form $y = ax^2 + bx + c$ to the form $y = a(x - h)^2 + k$.

The following example shows the steps to algebraically complete the square.

Example

Complete the square for $y = -2x^2 + 8x + 3$.

Solution

Step 1
Identify and remove the common factor from the x^2- and x-terms of the expression such that the coefficient of the x^2 term is 1.
In this example, the common factor is -2.
$y = -2(x^2 - 4x) + 3$

Step 2
Divide the coefficient of the x-term by 2, and then square it.

$y = -2(x^2 - 4x) + 3 \qquad \left(\frac{-4}{2}\right)^2 = 4$

Step 3
Both add and subtract this value (4) inside the brackets in order to keep the value of the expression the same.
$y = -2(x^2 - 4x + \underline{4 - 4}) + 3$

Step 4

Move the value that will not contribute to a perfect square trinomial outside the brackets. Remember to multiply the value by the coefficient in front of the brackets.

$y = -2(x^2 - 4x + 4 - 4) + 3$

$y = -2(x^2 - 4x + 4) + 8 + 3$

Step 5

Factor the perfect square trinomial inside the brackets and collect like terms outside the brackets.

$y = -2(x - 2)^2 + 11$

Determining the Maximum or Minimum Value of a Quadratic Function

When the quadratic function $f(x) = ax^2 + bx + c$ is converted into the completed square form $f(x) = a(x - h)^2 + k$, the coordinates of the vertex (h, k) can be quickly identified. Since the vertex is the maximum point if $a < 0$ or the minimum point if $a > 0$, the maximum or minimum value of the function, k, is also identified.

Example

Determine the maximum or minimum value of the quadratic function $f(x) = \frac{1}{2}x^2 - 4x + 2$, and identify whether it is a maximum or a minimum.

Solution

The function $f(x) = \frac{1}{2}x^2 - 4x + 2$ has a minimum because $a > 0$. Complete the square.

$$\begin{aligned} f(x) &= \frac{1}{2}x^2 - 4x + 2 \\ &= \frac{1}{2}(x^2 - 8x) + 2 \\ &= \frac{1}{2}(x^2 - 8x + 16 - 16) + 2 \\ &= \frac{1}{2}(x^2 - 8x + 16) - 8 + 2 \\ &= \frac{1}{2}(x - 4)^2 - 6 \end{aligned}$$

The minimum value is −6.

The maximum or minimum value can also be determined by partially factoring a quadratic formula and using symmetry.

Example

To determine the maximum value of $f(x) = -2x^2 - 24x - 67$, partially factor the function.

$f(x) = -2x(x + 12) - 67$

The values of $f(0)$ and $f(-12)$ are both −67, so by the symmetry of the parabola, the maximum must be at $x = -6$ (midway between $x = 0$ and $x = -12$).

The maximum is calculated as follows:

$$\begin{aligned} f(-6) &= -2(-6)^2 - 24(-6) - 67 \\ f(-6) &= -72 + 144 - 67 \\ f(-6) &= 5 \end{aligned}$$

Determining the Maximum or Minimum of a Quadratic Function in Standard Form

The maximum or minimum value of a quadratic function can be determined by inspecting the standard form equation of the quadratic function. The standard form equation for a quadratic function is $y = a(x - h)^2 + k$.

Use the following steps to determine the maximum or minimum value:

1. Use the a-value to determine whether the function has a maximum or a minimum.
   - If $a > 0$, the parabola opens up and has a minimum.
   - If $a < 0$, the parabola opens down and has a maximum.
2. Use the k-value to determine the value of the maximum or minimum.
   - The value of k is equal to the maximum or minimum value.

Example

What is the maximum or minimum value of the graph represented by the equation

$y = -3(x+7)^2 + 25$?

Solution

Step 1

Use the *a*-value to determine whether the function has a maximum or a minimum.

From the equation, $a = -3$. Since $a < 0$, the function has a maximum.

Step 2

Use the *k*-value to determine the maximum value.

From the equation, $k = 25$. Therefore, the maximum value is 25.

A-SSE.3c Choose and produce an equivalent form of an expression to reveal and explain properties of the quantity represented by the expression. Use the properties of exponents to transform expressions for exponential functions.

Simplifying Numerical Expressions Using the Zero Exponent Law

Any number (except 0) or variable to the exponent of zero is equal to 1. This is often referred to as the zero exponent rule and is stated as $x^0 = 1$, where $x \neq 0$.

This rule is an application of other rules of exponents.

For example, you can evaluate the expression $3^2 \times 3^{-2}$ using the negative exponent rule as well as the product rule for exponents to show that $3^0 = 1$.

Apply the negative exponent rule.

$3^2 \times 3^{-2} = 3^2 \times \frac{1}{3^2} = 9 \times \frac{1}{9} = 1$

Apply the product rule for exponents.

$3^2 \times 3^{-2} = 3^{2+(-2)} = 3^0$

Thus, $3^0 = 1$.

Example

Evaluate the expression $6(2^3 + 4^0)$.

Solution

Step 1

Evaluate 4^0.

$4^0 = 1$

Step 2

Substitute 1 for 4^0 in the given expression, and then simplify.

$$\begin{aligned} 6(2^3 + 4^0) &= 6(2^3 + 1) \\ &= 6(8 + 1) \\ &= 6(9) \\ &= 54 \end{aligned}$$

Example

Evaluate $(2^0 - 3^0)^0$.

Solution

Step 1

Apply the zero exponent rule to the terms inside the brackets and then simplify.

Remember to follow the order of operations (BEDMAS) in the process of evaluation.

$$\begin{aligned} (2^0 - 3^0)^0 &= (2^0 - (3)^0)^0 \\ &= (1 - 1)^0 \\ &= 0^0 \end{aligned}$$

Step 2

Evaluate.

Since the final expression has 0 as a base, the expression 0^0 is undefined.

Thus, the expression $(2^0 - 3^0)^0$ is undefined.

IDENTIFYING COMPOUND INTEREST AS AN EXPONENTIAL FUNCTION

The compound interest formula can be expressed as $FV = PV(1 + i)^n$ or $A = P(1 + i)^n$.
These formulas can be used to find the future value, *FV* or *A*, or the present value, *PV* or *P*, as follows:

$FV = PV(1 + i)^n \Rightarrow$ Given the value of *PV*

$PV = \dfrac{FV}{(1 + i)^n} \Rightarrow$ Given the value of *FV*

Note: Using the exponent law $\dfrac{1}{x^n} = x^{-n}$, the present value formula can be rewritten in the following ways:

$$PV = \frac{FV}{(1 + i)^n} \text{ or}$$

$$PV = FV\left(\frac{1}{1 + i}\right)^n \text{ or}$$

$$PV = FV(1 + i)^{-n}$$

Each variation of the compound interest formula can be represented as an exponential function of the form $f(x) = a(b)^x$.

Example

Jake invested \$2,000 into a GIC account that earned 12% interest per year compounded semi-annually. Use a table of values to show that the growth in the final amount, *FV*, can be represented as an exponential function $f(x) = a(b)^x$, where *b* reflects the compound interest rates.

Solution

Note: The interest per compounding period is $i = \dfrac{12\%}{2} = 6\%$, and the number of compounding periods, *n*, is 2 times per year.

Semi-Annual Periods	Final Amount (*FV*)	Growth Factor
0	\$2,000	—
1	$\$2,000(1 + 0.06)^1$ = \$2,120	2,120 ÷ 2,000 = 1.06
2	$\$2,000(1 + 0.06)^2$ = \$2,247.20	2,247.20 ÷ 2,120 = 1.06
3	$\$2,000(1 + 0.06)^3$ = \$2,382.03	2,382.03 ÷ 2,247.20 ≈ 1.06
4	$\$2,000(1 + 0.06)^4$ = \$2,524.95	2,524.95 ÷ 2,382.03 ≈ 1.06
5	$\$2,000(1 + 0.06)^5$ = \$2,676.45	2,676.45 ÷ 2,524.95 ≈ 1.06
6	$\$2,000(1 + 0.06)^6$ = \$2,837.04	2,837.04 ÷ 2,676.45 ≈ 1.06

The table shows that the growth factor is constant at 1.06. This is a characteristic of an exponential function. The exponential function $f(x) = 2{,}000(1.06)^x$ would therefore describe this scenario, where 2,000 represents the original present value and 1.06 is the growth factor.

The interest rate per compounding period, *i*, is represented by the value after the decimal point of the growth factor (1.6 ⇒ 6%).

Example

Stephanie needed to determine the present value, *PV*, that she needed to put into a bank account now at an interest rate of 10% per annum compounded annually so that she had $1,610 spending money for a planned holiday in 5 years. Determine the decreasing present value, *PV*, each year. Then, graph this data on your graphing calculator, and show that the graph represents an exponential function $f(x) = a(b)^x$, where b reflects the annual interest rate.

Solution

Use the formula $PV = FV(1 + i)^{-n}$ to determine the present values for the years 0 to 5.

Year (x)	Present Value (y)
0	$1,610
1	$1{,}610(1 + 0.10)^{-1}$ = $1,463.63
2	$1{,}610(1 + 0.10)^{-2}$ = $1,330.58
3	$1{,}610(1 + 0.10)^{-3}$ = $1,209.62
4	$1{,}610(1 + 0.10)^{-4}$ = $1,099.65
5	$1{,}610(1 + 0.10)^{-5}$ = $999.68

Enter this data as lists L_1 and L_2 on your graphing calculator, set the WINDOW to x:[−2, 6, 1], y:[0, 2,000, 100], and then graph the data using the 2nd[Y =] or STAT PLOT feature, as shown below.

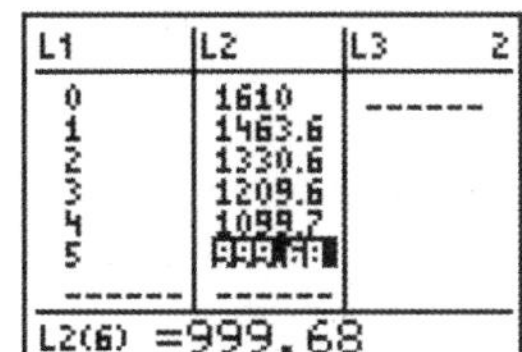

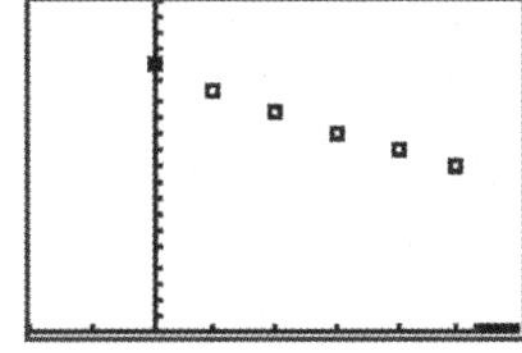

Do an exponential regression on the data by using the STAT CALC 0 or Exp Reg feature to get the following exponential equation on your screen.

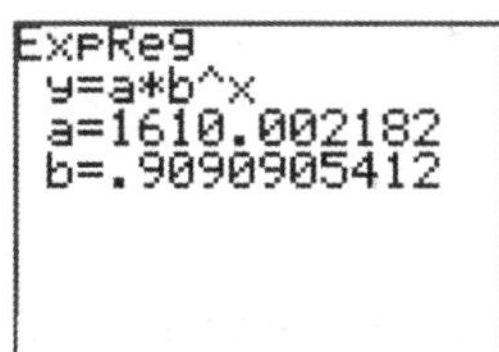

Finally, enter this equation in $[Y_1 =]$ as $Y_1 = 1{,}610 \times 0.909091^{\wedge}x$, and graph it to show it passing through the plotted points.

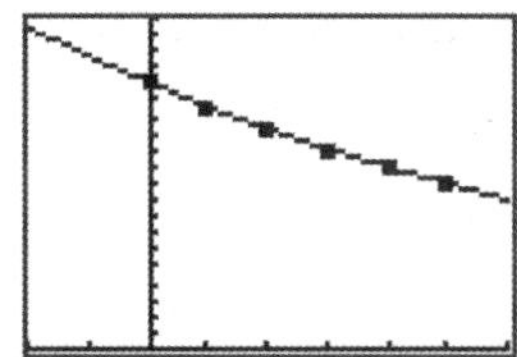

This graph shows that the exponential function $f(x) = 1{,}610(0.909091)^x$ represents the decreasing present value, y, over the annual compounding periods, x.

Since $PV = FV(1 + i)^{-n}$ can also be written as $PV = FV\left(\frac{1}{1+i}\right)^n$, then the value of $\frac{1}{b}$ in the exponential function $f(x) = a(b)^x$ should reflect the interest rate, i. Notice that this holds true in this scenario.

$$\begin{aligned}\frac{1}{b} &= \frac{1}{0.909091}\\ &= 1.09999989\\ &\approx 1.10\end{aligned}$$

The value after the decimal point in the reciprocal of the decay factor (1.10 ⇒ 10%) represents the interest rate per compounding period, i.

Simplifying Numerical Expressions Using the Product Law of Exponents

Numerical expressions can be simplified using the product law of exponents.

The product rule is $x^m \times x^n = x^{m+n}$.

Example

Use the product law of exponents to simplify the numerical expression $(2^3)(2^6)$.

Solution

Use the product rule which states when the bases are the same, add the exponents.
$(2^3)(2^6) = 2^{3+6} = 2^9$

Simplified as a single power, the numerical expression is 2^9.

To verify the solution with the original expression, a calculator could be used to determine the expressions separately.
$2^3 \times 2^6 = 512$ and $2^9 = 512$

Example

Simplify the expression $3^2 \times 3^5 \times 3^4$.

Solution

Use the product rule.

To multiply powers with the same base, add the exponents together.

$$3^2 \times 3^5 \times 3^4 = 3^{2+5+4} = 3^{11}$$

Example

Simplify the expression $5^3 \times 5^6 \times 5^4$ by writing it as a single power.

Solution

Use the product rule to simplify the given expression. Since the powers have the same base, add the exponents together.

$$5^3 \times 5^6 \times 5^4 = 5^{3+6+4} = 5^{13}$$

Written as a single power, the given expression is 5^{13}.

Simplifying Numerical Expressions by Applying the Exponent Laws

Exponent laws can be used to simplify an expression that involves operations of multiplication or division of powers with a common base. The exponent laws make it possible to simplify the expression by adding and subtracting the exponents of the powers with a common base.

Example

Simplify and evaluate the expression

$$\frac{5^3}{5^2} \times \frac{4^6 \times 4^{-2}}{(4^2)^2}.$$

Solution

Step 1

Apply the quotient law to the first expression.

$$\frac{5^3}{5^2} = 5^{3-2} = 5^1 = 5$$

Step 2

Apply the product law to the numerator and the power of a power law to the denominator of the second expression.

$$\frac{4^{6-2}}{4^{2\times 2}} = \frac{4^4}{4^4}$$

The expression so far is $5 \times \frac{4^4}{4^4}$.

Step 3

Apply the quotient law to the fraction.

$4^{4-4} = 4^0$

Step 4

Apply the zero exponent law to 4^0.

$4^0 = 1$

Step 5

Calculate the solution.

$5 \times 1 = 5$

Example

Simplify the expression $\dfrac{\left(\frac{2}{5}\right)^5}{\left(\frac{2}{5}\right)^4} \times \dfrac{\left(\frac{2}{3}\right)^6 \times \left(\frac{2}{3}\right)^{-2}}{\left(\frac{2}{3}\right)^2}$ using exponent rules.

Solution

Step 1

Apply the quotient law to the first expression.

$$\frac{\left(\frac{2}{5}\right)^5}{\left(\frac{2}{5}\right)^4} = \left(\frac{2}{5}\right)^{5-4} = \left(\frac{2}{5}\right)^1 = \frac{2}{5}$$

The expression is now $\dfrac{2}{5} \times \dfrac{\left(\frac{2}{3}\right)^6 \times \left(\frac{2}{3}\right)^{-2}}{\left(\frac{2}{3}\right)^2}$.

Step 2

Apply the product law to the second expression.

$$\frac{\left(\frac{2}{3}\right)^6 \times \left(\frac{2}{3}\right)^{-2}}{\left(\frac{2}{3}\right)^2} = \frac{\left(\frac{2}{3}\right)^{6+(-2)}}{\left(\frac{2}{3}\right)^2} = \frac{\left(\frac{2}{3}\right)^4}{\left(\frac{2}{3}\right)^2}$$

Apply the quotient law to the second expression.

$$\frac{\left(\frac{2}{3}\right)^4}{\left(\frac{2}{3}\right)^2} = \left(\frac{2}{3}\right)^{4-2} = \left(\frac{2}{3}\right)^2$$

The simplified expression is now $\frac{2}{5} \times \left(\frac{2}{3}\right)^2$.

Step 3

Expand and solve.

$$\frac{2}{5} \times \left(\frac{2}{3}\right)^2 = \frac{2}{5} \times \frac{2}{3} \times \frac{2}{3} = \frac{2 \times 2 \times 2}{5 \times 3 \times 3} = \frac{8}{45}$$

The expression simplifies to

$$\frac{\left(\frac{2}{5}\right)^5}{\left(\frac{2}{5}\right)^4} \times \frac{\left(\frac{2}{3}\right)^6 \times \left(\frac{2}{3}\right)^{-2}}{\left(\frac{2}{3}\right)^2} = \frac{8}{45}.$$

The simplified expression is $\frac{8}{45}$.

If the expression involves operations other than multiplication and division, the work must be done using **BEDMAS**. Apply exponent laws where possible to simplify the expression.

Example

Simplify and evaluate the expression

$6^{-3} \times 6^2 + \dfrac{4^2 + 4^3}{(2^2)^2}$.

Solution

Step 1

Simplify the first expression by applying exponent laws.

Apply the product law to the numerator of the first expression.

$$\begin{aligned} 6^{-3+2} &= 6^{-1} \\ &= \frac{1}{6} \end{aligned}$$

Step 2

Simplify the second expression.

The numerator of the second expression is formed by adding the two powers. Calculate the powers and add.

$$\begin{aligned} 4^2 + 4^3 &= 16 + 64 \\ &= 80 \end{aligned}$$

The second expression is now $\dfrac{80}{(2^2)^2}$.

The denominator of the second expression is a power of a power. Apply the power of a power law.

$$\begin{aligned} (2^2)^2 &= 2^{2\times 2} \\ &= 2^4 \\ &= 16 \end{aligned}$$

The second expression is now $\dfrac{80}{16}$.

Reduced to lowest terms, $\dfrac{80}{16} = 5$.

Step 3

Calculate the solution.

The expression so far is $\dfrac{1}{6} + 5$.

$$\frac{1}{6} + 5 = 5\frac{1}{6}$$

$$6^{-3} \times 6^2 + \frac{4^2 + 4^3}{(2^2)^2} = 5\frac{1}{6}$$

When the expression involves powers with rational bases, apply exponent rules first and then simplify.

Simplifying Algebraic Expressions with Exponents

An algebraic expression involving exponents is in simplified form when the given expression is written with a single coefficient and the appropriate laws of exponents have been applied.

For example, the algebraic expression $25x^2y^4z^3$ is in a simplified form.

When simplifying an algebraic expression involving exponents where the multiplication of two expressions is involved it is necessary to apply the **product law** of exponents. This law requires adding the exponents of common bases. For example, $(Mx^ay^b) \times (Nx^py^q) = (M \times N)x^{a+p}y^{b+q}$ where M and N are real numbers.

Example

Simplify the algebraic expression $(8x^3y^5)(9x^2y^3)$.

Solution

Step 1

Group the coefficients as well as the like bases.

$$\begin{aligned} &(8x^3y^5)(9x^2y^3) \\ &= (8 \times 9)(x^3 \times x^2)(y^5 \times y^3) \end{aligned}$$

- The first set of brackets illustrates the product of the coefficient of the first expression (8) and the coefficient of the second expression (9).
- The second set of brackets illustrates collecting the x variables.
- The third set of brackets illustrates collecting the y variables.

Step 2

Evaluate the coefficient, and apply the product law of exponents (add the exponents).

$$\begin{aligned} &(8 \times 9)(x^3 \times x^2)(y^5 \times y^3) \\ &= (72)(x^{3+2})(y^{5+3}) \end{aligned}$$

Step 3

State the final simplified algebraic expression.

$$\begin{aligned} &(72)(x^{3+2})(y^{5+3}) \\ &= 72x^5y^8 \end{aligned}$$

Simplifying an algebraic expression formed by raising an expression to an exponent requires the **power of a product law** to be used. This law involves the multiplication of exponents.

$(Mx^ay^bz^c)^k = M^kx^{a\times k}y^{b\times k}z^{c\times k}$

Example

Simplify the algebraic expression $(4x^4y^5z^2)^3$.

Solution

Step 1

Apply the power law of exponents (multiply the exponents).

Remember to include the coefficient.

$(4x^4y^5z^2)^3$

$= 4^{1\times 3}x^{4\times 3}y^{5\times 3}z^{2\times 3}$

Step 2

Evaluate the coefficient and exponents.

State the final simplified algebraic expression.

$= 4^3x^{4\times 3}y^{5\times 3}z^{2\times 3}$

$= 64x^{12}y^{15}z^6$

Simplifying an algebraic expression formed by the division of two expressions requires the **quotient law** to be used. This law involves subtracting the exponents of common bases.

$\dfrac{Mx^ay^bz^c}{Nx^py^qz^r} = (M \div N)x^{a-p}y^{b-q}z^{c-r}$

In the most simplified form, all exponents of an algebraic expression must be positive. There are two possibilities for the **law of negative exponents**.

$x^{-n} = \dfrac{1}{x^n}$ or $\dfrac{1}{x^{-n}} = x^n$

Example

Simplify the algebraic expression $\dfrac{(6x^4y^2)^2}{4xy^6}$.

Solution

Step 1

Apply the power law of exponents in the numerator.

$\dfrac{(6x^4y^2)^2}{4xy^6}$

$= \dfrac{6^2x^{4\times 2}y^{2\times 2}}{4xy^6}$

Step 2

Evaluate the coefficient and exponents in the numerator.

$= \dfrac{6^2x^{4\times 2}y^{2\times 2}}{4xy^6}$

$= \dfrac{36x^8y^4}{4xy^6}$

Step 3

Divide to determine the coefficient of the final expression, and apply the quotient law of exponents (subtract exponents).

$= \dfrac{36x^8y^4}{4xy^6}$

$= (36 \div 4)(x^{8-1})(y^{4-6})$

Step 4

Evaluate the coefficient and exponents.

$= (36 \div 4)(x^{8-1})(y^{4-6})$

$= 9x^7y^{-2}$

Step 5

Apply the negative exponent law, and state the final simplified algebraic expression.

$= 9x^7y^{-2}$

$= \dfrac{9x^7}{y^2}$

The **zero exponent law** states that when raising any base to the exponent zero, the result is always 1.

$x^0 = 1$

Simplifying algebraic expressions may involve applying one or more of the exponent laws; in some cases, all five exponent laws may need to be used.

Example

Simplify the algebraic expression

$\dfrac{(5p^3q^7r^2)(9p^4qr^3)}{(3pq^2r^3)^4}$.

Solution

Step 1

Simplify the numerator to a single expression by applying the product law of exponents.

$\dfrac{(5p^3q^7r^2)(9p^4qr^3)}{(3pq^2r^3)^4}$

$= \dfrac{(5\times 9)(p^{3+4})(q^{7+1})(r^{2+3})}{(3pq^2r^3)^4}$

Step 2
Apply the power law of exponents in the denominator.

$$= \frac{(5 \times 9)(p^{3+4})(q^{7+1})(r^{2+3})}{(3pq^2r^3)^4}$$
$$= \frac{(5 \times 9)(p^{3+4})(q^{7+1})(r^{2+3})}{3^4 p^{1\times4} q^{2\times4} r^{3\times4}}$$

Step 3
Evaluate the coefficients and exponents in both the numerator and denominator.

$$= \frac{(5 \times 9)(p^{3+4})(q^{7+1})(r^{2+3})}{3^4 p^{1\times4} q^{2\times4} r^{3\times4}}$$
$$= \frac{45p^7q^8r^5}{81p^4q^8r^{12}}$$

Step 4
Apply the quotient law of exponents.

$$= \frac{45p^7q^8r^5}{81p^4q^8r^{12}}$$
$$= \frac{45}{81}p^{7-4}q^{8-8}r^{5-12}$$

Step 5
Reduce the fractional coefficient by dividing both the numerator and denominator by the greatest common factor (9), and then evaluate the exponents.

$$= \frac{45}{81}p^{7-4}q^{8-8}r^{5-12}$$
$$= \frac{5}{9}p^3q^0r^{-7}$$

Step 6
Apply the zero exponent law and negative exponent law, and state the final simplified algebraic expression.

Recall that $q^0 = 1$.

$$= \frac{5}{9}p^3q^0r^{-7}$$
$$= \frac{5p^3}{9r^7}$$

Simplifying Numerical Expressions Using the Power of a Product Law

The power of a product law, $(ab)^m = a^mb^m$, can be used to simplify numerical expressions.

To apply the power of a product law, the exponent of each term inside the brackets of an expression must be multiplied by the exponent located outside the brackets. The law can be applied to terms that have either a positive or a negative base.

Example

Use the power of a product law to evaluate the expression $(2 \times 5)^3$.

Solution

Step 1
Distribute the exponent located outside the brackets of the expression to each term located inside the brackets.
$(2 \times 5)^3 = (2)^3 \times (5)^3$

Step 2
Evaluate the simplified expression.
$2^3 \times 5^3 = 8 \times 125 = 1{,}000$

Example

Evaluate the expression $(3^4 \times (-5)^2)^2$.

Solution

Step 1
Apply the power of a product law.
Distribute the exponent located outside the brackets of the expression to each term located inside the brackets.
$(3^4 \times (-5)^2)^2 = (3^4)^2 \times ((-5)^2)^2$

Step 2
Apply the power of a power law.
Multiply the exponent of each term by the distributed exponent.

$$\begin{aligned}(3^4)^2 \times ((-5)^2)^2 &= 3^{4\times2} \times (-5)^{2\times2}\\ &= 3^8 \times (-5)^4\end{aligned}$$

Step 3
Evaluate the simplified expression.

$$\begin{aligned}3^8 \times (-5)^4 &= 6{,}561 \times 625\\ &= 4{,}100{,}625\end{aligned}$$

Simplifying Numerical Expressions Using the Power of a Quotient Law

The power of a quotient law, $\left(\frac{a}{b}\right)^n = \frac{a^n}{b^n}$, $b \neq 0$, can be used to simplify numerical expressions.

To apply the power of a quotient law, the exponent of each term inside the brackets of an expression must be multiplied by the exponent located outside the brackets.

Example

Evaluate the expression $\left(\frac{3}{7}\right)^2$.

Solution

Step 1

Apply the power of a quotient law.

Distribute the exponent located outside the brackets of the expression to each term located inside the brackets.

$$\left(\frac{3}{7}\right)^2 = \frac{(3)^2}{(7)^2}$$

Step 2

Apply the power of a power law.

Multiply the exponent of each term by the distributed exponent.

$$\frac{(3)^2}{(7)^2} = \frac{3^{1\times2}}{7^{1\times2}} = \frac{3^2}{7^2}$$

Step 3

Evaluate the new expression using repeated multiplication.

$$\frac{3^2}{7^2} = \frac{3\times3}{7\times7} = \frac{9}{49}$$

Example

Evaluate the expression $\left(\frac{3^4}{2^6}\right)^3$ to the nearest thousandth.

Solution

Step 1

Apply the power of a quotient law.

Distribute the exponent located outside the brackets of the expression to each term located inside the brackets.

$$\left(\frac{3^4}{2^6}\right)^3 = \frac{(3^4)^3}{(2^6)^3}$$

Step 2

Apply the power of a power law.

Multiply the exponent of each term by the distributed exponent.

$$\frac{(3^4)^3}{(2^6)^3} = \frac{3^{4\times3}}{2^{6\times3}} = \frac{3^{12}}{2^{18}}$$

Step 3

Evaluate the new expression, and express the result as a decimal rounded to the nearest thousandth.

$$\frac{3^{12}}{2^{18}} = \frac{531{,}441}{262{,}144} = 2.027$$

Simplifying Numerical Expressions Using the Quotient Law of Exponents

The exponent laws dictate how to simplify exponents in operations involving powers.
To divide powers with the same base, subtract the exponents.

This the quotient law, which is stated as given:

$$\frac{x^m}{x^n} = x^{m-n}$$

Example

Simplify the expression $\frac{10^5}{10^3}$ by writing as a single power.

Solution

The expression contains two powers being divided. Since their bases are the same, the exponents can be subtracted. This simplifies the expression to a single power with a base of 10.

In this case, $\frac{10^5}{10^3} = 10^{5-3} = 10^2$

Example

Simplify the expression $4^8 \div 4^2$.

Solution

The expression contains two powers being divided. Since their bases are the same, the exponents can be subtracted. This simplifies the expression to a single power with a base of 4.

The quotient law states that $x^m \div x^n = x^{m-n}$.

In this case, $4^8 \div 4^2 = 4^{8-2} = 4^6$.

Simplifying Numerical Expressions Using the Power of a Power Law

If a power is raised to another power by the use of brackets, it is called a **power of a power**.

For example, $(3^2)^4$ is a power of a power.
The exponent outside the brackets indicates how many times the power inside the brackets is multiplied by itself.

The example $(3^2)^4$ can be expanded and simplified using the product law.

$$\begin{aligned}(3^2)^4 &= (3^2)(3^2)(3^2)(3^2)\\ &= 3^{2+2+2+2}\\ &= 3^8\end{aligned}$$

Alternatively, this power can be simplified using the power of a power law. **The power of a power law** states that $(a^m)^n = a^{mn}$.

To take a power to another power, multiply the exponents together while keeping the base the same.

$(3^2)^4 = 3^{2\times4} = 3^8$

Example

Evaluate the expression $(5^2)^3$.

Solution

Use the power of a power law to evaluate the given expression.

Step 1
Multiply the exponents to reduce the expression to a single power.

$$\begin{aligned}&(5^2)^3\\ &= 5^{2\times3}\\ &= 5^6\end{aligned}$$

Step 2
Evaluate the power.

$5^6 = 15,625$

When the expression $(5^2)^3$ is evaluated, the result is 15,625.

The power of a power law also applies to powers with negative bases.

Example

Evaluate the expression $((-9)^2)^4$.

Solution

Use the power of a power law to evaluate the given expression.

Step 1
Multiply the exponents to reduce the expression to a single power.

$$\begin{aligned}&((-9)^2)^4\\ &= (-9)^{2\times4}\\ &= (-9)^8\end{aligned}$$

Step 2
Evaluate the power.
$(-9)^8 = 43{,}046{,}721$

When the expression $((-9)^2)^4$ is evaluated, the result is 43,046,721.

EXERCISE #1—EXPRESSIONS IN EQUIVALENT FORMS

Use the following information to answer the next question.

Ozzie was asked by his teacher to solve the equation $-2x^2 - 3x + 19 = -10x^2 - 25x + 5$ by factoring. Ozzie's partial solution to the equation is shown.

1. $-8x^2 + 22x + 14 = 0$
2. $-2(4x^2 - 11x - 7) = 0$
3. $-2(4x^2 - 4x - 7x - 7) = 0$
4. $-2((4x^2 - 4x) + (-7x - 7)) = 0$
5. $-2(4x(x - 1) - 7(x - 1)) = 0$

352. Which of the following statements about Ozzie's partial solution is **true**?

A. Ozzie's partial solution is correct.

B. Ozzie made his first error in step 1.

C. Ozzie made his first error in step 3.

D. Ozzie made his first error in step 5.

353. The *x*-intercepts of the quadratic equation $y = 3x^2 - 27x - 210$ are

A. $x = -5$ and $x = 14$

B. $x = -7$ and $x = 12$

C. $x = -9$ and $x = 3$

D. $x = -10$ and $x = 17$

354. The number of different real zeros of the quadratic function $y = (3x + 2)(x - 2)$ is __________.

355. If the equation $y = 3x^2 + 42x + 142$ is expressed in completed square form $y = a(x - h)^2 + k$, the value of k is

A. –7 B. –5

C. 5 D. 7

356. For which of the following quadratic functions does the minimum value of its graph occur at the point (–2, –2)?

A. $y = 3x^2 + 12x + 10$

B. $y = 3x^2 + 12x + 8$

C. $y = 3x^2 + 12x + 6$

D. $y = 3x^2 + 12x + 4$

357. Which of the following statements about the function $y = -\frac{1}{3}(x + 9)^2 + 45$ is **true**?

A. The function has a minimum value of –9.

B. The function has a maximum value of –9.

C. The function has a minimum value of 45.

D. The function has a maximum value of 45.

Use the following information to answer the next question.

An expression is simplified as shown.

$$\frac{(4)^8(4)^{-4}}{(4)^4} = \frac{4^a}{4^4} = 4^b = c$$

358. The sum of $a + b + c$ is

A. 9 B. 8

C. 5 D. 4

359. Which of the following investments could be represented by the function $f(x) = 3{,}000(1.02)^{4x}$ if x represents the number of years the money is invested?

A. \$3,000 invested at 2%/*a*, compounded quarterly

B. \$3,000 invested at 8%/*a*, compounded quarterly

C. \$3,000 invested at 2%/*a*, compounded yearly

D. \$3,000 invested at 8%/*a*, compounded yearly

360. Simplified as a single power, the expression $5^3 \times 5^6 \times 5^4$ is

A. 5^{13}
B. 5^{12}
C. 5^5
D. 5^{-1}

361. Use the exponent rules to simplify the expression $\left(\frac{1}{4}\right)^{-2} \div \left(\frac{1}{4}\right)^3$.

362. The simplified form of $\left(x^4y^8\right)^{-\frac{1}{2}}$ is

A. $-x^2y^4$
B. $x^{\frac{7}{2}}y^{\frac{15}{2}}$
C. $\frac{1}{x^2y^4}$
D. $\frac{1}{x^8y^{16}}$

363. When the expression $\left(6^2 \times 3^4 \times -7\right)^2$ is simplified, an equivalent expression is

A. $6^4 \times 3^8 \times (-7)^2$
B. $6^4 \times 3^6 \times (-7)^3$
C. $(-126)^2$
D. 378^2

364. When the expression $\left(\frac{4^4}{5^6}\right)^3$ is simplified, it is equal to

A. $\frac{4^1}{5^3}$
B. $\frac{4^7}{5^9}$
C. $\frac{4^{12}}{5^{18}}$
D. $\frac{4^{18}}{5^{12}}$

365. Simplify $7^{11} \div 7^8$.

A. 7^{19}
B. 7^6
C. 7^3
D. 7^{-3}

366. An equivalent numerical expression to $\left(84^3\right)^0$ is

A. 0
B. 1
C. 84^1
D. 84^3

EXERCISE #1—EXPRESSIONS IN EQUIVALENT FORMS ANSWERS AND SOLUTIONS

352. B	356. A	360. A	364. C
353. A	357. D	361. See solution	365. C
354. 2	358. C	362. C	366. B
355. B	359. B	363. A	

352. B

Ozzie's first error occurred in step 1:
$-2x^2 - 3x + 19 = -10x^2 - 25x + 5$ simplifies to $8x^2 + 22x + 14 = 0$. The steps Ozzie should have followed are given below.

Step 1
Factor 2 from the trinomial.
$2(4x^2 + 11x + 7) = 0$

Step 2
Decompose the middle term of the trinomial.
$2(4x^2 + 4x + 7x + 7) = 0$

Step 3
Group the terms into two pairs of two.
$2((4x^2 + 4x) + (7x + 7)) = 0$

Step 4
Remove the greatest common factor from each pair.
$2(4x(x + 1) + 7(x + 1)) = 0$

353. A

Step 1
Factor out the greatest common factor from the trinomial.
$y = 3x^2 - 27x - 210$
$y = 3(x^2 - 9x - 70)$

Step 2
Factor the trinomial.
$y = 3(x^2 - 9x - 70)$
$y = 3(x - 14)(x + 5)$

Step 3
Set $y = 0$ and solve the equation by equating each factor to zero.
$0 = 3(x - 14)(x + 5)$
$0 = x - 14$
$14 = x$
$0 = x + 5$
$-5 = x$

The x-intercepts of $y = 3x^2 - 27x - 210$ occur at $x = -5$ and $x = 14$.

354. 2

The given quadratic function has two unique factors, and each factor will yield one real zero.

Determine the zeros of the function
$y = (3x + 2)(x - 2)$.
$3x + 2 = 0$
$3x = -2$
$x = -\frac{2}{3}$
$x - 2 = 0$
$x = 2$

Therefore, the function has two different real zeros.

355. B

Step 1
Identify and remove the common factor from the x^2- and x-terms of the expression.
In this case, the common factor is 3.
$y = 3(x^2 + 14x) + 142$

Step 2
Divide the resulting coefficient for the x-term by 2, and then square it.
$y = 3(x^2 + \underline{14x}) + 142$
$\left(\frac{14}{2}\right)^2 = 49$
Both add and subtract this value inside the brackets.
$y = 3(x^2 + 14x + \underline{49 - 49}) + 142$

Step 3
Move the value that will not contribute to a perfect square outside the brackets.
When -49 is moved outside the brackets, it becomes $3(-49) = -147$ because of the distributive property.
$y = \underline{3}(x^2 + 14x + 49\underline{- 49}) + 142$
$y = 3(x^2 + 14x + 49)\underline{- 147} + 142$

Step 4
Factor the trinomial inside the brackets to form a perfect square, and collect like terms outside the brackets.

$y = 3(x+7)^2 - 5$

When the equation $y = 3x^2 + 42x + 142$ is written in the completed square form $y = a(x-h)^2 + k$, it becomes $y = 3(x+7)^2 - 5$.
The k-value is –5.

356. A

For each of the given quadratic equations, $a > 0$ (because $a = 3$). This means the graph will have a minimum and not a maximum.

Step 1
Write the general quadratic equation that represents the equations, and complete the square.
Since the equations differ only in the value of their constants, the general quadratic equation is
$y = 3x^2 + 12x + k$.
Complete the square.

$$\begin{aligned} 3x^2 + 12x + k &= 3(x^2 + 4x) + k \\ &= 3(x^2 + 4x + 4 - 4) + k \\ &= 3(x^2 + 4x + 4) - 12 + k \\ &= 3(x+2)^2 - 12 + k \end{aligned}$$

Step 2
Determine the value of k that will make the vertex of the equation's graph (–2, –2).

The quadratic $y = 3(x+2)^2 - 12 + k$ is written in the form $y = a(x-h)^2 + k$. The vertex of a quadratic equation of the form $y = a(x-h)^2 + k$ is (h, k), which means the vertex of $y = 3(x+2)^2 - 12 + k$ is $(2, (-12+k))$.
Given that $(2, (-12+k))$ must equal (–2, –2), solve for k.

$$\begin{aligned} -12 + k &= -2 \\ k &= 10 \end{aligned}$$

The quadratic equation that has a minimum value at the point (–2, –2) is $y = 3x^2 + 12x + 10$.

357. D

Step 1
Use the a-value to determine whether the function has a maximum or a minimum.

In this function, $a = -\frac{1}{3}$. Since $a < 0$, the function has a maximum.

Step 2
Use the k-value to determine the maximum value. In the function, $k = 45$. Therefore, the function has a maximum value of 45.

358. C

Determine the values of a, b, and c by using the appropriate exponent rules.

Step 1
To determine the value of a, apply the product rule, $(x^m)(x^n) = x^{m+n}$, to simplify the expressions in the numerator.

$$\begin{aligned} \frac{(4)^8(4)^{-4}}{(4)^4} &= \frac{(4)^{8-4}}{(4)^4} \\ &= \frac{4^4}{4^4} \end{aligned}$$

The value of a is 4.

Step 2
To determine the value of b, apply the quotient rule, $\frac{x^m}{x^n} = x^{m-n}$.

$$\begin{aligned} \frac{4^4}{4^4} &= 4^{4-4} \\ &= 4^0 \end{aligned}$$

The value of b is 0.

Step 3
To determine the value of c, apply the zero exponent rule, $x^0 = 1$, where $x \neq 0$.

$4^0 = 1$

The value of c is 1.
Therefore, the sum of $a + b + c$ is $4 + 0 + 1 = 5$.

359. B

Compare the equation $f(x) = 3{,}000(1.02)^{4x}$ with the formula $A = P(1+i)^n$ to find that $n = 4x$, $1 + i = 1.02$, and $P = 3{,}000$.

Since the compounding period is $4x$, the money is compounded quarterly. The quarterly interest rate is 2%, so the yearly interest rate is 2% × 4 = 8%. P is the initial investment, so the initial investment is $3,000.

The equation $f(x) = 3{,}000(1.02)^{4x}$ represents $3,000 invested at 8%/$a$, compounded quarterly.

360. A

Apply the product law.

The product law states that the exponents of powers can be added when the bases are the same.

$$5^3 \times 5^6 \times 5^4 = 5^{3+6+4} = 5^{13}$$

361.

The expression contains two powers being divided. Since their bases are the same, the exponents can be subtracted. This simplifies the expression to a single power with a base of $\left(\frac{1}{4}\right)$. Subtract the exponents.

$$\left(\frac{1}{4}\right)^{-2} \div \left(\frac{1}{4}\right)^{3} = \left(\frac{1}{4}\right)^{-2-3} = \left(\frac{1}{4}\right)^{-5}$$

To convert a power with a negative exponent to a power with a positive exponent, take the reciprocal of the base, and change the exponent to a positive value.

$$\left(\frac{1}{4}\right)^{-5} = \frac{1}{\left(\frac{1}{4}\right)^{5}} = 4^5$$

Therefore, $\left(\frac{1}{4}\right)^{-2} \div \left(\frac{1}{4}\right)^{3} = 4^5$

362. C

Apply the laws of exponents to the given expression.

$$\left(x^4y^8\right)^{-\frac{1}{2}} = \frac{1}{\left(x^4y^8\right)^{\frac{1}{2}}} = \frac{1}{\left(x^4\right)^{\frac{1}{2}}\left(y^8\right)^{\frac{1}{2}}} = \frac{1}{x^{4\times\frac{1}{2}}y^{8\times\frac{1}{2}}} = \frac{1}{x^2y^4}$$

363. A

Step 1

Apply the power of a product law.

Rewrite the expression by applying the exponent outside the brackets to each part of the product inside the brackets.

$$\left(6^2 \times 3^4 \times -7\right)^2 = \left(6^2\right)^2 \times \left(3^4\right)^2 \times (-7)^2$$

Step 2

Apply the power of a power law.

Multiply the exponent of each term by the distributed exponent.

$$\left(6^2\right)^2 \times \left(3^4\right)^2 \times (-7)^2 = 6^4 \times 3^8 \times (-7)^2$$

364. C

Step 1

Apply the power of a quotient law, which states that $\left(\frac{a}{b}\right)^m = \frac{a^m}{b^m}$.

$$\left(\frac{4^4}{5^6}\right)^3 = \frac{\left(4^4\right)^3}{\left(5^6\right)^3}$$

Step 2

Apply the power of a power law, which states that $\left(a^m\right)^n = a^{m\times n}$.

$$\frac{\left(4^4\right)^3}{\left(5^6\right)^3} = \frac{4^{4\times3}}{5^{6\times3}} = \frac{4^{12}}{5^{18}}$$

365. C

According to the quotient law of exponents, $a^m \div a^n = a^{m-n}$.

Substitute the known values into the equation simplify.

$$7^{11} \div 7^8 = 7^{11-8} = 7^3$$

366. B

Simplify the expression using the power of a power law of exponents, $\left(a^m\right)^n = a^{mn}$.

$$\left(84^3\right)^0 = 84^{3\times0} = 84^0$$

The zero exponent law states that $a^0 = 1,\ a \neq 0$.

$84^0 = 1$

EXERCISE #2—EXPRESSIONS IN EQUIVALENT FORMS

367. The solutions to the quadratic equation $13 - x = 4x^2 + 3x - 35$ are

A. $x = 3,\ x = -4$

B. $x = 5,\ x = -3$

C. $x = 7,\ x = -5$

D. $x = 13,\ x = -7$

368. What are the coordinates of the x-intercepts of the quadratic function $y = x^2 + 13x + 36$?

A. (0, 9) and (0, 4)

B. (9, 0) and (4, 0)

C. (−9, 0) and (−4, 0)

D. (0, −9) and (0, −4)

Use the following information to answer the next question.

For the quadratic expression $y = x^2 - 2x - 15$, a student factored the equation to obtain $y = (x + 3)(x - 5)$.

369. The factored form that the student used leads to the determination of the

A. vertex of the graph of a parabola

B. minimum value of a parabola

C. x-intercepts of a parabola

D. y-intercept of a parabola

370. The quadratic function $y = x^2 - 8x + 23$ can be expressed in the form $y = a(x - h)^2 + k$ as

A. $y = (x - 7)^2 + 4$

B. $y = (x - 4)^2 + 7$

C. $y = (x - 8)^2 + 23$

D. $y = (x - 4)^2 + 23$

371. Find the minimum value of the function $f(x) = 2x^2 - 8x - 3$ by partially factoring the first two terms.

Use the following information to answer the next question.

Four different forms of the same quadratic function are shown.

Form I: $y = 2x^2 - 3x - 9$

Form II: $y = (x - 3)(2x + 3)$

Form III: $y = 2x\left(x - \frac{3}{2}\right) - 9$

Form IV: $y = 2\left(x - \frac{3}{4}\right)^2 - \frac{81}{8}$

372. Which form allows for the range to be identified by inspection?

A. I **B.** II

C. III **D.** IV

373. If $x \neq 0$, then the simplest form of $2(-3)^0 - 3^0 + (3x)^0$ is

A. 1 **B.** 2

C. $3x$ **D.** $1 + x$

Use the following information to answer the next question.

Rebecca wants to earn \$8,000 in 5 years. She needs to know how much she should put into an account earning interest at 8%/*a* compounded annually. She used the formula $PV = FV(1 + i)^{-n}$ to calculate the present values over 5 years. Then she entered her data as lists on her graphing calculator as shown and did an exponential regression on the data.

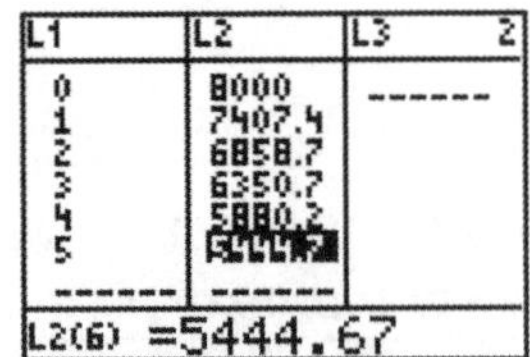

374. According to her exponential regression, the exponential function describing this pattern of decay and present values over x years is

A. $f(x) = 5{,}444.67(0.926)^{-x}$

B. $f(x) = 5{,}444.67(1.08)^{-x}$

C. $f(x) = 8{,}000(0.926)^{x}$

D. $f(x) = 8{,}000(1.08)^{x}$

375. To be applied correctly, the product law of exponents requires

A. variables of terms with the same base to be multiplied

B. coefficients of terms with the same base to be added

C. exponents with the same base to be added

D. powers taken to a power to be multiplied

376. The simplified form of the expression $\dfrac{(-2x^{-3})^{-3}}{(-2x^{-2})^{-4}}$ is

A. $-\dfrac{1}{2x^{17}}$

B. $-2x$

C. $\dfrac{1}{2x^{17}}$

D. $2x$

377. What is the simplified form of the coefficient in the expression $\dfrac{12x^2y^4}{18wxy^2}$?

A. $\dfrac{2}{3}$

B. $\dfrac{3}{4}$

C. $\dfrac{4}{3}$

D. $\dfrac{3}{2}$

378. When the expression $(3b^4)^3$ is simplified, what is the result?

A. $3b^{12}$

B. $27b^{12}$

C. $(3b)^{12}$

D. $(12b)^{12}$

379. The expression $\left(\dfrac{9}{5}\right)^2$ is equivalent to

A. $\dfrac{9}{5}$

B. $\dfrac{81}{5}$

C. $\dfrac{18}{10}$

D. $\dfrac{81}{25}$

Use the following information to answer the next question.

When simplified using the quotient law of exponents, $\dfrac{17^8}{17^5}$ can be written in the form a^b.

380. The value of $a + b$ is __________.

381. What is the value of the expression $(8^3)^3 - (6^5)^2$? __________

EXERCISE #2—EXPRESSIONS IN EQUIVALENT FORMS ANSWERS AND SOLUTIONS

367. A	371. See solution	375. C	379. D
368. C	372. D	376. B	380. 20
369. C	373. B	377. A	381. 73751552
370. B	374. C	378. B	

367. A

Step 1

Express the equation in the form $0 = ax^2 + bx + c$.

$13 - x = 4x^2 + 3x - 35$

$13 = 4x^2 + 4x - 35$

$0 = 4x^2 + 4x - 48$

Step 2

Factor the equation.

$0 = 4x^2 + 4x - 48$

$0 = 4\left(x^2 + x - 12\right)$

$0 = 4(x - 3)(x + 4)$

Step 3

Solve the equation by equating each binomial factor to zero.

$0 = x + 4$

$-4 = x$

$0 = x - 3$

$3 = x$

The solutions for $13 - x = 4x^2 + 3x - 35$ are $x = 3$ and $x = -4$.

368. C

Method 1

Find the x-intercepts by factoring and solving the equation $0 = x^2 + 13x + 36$.

$0 = x^2 + 13x + 36$

$0 = (x + 9)(x + 4)$

$0 = x + 9$

$x = -9$

$0 = x + 4$

$x = -4$

The x-intercepts are –9 and –4.

Method 2

Use the quadratic formula, $x = \dfrac{-b \pm \sqrt{b^2 - 4ac}}{2a}$, to find the x-intercepts.

$x = \dfrac{-b \pm \sqrt{b^2 - 4ac}}{2a}$

$x = \dfrac{-(13) \pm \sqrt{(13)^2 - 4(1)(36)}}{2(1)}$

$x = \dfrac{-13 \pm \sqrt{169 - (144)}}{2}$

$x = \dfrac{-13 \pm \sqrt{25}}{2}$

$x = \dfrac{-13 \pm 5}{\square}$

$x = \dfrac{-13 + 5}{2}$ or $x = \dfrac{-13 - 5}{2}$

$x = \dfrac{-8}{2}$ or $x = \dfrac{-18}{2}$

$x = -4$ or $x = -9$

Both methods provide the same answer, so the x-intercepts of the function $y = x^2 + 13x + 36$ are –9 and –4.

The y-values of the x-intercepts are equal to 0. Therefore, the coordinates of the x-intercepts are (–9, 0) and (–4, 0).

369. C

Recall that when a quadratic equation is expressed in the factored form $y = a(x - m)(x - n)$, the x-intercepts of the graph of the quadratic function will occur at $x = m$ and $x = n$.

370. B

Step 1

Identify and remove the common factor from the x^2- and x-terms in the equation.

In this case, the common factor is 1.

$y = 1\left(x^2 - 8x\right) + 23$

Step 2
Identify the resulting coefficient for the x-term. Divide this value by 2, and then square it.

$y = (x^2 \underline{- 8x}) + 23$

The coefficient of the x-term is −8.

$\left(\frac{-8}{2}\right)^2 = 16$

Step 3
Add and subtract this value inside the brackets.

$y = (x^2 - 8x + \underline{16 - 16}) + 23$

Step 4
Move the value that will not contribute to a perfect square outside the brackets.

$y = (x^2 - 8x + 16\underline{-16}) + 23$
$y = (x^2 - 8x + 16)\underline{-16} + 23$

Step 5
Factor the trinomial inside the brackets to form a perfect square, and collect like terms outside the brackets.

$y = (x - 4)^2 + 7$

The equation can be expressed as $y = (x - 4)^2 + 7$.

371.

The graph of the given function is a parabola opening upwards, which means the function will indeed have a minimum value, at its vertex.

The partially factored form of $f(x) = 2x^2 - 8x - 3$ is $f(x) = 2x(x - 4) - 3$. The values of $f(0)$ and $f(4)$ are both −3. Since the graph of a quadratic function is a parabola symmetrical about a vertical line passing through its vertex, the x-coordinate of the vertex must be at $x = 2$, which is halfway between $x = 0$ and $x = 4$.

Determine the minimum value of the function.

$$\begin{aligned} f(2) &= 2(2)^2 - 8(2) - 3 \\ &= 8 - 16 - 3 \\ &= -11 \end{aligned}$$

The minimum value is −11.

372. D

The only form of a quadratic function that allows you to determine the range by inspection is the vertex form $f(x) = a(x - h)^2 + k$, since the range is defined as $y \le k$, when $a < 0$, and $y \ge k$, when $a > 0$. This form of the function is given in Form IV: $y = 2\left(x - \frac{3}{4}\right)^2 - \frac{81}{8}$, where the range is $y \ge -\frac{81}{8}$.

373. B

Apply the zero exponent rule of $x^0 = 1$, where $x \ne 0$ the terms inside the brackets. Then, simplify by following the order of operations (BEDMAS).

$$\begin{aligned} &2(-3)^0 - 3^0 + (3x)^0 \\ &= 2(1) - 1 + 1 \\ &= 2 - 1 + 1 \\ &= 1 + 1 \\ &= 2 \end{aligned}$$

The simplest form of the expression $2(-3)^0 - 3^0 + (3x)^0$ is 2.

374. C

When the data is entered as lists L_1 and L_2 as shown in the STAT EDIT mode and the exponential regression is done on the data, the following screen on your calculator should appear:

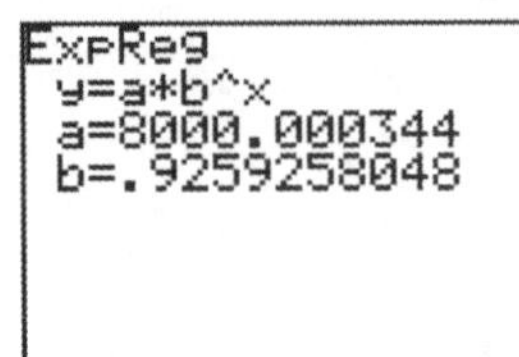

Therefore, the exponential regression function is $f(x) = 8{,}000(0.926)^x$.

375. C

The product law of exponents requires that the exponents must have the same base in order to add the exponents together.

376. B

Step 1
Use the negative exponent principle to convert each power into a power with a positive exponent.

$$\frac{(-2x^{-3})^{-3}}{(-2x^{-2})^{-4}} = \frac{(-2x^{-2})^4}{(-2x^{-3})^3}$$

Step 2
Apply the power of a product law to the powers in the numerator and denominator.

$$\begin{aligned} \frac{(-2x^{-2})^4}{(-2x^{-3})^3} &= \frac{(-2)^4 x^{-2\times4}}{(-2)^3 x^{-3\times3}} \\ &= \frac{(-2)^4 x^{-8}}{(-2)^3 x^{-9}} \end{aligned}$$

Step 3
Apply the quotient of powers law to simplify the expression.

$$\frac{(-2)^4x^{-8}}{(-2)^3x^{-9}} = (-2)^{4-3}x^{-8-(-9)}$$
$$= (-2)^1x^1$$
$$= -2x$$

The simplified form of the given expression is $-2x$.

377. A

Coefficients are numbers that are multiplied by the bases. They are located in front of the variable bases.

In this expression, 12 is located in the numerator in front of the variables x^2y^4, and 18 is located in the denominator in front of the variables wxy^2.

If the greatest common factor of 12 and 18 is 6, then $\frac{12}{18}$ when simplified is $\frac{2}{3}$.

378. B

Step 1
Determine the appropriate law of exponents.
Use the power of products law to solve this problem.

The power of products law states $(ab)^m = a^mb^m$.

Step 2
Apply the power of products law to simplify the expression.
Multiply the exponent outside the brackets by each term inside the brackets.

$$(3b^4)^3 = 3^3b^{4\times3}$$

Simplify.

$$3^3b^{4\times3}$$
$$= (3\times3\times3)b^{12}$$
$$= 27b^{12}$$

379. D

Step 1
Simplify the expression using the quotient law.

The power of a quotient law states $\left(\frac{x}{y}\right)^m = \frac{x^m}{y^m}$.

$$\left(\frac{9}{5}\right)^2 = \frac{9^2}{5^2}$$

Step 2
Evaluate the powers.

$$\frac{9^2}{5^2} = \frac{9\times9}{5\times5}$$
$$= \frac{81}{25}$$

380. 20

The quotient law of exponents states that to divide powers with the same base, subtract the exponents.

$$\frac{17^8}{17^5} = 17^{8-5} = 17^3$$

Since $a = 17$ and $b = 3$, it follows that $a + b = 17 + 3 = 20$.

381. 73751552

Step 1
Evaluate each power.
The power of a power law of exponents states that $(a^m)^n = a^{mn}$.

$$(8^3)^3 = 8^{3\times3}$$
$$= 8^9$$
$$= 134{,}217{,}728$$

$$(6^5)^2 = 6^{5\times2}$$
$$= 6^{10}$$
$$= 60{,}466{,}176$$

Step 2
Find the difference.

134,217,728 – 60,466,176 = 73,751,552

The value of the expression $(8^3)^3 - (6^5)^2$ is 73,751,552.

NOTES

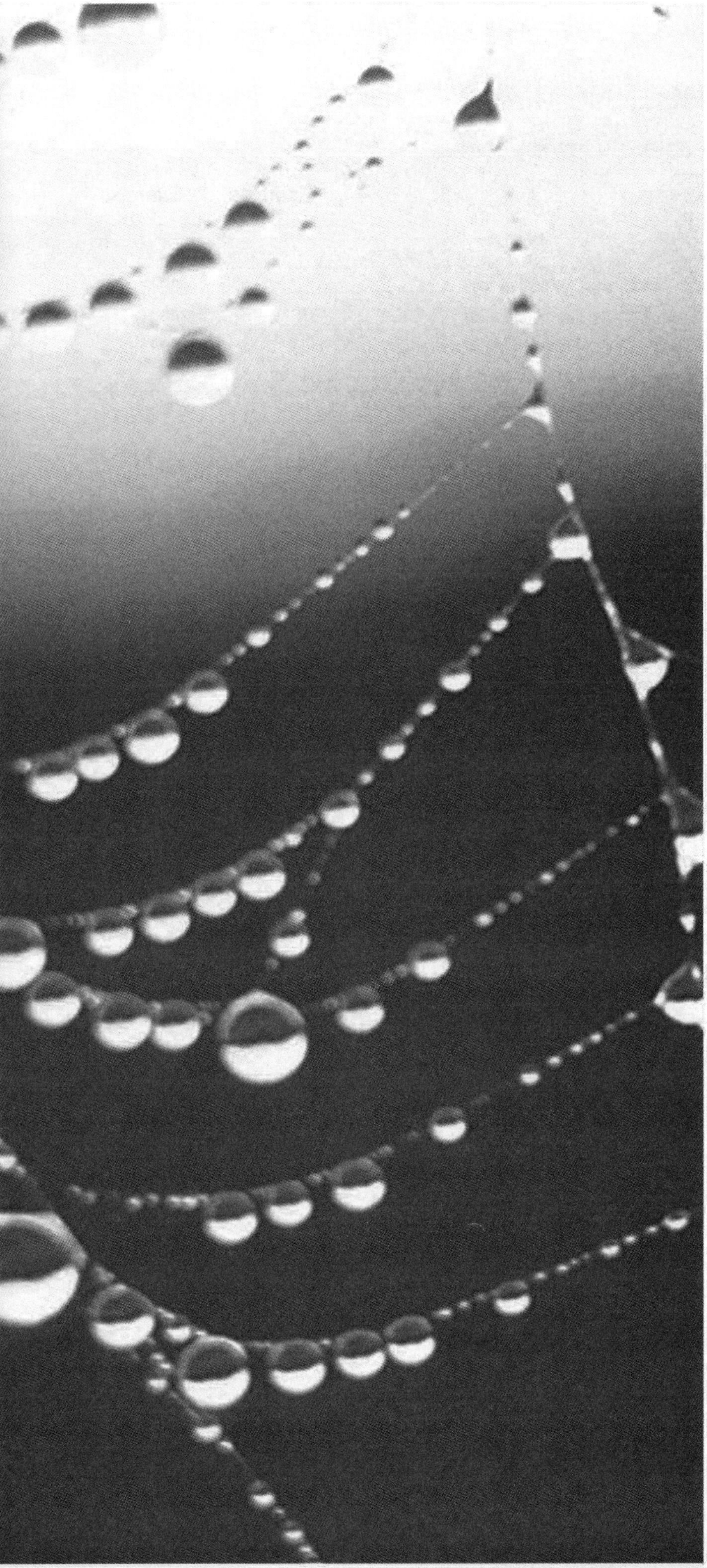

Polynomials

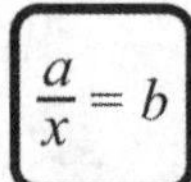

POLYNOMIALS

Table of Correlations				
Standard		Concepts	Exercise #1	Exercise #2
Unit4.3	Perform arithmetic operations on polynomials.			
A-APR.1	*Understand that polynomials form a system analogous to the integers, namely, they are closed under the operations of addition, subtraction, and multiplication; add, subtract, and multiply polynomials.*	Multiplying Two Monomials	382	387
		Multiplying Two Binomials	383	388
		Subtracting Polynomials Algebraically	384	389
		Adding Polynomials Algebraically	385	390
		Multiplying a Polynomial by a Monomial	386	391

$\frac{a}{x} = b$

A-APR.1 Understand that polynomials form a system analogous to the integers, namely, they are closed under the operations of addition, subtraction, and multiplication; add, subtract, and multiply polynomials.

Multiplying Two Monomials

Mono means "one," and *nomial* means "term." Multiplying two monomials means multiplying two terms together.

To multiply two monomials, follow these steps:

1. Break the term into the coefficient and variable.
2. Group the like components.
3. Combine like terms.

Example

Multiply the monomials $(2x)$ and $(3x^2)$.

Solution

Step 1
Break the terms into coefficients and powers.
$(2)(x)(3)(x^2)$

Step 2
Group the components. Group the coefficients together first. Group the variables second.
$= (2)(3)(x)(x^2)$

Step 3
Combine like terms. Multiply the coefficients together. Add exponents of the same base together.
$= (2 \times 3)(x^{1+2})$
$= 6x^3$

Apply the same procedure for monomials with more than one variable.

Example

Multiply the monomials $(2yx)$ and $(3x^2y^3)$.

Solution

Step 1
Break the terms into coefficients and powers.
$(2)(y)(x)(3)(x^2)(y^3)$

Step 2
Group the like components. Group the coefficients together first. Group the powers by variable second. Keep the variables in the same order they appear in the terms.
$= (2)(3)(x \cdot x^2)(y \cdot y^3)$

Step 3
Combine like terms. Multiply the coefficients together. Add exponents of the same base together.
$= (2 \times 3)(x^{1+2})(y^{1+3})$
$= 6x^3y^4$

Multiplying Two Binomials

To expand a product of binomials means multiplying the first binomial by the second binomial. To simplify the result requires the collection of like terms. There are three strategies commonly used to complete this process: the distributive property strategy, the FOIL strategy, and the vertical multiplication strategy.

To use the distributive property strategy, follow these steps:

1. Break the first binomial into its terms.
2. Multiply each term of the first binomial by each term of the second binomial.
3. Combine like terms.

Example

Expand and simplify $(x + 2)(x - 3)$.

Solution

Step 1
Break the first binomial into its terms.
$x + 2$

Step 2
Multiply each term of the first binomial by each term of the second binomial. This eliminates the brackets that surround each of the two binomials.
$= (x)(x - 3) + (2)(x - 3)$
$= (x)(x) + (x)(-3) + (2)(x) + (2)(-3)$
$= x^2 - 3x + 2x - 6$

Step 3
Combine like terms and simplify, writing the terms in descending order by degree.
$= x^2 + (-3x + 2x) - 6$
$= x^2 - 1x - 6$

FOIL:
$(x + a)(x + b) = x^2 + ax + bx + ab$
$= x^2 + (a + b)x + ab$

To use the **FOIL** strategy, follow these steps:

1. Multiply the terms following the acronym FOIL (First Outside Inside Last).
2. Gather up all the terms from the calculations.
3. Combine like terms and simplify, writing the terms in descending order by degree.

Example

Multiply the binomials $(x + 2)(x - 3)$.

Solution

Step 1
Multiply the terms following the acronym FOIL.

1. First
$(x + 2)$ $(x - 3)$
↑ ↑
$x \times x = x^2$
2. Outer
$(x + 2)$ $(x - 3)$
↑ ↑
$x \times -3 = -3x$
3. Inner
$(x + 2)$ $(x - 3)$
↑ ↑
$2 \times x = 2x$
4. Last
$(x + 2)$ $(x - 3)$
↑ ↑
$2 \times -3 = -6$

Step 2
Gather up all the terms from the calculations.
$x^2 - 3x + 2x - 6$

Step 3
Combine like terms and simplify, writing the terms in descending order by degree.
$= x^2 - x - 6$

The last strategy is the vertical multiplication strategy. This strategy places the polynomials vertically. Multiply it out similar to multiplying multi-digit numbers.

Example

Expand and simplify the expression $(x + 2)(x - 3)$.

Solution

Step 1
Write the two binomials, one on top of the other.

$$\begin{array}{r} x + 2 \\ \underline{\times\ x - 3} \end{array}$$

Step 2
Multiply the first term from the bottom row by each term in the top row.

$$\begin{array}{r} x + 2 \\ \underline{\times\ x - 3} \\ -3x - 6 \end{array}$$

Step 3
Multiply the second term from the bottom row by each term in the top row. Write the terms one on top of the other to make adding easier in the next step.

$$\begin{array}{rr} & x + 2 \\ & \underline{\times\ x - 3} \\ & -3x - 6 \\ x^2 + 2x & \end{array}$$

Step 4
Add like terms together.

$$\begin{array}{r} x + 2 \\ \underline{\times\ x - 3} \\ -3x - 6 \\ \underline{+x^2 + 2x\quad\ \ } \\ x^2 - 1x - 6 \end{array}$$

$\frac{a}{x} = b$

Subtracting Polynomials Algebraically

When subtracting polynomials, follow these steps:

1. Write the additive inverse of the expression.
2. Remove the brackets.
3. Organize the terms by writing them in descending order by degree.
4. Combine like terms.

Example

Simplify the polynomial $(2x^2 - 4x + 6) - (4x^2 - 4x + 1)$.

Solution

Step 1

Change the subtraction sign to an addition sign. Switch the signs of the terms located in the second set of brackets to their opposites.

$(2x^2 - 4x + 6) + (-4x^2 + 4x - 1)$

Step 2

Remove the brackets.

$= 2x^2 - 4x + 6 - 4x^2 + 4x - 1$

Step 3

Organize the terms by writing them in descending order by degree, with the constants coming last.

The degree of a term is the sum of the exponents of all its variables. Recall that if there is no exponent on the variable, it has a degree of 1.

$= 2x^2 - 4x^2 - 4x + 4x + 6 - 1$

Step 4

Combine like terms.

Add or subtract the coefficients of like terms while keeping the variable the same. Like terms have the same variable and exponent.

$= -2x^2 + 5$

Adding Polynomials Algebraically

To add polynomials algebraically, follow these steps:

1. Remove the brackets.
2. Organize the terms by writing them in descending order by degree.
3. Combine like terms.

Example

Add the polynomials $(-x^2 - 7x - 4) + (5x^2 + 8x - 1)$.

Solution

Step 1

Remove the brackets.

$-x^2 - 7x - 4 + 5x^2 + 8x - 1$

Step 2

Organize the terms by writing them in descending order by degree, with the constants as the last term. The degree of a term is the sum of the exponents of all its variables. Recall that if there is no exponent on the variable, it has a degree of 1.

$= -x^2 + 5x^2 - 7x + 8x - 4 - 1$

Step 3

Combine like terms. Add or subtract the coefficients of like terms while keeping the variable the same. Like terms have the same variable and exponent.

$= 4x^2 + x - 5$

Multiplying a Polynomial by a Monomial

The following mathematical processes can be used when multiplying a polynomial and a monomial:

- The distributive property: $a(x + y) = ax + ay$
- The product law of exponents: $(x^m)(x^n) = x^{m+n}$
- Collecting and simplifying all like terms.

To multiply a monomial by a polynomial, follow these steps:

1. Distribute the term outside the brackets to each term inside the brackets. This process is called using the **distributive property**.
2. Multiply each pair of terms.
3. Write the resulting terms in descending order by degree, with the constant being the last term. The **degree** of a term is the sum of the exponents of all its *variables*. Recall that if there is no exponent on the variable, the exponent is one.

Examples of terms of varying degree are shown.

- First degree terms (degree 1) → x, $2x$, $-5y$
- Second degree terms (degree 2) → x^2, $2x^2$, $2xy$, xy
- Third degree terms (degree 3) → x^3, $3x^3$, $2xy^2$, $2xyz$, x^2y, xyz

Example

Expand and simplify $3(2x^2 - 6x + 4)$.

Solution

To expand an expression means to multiply each term inside the brackets by the term outside the brackets.

Step 1
Distribute the term outside the brackets to each term inside the brackets.
$(3)(2x^2) + (3)(-6x) + (3)(4)$
Notice the addition signs are written between each group being multiplied. Minus six (–6) is written negative six (–6) in the expansion when applying the distributive property.

Step 2
Multiply each pair of terms. Multiply the coefficients. Add the exponents of like bases.
$= (3 \times 2)(x^2) + (3 \times -6)(x) + (3)(4)$
$= 6x^2 - 18x + 12$
or

$$\begin{array}{r} 2x^2 - 6x + 4 \\ \times \qquad\qquad 3 \\ \hline 6x^2 - 18x + 12 \end{array}$$

Example

Simplify the expression $2xy(3x - 1)$.

Solution

Step 1
Apply the distributive property to expand the expression.

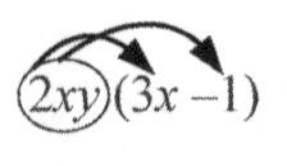

$= 2xy(3x) + 2xy(-1)$

Step 2
Simplify the expression.
Apply the product law, and collect like terms.
$= 2xy(3x) + 2xy(-1)$
$= 6x^2y - 2xy$

$\frac{a}{x} = b$

EXERCISE #1—POLYNOMIALS

382. Find the product of $(3x)(-4x)(-2)$.

383. What is the product of $(2x + 3)$ and $(7x + 10)$?

A. $14x^2 + 30$

B. $14x + 41x + 30$

C. $14x^2 + 41x + 30$

D. $14x^3 + 41x + 30$

384. When $2x - 3y$ is subtracted from $-x + 3y - 1$, the resulting expression is

A. $-3x + 6y - 1$

B. $3x - 6y + 1$

C. $-3x - 1$

D. $3x + 1$

Use the following information to answer the next question.

Selma is asked to determine the sum of the expressions $8a + 5b - 7$ and $6a - b + 10$. Her solution is as shown.

1. $(8a + 5b - 7) + (6a - b + 10)$
   $= (8a + 5b - 7) + (6a - 1b + 10)$
2. $= 8a + 5b - 7 + 6a - 1b + 10$
3. $= 8a + 6a + 5b - 1b - 7 + 10$
4. $= 14a + 4b - 3$

385. In which step did Selma make an error?

A. Step 1 B. Step 2

C. Step 3 D. Step 4

386. When the expression $5x + 3$ is multiplied by $7x$, the resulting expression is

A. $5x^2 + 10x$

B. $35x^2 + 21$

C. $35x^2 + 21x$

D. $5x^2 + 119x$

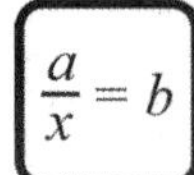

EXERCISE #1—POLYNOMIALS ANSWERS AND SOLUTIONS

382. See solution	384. A	386. C
383. C	385. D	

382.

Step 1
Break the terms into coefficients and variables.
$(3)(x)(-4)(x)(-2)$

Step 2
Group the like components.

Group the coefficients together first. Group the powers by variable second.
$(3)(x)(-4)(x)(-2)$
$= (3)(-4)(-2)(x)(x)$

Step 3
Combine like terms.

Multiply the coefficients together. Add exponents of the same base together.
$(3)(-4)(-2)(x)(x)$
$= (3 \times -4 \times -2)(x^{1+1})$
$= 24x^2$

383. C

Step 1
Multiply each term of the first binomial by each term of the second binomial.
$= (2x+3)(7x+10)$
$= 2x(7x+10)+3(7x+10)$
$= 14x^2+20x+21x+30$

Step 2
Collect like terms and simplify.
$= 14x^2+20x+21x+30$
$= 14x^2+41x+30$

384. A

Step 1
Place each expression in a set of brackets separated by the correct symbol.
$(-x+3y-1)-(2x-3y)$

Step 2
Follow the order of operations, and simplify.
$(-x+3y-1)-(2x-3y)$
$= (-x+3y-1)+(-2x+3y)$
$= -x+3y-1-2x+3y$
$= -x-2x+3y+3y-1$
$= -3x+6y-1$

385. D

Selma made an error in step 4 of her solution. The value of $-7+10$ is 3, not –3.

Instead, Selma should have written
$(8a+5b-7)+(6a-b+10) = 14a+4b+3$.

386. C

Step 1
Distribute the term outside the brackets to each term inside the brackets.
$7x(5x+3)$
$= 7x(5x)+7x(3)$

Step 2
Multiply the coefficients, and add the exponents of the same base together.
$7x(5x)+7x(3)$
$= (7 \times 5)(x^{1+1})+(7 \times 3)(x)$
$= 35x^2+21x$

$\frac{a}{x} = b$

EXERCISE #2—POLYNOMIALS

387. The expression $(2x)(5xy)(3y)$ is equivalent to

A. $10xy^2$
B. $10x^2y^2$
C. $30x^2y^2$
D. $150x^2y^2$

388. The expression $(2x+7)(3x-4)$ is equal to

A. $6x^2+13x-28$
B. $6x^2+21x+3$
C. $5x^2+13x+3$
D. $5x^2+7x-4$

389. Simplify the expression $(-9x^2+2x+4)-(6x^2+1-7x)$.

390. What are the like terms in the expression $3x^2-2x+3x-2y^2$?

A. $3x^2$ and $3x$
B. $-2x$ and $3x$
C. $3x^2$ and $-2y^2$
D. $-2x$ and $-2y^2$

391. When the expression $3y-4x-6$ is multiplied by $-5x$, the result is

A. $15xy-20x^2-30x$
B. $15xy-20x^2+30x$
C. $-15xy+20x^2+30x$
D. $-15xy+20x^2-30x$

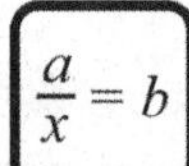

EXERCISE #2—POLYNOMIALS ANSWERS AND SOLUTIONS

387. C	389. See solution	391. C
388. A	390. B	

387. C

Step 1
Break the terms into coefficients and powers.
$(2x)(5xy)(3y)$
$= (2)(x)(5)(x)(y)(3)(y)$

Step 2
Group the coefficients together first. Group the variables second.
$(2)(x)(5)(x)(y)(3)(y)$
$= (2)(5)(3)(x)(x)(y)(y)$

Step 3
Combine like terms. Multiply the coefficients together. Add exponents of the same base together.
$(2)(5)(3)(x)(x)(y)(y)$
$= (2 \times 5 \times 3)(x^{1+1})(y^{1+1})$
$= 30x^2y^2$

388. A

Step 1
Multiply each term of the first binomial by each term of the second binomial.
$= (2x + 7)(3x - 4)$
$= 2x(3x - 4) + 7(3x - 4)$
$= 6x^2 - 8x + 21x - 28$

Step 2
Collect like terms and simplify.
$= 6x^2 - 8x + 21x - 28$
$= 6x^2 + 13x - 28$

389.

Step 1
Change the subtraction sign to an addition sign. Switch the signs of the terms inside the second set of brackets to their opposites.
$(-9x^2 + 2x + 4) + (-6x^2 - 1 + 7x)$

Step 2
Remove the brackets.
$= -9x^2 + 2x + 4 - 6x^2 - 1 + 7x$

Step 3
Organize the terms by writing them in descending order of degree.
$= -9x^2 - 6x^2 + 2x + 7x + 4 - 1$

Step 4
Combine like terms.
$= -15x^2 + 9x + 3$

390. B

Like terms are terms that contain the same variable raised to the same power. The only difference is their coefficients. In an expression, only like terms can be combined. A term with no variable (just a number) is called a constant.

The polynomial $3x^2 - 2x + 3x - 2y^2$ consists of one x^2 term, two x terms, and one y^2 term.
The two x terms ($-2x$ and $3x$) are the like terms.

391. C

Step 1
Distribute the term outside the brackets to each term inside the brackets.
$-5x(3y - 4x - 6)$
$= -5x(3y) - 5x(-4x) - 5x(-6)$

Step 2
Multiply the coefficients together, and add the exponents of the same base together.
$-5x(3y) - 5x(-4x) - 5x(-6)$
$= (-5 \times 3)(x)(y) + (-5 \times -4)(x^{1+1})$
$+ (-5 \times -6)(x)$
$= -15xy + 20x^2 + 30x$

One Variable Quadratic Equations

ONE VARIABLE QUADRATIC EQUATIONS

Table of Correlations

Standard		Concepts	Exercise #1	Exercise #2
Unit4.5	Solve equations and inequalities in one variable.			
A-REI.4a	*Solve quadratic equations in one variable. Use the method of completing the square to transform any quadratic equation in x into an equation of the form $(x-p)^2 = q$ that has the same solutions. Derive the quadratic formula from this form.*	Expressing $y = ax^2 + bx + c$ in the Form $y = a(x-h)^2 + k$ by Completing the Square	355	370
		Developing the Quadratic Formula	392	396
A-REI. 4bii	*Solve quadratic equations in one variable. Solve quadratic equations by inspection, taking square roots, completing the square, the quadratic formula and factoring, as appropriate to the initial form of the equation. Recognize when the quadratic formula gives complex solutions and write them as $a \pm bi$ for real numbers a and b.*	Solving Quadratic Equations Using Technology	102	107
		Solving Quadratic Equations by Factoring	352	367
		Using the Discriminant to Determine the Nature of the Roots of a Quadratic Equation	393	397
		Solving Quadratic Equations by Completing the Square	394	398
		Solving Quadratic Equations Using the Quadratic Formula	395	399

A-REI.4a Solve quadratic equations in one variable. Use the method of completing the square to transform any quadratic equation in x into an equation of the form $(x-p)^2 = q$ that has the same solutions. Derive the quadratic formula from this form.

Developing the Quadratic Formula

The **quadratic formula** can be used to determine the exact value and the approximate value of the roots of a quadratic equation that is either not factorable or not easily factorable.

The formula can be developed by isolating x in the equation $ax^2 + bx + c = 0$ by completing the square.

Factor out a from the x^2- and x-terms.

$$ax^2 + bx + c = 0$$
$$a\left(x^2 + \frac{b}{a}x\right) + c = 0$$

Using the coefficient of the x-term in the brackets (denoted by $\frac{b}{a}$), divide this value by 2, and then square it.

$$\left(\frac{b}{2a}\right)^2 = \frac{b^2}{4a^2}$$

Add and subtract the resulting value, $\frac{b^2}{4a^2}$, inside the brackets to maintain equality.

$$a\left(x^2 + \frac{b}{a}x + \frac{b^2}{4a^2} - \frac{b^2}{4a^2}\right) + c = 0$$

Move the value that will not contribute to a perfect square outside the brackets, remembering to multiply the value by a to maintain equality.

$$a\left(x^2 + \frac{b}{a}x + \frac{b^2}{4a^2}\right) - \frac{ab^2}{4a^2} + c = 0$$

Simplify the equation.

$$a\left(x^2 + \frac{b}{a}x + \frac{b^2}{4a^2}\right) - \frac{b^2}{4a} + c = 0$$

Factor the perfect trinomial inside the brackets.

$$a\left(x + \frac{b}{2a}\right)^2 - \frac{b^2}{4a} + c = 0$$

Isolate x.

$$a\left(x + \frac{b}{2a}\right)^2 = \left(\frac{b^2}{4a} - c\right)$$
$$\left(x + \frac{b}{2a}\right)^2 = \frac{b^2}{4a^2} - \frac{c}{a}$$
$$\left(x + \frac{b}{2a}\right)^2 = \frac{b^2}{4a^2} - \frac{4ac}{4a^2}$$
$$\left(x + \frac{b}{2a}\right)^2 = \frac{b^2 - 4ac}{4a^2}$$
$$\sqrt{\left(x + \frac{b}{2a}\right)^2} = \pm\sqrt{\frac{b^2 - 4ac}{4a^2}}$$
$$x + \frac{b}{2a} = \pm\frac{\sqrt{b^2 - 4ac}}{2a}$$
$$x = -\frac{b}{2a} \pm \frac{\sqrt{b^2 - 4ac}}{2a}$$
$$x = \frac{-b \pm \sqrt{b^2 - 4ac}}{2a}$$

The exact roots, as well as the approximate roots of the quadratic equation $ax^2 + bx + c = 0$, in which $a \neq 0$, can be determined using the quadratic formula.

$$x = \frac{-b \pm \sqrt{b^2 - 4ac}}{2a}$$

A-REI.4bii Solve quadratic equations in one variable. Solve quadratic equations by inspection, taking square roots, completing the square, the quadratic formula and factoring, as appropriate to the initial form of the equation. Recognize when the quadratic formula gives complex solutions and write them as a ± bi for real numbers a and b.

Using the Discriminant to Determine the Nature of the Roots of a Quadratic Equation

The nature of the roots of a quadratic equation can be determined using the radicand $b^2 - 4ac$ in the quadratic formula $x = \frac{-b \pm \sqrt{b^2 - 4ac}}{2a}$, which is called the **discriminant**.

The value of the discriminant determines whether the quadratic equation $ax^2 + bx + c = 0$, $a \neq 0$ has no real roots, two real and equal roots, or two real and different roots.

- If $b^2 - 4ac < 0$, then the quadratic equation $ax^2 + bx + c = 0$, $a \neq 0$, has no real roots.
- If $b^2 - 4ac = 0$, then the quadratic equation, $ax^2 + bx + c = 0, a \neq 0$, has two real and equal roots.
- If $b^2 - 4ac > 0$, then the quadratic equation, $ax^2 + bx + c = 0, a \neq 0$, has exactly two real and different roots.

Example

For the quadratic equation $3x^2 - 2x + 4 = 0$, use the discriminant to describe the nature of the roots.

Solution

Step 1
Identify the values of a, b, and c in the quadratic equation of the form $ax^2 + bx + c = 0$, $a \neq 0$.
$a = 3$, $b = -2$, and $c = 4$

Step 2
Determine the value of the discriminant $b^2 - 4ac$.

Substitute the values of a, b, and c into the discriminant $b^2 - 4ac$.

For $3x^2 - 2x + 4 = 0$,

$$\begin{aligned} b^2 - 4ac &= (-2)^2 - 4(3)(4) \\ &= 4 - 48 \\ &= -44 \end{aligned}$$

Since $b^2 - 4ac = -44$, $b^2 - 4ac < 0$ and the given equation has no real roots.

Solving Quadratic Equations by Completing the Square

A **quadratic equation** is any equation in the form $0 = ax^2 + bx + c$, where a, b, and c are real numbers and $a \neq 0$.

Quadratic equations cannot always be solved by factoring. However, just because a quadratic equation cannot be factored does not necessarily mean that the equation does not have solutions. When a quadratic equation cannot be solved by factoring, the method of **completing the square** can be employed.

In completed square form, the quadratic equation $0 = ax^2 + bx + c$ is expressed as $0 = a(x - p)^2 + q$.

The goal in completing the square is to generate a perfect square trinomial that can be factored as $(x - p)^2$ from the equation $0 = a(x - p)^2 + q$.

The following example illustrates the process involved in solving a quadratic equation by completing the square.

Example

Solve the quadratic equation $0 = x^2 - 4x - 45$ by completing the square.

Solution

Step 1
Factor the coefficient from the x^2- and x-terms.

Since $a = 1$ in the given equation, no factoring is required.

$0 = x^2 - 4x - 45$

Step 2
Divide the coefficient of the x-term (b) by 2, and then square it.
$\left(\frac{-4}{2}\right)^2 = 4$

Step 3
Both add and subtract this value (4) to keep the value of the expression the same, and collect like terms.

Note that the expression in the brackets is a perfect square trinomial.
$0 = \left(x^2 - 4x + 4\right) - 4 - 45$
$0 = \left(x^2 - 4x + 4\right) - 49$

Step 4
Factor the perfect square trinomial, and add 49 to both sides of the equation.
$49 = (x - 2)^2$

Step 5
Take the square root of both sides of the equation, and solve for x.
$\pm 7 = x - 2$

Add 2 to both sides.
$2 \pm 7 = x$

The solutions are $x = 2 + 7 = 9$ or $x = 2 - 7 = -5$.

Sometimes, some small modifications to the routine method of completing the square is helpful when $a \neq 1$. These modifications may include multiplying both sides of an equation by -1 to make the value of a positive, or factoring out a common factor from each term.

Example

Solve the quadratic equation $-3k^2 + 24k + 11 = 0$ by completing the square.

Solution

Step 1
Multiply both sides of the equation $-3k^2 + 24k + 11 = 0$ by -1.

Multiplying by -1 eliminates the need to work with a negative leading coefficient (negative a-value).
$3k^2 - 24k - 11 = 0$

Step 2
Add 11 to both sides of the equation
$3k^2 - 24k - 11 = 0$.
$3k^2 - 24k = 11$

Step 3
Divide both sides of the equation by 3.
$k^2 - 8k = \frac{11}{3}$

Step 4
Complete the square.
Remember that the goal of completing the square is to generate a perfect square trinomial. Note that 16 must be added to both sides of the equation.

$$k^2 - 8k + \_\_ = \frac{11}{3}$$
$$k^2 - 8k + 16 = \frac{11}{3} + 16$$
$$(k - 4)^2 = \frac{59}{3}$$

Step 5
Take the square root of both sides.
$$k - 4 = \pm\frac{\sqrt{59}}{\sqrt{3}}$$

Step 6
Simplify, and solve for k.
Multiply the numerator and denominator by $\sqrt{3}$ to rationalize the denominator.

$$k - 4 = \pm\frac{\sqrt{177}}{3}$$
$$k = 4 \pm \frac{\sqrt{177}}{3}$$
$$k = \frac{12 \pm \sqrt{177}}{3}$$

After completing the square, the solution to the quadratic equation $-3k^2 + 24k + 11 = 0$ is $k = \frac{12 \pm \sqrt{177}}{3}$.

Solving Quadratic Equations Using the Quadratic Formula

The roots of a quadratic equation, $ax^2 + bx + c = 0$, in which $a \neq 0$, can be found using the **quadratic formula**, $x = \dfrac{-b \pm \sqrt{b^2 - 4ac}}{2a}$.

Example

Solve the equation $x^2 - 4x - 45 = 0$ using the quadratic formula.

Solution

Step 1

Identify the values of a, b, and c.

$a = 1\, b = -4\, c = -45$

Step 2

Substitute the values for a, b, and c into the quadratic formula, and solve for x.

$$x = \frac{-b \pm \sqrt{b^2 - 4ac}}{2a}$$

$$x = \frac{-(-4) \pm \sqrt{(-4)^2 - 4(1)(-45)}}{2(1)}$$

$$x = \frac{4 \pm \sqrt{16 + 180}}{2}$$

$$x = \frac{4 \pm \sqrt{196}}{2}$$

$$x = \frac{4 \pm 14}{2}$$

Therefore,

$$x = \frac{4 + 14}{2} = 9 \text{ or } x = \frac{4 - 14}{2} = -5.$$

Example

Determine the exact roots to the equation $x^2 - 8x + 5 = 0$ by applying the quadratic formula.

Solution

Step 1

Identify the values of a, b, and c.

$a = 1 \quad b = -8 \quad c = 5$

Step 2

Substitute the values for a, b and c into the quadratic formula, and solve for x.

$$x = \frac{-b \pm \sqrt{b^2 - 4ac}}{2a}$$

$$= \frac{-(-8) \pm \sqrt{(-8)^2 - 4(1)(5)}}{2(1)}$$

$$= \frac{8 \pm \sqrt{64 - 20}}{2}$$

$$= \frac{8 \pm \sqrt{44}}{2}$$

$$= \frac{8 \pm \sqrt{4 \times 11}}{2}$$

$$= \frac{8 \pm 2\sqrt{11}}{2}$$

$$= \frac{2(4 \pm \sqrt{11})}{2}$$

$$= 4 \pm \sqrt{11}$$

The roots of the given equation are $4 + \sqrt{11}$ and $4 - \sqrt{11}$.

Example

Solve the equation $\frac{3}{4}x^2 + 2x = 5$ using the quadratic formula.

Solution

Step 1

Rearrange the equation $\frac{3}{4}x^2 + 2x = 5$ to identify the values of a, b, and c.

In cases in which the values are rational, it is also helpful to multiply both sides of the equation by a multiple of the denominators to make the values integral.

$$\frac{3}{4}x^2 + 2x = 5$$

$$(4)\left(\frac{3}{4}x^2\right) + (4)(2x) = (4)(5)$$

$$3x^2 + 8x - 20 = 0$$

$a = 3\, b = 8\, c = -20$

(x,y)

Step 2
Substitute the values into the quadratic formula.

$$x = \frac{-b \pm \sqrt{b^2 - 4ac}}{2a}$$

$$x = \frac{-8 \pm \sqrt{8^2 - 4(3)(-20)}}{2(3)}$$

$$x = \frac{-8 \pm \sqrt{64 + 240}}{6}$$

$$x = \frac{-8 \pm \sqrt{304}}{6}$$

Step 3
Convert to a mixed radical.

$$x = \frac{-8 \pm \sqrt{(16)(19)}}{6}$$

$$x = \frac{-8 \pm 4\sqrt{19}}{6}$$

Divide each term in the numerator and denominator by 2.

$$x = \frac{-4 \pm 2\sqrt{19}}{3}$$

EXERCISE #1—ONE VARIABLE QUADRATIC EQUATIONS

Use the following information to answer the next question.

> The first three steps in the algebraic development of the quadratic formula $ax^2 + bx + c = 0$ are given as follows:
>
> 1. $a\left(x^2 + \frac{b}{a}x\right) + c = 0$
> 2. $a\left(x^2 + \frac{b}{a}x + \frac{b^2}{4a^2} - \frac{b^2}{4a^2}\right) + c = 0$
> 3. $a(x + K)^2 - \frac{b^2}{4a} + c = 0$

392. Which expression is represented by the variable K?

A. $\frac{b^2}{4a^2}$ B. $\frac{b^2}{2a^2}$

C. $\frac{b}{4a}$ D. $\frac{b}{2a}$

393. Determine the equations of the family of lines that have a slope of 2 and that intersect the graph of the quadratic function $f(x) = -x^2 + 8x$ once, twice, or never.

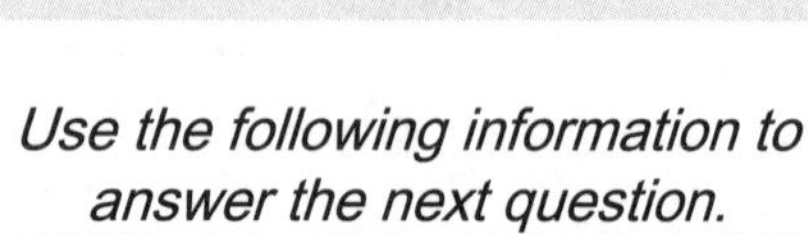

Use the following information to answer the next question.

> When the equation $x^2 + 8x + 3 = 0$ is solved by completing the square, the solution has the form of $x = -4 \pm \sqrt{a}$.

394. What is the value of a? __________

395. Determine the real number solutions for $2y^2 + 11y = -15$ using the quadratic formula.

EXERCISE #1—ONE VARIABLE QUADRATIC EQUATIONS ANSWERS AND SOLUTIONS

392. D	393. See solution	394. 13	395. See solution

392. D

In step 3, the value that does not contribute to a perfect square is moved outside the brackets.

Applying the distributive property, multiply $\frac{b^2}{4a^2}$ by the a in front of the brackets so the value outside the brackets becomes $\frac{b^2}{4a}$ which agrees with what is shown.

Now, factor the remaining perfect square trinomial inside the brackets.

Divide the term $\frac{b}{a}$ by 2 to give $\frac{b}{2a}$ which can be used to express the perfect square trinomial in factored form as the following shows.

$a\left(x+\frac{b}{2a}\right)^2-\frac{b^2}{4a}+c=0.$

The variable K represents the expression $\frac{b}{2a}$.

393.

Step 1

Determine the equations of the family of lines that have a slope of 2.

All lines with a slope of 2 have an equation of the form $y=2x+k$, where k is the y-intercept.

Step 2

To determine the number of points of intersection, equate the two functions, and put the resulting equation in the form $ax^2+bx+c=0$.

$2x+k=-x^2+8x$

$x^2-6x+k=0$

Step 3

The value of the discriminant, b^2-4ac, dictates the number and nature of the solutions to an equation of the form $ax^2+bx+c=0$.

Substitute the known values into b^2-4ac.

$b^2-4ac=(-6)^2-4(1)k$
$=36-4k$

Step 4

Determine the value of k if there is one intersection.

If $b^2-4ac=0$, there are two real, yet equal solutions to the equation, so there is one point of intersection.

$36-4k=0$
$36=4k$
$9=k$

The line $y=2x+9$ will intersect the parabola $f(x)=-x^2+8x$ at only one point.

Step 5

Determine the value of k if there are two intersections.

If $b^2-4ac>0$, there are two real and different solutions to the equation and thus two points of intersection.

$36-4k>0$
$36>4k$
$9>k$

All lines with a slope of 2 and a y-intercept less than 9 will intersect the parabola $f(x)=-x^2+8x$ at two points.

Step 6

Determine the value of k if there is no intersection.

If $b^2-4ac<0$, there are no real solutions to the equation and thus no points of intersection.

$36-4k<0$
$36<4k$
$9<k$

All lines with a slope of 2 and a y-intercept greater than 9 will not intersect the parabola $f(x)=-x^2+8x$ at any point.

394. 13

Step 1

Subtract 3 from each side of the equation.

$x^2+8x+3=0$

$x^2+8x=-3$

Step 2

Complete the square.

x^2+8x+ __________ $=-3$

Since $\left[\frac{1}{2}(8)\right]^2=16$, add 16 to each side of the equation. Then, factor the perfect square trinomial.

$x^2+8x+16=-3+16$
$(x+4)^2=13$

Step 3
Take the square root of both sides.
$x + 4 = \pm\sqrt{13}$

Step 4
Solve for x.
$x = -4 \pm \sqrt{13}$

It is given that the solution is $x = -4 \pm \sqrt{a}$; therefore, the value of a is 13.

395.

Step 1
Write the equation in the general form, $ax^2 + bx + c = 0$.

$$2y^2 + 11y = -15$$
$$2y^2 + 11y + 15 = 0$$

Step 2
Use the quadratic formula to solve the equation.

For a general quadratic equation, $ax^2 + bx + c = 0$, the value of x is given by the formula

$$x = \frac{-b \pm \sqrt{b^2 - 4ac}}{2a}.$$

Use the formula to determine the value of y.

$$y = \frac{-11 \pm \sqrt{11^2 - 4(2)(15)}}{2(2)}$$
$$y = \frac{-11 \pm \sqrt{121 - 120}}{4}$$
$$y = \frac{-11 \pm \sqrt{1}}{4}$$
$$y = \frac{-11 \pm 1}{4}$$

Therefore, $y = -\frac{5}{2}$ or $y = -3$.

(x,y)

EXERCISE #2—ONE VARIABLE QUADRATIC EQUATIONS

Use the following information to answer the next question.

A student's attempt at developing the quadratic formula is partially shown.

$ax^2 + bx + c = 0$

1. $x^2 + \frac{b}{a}x + \frac{c}{a} = 0$
2. $x^2 + \frac{b}{a}x = -\frac{c}{a}$
3. $x^2 + \frac{b}{a}x + \frac{b^2}{4a^2} - \frac{b^2}{4a^2} = -\frac{c}{a}$
4. $x^2 + \frac{b}{a}x + \frac{b^2}{4a^2} = \frac{b^2}{4a^2} - \frac{c}{a}$
5. $\left(x + \frac{b}{2a}\right)^2 = \frac{b^2}{4a^2} - \frac{c}{a}$

396. If steps 1 to 5 are correct, what is the next correct step?

A. $x + \frac{b}{2a} = \frac{b}{2a} - \frac{c}{a}$

B. $x + \frac{b}{2a} = \frac{b}{2a} - \sqrt{\frac{c}{a}}$

C. $\left(x + \frac{b}{2a}\right)^2 = \frac{b^2 - 4ac}{4a^2}$

D. $\left(x + \frac{b}{2a}\right)^2 = \frac{b^2 - 4ac}{2a}$

397. How many real zeros does the quadratic function $y = 3x^2 + 2x + 4$ have?

398. A student solves $2x^2 - 8x = 15$ by completing the square. One of the solutions to the equation is

A. $2 + \sqrt{23}$ B. $\frac{4 - \sqrt{46}}{2}$

C. $\frac{4 - \sqrt{23}}{2}$ D. $\frac{2 + \sqrt{46}}{2}$

399. Correct to the nearest tenth, what is one of the roots of the quadratic equation $5x^2 - 6x = 2$?

A. −1.5 B. −0.3

C. 5.1 D. 6.9

EXERCISE #2—ONE VARIABLE QUADRATIC EQUATIONS ANSWERS AND SOLUTIONS

396. C	397. See solution	398. B	399. B

396. C

Step 5 is as follows:

$$\left(x+\frac{b}{2a}\right)^2=\frac{b^2}{4a^2}-\frac{c}{a}$$

The next correct step involves placing the two terms on the right side of the equation over a common denominator.

$$\left(x+\frac{b}{2a}\right)^2=\frac{b^2-4ac}{4a^2}$$

397.

The nature of the zeros of a quadratic function can be determined by finding the value of the discriminant, b^2-4ac, given a quadratic of the form ax^2+bx+c.

Determine the value of the discriminant.

$$\begin{aligned}&b^2-4ac\\&=(2)^2-4(3)(4)\\&=4-48\\&=-44\end{aligned}$$

Since the discriminant is less than zero, the function has no real zeros.

398. B

$$2x^2-8x=15$$

Divide each side of the equation by 2.

$$x^2-4x=\frac{15}{2}$$

Complete the square.

$$x^2-4x+\underline{\qquad\qquad}=\frac{15}{2}$$

$$x^2-4x+4=\frac{15}{2}+4$$

$$(x-2)^2=\frac{23}{2}$$

Take the square root of each side of the equation.

$$x-2=\pm\frac{\sqrt{23}}{\sqrt{2}}$$

Multiply the numerator and denominator by $\sqrt{2}$ to rationalize the denominator.

$$x-2=\pm\frac{\sqrt{46}}{2}$$

Solve for x.

$$x=2\pm\frac{\sqrt{46}}{2}$$

Simplify.

$$x=\frac{4\pm\sqrt{46}}{2}$$

The solutions to the equation are $4+\frac{\sqrt{46}}{2}$ and $4-\frac{\sqrt{46}}{2}$.

399. B

Step 1

Rewrite the equation in $ax^2+bx+c=0$ form.

$$5x^2-6x=2$$

$$5x^2-6x-2=0$$

Step 2
Use the quadratic formula if factoring is not possible. Identify the values of a, b, and c, and substitute them into the quadratic formula.

$a = 5$
$b = -6$
$c = -2$

$$x = \frac{-b \pm \sqrt{b^2 - 4ac}}{2a}$$

$$x = \frac{-(-6) \pm \sqrt{(-6)^2 - 4(5)(-2)}}{2(5)}$$

Step 3
Simplify.

$$x = \frac{6 \pm \sqrt{36 + 40}}{10}$$

$$x = \frac{6 \pm 2\sqrt{19}}{10}$$

$$x = \frac{6 + 2\sqrt{19}}{10} \approx 1.471779$$

or

$$x = \frac{6 - 2\sqrt{19}}{10} \approx -0.271779$$

Step 4
Round the solutions to the nearest tenth.
The solutions are 1.5 and −0.3.
Therefore, one root of the quadratic equation is −0.3.

NOTES

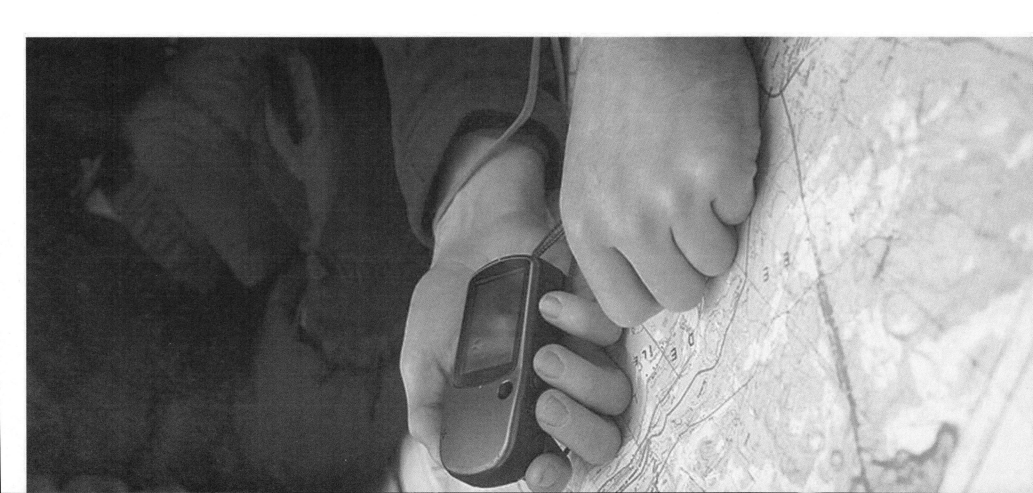

Solving Systems of Equations

SOLVING SYSTEMS OF EQUATIONS

Table of Correlations

Standard		Concepts	Exercise #1	Exercise #2
Unit4.6	Solve systems of equations.			
A-REI.7	*Solve a simple system consisting of a linear equation and a quadratic equation in two variables algebraically and graphically.*	Solving a Linear-Quadratic System of Equations with Two Variables by Substitution	400	402
		Solving Systems of Linear and Quadratic Equations Graphically	401	403

A-REI.7 Solve a simple system consisting of a linear equation and a quadratic equation in two variables algebraically and graphically.

Solving a Linear-Quadratic System of Equations with Two Variables by Substitution

Algebraic methods of solving a system of equations allow for exact value solutions. A solution to the system is an ordered pair (x, y) that satisfies both equations.

A linear-quadratic system of equations can be solved by substitution by following these steps:

1. Isolate one variable from one of the equations.
2. Substitute the isolated variable into the second equation, and simplify.
3. Factor the equation, and solve for the variable.
4. Substitute the solved value into either one of the original equations, and then solve for the unknown variable.
5. Write the solutions as ordered pairs in set notation.

A linear-quadratic system may have two, one, or no solutions.

Example

A system of equations is given.

① $y = x^2 - x + 5$
② $y = 3 - 4x$

Determine all the possible solutions of the system.

Solution

Step 1
Isolate one variable from equation (1) or (2). In this case, both equations already have a variable isolated.

Step 2
Substitute the isolated variable into the second equation, and simplify.
Substitute $3 - 4x$ for y in equation (1).

$3 - 4x = x^2 - x + 5$
$0 = x^2 + 3x + 2$

Step 3
Factor the equation, and solve for the variable.

$0 = x^2 + 3x + 2$
$0 = (x + 2)(x + 1)$

$0 = x + 2$
$-2 = x$

$0 = x + 1$
$-1 = x$

$x = -2$ or -1

Step 4
Substitute the solved values into equation (1) or (2), and solve for the unknown variable.

$y = 3 - 4x$
$y = 3 - 4(-2)$
$y = 11$

$y = 3 - 4x$
$y = 3 - 4(-1)$
$y = 7$

Step 5
Write the solutions as ordered pairs in set notation.
$\{(-2, 11), (-1, 7)\}$

A system of equations is given.

① $0 = x^2 + x - y$
② $0 = 6x - 2y - 2$

Determine all the possible solutions of the system.

Solution

Step 1
Isolate one variable from equation (1) or (2).

② $0 = 6x - 2y - 2$
$2y = 6x - 2$
$y = 3x - 1$

Step 2
Substitute the isolated variable into the second equation, and simplify.
Substitute $3x - 1$ for y in equation (1).

$0 = x^2 + x - (3x - 1)$
$0 = x^2 + x - 3x + 1$
$0 = x^2 - 2x + 1$

Step 3
Factor the equation, and solve for the variable.

$0 = x^2 - 2x + 1$
$0 = (x - 1)(x - 1)$
$0 = x - 1$
$1 = x$

Step 4
Substitute the solved value into equation (1) or (2), and solve for the unknown variable.

② $0 = 6x - 2y - 2$
$0 = 6(1) - 2y - 2$
$0 = 6 - 2y - 2$
$0 = 4 - 2y$
$2y = 4$
$y = 2$

Step 5
Write the solution as an ordered pair in set notation.
$\{(1, 2)\}$

Solving Systems of Linear and Quadratic Equations Graphically

Solving systems with linear and quadratic equations graphically involves showing all points common to both graphs. This occurs where the graphs of the equations intersect.

To solve systems of linear and quadratic equations graphically, graph the equations and find all points of intersection.

Example

A system of equations is given.
$y = -x$
$y = x^2 - 2$

Determine the solutions to the system of equations graphically.

Solution

Step 1
Graph the equations.

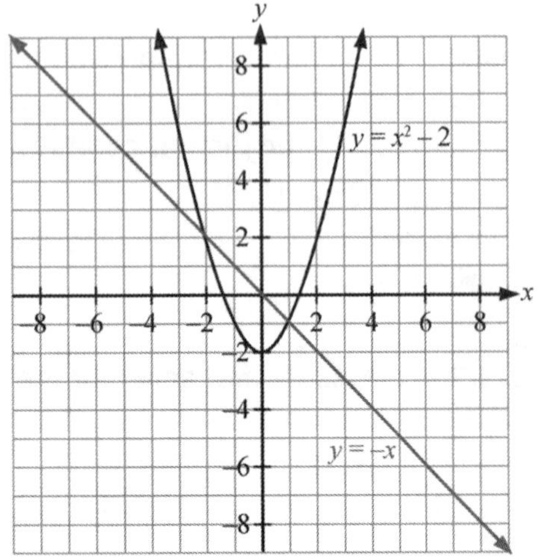

Step 2
Determine the points of intersection.

From the graph, it can be seen that the points of intersection are $(1, -1)$ and $(-2, 2)$.

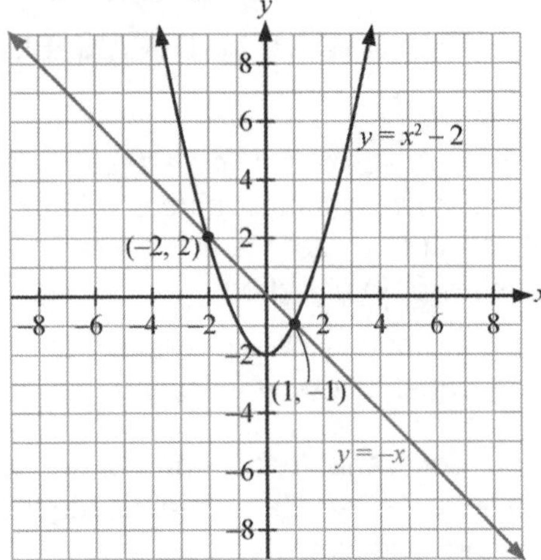

The solution set to the system is $\{(1, -1), (-2, 2)\}$.

Example

$4x - y = 5$
$y = x^2 - 2$

Solve the given system using a graphing calculator.

Solution

Step 1
Write the first equation in function form.
$y = 4x - 5$

Step 2
Graph the equations using a graphing calculator.

Press Y =, and input each function.

$Y_1 = 4X - 5$

$Y_2 = X^2 - 2.$

Press GRAPH. The window setting used to display the two graphs is x:[−5, 5, 1] y:[−5, 10, 1].

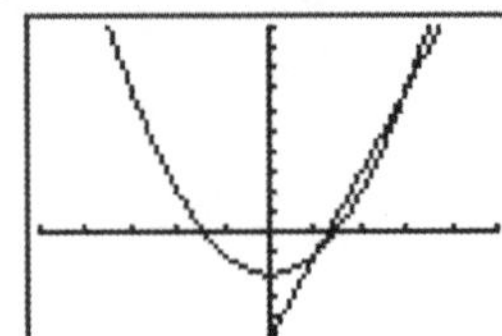

Step 3

Find the points of intersection.

Press 2nd TRACE, and choose 5:intersect.

For "First curve?", position the cursor just left or right of the intersection point that is farthest to the left, and press ENTER.

For "Second curve?", position the cursor just left or right of the intersection point that is farthest to the left, and press ENTER.

For "Guess?", press ENTER.

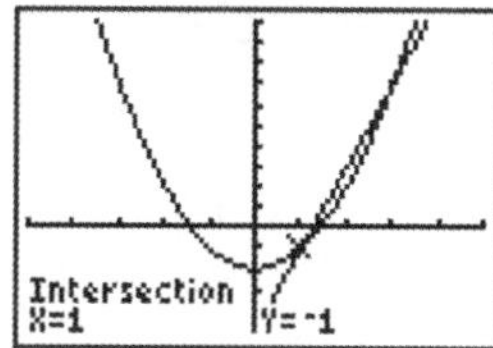

Repeat the process with the intersection point that is farthest to the right.

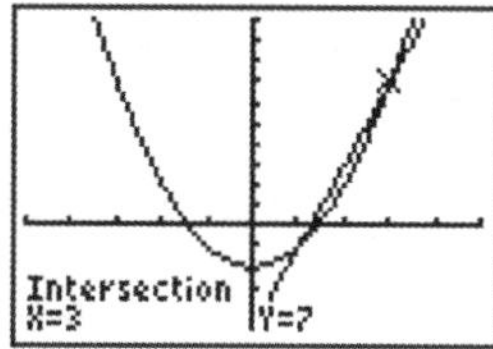

The solution to the system of equations is $\{(1, -1), (3, 7)\}$.

The calculator indicates that the two points of intersection of the curve and the line are at $(1, -1)$ and $(3, 7)$.

EXERCISE #1—SOLVING SYSTEMS OF EQUATIONS

Use the following information to answer the next question.

A system of equations is given.
① $5x + 316 = y$
② $2x - y = -3x^2 - 100$

400. What is the solution set of this system of equations?
A. {(3, 278), (−6, 159)}
B. {(3, −278), (6, 159)}
C. {(9, −361), (8, 276)}
D. {(9, 361), (−8, 276)}

Use the following information to answer the next question.

Two different systems of equations are given.

System A	System B
$y = 3x^2 - 12$ $6x - y = 3$	$2x^2 - 12x - y = 0$ $4x + y = 10$

Carl and Cara are asked to solve the solution sets graphically.

To find the solution set to system A, Carl graphs the equations $y = 3x^2 - 12$ and $6x - y = 3$.

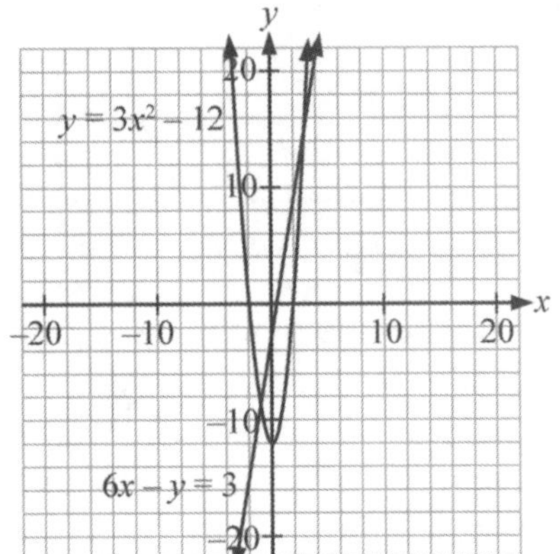

He determines that since the graphs of $y = 3x^2 - 12$ and $6x - y = 3$ intersect at the points (15, 3) and (−9, −1), the solution set to system A is {(15, 3), (−9, −1)}.

To find the solution set to system B, Cara graphs the equations $2x^2 - 12x - y = 0$ and $4x + y = 10$.

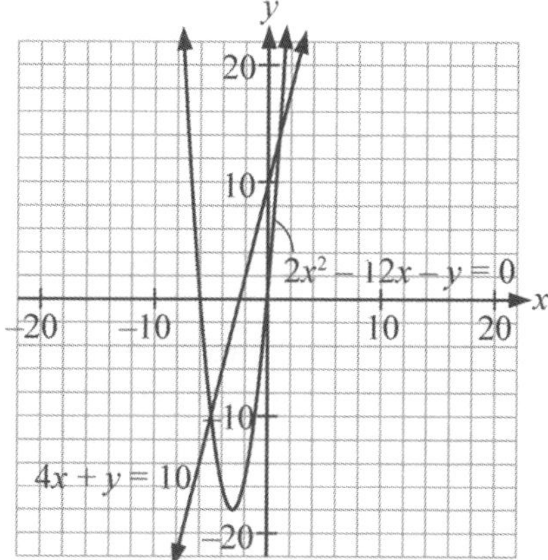

She determines that since the graphs of $2x^2 - 12x - y = 0$ and $4x + y = 10$ intersect at the points (−5, −10) and (1, 14), the solution set to system B is {(−5, −10), (1, 14)}.

401. Which of the following statements about the students' solutions is **true**?

A. Both Carl's and Cara's solutions are correct.

B. Both Carl's and Cara's solutions are incorrect.

C. Carl's solution is correct, and Cara's solution is incorrect.

D. Carl's solution is incorrect, and Cara's solution is correct.

EXERCISE #1—SOLVING SYSTEMS OF EQUATIONS ANSWERS AND SOLUTIONS

400. D	401. B

400. D

Step 1
Isolate one variable from equation 1 or 2.
Isolate y in equation 2.

$$2x - y = -3x^2 - 100$$
$$-y = -3x^2 - 2x - 100$$
$$y = 3x^2 + 2x + 100$$

Step 2
Substitute the isolated variable into the second equation, and simplify.

Substitute $3x^2 + 2x + 100$ for y in equation 1.

$$5x + 316 = y$$
$$5x + 316 = 3x^2 + 2x + 100$$
$$0 = 3x^2 - 3x - 216$$
$$0 = 3(x^2 - x - 72)$$
$$0 = x^2 - x - 72$$

Step 3
Factor the equation, and solve for x.

$$0 = x^2 - x - 72$$
$$0 = (x - 9)(x + 8)$$
$$x - 9 = 0$$
$$x = 9$$
$$x + 8 = 0$$
$$x = -8$$

Therefore, $x = 9$ or $x = -8$.

Step 4
Substitute the solved values into equation 1 or 2, and solve for the unknown variable.

$$5x + 316 = y$$
$$5(9) + 316 = y$$
$$45 + 316 = y$$
$$y = 361$$
$$5x + 316 = y$$
$$5(-8) + 316 = y$$
$$-40 + 316 = y$$
$$y = 276$$

Step 5
Write the solutions as ordered pairs in set notation.
{(9, 361), (−8, 276)}

401. B

Both Carl's and Cara's solutions are incorrect.

Carl reversed the x- and y-coordinates in each ordered pair when writing the points of intersection of the graphs of $y = 3x^2 - 12$ and $6x - y = 3$. These two graphs intersect at the points (3, 15) and (−1, −9), rather than (15, 3) and (−9, −1). Thus, the solution set to system A should have been {(3, 15), (−1, −9)}.

Cara did not draw the graphs of $2x^2 - 12x - y = 0$ and $4x + y = 10$ correctly. The graph of $2x^2 - 12x - y = 0$ and $4x + y = 10$ is given.

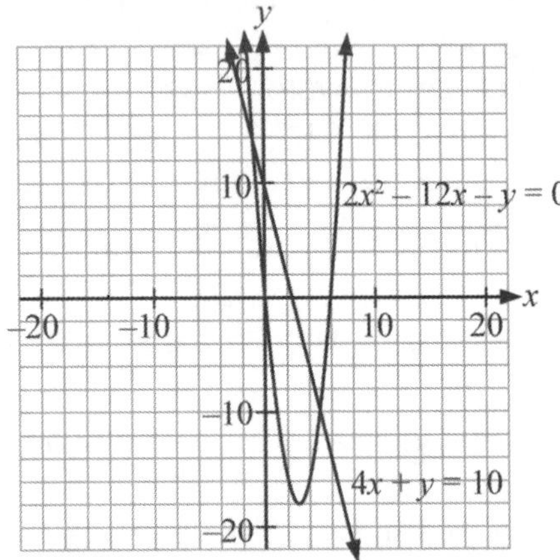

The correct graph shows that equations $2x^2 - 12x - y = 0$ and $4x + y = 10$ intersect at the points (−1, 14) and (5, −10). Therefore, the solution set to system B should have been {(−1, 14), (5, −10)}.

EXERCISE #2—SOLVING SYSTEMS OF EQUATIONS

Use the following information to answer the next question.

A system of equations is given:
① $0 = 6x^2 + 22x - 2y + 4$
② $0 = 5x - y + 2$

402. What are the solutions to the system?

A. {(−2, −8), (0, 2)}

B. {(−3, −4), (0, 2)}

C. {(−4, 6), (−2, −8)}

D. {(−4, 6), (−3, −4)}

Use the following information to answer the next question.

Two different systems of equations are given.

System A	System B
$y = 3 - 2x$ $y = -x^2 + 2x + 15$	$y = 3x + 8$ $y = x^2 + 4x - 12$

Selma and Julio are each asked to determine the solution set to a system graphically.

To find the solution set for system A, Selma graphs the equations $y = 3 - 2x$ and $y = -x^2 + 2x + 15$.

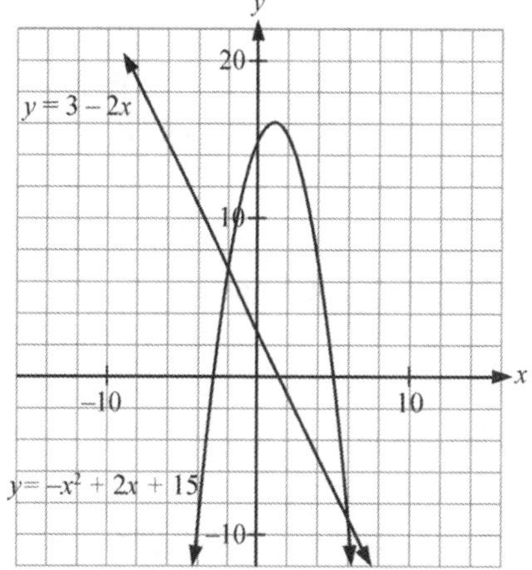

She determines that since the graphs of $y = 3 - 2x$ and $y = -x^2 + 2x + 15$ intersect at the points (−2, 7) and (6, −9), the solution set to system A is {(−2, 7), (6, −9)}.

To find the solution set for system B, Julio graphs the equations $y = 3x + 8$ and $y = x^2 + 4x - 12$.

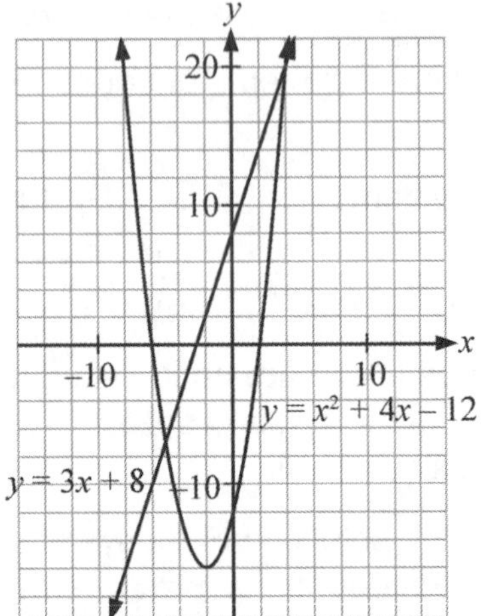

He determines that since the graphs of $y = 3x + 8$ and $y = x^2 + 4x - 12$ intersect at the points (−5, −7) and (2, 20), the solution set to system B is {(−5, −7), (2, 20)}.

403. Which of the following statements about the students' solutions is **true**?

A. Both Selma's and Julio's solutions are correct.

B. Both Selma's and Julio's solutions are incorrect.

C. Selma's solution is correct, and Julio's solution is incorrect.

D. Selma's solution is incorrect, and Julio's solution is correct.

EXERCISE #2—SOLVING SYSTEMS OF EQUATIONS ANSWERS AND SOLUTIONS

402. A	403. C

402. A

Step 1

Isolate one variable from one of the equations.

② $0 = 5x - y + 2$

$y = 5x + 2$

Step 2

Substitute the isolated variable into the second equation, and simplify.

Substitute $5x + 2$ for y in equation 1.

$0 = 6x^2 + 22x - 2(5x + 2) + 4$

$0 = 6x^2 + 22x - 10x - 4 + 4$

$0 = 6x^2 + 12x$

$0 = x^2 + 2x$

Step 3

Factor the equation, and solve for one variable.

$0 = x^2 + 2x$

$0 = x(x + 2)$

$x = 0$

$x + 2 = 0$

$x = -2$

$x = 0$ or $x = -2$

Step 4

Substitute the solved values into equation 1 or 2, and solve for the unknown variable.

$0 = 5x - y + 2$

$0 = 5(-2) - y + 2$

$0 = -10 - y + 2$

$y = -8$

$0 = 5x - y + 2$

$0 = 5(0) - y + 2$

$0 = -y + 2$

$y = 2$

Step 5

Write the solutions as an ordered pair in set notation.

$\{(-2, -8), (0, 2)\}$

403. C

Selma's solution is correct, but Julio's solution is incorrect. Julio incorrectly read the graph of the equations $y = 3x + 8$ and $y = x^2 + 4x - 12$. They intersect at the points $(-5, -7)$ and $(4, 20)$, rather than $(-5, -7)$ and $(2, 20)$. The solution set to system B should have been $\{(-5, -7), (4, 20)\}$.

NOTES

Rational and Irrational Numbers

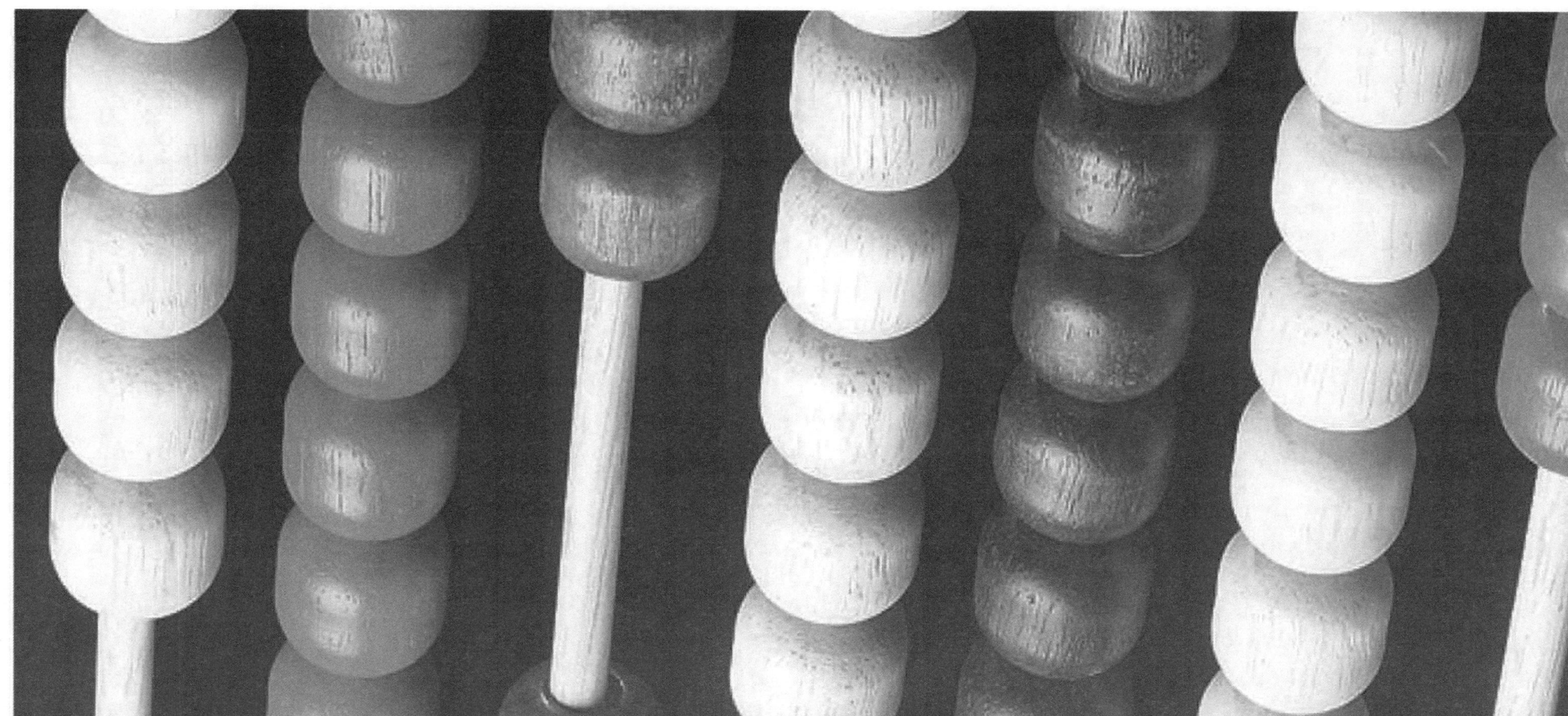

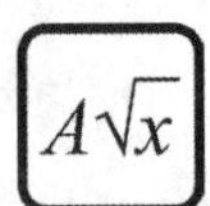

RATIONAL AND IRRATIONAL NUMBERS

Table of Correlations				
Standard		Concepts	Exercise #1	Exercise #2
Unit5.1	Use properties of rational and irrational numbers.			
N-RN.3	*Explain why the sum or product of two rational numbers is rational; that the sum of a rational number and an irrational number is irrational; and that the product of a nonzero rational number and an irrational number is irrational.*	Number Sets	404	408
		Operations with Irrational Numbers	405	409
		Adding Rational Numbers	406	410
		Multiplying Rational Numbers	407	411

$A\sqrt{x}$

N-RN.3 Explain why the sum or product of two rational numbers is rational; that the sum of a rational number and an irrational number is irrational; and that the product of a nonzero rational number and an irrational number is irrational.

Number Sets

Sometimes, it is not enough to say that a number is just a number. Mathematicians have placed all numbers in categories, from the everyday counting numbers 1, 2, 3,... to numbers that are non-terminating, such as π (pi).

All the number sets listed are included within the real number system. Each number set has its own symbol (or symbols) as well as restrictions on membership in that set. As in real life, it is possible for a member of one club to be a member of another club as well. Indeed, entire sets are nested within other sets. Keep this in mind as the number sets are introduced.

Natural Numbers ($\mathbb{N}$)

The natural numbers are often called the counting numbers. The set includes {1, 2, 3, 4, ...}.

Whole Numbers (W)

Whole numbers include all the counting numbers, as well as zero. The natural number set is nested within the set of whole numbers. The set includes {0, 1, 2, 3, 4, ...}.

If the natural number set is represented as being contained within a circle, a larger circle surrounding it would represent the whole numbers.

Integers ($\mathbb{Z}$ or I)

Although an uppercase I is often used to denote integers, another symbol used is an uppercase Z, which is derived from the German word *zahlen* meaning to count. The integers include all the counting numbers, their additive inverses (negative counterparts), and zero. The set includes {...−4, −3, −2, −1, 0, 1, 2, 3, 4, ...}.

The set of natural numbers and the slightly larger set of whole numbers are both nested within the set of integers.

Rational Numbers (Q)

The symbol Q is from the German word for quotient, which can be defined as a ratio. Any number that can be expressed by the quotient $\left(\frac{a}{b}\right)$, where both a and b are integers and b is not zero, is a rational number.

The restriction on b is to avoid division by zero, which is undefined. For example, since the number 6 can be expressed as $\frac{6}{1}$, where the numerator and denominator are both integers, 6 is a rational number. It is also a natural number, a whole number, and an integer.

Rational Numbers Written in Decimal Form

Up to this point, it is relatively easy to place a given number into a set that it belongs to or even to list all the sets that it belongs to. Rational numbers include a whole set of decimal numbers that do not belong to any previously listed set. Recall that if there is a quotient $\left(\frac{a}{b}\right)$, where a and b are integers and $b \neq 0$, the result is a rational number. Decimals can easily result from this quotient.

Example

Written in decimal form, the fraction $\frac{1}{8}$ is ________.

Solution

Divide 1 by 8.

$\frac{1}{8} = 0.125$

This is a terminating decimal. It stops at a clear point.

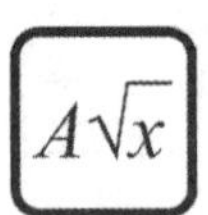

There are decimals that do not terminate, but instead repeat. Consider the following example.

Example

Without using technology, convert the repeating decimal 0.3333… into a fraction, if possible. Determine if this is a rational number.

Solution

Step 1

Let ① $a = 0.3333\ldots$

The number 0.3333… repeats after one decimal place, so multiply both sides of equation 1 by 10.

② $10a = 3.3333\ldots$

Step 2

Subtract equation 1 from equation 2.

$$\begin{aligned} 10a &= 3.3333\ldots \\ \underline{a} &= \underline{0.3333\ldots} \\ ③\ 9a &= 3 \end{aligned}$$

Isolate the variable in equation 3.

$$9a = 3$$

$$a = \frac{3}{9}$$

$$a = \frac{1}{3}$$

By this method, the repeating decimal number 0.3333… has been converted to a quotient of integers $\left(\frac{1}{3}\right)$.

The repeating decimal number 0.3333…, which can be written as $0.\overline{3}$, is a rational number.

Example

A student wishes to see if any repeating decimal number is a rational number, so the student tests 0.1212…

What fraction can the student create that is equivalent to 0.1212…?

Solution

Let ① $a = 0.1212\ldots$

The decimal 0.1212… repeats after two decimal places, so multiply both sides of equation 1 by 100.

② $100a = 12.1212\ldots$

Subtract equation 1 from equation 2.

$$\begin{aligned} 100a &= 12.1212\ldots \\ \underline{a} &= \underline{0.1212\ldots} \\ ③\ 99a &= 12 \end{aligned}$$

Isolate the variable in equation 3.

$$99a = 12$$

$$a = \frac{12}{99}$$

$$a = \frac{4}{33}$$

The fraction $\frac{4}{33}$ is equivalent to the repeating decimal 0.1212….

In the previous example, the student has correctly guessed that any repeating decimal is a rational number.

Irrational Numbers ($\overline{Q}$)

Any number when written in decimal form that results in a decimal number that does not terminate or does not repeat is an irrational number.

Examples of irrational numbers include π and $\sqrt{2}$.

Whereas the rational numbers have every other previously described number set nested within its set, the irrational numbers have only their own members.

Real Numbers (R)

The bold uppercase R is the symbol for the set of real numbers, which includes all rational and irrational numbers.

Operations with Irrational Numbers

A graphing calculator can be used to determine the value of a given root for a particular number. The resulting value will either be an exact value or an approximate value.

Example

Use a graphing calculator to determine the cube root of 4,913.

Solution

The following sequence of key strokes on a graphing calculator can be used to evaluate $\sqrt[3]{4{,}913}$:

MATH → 4 → 4 9 1 3 →) → ENTER

$\sqrt[3]{4{,}913} = 17$

Although it is not necessary to include (and) as key strokes, it is a good habit to include these key strokes because they are required when evaluating more complex expressions.

The value of a complex radical expression can be determined by using a graphing calculator and following the order of operations, as illustrated in the following example.

Example

Rounded to the nearest hundredth, what is the value of $\sqrt[4]{245 + 783}$?

Solution

Step 1

Determine the sum of 245 and 783.
$245 + 783 = 1{,}028$

Step 2

Evaluate $\sqrt[4]{1{,}028}$.

A possible sequence of key strokes is as follows:

4 → MATH → 5 → (→ 1 0 2 8 →) → ENTER

Rounded to the nearest hundredth, the value of $\sqrt[4]{1{,}028}$ is 5.66.

The approximate value of $\sqrt[4]{245 + 783}$ can also be determined in one step by using the following sequence of key strokes on a graphing calculator:

4 → MATH → 5 → (→ 2 4 5 → + → 7 8 3 →) → ENTER

The following example shows how to add irrational numbers.

Example

Rounded to the nearest hundredth, what is the value of $\sqrt{163} + 7\sqrt[3]{185}$?

Solution

Step 1

Evaluate $\sqrt{163}$.

A possible set of key strokes is as follows:

2nd → x^2 → 1 6 3 →) → ENTER

$\sqrt{163} \approx 12.76715$

Step 2

Evaluate $\sqrt[3]{185}$.

A possible set of key strokes is as follows:

MATH → 4 → 1 8 5 →) → ENTER

$\sqrt[3]{185} \approx 5.69802$

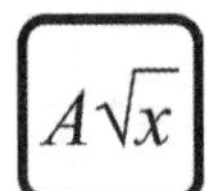

Step 3

Determine the value of $\sqrt{163} + 7\sqrt[3]{185}$ by making use of the derived values in steps one and two and following the order of operations.

$\sqrt{163} + 7\sqrt[3]{185} \approx 12.76715 + 7 \times 5.69802$
$\approx 12.76715 + 39.88614$
≈ 52.65364

Rounded to the nearest hundredth, the value of $\sqrt{163} + 7\sqrt[3]{185}$ is 52.65.

The approximate value of $\sqrt{163} + 7\sqrt[3]{185}$ can be determined in one step by using the following sequence of key strokes on a graphing calculator:

[2nd] → [x^2] → [1][6][3] → [)] → [+] → [7] → [×] → [MATH] → [4] → [1][8][5] → [)] → [ENTER]

The following example shows how to evaluate irrational numbers that involve taking more than one root. Treat the number underneath the first root sign as if it were in brackets. The order of operations still applies.

Example

Rounded to the nearest hundredth, what is the value of $\sqrt[5]{\sqrt{17,842}}$?

Solution

Step 1

Evaluate $\sqrt{17,842}$.

A possible set of key strokes is as follows:

[2nd] → [x^2] → [1][7][8][4][2] → [)] → [ENTER]

$\sqrt{17,842} \approx 133.57395$

Step 2

Evaluate $\sqrt[5]{133.57395}$.

A possible set of key strokes is as follows:

[5] → [MATH] → [5] → [(] → [1][3][3][.][5][7][3][9][5] → [)] → [ENTER]

$\sqrt[5]{133.57395} \approx 2.66161$

Rounded to the nearest hundredth, the value of $\sqrt[5]{\sqrt{17,842}}$ is 2.66.

The following sequence of key strokes on a graphing calculator can be used to determine the approximate value of $\sqrt[5]{\sqrt{17,842}}$ in one step.

[5] → [MATH] → [5] → [(] → [2nd] → [x^2] → [1][7][8][4][2] → [)] → [)] → [ENTER]

Adding Rational Numbers

Adding Integers

When adding two integers, pay careful attention to the signs attached to each number and follow the given integer addition rules.

1. If the signs are the same on both integers, add the two numerical values (the **absolute values**) and keep the sign the same.

Example

Solve the equation $-2 + (-5) = ?$.

Solution

Both numbers are negative. Add the two absolute values $(2 + 5)$ to get a value of 7. Express the answer as 7 with a negative sign in front of it.

$-2 + (-5) = -7$

---

2. If the signs are different on two integers, subtract the smaller absolute value from the larger absolute value. Then, take the sign of the larger absolute value.

Example

Solve the equation $-5 + 9 = ?$.

Solution

The signs of the two integers are different. The absolute value of −5 is 5. The absolute value of 9 is 9. Subtract the smaller absolute value (5) from the larger absolute value (9) to get a value of 4. Then, take the sign of the larger absolute value (9) for the final answer.
$-5 + 9 = 4$

A number line can also be used to add integers.

In order to use a number line to add integers, position your pencil on the first integer (−5) in the equation. Since the second integer in this example (9) is positive, move your pencil 9 places to the right of −5, ending on 4. The number of places your pencil moves is equal to the absolute value of the second integer.

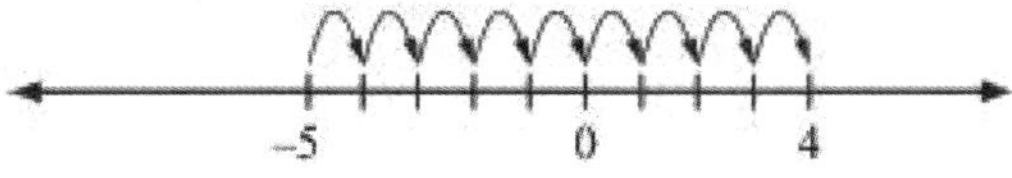

Adding Fractions

To add fractions that have the same denominator, add the numerators. The sum of the numerators becomes the numerator of the resulting fraction, while the denominator remains the same.
If possible, reduce the resulting fraction to its lowest terms.

Example

Add the fractions $\frac{1}{4} + \frac{1}{4}$.

Solution

Add the numerators and reduce the result to lowest terms.

$\frac{1}{4} + \frac{1}{4} = \frac{1+1}{4} = \frac{2}{4} \rightarrow \frac{2 \div 2}{4 \div 2} = \frac{1}{2}$

Therefore, $\frac{1}{4} + \frac{1}{4} = \frac{1}{2}$.

To add fractions with different denominators, find the lowest common denominator (LCD) of the given fractions. Use the LCD to create new equivalent fractions. Then, add the numerators while keeping the denominators the same.
If possible, reduce the resulting fraction to its lowest terms.

Example

Add the fractions $\frac{1}{4} + \frac{2}{3}$.

Solution

Step 1

Find the lowest common denominator (LCD).
Write the multiples of each denominator until a common denominator appears.
Multiples of 3: 3, 6, 9, **12**, 15
Multiples of 4: 4, 8, **12**, 16, 20
The LCD of 3 and 4 is 12. Therefore, the fractions in this example should be changed into equivalent fractions using a denominator of 12. To create equivalent fractions, multiply the numerator by the same number as the denominator.

$$\frac{1 \times 3}{4 \times 3} + \frac{2 \times 4}{3 \times 4}$$
$$\downarrow \qquad \downarrow$$
$$\frac{3}{12} + \frac{8}{12}$$

Step 2

Add the numerators while keeping the denominators the same.

$\frac{3+8}{12} = \frac{11}{12}$

The resulting fraction cannot be reduced.

Therefore, $\frac{1}{4} + \frac{2}{3} = \frac{11}{12}$.

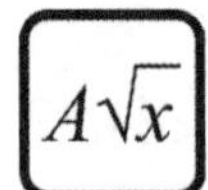

To add fractions involving mixed numbers in the form $a\frac{b}{c}$, use the following steps:

1. Convert mixed numbers into improper fractions.
2. Find the lowest common denominator.
3. Add the numerators while keeping the denominators the same.
4. If necessary, convert an improper fraction back to a mixed number

Example

Add the fractions $2\frac{1}{4}+1\frac{2}{3}$.

Solution

Step 1

Convert mixed numbers into improper fractions.

The procedure to convert mixed fractions into improper fractions is as follows:

whole number × denominator+numerator
= numerator for improper fraction

In other words, the mixed fraction $a\frac{b}{c}$ becomes $\frac{a\times c+b}{c}$.

$$2\frac{1}{4}\rightarrow\frac{2\times4+1}{4}=\frac{9}{4}$$

$$1\frac{2}{3}\rightarrow\frac{1\times3+2}{3}=\frac{5}{3}$$

Step 2

Find the lowest common denominator.

$$\frac{9\times3}{4\times3}+\frac{5\times4}{3\times4}$$

$$\downarrow \quad \downarrow$$

$$\frac{27}{12}+\frac{20}{12}$$

Step 3

Add the numerators while keeping the denominators the same.

$$\frac{27+20}{12}=\frac{47}{12}$$

Step 4

Convert an improper fraction back into a mixed number.

To convert an improper fraction to a mixed number, reverse the operations of step 1.

numerator of improper fraction ÷ denominator

$$=\text{quotient}+\frac{\text{remainder}}{\text{denominator}}$$

The quotient becomes the whole number in front of the fraction. The remainder becomes the numerator of the mixed number.

The denominator remains the same.

$47\div12=3$ remainder $11\rightarrow3\frac{11}{12}$

Therefore, $2\frac{1}{4}+1\frac{2}{3}=3\frac{11}{12}$.

Adding Integers, Decimals, and Fractions

To add integers, decimals, and fractions use the following steps:

1. Add the integers and decimals together.
2. Convert decimals to fractions.
3. Add the fractions and reduce to lowest terms if necessary.

Example

What is the sum of the rational numbers $3.\bar{2} + 1.6 + \frac{3}{8}$?

Solution

Step 1

Convert the decimals to fractions in lowest terms.

Since $3.\bar{2}$ is a repeating decimal and there is one digit repeating, convert the repeated part as a fraction out of 9.

$$3.\bar{2} = 3\frac{2}{9}$$

Since 1.6 is a non-repeating decimal and the decimal number is in the tenth position, convert the decimal part as a fraction out of 10 and reduce it to lowest terms.

$$\begin{aligned} 1.6 &= 1\frac{6}{10} \\ &= 1\frac{6 \div 2}{10 \div 2} \\ &= 1\frac{3}{5} \end{aligned}$$

Step 2

Convert the mixed fractions to improper fractions.

$$3\frac{2}{9} = \frac{3 \times 9 + 2}{9} = \frac{29}{9}$$

$$1\frac{3}{5} = \frac{1 \times 5 + 3}{5} = \frac{8}{5}$$

Step 3

Find the lowest common denominator (LCD) for all fractions.

For 8, 9, and 5, the LCD is 360.

Step 4

Convert the denominators of all fractions to the LCD, and add the numerators.

$$\frac{29 \times 40}{9 \times 40} + \frac{8 \times 72}{5 \times 72} + \frac{3 \times 45}{8 \times 45}$$

$$\frac{1{,}160}{360} + \frac{576}{360} + \frac{135}{360} = \frac{1{,}871}{360}$$

Step 5

Convert the improper fraction back into a mixed number.

$$\frac{1{,}871}{360} \rightarrow 5\frac{71}{360}$$

Therefore, the sum of the rational numbers $3.\bar{2} + 1.6 + \frac{3}{8}$ is $5\frac{71}{360}$.

Multiplying Rational Numbers

While it is always a good idea to use mental math, you may work through problems involving rational numbers with the aid of a calculator as a tool to check. Just remember that having an estimate of what the answer *should be* will help you to identify if you have made an error, either on paper or using your calculator.

Multiplying Integers

There are four rules to follow when multiplying integers.

Rule 1: When multiplying two integers with the *same signs* (two positive or two negative), the solution is positive.

Example

What is the solution when the integers (+4) and (+6) are multiplied? __________

Solution

Both integers are positive; therefore, the solution will be positive.

Multiply the numbers 4 and 6.

The solution is (+4)(+6) = +24.

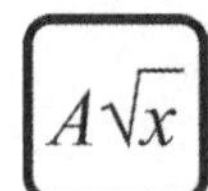

Rule 2: When multiplying or dividing two integers with *different signs* (one positive and one negative), the solution is negative.

Example

(+4)(−6) = ?

Multiply the given integers.

Solution

One of the integers is positive, and the other is negative.

Multiply the numbers 4 and 6, and keep the solution negative.
(+4)(−6) = −24

Rule 3: If there is an even number of negative signs, the answer is positive.

Example

Evaluate(−4)(+3)(−8)(+2).

Solution

There are two negative integers in this expression (an even number of negative signs).

Multiply the 4, 3, 8, and 2 together, and keep the solution positive.
(−4)(+3)(−8)(+2) = +192

Rule 4: If there is an odd number of negative signs, the answer is negative.

Example

Evaluate(−2) × (−3) × (−4).

Solution

This expression has three negative integers (an odd number of negative signs). Multiply the 2, 3, and 4 together, and keep the solution negative.
(−2) × (−3) × (−4) = −24

Multiplying Fractions

When multiplying fractions, common denominators are not needed. Common denominators are only needed to add or subtract fractions.

When multiplying fractions, follow these steps:

1. Convert any mixed numbers into improper fractions.
2. Multiply the numerators together, and place the result over the product of the denominators.
3. Finally, reduce the resulting fraction to lowest terms if possible.

Example

Evaluate the expression $\frac{2}{3} \times \frac{3}{5}$.

Solution

Multiply the numerators together, and place the result over the product of the denominators.

$\frac{2}{3} \times \frac{3}{5} = \frac{2 \times 3}{3 \times 5} = \frac{6}{15}$

Therefore, $\frac{2}{3} \times \frac{3}{5} = \frac{6}{15}$

Example

Evaluate the expression $3\frac{2}{5} \times 1\frac{3}{4}$.

Solution

Step 1
Convert the mixed numbers into improper fractions.

$3\frac{2}{5} \times 1\frac{3}{4} \rightarrow \frac{17}{5} \times \frac{7}{4}$

Step 2
Multiply the numerators together, and place the result over the product of the denominators.

$\frac{17}{5} \times \frac{7}{4} = \frac{17 \times 7}{5 \times 4} = \frac{119}{20}$

Step 3
Because the result is an improper fraction, convert it into a mixed number.

$119 \div 20 = 5$, remainder $19 \rightarrow 5\frac{19}{20}$

Therefore, $3\frac{2}{5} \times 1\frac{3}{4} = 5\frac{19}{20}$

$A\sqrt{x}$

Multiplying Decimals and Fractions

When multiplying integers, decimals, and fractions, follow these steps:

1. Multiply integers and decimals.
2. Convert decimals to fractions.
3. Multiply the fractions and reduce to lowest tems when necessary.

Example

Multiply the rational numbers $4.\overline{45}$ and $2\frac{5}{8}$.

Solution

Step 1

Convert decimals to fractions in lowest terms.

Since $4.\overline{45}$ is a repeating decimal and there are two digits repeating, convert the repeated part as a fraction out of 99 and reduce to lowest terms.

$$\begin{aligned} 4.\overline{45} &= 4\frac{45}{99} \\ &= 4\frac{45 \div 9}{99 \div 9} \\ &= 4\frac{5}{11} \end{aligned}$$

Step 2

Convert the mixed numbers into improper fractions.

$$4\frac{5}{11} \times 2\frac{5}{8} \rightarrow \frac{49}{11} \times \frac{21}{8}$$

Step 3

Multiply the numerators together, and place the result over the product of the denominators.

$$\frac{49}{11} \times \frac{21}{8} = \frac{49 \times 21}{11 \times 8} = \frac{1,029}{88}$$

Step 4

Because the result is an improper fraction, convert it into a mixed number.

$$\frac{1,029}{88} = 11\frac{61}{88}$$

Therefore, the product of $4.\overline{45}$ and $2\frac{5}{8}$ is $11\frac{61}{88}$.

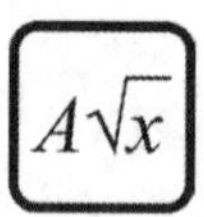

EXERCISE #1—RATIONAL AND IRRATIONAL NUMBERS

404. Which of the following sets of numbers both contain $-\sqrt{13}$?

A. Irrational numbers and real numbers
B. Natural numbers and real numbers
C. Integers and irrational numbers
D. Integers and rational numbers

Use the following information to answer the next question.

Jane is asked to determine the approximate value of $\left(\sqrt[3]{75}+\frac{\sqrt{60}}{4}\right)^2$. The steps in her solution are shown.

1. $\left(\sqrt[3]{75}+\frac{\sqrt{60}}{4}\right)^2 \approx (\sqrt[3]{75}+1.9365)^2$
2. $\approx (4.2172+1.9365)^2$
3. $\approx (4.2172)^2+(1.9365)^2$
4. $\approx 17.7848+3.7500$
5. ≈ 21.5348

405. Jane made her first error in step

A. 1
B. 2
C. 3
D. 4

Use the following information to answer the next question.

A local radio station has to give a skill-testing question to the winners of its on-air contests. The winners can only claim their prize by solving the given expression.

$$2\frac{3}{5}+4.4+(-5.2)+\left(-1\frac{3}{10}\right)$$

406. In order to claim the prize, a winning contestant must provide the fraction

A. $-\frac{1}{10}$
B. $-\frac{1}{2}$
C. $\frac{1}{2}$
D. $1\frac{1}{10}$

407. What is the product of $-1.4 \times \frac{5}{7} \times -\frac{27}{35}$?

A. $\frac{3}{4}$
B. $\frac{27}{35}$
C. $-1\frac{6}{35}$
D. $-2\frac{5}{7}$

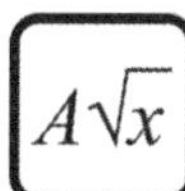

EXERCISE #1—RATIONAL AND IRRATIONAL NUMBERS ANSWERS AND SOLUTIONS

404. A	405. C	406. C	407. B

404. A

Step 1
Evaluate $-\sqrt{13}$.
$-\sqrt{13} = -3.605551275\ldots$

Step 2
Classify $-\sqrt{13}$ as a rational or irrational number.
Since $-3.605551275\ldots$ cannot be written in the fractional form $\frac{a}{b}$, where $b \neq 0$, $-\sqrt{13}$ is an irrational number.

Step 3
Determine the correct alternative.
All the irrational numbers are real numbers; therefore, the number $-\sqrt{13}$ can be classified as an irrational number and a real number.

405. C

Step 1
Check Jane's calculation in step 1.

Evaluate $\frac{\sqrt{60}}{4}$.

$$\frac{\sqrt{60}}{4}$$
$$\approx \frac{7.74597}{4}$$
$$\approx 1.9365$$

The expression $\left(\sqrt[3]{75} + \frac{\sqrt{60}}{4}\right)^2$ therefore become $\left(\sqrt[3]{75} + 1.9365\right)^2$.
So far, the solution is correct.

Step 2
Check Jane's calculation in step 2.

Evaluate $\sqrt[3]{75}$.
$\sqrt[3]{75} \approx 4.2172$

The expression $\left(\sqrt[3]{75} + 1.9365\right)^2$ therefore becomes $(4.2172 + 1.9365)^2$.
So far, the solution is correct.

Step 3
Check Jane's calculation in step 3.

Evaluate $(4.2172 + 1.9365)^2$.
$$(4.2172 + 1.9365)^2$$
$$\approx (6.1537)^2$$
$$\approx 37.8680$$

Alternatively, you can evaluate $(4.2172 + 1.9365)^2$ by using the formula for binomial expansion, $(a + b)^2 = a^2 + 2ab + b^2$.
$$(4.2172 + 1.9365)^2$$
$$\approx \left(\begin{array}{l} 4.2172^2 \\ + \ 2(4.2172 \times 1.9365) \\ + \ 1.9365^2 \end{array}\right)$$
$$\approx \left(\begin{array}{l} 17.7848 \\ + \ 16.3332 \\ + \ 3.7500 \end{array}\right)$$
$$\approx 37.8680$$

In step 3, Jane made her first error by not following the rules of binomial expansion: the values would first need to be added before they are squared. Alternatively, Jane could have applied the formula for binomial expansion, $(a + b)^2 = a^2 + 2ab + b^2$.

406. C

Step 1
Convert all the decimal numbers into fractions.
$$4.4 = 4\frac{4}{10} = 4\frac{2}{5}$$
$$-5.2 = -5\frac{2}{10} = -5\frac{1}{5}$$

Step 2
Convert the mixed fractions to improper fractions.
$$2\frac{3}{5} \rightarrow \frac{2 \times 5 + 3}{5} = \frac{13}{5}$$
$$4\frac{2}{5} \rightarrow \frac{4 \times 5 + 2}{5} = \frac{22}{5}$$
$$-5\frac{1}{5} \rightarrow -\frac{5 \times 5 + 1}{5} = -\frac{26}{5}$$
$$-1\frac{3}{10} \rightarrow -\frac{1 \times 10 + 3}{10} = -\frac{13}{10}$$

Step 3
Find the lowest common denominator (LCD) for all fractions.

For 5 and 10, the LCD is 10.

Step 4
Convert the denominators of all fractions to the LCD and add the numerators.

$$= \frac{13 \times 2}{5 \times 2} + \frac{22 \times 2}{5 \times 2} + \left(\frac{-26 \times 2}{5 \times 2}\right) + \left(\frac{-13}{10}\right)$$
$$= \frac{26}{10} + \frac{44}{10} - \frac{52}{10} - \frac{13}{10}$$
$$= \frac{26 + 44 - 52 - 13}{10}$$
$$= \frac{5}{10}$$

Step 5
Reduce the fraction to lowest terms.

$$\frac{5 \div 5}{10 \div 5} = \frac{1}{2}$$

Therefore, $2\frac{3}{5} + 4.4 + (-5.2) + \left(-1\frac{3}{10}\right) = \frac{1}{2}$.

407. B

Step 1
Convert −1.4 into a fraction in lowest terms.
Since −1.4 is a non-repeating decimal, and the decimal number is in the tenth position, convert the decimal part as a fraction out of 10 and reduce it to lowest terms.

$$\begin{aligned} -1.4 &= -1\frac{4}{10} \\ &= -1\frac{4 \div 2}{10 \div 2} \\ &= -1\frac{2}{5} \end{aligned}$$

Step 2
Convert the mixed number into an improper fraction.

$$-1\frac{2}{5} \times \frac{5}{7} \times -\frac{27}{35} \rightarrow \frac{-7}{5} \times \frac{5}{7} \times \frac{-27}{35}$$

Step 3
Multiply the numerators together, and place the result over the product of the denominators.

$$\frac{-7}{5} \times \frac{5}{7} \times \frac{-27}{35} = \frac{-7 \times 5 \times -27}{5 \times 7 \times 35} = \frac{945}{1{,}225}$$

Step 4
Reduce the fraction into lowest terms.

$$\frac{945}{1{,}225} \rightarrow \frac{945 \div 35}{1{,}225 \div 35} \rightarrow \frac{27}{35}$$

Therefore, the product of $-1.4 \times \frac{5}{7} \times -\frac{27}{35}$ is $\frac{27}{35}$.

$A\sqrt{x}$

EXERCISE #2—RATIONAL AND IRRATIONAL NUMBERS

408. Which of the following numbers can be classified as an integer but not as a whole number?

A. 0 **B.** 1

C. $\sqrt[3]{8}$ **D.** –5

Use the following information to answer the next question.

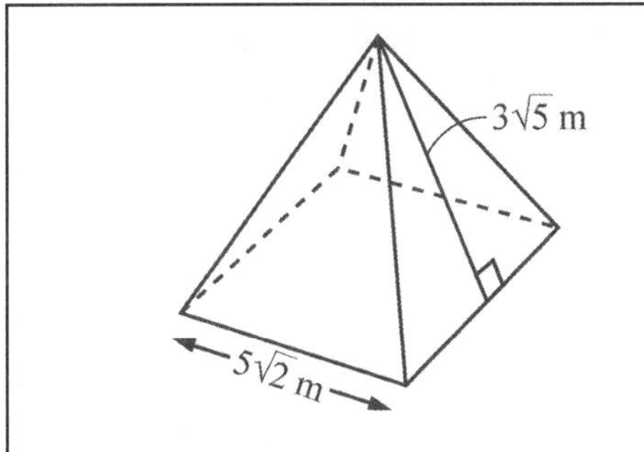

A pyramid with a square base

409. If each side of the pyramid's base is $5\sqrt{2}$ m in length and the slant height is $3\sqrt{5}$ m, as illustrated in the diagram, then what is the surface area of the pyramid to the nearest square meter? __________ m^2

Use the following information to answer the next question.

In order to claim a prize that she won, Becky had to answer the given skill-testing question.

$$-3.\bar{1} + 6 + 2\frac{1}{9} + 4\frac{5}{9}$$

410. If she received the prize after answering the question, the answer that Becky **most likely** gave to claim her prize was

A. $15\frac{1}{9}$ **B.** $10\frac{2}{9}$

C. $9\frac{7}{9}$ **D.** $9\frac{5}{9}$

411. When the numbers $2.\bar{3}$ and $2\frac{1}{4}$ are multiplied, what is the product?

A. $4\frac{1}{12}$ **B.** $4\frac{3}{4}$

C. $5\frac{1}{4}$ **D.** $5\frac{7}{40}$

EXERCISE #2—RATIONAL AND IRRATIONAL NUMBERS ANSWERS AND SOLUTIONS

408. D	409. 145	410. D	411. C

408. D

Whole numbers include all the counting numbers and 0. In set notation, this statement can be written as {0, 1, 2, 3, 4,...}.

Given that $\sqrt[3]{8} = 2$, $\sqrt[3]{8}$ is in the set of whole numbers {0, 1, 2, 3, 4,...}.

Although −5 is an integer, it is not in the set of whole numbers.

409. 145

Step 1
Determine the number of squares and congruent triangles in the given square pyramid.

There are four congruent triangles and one square in the given square pyramid.

Step 2
Determine the area of the square.

The area of a square with side length s is given by the formula $A = s^2$.

$A = s^2$

Substitute $5\sqrt{2}$ for s, and solve for A.

$$\begin{aligned} A &= (5\sqrt{2})^2 \\ &= (5)^2(\sqrt{2})^2 \\ &= (25)(2) \\ &= 50 \text{ m}^2 \end{aligned}$$

Step 3
Determine the total area of the four congruent triangles.

The area of a triangle with base b and height h is given by the formula $A = \frac{1}{2}bh$.

$A = \frac{1}{2}bh$

Substitute $5\sqrt{2}$ for b and $3\sqrt{5}$ for h.

$A = \frac{1}{2}(5\sqrt{2})(3\sqrt{5})$

$A = \frac{(5 \times 3)\sqrt{2 \times 5}}{2}$

$A = \frac{15\sqrt{10}}{2}$

The total area of the four congruent triangles is $4 \times \frac{15\sqrt{10}}{2} = 30\sqrt{10} \text{ m}^2$.

Step 4
Determine the surface area, SA, of the pyramid.
SA = the area of the base (square) + the total area of the four congruent triangles

$SA = 50 + 30\sqrt{10}$
$SA \approx 50 + 94.8683\ldots$
$SA \approx 144.8683\ldots \text{ m}^2$

The surface area of the pyramid to the nearest square meter is 145 m^2.

410. D

Step 1
Add $6 + 2\frac{1}{9}$ to get $8\frac{1}{9}$.

Step 2
Convert $-3.\overline{1}$ to a fraction in lowest terms.

Since $-3.\overline{1}$ is a repeating decimal, and there is one repeating digit, convert the decimal part as a fraction out of 9.

$-3.\overline{1} = -3\frac{1}{9}$

Step 3
Convert the mixed fractions to improper fractions.

$$-\left(3\frac{1}{9}\right) = -\left(\frac{3 \times 9 + 1}{9}\right) = -\frac{28}{9}$$
$$8\frac{1}{9} = \frac{8 \times 9 + 1}{9} = \frac{73}{9}$$
$$4\frac{5}{9} \rightarrow \frac{4 \times 9 + 5}{9} = \frac{41}{9}$$

Step 4
Find the lowest common denominator (LCD) for all fractions.

Since all denominators are the same, the LCD is 9.

Step 5
Add the numerators.

$$\frac{-28}{9} + \frac{73}{9} + \frac{41}{9} = \frac{86}{9}$$

Step 6
Convert the improper fraction back into a mixed number.

$\frac{86}{9} = 9\frac{5}{9}$

Therefore, the answer to the skill-testing question $-3.\overline{1} + 6 + 2\frac{1}{9} + 4\frac{5}{9}$ is $9\frac{5}{9}$.

411. C

Step 1

Convert $2.\bar{3}$ to a fraction in lowest terms.

Since $2.\bar{3}$ is a repeating decimal, and there is one digit repeating, convert the repeated part as a fraction out of 9, and reduce the fraction to lowest terms.

$$\begin{aligned} 2.\bar{3} &= 2\frac{3}{9} \\ &= 2\frac{3 \div 3}{9 \div 3} \\ &= 2\frac{1}{3} \end{aligned}$$

Step 2

Convert the mixed numbers into improper fractions.

$$2\frac{1}{3} \times 2\frac{1}{4} \rightarrow \frac{7}{3} \times \frac{9}{4}$$

Step 3

Multiply the numerators together, and place the result over the product of the denominators.

$$\frac{7}{3} \times \frac{9}{4} = \frac{7 \times 9}{3 \times 4} = \frac{63}{12}$$

Step 4

Convert the improper fraction into mixed form to lowest terms.

$$\frac{63}{12} \rightarrow 5\frac{3}{12} \rightarrow 5\frac{3 \div 3}{12 \div 3} \rightarrow 5\frac{1}{4}$$

Therefore, $2.\bar{3} \times 2\frac{1}{4}$ is equivalent to $5\frac{1}{4}$.

NOTES

The Pythagorean Theorem

THE PYTHAGOREAN THEOREM

Table of Correlations

Standard		Concepts	Exercise #1	Exercise #2
Unit5.2	Understand and apply the Pythagorean theorem.			
8.G.6	*Explain a proof of the Pythagorean theorem and its converse.*	Developing the Pythagorean Theorem Using Diagrams	412	417
		Investigating the Converse of the Pythagorean Theorem		
8.G.7	*Apply the Pythagorean theorem to determine unknown side lengths in right triangles in real-world and mathematical problems in two and three dimensions.*	Problem Solving Using the Pythagorean Theorem	413	418
		Solving Measurement Problems Using the Pythagorean Theorem	414	419
8.G.8	*Apply the Pythagorean theorem to find the distance between two points in a coordinate system.*	Developing the Distance Formula		
		Applying the Distance Formula	415	420
		Problem Solving Using the Distance Formula	416	421

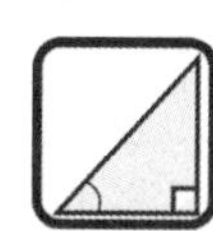

8.G.6 Explain a proof of the Pythagorean theorem and its converse.

Developing the Pythagorean Theorem Using Diagrams

The Pythagorean theorem describes the relationship between three sides of a right triangle. The theorem may be used to find the length of one side of any right triangle when the other two sides are given. This theorem is called the Pythagorean theorem because it was developed by Pythagoras, a Greek mathematician, in the 6th century BC.

Pythagoras drew the following triangle:

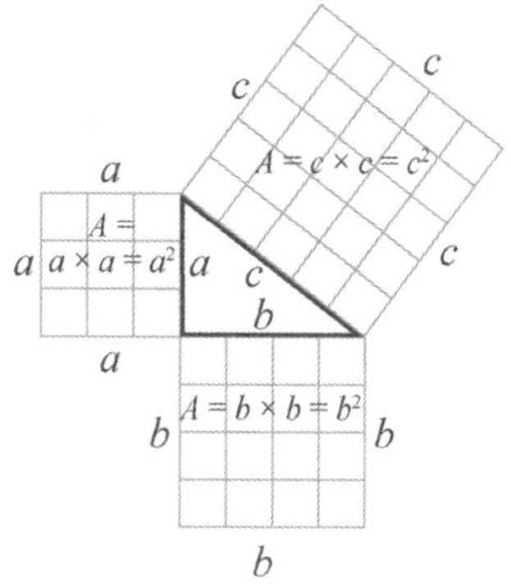

He used each side length of a triangle to make squares along each edge. He discovered that when the area of the square with the same side lengths as one leg of the triangle is added to the area of the square of the other leg of the triangle, they add up to the area of the square located along the hypotenuse.

He came up with what is now known as the Pythagorean theorem: $a^2 + b^2 = c^2$. Although the Pythagorean theorem equation is readily available on many formula sheets, it is so frequently used that it is a good idea to remember it. Therefore, most people memorize it as:
The square **on** the hypotenuse is equal to the sum of squares **on** the other two sides.
Notice that we say "on" as the squares are literally drawn on top of the sides.

Although the sides adjacent the right angle, called **legs**, are frequently labeled with letters *a* and *b*, and the *hypotenuse* is frequently labeled as *c*, any lower-case letters representing the hypotenuse and the legs may be used to write the Pythagorean theorem equation.

Here are some examples of right triangles with the sides properly labeled.

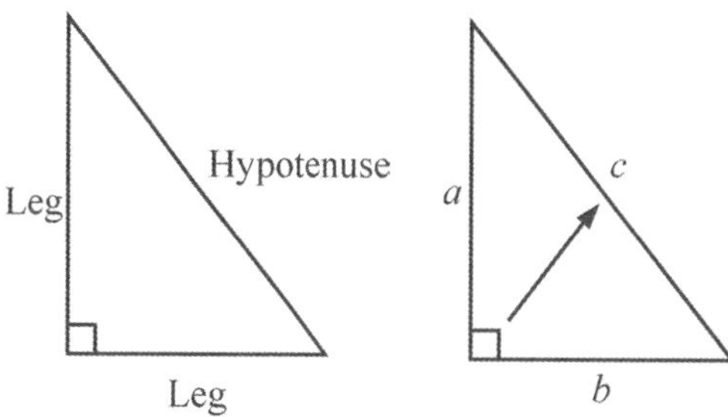

The sides *a* and *b* are interchangeable. As long as the two sides are the legs that make up the right angle, it does not matter which side is labeled *a* and which is labeled *b*.

Here are two more examples of right triangles.

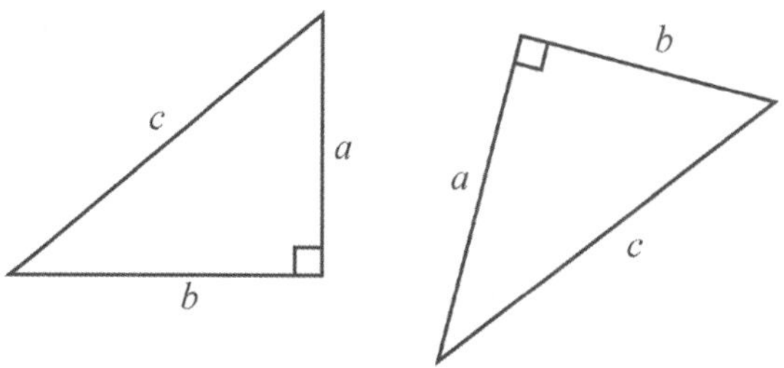

The **Pythagorean theorem** states that the area of the square on the hypotenuse is equal to the area of the squares on the legs added together.

To model the Pythagorean theorem, follow these steps:

1. Make a square using the length of one leg of the triangle (for example, *a*).
2. Make a square using the length of one leg of the triangle (for example, *b*).
3. Make a square using the length of the hypotenuse *c*.

Example

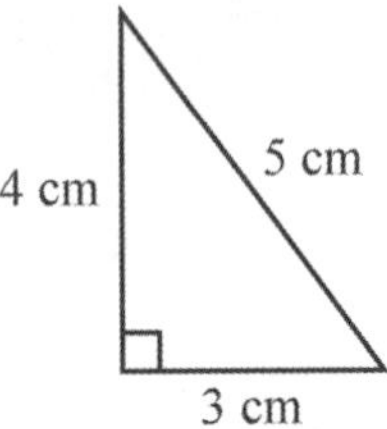

Show that the sum of the areas of the squares on the legs is equal to the area of the square on the hypotenuse.

Solution

Step 1
Make a square using the length of side *a*. Choose either of the two shorter sides to be side *a*.

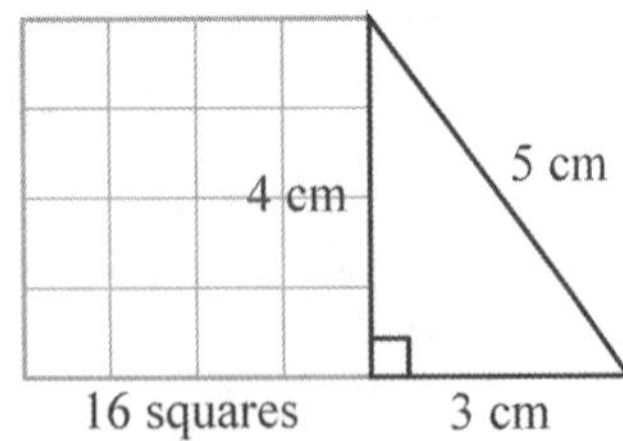

This square will have an area of 16 square centimeters.

Step 2
Make a square using the length of side *b*.

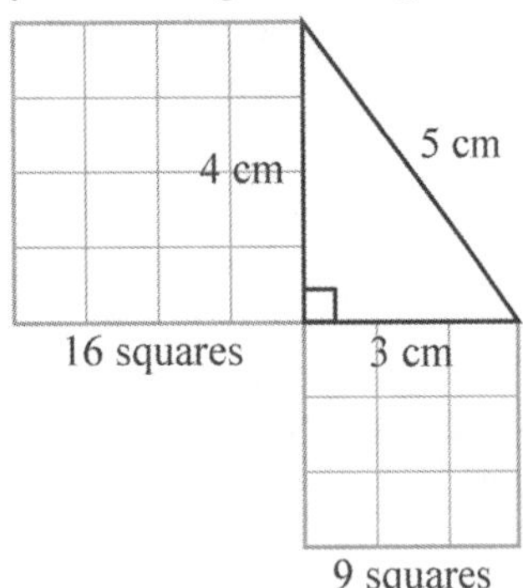

This square will have an area of 9 square centimeters.

Step 3
Make a square using the length of side *c*.

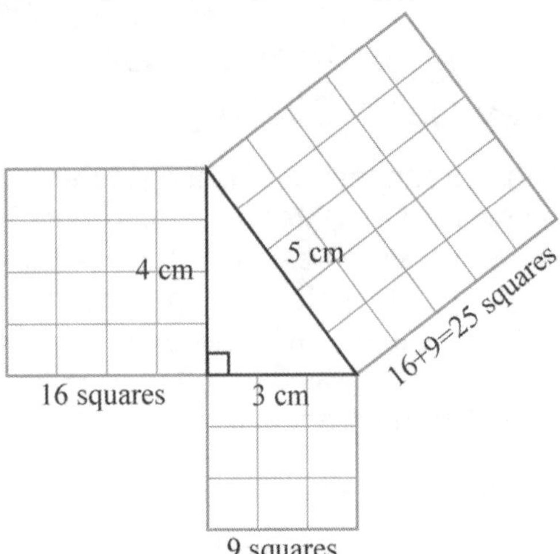

This square will have an area of 25 cm^2. 25 squares is equal to 16 squares and 9 squares added together. So, the area of the square on the hypotenuse is equal to the sum of the squares on the two legs of the right triangle.

The Pythagorean theorem may be used to determine whether a triangle is a right triangle.

Example

A triangle has sides lengths of 5 units, 11 units and 13 units.

Use the Pythagorean theorem to determine whether the triangle is a right triangle.

Solution

If the triangle is a right triangle, then by the Pythagorean theorem, the area of the square on the hypotenuse will equal to the sum of areas of squares on the other two sides.

The square on the side with 5 units length will have area of $5^2 = 25$ units^2 and the square on the side with 11 units will have area of $11^2 = 121$ units^2. The square on the hypotenuse has area of $13^2 = 169$ units^2. Check if the Pythagorean theorem holds:

$$5^2 + 11^2 = 13^2$$
$$25 + 121 = 169$$
$$146 \neq 169$$

The two sides of the equation are not equal, so the triangle is not a right triangle.

Example

Use the Pythagorean theorem to determine whether a right triangle can have sides of 5, 12, and 13 units.

Solution

If it is a right triangle, $5^2 + 12^2$ should equal 13^2. Check:

$$5^2 + 12^2 = 13^2$$
$$25 + 144 = 169$$
$$169 = 169$$

The two sides of the equation are equal, so this makes a right triangle.

Example

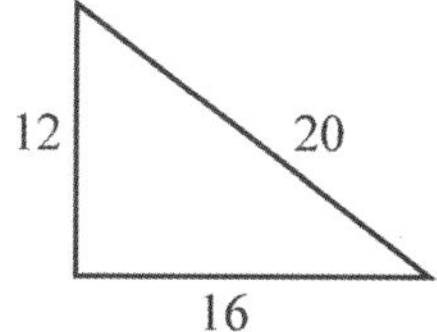

Use the Pythagorean theorem to determine whether the triangle is a right triangle.

Solution

Step 1

Label the sides.

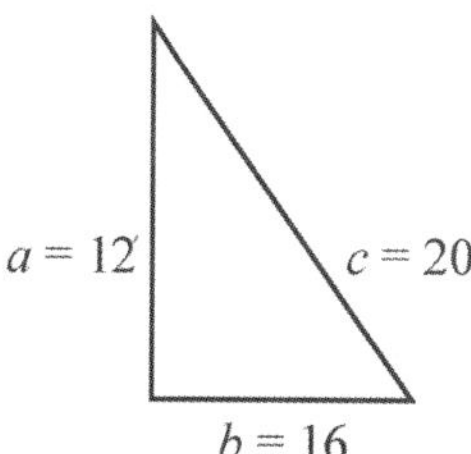

Step 2

Substitute the given values into the Pythagorean theorem, and simplify.

$$a^2 + b^2 = c^2$$
$$12^2 + 16^2 = 20^2$$
$$144 + 256 = 400$$
$$400 = 400$$

Since the two sides of the equation are equal, this is a right triangle.

Example

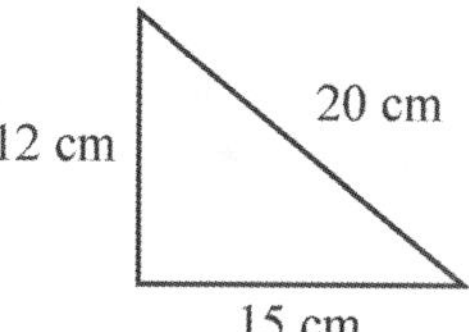

Use the Pythagorean theorem to determine whether the triangle is a right triangle.

Solution

Step 1

Label the sides.

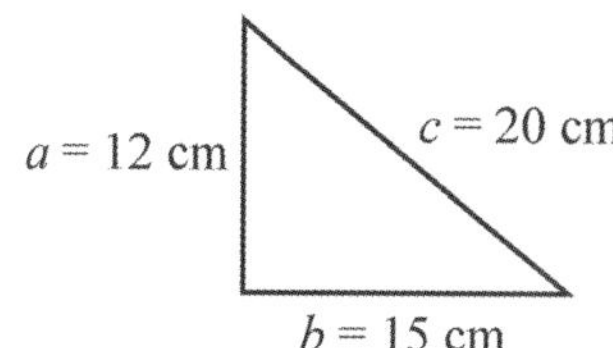

Step 2
Substitute the given values into the Pythagorean theorem, and simplify.

$$a^2 + b^2 = c^2$$
$$12^2 + 15^2 = 20^2$$
$$144 + 225 = 400$$
$$369 \neq 400$$

Since the two sides of the equation are not equal, this is not a right triangle.

Example

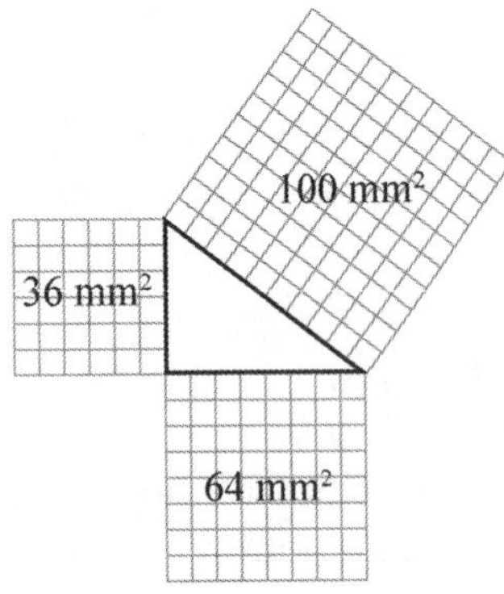

Use the Pythagorean theorem to determine whether the triangle is a right triangle.

Solution

Add the areas of the legs to see if their sum is equal to the area of the hypotenuse.

The largest value is always the hypotenuse.

$$36 + 64 = 100$$
$$100 = 100$$

The triangle is a right triangle because the sum of the area of the two legs is equal to the area of the hypotenuse.

Investigating the Converse of the Pythagorean Theorem

The Pythagorean theorem states that if a triangle is a right triangle, the side lengths of the triangle must have the relationship $a^2 + b^2 = c^2$.
The converse of this theorem is that if a triangle satisfies the formula $a^2 + b^2 = c^2$, the triangle must be a right triangle. The Pythagorean theorem is used in the proof of its converse.

Example

Triangle *EDF* has side lengths where $e^2 + d^2 = f^2$. It is uncertain if *EDF* is a right triangle.

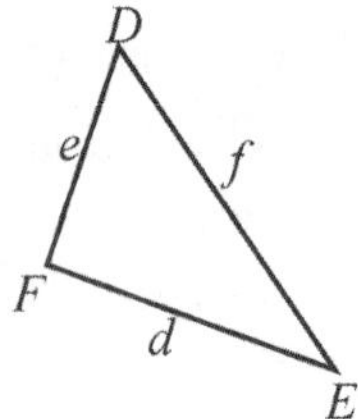

It is possible to construct a right triangle, *EDG*, using the known lengths *e* and *d*, as well as the unknown length of the hypotenuse, *g*.

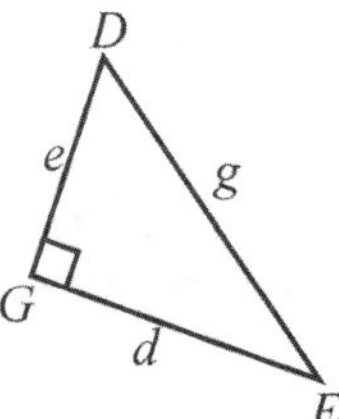

Since ΔEDG is a right triangle, it follows that $e^2 + d^2 = g^2$. Since lengths *e* and *d* are common to both triangles and sides *f* and *g* are equal in length, both triangles have the same three side lengths. According to the side-side-side condition, or SSS, ΔEDF is congruent to ΔEDG and is, therefore, a right triangle.

8.G.7 Apply the Pythagorean theorem to determine unknown side lengths in right triangles in real-world and mathematical problems in two and three dimensions.

Problem Solving Using the Pythagorean Theorem

When solving problems using the Pythagorean theorem, it is important to label all the sides of a right-angled triangle correctly. The legs of the triangle are the two sides that join to form the right angle. These are often labeled a and b.
The hypotenuse is the longest side of the triangle and is always opposite the right angle.
The hypotenuse is often labeled c.

To find the missing side of a right triangle, follow these steps:

1. Substitute the known values into the Pythagorean Theorem equation.
2. Solve for the missing side.

Example

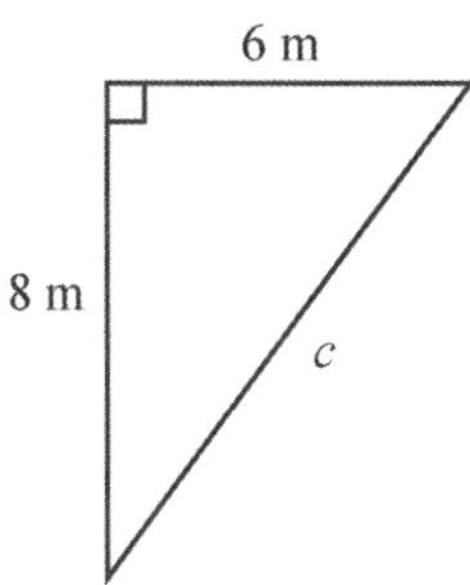

Use the Pythagorean theorem to solve for the missing side of the triangle.

Solution

Step 1
Substitute the known values into the Pythagorean theorem.
Label one side a and the other side b.
Substitute the values into the equation.
$a^2 + b^2 = c^2$
$6^2 + 8^2 = c^2$

Step 2
Solve for the missing side.
Follow the order of operations.
Calculate the exponents.
$36 + 64 = c^2$
$100 = c^2$

Take the square root of both sides to solve for c.
$\sqrt{100} = \sqrt{c^2}$
$10 = c$
$c = 10$ m

Example

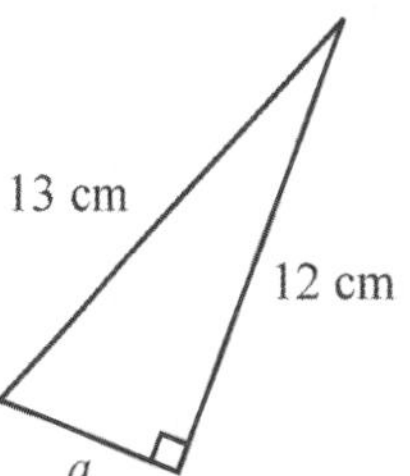

Use the Pythagorean theorem to solve for the missing side of the right triangle.

Solution

Step 1
Substitute the known values into the Pythagorean Theorem equation.
Substitute the values in for b and c.
$a^2 + b^2 = c^2$
$a^2 + 12^2 = 13^2$
$a^2 + 144 = 169$

Step 2
Solve for the missing side.
Subtract 144 from both sides of the equation to isolate a^2.
$a^2 + 144 - 144 = 169 - 144$
$a^2 = 25$

Take the square root of both sides to solve for a.
$\sqrt{a^2} = \sqrt{25}$
$a = 5$
Side a is 5 cm.

Example

A ladder is leaning against the side of a wall. The top of the ladder is 1.5 m from the ground. The base of the ladder is 2 m from the wall. The wall is **perpendicular** to the ground.

Use the Pythagorean theorem to determine the length of the ladder.

Solution

Step 1
Draw and label a figure that illustrates the problem.
Label the wall a and the ground b (or vice versa). The ladder will be side c because it is opposite the right angle.

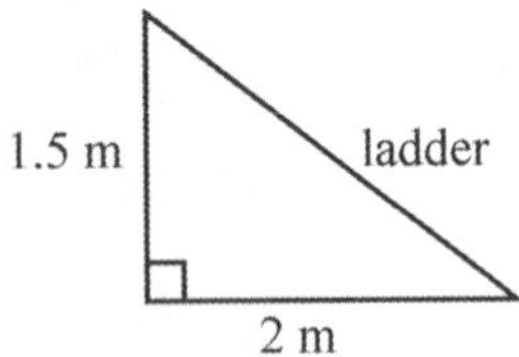

Note: Although we will use the common representation of the Pythagorean Theorem using variables a, b, and c, you may also label the triangle as w for the wall, g for the ground, and l for the ladder. In this case, the Pythagorean Theorem will lead to an expression: $w^2 + g^2 = l^2$.

Step 2
Substitute the known values into the Pythagorean theorem, and solve for the unknown.
Simplify by following the order of operations.

$$a^2 + b^2 = c^2$$
$$1.5^2 + 2^2 = c^2$$
$$2.25 + 4 = c^2$$
$$6.25 = c^2$$
$$\sqrt{6.25} = \sqrt{c^2}$$
$$2.5 = c$$
$$c = 2.5 \text{ m}$$

The ladder is 2.5 m long.

Example

A square field has a path running diagonally across it. The sides of the field measure 4.2 m long.

Rounded to the tenth of a meter, how long is the path?

Solution

Step 1
Draw and label a figure that illustrates the problem.
Label the sides a and b; label the diagonal path c.

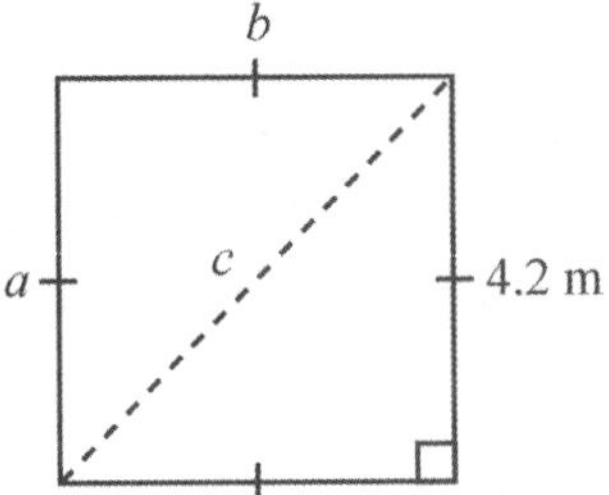

Note: In this diagram, one may choose to label sides of the square field using letter s representing "side", and the diagonal path using letter p for "path" or d for diagonal. Using letters s and p, the Pythagorean Theorem equation will be $s^2 + s^2 = p^2$ since both sides of the square are equal in length and represented by the same variable.

Step 2
Substitute the known values into the Pythagorean theorem, and solve for the unknown.

$$a^2 + b^2 = c^2$$
$$4.2^2 + 4.2^2 = c^2$$
$$17.64 + 17.64 = c^2$$
$$35.28 = c^2$$
$$\sqrt{35.28} = \sqrt{c^2}$$
$$5.93969692 = c$$
$$c = 5.9 \text{ m}$$

The path across the field is 5.9 m long.

Solving Measurement Problems Using the Pythagorean Theorem

To solve a problem involving perimeter, area, surface area, or volume of a figure, the use of the Pythagorean theorem, $c^2 = a^2 + b^2$, may be applied in order to find a missing length of the figure before the final solution can be calculated.

Example

The figure shown is an irregular polygon.

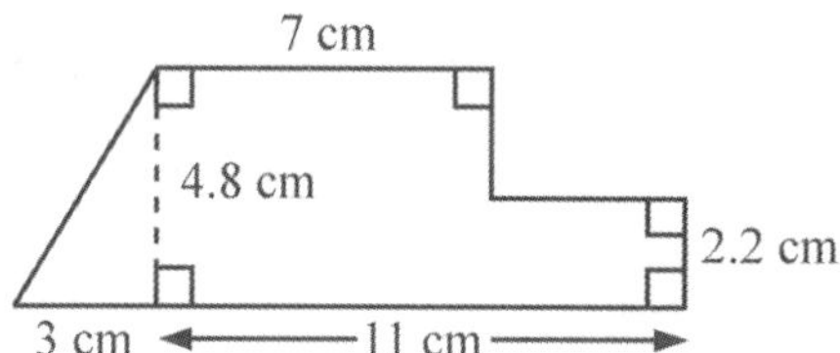

Determine the perimeter of the polygon, *P*, to the nearest tenth of a centimeter.

Solution

Step 1

Label the unknown sides as *x*, *y*, and *z*. Then, determine the measures of the unknown sides.

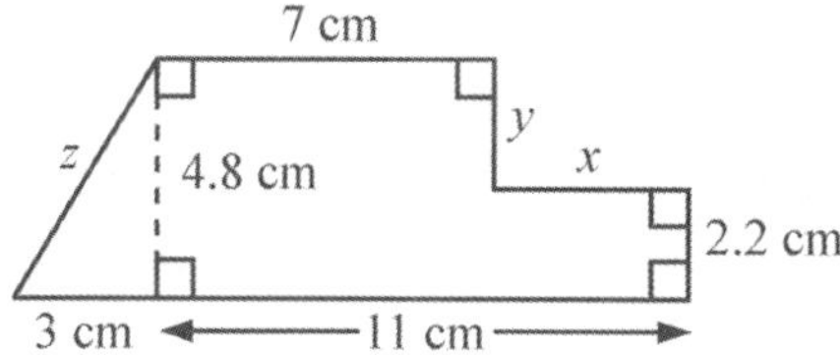

$x = 11 - 7$
$= 4$ cm
$y = 4.8 - 2.2$
$= 2.6$ cm

Use the Pythagorean theorem to determine *z*.

$c^2 = a^2 + b^2$
$z^2 = (3)^2 + (4.8)^2$
$z = \sqrt{(3)^2 + (4.8)^2}$
$= 5.66$ cm

Step 2

Determine the perimeter by adding all the lengths of the sides.

$P = 3 + 11 + 2.2 + 4 + 2.6 + 7 + 5.66$
$= 35.46$ cm

Therefore, the perimeter of the polygon, to the nearest tenth, is 35.5 cm.

Example

The base radius and slant length of a right circular cone are 6 cm and 10 cm, respectively.

Determine the volume of this cone to the nearest tenth of a cubic centimeter.

Solution

Step 1

Determine the height, *h*, of the right circular cone.

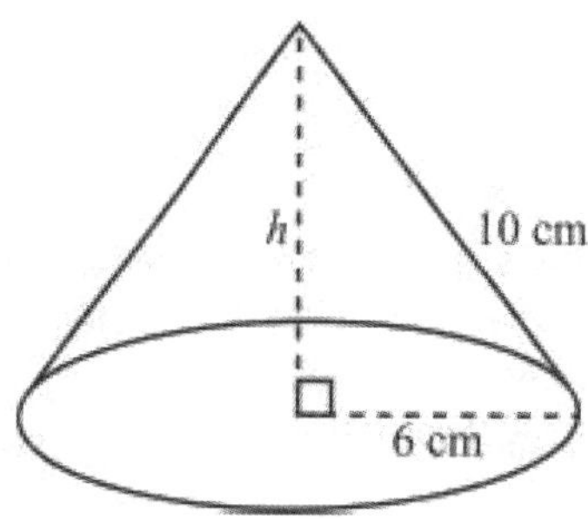

$c^2 = a^2 + b^2$
$(10)^2 = h^2 + (6)^2$
$100 = h^2 + 36$
$100 - 36 = h^2 + 36 - 36$
$64 = h^2$
$\sqrt{h^2} = \sqrt{64}$
$h = 8$ cm

Step 2

Determine the volume, *V*, of the cone.

$V_{cone} = \frac{1}{3}\pi r^2 h$
$= \frac{1}{3}\pi(6)^2(8)$
$= \frac{1}{3}\pi(36)(8)$
$\approx 301.5929 \text{ cm}^3$

Therefore, the volume of the right circular cone, to the nearest tenth, is 301.6 cm^3.

Note: If 3.14 is used for π, then the volume would be 301.4 cm^3.

8.G.8 Apply the Pythagorean theorem to find the distance between two points in a coordinate system.

Developing the Distance Formula

The mathematical formula of the distance between two points is $d_{AB} = \sqrt{(x_2 - x_1)^2 + (y_2 - y_1)^2}$.

This formula can be used to determine the length of a line segment. Thus, the length of a line segment is the distance between the two endpoints of that line segment.

To develop the distance formula between two points, *A* and *B*, you can plot a third point, *C*, that produces a horizontal line, *BC*, and a vertical line, *AC*. The three line segments will form a triangle.

In the given graph, the coordinates of point *A* are (x_1, y_1), and the coordinates of point *B* are (x_2, y_2).

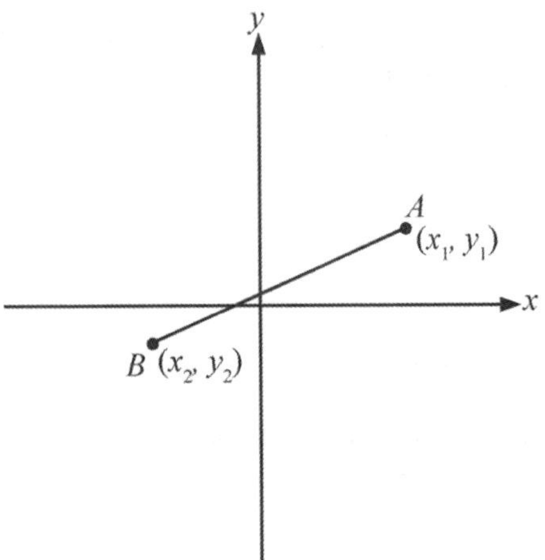

Given this information, the length of segment *AB* can be determined by drawing a vertical line from point *A* and a horizontal line from point *B* that intersect with one another at the labeled point *C*, as shown in this diagram.

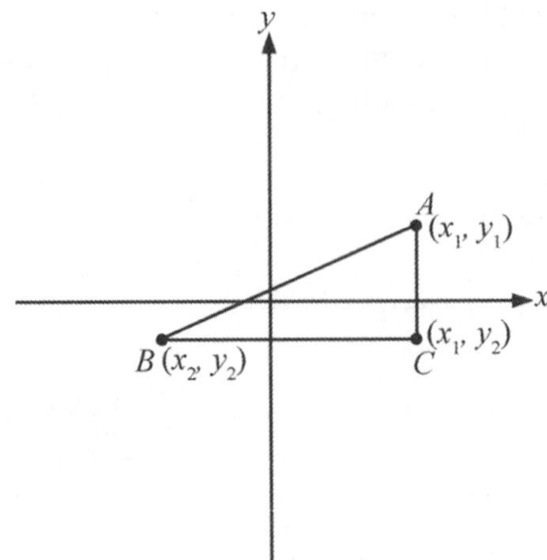

Notice that the coordinates for point *C* are (x_1, y_2) and that the triangle formed is a right triangle. You can easily calculate the lengths of the two legs of the triangle, segments *AC* and *BC*, since they are vertical and horizontal line segments. Thus, by applying the Pythagorean theorem, you can determine the length of the hypotenuse of the right triangle, segment *AB*.

To determine the length of the horizontal line segment *BC*, subtract the *x*-coordinates of point $B(x_2, y_2)$ and point $C(x_1, y_2)$.

$BC = x_2 - x_1$

To determine the length of the vertical line segment *AC*, subtract the *y*-coordinates of point $C(x_1, y_2)$ and point $A(x_1, y_1)$.

$AC = y_2 - y_1$

The length of the hypotenuse (segment *AB*) can be determined by applying the Pythagorean theorem.

$$c^2 = a^2 + b^2$$
$$(AB)^2 = (BC)^2 + (AC)^2$$
$$(AB)^2 = (x_2 - x_1)^2 + (y_2 - y_1)^2$$
$$\sqrt{(AB)^2} = \sqrt{(x_2 - x_1)^2 + (y_2 - y_1)^2}$$
$$AB = \sqrt{(x_2 - x_1)^2 + (y_2 - y_1)^2}$$

To write the distance formula, replace AB with d_{AB}.

$d_{AB} = \sqrt{(x_2 - x_1)^2 + (y_2 - y_1)^2}$

Applying the Distance Formula

The **distance formula**,
$d_{AB} = \sqrt{(x_2 - x_1)^2 + (y_2 - y_1)^2}$, can be used to calculate the distance, d_{AB}, between two points, $A(x_1, y_1)$ and $B(x_2, y_2)$, on a coordinate grid. To use the formula, begin by subtracting the x-coordinates of both points from each other and the y-coordinates from each other. Then, square both results, add the squared values together, and calculate the square root of the sum.

There are a couple of common mistakes to avoid when using the distance formula. The most common mistake is accidentally mismatching the x- and y-values, so ensure that the numbers are paired correctly. Another common problem is found in the square root operation. Often, the very last step of finding the square root of the sum of the squared values will be forgotten.

Example

Determine the distance between point $D(4, -3)$ and point $E(-1, -9)$.

Solution

To determine the length of the line segment joining points D and E, use the distance formula $d = \sqrt{(x_2 - x_1)^2 + (y_2 - y_1)^2}$.

Let $E(-1, -9)$ represent the point (x_2, y_2), and let $D(4, -3)$ represent the point (x_1, y_1). Substitute -1 for x_2, 4 for x_1, -9 for y_2, and -3 for y_1.

$$d_{DE} = \sqrt{(x_2 - x_1)^2 + (y_2 - y_1)^2}$$
$$d_{DE} = \sqrt{((-1) - 4)^2 + ((-9) - (-3))^2}$$
$$d_{DE} = \sqrt{(-5)^2 + (-6)^2}$$
$$d_{DE} = \sqrt{25 + 36}$$
$$d_{DE} = \sqrt{61}$$
$$d_{DE} \approx 7.81$$

To the nearest hundredth, the distance between points D and E is approximately 7.81 units.

Problem Solving Using the Distance Formula

To solve a problem where you have to calculate the distance between two points, use the distance formula, $d_{AB} = \sqrt{(x_2 - x_1)^2 + (y_2 - y_1)^2}$, for two points, $A(x_1, y_1)$ and $B(x_2, y_2)$, on a coordinate grid.

Example

A ship is 5 km east and 7 km south of a lighthouse. Assuming that (1 grid unit = 1 kilometer) the location of the ship can be expressed as (5, –7) and the light house as (0, 0) on a Cartesian plane.

What is the distance, to the nearest tenth kilometer, between the ship and the lighthouse?

Solution

Apply the distance formula. In terms of the formula, the coordinates of the lighthouse, (0, 0), would provide values for (x_1, y_1), and the coordinates of the ship, (5, –7), would provide the values for (x_2, y_2).

$$\begin{aligned} d &= \sqrt{(x_2 - x_1)^2 + (y_2 - y_1)^2} \\ &= \sqrt{(5 - 0)^2 + (-7 - 0)^2} \\ &= \sqrt{(5)^2 + (-7)^2} \\ &= \sqrt{(25) + (49)} \\ &= \sqrt{74} \\ &\approx 8.6 \end{aligned}$$

Therefore, the ship is approximately 8.6 km from the lighthouse.

Example

The corners of a square garden are located at (0, 0), (5, –2), (3, –7), and (–2, –5).

What is the area of the garden?

Solution

Step 1

Determine the length of each side of the square garden.

Since it is given that the garden is a square, all the sides are of equal length. Therefore, the length of only one side has to be found.

Use the points (0, 0) and (5, –2), and substitute them into the distance formula $d = \sqrt{(x_2 - x_1)^2 + (y_2 - y_1)^2}$.

$$\begin{aligned} d &= \sqrt{(x_2 - x_1)^2 + (y_2 - y_1)^2} \\ &= \sqrt{(5-0)^2 + ((-2)-0)^2} \\ &= \sqrt{(5)^2 + (-2)^2} \\ &= \sqrt{25+4} \\ &= \sqrt{29} \text{ units} \end{aligned}$$

The length of each side of the square garden is $\sqrt{29}$ units.

Step 2

Calculate the area of the garden.

$$\begin{aligned} A_{\text{square}} &= b \times h \\ &= \sqrt{29} \times \sqrt{29} \\ &= 29 \text{ units}^2 \end{aligned}$$

Therefore, the area of the square garden is 29 units^2.

EXERCISE #1—THE PYTHAGOREAN THEOREM

412. Which of the following sets of numbers could be the sides of a right triangle?

A. 12, 48, 52 **B.** 16, 63, 65

C. 23, 72, 74 **D.** 26, 81, 85

Use the following information to answer the next question.

The hypotenuse of a right triangle is 23 mm, and the length of one side is 15 mm.

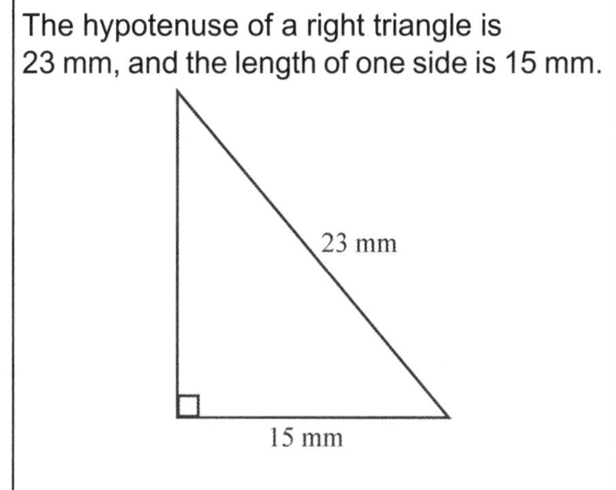

413. To the nearest tenth, the length of the missing side is __________ mm.

Use the following information to answer the next question.

A toy block in the shape of a triangular prism is illustrated in the given diagram.

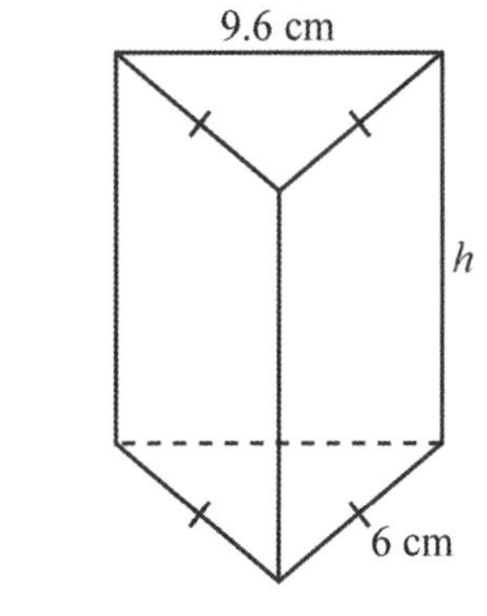

414. If the volume of the toy block is 216 cm^3, then the height, h, of the block is

A. 7.5 cm **B.** 12.5 cm

C. 15.0 cm **D.** 25.0 cm

415. A line passes through the points $A(-4, -7)$, $B(-1, 2)$, and $C(4, 17)$. Which of the following expressions does **not** represent the length of segment AC?

A. $\sqrt{640}$ units

B. $\sqrt{90}+\sqrt{250}$ units

C. $(3\sqrt{10})^2+(5\sqrt{10})^2$ units

D. $\sqrt{(-3)^2+(-9)^2}+\sqrt{(-5)^2+(-15)^2}$ units

Use the following information to answer the next question.

Points $A(-2, 2)$, $B(1, -4)$, and $C(2, 6)$ are shown on the given coordinate plane.

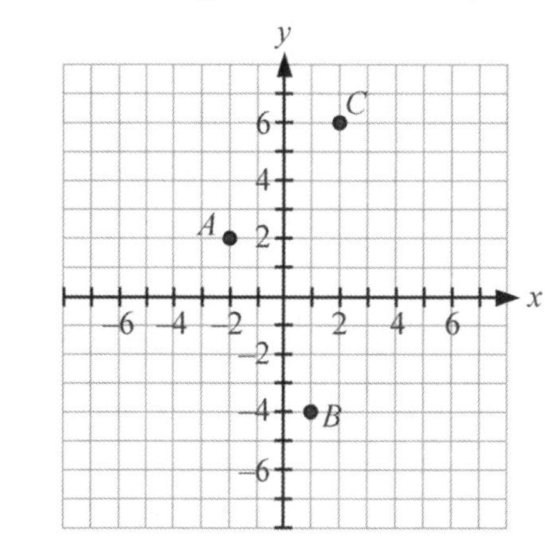

416. The perimeter of triangle ABC is equal to

A. $\sqrt{178}$

B. $\sqrt{784}$

C. $\sqrt{5}+\sqrt{13}+8$

D. $3\sqrt{5}+4\sqrt{2}+\sqrt{101}$

EXERCISE #1—THE PYTHAGOREAN THEOREM ANSWERS AND SOLUTIONS

412. B	414. B	416. D
413. 17.4	415. C	

412. B

Evaluate each set of numbers using the Pythagorean theorem.

Step 1
Evaluate the set of numbers 12, 48, and 52.

$$a^2 + b^2 = c^2$$
$$12^2 + 48^2 = 52^2$$
$$144 + 2{,}304 = 2{,}704$$
$$2{,}448 \neq 2{,}704$$

Step 2
Evaluate the set of numbers 16, 63, and 65.

$$a^2 + b^2 = c^2$$
$$16^2 + 63^2 = 65^2$$
$$256 + 3{,}969 = 4{,}225$$
$$4{,}225 = 4{,}225$$

Step 3
Evaluate the set of numbers 23, 72, and 74.

$$a^2 + b^2 = c^2$$
$$23^2 + 72^2 = 74^2$$
$$529 + 5{,}184 = 5{,}476$$
$$5{,}713 \neq 5{,}476$$

Step 4
Evaluate the set of numbers 26, 81, and 85.

$$a^2 + b^2 = c^2$$
$$26^2 + 81^2 = 85^2$$
$$676 + 6{,}561 = 7{,}225$$
$$7{,}237 \neq 7{,}225$$

The set of numbers 16, 63, and 65 could be the sides of a right triangle.

413. 17.4

Step 1
Substitute the known values into the Pythagorean theorem.

$$a^2 + b^2 = c^2$$
$$a^2 + 15^2 = 23^2$$
$$a^2 + 225 = 529$$

Step 2
Solve for the missing side.
Subtract 225 from both sides of the equation to isolate a^2.

$$a^2 + 225 = 529$$
$$a^2 + 225 - 225 = 529 - 225$$
$$a^2 = 304$$

Take the square root of both sides to solve for a.

$$\sqrt{a^2} = \sqrt{304}$$
$$a \approx 17.4356$$

The length of the missing side to the nearest tenth is 17.4 mm.

414. B

In order to determine the volume of the toy block, it is necessary to consider one of the triangular faces as the base of the block.

Step 1
Draw a sketch of one of the triangular faces, and label the height of the triangle as x.
A possible sketch is shown here.

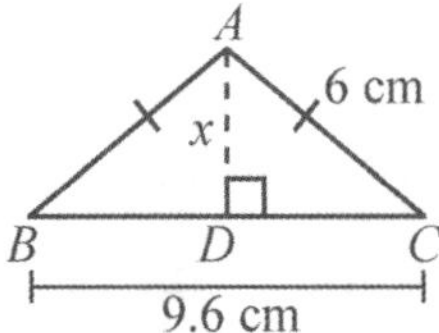

Step 2
Determine the value of x.
Notice that the triangle shown is an isosceles triangle, so the distance from C to D is $9.6 \div 2 = 4.8$ cm. Use the Pythagorean theorem to solve for x.

$$4.8^2 + x^2 = 6^2$$
$$23.04 + x^2 = 36$$
$$x^2 = 12.96$$
$$x = \sqrt{12.96}$$
$$x = 3.6$$

The height of the triangle is 3.6 cm.

Step 3
Determine the area of the base of the toy block by applying the formula for the area of a triangle, $A = \frac{bh}{2}$.

Substitute 9.6 for b and 3.6 for h, and then solve for A.

$$A = \frac{bh}{2}$$
$$A = \frac{9.6 \times 3.6}{2}$$
$$A = \frac{34.56}{2}$$
$$A = 17.28 \text{ cm}^2$$

Step 4
Solve for h, the height of the toy block, by applying the formula for the volume of a triangular prism, $V = A_{base} \times h$.

Substitute 17.28 cm^2 for the area of the base and 216 cm^3 for V, and then solve for h.

$$V = A_{base} \times h$$
$$216 = (17.28) \times (h)$$
$$216 = 17.28h$$
$$12.5 = h$$

The height of the toy block is 12.5 cm.

415. C

Apply the distance formula $d = \sqrt{(x_2 - x_1)^2 + (y_2 - y_1)^2}$.

Use the points (4, 17) for P_2 and (−4, −7) for P_1 in the formula. Substitute 4 for x_2, −4 for x_1, 17 for y_2, and −7 for y_1.

$$d = \sqrt{(4-(-4))^2 + (17-(-7))^2}$$
$$= \sqrt{64 + 576}$$
$$= \sqrt{640} \text{ units}$$

The expression $\sqrt{640}$ units does represent the length of segment AC.

Alternatively, the length of segment AC can be determined by adding the length of AB and the length of BC. Determine the length of AB using the distance formula.

$$d_{AB} = \sqrt{(x_A - x_B)^2 + (y_A - y_B)^2}$$
$$= \sqrt{(-4-(-1))^2 + (-7-(2))^2}$$
$$= \sqrt{(-3)^2 + (-9)^2} \text{ units}$$

Determine the length of BC using the distance formula.

$$d_{BC} = \sqrt{(x_B - x_C)^2 + (y_B - y_C)^2}$$
$$= \sqrt{(-1-(4))^2 + (2-17)^2}$$
$$= \sqrt{(-5)^2 + (-15)^2} \text{ units}$$

Calculate the length of AC by adding the lengths of AB and BC.

$$d_{AC} = d_{AB} + d_{BC}$$
$$= \sqrt{(-3)^2 + (-9)^2} + \sqrt{(-5)^2 + (-15)^2}$$
$$= \sqrt{90} + \sqrt{250} \text{ units}$$

The expressions $\sqrt{90} + \sqrt{250}$ units and $\sqrt{(-3)^2 + (-9)^2} + \sqrt{(-5)^2 + (-15)^2}$ units also represent the length of segment AC.

416. D

Step 1
Using the distance formula $d = \sqrt{(x_2 - x_1)^2 + (y_2 - y_1)^2}$, find the distances d_{AC}, d_{AB}, and d_{BC}.

$$d_{AC} = \sqrt{(-2-2)^2 + (2-6)^2}$$
$$= \sqrt{(-4)^2 + (-4)^2}$$
$$= \sqrt{16 + 16}$$
$$= \sqrt{32}$$
$$= \sqrt{16(2)}$$
$$d_{AC} = 4\sqrt{2}$$

$$d_{AB} = \sqrt{(-2-1)^2 + [2-(-4)]^2}$$
$$= \sqrt{(-3)^2 + 6^2}$$
$$= \sqrt{9 + 36}$$
$$= \sqrt{45}$$
$$= \sqrt{9(5)}$$
$$d_{AB} = 3\sqrt{5}$$

$$d_{BC} = \sqrt{(1-2)^2 + (-4-6)^2}$$
$$= \sqrt{(-1)^2 + (-10)^2}$$
$$= \sqrt{1 + 100}$$
$$d_{BC} = \sqrt{101}$$

Step 2
Find the perimeter by adding the distances d_{AC}, d_{AB}, and d_{BC}.

$$d_{AC} + d_{AB} + d_{BC} = 4\sqrt{2} + 3\sqrt{5} + \sqrt{101}$$

The perimeter is equal to $3\sqrt{5} + 4\sqrt{2} + \sqrt{101}$.

EXERCISE #2—THE PYTHAGOREAN THEOREM

417. If ΔABC has a right angle at B, the measures of sides AB, BC, and CA respectively could be

A. 12 cm, 13 cm, and 17 cm

B. 9 cm, 11 cm, and 15 cm

C. 8 cm, 15 cm, and 17 cm

D. 17 cm, 19 cm, and 24 cm

Use the following information to answer the next question.

The rope that attaches to the top of a tent pole is 170 cm long, and it is fastened to the ground 80 cm away from the foot of the pole.

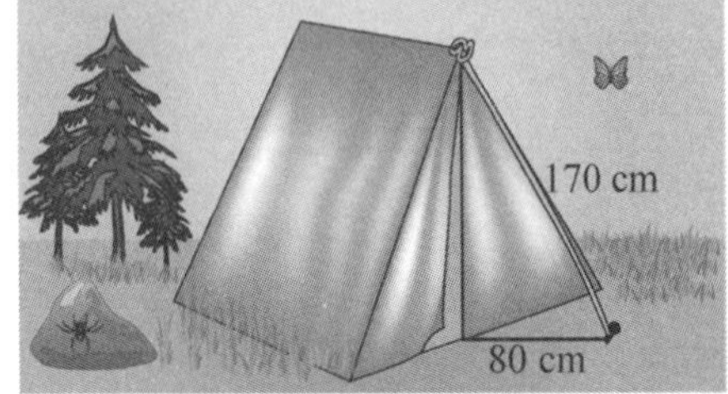

418. How tall is the tent pole? __________ cm

Use the following information to answer the next question.

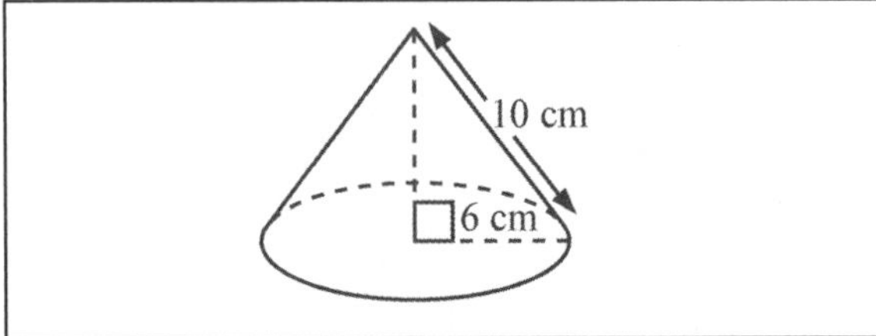

419. The volume of the given cone, to the nearest tenth of a cubic centimeter, is __________ cm^3.

420. The length of the line segment that joins point $P(-6, 7)$ and point $Q(9, -11)$, correct to the nearest tenth, is __________units.

421. What is the perimeter of a triangle with vertices at points (2, 3), (6, 0), and (5, 7)?

A. $(10 + 5\sqrt{3})$ units

B. $(5 + 10\sqrt{3})$ units

C. $(10 + 5\sqrt{2})$ units

D. $(5 + 10\sqrt{2})$ units

EXERCISE #2—THE PYTHAGOREAN THEOREM ANSWERS AND SOLUTIONS

417. C	419. 301.4	421. C
418. 150	420. 23.4	

417. C

Use the Pythagorean theorem of $a^2 + b^2 = c^2$ to evaluate each option.

Step 1
Substitute the values of the measures 12 cm, 13 cm, and 17 cm into the formula.

$$a^2 + b^2 = c^2$$
$$12^2 + 13^2 = 17^2$$
$$144 + 169 = 289$$
$$313 \neq 289$$

Since the two sides of the equation are not equal, this could not be the answer.

Step 2
Substitute the values of the measures 9 cm, 11 cm, and 15 cm into the formula.

$$a^2 + b^2 = c^2$$
$$9^2 + 11^2 = 15^2$$
$$81 + 121 = 225$$
$$202 \neq 225$$

Since the two sides of the equation are not equal, this could not be the answer.

Step 3
Substitute the values of the measures 8 cm, 15 cm, and 17 cm into the formula.

$$a^2 + b^2 = c^2$$
$$8^2 + 15^2 = 17^2$$
$$64 + 225 = 289$$
$$289 = 289$$

Since the two sides of the equation are equal, this is the answer.

Step 4
Substitute the values of the measures 17 cm, 19 cm, and 24 cm into the formula.

$$a^2 + b^2 = c^2$$
$$17^2 + 19^2 = 24^2$$
$$289 + 361 = 576$$
$$650 \neq 576$$

Since the two sides of the equation are not equal, this could not be the answer.

418. 150

The rope attached to the tent represents the hypotenuse of a right triangle. The height of the tent and the distance the rope is from the foot of the pole represent the legs of a right triangle.

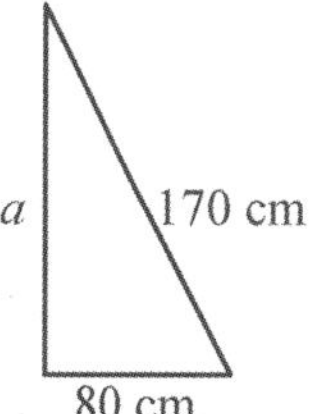

Step 1
Substitute the known values into the Pythagorean theorem.

$$a^2 + b^2 = c^2$$
$$a^2 + 80^2 = 170^2$$
$$a^2 + 6{,}400 = 28{,}900$$

Step 2
Rearrange the formula to solve for the missing side.

$$a^2 + 6{,}400 = 28{,}900$$
$$a^2 + 6{,}400 - 6{,}400 = 28{,}900 - 6{,}400$$
$$a^2 = 22{,}500$$

Take the square root of both sides to solve for a.

$$\sqrt{a^2} = \sqrt{22{,}500}$$
$$a = 150$$

The height of the tent pole is 150 cm.

419. 301.4

Step 1
Use the Pythagorean theorem to find the height, h, of the cone.
Substitute 6 for b, 10 for c, and h for a.

$$a^2 + b^2 = c^2$$
$$h^2 + (6)^2 = (10)^2$$
$$h^2 = (10)^2 - (6)^2$$
$$h^2 = 100 - 36$$
$$h^2 = 64$$
$$\sqrt{h^2} = \sqrt{64}$$
$$h = 8 \text{ cm}$$

Step 2
Calculate the volume of the cone using the volume formula for a cone.

$$V_{cone} = \frac{(\text{area of base})(\text{height})}{3}$$
$$= \frac{(\pi r^2)(h)}{3}$$

Substitute 6 for r and 8 for h.

$$V_{cone} = \frac{\pi(6)^2(8)}{3}$$
$$= \frac{3.14(36)(8)}{3}$$
$$= \frac{904.32}{3}$$
$$= 301.44 \text{ cm}^3$$

The volume of the given cone, to the nearest tenth of a cubic centimeter, is 301.4 cm^3.

420. 23.4

The length of the line segment is the distance between the two points.

Apply the distance formula $d = \sqrt{(x_2 - x_1)^2 + (y_2 - y_1)^2}$ using the points (−6, 7) and (9, −11).

$$d = \sqrt{(9 - (-6))^2 + ((-11) - 7)^2}$$
$$d = \sqrt{(15)^2 + (-18)^2}$$
$$d = \sqrt{(15)^2 + (-18)^2}$$
$$d = \sqrt{549}$$
$$d \approx 23.4$$

Correct to the nearest tenth, the length of the line segment that joins point $P(-6, 7)$ and point $Q(9, -11)$ is 23.4 units.

421. C

Let the triangle be ΔABC, and let $A(2, 3)$, $B(6, 0)$, and $C(5, 7)$ be the vertices of the triangle.

Step 1
Calculate the length of each side using the distance formula $d = \sqrt{(x_2 - x_1)^2 + (y_2 - y_1)^2}$.

Calculate the length of side AB.

$$AB = \sqrt{(6-2)^2 + (0-3)^2}$$
$$AB = \sqrt{4^2 + (-3)^2}$$
$$AB = \sqrt{16 + 9}$$
$$AB = \sqrt{25}$$
$$AB = 5 \text{ units}$$

Calculate the length of BC.

$$BC = \sqrt{(5-6)^2 + (7-0)^2}$$
$$BC = \sqrt{(-1)^2 + 7^2}$$
$$BC = \sqrt{1 + 49}$$
$$BC = \sqrt{50}$$
$$BC = 5\sqrt{2} \text{ units}$$

Calculate the length of CA.

$$CA = \sqrt{(2-5)^2 + (3-7)^2}$$
$$CA = \sqrt{(-3)^2 + (-4)^2}$$
$$CA = \sqrt{9 + 16}$$
$$CA = \sqrt{25}$$
$$CA = 5 \text{ units}$$

Step 2
Determine the perimeter of ΔABC.

$$\Delta ABC = AB + BC + CA$$
$$\Delta ABC = 5 + 5\sqrt{2} + 5$$
$$\Delta ABC = (10 + 5\sqrt{2}) \text{ units}$$

The perimeter of the given triangle is $(10 + 5\sqrt{2})$ units.

Using Representations To Analyze Functions

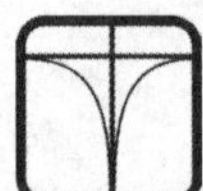

USING REPRESENTATIONS TO ANALYZE FUNCTIONS

Table of Correlations

Standard		Concepts	Exercise #1	Exercise #2
Unit5.4	Analyze functions using different representations.			
F-IF.7bi	*Graph functions expressed symbolically and show key features of the graph, by hand in simple cases and using technology for more complicated cases. Graph square root, cube root, and piecewise-defined functions, including step functions and absolute value functions.*	Absolute Value Function	422	431
		Defining Piecewise Functions	423	432
F-IF.8a	*Write a function defined by an expression in different but equivalent forms to reveal and explain different properties of the function. Use the process of factoring and completing the square in a quadratic function to show zeros, extreme values, and symmetry of the graph, and interpret these in terms of a context.*	Sketching the Graph of $y = a(x - r)(x - s)$ Using the Key Features	188	196
		Graphing Quadratic Functions by Hand by Completing the Square	192	200
		Determining the x-intercepts of a Graph Given its Quadratic Equation in the Form $y = ax^2 + bx + c$	353	368
		Determining the x-Intercepts of the Graph of a Quadratic Function Given in Factored Form	354	369
		Expressing $y = ax^2 + bx + c$ in the Form $y = a(x - h)^2 + k$ by Completing the Square	355	370
		Using Algebra to Complete the Square	424	433
		Solving Real-World Quadratic Problems Given a Graph	425	434
		Solving Real-World Quadratic Problems Graphically when Given an Equation	426	435
		Algebraically Solving Real-World Quadratic Problems Given an Equation	427	436
		Determining the Vertex of a Quadratic Function's Graph $y = ax^2 + bx + c$	428	437
		Determining the Vertex of a Quadratic Function's Graph in Factored Form	429	438
F-IF.8b	*Write a function defined by an expression in different but equivalent forms to reveal and explain different properties of the function. Use the properties of exponents to interpret expressions for exponential functions.*	Modeling Exponential Functions of Growth	41	59
		Modeling Exponential Functions of Decay	42	60
		Properties of Exponential Functions	165	177
		Gathering Information from Exponential Functions	430	439

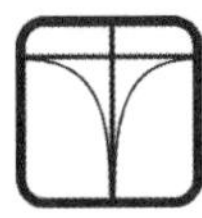

F-IF.7bi Graph functions expressed symbolically and show key features of the graph, by hand in simple cases and using technology for more complicated cases. Graph square root, cube root, and piecewise-defined functions, including step functions and absolute value functions.

Absolute Value Function

If a function $f(x)$ is given, the absolute value function is defined by the equation $y = |f(x)|$. When the graph of $y = f(x)$ is transformed to the graph of the absolute value function $y = |f(x)|$, the part of the graph that is below the x-axis on the graph of $y = f(x)$ is reflected above the x-axis on the graph of $y = |f(x)|$, and the part of the graph that is above the x-axis on the graph of $y = f(x)$ remains the same.

To sketch the graph of $y = |f(x)|$ given the graph of $y = f(x)$, follow these steps:

1. Sketch the graph of $y = f(x)$.
2. Identify points where the graph of $y = f(x)$ is zero or positive (above the x-axis) and where the graph of $y = f(x)$ is negative (below the x-axis).
3. Reflect the negative parts of $y = f(x)$ about the x-axis.

The graph of $y = |f(x)|$ will consist of the parts of the graph of $y = f(x)$ that are above the x-axis and the parts that were reflected about the x-axis, as illustrated in the following example.

Example

Given the function $f(x) = x + 2$, sketch the graph of $y = |f(x)|$.

Solution

Step 1

Sketch the graph of $f(x) = x + 2$.

The graph of $f(x) = x + 2$ is a line with a slope of 1 and a y-intercept at 2.

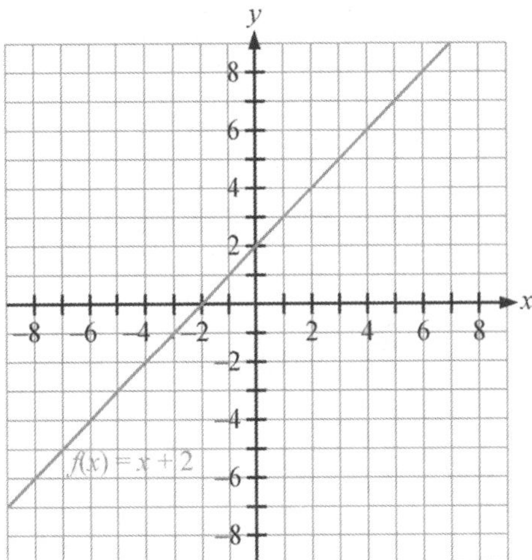

Step 2

Identify points where the function $f(x)$ is zero or positive (above the x-axis) and where the function $f(x)$ is negative (below the x-axis).

The function $f(x)$ is zero or positive for x-values greater than or equal to −2 or $x \geq -2$.

The function $f(x)$ is negative for x-values less than −2 or $x < -2$.

Step 3
Reflect the negative part of the graph of $y = f(x)$ about the x-axis.

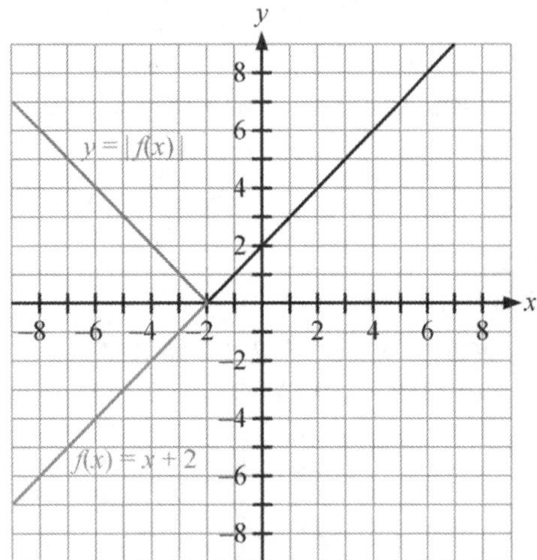

Step 4
Show the sketch of $y = | f(x) |$.

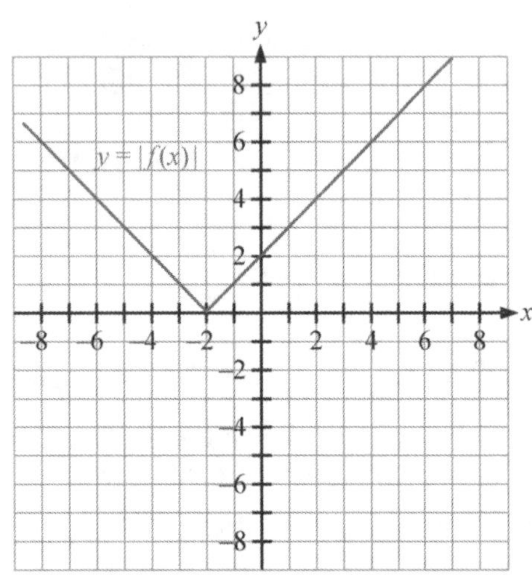

Defining Piecewise Functions

A **piecewise function** is a function that is defined on a sequence of intervals. The most common case of a piecewise function is an absolute value function. For example, the definition of an absolute value of the variable x is a piecewise function, which is given as follows: $|x| = x$ when $x \geq 0$, and $|x| = -x$ when $x < 0$.

You can obtain the graph of $y = |x|$ by using the definition of an absolute value to write $y = |x|$ as two distinct functions.

Example

Use tables of values and the definition of absolute value to sketch the graph of $y = |x|$.

Solution

Step 1
Create a table of values.
The function $y = |x|$ can be written as two functions: $y = x$ when $x \geq 0$ and $y = -x$ when $x < 0$.
Construct a table of values using these two functions.

$y = x,\ x \geq 0$		$y = -x,\ x < 0$		
x	y	x	y	
0	0			
1	1	−1	1	
		−2	2	2
		−3	3	3
		−4	4	4

Step 2
Sketch the graph.
Plotting the ordered pairs from the table of values on the Cartesian plane and drawing lines through the points gives a graph of the function. Since the values for x and y can be any real numbers, ordered pairs, such as (7.4, 7.4) and $(-\sqrt{5}, \sqrt{5})$, are part of the graph. Therefore, the lines are continuous and without end for extreme values.

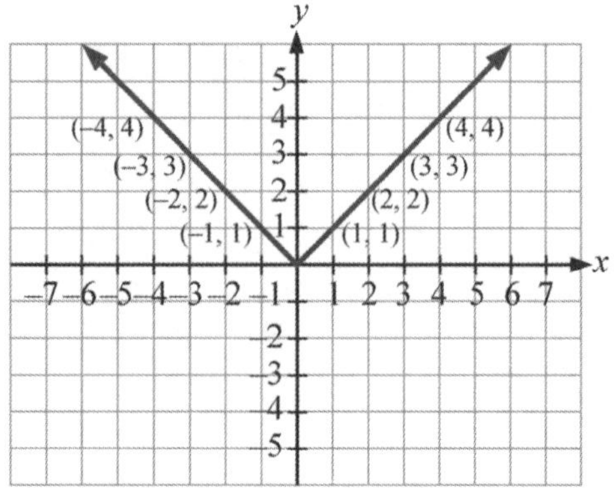

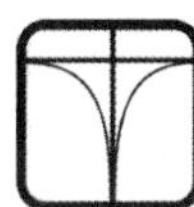

Piecewise functions are not limited to absolute value functions. They can be made up of different kinds of functions on different intervals. Pay close attention to the intervals included for the values of each function. If you are given $x > 5$ as an interval, it does not include the value of 5. You can graph this function by drawing the graph up to the point and placing a empty point at the coordinate $(5, y)$. Similarly, if $x \leq -3$, the value of -3 is included. You can graph this function by drawing the graph up to the point and placing a solid point at the coordinate $(-3, y)$.

Example

Function	Interval
$y = x + 5$	$x < -2$
$y = x^3$	$-2 \leq x \leq 2$
$y = x^2 - 3x - 1$	$x > 2$

Graph the given piecewise function.

Solution

Step 1

Construct a table of values for the function $y = x + 5$ in the interval $x < -2$.

x	y
−5	0
−4	1
−3	2
−2	3

Step 2

Construct a table of values for the function $y = x^3$ in the interval $-2 \leq x \leq 2$.

x	y
−2	−8
−1	−1
0	0
1	1
2	8

Step 3

Construct a table of values for the function $y = x^2 - 3x - 1$ in the interval $x > 2$.

x	y
2	−3
3	−1
4	3
5	9

Step 4

Sketch the piecewise function.

The interval of $y = x^3$ includes the values −2 and 2; the other two functions do not.

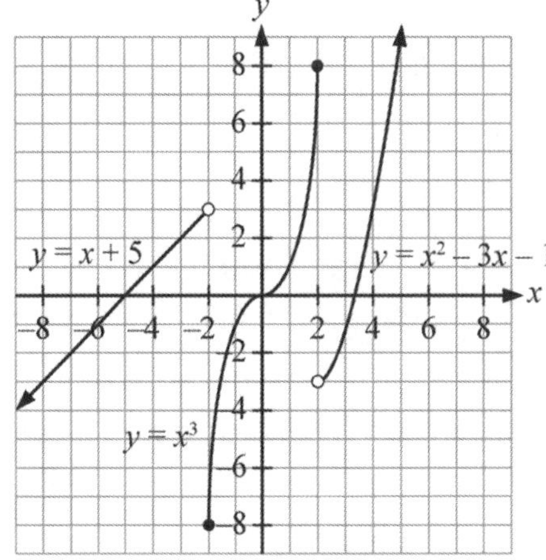

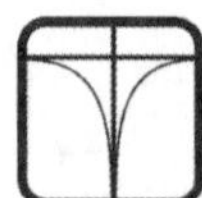

F-IF.8a Write a function defined by an expression in different but equivalent forms to reveal and explain different properties of the function. Use the process of factoring and completing the square in a quadratic function to show zeros, extreme values, and symmetry of the graph, and interpret these in terms of a context.

Using Algebra to Complete the Square

The following example shows the steps for algebraically completing the square.

Example

Complete the square for $y = 2x^2 + 5x - 3$.

Solution

Identify and remove the common factor of a from the x^2- and x-terms of the expression. In this example, the common factor is 2.

$y = 2(x^2 + 2.5x) - 3$

Identify the coefficient of the x-term to be 2.5, divide this value by 2, and square it.

$y = 2(x^2 + 2.5x) - 3 \qquad \left(\frac{2.5}{2}\right)^2 = 1.5625$

Both add and subtract this value of 1.5625 inside the brackets in order to keep the algebraic expression unchanged.

$y = 2(x^2 + 2.5x + 1.5625 - 1.5625) - 3$

Move the negative value −1.5625 out of the brackets by multiplying it by the leading coefficient.

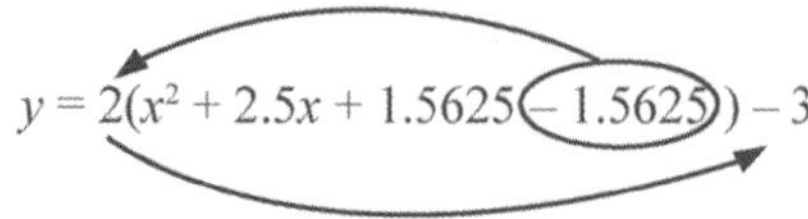

$y = 2(x^2 + 2.5x + 1.5625) - 3.125 - 3$

Factor the perfect square trinomial inside the brackets, and collect the constant terms outside the brackets.

$y = 2(x + 1.25)^2 - 6.125$

Note: The numerical part of the binomial in the final bracket is always $\frac{1}{2}$ of the coefficient on the x-term of the perfect square trinomial $\left(\text{i.e., } +1.25 = \frac{+2.5}{2}\right)$.

You can verify that the two forms of the quadratic function represent the same graph on your graphing calculator by following the same steps as mentioned in the previous section.

Enter:

$Y_1 = 2x^2 + 5x - 3$

$Y_2 = 2(x + 1.25)^2 - 6.125$

WINDOW	ZOOM	6	ENTER	GRAPH:

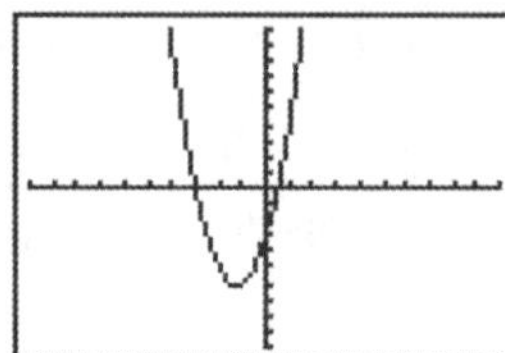

Solving Real-World Quadratic Problems Given a Graph

Quadratic functions can be used to model real-world situations and solve problems that require an analysis of the graph of the given quadratic function.

Most real-world problems involving quadratic functions can be solved by analyzing the graph of the corresponding parabola and identifying the y-intercept, the x-intercept, the coordinates of the vertex, or another particular point on the parabola.

Example

The trajectory of a baseball is represented by the given graph.

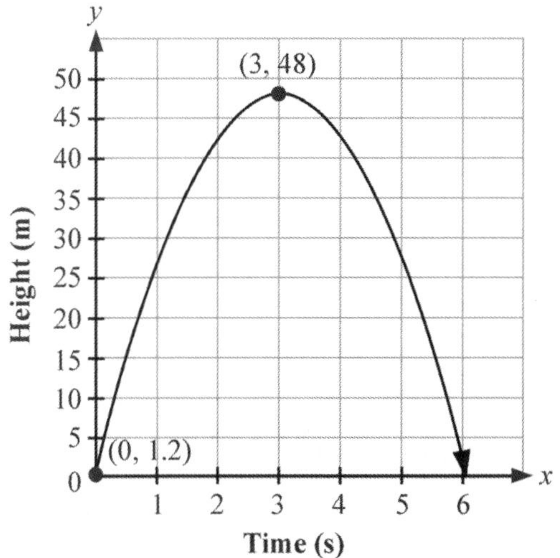

What is the maximum height of the baseball's trajectory?

Solution

The given parabola opens downward and has a vertex at (3, 48).

The maximum value (since the parabola opens downwards) of the quadratic function represented by the given parabola is equal to the *y*-coordinate of the vertex of the parabola.

Therefore, the maximum height of the baseball is 48 m.

What was the initial height of the baseball when it was hit?

Solution

At 0 s, the baseball was at its initial height. This corresponds to the ordered pair (0, 1.2) on the parabola.

Thus, the baseball was hit from an initial height of 1.2 m.

How long does the baseball remain in the air?

Solution

The ball remains in the air until it hits the ground. This occurs at the point where the parabola intersects the *x*-axis after reaching its maximum value.

Since the graph intersects the *x*-axis at 6, the ball remains in the air for 6 s.

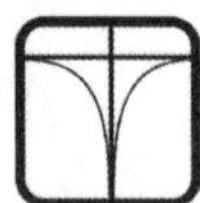

Solving Real-World Quadratic Problems Graphically when Given an Equation

Quadratic functions can be used to describe real-world situations.

The problems related to the equation can be solved graphically.

Example

A city's population can fluctuate. A small Ontario city that has a declining population is expecting the population to begin increasing in the near future because of the introduction of several industrial development initiatives.

The city planners predict that the city's population can be modeled by the quadratic function $P = 150t^2 - 1,200t + 14,900$, $t \geq 0$, in which t represents the time in years since January 1st, 2006, and P represents the population.

Using a graphing calculator, determine the year the city's population will be the lowest.

Solution

Press the Y= button on your calculator, and enter the equation $P = 150t^2 - 1,200t + 14,900$ into the Y_1 = value as follows:
$Y_1 = 150X^2 - 1,200X + 14,900$.

Press WINDOW, and use settings such as x: [−5, 12, 2] and y: [7,500, 20,000, 2,500].

Use the Minimum feature of your calculator. Press 2nd TRACE to access the CALC menu.

Choose 3:minimum from the list. Follow the prompts given by the calculator. Provide a left bound, a right bound, and press ENTER when prompted for a guess.

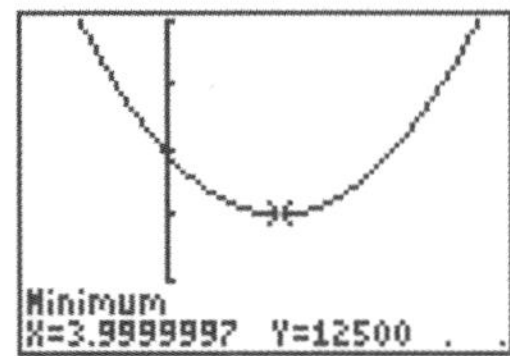

Since the graphing calculator's cursor is at $x \approx 4$, the minimum population will occur at the beginning of $t = 4$, or 2,006 + 4 = 2,010.

Using a graphing calculator, determine the first year that the city's population will be more than 24,000.

Solution

Press the Y= button on your calculator, and enter the equation $P = 150t^2 - 1,200t + 14,900$ into the Y_1 = value as follows:
$Y_1 = 150X^2 - 1,200X + 14,900$.

Use the Intersection feature of your calculator to find the first positive intersection point between this line and the line of the quadratic function, $Y_1 = 150X^2 - 1,200X + 14,900$.

Enter the line referring to the population of 24,000 into the Y_2 = value as follows:
$Y_2 = 24,000$.

Press WINDOW, and use settings such as x: [−5, 20, 2] and y: [7,500, 35,000, 2,500].

Press 2nd TRACE to access the CALC menu.

Choose 5:intersect from the list. Follow the prompts given by the calculator. Choose a point near the intersection on the first function (the quadratic function), and a point near the intersection on the second function (the line). Press ENTER when prompted for a guess.

The first positive intersection point occurs when $x = 12.76$, as shown in the given diagram.

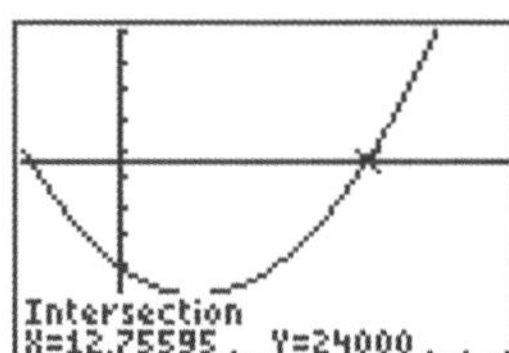

The first year that the population will be more than 24,000 is 2,006 + 12.76 = 2,018.76, or 2019.

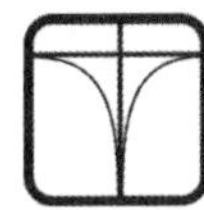

ALGEBRAICALLY SOLVING REAL-WORLD QUADRATIC PROBLEMS GIVEN AN EQUATION

Quadratic functions can describe real-world situations. You can use these quadratic functions to solve problems related to these real-world situations. If you know the equation, you can use algebra to solve the problem.

Example

A city's population can fluctuate. The population of a small Ontario city has declined in recent years, but it is expected to increase because of the introduction of several industrial development initiatives. The city planners predict that the city's population can be modeled by the quadratic function $P = 150t^2 - 1{,}200t + 14{,}900$, $t \geq 0$, where t is the time in years since January 1, 2006, and P is the population.

What was the city's population on January 1, 2008?

Solution

On January 1, 2008, exactly 2 years have passed since January 1, 2006.

Substitute the value of 2 for t, and solve for P.

$$P = 150t^2 - 1{,}200t + 14{,}900$$
$$P = 150(2)^2 - 1{,}200(2) + 14{,}900$$
$$P = 600 - 2{,}400 + 14{,}900$$
$$P = 13{,}100$$

The population on January 1, 2008, was 13,100.

At the beginning of what year will the city's population be the lowest?

Solution

The minimum population can be found when the function is rewritten in the vertex form $f(x) = a(x - h)^2 + k$.

Complete the square of the function.

$$P = 150t^2 - 1{,}200t + 14{,}900$$
$$P = 150\left(t^2 - 8t\right) + 14{,}900$$
$$P = 150\left(t^2 - 8t + 16 - 16\right) + 14{,}900$$
$$P = 150(t - 4)^2 + 12{,}500$$

The minimum population of 12,500 occurs when $t = 4$ since the vertex is (4, 12,500). Since 2,006 + 4 = 2,010, the city's population will be at its lowest at the beginning of 2010.

What is the first year that the city's population will be greater than 24,000?

Solution

Substitute the value 24,000 for P, and solve for t using the quadratic formula.

$$P = 150t^2 - 1{,}200t + 14{,}900$$
$$24{,}000 = 150t^2 - 1{,}200t + 14{,}900$$
$$0 = 150t^2 - 1{,}200t - 9{,}100$$

Solve for t using an algebraic method such as the quadratic formula.

$$t = \frac{-b \pm \sqrt{b^2 - 4ac}}{2a}$$
$$t = \frac{1{,}200 \pm \sqrt{(-1{,}200)^2 - 4(150)(-9{,}100)}}{2(150)}$$
$$t = \frac{1{,}200 \pm 2{,}626.785107\ldots}{300}$$
$$t \approx 12.76 \text{ or } -4.76$$

The function is not defined for years before 2006. Since −4.76 refers to a time before 2006, the value $t = 12.76$ is the solution to this question.

The first year that the population will be more than 24,000 is 2006 + 12.76 = 2018.76, or 2019.

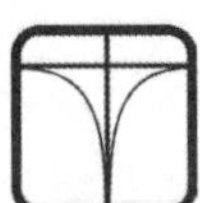

Determining the Vertex of a Quadratic Function's Graph $y = ax^2 + bx + c$

In order to determine the vertex of the function $y = ax^2 + bx + c$, the form of the function must first be changed by either completing the square or factoring.

In factored form, the x-coordinate of the vertex is found using the midpoint formula and then substituted into the equation to solve for the y-coordinate of the vertex.

Another method to find the vertex is to apply the formula for the vertex, which is found by completing the square of the generic equation $y = ax^2 + bx + c$.

The coordinates of the vertex of any quadratic function of the form $y = ax^2 + bx + c$ are $\left(-\frac{b}{2a}, -\frac{b^2}{4a} + c\right)$.

Example

Determine the vertex of the function $y = 2x^2 + 4x + 5$.

Solution

The coordinates of the vertex of any quadratic function in the form $y = ax^2 + bx + c$ are $\left(-\frac{b}{2a}, -\frac{b^2}{4a} + c\right)$. The vertex of the function $y = 2x^2 + 4x + 5$ can be found by substituting the appropriate values into the variables $\left(-\frac{b}{2a}, -\frac{b^2}{4a} + c\right)$.

$$\left(-\frac{b}{2a}, -\frac{b^2}{4a} + c\right)$$
$$= \left(-\frac{4}{2(2)}, -\frac{4^2}{4(2)} + 5\right)$$
$$= \left(-\frac{4}{4}, -\frac{16}{8} + 5\right)$$
$$= (-1, -2 + 5)$$
$$= (-1, 3)$$

The vertex of the function $y = 2x^2 + 4x + 5$ is $(-1, 3)$.

Determining the Vertex of a Quadratic Function's Graph in Factored Form

To determine the vertex of the function $y = a(x - r)(x - s)$, first find the x-coordinate of the vertex. When the function is written in this form, the x-intercepts can be easily determined from the equation. Since the graph will be symmetrical, the x-coordinate of the vertex will be exactly halfway between the x-intercepts. This position can be found by using the midpoint formula $M = \left(\frac{x_1 + x_2}{2}, \frac{y_1 + y_2}{2}\right)$. The x-coordinate can then be substituted back into the equation to solve for the y-coordinate.

To find the vertex of $y = a(x - r)(x - s)$, follow these steps:

1. Determine the x-intercepts.
2. Determine the midpoint of the x-intercepts.
3. Substitute the x-coordinate from the midpoint into the equation to solve for y.

Example

Determine the vertex of the function $y = \frac{1}{2}(x - 2)(x + 5)$.

Solution

Step 1

Determine the x-intercepts.

Set the equation equal to 0, and apply the zero product property.

$$0 = \frac{1}{2}(x - 2)(x + 5)$$
$$0 = x - 2$$
$$2 = x$$
$$0 = x + 5$$
$$-5 = x$$

Step 2

Determine the midpoint of the x-intercepts.

$$M = \left(\frac{x_1 + x_2}{2}, \frac{y_1 + y_2}{2}\right)$$
$$M = \left(\frac{-5 + 2}{2}, \frac{0 + 0}{2}\right)$$
$$M = \left(\frac{-3}{2}, \frac{0}{2}\right)$$
$$M = \left(-\frac{3}{2}, 0\right)$$

Step 3
Substitute the x-coordinate from the midpoint into the equation to solve for y.

$$y = \frac{1}{2}(x-2)(x+5)$$
$$y = \frac{1}{2}\left(-\frac{3}{2}-2\right)\left(-\frac{3}{2}+5\right)$$
$$y = \frac{1}{2}\left(-\frac{7}{2}\right)\left(\frac{7}{2}\right)$$
$$y = -\frac{49}{8}$$

The coordinates of the vertex of the function $y = \frac{1}{2}(x-2)(x+5)$ are $\left(-\frac{3}{2}, -\frac{49}{8}\right)$.

F-IF.8b Write a function defined by an expression in different but equivalent forms to reveal and explain different properties of the function. Use the properties of exponents to interpret expressions for exponential functions.

Gathering Information from Exponential Functions

The graphs of exponential functions of the form $f(x) = a^x$, where $a > 0$ and $a \neq 1$, have some unique characteristics.

Four examples of the graphs of the exponential functions $f(x) = \left(\frac{1}{3}\right)^x$, $f(x) = \left(\frac{1}{2}\right)^x$, $f(x) = (1.5)^x$, and $f(x) = 3^x$ are shown in the diagram.

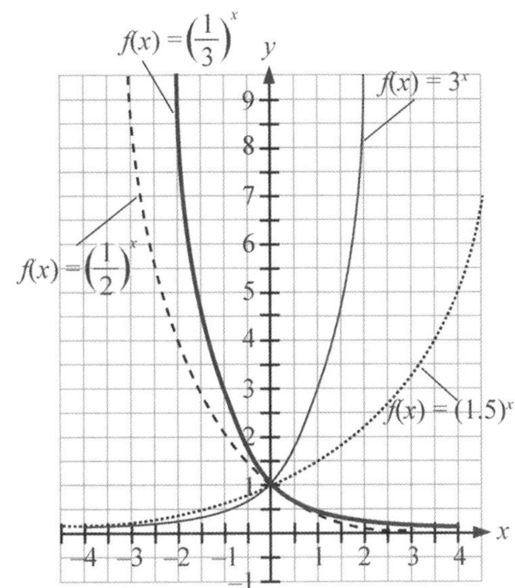

By examining these four graphs, you can make some generalizations about all graphs of exponential functions of the form $f(x) = a^x$.

Domain: $x \in \mathbb{R}$, since all x-values are permissible.

Range: $y > 0$, since each graph has y-values that get closer and closer to the y-axis, but never become 0.

Horizontal asymptote: $y = 0$

Note: An asymptote is the line a curve approaches but never touches, which in this case, is the x-axis defined by the equation $y = 0$.

y-intercept: (0, 1) or 1, since for all exponential functions $f(x) = a^x$, $a^0 = 1$.

x-intercept: None, since the graph never touches the x-axis.

When $a > 1$:

- The graph is an *increasing* function as you move from left to right through the domain, as is shown by the graph of $f(x) = 1.5^x$ and $f(x) = 3^x$.
- The graph is also *flatter* on the left side of the y-axis, and is *steeper* or increases more rapidly on the right side of the y-axis as the value of *a increases*.

When $0 < a < 1$:

- The graph is a *decreasing* function as you move from left to right through the domain, as is shown by the graph of $f(x) = \left(\frac{1}{2}\right)^x$ and $f(x) = \left(\frac{1}{3}\right)^x$.
- The graph is also *flatter* on the right side of the y-axis, and is *steeper* or decreases more rapidly on the left side of the y-axis as the value of *a decreases* or gets closer to 0.

Example

For each representation of an exponential function of the form $f(x) = a^x$ shown below, determine whether it is an increasing or decreasing function, and explain why.

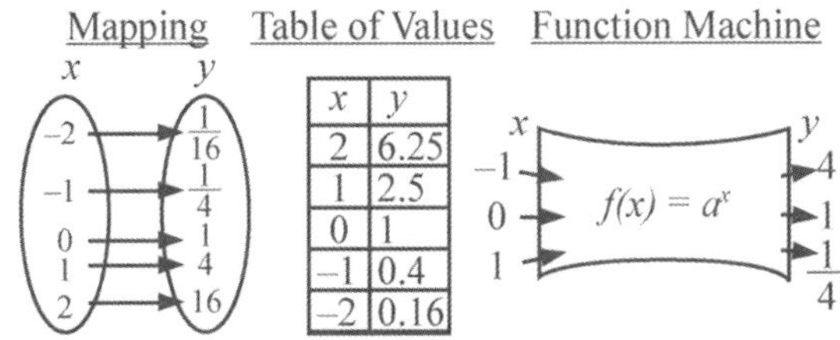

x	y
2	6.25
1	2.5
0	1
−1	0.4
−2	0.16

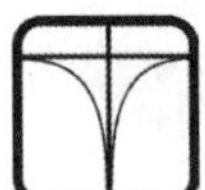

Solution

Mapping: As the *x*-values move from the top (–2) to the bottom (2), the *y*-values increase $\left(\frac{1}{16} \to 16\right)$.

The function is $f(x) = 4^x$, since $f(1) = a^1 = a = 4$.

Therefore, since $a > 1$, this is an increasing function.

Table of values: As the *x*-values move from the bottom (–2) to the top (2), the *y*-values increase $(0.16 \to 6.25)$. The function is $f(x) = 2.5^x$, since $f(1) = a^1 = a = 2.5$.

Therefore, since $a > 1$, this is an increasing function.

Function machine: As the *x*-values move from the top (–1) to the bottom (1), the *y*-values decrease $\left(4 \to \frac{1}{4}\right)$. The function is $f(x) = \left(\frac{1}{4}\right)^x$, since $f(1) = a^1 = a = \frac{1}{4}$.

Therefore, since $0 < a < 1$, this is a decreasing function.

EXERCISE #1—USING REPRESENTATIONS TO ANALYZE FUNCTIONS

422. If the range of the function $y = f(x)$ is $-3 \le y \le 5$, then the range of the function $y = |f(x)|$ is

A. $-3 \le y \le 5$ B. $0 \le y \le 3$

C. $0 \le y \le 5$ D. $3 \le y \le 5$

Use the following information to answer the next question.

A function, $f(x)$, is defined as follows:

$$f(x) = \begin{cases} -(x+2) \text{ when } x \le 0 \\ |2 - x| \text{ when } x > 0 \end{cases}$$

423. Which of the following graphs shows the given function?

A.

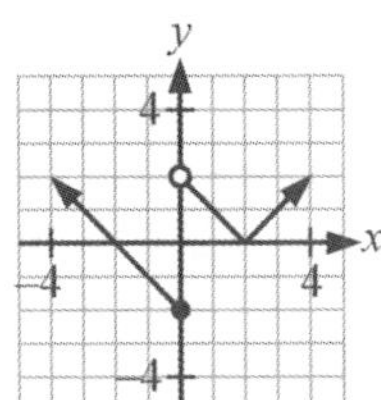

B.

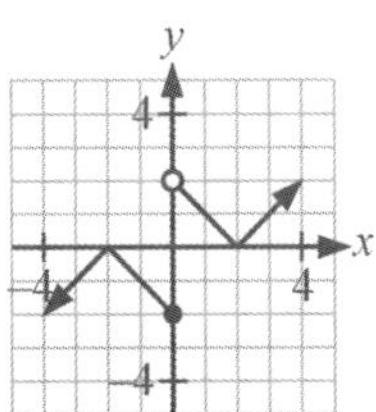

C.

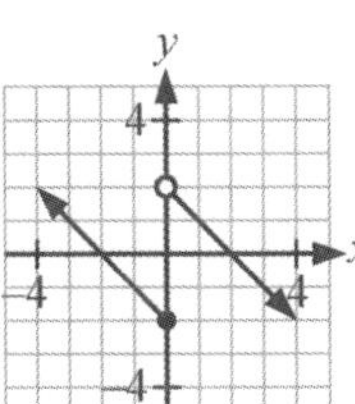

D.

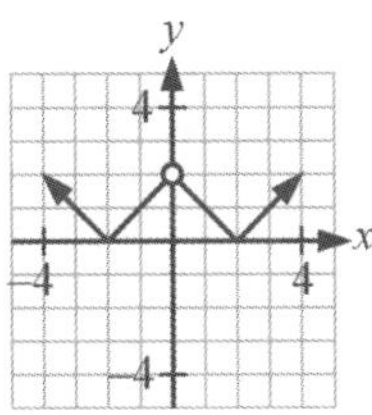

424. By completing the square, it can be determined that the quadratic function $f(x) = -3x^2 + 12x - 4$ has a

A. maximum value of –16

B. minimum value of –16

C. maximum value of 8

D. minimum value of 8

Use the following information to answer the next question.

A small model rocket is launched from a second-story balcony deck. The path of the rocket is represented by the given graph.

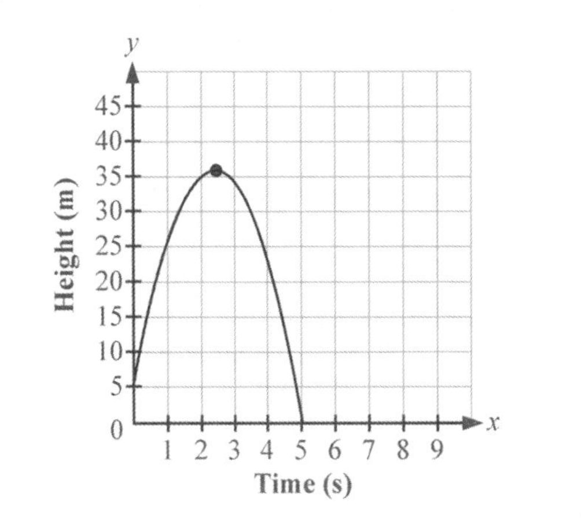

425. Once it is launched, how much time does the rocket take to strike the ground?

A. 3 s B. 4 s

C. 5 s D. 6 s

Use the following information to answer the next question.

A football kicked during a football game followed a parabolic path. This path can be modeled by graphing the equation $h = -2t^2 + 11t - 3$, $t \ge 1$, where t is the number of seconds that have elapsed since the football was kicked and h is the height of the football above the ground in yards.

426. How long did it take the football to reach a height of 12 yards above the ground after it was kicked?

A. 2.0 seconds B. 2.5 seconds

C. 3.0 seconds D. 3.5 seconds

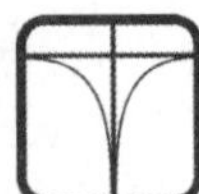

Use the following information to answer the next question.

A baseball is thrown vertically upward with an initial velocity of 30 m/s. Its height, h (in meters), above the ground at any time, t (in seconds), is approximated by the function $h(t) = 30t - 5t^2$.

427. The maximum height above the ground that the ball will reach is __________m.

Use the following information to answer the next question.

Shannon's teacher asked her to determine the vertex of $y = -\frac{1}{2}x^2 + 2x + 3$.

She decided to find the vertex of the function by substituting the appropriate values into the variables $\left(-\frac{b}{2a}, -\frac{b^2}{4a} + c\right)$. The steps in Shannon's solution are shown.

1. $\left(-\frac{b}{2a}, -\frac{b^2}{4a} + c\right)$
2. $= \left(-\frac{2}{2\left(-\frac{1}{2}\right)}, -\frac{2^2}{4\left(\frac{1}{2}\right)} + 3\right)$
3. $= \left(-\frac{2}{-1}, -\frac{4}{2} + 3\right)$
4. $= (2, 1)$

428. In which step of Shannon's solution did she make her first error?

A. 1 **B.** 2

C. 3 **D.** 4

429. What is the y-coordinate of the vertex of the function $y = -(x + 4)(x + 1)$?

A. $\frac{9}{4}$ **B.** $\frac{3}{2}$

C. $-\frac{7}{4}$ **D.** $-\frac{5}{2}$

430. Which of the following tables of values does **not** represent an exponential function?

A.

x	1	2	3	4	5
y	2	8	32	128	512

B.

x	1	2	3	4	5
y	729	486	324	216	144

C.

x	1	2	3	4	5
y	0.8	1.2	1.8	2.7	4.05

D.

x	1	2	3	4	5
y	0.5	2.0	4.5	8.0	12.5

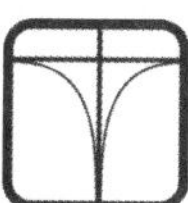

EXERCISE #1—USING REPRESENTATIONS TO ANALYZE FUNCTIONS ANSWERS AND SOLUTIONS

422. C	425. C	428. B
423. A	426. B	429. A
424. C	427. 45	430. D

422. C

The graph of the absolute function $y = |f(x)|$ will reflect in the x-axis any portion of the graph of $y = f(x)$ that is below the x-axis. For example, let $y = f(x)$ be represented by the graph shown.

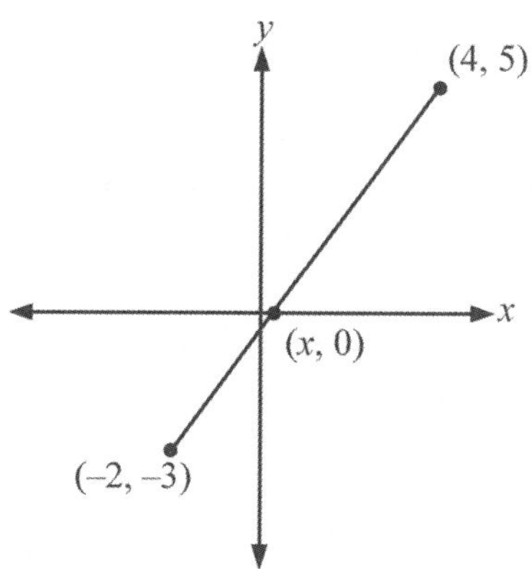

The graph of $y = |f(x)|$ will then appear as shown here.

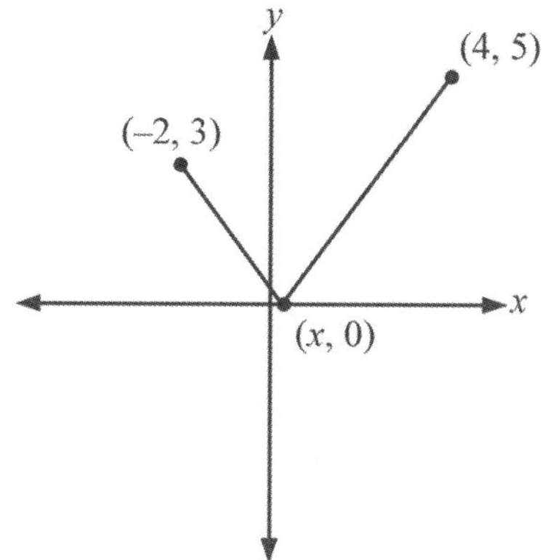

The range of $y = |f(x)|$ is therefore $0 \le y \le 5$.

423. A

Step 1
Construct a table of values for the function $f(x) = -(x+2)$ when $x \le 0$.

x	$f(x)$
–3	1
–2	0
–1	–1
0	–2

Step 2
Construct a table of values for the function $f(x) = |2 - x|$ when $x > 0$.

x	$f(x)$
0	2
1	1
2	0
3	1

Step 3
Sketch the piecewise function using the coordinates from the tables of values. Only the piece of the function defined by $f(x) = -(x+2)$ is defined for an x-value of 0.

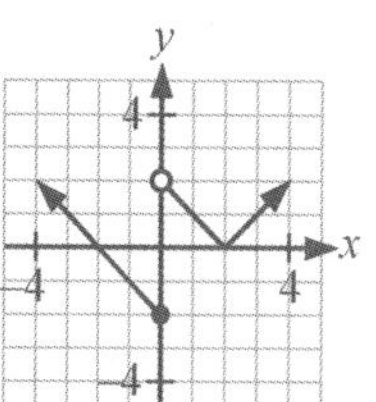

424. C

The function $f(x) = -3x^2 + 12x - 4$ has a maximum value since parameter $a < 0$.
Complete the square.

$$\begin{aligned} f(x) &= -3x^2 + 12x - 4 \\ &= -3(x^2 - 4x) - 4 \\ &= -3(x^2 - 4x + 4 - 4) - 4 \\ &= -3(x^2 - 4x + 4) + 12 - 4 \\ &= -3(x-2)^2 + 8 \end{aligned}$$

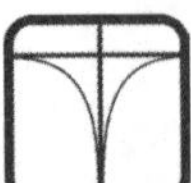

The vertex of the graph of the function is located at (2, 8). As such, the maximum value of the function is 8.

425. C

The rocket will strike the ground where the parabola intersects the x-axis after it has reach the vertex. The parabola intersects the x-axis at 5 s, so it takes the rocket 5 s to strike the ground.

Thus, the time it takes the rocket to hit the ground is 5 seconds.

426. B

Use the TI-83 Plus graphing calculator to plot the line $y = 12$ and the parabola $y = -2x^2 + 11x - 3$. Then use the INTERSECTION feature to find the intersection points of the two graphs.

The first intersection point is: (2.5, 12)

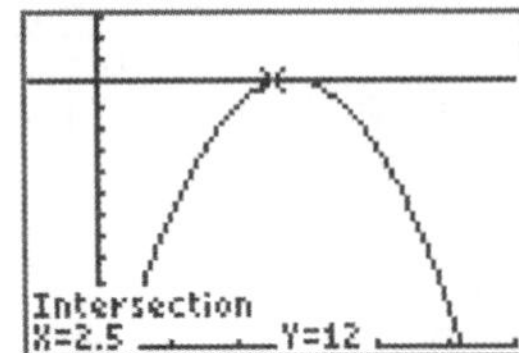

The second intersection point is: (3, 12)

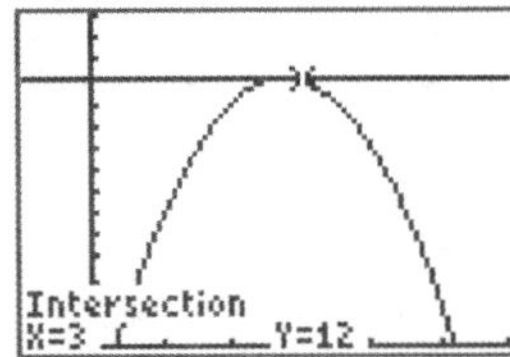

The first value of x is closest to the moment of the kick, so the first value of x is the time taken for the ball to reach a height of 12 m. Therefore, the least number of seconds it took the football to reach a height of 12 yards above the ground is 2.5 seconds.

427. 45

Step 1
Determine the vertex of the parabola represented by the given function.
To determine the vertex, write the function in completed square form.
Factor out –5.

$$\begin{aligned} h(t) &= 30t - 5t^2 \\ &= -5t^2 + 30t \\ &= -5(t^2 - 6t) \end{aligned}$$

Step 2
Add and subtract $\left(\frac{-6}{2}\right)^2 = 9$ inside the brackets.

$h(t) = -5(t^2 - 6t + 9 - 9)$
Move –9 outside the brackets, and multiply it by –5.
$h(t) = -5(t^2 - 6t + 9) - 9(-5)$
Factor the perfect square trinomial in the brackets, and simplify.
$h(t) = -5(t - 3)^2 + 45$

Step 3
Determine the vertex.
A function of the form $y = a(x - p)^2 + q$ has the vertex (p, q).
The vertex is (3, 45).

Step 4
Determine the maximum height the ball reaches and the time it takes to reach the maximum height.
Since the a-value $-5 < 0$, the graph of the function $h(t) = -5(t - 3)^2 + 45$ is a parabola opening downward, and thus has a maximum value.
The y-coordinate of the vertex represents the maximum height the ball will reach, and the x-coordinate of the vertex is the time the ball takes to reach the maximum height.
Therefore, a maximum height of 45 m is reached after 3 s.

428. B

Shannon's first error occurred in step 2: she forgot a negative sign when she substituted one of the values of a.

The correct solution is as follows:

1. $\left(-\frac{b}{2a}, -\frac{b^2}{4a} + c\right)$
2. $= \left(-\frac{2}{2\left(-\frac{1}{2}\right)}, -\frac{2^2}{4\left(-\frac{1}{2}\right)} + 3\right)$
3. $= \left(-\frac{2}{-1}, -\frac{4}{-2} + 3\right)$
4. $= (2, 5)$

429. A

Step 1

Determine the x-intercepts.

Set the equation equal to 0, and apply the zero product property.

$y = -(x+4)(x+1)$

$0 = x+4$

$-4 = x$

$0 = x+1$

$-1 = x$

Step 2

Determine the midpoint of the x-intercepts.

$$M = \left(\frac{x_1 + x_2}{2}, \frac{y_1 + y_2}{2}\right)$$

$$M = \left(\frac{(-4)+(-1)}{2}, \frac{0+0}{2}\right)$$

$$M = \left(\frac{-5}{2}, \frac{0}{2}\right)$$

$$M = \left(-\frac{5}{2}, 0\right)$$

Step 3

Substitute the x-coordinate from the midpoint into the equation to solve for y.

$y = -(x+4)(x+1)$

$$y = -\left(-\frac{5}{2}+4\right)\left(-\frac{5}{2}+1\right)$$

$$y = -\left(-\frac{5}{2}+\frac{8}{2}\right)\left(-\frac{5}{2}+\frac{2}{2}\right)$$

$$y = -\left(\frac{3}{2}\right)\left(-\frac{3}{2}\right)$$

$$y = \frac{9}{4}$$

The coordinates of the vertex of the function $y = -(x+4)(x+1)$ are $\left(-\frac{5}{2}, \frac{9}{4}\right)$. The y-coordinate of the vertex is $\frac{9}{4}$.

430. D

A function is an exponential function if successive y-values in a table have ratios that are constant. R stands for ratio.

Alternative A: This is an exponential function with a constant ratio of 4.

x	1	2	3	4	5
y	2	8	32	128	512
R	$\frac{8}{2} = 4$	$\frac{32}{8} = 4$	$\frac{128}{32} = 4$	$\frac{512}{128} = 4$	

Alternative B: This is an exponential function with a constant ratio of 0.67.

x	1	2	3	4	5
y	729	486	324	216	144
R	$\frac{486}{729} = 0.67$	$\frac{324}{486} = 0.67$	$\frac{216}{324} = 0.67$	$\frac{144}{216} = 0.67$	

Alternative C: This is an exponential function with a constant ratio of 1.5.

x	1	2	3	4	5
y	0.8	1.2	1.8	2.7	4.05
R	$\frac{1.2}{0.8} = 1.5$	$\frac{1.8}{1.2} = 1.5$	$\frac{2.7}{1.8} = 1.5$	$\frac{4.05}{2.7} = 1.5$	

Alternative D: This is not an exponential function since the ratio is not constant.

x	1	2	3	4	5
y	0.5	2.0	4.5	8.0	12.5
R	$\frac{2.0}{0.5} = 4$	$\frac{4.5}{2.0} = 2.25$	$\frac{8.0}{4.5} = 1.78$	$\frac{12.5}{8.0} = 1.56$	

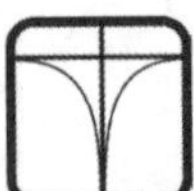

EXERCISE #2—USING REPRESENTATIONS TO ANALYZE FUNCTIONS

Use the following information to answer the next question.

The point with coordinates (2, −6) lies on the graph of the function $y = f(x)$.

431. What are the coordinates of the corresponding point on the graph of $y = |f(x)| + 2$?

A. (2, 4) B. (2, 8)
C. (−2, 4) D. (−2, −8)

Use the following information to answer the next question.

A function, $f(x)$, is defined as follows:

$$f(x) = \begin{cases} x^2 \text{ when } x < 0 \\ x \text{ when } 0 \le x \le 1 \\ \dfrac{1}{x} \text{ when } 1 < x < \infty \end{cases}$$

432. Which of the following graphs shows the given function?

A.

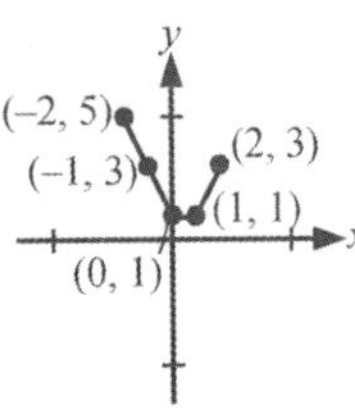

B.

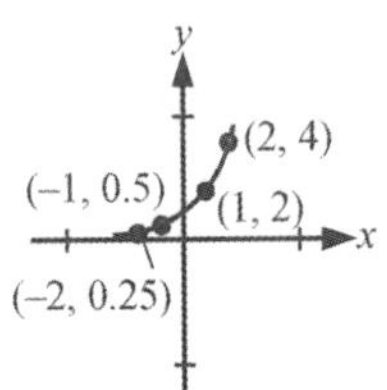

C.

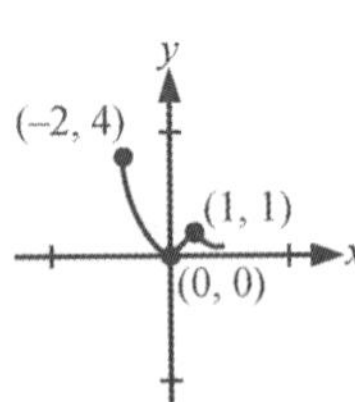

D.

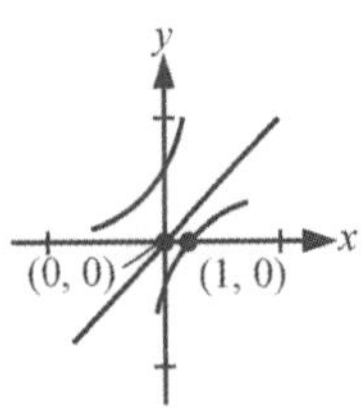

433. The vertex form of the quadratic function $f(x) = -\frac{1}{2}x^2 + 4x + c$ is

A. $f(x) = -\frac{1}{2}(x-1)^2 + \left(c + \frac{1}{2}\right)$

B. $f(x) = -\frac{1}{2}(x-1)^2 + (c+1)$

C. $f(x) = -\frac{1}{2}(x-4)^2 + (c+8)$

D. $f(x) = -\frac{1}{2}(x-4)^2 + (c+16)$

Use the following information to answer the next question.

The unit value of a particular stock, in Japanese yen (JPY), followed a quadratic pattern over a period of 20 consecutive days. Part of this trend is portrayed in the bar graph shown below.

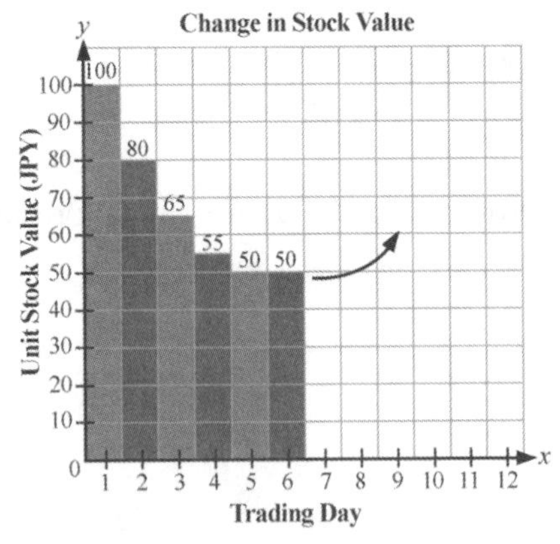

434. Based on the trend, the stock would recover to its original value of 100 JPY on day __________.

Use the following information to answer the next question.

The flight path of a flare fired from the top of a cliff to the ground can be described by the graph of the quadratic function $h(t) = -4.9t^2 + 29.4t + 352.8$, where $h(t)$ is the height, in meters, of the flare above the ground at a time, t, in seconds. Yosef wanted to use his graphing calculator to find the time, in seconds, when the flare hit the ground at $h(t) = 0$, namely the t-intercept.

435. The window Yosef used to display the whole flight of the flare to the ground ($h(t) = 0$) was ___i___, and the t-intercept was ___ii___.

Which of the following rows correctly completes this statement?

A.

i	ii
x:[−10, 10, 1] y:[−10, 10, 1]	6.0 seconds

B.

i	ii
x:[−10, 20, 1] y:[−10, 500, 1]	6.0 seconds

C.

i	ii
x:[−10, 10, 1] y:[−10, 500, 1]	12.0 seconds

D.

i	ii
x:[−10, 20, 1] y:[−10, 500, 1]	12.0 seconds

Use the following information to answer the next question.

A rocket is launched from a platform. Its height, h, in meters is given as a function of the time, t, in seconds by the equation $h = -4.9t^2 + 98t + 5$.

436. To the nearest meter, what is the maximum height above the ground that can be reached by the rocket? __________ m

437. What is the vertex of the function $y = x^2 + 3x - 5$?

A. $\left(-\frac{3}{2}, -\frac{29}{4}\right)$

B. $\left(-\frac{3}{2}, -\frac{7}{2}\right)$

C. $\left(-\frac{3}{2}, \frac{11}{4}\right)$

D. $\left(-\frac{3}{2}, \frac{13}{2}\right)$

438. What is the vertex of the function $y = 2(x - 3)(x - 7)$?

A. (3, 7)
B. (5, −8)
C. (−5, 8)
D. (−3, −7)

439. Which of the following features does **not** describe the graph of $f(x) = 10^x$?

A. The range is $y > 0$.

B. The horizontal asymptote is $y = 0$.

C. The graph is flatter on the left side of the y-axis than the graph of $f(x) = 8^x$.

D. The graph is steeper on the right side of the y-axis than the graph of $f(x) = 12^x$.

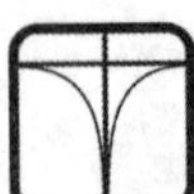

EXERCISE #2—USING REPRESENTATIONS TO ANALYZE FUNCTIONS ANSWERS AND SOLUTIONS

431. B	434. 10	437. A
432. C	435. D	438. B
433. C	436. 495	439. C

431. B

To sketch the graph of the absolute value of $y = f(x)$, the part of the graph that lies below the x-axis on the graph of $y = f(x)$ is reflected in the x-axis; that is, it is reflected to lie above the line $y = 0$.
Thus, the point (2, −6) becomes (2, 6) on the graph of $y = |f(x)|$.
The graph of $y = |f(x)| + 2$ is then obtained by translating the graph of $y = |f(x)|$ up 2 units.

The point (2, 6) becomes the point (2, 8).
Therefore, the corresponding point on the graph of $y = |f(x)| + 2$ has the coordinates (2, 8).

432. C

Step 1
Construct a table of values for the function $f(x) = x^2$ in the interval $x < 0$.

x	$f(x)$
0	0
−1	1
−2	4
−3	9

Step 2
Construct a table of values for the function $f(x) = x$ in the interval $0 \le x \le 1$.

x	$f(x)$
0	0
1	1

Step 3
Construct a table of values for the function $f(x) = \frac{1}{x}$ in the interval $1 \le x \le \infty$.

x	$f(x)$
1	1
2	$\frac{1}{2}$
3	$\frac{1}{3}$
4	$\frac{1}{4}$
5	$\frac{1}{5}$

Step 4
Sketch the piecewise function by using the coordinates from the tables of values.

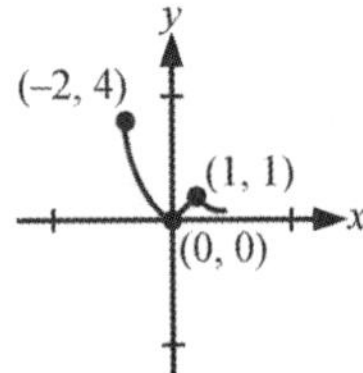

433. C

Convert $f(x) = -\frac{1}{2}x^2 + 4x + c$ into the vertex form $f(x) = a(x - h)^2 + k$ as follows:

Factor out $-\frac{1}{2}$.

$$f(x) = -\frac{1}{2}x^2 + 4x + c$$

$$f(x) = -\frac{1}{2}(x^2 - 8x) + c$$

Find the perfect square value, and put this as both a negative and a positive value in the brackets.

$$f(x) = -\frac{1}{2}(x^2 - 8x + 16 - 16) + c$$

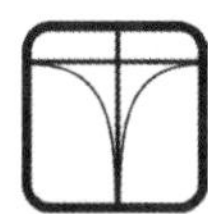

Multiply −16 by $-\frac{1}{2}$ and bring this value outside the brackets.

$f(x) = -\frac{1}{2}(x^2 - 8x + 16) + 8 + c$

Factor the perfect square trinomial, and combine the constant terms.

$f(x) = -\frac{1}{2}(x-4)^2 + (8 + c)$

The vertex form of the function is

$f(x) = -\frac{1}{2}(x-4)^2 + (c + 8)$.

434. 10

A quadratic pattern is symmetrical in that it decreases and increases from its minimum point in equivalent steps. The drops on the left side of the minimum over the first 5 days are

$100 \xrightarrow{-20} 80 \xrightarrow{-15} 65 \xrightarrow{-10} 55 \xrightarrow{-5} 50$. Therefore, the increases on the right side of the graph from day 6 onward will follow the same pattern of

$50 \xrightarrow{+5} 55 \xrightarrow{+10} 65 \xrightarrow{+15} 80 \xrightarrow{+20} 100$.

This increased pattern of the stock can be represented in the completed graph below.

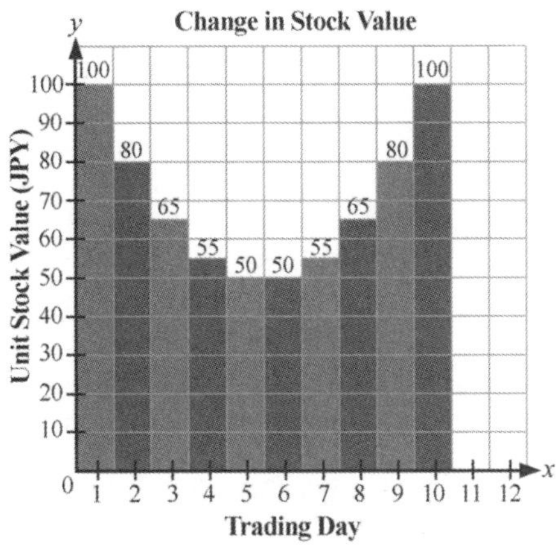

According to the completed pattern shown in the graph, the stock recovers to its original value of 100 JPY on day 10.

435. D

Enter the function $h(t) = -4.9t^2 + 29.4t + 352.8$ into your $[Y_1 =]$ button on your graphing calculator. Then, press GRAPH and use WINDOW (ZOOM 6).

$Y_1 = -4.9x^2 + 29.4x + 352.8$

The graph only shows the negative x-intercept which does not apply to this question. Also, the top (maximum) of the graph is not visible. Therefore, the WINDOW needs to be made larger to the right (x_{max}) and moved up (y_{max}) a lot. The window that seems appropriate is given in alternatives B or D as:

x:[−10, 20, 1]
y:[−10, 500, 1]

When this WINDOW setting is used, the whole graph is shown with its maximum and the positive x-intercept, namely the point representing when the flare hits the ground. Then, carry out the 2nd TRACE ZERO feature to determine that this x-intercept is 12.0, as shown below:

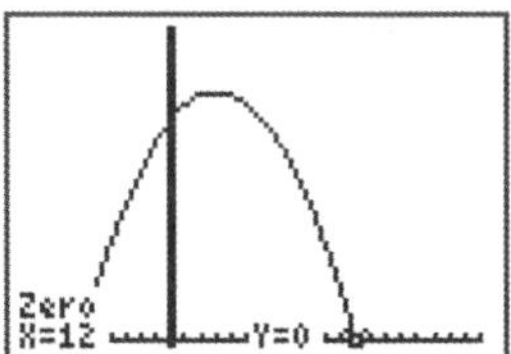

436. 495

Step 1

To determine the maximum height, rewrite the given equation using the completing the square method.

The given equation is $h = -4.9t^2 + 98t + 5$.

Factor −4.9 out of the t^2- and t-terms.

$h = -4.9(t^2 - 20t) + 5$

Step 2

Divide the coefficient of t by 2, and then add and subtract the square of the result within the brackets.

$\left(-\frac{20}{2}\right)^2 = 100$

$h = -4.9(t^2 - 20t + 100 - 100) + 5$

Step 3

Move the term that will not contribute to the perfect square outside the brackets. To move −100 outside the brackets, multiply it by −4.9.

$h = -4.9(t^2 - 20t + 100) - 100(-4.9) + 5$

Write the trinomial in brackets as the square of a binomial, and simplify the equation.

$h = -4.9(t - 10)^2 + 495$

This equation is in the form $y = a(x - p)^2 + q$, where q is the maximum function value when $a < 0$. The maximum height is 495 m.

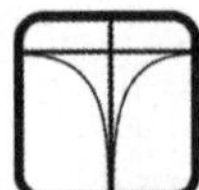

437. A

The coordinates of the vertex of any quadratic function of the form $y = ax^2 + bx + c$ are $\left(-\frac{b}{2a}, -\frac{b^2}{4a} + c\right)$. The vertex of the function $y = x^2 + 3x - 5$ can be found by substituting the appropriate values into the variables $\left(-\frac{b}{2a}, -\frac{b^2}{4a} + c\right)$.

$$\left(-\frac{3}{2(1)}, -\frac{3^2}{4(1)} + (-5)\right)$$
$$= \left(-\frac{3}{2}, -\frac{9}{4} - 5\right)$$
$$= \left(-\frac{3}{2}, -\frac{9}{4} - \frac{20}{4}\right)$$
$$= \left(-\frac{3}{2}, -\frac{29}{4}\right)$$

438. B

Step 1
Determine the x-intercepts.
Set the equation equal to 0, and apply the zero product property.

$y = 2(x - 3)(x - 7)$
$0 = x - 3$
$3 = x$
$0 = x - 7$
$7 = x$

Step 2
Determine the midpoint of the x-intercepts.

$$M = \left(\frac{x_1 + x_2}{2}, \frac{y_1 + y_2}{2}\right)$$
$$M = \left(\frac{3 + 7}{2}, \frac{0 + 0}{2}\right)$$
$$M = \left(\frac{10}{2}, \frac{0}{2}\right)$$
$$M = (5, 0)$$

Step 3
Substitute the x-coordinate from the midpoint into the equation to solve for y.

$y = 2(x - 3)(x - 7)$
$y = 2(5 - 3)(5 - 7)$
$y = 2(2)(-2)$
$y = -8$

The coordinates of the vertex of the function $y = 2(x - 3)(x - 7)$ are $(5, -8)$.

439. C

As the value of a increases, the graph gets flatter on the left side of the y-axis and gets steeper on the right side.

Since $a = 8$ in $f(x) = 8^x$ is smaller (not greater) than $a = 10$ in the original function $f(x) = 10^x$, this statement is incorrect.

The range is $y > 0$, and the horizontal asymptote is $y = 0$.

The value of $a = 12$ in $f(x) = 12^x$ is greater than $a = 10$ in the original function $f(x) = 10^x$, so this statement is also correct.

Building New Functions

BUILDING NEW FUNCTIONS

Table of Correlations

Standard		Concepts	Exercise #1	Exercise #2
Unit5.6	Build new functions from existing functions.			
F-BF.4a	*Find inverse functions. Solve an equation of the form f(x) = c for a simple function f that has an inverse and write an expression for the inverse.*	Determining the Equation of the Inverse of a Function Algebraically	440	442
		Defining the Inverse of a Function	441	443

F-BF.4a Find inverse functions. Solve an equation of the form f(x) = c for a simple function f that has an inverse and write an expression for the inverse.

Determining the Equation of the Inverse of a Function Algebraically

A **function** is a set of ordered pairs in which every element of the domain is paired with exactly one element of the range. The **inverse** of a function is the relation that exists from interchanging the values in the ordered pairs of the function.
The function notation for the inverse of a function is $f^{-1}(x)$, and it is read "*f* inverse."

Note that −1 is not an exponent—it is just part of the symbol. The $f^{-1}(x)$ form can only be used when the inverse is a function.

Follow these steps when determining the equation of the inverse of a function:

1. Replace $f(x)$ with y.
2. Interchange x and y.
3. Resolve for y.
4. Replace y with $f^{-1}(x)$ if the inverse of the original function is also a function.

Example

Write the inverse of $f(x) = \frac{1}{3}x + 4$.

Solution

Step 1
Replace $f(x)$ with y.
$y = \frac{1}{3}x + 4$

Step 2
Interchange x and y.
$x = \frac{1}{3}y + 4$

Step 3
Solve for y.

$$\begin{aligned} x &= \frac{1}{3}y + 4 \\ 3x &= y + 12 \\ 3x - 12 &= y \\ y &= 3x - 12 \end{aligned}$$

Step 4
Replace y with $f^{-1}(x)$.
Since $y = 3x - 12$ is a linear function, it can be written using function notation.
$f^{-1}(x) = 3x - 12$

Example

Write the inverse of $f(x) = -(x+2)^2$.

Solution

Step 1
Replace $f(x)$ with y.

$$\begin{aligned} f(x) &= -(x+2)^2 \\ y &= -(x+2)^2 \end{aligned}$$

Step 2
Interchange x and y.
$x = -(y+2)^2$

Step 3
Resolve for y.

$$\begin{aligned} x &= -(y+2)^2 \\ -x &= (y+2)^2 \\ \pm\sqrt{-x} &= y + 2 \\ -2 \pm \sqrt{-x} &= y \\ y &= -2 \pm \sqrt{-x} \end{aligned}$$

Since the inverse of $f(x)$ is not a function, the equation of the inverse remains as $y = -2 \pm \sqrt{-x}$.

The inverses of other functions are determined using the same procedures as for linear and quadratic functions. The important thing is that the domain and range are exactly interchanged between any function or relation and its inverse.

Example

Determine the inverse of $f(x) = \frac{3}{x-4}$, writing the inverse in function notation if appropriate.

Solution

Step 1
Replace $f(x)$ with y.

$$\begin{aligned} f(x) &= \frac{3}{x-4} \\ y &= \frac{3}{x-4} \end{aligned}$$

Step 2
Interchange x and y.

$$x = \frac{3}{y-4}$$

Step 3
Resolve for y.

$$(y-4)x = 3$$
$$y-4 = \frac{3}{x}$$
$$y = \frac{3}{x} + 4$$
$$y = \frac{3}{x} + 4 \text{ or } y = \frac{3+4x}{x}$$

Since the inverse is a function, it can be written as $f^{-1}(x) = \frac{3}{x} + 4$ or $f^{-1}(x) = \frac{3+4x}{x}$.

Example

Write the inverse of $f(x) = \sqrt{x-2}$, writing the inverse in function notation if appropriate.

Solution

Step 1
Replace $f(x)$ with y.

$$f(x) = \sqrt{x-2}$$
$$y = \sqrt{x-2}$$

Step 2
Interchange x and y.

$$x = \sqrt{y-2}$$

Step 3
Resolve for y.

$$x = \sqrt{y-2}$$
$$x^2 = y-2$$
$$x^2 + 2 = y$$
$$y = x^2 + 2$$

In the original function $f(x) = \sqrt{x-2}$, the range is $y \geq 0$.

Thus, the domain of the inverse, $y = x^2 + 2$, must be $x \geq 0$.

Since the inverse is a function, it can be written as $f^{-1}(x) = x^2 + 2,\ x \geq 0$.

Defining the Inverse of a Function

The inverse of a function can be obtained through an **inverse procedure**, which is a reverse process. The inverse of a function can be compared to a machine: if there were a machine that could take a finished product and recreate the raw materials that made it, then this machine would be the inverse of the one that created the finished product from the raw materials.

An example from basic mathematics is factoring. Factoring is the inverse process of expanding, and vice versa.

Example

When the factored expression $2(x+4)$ is expanded, it is written as $2x+8$. You expand the expression by multiplying both terms inside the brackets by the term outside the brackets.

When the expanded expression $3x+9$ is factored, it is written as $3(x+3)$. You factor the expression by dividing each term by the same value and placing that value outside the brackets.

A function is a set of ordered pairs in which every element of the domain (input) is paired with exactly one element of the range (output). The first set of values in the ordered pairs that define a function is the **domain** of the function. The second set of values in the ordered pairs that define a function is the **range** of the function.

The inverse of a function, $f(x)$, is formed by interchanging the variables x and y in the equation that defines the function. Every value that is a range value in the original function will become a domain value in the inverse function. Every value that is a domain value in the original function will become a range value in the inverse function. If an ordered pair is represented by (s, t) in the original function, it would be represented by (t, s) in the inverse of that function.

If the inverse is a function, it can be represented in function notation as $f^{-1}(x)$.

Example

Write the inverse of $f(x) = \frac{1}{3}x + 4$.

Solution

Step 1

Replace $f(x)$ with y.

$y = \frac{1}{3}x + 4$

Step 2

Interchange x and y.

$x = \frac{1}{3}y + 4$

Step 3

Solve for y.

$$x = \frac{1}{3}y + 4$$
$$3x = y + 12$$
$$3x - 12 = y$$
$$y = 3x - 12$$

Step 4

Replace y with $f^{-1}(x)$.

Since $y = 3x - 12$ is a linear function, it can be written using function notation.

$f^{-1}(x) = 3x - 12$

Example

Sketch the graph of the function $y = 2x - 4$ and the graph of its inverse function, $x = 2y - 4$.

Solution

Step 1

Set up an appropriate table of values for the graph of $y = 2x - 4$. One possible table of values is shown.

x	–4	–2	0	2	4
y	–12	–8	–4	0	4

Step 2

Determine the table of values for the inverse graph by interchanging the x- and y-values of each ordered pair in the table of values for $y = 2x - 4$.

x	–12	–8	–4	0	4
y	–4	–2	0	2	4

Step 3

Sketch the graph of $y = 2x - 4$ and its inverse on the same Cartesian plane by using the tables of values. The equation of the inverse, $x = 2y - 4$, can be written in terms of y as $y = \frac{1}{2}x + 2$.

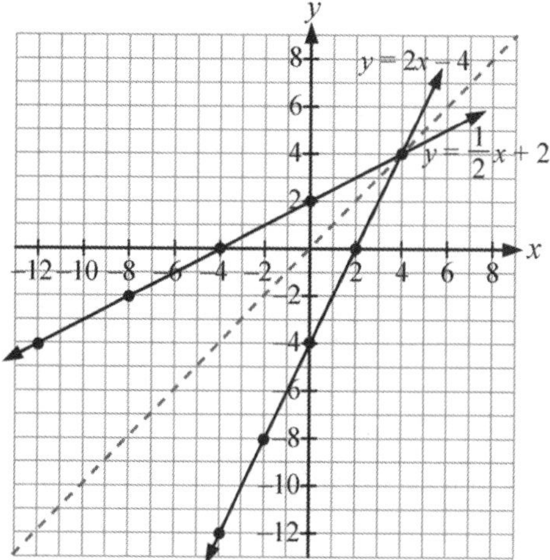

Observe that the second graph is the graph of $y = 2x - 4$ reflected in the line $y = x$.

EXERCISE #1—BUILDING NEW FUNCTIONS

440. The inverse of the quadratic function $f(x) = \frac{1}{2}(x+6)^2 - 5$ is

A. $y = \pm\sqrt{2x+5} - 6$

B. $y = \pm\sqrt{2x+10} - 6$

C. $y = \pm 2\sqrt{x+5} - 6$

D. $y = \pm 2\sqrt{x-6} + 5$

441. A function, $f(x)$, is defined as $f(x) = \sqrt{3x+1}$. What is the correct order of operations to obtain the inverse of $f(x)$?

A. Square the input, subtract 1, and divide the difference by 3.

B. Divide the input by 3, subtract 1, and square the difference.

C. Multiply the input by 3, add 1, and take the square root of the sum.

D. Take the square root of the input, add 1, and multiply the sum by 3.